Critical Thinking

EXERCISES

Psychology
in Action

Psychology in Action

THIRD EDITION

Karen Huffman

Palomar College

Mark Vernoy

Palomar College

Judith Vernoy

JOHN WILEY & SONS, INC.

New York   Chichester   Brisbane   Toronto   Singapore

Acquisitions Editor	Karen Dubno
Developmental Editor	Kathleen Dolan
Marketing Manager	Catherine Faduska
Production Supervisor	Charlotte Hyland
Designer	Laura Nicholls
Manufacturing Manager	Susan Stetzer
Director of Photo Department	Stella Kupferberg
Photo Researcher/Editor	Jennifer Atkins
Illustration Coordinator:	Anna Melhorn
Electronic Illustrations:	Precision Graphics
Anatomical Illustrations:	Network Graphics
Cover Photo:	David Barnes/The Stock Market

This book was set in 10/12 ITC Clearface by Progressive Typographers and printed and bound by Von Hoffmann Press. The cover was printed by Phoenix.

Library of Congress Cataloging-in-Publication Data:
Huffman, Karen.
    Psychology in action / Karen Huffman, Mark Vernoy, Judith Vernoy.
    — 3rd ed.
        p.   cm.
    Rev. ed. of: Psychology in action / Karen Huffman . . . [et al.].
2nd ed. c1991.
    Includes bibliographical references and index.
    ISBN 0-471-58409-6 (cloth)
    1. Psychology. I. Vernoy, Mark W.   II. Vernoy, Judith.
III. Title
BF121.H78   1994
150—dc20   93-2269
                                                  CIP
Printed in the United States of America

10   9   8   7   6   5   4   3   2   1

Preface

Welcome to the third edition of *Psychology in Action*. The world was very different when we began work on the first edition in 1984. Communism and the Berlin Wall were still in place, Ronald Reagan had just been reelected to a second term as president of the United States, and the dominant theme in politics was protecting ourselves against the "evil empire." In one decade we have witnessed the collapse of communism, devastating famine and outbreaks of terrorism and war, high unemployment and one of the worst race riots in American history, and the election of a new U.S. president whose main campaign promise was change.

Just as the world and our nation have undergone significant changes, so too has psychology. In today's global village, the demand for gender equality and respect for cultural diversity has increased. Therefore, any serious survey of human behavior must include male and female issues and a cross-cultural perspective. We have added both as an integral part of every chapter of *Psychology in Action*. We have also extensively streamlined, updated, and improved the third edition with several new features. Naturally, we have retained key features of earlier editions, such as the SQ4R method, the focus on critical thinking, and our student-oriented writing style. Let us tell you a little more about what we have done.

NEW TO THIS EDITION

Increased Focus on Active Learning

As reflected in the title of our text, we promote learning as an *activity* of the reader. Too often students adopt a passive approach to learning, but research shows that educational achievement improves with active participation (Bonwell and Eison, 1991). To this end, we have incorporated special "Try This Yourself" activities into every chapter (identified by the 🏃 icon). These high-interest and simple-to-do experiments, demonstrations, and personality tests give students an opportunity to apply basic principles and concepts of psychology. In Chapter 15, for example, one "Try This Yourself" activity debunks myths about mental illness and another presents a checklist for recognizing serious depression.

Gender and Cultural Diversity Coverage

For years, psychological research and introductory texts focused on white American and Western European males. But as the world has shrunk and understanding has grown, more attention has been directed to the cultural and gender contexts of behavior. We reflect that welcome change in this edition in four ways. First, the field of cultural psychology is introduced in Chapter 1 with a discussion of ethnocentrism, individualism–collectivism, and universal and culturally specific behaviors. Second, topic coverage routinely takes into account cultural and gender research. Third, photographs, figures, and physiological art were carefully selected or drawn to reflect both cultural and gender diversity. If photos (and illustrations) are truly "worth a thousand words," then it is essential that they include women and members of diverse ethnic groups. Finally, every chapter includes one or more Gender and Cultural Diversity sections (identified by the ♀ icon). These sections highlight particularly interesting or current topics. In all cases, though, the material is *embedded* in the text narrative, not set off in boxes or a separate chapter. We hope this conveys to students the integral importance of gender equality and cultural diversity to the field of psychology and in everyday life.

Increased Emphasis on the Science of Psychology

While attention to diversity is crucial to modern psychology, it is also important to recognize that a century of psychological research has advanced tremendously our understanding of human behavior. Therefore, in preparing this third edition, we have tried to enhance students' appreciation of psychology as an empirical study of human experience and demonstrate the advantages of the scientific method over speculation and common sense. To do this, we have increased significantly our emphasis on the science of psychology. For example, in Chapter 1 we expanded our discussion of the scientific method, bias in research, and types of correlation. We have also included extended research examples, both recent and classic, in every chapter. Students not only enjoy but learn from the detail of such newly added experiments as the "knockout mice" in Chapter 7 and the blue-eyed/brown-eyed study in Chapter 18. In addition, we increased our coverage of the biological and cognitive perspectives. For instance, in Chapter 5 we explain how psychoactive drugs work as agonists or antagonists to the body's natural neurotransmitters. This helps students understand the biology of drugs, and it builds on their knowledge of the brain and nervous system from Chapter 2. The discussion of cognition in Chapter 8 now opens with an overview of the two basic approaches to cognition: the information processing approach and the connectionist approach. We have also reconceptualized and redrawn in full color *all* of the biological figures and added many new ones to clarify difficult concepts, such as neurotransmitter reuptake at the synapse.

Updating and Revising Throughout

The third edition of *Psychology in Action* includes over 700 new citations from 1992, 1993, and 1994. In addition, Chapter 15 has been rewritten extensively to reflect changes in the DSM-IV. Also, while not slighting core concepts, we have attempted to present topics of interest in the 1990s. Chapter 11, for example, contains a new section on coercive sex: rape, incest, and sexual harassment. Chapter 13 has a new section on self-care to reduce stress when it is occurring.

During revisions of previous material, we made a conscious effort to crystallize discussions rather than merely list facts and theories. For example, in Chapters 14, 15, and 16 (personality, abnormal behavior, and therapy), every theory concludes with an "evaluating" section of strengths and weaknesses to help students weigh what they have learned. Finally, we have selectively chosen each photo and figure to reinforce and clarify key concepts, and the entire text has been carefully rewritten for greater readability.

Reorganization for Greater Clarity

We have completely reorganized and rewritten Chapters 9 and 10 (Lifespan Development I and II). These chapters are now arranged topically, rather than chronologically. This allows the reader to explore all four of Piaget's stages at one time (Chapter 9) and all eight of Erikson's stages at one time (Chapter 10), rather than splitting treatment of both between chapters. We also completely revised and reorganized the social psychology chapters to group topics under "Social Behavior and Cognition" (Chapter 17) and

"Social Interactions" (Chapter 18). Material on applied psychology (environmental and Industrial/Organizational) was expanded to occupy its own appendix.

We also restructured within some chapters for greater clarity. The psychoactive drug section of Chapter 5 now reflects the categorization typical of most drug researchers—depressants, stimulants, narcotics, and hallucinogens. Chapter 12 covers motivation and emotion in two parallel sections, and the coverage of personality in Chapter 14 was reorganized into smaller, more manageable units. In every chapter, we added many third-level heads to help students structure their reading.

ENHANCED FEATURES

Critical Thinking Activities

Critical thinking has received considerable attention from education specialists and textbook authors. Unfortunately, many texts that advocate critical thinking do little more than exhort students to "think critically." They give no specific suggestions or activities that will develop critical thinking skills. In line with our focus on active learning, we have tried to take the student out of this passive role by developing highly focused exercises based on the most recent research. In every chapter we include an exercise called "Critical Thinking: Psychology in Action." For example, in Chapter 5, students get practice in distinguishing fact from opinion on the topic of drug use and abuse. Chapter 12 offers practice in recognizing emotional appeals. Additional specific exercises and activities that promote critical thinking are provided in the Student Study Guide and the Instructor's Manual, which are available from the publisher. The 21 basic components of critical thinking are introduced and explained in the prologue of this text and summarized on the inside front cover.

SQ4R Learning Activities

We have also tried to overcome the passive-learner syndrome by structuring our text around the SQ4R (Survey, Question, Read, Recite, Review, and "wRite") method of learning:

Survey and Question   To facilitate the student's surveying technique, we begin each chapter with an outline, an opening vignette, and an introductory paragraph that presents an overview of the chapter. To encourage questioning, we have written the text in a "question/answer" format rather than the traditional author-directed straight narrative. This facilitates an active learning experience for readers, while also modeling the types of questions readers should be asking themselves while they read.

In this third edition, we have strengthened the survey and question components by presenting a list of survey questions following the introductory paragraph. For reinforcement, we repeat the questions in the margin at the place in the chapter where they are discussed.

Read   Each chapter has been carefully evaluated for clarity, conciseness, and student reading level. To further facilitate comprehension, we do not have the boxed essays that are commonly found in other texts. Such boxes interrupt the continuity of the text narrative, and many students find it difficult to decide "what part is important to read." Their complaints support our belief that setting off specific studies or applications from the main text narrative conveys the impression that these topics are less important. If something is worth discussing, we integrate it into our presentation.

Recite and Review   To encourage recitation and review, we offer Review Questions after each major section. These Review Questions provide still another opportunity for active participation. On the advice of users of previous editions, we have added more higher-order questions and moved the answers to the back of the book, where they are identified by a guide in the margin for easy location. This removes the temptation to peek, while still allowing access to the correct answers. To further encourage reviewing, each chapter concludes with a "Review of Major Concepts" that summarizes key terms and concepts.

wRite   As part of the fourth R to the SQ4R method, this book is also designed to incorporate writing as a way of improving student retention. In addition to the writing students will do in the survey, question, and review sections, we encourage note-taking in the margin of each page. We have attempted to keep the margins as clear as possible, and the Instructor's Manual, which accompanies this text, describes a special "marginal marking" technique that can be easily taught to students.

The Owner's Manual, "How to Use this Book," which begins on page *xxi*, and the accompanying Student Study Guide both discuss the SQ4R method in more detail.

Numerous Learning Aids

In addition to the SQ4R techniques, we have incorporated other learning aids that are known to increase comprehension and retention. New terms are put in boldface type and immediately defined in the text and in the margin. Calling out and defining key terms in the margin increases overall comprehension and provides a useful review tool. All terms are also gathered in a complete, cumulative glossary at the end of the text. We have added many new tables, such as the table on drug actions and neurotransmitters in Chapter 5, which also contains an important illustration. The added tables that compare cross-sectional and longitudinal research designs in Chapter 9 and personality theories in Chapter 14 also serve as important educational tools. In addition, we have added a new photo timeline in Chapter 1 that provides an overview of the history of psychology. As a further aid to learning, an annotated list of suggested readings, popular and academic, is given at the end of each chapter.

Supplements

Psychology in Action is accompanied by a host of ancillary materials designed to facilitate active learning and teaching. The student supplements are described more fully on the back cover of this textbook. The instructor's supplements include an instructor's manual, a completely revised and magnificently improved test bank with user-friendly testing software, and much, much more. Information about these supplements can be found on the dust jacket of this text, in the Supplement Sampler sent with your examination copy, or by contacting your local Wiley sales representative.

ACKNOWLEDGMENTS

Our writing of this text has been a group effort involving the input and support of our families, friends, and colleagues. To each person we offer our sincere thanks. A special note of appreciation goes to Jay Alperson, Bill Barnard, Julia Bassett, Haydn Davis, Ann Haney, Herb Harari, Terry Humphrey, Rob Miller, and Kate Townsend-Merino.

To the reviewers, focus group, and telesession participants who gave their time and constructive criticism, we offer our sincere appreciation. We are deeply indebted to the following individuals and trust that they will recognize their contributions throughout the text.

Reviewers for Third Edition

Joyce Allen
Lakeland College

Emir Andrews
Memorial University of Newfoundland

Richard Anglin
Oklahoma City Community College

Susan Anzivino
University of Maine at Farmington

Daniel Bellack
College of Charleston

Linda Bosmajian
Hood College

Meg Clark
California State Polytechnic University– Pomona

Dennis Cogan
Texas Tech University

Kathryn Jennings Cooper
Salt Lake Community College

Linda Scott DeRosier
Rocky Mountain College

Robert Glassman
Lake Forest College

Patricia Marks Greenfield
University of California–Los Angeles

Sam Hagan
Edison County Community College

Algea Harrison
Oakland University

Linda Heath
Loyola University of Chicago

Dennis Jowaisis
Oklahoma City Community College

Kevin Keating
Broward Community College

Marsha Laswell
California State Polytechnic University– Pomona

Maria Lopez-Treviño
Mount San Jacinto College

Edward McCrary III
El Camino Community College

Yancy McDougal
University of South Carolina– Spartanburg

David Miller
Daytona Beach Community College

Kathleen Navarre
Delta College

Leslie Neumann
Forsyth Technical Community College

Linda Palm
Edison Community College

Leslee Pollina
Southeast Missouri State University

Edward Rinalducci
University of Central Florida

Michael Scozzaro
State University of New York at Buffalo

Larry Smith
Daytona Beach Junior College

Debra Steckler
Mary Washington College

Cynthia Viera
Phoenix College

Benjamin Wallace
Cleveland State University

Mary Wellman
Rhode Island College

Fred Whitford
Montana State University

Mary Lou Zanich
Indiana University of Pennsylvania

Focus Group and Telesession Participants for Third Edition

Brian Bate, Cuyahoga Community College; Hugh Bateman, Jones Junior College; Ronald Boykin, Salisbury State University; Jack Brennecke, Mount San Antonio College; Ethel Canty, University of Texas–Brownsville; Joseph Ferrari, Cazenovia College; Allan Fingaret, Rhode Island College; Richard Fry, Youngstown State University; Roger Harnish, Rochester Institute of Technology; Richard Harris, Kansas State University; Tracy B. Henley, Mississippi State University; Roger Hock, New England College; Melvyn King, State University of New York at Cortland; Jack Kirschenbaum, Fullerton College; Cynthia McDaniel, Northern Kentucky University; Deborah McDonald, New Mexico State University; Henry Morlock, State University of New York at Plattsburgh; Kenneth Murdoff, Lane Community College; William Overman, University of North Carolina at Wilmington; Steve Platt, Northern Michigan University; Janet Proctor, Purdue University; Dean Schroeder, Laramie Community College; Michael Schuller, Fresno City College; Alan Schultz, Prince George Community College; Peggy Skinner, South Plains College; Charles Slem, California Polytechnic State University–San Luis Obispo; Eugene Smith, Western Illinois University; David Thomas, Oklahoma State University; Cynthia Viera, Phoenix College; Matthew Westra, Longview Community College

Reviewers of Previous Editions

Worthon Allen, Utah State University; Peter Bankart, Wabash College; Patricia Barker, Schenectady County Community College; Daniel Bellack, Lexington Community College; Terry Blumenthal, Wake Forest University; Theodore N. Bosack, Providence College; Bernado J. Carducci, Indiana University Southeast; Charles S. Carver, University of Miami; Marion Cheney, Brevard Community College; Steve S. Cooper, Glendale Community College; Mark Covey, University of Idaho; Grace Dyrud, Augsburg College; Thomas Eckle, Modesto Junior College; James A. Eison, Southeast Missouri State University; Eric Fiazi, Los Angeles City College; Sandra Fiske, Onondaga Community College; Pamela Flynn, Community College of Philadelphia; William F. Ford, Bucks City Community College; Harris Friedman, Edison Community College; Paul Fuller, Muskegon Community College; Frederick Gault, Western Michigan University; Russell G. Geen, University of Missouri, Columbia; Joseph Giacobbe, Adirondack Community College; David A. Griese, SUNY Farmingdale; Sylvia Haith, Forsyth Technical College; Frederick Halper, Essex County Community College; George Hampton, University of Houston–Downtown; Mike Hawkins, Louisiana State University; Sidney Hochman, Nassau Community College; Kathryn Jennings, College of the Redwoods; Richard D. Honey, Transylvania University; Seth Kalichman, University of South Carolina; Paul Kaplan, Suffolk County Community College; Bruno Kappes, University of Alaska; Allan A. Lippert, Manatee Community College; Thomas Linton, Coppin State College; Virginia Otis Locke, University of Idaho; Tom Marsh, Pitt Community College; Nancy Meck, University of Kansas Medical Center; Michael Miller, College of St. Scholastica; Phil Mohan, University of Idaho; John Near, Elgin Community College; Steve Neighbors, Santa Barbara City College; Sarah O'Dowd, Community College of Rhode Island; Joseph J. Palladino, University of Southern Indiana; Richard S. Perroto, Queensborough Community College; Larry Pervin, Rutgers University, New Brunswick; Valerie Pinhas, Nassau Community College; Howard R. Pollio, University of Tennessee–Knoxville; Christopher Potter, Harrisburg Community College; Derrick Proctor, Andrews University; Antonio Puete, University of North Carolina–Wilmington; Joan S. Rabin, Towson State University; Michael J. Reich, University of Wisconsin–River Falls; Leonard S. Romney, Rockland Community College; Thomas E. Rudy, University of Pittsburgh; Carol D. Ryff, University of Wisconsin–Madison; Neil Salkind, University of Kansas–Lawrence; Richard J. Sanders, University of North Carolina–Wilmington; Steve Schneider, Pima College; Tizrah Schutzengel, Bergen Community College; Lawrence Scott, Bunker Hill Community College; Fred Shima, California State University–Dominquez Hills; Art Skibbe, Appalachian State University; Michael J. Strube, Washington University; Ronald Testa, Plymouth State College; John T. Vogel, Baldwin Wallace College; Mary Wellman, Rhode Island College; Paul J. Wellman, Texas A & M University; I. Eugene White, Salisbury State College; Delos D. Wickens, Colorado State University–Fort Collins; Charles Wiechert, San Antonio College; Jeff Walper, Delaware Technical and Community College; Bonnie S. Wright, St. Olaf College; Brian T. Yates, American University

Special thanks also go to the staff at John Wiley and Sons. This project benefited from the wisdom and insight of Andrea Bryant, Kathleen Dolan, Catherine Faduska,

Charlotte Hyland, Laura Nicholls, Lucille Buonocore, Stella Kupferberg, and others. In particular, we thank Karen Dubno who orchestrated this third edition and whose dedication and commitment to excellence greatly improved the project. Our developmental editor, Harriett Prentiss, has also been an essential contributor. Her careful attention, long hours of rewriting, thoughtful feedback, and necessary criticism were invaluable.

We also would like to extend our appreciation to Walter Lonner and his fellow cross-cultural specialists who conducted an intensive workshop at Western Washington University on "Making basic texts in psychology more culture-inclusive and culture-sensitive." Our attendance at this workshop greatly increased our knowledge and exposure to the field of cultural psychology. Following this workshop, we consulted further with Patricia Marks Greenfield, and her expertise in this field and specific suggestions were indispensable.

Finally, we would like to express our continuing appreciation to our students. They taught us what students want to know and inspired us to write the book. Two students deserve special recognition for their research assistance, Richard Hosey and Tom Anderson. Our warm appreciation is also extended to Kandis Mutter for her tireless efforts, library research, and unique sense of what should and should not go into an introduction to psychology text.

Contents in Brief

Contents

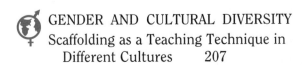

How To Use This Book

Thank you for buying our text. We, the authors, would like to help you get the most from your purchase. We want to help you master the material in this text and get high grades in your introductory psychology course. You can reach both of these goals—mastery and demonstrating your mastery—if you take time now to do three things:

1. Familiarize yourself with the parts of the book.
2. Accept a little advice on how to read a chapter.
3. Keep three study tips in mind.

If you need more specific help, talk to your instructor and/or visit your college's counseling center. The Student Study Guide that accompanies this text is another important resource. It provides additional review and opportunities to apply what you have learned. This Guide and other student supplements are described on the back cover of this textbook.

FAMILIARIZING YOURSELF WITH THE TEXT

Psychology in Action has been carefully designed to help you learn the material. Take time now to examine the parts of this text and benefit from the help each offers.

- *Preface.*   If you have not already done so, read the preface. It is a road map for the rest of the text.

- *Prologue.*   This section presents the 21 basic components of critical thinking. Learn what critical thinking is and why it is important to improve your critical thinking skills.

- *Table of Contents.*   Scan the table of contents for a bird's eye view of what you will study in this course. Get the big picture from the titles of chapters and the major topics within each chapter.

- *Appendixes.*   Two Appendixes—Statistics and Applied Psychology—present important information about specific areas of study within the field of psychology. The Statistics appendix may be particularly helpful when studying Chapter 1 of the text. Consult your instructor regarding the use of the Applied Psychology appendix. A third appendix contains answers to the review questions.

- *End-of-Book Glossary.*   There are two glossaries in this textbook. A "running glossary" appears in the margin of each chapter where key terms and concepts are defined when they are introduced. There is also an end-of-book glossary that gathers all of the terms from the running chapter glossaries in one place. Use the end-of-book glossary to review terms from other chapters.

- *References.*   As you read a chapter assignment, you will find numerous studies cited (e.g., Jones et al., 1994). The reference section at the end of the book gives the complete data for all these citations. Use these sources for further reading on specific topics or for term paper research.

- *Name Index and Subject Index.*   If you are interested in learning more about a particular individual, look for his or her name in the name index. The page numbers refer you to every place in the text where the individual is mentioned. If you are interested in a specific subject (e.g., anorexia nervosa or stress), check the subject index for page references.

HOW TO READ A CHAPTER

Every chapter of *Psychology in Action* contains specific learning aids to help you master the material:

CHAPTER

1

Introducing Psychology

CHAPTER OUTLINE
Every chapter begins with an outline of major topics and subtopics that will be discussed. The major topics are boldfaced and fully capitalized. Under each are approximately three to five subtopics. Only the first letter of each word of these headings is capitalized. This pattern of headings is repeated within the chapter itself. The chapter outline and the corresponding headings within the chapter give you a mental scaffold upon which to arrange the new information you are learning.

OUTLINE

UNDERSTANDING PSYCHOLOGY
The Goals of Psychology
Areas of Psychology
  GENDER AND CULTURAL DIVERSITY
  Cultural Psychology
Psychology in Your Life
PSYCHOLOGICAL RESEARCH
Experimental Research
Nonexperimental Research Techniques
Correlation versus Experimental Methods
Evaluating Research
  CRITICAL THINKING
  Applying Abstract Terminology
ETHICS IN PSYCHOLOGY
Research Ethics
Animals in Research
Clinical Practice Ethics
SCHOOLS OF PSYCHOLOGY
Structuralism and Functionalism
The Psychoanalytic and Gestalt Schools
Behaviorism
Humanistic Psychology
Cognitive Psychology
Psychobiology
Psychology Today

OPENING VIGNETTE

Following the outline is a brief story from real life or an anecdotal retelling of a classic experiment that introduces the theme of the chapter. These opening vignettes were carefully chosen both for their interest and their application to the chapter material. You will find references throughout the chapter to the opening vignette. Drawing on the vignette for examples helps you organize and remember key concepts.

I have just touched my dog. He was rolling on the grass, with pleasure in every muscle and limb. I wanted to catch a picture of him in my fingers, and I touched him as lightly as I would cobwebs. . . . He pressed close to me, as if he were fain to crowd himself into my hand. He loved it with his tail, with his paw, with his tongue. If he could speak, I believe he would say with me that paradise is attained by touch. (pp. 3–4)

Thus Helen Keller began her book *The World I Live In*. Her world was totally different from that of most people: She couldn't see it or hear it because she was blind and deaf, but she learned to know it through her sense of touch. Although deprived of two senses, she was as capable and as appreciative of life—if not more so—as any person with all five senses. This was because she made the most of the senses she did have. Excerpts from her book describe how she used these senses:

Through the sense of touch I know the faces of friends, the illimitable variety of straight and curved lines, all surfaces, the exuberance of the soil, the delicate shapes of flowers, the noble forms of trees, and the range of mighty winds. Besides objects, surfaces, and atmospherical changes, I perceive countless vibrations. . . . Footsteps, I discover, vary tactually according to the age, the sex, and the manners of the walker. . . . When a carpenter works in the house or in the barn near by, I know by the slanting, up-and-down, toothed vibration, and the ringing concussion of blow upon blow, that he is sawing or hammering. . . . In the evening quiet there are fewer vibrations than in the daytime, and then I rely more largely upon smell. . . . Sometimes, when there is no wind, the odors are so grouped that I know the character of the country and can place a hayfield, a country store, a garden, a barn, a grove of pines, a farmhouse with the windows open. . . . I know by smell the kind of house

munication with others. This isolation was a constant source of frustration and anger, leading her to violent temper tantrums. In fact, she noted that "after awhile the need of some means of communication became so urgent that these outbursts occurred daily, sometimes hourly" (1902, p. 32).

Helen's parents realized they had to find help for their daughter, and after diligently searching they found Anne Sullivan, a young teacher who was able to break through Helen's barrier of isolation by taking advantage of her sense of touch. From the moment she arrived, Anne began finger-spelling names of objects by placing her hand in Helen's and forming letters used in sign language. Although Helen learned to finger-spell many words, she didn't understand that these finger movements could signify names for things. Then one day, Anne took Helen to the pumphouse and, as Anne (1902) wrote:

I made Helen hold her mug under the spout while I pumped. As the cold water gushed forth, filling the mug, I spelled "w-a-t-e-r" in Helen's free hand. The word coming so close upon the sensation of cold water rushing over her hand seemed to startle her. She dropped the mug and stood as one transfixed. A new light came into her face. (p. 257)

From that moment on, Helen had an unquenchable desire to learn the names of everything and everybody, to interact and communicate with everyone. That one moment, brought on by the sensation of cold water on her hand, was the impetus for a lifetime of learning about, understanding, and appreciating the world through her remaining senses. In 1904, Helen Keller graduated cum laude from Radcliffe, one of the most respected women's colleges in the world, and following her graduation went on to become a famous author and lecturer, inspiring hope and encouragement to the handicapped throughout the world.

The story of Helen Keller has been told and retold as an example of how people can overcome sensory deficiencies by using their other senses to the optimum. In this chapter, we will discuss each sense in detail and examine the sensory mechanisms by which each operates. We will describe, for instance, how environmental stimuli—light from a flashlight, the odor of a skunk, heat from a campfire—are received by sensory receptors, converted into a language the brain can understand, then transmitted to the brain. This process of receiving, converting, and transmitting information from the outside world ("outside" the brain, not necessarily outside the body) is called sensation. Our study of sensation covers not only what are commonly known as the five senses—vision, hearing, taste, smell, and touch—but also those senses that provide the brain with data from inside the body. These internal senses are the vestibular sense (the sense of balance) and kinesthesis (the sense of bodily position and movement).

As you read Chapter 3, keep the following **Survey** questions in mind and answer them in your own words:

- How do our sensory organs gather sensory information and convert it into signals the brain can understand?
- What is light, and how do our eye structures work to enable us to see?
- What is sound, and how do our ear structures work to enable us to hear?
- How do we smell different odors and taste different flavors?
- How do we feel pressure, temperature, and pain? How are we able to keep our balance? And how do we know what our body is doing without watching it?
- What happens if we are deprived of all sensory information?

Sensation: The process of receiving, translating, and transmitting information to the brain from the external and internal environments.

EXPERIENCING SENSATIONS

To experience sensations, we must have both a means of detecting stimuli and a means of converting them into a language the brain can understand. By their nature, our sensory organs accomplish both goals. They are effective in detecting light, sound, tastes, odors, heat, and other stimuli that they then convert into signals that are sent to the brain.

• How do our sensory organs gather sensory information and convert it into signals the brain can understand?

Sensory Processing: Transduction, Reduction, and Coding

Our sense organs contain cells called receptors that receive and process sensory information from the environment. For each sense, these specialized cells respond to a distinct stimulus, such as sound waves and odor molecules. Through a process called transduction, the receptors convert the stimulus into neural impulses, which are sent to the brain. In hearing, for example, tiny receptor cells in the inner ear transduce mechanical vibrations (from sound waves) into electrochemical signals. These signals are carried by neurons to the brain. Each type of sensory receptor is designed to detect a wide variety of stimuli and a wide range of stimulation. However, also built into our sensory systems are structures that purposefully reduce the amount of stimuli we receive.

Why would we want to reduce the amount of sensory information we receive? Can you imagine what would happen if you did not have some natural filtering of stimuli? You would constantly hear blood rushing through your veins and continually feel your clothes brushing against your skin. Obviously, some level of filtering is needed so the brain is not overwhelmed with unnecessary information. It needs to be free to respond to those stimuli that have meaning for survival. Each of our senses is therefore custom-designed to respond to only a select range of potential sensory information. All species have evolved selective receptors that suppress or amplify information in order to survive. For example, hawks have an acute sense of vision but a poor sense of smell. Similarly, although we humans cannot sense many stimuli (such as ultraviolet or infrared light),

Receptors: Body cells specialized to detect and respond to stimulus energy.

Transduction: The process by which energy stimulating a receptor is converted into neural impulses.

75

INTRODUCTORY PARAGRAPH AND SURVEY QUESTIONS

After the opening vignette is a paragraph of commentary that also presents the major topics that will be discussed in the chapter. It concludes with a list of four to six Survey Questions. These are general questions you should be asking yourself as you read the chapter. For reinforcement, they are repeated in the margin at the place they are discussed. These questions are an important part of the SQ4R method described in the preface and in the Student Study Guide that accompanies this text.

RUNNING GLOSSARY

Key terms and concepts, which are bold-faced in the text the first time they appear, are defined. They are also printed again in the margin and defined in a "running glossary." The running glossary provides a helpful way of reviewing key terms before tests. If you want to check the meaning of a key term from another chapter, use the end-of-book glossary.

TRY THIS YOURSELF ACTIVITIES

In each chapter you will find several opportunities to apply what you are learning. These "Try This Yourself" sections are identified with the special icon shown above. These brief activities are fun to do, and research shows that actively involving yourself in learning increases comprehension and retention.

ILLUSTRATIONS

Don't skip over the photos, figures, and tables. They visually reinforce important concepts and therefore often contain material that may appear on exams.

---

we can see a candle burning 30 miles away on a dark, clear night, hear the tick of a watch at 20 feet under quiet conditions, and smell one drop of perfume in a six-room apartment (Galanter, 1962).

In the process of sensory reduction, we not only filter incoming sensations, we also analyze the sensations sent through before a neural impulse is finally sent to the cortex of the brain. This analysis is performed by cells in the reticular activating system (RAS) within the brain stem (see Chapter 2). The RAS determines whether or not incoming sensory information is important. If important, it passes the information on to the cerebral cortex. Because of this screening process, parents of a newborn, for example, can sleep through passing sirens and blaring stereos yet awaken to the slightest whimper of their baby.

How does the brain differentiate between various incoming sensations, such as sounds and smells? It does so through a process called coding. Coding for a specific sensation depends on the number and type of sensory cells that are activated, on the precise nerve that is stimulated, and ultimately on the part of the brain that the nerve stimulates. In other words, sounds and smells are interpreted as distinct sensations not because of the environmental stimuli that activate them but because their respective neural impulses travel by different routes and arrive at different parts of the brain. Figure 3.1 illustrates the parts of the brain involved in sensory reception.

Coding: The three-part process that converts a particular sensory input into a specific sensation.

 Try This Yourself

To personally experience coding, close your eyes and with your fingertips press *gently* on your eyelids for about 30 seconds. The visual sensations you experience (circles; streams of light) reflect the fact that the receptor cells at the backs of your eyes are prepared to code any kind of stimulation, including pressure, into visual patterns. So even though you aren't looking at anything, you still "see" something because your visual receptors have been stimulated. ∎

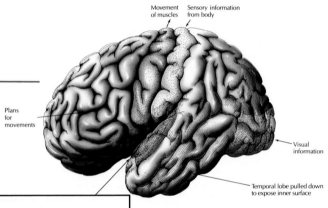

Movement of muscles

Sensory information from body

Plans for movements

Visual information

Temporal lobe pulled down to expose inner surface

...reas of the brain. Neural impulses travel from the sensory receptors to various parts of

---

Critical Thinking
PSYCHOLOGY IN ACTION
CONDUCTING SOCRATIC DISCUSSIONS
Thinking about Sensation

At the heart of critical thinking is critical questioning. The ability to delve beneath the superficial or rise above mere appearances by considering logical consequences and possible boundaries is the core of critical thinking. Socrates, an ancient Greek philosopher, modeled this type of thinking in his question-and-answer method of teaching. In a Socratic discussion, the questioner uses probing questions to learn what the other person thinks, to help the respondent develop his or her ideas, and to mutually explore the implications, consequences, and values of an idea. In turn, the respondent is comfortable and doesn't become offended, defensive, or intimidated, because he or she knows the *shared* purpose is to clarify and evaluate a line of reasoning.

In this exercise, we offer several questions related to Chapter 3 that will help you practice the method of Socratic discussion. Select a good friend or classmate to simulate the roles of "questioner" and "respondent." One of you should play Socrates and question the other for half the questions; then reverse roles for the remaining questions. We are providing sample questions that Socrates might ask, and the respondent's answers should be followed up with questions such as: "Why?" "How do you know?" "What is your reason for saying that?" "For example?" "Can I summarize your point as . . . ?" Relax and enjoy your role as both the questioner and respondent. Critical, Socratic questioners do not attempt to make the other person look stupid. This should be a fun "mind game" that stretches your intellectual capacity and de-velops your critical thinking skills. (A by-product of this exercise is that it will help you master the chapter material.)

Sample Socratic Questions

1. Is there a sound if no one is there to hear it? Does a hamburger have a taste if no one is there to taste it?

2. What would the world be like if the absolute thresholds for sensation were changed? If we could see X rays and ultraviolet light or infrared rays and radar? If we were like bats and dolphins and could hear sounds up to 100,000 hertz?

3. What would happen if each sensory receptor (e.g., eyes, ears, skin) were receptive to every type of incoming stimuli? If your eyes were also sensitive to sound waves and odor molecules, could the brain distinguish and integrate this information?

4. William James, a famous early psychologist, suggested that, "If a master surgeon were to cross the auditory and optic nerves, then we would hear lightning and see thunder." How do you explain this statement?

5. How do you explain the fact that blind people tend to be better adjusted psychologically and less subject to emotional difficulties than deaf people?

6. If you had to choose between losing vision, hearing, or touch, which would it be? Why? What effect would it have on your life?

Intentional Deprivation: The Benefits of Boredom

Considering the extreme boredom, hallucinations, and occasional panic experienced by the students in the original studies of sensory deprivation, it is surprising that researchers have found beneficial uses for it. In the early 1960s, a psychiatrist named John C. Lilly set out to study deprivation effects by donning a diving helmet and immersing himself in a dark, soundproof tank of highly saline, buoyant water. During his immersion, Lilly reported experiencing "out of body" sensations, mind trips to other dimensions, and a general sense of being born again (Lilly, 1972). Other proponents of "tanking" claim that it produces a blissful, relaxed state of mind and vivid, enjoyable hallucinations.

Why did Bexton, Heron, and Scott's subjects experience such an unpleasant state if people who engage in tanking find it so enjoyable? One of the major reasons for the difference may be the power of suggestion. In Bexton, Heron, and Scott's studies, participants were unwittingly led to expect negative experiences, since they were given medical release forms to sign and "panic buttons" to push if they became too stressed. However, the results may also be due to a time factor. Whereas the McGill students experienced deprivation for many hours or even days, people in isolation tanks stay for, at the most, a few hours.

CRITICAL THINKING EXERCISE

Each chapter contains a special critical thinking exercise. These exercises provide important insights into the chapter material, while also improving your basic critical thinking skills.

NARRATIVE QUESTIONS

These imbedded, narrative questions model for you the process of active learning and the questioning goal for the SQ4R method. This helps focus your reading and increases comprehension.

106   CHAPTER 3 / SENSATION

Gender and Cultural Diversity

SEEKING SENSORY DEPRIVATION

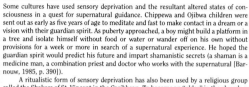

Some cultures have used sensory deprivation and the resultant altered states of consciousness in a quest for supernatural guidance. Chippewa and Ojibwa children were sent out as early as five years of age to meditate and fast to make contact in a dream or a vision with their guardian spirit. As puberty approached, a boy might build a platform in a tree and isolate himself without food or water or wander off on his own without provisions for a week or more in search of a supernatural experience. He hoped the guardian spirit would predict his future and impart shamanistic secrets (a shaman is a medicine man, a combination priest and doctor who works with the supernatural [Barnouw, 1985, p. 390]).

A ritualistic form of sensory deprivation has also been used by a religious group called the Shakers of St. Vincent in the Caribbean. To become an "elder" in the church, a person must participate in a sensory deprivation ceremony called *mourning*. (The elders need not be old and the mourning is for their own sins.) Mourning involves a week or two of sensory isolation during which the prospective elder lies blindfolded on a pallet and discusses any spiritual experiences with a church official. It is possible that many of these experiences are similar to those experienced by John C. Lilly and the subjects in the Bexton, Heron, and Scott experiments at McGill University. ∎

A Chippewa Indian

Sensory Substitution: Natural and Artificial Compensation

Another interesting finding from deprivation research is that when sensory stimulation is blocked for one sense, the body compensates by increasing sensitivity in other senses. In a study by Bross, Harper, and Sicz (1980), the visual sensitivity of experimental subjects made artificially deaf first dropped and then rebounded to above starting levels. Researchers have also been successful in developing sensory substitution systems with devices that substitute vibrations on the skin for sensory impairments (Lechet, 1986).

Helen Keller similarly learned to "see" and "hear" with her sense of touch, and she often recognized visitors by their smell or by vibrations from their walk. Despite the heightened sensitivity of her functioning senses, however, Helen professed a lifelong yearning to experience a normal sensory world. She gave this advice to those whose senses are "normal":

> *I who am blind can give one hint to those who see: use your eyes as if tomorrow you would be stricken blind. And the same method can be applied to the other senses. Hear the music of voices, the song of a bird, the mighty strains of an orchestra as if you would be stricken deaf tomorrow. Touch each object as if tomorrow your tactile sense would fail. Smell the perfume of flowers, taste with relish each morsel as if tomorrow you could never smell and taste again. Make the most of every sense, glory in all the facets of pleasure and beauty which the world reveals to you through the several means of contact which nature provides.*
> (1962, p. 23)

Review Questions

1. What are some of the effects of sensory deprivation?
2. The technique termed REST, which is based on sensory deprivation, has been successful in treating ——————, a severe childhood psychological disorder.
3. What is meant by "sensory substitutio

Answers to Review Questions c

GENDER AND CULTURAL DIVERSITY SECTIONS

These sections embedded in the running narrative of each chapter are identified with a separate heading and a special icon, shown above. To succeed in today's world, you must be aware of other cultures and important gender issues.

REVIEW QUESTIONS

Each major section of a chapter concludes with 4 to 10 self-test comprehension questions. These review questions give you feedback on whether you have "drifted off" or fully mastered the major concepts in that section. Use these questions to review for exams, too. The answers for all questions are found in an appendix at the back of the text.

SUGGESTED READINGS   35

6. Psychological findings can be applied to improve our personal lives. The study of psychology leads to an appreciation for scientific methods of research, as opposed to pseudo-scientific methods.

PSYCHOLOGICAL RESEARCH

7. Research methodology includes experimental techniques designed to investigate cause-and-effect relationships and nonexperimental techniques that provide descriptions of behavior.

8. An experiment begins with a hypothesis or possible explanation for behavior. Independent variables are the factors the experimenter manipulates and dependent variables are measurable behaviors of the subjects. Experimental control includes assigning subjects to groups and holding extraneous variables constant.

9. Nonexperimental research techniques are used to obtain descriptions of behavior. Naturalistic observation is used to study behavior in its natural habitat. Surveys use interviews or questionnaires to obtain information on a sample of subjects. Individual case studies are in-depth studies of single subjects.

10. Experiments enable us to determine causes for behaviors, whereas correlational relationships only enable us to predict behaviors.

11. Psychologists use statistics to judge whether research findings are significant or due to chance.

ETHICS IN PSYCHOLOGY

12. Psychologists are expected to maintain high ethical standards in their relations with human and animal research subjects and in therapeutic relationships with clients. The APA has published specific guidelines detailing these ethical standards.

SCHOOLS OF PSYCHOLOGY

13. Psychologists have grouped together to form various schools of psychology with distinct approaches to the study of behavior. Structuralists attempted to identify elements of consciousness and how these elements form the structure of the mind. Functionalists studied the functions of mental processes in adapting the individual to the environment. They broadened the scope of psychology and extended its influence to such fields as education and industry.

14. Freud's psychoanalytic theory examined psychological problems that were presumed to be caused by unconscious conflicts. The Gestalt school studied organizing principles of perceptual processes and paved the way for an eclectic approach.

15. Behaviorism emphasizes observable behaviors and the ways they are learned. Humanistic psychology focuses on inner meanings and assumes our nature is positive and growth-seeking. Cognitive psychology examines reasoning and mental processes.

16. Psychobiology attempts to explain behavior as complex chemical and biological events within the brain.

REVIEW OF MAJOR CONCEPTS

At the end of each chapter, the entire chapter is summarized in sentence outline form. The summary provides an additional opportunity to see how all the topics and subtopics within the chapter are interrelated. This section also reinforces the key terms and concepts from the chapter, but it does not explain them. Therefore, it is not an alternative to reading the chapter.

SUGGESTED READINGS

The list of suggested readings at the end of each chapter is useful for term paper research, as well as general interest and personal growth. Some are academic sources, and others are popular books and articles, but all are readable and informative.

SUGGESTED READINGS

AMERICAN PSYCHOLOGICAL ASSOCIATION. (1986). *Careers in psychology.* Washington, DC: APA. This booklet is available free to students from the American Psychological Association, 1200 17th Street NW, Washington, DC 20036.

AMERICAN PSYCHOLOGICAL ASSOCIATION. (1990). Ethical principles of psychologists. *American Psychologist, 45*, 390–395. This article lists and discusses the ethical principles involved with clinical practice, research with human subjects, and research with animals.

BRISLIN, R. (1993). *Understanding culture's influence on behavior.* Orlando, FL: Harcourt Brace Jovanovich. A fun book to read, especially for people who like people.

COZBY, P. C. (1989). *Methods in behavioral research.* (4th ed.) Palo Alto, CA: Mayfield. An introduction to the use of research methods in psychology.

MILGRAM, S. (1974). *Obedience to authority.* New York: Harper & Row. In this book, Milgram describes his original experiments.

SCHULTZ, D. P., & SCHULTZ, S. E. (1992). *A history of modern psychology* (5th ed.). Orlando, FL: Harcourt, Brace, Jovanovich. A short history of psychology.

STANOVICH, K. E. (1991). *How to think straight about psychology.* New York: HarperCollins. An interesting book on how to evaluate psychological and pseudopsychological research.

THREE STUDY TIPS

Now that you have a sense of the book as a whole and how to approach each chapter, you are on your way to meeting your twin goals—mastering the material and demonstrating your mastery. We'd like to send you off with three guaranteed-to-work study tips:

1. **Use the SQ4R method.** These initials stand for the six steps in effective reading: Survey, Question, Read, Recite, Review, and wRite. Here's how to apply SQ4R to this textbook.

   - *Survey* the chapter using the outline, opening vignette, introductory paragraph, and survey questions.

   - To maintain your attention and increase comprehension as you read, turn the heading of each section into a *question*. The survey questions listed at the beginning of the chapter and repeated in the margin do this for the main sections. Use them as a model for turning the second- and third-level headings into questions.

   - As you *read* the chapter, attempt to answer the questions you form from the headings.

   - After you have read and looked for answers to your questions, stop and *recite* your answers. Either say them quietly to yourself or write them down.

   - Answer the *review* questions at the end of each major section. Write down your responses and check your answers at the back of the book.

   - In addition to the writing you do in the above steps, add to the *wRiting* component of the SQ4R method by taking brief notes to yourself in the text margins about points that are unclear. Use these notes to ask questions during class lectures. The SQ4R method may sound time consuming, but our students have found that it actually saves time while also increasing their understanding of the material.

2. **Distribute your study time.** While it is important to review before a quiz or exam, if you wait until the last minute to cram a lot of material into a short, intensive study period you are not likely to do well in any college class. One of the clearest findings in psychology is that spaced practice is a much more efficient way to study and learn than massed practice (see Chapter 7). Just as you wouldn't wait until the night before a big basketball game to begin practicing your freethrows, you can't begin to study the night before an exam.

3. **Actively listen to class lectures.** Arrive on time and don't leave class early—you may miss important notes and assignments. Listen *actively* during lecture. Ask questions if you don't understand. Look at the instructor while he or she is talking. Focus your attention on what is being said by asking yourself, "What is the main idea?" Write down the key ideas and supporting details and examples. Include important names, dates, and new terms. But don't try to write everything the instructor says word for word. This is passive, rote copying, not active listening. Leave enough space in your notes so you can add material if the lecturer goes back to a topic or expands on the discussion. Pay particular attention to anything the instructor writes on the board. Lecturers generally take the time to write on the board those concepts they feel are most important to your learning.

If you would like more information on study skills, consult any of the following books. CARMAN, R. A., & ADAMS, W. R. (1985). *Study skills: A student's guide for survival.* New York: Wiley.

WALTER, T. L., & SIEBERT, A. (1993). *Student success: How to succeed in college and still have time for your friends.* Orlando, FL: Harcourt Brace Jovanovich.

YOUNG, S. (1991). *Straight talk on college: A real world perspective.* Nashville, TN: Straight Talk Publications.

We hope that you will enjoy reading our third edition of *Psychology in Action.* As the name implies, we believe that psychology is a vital science that is fascinating to learn and of practical use throughout your life. You will be the best judge of how well we have reached our goals. Please send us your comments, complaints, and questions while you are reading the text. We value your opinion and would appreciate your feedback.

Address correspondence to:

Karen Huffman, Mark Vernoy, or Judy Vernoy
Behavioral Sciences Department
Palomar College
San Marcos, CA 92069

Critical Thinking

A great many people think they are thinking when they are merely rearranging their prejudices.

William James

Although the ability to think critically has always been important, it is now imperative. The world has greatly increased its complexity and cultural diversity. The choices we make today about endangered species, diminishing rain forests, homelessness, urban crime, the world's rapidly expanding population, and hotspots of war and conflict will affect not only us and our families but future generations as well. How do we make decisions on such important issues?

There is no shortage of information available to help us in life decisions. In fact, as a college student, you have ready access to mountains of information. Think about the last research paper you did. You could go beyond your library by using a personal computer and modem to search thousands of daily newspapers, research journal articles, and encyclopedia services.

The problem is not a lack of data but knowing what to do with the information explosion. Information must be interpreted, evaluated, digested, synthesized, and applied logically and rationally. In short, as a student and as a citizen, you must be a critical thinker.

WHAT IS "CRITICAL THINKING"?

Critical thinking has many meanings and some books dedicate entire chapters to defining the term. The word *critical* comes from the Greek word *kritikos,* which means to question, make sense of, be able to analyze. *Thinking* is the cognitive activity involved in making sense of the world around us. *Critical thinking,* therefore, is defined as thinking about and evaluating our thoughts, feelings, and behavior so that we can clarify and improve them (adapted from Chaffee, 1988, p. 29).

Critical thinking is a process. As a process—something you *do*—you can do it *better.* You can develop your critical thinking skills. Each chapter of *Psychology in Action* (and corresponding chapters in the Student Study Guide and Instructor's Manual) includes a specific critical thinking exercise devoted to improving one or more of the specific components of critical thinking. To learn more about each of these components, study the following three lists. They present the affective (emotional), cognitive (thinking), and behavioral (action) components of critical thinking. You will no doubt find that you already employ some of these skills. You will also no doubt recognize areas that need strengthening through practice. We hope you will also see opportunities to apply critical thinking to areas of your life where strong emotional reactions to issues have hampered your decision-making abilities.

THE CRITICAL THINKING PROCESS

Affective Components—the emotional foundation that either enables or limits critical thinking.

- *Valuing truth above self-interest.*   Critical thinkers must hold themselves and those they agree with to the same intellectual standards to which they hold their opponents.
- *Accepting change.*   Critical thinkers remain open to the need for adjustment and adaptation throughout the life cycle. Because critical thinkers fully trust the processes of reasoned inquiry, they are willing to use these skills to examine even their most deeply held values and beliefs, and to modify these beliefs when evidence and experience contradict them.
- *Empathizing.*   Critical thinkers appreciate and try to understand others' thoughts, feelings, and behaviors. Noncritical thinkers view everything and everyone in relation to the self.
- *Welcoming divergent views.*   Critical thinkers value examining issues from every angle, and know that it is especially important to explore and understand positions with which they disagree.
- *Tolerating ambiguity.*   Although formal education often trains students to look for a single "right" answer, critical thinkers recognize that many issues are complex, intricate, and subtle, and that complex issues may not have a "right" answer. They recognize and value qualifiers such as "probably," "highly likely," and "not very likely."
- *Recognizing personal biases.*   Critical thinkers use their highest intellectual skills to detect personal biases and self-deceptive reasoning so they can design realistic plans for self-correction.

Cognitive Components—the thought processes actually involved in critical thinking.

- *Thinking independently.*   Critical thinking is autonomous, independent thinking. Critical thinkers do not passively accept the beliefs of others and are not easily manipulated.
- *Defining problems accurately.*   A critical thinker identifies the issues in clear and concrete terms, to prevent confusion and lay the foundation for gathering relevant information.
- *Analyzing data for value and content.*   By carefully evaluating the nature of evidence and the credibility of the source, critical thinkers recognize illegitimate appeals to emotion, unsupported assumptions, and faulty logic. This enables them to discount sources of information that lack a record of honesty, contradict themselves on key questions, or have a vested interest in selling a product or idea.
- *Employing a variety of thinking processes in problem solving.*   Among these are the ability to use each of the following skills: *inductive logic*—reasoning that moves from the specific to the general; *deductive logic*—reasoning that moves from the general to the specific; *dialogical thinking*—thinking that involves an extended verbal exchange between differing points of view or frames of reference; and *dialectical thinking*—thinking conducted in order to test the strengths and weaknesses of opposing points of view.
- *Synthesizing.*   Critical thinkers recognize that comprehension and understanding result from combining various elements into meaningful patterns.
- *Resisting overgeneralization.*   Overgeneralization is the temptation to apply a fact or experience to situations that are only superficially similar to the original context.
- *Employing metacognition.*   Metacognition, also known as reflective or recursive thinking, involves a review and analysis of your own mental processes—thinking about your own thinking.

Behavioral Components—the actions necessary for critical thinking.

- *Delaying judgment until adequate data is available.*   A critical thinker does not make snap judgments.

- *Employing precise terms.*   Precise terms help critical thinkers identify the issues clearly and concretely so they can be objectively defined and empirically tested.

- *Gathering data.*   Collecting up-to-date, relevant information on all sides of an issue is a priority before making decisions.

- *Distinguishing fact from opinion.*   Facts are statements that can be proven true. Opinions are statements that express how a person feels about an issue or what someone thinks is true.

- *Encouraging critical dialogue.*   Critical thinkers are active questioners who challenge existing facts and opinions and welcome questions in return. Socratic questioning is an important type of critical dialogue where the questioner deeply probes the meaning, justification, or logical strength of a claim, position, or line of reasoning.

- *Listening actively.*   Critical thinkers fully engage their thinking skills when listening to another.

- *Modifying judgments in light of new information.*   Critical thinkers are willing to abandon or modify previous judgments if later evidence or experience contradicts them.

- *Applying knowledge to new situations.*   When critical thinkers master a new skill or discover an insight, they transfer this information to new contexts. Noncritical thinkers can often provide correct answers, repeat definitions, and carry out calculations, yet be unable to transfer their knowledge to new situations because of a basic lack of understanding.

Psychology in Action

Introducing Psychology

OUTLINE

$\mathcal{P}$retend for the moment that you are one of the people responding to this ad. As you arrive at the Yale University laboratory, you are introduced to the experimenter and to another **subject** (another participant in the experiment). The experimenter explains that he is studying the effects of punishment on learning and memory, and that one of you will play the role of a learner and the other will play the role of a teacher. You draw lots, and on your paper is written "teacher." The experimenter leads you into a room where he straps the other subject—the "learner"—into an "electric chair" apparatus that looks escape-proof. The experimenter then applies some electrode paste to the learner's wrist "to avoid blisters and burns" and attaches an electrode that is connected to a shock generator.

You are then shown into an adjacent room and asked to sit in front of the shock generator, which is wired through the wall to the chair of the "learner." As you can see in Figure 1.1, the shock machine consists of 30 switches that represent succeedingly higher levels of shock in 15-volt increments. In addition, labels appear below each group of levers, ranging from "slight shock," to "danger: severe shock," all the way to "XXX." The experimenter explains that it is your job to teach the learner a list of word pairs and to punish any errors by administering a shock. With each wrong answer, you are to give a shock one level higher on the shock generator—for example, at the first wrong response, you give a shock of 15 volts; at the second wrong response, 30 volts; and so on.

As the experiment begins, the learner seems to be having problems with the task because the responses are often wrong. Thus, you find that before long you are inflicting shocks that must be extremely painful. Indeed, after you administer 150 volts, the learner begins to protest and demands, "Get me out of here . . . I refuse to go on."

You hesitate and wonder what you should do. The experimenter urges you to continue and insists that even if the learner makes no response, you must keep increasing the shock levels. But the other person is obviously in pain. What should you do? Should you keep giving the shocks or should you stop?

Actual subjects participated in a series of such experiments and suffered real conflict when confronted

with this problem. The following dialogue took place between the experimenter and a subject in one of these experiments (Milgram, 1974, pp. 73–74):

Subject: I can't stand it. I'm not going to kill that man in there. You hear him hollering?

Experimenter: As I told you before, the shocks may be painful, but [there is no permanent tissue damage].

Learner (screaming): Let me out of here, you have no right to keep me here. Let me out of here, let me out, my heart's bothering me, let me out! *(Subject shakes head, pats the table nervously.)*

Subject: You see, he's hollering. Hear that? Gee, I don't know.

Experimenter: The experiment requires . . .

Subject (interrupting): I know it does, sir, but I mean—hunh! He don't know what he's getting in for. He's up to 195 volts! *(Experiment continues through 210 volts, 225 volts, 240 volts, 255 volts, 270 volts, at which point the teacher, with evident relief, runs out of word-pair questions.)*

Experimenter: You'll have to go back to the beginning of that page and go through them again until he's learned them all correctly.

Subject: Aw, no I'm not going to kill that man. You mean I've got to keep going up with the scale? No sir. He's hollering in there. I'm not going to give him 450 volts.

SUBJECT: A participant in a research study.

What do you think happened? Did the man continue? It may surprise you that this particular subject continued to give shocks in spite of the learner's strong protests and even continued to the highest level when the learner refused to give any more answers.

As you may have guessed, the purpose of this experiment was not really to study the effects of punishment on learning. The psychologist who designed the experiment, Stanley Milgram, was investigating the question of obedience to authority. In fact, no shocks were administered at all—the "learner" was an accomplice of the experimenter

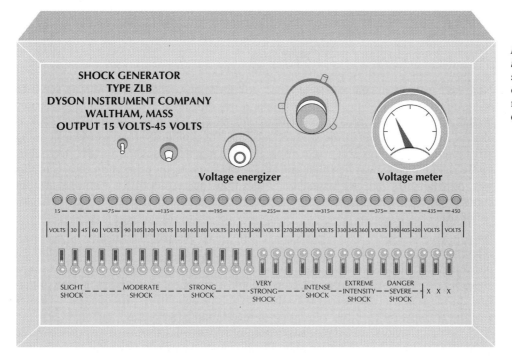

Figure 1.1 Milgram's shock generator. This is the apparatus Milgram's subjects used in the experiment on obeying authority. Note how clearly marked the effects are, from slight to dangerous.

and simply pretended to be shocked.

How obedient do you think you would have been? Milgram conducted a survey to determine how people expected they would perform in such an experiment. No one predicted that they would go past the 300-volt level, and less than 25 percent predicted that they would go beyond 150 volts. Even Milgram was surprised when a full 65 percent of the subjects actually administered the maximum shock intensity.

This book is an introduction to the study of psychology. As you read you will discover that most psychological research is not quite so "shocking" as Milgram's, but you will probably be pleasantly surprised to find that much of it is just as interesting. When asked what they expect from a course in psychology, students often say that they expect to find out "how the mind works," "what makes people break down and go crazy," "how to raise children," "the meaning of dreams and personality tests," and so on. We will discuss these topics. We will also answer such questions as: How do people learn? How do we remember things? What motivates some people to starve themselves to the point of death while others eat themselves into obesity? Should anger be controlled and suppressed, or should its expression be encouraged? How does stress affect our physical and psychological functioning? Why do we like some people and not others? What makes some people so influential and powerful, while others are mindless followers and socially ineffective?

In this chapter, we will define psychology and explain its goals, provide an overview of the fields in which psychologists are involved, introduce the types of psychological research, speak to the ethics expected of psychologists, and outline the schools of psychology that have led to its present perspectives.

As you read Chapter 1, keep the following **Survey** questions in mind and answer them in your own words:

- What is psychology and what are its goals? What are the different fields of psychology?

- What is the advantage of conducting an experiment to study a research question, and how do researchers conduct experiments?

- What are the nonexperimental research techniques, and what are their merits and limitations?

- How are research and clinical psychologists encouraged to uphold ethical behavior and procedure?

- What are the major perspectives from which psychologists have approached the study of psychology?

UNDERSTANDING PSYCHOLOGY

• *What is psychology and what are its goals? What are the different fields of psychology?*

Psychology: The scientific study of behavior.

Behavior: Anything a person or animal does, feels, thinks, or experiences.

Overt: Observable, not concealed.

Covert: Hidden or unobservable.

Milgram's experiment demonstrates that we cannot always rely on common sense to accurately predict behavior, whether it is our own or others'. Rather, to ensure reliable predictions, behavior needs to be studied objectively and scientifically. This book is about psychology, the *scientific* study of behavior. Psychologists study behavior by using strict scientific methods. They follow standardized scientific procedures to collect information about a particular behavior and to analyze and interpret the information. In this way, psychologists can be reasonably certain that the results of their studies are not contaminated by their own personal attitudes or by factors unrelated to the behavior being studied.

Isn't "behavior" a rather narrow area of study?   In everyday language behavior may refer primarily to the way people act, but in psychology it is used to describe anything a person or animal does, feels, thinks, or experiences. Behaviors range from depressing a shock lever to running a marathon, from solving a complicated math problem to forgetting the name of a longtime friend, from suffering the delightful thrill of a roller-coaster ride to experiencing the utter relaxation of meditation.

Some behaviors are overt—easily seen or identified. Others are covert—covered or hidden, and not directly observable. Psychologists have been quite clever in finding ways to measure not only overt but also covert behaviors. To measure unobservable, covert behaviors, researchers use a variety of creative techniques. If Milgram had wanted to study his subjects' anxiety levels, for example, he could have used electrocardiograph (EKG) and other apparatus to measure their heart rate, blood pressure, muscle tension, and so on.

The Goals of Psychology: Describe, Explain, Predict, and Change

The first step in understanding the complex world of psychology is to look at its four basic goals: to describe, explain, predict, and change behavior. In some studies, psychologists attempt merely to *describe* particular behaviors by making careful scientific observations. In other studies, psychologists also try to *explain* behaviors by conducting experiments to determine their causes. Psychologists often use research information to *predict* when the behavior being studied will occur in the future. They can also apply research findings to *change* inappropriate behavior or circumstances.

Milgram's study achieved all these goals. He was able to *describe* how his subjects behaved when an authority figure told them to do something that was opposed to their sense of right and wrong. He was able to *explain* why subjects acted in this way by systematically varying certain experimental conditions. For example, by varying whether or not the teacher and the learner were in the same room, Milgram found that remoteness from the "victim" (the learner) is a contributing cause of obedience.

By applying Milgram's results to the real world, it is possible to *predict* the behavior of people in similar situations. For example, officers in the armed forces might use Milgram's findings to predict that pilots would be more likely to obey orders to fire a missile at a distant obscure city than to kill someone with their bare hands.

Findings from Milgram's and similar research are being used today to *change* behavior. For example, parents and educators now teach children to question authority in critical or dangerous situations rather than to automatically obey. In an effort to prevent sexual molestation, many schools present special programs to young children. Puppet shows, role playing, class discussion, and other techniques are being used to teach children to say "no" when adults touch them inappropriately or do something they feel is uncomfortable. On a personal note, you might find ways to apply Milgram's results in changing your own behavior when someone insists that you do something questionable. For instance, you might seek a second opinion when your doctor says you need surgery.

Basic Research

Often researchers such as Stanley Milgram study some aspect of behavior with no thought of how their results can be applied to the real world. Known as basic research, this type of research is usually conducted in universities or in research laboratories to test new theories and models of behavior and may or may not have any immediate real-world applications. Basic research is conducted in all major subfields of psychology. Recent research on memory (Estes, 1991; Hintzman, 1990) testing mathematical models of how people acquire and retain information is an example of basic research. Memory is the subject of Chapter 7. Another example of basic research is a long-term study spanning the past quarter of a century that has been directed at delineating the differences between the right and left sides of the brain (Hellige, 1990). Split-brain research is detailed in Chapter 2. Perception, how we perceive the external world using our senses of touch, taste, smell, sight, and hearing, is a major area of basic research (Banks and Krajicek, 1991). All of Chapter 4 is dedicated to the topic of perception.

Basic Research: Research conducted to study theoretical questions without trying to solve a specific problem.

In basic research, then, we use the goals of psychology to study behavior for its own sake—simply for knowledge. When we want to use the goals of psychology to solve existing real-world problems, we need to conduct applied research.

Applied Research

Applied research is conducted to answer specific real-world questions about behavior. Although applied research is conducted in nearly all psychological disciplines, certain ones are known as applied research areas. These are industrial/organizational psychology, environmental psychology, sports psychology, consumer psychology, health psychology, and clinical psychology.

Applied Research: Research that utilizes the principles and discoveries of psychology for practical purposes, to solve real-world problems.

Industrial/organizational psychology applies the principles of psychology to the workplace (Aamodt, 1991, p. 4). It includes personnel psychology—personnel selection and evaluation; organizational psychology—the study of leadership, job satisfaction, employee motivation, and group processes within the organization; and training and development. Industrial/organizational psychology is discussed in more detail in Chapter 17.

Environmental psychology is the study of the behavioral reactions to changes in the environment. For example, environmental psychologists have found that recovery from stress is faster when subjects are exposed to natural rather than urban environments (Ulrich et al., 1991).

Sports psychology studies ways psychological principles can be applied to enhance athletic performance, such as using mental imagery and mental practice to improve athletic performance (Murphy, 1990).

Applying psychological principles to consumer behavior is the realm of consumer psychologists, who study the decision-making processes of consumers as well as their patterns of consumption (Cohen and Chakravarti, 1990). Many topics of interest to consumer psychologists are discussed in Chapter 17.

We devote entire chapters to health psychology (Chapter 13), in which we discuss how following recommended health practices such as exercising and not smoking contributes to good health, and clinical psychology (Chapter 16), in which we detail the various types of therapy techniques.

As you can guess from the diverse nature of applied areas, psychologists who conduct applied research work in many different settings. They might work for government agencies, large corporations, hospitals, or in academia.

Areas of Psychology: A Field of Diversity

Psychologists perform a wide variety of roles in a wide variety of areas. They serve as mental health providers, researchers, consultants, and university and college professors. Often wearing more than one hat, a psychologist might teach, conduct research, and be

Clinical and counseling psychologists help people with emotional problems.

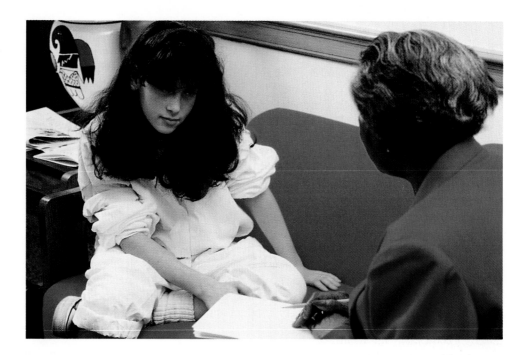

an industrial consultant at the same time, or have a private practice of clients in therapy while conducting ongoing research. Most psychologists specialize in one particular area. Some of these, but by no means all, are listed below:

Clinical and counseling psychologists work with mentally ill or emotionally disturbed people by doing therapy or counseling. Students often wonder about the difference between a psychiatrist and a clinical psychologist. Psychiatrists are true medical doctors in that they have gone to medical school and have received their M.D. degrees with a specialization in psychiatry; thus, they are licensed to prescribe medications and drugs. Clinical psychologists, on the other hand, have gone to graduate school and have received Ph.D. degrees after intense study of human behavior and methods of therapy.

Educational psychologists study the processes of education—how people learn and what teaching techniques work best.

School psychologists work with educators to promote the intellectual, social, and emotional development of children in the school environment.

Industrial/organizational psychologists are employed to help companies run more smoothly and productively.

Developmental psychologists study physical, social, cognitive, and personality development from conception to death.

Social psychologists are interested in the behavior of people in group situations.

Comparative psychologists study animal behavior to gain insights into how both animals and humans behave.

Educational psychologists study how people learn in an attempt to improve the quality of education for our children. Here, by using a one-way mirror, an educational psychologist observes an educational setting without being observed herself.

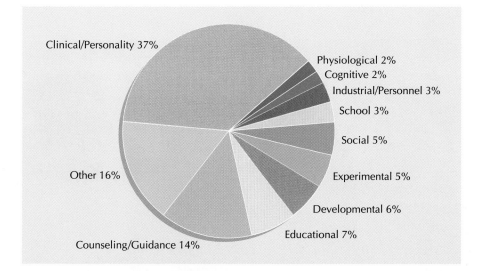

Physiological psychologists study the relationship of the brain and the rest of the nervous system to behavior.

Health psychologists are concerned with how psychology can contribute to maintaining good health and health care practices.

Cognitive psychologists study the mental processes involved in gathering and organizing information and processing and storing it. In other words, they study sensation, perception, learning, thinking processes, language usage, and memory.

To get an idea of the relative number of psychologists working in different fields of psychology, see Figure 1.2. This figure shows the percentages of doctorate degrees con-

Table 1.1   **The Divisions of the American Psychological Association**

1. General Psychology	27. Community Psychology
2. Teaching of Psychology	28. Psychopharmacology
3. Experimental Psychology	29. Psychotherapy
5. Evaluation and Measurement	30. Psychological Hypnosis
6. Physiological and Comparative Psychology	31. State Psychological Association Affairs
7. Developmental Psychology	32. Humanistic Psychology
8. Personality and Social Psychology	33. Mental Retardation
9. Society for the Psychological Study of Social Issues	34. Population and Environmental Psychology
10. Psychology and the Arts	35. Psychology of Women
12. Clinical Psychology	36. Psychologists Interested in Religious Issues
13. Consulting Psychology	37. Child, Youth, and Family Services
14. Society for Industrial and Organizational Psychology	38. Health Psychology
15. Educational Psychology	39. Psychoanalysis
16. School Psychology	40. Clinical Neuropsychology
17. Counseling Psychology	41. Psychology and Law
18. Psychologists in Public Service	42. Psychologists in Independent Practice
19. Military Psychology	43. Family Psychology
20. Adult Development and Aging	44. Society for the Psychological Study of Lesbian and Gay Issues
21. Applied Experimental and Engineering Psychologists	45. Society for the Psychological Study of Ethnic Minority Issues
22. Rehabilitation Psychology	46. Media Psychology
23. Consumer Psychology	47. Exercise and Sport Psychology
24. Theoretical and Philosophical Psychology	48. Peace Psychology
25. Experimental Analysis of Behavior	49. Group Psychology and Group Psychotherapy
26. History of Psychology	

When your friends are from cultures different from your own, they may behave in ways that seem strange to you. In today's world, as people from different cultures increasingly interact with each other, it becomes more and more important to understand the extent to which the customs and beliefs of their cultures influence their behavior.

ferred for most of the specialties described. Keep in mind that this is just a small sampling of the numerous areas within psychology. In fact, psychology is such a diverse field that the American Psychological Association, the largest professional psychological organization, has 47 separate divisions. These are listed in Table 1.1 (there are no Divisions 4 or 11).

Gender and Cultural Diversity

CULTURAL PSYCHOLOGY

Another area of psychology is becoming important today as our lives become more globally interconnected. This is the field of *cultural psychology*. Cultural psychologists study the influence of culture and ethnic practice on people's behavior in order to determine which behaviors are universal to all human beings and which are specific to individual cultures. Their ultimate goal is to help people from diverse cultures with diverse outlooks and habits live together peacefully and effectively in a world that is fast becoming a global community.

Unless we are specifically made aware of it, few of us realize the significant influence our culture has over our daily lives. As Segall et al. (1990) point out, when you go to school, you probably walk into a classroom at the same time on the same days, sit in a chair, and either listen to a trained teacher or participate in an activity directed by that teacher. This you do because it is the schooling system of your culture. In another culture, in a remote region of East Africa, for instance, your schooling might be quite different as you and your friends gather informally around a respected elder, some of you sitting and others standing, all of you listening to the elder tell stories of the history of the tribe.

In the next few pages, we discuss some of the more important concerns in the study of cultural influences on behavior. We talk about what we mean by the term *culture*, and then go on to discuss ethnocentrism, individualism-collectivism, and finally, culturally universal and culturally specific behaviors.

What Is Culture?

Culture: Values and assumptions about life and patterns of behavior that develop as a response to social and environmental factors and are passed on from generation to generation.

Berry et al. (1992) succinctly state that culture is the shared way of life of a group of people. This way of life includes ideals, values, and assumptions about life that guide behaviors (Brislin, 1993) and make it possible for people to survive in their environment (Segall et al., 1992). Each culture develops its own standards for dress, housing, and transportation, its own language, its own religions and worshipping practices, its own traditions, its own social customs. One hot summer while hiking in Yosemite National

Park, two of the authors came across a group of young men wearing white cotton shirts and long pants and young women wearing dresses. This was in contrast to *every* other person in the park who was wearing some variation of shorts and shirt. Merely the fact that the clothing was unusual for that situation signaled to us that these people must be from some other culture. You have probably had a similar experience when you've seen women wearing saris or men wearing turbans.

Each of the diverse cultures in the world has developed in response to a multitude of factors, both ecological and sociopolitical (Segall et al., 1990). Ecological factors include climate, natural resources, and geographical features such as terrain and soil conditions. In response to the importance of snow, cultures living near the Arctic circle have many words for shades of white in their languages but no words for the various hues of red and green (see Luria, 1976, p. 23). Sociopolitical factors include migration, invasion, and international trade. The early dwellings of North American Indians developed in response to sociopolitical factors. The Plains Indians developed the tepee, which they could readily put up and take down because their way of life was nomadic, following the buffalo that were their primary source of food, clothing, and shelter. The cliff dwellers of the Southwest, on the other hand, who farmed and were frequently attacked by other tribes, built adobe houses with pull-up ladders on the sides of cliffs for protection.

Ethnocentrism

In today's world, contact with people from other cultures is inevitable. Whether you are a businessperson, a teacher, a counselor, a lawyer, or any other professional, whether you are a world traveler or someone who never leaves home, you need to be able to get along with people from other cultures. And getting along means not only understanding how they are different, but appreciating and respecting those differences. People have a tendency toward ethnocentrism, which is considering your own culture's practices as "the" standard of comparison with other cultures. So we feel that our own culture's ways of dressing, speaking, or behaving are natural or correct and that those of other cultures are unnatural. We similarly tend to feel that our own culture's values and norms are right and when those of other cultures are different, they are wrong. Hence we judge people favorably if they are like us and unfavorably if they are not (Triandis, 1990). In fact, no culture is natural or unnatural, right or wrong; cultures are simply different. When someone from another culture behaves in a different way from us, it merely means that he or she was raised with a different set of cultural beliefs or customs. To avoid ethnocentrism, observe differences and respect them, but do not judge them.

By being aware of cultural differences, we can avoid major blunders in both personal and business transactions. Richard Brislin (1993) tells the story of a Japanese businessman who was asked to give a speech to a Fortune 500 company in New York. He was aware that Americans typically begin speeches by telling an amusing story or a couple of jokes. Japanese typically begin speeches by apologizing for the "inadequate" talk they are about to give. The businessman began his speech: "I realize that Americans often begin by making a joke. In Japan, we frequently begin with an apology. I'll compromise by apologizing for not having a joke" (p. 9). By appreciating cultural differences we can, like the Japanese businessman, learn to honor all cultures and feel comfortable in our intercultural exchanges.

Ethnocentrism: The feeling that one's own cultural group is superior to others and its customs and ways of life are the standards by which other cultures should be judged.

Individualism-Collectivism

To understand the behavior of people from other cultures, it is important to understand the concept of *individualism-collectivism*. People from individualist cultures, found primarily in Europe and North America, work toward their own goals and focus on themselves and their immediate families, with individual initiative encouraged. People from collectivist cultures, found throughout Asia, Africa, and Central and South America, work toward the goals of a valued group, which is often an extended family, and are willing to sacrifice their own interests for the sake of society. Knowing this may help teachers and employers understand why a Hispanic family living in the United States

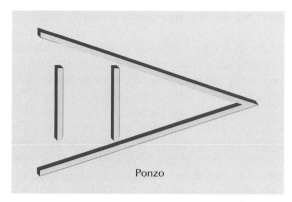

Figure 1.3 The Ponzo illusion. The vertical line at the right is more likely to be seen as farther away and therefore longer than the vertical line at the left by people from Western cultures. How we see illusions—and much else in the world—is culturally specific.

might abruptly disappear for months at a time. This happens frequently when migrant families return to their collectivist homeland to provide support to members of their extended families during a time of crisis, such as comforting a bereaved mother when a father passes away. In thinking critically about individualism and collectivism, can you see what makes the United States the most individualistic country in the world and why communism still has a strong hold in China?

Universal and Culturally Specific Behaviors

Cultural psychologists conduct research in all areas of psychology, primarily to determine which behaviors are universal to the entire human race and which are specific to individual cultures. Until relatively recently, most psychological research was conducted in Europe and North America. It is from this research that theories of human behavior have been formulated. What cultural researchers are finding is that when they repeat "classical" psychological research with people from other cultures, they do not always obtain the same research results. For instance, researchers in visual perception had assumed that all people were susceptible to visual illusions (shown in Figure 1.3 and discussed in Chapter 4). But when they conducted research with subjects in remote African villages, they found the people from these cultures to be much less susceptible to the distortions in illusions than people from Western cultures (Segall et al., 1990). Studies like this indicate that behaviors thought to be universal may actually be culturally specific to the Western cultures in which they were originally studied.

It is interesting to note, however, that when research is conducted to determine cultural diversities, it can lead to insights into universal truths. For instance, research into alternate states of consciousness uncovered the fact that, even though in some cultures people smoke marijuana or drink alcohol and in other cultures people chew coca leaves, there is a universal tendency in all cultures for people to engage in behaviors that bring them into alternate states of consciousness.

As you read this and other psychology books, keep in mind that most of the reported findings derive from research conducted with subjects living in traditional Western cultures and may not always apply to people from other cultures.

In this book we describe key research in cultural diversities and universals of behavior. Although we integrate this research throughout the text, each chapter includes a section that begins like this one, with the title *Gender and Cultural Diversity* and a special icon in the margin that looks like this:
These sections highlight particularly interesting cultural topics. Some are about a subfield of cultural psychology, the culture of men and women, hence the title *Gender and Cultural Diversity.* ■

Psychology in Your Life: Separating Fact from Fiction

Psychology is a compelling field of study because it deals with topics that you can apply to your everyday life. For example, by reading about how people learn and remember,

*Beware of the **pseudopsychologist**. Only scientific psychological research enables us to understand and predict behavior. Pseudopsychologists such as astrologers and psychics make many claims, but their unscientific methods and unfounded claims do not qualify them to accurately predict or understand human behavior.*

you might develop better study habits and create a better learning environment for yourself. By reading about interpersonal relationships, you might learn effective ways to maintain long-term friendships. By reading about motivation, you might be able to modify undesirable behaviors, such as overeating or smoking.

The study of psychology will also give you a greater awareness of the distinction between scientifically verified explanations of behavior and explanations based on mere subjective observation. Many "scientific" claims publicized in the popular press, for example, are in fact bogus—they do not follow from scientifically collected data.

Similarly, there is no scientific basis for the many popular pseudopsychologies, or "false psychologies," that attempt to explain behavior or personality differences using nonscientific methods. Pseudopsychologies include palmistry (reading people's character from the markings on the palms of their hands), psychometry (the ability to determine facts about an object by handling it), psychokinesis (the movement of objects by purely mental means), and astrology (the study of how the positions of the stars and planets influence people's personalities and affairs). Although these pseudopsychologies are entertaining (horoscopes are fun to read and great conversation starters), there is no documented proof that they legitimately explain complex human behavior.

In fact, horoscopes may at times be harmful. When Ronald Reagan was president of the United States, his wife Nancy would not allow him to make certain public appearances based solely on information from her astrologer. Many astrologers and other pseudopsychologists have been proven to be frauds by a magician named James Randi. In his book *Flim-Flam!* (1982), he describes how time and time again, under carefully controlled, standardized conditions, he has exposed their phony claims.

Psychology Today magazine poked fun at pseudopsychologies in September 1983 when it announced its first "Invent-a-Scam" contest. Readers were asked to invent a pseudopsychology similar to those mentioned above. Some of the winners included Interior Seating Therapy, which deals with psychological disorders associated with furniture, such as "anorexia newsofa"; Autozodiac, in which clients are asked to send in the make, model, year, and serial number of their car in return for an astrological chart containing such information as descriptions of the car's individual temperament and days on which it is safe to take trips; and Fetal Terpsicology, in which babies are taught to

Pseudopsychologies: "False psychologies"; popular systems that pretend to discover psychological information through nonscientific or deliberately fraudulent methods.

tap dance before birth. Although these "scams" were created to have fun, they illustrate the absurdity of the various pseudosciences and point out that we should be aware of the difference between false psychology and objective, scientific studies of behavior.

Review Questions

1. What is the definition of *psychology*?
2. What is the difference between overt and covert behaviors?
3. The goals of psychology are to _____ , _____ , _____ , and _____ behavior.
4. How are basic and applied research different?
5. The main criticism of _____ is that they attempt to explain behavior using nonscientific methods and cannot be proven true when objective, standardized methods are used.

Answers to Review Questions can be found in Appendix C.

PSYCHOLOGICAL RESEARCH

- *What is the advantage of conducting an experiment to study a research question, and how do researchers conduct them?*

Data: Facts, statistics, pieces of information.

Research Methodology: Standardized scientific procedures for conducting investigations.

Since psychology involves studying behavior *scientifically*, psychologists, like scientists in biology, chemistry, or any other scientific field, need to conduct investigations in which they methodically collect their data. They then piece it together bit by bit until they come to an objective conclusion. So that other people—laypeople as well as scientists—can understand, interpret, and repeat their research, psychologists must follow standardized scientific procedures, or methods, in conducting their studies. These procedures are collectively known as research methodology. A distinct methodology is used in each of the two basic approaches to research in psychology, experimental and nonexperimental research. In this section, we will discuss the distinguishing features and examine the methodology used in each approach.

Experimental Research: The Study of Cause and Effect

Experiment: A carefully controlled scientific procedure conducted to determine whether certain variables manipulated by the experimenter have an effect on other variables.

Every research study begins with an idea or question that inspires inquiry. Stanley Milgram, for example, wanted to know what causes people to obey authority figures who ask them to do something totally opposed to their moral values. The only way he could answer this question was to conduct an experiment. Only through an experiment can researchers isolate a single factor and examine the effect of that factor alone on a particular behavior (Cozby, 1985). For example, when you are studying for an upcoming test, you probably try a lot of methods—studying in a quiet room, rereading highlighted sections, repeating key terms with their definitions over and over to yourself, and so on—to help you remember the material. It is impossible to determine which study methods are truly effective because you probably use several at the same time. The only way you could discover which one is most effective would be to isolate each method in an experiment. (Numerous experiments have been conducted concerning memory and study techniques. If you're interested in how to develop better study habits, refer to the Study Guide and to Chapter 7, which discuss the findings from such research.)

An experiment has several critical components. In this section, we will discuss the major ones: the theory, the hypothesis, independent variables, dependent variables, and experimental controls. A more in-depth discussion of experiments and the analysis of experimental results is provided in the appendix at the end of the book.

The Theory

Theory: An interrelated set of concepts that is developed in an attempt to explain a body of data and generate testable hypotheses.

Most, but not necessarily all, experimental research is generated by a theory. A scientific theory is an interrelated set of concepts that explains a body of data and can be used to predict results of future experiments. Theories are *not* guesses or hunches or beliefs. Psychological theories are explanations of behavior that are developed after extensive research and scientific observation and, as cultural researchers insist, after carefully conducted research with diverse cultures.

The Hypothesis

After thorough study of existing theories about people's behavior and intensive study of the research, Stanley Milgram formulated questions about people's reactions to authority figures and predictions about how they would behave. During this process, he considered possible ways to study obedience to authority. Then, having gained the background needed to do so, he generated a *hypothesis* proposing why people obey authority figures.

A hypothesis is an "educated guess" or a possible explanation for a behavior being studied that is expressed as a prediction or a statement of cause and effect.

Hypothesis: A possible explanation for a behavior being studied that can be answered or affirmed by an experiment or a series of observations.

People generate informal hypotheses all the time. For example, we sometimes hear such statements as "Children today are illiterate because they watch too much TV" or "Cloudy days make people feel depressed." These are informal explanations for behaviors that are based only on personal observation or experience. A *scientific* hypothesis is based on facts and theories that have been gathered and investigated by previous researchers, as well as on personal experience and observations. It is posed in a way that indicates how the results can be measured. For example, experimental research on smoking cessation programs might state "Subjects in Group A will smoke fewer cigarettes than those in Group B when. . . ." A hypothesis may or may not be correct; it is merely a *possible* explanation for a behavior that is subject to verification through scientific study.

What was Milgram's hypothesis? Milgram had one basic hypothesis: When directed to do so by an authority figure, people will administer a higher level of shock to someone than when they act on their own initiative. However, he also developed and tested variations of this hypothesis, such as:

Group effects. Subjects will administer a higher level of shock when they are members of a group as opposed to when they are acting as individuals.

Subjects' perceived personal responsibility. When subjects feel less responsible, they will administer greater levels of shock.

Results of experiments conducted to test these hypothesis revealed that the first hypothesis—people *do* obey authority—was supported throughout the many variations

Reprinted courtesy Omni Magazine © 1990.

"I know how to get out, but I wouldn't give them the satisfaction."

of Milgram's basic experiment. Brief summaries of these variations as well as their results are given in Figure 1.4. As you may be able to tell from the figure, Milgram found that modeling, or imitation, of defiance and increased sense of responsibility are the two most important factors in obedience. You might keep these findings in mind when you are questioning whether your "one voice of dissent" can make a difference in the world.

Independent and Dependent Variables

Variables: Factors that can be varied and can assume more than one value.

After generating a hypothesis, an experimenter decides on an appropriate research design to test that hypothesis. A basic part of the design is to make a decision about which factors will be directly manipulated by the experimenter and which factors will be examined for possible changes. These factors are known as variables and are just that—factors that can vary, that can assume more than one value. Variables include such factors as weight, time, distance between people, scores on a test, number of responses, and so on. The two major types of variables used in an experiment are independent and dependent variables.

Independent Variable: A variable that is controlled by the experimenter and is applied to the subject to determine its effect.

An independent variable is a factor that is selected and manipulated by the experimenter and is totally independent of anything the subject does. Initially, Milgram obtained a basic measurement of obedience to authority by recording responses of subjects who had been directed by the experimenter to shock a learner in a separate room. He then manipulated various factors—the proximity of the learner to the subject, whether or not the experimenter was present, the gender of the subject, and several others—to determine their effect on obedience. These manipulated factors were Milgram's independent variables.

Dependent Variable: A measurable behavior that is exhibited by a subject and is affected by the independent variable.

In contrast to the independent variable, which is selected and manipulated by the experimenter, the dependent variable is a measurable behavior exhibited by the subject. It is a result of, or is dependent on, the independent variable. In Milgram's experiments, the dependent variable was always the same—the highest level of shock administered by any one subject.

Experimental Controls

Experimental design requires that there be at least two groups of subjects so that the performance of one group can be compared with that of another. Ideally, the only way these groups differ is in the amounts or levels of the independent variable. For example,

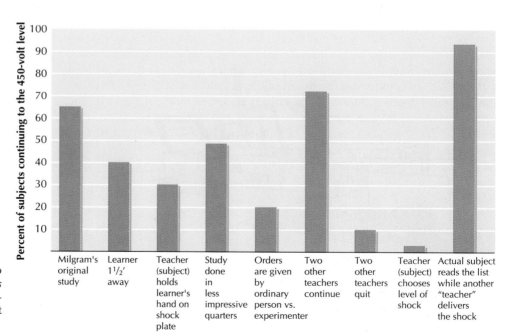

Figure 1.4 Degrees of obedience to different experimental conditions that Milgram posed. To test his hypothesis, Milgram set up different test conditions.

Helene Intraub (1979) conducted an experiment to determine whether rehearsal (repeating something over and over) improves memory for faces. Her independent variable was the amount of rehearsal time between presentation of the faces. Results of the experiment indicated that subjects in the groups allotted greater amounts of rehearsal time recognized more faces than those given lesser amounts. Since the only difference between the groups was rehearsal time, it can be concluded that increased rehearsal time *causes* better recognition of faces.

Often, one group of subjects will be assigned to a zero or control condition in which they are not exposed to any amount of the independent variable. If, in her memory experiment, Intraub had wanted to have a control group, she might have asked subjects to perform a totally unrelated task between presentations of the faces, such as counting backward from 998 by sevens as fast as possible. Thus, they would have had no opportunity to rehearse the faces. Having a control group allows the experimenter to make broader generalizations about the results of the experiment than can be made with experiments lacking a control group, but there are always at least two groups in an experiment for comparison purposes.

Often, in drug-related research, subjects in the control condition are given a pill or an injection that appears identical to the one given to subjects in the experimental condition. The pills or injections in the control condition, however, contain only inert substances such as sugar or distilled water. These fake pills and injections are called placebos. Researchers use placebos because they have found that the mere act of taking a pill or receiving an injection can change the behavior of a subject. Thus, to ensure that a particular effect is indeed due to the drug being tested and not to the placebo effect, control subjects must be treated exactly as the experimental subjects, even if this means going through the motions of giving them drugs or medications.

Assigning Subjects to Groups

When assigning subjects to the groups, the experimenter may randomly assign them and hope that subjects with similar characteristics do not all wind up in the same group. However, if there are factors that may have a bearing on the results, such as intellectual level in a memory experiment, the experimenter may decide to *match* subjects as closely as possible. This can be done with a pretest, a survey, or some other means. Milgram was particularly careful to match members of his groups according to age level (each group was composed of the same percentage of subjects in their twenties, thirties, and forties) and occupational background (each group had the same percentage of skilled and unskilled workers, sales and business people, and professional workers).

Cultural researchers must pay special attention to maintaining equivalency among the cultures being studied. This means that a conceptual understanding of what is being expected of them needs to be the same for all subjects, wording of the instructions needs to be equally as comprehensible to all subjects, and the stimuli need to be equally familiar to all subjects. (Stimuli are the objects presented for the subject's response.) The importance of this is illustrated in a study described by Serpell (1976) in which adults from a tribe living in a remove area of Ethiopia were presented with pictures and photographs printed on paper. In the initial study, they smelled, tasted, and rustled the papers and showed no response to the pictures. In a follow-up study using drawings on cloth, which was more familiar to them, they were not distracted by an unfamiliar stimulus and responded appropriately to the pictures.

In every experiment, the researcher takes care to assure that all extraneous variables (those that are not being directly manipulated or measured) are held *constant*. That is, factors that should have no bearing on the experimental results, such as the on-again, off-again noise of the air conditioner, need to be kept constant (the same) for all subjects so that they do not affect subjects' responses.

Milgram's experiment was particularly well controlled. For example, the instructions were the same for all conditions and the learner gave identical responses for the level of shock being administered. At 285 volts, he merely let out an agonized scream; at

Control Condition: The part of an experiment in which subjects are treated identically to subjects in the experimental condition, except that the independent variable is not applied to them.

Experimental Condition: The part of an experiment in which the independent variable is applied to the subjects.

Placebo: A substance that would normally produce no physiological effect that is used as a control technique, usually in drug research.

Placebo Effect: A change in subjects' behavior brought about because the subjects believe they have received a drug that elicits that change when in reality they have received a placebo, an inert substance.

300 volts, he let out an agonized scream, then said, "I absolutely refuse to answer any more. Get me out of here. You can't hold me here. Get me out. Get me out of here." At 315 volts, he let out an intensely agonized scream, then said, "*I told you I refuse to answer.* I'm no longer part of this experiment." Some variables, of course, are irrelevant to the research and can be ignored; there was no need for Milgram to control for subjects' eye color or handedness, for example. If the appropriate variables have been controlled, any change found in the dependent variable should be attributable *only* to the independent variable and the researcher should be reasonably able to assume that the independent variable is the *cause* of the change in behavior.

Bias in Research

Besides extraneous variables, there are other details that must be controlled. Experimenters, like everyone, have their own personal beliefs and expectancies. In the process of data collection they may inadvertently give subtle cues or treat subjects differently in accordance with these expectations. For example, an experimenter may breathe a sigh of relief when a subject gives a response supporting the hypothesis. This tendency of experimenters to influence the results in the expected direction is called experimenter bias.

Experimenter Bias: The tendency of experimenters to influence the results of a research study in the expected direction.

There are several ways experimenters can prevent experimenter bias. One technique is to run a double-blind experiment, in which both the experimenter and the subjects are unaware of which subjects are part of the control group and which are part of the experimental group. For instance, in a double-blind experiment testing a new drug, both the experimenter administering the drug and the subjects taking the drug are blind as to who is receiving a placebo and who is receiving the drug itself. Other techniques to prevent experimenter bias include using recording methods that are as objective as possible and enlisting neutral people other than the experimenter to interact with the subjects and collect the data. Milgram employed both of these techniques: he used an automatic recording device to record subjects' responses, and he hired a high school teacher to play the role of experimenter.

Double-Blind Experiment: An experiment in which neither the subject nor the experimenter knows which treatment is being given to the subject or to which group the subject has been assigned.

Another bias that cultural researchers need to control is *ethnocentrism.* Researchers cannot assume that just because a certain behavior is typical in their own culture, it is typical in all cultures. One way to avoid ethnocentrism is to have two researchers, one from one culture and one from another, conduct the same research study two times, once with their own culture and once with the other culture. By comparing the four studies, differences due to ethnocentrism can be isolated from actual differences in behavior between the two cultures (Berry et al., 1992).

Another type of bias is called sample bias. A sample is a group of experimental subjects selected to represent a larger group, or population. Sample bias is the tendency for the sample to be not truly representative, or typical, of the population being studied. For example, much research has been done on heart disease. The research, however, has been conducted almost exclusively with males. Doctors apply findings from this research to the treatment of all their patients, both male and female, with no regard to the male sample bias in the original research. Because the purpose of conducting experiments is to apply, or *generalize,* the results to a wide population, it is of considerable importance that the sample represent this general population.

Sample: A selected group of subjects that is representative of a larger population.

Population: The total of all possible cases from which a sample is selected.

Sample Bias: The tendency for the sample of subjects in a research study to be atypical of a larger population.

Ideally, research psychologists choose their subjects randomly from the population being measured. Proper random selection will likely produce a representative, unbiased sample. Random assignment of these subjects to the different experimental conditions will further control for any possible biases. It is also important that the sample be of sufficient size—the larger the sample, the more likely it will represent a cross-section of the entire population. Researchers generalizing results to the entire human population must take care to consider differences among the various world cultures and include subjects representative of many cultures in their studies.

Isn't a lot of research conducted with college students or with animals? How can you generalize these results to people in the real world?   This can present a problem. Milgram realized that Yale undergraduates represented only a small percentage of the general population, since they were highly intelligent, they were in their late teens or early twenties, and many had had some recent experience with psychological studies. Thus, Milgram recruited subjects ages 20 to 50 with a wide variety of occupational backgrounds from the community around Yale and paid them to participate in the experiment.

Not all researchers have funds to pay their subjects, however. This is why a large percentage of psychological research is conducted with animals and college students. Most often, these subjects are sufficiently similar to the general population in behaviors under investigation that the study results can validly be generalized to the population at large. For example, David Hubel (1984), who had conducted extensive research on brain physiology, has stated: "The principles of [nerve] function are remarkably similar in animals as far apart as the snail and man. . . . Even the major structures of the brain are so similar in, say, the cat and man that for most problems it seems to make little difference which brain one studies" (p. 4).

Review Questions

1. Why is an experiment the only way we can determine the cause of a behavior?

2. A _____ is a tentative explanation for behavior.

3. _____ are factors that can change or vary.

4. When Milgram varied the distance between the "learner" and the subject in one of his experiments, the distance was the _____ variable, and the highest level of shock administered by the subject was the _____ variable.

5. Subjects in a _____ condition are exposed to a zero level of the independent variable.

6. Why do many researchers use computers to record subjects' responses and hire uninformed people to run their experiments?

Answers to Review Questions can be found in Appendix C.

Nonexperimental Research Techniques: Studying the Correlates of Behavior

Sometimes it is not feasible for ethical or practical reasons to study behavior experimentally, so a number of nonexperimental techniques have been devised. These techniques include naturalistic observation, surveys, and individual case studies. Although none of these methods can be used to determine the causes of behavior, they can be quite valuable in determining relationships between variables and in providing information vital to making predictions of future behavior.

* *What are the nonexperimental research techniques, and what are their merits and limitations?*

Naturalistic Observation

When using naturalistic observation, researchers systematically record the behavior of subjects in their natural state or habitat. This habitat may be the jungle in a study of chimpanzees, a classroom in a study of third graders (Josephson, 1987), or the streets of Recife, Brazil, in the study of child street vendors (Saxe, 1991). Cheney and Foss (1984) used naturalistic observation in a study of social problems encountered by mentally impaired workers. They recorded observations of mentally retarded people in their work setting. These observations revealed 355 distinct social problems encountered by mentally retarded workers. Most of them involved interpersonal problems with supervisors or coworkers or disruptive and distractive behavior patterns on the part of the mentally

Naturalistic Observation: The systematic recording of behavior in the subject's natural state or habitat.

Jane Goodall has used naturalistic observation to amass a great deal of information about the behavior of chimpanzees in the wild.

retarded workers. Analysis of the nature of such problems can yield valuable information in the assessment and training of mentally retarded people.

Ideally, a researcher using naturalistic observation tries to prevent subjects from detecting that they are being observed because their behavior becomes unnatural when they know they are being watched. For example, have you ever been driving down the street, singing along with a song on the radio, only to stop in the middle of a phrase as you realized that the person in the next car was watching? The same type of thing normally happens when subjects of scientific studies realize they are being observed.

The chief advantage of using naturalistic observation is that researchers are able to obtain data about a truly natural behavior rather than a behavior that is a reaction to a contrived experimental situation. If the Cheney–Foss study had taken place in a lab, the workers would probably have acted quite differently from how they behaved in their actual workplace. On the other hand, naturalistic observation can be difficult and time-consuming, controls are lacking, it is difficult to generalize the results of the research, and scientific objectivity may be lost if the experimenters somehow interact with their subjects.

Surveys

Surveys: Nonexperimental research techniques that sample behaviors and attitudes of a population.

Surveys, tests, questionnaires, and interviews (we will refer to them all as "surveys") are similar techniques that sample a wide variety of behaviors and attitudes. They range from personality inventories that probe the makeup of individuals to public opinion surveys such as the well-known Gallup and Harris polls.

The survey technique was used in a study conducted by S. Plous, who wanted to produce an accurate portrait of animal rights activists in the United States. At a large animal rights rally in Washington, D.C., in June 1990, he surveyed 574 people. After

Table 1.2   **What Should the Animal Rights Movement Focus on Most?**

The Treatment of:	Activists[a]	Nonactivists
Animals used in research	54	26
Animals used for food	24	8
Animals used for clothing or fashion	12	22
Animals in the wild	5	30
Animals used in sports or entertainment	4	14
Animals used in education	1	0

[a] Figures indicate the percentage of respondents giving each answer.

asking them whether they considered themselves animal rights activists (402 were) or nonactivists (172), he had them express their opinion about what they felt should be the agenda of the animal rights movement. Table 1.2 (Plous, 1991) shows a portion of the survey results. As you can see, just over half the activists felt that the single highest priority of the animal rights movement should be animals used in research, while only one-quarter of the nonactivists agreed.

Surveys enable researchers to describe the characteristics of a relatively small sample, say, a few hundred people, and then generalize that information to a larger population. For example, by surveying only 402 animal rights activists, Plous might generalize his results to the entire animal rights movement. For surveys to be effective research tools, it is critical that the wording of questions is as unambiguous and un-biased as possible. Considerable attention must also be given to such details as ensuring that the sample is representative of the population. To get a random representative sample of activists, Plous deployed his research team at several different street corners and they randomly approached people on the way to the rally.

Survey techniques cannot, of course, be used to explain causes of behavior, but they can be used to predict behavior. Plous could not pinpoint the causes of the activists' beliefs, but the results of his survey can be used to predict the attitudes and goals of animal rights activists in the United States.

 Try This Yourself

Why don't you conduct your own survey? Station yourself at a conspicuous spot on campus, in your dorm, or some other place. Ask random passersby whether they consider themselves animal rights activists or nonactivists. Then ask them the question in Table 1.2 and indicate their response next to the appropriate item. How do your survey results compare with Plous's? ▪

Case Studies

Suppose a researcher wanted to investigate the problem of "photophobia," fear of light. Most people are not afraid of light, so it would be next to impossible to gather enough subjects to conduct an experiment or to use surveys or naturalistic observation. In the case of such rare disorders, researchers usually find a single person who has the problem and study him or her intensively. Such an in-depth study of a single research subject is called a case study.

In a case study, many aspects of a single subject's life are examined in depth in an attempt to describe the person's behavior and to evaluate any treatment techniques that are used. Consider, for example, the case of H. M., a man who underwent brain surgery to

Case Study: An in-depth study of a single research subject.

"Just pretend we're not here, Ms. Robinson..."

Drawing by David Sipress.

alleviate severe epilepsy (Milner, 1959). The surgery was successful in that it lessened the severity of the epilepsy, but it had an unexpected side effect. H. M. could not form *new* memories. He could remember things from the past before the surgery but could not remember things that happened after the surgery. (This case is described in more detail in Chapter 7.) Because of Milner's study, surgeons faced with similar cases have avoided destroying the brain areas that seem to be involved in the formation of new memories.

Correlation versus Experimental Methods: Which Is Appropriate?

Having studied both experimental and nonexperimental research techniques, let's look at the advantages and disadvantages of each. As we discovered in the previous section, carefully controlled experiments are very powerful tools for discovering the *causes* of behavior. In her research on H. M., however, Milner used the case study because it was the only appropriate technique. In many instances, the only appropriate research technique is a nonexperimental one, especially when studying human behavior. In fact, it would be impossible to study some variables in any other way. For example, it would be unethical to administer a drug to one group of pregnant women and none to another group to see whether the drug causes birth defects. The only way to study such topics as suicide, mental illness, alcoholism, divorce, and drug abuse is to observe them as they occur naturally (Cozby, 1989).

Correlation: The relationship between variables.

Although nonexperimental techniques do not allow researchers to determine the causes of behavior, they enable researchers to determine the correlation, or relationship, between variables being studied. When any two variables are correlated, a change in one variable is accompanied by a concurrent change in the other.

Types of Correlation

Variables may be correlated in any one of three ways. If both variables vary in the same direction—both go up or both go down—the relationship is described as *positive*. For instance, salary and years of education are positively correlated because the people making the highest salaries tend to be the ones who have gone to school the longest. Conversely, if two variables vary in the opposite direction—as one goes up, the other goes down—the relationship is *negative*. For example, grade point average and the number of hours of television watched per day are negatively correlated because people who watch a lot of television tend to get lower grades. Finally, variables that are not at all related have a *zero correlation*. The relationship between personality and the movement of distant stars illustrates a zero correlation. Contrary to strong beliefs in astrology held by a surprising number of people, bona fide studies show absolutely zero correlation between the position of stars at the time you are born and the true nature of your personality.

Correlational Studies

Correlational methods have produced important research. There is a well-known correlation between heredity and schizophrenia (a type of mental disorder characterized by disorganized thinking and disturbed emotions—see Chapter 15). Studies have been done comparing the development of schizophrenia in identical twins with its development in fraternal twins. Identical twins inherit identical genes from the parents, whereas fraternal twins are no more alike than brothers and sisters born at different times. If one identical twin develops schizophrenia, the other twin has a 41–63 percent chance of also becoming schizophrenic; but when one fraternal twin is schizophrenic, the other twin has only a 12–21 percent chance (Bernheim and Lewine, 1979; Gottesman and Shields, 1982).

Do studies of twins prove that schizophrenia is inherited?   Absolutely not. Investigators may *guess* at the reasons for correlations between variables, but nonexperimental techniques provide no means for *proving* them. In the case of schizophrenia, correlational

Correlation studies have shown that schizophrenia tends to run in families. Each of the Genain quadruplets was diagnosed as schizophrenic.

studies indicate a strong genetic disposition toward its development. But environmental stresses, particularly family dysfunction, also play a significant role (see McGue, 1992; Torrey, 1992; Hans and Marcus, 1987; Ratner, 1982). Only through *experimental* research can we determine the true causes of schizophrenia.

A study conducted in Taiwan demonstrates how absurd it is to assume that when two factors are correlated, one must cause the other. Li (1975) wanted to determine which factors correlate with the use of birth control methods. Of the variables tested, it was found that the variable most strongly related to the use of contraceptives was the number of electric appliances (toasters, can openers, popcorn poppers, and so on) in the home. Does this mean, then, that Planned Parenthood should pass out toasters to cut down on teenage pregnancy? Of course not. Just because electrical appliances and the use of birth control methods are correlated, it does not follow that electrical appliances *cause* people to use birth control. We cannot state this strongly enough: *Correlation does not imply causation.*

This is not to say that nonexperimental studies are useless. The descriptions and correlations obtained from nonexperimental studies can lead to predictions of behavior, and these predictions can be of considerable value. For example, the Taiwan study may lead researchers to seek a variable that relates to both the number of appliances and contraceptive use, such as socioeconomic level. If a strong correlation exists between these three variables, we might be able to predict that the higher the socioeconomic level, the greater the contraceptive use. By knowing this, family planning agencies can target people of different socioeconomic levels when designing and distributing birth control information.

Evaluating Research: Are the Findings Significant?

How do researchers know whether the information they have collected really measures the behavior they are studying?   There are criteria to be followed to ensure that research results will be accurate, legitimate measures of the hypothesis. These criteria vary according to the type of study being conducted, but they include controlling for experimenter or researcher bias, controlling extraneous influences, ensuring that the sample size is substantial, and ensuring that the sample is representative of the population to which the results will apply. However, even though the proper procedures and controls have been used, the results need to be analyzed statistically. Statistics consist not only of the data (the numbers) that are recorded when some behavior is measured, but also analyses of these data according to specific rules and mathematical formulas. Statistical analysis is used to determine whether any relationships or differences among the variables are significant. A statistically significant relationship or difference is one that the experimenter has good reason to believe is true or real and not due merely to chance or coincidence. Statistics and the concept of significance are examined in detail in the appendix at the end of the book.

Statistics: Data collected in a research study and the mathematical procedures used to analyze the data.

Statistically Significant: A relationship believed not to be caused by chance.

Replicate: To conduct a research study again, following the same procedure.

Another way to determine whether research results are legitimate is to replicate the research project by conducting the same study again following the same procedure. Milgram's study has been replicated countless times, with similar results, both by Milgram himself and by other researchers (Kilham and Mann, 1974; Shanab and Yahya, 1977). Replication is often done as a means of substantiating research. As more and more replications confirm the results of the original research, it becomes more evident that the research findings are valid and can legitimately be applied to real-world situations. Replication is also conducted for other reasons. When examining research reports, psychologists might question some aspect of the research. For example, they may dispute results that are not consistent with other research findings or with common expectation. Or they may detect an error in methodology, in procedure, or in some other aspect of the study. As a result, they decide to replicate the study. The findings of such replications may either support or refute the original research. If replications do not support the research, it is necessary to study the problem further.

Review Questions

1. When researchers conduct studies by observing people's behavior through a one-way mirror, they are using the technique of _____ .

2. Surveys measure a relatively small sample in order to generalize the information to a larger _____ .

3. When are case studies used?

4. If two things are highly correlated, does that mean that one thing causes the other?

5. _____ consist of data that are gathered during an experiment as well as the analysis of the data using mathematical formulas and procedures.

6. Why would a researcher want to replicate a research study?

Answers to Review Questions can be found in Appendix C.

ETHICS IN PSYCHOLOGY

• *How are research and clinical psychologists encouraged to uphold ethical behavior and procedures?*

The American Psychological Association (APA), the largest professional organization of psychologists, recognizes the importance of maintaining high ethical standards in research, therapy, and all other areas of professional psychology. The preamble to their publication *Ethical Principles of Psychologists* (1990) admonishes psychologists to maintain their competence, to retain objectivity in applying their skills, and to preserve the dignity and best interests of their clients, colleagues, students, research participants, and society.

Research Ethics: Respecting the Rights of Subjects

Think back to Milgram's experiment for a moment. In that study subjects were led to believe that they were administering shocks to an unfortunate "learner." The learner was actually a confederate, or accomplice, of the experimenter, who only pretended to be in pain. The role was played by a 47-year-old accountant who delivered a believable performance as the desperate, protesting learner. Can you imagine how Milgram's subjects must have felt when they discovered they had been tricked and that the turmoil they had gone through had been purposely created?

Because of this deception, Milgram's experiment has been criticized on ethical grounds. Critics point out that subjects may have suffered from feelings of guilt and remorse after the experiment, as well as intense inner conflict and stress during the

Critical Thinking

PSYCHOLOGY IN ACTION

APPLYING ABSTRACT TERMINOLOGY
Becoming a Better Consumer of Scientific Research

The news media, advertisers, politicians, teachers, close friends, and other individuals frequently use research findings in their attempts to change your attitudes and behavior. How can you tell whether such information is accurate and worthwhile?

The following exercise will improve your ability to critically evaluate sources of information. It is based on the concepts you learned in the previous discussion of psychological research techniques. Read each "research" report and decide what the *primary* problem or research limitation is. In the space provided, make one of the following marks:

CC = The report is misleading because correlational data are used to suggest causation.

CG = The report is inconclusive since there was no control group.

EB = The results of the research were unfairly influenced by experimenter bias.

SB = The results of the research are questionable because of sample bias.

_____ 1. A clinical psychologist strongly believes that touching is an important adjunct to successful therapy. For two months he touches half his patients (Group A) and refrains from touching the other half (Group B). He then reports a noticeable improvement in Group A.

_____ 2. A newspaper reports that violent crime corresponds to phases of the moon. The reporter concludes that the gravitational pull of the moon controls human behavior.

_____ 3. A researcher interested in women's attitudes toward premarital sex sends out a lengthy survey to subscribers of *Playboy* and *Cosmopolitan* magazines.

_____ 4. An experimenter is interested in studying the effects of alcohol on driving ability. Prior to testing on an experimental driving course, Group A consumes 2 ounces of alcohol, Group B consumes 4 ounces of alcohol, and Group C consumes 6 ounces of alcohol. The researcher reports that alcohol consumption adversely affects driving ability.

_____ 5. After reading a scientific journal that reports higher divorce levels among couples who lived together before marriage, a college student decides to move out of the apartment she shares with her boyfriend.

_____ 6. A theater owner reports increased beverage sales following the brief flashing of a subliminal message to "Drink Coca-Cola" during the film showing.

Answers: 1. EB; 2. CC; 3. SB; 4. CG; 5. CC; 6. CG

experiment (Baumrind, 1985). Milgram (1974) argues that he took great care to assure both the short- and long-term psychological well-being of his subjects. In postexperimental sessions, Milgram informed subjects about the true nature of the experiment, discussed the research with them, and took pains to reassure them that whatever behavior they exhibited—obedient or defiant—was normal and in keeping with that of other subjects. He also sent a five-page summary of the research results to each subject.

Studies such as Milgram's raise a number of questions regarding ethics in psychological research. These questions are addressed in a special publication of the APA, *Ethical Principles of Psychologists* (1990).

One of the chief principles set forth in the APA document is that an investigator should obtain the subject's "informed consent" before initiation of an experiment. The researcher should fully inform the subject as to the nature of the study and come to an agreement with the subject on the responsibilities of each. Milgram, of course, did not obtain such "informed consent." He deceived subjects by telling them that they were involved in a study of learning and memory.

But if Milgram had told his subjects he was studying obedience, wouldn't they have behaved differently?   Yes, that's probably true. That's the reason why deception research is conducted. If subjects knew the true purpose behind some studies, they would almost certainly not respond normally. Therefore, APA acknowledges the need for some deception research. However, researchers conducting this research are expected to follow strict guidelines, which include debriefing subjects at the end of the experiment.

Considerable media attention has been paid to animal rights groups who continue to protest the use of animals in psychological and medical research.

Debriefing: Explaining the research process to subjects who participated.

When debriefing subjects, researchers explain the reasons for conducting the research and clear up any misconceptions or concerns on the part of the subject. It is expected that subjects will be debriefed at the end of all experiments. Milgram did indeed debrief his subjects and send them research results.

Animals in Research: Is it Ethical?

Although Milgram's learners were not really shocked, there has been some research in which electric shock or some other type of unpleasant or aversive treatment has been administered to animals. In recent years, this type of research has been brought to the public's attention by animal rights groups opposed to such research and to improper care of laboratory animals. Such research is extremely rare, however, and psychologists argue that it is conducted only when there is no alternative way to study the behavior or when applications of the research justify the nature of the experiment. Only about 7 to 8 percent of all psychological research is done on animals, and 90 percent of that is done with rats and mice (APA, 1984). In most institutions where animal research is conducted, animal care committees are established to ensure proper treatment of research animals, to review projects, and to set guidelines that are in accordance with the APA standards for the care and treatment of research animals.

Most studies involving animals consist of naturalistic observation or learning experiments using rewards rather than punishments (Mesirow, 1984; Gallup and Suarez, 1985). Animals are used instead of humans because "time requirements [as in studies of aging], risk, or other conditions make it impossible to use humans" (APA, 1984). Animal research has benefited humans in many ways (Johnson, 1991). Research on learning in rats and pigeons has led to the development of programmed learning materials. Research in teaching sign language to chimps and gorillas has led to a better understanding of the structure of human language. Research involving the effects of drugs on unborn animals has demonstrated the risks of maternal alcohol and other drug use for human babies. Animal research has also benefited animals. For example, more natural environments have been created for zoo animals, successful breeding techniques have been developed for endangered species, and more effective training techniques have been developed for pets and wild animals in captivity. However, despite the benefits of animal research, the use of animals in psychological research will continue to be an ethical problem for psychologists in the future (see Gallup and Suarez, 1985; Herzog, 1988; Miller, 1991; Ulrich, 1991).

Because of pressure from animal rights groups, psychological and medical researchers are waging media campaigns that promote the benefits of animal research.

Clinical Practice Ethics: Respecting the Rights of Clients

Successful psychotherapy requires that clients reveal their innermost thoughts and feelings during the course of treatment. Thus, clients need to develop a sense of trust in their therapists. This places a burden of responsibility on therapists to maintain the highest of ethical standards in upholding this trust.

Psychotherapy: Application of psychological principles and techniques to the treatment of mental disorders or to the problems of everyday adjustment.

Therapists are expected to conduct themselves in a moral and professional manner. They should remain objective while becoming sufficiently involved with the clients' problems to know how to best help the client. They should encourage the client to become involved not only in deciding the type of treatment to be given but also in the treatment process itself. A therapist is expected to make adequate measures of clients' progress and to report that progress to them.

All personal information and therapy records must be kept confidential, with records being available only to authorized persons of whom the client is aware. Such confidentiality can become an ethical issue when a client reveals something that might affect or possibly injure another person. For example, if you were a therapist, what would you do if a client revealed plans to commit murder—would you alert the police or uphold your client's trust? It is a difficult decision, but therapists have the responsibility not only of protecting clients' interests but protecting the interests of others as well; thus, they are expected to report such cases. Similarly, they are required by law to disregard their pledge of confidentiality when confronted with disclosures of child abuse by reporting such cases to appropriate authorities.

Is it ethical for psychologists to hand out advice to callers on radio and TV talk shows?   Ethical concerns also come into play when psychologists dispense diagnoses and advice over the radio or on TV. Many psychologists condemn such talk-show psychology because of the impossibility of accurately assessing people's problems in such a short period of time. They also disapprove of the practice on the grounds that listeners may apply to themselves advice bestowed on another, which may lead to problems since no two people or situations are alike. However, others argue that the nature of the on-air

Table 1.3   Major Schools of Psychology

	Structuralism	Functionalism	Psychoanalytic Theory	Gestalt Psychology
Prominent Figures	Wilhelm Wundt Edward Titchener	William James John Dewey	Sigmund Freud Carl Jung	Max Wertheimer Wolfgang Kohler Kurt Koffka
Major Emphases	The importance of thought processes and the structure of the mind Identification of the elements of thought	The importance of applying psychological findings to practical situations The function of mental processes in adapting to the environment	The influence of the unconscious on behavior The importance of early life experiences on personality development	The importance of organization and context in the perception of meaningful wholes
Techniques of Studying	Trained introspection	Introspection Experimental method Comparative method (comparing psychological functioning of people and animals)	Individual case studies of patients	Perception experiments

interview is supportive and rather general in nature, and talk-show psychologists maintain that when indicated, they refer the caller for direct counseling with a qualified therapist. They maintain that radio psychologists can benefit thousands of listeners by acquainting them with psychologists and with psychological principles and techniques that they might apply to their own personal problems (Schwebel, 1982).

Review Questions

1. If a friend of yours agreed to be an accomplice in your experiment and pretended to be another subject, your friend would be known as a _____ .

2. In the case of any necessary deceptive research, APA guidelines specify that at the end of the study subjects must be _____ , in which the experimenter explains the purpose and results of the study and answers questions.

3. Animals are used in psychological research only when _____ .

Answers to Review Questions can be found in Appendix C.

SCHOOLS OF PSYCHOLOGY

• *What are the major perspectives from which psychologists have approached the study of psychology?*

During the early 1800s research into biology, physiology, chemistry, and physics got under way, and such research led to an interest in the behavior of both animals and humans. Physiologists investigated the structure and function of the nervous system, while physicists studied relationships between physical stimuli and the sensations they evoke. However, it was not until the first psychological laboratory was founded in 1879 that psychology as a science officially began. As interest in the new field grew, psychologists took various approaches to their research. Eventually, the distinct approaches and beliefs regarding the study of behavior came to be grouped into schools of psychology (see Table 1.3).

Behaviorism	Humanistic Psychology	Cognitive Psychology	Psychobiology
John Watson B. F. Skinner Edward Thorndike	Carl Rogers Abraham Maslow	Jean Piaget Albert Ellis Albert Bandura Robert Sternberg	Johannes Müller Karl Lashley David Hubel Torsten Wiesel
The importance of objective, observable behavior in the study of psychology The importance of careful research methods The conviction that behaviors are mere responses to external stimuli	The importance of people's feelings The view of human nature as naturally positive and growth-seeking Faith in people's abilities to solve their own problems	Focus on thinking and reasoning processes Focus on the mental processing of information	Behavior as a result of complex chemical and biological processes within the brain
Experiments, primarily on learning and often done with animals	Interview techniques	Information processing approach	Brain scans Electrical stimulation and recording Chemical analysis of brain tissue

Structuralism and Functionalism: The Earliest Schools

Structuralism

Wilhelm Wundt is generally known as the founder of experimental psychology. Wundt offered the first formal psychology course (in physiological psychology) and wrote what is often considered the most important book in the history of psychology, *Principles of Physiological Psychology*. It was Wundt, too, who established the first psychological laboratory at the University of Leipzig, Germany in 1879 (Schultz, 1969). In this laboratory, Wundt and his followers undertook the study of psychology, which to them consisted of the study of experience. They went about this study by trying to break down conscious experiences into basic elements. Their chief method was termed introspection, monitoring and reporting on the contents of consciousness. If you were one of Wundt's subjects trained in introspection, you might be presented with the sound of a clicking metronome. You would focus solely on the clicks and report only your immediate reactions to them—your basic sensations and feelings.

Although Wundt never referred to his school of thought as "structuralism," Edward Titchener, one of Wundt's followers, brought Wundt's ideas to America, where he established a psychological laboratory and coined the term structuralism to embody Wundt's ideas.

Like Wundt, structuralists believed that, just as the elements hydrogen and oxygen combine to form the compound water, the "elements" of conscious experience combine to form the "compounds" of the mind. They sought to identify the elements of thought through introspection and then determine how these elements combined to form the whole of experience. Thus, their study focused on the investigation of thought processes and the structure of the mind.

Structuralists inaugurated psychology as a science and established the importance of studying mental processes. However, psychologists, especially those in America, became impatient with structuralism. They felt it was limited to only one area of behavior and had few practical applications. These American psychologists, feeling the need for

Structuralism: An early psychological school that focused on the sensations and feelings of perceptual experience.

Introspection: A technique for reporting the content of one's consciousness.

application of psychological findings to practical situations, began a new school of psychology known as functionalism.

Functionalism

By the end of the nineteenth century, Darwin's theory of evolution was beginning to have a significant impact on psychology. Of particular interest was his idea of the "survival of the fittest," which stressed the function of superior biological structures in adapting organisms to their environment. It was this idea that led several American psychologists to investigate the *function of mental processes* in adapting the individual to the environment—thus the name functionalism. Darwin's theory of evolution also suggested the possibility that mental processes of animals and people might be part of a continuum. Therefore, functionalists studied mental processes of both animals and humans to test their theories. Many then applied their research findings to practical situations.

Functionalism: The psychological school that investigates the function of mental processes in adapting the individual to the environment.

William James was the leading force in the functionalist school. In keeping with structuralism, he viewed psychology as the study of consciousness, but James did not believe consciousness could be separated into distinct elements. He felt that mental activities form a unit of experience—that they are continually changing while remaining interrelated, one thought flowing into another in a continuous "stream of consciousness."

Functionalism had a great impact on the development of psychology. Though it is no longer considered a formal "school," the functionalist tradition remains a major orientation of most modern psychologists. Functionalists expanded the scope of psychology to include research on emotions and observable behaviors. They initiated the psychological testing movement, changed the course of modern education, and were responsible for extending psychology's influence to diverse areas in industry.

The Psychoanalytic and Gestalt Schools: European Contributions

During the late 1800s and early 1900s, while functionalism was prominent in America, two new schools of psychological thought were forming in Europe: the psychoanalytic and the Gestalt schools. Psychoanalytic theory was developed by Sigmund Freud as a result of experiences with his medical patients and was not directly related to earlier approaches, but Gestalt psychology developed as a direct reaction to structuralism.

Psychoanalytic Theory

Sigmund Freud was an Austrian physician who was fascinated by the way the mind influences behavior. During the course of his normal medical practice, he periodically encountered patients who presented symptoms with no physiological basis. For example, one patient lost feeling not in the arm or wrist but only in the right hand, a condition known as "glove anesthesia." This condition is physiologically impossible. After encountering several such cases with no physiological basis, Freud assumed that their causes must be *psychological*. Further studies of these patients convinced Freud that such problems are caused by conflicts between what people believe to be acceptable behavior and their unacceptable motives, which are primarily of a sexual or aggressive nature. Freud considered these motives, the driving forces behind behavior, to be hidden in the unconscious, the part of the mind of which we are not aware.

Unconscious: The part of the mind whose contents people actively resist bringing into awareness.

Psychoanalytic Theory: Freud's theory of personality that emphasizes the influence of the unconscious mind.

Freud developed psychoanalytic theory to explain these conflicts and to provide a basis for a system of therapy known as *psychoanalysis*. Psychoanalysts (followers of Freud who perform psychoanalysis) use techniques such as hypnosis, dream analysis, and free association (where patients talk freely about whatever comes to mind) in an attempt to uncover unconscious conflicts, motives, and feelings. Psychoanalysts believe that when these unconscious forces are revealed, they can help patients resolve their conflicts and live well-integrated, competent lives.

Isn't there a lot of criticism of Freud?   Freud's theory has been the focus of a great deal of controversy over the years. One of the major criticisms is of his research methodology. Freud relied almost exclusively on the individual case-study technique, without comparing any of his data to "normal" people as a control. Therefore, critics contend that Freud's theory applies only to abnormal behavior—if it is applicable at all.

Although much of Freud's theory remains controversial, it has had a profound impact on psychotherapy and psychiatry; and Freud must be credited with expanding the impact of psychology throughout the world. His work revealed the potential benefits of studying the processes of the mind, especially the unconscious. It also led people to realize that the first few years of life are important for later personality development (see Chapter 14), and that psychological methods can be used to change behavior.

Gestalt Psychology

Gestalt psychology was founded by a group of German psychologists headed by Max Wertheimer. These psychologists were interested in conducting research on *perception,* the interpretation of information from the senses. While Wundt and the structuralists were also interested in perception, the underlying philosophy of the Gestaltists was quite different. Gestaltists rejected the notion that experiences can be broken down into elements. Rather, they insisted that experience can only be studied as a whole—that the whole experience is qualitatively different from the sum of the distinct elements of that experience (gestalt means roughly "organized whole" or "pattern" in German).

To illustrate their theory, Gestalt psychologists used their research on perception. One example is the perception of apparent movement when lights are lit at alternate times. We are all familiar with signs on bars and cafes that draw our attention using an arrow made of lights that are lit in succession, so that the arrow seems to move and point the way to the door. What our eyes *actually* see is a series of light bulbs lighting up at different times, but what our brain *perceives* is a moving lighted arrow. Thus, the whole experience exceeds the simple sum of its parts. Gestalt psychologists felt that psychology should study not only specific behaviors but also how those pieces fit together to create meaningful wholes or organizations of experience. They also emphasized the importance of the context or background of the experience in creating meaning for a specific event. The Gestalt influence can be seen in the modern eclectic approach in psychology that considers the whole person and utilizes any appropriate technique in both research and therapy.

Gestalt Psychology: A school of psychology that focuses on principles of perception and believes the whole experience is qualitatively different from the sum of the distinct elements of that experience.

Gestalt: An organized whole or pattern of perception.

Eclectic Approach: An approach to psychology that considers the whole person and utilizes techniques appropriate for the specific circumstance.

Behaviorism: The Study of Observable Behaviors

Behaviorists feel that a truly scientific research method must be limited to the study of objective, observable behaviors. In fact, they believe that all behavior can be viewed as a response to a stimulus (an object or event, either internal or external, that stimulates or causes an organism to respond). For example, a dog salivating to a bell is demonstrating a stimulus–response behavior: The bell is the stimulus and the salivation is the response.

Because animals are ideal subjects for studying objective, overt behaviors, the majority of behaviorist research has been done with animals or with techniques developed through animal research. Using dogs, rats, pigeons, and other animals, behaviorists such as John Watson in the early 1900s and more recently, B. F. Skinner have focused primarily on *learning*—on how behaviors are acquired. They formulated a number of basic principles about learning that are explained in Chapter 6.

It sounds like behaviorists are interested only in animals. Aren't any of them interested in humans?   Yes, behaviorists *are* interested in people. One of the most well-known behaviorists, B. F. Skinner, was convinced that we could use behaviorist approaches to actually "shape" human behavior and thereby change the present negative course (as he perceived it) of humankind. He did considerable writing and lecturing to convince

Behaviorism: The school of psychology that focuses on objective or observable behaviors.

Stimulus: An object or event that causes an organism to respond.

Wilhelm Wundt — Creates the first psychology laboratory at the University of Leipzig in Germany.

1879

G. Stanley Hall — Is the first American Ph.D in psychology. Initiates the study of educational psychology in a talk to the National Education Association.

1882

Margaret Washburn — Is the first woman to receive a Ph.D in psychology. Later writes several textbooks on comparative psychology.

1908

Ivan Pavlov — Publishes his learning research on the salivation response in dogs.

1906

Alfred Binet — Develops the first intelligence test in France.

1905

John Watson — Publishes his article "Psychology as the Behaviorist Views It", in which he describes his program of behaviorism.

1913

Carl Jung — Splits with Freud and forms an offshoot of psychoanalysis called analytical psychology.

1914

Solomon Asch — Demonstrates crucial factors in impression formation and later studied the effects of group pressure on independence and conformity.

1946

Karen Horney — Criticizes Freud's psychoanalytic viewpoint.

1945

B.F. Skinner — Publishes *Behavior of Organisms*.

1938

Erik Erikson — Publishes *Childhood and Society*, a revision of Freud's psychoanalytic theory.

1950

Abraham Maslow — Establishes the school of humanistic psychology.

1954

Lawrence Kohlberg — Demonstrates the sequence of moral development.

1963

Albert Bandura — Along with Richard Walters, writes *Social Learning and Personality Development* in which he describes the effects of observational learning on personality development.

1963

Carl Rogers — Publishes *On Becoming a Person*, in which he puts forth his ideas of humanistic psychology.

1961

Roger Sperry — Publishes his split-brain research. Later receives the Nobel Prize for this work.

1964

Stanley Milgram — Demonstrates conditions of obedience and disobedience to authority.

1965

William James — Writes *The Principles of Psychology*, in which he promotes his psychological ideas that are later grouped together under the term functionalism.

1890

Mary Calkins — Establishes a psychology laboratory at Wellesley and later becomes the first woman president of the American Psychology Association.

1891

Sigmund Freud — Publishes *Interpretation of Dreams* and presents his ideas on psychoanalysis.

1900

Edward Thorndike — One of the pioneers in animal learning, develops the "Law of effect" as a result of research on trial and error learning of animals using his *puzzle box*.

1898

Edward Titchener — Earns his doctorate and moves to the United States, where he continues his work with the structuralist technique of introspective analysis at Cornell.

1892

Leta Stetter Hollingworth — Receives her Ph.D and goes on to publish the first works on the psychology of women.

1916

Mary Cover Jones — Demonstrates how to use conditioning to remove a child's fear.

1924

Jean Piaget — Publishes *The Moral Judgement of the Child*, a precursor to cognitive psychology.

1932

Anna Freud — Publishes her first book *Introduction to the Technique of Child Analysis*, in which she expands her father's ideas to the realm of psychoanalysis with children.

1927

Wolfgang Kohler — Publishes *The Mentality of Apes*, in which he describes his theory of insight learning. Is a major proponent of the Gestalt school of psychology.

1925

Gordon Allport — Writes *The Nature of Prejudice*. Is widely known for his trait theory of personality.

1954

Kenneth B. Clark — Conducts research with his wife Mamie that is cited by the Supreme Court in their decision to overturn racial discrimination in schools. Becomes the first black president of the American Psychological Association in 1971.

1954

John Berry — Presents his ideas on the importance of cross-cultural research in psychology.

1961

Herbert Simon — Presents his views on information processing theory.

1958

Leon Festinger — Proposes the theory of cognitive dissonance.

1957

History of Psychology Timeline
1879 - 1965

Please note that due to space limitations and the decision to end this timeline at 1965, most contemporary psychologists, as well as many psychologists who have made significant contributions to psychology, could not be included.

others of this (Skinner, 1971, 1985). Skinner also had an intense interest in human learning and did research on programmed learning and the use of learning machines (computers), which he promoted for classroom use. Other behaviorists have been successful in treating people with behavior problems. For example, to treat people with phobias (irrational fears) and alcoholism, they have developed a therapy technique known as *behavior modification,* which is discussed in Chapter 16.

Humanistic Psychology: Emphasizing the Uniqueness of the Individual

Humanistic Psychology: A school of psychology that emphasizes the importance of the inner, subjective self and stresses the positive side of human nature.

Humanistic psychology is a relatively new but powerful force in psychology. Its proponents claim that the uniqueness and value of human experience are overlooked in the behaviorist approach. This criticism has been summarized by one of the best-known humanists, Carl Rogers (1964):

> *In this world of inner meanings, humanistic psychology can investigate all the issues which are meaningless for the behaviorist—purposes, goals, values, choice, perceptions of self, perceptions of others, the personal constructs with which we build our world, the responsibilities we accept or reject, the whole phenomenal world of the individual with its connective tissue of meaning. Not one aspect of this world is open to the strict behaviorist. Yet that these elements have significance for man's behavior seems certainly true. (p. 119)*

From Rogers's statement, it is evident that humanistic psychology emphasizes the importance of the inner, subjective self, of consciousness and feelings. Humanists stress that human nature is naturally positive, creative, and growth-seeking unless thwarted by experience. In humanistic therapy, people are viewed in a positive light, as "clients" rather than "patients," and are encouraged to express their feelings and find their own solutions to problems while engaged in a supportive relationship with their therapist.

In contrast to the behaviorist view of behavior as responses to stimuli, humanists emphasize the capacity of people to exercise free will in making their own choices and deciding how to behave. As a result, each person is seen as a unique individual. All people, according to humanist Abraham Maslow, have both the need and the ability to fulfill their unique and optimum potential.

Cognitive Psychology: The Return to Thought Processes

Cognitive Psychology: A school of psychology that focuses on reasoning and the mental processing of information.

Cognitive psychology focuses on the mental processing of information. It is concerned with the acquisition, storage, retrieval, and use of knowledge, whether that knowledge is how to split an atom or how to change a flat tire. Cognitive psychologists study how we gather, encode, and store information from our environment using such mental processes as perception, memory, imagery, concept formation, problem solving, reasoning, decision making, and language. If you were listening to a friend describe her whitewater rafting trip, a cognitive psychologist would be interested in how you decipher the meaning of her words, how you form mental images of the turbulent water, how you incorporate your impressions of her experience into your previous concepts of rafting, and so on.

Information Processing Approach: An approach to studying mental processes that views people and computers in similar terms, as processors of information that has been gathered from the environment, then encoded for memory storage and retrieval.

Cognitive psychologists take what is called an information processing approach in their studies. It is derived from the computer sciences. According to this approach, we gather information from the environment, then process it in a series of stages. A certain type of processing is performed at one level before the information is passed on to another level for a different kind of processing. The information processing approach is based on the idea that humans are like computers in that both take in information, process it, and produce a response. In fact, cognitive psychologists often express models of human thought processes with techniques used in the computer sciences, such as flowcharts (diagrams with arrows leading from one box to successive others) and mathematical formulas. For example, cognitive psychologists studying memory have devised a model (see Figure 7.1) that illustrates the sequence of stages in the acquisition of memory.

Psychobiology: The Brain and Behavior

During the last few decades, significant advances have been made in our understanding of the structure and function of the brain and nervous system. This new knowledge has given rise to an increasingly important school of psychology known as physiological psychology, or psychobiology. Psychobiologists explain behavior as a result of complex chemical and biological events within the brain. Recent research has explored the role of biological factors in sensation, perception, learning, memory, language, sexual behavior, and schizophrenia.

Psychobiology: The study of the biology of behavior.

The roots of psychobiology can be traced to the beginnings of experimental physiology and Johannes Müller, whose most important contribution was his *doctrine of specific nerve energies.* This doctrine stated that all nerves carry the same basic message, an electrical impulse. Other significant nineteenth-century physiologists and anatomists who made contributions to this area include Paul Broca, a French surgeon who studied patients with brain injuries; Luigi Galvani, the first to use electrical stimulation to study the workings of the brain; Hermann von Helmholtz, the first to attempt to measure the speed of the nerve impulse; and Charles Darwin, whose theory of evolution inspired research into comparative physiology. Unlike their predecessors, today's psychobiologists have access to modern technological equipment to help them study the functioning of individual nerve cells, the roles of various parts of the brain, the effects of drugs on brain functions, and so on. Chapter 2 is devoted to modern research into the biological basis of behavior. As you will discover, the biology of behavior is a theme that is woven into the discussion of many types of behavior throughout this text.

Psychology Today: An Eclectic View

Rather than speak of "schools of psychology," most modern psychologists talk about the five basic "perspectives" that influence the topics psychologists study, how they conduct their research, and what information they consider important. These are the *psychoanalytic, behavioristic,* and *humanistic,* as well as the increasingly important *cognitive* and *biological* perspectives. As you study this text and read generally about psychology, you will find numerous references to these perspectives.

In discussing the various schools or perspectives within psychology, we have necessarily examined them separately and made distinctions between their philosophies and practices. Today most psychologists recognize the value of each orientation, but at the same time concede that no one view has all the answers. The complex behaviors we humans exhibit require complex ways of dealing with them. Thus, most psychologists take an eclectic approach, using principles and techniques from different perspectives as they suit the situation at hand.

Is any one school of thought more "right" than the others?   Most students begin by agreeing with one major school, then another, and another, as they learn more about each one. Usually, most come to realize the value of different orientations for distinct situations as they look for ways to apply psychological concepts to their everyday lives. For example, they can see the value of behaviorism in training their dog not to jump up on people and the value of humanism in developing a sense of responsibility for their own lives.

Also keep in mind that human behavior is influenced by the sociocultural context in which it occurs. Factors as obvious as schooling or as seemingly meaningless as the shape of the houses in which people live can affect behavior. When parents were asked what they considered the most important things their children should learn in preschool, they responded exactly as the collectivist-individualist theme would predict. The number one response of Japanese parents was sympathy, empathy, and concern for others; the number one response of American parents was self-reliance and self-confidence (Tobin, Wu, and Davidson, 1989). As for the shape of our houses, people who live in houses with straight lines respond differently to certain optical illusions than people who live in round houses, so they actually perceive the world differently. By being aware of cultural influences on behavior, the psychologist in all of us can better describe, explain, predict, and change behavior.

A Final Note

One final note as you begin your study of psychology: You will learn a great deal about psychological functioning, but take care that you don't overestimate your expertise. Once friends and acquaintances know that you're taking a course in psychology, they may ask you to interpret their dreams, help them to discipline their children, or even offer your opinion on whether they should break up their relationships. As David L. Cole, a recipient of the APA Distinguished Teaching in Psychology Award, stated, "Undergraduate psychology can, and I believe should, seek to liberate the student from ignorance, but also the arrogance of believing we know more about ourselves and others than we really do" (1982). Remember that the ideas, philosophies, and even experimental findings of the science of psychology are continually being revised. At the same time, psychological findings and ideas developed through careful research and study can make important contributions to our lives. As Albert Einstein once said, "One thing I have learned in a long life: that all our science, measured against reality, is primitive and childlike—and yet, it is the most precious thing we have."

Review Questions

1. The _____ school of psychology originated the method of introspection to examine thoughts and feelings.

2. _____ investigated the function of mental processes in adapting to the environment and many applied their findings to real-world situations.

3. Why is Freud's theory so controversial?

4. A _____ is an organized whole or pattern of perception.

5. Therapists using the _____ approach help clients examine themselves and their feelings and lend support while clients find ways to help themselves.

6. _____ focuses on how we process information, by gathering, encoding, storing, and retrieving it by using mental processes.

7. _____ attempts to explain behavior as complex chemical and biological events within the brain.

8. If you were a therapist, which approach would you use in dealing with disturbed individuals?

Answers to Review Questions can be found in Appendix C.

REVIEW OF MAJOR CONCEPTS

UNDERSTANDING PSYCHOLOGY

1. Psychology is the scientific study of behavior. Psychologists use scientific research methods to investigate overt, or observable, behaviors and covert behaviors such as thoughts and feelings.

2. The goals of psychology are to describe, explain, predict, and change behavior.

3. Psychologists perform research and can specialize in several areas, including clinical, counseling, educational, school, physiological, developmental, social, or industrial and organizational psychology.

4. Basic research involves the study of theoretical issues; applied research involves solving specific problems.

5. Cultural psychology is the study of the influences of culture on behavior with the purpose of distinguishing between culturally specific behavior and universal behavior. People tend to be ethnocentric with the belief that their own culture's practices are normal and practices of other cultures, if different, are deficient or abnormal. To succeed in today's world, we need to learn not only about how people from other cultures are different but also how much they are the same.

6. Psychological findings can be applied to improve our personal lives. The study of psychology leads to an appreciation for scientific methods of research, as opposed to pseudo-scientific methods.

PSYCHOLOGICAL RESEARCH

7. Research methodology includes experimental techniques designed to investigate cause-and-effect relationships and nonexperimental techniques that provide descriptions of behavior.

8. An experiment begins with a hypothesis or possible explanation for behavior. Independent variables are the factors the experimenter manipulates and dependent variables are measurable behaviors of the subjects. Experimental control includes assigning subjects to groups and holding extraneous variables constant.

9. Nonexperimental research techniques are used to obtain descriptions of behavior. Naturalistic observation is used to study behavior in its natural habitat. Surveys use interviews or questionnaires to obtain information on a sample of subjects. Individual case studies are in-depth studies of single subjects.

10. Experiments enable us to determine causes for behaviors, whereas correlational relationships only enable us to predict behaviors.

11. Psychologists use statistics to judge whether research findings are significant or due to chance.

ETHICS IN PSYCHOLOGY

12. Psychologists are expected to maintain high ethical standards in their relations with human and animal research subjects and in therapeutic relationships with clients. The APA has published specific guidelines detailing these ethical standards.

SCHOOLS OF PSYCHOLOGY

13. Psychologists have grouped together to form various schools of psychology with distinct approaches to the study of behavior. Structuralists attempted to identify elements of consciousness and how these elements form the structure of the mind. Functionalists studied the functions of mental processes in adapting the individual to the environment. They broadened the scope of psychology and extended its influence to such fields as education and industry.

14. Freud's psychoanalytic theory examined psychological problems that were presumed to be caused by unconscious conflicts. The Gestalt school studied organizing principles of perceptual processes and paved the way for an eclectic approach.

15. Behaviorism emphasizes observable behaviors and the ways they are learned. Humanistic psychology focuses on inner meanings and assumes our nature is positive and growth-seeking. Cognitive psychology examines reasoning and mental processes.

16. Psychobiology attempts to explain behavior as complex chemical and biological events within the brain.

SUGGESTED READINGS

AMERICAN PSYCHOLOGICAL ASSOCIATION. (1986). *Careers in psychology.* Washington, DC: APA. This booklet is available free to students from the American Psychological Association, 1200 17th Street NW, Washington, DC 20036.

AMERICAN PSYCHOLOGICAL ASSOCIATION. (1990). Ethical principles of psychologists. *American Psychologist, 45,* 390–395. This article lists and discusses the ethical principles involved with clinical practice, research with human subjects, and research with animals.

BRISLIN, R. (1993). *Understanding culture's influence on behavior.* Orlando, FL: Harcourt Brace Jovanovich. A fun book to read, especially for people who like people.

COZBY, P. C. (1989). *Methods in behavioral research.* (4th ed.) Palo Alto, CA: Mayfield. An introduction to the use of research methods in psychology.

MILGRAM, S. (1974). *Obedience to authority.* New York: Harper & Row. In this book, Milgram describes his original experiments.

SCHULTZ, D. P., & SCHULTZ, S. E. (1992). *A history of modern psychology* (5th ed.). Orlando, FL: Harcourt, Brace, Jovanovich. A short history of psychology.

STANOVICH, K. E. (1991). *How to think straight about psychology.* New York: HarperCollins. An interesting book on how to evaluate psychological and pseudopsychological research.

The Biological Bases of Behavior

OUTLINE

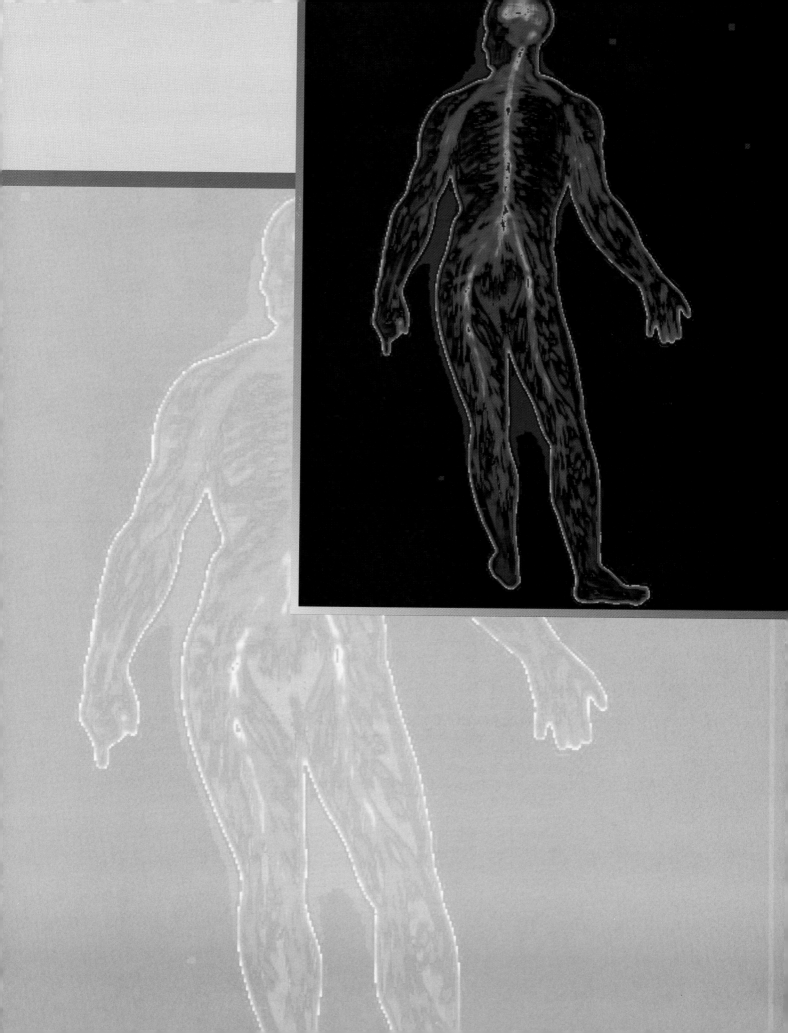

RED	YELLOW	YELLOW	GREEN	BLUE
BLUE	GREEN	RED	BLUE	YELLOW
GREEN	RED	GREEN	YELLOW	BLUE
YELLOW	RED	RED	YELLOW	RED
GREEN	RED	YELLOW	BLUE	GREEN
GREEN	BLUE	YELLOW	GREEN	RED
BLUE	BLUE	BLUE	RED	GREEN
BLUE	YELLOW	GREEN	BLUE	RED
YELLOW	GREEN	BLUE	BLUE	GREEN
RED	BLUE	RED	RED	BLUE
GREEN	BLUE	GREEN	YELLOW	YELLOW
RED	YELLOW	GREEN	YELLOW	GREEN
BLUE	RED	YELLOW	BLUE	YELLOW
YELLOW	GREEN	BLUE	GREEN	BLUE
GREEN	RED	GREEN	RED	RED
YELLOW	BLUE	RED	YELLOW	RED
RED	YELLOW	YELLOW	GREEN	BLUE
BLUE	GREEN	RED	BLUE	YELLOW
GREEN	RED	GREEN	YELLOW	BLUE
YELLOW	RED	RED	YELLOW	RED
GREEN	BLUE	YELLOW	BLUE	GREEN
GREEN	BLUE	BLUE	RED	GREEN
BLUE	YELLOW	GREEN	BLUE	RED
YELLOW	GREEN	BLUE	BLUE	GREEN

*L*ook at the list of words printed to the right. Try to read the entire list out loud as fast as you can, beginning with the left-hand column and reading down each column. That was easy, wasn't it? Now try again, but this time say aloud *not* the words themselves but the colors of the ink in which the words are printed.

Could you do it without making a mistake? Did you stutter and stammer, hesitate, get confused? It took you a lot longer to say the colors, didn't it? This is a version of the "Stroop effect" that has fascinated psychologists since 1935 when J. R. Stroop first studied the phenomenon in a learning experiment. How do you think the Stroop effect works? Why do you think it is so easy to read the words and so hard to say the colors of ink?

Whenever one of your five senses detects a stimulus—a stop sign, the voice of a friend, chocolate ice cream—the resulting sensation is changed into neural (nerve) signals that are sent to your brain. So when you read a word or identify a color on the Stroop list, your eyes sense the word or color and transcribe the sensation into neural signals, which are sent via nerves to your brain. After processing the information, your brain "decides" what you should say and sends a message to your mouth and vocal cords to produce it.

When you are directed to say the colors rather than the words in the list, confusion results somewhere within the maze of interconnected brain cells. Why? One plausible explanation is that your brain is so accustomed to reading words that reading any word, no matter what its color, is automatic. So when you try to name a color different from the word it forms, your deeply ingrained reading habit interferes, resulting in confusion in your brain.

When you think about it, it is astounding that our brain does not get confused more often than it does. The brain is an extraordinarily complex structure composed of billions of cells working in concert with one another to enable us to move, perceive, feel, and think. As if the brain itself is not complex enough, a system of thousands of nerves courses through the body carrying messages to and from the brain, enabling us to do anything from jump hurdles to memorize poems. The brain is ultimately responsible for all our actions and is the part of the body that makes each of us unique—even identical twins who have developed from the same fertilized egg do not have identical brains.

Unique as they are, all brains are made up of similar parts. Psychobiologists study brain anatomy and the rest of the nervous system to see how it affects our behavior. For example, they know what area of your brain is responsible for your feelings of frustration when you stumbled over the ink colors in the Stroop test. They even know along which neural pathways the color messages travel from your eyes to your brain, and how the messages are passed from one nerve cell to another.

In this chapter we discuss the major findings of psychobiologists, as well as the techniques they use to conduct their investigations. In our discussion, we examine the two major divisions of the nervous system: the *central nervous system (CNS)*, which consists of the brain and the spinal cord, and the *peripheral nervous system (PNS)*, which consists of all nerves in the body outside the CNS (see Figure 2.1). We also examine the *endocrine system,* which consists of glands that help regulate our behavior by secreting hormones, or chemicals.

As you read Chapter 2, keep the following **Survey** questions in mind and answer them in your own words:

- What are neurons and how do they convey electrochemical information throughout the body?
- How do the nervous and endocrine systems use chemicals to direct everything our bodies do?

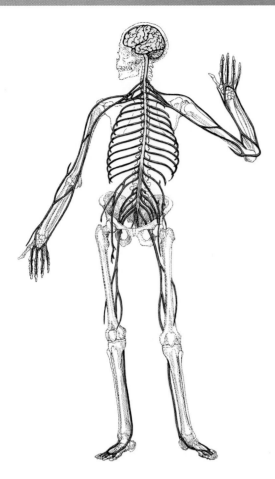

*Figure 2.1 **The nervous system**. The central nervous system (CNS) consists of the brain and spinal cord. The peripheral nervous system (PNS) consists of all nerves outside the CNS.*

- How do the two major subdivisions of the peripheral nervous system initiate bodily activity and regulate body functions?

- Why do we have a spinal cord? What are the major structures of the brain, and what are their roles in behavior?

- How do researchers study the brain, and what are some of their findings?

THE NEURON

The brain and the rest of the nervous system essentially consist of neurons. Neurons are cells that transmit information throughout the body, as well as within the brain. All behavior—everything you do, think, or feel—is a result of neuronal activity. Your every movement, every thought, and every heartbeat ultimately depends on what happens at the level of the neuron. Each neuron is a tiny information-processing system with thousands of connections for receiving and sending signals to other neurons. Although nobody knows for sure, it is estimated that the brain alone contains on the order of 100 billion neurons (Fischbach, 1992). Translated into more comprehensible terms, this means that if placed end to end, the body's neurons would reach to the moon and back.

Structure of a Neuron: Three Basic Parts

Just as no two people are alike, no two neurons are exactly alike, although most share three basic features: dendrites, a soma, and an axon (see Figure 2.2). Information from other cells normally enters the neuron through the numerous dendrites, passes through the soma, and is transmitted to other cells by the axon. Dendrites are branching structures that receive information from other neurons. Each neuron may have hundreds or

- *What are neurons and how do they convey electrochemical information throughout the body?*

Neurons: Individual nerve cells responsible for transmitting information throughout the body.

Dendrites: Branching neuron structures that receive neural impulses from other neurons and convey impulses toward the cell body.

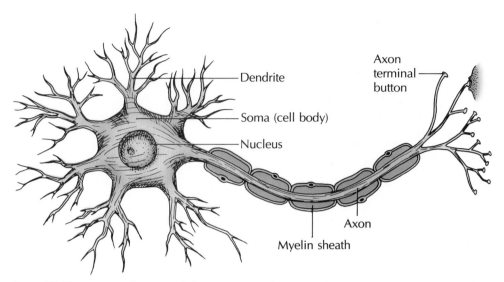

Figure 2.2 The structure of a neuron. Information enters the neuron through the dendrites, is integrated in the soma, and is transmitted to other neurons via the axon. The myelin is a fatty insulation that increases the speed at which the axon can transfer information. Neurotransmitter is stored in and released by the axon terminal buttons.

Soma: The cell body of the neuron; it integrates incoming information from the dendrites, absorbs nutrients, and produces the majority of the protein molecules needed by the neuron.

Axon: A long tubelike structure attached to the neuron cell body that conveys impulses away from the cell body toward other neurons.

Action Potential: An electrochemical impulse that travels down an axon to the axon terminal buttons.

Axon Terminal Buttons: Small structures at the ends of axons that release neurotransmitter chemicals.

Nerve: A bundle of axons that have a similar function.

thousands of dendrites. The cell body, or soma, serves several functions: It integrates the electrical information coming from the dendrites; it absorbs needed nutrients; and because it contains the nucleus, it produces the majority of protein molecules needed for normal functioning of the cell. The axon is a long tubelike structure specialized for transmitting neural information. It is highly sensitive to changes in the electrical charge of its membrane. If the electrical change is sufficient, an action potential (an electrochemical impulse) is initiated at the junction between the soma and the axon. This action potential travels down the length of the axon to its end, where it branches into small structures called axon terminal buttons. These terminal buttons form junctions with other neurons and with muscles, which in turn are activated by chemicals released by the terminal buttons.

Is a nerve the same thing as a neuron?   No. A neuron is a single cell consisting of three parts. A nerve is a bundle of axons that have a similar function (see Figure 2.3). This distinction is similar to the difference between a single telephone wire and a telephone cable containing thousands of wires. For example, the optic nerve has over a million axons transmitting visual information from the eye to the brain. When you were looking at the Stroop list, several thousand individual neurons were activated. Their messages were transmitted to your brain along thousands of axons bundled together within the two optic nerves, one leading from each eye. Thus, the loss of a single neuron would be insignificant compared to the loss of an entire nerve.

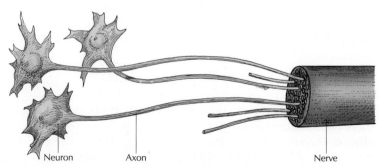

Figure 2.3 A nerve. A nerve is a bundle of axons from many neurons.

Resting Potential and Action Potential: To Transmit or Not to Transmit, That Is the Question

Neurons are activated through a rather complicated electrochemical process that produces an action potential. We will simplify our description of the process. Nevertheless, it will greatly help you to refer to Figures 2.4 and 2.5 at each step.

Picture the axon as a tube of membranous tissue filled with chemicals. This tube is floating within a liquid sea of still more chemicals. The chemicals both inside and outside the tube are **ions,** molecules that carry a particular electrical charge, either positive or negative. When nerve impulses are not being passed along the neural membrane, the chemical ions and their electrical charges outside and inside the membrane

Ions: Molecules that carry positive or negative electrical charges.

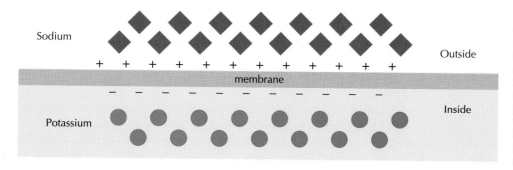

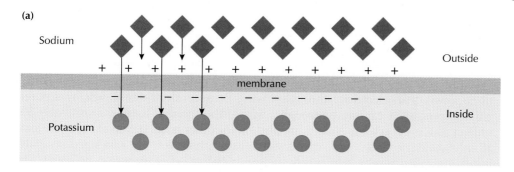

Figure 2.4 Resting potential. In this diagram of the axon membrane, the sodium ions are represented by diamonds and the potassium ions are represented by circles. Although the sodium and potassium ions are both positively charged, the inside of the membrane has a net negative charge because of the large number of negatively charged protein ions (not shown) inside the cell. No ions are moving and therefore the axon is said to be at rest.

(a)

(b)

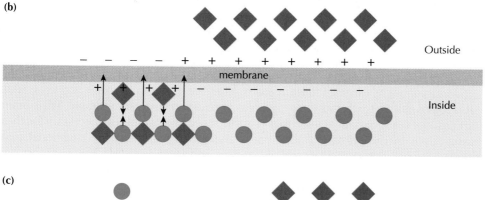

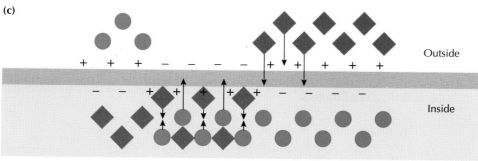

(c)

Figure 2.5 Action potential. (a) Stimulation of the axon causes the membrane barrier to break down and sodium begins to enter the cell. (b) As the sodium enters the cell, the charge inside the membrane goes from negative to positive. (c) Potassium exits the cell, restoring the inside of the cell to a negative charge. Meanwhile, sodium enters the next segment of the membrane as the sodium barrier breaks down there. Since the ions are moving, causing a nerve impulse to move down the axon, this is called an action potential.

Resting Potential: The resting state of the axon membrane, which consists of a high concentration of sodium molecules outside the axon and a high concentration of potassium and protein molecules inside the axon.

Sodium-Potassium Pump: An ongoing process whereby sodium ions are continually moved out and potassium ions are continually moved into the axon to restore and preserve the resting potential.

Myelin: Fatty insulation that serves to greatly increase the speed at which an action potential moves down an axon.

Many complex cognitive or motor tasks, such as reading or riding a bicycle, require continued development of the brain and nervous system.

are balanced in such a way that the neuron is in a state of rest. This is known as the resting potential. During the resting potential, sodium ions, which carry a positive electrical charge, lie predominantly outside the axon membrane. Inside the membrane are positively charged potassium ions and negatively charged protein ions. Overall, the outside of the membrane is more positively charged than the inside (see Figure 2.4).

An action potential is initiated when enough stimulation is received at the dendrites or soma to change the electrical properties of the soma and the axon membrane. When this happens, ion channels in the axon membrane open and sodium ions rush in, temporarily giving the inside of the cell a positive charge. Almost immediately, potassium ions leave the cell, restoring the negative internal charge. These events at one spot on the neuron membrane trigger ion channels to open in the next section of the membrane, allowing sodium to move in and potassium to move out (see Figure 2.5). In short, a chain reaction occurs, with the impulse traveling down the axon, one section at a time, until it reaches the terminal buttons at the end. Arrival of an action potential at the terminal buttons causes them to squirt a tiny amount of chemical into the space between their neuron and another neuron (or muscle). If the other neuron receives sufficient chemical stimulation, an action potential is initiated along its axon membrane and the process is repeated.

How does the axon return to its resting state?   Two processes are required to return the axon to its resting state: the closing of the sodium ion channels and the sodium-potassium pump. The electrical change from negative to positive resulting from the inrush of sodium ions during the action potential causes the sodium ion channels to close and prevents further inflow of sodium into the cell. Once this happens, the cell membrane swiftly returns to its original resting potential. In order for future action potentials to occur, however, any excess sodium that entered the cell during the action potential must be expelled. This is accomplished through the sodium-potassium pump, a process that continually moves sodium ions out of the axon and draws in potassium ions in an attempt to maintain the electrochemical balance essential to the resting potential.

How fast does a nerve impulse travel?   Actually, a nerve impulse moves slowly, much more slowly than electricity through a wire. Because electricity travels by a purely physical process, it can move through a wire at the speed of light, approximately 300 million meters per second. A nerve impulse, on the other hand, travels along a bare axon at only about 10 meters per second. Some axons, however, are enveloped in a fatty insulation called myelin that greatly increases the speed of an action potential. The myelin blankets the axon, with the exception of periodic nodes, points at which the myelin is very thin or absent (see Figure 2.2). The action potential jumps from node to node rather than traveling along the full membrane. An action potential in a myelinated axon moves about 10 times faster than a bare axon, at over 100 meters per second (Kalat, 1992, p. 49).

In humans, myelinization is not completed until about age 12. This means that children cannot be expected to learn and react as fast as nor in the same way as an adult. It is impossible to teach most two-year-olds to read and write, for example. Their brains are just not ready to handle information at the speed and complexity necessary for these tasks. Even in the primary grades, paper and pencil work and the traditional basal readers are not developmentally suitable for six- and seven-year olds. Educators are now developing more appropriate techniques and materials. On a different note, certain diseases such as multiple sclerosis can destroy the myelin sheath. The greatly slowed rate of conduction in action potentials affects the person's movement and coordination.

Review Questions

1. The nervous system is divided into two major parts: the _____ nervous system, which consists of _____ , and the _____ nervous system, which consists of _____ .

2. Draw and label the five major parts of a neuron.

3. An electrochemical impulse that travels down an axon is called an _____ .

4. How is a neuron different from a nerve?

5. When an action potential is first initiated, _____ ions rush into the axon and _____ ions move out.

6. What is the purpose of the sodium-potassium pump?

7. Fourteen-year-old Lisa can play scales on the piano twice as fast as her six-year-old sister. In terms of neurons, what is the reason for this?

Answers to Review Questions can be found in Appendix C.

CHEMICAL MESSENGERS

Before reading about the action potential, you may not have realized the extent to which your body depends on electrical and chemical processes. But if you stop a moment to think about it, you are in fact a conglomeration of chemicals. You think, you move, you feel because of information conveyed throughout your body by chemicals. These chemical actions are directed by the nervous system, in which case the chemicals are transmitted within and between neurons, and by the endocrine system, which distributes chemicals through the bloodstream.

• *How do the nervous and endocrine systems use chemicals to direct everything our bodies do?*

Endocrine System: A system of glands that, by releasing bodily chemicals into the bloodstream, is responsible for distributing chemical information throughout the body to effect behavioral change or to maintain normal bodily functions.

Nervous System Messengers: Neurotransmitters

Information from our senses or from our brain or spinal cord travels throughout our body from neuron to neuron. For example, when you looked at the first word on the Stroop list, neurons at the back of your eye were stimulated. They in turn stimulated other neurons in the optic nerve, which stimulated other neurons in your brain, which stimulated still other brain neurons, and so on. This successive neural stimulation, this relaying of information from one neuron to another, begins at the juncture between the neurons. This juncture is known as the synapse. Figure 2.6 shows the basic components of a synapse. When the action potential reaches the axon terminal buttons, it causes a minute amount of neurotransmitter to be released into the *synaptic gap*, the space between the two cells. Neurotransmitters are special chemicals that cross the gap and stimulate another cell.

When neurotransmitter is released into the synapse, it binds to receptor sites on the membrane of the receiving cell. These receptor sites are highly sensitive to neuro-

Synapse: The junction between two neurons where neurotransmitter passes from the axon of one neuron to the dendrite or soma of another.

Neurotransmitters: Special chemicals released from axon terminal buttons that cross the synaptic gap and bind to receptor sites on the membrane of another neuron.

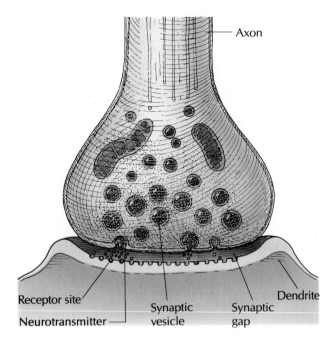

Figure 2.6 A synapse. In this schematic view of a synapse, neurotransmitter chemicals are found in small synaptic vesicles in the axon terminal button. When the action potential reaches the axon terminal button, these vesicles release the stored neurotransmitter into the synaptic gap. The neurotransmitter chemicals then diffuse across the synaptic gap and stimulate the receptor sites on the dendrite.

transmitters. As a result of this binding, there is a slight electrical change in the membrane. If enough receptors are bound, the electrical change will initiate an action potential in the receiving cell.

Action potentials do not always occur, however, even when enough receptor sites are bound, because some neurotransmitters inhibit action potentials from occurring. Basically, transmitters can have either excitatory or inhibitory effects on their target cells. When neurotransmitters are excitatory, they cause the receiving cell to be more likely to initiate an action potential; when they are inhibitory, they cause the receiving cell to be less likely to initiate one. Excitatory transmitters include acetylcholine, norepinephrine, serotonin, and dopamine. A major inhibitory transmitter is endorphin, which blocks neural signals in pain pathways. Neuroscientists believe that dozens of chemicals serve as neurotransmitters in the brain, with more being identified each year (Kalat, 1992, p. 68). They have found that even though a neurotransmitter such as acetylcholine or dopamine might be shown to be predominantly an excitatory transmitter in one area of the brain, it might have the opposite (inhibitory) effect in a different area.

Does the strength of an action potential depend on how much neurotransmitter reaches the neuron?   No. All action potentials that occur in any neuron are of the same intensity. The neuron either fires an action potential or it doesn't. This is known as the all-or-nothing principle. In a way, the conduction of an action potential in a neuron is similar to the firing of a bullet out of a gun. An action potential is fired by the binding of neurotransmitters; a gun is fired by pulling a trigger. In a gun, the only factor in ejecting the bullet is a certain amount of pressure on the trigger. Whether the pressure is exactly the amount required or 20 times the amount , the bullet comes out of the barrel with the same force. In a neuron, if the necessary amount of excitatory neurotransmitter is received at the receptor sites, an action potential is generated in the axon. If the neuron receives 20 times the required amount of neurotransmitter, it will still initiate an action potential of the same intensity as all other action potentials.

Although the strength of action potentials does not vary, the *rate* at which they are fired can differ. Generally, a high level of stimulation will cause a neuron to fire many action potentials in succession, whereas a low level of stimulation will produce only intermittent firing.

How do neurotransmitters cause action potentials?   Neurotransmitters bind to receptor sites in much the same way as a key fits into a lock. Just as different keys have distinct three-dimensional shapes, various chemical molecules, including neurotransmitters,

All-or-Nothing Principle: The principle whereby an axon either fires an action potential or does not—there are no gradations; if one is fired, it is of the same intensity as any other.

How the brain works.

Reprinted with special permission of King Features Syndicate.

have distinguishing three-dimensional characteristics. If a neurotransmitter has the proper three-dimensional shape, it will bind to the receptor site (see Figure 2.7*a*) and thereby influence the firing of the receiving cell (Bloom, 1983; S. H. Snyder, 1984). Molecules that do not have the correct three-dimensional shape will not fit into the receptor site and will therefore fail to affect the cell (see Figure 2.7*b*).

Psychoactive Drugs

Anything that causes neurotransmitters to be released or blocked at the synapse affects our perceptions or moods. For example, most psychoactive drugs (drugs that affect the nervous system in some way, like alcohol or caffeine) have their effect at the synapse by either decreasing or enhancing the amount of neurotransmitter released.

The "runner's high" is an example of how a person's pain perception can be reduced. As muscles become fatigued during a long run, pain pathways are activated. To counter this pain and enable the runner to keep going, the brain releases endorphins (inhibitory transmitters) that bind to receptor sites and slow the pain signals. These receptor sites are the same as those to which the opiate drugs morphine and heroin bind. Under certain circumstances, when enough endorphin is released, a natural euphoria such as the runner's high can be produced. This state is remarkably similar to one produced by heroin and morphine.

Psychoactive Drugs: Drugs that affect the nervous system and cause a change in perception or mood.

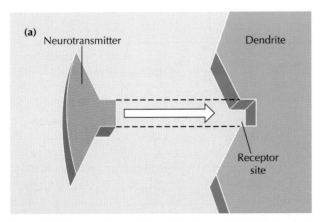
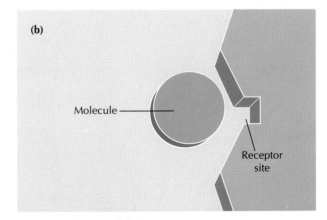

Figure 2.7 Receptor sites. (a) Receptor sites on the dendrite recognize neurotransmitters because of their three-dimensional shape. (b) Molecules without the correct shape will not fit the receptors and therefore will not stimulate the dendrite.

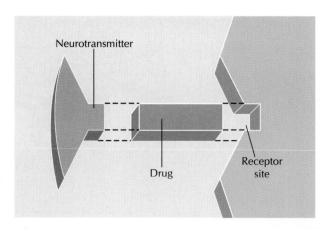

*Figure 2.8 **Possible drug action.*** Some drugs operate by filling a receptor site and thus not allowing the neurotransmitter to stimulate the receptor.

Some drugs, such as amphetamine, cocaine, and caffeine, act by increasing the amount of neurotransmitter in the synapse or by directly activating receptor sites on the dendrites. They can do this because they have a three-dimensional shape similar to that of the neurotransmitter. These drugs thus have a stimulating effect on the nervous system. Other drugs, such as barbiturates and alcohol, work by suppressing the release of neurotransmitter, increasing the release of inhibitory transmitters, or competing with the transmitter for the receptor sites on the dendrite (Carlson, 1992, p. 126). To use our lock-and-key analogy, these drugs fit into the lock but do not turn the tumblers. If the false "key" is taking up space in the lock, the lock will not open, and the real key will be prevented from getting into the lock (see Figure 2.8). These drugs thus depress nervous system functioning. Psychoactive drugs are discussed in further detail in Chapter 5.

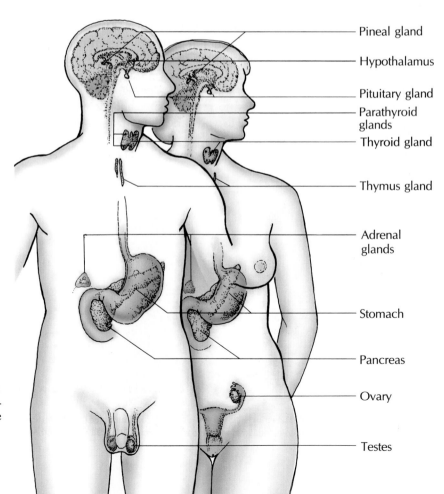

*Figure 2.9 **The endocrine system.*** The major endocrine glands are shown in color along with some internal organs to help you locate the glands.

Endocrine System Messengers: Hormones

The nervous system and the endocrine system work hand in hand to direct our behavior and maintain our body's normal functioning. The endocrine system consists of several glands that manufacture the chemicals we call hormones. Upon receiving signals from the brain, the glands release these hormones into the bloodstream, which circulates them throughout the body. The primary function of many endocrine glands, including the pituitary, the thyroid, the adrenals, and the pancreas (see Figure 2.9), is to maintain homeostasis, the normal functioning of bodily processes. They accomplish this by maintaining the tissue and blood levels of certain chemicals within a specific range. For example, sugar is a chemical that must remain within a certain concentration for the body to function normally. If too much sugar enters the bloodstream, the pancreas (an endocrine gland) will secrete the hormone insulin to lower the blood sugar level to a more normal, safer level.

Another major function of the endocrine glands, particularly the ovaries and the testes, is to secrete hormones that regulate reproductive functions and turn on the genes responsible for the development of such sexual characteristics as breast development and facial hair. The major endocrine glands, the hormones they secrete, and their functions are listed in Table 2.1.

The Hypothalamus

The major link between the endocrine system and the nervous system is the hypothalamus, a tiny brain structure that lies above the pituitary gland. The pituitary is usually considered the master endocrine gland because it releases hormones that activate the

Hormones: Chemicals manufactured within the body that are circulated in the bloodstream to produce bodily changes or to maintain normal bodily functions.

Homeostasis: The body's steady state of normal functioning.

Hypothalamus: A group of neuron cell bodies that ultimately controls the endocrine system and regulates such drives as hunger, thirst, sex, and aggression.

Table 2.1 The Endocrine System

Endocrine Gland	Hormone	Function
Anterior pituitary	Follicle-stimulating hormone	Ovulation, spermatogenesis
	Luteinizing hormone	Ovarian/spermatic maturation
	Thyrotropin	Thyroxin secretion
	Adrenocorticotropin	Corticosteroid secretion
	Growth hormone	Somatomedin secretion Protein synthesis
	Prolactin	Growth and milk secretion
Posterior pituitary	Vasopressin	Water retention Increase in blood pressure
	Oxytocin	Uterine contraction, milk production
Ovaries	Estrogens	Female secondary sex characteristics; female sex drive; ovulation
	Progesterone	Maintenance of pregnancy
Testes	Androgens	Male secondary sex characteristics; male sex drive; sperm production
Thyroid	Thyroxin	Increase in metabolic rate
Parathyroid	Calcitonin	Calcium retention
Adrenal cortex	Corticosteroids	Use of energy resources Inhibition of antibody formation and inflammation
	Aldosterone	Sodium retention
	Androgens	Male sex characteristics
	Estrogens	Female sex characteristics
Adrenal medulla	Epinephrine Norepinephrine	Activation of sympathetic responses
Pancreas	Insulin	Decrease in blood sugar; increase in glucose storage after conversion to fat
	Glucagon	Increase in blood sugar; conversion of stored fat to glucose

other endocrine glands. However, the hypothalamus is the part of the brain that controls the pituitary through direct neural connections and through the release of its own hormones into the blood supply of the pituitary. Thus, the real "master endocrine gland" is the hypothalamus. Specific endocrine functions of the hypothalamus are described in the chapters on sexuality (Chapter 11), eating and feeding behavior (Chapter 12), and health psychology (Chapter 13).

We have examined the workings of the individual neuron in passing neural information throughout the body. We have also noted the role of glands in sending hormonal information through the bloodstream. In the next section, we shall see how neurons and glands together form a coordinated system responsible for our most basic bodily movements and functions.

Review Questions

1. Neurotransmitters are bodily chemicals released at the _____ .

2. Suppose you burned your arm. You feel constant pain because the neurons in your pain pathways are releasing neurotransmitters that have _____ effects on the receiving neurons. When you exercise your body releases endorphins, which block pain signals; therefore, these endorphin neurotransmitters have _____ effects.

3. Basically, how does the endocrine system work?

4. What is *homeostasis*?

Answers to Review Questions can be found in Appendix C.

THE PERIPHERAL NERVOUS SYSTEM

* *How do the two major subdivisions of the peripheral nervous system initiate bodily activity and regulate body functions?*

Peripheral Nervous System (PNS): The part of the nervous system outside the central nervous system that consists of the nerves going to and from the brain and spinal cord.

Somatic Nervous System: A subdivision of the peripheral nervous system that consists of nerves carrying afferent sensory information and efferent motor information to and from the central nervous system, the sense organs, and the skeletal muscles.

Afferent: Incoming sensory information.

Efferent: Outgoing motor information.

The peripheral nervous system (PNS) includes all nerves going to and from the brain and spinal cord. The PNS has two major subdivisions—the somatic nervous system and the autonomic nervous system. The PNS works jointly with the central nervous system and the endocrine system in carrying out their functions. The somatic nervous system sends and receives sensory messages and controls motor (muscle) movements, whereas the autonomic nervous system regulates more automatic bodily functions, such as heart rate and breathing (see Figure 2.10).

The Somatic Nervous System: A Network for Sensory and Motor Messages

The somatic nervous system consists of all the nerves that carry incoming sensory information and outgoing motor information. Incoming (afferent) information comes toward the spinal cord or the brain from sense organs and muscles, with information

Figure 2.10 Subdivisions of the peripheral nervous system (PNS).

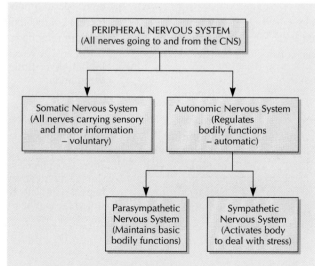

about external stimulation and the position of the skeletal muscles and limbs. Outgoing (efferent) information travels from the brain or spinal cord in the form of neural impulses with instructions for skeletal muscles to contract or relax. When you were saying the colors of the words in our chapter preview, afferent information traveled from your eyes to your brain and efferent information traveled from your brain to your mouth and vocal cords.

Depending on the origin and complexity of the stimulation, the somatic nervous system deals with neural information in one of three ways. First, information originating in the face and head enters and exits the brain through one of 12 cranial nerves. Second, in the case of a simple reflex, neural information is processed solely in the spinal cord. (A reflex is an involuntary reaction to a stimulus that is performed without involving the brain.) Finally, in more complex behavior requiring input from the brain, afferent information enters the spinal cord and is sent to the brain where it is analyzed. Then efferent messages are sent down the spinal cord and out to target muscles.

The somatic nervous system responds to external stimuli and regulates voluntary actions. However, the peripheral nervous system is also responsible for involuntary tasks, such as heart rate, digestion, and breathing. These involuntary actions and many others are carried out by the second half of the PNS, the autonomic nervous system.

The Autonomic Nervous System: Preparing for Fight or Flight

The primary function of the autonomic nervous system (ANS) is to maintain homeostasis, the body's steady state of normal functioning. It does this by regulating the endocrine glands, the heart muscle, and the smooth muscles of the blood vessels and internal organs. The autonomic nervous system is divided into two branches, the parasympathetic and the sympathetic. These tend to work in opposition to each other to regulate the functioning of such target organs as the heart, the intestines, and the lungs (see Figure 2.11).

When an athlete such as gymnast Svetlana Boginskaya performs, the neural information needed for body control moves through both afferent and efferent nerves of the somatic nervous system.

Autonomic Nervous System (ANS): A subdivision of the peripheral nervous system that maintains normal functioning of glands, heart muscles, and the smooth muscles of the blood vessels and internal organs.

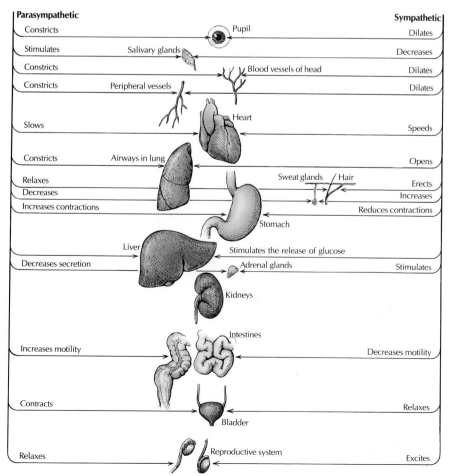

Parasympathetic		Sympathetic
Constricts	Pupil	Dilates
Stimulates	Salivary glands	Decreases
Constricts	Blood vessels of head	Dilates
Constricts	Peripheral vessels	Dilates
Slows	Heart	Speeds
Constricts	Airways in lung	Opens
Relaxes	Sweat glands / Hair	Erects
Decreases		Increases
Increases contractions		Reduces contractions
	Stomach	
	Liver Stimulates the release of glucose	
Decreases secretion	Adrenal glands	Stimulates
	Kidneys	
Increases motility	Intestines	Decreases motility
Contracts	Bladder	Relaxes
Relaxes	Reproductive system	Excites

Figure 2.11 Actions of the autonomic nervous system (ANS). This figure illustrates some of the actions of the parasympathetic and sympathetic branches of the ANS.

Both of these animals have activated the fight-or-flight response of the sympathetic nervous system.

Parasympathetic Nervous System: The part of the autonomic nervous system that is normally dominant when a person is in a relaxed, nonstressful physical and mental state.

The parasympathetic nervous system is normally dominant when a person is in a relaxed, nonstressful physical and mental state. The main function of the parasympathetic system is to slow heart rate, lower blood pressure, and increase digestive and eliminative processes. In short, it performs basic housekeeping and bodily maintenance. As Chapter 13 points out, it is definitely healthier to have the parasympathetic system dominant over the sympathetic system.

Sympathetic Nervous System: The part of the autonomic nervous system that dominates when a person is under mental or physical stress.

When a person is under some type of stress, mental or physical, the sympathetic nervous system takes over. The sympathetic nervous system stops digestive and eliminative processes, increases respiration, increases heart rate, increases blood pressure, and causes several hormones to be released into the bloodstream. The net result of sympathetic activation is to get more oxygenated blood to the skeletal muscles, thus making a person better able to deal with the source of stress. The sympathetic system is sometimes referred to as the *fight-flight system*—it prepares the body to fight or flee from whatever is causing the stress.

 Try This Yourself

To experience the takeover of your own sympathetic nervous system, arrange with your roommate or a family member to surprise you after you really "get into" studying. Make your plans a day in advance. Then he or she can sneak up behind you and beat on some pots and pans or make some other kind of loud, obnoxious noise when your parasympathetic system is fully in force. You can bet your sympathetic system will kick in with increased respiration, heart rate, blood pressure, and hormone levels. You'll want to do something active afterward before returning to your studies, to use up the excess hormones in your bloodstream. (You'll find out in Chapter 13 that they can lead to hypertension.) ■

Review Questions

1. What are the two major parts of the peripheral nervous system and what are their main functions?
2. Afferent nerves carry information _____ the brain or spinal cord; efferent nerves carry information _____ the brain or spinal cord.
3. A gazelle is standing quietly and grazing. Along comes a lioness who begins an attack. What part of the gazelle's autonomic nervous system is dominant before the lioness appears and what part becomes dominant after she attacks?

Answers to Review Questions can be found in Appendix C.

THE CENTRAL NERVOUS SYSTEM

The central nervous system (CNS) consists of the brain and the spinal cord. The brain is the control center for all voluntary behavior (such as driving a car) and some involuntary behavior (such as breathing). The spinal cord contains the structures responsible for reflex actions and the nerve fibers that link the brain and other parts of the body.

As you read about the central nervous system, keep track of which structures are major parts of the brain and which are components of major structures by referring to Figure 2.12.

The Spinal Cord: The Link Between the Brain and the Body

Beginning at the base of the brain and continuing down the back, the spinal cord is surrounded and protected by vertebrae, the bones of the spinal column. The spinal cord is involved in all voluntary and reflex responses of the body below the neck. Serving as a communications link between the brain and the body, it relays incoming sensory information to the brain and sends messages from the brain to muscles.

The spinal cord has two major components: gray matter and white matter (see Figure 2.13). The gray matter, found near the center of the spinal cord, contains mostly cell bodies. It is within the gray matter that information is processed. The white matter, found in the outer layers of the spinal cord, contains mostly myelinated axons. It is within the white matter that axons transmit information to and from the brain.

- *Why do we have a spinal cord? What are the major structures of the brain, and what are their roles in behavior?*

Central Nervous System (CNS): The part of the nervous system that consists of the brain and the spinal cord.

Brain: An extremely complex mass of nerve tissue organized into structures that control all voluntary and much involuntary behavior.

Spinal Cord: The part of the nervous system found within the spinal column that is involved in reflexes and the relay of neural information to and from the brain.

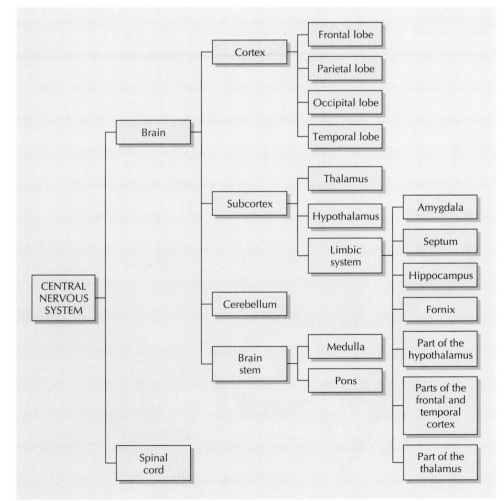

Figure 2.12 The central nervous system (CNS). A schematic diagram of the CNS listing the major subdivisions and the names of the brain structures associated with those subdivisions.

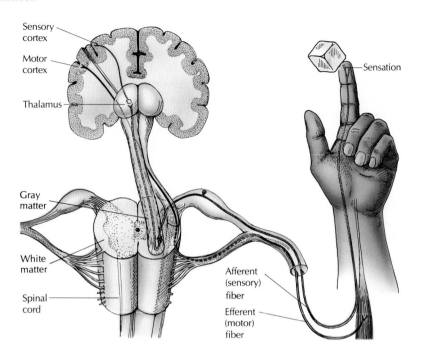

*Figure 2.13 **The spinal cord.*** The spinal cord and message pathways to (afferent) and from (efferent) the brain.

Imagine you are a child who has just seen your first icicle. Delighted, you rush to where it dangles and break it off. After a few licks you become aware of how cold your hand is growing. The cold receptors in your skin are being stimulated and are firing nerve impulses. This incoming afferent information from the receptors in your hand travels through neurons to your spinal cord where it enters the gray matter in the center of the cord. It then travels via axons in the white matter to your brain. Although researchers do not yet fully comprehend how, the brain analyzes this sensory information and may initiate a voluntary movement in response, such as dropping the icicle or putting on a mitten. This message is sent down axons in the white matter to the cell bodies of the appropriate motor nerves in the gray matter. The efferent motor information travels to the muscles, which contract and enable you to let go of the icicle or grab a mitten.

*Figure 2.14 **The reflex arc.*** In a simple reflex arc, a sensory receptor initiates a neural impulse in an afferent sensory nerve fiber. The impulse travels along the afferent fiber to the spinal cord. In the gray matter, the afferent fiber synapses with an interneuron and then with an efferent motor fiber. The efferent signal travels to the appropriate muscle which then contracts. Compare this figure and Figure 2.13. Action is immediate in a reflex because the signal only travels as far as the spinal cord, not all the way to the brain.

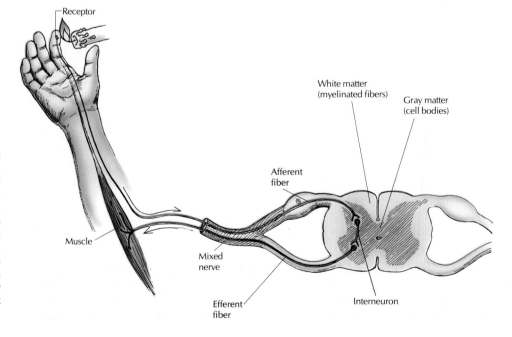

When a person suffers damage to the spinal cord, muscles served by sections of the spinal cord below the damaged area will not function normally and the person may be paralyzed.

Then people with damage to their spinal cord can't move at all?   That's not totally true. They can move parts of their body served by nerves above the injured area, and other areas of the spinal cord may still be able to provide reflex movement. Reflexes are important because they enable us to respond immediately to possibly dangerous or painful stimuli without involving the brain. Suppose you grabbed a hot pan and the pain signal had to travel from your hand to your brain and back to your hand. It might take several seconds, and meanwhile the tissue in your hand could be severely damaged. But by bypassing the brain and following a simple reflex arc through the spinal cord, the pain message speeds directly to an arm muscle. You withdraw your hand almost instantly, avoiding serious injury. Take the time to examine the simple reflex arc detailed in Figure 2.14.

 Try This Yourself

You can initiate an eyeblink reflex in a friend. All you need is a drinking straw. Tell your friend to be very still. Hold the end of the straw no closer than five or six inches from his or her eye and direct a quick, strong puff of air through the straw to the eye. Your friend will exhibit an involuntary, reflexive blink of the eye. Of if you have a dog, you can observe a scratching reflex. If you scratch the dog's trunk in just the right place, it will exhibit a reflexive scratching motion with one leg. ■

With a damaged spinal cord, information may not be able to travel to and from the brain, but many reflexes may still remain intact. For instance, you might not be able to voluntarily move your legs, but you may still exhibit a knee jerk reflex when tapped just below the kneecap.

Even though it is impossible for the brain to control muscles through a damaged spinal cord, recent research has made it possible for some patients who have lost the use of their legs to walk again. The photograph on this page shows a very determined woman, Jennifer Smith. Jennifer's spinal cord was severed by a sniper's bullet in 1980, paralyzing her legs. With the help of a computerized electronic muscle-stimulation system developed by the National Center for Rehabilitation Engineering at Wright State University in Dayton, Ohio, she was able to participate in the Honolulu Marathon in 1985.

The Brain: The Body's Control Center

The brain is an extremely complex bundle of billions of neurons organized to control what we think, feel, and do. Brain size and complexity vary significantly from species to species. Lower species such as fish and reptiles have smaller, less complex brains than those of higher species such as cats and dogs. The most complex brains belong to whales, dolphins, and higher primates such as chimps, gorillas, and humans.

In this chapter, we will discuss the physiology—the structure and functions—of the human brain. The major divisions of the human brain are the cerebrum, consisting of the cerebral cortex and subcortical areas, the cerebellum, and the brain stem.

The Cerebral Cortex

The bumpy convoluted outside surface of the brain is the cerebral cortex. The cortex is divided into two halves, the right and left hemispheres, that resemble the halves of a walnut. An interesting and significant fact is that each hemisphere processes information about the opposite side of the body. When you arrive home after dark, you probably fumble around in your pocket or purse for your door key. If you touch the key with your left hand, the sensation travels to your spinal cord and crosses over to your right hemisphere. On the other hand, if you insert the key into the lock with your right hand, the

Reflexes: Movements that are initiated by an external stimulus and do not require input from the brain.

Reflex Arc: The path that the neural impulse travels to initiate a reflex.

Researchers at Wright State University help a paraplegic walk by using a computer to directly stimulate the muscles in her legs. This is necessary because a spinal cord injury makes it impossible for the motor cortex to send nerve impulses to control these muscles.

Cerebral Cortex: The bumpy, convoluted area on the outside surface of the brain that contains primary sensory centers, motor control centers, and areas responsible for higher mental processes.

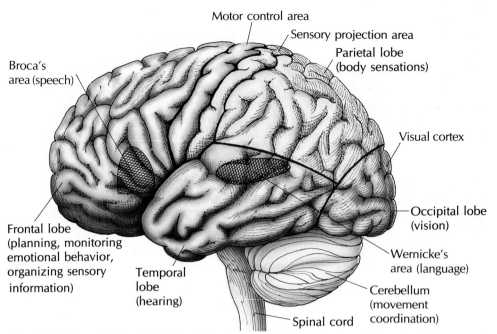

Figure 2.15 The cerebral cortex. The four lobes of the cerebral cortex, the frontal, the parietal, the occipital, and the temporal, along with their major functions, are shown in this figure.

motor information enabling your right hand to move has come from your left hemisphere.

Each of the two cerebral hemispheres is further divided into four areas, or lobes, according to their general functions and structure. These areas, shown in Figure 2.15, are known as the frontal, parietal, occipital, and temporal lobes. As we describe the functions of each lobe, it would be helpful for you to refer to this figure.

The Frontal Lobes

Frontal Lobes: The cortical lobes located at the front of the brain whose functions include motor and speech control, the ability to plan ahead, initiative, and self-awareness.

The frontal lobes are responsible for many of the functions that distinguish humans from most other animals, such as self-awareness, initiative, and the ability to plan ahead. For example, what are you going to be doing twenty minutes from now, two hours from now, tomorrow, next week, next year? These are questions that, as far as we currently know, only humans can answer, and we use the frontal lobes to do so. By far the largest of the cortical lobes, the frontal lobes are located at the top front portion of the two brain hemispheres.

Motor Control Area: The area located at the back of the frontal lobes of the cortex that is responsible for instigating voluntary movements.

At the very back of the frontal lobes lies the motor control area. All neural signals that instigate voluntary movement originate here. For instance, when you reach out to choose a candy bar from a vending machine, it is the motor control area of the frontal lobes that guides your hand in pulling the proper lever. A specialized area in the *left* frontal lobe, on the surface of the brain near the bottom of the motor control area, is Broca's area, which controls the muscles that produce speech. When you read aloud the words on the Stroop list, it was your Broca's area that sent the signals to your lips, tongue, jaws, and vocal cords to produce the words.

Broca's Area: A brain area found in the left frontal lobe that controls the muscles used to produce speech.

Association Areas: The areas in the cerebral cortex that are involved in such mental operations as thinking, memory, learning, and problem solving.

The remainder of the frontal lobes consists of association cortex. Association areas in the cortex have no specific motor or sensory functions but are thought to involve such mental operations as perception, emotion, memory, language, and thinking (Luria, 1973, 1980). We use these areas, which make up a large portion of the cortex, when we solve a complicated math problem, plan a weekend camping trip, or create a modern sculpture. Association areas organize and integrate sensory information received from other brain areas to enable us to perform specific functions. Recent evidence also suggests that a person's working memory is located in the very front of the frontal lobes (Goldman-Rakic, 1992). The working memory, which is the memory system that allows us to manipulate and access stored memories, is discussed in more detail in Chapter 7.

The association areas of the cerebral cortex are responsible for organizing sensory information coming from other areas of the brain and therefore allow humans to perform complex tasks such as creating a detailed sculpture.

THE FAR SIDE By GARY LARSON

"Whoa! *That* was a good one! Try it, Hobbs — just poke his brain right where my finger is."

Although we do not fully comprehend the mechanisms involved, we can deduce from what is known that association areas must play an important role in the Stroop effect. Color and word information from the list is converted to neural signals that are processed in the visual area of the brain. This neural information is then sent to association areas, where it is organized, integrated with other information, analyzed, and in the case of the Stroop effect, confused. It appears that the association areas then send signals to other parts of the brain, such as signals for speech production to Broca's area.

Recent research has found that the frontal lobes are especially important for planning or changing a course of action. When the solution to a problem involves planning, damage to the frontal lobes can severely limit a person's abilities (Damasio, 1979; Pines, 1983). Research also indicates that the frontal cortex monitors emotional behavior, and damage to this area can severely affect the emotionality of an individual (Nauta, 1972). These findings explain the famous case of Phineas Gage. Gage was a construction supervisor who in 1848 suffered a bizarre accident. An iron rod he was holding blew through his frontal lobes in an explosion (see Figure 2.16). He recovered fairly rapidly from the physical damage, but psychologically he was never again himself. He had difficulty making decisions and could not perform his duties as supervisor. His personality was also affected in that he became undependable, irritable, vulgar, and profane—a different person from the original Phineas Gage. From this case and from other research, it appears that much of our individual personality and much of what makes us uniquely human is regulated by our frontal lobes.

The Parietal Lobes

At the top of the brain just behind the frontal lobes are the parietal lobes, the seat of body sensations and much of our memory about the environment. At the front of the parietal lobes are the projection areas for body sensations (see Figure 2.17). These are areas that receive information about such bodily sensations as touch, pain, and heat from nerves throughout the body. For example, when you step on a tack, you don't feel the pain until the sensory information from the pain and pressure receptors in the skin of your foot reaches the sensory projection areas.

As in the frontal lobes, the remainder of the parietal lobes is made up of association areas which are involved chiefly with integrating information from the environment and reconciling tactile (touch) information with visual and auditory (hearing) information. In these association areas, therefore, lie such abilities as using memory to orient oneself in space and identifying objects within that space. For instance, if something touches your shoulder, identifying whether that touch is a friend's tap or an acorn dropping from

Figure 2.16 The skull of Phineas Gage. Gage's personality changed drastically after a tamping iron plunged through his skull during an explosion.

Parietal Lobes: The cortical lobes located at the top of the brain that are the seat of body sensations and memory of the environment.

Projection Areas: Parietal areas of the brain that receive incoming sensory information.

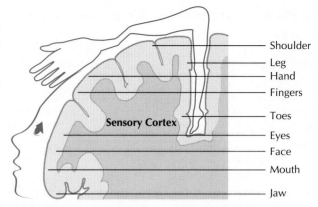

Figure 2.17 Proportions of sensory cortex devoted to body parts. In this drawing, the area of cortex responsible for processing sensory information from various parts of the body corresponds to the body part adjacent to the cortex.

a tree requires information not only from the sensory areas of the parietal lobes but also from the visual and auditory areas of the brain. If you see a friendly face and hear a familiar voice, the touch on the shoulder is probably from a friend rather than from nature.

The Occipital Lobes

Occipital Lobes: The cortical lobes located at the back of the brain that are dedicated entirely to vision and visual perception.

Located at the very back of the brain are the occipital lobes, dedicated entirely to vision and visual perception. When you were reading the Stroop list, visual information was processed in the occipital lobes before being sent to the association areas and possibly other parts of the brain.

Is that why I see stars when I'm hit on the back of the head—because the visual area of the brain is located there?   Absolutely. When you are hit on the back of the head, the blow activates the nerve cells in the occipital lobes of the cerebral cortex. Since this type of stimulation does not come from the normal sensory channels, you just see flashes of light, or "stars," not a meaningful image of something.

David Hubel and Torsten Wiesel (1962, 1968) extensively researched this brain area. They placed electrodes (small electrical wires) in the occipital lobes of cats and recorded how individual neurons in this lobe responded when the cats were presented with a simple stimulus, such as a picture of a horizontal bar. Their research demonstrated that the occipital cortex is organized in columns of neurons lying perpendicular to the surface of the cortex. All the neurons in the same column tend to respond only to similar visual stimuli. This type of organization seems to hold true for the rest of the cortex as well.

The Temporal Lobes

Temporal Lobes: The cortical lobes whose functions include auditory perception, language, memory, and some emotional control.

The last of the four major cortical lobes, the temporal lobes, are found on the sides of the brain. Their major functions are auditory perception (hearing), language, memory, and some emotional control. The auditory perception areas are located at the top front of the temporal lobe. On reaching this area of the cortex, incoming sensory information from the ears is processed and then sent to the parietal lobes, where it is combined with visual and other body sensation information.

Wernicke's Area: An area of the cerebral cortex responsible for the thinking and interpreting aspect of language production.

Wernicke's area is found at the top of the left temporal lobe near its junction with the parietal lobe. This area is responsible for the thinking and interpreting aspect of language production. Damage can cause severe difficulties in communication. For example, people with damage to Wernicke's area may not be able to read, write, speak, or interpret any kind of language at all, whether it is spoken, written, or signed.

Dyslexia: An inability or difficulty in reading.

Do people with dyslexia have a problem with this area of the brain?   People with dyslexia have normal intelligence and their ability to speak and understand spoken language is normal, but they have trouble reading. Often, they do not see letters in words or they inadvertently reverse letters. For example, they might read the word "read" and process it as "red," or they might read "rat" and process it as "tar." Obviously, this can present quite a problem.

Although there are several theories, no one is quite sure what causes dyslexia; it may in fact have several different causes (Bloom, Lazerson, and Hofstadter, 1988). Visual problems may not allow the person to see the words correctly. There may be problems with areas of the cortex that integrate visual and auditory information. This results in mismatching letter combinations with the sounds those combinations make. Finally, to answer the question, yes, there is evidence that abnormalities in Wernicke's area may sometimes cause dyslexia (Galaburda and Kemper, 1979). In the normal brain, the cells are arranged in columns, whereas in the dyslexic brain no such organization is evident. The good news is that most people with dyslexia can, through training, learn to process information in ways that enable them to read normally.

The temporal lobes are also important in the formation of new concepts and memories. The ability to form simple concepts, such as determining which of several stimuli is different from the others, is severely disrupted by damage to large areas of the temporal lobes (Mishkin and Pribram, 1954).

The temporal lobes also seem to be involved, along with several other brain structures, in emotional behavior. Research with cats and monkeys has shown that damage to areas of the brain attached to the temporal lobes known as the *amygdala* and the *hippocampus* can severely disrupt emotionality. Kluver and Bucy (1939) removed both temporal lobes of monkeys, including the amygdala and the hippocampus which are limbic areas adjacent to the temporal lobes. As might be expected, the monkeys were quite different after the surgery. Their emotional behavior was noticeably flat. For example, they showed no fear of snakes after the surgery, whereas they had previously been terrified of snakes. Similar results have been reported in humans whose temporal lobes have been damaged by illness (Marlowe, Mancall, and Thomas, 1975). The temporal lobes, as well as the other cortical lobes, are connected with other areas of the brain, including the subcortical areas.

Subcortical Brain Areas

What makes you feel like hitting something when you're angry? How does your body maintain a temperature of 98.6 degrees? What part of your brain is responsible for your sexual drives? Tucked into the center of the brain and surrounded by the cerebral cortex

David Hubel and Torsten Wiesel received the Nobel Prize for their work in mapping visual areas in the occipital cortex of the brain.

The size of the body parts of this model indicates the amount of cortex dedicated to the processing of sensory information from that part of the body.

Figure 2.18 The subcortex and the cerebellum. If your brain were sliced down the center, lengthwise, most of the subcortical areas and the cerebellum would be exposed.

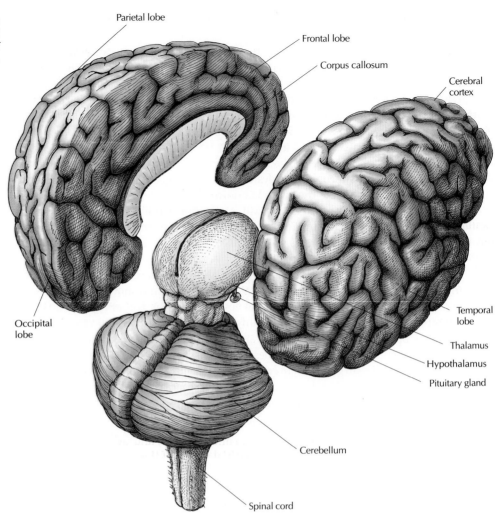

are the areas of the brain that hold the answers to these questions. Called *subcortical brain areas,* they include the corpus callosum, the thalamus, the hypothalamus, and a group of structures collectively known as the limbic system. Most of these structures can be viewed if the brain is sliced lengthwise down the middle (see Figure 2.18).

The corpus callosum serves as a bridge between the two cerebral hemispheres, making it possible for the hemispheres to communicate with each other. Severing the corpus callosum creates two separate brains that function independently of each other, as we will see later in the chapter when we discuss split-brain research techniques.

The thalamus lies below the corpus callosum. It looks like two little footballs, one on each side, connected by a thin group of nerve fibers (see Figure 2.17). Serving as the major sensory relay center for the brain, the thalamus receives input from nearly all the sensory systems, then projects this information to the appropriate cortical areas. Visual information from the words in the Stroop list, for example, first goes to the thalamus before it is projected to the occipital lobe for further processing. The thalamus also relays information from the primary sensory areas of the cerebral cortex to other cortical areas.

The thalamus may also play a role in learning and memory. Damage to the thalamus is known to cause memory problems as evidenced in a person whose thalamus was damaged when a fencing foil went up through his nose and entered his brain. The damage to his thalamus caused him to have severe difficulties in making new memories. For instance, he was unable to learn new phone numbers or remember new faces (Bloom, Lazerson, and Hofstadter, 1988).

The hypothalamus is a group of neuron cell bodies lying below the thalamus. Its general function is homeostasis, including temperature control, which it accomplishes

Corpus Callosum: A connecting bridge of nerve fibers between the left and right hemispheres of the cerebral cortex.

Thalamus: A subcortical area located below the corpus callosum that serves as the major relay area for incoming sensory information.

through regulating the endocrine system. Research has shown that when the hypothalamus is damaged or disconnected, mammals and birds no longer exhibit behaviors such as sweating or shivering to maintain normal body temperatures. Also, when outside temperatures remain constant, their internal body temperatures can fluctuate over a wide range (Satinoff, 1974; Satinoff, Liran, and Clapman, 1982).

The hypothalamus also controls hunger, thirst, sex, and aggression. It controls these drives directly, by generating some behaviors itself, and indirectly, by controlling parts of the autonomic nervous system. Animals exhibit increased or decreased eating and drinking patterns depending on what area of the hypothalamus is affected. More detailed discussion of the functions of the hypothalamus can be found in Chapters 11 and 12.

If the entire brain above the hypothalamus were disconnected or otherwise rendered nonfunctional but the hypothalamus remained functional, animals would still exhibit survival behaviors, although they would be particularly primitive and often without direction. The mechanisms prompting them to breathe, to eat and quench their thirst, to shiver when cold and pant when hot, to exhibit sexual behaviors, and to sleep and awaken would remain. They would still be able to move in a smooth, coordinated fashion. They would also be capable of some emotional reactions and aggressive behaviors, such as fear and attack behaviors, although these would be generalized—not directed toward any particular stimulus (Bard, 1934).

Gender and Cultural Diversity
SEXUAL ORIENTATION AND THE HYPOTHALAMUS

Some interesting research has been done on the hypothalamus regarding gender and sexual orientation. In 1989, research by Allen, Hines, Shryne, and Gorski showed that a particular area of the hypothalamus, the interstitial nuclei of the anterior (front part) of the hypothalamus, is twice as large in males as in females. In 1991, Simon LeVay, a neuroscientist at the Salk Institute in San Diego, documented a difference in this same portion of the hypothalamus between heterosexual and homosexual men.

LeVay obtained brain tissue from 41 subjects who died at seven metropolitan hospitals in New York and California. Of the 41 subjects, 19 were homosexual men who died of complications from AIDS. Of the other 22, 16 were heterosexual men and six were heterosexual women. LeVay found that the anterior hypothalamus was twice as large in heterosexual men as compared to homosexual men and heterosexual women. Does this mean the size of the anterior hypothalamus *determines* sexual orientation? Not necessarily. It could as logically be that size is the *result* of orientation. Or, just as logically, that *some unknown third variable* is involved. LeVay's research findings are fascinating and important for the new directions they inspire in research, but they are not at all conclusive. There may or may not be a direct causal relationship between the size of the hypothalamus and sexual orientation and if there is, we don't know what is cause and what is result. (See also Adler, 1991; Barinaga, 1991; and Gibbons, 1991.) ■

The limbic system is an interconnected group of structures involved with emotional behavior, particularly aggression (see Figure 2.19). The structures that make up the limbic system include the hypothalamus, the fornix, the hippocampus, the amygdala, the septum parts of the thalamus, and parts of the frontal and temporal cortical lobes. The areas of the limbic system most involved with aggression are the amygdala and the septum. Research on cats and rats shows that stimulating the amygdala increases aggressive behavior (Egger and Flynn, 1967). The septum, on the other hand, seems to have a moderating effect on aggression. Animals that have had their septum removed tend to attack anything that comes near them. The hypothalamus affects aggressive behavior through its regulation of the pituitary gland, which releases the male hormone testosterone—a hormone related to aggressiveness in several species. The more testosterone in the bloodstream, the more likely the animal will be aggressive.

Limbic System: An interconnected system of subcortical structures involved with many types of emotional behavior, particularly aggression.

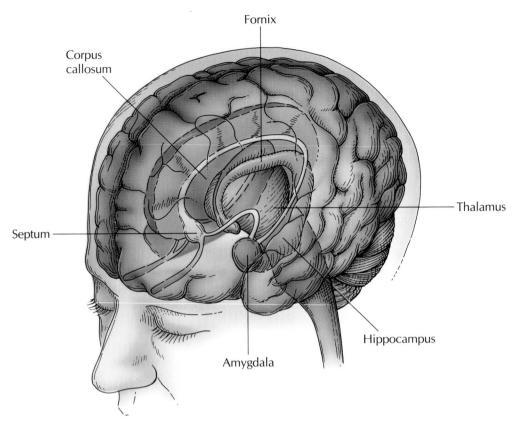

Figure 2.19 The major brain structures associated with the limbic system.

The cerebellum is responsible for coordinating movement and maintaining posture and balance, which are needed for this carpenter to perform his craft.

Cerebellum: The brain area responsible for the maintenance of smooth movement and for coordinated motor activity.

Brain Stem: An area of the brain below the subcortex and in front of the cerebellum that includes the pons, the medulla, and the reticular formation.

Cerebellum

The cerebellum is located at the base of the brain behind the brain stem (see Figures 2.18 and 2.20). In evolutionary terms, it is a very old structure. (Generally, the lower brain structures are older and more primitive than the higher structures.) The cerebellum is responsible for maintaining smooth movement and coordinating motor activity. Although the motor control area of the frontal lobe is involved in initiating voluntary movements, it is the cerebellum that makes these movements smooth, coordinated, and on target. For example, as we type words into our word processors, it is the cerebellum that enables us to hit the correct keys in succession.

The cerebellum also controls the automatic adjustments of posture that allow us to stay upright when we walk and that keep us from falling out of our chairs when we are listening to a lecture or reading a book. To know what postural adjustments to make, the cerebellum receives input from all areas of the brain, including the cortex, the subcortex, and the brain stem.

Brain Stem

You are sleeping. Your eyes dart back and forth as you begin your last dream of the night. Your heart rate, blood pressure, and respiration increase as the dream gets more exciting. Then your dream is shattered by your buzzing alarm clock. All your behaviors and responses in this situation have been either controlled or influenced by areas located in the brain stem. The brain stem lies below the subcortical brain areas and in front of the cerebellum. Three major brain stem areas are of interest to us: the pons, the medulla, and the reticular activating system.

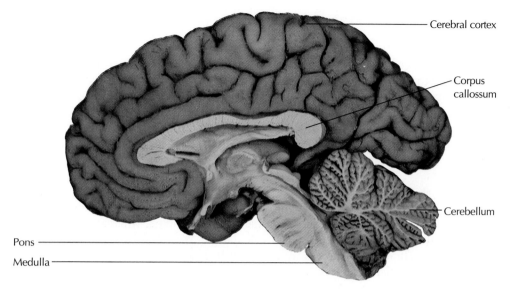

Cerebral cortex

Corpus callossum

Cerebellum

Pons

Medulla

Figure 2.20 The cerebellum. This section through the center of a whole human brain shows parts of the cortex, the subcortex, the brainstem, and the cerebellum. The heavily folded and grooved area at the top is the right hemisphere of the cerebral cortex. The white matter at the center of the photograph is the corpus callossum. The pons and medulla can be seen at the bottom of the photo and they appear white. The feathery sectioned structure at the bottom right is the cerebellum.

The pons is located in the upper portion of the brain stem below the subcortex. It is in front of the cerebellum. The pons contains several types of fibers. Some connect the two halves of the cerebellum, whereas others carry visual and auditory information either to the brain or to the cerebellum. Still other fibers are associated with respiration, movement, facial expression, and sleep, including initiation of the rapid eye movements associated with dream sleep (see Chapter 5).

The medulla is found below the pons at the bottom of the brain stem, just above the spinal cord. Its functions are similar to those of the pons. Because it is essentially an extension of the spinal cord, the medulla has many nerve fibers passing through it carrying information to and from the brain. The medulla also contains many nerve fibers that control automatic bodily functions such as respiration (Smith, Ellenberger, Ballanyi, Richter, and Feldman, 1991). Damage to the medulla can lead to failure of bodily functions and death.

The reticular activating system (RAS) is a diffuse set of cells in the medulla, pons, hypothalamus, and thalamus (see Figure 2.20). The RAS serves as a filter for incoming sensory information. After receiving input from most of the sensory systems, the RAS filters it and rejects unimportant or nonvital sensory input. Have you ever been to a party where you tried to hold a conversation with a friend over the din of other conversations? Your RAS was helping you make sense of what your friend was saying by allowing the sensory information from your friend to pass to other parts of the brain, while screening or blocking information from other conversations. Because the RAS serves as a sensory filter, it is also important for attention and arousal. For example, if someone across the room at the party says your name, the RAS will let that information through to your cortex, and you might try to zero in on that voice and hear what is being said about you.

In this brief discussion of the major brain structures, we have isolated each structure in detailing its functions. In a fully operational brain, each brain part has many interconnections with other parts—cortical areas with other cortical areas, cortical areas with subcortical areas, and so on. As you may have noticed when we pointed out the part played by various brain structures in the Stroop effect, several brain areas, both cortical and subcortical, contribute to it.

Pons: A brain structure located at the top of the brain stem that is involved with functions such as respiration, movement, and sleep.

Medulla: A structure in the brain stem responsible for automatic body functions, such as respiration.

Reticular Activating System: A diffuse set of cells in the medulla, pons, hypothalamus, and thalamus that serves as a filter for incoming sensory information.

Gender and Cultural Diversity

MALE AND FEMALE DIFFERENCES IN THE BRAIN

Often we hear people attribute differences in male and female behavior to social factors by claiming that girls play with dolls and boys play with cars because of parental influence or that girls are good at reading and boys are good at math because of societal expectations. Although no one can deny there are societal influences at work, it looks more and more as if male and female differences may ultimately stem from biological factors and in particular, from differing organizational patterns within the brain resulting from early hormonal influence (Kimura, 1992; Reinisch, Ziemba, and Sanders, 1991).

Look at Figures 2.21 and 2.22. These figures summarize recent research conducted to determine differences in cognitive abilities of men and women. As you can see, men tend to score higher on tests of mathematical reasoning, whereas women score higher on tests involving mathematical calculation. Men tend to perform better on spatial relationship tasks, whereas women tend to perform better on tasks requiring perceptual speed. Men tend to be more accurate in target-directed motor skills, while women tend to be more efficient in skills requiring fine motor coordination. What accounts for these differences?

According to recent research, the answer lies in the effect hormones have on brain development early in life. Immediately after conception, all developing embryos exhibit female sexual characteristics, but at approximately six weeks male embryos begin to develop testes. The testes then begin secreting androgens, or masculinizing hormones, chief of which is testosterone. (This is discussed in more detail in Chapter 11.) These androgens not only bring about the development of male genitals, they also appear to influence the structural development of the brain and permanently alter brain function. Based on research with rats conducted by Christine Vito and Thomas Fox (1981), it is believed that hormones act on the brain at a certain critical period near birth. If administered later in life, they do not have the same effect.

The extent of early hormonal influence is illustrated in studies involving children who have been exposed to excess amounts of hormones during the period before birth. One of these studies was done with 9- to 21-year-old boys who had been exposed to a type of estrogen (a female hormone) before birth. They exhibited lowered spatial ability as compared with their unexposed brothers (Reinisch and Sanders, 1992). Other studies have been conducted with girls affected with a genetic defect known as congenital adrenal hyperplasia (CAH), which is caused by an excess amount of androgens, male hormones, in the period just before or just after birth. Although physiological effects resulting from CAH—the development of male genitals and the overproduction of androgens—can be surgically or medically corrected, the hormonal influence on brain development cannot be reversed. CAH-affected girls grow up to be more tomboyish and aggressive than nonaffected girls, and when given a choice of toys they prefer typically masculine toys such as trucks and building toys rather than typically feminine toys such as dolls and tea sets. In fact, they play with cars for the same amount of time that boys do (Kimura, 1992). Moreover, they outperform nonaffected girls on cognitive tests of spatial ability on which males are known to excel, such as the mental rotation task shown in Figure 2.22 (Nass and Baker, 1991). Assuming that their parents would encourage feminine behavior patterns equally in CAH girls and in their nonaffected sisters, it seems that the affected girls' behavior must be due to the early androgen influence.

Hormonal levels may influence cognitive performance throughout our lifetime. Women's performance on certain tasks fluctuates according to estrogen levels during the menstrual cycle. High estrogen levels toward the beginning of the menstrual cycle are associated with increased articulation and motor capability but lowered spatial ability (Hampson, 1990). In men, seasonal fluctuations in spatial ability have been recorded by Doreen Kimura (1992). In the spring, with lowered testosterone levels, men tend to perform higher on spatial tasks.

Not only are there behavioral differences in males and females, there are differences in the anatomical structure of male and female brains. Most researchers agree that

---

Problem-Solving Tasks Favoring Women

Perceptual speed:
As quickly as possible identify matching items.

Displaced objects:
After looking at the middle picture, tell which item is missing from the the picture on the right.

Verbal fluency:
List words that begin with the same letter. (Women also tend to perform better in ideational fluency tests, for example, listing objects that are the same color.)

B – – –	Bat, big, bike, bang, bark, bank, bring, brand, broom, bright, brook bug, buddy, bunk

Precision manual tasks:
Place the pegs in the holes as quickly as possible.

Mathematical calculation:
Compute the answer.

72	$6(18+4)-78+\frac{36}{2}$

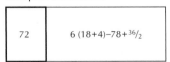

Figure 2.21 Problem-solving tasks favoring women.

females possess cerebral hemispheres that are more asymmetrical for speech and have an enlarged back part of the corpus collosum (Allen et al., 1991). This indicates that there may be more nerve fibers passing back and forth across the corpus collosum with possibly more communication among brain structures in the female brain than in the male brain.

There is also evidence that female and male brains are organized differently for various functions. In studies comparing aphasias (speech disorders) and apraxias (difficulties in selecting purposeful movement) in men and women, researchers have found that both disorders result from brain damage toward the front of the brain in women and toward the rear of the brain in men. These differences may explain some of the gender differences we previously mentioned. The close proximity of the "praxia," or motor selection, center in women to the motor cortex near the front of the brain may account for women's enhanced fine motor skills. Similarly, the close proximity of men's praxia center to the visual cortex toward the back of the brain may account for men's superior targeting ability (Kimura, 1992).

So it seems that male and female brains are organized differently from early in life due to hormonal influence. Although there seems to be no difference in overall intelligence levels, males and females do exhibit differences in patterns of cognitive functioning. There are certainly exceptions—many males perform well on tasks normally favoring women and likewise, many females perform well on tasks normally favoring men. But even these exceptions can be explained in terms of hormonal influence. Depriving newborns of normal hormonal influence during their critical period leads to males exhibiting female-like behavior and females exhibiting male-like behavior.

We need to keep in mind that the research conducted in hormonal influence on brain organization is correlational, so the mechanisms involved in the actual cause of certain adult behaviors have yet to be determined. There is no doubt, though, that this research shows the importance of early biological processes and their involvement in determining male and female differences in cognitive behavior patterns. ■

Review Questions

1. What is a reflex and why is it important?
2. The bumpy, convoluted area making up the outside surface of the brain is the _____ .
3. You are giving a speech. Name the cortical lobes involved when you engage in these behaviors:
   a. planning what to say next,
   b. identifying the faces in the audience,
   c. hearing and formulating answers to questions after the speech,
   d. remembering where your car is in the parking lot on your way home.
4. The connecting bridge that makes it possible for the hemispheres to communicate with each other is the _____ .
5. The subcortical brain structure that relays sensory input to other brain areas is the _____ .
6. The major function of the hypothalamus is _____ .
7. List the three major brain stem structures.

Answers to Review Questions can be found in Appendix C.

STUDYING THE BRAIN

Information about the brain presented in this chapter has come from research using various techniques. They include anatomical studies, lesion procedures, electrical recording, electrical stimulation, split-brain studies, computerized axial tomography (CAT), positron emission topography (PET), and magnetic resonance imaging (MRI).

Many of the differences between males and females can be traced to differences between male and female brains.

Problem-Solving Tasks Favoring Men

Spatial tasks:
Mentally rotate the 3-d object to identify its match.

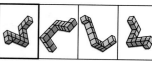

Spatial tasks:
Mentally manipulate the folded paper to tell where the holes will fall when it is unfolded.

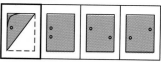

Target-directed motor skills:
Hit the bulls eye.

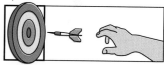

Disembedding tests:
Find the simple shape on the left in the more complex figures.

Mathematical reasoning:
What is the answer?

5 ½	If you bicycle 24 miles a day, how many days will it take to travel 132 miles?

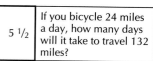

Figure 2.22 Problem-solving tasks favoring men.

- *How do researchers study the brain, and what are some of their findings?*

Anatomical Studies: From Cadavers to Computers

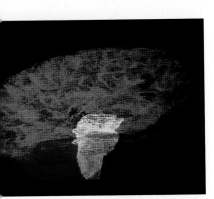

It is possible to learn a great deal about the structure of the human brain by generating computerized views of actual human brains.

Early data on nervous system structure and function came from the study of human anatomy. By the mid-1800s, cadaver dissection had produced a basic map of the peripheral nervous system and some of the brain. One of these early physiologists was Paul Broca (1861), who located an area of the brain (now known as Broca's area) that, when damaged, causes a partial or complete loss of the ability to use language. Broca identified this area by dissecting brains of deceased patients who had had language disabilities.

More recently, investigators have used sophisticated microscopes and advanced computer methods to study the fine detail of cadaver brains. A good example of the use of computers in research on brain structure is shown at the left. This computer-generated view of the human brain was produced by Robert Livingston at the University of California, San Diego. Livingston and his group produced this image by feeding a computer hundreds of images from slides of brain tissue. Using a computer graphics system, Livingston added color to certain parts of the brain and even made motion pictures of different areas of the brain.

But just as it is impossible to determine the function of a complex machine by looking at it, we cannot determine brain function merely by examining dead brain tissue. Researchers have, however, developed a number of techniques for examining the living brain.

Lesion Techniques: Studying the Brain Through Systematic Deactivation

Lesion Technique: Any brain research technique that systematically destroys brain tissue to observe the effect of the destruction on behavior.

The first techniques used to examine living brains were invasive; that is, researchers surgically damaged the brains of animals in some way so that the effect on behavior could be observed. Any technique that systematically destroys brain tissue to observe the effect of the destruction on behavior is a lesion technique. In the earliest experimental research using this approach, both large and small amounts of brain tissue were destroyed in order to better understand the function of the brain.

Although lesion techniques have helped researchers determine specific functions for some portions of the brain, these techniques have two severe drawbacks: (1) The researcher is doing permanent damage to the brain of a living, thinking animal; and (2) once part of the brain of an animal is destroyed, the researcher is no longer observing the brain of a normal animal. Researchers today prefer newer techniques that do not have these drawbacks, such as electrical recording techniques and electrical stimulation of the brain.

Electrical Recording: Measuring Electrical Changes in the Brain

Because the action potential that travels down an axon generates a small electrical current, it is possible to measure the electrical activity of a single neuron, a group of neurons, or an intact nerve. Such measurement requires a recording electrode, an

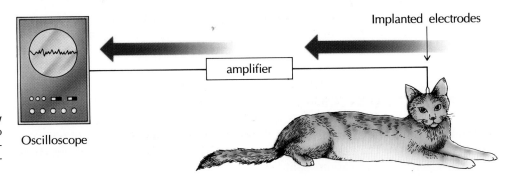

Figure 2.23 An electrical recording system. Such a system is used to monitor changes in individual neurons or groups of neurons in particular brain areas.

Oscilloscope

amplifier

Implanted electrodes

Critical Thinking

PSYCHOLOGY IN ACTION

CLARIFYING TERMS AND CONCEPTS
Understanding Brain Anatomy and Function

Being able to define a term or concept doesn't necessarily mean you fully comprehend it. Critical thinkers look at key terms from different angles. They not only ask "What does this mean?"; they let their curiosity roam. They also ask "What would happen if . . . ?" and "Suppose this were different, would . . . ?" They explore key terms and concepts. Such free-wheeling exploration not only improves comprehension of the original term but also encourages the development of general critical thinking skills.

The following exercise will help to clarify your understanding of brain terminology and function. While so doing, it provides a model for the types of questions that lead to critical thinking.

Situation #1
A neurosurgeon is about to perform brain surgery. The surgeon touches (stimulates with an electrode) a tiny portion of the patient's brain, and the patient's right finger moves. After noting the reaction, the surgeon stimulates a portion of the brain a short distance away and the patient's right thumb moves.

Questions to Answer

1. What section of the brain has been stimulated? _____ What lobe is this in? _____

2. What hemisphere of the brain is being stimulated? _____

3. During this stimulation, would the patient experience feelings of pain? Why or why not? _____

4. Given that some parts of the brain are specialized for certain functions (e.g., receiving sensory information, controlling motor output), what would happen if the brain were disconnected from the rest of the body? Does brain functioning require feedback from the receptors in the body? If your brain could be kept alive outside your body, what could it do? Would you be able to think without sensory input or motor output?

Situation #2
The scene: An emergency room in a hospital. Two interns are talking about a car crash victim who has just been wheeled in.

First Intern: "Good Grief! The whole cerebral cortex is severely damaged; we'll have to remove the entire area."

Second Intern: "We can't do that. If we remove all that tissue the patient will die in a matter of minutes."

First Intern: "Where did you get your medical training—watching "General Hospital"? The patient won't die if we remove his whole cerebral cortex."

Second Intern: "I resent your tone and insinuation. I went to one of the finest medical schools, and I'm telling you the patient *will* die if we remove his whole cerebral cortex."

Questions to Answer

1. If the whole cerebral cortex is removed, will the patient die? Explain your answer.

2. If the patient is kept alive without a cerebral cortex, what kinds of behaviors or responses would be possible? What changes would you expect in personality, memories, and emotions?

3. What behaviors could be expected with only the subcortex, medulla, and spinal cord intact? What if only the medulla and spinal cord were functioning? Only the spinal cord?

4. If a patient could be kept alive without a cerebral cortex, would life be worth living? What parts of your brain could be removed before you would want to stop living?

---

amplifier, and an output (or recording) device (see Figure 2.23). Electrodes are small devices that conduct electricity. Of many shapes and sizes, most electrodes used in recording neural activity are similar to thin wires. Amplifiers intensify the tiny electrical currents into signals that can be recorded on an output device. The recording device can be electronic, such as an oscilloscope, or mechanical, such as a polygraph (paper chart recorder).

Do you have to put the electrodes inside the brain of a person or an animal to record brain activity?   No. It is possible to record large changes in brain activity with electrodes attached to a person's skin or scalp. Brain activity is measured by an electroencephalograph (EEG) machine, which can be used to monitor a person's general state of consciousness. This type of recording is widely used with humans because it requires no surgery. EEG recording is used in the study of sleep and dreaming, as we will see in Chapter 5.

Electrodes: Small devices (normally wires) used to conduct electricity to or from brain tissue.

Electroencephalograph (EEG): A machine that monitors large changes in brain activity with electrodes attached to a person's scalp.

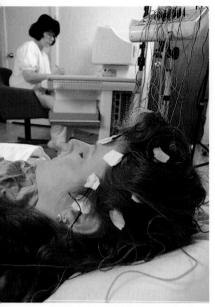

The electrical activity of the brain can be recorded using the electroencephalograph (EEG). The electrodes are attached to the patient's scalp and the electrical activity of the brain is often displayed on a computer monitor or recorded on a paper chart.

Reward Centers: Areas in the brain that, when stimulated, invoke a highly satisfying feeling.

Electrical Stimulation: Eliciting Brain Activity

A researcher can activate certain areas of the brain by using electrodes to deliver small electrical currents to those areas. These electrical currents will then cause the person or animal to move a muscle, experience a feeling, remember something, or perhaps see or hear something. This type of research is usually done with humans, since animals can give us only a limited amount of information. For example, if a rat is stimulated in the visual area, it cannot say, "Oh, wow, what a beautiful blue!" Most of the functional mapping of the brain using electrical stimulation has been done with people undergoing brain surgery for some reason. In cases where the surgeon needed to determine the functions of brain areas to be lesioned or removed, mapping the surrounding area was part of the process.

The neurosurgeon and researcher Wilder Penfield has published his findings. Since the brain itself does not feel pain, it is possible for people to be aware and alert during brain surgery. When Penfield stimulated particular brain areas, his subjects reported feeling various sensations, seeing visual images, hearing musical passages, experiencing memories from the past, and so on. One patient told him that she felt she was in her kitchen listening to the voice of her little boy playing outside in the yard. Another reported that he was watching a small town baseball game and saw a young boy crawl under the fence and join the other spectators (1975, pp. 21–22).

One researcher who successfully used animals in brain stimulation research was James Olds. In the early 1950s, Olds designed an experiment that allowed him to determine whether a rat liked or disliked a particular brain stimulation (Olds and Milner, 1954). Within the rat's brain, he implanted a permanent electrode that was hooked up to a stimulator connected to a bar in the rat's cage. The rat was then taught to press the bar to receive an electrical stimulation of the brain. Olds found that rats would rapidly press the bar when the electrode was placed in specific brain areas. The areas that caused the most vigorous bar pressing were called reward centers. Of course, it is not clear exactly what the rats felt or why they pressed the bar. Whatever the reason, the brain stimulation was apparently very rewarding. In some cases, hungry rats preferred the electrical stimulation to food.

Split-Brain Research: Two Brains Rather Than One

Some fascinating aspects of brain functioning have been uncovered from split-brain research. This research had its beginnings in 1961, when Joseph Bogen, a neurosurgeon, severed the corpus callosum of a patient with severe epilepsy, a chronic disease of the nervous system in which patients suffer from seizures. This was a radical step, but previous research led him to believe it would greatly reduce or completely eliminate the seizures. Since the corpus callosum connects the two cerebral hemispheres, after surgery, the two halves of the brain would no longer be able to communicate with each other. Each hemisphere will operate independently. Although fewer than 100 split-brain operations have been done since 1961, the resulting research has profoundly improved our understanding of how the two halves of the brain function.

Split-brain patients show no outward change in their behavior. They talk, walk, play catch, and perform complicated mental tasks. Nor do they behave as if they have a "split personality." However, testing has revealed subtle differences in functioning. Because split-brain patients cannot transfer information from one half of the brain to the other, tasks that require this sharing of information are difficult or impossible for them to perform.

The following example illustrates this difficulty. Two split-brain people are blindfolded. Subject L picks up a key with his left hand. Because information from the left side of the body crosses over and is received in the right brain, the information about the key travels to L's right hemisphere (see Figure 2.24). Subject R picks up a key with her right hand; this information is received and processed in the left hemisphere. Thus, for each

James Olds implanted electrodes into the brains of rats to study reward centers in the brain.

subject, information about the key travels from one side of the body to the opposite brain hemisphere but cannot be shared with the other hemisphere because of the severed corpus callosum.

When the subjects are asked to say what is in their hands, subject L cannot verbally say, "a key," whereas subject R can. However, if the blindfolds are removed and the subjects are asked to point out the object they were holding from among other objects, both subjects are able to do so. The right brain (which receives information from the left hand) knows what the key is but cannot verbally identify it. The left brain also knows what the key is and *can* verbally identify it. The reason for this discrepancy is that language areas are in the left hemisphere; thus, the left brain can talk but the right brain is mute.

Left Brain–Right Brain Specialization

Research on split-brain patients (Gazzaniga, 1970; Sperry, 1968; Zaidel, 1975) has given a clear picture of the differences between the two brain hemispheres (summarized in Figure 2.25). The left hemisphere is specialized for language functions—speaking, reading, writing, and understanding language—and for analytical functions, such as mathematics. The right hemisphere is specialized for nonverbal abilities. These include musical abilities and perceptual and "spatio-manipulative" skills, such as maneuvering through space, drawing or building geometric designs, working puzzles, painting pictures and recognizing faces (Springer and Deutsch, 1981). Split-brain research has also helped point out the interdependence of the two cerebral hemispheres. For example, subjects who can solve the block design subtest of the Wechsler Intelligence Scale (see Chapter 8) take more time to solve the problems after the split-brain surgery. This indicates that the solution requires integration of information from both sides of the brain (Gazzaniga, 1989).

Is this left- and right-brain specialization reversed in left-handed people? Not necessarily. Most people who use their left hands to write, hammer a nail, and throw a ball still have their language areas on the left side of the brain. Springer and Deutsch (1981) describe a study in which 95 percent of right-handers were found to have speech local-

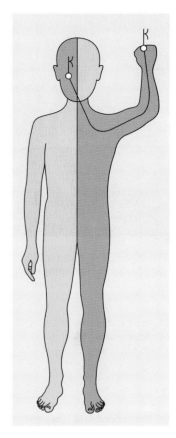

Figure 2.24 Information crossover. Information from the left side of the body crosses over to the right brain.

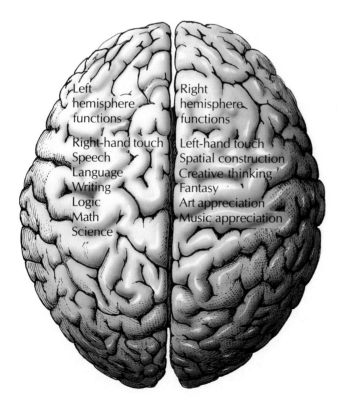

Left hemisphere functions

Right-hand touch
Speech
Language
Writing
Logic
Math
Science

Right hemisphere functions

Left-hand touch
Spatial construction
Creative thinking
Fantasy
Art appreciation
Music appreciation

Figure 2.25 Functions of the left and right hemispheres. The left hemisphere *tends* to specialize in verbal and analytical functions; the right hemisphere *tends* to specialize in nonverbal abilities such as spaciomanipulative skills and musical abilities.

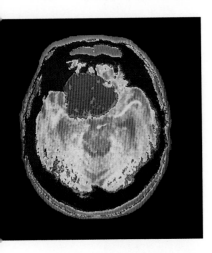

This false color CAT scan used X rays to locate a brain tumor that appears as the deep purple mass at the top left.

ized on the left side of their brain and 70 percent of left-handers showed the same pattern. This research suggests that even though the right side of the brain is the dominant hemisphere for movement in left-handers, other types of skills are often localized in the same brain areas as for right-handers.

Although it is true that left-handers are generally penalized for living in a right-handed world, there may be some benefits to being left-handed. Statistics show that left-handed people tend to recover better from strokes that damage the language areas in their brain (Seamon and Gazzaniga, 1973). This may be because the nonspeech hemisphere in left-handers is better able to take over speech functions if the primary speech areas are damaged.

Research into hemispheric specialization has provided possible answers to many psychological puzzles. For example, a possible explanation for the confusion experienced in the Stroop effect is that the words and the colors are processed in separate hemispheres, the words in the left hemisphere and the colors in the right. For people to name the color, the right brain must first identify it and send this information to the left brain, which takes time. Meanwhile, the left hemisphere might mistakenly process and speak the printed word.

CAT, PET, and MRI: Techniques That Scan the Brain

Advances in brain research depend on both the creativity of the researcher and the available technology. New technology now allows researchers to study intact, functioning brains by taking pictures of them. New techniques include CAT scans, PET scans, and magnetic resonance imaging.

CAT stands for computerized axial tomography. The CAT scan uses X rays to take pictures of internal organs, including the brain. CAT scans are more useful than regular X rays because they pinpoint exact locations of tumors or other problem areas quite clearly, whereas normal X rays are not nearly as clear and accurate. CAT scans can reveal structural problems with the brain, but they cannot provide information about the function of any particular brain area.

CAT (Computerized Axial Tomography) Scan: X-ray pictures of internal organs that are clearer and more accurate than normal X rays.

PET scans, on the other hand, yield information that is helpful in determining brain function. PET stands for positron emission tomography. In a PET scan, glucose is made radioactive and is injected into the bloodstream of the subject. This radioactive glucose emits positively charged particles called "positrons." The positrons react with other particles to generate gamma rays, which are detected by the PET scanner (Li and Shen, 1985). The more gamma rays detected in a certain area of the brain, the more glucose is being used in that area and the more neural activity is occurring in that brain area (Phelps and Mazziotta, 1985). PET scans, then, can clearly show which areas of the brain are active and which are not (see the photograph on this page). This can be particularly helpful when studying mental disorders and problems associated with strokes (Andreasen, 1988).

PET (Positron Emission Tomography) Scan: A type of brain scan in which radioactive glucose is injected into the bloodstream in order to see brain activity in an intact, living brain.

MRI (Magnetic Resonance Imaging): A research technique utilizing radio waves instead of X rays to allow researchers to see structures within the brain.

A more recent technique that shows the structure of a living brain much more clearly even than CAT scans is magnetic resonance imaging, or MRI. It uses radio waves instead of X rays (see the photograph on this page). MRI reveals the distribution of specific types of atoms within a brain area (Pykett, 1982) by utilizing the magnetic properties of the nuclei of different atoms to make clear pictures of the structure of the brain. MRI techniques have been improved by the use of echo-planar imaging (EPI). EPI has greatly decreased the time necessary to complete a brain scan so that it is now possible to take an MRI "snapshot" of the brain in a fraction of a second, whereas previously it might have taken several minutes (Stehling, Turner, and Mansfield, 1991).

As we have seen in this chapter, behavior is a complex process that has its roots in the nervous and endocrine systems. Slowly, these body systems are revealing their secrets to teams of psychologists, physiologists, and medical researchers. The more we learn about the brain and the nervous system, the better we will understand why people and animals behave the way they do.

Drawing by John Chase.

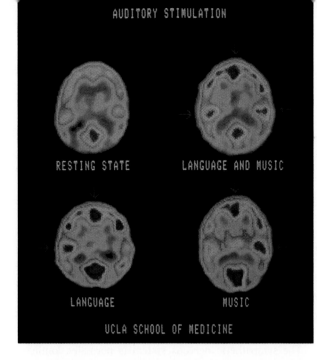

A PET scan can be used to indicate the function of different brain areas. As you can see in these four scans, the right side of the brain shows more activity when we listen to music and the left side of the brain is more active when we process language. Both sides of the brain are active when we hear both language and music at the same time.

Review Questions

1. Dissection of cadaver brains is an example of _____ techniques.

2. What are the drawbacks of using lesion techniques?

3. Small wires inserted into the brain to record electrical activity of different brain structures are called _____ .

4. How is electrical stimulation done?

5. Severing the corpus callosum of a patient results in a person with a _____ brain.

6. Research conducted with split-brain patients indicates that when we converse or work a calculus problem, we use primarily the _____ hemisphere of the brain; when we play the violin or draw blueprints, we use primarily the _____ hemisphere.

7. The three major techniques used for scanning the brain are _____ , _____ , and _____ ; the one that gives the clearest images is _____

Answers to Review Questions can be found in Appendix C.

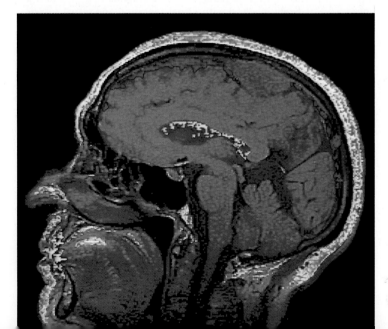

Magnetic resonance imaging (MRI) enables researchers to see the internal structures of the brain. Here, one can clearly see the fissures and internal structures of the cerebral cortex, as well as the cerebellum and the brainstem. The throat, nasal airways, and cerebrospinal fluid surrounding the brain are dark.

REVIEW OF MAJOR CONCEPTS

THE NEURON

1. **Neurons** are cells that are responsible for transmitting information throughout the body. The main parts of the neuron are the dendrites, which receive information from other neurons; the soma, or cell body; and the axon, which sends neural information. At the end of the axon are small structures called axon terminal buttons that form synapses with other nerve cells and that secrete neurotransmitters.

2. Nerves are bundles of axons from neurons having similar functions.

3. The axon is a tubelike structure that may be covered with an insulating substance called myelin. The axon is specialized for transmitting neural impulses, or action potentials. During times when no action potential is moving down the axon, the axon is at rest. The resting potential gives way to the action potential when a stimulus causes chemical ions to move across the axon membrane. All action potentials in a given neuron are of the same intensity.

CHEMICAL MESSENGERS

4. Information is transferred from one neuron to another at the synapse via chemicals called neurotransmitters. Neurotransmitters are released by axon terminal buttons when an action potential reaches the buttons. Most psychoactive drugs have their effect on the nervous system by affecting the amount of neurotransmitter that crosses the synapse.

5. Closely associated with the autonomic nervous system is the endocrine system, a system of glands that release hormones into the bloodstream to regulate the level of critical chemicals within the body. The major link between the endocrine and nervous systems is the hypothalamus.

THE PERIPHERAL NERVOUS SYSTEM

6. The peripheral nervous system incudes all nerves going to and from the brain and spinal cord. Its two major subdivisions are the somatic nervous system and the autonomic nervous system.

7. The somatic nervous system includes all nerves carrying afferent (incoming) sensory information and efferent (outgoing) motor information to and from the sense organs and skeletal muscles.

8. The autonomic nervous system includes those nerves outside the brain and spinal cord that maintain normal functioning of glands, heart muscle, and the smooth muscles of the blood vessels and internal organs. The autonomic nervous system is divided into two branches, the parasympathic and the sympathetic, which tend to work in opposition to one another.

9. The parasympathetic nervous system is normally dominant when a person is relaxed and not under any physical or mental stress. Its main function is to slow heart rate, lower blood pressure, and increase digestion and elimination.

10. The sympathetic nervous system is normally dominant when a person is under physical or mental stress. It functions to increase heart rate and blood pressure and slow digestive processes, mobilizing the body for fight or flight.

THE CENTRAL NERVOUS SYSTEM

11. The central nervous system is composed of the brain and the spinal cord.

12. The spinal cord is the communications link between the brain and the rest of the body below the neck. It is involved in all voluntary and reflex responses of the body below the neck. Its major components are gray matter and white matter. Gray matter contains cell bodies and synapses where information is transferred and processed in the spinal cord. White matter is made up wholly of axons carrying information to and from the brain.

13. The major divisions of the brain are the cerebral cortex, the subcortical areas, the cerebellum, and the brain stem.

14. The cerebral cortex, the bumpy, convoluted area making up the outside surface of brain, is divided into four lobes: frontal, parietal, occipital, and temporal. The frontal lobes control movement and speech and are involved with self-awareness and the ability to plan ahead. The parietal lobes function as the receiving area for sensory information from the limbs and skin. The occipital lobe is almost entirely involved with visual sensation and visual informa-

tion processing. The major functions of the temporal lobes include hearing and language.

15. The subcortex lies in the middle of the brain under the cerebral cortex and includes many different areas; the most important are the corpus callosum, the thalamus, the hypothalamus, and the limbic system. The corpus callosum is a connecting bridge of axons between the two cerebral hemispheres. The thalamus is the major incoming sensory relay area of the brain. The hypothalamus regulates functioning of the endocrine system and is the major brain center for regulating temperature, thirst, hunger, sex, and aggression. The limbic system is an interconnected group of brain structures involved with emotional behavior.

16. Research shows relationships between hypothalamus, gender, and sexual orientation, but we do not know what is cause and what is effect. Recent research also seems to indicate that male and female differences may ultimately stem from biological factors. Early hormonal influence and anatomical differences in brain structure are being further investigated.

17. The cerebellum is located at the base of the brain behind the brain stem. It is responsible for smooth movement and coordinated motor activity.

18. The brain stem lies below the subcortex and in front of the cerebellum. Its major areas are the pons, the medulla, and the reticular formation. The pons is involved with respiration, movement, facial expression, and sleep. The main function of the medulla is control of respiration. The reticular formation is a diffuse set of neurons that are associated with attention and arousal.

STUDYING THE BRAIN

19. Anatomical research techniques refer to studying the brain's structure through direct observation, such as examining the brains of cadavers or studying slices of brain tissue under a microscope.

20. Lesion techniques involve destroying part of an animal's brain and studying resultant changes in the animal's behavior.

21. Electrical recording techniques involve implanting electrodes into the brain or on its surface to study the brain's electrical activity.

22. Electrical stimulation techniques involve passing small electrical currents through parts of the brain to activate neurons in a particular area. One finding from this research has been the discovery of reward centers in the brain.

23. In split-brain research, patients who have had their corpus callosum severed are studied to determine the differences in functional abilities between the left and right brain hemispheres.

24. Split-brain research has led to findings suggesting that the left hemisphere is specialized for language and analytical functions, whereas the right hemisphere is specialized for nonverbal abilities, including musical abilities and perceptual and spatiomanipulative skills.

25. CAT, PET, and MRI scans are used to study the structures and function of intact, living brains without having to place electrodes in the brain or destroy normal brain tissue.

SUGGESTED READINGS

BLOOM, F. E., LAZERSON, A., & HOFSTADTER, L. (1988). *Brain, mind, and behavior* (2nd ed.). New York: Freeman.

BRIDGEMAN, B. (1988). *The biology of behavior and mind.* New York: Wiley. An introduction to physiological psychology.

CARLSON, N. R. (1991). *Foundations of physiological psychology* (2nd ed.). Boston: Allyn & Bacon. An interesting introduction to physiological psychology.

KALAT, J. W. (1991). *Biological psychology* (4th ed.). Belmont,

CA: Wadsworth. A readable introduction to physiological psychology.

PIEL, J. (ED.). (1992). Mind and brain (Special Issue). *Scientific American, 267*(3).

SPRINGER, S. P., & DEUTSCH, G. (1989). *Left brain, right brain* (3rd ed.). San Francisco: Freeman. A book about the research on split-brain surgery and the difference between the left and right hemispheres of the cerebral cortex.

Sensation

OUTLINE

I have just touched my dog. He was rolling on the grass, with pleasure in every muscle and limb. I wanted to catch a picture of him in my fingers, and I touched him as lightly as I would cobwebs. . . . He pressed close to me, as if he were fain to crowd himself into my hand. He loved it with his tail, with his paw, with his tongue. If he could speak, I believe he would say with me that paradise is attained by touch. (pp. 3–4)

Thus Helen Keller began her book *The World I Live In.* Her world was totally different from that of most people: She couldn't see it or hear it because she was blind and deaf, but she learned to know it through her sense of touch. Although deprived of two senses, she was as capable and as appreciative of life—if not more so—as any person with all five senses. This was because she made the most of the senses she did have. Excerpts from her book describe how she used these senses:

> Through the sense of touch I know the faces of friends, the illimitable variety of straight and curved lines, all surfaces, the exuberance of the soil, the delicate shapes of flowers, the noble forms of trees, and the range of mighty winds. Besides objects, surfaces, and atmospherical changes, I perceive countless vibrations. . . . Footsteps, I discover, vary tactually according to the age, the sex, and the manners of the walker. . . . When a carpenter works in the house or in the barn near by, I know by the slanting, up-and-down, toothed vibration, and the ringing concussion of blow upon blow, that he is sawing or hammering. . . .
>
> In the evening quiet there are fewer vibrations than in the daytime, and then I rely more largely upon smell. . . . Sometimes, when there is no wind, the odors are so grouped that I know the character of the country and can place a hayfield, a country store, a garden, a barn, a grove of pines, a farmhouse with the windows open. . . . I know by smell the kind of house we enter. I have recognized an old-fashioned country house because it has several layers of odors, left by a succession of families, of plants, perfumes, and draperies. (pp. 43–44, 46, 68–69)

Helen Keller wasn't born deaf and blind. When she was 19 months old, she suffered a fever that left her without sight or hearing and thus virtually isolated from the world. As a young child, Helen learned to function by substituting her other senses for those she lacked. She discovered her father's facial features not through sight, but by feeling them; she knew when the door slammed not through hearing it, but by feeling the resulting vibrations; she found out where she had wandered not by looking around, but by smelling the fragrances in that part of the yard.

Although Helen did manage to maneuver through her silent world, she remained isolated from any communication with others. This isolation was a constant source of frustration and anger, leading her to violent temper tantrums. In fact, she noted that "after awhile the need of some means of communication became so urgent that these outbursts occurred daily, sometimes hourly" (1902, p. 32).

Helen's parents realized they had to find help for their daughter, and after diligently searching they found Anne Sullivan, a young teacher who was able to break through Helen's barrier of isolation by taking advantage of her sense of touch. From the moment she arrived, Anne began finger-spelling names of objects by placing her hand in Helen's and forming letters used in sign language. Although Helen learned to finger-spell many words, she didn't understand that these finger movements could signify names for things. Then one day, Anne took Helen to the pumphouse and, as Anne (1902) wrote:

> I made Helen hold her mug under the spout while I pumped. As the cold water gushed forth, filling the mug, I spelled "w-a-t-e-r" in Helen's free hand. The word coming so close upon the sensation of cold water rushing over her hand seemed to startle her. She dropped the mug and stood as one transfixed. A new light came into her face. (p. 257)

From that moment on, Helen had an unquenchable desire to learn the names of everything and everybody, to interact and communicate with everyone. That one moment, brought on by the sensation of cold water on her hand, was the impetus for a lifetime of learning about, understanding, and appreciating the world through her remaining senses. In 1904, Helen Keller graduated cum laude from Radcliffe, one of the most respected women's colleges in the world, and following her graduation went on to become a famous author and lecturer, inspiring hope and encouragement to the handicapped throughout the world.

The story of Helen Keller has been told and retold as an example of how people can overcome sensory deficiencies by using their other senses to the optimum. In this chapter, we will discuss each sense in detail and examine the sensory mechanisms by which each operates. We will describe, for instance, how environmental stimuli—light from a flashlight, the odor of a skunk, heat from a campfire—are received by sensory receptors, converted into a language the brain can understand, then transmitted to the brain. This process of receiving, converting, and transmitting information from the outside world ("outside" the brain, not necessarily outside the body) is called sensation. Our study of sensation covers not only what are commonly known as the five senses—vision, hearing, taste, smell, and touch—but also those senses that provide the brain with data from inside the body. These internal senses are the vestibular sense (the sense of balance) and kinesthesis (the sense of bodily position and movement).

Sensation: The process of receiving, translating, and transmitting information to the brain from the external and internal environments.

As you read Chapter 3, keep the following **Survey** questions in mind and answer them in your own words:

- How do our sensory organs gather sensory information and convert it into signals the brain can understand?

- What is light, and how do our eye structures work to enable us to see?

- What is sound, and how do our ear structures work to enable us to hear?

- How do we smell different odors and taste different flavors?

- How do we feel pressure, temperature, and pain? How are we able to keep our balance? And how do we know what our body is doing without watching it?

- What happens if we are deprived of all sensory information?

EXPERIENCING SENSATIONS

To experience sensations, we must have both a means of detecting stimuli and a means of converting them into a language the brain can understand. By their nature, our sensory organs accomplish both goals. They are effective in detecting light, sound, tastes, odors, heat, and other stimuli that they then convert into signals that are sent to the brain.

- *How do our sensory organs gather sensory information and convert it into signals the brain can understand?*

Sensory Processing: Transduction, Reduction, and Coding

Our sense organs contain cells called receptors that receive and process sensory information from the environment. For each sense, these specialized cells respond to a distinct stimulus, such as sound waves and odor molecules. Through a process called transduction, the receptors convert the stimulus into neural impulses, which are sent to the brain. In hearing, for example, tiny receptor cells in the inner ear transduce mechanical vibrations (from sound waves) into electrochemical signals. These signals are carried by neurons to the brain. Each type of sensory receptor is designed to detect a wide variety of stimuli and a wide range of stimulation. However, also built into our sensory systems are structures that purposefully reduce the amount of stimuli we receive.

Receptors: Body cells specialized to detect and respond to stimulus energy.

Transduction: The process by which energy stimulating a receptor is converted into neural impulses.

Why would we want to reduce the amount of sensory information we receive? Can you imagine what would happen if you did not have some natural filtering of stimuli? You would constantly hear blood rushing through your veins and continually feel your clothes brushing against your skin. Obviously, some level of filtering is needed so the brain is not overwhelmed with unnecessary information. It needs to be free to respond to those stimuli that have meaning for survival. Each of our senses is therefore custom-designed to respond to only a select range of potential sensory information. All species have evolved selective receptors that suppress or amplify information in order to survive. For example, hawks have an acute sense of vision but a poor sense of smell. Similarly, although we humans cannot sense many stimuli (such as ultraviolet or infrared light), we can see a candle burning 30 miles away on a dark, clear night, hear the tick of a watch at 20 feet under quiet conditions, and smell one drop of perfume in a six-room apartment (Galanter, 1962).

In the process of sensory reduction, we not only filter incoming sensations, we also analyze the sensations sent through before a neural impulse is finally sent to the cortex of the brain. This analysis is performed by cells in the reticular activating system (RAS) within the brain stem (see Chapter 2). The RAS determines whether or not incoming sensory information is important. If important, it passes the information on to the cerebral cortex. Because of this screening process, parents of a newborn, for example, can sleep through passing sirens and blaring stereos yet awaken to the slightest whimper of their baby.

How does the brain differentiate between various incoming sensations, such as sounds and smells?   It does so through a process called coding. Coding for a specific sensation depends on the number and type of sensory cells that are activated, on the precise nerve that is stimulated, and ultimately on the part of the brain that the nerve stimulates. In other words, sounds and smells are interpreted as distinct sensations not because of the environmental stimuli that activate them but because their respective neural impulses travel by different routes and arrive at different parts of the brain. Figure 3.1 illustrates the parts of the brain involved in sensory reception.

 *Try This Yourself*

To personally experience coding, close your eyes and with your fingertips press *gently* on your eyelids for about 30 seconds. The visual sensations you experience (circles; streams of light) reflect the fact that the receptor cells at the backs of your eyes are prepared to code any kind of stimulation, including pressure, into visual patterns. So even though you aren't looking at anything, you still "see" something because your visual receptors have been stimulated. ■

Coding: The three-part process that converts a particular sensory input into a specific sensation.

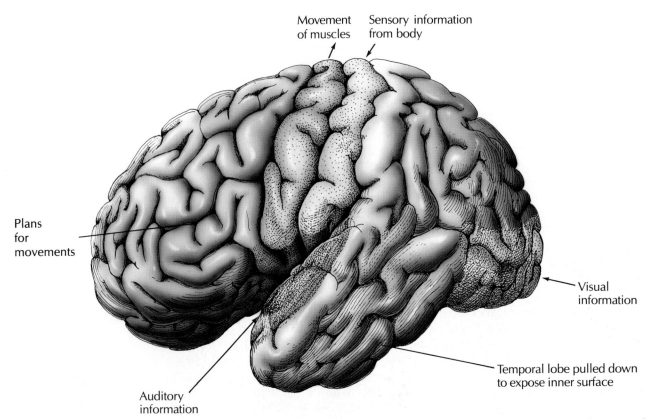

Figure 3.1 Sensory areas of the brain. Neural impulses travel from the sensory receptors to various parts of the brain.

Sensory Thresholds: Testing the Limits and Changes

Suppose you are the parent of a schoolage daughter who, like Helen Keller, has just suffered from a serious illness accompanied by high fever. During her period of recovery, you notice that she does not seem to hear as well as before her illness, so you take her to a hearing specialist. The specialist administers a series of tests based on principles of psychophysics, which is the study of the relationships between physical stimuli and the sensations they evoke.

In a test for hearing loss, the specialist uses a tone generator that produces sounds of differing pitches and intensities. Your daughter listens to the sounds over earphones and is asked to indicate the earliest point at which she can hear a tone. She thereby indicates her absolute threshold, or the smallest magnitude of sound she can detect. To test your daughter's difference threshold, the examiner presents a small change in volume and asks the child to respond when she notices a difference. By noting your daughter's thresholds and comparing them to those of people with normal hearing, the specialist is able to determine whether your daughter has a hearing loss and, if so, the extent of the loss.

Sensory thresholds exist not only for hearing but also for vision, taste, smell, and the skin senses. In fact, much of the research done in all areas of sensation originally began by studying various thresholds.

Do people's thresholds vary?   People with sensory impairments obviously have thresholds that differ from the norm. But even among individuals with no sensory difficulties there is a considerable range in sensitivities. Moreover, the sensitivity of an individual can vary from moment to moment, depending on his or her physiological state. Lack of food and certain drugs, for example, can change a person's normal threshold. Also, if you have gone through any type of sensory deprivation (a condition where use of the senses is restricted), your thresholds will be lower than normal. (We will discuss sensory deprivation in detail later in the chapter.)

Sensory Adaptation: Weakening the Response

An interesting thing happens when a constant stimulus is presented to a person for a length of time: The sensory structures involved diminish our awareness of that stimulus,

Psychophysics: The study of the relationships between physical stimulation and the sensations evoked by such stimulation.

Absolute Threshold: The smallest magnitude of a certain stimulus energy that can be detected.

Difference Threshold: The smallest magnitude of difference in stimulus energy that a person can detect.

Sensory Deprivation: A state in which all sensory stimulation is diminished as much as possible.

One of the major goals of a hearing test is to measure a person's absolute threshold for sound.

People exposed to constant noise readily adapt to it.

Sensory Adaptation: A decrease in response of a sensory system to continuous stimulation.

a process known as <u>sensory adaptation</u>. For example, if you are presented with a constant tone for a long time, your hearing receptors will decrease their firing rates and you will perceive the tone as less loud. In effect, we turn it down or even off.

All sensory systems display adaptation, but some, such as smell and touch, adapt quickly whereas others, such as the sense of pain, adapt more slowly. By deemphasizing repetitive information, the process of sensory adaptation allows us to operate efficiently within a wide range of stimulus intensities and makes us more alert to novel stimuli. Thus, when you walk into a kitchen, the aroma from freshly baked cookies can be delightfully overwhelming, but the baker, who has been in the kitchen for some time, hardly notices the smell.

 Try This Yourself

In some instances, adaptation can also distort sensation. To fully appreciate this, place one hand in icy water and the other in very warm water. After you have adapted to the two temperatures, place both hands in a pail of lukewarm water. If you are like most people, you will find that the water feels hot to the hand that had been in ice water but cold to the hand that had been in warm water. This phenomenon applies not only to touch, but to all our senses. For example, a friend's voice sounds much louder when we have adapted to silence than when we have adapted to the blaring music of a rock band. Thus, our sensory experiences are relative, depending on our level of adaptation. ∎

Each of the sensory principles we've discussed thus far—reduction, transduction, coding, thresholds, and adaptation—applies to all the senses. Yet each sense is uniquely different, as we shall see in the remainder of the chapter.

Review Questions

1. The process of receiving, translating, and transmitting information from the "outside" to the brain is called _____ .

2. What happens in the process of transduction?

3. Which part of your brain would alert you if suddenly the professor said your name in the midst of a seemingly endless monologue?

4. If a researcher were testing to determine the dimmest light a subject could perceive, the researcher would be measuring the _____ .

5. You can't smell your own perfume or aftershave a few minutes after you douse yourself because _____ is at work.

Answers to Review Questions can be found in Appendix C.

VISION

While on a long train trip, Helen Keller's aunt improvised a doll for six-year-old Helen out of a few towels. It had no nose, no mouth, no ears, no eyes—nothing to indicate a face. Helen found this disturbing. Most disturbing, though, was the lack of eyes. In fact it agitated her so much that she was not content until she found some beads and her aunt attached them for eyes.

Uncomprehending as she was of the myriad sensations our eyes bring us, Helen still seemed to know the importance of having eyes. Have you ever taken the time to consider the fantastic capabilities of our visual systems? At a football game, you can watch a distant action on the field and in the next instant consult the program in your lap. You can see a whole range of brightness, from pure white to jet black, and all the colors of the rainbow unless, of course, you're color-blind.

To fully appreciate the marvels of sight, we first need to examine the properties of light, since without it we wouldn't be able to see. We will then examine the structure and function of the eye, and finally the way in which visual input is processed.

Light: Electromagnetic Energy

Light is a form of electromagnetic energy. Electromagnetic energy is made up of tiny packets of energy called photons that move in waves similar to the movement of waves in the ocean. There are many different types of electromagnetic waves, from short X rays to long radio waves. Together they form the electromagnetic spectrum (see Figure 3.2). Most wavelengths are invisible to the human eye; only a small part of the spectrum, known as visible light, can be detected by our visual receptors. Visible light can be emitted by a source such as the sun or a light bulb, or it can be reflected from an object. Most often, it is by reflected light that we see our world.

Light waves vary in length and height, each with a distinct effect on vision (see Figure 3.3). The wavelength—the distance between the crest of one wave and the crest of the next—determines its hue, or color. When white light strikes a prism or water droplets, it is separated into the individual colors found in the visible spectrum. The amplitude, or height, of a light wave determines its brightness—the higher a wave, the greater the amplitude, and the brighter the color.

The Eye: The Anatomy of Vision

The eye is uniquely designed to capture light and focus it on receptors at the back of the eyeball. The receptors in turn convert light energy into neural signals to be interpreted

> • *What is light, and how do our eye structures work to enable us to see?*

Electromagnetic Spectrum: The band of radiant energy generated by the sun; visible light is only a small part of this spectrum.

Wavelength: The length of a sound or light wave, measured from the crest of one wave to the crest of the next.

Hue: The visual dimension seen as a particular color; determined by the length of a light wave.

Amplitude: The height of a light or sound wave; pertaining to light, it refers to brightness.

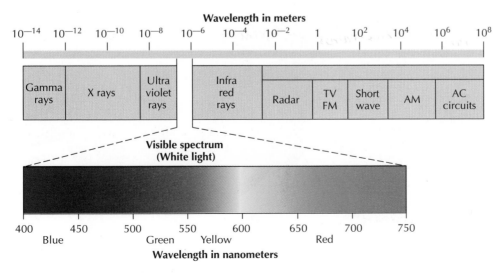

Figure 3.2 The electromagnetic spectrum. (a) Gamma radiation and X radiation have short wavelengths, visible light has medium wavelengths, and TV and AC circuits have long wavelengths. (b) The human eye can see only a small part of the full spectrum, visible light. Short wavelength visible light is blue, the middle visible wavelengths are green and yellow, and long wavelength visible light is red.

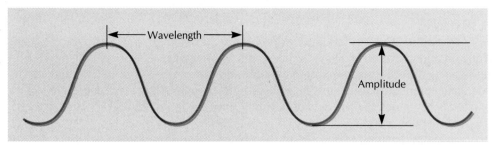

Figure 3.3 Wavelength and amplitude. The two major physical properties of light waves are wavelength (the distance from peak to peak) and amplitude (the distance from trough to peak).

by the brain. Several structures in the eye contribute to the vision process. To explain how light is converted into neural signals, we will trace the path of light through these structures. As we do, please take the time to refer to Figure 3.4.

The Cornea

Cornea: The transparent bulge at the front of the eye where light enters.

Sclera: The white opaque outer wall of the eye.

Aqueous Humor: The clear fluid that fills the front chamber of the eye.

Light waves enter the eye through a tough transparent shield called the cornea. Its bulging shape bends the entering light rays to fix an image on the receptors at the back of the eye. The cornea is attached to the sclera, the white, opaque outer wall of the eye. Within the cornea is a clear fluid known as the aqueous humor, which nourishes the cornea. At times, you may have noticed "spots" floating before your eyes. These spots are impurities floating in the aqueous humor. Since this fluid is recycled about once every four hours, the "floaties" are sometimes brought in and then carried away in the recycling process.

The Pupil

Pupil: An opening surrounded by the iris through which light passes into the eye.

Iris: The colored part of the eye consisting of muscles that control the size of the pupil.

Light passes from the cornea through the pupil, an opening that can enlarge or reduce to regulate the amount of light entering the eye. The muscles that control the size of the pupil are known as the iris. The iris is the colored part of the eye.

The Lens

Lens: The transparent elastic structure in the eye that focuses light on the retina by changing shape.

Accommodation: The bulging and flattening of the lens in order to focus an image on the retina.

After passing through the pupil, light travels through the lens, a transparent elastic structure that focuses light on the back of the eye by changing its shape—by bulging and flattening. This focusing process is known as accommodation (see Figure 3.5). When you look at a faraway object, your lens accommodates by flattening to focus; when your

Figure 3.4 Anatomy of the eye. Trace the path of light from the point where it enters the eye at the cornea, passes through the pupil and lens to the retina where it is transduced into neural impulses, and then travels along the optic nerve to the brain.

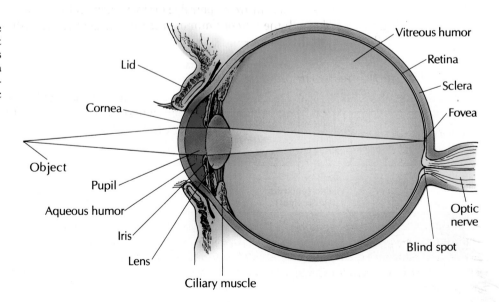

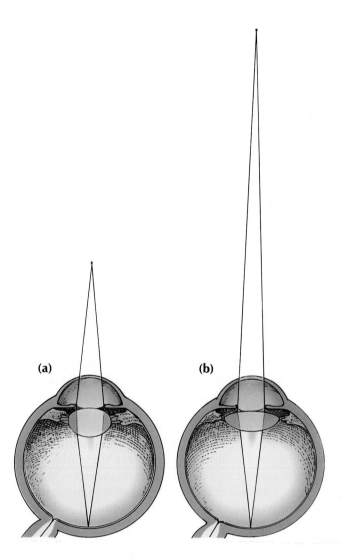

(a)   **(b)**

Figure 3.5 Accommodation. The lens (a) bulges to focus on a near object and (b) flattens to focus on a distant object.

glance shifts back to a near object, such as the book you're reading, your lens accommodates by bulging. The muscles responsible for changing the shape of the lens during accommodation are the ciliary muscles, which attach the lens to the sclera. Muscles attached to the outer surface of the sclera are responsible for movement of the eye itself. From the lens, light passes through the vitreous humor, a semiliquid gel that nourishes the eye and gives the eye a spherical shape.

The Retina

Ultimately, incoming light waves fall on the retina. This is an area at the back of the eye that contains light receptors (in the shape of rods and cones), blood vessels, and a network of neurons that transmit neural information to the occipital lobes of the brain. In the center of the retina is the fovea, a tiny pit in which are concentrated specialized receptor cells called cones. The fovea is responsible for our sharpest vision. In contrast to the fovea, there is an area called the blind spot that has no visual receptors at all because it is the point where blood vessels and nerve pathways enter and exit the eyeball.

We are not normally aware of the existence of our blind spot because our eyes are always moving, and we fill in the information missing from the blind spot of one eye with information sent to adjacent spots on the retina or with images from the other eye. After the retinal receptors convert incoming light waves to neural signals, they travel via the optic nerve to the brain for interpretation (a process we discuss in the next chapter on perception).

Ciliary Muscles: Muscles attached to the lens that stretch and relax it in order to focus images on the retina.

Vitreous Humor: A semiliquid gel that nourishes the inside of the eye and is responsible for maintaining the eye's shape.

Retina: An area at the back of the eye containing light receptors in the shape of rods and cones.

Fovea: The point on the retina containing only cones, where light from the center of the visual field is focused; the point responsible for our clearest vision.

Blind Spot: A part of the retina containing no receptors; the area where the optic nerve exits the eye.

Optic Nerve: The cranial nerve that carries visual information from the retina to the brain.

 *Try This Yourself*

To experience your blind spot, hold the book about one foot in front of you, close your right eye, and stare at the X below with your left eye. Very slowly, move the book closer to you. You should see the worm disappear and the apple become whole. ■

Photoreceptors: Receptors for vision, the rods and cones.

When light reaches the retina, it stimulates the photoreceptors. These are light-sensitive cells, called rods and cones, that are named for their distinctive shapes (see Figures 3.6 and 3.7). Photoreceptors are filled with chemicals that react to the characteristics of light (Schoelein, Peteanu, Mathies, and Shank, 1991). There are about 6 million cones and 120 million rods packed tightly together at the back of the retina (Carlson, 1992).

Rods: Receptors in the retina that are most sensitive in dim light; they do not respond to color.

The rods, besides being much more numerous, are also more sensitive to light than the cones. They enable us to see in dim light. This greater sensitivity, however, is achieved at the expense of fine detail and acuity in space and time—the job of the cones. You've probably noticed how increasingly difficult it becomes to play tennis, say, or basketball as the afternoon sun fades into early twilight. At such times, your vision relies more and more on the rods. When rods are being used, there is a measurable delay in the message going from the eye to the brain and a consequent decline in the precise localization of moving objects. This is not to say that rods do not detect movement—they are very sensitive to motion—but only that the fine detail and timing of the movement are impeded. You can demonstrate this for yourself by extending your arms out at shoulder height and staring straight ahead while wiggling your fingers. Without moving your head, you can readily detect the movement of your fingers but can see little detail and no color. This is because the outer parts of your eyes—the periphery of the retina—contain only rods and no cones.

*Figure 3.6 **The retina.** The retina of the eye is a complicated structure with many different types of cells. The most important are the rods and cones.*

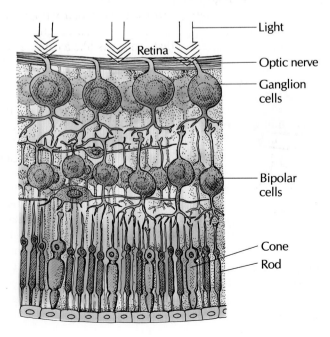

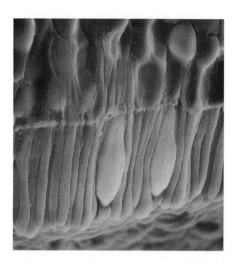

Figure 3.7 Rods and cones. In this photomicrograph, the two large yellow cone-shaped objects are retinal cones, and the long reddish rod-shaped objects are the retinal rods. The bipolar cells are located directly above the rods and cones.

Cones become more numerous toward the center of the retina. In fact, in the exact center, the fovea, only cones are found. When you are reading and you detect something moving in your peripheral vision, you immediately turn your head to focus the object on your fovea. You do so because it is the cones that enable you to see the object in fine detail. Cones function better in bright light and diminish in function as the light dims. Cones not only enable us to see things in fine detail, they also enable us to see in color. All cones are sensitive to many wavelengths, but each is maximally sensitive to one color—red, green, or blue (Boynton, 1988). We will discuss color vision in the section on color perception in Chapter 4.

When the brightness level suddenly changes, how do the rods "take over" from the cones, and vice versa? You've probably noticed when walking into a dark movie theater on a sunny afternoon that you are momentarily blinded. This happens because in bright light, the pigment inside the rods is bleached and they are temporarily nonfunctional. Going from a very light to a very dark setting requires a rapid shift from cones to rods. During the changeover, there is a second or two before the rods are functional enough for you to see. They continue to adjust for longer than half an hour, until your maximum light sensitivity is reached. This process is known as dark adaptation (Hecht, Haig, and Wald, 1935). The visual adjustment that takes place when you leave the theater and go back into the sunlight—light adaptation—takes about seven minutes and is the work of the cones. This adaptation process is particularly important to remember when driving your car from a brightly lit garage into a dark night.

You may have heard that the eye is like a camera. This is true to a certain extent. Like a camera, the eye admits light through a small hole that adjusts in size to various light intensities. Also like a camera, the eye passes the light through to a lens that focuses an image on a photosensitive surface. However, unlike the camera lens, which moves forward or backward in the focusing process, the human lens focuses by bulging and flattening. Furthermore, the eye does not produce an actual "image" on the retina but rather sends information to the brain in the form of electrical impulses. In this regard, the eye is more like a video camera than a still camera.

The eye also differs from a camera in that a camera must be held steady when shooting, whereas the eye works quite well during bodily movement. In fact, the eyeball itself is in constant motion. This motion is necessary to prevent fatigue of the receptor cells in the retina. When nerve cells are continually stimulated, their receptivity tends to "fade" (an adaptation process). Thus, if the muscles of the eye weren't continually in motion and weren't shifting the image to neighboring cells when we looked at something for more than a few seconds, the image would disappear. You can check this for yourself by placing a finger at the corner of each eye and gently, being very careful, pressing on your eyeball for a few seconds to hold the eye still. Your visual field will soon fade to black.

Cones: Receptors in the retina that respond to color and fine detail.

Dark Adaptation: Visual adjustment that increases the sensitivity of the rods and cones and allows us to see better in dim light.

Light Adaptation: The visual adjustment of the rods and cones that reduces sensitivity to bright light.

Vision Problems: Eyes That Are Too Long, Too Short, or Too Old

Our visual system, when all its structures are intact and working properly, enables us to see forms and shapes, colors, brightness levels, moving objects—everything necessary to function in our world. However, numerous things can affect vision. For example, many people are born with or develop eyes that are too long or too short, yet their lenses function as if they had normal-shaped eyes. Thus, light is focused in front of the retina if the eye is too long and at the back of the retina if the eye is too short. People whose eyes are longer than normal are myopic.

Myopia: Nearsightedness; the eye is longer than normal and the image falls in front of the ideal position on the retina.

Myopia is commonly called "nearsightedness." People who are myopic have trouble focusing on distant objects, although they can see normally when they view the same objects from a near position. The opposite of myopia is hyperopia, or "farsightedness." Hyperopic people have trouble focusing on near objects because their eyes are shorter than normal, but they can see things in the distance clearly. Both myopia and hyperopia can be corrected with eyeglasses or contact lenses that refocus the incoming light so that it falls in the right place on the retina (see Figure 3.8).

Hyperopia: Farsightedness; the eye is shorter than normal and the image falls behind its ideal position on the retina.

Do all people get farsighted when they get old?   As we grow older, we do tend to have trouble viewing close objects while we still see faraway objects relatively well. But the

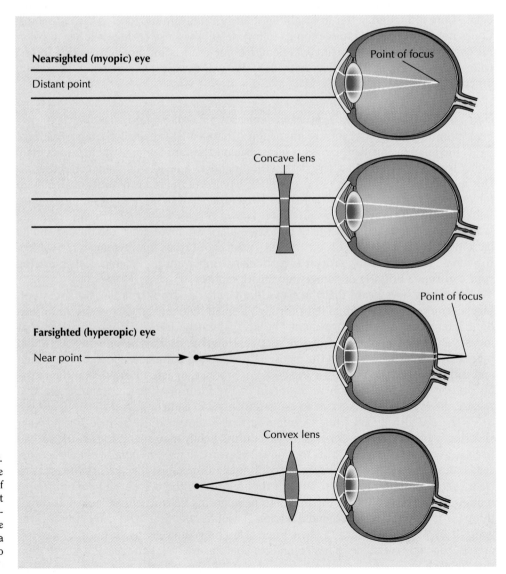

Figure 3.8 Myopia and hyperopia. Since the myopic (nearsighted) eye focuses a distant image in front of the retina it is necessary to correct this with a concave lens. The hyperopic (farsighted) eye focuses the image behind the retina and needs a convex lens to bring the image into focus on the retina.

The photo on the left shows what things would look like if you were myopic—close objects would be clear, and far objects would be blurry. The photo on the right shows what things would look like if you were hyperopic—close objects would be blurry, and far objects would be clear.

cause of this farsightedness is different from hyperopia. Our lenses grow stiffer as we age and therefore do not bulge as easily as they once did. Consequently, older people have trouble focusing on near objects and need to hold things such as books farther and farther away to see them clearly. Eventually, the time comes when their arms are not long enough and they must wear reading glasses if they want to look at something close. Farsightedness due to age is called presbyopia.

Presbyopia: Farsightedness due to age.

Other Vision Problems

Other vision problems may arise from disorders of the retina or the optic nerve. Problems involving the retina normally develop as a result of disease or trauma (some type of violent blow or action). Trauma to the retina may result in a partial loss of vision in the form of a blind spot. Many times the brain will ignore the blind spot if it is not too large, and the person will almost never notice the small absence of vision. Sometimes trauma may result in a detached retina. A sudden severe jolt to the head that disconnects the retina can cause total or partial blindness in that eye. Treatment involves surgically

Detached Retina: A disconnection of the retina from the back of the eye, which causes total or partial blindness of that eye.

As people age, the lenses in their eyes do not bulge as easily as they did when they were younger, so they need to wear glasses to see normally.

reattaching the retina to the back of the eye by "spot welding" it many times with a laser. World champion boxer Sugar Ray Leonard had his career and eyesight jeopardized by a detached retina.

Damage to the optic nerve or to the visual cortex of the brain can cause various problems, from partial loss of sight to total blindness. Although we cannot know for certain the cause of Helen Keller's blindness, it was probably due to some type of brain damage from her high fever. We still do not have an effective treatment for nerve cell damage, so visual problems resulting from damage to these areas are permanent.

Several artificial visual systems have been developed to help those who are totally blind distinguish basic forms and outlines. One of these allows a person to "see" with the sense of touch through televised images projected onto their skin (Collins, 1970). A television camera translates images into electrical signals, and the individual learns to interpret the patterns of vibrations created by the signals as representations of objects. Using this system, blind students have been able to find and retrieve objects around a room, read meters, and even use an oscilloscope (Hechinger, 1981).

Review Questions

1. What is the difference between the wavelength and the amplitude of light?

2. Light waves entering the eye pass through the outer transparent _____ and the opening called the _____ and are focused by the elastic _____ on the _____ at the back of the eye.

3. The lens of the eye focuses by _____ and _____ . The focusing process is known as _____ .

4. There are two kinds of photoreceptors found on the retina. Which kind do you use to read with, and why? Which kind do you use outside after the sun is down, and why?

5. An increased sensitivity to light after being in the dark for several minutes is called _____ .

6. Match the letters of the terms and definitions that go together:

    a. myopia   d. farsighted   f. lens stiffens with age
    b. presbyopia   e. nearsighted   g. eyeball shorter than normal
    c. hyperopia   h. eyeball longer than normal

Answers to Review Questions can be found in Appendix C.

HEARING

• *What is sound, and how do our ear structures work to enable us to hear?*

Audition: The sense of hearing.

In this section, we examine audition, the sense of hearing, which we use nearly as much as our sense of vision. Our auditory sense is as remarkable as our visual sense. In listening to music, we can identify different instruments by their subtle differences in tonal quality. Our hearing receptors can accommodate wide differences in volume, from the delicate sound of a mouse nibbling at a sunflower seed to the sharp bark of Rover sitting at our feet.

Helen Keller couldn't hear sounds like these, but she recalled the time during her childhood when she went upstairs to dress in "company clothes" because she had sensed the door shutting and figured that company had just arrived. How could she know the door had shut without being able to hear it? What is it about sound that allows hearing people to discriminate between a flute and a violin and enables a deaf person to tell that a door has been closed?

Sound: Movement of Air Molecules

Sound is the movement of air molecules in a particular wave pattern. The waves produced are called sound waves. They result from rapid changes in air pressure caused by vibrating objects, such as vocal cords or guitar strings. It was differences in the patterns of vibration that enabled Helen Keller to sense the "sound" of the door.

The vibrations from people's voices or musical instruments cause air to move like the ripples in a pond created by a bobbing cork on a fishing line. As vocal cords vibrate back and forth, they make ripples in the air around them. The sound waves then travel through the air, just as the ripples from a cork travel across the surface of a pond.

Like light waves, sound waves vary in two basic ways, frequency and amplitude, each with a distinct sensory effect (see Figure 3.9). Frequency refers to the number of sound waves emitted per second. Sounds of different frequencies are perceived as being high or low. This is known as pitch. For instance, the faster a particular vocal cord vibrates (the more waves per second), the higher the pitch of a person's voice. Frequency is measured in *hertz,* which is the number of sound wave cycles per second. Just as the eye responds only to light waves within a particular range, the ear responds only to frequencies from about 15 hertz (cycles per second) to 20,000 hertz (Kalat, 1992, p. 194). Dogs can detect sounds up to 30,000 hertz, and bats and dolphins up to 100,000 hertz. Humans are most sensitive to sounds that fall in the range of speech, about 500 to 3,000 hertz.

Amplitude refers to the amount of pressure (height) of sound waves. The amplitude of the wave determines loudness, which is measured in units termed decibels. Figure 3.10 gives decibel ratings for various sounds.

Sound Waves: The movement of air molecules produced by a vibrating object.

Frequency: The number of sound pressure waves per second, perceived as the pitch of a sound.

Pitch: The highness or lowness of tones or sounds, depending on their frequency.

Amplitude: The height of a light or sound wave; pertaining to sound, it refers to loudness.

The Ear: The Anatomy of Hearing

The ear is composed of three major sections: the outer ear, the middle ear, and the inner ear. The outer ear gathers and focuses sound waves. The middle ear amplifies and concentrates sounds. The inner ear contains the receptor cells that ultimately transduce the mechanical energy created by sounds into neural impulses. As we trace the path of sound waves through the ear, it will help to refer to Figure 3.11.

The Outer Ear

Sound waves are gathered and funneled into the outer ear by the pinna, the external, visible part of the ear that we automatically envision when we think of an "ear." The

Pinna: The fleshy part of the outer ear that we think of as "the ear."

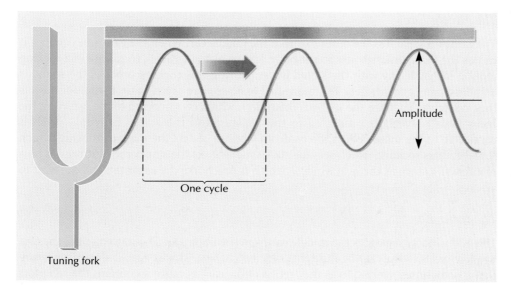

Figure 3.9 Sound. Sound is caused by the vibration of objects, which produces sound pressure waves of varying frequency and amplitude. The number of cycles per second determines the frequency, or pitch, of the sound, and the amplitude, or height of the wave, determines the loudness.

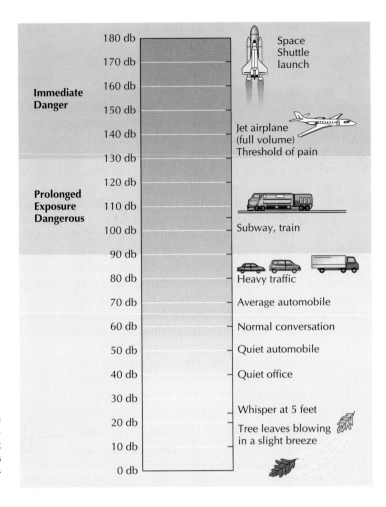

Figure 3.10 Loudness. The loudness of a sound is measured in decibels. This figure lists some familiar sounds and the corresponding decibel level for that sound. One decibel is the faintest sound a normal person can hear. Normal conversation takes place at about 60 decibels. Constant noise above about 90 decibels can cause permanent nerve damage to the ear.

Auditory Canal: A tubelike structure into which sound is channeled by the pinna.

Eardrum (Tympanic Membrane): The membrane located between the auditory canal and the middle ear that vibrates in response to sound waves.

Ossicles: Three small bones of the middle ear: the malleus, the incus, and the stapes.

Malleus: The first of the ossicles, attached to the eardrum and the incus.

Incus: The middle ossicle, attached to the malleus and the stapes.

Stapes: The last of the ossicles, attached to the incus and to the oval window.

Oval Window: The membrane of the cochlea that is moved by the stapes.

Cochlea: The inner ear structure that contains the receptors for hearing.

pinna channels the sound waves into the auditory canal, a tubelike structure that focuses the sound. At the end of the auditory canal is a thin, tautly stretched membrane known as the eardrum, or tympanic membrane. As sound waves hit the eardrum, it vibrates. The eardrum is so sensitive and elastic that it matches any incoming sound waves in exact frequency and amplitude.

The Middle Ear

The eardrum separates the outer ear from the middle ear. When the eardrum vibrates, it causes the three tiniest bones in the body, known as the ossicles, to vibrate in a rocking motion in synchrony with the sound waves. During this rocking process, the sound is amplified and concentrated. The individual ossicles were given Latin names for objects they resemble. They are the malleus (hammer), which is connected to the eardrum; the incus (anvil), which is connected to the malleus; and the stapes (stirrup), which is connected to the incus. When the eardrum vibrates, it sets the malleus rocking, which sets the incus rocking, which sets the stapes rocking. As the stapes rocks, it presses on a membrane known as the oval window, which is much like the eardrum, and causes it to vibrate.

The Inner Ear

The oval window separates the middle ear from the inner ear. The movement of the oval window creates waves in the fluid that fills the cochlea. This is a snail-shaped structure that is sometimes referred to as the "retina of the ear" because it contains the receptors for hearing. The hearing receptors are known as hair cells and they do in fact resemble

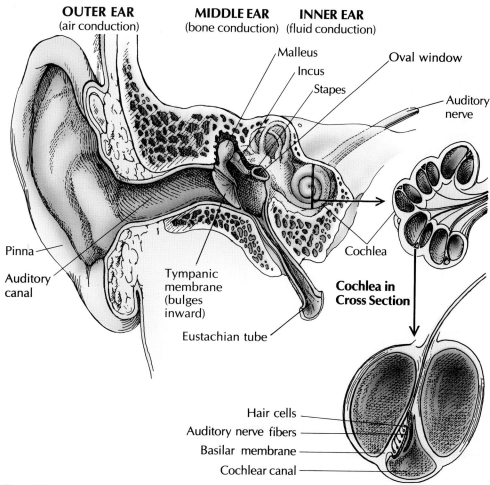

OUTER EAR (air conduction) **MIDDLE EAR** (bone conduction) **INNER EAR** (fluid conduction)

Malleus
Incus
Stapes
Oval window
Auditory nerve
Pinna
Auditory canal
Tympanic membrane (bulges inward)
Eustachian tube
Cochlea
Cochlea in Cross Section
Hair cells
Auditory nerve fibers
Basilar membrane
Cochlear canal

Figure 3.11 Anatomy of the ear. Sound waves enter the outer ear, are amplified and concentrated in the middle ear, and are transduced in the inner ear.

hairs. As the waves travel through the cochlear fluid, they displace the basilar membrane, to which the hair cells are attached. This displacement causes the hair cells to bend from side to side. It is at this point that the mechanical energy of the wave is transduced into electrochemical impulses that are carried via the auditory nerve to the brain.

How do we know what direction a sound is coming from?　Locating sounds in space is aided by the slight time difference necessary for sounds to reach the two ears (Spitzer and Semple, 1991). When a bell rings somewhere to the right of us, the sound will reach the right ear slightly before it reaches the left (see Figure 3.12). Also, the sound reaching the right ear will be slightly louder than the sound reaching the left ear. We often have difficulty locating a sound that is directly in front of or directly behind us because the sound enters both ears at the same time. Sometimes a turn of the head will allow enough of a time or loudness differential to determine whether the sound is in front of or behind us.

Pitch and Loudness

We hear different pitch and loudness levels by a combination of mechanisms, depending on the frequency of the sound. First, let's discuss how we hear various pitches of sounds. It seems that we hear high-pitched sounds according to the place along the basilar membrane that is most stimulated. When we hear a particular sound, it causes the eardrum, the ossicles, and the oval window to vibrate, which in turn produces a "travel-

Hair Cells: Auditory receptors in the cochlea.

Basilar Membrane: The membrane in the cochlea that contains the hearing receptors.

Auditory Nerve: The cranial nerve that carries auditory information from the hair cells to the brain.

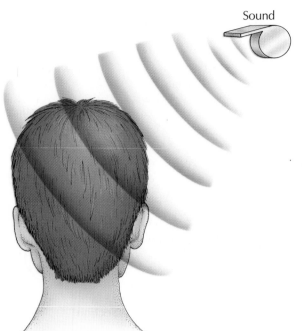

Sound

Figure 3.12 Sound localization. When a sound is generated to a person's right, the sound waves reach the right ear before they reach the left ear. This difference in arrival time helps us localize a sound.

ing wave" through the fluid in the cochlea. This wave causes some bending of hair cells all along the basilar membrane, but there is a single point where the hair cells are maximally bent for each distinct pitch. This maximal bending is described by the *place theory,* which explains how we hear higher-pitched sounds (Carlson, 1992, p. 183).

How we hear lower-pitched sounds is explained by the *frequency theory.* According to this theory, we hear a particular low sound because it causes hair cells along the basilar membrane to bend and fire action potentials at the same rate as the frequency of that low sound (Carlson, 1992, p. 183). For example, a sound with a frequency of 90 hertz would produce 90 action potentials per second in the auditory nerve.

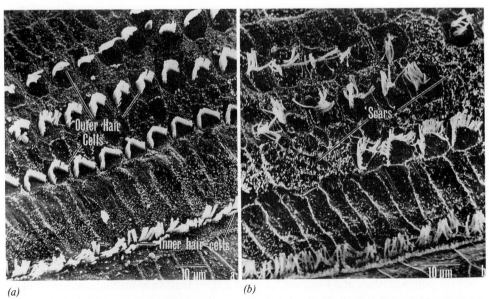

(a)   (b)

Intense sound can cause damage to the hair cells of the inner ear. (a) depicts part of the cochlea of a normal guinea pig, showing three rows of outer hair cells and one row of inner hair cells. (b) depicts part of the cochlea after a 24-hour exposure to sound at a level approached by loud rock music. Note the loss of hair cells that have been replaced by scars.

How we detect loudness levels also differs according to the frequency of the sounds. When a sound has a high pitch, we hear it as louder because the neurons fire at a faster rate. Louder sounds produce more intense vibrations, which result in a greater bending of the hair cells, a greater release of neurotransmitter, and consequently a higher firing rate of action potentials. However, there must be an alternate explanation for the perception of the loudness of low sounds, because as just described, rate of firing explains how we hear the pitch of a low sound. Most researchers think that the loudness of lower-pitched sounds is detected by the number of axons that are firing at any one time (Carlson, 1992).

Hearing Problems: When Things Go Wrong

Hearing problems vary according to their cause and location. For example, people suffering from a problem in the eardrum or the middle ear (a conductive hearing loss) might ask you to "speak louder." People suffering from an inner ear problem (nerve deafness) might ask you to "speak more clearly." And people suffering from damage to the auditory areas of the brain either cannot hear at all or cannot interpret the sounds that are sent to the cerebral cortex.

Conduction Deafness

In conduction deafness, sound waves are unable to reach the inner ear. The most common cause of conduction deafness is a middle ear infection involving a buildup of fluid that prevents the eardrum and ossicles from vibrating. If ear infections in young children are left untreated, the hearing loss during this critical time of cognitive and language development can lead to severe speech impairments, problems in cognitive development, and impeded social development. Another cause of conduction deafness is a bony growth that develops where the stapes connects to the oval window, which prevents the stapes from rocking freely. This condition is normally corrected with a hearing aid (although hearing with hearing aids is distorted and is not the same as normal hearing). It can also be treated through a surgical technique that frees the stapes.

Nerve Deafness

Hearing losses due to inner ear problems are much more serious than those due to conduction problems, since they stem from damage to the nerve cells in the cochlea. These nerve cells cannot regenerate, so any damage done to them is irreversible. Nerve deafness is normally a result of disease, birth defects, frequent exposure to loud sounds, or the simple process of aging. Many older people can no longer hear higher-pitched sounds, so you might remember that instead of shouting when talking to older people who have hearing difficulties, first try lowering the pitch of your voice.

Is it true that loud music can damage your hearing?   Yes. One of the most common causes of nerve deafness is a condition known as stimulation deafness, in which continuous exposure to loud sounds damages the hair cells. If a noise is loud—150 decibels or more, such as blaring music or a jet airplane engine—even a brief exposure can cause permanent deafness. Daily exposure to approximately 85 decibels (such as heavy traffic or motorcycles) may lead to permanent hearing loss.

Because nerve deafness is caused by irreversible damage to the nerve or receptor cells, the only treatment is prevention. That means avoiding exceptionally loud noises (rock concerts, jackhammers, stereo headphones at full blast), wearing ear plugs when such situations cannot be avoided, and paying attention to bodily warnings. These warnings include a change in your normal hearing threshold or tinnitus, a whistling or ringing sensation in the ears.

An artificial ear has been developed that may restore the hearing of about 70 percent of the 500,000 people in the United States with nerve deafness who cannot benefit from traditional hearing aids. This "bionic" ear attempts to electronically dupli-

Long term exposure to loud noise such as rock music can cause nerve deafness. These members of the "Grateful Dead" and their audience are potential victims of nerve deafness induced by loud noise.

cate the function of the cochlea. A tiny microphone worn around the pinna picks up sounds and transmits them to a microprocessor worn around the waist. The microprocessor then transduces the information into electrical impulses that are sent to a small number of tiny electrodes that are surgically implanted in the cochlea. This device has enabled some patients to understand spoken words, although when listening to several people talking, they can understand only one voice at a time.

Review Questions

1. _____ result from rapid changes in air pressure caused by vibrating objects.
2. A 20,000-hertz tone has a _____ pitch, whereas a 100-hertz tone has a _____ pitch.
3. Loudness is related to the _____ of a sound wave.
4. Trace a sound wave from its source, a car horn, through the structures of the ear to the brain.
5. The receptors for sound are the _____, which are located in the _____ .
6. We hear _____-pitched sounds according to the place on the basilar membrane that is most stimulated; we hear _____-pitched sounds according to the rate action potentials are fired.
7. What can you do to minimize your chances of developing stimulation deafness?

Answers to Review Questions can be found in Appendix C.

SMELL AND TASTE

• *How do we smell different odors and taste different flavors?*

Smell and taste are sometimes referred to as the chemical senses because they both involve chemoreceptors. These are receptors that are sensitive to certain chemical molecules rather than to electromagnetic or mechanical energy. Chemical stimulation of these receptors initiates transduction and the transmission of nerve impulses to the brain.

Smell and taste receptors are located near each other and often interact so closely that we have difficulty separating the sensations. Have you ever noticed how food seems bland when your nose is blocked by a cold and you cannot smell your food? The interaction between taste and smell is also affected by the temperature of food. Pizza and pancakes are much tastier when hot than cold. The steam from hot foods stimulates the smell receptors and enhances our sense of taste.

 Try This Yourself

To experience what a major role smell plays in the sense of taste, close your eyes, hold your nose, and bite into an onion, an apple, and a potato. You will find that without the help of your smell receptors, it is hard to tell which is which. ■

Olfaction: The Sense of Smell

The sense of smell, or olfaction, results from stimulation of receptor cells in the nose (see Figure 3.13). These receptors are embedded in a mucus-coated membrane called the olfactory epithelium. The olfactory epithelium is accessible from the mouth, through the oral-nasal connection at the top of the throat, which accounts for the strong contribution of smell to taste. The olfactory receptors are actually modified neurons, with a

Olfaction: The sense of smell.

Olfactory Epithelium: The mucus-coated membrane lining the top of the nasal cavity and containing the receptors for smell.

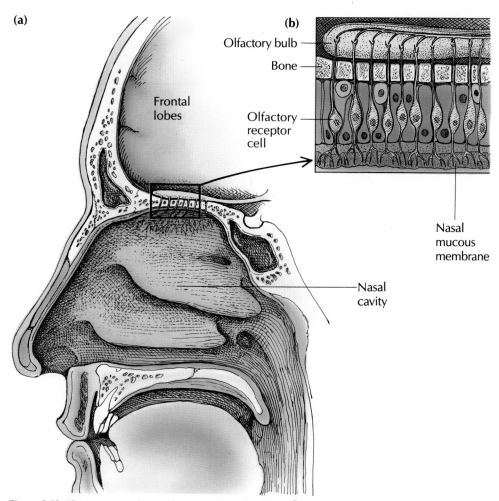

Figure 3.13 The anatomy of the olfactory system. (a) The nasal cavity showing the location of olfactory receptors. (b) Detail of the olfactory receptor system.

branched set of dendrites extending out of the epithelium. When air molecules in the nasal cavity come in contact with the dendrites, they initiate a neural impulse. The impulse travels along the neuron's axon directly to the olfactory bulb just below the frontal lobes. Most of the olfactory information is processed in the olfactory bulb before being sent to other parts of the brain.

Pevsner, Reed, Feinstein, and Snyder (1988) have identified an odorant-binding protein in the nasal epithelium of several animals. This protein attaches to odorant molecules and then transports them to olfactory receptors. Since the major function of the protein is to concentrate odorant molecules, its presence may explain why we can smell some odors at extremely low concentrations.

Distinguishing Odors

Lock-and-Key Theory: The idea that each odor molecule will fit into only one type of smell receptor cell according to shape.

Although researchers have proposed a number of explanations, there are two major theories that explain how we distinguish different odors. One suggests that all the complex odors are made up of between 6 and 32 primary qualities, such as camphor (mothball), floral, peppermint, ether (dry-cleaning fluid), musk, pungent (spices), putrid (rotten eggs), fishy, malty, and sweaty (Amoore, Johnston, and Rubin, 1964; Amoore, 1977). The complex molecules responsible for each of these odors differ in shape and size. According to this lock-and-key theory, each odor fits into only one type of receptor cell, like a key into a lock. Some molecules, such as carbon monoxide, have a shape that does not fit into any receptor and are therefore odorless.

The other major theory proposes that, as opposed to specific receptors responding only to distinct odors, all receptors contribute to the detection of all odors. Any one receptor may respond more to some odors than to others, but most receptors respond in varying degrees to a wide range of odors (Tanabe, Iino, and Takagi, 1975). According to this theory, we perceive any particular odor because it excites a certain *pattern* of activity within all the olfactory receptors.

Adaptation

Whatever the mechanism by which we distinguish odors, there is no question that smell receptors adapt quickly. Odors that initially seem overpowering soon seem to wear off. Furthermore, some people adapt to smells more quickly than others. (It's too bad that many of us didn't know this when we were first learning to use aftershave lotion and cologne.) Also, smell acuity is generally keen—we can detect up to tens of thousands of different odors—but, again, there is variation among individuals. Some of us are totally "blind" to certain odors (such as musk and sweat). Older people sometimes suffer a complete loss of smell (Cohen, 1981). The exact reasons for these variations are unclear, but current research is looking at the roles of heredity, hormones, and learning.

Does smell really have an effect on sexual attraction?   Since ancient times, people have been interested in finding ways to increase their sexual attractiveness. One popular means has been the use of perfumes, aftershave lotions, and other odorous substances to enhance attraction. Is there any scientific basis to such practices? One line of research has focused on pheromones—chemical odors we give off that are thought to affect the behavior of others, including their sexual behavior.

Pheromones: Bodily chemicals that affect others' behavior.

Pheromones have been found in a number of animal species. Michael and Keverne (1970) found, for example, that female monkeys secrete chemicals called copulins that are sexually attractive to males. Similarly, Morris and Udry (1978) found that when human females were instructed to rub perfume containing copulins on their chests, a definite increase occurred in the sexual behavior of both their partners and themselves. Researchers looking for male copulins have found that ovulating women are much better than men or children at detecting the musky fragrance of a synthetic substance called exaltolide, which chemically resembles a substance found in human urine. Males secrete twice as much of this substance in their urine as women, and children secrete none. Perhaps exaltolide is a male pheromone that attracts females at the very time when they are most likely to conceive (Hassett, 1978).

At the other extreme, Gustavson, Dawson, and Bonett (1987) have suggested that women may secrete a "spacing" pheromone that acts as a sexual deterrent. These researchers report that men are likely to avoid areas treated with a female pheromone called androstenol. It is possible that androstenol is secreted during times when women's fertility rates are at their lowest. Perfume companies are very interested in pheromone research, of course, but the studies done need further validation.

Gustation: The Sense of Taste

Today, taste, or gustation, may be the least critical of our senses. In our primate past, however, it probably contributed to our survival. The major function of taste is to provide information about substances that are entering our digestive tract and screen out those that may be harmful. This function is aided by the sense of smell.

Gustation: The sense of taste.

When the sense of smell is eliminated, the enormous variety of tastes can be reduced to four: sweet, sour, salty, and bitter. Like smell receptors (in the lock-and-key theory), taste receptors respond differentially to the varying shapes of food and liquid molecules. Some research has found that the four basic taste sensations can be mimicked by artificial substitutes. Aspartame, for example, is a derivative from the artichoke plant that appears to mimic the molecular shape of sweet substances. Both Nutrasweet and saccharin can act as artifical sweeteners in many diet products because they have a molecular shape that is similar enough to sugar that they can stimulate sweet receptors.

The Tongue Map

Unlike smell receptors, taste receptors for the four basic sensations have specific locations (see Figure 3.14). We generally don't notice this division of taste cells because food usually reaches all parts of the tongue while we eat. But if you want to avoid tasting a pill, throw a salty pill on the back of your tongue and place a bitter pill on the exact center. If you want to savor a sweet treat, roll it around on the tip of your tongue. Note in Figure 3.14 that the major taste buds are clustered together within little bumps, called papillae, that you can see on the surface of your tongue. When liquids enter the mouth or food is chewed and dissolved, the fluid runs over the papillae and into the pores to the taste buds. This is why we should chew our food slowly and completely to get maximum taste satisfaction.

Why are children so "picky" about food? In young people, taste buds die and are replaced about every seven days. As we age, the buds are replaced more slowly, so taste

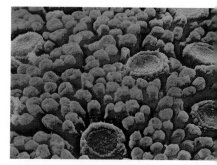

The surface of the human tongue magnified 47 times. The lavendar circular areas are the papillae, which contain the taste buds.

Papillae: Small bumps on the surface of the tongue that contain the taste receptors.

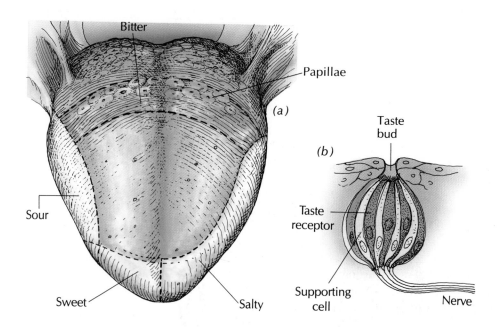

*Figure 3.14 **The tongue.** (a) Taste regions of the tongue. The front of the tongue is most sensitive to sweet and salty while the sides are most sensitive to sour and the back of the tongue responds to bitter. (b) This drawing is a detail of a taste bud.*

Many food and taste preferences are the result of childhood experiences and cultural influences. These Japanese children are eating octopus on a stick, while the American children are eating corn dogs on a stick. Due to their cultural upbringing, the American children might not share the zest for the Japanese children's octopus, and vice versa.

declines as we grow older. Thus, children, who have abundant taste buds, often dislike foods with strong or unusual tastes (such as liver and spinach), but as they grow older and lose taste buds, they may come to like these foods.

Pickiness also relates to the fact that the sense of taste enables humans and animals to discriminate between foods that are safe to eat and foods that are poisonous. Because most plants that taste bitter contain toxic chemicals, an animal is more likely to survive if it avoids bitter-tasting plants (Akabas, Dodd, and Al-Awqati, 1988). On the other hand, humans and animals have a preference for sweet foods because they are generally nonpoisonous and are good sources of energy.

Some pickiness is related to learning. Many food and taste preferences result from childhood experiences and cultural influences. For example, Japanese children eat raw fish and Chinese children eat chicken feet as part of their normal diet, whereas American children consider these foods "yucky." Likewise, smells we perceive as offensive or alluring are learned and often are culturally defined, as evidenced by the extreme measures Americans take to disguise their body odors.

Review Questions

1. The chemical senses are _____ and _____, otherwise known as _____ and _____ .
2. Explain the lock-and-key theory of smell.
3. Bodily chemicals that may affect the behavior of others are called _____ .
4. The four basic taste sensations are _____ , _____ , _____ , and _____ .
5. Describe how you taste orange juice.

Answers to Review Questions can be found in Appendix C.

THE BODY SENSES

• *How do we feel pressure, temperature, and pain? How are we able to keep our balance? And how do we know what our body is doing without watching it?*

Imagine for a moment that you are an Olympic skier, and you're anxiously awaiting the starting signal that will begin your once-in-a-lifetime race for the gold medal in the giant slalom. What senses will you need to manage the subtle and ever-changing balance adjustments required for Olympic-style skiing? How will you make your skis carve the cleanest, shortest, fastest line from start to finish? What will enable your arms, legs, and trunk to work in perfect harmony so that you can record the shortest time and win the gold? The senses that will allow you to do all this, and much more, are the body senses.

The body senses tell the brain how the body is oriented, where and how the body is moving, the things it touches or is touched by, and so on. These senses include the skin senses, the vestibular sense, and the kinesthetic sense.

Body Senses: These include the skin senses of pressure, warmth and cold, and pain; the vestibular sense of balance; and the kinesthetic sense of body position and movement.

The Skin Senses: More Than Just Touch

The skin senses are extremely vital. Skin not only protects the internal organs but also provides the brain with basic survival information. With their nerve endings in the various layers of skin, our skin senses tell us when a pot is dangerously hot, when the weather is freezing cold, when we have been hurt. Helen Keller broke out of her isolated existence through her skin senses. It was through feeling the cool gush of water over her hand that Helen was able to understand the "mystery of language" by associating objects with finger-spelled words.

Researchers have "mapped" the skin by applying probes to all areas of the body. Mapping shows there are four basic skin sensations: pressure, warmth and cold, and pain. Receptors for these sensations lie at various depths in the skin and connect to neurons that transmit the sensory information to the appropriate parts of the brain (see Figure 3.15). At present, the relationship between the types of receptors and the different sensations is not clear. It used to be thought that each receptor responded to only one type of stimulation, but recent research shows that some receptors respond to more than

Skin Senses: The sensory system for detecting pressure, temperature, and pain.

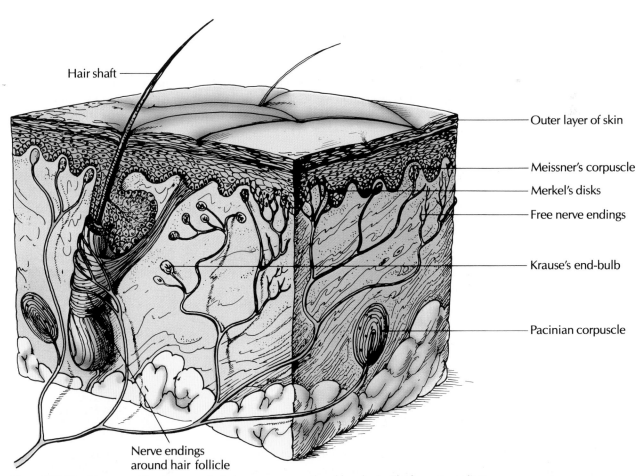

Hair shaft

Outer layer of skin

Meissner's corpuscle

Merkel's disks

Free nerve endings

Krause's end-bulb

Pacinian corpuscle

Nerve endings around hair follicle

Figure 3.15 The skin senses. The skin senses include pressure, warmth, cold, and pain. The free nerve endings are sensitive to pressure and pain. The Pacinian corpuscles, Meissner's corpuscles, and Merkel's disks, as well as some free nerve endings, are sensitive to touch and pressure. Temperature is sensed by myelinated axons located in the upper layers of the skin.

one. For example, pressure receptors also respond to certain sound waves (Green, 1977), and itching, tickling, and vibrating sensations seem to be produced by light stimulation of both pressure and pain receptors. Nevertheless, each of the four skin senses has been studied separately, and research has revealed some interesting facts about them.

Pressure

Pressure receptors are not evenly distributed. For example, the fingertips, lips, tip of the tongue, inner forearm, and genitals contain densely packed receptors and are extremely sensitive to pressure or touch, whereas portions of the back are relatively insensitive. Like Helen Keller, many blind people use their fingertip sensitivity to "see" the world. They can recognize people and objects through their sense of touch and can read books by using the Braille alphabet.

Interestingly, newborn boys and girls seem equally sensitive to touch—both are quieted when soothed with a blanket or soft fabric (Richmond-Abbott, 1983). But both parents tend to touch, as well as talk to, their girl babies more than their boy babies, and by adulthood women test out as more sensitive to touch stimuli than men (Tavris and Offir, 1984).

Is touch really necessary to the bonding between parent and child?   The popular press has given a great deal of attention to research on the importance of touch in the early bonding process between parent and child (Minde, 1986; Montagu, 1971). The research has suggested that skin contact in the first few hours of life could, among other things, increase the amount of time mothers spend with their babies, their success in nursing, the babies' intellectual development, and so on. Other studies have refuted this bonding research. They conclude that a strong bond between parent and child develops not because of skin contact immediately after birth but by continual contact between parent and child throughout infancy and subsequent childhood (Lamb, 1982; Reed and Leiderman, 1983). These later findings can do much to alleviate the guilt that might have been experienced by parents who adopted, by mothers who had cesarean deliveries, and by parents who gave birth before the bonding research was done. As we noted in Chapter 1, psychological research often has wide-ranging influences on public opinion, and this is a good example of why we all need to be alert to both supportive and refutational findings.

Warmth and Cold

The average square centimeter of skin contains about six cold spots where only cold can be sensed, and one or two warm spots where only warmth can be felt. Researchers have found no "hot" receptors, but by using a device called a "heat grill" (see Figure 3.16), they have found that the sensation of "hot" is created by stimulation of both warm and cold receptors at the same time.

As discussed earlier in this chapter, skin adapts quite readily to temperature changes, so that the same bucket of water can be perceived as warm or cold depending on

Continued contact between parent and child throughout infancy is important for the bonding process.

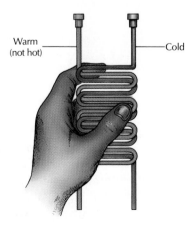

Warm (not hot) ———— Cold

Figure 3.16 The heat grill. When you grasp the heat grill you get the sensation of intense heat.

skin temperature. In other words, we can tell when something is hotter or colder than our skin, but not how hot or cold it is on an absolute scale. When conducting studies involving temperature receptors, researchers must therefore establish the subject's normal temperature in the skin area under study. This baseline temperature is referred to as *physiological zero.* They then record sensory reactions to changes from this baseline.

Pain

Many kinds of stimuli can initiate pain—scratches, cuts, burns, abscessed teeth, even hungry stomachs. We feel pain as a result of the overstimulation of sensory receptors (when we burn our mouth on piping hot pizza) and as a result of the stimulation of specific pain receptors (when we prick our finger with a needle). Although classified as a skin sense, the sense of pain is not restricted to the skin. Pain that is perceived as "dull and achy" can be felt in the internal organs as well as in the deeper layers of the skin. On the other hand, pain experienced as "sharp" or "bright" is felt in the superficial layers of the skin.

The common function for all types of pain is to serve as a warning for real or potential damage to bodily tissues. During a long-lasting headache, we would like to trade away our ability to sense pain, but this would be a dangerous move. People with diseases or injuries that reduce or eliminate pain perception are in constant danger. These individuals often suffer extensive burns and deep cuts without even noticing them—one woman even chewed off the tip of her tongue without feeling a thing (Cohen et al., 1955; McMurray, 1950).

At the other end of the pain continuum are those who suffer from chronic pain as a result of cancer, arthritis, or other causes. Chronic pain is the most common reason both for going to the doctor and for taking medication, yet it has received relatively little attention in research and in the training of doctors.

Contrary to how we react to the senses of smell and taste, we do not adapt to pain. The sensation of pain is transmitted along both rapid and slow neural pathways in the spinal cord. Thus, we tend to experience "first and second pain" (Sternbach, 1978). The initial pain you feel when you touch a hot stove is a clear, localized feeling that is carried over rapid pathways to the brain. This warning pain fades quickly. The pain that doesn't fade is the second, follow-up pain. This pain is more diffuse and long-lasting and is carried by slower neural pathways. The fact that we don't adapt to pain is quite functional—it is a reminder to do something about the tissue that has been hurt, such as put some ice on that burned hand.

If we don't adapt to pain, how do athletes keep playing despite painful injuries, and soldiers keep fighting after they've been wounded? In certain situations, the body releases natural pain killers called endorphins. Endorphins are chemicals that act in the same way as morphine to relieve pain by inhibiting pain perception. An extremely painful injury, along with the motivation to win an athletic contest or the sense of danger during battle, can cause the release of these endorphins and the closing of the pain pathways.

Endorphins: Morphinelike chemicals occurring naturally in the brain that can lessen pain responses.

There are many theories explaining pain transmission and perception, but no one theory adequately explains every type of pain. One of the most accepted and useful (useful as it applies to pain relief) is the gate-control theory, developed by Ronald Melzack and Patrick Wall (1965) (see Figure 3.17). As mentioned earlier, there are both large, fast nerve fibers and smaller, slower fibers that transmit sensory information from receptors to the brain via the spinal cord. The large fibers are responsible for sensations of touch, pressure, and dull pain; the smaller fibers are responsible solely for pain sensations. According to the gate-control theory, if a person receives some type of painful stimulation (e.g., a bee sting), the small fibers carry the pain information to the spinal cord and open a pain "gate" that allows this information to be sent on to the brain. If the person receives some type of alternate stimulation (such as pressing on or rubbing the bee sting), information from the larger, faster nerve fibers will arrive sooner than pain information from the small, slow fibers. This closes the gate, thereby reducing the amount of pain information sent to the brain (Warga, 1987).

Gate-Control Theory of Pain: The idea that pain sensations are processed and altered by mechanisms within the spinal cord.

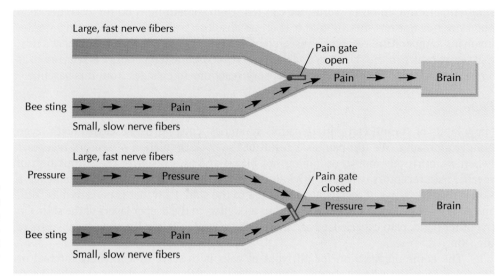

Figure 3.17 The gate-control theory of pain. Small, slow nerve fibers carry pain information to the brain unless large slow nerve fibers are activated by pressure to close the pain gate and allow only pressure information to be carried to the brain.

Recent research suggests that the gate may be chemically controlled, that a neurotransmitter called substance P works as a chemical opener for the pain gate and that endorphins close it. Although the gate-control theory has generated a good deal of debate (Nathan, 1976), it does explain why several pain control techniques are successful. These techniques include back rubs and massages, applications of heat, acupuncture, and the use of electrical nerve-stimulating devices. According to the gate-control theory, these procedures stimulate the touch and pressure fibers, thereby causing the gate to close on pain information.

The Vestibular Sense: The Sense of Balance

Vestibular Sense: The sense of how the body is oriented in relation to the pull of gravity; the sense of balance.

The vestibular sense is the sense of body orientation and position with respect to gravity and three-dimensional space (in other words, the sense of balance). Even the most routine activities—riding a bike, walking, or even sitting up—would be impossible without this sense. The vestibular apparatus is located in the inner ear and is composed of two small organs: the vestibular sacs, consisting of the saccule and the utricle, and the semicircular canals (see Figure 3.18).

Semicircular Canals: Three arching structures in the inner ear containing the hair receptors that provide balance information from head movements.

The semicircular canals are three arching structures located above and attached to the entrance to the cochlea. They provide the brain with balance information, particularly information about the rotation of the head. Because space has three dimensions—length, breadth, and height—the semicircular canals are arranged in three planes to detect movement in each dimension. As the head moves, liquid in the canals moves and bends hair cell receptors. At the end of the semicircular canals are the vestibular sacs, which contain hair cells sensitive to the specific angle of the head—straight up and down or tilted. Information from the semicircular canals and the vestibular sacs is converted to neural impulses that are then carried to the appropriate section of the brain.

Vestibular Sacs: Inner ear structures containing hair receptors that respond to the specific angle of the head, to provide balance information.

What causes motion sickness? Information from the vestibular sense is used by the eye muscles to maintain visual fixation and sometimes by the body to change body orientation. If the vestibular sense gets overloaded or becomes confused by boat, airplane, or automobile motion, the result is often dizziness and nausea. Research has found that random versus expected movements are more likely to produce motion sickness (Geeze and Pierson, 1986). Thus, automobile drivers are better prepared than passengers for upcoming movement and are less likely to feel sick. Motion sickness seems to vary with age: Infants are generally immune, children from 2 to 12 have the highest susceptibility, and the incidence declines in adulthood.

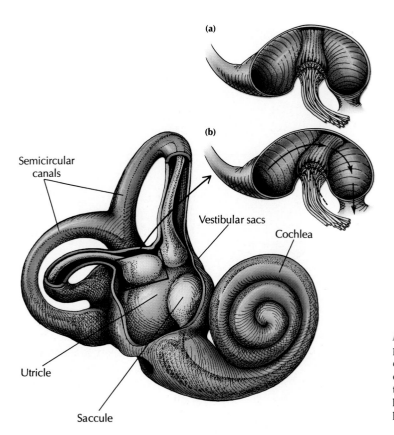

Figure 3.18 *Vestibular apparatus.* The receptor cells for body position are located in the vestibular sacs and the semicircular canals, which are shown in the cutaways above. **(a)** The position of the vestibular hair cells when the head is upright. **(b)** Tilting the head causes the fluid in the semicircular canals to move and bend the hair cells, allowing us to determine which way the head has tilted.

The vestibular sense and the kinesthetic sense work in harmony to enable us to move and maintain our balance. World class skiers such as Alberto Tomba use the vestibular and kinesthetic senses to their limits.

Random, unpredictable movement can cause motion sickness.

Motion sickness has been a particular problem for space travelers (Kohl, 1987). Conditions such as a gravity-free environment, rapid changes in altitude, and loss of visual reference with respect to the ground and horizon all contribute to the motion sickness often experienced by astronauts. Research by NASA, the Air Force, and the Navy has yielded several preventive treatments, however. There are drugs and antinausea patches that are worn behind the ear, which reduce sensitivity within the semicircular canals. It also helps to close your eyes and imagine you are fixing your gaze on a stable object. Relaxation techniques such as lying down, slowly and rhythmically tensing and untensing muscles, and open-mouth deep breathing also seem to help (Fromer, 1983).

The Kinesthetic Sense: The Sense of Movement

Kinesthesis: The sensory system that provides information on body posture and orientation.

Kinesthesis (from the Greek word for "motion") is the sense that provides the brain with information about bodily posture and orientation, as well as bodily movement. Unlike the receptors for sight, hearing, smell, taste, and balance, which are clumped together in one organ or area, the kinesthetic receptors are found throughout the muscles, joints, and tendons of the body. As we sit, walk, bend, lift, turn, and so on, our kinesthetic receptors respond by sending messages to the brain. They tell which muscles are being contracted and which relaxed, how our body weight is distributed, where our arms and legs are in relation to the rest of our body. Without these sensations, we would literally have to watch every step we make.

We generally take our kinesthetic sense for granted. Helen Keller certainly did. She praised her senses of smell, taste, and touch in compensating for her lack of vision and hearing, but she never mentioned the value of her kinesthetic sense. However, she relied on kinesthesis heavily when climbing trees (which she did frequently), paddling a rowboat (she could feel by the resistance of the water if she was holding the oars correctly), writing or typing a letter or a lesson, or making any kind of movement.

Sighted and hearing people likewise rely on kinesthesis constantly, yet seldom acknowledge it, since this sense is rarely disturbed in their everyday lives. In one study, an experimenter intentionally disturbed subjects' wrist tendon receptors by producing certain vibrations. Subjects reported sensations of having multiple forearms and impossible positions of their arms (Craske, 1977). But we don't have to go through experimental procedures to appreciate our kinesthetic sense. All we have to do is observe children learning new skills and remember when we were just learning to ride a bike, jump rope, or catch a football. During the learning process, we consciously move certain body parts and certain muscles, but gradually we learn to operate on "automatic pilot." Thus, just as wine tasters need training in knowing what smells and tastes to notice, our kinesthetic sense needs training in recognizing how various postures and movements should feel.

Review Questions

1. Name the body senses and briefly describe each.
2. There are four basic types of skin receptors: _____ , _____ , _____ , and _____ .
3. The _____ theory of pain suggests that pain-related information is let through to the brain when small, slow fibers are stimulated and is prevented from getting through when large, fast fibers are stimulated.
4. What is the advantage of feeling pain?
5. Endorphins are chemicals that _____ the pain gate, whereas substance P _____ the pain gate.
6. The _____ _____ in the inner ear provide the brain with information about the body's balance.

Answers to Review Questions can be found in Appendix C.

SENSORY DEPRIVATION

Although Helen Keller was deprived of two critical senses, she compensated for her deficiencies with her other senses and thus lived a successful, satisfying life. What would it be like, however, to be deprived of all our senses? in 1954, Bexton, Heron, and Scott conducted a classic study of such sensory deprivation. They offered $20 a day (a good wage at that time) to students at McGill University to do nothing more than rest on a comfortable bed, shielded from any stress or distractions. Sensations from outside their bodies were diminished as much as possible. The subjects wore translucent plastic visors that prevented recognition of any type of visual patterns. They heard the continuous hum of an air conditioner that muffled any incoming sounds, and they lay on a U-shaped foam pillow and wore cotton gloves and cardboard cuffs to prevent any sensation of touch.

• What happens if we are deprived of all sensory information?

After just a few hours, students began to feel bored and irritable, and most of them began to experience "blank periods" when they couldn't focus their attention on anything. Continued lack of sensory stimulation led several subjects to embark on drugless "trips" in which they experienced visual, tactile, and auditory hallucinations. The visual hallucinations chiefly took the form of simple geometrical patterns or dots of light. However, one subject saw little yellow men wearing black caps parading past with open mouths; another saw distorted eyeglasses marching down a street; and another, squirrels hurrying by, carrying sacks over their shoulders.

Many subjects quit during the first day, with few remaining after two days, despite the financial incentive to continue. Apparently, our bodies need some sort of sensory stimulation to function normally, and deprivation of stimulation for long periods of time is very unpleasant and can lead to adverse effects.

Critical Thinking
PSYCHOLOGY IN ACTION
CONDUCTING SOCRATIC DISCUSSIONS
Thinking about Sensation

At the heart of critical thinking is critical questioning. The ability to delve beneath the superficial or rise above mere appearances by considering logical consequences and possible boundaries is the core of critical thinking. Socrates, an ancient Greek philosopher, modeled this type of thinking in his question-and-answer method of teaching. In a Socratic discussion, the questioner uses probing questions to learn what the other person thinks, to help the respondent develop his or her ideas, and to mutually explore the implications, consequences, and values of an idea. In turn, the respondent is comfortable and doesn't become offended, defensive, or intimidated, because he or she knows the *shared* purpose is to clarify and evaluate a line of reasoning.

In this exercise, we offer several questions related to Chapter 3 that will help you practice the method of Socratic discussion. Select a good friend or classmate to simulate the roles of "questioner" and "respondent." One of you should play Socrates and question the other for half the questions; then reverse roles for the remaining questions. We are providing sample questions that Socrates might ask, and the respondent's answers should be followed up with questions such as: "Why?" "How do you know?" "What is your reason for saying that?" "For example?" "Can I summarize your point as . . . ?" Relax and enjoy your role as both the questioner and respondent. Critical, Socratic questioners do not attempt to make the other person look stupid. This should be a fun "mind game" that stretches your intellectual capacity and de-velops your critical thinking skills. (A by-product of this exercise is that it will help you master the chapter material.)

Sample Socratic Questions

1. Is there a sound if no one is there to hear it? Does a hamburger have a taste if no one is there to taste it?

2. What would the world be like if the absolute thresholds for sensation were changed? If we could see X rays and ultraviolet light or infrared rays and radar? If we were like bats and dolphins and could hear sounds up to 100,000 hertz?

3. What would happen if each sensory receptor (e.g., eyes, ears, skin) were receptive to every type of incoming stimuli? If your eyes were also sensitive to sound waves and odor molecules, could the brain distinguish and integrate this information?

4. William James, a famous early psychologist, suggested that, "If a master surgeon were to cross the auditory and optic nerves, then we would hear lightning and see thunder." How do you explain this statement?

5. How do you explain the fact that blind people tend to be better adjusted psychologically and less subject to emotional difficulties than deaf people?

6. If you had to choose between losing vision, hearing, or touch, which would it be? Why? What effect would it have on your life?

Intentional Deprivation: The Benefits of Boredom

Considering the extreme boredom, hallucinations, and occasional panic experienced by the students in the original studies of sensory deprivation, it is surprising that researchers have found beneficial uses for it. In the early 1960s, a psychiatrist named John C. Lilly set out to study deprivation effects by donning a diving helmet and immersing himself in a dark, soundproof tank of highly saline, buoyant water. During his immersion, Lilly reported experiencing "out of body" sensations, mind trips to other dimensions, and a general sense of being born again (Lilly, 1972). Other proponents of "tanking" claim that it produces a blissful, relaxed state of mind and vivid, enjoyable hallucinations.

Why did Bexton, Heron, and Scott's subjects experience such an unpleasant state if people who engage in tanking find it so enjoyable? One of the major reasons for the difference may be the power of suggestion. In Bexton, Heron, and Scott's studies, participants were unwittingly led to expect negative experiences, since they were given medical release forms to sign and "panic buttons" to push if they became too stressed. However, the results may also be due to a time factor. Whereas the McGill students experienced deprivation for many hours or even days, people in isolation tanks stay for, at the most, a few hours.

When "tanking," people float in a water-filled chamber. They claim this produces a blissful, relaxed state of mind.

 Try This Yourself

You can simulate sensory deprivation with meditation. Seclude yourself in a quiet room with, ideally, no distractions. Sit in a relaxed, comfortable position, close your eyes, practice rhythmical, deep breathing, and touch nothing but the chair on which you are sitting. Do this at a time when you are not likely to go to sleep and you have plenty of time (perhaps a three-day weekend or a holiday). Compare your experiences with those of Lilly and the McGill students. ■

Despite the discrepancies in the effects of sensory deprivation, it has proven beneficial when applied to certain clinical situations involving problem behaviors. Many psychologists have used a sensory deprivation approach called *restricted environmental stimulation therapy* (REST) as a treatment for clients with phobias or motivational problems in overeating, smoking, or drinking (Suedfeld, 1975; Suedfeld and Baker-Brown, 1986). One of the most interesting applications of the REST technique is with autistic children. Autism is a severe childhood psychological disorder. It is characterized by self-imposed isolation, language difficulties, intellectual impairment, insistence on sameness in the environment, and violent, self-destructive behavior. The autistic child withdraws into a private world and appears to have no need for affection or interaction with others. There is considerable debate over the cause and treatment of autism (see Chapter 15), but use of REST is based on the idea that autism may be the result of sensory overload. Autistic children may be unable to selectively reduce the normal bombardment of sensory stimuli. Acting on this theory, many therapists have had some success in treating the violent temper tantrums and other maladaptive behaviors of autistic children with two or three days of sensory isolation (Suedfeld, 1977).

Another treatment based on the sensory overload theory of autism involves an input-control device called a phonic ear, which consists of a set of earphones connected to an FM radio and a wireless microphone that broadcasts to the radio (Smith et al., 1981). The device allows autistic children to select and control their own audio input. They simply adjust the volume and point the microphone toward any sound they wish to hear. The phonic ear has been enthusiastically received by autistic children, as well as by their parents and teachers. In some children, inappropriate behavior is dramatically reduced, while spontaneous speech is greatly increased. These benefits arise, it seems, because the child can now control the previous sensory overload. Thus, limited sensory deprivation can be beneficial for some people.

Gender and Cultural Diversity

SEEKING SENSORY DEPRIVATION

Some cultures have used sensory deprivation and the resultant altered states of consciousness in a quest for supernatural guidance. Chippewa and Ojibwa children were sent out as early as five years of age to meditate and fast to make contact in a dream or a vision with their guardian spirit. As puberty approached, a boy might build a platform in a tree and isolate himself without food or water or wander off on his own without provisions for a week or more in search of a supernatural experience. He hoped the guardian spirit would predict his future and impart shamanistic secrets (a shaman is a medicine man, a combination priest and doctor who works with the supernatural [Barnouw, 1985, p. 390]).

A ritualistic form of sensory deprivation has also been used by a religious group called the Shakers of St. Vincent in the Caribbean. To become an "elder" in the church, a person must participate in a sensory deprivation ceremony called *mourning*. (The elders need not be old and the mourning is for their own sins.) Mourning involves a week or two of sensory isolation during which the prospective elder lies blindfolded on a pallet and discusses any spiritual experiences with a church official. It is possible that many of these experiences are similar to those experienced by John C. Lilly and the subjects in the Bexton, Heron, and Scott experiments at McGill University. ■

A Chippewa Indian

Sensory Substitution: Natural and Artificial Compensation

Another interesting finding from deprivation research is that when sensory stimulation is blocked for one sense, the body compensates by increasing sensitivity in other senses. In a study by Bross, Harper, and Sicz (1980), the visual sensitivity of experimental subjects made artificially deaf first dropped and then rebounded to above starting levels. Researchers have also been successful in developing sensory substitution systems with devices that substitute vibrations on the skin for sensory impairments (Lechet, 1986).

Helen Keller similarly learned to "see" and "hear" with her sense of touch, and she often recognized visitors by their smell or by vibrations from their walk. Despite the heightened sensitivity of her functioning senses, however, Helen professed a lifelong yearning to experience a normal sensory world. She gave this advice to those whose senses are "normal":

> I who am blind can give one hint to those who see: use your eyes as if tomorrow you would be stricken blind. And the same method can be applied to the other senses. Hear the music of voices, the song of a bird, the mighty strains of an orchestra as if you would be stricken deaf tomorrow. Touch each object as if tomorrow your tactile sense would fail. Smell the perfume of flowers, taste with relish each morsel as if tomorrow you could never smell and taste again. Make the most of every sense, glory in all the facets of pleasure and beauty which the world reveals to you through the several means of contact which nature provides.
>
> *(1962, p. 23)*

Review Questions

1. What are some of the effects of sensory deprivation?
2. The technique termed REST, which is based on sensory deprivation, has been successful in treating _____, a severe childhood psychological disorder.
3. What is meant by "sensory substitution"?

Answers to Review Questions can be found in Appendix C.

REVIEW OF MAJOR CONCEPTS

EXPERIENCING SENSATION

1. Sensory processing includes reduction, transduction, and coding. The reticular activating system is responsible for much of the sensory reduction that takes place. Transduction, or the conversion of physical stimuli into neural impulses, occurs at the receptors in our sense organs. Each sensory system is specialized to code its stimuli into unique sets of neural impulses that the brain interprets as light, touch, and so on.

2. Psychophysics is the study of the relationships between physical stimuli and the sensations they evoke, including the study of thresholds. The absolute threshold is the smallest magnitude of a stimulus we can detect. The difference threshold is the smallest change in a stimulus we can detect.

3. The process of sensory adaptation allows us to operate efficiently in a wide range of stimulus intensities by decreasing our sensitivity to constant, unchanging stimuli.

VISION

4. Light is a form of energy that is part of the electromagnetic spectrum. The wavelength of a light determines its hue, or color; the amplitude, or the height of a light wave, determines its intensity.

5. The function of the eye is to capture light and focus it on the visual receptors that convert light energy to neural impulses.

6. The major parts of the eye include the cornea, the clear bulge at the front of the eye where light enters; the sclera, the white outer covering of the eye; the pupil, the hole through which light passes into the eye; the iris, the colored muscles that surround the pupil; the lens, the elastic structure that bulges and flattens to focus an image on the retina; and the retina, the back part of the eye that contains the visual receptor cells.

7. The visual receptors, called photoreceptors, are the rods and cones. The rods are very sensitive to light and enable us to see at night. The cones are specialized for bright light conditions and enable us to see close and fine detail.

8. The major visual problems are myopia, hyperopia, and presbyopia. Myopia occurs when the lens focuses the image in front of the retina, resulting in nearsightedness. Hyperopia occurs when the lens focuses the image in back of the retina, resulting in farsightedness. Presbyopia occurs when the lens in the eye ages and hardens and is no longer able to focus on near objects.

HEARING

9. The sense of hearing is known as audition.

10. Sound waves result from rapid changes in air pressure caused by vibrating objects. The frequency of these sound waves is sensed as the pitch of the sound and is measured in cycles per second, whereas the amplitude of the waves is perceived as loudness and is measured in decibels.

11. The structures of the ear include the pinna, the external visible part of the ear; the eardrum, or tympanic membrane, that vibrates when hit by sound waves; the ossicles —the malleus, incus, and stapes—that transmit the sound vibrations through the middle ear; the oval window, the membrane separating the middle ear from the inner ear; and the cochlea, the structure that forms the inner ear. The major structures of the cochlea are the basilar membrane and the auditory receptor cells (hair cells).

SMELL AND TASTE

12. The sense of smell (olfaction) and the sense of taste (gustation) are called the chemical senses and are closely interrelated.

13. The receptors for olfaction are in the olfactory epithelium located at the top of the nasal cavity. According to the lock-and-key theory, we can smell diverse odors because each three-dimensional odor molecule fits only into one type of receptor.

14. The receptors for taste are located on the tongue and throat. Taste receptors are sensitive to the four major tastes: salty, sweet, sour, and bitter.

THE BODY SENSES

15. The body senses are the skin senses, the vestibular sense, and the kinesthetic sense.

16. The skin senses, which include pressure, temperature, and pain, not only protect the internal organs but also provide basic survival information.

17. The vestibular sense is the sense of body orientation and position with respect to gravity and three-dimensional space. It is our sense of balance. The vestibular apparatus is located in the inner ear and is composed of two small sensory organs: the semicircular canals and the vestibular sacs.

18. The kinesthetic sense provides the brain with information about bodily posture and orientation, as well as bodily movement. The kinesthetic receptors are spread throughout the body in muscles, joints, and tendons.

SENSORY DEPRIVATION

19. Sensory deprivation is the restricting of incoming sensory information to the brain. This phenomenon has been studied by isolating people from external sensory stimulation.

20. Sensory substitution occurs when one sensory system takes over for an impaired sensory system.

SUGGESTED READINGS

GREGORY, R. L. (1977). *Eye and brain: The psychology of seeing* (3rd ed.). New York: World University Library. A wonderful book on the wonders of seeing.

SCHIFFMAN, H. R. (1990). *Sensation and perception: An integrated approach* (3rd ed.). New York: Wiley. An introduction to the study of sensation and perception.

CHAPTER

4

Perception

OUTLINE

$\mathcal{S}$uppose you put on some glasses that inverted your world so it looked like the picture above. How do you think you would react? Could you still walk? write? ride a bike? take a shower? Do you think you would get used to your new way of seeing things? Would you "adapt"?

To answer just such questions psychologist George Stratton (1896) wore a special lens over one eye and a patch over the other for eight days. Whenever he removed the lens he covered both eyes. For the first few days, Stratton had a great deal of difficulty navigating his environment and coping with everyday tasks. His arms and legs seemed to be in the wrong places and the world had an unreal feeling about it. But by the third day he noted:

> Walking through the narrow spaces between pieces of furniture required much less care than hitherto. I could watch my hands as they wrote, without hesitating or becoming embarrassed thereby.

By the fifth day Stratton's adjustment to this strange perceptual environment was almost complete, and he could walk around his house with ease. When he removed the lens on the eighth day of his experiment, he was surprised to find that even though his vision had been restored to "normal," his world didn't feel entirely normal. Stratton wrote:

. . . the scene had a strange familiarity. The visual arrangement was immediately recognized as the old one of pre-experimental days; yet the reversal of everything from the order to which I had grown accustomed during the last week gave the scene a surprising bewildering air which lasted for several hours. It was hardly the feeling, though, that things were upside down.

Stratton's experiment is considered a classic today because he demonstrated for the first time the crucial role of learning in perception. You can gain a sense of what Stratton experienced from the inverted photograph, which shows what you would see if your visual field were inverted, and from trying to read the following passage:

This is how a written text would have appeared to George Stratton when he was wearing his spectacles. Although it may be hard for you, you can probably read this. If you had been taught to read words upside down and backward, this would appear normal.

ジョージ・ストラットン氏が
眼鏡を掛けていた時
文書が 氏には
こんな風に
見えたでしょう。たとえ
難しくても、おそらく
読むことができます。
もし文字をさかさまや
逆から 読むように
習えば、たぶんこれは.
普通と思われる
でしょう。

With some difficulty, or by turning the book upside down and holding it up to a mirror, you can decipher the picture and decode the inverted passage. But can you interpret the passage at the left?

Understanding this passage depends on your experience with, or prior learning of, Japanese characters. If you read Japanese, you know that this passage says the same thing as the inverted English paragraph above. Without learning and experience, raw sensory data such as these Japanese characters are just meaningless jumbles of lines that cannot be *perceived* by the brain.

In this chapter, you will learn the difference between merely receiving sensory input and actually perceiving, or making sense of, stimuli. You may be surprised to learn that before we hear sound waves, see points of light, or smell an odor, we must not only pay attention to the stimuli, but also organize the stimulus input, and then interpret the neural signals that are sent to the brain. You will also discover how we perceive distance and movement, how we see different colors, and whether there is any scientific evidence to support ESP. As you read Chapter 4, keep the following **Survey** questions in mind and answer them in your own words:

- What is the difference between sensation and perception?
- How do we decide what to pay attention to in our environment?
- How do we organize stimuli in order to perceive form, depth, color, and motion?
- What factors influence how we interpret sensations?

SENSATION AND PERCEPTION

Sensation and perception are intimately related and difficult to separate, but there is a distinct difference. Figure 4.1 may help you to understand this difference. Sensation generally refers to the process of detecting and transducing raw sensory information, whereas perception refers to the process of selecting, organizing, and interpreting sensory data into usable mental representations of the world.

To better understand how perception differs from sensation, look at Figure 4.2. Do you see a downward curving spiral? Now try putting your finger on the outermost circle

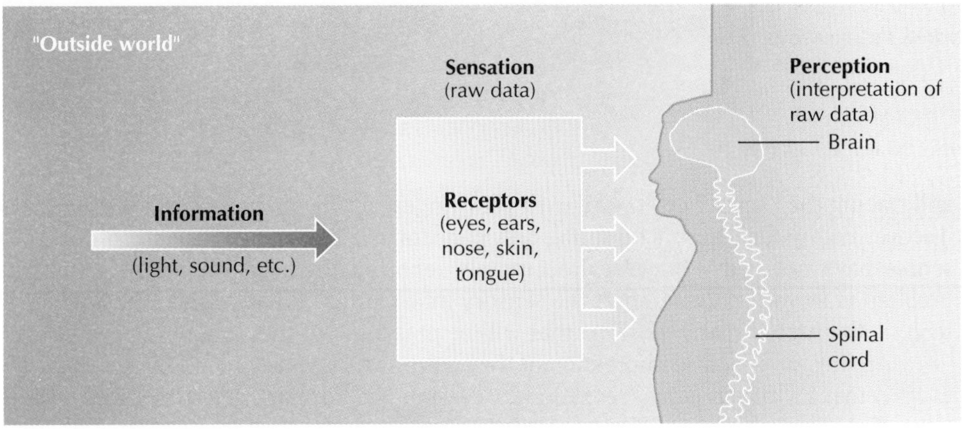

• *What is the difference between sensation and perception?*

Sensation: The process of detecting and transducing raw sensory information.

Perception: The process of selecting, organizing, and interpreting sensory data into usable mental representations of the world.

"Outside world"

Sensation
(raw data)

Perception
(interpretation of raw data)
— Brain

Information
(light, sound, etc.)

Receptors
(eyes, ears, nose, skin, tongue)

— Spinal cord

Figure 4.1 Sensation and perception. Sensation is the entering of raw data from the senses into the brain. Perception is the interpretation of that raw sensory data.

Figure 4.2 Spiral? Is this a spiral or a series of concentric circles?

The art of M. C. Escher uses illusions to trick the brain and produce "impossible images."

Illusion: A false impression of the environment.

Highway guidelines appear much shorter to the driver than they actually are.

and tracing the "spiral" downward with your fingertips. If you do this carefully, you will discover that in fact there is no spiral, only concentric circles, one inside the other. Your senses have not lied—they have accurately reported the available information. The problem is in your perception of the sensory information. What you have just encountered is the first of many *illusions* that will be presented in this chapter.

An illusion is a false impression of the environment. Our perceptions are normally in agreement with our actual sensations. Occasionally, however, sensations and perceptions do not match and an illusion results. Illusions can be produced by actual physical distortion of stimuli, as is the case of a desert mirage caused by refracted light. Illusions can also be caused by distortions in the perceptual process, as in the spiral illusion (Figure 4.2) or an M. C. Escher print. Illusions offer psychologists an indirect method for studying the normal modes of perception. By studying how and where the perceptual system breaks down, they can obtain valuable information on perceptual processes.

Psychologists also study illusions found in everyday situations. For instance, we commonly misperceive the length of the dashed guidelines that separate lanes on streets and highways as shorter than they actually are. Most people estimate that the lines are 2 to 5 feet long; in reality, they are longer than 10 feet, and some are as long as 18 feet (Harte, 1975). Information from this type of research can be applied to improving conditions in everyday life. In this case, the findings can be used to determine the best placement of safety features along our highways, such as the optimum height of lettering painted on roadways.

 Try This Yourself

Most of the illusions you will encounter in this chapter involve the visual sense. But illusions do occur in all the senses. For an example of a touch illusion, try this: With the tip of your *retracted* ball-point pen, trace a letter or numeral on the palm of your hand as it faces you. Then turn your palm away from you and ask a friend to do the same tracing. If you are like many subjects, the second tracing will seem backward (Kaufman, 1974). ∎

Whichever senses are involved, perception consists of three basic processes: (1) selection, in which we select which stimuli to focus on while disregarding the rest; (2) organization, in which we assemble selected sensations into common patterns and shapes; and (3) interpretation, in which we attempt to explain the selected and organized sensations and make reasonable judgments from them.

We can see these three processes operating in a major league baseball player, like Tony Gwynn or Roberto Alomar, coming up to bat. The first thing he does is *select* the sensory input: He directs his attention to the players on the field rather than the people in the stands and listens to the directions from his coach rather than the cheers, boos, or comments from the fans. As he takes his stance, he *organizes* his sensory input. He notes positions of the players on both teams and gaps in the opposing team's defense. As he gets ready to swing, he *interprets* the information he has selected and organized to judge where he should hit the ball and how hard he should swing.

In the rest of the chapter we will examine each of these steps in perception (selection, organization, and interpretation) and present some facts and theories about how perception works and why people often differ in their view of the world.

Zina Garrison is selecting, organizing, and interpreting information about the tennis ball that is approaching her at a speed that is faster than 100 miles per hour.

SELECTION

The first step in perception is *selection,* in which we select the stimuli to which we will pay attention. Imagine that you are at a three-ring circus, with dancing bears and clowns in ring one, a troupe of high-wire trapeze artists in ring two, and a lion-taming act in ring three. With such an array of stimuli, how can you keep from being overwhelmed? In almost every situation there is an excess of sensory information, but the brain manages to sort out the important messages and discard the rest. This process is known as selective attention. While watching the circus, for example, you generally direct your attention to only one of the three rings at a time and ignore the others. You can also listen to your friends sitting next to you at the circus while watching the clowns in ring one, although it may be difficult to accurately attend to both at the same time. But it is nearly impossible to simultaneously watch both the clowns in ring one and the trapeze artist in ring two. While it is possible to ignore information coming in from one of your senses and attend to information from one of your other senses, multiple messages entering the same sensory apparatus become confused.

Why does the brain decide to pay attention to some sensory stimuli but not to others? There are three major factors involved in a selection decision: physiological factors, stimulus factors, and psychological factors.

Physiological Factors: Biological Influences on Selection

One of the major physiological factors in selection is the presence of specialized cells in the brain called feature detectors (or feature analyzers) that respond only to certain sensory information. In 1959 researchers discovered specialized nerve cells, which they called "bug detectors," in the optic nerve of the frog that responded only to moving bugs (Lettvin, Maturana, McCulloch, and Pitts, 1959). In the early 1960s, David Hubel and Torsten Wiesel, in studies of the visual system of cats, found feature detectors that respond to specific lines and angles in the visual field (Hubel, 1963; Hubel and Wiesel, 1965). In addition to these specialized cells that select for visual movement and patterns, cells have also been found in the auditory area of animal brains that respond to different and changing pitches of sound (Whitfield and Evans, 1965).

Visual Deprivation

The basic mechanisms for perceptual selection are thus built into the brain, but a certain amount of interaction with the environment is apparently necessary for feature detector

* *How do we decide what to pay attention to in our environment?*

Selective Attention: The process whereby the brain manages to sort out and attend only to the important messages from the senses.

Feature Detectors: Specialized cells in the brain that respond only to certain sensory information.

cells to develop normally. In one well-known study it was found that early visual deprivation can lead to permanent degeneration of the retina in chimpanzees (Riesen, 1950). Another study demonstrated that kittens raised in a cylinder with vertically or horizontally striped walls develop severe behavioral and neurological impairments (Blakemore and Cooper, 1970). When "horizontal cats"—those cats raised with only horizontal lines in their environment—were removed from the cylinder and allowed to roam, they could easily jump onto horizontal surfaces but had great difficulty negotiating objects with vertical lines, such as chair legs. The reverse was true for the "vertical cats": They could easily avoid table and chair legs but never attempted to jump onto horizontal structures. Examination of the visual cortex of these cats revealed that because of their restricted environment they had failed to develop their potential feature detectors for either vertical or horizontal lines and angles. Unlike these cats, however, George Stratton was able to adjust to his new environment because, during development, his brain had been organized along principles that applied to both his normal and his distorted environments.

Visual deprivation research has several practical applications. For one thing, it gives scientific backing to the idea, long advocated by both pediatricians and psychologists, that infants need a certain amount of sensory stimulation even in the earliest days of life. Furthermore, such research suggests that certain childhood visual defects, such as squinting or astigmatism, must be corrected early in life. If treatment is delayed, they may not be correctable, since the perceptual "wiring" within the brain will then be at fault, not the sensory processes in the eye.

Habituation

Habituation: The tendency of the brain to ignore environmental factors that remain constant.

An additional physiological factor important in selecting sensory data is habituation, the tendency to ignore environmental factors that remain constant. The brain seems "prewired" to pay more attention to *changes* in the environment than to stimuli that remain constant. Have you ever gotten a new clock and thought it had a very loud tick, but in a short time you realized you weren't aware of it ticking at all? This happens because you become *habituated* to the regularity of the sound. If the sound changed every few minutes, you would notice every change because you would not have enough time to become habituated each time.

Is habituation the same as sensory adaptation?   No. Both are adaptive responses, but one has to do with sensation and the other, with perception. As you may remember from Chapter 3, sensory receptors respond to a constant stimulus by slowing down their firing rates. This process is called *adaptation*. When the brain "decides" not to pay attention to the constant stimulus, it is called *habituation*. To illustrate the difference, picture yourself walking into a room full of people smoking. The smell of smoke is overwhelming at first but your smell receptors *adapt* after you have been in the room for a while. The smoke will still burn your eyes and affect your breathing, but less so after the first few minutes. However, if you become engrossed in some hot topic of conversation, your brain will completely ignore the discomfort caused by the smoke—you will habituate to it.

Stimulus Factors: Environmental Influences on Selection

When given a wide variety of stimuli to choose from, we automatically select the stimuli that are intense, novel, moving, contrasting, or repetitious. Parents and teachers often use these attention-getting principles, but advertisers have developed them to a fine art.

 Try This Yourself

The next time you're watching TV, take the time to notice what techniques advertisers use to get your attention. Is a commercial louder or brighter than the show you've been watching? Does it use dancing cats, singing raisins, or some other novelty effect? Does it employ repetition to the point that you feel like throwing something at the tube to make it stop? ∎

Surprisingly, obnoxious advertising does not deter people from buying the advertised product. Advertisers are well aware of the potential for irritating their audience, but they have found that the single most important factor in sales is getting people's attention. For sheer volume of sales, the question of whether you *like* a commercial or an ad is irrelevant. What matters is whether you *notice* the product being promoted.

Psychological Factors: Intrapsychic Influences on Selection

In addition to physiological and stimulus factors, certain psychological factors also explain why you attend to some stimuli and not to others. Motivation and personal needs are two of these. What you choose to perceive is determined largely by your current level of satisfaction or deprivation. For example, when you are hungry, you are much more likely to notice television commercials for doughnuts, hamburgers, or pizza than those for cars or detergent. Similarly, in everyday life, when you're lonely, your perceptions are affected so that it seems everyone is part of a happy couple except you.

In addition to the strong influence of needs and motivations on perceptual selection, personality and interests play a role. At a college football game, for example, an ex-quarterback may be paying close attention to plays being called on the field, while his friend, a musician, may be listening to the band, and a broadcasting major sitting next to them may be focusing on the announcer's vocal qualities.

Subliminal Stimuli

Is it possible to perceive something without paying attention to it, such as hidden advertising messages or backward messages on records? Can subliminal stimuli (stimuli that are below the threshold of our conscious awareness) somehow make us do things without our being aware of it? In fact, a great deal of research has been conducted in this area (Zanot, Pincus, and Lamp, 1983). One researcher, Lloyd Silverman (1980; Silverman and Lachmann, 1985) has proposed that subliminal messages are perceived by our unconscious mind, where they can affect personality and behavior. However, research has not shown any support for this idea.

Subliminal: Pertaining to any stimulus presented below the threshold of conscious awareness.

Whether or not the unconscious mind can really perceive these messages, it is clear from the research that they have little or no influence on consumer behavior. In 1956 managers of a New Jersey theater allegedly inserted the messages "Drink Coca-Cola" and "Hungry? Eat popcorn" on the screen every five seconds. They flashed the messages so fast that people were unable to "see" them, but the managers claimed that their sales of Coke and popcorn increased. This claim was never supported by any data, and subsequent research has been unable to document any significant change in buying behavior (Moore, 1982).

More recently, subliminal self-help audio tapes have come on the market. Although most psychologists working in the field agree that some perception occurs without awareness (Kent, 1991; Merikle and Reingold, 1990), there is also near-unanimous agreement that these tapes do not influence behavior (Greenwald, Spangenberg, Pratkanis, and Eskenazi, 1991; Kent, 1991). Using a double-blind research design Greenwald, et al. asked their subjects to listen to two different commercially available subliminal self-help audiotapes. One tape claimed to increase self-esteem, and the other, to improve memory. The results of the experiment were very interesting. Not only did the tapes not produce the promised results, they had a placebo effect. Memory improved slightly when the tape was labeled "memory" even though it was originally marketed as a self-esteem tape, and vice versa.

Review Questions

1. What is *perception?*
2. What is an illusion?
3. Tell which of the three basic processes of perception is involved as you're lying in the grass watching clouds move past:
   _____ You recognize the shape of a sailboat.
   _____ You ignore the birds flying around and focus on the clouds.
   _____ You see white shapes against a blue background.
4. The process that allows us to sort out the important sensory information from the unimportant is _____ .
5. Specialized cells in the brain called _____ respond only to certain types of sensory information.
6. You write a reminder on a post-it and stick it on the door where you see it every day. A month later, you forget your appointment because of the tendency to ignore constant stimuli, which is known as _____ .

Answers to Review Questions can be found in Appendix C.

ORGANIZATION

• How do we organize stimuli in order to perceive form, depth, color, and motion?

Having selected incoming information, we must organize it into patterns and principles that will help us to understand the world. Raw sensory data are like the parts of a watch—they must be assembled in a meaningful way before they are useful. The *organization* of sensory data can be divided into five areas: form perception, perceptual constancies, depth perception, color perception, and motion perception.

Form Perception: Organizing Stimuli into Patterns or Shapes

Gestalt: A German word meaning "whole" or "pattern."

Gestalt psychologists were among the first to study how sensory impressions are organized by the brain. The German word gestalt means "whole" or "pattern." Accordingly, Gestaltists emphasized the importance of organization and patterning in enabling us to perceive the *whole* stimulus rather than perceiving its discrete parts as separate entities. The Gestaltists proposed laws of organization that specify how people perceive form. These basic laws are summarized in Figure 4.3. Although these examples are all visual, each law applies to other modes of perception as well.

Figure and Ground

Figure and Ground: A Gestalt law of perceptual organization stating that our perceptions consist of two aspects: the figure, which stands out and has a definite contour or shape, and the ground, which is more indistinct.

Reversible Figure: An ambiguous figure that has more than one possible figure and ground organization.

The most fundamental Gestalt principle or law of organization is that we tend to distinguish between figure and ground. For example, while reading this material your eyes are receiving sensations of black lines and white paper, but your brain is organizing these sensations into letters and words that are perceived against a backdrop of white pages. The letters constitute the figure and the pages, the ground. The discrepancy between figure and ground is sometimes so vague that we have difficulty in perceiving which is which, as can be seen in the photograph on p. 133 at the end of this chapter. This is known as a reversible figure. It is also possible to "see" a figure and background where none actually exist. The figure–ground principle is the basis for explaining why people wear makeup. Makeup highlights the figures of the face, making the eyebrows, eyes, cheeks, and lips stand out against the background of the skin. This principle also illustrates why camouflage works. The similarity between the color and/or shape of the figure and its background makes the contour of the figure nearly indistinguishable—hence

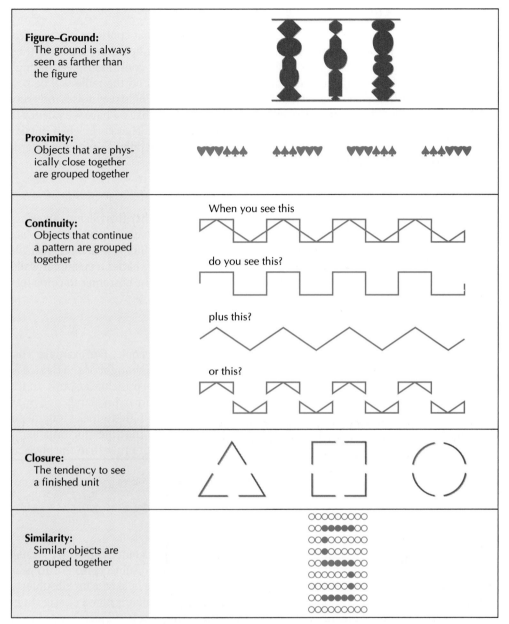

Figure 4.3 Some basic Gestalt principles of organization. The Gestalt principles of figure–ground, proximity, continuity, closure, and similarity are shown here. The Gestalt principle of contiguity cannot be shown because it involves nearness in time, not visual nearness.

the difficulty in distinguishing tigers from their natural surroundings. Since camouflage often depends on color blending, many "color-blind" soldiers were employed during World War II to detect camouflaged enemy targets (color blindness is discussed later in this chapter).

Proximity

According to the principle of proximity, elements that are physically close together will be grouped together and perceived as a single unit. Most young children in the United States initially learn the alphabet by singing it to the tune of "Twinkle, Twinkle, Little Star." The principle of proximity explains why these children often conclude that L, M, N, O, and P are one letter, since in the song those letters are sung as a phrase and sound like the name of one letter, elamenopee.

Proximity: The Gestalt principle proposing that elements that are physically close together will be grouped together and perceived as a single unit.

Continuity and Closure

Continuity: The Gestalt principle proposing that patterns or objects that continue in one direction, even if interrupted by another pattern, tend to be perceived as being grouped together.

According to the principle of continuity, patterns or objects that continue in one direction, even if interrupted by another pattern, are perceived as being grouped together. Thus, the contour of distant hills will be perceived as being continuous even though interrupted by intervening trees and buildings. Sounds heard on the radio will be perceived as part of the same song even if horns honking and blaring street noises interrupt them occasionally. The similar principle of closure proposes that we have a tendency to perceive a finished or whole unit even if there are gaps in it. Therefore, when outside noises blot out some words of a song on the radio, you can generally fill in missing words via the principle of closure.

Closure: The Gestalt principle proposing that people have a tendency to perceive a finished unit even if there are gaps in it.

Contiguity

Many Gestalt principles of organization involve perceptions other than vision. An example is the law of contiguity, which states that when two events happen at a time and place near to each other, one is perceived as causing the other. Suppose a three-year-old playing in her mother's store observes that every time her dog barks, a customer walks in. She could very well conclude that the barking dog *causes* the customer to come into the store.

Contiguity: The Gestalt principle stating that when two events happen at a time and place near to each other, one is perceived as causing the other.

Similarity

Gestalt principles also apply to perceptions involving other people. For example, Hispanics, women, senior citizens, and Native Americans are often thought of and treated as members of a group rather than as individuals—the similarity principle at work. In the same way, the figure–ground principle explains why a white person stands out in an all-black group. And the proximity principle suggests that we tend to make judgments about others on the basis of the company they keep. Thus, the rules for organizing stimuli can also help us to understand areas of human behavior other than the physical modes of perception (see Chapters 17 and 18).

Similarity: The Gestalt principle proposing that things that appear similar or act in a similar fashion are perceived as being the same.

Gender and Cultural Diversity

ARE THE GESTALT LAWS UNIVERSALLY TRUE?

Are the Gestalt laws of perception universally true for all people? Since the Gestalt psychologists conducted most of their work with well-educated subjects from European urban cultures, A. R. Luria (1976) wondered whether their laws held true for all subjects, no matter what their educational level or cultural setting. In what is now a classic study, Luria recruited subjects living in what was then the USSR. These subjects ranged from illiterate Ichkari women from remote villages to semiliterate collective farm activists to educated women students enrolled in a teachers' school.

Luria found that when presented with the stimuli shown in Figure 4.4, the literate women students were the only ones who identified the shapes by their categorical names. That is, whether triangles were made of solid lines, dotted lines, or Xs, they called them all triangles. The other subjects named the shapes according to objects they resembled. They called a circle a watch, a plate, or a moon; they called a square a mirror, a house, or an apricot-drying board. As may be expected, when asked to classify the stimuli in Figure 4.4, the educated women students readily grouped similar shapes into geometrical categories, whereas the illiterate Ichkari women classified the shapes according to objects they were perceived to represent. When asked if numbers 12 and 13 were alike, one woman answered, "No, they're not alike. This one's not like a watch, but that one's a watch because there are dots" (p. 37).

So it appears, concludes Luria, that the Gestalt laws of perceptual organization are valid for people who have been schooled in geometrical concepts, but they do not apply to illiterate people who perceive shapes in an object-oriented fashion and who classify shapes according to the objects they are perceived to represent. ■

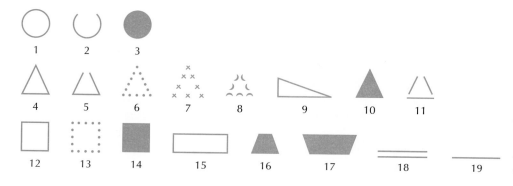

Figure 4.4 *Luria's stimuli.* When presented with these stimuli, literate subjects perceive geometric shapes, whereas illiterate subjects perceive objects that the stimuli resemble.

Perceptual Constancies: Stabilizing a Changing World

Although we are particularly alert to changes in our sensory input, we also manage to perceive a great deal of consistency in the environment, thanks to the principle of perceptual constancy. Although the visual sensory input of George Stratton was drastically altered by his inverting lens, his world was not completely foreign to him since, through prior experience, he had learned certain consistencies that transferred to his distorted world. Without perceptual constancies, our world would be totally chaotic. Things would seem to grow as we got closer to them, to change shape as our viewing angle changed, and to change color as light levels changed.

Constancy: The tendency for the environment to be perceived as remaining the same even with changes in sensory input.

Size Constancy

Most perceptual constancies are based on prior experience and learning. For example, preschoolers express wonder at the fact that the car parked down the street is only "this high" (as they show about two inches between their fingers), while the car they are standing next to is taller than they are. Their size judgment is mistaken because they haven't yet had the experiences necessary for learning size constancy. According to this principle, the perceived size of an object remains the same even though the size of its retinal image changes. Research shows that adults consistently outperform young children in tasks involving size constancy. But when children reach about age six or seven they have had enough experience with relative sizes that their size judgments remain constant with varying distances and their size constancy skills match those of adults (Teghtsoonian and Beckwith, 1976).

Size Constancy: The process in which the perceived size of an object remains the same, even though the size of the retinal image changes.

An example of an adult who had never developed a sense of size constancy was provided by anthropologist Colin Turnbull (1961). While he was studying pygmies living in the dense rain forest of the Congo River Valley in Africa, Turnbull took a native named Kenge for a jeep ride to the African plains. Kenge had lived his entire life in an area so dense with foliage that he had never seen distances farther than about 100 yards. Now he was suddenly able to see for almost 70 miles. Lacking perceptual experience with such wide open spaces, Kenge had great difficulty judging sizes. When he first saw a herd of water buffalo in the distance, he thought they were insects. When Turnbull insisted they were buffalo that were very far away, Kenge was insulted and asked, "Do you think that I am ignorant?" To Kenge's surprise, as they drove toward the "insects" the creatures seemed to grow into buffalo. He concluded that witchcraft was being used to fool him, and after Turnbull showed him a lake so large that its opposite shore couldn't be seen, he asked to be taken back to his rain forest.

Shape Constancy

Other constancies also develop through individual experience. When you look at a chair directly from the front or the back, it has a rectangular shape. When you look at it directly from the side, it has an "h" shape. Yet you still perceive the chair as having a single shape because your brain remembers past experiences with objects that only

The Ames room illusion. In the top photo, the woman on the right is seen as substantially taller than the boy on the left. In the bottom photo, the boy on the right is seen as taller than the woman on the left. The woman is actually much taller than the boy. For an explanation of how this is possible, see Figure 4.4.

Shape Constancy: The process in which the perceived shape of an object remains the same, even though the retinal image of that object changes.

seemed to change shape as you moved but actually remained constant. This is known as shape constancy. Without shape and size constancy, a romantic kiss would become a nightmare as your partner's nose and eyes grew larger and more prominent as he or she approached you.

A perceptual psychologist named Adelbert Ames demonstrated the power of shape and size constancies by creating what is now known as the *Ames room* (see photograph on this page). Upon examining this photograph, you might conclude that the person on the left is a midget and the person on the right is a giant. In actuality, both people are of normal size. This illusion is based on the unusual construction of the room. As can be seen in the diagram in Figure 4.5, linear perspective tricks the observer into perceiving the room as square when it is actually shaped like a trapezoid. The illusion is so strong that when a person walks from the left corner to the right, the observer perceives the person to be "growing," even though that is not possible.

If we know the truth of this illusion, why does it still work?   Our brain has had a lifetime of interaction with normally constructed rooms, and our desire to perceive the room according to our experience is so powerful that we overrule the truth. This is not a breakdown in perception but rather a result of trying to apply the standard perceptual processes of shape and size constancy to an unusual situation. You *can* learn not to see such illusions, but it takes lots of practice and experience in the distorted environment.

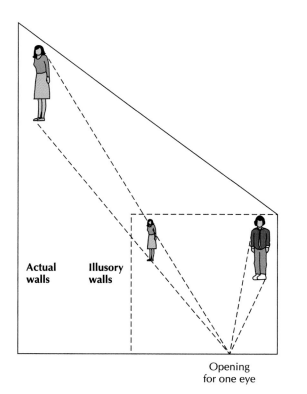

Actual place
and size
of woman

Illusory place
and size
of woman

Actual place
and size
of boy

**Actual
walls**

**Illusory
walls**

Opening
for one eye

Figure 4.5 An explanation for the Ames room illusion. This drawing illustrates why the boy in the bottom photo appears to be taller than the woman. We assume that both the boy and the woman are equidistant from the front wall. In actuality, however, the woman is standing twice as far away.

Although Stratton did not have to overcome illusions of constancy, he did have to adjust to a distorted environment, which he accomplished only after wearing the lens for several days. Similarly, divers wearing masks underwater experience severe distortions of their normal visual fields, yet they can learn to adapt to these distortions, given enough practice (Vernoy, 1990; Vernoy and Luria, 1977).

Color and Brightness Constancy

A third form of constancy that adds stability to our world is color and brightness constancy. This enables us to perceive things as retaining the same color or brightness level even though the amount of light may vary. For example, if you place a piece of gray paper in bright sunlight and a piece of white paper in shade, you will still perceive the white as lighter and the gray as darker. This is true regardless of the amount of reflected light actually coming from their surfaces. If you know an object from prior experience, you expect it will be the same color in bright light as in low light. That is, you expect it to be its "right" color.

As is the case with shape and size constancy, color constancy is the result of learning and experience and occurs primarily with familiar objects. If an object is unfamiliar, its color will be determined by the *actual* wavelength of reflected light—it will not be affected by prior experience with the object.

Brightness Constancy: The phenomenon in which objects tend to maintain their appropriate brightness, even when illumination varies.

Color Constancy: The tendency for the color of objects to be perceived as remaining the same even when illumination varies.

Review Questions

1. What is the Gestalt figure–ground principle?
2. Name the Gestalt principle that is being described:
   _____ You see a black line on the concrete and realize that it is a single trail of ants.
   _____ You can read a sentence on a bulletin board even if there are people standing in front of it.
   _____ You see a circle even though part of its curve is erased in three spots.

3. The principle of _____ is at work when, as your brother walks away from you, you don't perceive him to be shrinking.

4. _____ allows us to see a white blouse as white both in sunlight and in shade.

Answers to Review Questions can be found in Appendix C.

Depth Perception: Seeing the World as Three Dimensional

Depth Perception: The ability to perceive distance and therefore perceive space in three dimensions.

Evidence for the role of experience and learning in the organization of perceptions is particularly clear in the sense of depth perception, the ability to accurately estimate the distance of perceived objects and thereby perceive the world in three dimensions. It is possible to judge the distance of objects with nearly all senses. For example, if a woman who enters a dark room walks toward you, her voice gets louder, the smell of her perfume gets stronger, and if you can't see her at all, you can reach out to feel how close she is to you (Chan and Turvey, 1991). However, you rely most heavily on vision to perceive distance. When you add the ability to accurately perceive distance to the ability to judge the height and width of an object, you are able to perceive the world in three dimensions. But no matter which sense you use to perceive the three-dimensional world, this ability is learned.

Take the example of a patient known as S. B., blind since the age of 10 months, whose sight was restored at the age of 52. Following the operation that removed cataracts from both eyes, S. B. had great difficulty learning to use his newly acquired vision for judging distance and depth. On one occasion, he was found trying to crawl out of the window of his hospital room. He thought he would be able to lower himself by his hands to the ground below, even though the window was on the fourth floor.

Didn't S. B. have some inborn depth and distance perception? The answer is not clear. The question of innate depth perception has been the subject of general debate for many years, with the *nativists* arguing that depth perception is inborn and the *empiricists* insisting that it is learned. As is often the case, most psychologists have concluded that there is truth in both viewpoints.

The visual cliff. Once children can crawl, they refuse to cross the "deep" side, even to get to their parent.

Evidence for the innate position comes from a set of interesting experiments with an apparatus called the *visual cliff,* which can be seen in the photograph to the left. The apparatus consists of a table top with a slightly raised platform across the middle. On one side of the platform the table top is clear glass, with a red-and-white-checked pattern running down the side of the table and onto the floor several feet below the glass, simulating a steep cliff. The other side of the table top has the checked pattern directly on it. When an infant is placed on the platform and is coaxed by his or her mother to crawl to one side of the table, the infant will readily move to the "shallow" side but will hesitate or refuse to move to the "deep" side (Gibson and Walk, 1960). This reaction is given as evidence of innate depth perception—the infant's hesitation is attributed to fear of the apparent cliff.

The empiricists argue, however, that by the time infants are crawling and old enough to be tested, they may have *learned* to perceive depth. Nevertheless, similar research with baby chickens, goats, and lambs—animals that walk almost immediately after birth—supports the hypothesis that some depth perception is inborn, since these animals hesitate in stepping onto the steep side. The question is further complicated by two separate studies in which infants as young as two months of age have been lowered face-down on both the deep and shallow sides of the visual cliff. In a study done by Campos et al. (1978), the infants showed a change in heart rate only when lowered on the deep side, whereas a study done by Campos et al. (1982) generated conflicting results.

Although the nativist versus empiricist debate remains unsettled, there is no doubt that in our three-dimensional world, the ability to perceive depth and distance is essential. But how do we perceive a three-dimensional world with a two-dimensional receptor system? The rods and cones do not respond to depth and distance, but we have two other mechanisms that provide depth cues. One mechanism is the interaction of both eyes to produce *binocular* depth cues; the other involves *monocular* depth cues, which work with each eye separately.

Binocular Cues

One of the most important cues to depth and distance perception comes from retinal disparity. Because of the separation of the two eyes, each retina receives a slightly different view of the world. You can demonstrate this for yourself by pointing at some distant object across the room with your arm extended straight in front of you. Holding your pointing finger steady, close your left eye and then your right. You will notice that your finger seems to jump around in relation to the rest of the room as you change eyes, because of retinal disparity (Kaufman, 1974).

Retinal Disparity: A binocular cue to distance in which the separation of the eyes causes different images to fall on each retina.

The brain fuses the different images received by the two eyes into one overall visual image so that an accurate sensation of depth occurs (see Figure 4.6). Such stereoscopic vision offers a distinct depth perception advantage over animals that have only monocular cues for depth. But animals such as horses, deer, and fish with eyes set on each side of their heads have nearly a 360° field of view. This broad view gives them a better chance of detecting predators. Their predators, on the other hand, have eyes set in the front of their heads, like ours, and can use their superior ability to judge depth for distinguishing their prey from surrounding camouflage.

Stereoscopic Vision: Three-dimensional vision that results from the brain fusing the two different images received from the eyes into one image.

 Try This Yourself

As we move closer and closer to an object, another binocular cue helps us judge depth and distance. The closer the object, the more our eyes are turned inward, toward our noses (see Figure 4.7). Hold your index finger at arm's length in front of you and watch it as you bring it closer and closer until it is right in front of your nose. The amount of muscular strain in your eyeball created by the convergence, or turning inward of the eyes, is used as a cue by your brain to interpret distance. ■

Convergence: A binocular depth cue in which the closer the object, the more the eyes converge, or turn inward.

Knowing how convergence operates might help you improve your performance in athletic endeavors. Allen Souchek (1986) found that depth perception is better when looking directly at an object, rather than out of the corner of your eye. Thus, if you turn your body or your head so that you look straight at your tennis opponent or the pitcher, you will more accurately judge the distance of the ball and thereby more likely swing at the right time.

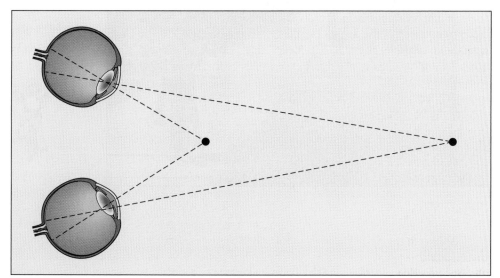

Figure 4.6 Retinal disparity. Through the process of retinal disparity objects at different distances project their images on different parts of the retina. Far objects project on the retinal area near the nose, whereas near objects project farther out, closer to the ears.

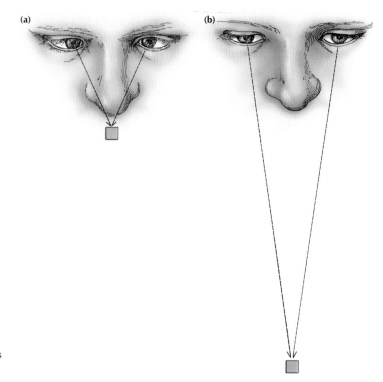

Figure 4.7 Convergence. Your eyes turn in to view close objects
(a) and turn out to view distant objects (b).

Monocular Cues

Retinal disparity and convergence are inadequate in judging distances farther than the
length of a football field. According to R. L. Gregory (1969), "we are effectively one-eyed
for distances greater than perhaps 100 meters" (p. 67). Luckily, we have several *monocular cues* available separately to each eye. Artists use these same monocular cues to

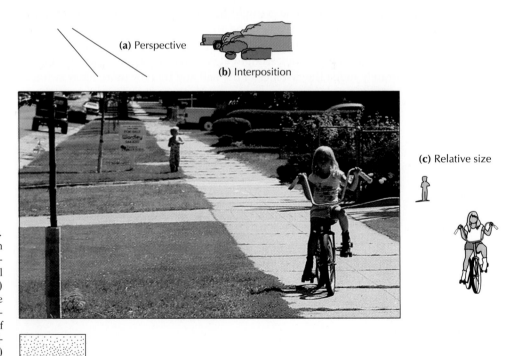

Figure 4.8 Monocular depth cues.
Several monocular depth cues can
be seen in this photograph. (a) Linear perspective occurs when parallel
lines converge in the distance. (b)
Interposition occurs when a close
object obscures part of a distant object. (c) Relative size is the result of
close objects projecting a larger retinal image than distant objects. (d)
Texture gradient results from the
change in perceived texture as the
background recedes into the distance.

Drawing by Chase.

create an illusion of depth on a flat canvas, a three-dimensional world on a two-dimensional surface. These monocular cues, illustrated in Figure 4.8, include:

1. Linear perspective. As two parallel lines recede from us, they appear to come together at the horizon. Any time you have a long, unobscured view of a street, a tall building, railroad tracks, or anything that is delineated by two parallel lines, you experience this cue. See Figure 4.8a. The Ponzo illusion shown in Figure 4.9 is based on linear perspective.

2. Aerial perspective. Objects that are far away look "fuzzy" and blurred in comparison to near objects because of intervening particles of dust, haze, or smoke in the atmosphere. This becomes noticeable when there is an absence of haze or smog. On a really clear day, we are often startled at the seeming nearness of skyscrapers, silos, or mountains that normally appear far away.

3. Texture gradients. Close objects appear to have a rough or detailed texture; as distance increases, the texture appears to become finer and finer — see Figure

Linear Perspective: The principle that as parallel lines recede, they appear to come together at the horizon.

Aerial Perspective: A monocular depth cue based on the fact that more distant objects appear less distinct than closer objects because of dust or haze in the air.

Texture Gradients: Monocular cue to distance based on the fact that texture changes from coarse to fine as the distance of an object increases.

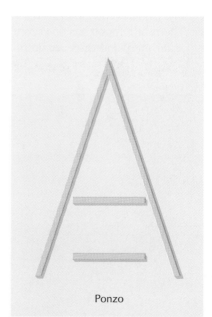

Ponzo

Figure 4.9 ***The Ponzo illusion.*** The horizontal line on the top is seen as farther away and therefore longer than the horizontal line on the bottom. This is due to the linear perspective created by the converging lines.

Interposition: A monocular depth cue in which an object that partially obscures another object is seen as closer.

Relative Size: A monocular cue to distance in which smaller objects appear more distant than larger objects.

Light and Shadow: A monocular depth cue in which brighter objects are perceived as closer, whereas darker, dimmer objects are perceived as farther away.

Accommodation: A change in the shape of the lens to focus on near or far objects.

Motion Parallax: A monocular depth cue that occurs when a moving observer perceives that objects at various distances move at different speeds across the retinal field.

4.8*d*. You may have noticed this effect when driving on a gravel road. The road in the distance looks much smoother than the road directly in front of you.

4. Interposition. An object that partially obscures another is perceived as being closer. See Figure 4.8*b*. As your professor moves behind the lectern, the lectern obscures part of his or her body, but you don't notice part of your professor as disappearing; you just see the lectern as closer than your professor.

5. Relative size. Objects that are far away look smaller than close objects of the same size. See Figure 4.8*c*. This principle is exploited by the Ames room illusion.

6. Light and shadow. Brighter objects are perceived as closer, whereas darker, dimmer objects are perceived as farther away. The variations in light produced by irregular surfaces also give cues for depth and distance as well as for shapes of objects (Ramachandran, 1988).

Two additional monocular cues—ones that cannot be used by artists—are accommodation of the lens of the eye and motion parallax. As you may remember from the previous chapter, accommodation refers to changes in the shape of the lens of the eye in response to the distance of the object being focused. For near objects the lens bulges; for far objects it flattens. Information from the muscles that move the lens is sent to the brain, which interprets the signal and perceives the distance of the object.

Motion parallax (also known as relative motion) refers to the fact that when an observer is moving, objects at various distances move at different speeds across the retinal field. Close objects appear to whiz by, farther objects appear to move past slowly, and very distant objects appear to remain stationary. This effect can easily be seen when traveling by car or train, as telephone poles and fences next to the road or track seem to move by very rapidly, houses and trees in the midground seem to move by relatively slowly, and the mountains in the distance seem not to move at all.

One of the most interesting everyday experiences that result from inappropriate use of monocular cues is the distortion in perception known as the *moon illusion* (Baird, 1982; Baird and Wagner, 1982). Perhaps you've noticed that a full moon looks gigantic when seen on the horizon but tiny by comparison when at its zenith, straight overhead. Nevertheless, the moon's physical distance from the earth and the size of its image remain constant.

Why, then, does the moon look larger on the horizon? One possible explanation is that when we look at the moon on the horizon, we use the monocular depth cue interposition in judging that intervening objects, such as houses, trees, and hills, are rather close, as compared to the moon, which we perceive as very far away. Because the moon seems so far away, our brain assumes that it must be quite large. The zenith moon has no accompanying depth cues, so we do not perceive it as being as far away and thus, we do not

The moon illusion. The moon appears larger on the horizon because of the many cues to distance.

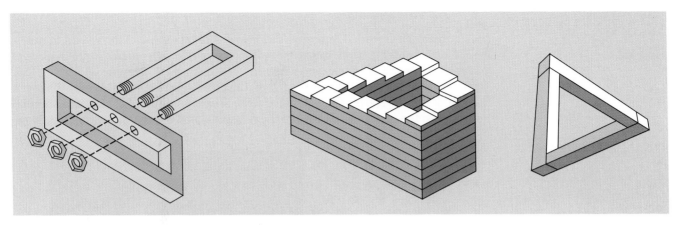

Figure 4.10 Some examples of impossible figures.

judge it to be as large. You can demonstrate this difference for yourself by looking at a horizon moon through a rolled-up paper tube—the moon will "shrink" when observed without its accompanying depth cues.

Distance and depth cues can also be used to explain certain visual illusions known as impossible figures (see Figure 4.10). In these instances, we initially perceive the figures as real objects, but as we examine them, we realize they can't really exist. Can you explain these impossible figures in terms of the cues we've just discussed?

Color Perception: Discriminating among Hues

We humans may be able to discriminate among seven million different hues (Indow, 1991). Such color perception seems to be inborn. Studies of infants old enough to focus and move their eyes have shown that they are able to see color nearly as well as adults (Teller, Peeples, and Sekel, 1978; Werner and Wooten, 1979). So, practically from the moment of birth, we are able to see a world of greens and oranges, blues and reds, yellows and purples.

As mentioned in Chapter 3, color is produced by different wavelengths of light, ranging from the short wavelengths of purple and blue to the long wavelengths of orange and red. The actual way in which we perceive color, however, is a matter of scientific debate. Traditionally, there have been two theories of color vision, the trichromatic (three-color) theory and the opponent-process theory. The trichromatic theory was first proposed by Thomas Young in the early nineteenth century and was later refined by Hermann von Helmholtz and others. It states that there are three "color systems," as they called them—one system that is maximally sensitive to blue, another maximally sensitive to green, and another maximally sensitive to red (Young, 1802). The proponents of this theory demonstrated that mixing lights of these three colors could yield the full spectrum of colors we perceive. Unfortunately, this theory has two major flaws. One is that it doesn't explain color weakness; the other is that it doesn't explain color aftereffects.

The opponent-process theory, proposed by Ewald Hering later in the nineteenth century, also claims there are three color systems but that each is sensitive to two opposing colors—blue and yellow, red and green, black and white—in an "on–off" fashion. In other words, each color receptor responds to either blue *or* yellow, red *or* green, with the black and white system responding to differences in brightness levels. This theory makes a lot of sense, since when different colored lights are combined, people are unable to see reddish greens and bluish yellows; in fact, when red and green lights or blue and yellow lights are mixed in equal amounts, we see white. The opponent-process theory also accounts for the phenomenon of color aftereffects, images that are perceived after staring at a particular colored pattern for a period of time.

Trichromatic Theory: The theory of color vision first proposed by Thomas Young stating that there are three color systems—red, green, and blue.

Opponent-Process Theory: The theory of color vision first proposed by Ewald Hering that claims that there are three color systems—blue–yellow, red–green, and black–white.

Color Aftereffects: Color images that are seen after staring at a particular colored pattern for a long time.

Try This Yourself

Look at the color-distorted American flag below. After staring at it for several minutes, look at a plain sheet of white paper. You will perceive color aftereffects—red in place of green, blue in place of yellow, and white in place of black, a "genuine" American flag. What happened? As you stared at the figure, the green stripes stimulated only the green channel of the red-green opponent color cells. Several minutes of continuous stimulation fatigued the green channel, while the nonstimulated red channel was not fatigued.

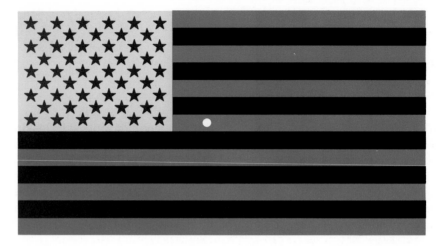

When you looked at the blank piece of paper, the white stimulated both the red and the green channels equally. Under normal viewing conditions, the red and green channels would have canceled each other out and you would have seen white. However, because the green channel was fatigued, the red channel fired at a higher rate and you therefore saw a red color aftereffect. ■

The opponent-process theory also adequately explains color vision defects, since most people who have a color weakness are unable to see *either* red and green *or* blue and yellow. Have you ever tested yourself to see if you're color-blind? Try it. Figure 4.11 is a color vision test.

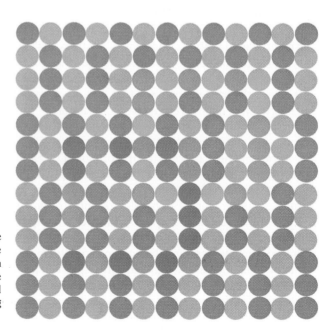

Figure 4.11 Color vision test. People with red-green color weakness see only the upper square. People with blue-yellow color weakness see the lower square. If you have normal color vision you see two interlocking squares.

Two Correct Theories

Judging from the discussion so far, it would seem the opponent-process theory is the correct one. Actually, however, both theories are correct. In 1964, George Wald demonstrated that there are indeed three different types of cones in the retina, each with its own type of photopigment. One type of pigment is sensitive to blue light, one is sensitive to green light, and the third is sensitive to red light (see Figure 4.12). At nearly the same time that Wald was doing his research on cones, R. L. DeValois (1965) was doing electro-physiological recording of cells in the optic nerve and optic pathways to the brain. DeValois discovered cells that responded to color in an *opponent* fashion in the thalamus. Thus, it appears that the two theories have been correct all along. Color is processed in a trichromatic fashion at the level of the retina (in the cones) and in an opponent fashion at the level of the optic nerve and the thalamus (in the brain).

You mentioned that we see white light when blue and yellow lights are mixed—why is this? Shouldn't we see green?   When blue and yellow paint pigments are mixed together, they do indeed produce the color green. However, mixing lights is different from mixing pigments. The reason we perceive the red from a red stop light is that a long wavelength of light (red light) is projected into our eyes. On the other hand, the reason we perceive the red from a stop sign is that the pigments in the red paint absorb all colors except red, which is reflected into our eyes. So we see colored light by an *additive* process because our visual system adds the colors together. We see colored pigments by a *subtractive* process because some colors are reflected and others are subtracted, or absorbed, by the object.

As you know, not all people can see color. Some people are color-blind. People who are totally color-blind, known as monochromats (meaning "one color"), have just rods and no cones and can therefore see things only in black and white and shades of gray. What they see is similar to what we see when we are watching a black-and-white television show. Monochromats are rare; much more common are people with a color weakness. Known as dichromats (meaning "two colors"), these people are missing one type of cone pigment and thus are either unable to distinguish red and green or, less commonly, blue and yellow (Nathans, 1989; Nathans et al., 1986; Nathans et al., 1986). Because people with a color weakness are unable to distinguish between certain colors by using wavelength (hue) information, they must rely on brightness information. For example, a red–green dichromat cannot distinguish a green traffic light from a red one on the basis of color, and so must distinguish between the brighter (green) and the darker (red) light or read the signal by the position of the lights.

Color blindness and color weakness can create problems in everyday life. People who are unable to discriminate between red and green are restricted to certain ranks and duties within the armed forces. They would be unable to tell at night whether another airplane or ship was approaching or receding. (This is determined by noting the colors of

Monochromat: A person who is truly color-blind because he or she has only rods and no cones.

Dichromat: A person having the type of color weakness in which only two types of cones are present, rather than the normal three.

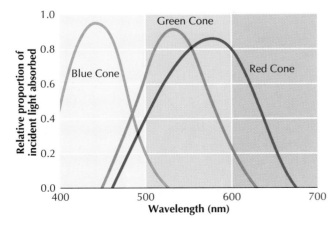

Figure 4.12 Cone response graphs. The three types of cones in the human retina absorb different wavelengths of light. The "blue" cone is most sensitive to blue light and therefore absorbs very little green and no red light. The "green" cone is most sensitive to green light but also absorbs some blue and some red light. The "red" cone absorbs mostly red and green light and is relatively insensitive to blue light.

lights on the wings or the sides of the ship—green lights denote the right side, whereas red lights denote the left.) You can probably imagine some of the inconveniences faced by a red–green dichromat in trying to choose clothing that matches or in picking out red apples from green ones at the supermarket.

Color Perception Studies

Research into color perception has had important practical applications. For example, what color do you think of when the word "fire engine" is mentioned? Most people respond with "red." However, many new fire engines are being painted light green, yellow, or white because research has found that these colors are seen equally well at night and during the day. Another study found that it is easier to see and estimate the distance of lights when one light is red and the other blue, as opposed to both lights being the same color (Berkhout, 1979). This research supports the current practice of placing one red and one blue light on top of emergency vehicles. There is an additional safety reason for the placement of these lights: Red shows up better in low light, blue better in brighter conditions. Other studies have been done involving the color of the print on computer video screens. It has been found that, contrary to the white-on-black that many people expect, amber or green on a black background or white letters on a blue background are more readable. These and many other perceptual studies have made our lives safer and more comfortable.

Motion Perception: Seeing Movement, Both Real and Apparent

Another factor in perceptual organization and everyday survival is the perception of movement. Each day we avert disaster by responding to movement in our environment —we move out of the way of oncoming trucks, we avoid collisions with hurrying shoppers in the mall, and so on. Occasionally, our perceptual processes are fooled by objects that look as if they're moving when they really aren't. It is important, therefore, to differentiate between real and apparent motion.

Real Motion

The perception of real movement is the result of an actual change in the object's position in space. There are basically two ways that we perceive real motion: (1) An image moves across the retina, and (2) the eye moves in the head to follow the path of the moving object (see Figure 4.13).

Much real movement perception has been explained by the work of Hubel and Wiesel (1968). Their research has shown that, just as there are line and angle detectors in the visual cortex, there are also motion detectors that respond specifically to the movement of an object across the retina. Another explanation for movement perception stems

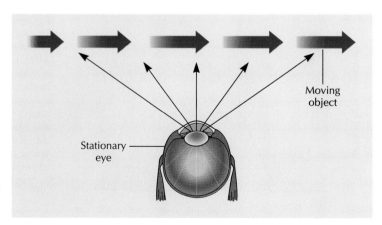

Figure 4.13 Motion perception. Real motion is perceived when objects move across the field of vision and the retina is stimulated in different places.

from the fact that when the eyes move to follow an object, the brain sends signals to the eye muscles to keep the image on the fovea, at the center of the retina. This tracking motion thereby provides additional cues for motion perception (Kasamatsu, 1976).

Have you ever wondered why so many people are killed in car and train accidents when virtually every railroad crossing has a warning device to signal approaching trains? You might think that the people don't hear the train whistle or see the flashing lights. However, through analysis of accidents it has been found that, although most drivers probably did see the approaching trains and were well aware of the warning signals, they chose to ignore them. Leibowitz (1985) suggests that aspects of motion perception could explain these accidents. Large objects are perceived as moving more slowly than small objects and objects seem to move more slowly when tracked, as opposed to keeping the head and eyes still. Thus, the drivers apparently perceived the trains as moving slower than they really were. These proved to be fatal misperceptions.

Apparent Motion

It is possible to perceive movement in the absence of any real motion. If you are seated in a darkened room and look at two adjacent lights being turned on, one after the other, it will seem that a single light is jumping back and forth. This is known as stroboscopic motion, or the "phi phenomenon." This illusion makes it possible to construct "moving arrows" on electric signs and to put "motion" into motion pictures. What you see on the movie screen is actually a series of still images illuminated in rapid succession. Old black-and-white movies and home movies sometimes seem jerky because only 16 still pictures are projected per second, whereas modern movie films flash 24 pictures per second. Even at this speed, some flicker would occur were it not that projectors have a three-bladed shutter that rotates in front of the light source. This shutter causes each frame of film to be projected three times for an effective projection rate of 72 pictures a second.

Stroboscopic Motion: The illusion of motion in which alternating lights are seen as one moving light.

Another form of apparent movement is the autokinetic effect—perceived motion of a single stationary light or object. You can experience this illusion by looking at a small dim light at the far end of a completely dark room (a small glow-in-the-dark sticker is a good target). If you stare at the light for a few seconds, it will appear to wander around erratically. This apparent movement occurs because there are no cues to tell you that the light is really stationary, and the slight constant movement of the eye (mentioned in Chapter 3) makes the light appear to move. Another explanation for the autokinetic effect is that the eye muscles fatigue from their effort to obey the commands of the brain to maintain their fixation on the spot of light (Gregory, 1977).

Autokinetic Effect: The perceived motion of a single stationary light in the dark.

In the past, this illusion created a safety problem for night-flying pilots trying to judge the position of beacon lights or of tail and wing lights on other airplanes. You may have noticed that lights on airplanes and beacons now flash on and off, which helps reduce the autokinetic illusion. The autokinetic effect could also explain some unidentified flying object (UFO) sightings. A common element in the description of UFOs is their "erratic" movements and strange abilities to "hover." Can you see how a simple steadily beaming light on a dark night and the autokinetic illusion could lead to a UFO "sighting"?

Review Questions

1. Binocular cues to distance require _____ eye(s), whereas monocular cues require _____ eye(s).
2. Compare and contrast retinal disparity and convergence.
3. List the eight monocular cues to distance.
4. The color theory that states that there are three color systems—red, green, and blue—is known as the _____ theory.

5. The color theory that claims that there are red–green, blue–yellow, and black–white color systems is the _____ theory.

6. Which color theory is correct? Explain.

7. We perceive movement in motion pictures because of _____ motion.

Answers to Review Questions can be found in Appendix C.

INTERPRETATION

• *What factors influence how we interpret sensations?*

After selectively sorting through incoming sensory information and organizing it into patterns, the brain uses this information to explain and make judgments about the external world. This final stage of perception, *interpretation,* is influenced by several factors, including early life experiences, perceptual expectations, cultural factors, and personal motivations and frame of reference.

Early Life Experiences: The Effects of Environmental Interaction

As we discovered in the section on selection, early life experiences can have a dramatic effect on the biological development of perceptual systems. Early experiences also influence the process of interpretation. Held and Hein (1963) conducted a famous experiment that dramatically demonstrated the influence of early learning on perceptual development. These researchers raised 20 kittens in total darkness except for one hour a day when they were allowed to see. During that one hour, one group of kittens was placed in body harnesses that allowed them to walk in a circular path around a patterned "kitty carousel." Another group of kittens was suspended passively above the floor of the carousel in a gondola that could be pulled by the movement of the active kittens (see the photograph below). When all kittens were later released, the active kittens displayed normal visual perception (avoiding the deep side of a visual cliff, blinking when faced with an approaching object, and so on), but the passive kittens displayed none of these behaviors. After several days of being allowed to move about freely, the kittens who rode passively in the gondola did finally catch up to their active partners.

The importance of being able to actively explore and experiment with the environment can also be seen in the experiences of George Stratton. On the first day of his

In the "kitty carousel," both kittens receive the same visual stimulation, but only the free-moving kitten develops normal depth perception.

experiment, he was unable to manage the simple act of pouring and drinking a glass of milk, but by the third day he could sit down and enjoy a full meal.

Perceptual Expectancy: The Effects of Prior Experience

Imagine what it was like for George Stratton when he first put on his inverting lens. To function during the initial period, Stratton most likely relied on his expectations of the way objects in his environment *ought* to look, based on his prior experiences with them. Similarly, in our normal, everyday world, our expectations often bias our perceptions. If batter Tony Gwynn is thrown three fast balls in a row, he will expect another fast ball and will not be prepared to hit a curve ball. In fact, he may even misperceive the next pitch and actually see it as a fast ball when indeed it is a curve. The incoming sensory information will be correct, but the perception of that information may be influenced by his *perceptual expectations*.

 Try This Yourself

You can test your reliance on perceptual expectations with the photograph below. Do you notice anything unusual in this photo? All the facial features seem to be in the correct positions for an upside-down face. But when you turn the face right side up, you'll be surprised to find that your expectations are wrong. The strong influence of

When you look at this photo do you see a vase or a silhouette of the British royal couple? The answer depends on whether your perceptual expectations force you to see the vase as figure or as ground.

Do either of these pictures of Bill Clinton bother you? You expect that the pictures have just been printed upside down and will be similar when they are righted. Now turn the book so that the pictures are both rightside up, and you will see that your expectations are mistaken.

perceptual expectancies can especially be noted when viewing ambiguous figures. If someone had been discussing the Royal Family and then showed you the picture of the vase in the margin, you would probably see the faces first, rather than the vase. ∎

Gender and Cultural Diversity

CAN EVERYONE SEE ILLUSIONS?

Different cultures have different holidays, customs, religions, social roles and organizations, and economic institutions. But surely, whether you come from a rain forest, a remote Russian village, or New York City, you—and everyone else in the world—must

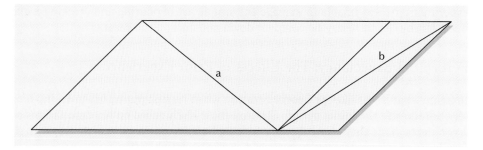

Figure 4.14 *The Sander parallelogram illusion.* Which of the diagonal lines from the bottom of the parallelogram is longer, a or b? People living in a carpentered environment see the obtuse and acute angles as buildings in their environment and are fooled into thinking that line a is longer than line b.

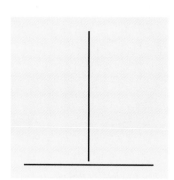

Figure 4.15 *The horizontal-vertical illusion.* Which is longer: the horizontal or vertical line? People living in areas where they can see long straight lines on the ground, such as roads and shadows of telephone poles, perceive the horizontal line as shorter because of the foreshortening effect.

Figure 4.16 *The Müller-Lyer illusion.* Which vertical line is longer? Both are actually the same length, but people who live in urban environments normally see the vertical line on the right as longer than the vertical line on the left. This is because they are used to making size and distance judgments from perspective cues created by right angles and horizontal and vertical lines of buildings and streets.

see the same thing when you look at a visual illusion. Or do you? No, you don't, say many psychologists. Cultural factors strongly influence how we perceive the world, even visual illusions (Segall, Dasen, Berry, and Poortinga, 1990).

Look at Figures 4.14, 4.15, and 4.16. These are three well-known visual illusions. In the Sander parallelogram, the two diagonals extending from the bottom point to the upper corners are exactly the same length, but most people throughout the world perceive the left diagonal as longer. In the horizontal–vertical illusion, most people perceive the vertical line as longer than the horizontal line, when they are actually equal. In the Müller-Lyer illusion, the vertical lines are equal in length, but most people perceive the right as longer.

In a study comparing the effect of culture on how we see illusions, Segall, Dasen, Berry, and Poortinga (1990) found that urban cultures differed from rural cultures. Subjects living in cities perceived more of a difference between the lines than did subjects living in rural areas of Africa and the Philippines. Segall and his colleagues explained the results by applying three previously developed hypotheses (1966): (1) the carpentered world hypothesis, (2) the front-horizontal foreshortening hypothesis, and (3) the two-dimensional media hypothesis.

The carpentered world hypothesis explains why urban subjects perceive a greater distortion in the Sander parallelogram. Subjects who grow up in an urban carpentered world—one with many horizontal and vertical lines and right angles—are susceptible to the illusion because they perceive acute and obtuse angles as representing real-world objects (road intersections, rectangular buildings) that they constantly view from various vantage points. People who grow up in a rural, uncarpentered world perceive the acute and obtuse angles for what they are, lines in an abstract drawing. They do not mistakenly perceive one diagonal as longer than the other because they do not have the same previous experience as their urban counterparts.

The front-horizontal foreshortening theory explains why the lines in the horizontal-vertical illusion are misperceived. People living in urban environments who regularly see long straight lines along the ground (highway divider lines, for example, or scenic views on television or in magazines) have learned that even short vertical lines may actually represent extremely long lines. Thus, a line on the ground extending away from them produces a retinal image that is greatly foreshortened compared with the actual length of that line. They tend to perceive a vertical line as being longer than an equal-length horizontal line and are more susceptible to this illusion than people who live in rain forests or canyons.

The third hypothesis derives from the fact that urbanized cultures use paper and other flat display media such as TV screens to depict three-dimensional objects. The Müller-Lyer figure looks the way corners are depicted on flat surfaces: The left one looks like a corner with wall lines receding away from the observer, and the right one looks like a corner with wall lines extending toward the observer. Because close figures are usually drawn larger than faraway figures and because both corners in this illusion produce the same retinal image, people from urbanized cultures perceive the "farther" one on the right as being longer than the "closer" one on the left. Moreover, the more experience a person has with pictures and photographs, the more susceptible he or she is to illusions such as the Müller-Lyer. ■

People brought up in a carpentered environment, such as Paris with its square and rectangular buildings and long, straight streets running at right angles to each other, are susceptible to illusions that exploit their perceptual expectations. People brought up in an environment that has very few straight lines, such as this African village, are much less susceptible to illusions that exploit their perceptual expectations.

Other Influences on Interpretation: Personal Motivations and Frames of Reference

Among other factors that influence our interpretations of what we perceive are our personal interests and needs that influence our perceptions and the frame of reference, or context, of what is being perceived. As we discovered in the process of selection, our individual needs and interests can affect what we selectively attend to; they can also affect how we judge or interpret the information selected. For example, Stephan, Berscheid, and Walster (1971) found that sexually aroused men judged photographs of women as more attractive than did nonaroused males, and this reaction was particularly strong when the men believed they would actually have a date with the women. Thus, when men's sexual needs were stimulated and their interests were piqued because of an impending date, the men perceived the photographs more favorably.

Our perceptions of people, objects, or situations are also affected by their frame of reference. A man might judge a woman's photograph attractive when seen by itself, but he might judge it unattractive when seen next to a photo of Miss America.

Extrasensory Perception: Strange But Not True

In the third step of perception, when we interpret external stimuli and the patterns they form, we are trying to make sense of our world. But what about the things that happen that cannot be explained? Some people have such a strong need to understand their experiences and events in the world that they believe in extrasensory perception (ESP). ESP is the alleged ability to perceive things that cannot be perceived with the normal five senses. People who claim to have ESP, or psychics, profess to be able to read other people's minds (telepathy), perceive objects or events that are inaccessible to their normal senses (clairvoyance), predict the future (precognition), or move or affect objects without touching them (psychokinesis). Popular tabloids are filled with accounts of psychics claiming to be able to find lost children or predict assassinations.

Psychics use magic and perceptual illusions to mislead general audiences, including scientific observers. James ("The Amazing") Randi, a magician and self-proclaimed "professional charlatan," has offered $10,000 to anyone who can perform even *one* example of psychic abilities under previously agreed on standards of control. After over 600 would-be psychic inquiries and more than 20 years, Randi still has his money (Morris, 1980; Randi, 1980).

ESP Research

Scientific investigations of ESP began in the early 1900s when Joseph B. Rhine conducted experiments to test psychic abilities in his subjects. Many of his experiments, as well as those done by subsequent ESP researchers, involved *Zener cards,* a deck of 25 cards that bear five different symbols—a plus sign, a square, a star, a circle, and wavy lines. When experimenters want to study telepathy, for instance, they ask a "sender" to concentrate on a card; then they ask the "receiver" to try to "read the mind" of the sender. With luck alone, the receiver will guess the symbols on about five cards correctly. A subject who consistently scores above "chance" is credited with having ESP.

Rhine's findings were impressive, but critics have since found fault with much of his scientific methodology, particularly in the area of experimental control. In many early experiments, for example, the Zener cards were so cheaply printed that a faint outline of the symbol could be seen from the back. Also, since experimenters knew which cards were correct, they could unknowingly give subjects cues through subtle facial gestures. Later experiments that used necessary controls, such as double-blind procedures, reported contradictory results (Hansel, 1980).

Another criticism of studies indicating the existence of ESP is their lack of stability and replicability. Findings in ESP are notoriously "fragile" (Gardner, 1977). Not only do different researchers find conflicting evidence, but the same subject will show psychic abilities in some laboratories but not others. Rhine himself stated that he never found a subject whose ESP powers did not disappear over time (Rhine, 1972).

The Need to Believe

When people hear about or personally experience something unusual that cannot be easily explained, they grab hold of any explanation that sounds feasible. Because ESP is

Extrasensory Perception (ESP): Perceptual, or "psychic," abilities that go beyond the "known" senses, including telepathy, clairvoyance, precognition, and telekinesis.

Telepathy: The ability to read other people's minds.

Clairvoyance: The ability to perceive objects or events that are inaccessible to the normal senses.

Precognition: The ability to predict the future.

Psychokinesis: The ability to move or affect objects without touching them.

Critical Thinking
PSYCHOLOGY IN ACTION
RECOGNIZING FAULTY REASONING
Problems with Believing in ESP

The subject of ESP often generates great interest and emotional responses in people, and individuals who feel strongly about an issue sometimes fail to recognize the faulty reasoning underlying their beliefs. Belief in ESP is particularly susceptible to illogical, noncritical thinking.

In this exercise, you have a chance to examine common reports of ESP and practice identifying possible faulty reasoning. Begin by studying the following list of "common problems with ESP."

1. *Fallacy of Positive Instances* Noting and remembering events that confirm personal expectations and beliefs (the "hits") and ignoring nonsupportive evidence (the "misses").

2. *Innumeracy* Failing to recognize chance occurrences for what they are due to a lack of training in statistics and probabilities. Unusual events are misperceived as statistically impossible, and extraordinary explanations, such as ESP, are seen as the logical alternative.

3. *Willingness to Suspend Disbelief* Refusing to engage one's normal critical thinking skills because of a personal need for power and control. Although few people would attribute a foreign country's acquisition of top-secret information to ESP, some of these same individuals would willingly believe that a psychic could help them find their lost child.

4. *The "Vividness" Problem* Human information processing and memory storage and retrieval are often based on the initial "vividness" of the information. Sincere personal testimonials, theatrical demonstrations, and detailed anecdotes easily capture our attention and tend to be remembered better than rational, scientific descriptions of events.

Now read the following ESP reports and decide which "problem with ESP" is MOST appropriate. More than one problem may be applicable, but try to limit your choice. Enter only one number beside each report, and then compare your answers with those of your classmates or friends. Comparing results will help sharpen your critical thinking skills.

_____ John hadn't thought of Paula, his old high school sweetheart, for years. Yet one morning he woke up thinking about her. He was wondering what she looked like and whether she was married now, when suddenly the phone rang. For some strange reason, he felt sure the call was from Paula. He was right. John now cites this call as evidence for his personal experience with extrasensory perception.

_____ A psychic visits a class in introductory psychology. He predicts that, out of this class of 23 students, two individuals will have birthdays on the same day. When a tally of birthdays is taken, his prediction is supported and many students leave class believing that ESP has been supported.

_____ A National League baseball player dreams of hitting a bases-loaded triple. Two months later, during the final game of the World Series, he gets this exact triple and wins the game. He informs the media of his earlier dream and the possibility of ESP.

_____ A mother is sitting alone in her office at work and suddenly sees a vivid image of her home on fire. She immediately calls home and awakens the sitter who excitedly reports smoke coming under the door. The sitter successfully extinguishes the fire, and the mother later attributes her visual images to ESP.

by nature subjective and *extra*ordinary, people tend to accept it as an explanation for out-of-the-ordinary experiences. Moreover, as was mentioned earlier in the chapter, people's motivations and interests can influence their perceptions. They tend to pay extra attention to things they want to see or hear. Often both subjects and researchers exhibit this strong motivation to believe in ESP. People generally have difficulty processing and evaluating complex scientific information. In the case of psychic abilities it is hard to distinguish chance and coincidental events from the multitude of experiences in daily life. But the most important underlying reason for why people believe in ESP is that they *want* to. A quick glance at children's fairy tales, comic books, and popular movies finds an abundance of superhuman characters and violations of the laws of physics. It seems that release from natural law is one of the most common and satisfying human fantasies (Moss and Butler, 1978). When it comes to ESP, people eagerly engage in a process known as "the willing suspension of disbelief." We seem to have a hard time accepting our finiteness, and a belief in psychic phenomena offers an increased feeling of power and control.

In addition to personal motivation, there are several social reasons why people believe in ESP. Singer and Benassi (1981) point out that the public generally tends to believe what they see in print or on TV. Yet most newspapers and TV programs that report stories about ESP seldom demand scientific proof. This media belief is particularly strong when the source is perceived as "scientific" or as a "documentary," but Singer and Benassi found that many college students listed *Reader's Digest,* the *National Enquirer,* and movies such as *Star Wars* as examples of "scientific sources." Finally, our fast-paced technological world reinforces a belief in ESP. Our rapid scientific progress leads many people to believe that virtually anything is possible, and possible is often translated as "probable."

In this chapter we have seen that a number of internal and external factors affect all three stages of perception—selection, organization, and interpretation. In upcoming chapters, we will continue our study of perception by examining how incoming sensory information is processed and retrieved in the different types of memory (Chapter 7), how perception develops in infants (Chapter 9), and how we perceive ourselves and others (Chapter 17).

Review Questions

1. Why is Held and Hein's "kitty carousel" experiment so significant?
2. _____ occurs when what we anticipate influences what we perceive.
3. Would you expect that someone raised in New York City would perceive visual illusions in the same way as someone raised in the middle of the African grasslands?
4. What controlled scientific research supports a belief in extra sensory perception?

Answers to Review Questions can be found in Appendix C.

REVIEW OF MAJOR CONCEPTS

1. Whereas sensation is the process of detecting and transducing raw sensory information, perception is the process of selecting, organizing, and interpreting this data into a usable mental representation of the world.

2. Illusions can be used to study the process of perception because they represent a situation where sensory information is organized or interpreted improperly.

3. The three basic processes of perception are selection, organization, and interpretation.

SELECTION

4. The selection process allows us to choose which of the billions of separate sensory messages will eventually be processed.

5. Selective attention allows us to direct our attention to the most important aspect of the environment at any one time.

6. Feature detectors are specialized cells in the brain that distinguish between different sensory inputs. Early deprivation may lead to problems with feature detectors.

7. The selection process is very sensitive to changes in the environment. Those stimuli that remain the same can cause either sensory adaptation, in which the receptors slow down their firing rates, or perceptual habituation, in which the brain ignores the constant stimuli.

ORGANIZATION

8. The process of organization was studied intensely by the Gestalt psychologists, who set forth laws of organization explaining how people perceive form. Their most fundamental principle is the distinction between figure and ground. Other principles include proximity, continuity, closure, contiguity, similarity, and contrast.

9. According to a study by Luria, the Gestalt laws of perceptual organization are not universally true; they are only valid for people who have been schooled in geometrical concepts, not for illiterate people who perceive shapes in an object-oriented world.

10. Through the perceptual constancies—size constancy, shape constancy, and brightness constancy—we are able to perceive consistencies in our environment, even though the actual sensory information we receive may be constantly changing. These constancies are based on our prior experiences and learning.

11. There are two major types of cues to size and distance: binocular cues, which require two eyes, and monocular cues, which only require one eye. The binocular cues are retinal disparity and convergence. Monocular cues include linear perspective, aerial perspective, texture gradients, interposition, light and shadow, relative size, accommodation, and motion parallax.

12. The perception of color is explained by a combination of the two traditional color theories, the trichromatic theory and the opponent-process theory. The trichromatic theory proposes that there are three kinds of color systems maximally sensitive to blue, green, and red. The opponent-process theory also proposes three color systems but that each is sensitive to two opposing colors—blue and yellow, red and green, and black and white—and that they operate in an on–off fashion. It appears that the trichromatic system operates at the level of the retina, whereas the opponent-process system occurs at the level of the brain.

13. Some people cannot perceive color normally. Monochromats have only rods and no cones and see things only in black and white and shades of gray. Dichromats are missing only one type of cone system and cannot distinguish between red and green or blue and yellow.

14. We are able to perceive both real motion and apparent motion. The perception of real motion is due to the movement of an object across the retina or the movement of the eye to follow a moving object. The perception of apparent motion can be due to stroboscopic motion, in which two stimuli are presented in close succession, or the autokinetic effect, the apparent movement of a single light in a dark room.

15. Cultural factors strongly influence how we perceive the world, even visual illusions. Urban cultures differ from rural cultures in perceiving visual illusions; the carpentered world hypothesis partly explains the difference.

INTERPRETATION

16. Interpretation, the final stage of perception, can be influenced by early life experiences, perceptual expectancy, cultural factors, needs and interests, and frames of reference.

17. Extrasensory perception (ESP) is the supposed ability to perceive things through senses that go beyond the "known" senses. ESP research has produced "fragile" results, and critics condemn its scientific validity because it lacks experimental control and replicability.

SUGGESTED READINGS

GREGORY, R. L. (1977). *Eye and brain: The psychology of seeing* (3rd ed.). New York: World University Library. A wonderful book on the wonders of seeing.

HANSEL, C. E. M. (1980). *ESP and parapsychology.* Buffalo, NY: Prometheus. This book takes a critical look at research into ESP and parapsychology.

RANDI, J. (1982). *Flim-flam.* Buffalo, NY: Prometheus. The "Amazing Randi" takes on all kinds of pseudoscientists and con artists in demonstrating how the claims and accomplishments of famous psychics are based on mere magicians' tricks.

SCHIFFMAN, H. R. (1990). *Sensation and perception: An integrated approach* (3rd ed.). New York: Wiley. An introduction to the study of sensation and perception.

Consciousness

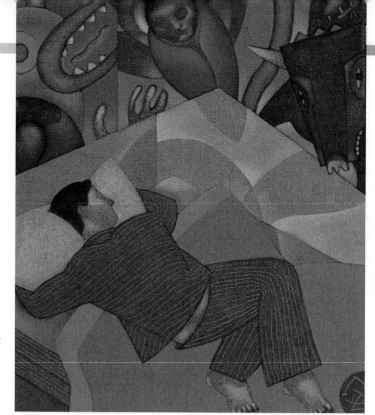

*H*alf an hour after swallowing the drug, I became aware of a slow dance of golden lights. A little later there were sumptuous red surfaces swelling and expanding from bright nodes of energy that vibrated with a continuously changing, patterned life. I saw the books . . . all of them glowed with living light and in some the glory was more manifest than in others. The legs . . . of that chair . . . how miraculous their tubularity, how supernatural their polished smoothness! I spent several minutes—or was it several centuries?—not merely gazing at those bamboo legs, but actually being them—or rather being myself in them: or, to be still more accurate . . . being my Not-self in the Not-self which was the chair.

Aldous Huxley, 1954,
The Doors of Perception, p. 45

This is the British author Aldous Huxley's account of his personal experience with a chemically induced state of consciousness. Compare that description with the experiences of Peter Tripp, a New York disc jockey who stayed awake in a 200-hour "wake-a-thon" to benefit charity.

After little more than two days [without sleep] as he changed shoes in the hotel, he pointed out [to a psychiatrist] a very interesting sight. There were cobwebs in his shoes—to the eyes at least. . . . Specks on the table began to look like bugs. . . . He was beginning to have trouble remembering things. By 110 hours there were signs of delirium. . . . A doctor walked into the recording booth in a tweed suit that Tripp saw as a suit of furry worms. On the morning of the final day [of the 200-hour period] a famous neurologist arrived to examine him . . . [Tripp] came to the morbid conclusion that this man was an undertaker, there for the purpose of burying him [and] leapt for the door with several doctors in pursuit.

Luce and Segal, 1966, p. 91

To a reader in a "normal" state of consciousness, these passages seem bizarre and confusing—what is a "Not-self in a Not-self," and why would a tweed suit look like "furry worms"?

To understand Huxley's drug experience and Tripp's sleep deprivation reactions, we turn to the area of psychological study known as *consciousness*. We begin with a general look at the structure of consciousness and at some ways cultures have sought alternate states of consciousness throughout history. Next we examine the changes in consciousness associated with sleep and dreaming, and with the use of psychoactive drugs. The chapter concludes with a look at how daydreams, hypnosis, and meditation affect consciousness.

As you read Chapter 5, keep the following **Survey** questions in mind and answer them in your own words:

- What is consciousness? How do alternate states of consciousness differ from normal consciousness?

- What is the function of sleep and dreaming?

- How is consciousness affected by drugs?

- How do daydreams, hypnosis, and meditation create alternate states of consciousness?

STUDYING CONSCIOUSNESS

- *What is consciousness? How do alternate states of consciousness differ from normal consciousness?*

In the late nineteenth century, when psychology first established itself as a scientific discipline separate from philosophy, it was defined as "the study of human consciousness." The difficulty of *scientifically* studying consciousness, however, caused many psychologists to become disenchanted. In particular, the behaviorists, led by John Watson, believed that consciousness was not the proper focus of psychology. In fact, he declared that "the time seems to have come when psychology must discard all references to consciousness; when it need no longer delude itself into thinking that it is making mental states the object of observation" (1913, p. 164). The behavioristic approach dominated the field of psychology during the first half of the twentieth century, and the goal of establishing a science of consciousness was nearly abandoned (Crick and Koch, 1992).

In recent times, psychology has experienced a quiet return to the study of consciousness. This revived interest is due in part to advances in scientific technology that provide objective means of measuring states of consciousness (such as through brain wave monitoring). The development of the humanistic branch of psychology and the work of cognitive psychologists have also helped refuel scientific interest in consciousness (Baars and Banks, 1992; Hilgard, 1992).

Today, consciousness is generally defined as the awareness of external and internal stimuli. At the present moment, for example, you are conscious of the words on this page. Perhaps you are also conscious of other external stimuli, such as the sound of the radio or television in the next room. Your consciousness also includes internal stimuli, such as thoughts about how your instructor will test you on this chapter or sensations of hunger or feelings of sleepiness. Additionally, your *internal monitor,* a special part of consciousness, is aware of your *self* as a being who is experiencing hunger, sleepiness, thoughts, and so on.

Consciousness is a complex phenomenon, and like other psychological terms, such as *intelligence* and *personality,* it eludes simple definition. To help you fully understand it, we will discuss three key concepts: stream of consciousness, levels of awareness, and states of consciousness.

Consciousness: The general state of being aware and responsive to stimuli in the external and internal environment.

Stream of Consciousness: The Continuously Changing Nature of Consciousness

As you probably have noticed, your consciousness sometimes seems to have a "mind of its own." Instead of staying focused on a task like driving in traffic or listening to a lecture, your mind frequently shifts between external and internal worlds, from event to event, from stimuli to stimuli, and from past to present to future. William James (1890) observed that normal waking consciousness is seldom fixed on any one event for any length of time. Instead, it seems to consist of a continuously changing flow of awareness, a *stream of consciousness.* (Note that this concept of "stream of consciousness" differs from everyday usage, which implies a train of loosely related thoughts.)

Why does this happen?   As you may recall from Chapter 4, the brain readily *habituates* or becomes less responsive to unchanging stimuli, and the meanderings of the stream of consciousness keep the brain responsive and functional.

Levels of Awareness: A Continuum of Alertness

A second important aspect of consciousness is *levels of awareness.* Consciousness is not an all-or-nothing phenomenon. Instead, it exists on a continuum ranging from high awareness and sharp, focused alertness to coma and death (see Figure 5.1). Level of awareness is modified by internal factors such as interest and fatigue, and by external factors such as stimulant drugs (caffeine, amphetamines, cocaine) and depressant drugs (alcohol, barbiturates).

Using our original definition of consciousness (awareness of external and internal stimuli), "unconsciousness" would refer to a lack of awareness of both types of stimuli, such as when under general anesthesia during surgery. Note that when people use the term "unconscious" to refer to being unaware of hidden hostilities or repressed desires that unknowingly affect behavior, they are referring to a type of lowered awareness first

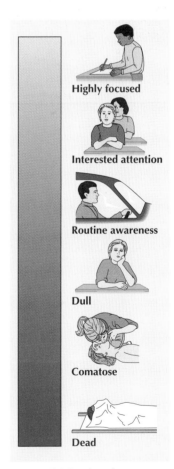

Figure 5.1 Levels of awareness. Consciousness is not an all-or-nothing phenomenon. Instead, it exists along a continuum, with highly focused awareness at the top and lowered awareness and death at the other.

described by Sigmund Freud. We will save our discussion of this type of consciousness for Chapter 14, where we fully explore what Freud meant when he used the terms "conscious," "preconscious," and "unconscious."

States of Consciousness: Normal versus Alternate States

We experience the contents of our consciousness in a continuously flowing stream and at various levels of awareness. When you are wide awake in a college classroom, your consciousness is at a moderate to high level of awareness, and your stream of consciousness might shift from the itch on your back, to what the instructor is saying, to the noise out in the hall, to a memory of last night's party, and back to the lecture. But what happens if you get so caught up in reminiscing about last night that you drift completely away from what's going on in the class and begin actively daydreaming? Is your consciousness different now? What if you fall asleep in class? Consciousness exists in several dimensions or categories known as *states of consciousness*, which are generally divided into normal, ordinary consciousness (waking states) and alternate, out-of-the-ordinary consciousness (drug-induced states, sleep, dreaming, etc.).

Normal Consciousness

In addition to the normal, waking state of consciousness described in our example of listening to a lecture, we also have normal states of consciousness called *controlled* and *automatic* processing (Logan, 1988; Posner and Snyder, 1975). Controlled processes require alert, high awareness and control of behavior. When you are taking an exam, playing an important soccer game, or learning to drive a car, your intense concentration consumes significant attentional capacity in your brain. As a result, you are normally restricted to one task requiring controlled processing at a time. Thus, you would find it difficult to listen to a radio while taking an exam.

In automatic processing, on the other hand, you perform activities with relatively little conscious awareness and simultaneously with other activities. Once you have learned to drive a car, for example, you become so comfortable that you are almost on "automatic pilot." You can listen to tapes, think about your classes, or talk to friends all while you're driving across town.

Can't this lowered awareness sometimes cause problems?   While you may occasionally forget to monitor your speed, the process of *selective attention* generally prevents serious dangers such as running into the car in front of you. As you may recall from Chapter 4, selective attention allows our brain to sort out and attend to only the most important messages from our senses.

While automatic, unconscious processes are generally not dangerous, there *are* times we are automated when we don't want to be. For example, do you find yourself "unconsciously" biting your nails or "automatically" reaching for a second helping at the table? Novelist Colin Wilson (1967) provides a humorous look at what he calls his "inner robot":

> *When I learned to type, I had to do it painfully and with much nervous wear and tear. But at a certain stage a miracle occurred, and this complicated operation was "learned" by a useful robot whom I conceal in my subconscious mind. Now I only have to think about what I want to say; my robot secretary does the typing. He is really very useful. He also drives the car for me, speaks French (not very well), and occasionally gives lectures at American universities. [My robot] is most annoying when I am tired, because then he tends to take over most of my functions without even asking me. I have even caught him making love to my wife.* (p. 98)

In Chapters 6 and 16 we will look at some ways of dismissing or controlling your "inner robot."

Alternate States of Consciousness

In addition to normal, waking consciousness, we also experience out-of-the-ordinary alternate states of consciousness as a result of sleep, dreaming, drugs, hypnosis, and meditation. (In recent years, the term "altered" has come to be used for changed states of consciousness that are deliberately evoked through drugs, hypnosis, or meditation. Changes that occur naturally, such as sleeping and dreaming are then called "alternate states." However, the term "altered" has been criticized for implying a single "desirable" state of consciousness. Therefore, we will use "alternate" to refer to all states that differ from "normal" consciousness.)

William James (1902/1936), widely considered the father of psychology, was fascinated by alternate states of consciousness. After inhaling nitrous oxide, sometimes called "laughing gas," he wrote, "Our normal waking consciousness, rational consciousness as we call it, is but one special type of consciousness, whilst all about it, parted from it by the filmiest of screens, there lie potential forms of consciousness entirely different" (p. 64).

How are alternate states of consciousness different from normal consciousness? Alternate states of consciousness (ASCs) differ from normal, waking states of consciousness primarily in the dimensions of *awareness* and *control*. When a person is in a drug-induced ASC, for example, his or her awareness of the world is lessened or distorted, as Aldous Huxley saw his books glowing with a "living light." The dimension of control (or actually lack of control) is similar to being in a dream where we desperately need to run but can't get our legs to move.

Alternate States of Consciousness (ASCs): Any state of consciousness other than normal waking consciousness.

Although ASCs are hard to describe precisely, they generally have one or more of the following characteristics (Ludwig, 1966; Nideffer, 1976; Smith, 1982; Tart, 1975):

1. Distortions of perceptual processes, sense of time, and body image (such as Huxley's loss of time while staring at the "supernatural smoothness" of the chair legs).

2. Emotional intensity ranging from quiet, profound peace or depression to rapturous joy or extreme anger and paranoia (such as the paranoia in Peter Tripp's belief that the examining doctor was an undertaker coming for his body).

3. Disruptions in normal thinking and memory (as when people drink too much and can't remember what happened the next morning).

4. Inability to communicate the experience, particularly in the language understood by the normal type of consciousness.

5. Feelings of unity and fusion, with a loss of boundaries between self and others and loss of physical constraints such as time and space (as evidenced by Huxley's feelings of being a "Not-self in the Not-self which was the chair").

Some of these changes in normal consciousness also characterize high fever and intense religious experiences, as well as the runner's high (Chapter 2), sensory deprivation (Chapter 3), and biofeedback (Chapter 6).

Gender and Cultural Diversity

CONSCIOUSNESS ACROSS CULTURES

Throughout recorded history, people have sought ways to alter their consciousness. As early as 2500 B.C., the Sumerians recorded their reactions to the drug *opium* with a symbol that archeologists translate as "joy" or "rejoicing" (Davis, 1990). The oldest known code of laws, that of Hammurabi of Babylonia (ca. 1700 B.C.), regulated the sale of wine.

In a modern survey of 488 societies in all parts of the world, 90 percent were found to practice institutionally recognized methods of changing consciousness (Bourguignon, 1973). These methods include taking drugs, ritualistic fasting, dancing, chanting,

Meditation and religious chants, drugs such as alcohol, and childhood experiments with swings are common ways of changing consciousness.

and inducing a trance. Moreover, very young children in almost all cultures have been observed engaging in practices designed to alter their consciousness. According to Harvard researcher and physician Andrew Weil (1972): "Three- and four-year-olds commonly whirl themselves into vertiginous stupors, hyperventilate, and have other children squeeze them around the chest until they faint. They also choke each other to produce loss of consciousness" (p. 19). Such historical and cultural commonalities have led some researchers to suggest there is a basic, inborn human need to experience nonordinary reality (Siegel, 1989; Weil and Rosen, 1993).

A drink made from the kava plant was once used as a means for communicating with the gods. Today, many South Pacific islanders visit local kava bars to relax after a hard day at work.

Why are people so interested in altering their consciousness? A recent study of *kava,* a drink made from the dried roots of a South Pacific Island plant that creates an alternate state of consciousness, offers three answers to this question (Merlin, Lebot, and Lindstrom, 1992). Though other cultures use different substances or means, most attempts to achieve ASCs serve the same functions as kava does for the Pacific Islanders:

1. Sacred rituals Many cultures seek an alternate state of consciousness as a pathway to spiritual enlightenment. The earliest use of kava was as a means of communicating with the gods. Spiritual seekers believed that the voices of their ancestors could be heard in the nonordinary reality induced by the kava. Using psychoactive drugs for spiritual purposes has a long history among peoples around the world. Tobacco, for example, has always been an integral part of Native American religions (Robicsek, 1992). It serves as a ritual fumigant, a goodwill offering, a sacrifice, and a sacrament. In addition to drug use, individuals in many cultures voluntarily undergo long fasts, isolation, chanting, whirling, and sensory deprivation in search of spiritual guidance (Barnouw, 1985; Kehoe, 1992).

2. Social/political functions Alternate states of consciousness are also an integral part of most cultures' social and political functions. Pacific Islanders often exchange large, elaborately decorated kava plants at festivals and weddings. And political meetings often start with a ritual cup of kava. In small amounts, the drink relaxes the muscles and produces a mild euphoria, while leaving the mind alert. Thus, kava is favored both for celebrations and as a means of reducing the frictions of village life (Fackelmann, 1992).

In our North American culture, the use of alcohol is a prominent feature of many social occasions. Have you noticed how often champagne is used to celebrate weddings, births, and New Year's Eve? Alcohol is also commonly available during many business lunches and political meetings.

3. Individual rewards In addition to the spiritual and social/political functions, many alternate states of consciousness are desirable on an individual level because they provide pleasure and escape from anxiety or stress. In New Guinea and Figi, islanders commonly visit kava bars after work for a relaxing cup of kava. The stresses of the day are replaced with a sense of well-being. In Western societies, alcohol serves a similar purpose. (The stimulant, depressant, narcotic, and hallucinogenic properties of the most common drugs in North America are discussed later in this chapter.) ■

Review Questions

1. Why were early psychologists reluctant to study consciousness?

2. Give a brief definition of consciousness.

3. Through the process of _____, we gain control over our stream of consciousness.

4. Alternate states of consciousness differ from normal, waking states of consciousness primarily in the dimensions of _____ and _____ .

5. Throughout history and across all cultures, there has been a strong interest in alternate states of consciousness. Can you explain this?

6. List the three major functions that are served by alternate states of consciousness.

Answers to Review Questions can be found in Appendix C.

SLEEP AND DREAMING

Sleep has always been a welcome but mysterious and sometimes elusive guest in our lives. The ancient Greeks believed the god Morpheus granted—or refused—sleep to mortals. In other words, sleep was a gift. Although each of us will spend almost 25 years in the alternate states of sleep and dreaming (Dement, 1974, 1992), these two states of consciousness are widely misunderstood.

• *What is the function of sleep and dreaming?*

 Try This Yourself

Before reading on, you might test your personal knowledge of sleep and dreaming by reviewing the common myths below. ■

Myth: Everyone needs eight hours of sleep a night to maintain sound mental and physical health. While most of us average 7.6 hours of sleep a night, some people seem to get by on less than 15 to 30 minutes of sleep a night, while others may need as much as 11 hours (Ellman et al., 1991; Meddis et al., 1973).

Myth: It is easier to learn complicated things, like foreign languages, while asleep. Although *some* learning can occur during the lighter stages (1 and 2) of sleep, the processing and retention of this material is minimal (Aarons, 1976; Ogilvie, Wilkinson, and Allison, 1989). Wakeful learning is much more effective and efficient (see Chapter 7 for more details).

Myth: Some people never dream. Even people who firmly believe they never experience dreaming will report dreams if they are awakened during a *rapid-eye-movement* (REM) period (Goodenough, 1991; Hall and Nordby, 1972). Apparently everyone dreams, but some people don't remember their dreams.

Myth: Dreams only last a few seconds. Research has shown that dreams seem to occur in "real time"; that is, the longer they seem to last, the longer they really are (Dement and Wolpert, 1958).

Myth: When a man or woman experiences genital arousal during sleep, it means they are having a sexual dream. When sleepers are awakened during this time, they are no more likely to report dreams with sexual content than they do at other times (Hall and Van de Castle, 1966; Pivik, 1991).

Myth: Dreaming of dying can be fatal. This is a good opportunity to exercise your critical thinking skills. Take time to critically evaluate this common belief. Where did this myth come from? Has anyone ever personally experienced and recounted a fatal dream? Could we ever scientifically prove or disprove this belief?

Sleep as a Biological Rhythm: Chronobiology and the Four Biological Rhythms

Chronobiology: The study of biological rhythms.

Have you ever wondered why some people love to stay up late at night and sleep-in the next day, while others spring out of bed in the morning and fade by nine o'clock at night? Or have you wondered whether the pilot on your airplane is suffering from sleepiness and jet lag? If so, the science of chronobiology, the study of biological rhythms, will interest you.

One of the intriguing findings in chronobiology is that human behavior appears to be affected by four basic biological rhythms: (1) the yearly or seasonal cycle, which is related to patterns of sexual activity and certain types of depression (see Chapter 15); (2) the monthly or 28-day lunar cycle, which corresponds to the female menstrual cycle; (3) the 24-hour daily cycle, which is related to our sleep and waking cycle, and (4) the 90-minute rest-activity cycle, which is related to variations in alertness and daydreaming. Of these four cycles, the 24-hour daily cycle (also known as *circadian rhythms*) has the clearest effect on human behavior.

Circadian Rhythms

Circadian Rhythms: Biological changes that occur on a 24-hour cycle.

During each 24-hour period of each day, our world cycles continually from light to dark and back again. Most animals have adapted to this change by developing a variety of circadian rhythms —*circadian* means *diurnal* or lasting about a day.

While noctural animals, such as rats, sleep most of the day and stay awake at night, humans and most other animals are awake during the light times of the 24-hour period and asleep during the dark periods. For humans, circadian rhythms influence not only sleep and waking, but also fluctuations in blood pressure, pulse rate, body temperature, blood sugar level, and cell growth. These daily rhythms help explain why most people's sleep/waking cycle is relatively regular and why we may feel irritable, hungry, listless, or energetic at different times of the day. These daily rhythms vary from person to person. For example, "morning people" tend to reach their peak body temperature and corresponding alertness and efficiency at midmorning, whereas "night people" have higher temperatures and function better in the evening (Luce, 1971).

Disrupted Circadian Rhythms

Under normal conditions, disruptions in circadian rhythms do not pose a significant problem for most people. If you are a typical college student, your late night study sessions, early morning classes, and full or part-time work often cause disturbances in your biological clock. And you may experience bouts of extreme sleepiness during the day, difficulty sleeping at night, and a strong need to sleep-in during the weekend. But by adjusting your work schedule and social life, you can cope with these disruptions. "Morning people" and "night people" can try to match their class schedules and study time to their daily fluctuations in mood and energy to improve their overall college functioning.

There are circumstances, however, when we cannot ameliorate the effects of disrupted circadian rhythms. For example, about 20 percent of workers in the United States are on rotating shift schedules that force them to keep changing their sleep and waking cycles (Moorcroft, 1989). Studies show that shift workers typically suffer from increased fatigue and sleep disorders due to disruptions in their normal circadian rhythms. Shift workers are also much less productive and more accident-prone while on the job (Chollar, 1989; Coleman, 1986). It is interesting to note that the Union Carbide chemical accident in Bhopal, India, the nuclear power plant disaster in Chernobyl, and the Alaskan oil spill from the Exxon Valdez all occurred during the night shift. Although this may be a simple coincidence, it could also indicate that the circadian cycle of these workers was oriented toward sleep at a time when full alertness was required.

In addition to rotating work schedules, you can also get out of sync with your circadian rhythms by flying across several time zones. Have you ever taken a long airline flight and felt fatigued, sluggish, and irritable for the first few days on arriving? If so, you have experienced what is commonly known as *jet lag*. Like rotating shift work, jet lag has been found to correlate with decreased alertness, decreased mental agility, and overall reduced efficiency (Hilts, 1984). In response to such findings, airlines allow pilots additional adjustment time on international flights.

I've heard that it is easier to fly westward than eastward. Is this true?   Yes. Studies show that it is usually more difficult to adapt to *phase advances* (accelerations of circadian rhythms) than to *phase delays* (decelerations of circadian rhythms). Therefore, most people take longer to adjust to eastern flights and to changes in shift work that require earlier rising.

 Try This Yourself

Whether you are flying eastward or toward the west, if you want to reduce jet lag you may want to follow the "anti-jet-lag" diet and behavior suggestions developed by Dr. Charles Ehret (Perry, 1982):

1. Eat lightly the day before a long flight, and stick to low-calorie, low-carbohydrate foods such as eggs, fish, salad, and fruit.

2. When you board the plane, set your watch to correspond to the time zone of your planned destination and then eat and sleep according to this new timetable.

3. On the plane and at your destination, avoid alcohol and eat a high-protein breakfast and lunch and a high-carbohydrate dinner.

4. At your destination, go to bed early and according to the new time zone. ■

How Scientists Study Sleep: Using the EEG and Sleep Labs

How do scientists study private, mental events like sleep and dreaming? Although surveys and interviews can provide a great deal of information about the nature of sleep (Antrobus et al., 1991), a real breakthrough in sleep research came with the development of the *electroencephalograph* (EEG). As a person moves from a waking state to deep sleep, the brain shows complex and predictable changes in electrical activity. The EEG records these brain wave changes by means of small disklike electrodes placed on the scalp. In addition to the EEG, sleep researchers also rely on the *electromyograph* (EMG) to record changes in muscular activity, the *electrooculograph* (EOG) to measure eye movements, and the *electrocardiograph* (EKG) to record contractions of the heart. Other devices allow investigators also to record respiration rate, blood pressure, and even the degree of genital arousal.

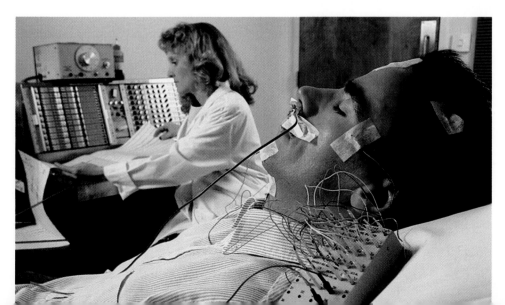

Figure 5.2 How sleep is studied. Researchers in a sleep laboratory use sophisticated equipment to record physiological changes during sleep. Electroencephalograph (EEG) electrodes are taped to the scalp to measure brainwave activity. Electromyograph (EMG) electrodes are applied to the chin and mouth to measure muscular activity. Electrooculograph (EOG) electrodes are taped near the eyes to record eye movements. Other devices not shown in this photo record heart rate, respiration rate, and genital arousal.

Cycling through the Stages of Sleep

Perhaps the best way to appreciate the methods and findings of sleep researchers is to pretend for a moment that you are a subject in a sleep experiment. When you arrive at the sleep lab, you are assigned one of several "bedrooms." The researcher hooks you up to various physiological recording devices, such as the EEG, EMG, and EOG (see Figure 5.2). If you are like other subjects, you probably need a night or two to adapt to the equipment and return to a normal mode of sleeping (Browman and Cartwright, 1980).

Having adapted to the strange equipment and environment, you are ready for the researchers to monitor your typical night's sleep. As your eyes close and you begin to relax, the researcher in the next room notices that your EEG recordings have moved from *beta waves,* associated with normal wakefulness, to *alpha waves,* which indicate drowsy relaxation (see Figure 5.3). This period is considered a special type of ASC and is known as the hypnogogic state. You may experience visual images (such as flashing lights or colors) or swift, jerky movements and a corresponding feeling of slipping or falling. Such experiences are common during the hypnogogic state.

As you continue relaxing, your brain's electrical activity slows even further and *theta waves* begin to dominate your EEG. You are now in *Stage 1* sleep in which your breathing becomes more regular, your heart rate slows, and your blood pressure decreases. At this stage you could still be readily awakened. No one wakens you, though, so you relax more deeply and slide gently into *Stage 2* sleep. This stage is noted on your EEG by the appearance of occasional short bursts of rapid, high-amplitude brain waves known as *sleep spindles.* During Stage 2 sleep you become progressively more relaxed and less responsive to the external environment. Stage 2 sleep is followed by even deeper levels of sleep—*Stages 3* and *4.* As shown in Figure 5.3, these stages are marked by the appearance of slow, high-amplitude *delta waves.*

In about an hour, you progress through all four stages of sleep. Then the sequence begins to reverse itself. As can be seen in Figure 5.4, during the course of a night people usually complete four to five cycles of light to deep sleep. Since each cycle lasts about 90 minutes, this sleep pattern is an example of the 90-minute rest-activity biological rhythm.

Figure 5.4 also shows an interesting phenomenon that occurs at the end of the first cycle. You go back through Stage 3, then to Stage 2, but instead of reentering the calm, relaxed *theta* state of Stage 1, something totally different happens. Quite abruptly, your scalp recordings display a pattern of small-amplitude, fast activity similar in many ways to that of an awake, vigilant person (see Figure 5.3). Your breathing and pulse rates become fast and irregular and your genitals very likely show signs of arousal (either an erection or vaginal lubrication). Although your brain and body are giving many signs of active arousal, your musculature is deeply relaxed and unresponsive. Because of this seeming contradiction, one name for this stage is *paradoxical sleep.*

REM Sleep

During the paradoxical sleep stage, rapid eye movements occur under your closed lids. Thus, another—and more common—name for paradoxical sleep is rapid-eye-movement (REM) sleep. REM sleep signals that dreaming is taking place. When researchers systematically awaken subjects to ask them whether they have been dreaming, REM awakenings produce dream recall 78 percent of the time, while the other stages of sleep are accompanied by dream recall only 14 percent of the time (Dement, 1974, 1992). Dreams during REM sleep are not only more frequent, but also more vivid, emotional, and storylike (Farthing, 1992).

REM sleep and its connection to dreaming were discovered accidentally in the 1950s by Eugene Aserinsky, a graduate student working in Nathaniel Kleitman's lab at the University of Chicago (Aserinsky and Kleitman, 1953; Dement and Kleitman, 1957). REM sleep is such a special stage that the other four stages are often grouped together and referred to as non-rapid-eye-movement sleep (NREM).

Hypnogogic State: A state of consciousness at the beginning of sleep in which many people experience visual, auditory, and kinesthetic sensations.

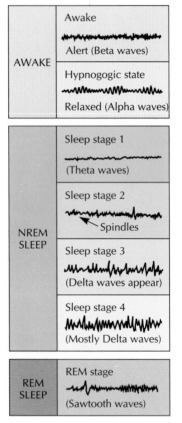

Figure 5.3 EEG patterns during sleep. As you move from being awake to deeply asleep, your brain waves decrease in frequency (cycles per second) and increase in amplitude (height).

Rapid-Eye-Movement (REM) Sleep: A stage of sleep marked by rapid eye movements, high-frequency brain waves, and dreaming.

Non–Rapid-Eye-Movement (NREM) Sleep: Sleep stages 1 through 4, which are marked by an absence of rapid eye movements, relatively little dreaming, and variations in EEG activity.

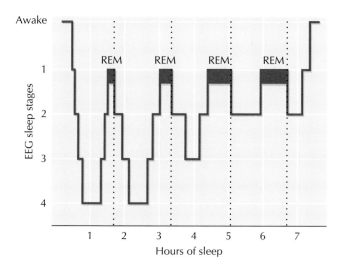

Figure 5.4 Stages in a typical night's sleep. During a normal night's sleep, the sleeper moves in and out of various stages of sleep. Starting off alert, the sleeper gradually shifts downward into Stage 1, then Stages 2, 3, and 4. The sleep cycle then reverses. At the peak of the return trip, the sleeper spends some time in REM and then the cycle starts downward again. As the night continues, the sleeper repeats the general cycle four to five times. (The dashed lines indicate the boundaries of each cycle.) Note that the periods of Stage 4 and then Stage 3 sleep diminish during the night, while REM periods increase in duration.

What is the purpose of REM sleep?   Although the exact function of REM sleep is controversial, there is general agreement that it serves an important biological need. When researchers selectively deprive sleepers of REM sleep (by waking them each time they enter the state), most people show a *rebound effect*. That is, they try to "catch up" on REM sleep on subsequent occasions by spending more time than usual in this state (Brunner et al., 1990).

Non-REM Sleep

While REM sleep is important to our biological functioning, the need for Non-REM sleep may be even greater. When people are deprived of *total* sleep, rather than just REM sleep, their recovery sleep on the first uninterrupted night has a greater proportion of Non-REM sleep (Borbely, 1982). It seems that nature's first need is for Non-REM sleep. As you may remember from Figure 5.4, when you initially begin to sleep you spend more time in Stages 1–4 (Non-REM) sleep. After this need has been satisfied, the latter parts of the night are devoted more to REM sleep.

The idea that nature first satisfies its need for Non-REM sleep before going on to REM sleep is also supported by studies showing that adults who are "short sleepers" (five hours or less each night) spend less time in REM sleep than "long sleepers" (nine hours or more each night). Similarly, infants get more sleep and have a higher percentage of REM sleep than adults (see Figure 5.5). Apparently, the greater the total amount of sleep, the greater is the percentage of REM sleep.

To sum up, both REM and Non-REM sleep serve important biological needs. We do not, however, fully understand their specific functions, and further research is necessary. We now turn to the larger question, "What is the function of sleep?"

Why Do We Sleep? Repair or Evolutionary Advantage?

There are currently two major theories that attempt to explain why we sleep. The repair/restoration theory suggests that sleep serves an important recuperative function, allowing us to recover not only from physical fatigue but also from emotional and intellectual demands (Webb, 1992). The evolutionary/circadian theory emphasizes the relationship of sleep to basic circadian rhythms. According to this view, sleep is merely a neural mechanism that evolved so animals could conserve energy during the time of day they are not foraging for food or seeking mates. It also serves to keep them still at times when predators are active (Allison and Cicchetti, 1976; Hobson, 1989). The repair/restoration theory may be likened to a gentle parent—"Go to sleep. You need your rest." And the evolutionary/circadian theory can be compared to a harsh parent—"Go to sleep. You need to stay out of trouble."

Repair/Restoration Theory: A theory suggesting that sleep serves a restorative function, allowing organisms to recuperate from physical, emotional, and intellectual demands.

Evolutionary/Circadian Theory: A theory suggesting that sleep is a part of circadian rhythms and evolved as a means of conserving energy and protecting individuals from predators.

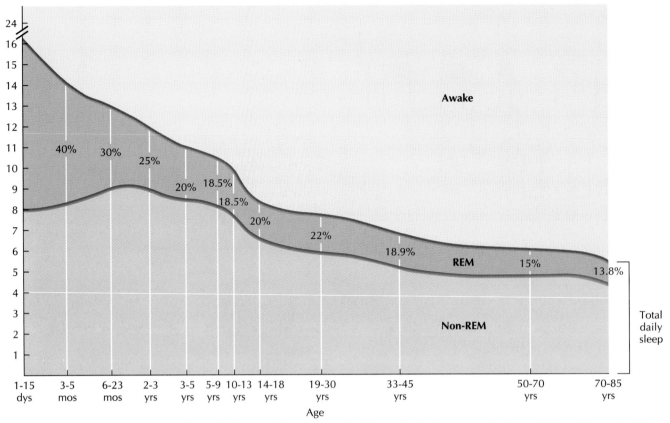

Figure 5.5 Sleep and dreaming over the life span. Notice that as you get older both the total amount of sleep per night and the portion of REM sleep decrease. The most dramatic changes occur during the first two to three years of life. Note how as an infant you spent almost eight hours a day in REM sleep, and at the age of seventy you spend less than an hour.

Repair/Restoration Theory

Support for the repair/restoration theory comes from research showing increased production of new proteins during sleep (Adam, 1980). This theory also seems consistent with our subjective impressions: Most of us do feel more refreshed and "repaired" after a good night's sleep.

There are at least two reasons, however, to doubt that we sleep only for repair and restoration. First, sleep, especially REM sleep, is often far from being restful and recuperative. Recall that during REM sleep, many internal physiological processes (like heart rate and brain waves) are as active as when we are fully awake. Second, if sleep restores energy and repairs bodily damage, loss of sleep should result directly in significant energy loss and bodily damage.

While experiments with severe sleep deprivation in rats can produce serious side effects and even death (Dement, 1992; Rechtschaffen et al., 1983), research with human subjects suggests that it may not be as detrimental as most people think it must be. Studies of extreme sleep loss, such as Peter Tripp's 200-hour wake-a-thon, have shown that some people can tolerate up to 60 hours or so of complete sleeplessness without measurable ill effects (Borbely, 1986; Horne, 1989). In 1965, a 17-year-old student named Randy Gardner who wanted to earn a place in the *Guinness Book of Records* stayed awake for 264 consecutive hours. He remained relatively alert and active throughout the entire period and showed none of the bizarre hallucinations and disturbances experienced by Peter Tripp. After the ordeal, Randy slept a mere 14 hours and then returned to his usual 8-hour cycle (Dement, 1978). Although Peter Tripp did suffer from a temporary form of *sleep-deprivation psychosis* (e.g., seeing the "coat of furry worms"),

Would the repair/restoration theory or the evolution/circadian theory best explain this type of sleep?

neither he nor Randy Gardner seemed to suffer lasting physical or psychological harm from their extended sleep deprivation.

Evolutionary/Circadian Theory

While the evolutionary/circadian theory agrees that sleep serves a recuperative function, it goes further to suggest that evolution has programmed us to sleep when activity is most ineffective and possibly dangerous. This theory also reconciles the differences in sleep patterns across species (see Figure 5.6). Animals like armadillos and opossums sleep even more than humans because they are relatively unthreatened by their environment and are able to easily find food and shelter. In comparison, because of their vegetarian diets, horses and sheep must spend almost all their waking hours foraging for food. Also, their only defense against predators is vigilance so they can run away.

Which theory is correct?   Actually, the theories do not contradict each other and most theorists think both may be correct (Borbely, 1986; Webb, 1992).

Figure 5.6 Average daily hours of sleep for different mammals. According to the evolutionary/circadian theory of sleep, animals that sleep the longest are those that are not threatened by the environment and can easily find food and shelter. Note how the opossum and cat spend longer hours in sleep than the horse and sheep, presumably because of differences in diet and number of predators.

The Biology of Sleep: What Causes This ASC?

Some researchers have looked for a specific neurotransmitter or part of the brain as the cause of sleep. As you may suspect, there is no *one* single neurotransmitter that serves as a "sleeping pill." (As noted in Chapter 2, neurotransmitters are chemical substances that carry neurological messages from one neuron to the next.) Serotonin, for example, tends to promote sleep and to suppress REM, while acetylcholine promotes REM sleep. Norepinephrine and dopamine, on the other hand, promote wakefulness, and a number of sleeping pills operate in part by blocking production of these neurotransmitters (Garcia-Arraras and Pappenheimer, 1983; Koella, 1985).

A similar state of affairs exists with research on the role of the brain in sleep. Many areas have been identified as having a role in the production or maintenance of sleep—the pons, the ascending reticular activating system (ARAS), the basal forebrain, the medulla, the thalamus, the hypothalamus, and the limbic system. But there seems to be no single "Morpheus area" for sleep as there is, for example, a Broca's area for language. (If any of these terms are unfamiliar, you may wish to review the Chapter 2 discussion of neurotransmitters and brain structures.)

Review Questions

1. What are the four basic biological rhythms for humans?
2. Biological rhythms that occur on a daily basis are called _____ rhythms.
3. The machine that measures the voltage (or brain waves) that the brain produces is the _____ .
4. As a person relaxes before going to sleep, the brain waves move from _____ waves associated with normal wakefulness to _____ waves that indicate drowsy relaxation.
5. Dreaming occurs primarily during _____ sleep.
6. Explain how the repair/restoration theory of sleep differs from the evolutionary/circadian theory.

Answers to Review Questions can be found in Appendix C.

Why Do We Dream? Two Theories

One of the most mysterious aspects of sleep is dreaming. The average dream reflects normal fears, frustrations, and personal desires, as well as events that violate laws of physics, principles of logic, and personal codes of morality. One survey of dream content found that dreams about being chased or about falling were the most common, followed by dreams of returning to a childhood home, flying, appearing naked or scantily clad in a public place, and being unprepared for an exam (Stark, 1984). Thirty-nine percent of dreamers in this survey also claimed to be able to control the course of their dreams.

A number of theories attempt to explain the purpose of dreams (Hunt, 1989). We will discuss two major ones: wish-fulfillment and activation synthesis.

Wish-Fulfillment Theory

One of the oldest and most scientifically controversial explanations for why we dream is Freud's wish-fulfillment theory. Wish-fulfillment theory says dreams are disguised symbols of repressed desires. In one of his first books, *The Interpretation of Dreams* (1900), Freud argued that dreams are "the royal road to the unconscious," because dreaming is

Have you ever had dreams like this? In this painting, I and the Village, *artist Marc Chagall captures images common to the state of dreaming.*

Wish-Fulfillment Theory: Freud's theory of dream interpretation that emphasizes the roles of manifest and latent content.

one of the few times when forbidden and personally unacceptable desires rise to the surface of consciousness. Using this reasoning, it may explain why we sometimes dream of food when we're hungry or of having sex with someone other than our spouse.

According to Freud and psychoanalysts, dreams sometimes offer us direct insight into the unconscious but more often, the dream content is so threatening and anxiety producing that it must be couched in symbols. Freud referred to these symbols as the manifest content of dreams, and the underlying, true meaning as the latent content.

Activation-Synthesis Hypothesis

In contrast to the Freudian model of dreaming is the activation–synthesis hypothesis advanced by J. Alan Hobson and Robert W. McCarley (1977) of Harvard Medical School. In their view, dreams have no real significance. On the basis of research conducted on the brain activity of cats during REM sleep, these investigators proposed that dreaming is a simple and unimportant by-product of random stimulation of brain cells. According to this theory, certain cells in the sleep center of the brain stem are activated during REM sleep. The brain struggles to "synthesize" or make sense out of this random stimulation by searching through stored memories and manufacturing dreams.

Can people sometimes tell that they're dreaming while the dream is going on? Lucid dreaming, in which the dreamer recognizes the dream as a dream, has been reported for many years and has recently been documented in studies where sleepers are trained to signal when they were dreaming by voluntarily moving their eyes and clenching their fists (La Berge, 1992; Weinstein, Schwartz, and Arkin, 1991). Since this type of training also allows "on the scene" reporting versus after-the-fact recall, scientists are especially interested in this reporting technique. Lucid dreamers have been found to be able to not only evaluate their dreams as they are occurring but on occasion to even influence the outcome. If you would like to learn how to lucid-dream, consult the book *Control Your Dreams,* which is listed at the end of this chapter.

Controlling your dreams might be particularly useful when they're bad. In fact, the problem of nightmares and other sleep disorders has gained considerable research attention in recent years.

Sleep Disorders: When Sleep Becomes a Problem

For approximately 50 million Americans, sleep is an enemy. These people have the problem of sleeping too little (insomnia), sleeping too much (hypersomnia), or having troubled sleep (nightmares and night terrors).

Insomnia

People with insomnia have repeated difficulty falling asleep (taking longer than 20 minutes), staying asleep, or waking wake up too early. Although many people often think they have insomnia because they wrongly assume that everyone *must* sleep eight hours a night or because they think they aren't sleeping when they really are, a large percentage of the population (as much as 30 percent) does suffer from this disorder (Hartmann, 1985). Insomnia is associated with alcohol and other drug abuse, with emotional disturbances (such as anxiety and depression), and with a variety of physiological conditions (Spielman and Herrera, 1991). Unfortunately, the most popular treatment for insomnia is drugs—either over-the-counter pills such as Sominex and Sleep-eze or prescription drugs such as tranquilizers and barbiturates. The problem with nonprescription pills is that they generally don't work (Kales and Kales, 1973). Prescription pills, on the other hand, create a type of artificial sleep—they put you to sleep but they decrease Stage 4 and REM sleep, thereby seriously affecting the quality of sleep. People who regularly use sleeping pills also run the risk of psychological and physical drug dependence (Roth and Zorick, 1983; Spielman and Herrera, 1991). (We will discuss these terms in the next section, on chemical alterations of consciousness.)

Manifest Content: The surface content of a dream, containing dream symbols that distort and disguise the true meaning of the dream, according to Freudian dream theory.

Latent Content: The true, unconscious meaning of a dream, according to Freudian dream theory.

Activation–Synthesis Hypothesis: The idea that dreams have no real significance, but in fact are simply unimportant by-products of random stimulation of brain cells.

Lucid Dreaming: The ability to be aware that one is dreaming and to direct one's dreams.

Insomnia: A sleep disorder in which a person has repeated difficulty in falling asleep or staying asleep or awakens too early.

What is recommended instead of drugs? If you're having difficulty falling asleep at night, try concentrating on simple relaxation. Instead of monitoring the clock and nervously waiting to fall asleep, close your eyes and try to systematically relax each part of your body. Or, you may want to try some of the techniques listed in Table 5.1.

Sleep Apnea

Sleep Apnea: A temporary cessation of breathing during sleep; one of the causes of snoring and a suspected cause of sudden infant death syndrome.

A sleep disorder that is more serious and difficult to treat than general insomnia is sleep apnea, a temporary cessation of breathing. It is one of the causes of snoring and is a suspected factor in the *sudden infant death syndrome* (*SIDS,* or "crib death") (Carlson, 1992; Guilleminault, 1979; Harper, 1983). Sleep apnea seems to result from blocked upper air passages or from the brain ceasing to send signals to the diaphragm, thus causing breathing to stop. Obstruction of the breathing passages is sometimes treated with reducing diets for obese patients. For others, surgery may be the answer. If you have friends who snore loudly, they may be suffering from sleep apnea and should be encouraged to seek medical attention, since the condition may eventually lead to heart damage. Babies with a suspected risk of SIDS can be monitored with a special device mounted above the crib that sounds an alarm when breathing weakens (Naeye, 1980). Since many adult sufferers are often unaware that sleep apnea is the cause of their sleep disturbances, they often seek help from doctors who may prescribe drugs to help them sleep more soundly. Such medications, as well as alcohol and other depressant drugs, are potentially dangerous since they also suppress the normal reflexes that would otherwise awaken the sleeper when breathing stops (Kalat, 1992).

Table 5.1   Methods for Enhancing Sleep

You can help yourself to a good night's sleep by preparing during the day and at bedtime. These suggestions come from the Better Sleep Council, a nonprofit educational organization in Burtonsville, MD.

During the day:

Exercise. Daily physical activity works away tension. But don't exercise vigorously late, or you'll get fired up instead.

Keep regular hours. An erratic schedule can disrupt biological rhythms. Get up at the same time each day.

Avoid stimulants. Coffee, tea, soft drinks, chocolate, and some medications contain caffeine. Nicotine may be an even more potent sleep disrupter.

Avoid late meals. Heavy or spicy meals at bedtime keep you awake. Have light snacks.

Avoid heavy drinking. Overindulgence can shatter your normal sleep pattern.

Stop worrying. Focus on your problems at a set time earlier in the day. If you worry in bed, tell yourself you'll resolve the problems tomorrow.

Use presleep rituals. Follow the same routine every evening: listen to music, write in a diary, meditate.

In bed:

Use progressive muscle relaxation. Alternately tense and relax various muscle groups.

Apply yoga. These gentle exercises help you relax.

Light a candle in your mind. Focus on the flame to get rid of distracting thoughts.

Try sandman's snacks. Eggs, tunafish, chicken, turkey, and soy beans contain L-tryptophan, an amino acid called nature's sleeping pill.

Have a nightcap. Warm milk and herbal teas can promote sleep.

Use fantasies. Imagine yourself in a tranquil setting. Feel yourself relax.

Use deep breathing. Take deep breaths, telling yourself you're falling asleep.

Try a splashdown. A warm bath can induce drowsiness because it sends blood away from the brain to the skin surface.

Use mind games. Imagine you're writing 6-foot-high numbers. Start at 100 and count backwards.

Count sheep. It works by relaxing both sides of the brain.

Narcolepsy

A serious sleep disorder that is somewhat the opposite of insomnia is narcolepsy—excessive daytime sleepiness characterized by sudden and irresistible demands for sleep. During an attack, the narcoleptic's muscles unexpectedly go limp and he or she drops directly into the REM state of sleep. These attacks are obviously dramatic and incapacitating. Can you imagine what it would be like to be driving along the highway or walking across campus and suddenly have an attack? Although stimulant or antidepressant drugs may help reduce the frequency of attacks, the causes and cure of narcolepsy are still unknown (Spielman and Herrera, 1991). Researchers at Stanford University's Sleep Disorders Center have selectively bred a group of narcoleptic dogs, which suggests a genetic basis for the disorder and a promising avenue for future research (Dement, 1983).

Narcolepsy: A disease marked by sudden and irresistible onsets of sleep during normal waking hours.

Nightmares and Night Terrors

Nightmares, or bad dreams, occur toward the end of the sleep cycle during REM sleep. They are also more likely to occur toward morning and when the REM period is longer. Nightmares occur more often in childhood and seem to decrease with age. Less common but more frightening are night terrors, which occur early in the cycle during Stage 4 of NREM. With night terrors, the dreamer awakens suddenly, in a state of panic, with no recollection of any dream. Night terrors are most prevalent among pre-schoolage children but can also occur in adults (Hartmann, 1983; Kahn, Fisher, and Edwards, 1991). Sleepwalking and sleeptalking tend to accompany night terrors and generally occur during NREM sleep (which explains the movement).

Nightmares: Anxiety-arousing dreams that generally occur near the end of the sleep cycle, during REM sleep.

Night Terrors: Abrupt awakenings from NREM sleep accompanied by intense physiological arousal and feelings of panic.

Nightmares, night terrors, sleepwalking, and sleeptalking all seem to be found more often in young children, and when in adults, during times of stress. Thus, patience and soothing reassurance at the time of the sleep disruption are the only treatment usually recommended (Arkin, 1991).

Review Questions

1. Freud believed that dreams were the "royal road to the _____."
2. In the Freudian interpretation of dreams, how does the *manifest content* differ from the *latent content?*
3. Which theory of dreams states that dreams are an unimportant by-product of random stimulation of brain cells?
4. Following are three descriptions of people suffering from sleep disorders. Label each type.
   a. While sleeping, Joan often snores loudly and frequently stops breathing temporarily. _____
   b. Tyler is a young child who often wakes up terrified and cannot describe what has happened. These episodes occur primarily during NREM sleep.

   _____

   c. George complains to his physician about sudden and irresistible onsets of sleep during his normal workday. _____

Answers to Review Questions can be found in Appendix C.

DRUGS AND CONSCIOUSNESS

* *How is consciousness affected by drugs?*

Since the beginning of civilization, people of all cultures have used—and abused—psychoactive drugs (Julien, 1992; Weil and Rosen, 1993). Psychoactive drugs are defined as chemicals that affect the nervous system and cause a change in behavior, mental

Psychoactive Drugs: Chemicals that affect the nervous system and cause a change in behavior, mental processes, and conscious experience.

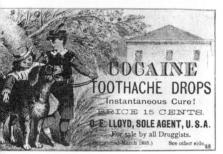

Before the Food and Drug Administration began to regulate the sale of drugs, heroin, opium, cocaine, and similar substances were readily available in over-the-counter, nonprescription drugs.

Agonist: A chemical (or drug) that mimics the action of a specific neurotransmitter.

Antagonist: A chemical (or drug) that opposes or blocks the action of a neurotransmitter.

processes, and conscious experience. As an adult in contemporary times, you may use drugs like caffeine (in coffee, tea, chocolate, or cola) and nicotine (in cigarettes) to pick you up. You may also use drugs like alcohol (in beer, wine, and cocktails) to relax you and lessen your inhibitions. How use differs from abuse and how chemical alterations in consciousness affect a person both psychologically and physically are important topics in psychology. In this section, we begin by discussing how drugs work and clarifying differences in terminology. We then go on to look at the four major categories of psychoactive drugs that affect our consciousness. (How drugs affect prenatal development is discussed in Chapter 9 and how drugs are used to treat mental disorders is covered in Chapter 16.)

Understanding Drugs: How Drugs Affect Consciousness

Have you noticed how difficult it is to have a logical, nonemotional discussion about drugs? In our society, where the "drugs of choice" are caffeine, tobacco, and ethyl alcohol, we often become very defensive when these drugs are grouped with illicit drugs such as marijuana and heroin. Similarly, users of marijuana are disturbed that their drug of choice is grouped with "hard" drugs like heroin. Psychologists generally believe that all psychoactive drugs can be used and abused. To facilitate our discussion and understanding of drugs, we need to examine three major concepts: how drugs affect neurotransmitters, how abuse differs from addiction, and how drug effects are influenced by both the drug itself and characteristics of the user.

Drugs and Neurotransmitters

Psychoactive drugs influence the nervous system in a variety of ways. Alcohol, for example, has a diffuse effect on neural membranes throughout the entire central nervous system. But most psychoactive drugs act in a more specific way—they work by changing the effect of neurotransmitters in the brain.

Drugs can alter the effect of neurotransmitters in two basic ways: They facilitate it, or they inhibit it. Drugs that mimic the action of a particular neurotransmitter, and in so doing increase the effectiveness of synaptic transmission, are called agonists. Drugs that block the action of specific neurotransmitters are called antagonists. As can be seen in Figure 5.7, agonist and antagonist drugs work at four major steps in the transmission by (1) altering the production or synthesis of neurotransmitters, (2) changing the amount of neurotransmitter stored or released by a neuron, (3) altering the effect of neurotransmitters on the receptor sites of the receiving neuron, or (4) blocking inactivation of the neurotransmitter in the synapse.

Perhaps a few examples will help to clarify drug action at these four steps:

(Step 1). **Production or synthesis.** Patients with Parkinson's disease have decreased activity in cells that produce dopamine. Usually the treatment is the drug L-DOPA because it is converted in the brain to dopamine. Producing what the brain itself can't, the drug sometimes relieves the tremors, rigidity, and difficulty in movement characteristic of patients with Parkinson's disease.

(Step 2). **Storage and release.** Venom from a black widow spider increases the release of the neurotransmitter acetylcholine. This causes more acetylcholine to be available to the receiving neurons, thereby creating an exaggerated stimulant effect.

(Step 3). **Reception.** Some drugs, called *receptor agonists,* have a molecular structure very similar to the body's own neurotransmitters (see Figure 5.8). Nicotine is similar to the neurotransmitter acetylcholine and when it fills the acetylcholine receptors it produces similar effects (increased stimulation). Some drugs are similar enough to occupy the same sites as the neurotransmitter, but they are dissimilar enough that they don't cause a response on the receiving neuron. They are called

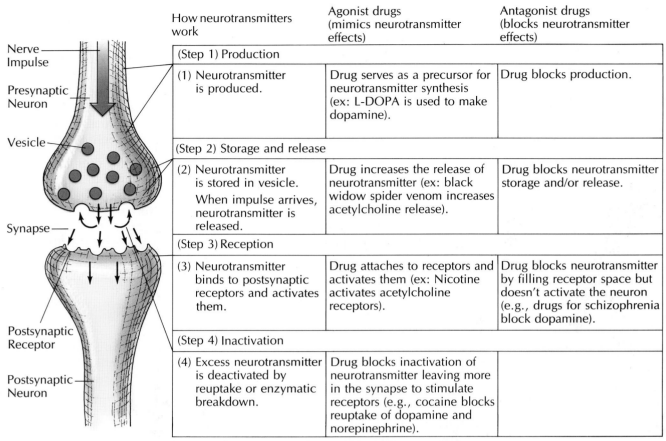

	How neurotransmitters work	Agonist drugs (mimics neurotransmitter effects)	Antagonist drugs (blocks neurotransmitter effects)
(Step 1) Production			
(1)	Neurotransmitter is produced.	Drug serves as a precursor for neurotransmitter synthesis (ex: L-DOPA is used to make dopamine).	Drug blocks production.
(Step 2) Storage and release			
(2)	Neurotransmitter is stored in vesicle. When impulse arrives, neurotransmitter is released.	Drug increases the release of neurotransmitter (ex: black widow spider venom increases acetylcholine release).	Drug blocks neurotransmitter storage and/or release.
(Step 3) Reception			
(3)	Neurotransmitter binds to postsynaptic receptors and activates them.	Drug attaches to receptors and activates them (ex: Nicotine activates acetylcholine receptors).	Drug blocks neurotransmitter by filling receptor space but doesn't activate the neuron (e.g., drugs for schizophrenia block dopamine).
(Step 4) Inactivation			
(4)	Excess neurotransmitter is deactivated by reuptake or enzymatic breakdown.	Drug blocks inactivation of neurotransmitter leaving more in the synapse to stimulate receptors (e.g., cocaine blocks reuptake of dopamine and norepinephrine).	

Figure 5.7 Psychoactive drugs and neurotransmitters. Most psychoactive drugs produce their effects by disrupting the body's supply of neurotransmitters at one of the steps in transmission. Drugs can alter the production or synthesis of neurotransmitters (Step 1), they can affect the storage and release (Step 2), or they can disrupt the reception by the next neuron (Step 3). Once neurotransmitters carry a message across the synapse, the sending neuron normally reabsorbs (reuptakes) the excess neurotransmitters or enzymes are released to destroy the excess neurotransmitter (Step 4). Psychoactive drugs, like cocaine, produce their effect primarily by blocking the reuptake. Since the extra neurotransmitters remain in the synapse, the neurons continue to fire and the mood-altering effects are intensified.

receptor antagonists. As long as they are attached to the receptors, they prevent the "real" neurotransmitter from getting its message through. As you will see in Chapters 15 and 16, many people believe schizophrenia is caused by an excess of dopamine, so it is often treated with drugs that act as receptor antagonists. They fill up the sites and block the

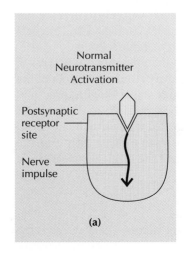

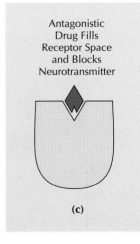

Figure 5.8 How agonists and antagonists work. In normal neurotransmitter activation (a), the neurotransmitter fits into the receptor and stimulates the receiving neuron. If, as shown in (b), a drug is ingested that contains the same molecular shape as a naturally occurring neurotransmitter, it works as an *agonist,* mimicking the neurotransmitter's action. In (c), note that the *antagonist* drug is similar enough in shape to the neurotransmitter that it can fill the same site, but its slight dissimilarity causes no stimulation of the receiving neuron. Antagonist drugs are important because they block the action of neurotransmitters by filling their normal receptor spaces.

action of the schizophrenic person's excess dopamine—thus relieving the major symptoms of the disorder.

(Step 4).   *Inactivation.* After neurotransmitters carry their message across the synapse, the sending neuron normally removes the excess in two ways: reabsorption (or reuptake) and enzymatic breakdown. If the excess is not removed the receiving neurons continue to respond as if they were receiving fresh messages. Cocaine primarily works by blocking the reuptake of dopamine and norepinephrine. The normal mind-altering effects of these two neurotransmitters are thereby enhanced.

Knowing how psychoactive drugs create their effects by altering neurotransmitter action, you can understand that the apparent high energy attributed to drugs such as cocaine comes not from the drug itself but from an accelerated use of the brain's own energy stores. As the effects of the drug wear off, this depletion of energy causes a relative depression of brain function and mood. There is then a strong motivation to regain the high state by taking the drug again, perhaps in a larger dose. After repeated "trips" and increasingly severe "crashes," the user may be tempted to take a stronger drug. Eventually it may be multiple drugs in dangerous, even deadly, combinations. Obviously this is harmful and abusive drug use.

Abuse versus Addiction

Is drug abuse the same as drug addiction? The term "drug abuse" is generally used to refer to drug taking that causes emotional or physical harm to the individual or others. The drug consumption is also typically compulsive and follows a high-frequency, intense pattern. The term "addiction" was initially used to describe heavy and compulsive drug use, but in recent times it has come to be used for almost any type of compulsive activity. Psychologist Stanton Peele (1984), for example, suggests that people may become "addicted" to television watching, work, or physical exercise programs like jogging, weightlifting, or aerobics. Two of the supposedly strongest addictions are romantic love and gambling (Blume, 1992).

Psychological Dependence: A desire or craving to achieve the effects produced by a drug.

Physical Dependence: A condition in which bodily processes have been so modified by repeated use of a drug that continued use is required to prevent withdrawal symptoms.

Withdrawal: Unpleasant, painful, or agonizing physical reactions resulting from discontinued use of a drug.

Because of the problems associated with such an all-encompassing definition, most drug researchers no longer use the term. Instead they use psychological dependence to refer to the mental desire or craving to achieve the effects produced by a drug and physical dependence to refer to the modifications of bodily processes that require use of the drug for minimum daily functioning. The state of physical dependence is shown most clearly when the drug is withheld, as the user undergoes painful physical reactions known as withdrawal.

Although psychological dependence is sometimes considered less dangerous than physical dependence, the effects on the drug user's life can be just as damaging. The desire or craving in psychological dependence can be so strong that the user ingests the drug regularly and maintains a constant drug-induced state. In addition, the psychological aspects of drug taking are often so powerful that an "addict" will return to his or her habit even after all signs of physical dependence are removed. Psychological and physical dependence may or may not occur together, as can be seen in Table 5.2.

Tolerance: A decreased sensitivity to a drug that requires larger and more frequent doses to produce the desired effect.

The term *addiction* is also commonly confused with the physiological process of tolerance, in which larger and more frequent doses of a drug are required to produce the desired effect. After repeated use of a drug, many of the body's physiological processes adjust to higher and higher levels of the drug (Poulos and Cappell, 1991). Amounts far above what might be a lethal dose for nonusers can be ingested with virtually no effect, pleasurable or adverse. Tolerance is also what leads many users to escalate their drug use and to experiment with other drugs in an attempt to recreate the originally pleasurable altered state.

Drug Effects

How a drug affects a particular individual depends on several factors, one of which is the route by which it enters the body (through the nasal membranes, the lungs, the digestive

Table 5.2   Effects of the Major Psychoactive Drugs

Category	Desired Effects	Undesirable Effects	Physical Dependence	Psychological Dependence	Tolerance
Depressants (Sedatives) Alcohol, barbiturates, antianxiety drugs (Valium)	Tension reduction, euphoria, disinhibition, drowsiness	Anxiety, nausea, disorientation, impaired reflexes and motor functioning, loss of consciousness, shallow respiration, convulsions, coma, death	Yes	Yes	Yes
Stimulants Cocaine, amphetamines	Exhilaration, euphoria, high physical and mental energy, perceptions of power and sociability, loss of appetite	Irritability, anxiety, paranoia, hallucinations, psychosis, convulsions, death	Yes	Yes	Yes
Caffeine	Increased alertness	Insomnia, restlessness, increased pulse rate, sleep disruption, mild delirium, ringing in the ears, rapid heartbeat	Yes	Yes	Some
Nicotine	Relaxation, increased alertness, sociability	Irritability, raised blood pressure, stomach pains, vomiting, dizziness, cancer, heart disease, emphysema, death	Yes	Yes	Some
Narcotics (Opiates) Morphine, heroin, codeine	Euphoria, "rush" of pleasure, pain relief, prevention of withdrawal discomfort	Nausea, vomiting, constipation, painful withdrawal, shallow respiration, convulsions, coma, death	Yes	Yes	Yes
Hallucinogens (Psychedelics) LSD (lysergic acid diethylamide)	Delusions, hallucinations, distorted perceptions and sensations	Longer and more extreme delusions, hallucinations, and perceptual distortions ("bad trips"), psychosis, death	No	No	Yes
Marijuana	Relaxation, mild euphoria, increased appetite	Perceptual and sensory distortions, hallucinations, fatigue, lack of motivation, paranoia, possible psychosis	No	Yes	Yes

Sources: Groves and Rebec (1988); Julien (1992); Leavitt (1984).

tract, or a vein. Drug effects come on much more quickly and powerfully (with a "rush") when drugs are taken through the lungs or intravenously, whereas absorption is delayed and prolonged in the digestive tract. Several routes of administration may be used for a given drug because it is available in different forms (leaf, pill, powder, or liquid).

Drug effects also depend on physical and psychological characteristics of the individual—"some people experience nothing even at high doses, while many others describe overwhelming sensations" (Snyder, 1980, p. 99). Physical characteristics that

Set: The internal state (beliefs and expectations) of a drug user that influences the overall effects of any drug.

Setting: The physical and interpersonal environment that surrounds a drug user and influences the effects of the drug.

influence drug effects include metabolic rate, disease conditions, and body weight and structure. The effects of alcohol, for example, can vary dramatically on the simple basis of body weight. As a general rule of thumb, the greater a person's body weight, especially if the body has more muscle than fat, the more alcohol the person can drink without feeling the effects (Leavitt, 1982).

Among the most important psychological determinants of a drug's effects are the set, or internal state of the drug taker (including his or her beliefs and expectations), and the setting, or physical and interpersonal environment surrounding the individual at the time the drug is being taken. According to Andrew Weil (1980), "drugs do not work unless set and setting encourage us to interpret their direct physical effects in ways that allow us to be high" (p. 41).

Gender and Cultural Diversity

A CULTURAL LOOK AT MARIJUANA AND COCAINE

A look at other cultures' experience with drugs demonstrates the effects of form and route of drug administration and set and setting. Recent anthropological studies of cocaine indicate that cultural variations in the form and route of drug ingestion have an enormous impact on the physiological process of addiction (Allen, 1989; Davis, 1990; Hamid, 1990). Many native Peruvians, for example, chew a wad of lime-treated coca leaves during their workday and throughout their lifetime. Yet few ever show signs of addiction. In cultures where the coca leaves are refined into cocaine, which is then smoked or snorted, a much higher dose of the drug reaches the brain and nervous system. The physiological response is entirely different in this case, and addiction is common.

When the National Institutes of Mental Health sponsored a comprehensive cross-cultural study of cannabis (marijuana) use, they discovered that its use and effects varied according to cultural expectations (Nanda, 1991). Participating in this cross-cultural project, William Partridge reported that in Colombia cannabis is smoked out in the fields in the context of work. It is thought by its users to make them better workers. Perceptions of cannabis as an energizer were also found in Jamaica.

These findings stand in dramatic contrast to the Western European and North American responses to marijuana where users typically report decreased energy and

North Americans and Western Europeans often experience a mellow relaxation after smoking marijuana. Some cultures, however, report that marijuana energizes them and makes them better workers.

motivation. With chronic use, some individuals become so listless and unmotivated that health professionals describe their condition as the *amotivational syndrome*.

It is easy to see why research in the field of cultural psychology has increased in recent years. By examining the practices and beliefs of people in other cultures, we not only gain insights into their world, we also raise important questions about our own beliefs and practices. ■

In the next section, we discuss specific groups of psychoactive drugs. For convenience, psychologists divide psychoactive drugs into four broad categories: depressants, stimulants, narcotics, and hallucinogens. Because most of the research cited is based on Western European and American responses, remind yourself of the importance of factors such as form and route and set and setting.

Depressants: Drugs That Suppress the Central Nervous System

Depressants, which include ethyl alcohol, barbiturates (e.g., Seconal), and antianxiety drugs (e.g., Valium), act on the central nervous system (CNS) to depress behavior, causing relaxation, sedation, or even loss of consciousness. Because tolerance and dependence (both physical and psychological) are rapidly acquired with these drugs, there is a strong potential for abuse.

Depressants: Psychoactive drugs that act on the central nervous system to suppress or slow down bodily processes and reduce overall responsiveness.

Understanding Alcohol

Alcohol is unquestionably the most widely used drug in Western society. Although it does have an overall sedative, depressant effect, it has a reputation for being a "party drug." Initially, it does seem to put people in a party mood. But with an increasing number of drinks and rising blood alcohol level, the sedative effects become obvious (see Table 5.3). With higher doses, the initial relaxed state is replaced with increasing degrees of cognitive, perceptual, verbal, and motor impairment. At the highest doses, the depressant effects can make the drinker "out of control" and incapable of voluntary action. If blood levels reach 0.5 percent, there is risk of coma and even death from respiratory depression (Julien, 1992).

What causes these effects? As mentioned, alcohol has a diffuse, destabilizing effect on cell membranes throughout the nervous system, which decreases neural firing—hence the term "depressant." In addition to this nonspecific effect, alcohol increases sensitivity to the neurotransmitter known as GABA, which promotes the initial feelings of relaxation and decreased anxiety.

The GABA connection is particularly interesting in light of our earlier discussion of drugs and their effect on neurotransmitters. The same researchers who found that alcohol makes GABA receptors more sensitive (Suzdak et al., 1986) also discovered a

Table 5.3   Alcohol's Effect on the Body and Behavior

Blood Alcohol Content (%)	Effect
.05	Relaxed state; judgment not as sharp
.08	Everyday stress lessened
.10[a]	Movements and speech become clumsy
.20	Very drunk; loud and difficult to understand; emotions unstable
.40	Difficult to wake up; incapable of voluntary action
.50	Coma and/or death

[a]Most states use .10 as the lowest indicator of driving while intoxicated. A few states use .08, while some go as high as .12.

drug that works as an alcohol antagonist. It *reverses* alcohol intoxication, presumably by blocking the GABA receptor sites. Don't become too excited about the possibilities of this "wonder drug," however. While it can block the intoxicating effects of alcohol, it does not reverse the effects on the hindbrain's breathing centers. Thus, a person could drink himself or herself to death without becoming drunk in the process. Drug companies have chosen to discontinue work on this drug because of moral and legal concerns.

Before leaving this discussion of the physiological effects of alcohol, it is important to point out that alcohol's effect is determined primarily by the amount that reaches the brain. Since the liver breaks down alcohol at the rate of about one ounce per hour, the number of drinks and the speed of consumption are very important. High school and college students have died after drinking extremely high amounts of alcohol in a short period of time. In addition, research shows that men's bodies are more efficient at breaking down alcohol (Frezza et al., 1990). Even after accounting for differences in size and muscle-to-fat ratio, women have a higher blood alcohol level than men following equal doses of alcohol.

Alcohol as a Social Concern

In addition to the effects of alcohol on the individual user, alcohol also plays a role in our most serious social problems. Did you know, for example, that alcohol is a factor in nearly half of all murders, suicides, and accidental deaths in the United States ("Alcohol's toll," 1993; Lord et al., 1987)? Or did you know that drinking drivers account for about one-half of all highway fatalities (Leavitt, 1982)? Medical authorities also list alcohol as the third leading cause of birth defects (Julien, 1992). When we add in the fact that about 7 percent of all adults in the United States are considered *problem drinkers*—people who get drunk at least once a month—we can see that alcohol abuse is an extremely important social issue.

Despite the aforementioned facts, many people do not consider alcohol a drug. Although the American Medical Association has long considered alcohol the most dangerous and physically damaging of all psychoactive drugs, drinking still enjoys wide social acceptance. Most people would undoubtedly be shocked and outraged by someone publicly "shooting up" a dose of heroin, yet they calmly accept alcohol consumption at major sporting events, parties, business lunches, and dinner get-togethers. Many parents express relief when they discover that their teenagers are "only drinking," yet surveys show this group is one of the largest of alcohol abusers (Foderaro, 1989; Leary, 1988). And teens, like most problem drinkers, usually deny that they have a problem.

Did you know that drunk drivers account for almost 50 percent of all highway fatalities? Because alcohol disrupts cognitive, perceptual, verbal, and motor skills, the driver's judgment and reaction time are seriously affected when under the influence of alcohol.

 *Try This Yourself*

If you are concerned about your own drinking, or that of a friend, you may want to ask yourself the following questions:

1. Are you frequently preoccupied with alcohol?
2. Do you often drink more than you intend?
3. Do you need more and more alcohol to get drunk?
4. Do you suffer withdrawal symptoms?
5. Despite repeated attempts, do you fail to cut down on drinking?
6. Are you frequently drunk or impaired when expected to fulfill social or occupational obligations?
7. Are you willing to give up important social, occupational, or recreational opportunities to drink?
8. Do you drink despite a significant social, occupational, or legal problem, or a physical disorder worsened by alcohol?

According to the American Psychiatric Association (1994), you have an alcohol dependency if you answered "yes" to three or more of these questions. ∎

Why do authorities warn us about mixing alcohol and barbiturates?   Combining alcohol and barbiturates is dangerous because of the synergistic effect, which means that the two drugs interact in such a way that the combined effects are much stronger than a simple summation of their individual doses. The combination of alcohol and barbiturates in particular can easily become fatal because it causes the diaphragm muscles to relax to such a degree that the person literally suffocates. Actress Judy Garland is among celebrities known to have died from barbiturate and alcohol mixture.

Synergistic Effect: The interaction of two or more drugs such that the combined effects are much stronger than a simple summation of their individual doses.

Review Questions

1. Drugs that change conscious awareness or perception are called _____ .
2. What are the four major ways psychoactive drugs act on neurotransmitters?
3. Drug taking that causes emotional or physical harm to the individual or others is known as _____ .
4. How does physical dependence differ from psychological dependence?
5. Among the most important psychological determinants of a drug's effects are the _____ and the _____ .
6. When two drugs interact in such a way that the combined effects are much stronger than a simple summation of their individual doses, they are said to have a _____ .

Answers to Review Questions can be found in Appendix C.

Stimulants: Drugs That Activate the Central Nervous System

Whereas depressants are "downers," stimulants are "uppers." Stimulant drugs act on the central nervous system to increase its overall activity and responsiveness. Nicotine, caffeine, amphetamines, and cocaine are the most common uppers used and abused in our society. Table 5.4 lists the caffeine content in common foods and over-the-counter drugs.

Stimulants: Drugs that act on the brain and nervous system, increasing their overall activity and general responsiveness.

Table 5.4 Common Sources of Caffeine

	Average (milligrams)
Coffee (5-ounce cup)	
Drip	145
Percolated	108
Instant	64
Tea (5-ounce cup)	50
Soft drinks (12 ounces)	40
OTC[a] stimulants (per tablet)	
Vivarin	200
No-Doz	100
OTC[a] analgesics (per tablet)	
Excedrin	65
Anacin, Midol, Vanquish	33
OTC[a] cold remedies (per teaspoon)	
Coryban-D, Triaminicin	30

[a]OTC = over the counter

Source: Adapted from Julien, 1992.

In low initial doses, the stronger stimulants (amphetamines and cocaine) promote feelings of high physical and mental energy and perceptions of power and invulnerability. This alternate state is highly reinforcing, leading the person to repeatedly try to recapture the high and avoid the inevitable comedown. The inevitable low that accompanies stimulant abuse is seldom acknowledged by the general public. Instead of recognizing that the high is the result of using bodily stores of energy to the point of depletion, many people falsely attribute the extra energy to something magical in the drug. Just as credit card purchases sometimes seem like an easy source of extra money, stimulants also seem to offer an easy source of extra energy. But after continued use of stimulants and higher doses, the "bills" come in: irritability, anxiety, paranoia, and auditory or visual hallucinations.

Cocaine Abuse

Cocaine was once considered a relatively harmless "recreational drug," and its potential for physical damage and severe psychological dependence was grossly underestimated (Fackelmann, 1989; Long, 1989). Sigmund Freud is often cited as a supporter of cocaine use, but few people know that in his later writings Freud warned that overuse could lead to severe depression and psychosis. But even small initial doses can be fatal, as the tragic death of the college basketball star Len Bias showed (Leo, 1986). Death can occur because cocaine interferes with the electrical system of the heart causing irregular heartbeats and resultant heart failure. It can also produce heart attacks by temporarily constricting blood supplies.

Animals who are allowed unlimited access to cocaine will self-administer the drug in long binges, and a significant number will self-administer a lethal dose (Koob and Bloom, 1988). Cocaine seems to have similar ill effects on human users. Some individuals may remain "social sniffers" who restrict their use to occasional recreational purposes, yet many individuals become "cokeaholics" who lose control over their consumption and jeopardize everything for the drug (Stone et al., 1985). The potential dangers for cocaine abuse used to be somewhat limited by its relatively high cost. In recent years, however, increased production and supply have lowered the cost and the development of cheaper forms (such as "crack") has made it widely available to all groups.

One of the primary reasons for cocaine's increasing popularity is that it reportedly induces strong feelings of power, security, and individual dynamism—emotions that are highly valued in our culture (Gawin, 1991; Stone et al., 1985). Repeated use of cocaine seems to create an inability to feel pleasure without the drug. Drug researchers Frank Gawin and Herbert Kleber (1984) have found that cocaine abusers "can't get off on the real world." They take the drug initially to feel powerful and dynamic but then find they can no longer feel even the small satisfactions of life.

Don't most drugs become addictive because the user can't enjoy life without them? Although every psychoactive drug alters the user's "normal" state of consciousness, which may affect their enjoyment of everyday life, cocaine seems to be one of the most rewarding of all known chemicals. Rats apparently find cocaine so irresistible they will self-administer to the point of death. Wise (1984) suggests that this may be due to cocaine's unique effect on the reward or pleasure centers of the brain (see Chapter 2). It is also known that cocaine and amphetamines increase feelings of energy and power largely because they increase the amount of available neurotransmitters in the synapse (depressants decrease the amount or block the transmission). The initial high is due to prolonging the neurotransmitters' effects, and the crash afterward is due to the depletion of these neurotransmitters. Some treatment programs help cocaine abusers kick their habit by administering certain drugs that mimic the effect of cocaine but are not habit forming and do not cause the same overall depletion of neurotransmitters.

An additional reason for cocaine's current popularity is its reputation as a "love drug." Throughout history, people have gone to great lengths in search of aphrodisiacs, substances that increase sexual desire. But cocaine, like alcohol, probably maintains its sexual reputation because it lowers inhibitions and because of the self-fulfilling nature of expectations. If people believe cocaine or any other substance will improve their sexual performance and enjoyment, they may act in such a way that they will make this belief come true. Current research is inconclusive regarding the exact relationship between cocaine and sexual desire.

Aphrodisiacs: Substances that supposedly increase sexual desire.

Narcotics: Drugs That Relieve Pain

Narcotics, which include morphine and heroin, numb the senses and thus are used medically to relieve pain (Julien, 1992). Narcotics are also called *opiates* because they are all derived from opium, the juice of the opium poppy. They are attractive to people seeking an alternate state of consciousness because they produce feelings of relaxation and euphoria. The euphoria generally results from relief of pain, tension, anxiety, and feelings of inferiority. Users report a happy glow of contentment and a rosy perception of reality. The reaction to heroin sometimes includes a "rush," or ecstatic thrill of pleasure that reportedly resembles sexual experiences—an "abdominal orgasm."

Narcotics: Drugs that are derived from opium and function as an analgesic or pain reliever.

If the opiate drugs are removed or withheld, the user experiences a very painful withdrawal. As we noted in Chapter 2, the brain produces chemicals closely resembling opiates (endorphins) and contains special receptor sites for them. Regular opiate use overloads the endorphin receptor sites, and the brain soon stops producing these substances. When the drugs are no longer taken, neither opiates nor endorphins are available for regulating pain and discomfort. Thus, the user experiences excruciating pains of withdrawal (Platt, 1986).

Hallucinogens: Drugs That Alter Perception

One of the most intriguing alterations of consciousness is through the use of hallucinogens, drugs that produce visual, auditory, or other sensory hallucinations. According to some reports, colors are brighter and more luminous, patterns seem to pulsate and rotate, and senses may seem to fuse—colors are "heard" or sounds "tasted." Perhaps as a result of these changes in normal sensory or perceptual experiences, hallucinogens are highly valued by some artists as a way of increasing creativity (Leavitt, 1982). Some

Hallucinogens: Drugs that produce visual, auditory, or other sensory hallucinations.

cultures have also used these drugs for religious purposes, as a way to experience "other realities" or to communicate with the supernatural. In Western societies, most people use hallucinogens for their reported "mind-expanding" potential, but it is not always a positive experience. Terror-filled "bad trips" and dangerous *flashbacks,* where the effects of the drug spontaneously reoccur long after the initial ingestion, can occur unpredictably.

Hallucinogens are also commonly referred to as *psychedelics* (from the Greek for "mind manifesting"). Hallucinogens include mescaline (derived from the peyote cactus, its effects on Aldous Huxley are described in the opening example), psilocybin (from mushrooms), phencyclidine (chemically derived), and LSD (derived from ergot, a rye mold). Marijuana ("pot," "grass," or hashish) is sometimes classified as a hallucinogen since in sufficient dosages it can produce mental effects similar to the stronger hallucinogens. We will focus on LSD and marijuana in our discussion because they are the most widely used of these drugs.

Visions from an LSD trip? According to psychologist Ronald Siegel, white lights that explode from the center to the periphery and spiral tunnels that pulsate and rotate are often reported during drug-induced hallucinations.

LSD

Lysergic acid diethylamide (LSD), an odorless, tasteless, and colorless substance, is one of the most potent drugs known. As little as 10 micrograms of LSD can produce a measurable effect in one individual, while an amount the size of a five-grain aspirin is enough to produce effects in 3,000 people. In 1943 Albert Hofman, the Swiss chemist who first synthesized LSD in a laboratory, accidentally licked some of the drug off his finger and later recorded in his journal:

> *Last Friday, April 16, 1943, I was forced to stop my work in the laboratory in the middle of the afternoon and to go home, as I was seized by a peculiar restlessness associated with a feeling of mild dizziness. Having reached home, I lay down and sank in a kind of drunkenness which was not unpleasant and which was characterized by extreme activity of imagination. As I lay in a dazed condition with my eyes closed (I experienced daylight as disagreeably bright) there surged upon me an uninterrupted stream of fantastic images of extraordinary plasticity and vividness and accompanied by an intense, kaleidoscope-like play of colors. This condition gradually passed off after about two hours.*
>
> Hofman (1968), pp. 184–185

Perhaps because the LSD experience is so powerful, few people actually "drop acid" on a regular basis, which may account for the fact that it has a relatively low reported abuse rate ("Psychedelic drugs," 1990). Because the LSD experience is so powerful, it is an extremely dangerous drug if the user is not prepared. Serious psychological reactions and even suicide can result if the user fails to interpret the LSD trip in the "appropriate" manner. Even if you are prepared, a "bad trip" can occur.

Marijuana

Marijuana is a hard drug to classify. It has some of the properties of depressants, as well as stimulants and hallucinogens. Regardless of its classification, it is one of the most popular of all illegal consciousness-altering drugs today. In low doses it induces a sense of relaxation and mild euphoria sometimes characterized by detachment or uncontrollable giggles. With higher doses subjects often report disruptions in time perception and sensory experiences and, with very high doses, visual or auditory hallucinations.

With the exception of alcohol during the time of Prohibition, there has never been a drug more hotly debated than marijuana—or more heavily researched (Weil and Rosen, 1983). For every study that lists no ill effects with moderate usage, there exists a conflicting study that lists dangers. These dangers include throat and respiratory disorders, impaired lung functioning and immune response, declines in testosterone levels, reduced sperm count, impairment of short-term memory, disruption of the menstrual cycle and ovulation, and brain atrophy (Bower, 1988; Fackelmann, 1989; Julien, 1992; Wallace and Fisher, 1983).

Arguments over the short-term and long-term dangers associated with marijuana use will undoubtedly continue for many years. However, some research has found marijuana to be therapeutic in the treatment of glaucoma, in alleviating the nausea and vomiting associated with chemotherapy, in increasing appetite, and in treating asthma, seizures, and anxiety (Julien, 1992; Leavitt, 1982). One anonymous survey of 1,035 cancer specialists found that 44 percent had recommended marijuana to at least one patient, 63 percent said that it was effective in the control of nausea and vomiting, and 48 percent said they would prescribe it if it were legal (Doblin and Kleiman, 1991).

A Concluding Note

We have just completed our whirlwind trip through the drugs people use to induce alternate states of consciousness. Before we go on, we'd like to offer a brief warning. We've tried to be as factual as possible in our presentation of this material, but the information is obviously limited and will quickly become dated. With all drug consumption, both prescription and "recreational," the consumer must assume the responsibility for maintaining a complete and up-to-date drug education. This warning is particularly important for illicit "street drugs." Since there are no truth-in-packaging laws to protect drug buyers from unscrupulous practices, sellers often substitute unknown, cheaper, and potentially even more dangerous substances for the ones they claim to be selling. The cocaine-related deaths of sports stars like Don Rogers can be traced to very potent or adulterated forms of the drug (Gold, Gallanter, and Stimmel, 1987). When you add in the danger of transmission of deadly infectious diseases such as AIDS and hepatitis, which can be passed through the sharing of nonsterile needles, the dangers of drug use go far beyond the ones associated with the particular drug itself.

In addition to these "old" problems that have been with us for years, we also face some new ones. New and untried drugs, like clove cigarettes and the so-called designer drugs created by "street chemists," pose unknown threats. A synthetic drug that has caused particular concern is crystal methamphetamine (a form of amphetamine). This drug, the cheapest form is known as "ice," produces insomnia, anxiety, depression, and serious psychotic symptoms that are sometimes indistinguishable from paranoid schizophrenia (Largent, 1989).

Designer Drugs: Drugs produced by slightly altering the molecular structure of psychoactive drugs, thereby creating a new drug that has similar effects.

Given the basic human desire to experiment with other states of consciousness, we would like to offset the serious concerns associated with drugs by encouraging more positive routes to alternate states. The fact is that many benefits associated with drugs, such as relaxation and improved mood, can be achieved through nondrug methods such as daydreams or fantasies, hypnosis, meditation, and physical exercise. We discuss these psychological methods in the next section.

Review Questions

1. What are the four major categories of psychoactive drugs and how do they differ?

2. The strongest illegal stimulants most commonly abused are _____ and _____ .

3. The use of _____ leads to a powerful experience characterized mostly by visual hallucinations.

4. When street chemists take a known drug and slightly alter its molecular structure, they create a _____ .

Answers to Review Questions can be found in Appendix C.

Critical Thinking
PSYCHOLOGY IN ACTION
DISTINGUISHING FACT FROM OPINION
Understanding Claims about Drug Use and Abuse

The topic of drugs often generates heated debate between people with different perspectives. When discussing controversial issues, it is helpful to make a distinction between statements of *fact* and statements of *opinion*. A fact is a statement that can be proven true or false. An opinion is a statement that expresses how a person feels about an issue or what someone thinks is true. Although it is also important to determine whether the facts *are* true or false, in this exercise simply mark "O" for opinion and "F" for fact to test your ability to distinguish between the two.

_____ 1. Marijuana is now one of America's principal cash crops.

_____ 2. Friends don't let friends drive drunk.

_____ 3. People who use drugs aren't hurting anyone but themselves.

_____ 4. Legalizing drugs such as cocaine, marijuana, and heroin would make them as big a problem as alcohol and tobacco.

_____ 5. The number of cocaine addicts is small compared with the number of alcoholics.

_____ 6. The American Medical Association considers alcohol to be the most dangerous of all psychoactive drugs.

_____ 7. Random drug tests are justified for personnel involved with public safety (e.g., air traffic controllers, police officers, etc.).

_____ 8. If parents use drugs, their children are more likely to use drugs.

_____ 9. Mothers who deliver cocaine-addicted babies are guilty of child abuse.

_____ 10. Alcohol abuse by pregnant mothers is one of the most important factors in mental retardation.

from Bach, 1988.)

ANSWERS: 1. F; 2. O; 3. O; 4. O; 5. F. Rather than offering specific answers to the remaining questions, we suggest that you discuss your answers with your classmates and friends. Listening to the reasons others give for their answers often provides valuable insights in distinguishing between fact and opinion. (Adapted

ADDITIONAL ROUTES TO ALTERNATE STATES

• *How do daydreams, hypnosis, and meditation create alternate states of consciousness?*

As we have discovered thus far in this chapter, alternate states of consciousness may be reached through everyday means such as sleep and dreaming or through the chemical channel of drugs. In this section we explore three additional routes for changing consciousness: daydreaming, hypnosis, and meditation.

Daydreaming: A Special Type of Alternate State

Daydreaming: An alternate state of consciousness characterized by internal reverie or inwardly focused thought.

Daydreaming, or fantasizing, is a personal form of reverie or inwardly focused thought. It is one of the most commonly experienced ASCs. Scientists have found that during a typical 24-hour period we spend as much as one-third of our waking hours daydreaming (Foulkes and Fleisher, 1975; Webb and Cartwright, 1978).

Why do we daydream? Most people daydream during quiet, private moments when outside events are boring or automatized, such as while waiting at bus stops or washing dishes. It appears that our consciousness responds to an unchanging external world by turning inward and creating more interesting thoughts and images. Daydreaming while sitting in a lecture or driving a car may be counterproductive and potentially dangerous, but under other circumstances it can be helpful. Daydreaming not only helps us cope with boring tasks and difficult situations, it also seems to allow mental relaxation, improve intellectual functioning, and release creative abilities (Klinger, 1987; Starker, 1982).

Sexual Fantasies

Daydreams or fantasies also seem to be important to our sexual functioning (Klinger, 1990). Studies have shown that self-created sexual fantasies allow individuals to control or "fine tune" their excitement and arousal (Davidson and Hoffman, 1986). Also, when long-term relationships begin to seem boring, couples have used fantasies to provide novelty and renewed excitement.

While studies have shown that fantasies about sex with strangers, group sex, or forced sex are common (Ellis and Symons, 1990; Hunt, 1974), it is important to recognize that our sexual fantasies do not necessarily reflect what we would like to happen in reality. For example, sex educators Kathryn Kelley and Donn Byrne (1992) offer an important insight into rape fantasies:

> *Women do not want to be raped, but rape fantasies are often enjoyable and arousing. Being a victim of a rapist is neither enjoyable nor arousing. An analogy might help clarify the distinction. Many people enjoy murder mysteries and horror movies, but this does not indicate that they wish to murder anyone, be murdered, or interact with flesh-eating creatures from outer space. (p. 308)*

Hypnosis: Alternate Consciousness or Role Playing?

Many students are initially surprised to find that hypnosis is a respectable topic for a college textbook. Because of its "shady" past and its association with quackery and magic, hypnosis has often been glibly dismissed. It can be, however, a legitimate psychological phenomenon and medical technique.

What exactly is hypnosis?   Hypnosis is an alternate state of consciousness characterized by one or more of the following: (1) heightened suggestibility (increased willingness to respond to proposed changes in perceptions—"this onion is an apple"); (2) narrowing and focusing of attention (the subject is able to "tune out" competing sensory stimuli); (3) an effortless use of imagination and hallucinations (in the case of visual hallucinations, subjects may see things that aren't there or not see things that are); (4) a passive and receptive attitude; and (5) decreased responsiveness to pain (Hilgard, 1986, 1992; Plotnick, Payne, and O'Grady, 1991).

Hypnosis: An alternate state of heightened suggestibility characterized by relaxation and intense focus.

The characteristic of increased suggestibility is often used to argue that hypnosis is *not* a separate and distinct state of consciousness. Barber (1969, 1986) and Sarbin (1988, 1992), for example, suggest that hypnosis is simply the result of experimental (1) *demand characteristics* (the subject attempts to please the experimenter and tries not to "ruin the show"), (2) *role playing* (the subject plays the role he or she believes a "hypnotized" person is expected to play), and (3) *personal expectancy* of how easily he or she can be hypnotized or of what hypnosis is like. The other argument against hypnosis as an ASC is that it has been difficult to demonstrate physiological differences between hypnotized and unhypnotized subjects in terms of eye movements, brain wave patterns, respiration, and heart rate.

Dissociation

One of the most convincing theories supporting the idea that hypnosis *is* a unique and separate state of consciousness is dissociation. In dissociation one part of your mind is conscious of certain experiences (and can report on them) and another part is not (Hilgard, 1992). Have you ever arrived at your destination and realized that you didn't remember a single detail of the drive? The fact that you managed to make all the right turns, stopped at stop signs, and maneuvered through traffic is evidence of your own experience with dissociation or the automatic processing mentioned earlier in this chapter. In a similar fashion, people can be hypnotized and one part of their mind will be

Dissociation: A splitting or separating of consciousness. Under hypnosis, one part of consciousness seems to be aware and observing hypnotic suggestions, while another part is responding to the suggestion.

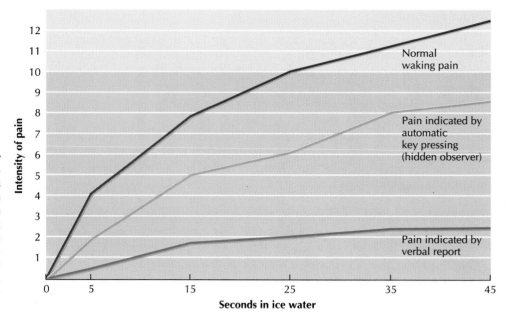

Figure 5.9 Pain perception under hypnosis. Compared with unhypnotized subjects, hypnotized subjects will verbally report little pain while their hands are submerged in ice water (the bottom blue line). When asked to report the pain through the "eyes" of the *hidden observer,* however, the subjects will press a key indicating a higher level of pain. [Source: Hilgard, E. R. (1977). Reprinted with permission.]

unaware of strong sensations of pain while another part seems to be watching and monitoring. This "hidden observer" is easily seen in research where subjects are hypnotized not to feel pain while their hands are in ice water for 45 seconds, a situation that normally produces intense pain (Hilgard, 1978). However, when these same subjects are asked to report the pain through "the eyes" of the hidden observer, they will press a key that indicates a higher level of pain. As shown in Figure 5.9, one part of the mind is apparently aware of the pain while the other is fully hypnotized and unaware.

Dissociation theory is an intriguing explanation of hypnosis, but it is not universally accepted (Sarbin, 1988, 1992; Spanos et al., 1992). Some critics argue that the "hidden observer" in dissociation is also engaging in a subtle form of role playing. While psychologists continue to debate whether hypnosis *is* or is *not* a separate form of consciousness, magicians and entertainers continue to amuse large audiences by asking volunteers to impersonate the opposite sex and cluck like a chicken.

Four Popular Myths

1. Forced hypnosis   One of the most common misconceptions is that people can be hypnotized against their will. Because hypnosis requires the subject to make a conscious decision to relinquish control of his or her consciousness to another person, it is virtually impossible to hypnotize an unwilling subject. As a matter of fact, about 8 to 9 percent of the population *cannot* be hypnotized even when they are willing and trying very hard to cooperate. The best potential subjects are able to focus attention, open to new experience, and capable of imaginative involvement or fantasy (Lynn and Rhue, 1988; Nadon et al., 1991).

2. Unethical behavior   A related misconception is that hypnosis can make a person behave immorally or take dangerous risks against his or her will. Generally, people will not go against their strongest and most basic values. However, stage hypnotists have persuaded individuals to disrobe in public, and in experiments, hypnotized subjects have thrown what they believed to be *acid* in a research assistant's face (Orne and Evans, 1965). Before concluding that hypnosis *does* have unusually powerful effects, it is important to point out that when Orne and Evans also asked a control group of subjects to simply *pretend* that they had been hypnotized, they achieved the same results.

Although many believe that people can be hypnotized against their will, it is virtually impossible to hypnotize an unwilling subject. Stage hypnotists solicit volunteers from the audience who eagerly co-operate and generally want to be hypnotized.

How would you explain this? There are at least three possible explanations. First, since both the hypnotized and the nonhypnotized subjects behaved in a similar fashion, hypnosis may *not* be a special, separate form of consciousness. All subjects may have simply conformed to the "role" they thought was expected of them as a hypnotized person. Second, hypnosis may be real, but it may act only as a *disinhibitor* of behavior. Like alcohol and other drugs, hypnosis may relax or reduce normal inhibitions that generally restrain individuals from acting in socially undesirable ways. Hypnotized subjects may have felt that they could not be held responsible for their actions while they were hypnotized, and the pretend subjects may have mimicked this disinhibited behavior. Finally, the hypnotist/experimenter may have been seen as an authority figure and the experiment as a legitimate context for obedience. As shown in Chapter 1, people have been induced to do things they wouldn't think they would do when they perceived the experimenter as a legitimate authority.

3. Superhuman strength   It is also a misconception that under hypnosis people can perform acts of special, superhuman strength. When nonhypnotized subjects are simply asked to try their hardest on tests of physical strength, they can generally do anything that a hypnotized subject can do (Barber, 1976). You can recreate a common demonstration of superhuman strength used by stage hypnotists. Simply get two chairs and a willing friend (see Figure 5.10).

4. Exceptional memory   On rare occasions, the relaxed state of hypnosis has allowed witnesses and victims of violent crimes to remember crucial facts that have led authorities to the criminals. Exactly what role hypnosis played in solving these cases remains controversial. Would the facts eventually have been remembered? What is certain is that using hypnosis to solve crimes creates problems for the legal process. Memories are imperfect, personal constructions (Loftus, 1980, 1992; see also Chapter 7). Researchers have found that some parts of recall memory are improved under hypnosis because the subject is able to relax and focus intently, but they have also found that the number of errors increased. When pressed to recreate details, hypnotized subjects have more difficulty separating fact and fantasy and are more willing to guess (Dywan, 1984). Consequently, a growing number of judges and state bar associations ban the use of

Figure 5.10 Magician's tricks versus hypnosis. This is a favorite trick of stage hypnotists that is supposed to convince the audience that hypnosis confers superhuman strength. If you try this at home with a willing friend, however, you will see hypnosis isn't necessary.

hypnosis and the testimony of hypnotized subjects from the courtroom (Spiegel, 1985; Stark, 1984).

Therapeutic Uses

Hypnosis has been widely used in both medical and psychotherapy settings (Fromm, 1992; Weir, 1990). Before the discovery of anesthetics like ether and cloroform, hypnosis was commonly used with surgical patients. It is still occasionally used today when anesthetics cannot be used and in the treatment of chronic pain (see Chapter 13). Hypnosis has found its best use in medical areas where patients have a high degree of fear and misinformation, such as dentistry and obstetrics. Because pain is strongly affected by tension and anxiety, any technique that helps relax the patient is medically useful.

In psychotherapy, hypnosis can help patients relax, remember, or reduce anxiety. It has had limited success in the treatment of phobias, and in attempts to lose weight, stop cigarette smoking, and improve study habits (Long, 1986). Many athletes use self-hypnosis techniques of mental imagery and focused attention. Long-distance runner Steve Ortiz, for example, mentally relives all his best races before a big meet. By the time the race actually begins he says, "I'm almost in a state of self-hypnosis. I'm just floating along" (cited in Kiester, 1984, p. 23).

Meditation: A "Higher" State of Consciousness?

Meditation: A group of techniques designed to focus attention and produce a heightened state of awareness.

Meditation refers to a group of techniques designed to focus attention and produce a heightened state of awareness. Success in meditation requires control of the mind's natural tendency to wander (the previously mentioned "stream of consciousness").

Some meditation techniques focus on body movements and postures, as in T'ai Chi and Hatha Yoga. In other techniques, the meditator remains motionless, attending to a single focal point—gazing at a stimulus (such as a candle flame), observing the breath, or silently repeating a mantra. (A mantra is a specially designed sound, word, or phrase used for mind concentration or spiritual worship.)

Meditation has only recently gained acceptance and popularity in America, primarily for its relaxation and anxiety reduction value. It has, however, been practiced in some parts of the world for centuries, primarily as a means of spiritual development. Among the most interesting claims for meditation is that it offers a "higher" and more enlightened form of consciousness, superior to that of all other levels, and that it allows meditators to have remarkable control over bodily processes.

What can be achieved with meditation? In the beginning stages of meditation, subjects often report a mellow type of relaxation, followed by a mild euphoria. With long practice, some advanced meditators report experiences of profound rapture and joy or strong hallucinations (Smith, 1982). A particularly vivid description is provided by Gopi Khrishna (1971):

> *Suddenly, with a roar like that of a waterfall, I felt a stream of liquid light entering my brain through the spinal cord. The illumination grew brighter and brighter, the roaring louder. I experienced a rocking sensation and then felt myself slipping out of my body, entirely enveloped in a halo of light. I felt the point of consciousness that was myself growing wider, surrounded by waves of light. (pp. 12–13)*

With sophisticated electronic equipment, researchers have verified that meditation can produce dramatic changes in basic physiological processes such as brain waves, heart rate, oxygen consumption, and sweat gland activity (Benson, 1988; Pagano and Warrenberg, 1983). For the one out of four Americans who suffers from high blood pressure, it may be useful to know that meditation has proven successful in reducing stress and lowering blood pressure (Alexander et al., 1989; Gaylord, Orme-Johnson, and

Travis, 1989). Blood pressure, visual acuity, and auditory threshold are often used to calculate an individual's biological age, and on all three measures long-term meditators have been found significantly younger than a chronologically matched age group (Wallace et al., 1982). Meditation has also been helpful in reducing substance abuse (Gelderloos et al., 1991) and recidivism among maximum security prisoners (Bleick and Abrams, 1987).

 Try This Yourself

You can experience many of the benefits of meditation by practicing the relaxation technique developed by Herbert Benson (1977).

1. Pick a focus word or short phrase that is firmly rooted in your personal value system (such as "love," "peace," "one," "shalom," "Hail, Mary, full of grace").

2. Sit quietly in a comfortable position, close your eyes, and relax your muscles.

3. Focusing on your breathing, breathe through your nose, and as you breathe out say your focus word or phrase silently to yourself. Continue for 10 to 20 minutes. You may open your eyes to check the time, but do not use an alarm. When you have finished, sit quietly for several minutes, at first with closed eyes and later with opened eyes.

4. Maintain a passive attitude throughout the exercise—permit relaxation to occur at its own pace. When distracting thoughts occur, ignore them and gently return to your repetition.

5. Practice the technique once or twice daily, but not within two hours after a meal—the digestive processes seem to interfere with a successful relaxation response. ■

Review Questions

1. Why do we daydream?

2. _____ is an alternate state of heightened suggestibility characterized by relaxation and intense focus.

3. During _____ one part of the mind is conscious of certain experiences and another part is unconscious.

4. Why is it almost impossible to hypnotize an unwilling subject?

5. Unlike hypnosis, _____ produces verifiable changes in basic physiological processes.

Answers to Review Questions can be found in Appendix C.

REVIEW OF MAJOR CONCEPTS

STUDYING CONSCIOUSNESS

1. Consciousness is the general state of being aware and responsive to stimuli and events in both the external and internal environments. Our consciousness consists of a continuously changing flow of awareness known as the *stream of consciousness*. It also exists along a continuum of awareness. Alternate states of consciousness (ASCs) differ from normal waking consciousness in the dimensions of awareness and control.

2. While the study of consciousness has waxed and waned among psychologists, the general public has historically been very interested—particularly in the ASCs. Among

peoples of all cultures, ASCs (1) are part of sacred rituals, (2) serve social and political needs, and (3) provide individual rewards.

SLEEP AND DREAMING

3. Biological rhythms affect many aspects of our lives. Circadian rhythm has a particular effect on our sleep and waking cycle, and disruptions in this rhythm can cause problems, such as fatigue from shift work and jet lag.

4. A typical night's sleep consists of four to five 90-minute cycles. The cycle begins in Stage 1 and then moves through Stages 2, 3, and 4. After reaching the deepest level of sleep, the cycle reverses up to the REM state. In REM (rapid eye movement) sleep, the eyes dart rapidly about under the eyelids. During REM sleep, the brain pattern of the sleeper is similar to the waking state and the person often is dreaming.

5. The exact function of sleep is not known, but it is thought to be necessary for its restorative value, both physically and psychologically. It also has some adaptive, evolutionary functions. Sleep seems to be controlled by various areas of the brain and by several neurotransmitters.

6. There are two major theories that attempt to explain why we dream. The wish-fulfillment theory says dreams are disguised symbols of repressed desires. The activation–synthesis hypothesis argues that dreams are simply unimportant by-products of random stimulation of brain cells.

7. There are several different types of dreams: lucid dreams, in which the person knows that he or she is dreaming; nightmares, which are bad dreams experienced during REM; and night terrors, which are terrifying dreams usually experienced in Stage 4 of NREM sleep.

8. Sleep problems include insomnia, sleep apnea, and narcolepsy. Insomnia is experienced by people who have repeated difficulty in falling asleep. Sleep apnea is a condition in which a person temporarily stops breathing during sleep, causing loud snoring or poor quality sleep. Narcolepsy is excessive daytime sleepiness characterized by sudden sleep attacks.

DRUGS AND CONSCIOUSNESS

9. Psychoactive drugs are those drugs that change conscious awareness or perception. The major categories of psychoactive drugs are depressants, stimulants, narcotics, and hallucinogens. Depressant drugs slow down the central nervous system, whereas stimulants activate it. Narcotics relieve pain, and hallucinogens or psychedelics alter perceptions.

10. Psychoactive drug use can lead to psychological dependence or physical dependence or both. Psychological dependence is a desire or craving to achieve the effects produced by a drug. Physical dependence is a change in bodily processes due to continued drug use that results in withdrawal symptoms when the drug is withheld. Tolerance to a drug is a physiological process that creates the need for larger and more frequent doses of a drug to produce the desired effect. The effects of a particular drug depend on many factors, including the setting and the person's psychological set.

11. Cross-cultural studies reveal not only the importance of form and route, but that use and effects of drugs vary according to cultural expectations. In Colombia, for example, marijuana is considered an energizer, in contrast to the North American view that marijuana decreases motivation.

ADDITIONAL ROUTES TO ALTERNATE STATES

12. One of the most commonly experienced ASCs is daydreaming or fantasizing. Most people daydream frequently during private quiet moments. Daydreams and sexual fantasies serve important functions in our lives.

13. Hypnosis is an alternate state of heightened suggestibility characterized by relaxation and intense focus. Hypnosis has been used to reduce pain and increase concentration. Some researchers argue that hypnosis is not a separate state of consciousness, whereas others argue that it is a distinct dissociative state.

14. Meditation is a group of techniques designed to focus attention and produce a heightened awareness. Meditation can produce dramatic changes in physiological processes, including heart rate and respiration.

SUGGESTED READINGS

DEMENT, W. C. (1976). *Some must watch while some must sleep*. New York: Norton. Intended for nonprofessional readers, this paperback offers a survey of major sleep disorders, as well as normal sleeping and dreaming.

ELLMAN, S. J., & ANTROBUS, J. S. (EDS.). (1991). *The mind in sleep: Psychology and psychophysiology*. New York: Wiley. An excellent review of research on many aspects of sleep and dreams.

GACKENBACK, J., & BOSVELD, J. (1989). *Control your dreams*. New York: Harper & Row. An entertaining and interesting look at the "how-to's" of lucid dreaming.

JULIEN, R. (1992). *A primer of drug action* (6th ed.). San Francisco: Freeman. An excellent resource for the background, mechanisms of action, and effects of psychoactive drugs.

KELLY, S. F., & KELLY, R. J. (1985). *Hypnosis: Understanding how it can work for you*. Reading, MA: Addison-Wesley. An interesting and helpful text that describes the use of hypnosis in overcoming common problems (such as anxiety, smoking, and overeating) and how it is used and misused in detective work and the courtroom.

SIEGEL, R. (1989). *Intoxication: Life in pursuit of artificial paradise*. New York: Dutton. Psychopharmacologist Dr. Ronald

Siegel explains his controversial theory that the desire for intoxication is actually a fourth drive, as unstoppable as hunger, thirst, and sex.

TRIMBLE, J. E., BOLCK, C. S., & NIEMERYK, S. J. (EDS). (1993). *Ethnic and multicultural drug abuse: Perspectives on current research.* Binghamton, NY: Haworth Press. A compilation of cutting-edge research in drug abuse with specific ethnic-minority groups.

WALLACE, B., & FISHER, L. E. (1991). *Consciousness and behavior* (3rd ed). Boston: Allyn & Bacon. A far-ranging discussion of the general topic of consciousness.

Learning

OUTLINE

When you visit the gorillas, orangutans, and chimpanzees at the zoo, do you have the feeling that they are looking at you just as much as you are looking at them? Do their behaviors strike you as being amazingly humanlike? Have you ever felt like crossing over the wall separating you and trying to see if you could somehow communicate with them? Francine (Penny) Patterson did cross barriers to do just this. Thanks to the San Francisco Zoo, she acquired a gorilla, Koko, whom she taught to communicate through American Sign Language. After less than a month of watching people use sign language and only two days of formal training, Koko signed her first word. As Patterson describes the experience:

> [Koko] consistently responded with close approximations of the *food* sign when I offered her tidbits of fruit. Most frequently she put her index finger to her mouth, but she also made the sign correctly—putting all the fingers of one hand, held palm down, to her mouth. As it dawned on me that for the first time she was consistent and deliberate in her signing, I wanted to jump for joy. Finally she seemed to have made the connection between the gesture and the delivery of food, to have discovered that she could direct my behavior with her own.
>
> *Patterson and Linden, 1981, p. 28*

Thus, Koko learned to associate a specific gesture with the object it represented. How did she learn this? How could an ape learn to use hand symbols to communicate her needs to others when neither she nor her predecessors had ever done this? Below, Patterson explains the procedure she used to teach Koko the *food* sign.

> I praised Koko profusely and seized every chance to get her to sign *food,* showering her with treats in the process. Whenever she reached for some food, I would prompt her by signing *food,* and almost every time she responded. I made sure that she realized she was supposed to ask for things by name by pushing her hand away and signing *no* when she did not make the sign. On several occasions Koko signed *food* without any prompting on my part. After her nap I gave Koko another twenty or so opportunities to sign *food,* and she responded incorrectly only toward the end of the afternoon, by which time the stuffed gorilla had no interest in food whatsoever.
>
> *Patterson and Linden, 1981, p. 28*

At first, Penny Patterson rewarded Koko with pieces of fruit if the gorilla made any sign that even resembled the correct one. Gradually, Patterson rewarded only those gestures that were formed correctly. It was through a system of reinforcements that Koko learned sign language. Patterson has continued to work with Koko on using reinforcement, and today Koko knows over 600 different signs and continues to learn new ones.

There is no doubt that Koko has learned to communicate with humans. That is not to imply the language abilities of gorillas are comparable to those of humans: They very decidedly are not. Human language is exceedingly complex and involves much more than simple associations of signs or sounds with objects (see Chapter 8). The *learning* of human language is likewise exceedingly complex. Language is not learned in the simple way Koko learned sign language. Nevertheless, people and animals do learn many behaviors through systems of rewards and punishment. Rewards and punishments are effective in teaching seals to honk horns for tidbits of fish, students to study hard for A's on final exams, and drivers to stay within the speed limit in order to not get a ticket.

In this chapter, we will examine the major theories that explain how we learn. People learn through association, through mental operations, and through observing others. We will discuss techniques psychologists such as Pavlov and B. F. Skinner have used in learning research. We will explore the many factors that can affect how readily people learn things. Finally, we will show you how to apply what you learn about learning to your own life.

As you read Chapter 6, keep the following **Survey** questions in mind and answer them in your own words:

- What are the different kinds of learning?
- How does pairing a reflex to a neutral stimulus lead to the type of learning known as classical conditioning? How do extinction, spontaneous recovery, generalization, and discrimination occur?
- How do consequences lead to the type of learning known as operant conditioning? How do extinction, spontaneous recovery, generalization, and discrimination occur?
- How do we learn according to cognitive learning theory?
- Can people learn merely by watching other people?

LEARNED AND INNATE BEHAVIORS

Not all animal behaviors are learned. Although the extent depends on the species, at least some behavior is innate, or inborn, in the form of either reflexes or instincts. It appears that all animals are "preprogrammed" to engage in certain innate behaviors at a predetermined point in their maturation. Often, an innate behavior emerges when some type of environmental stimulus triggers the behavior. We have all experienced reflexive reactions. When a gnat flies too close to our eyes, we automatically blink. When we touch a hot pan, we reflexively pull our hand away. When infants feel a light touch on the cheek, they turn their heads toward the touch, with their mouths searching for that milk-giving nipple. Reflexes allow animals to deal with specific stimuli that are critical to their survival with rigid, automatic responses.

Although humans do exhibit reflexive behaviors, it is generally agreed that we do not engage in instinctive behaviors. Whereas a reflex consists of a single response, an instinct comprises a complex sequence of responses, such as the elaborate mating rituals of some species of birds or the instinctive paddling responses of dogs thrown into deep water. For many years, it was thought that instincts were totally genetically determined and were completely independent of environmental influence. More recent research has shown, however, that many behaviors, such as singing in birds, arise from a combination of genetic factors and environmental influences (Gordon, 1989; Marler and Mundinger, 1971).

- *What are the different kinds of learning*

Innate: Referring to any inborn behavior that emerges during a predetermined period of an organism's life as a result of maturation only and not as a result of practice.

Learned Behavior: A Result of Experience

In stark contrast to innate behavior is learned behavior. We engage in learned behavior as a result of environmental influence, as opposed to some type of genetic programming. We learn through actively doing things, we learn through associating one item with another, and we learn through observing others. In other words, the behaviors we learn result from interactions with people, events, or objects in our environment.

Learning is defined as a relatively permanent change in behavior or behavioral potential as a result of practice or experience. Let's take a moment to examine this definition bit by bit. Because learning is a *change* in behavior or *behavioral potential*, it might consist of changes in immediate behavior (e.g., changing your breaststroke immediately after your swim instructor suggests an improvement). Or it might consist of behavioral changes that occur much later but are the result of experience (changing your breaststroke after watching the moves of a champion swimmer on TV). It could even consist of changes that could potentially be initiated but never are because the opportunity never arises (by watching that champion swimmer, you know how to improve your stroke but never again go swimming).

Learning: A relatively permanent change in behavior or behavioral potential as a result of practice or experience.

These tigers have learned to perform a variety of tricks in response to the commands of their trainer.

Note in this definition that learning is *relatively* permanent. This means that any learned behavior is not necessarily permanent and can possibly be unlearned. Also, learning is a *result of practice or experience.* This reflects the fact that learning can result from actively performing a behavior or merely from passively experiencing (watching or hearing) someone or something else.

How Do We Learn Things? Let Us Count the Ways

Most psychologists and educators agree that we learn our myriad behaviors through a variety of methods. However, there are some learning theorists who staunchly proclaim one type of learning as the method by which we learn everything we know. In our overview of learning principles, we will isolate the major types of learning and discuss them separately, but keep in mind that most of our complex human behaviors are not learned solely by one method.

In the opening preview to this chapter, you read how Koko learned the appropriate gesture for food by receiving a bite to eat after associating the *food* sign with actual food. One theory of learning views learning solely in this way: as an association between some external stimulus (food, a bell, a snake) and a response (salivation, an eyeblink, a change in blood pressure). Learning an association between a stimulus and a response is called conditioning. One type of conditioning, called classical conditioning, involves learning reflexive, involuntary responses to stimuli that don't normally cause such responses. Another type of conditioning, called operant conditioning, the one by which Koko learned the *food* sign, involves learning voluntary responses to stimuli through the consequences of previous responses.

Another theory of learning is more concerned with the thinking processes involved in learning. Known as cognitive learning theory, it proposes that learning involves more than observable responses to stimuli. Proponents of this theory believe there is an inner, subjective element in learning that sometimes cannot be directly observed or measured. Consequently, they study the thought processes underlying the observable behaviors of their subjects.

Observational learning theory combines elements of conditioning and cognitive learning theories. It explains how we can learn certain behaviors through watching

Conditioning: The type of learning involving stimulus–response connections, in which the response is conditional on the stimulus.

Classical Conditioning: Learning a response to a neutral stimulus when that neutral stimulus is paired with a stimulus that causes a reflex response.

Operant Conditioning: Learning that occurs when a response to an environmental cue is reinforced.

Cognitive Learning Theory: The idea that learning involves more than an observable response, that it often involves thought processes that may not be directly observed or objectively measured.

Observational Learning Theory: The idea that we learn certain behaviors merely by watching someone else perform them.

models perform them. Depending on our esteem for the model or the consequences of the behavior we observe, we learn to mimic or not to mimic the model's behavior.

Now that we have briefly introduced the major approaches to the study of learning, let us look at each one in greater detail. Remember as you read that few psychologists adhere strictly to any one theory as the explanation for all learning.

Review Questions

1. Compare and contrast reflexes with instincts.
2. A change in behavior that is relatively permanent, results from practice or experience, and is *solely* a result of environmental influence is called _____ .
3. Do we learn each type of behavior by one certain learning method? Explain.

Answers to Review Questions can be found in Appendix C.

CONDITIONING

As explained, *conditioning* is a type of learning that occurs when an association is made between a stimulus and a behavioral response. The two major types of conditioning are classical conditioning and operant conditioning.

• How does pairing a reflex to a neutral stimulus lead to the type of learning known as classical conditioning? How do extinction, spontaneous recovery, generalization, and discrimination occur?

Classical Conditioning: Learning through Stimulus Pairing

Have you ever noticed that when you are hungry and see a large slice of chocolate cake or a juicy steak, your mouth starts to water? It seems natural that your mouth should water if you put food into it, but why should your mouth water simply when you see food or sometimes merely think of food? This is a question Ivan Pavlov contemplated over 80 years ago. Pavlov was a Russian physiologist who conducted pioneering work on the digestive system, work for which he was eventually awarded the first Russian Nobel Prize for physiology and medicine.

One of Pavlov's experiments involved salivary responses in dogs. In studying how the salivary glands respond to different types of food, Pavlov attached to a dog's salivary gland a glass funnel that directed the saliva into a container where it could be measured. In this way, Pavlov was able to determine that dry food required more saliva than moist food and that nonfood objects required varying amounts of saliva, depending on how hard it was to spit them out. During this research, Pavlov noticed that many of his dogs would begin to salivate as soon as they entered the experimental room or saw the people who normally fed them. Although this "unscheduled" salivation originally irritated him because it interfered with his original research design, Pavlov eventually decided to conduct a systematic investigation into the reason behind it.

Pavlov designed an experiment (see Figure 6.1) in which he could measure and record the amount of saliva produced when a neutral stimulus was paired with the presentation of food. He used a bell as the neutral stimulus, since a bell was something that wouldn't normally elicit salivation when presented by itself. He paired the bell with meat powder, which when presented to the dogs *would* naturally produce a salivation reflex. Pavlov's experimental procedure went as follows:

Neutral Stimulus: An external stimulus that does not ordinarily cause a reflex response or an emotional response.

1. The bell was rung (neutral stimulus).
2. Meat powder was given to the dog (a stimulus that elicits a reflex).
3. The dog salivated (reflex response).

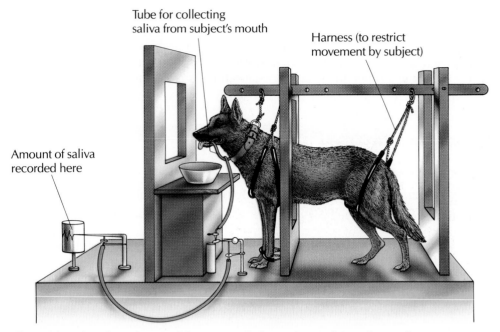

Figure 6.1 Pavlov's dog. A drawing of the apparatus Pavlov used to condition a dog to salivate.

Drawing by John Chase.

Unconditioned Stimulus (UCS): Any stimulus that causes a reflex or emotional response without the necessity of learning or conditioning.

Unconditioned Response (UCR): The reflex response evoked by a stimulus without the necessity of learning.

After several trials of pairing the bell with the meat powder, Pavlov found that the mere ringing of the bell would elicit salivation. In this way, the dog had been *conditioned*—it had *learned*—to salivate to the bell in the same way that the other dogs had unintentionally been conditioned to salivate to the sight of the experimental room.

This stimulus–response type of learning acquired by Pavlov's dogs is known as *classical conditioning*. It involves learning reflexive, involuntary responses to stimuli that do not usually cause such responses. In classical conditioning, a subject is initially presented with a neutral stimulus such as a bell. This neutral stimulus is anything that does not ordinarily elicit a particular reflexive or emotional response from the subject. For example, dogs do not naturally salivate to a bell; Pavlov's dogs had to be conditioned, or taught, to do so. Immediately after being introduced, the neutral stimulus is paired with a stimulus that *does* elicit a reflex or emotional response. This reflex-producing stimulus is known as the unconditioned stimulus (UCS). It is called "unconditioned" because it involves no learning. It always causes a specific *unlearned* reflex-type response, which is called an unconditioned response (UCR). Figure 6.2 summarizes the classical conditioning procedure. It would be helpful for you to refer to it as we continue our discussion.

After several pairings of the neutral stimulus (the bell) with the UCS (the meat powder), the neutral stimulus becomes associated with the UCS, and the subject makes

Figure 6.2 A summary of classical conditioning. Before conditioning, the neutral stimulus causes no relevant response while the unconditioned stimulus always causes the unconditioned response. During conditioning, the neutral stimulus is paired with the unconditioned stimulus. After conditioning, the previously neutral stimulus has become a conditioned stimulus and now causes a conditioned response.

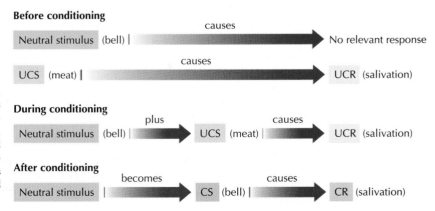

the same response to the neutral stimulus as it does to the UCS. At this point, the neutral stimulus comes to be known as the conditioned stimulus (CS), since the subject has been conditioned to respond to it, and the response the subject has been conditioned to make is called the conditioned response (CR). The CR (in this case, salivation) is normally the same or very similar to the unconditioned response (also salivation). However, it is now considered a conditioned response because the stimulus that elicits it (the bell) has been learned, or conditioned.

Conditioned Emotional Responses

Though it may not be immediately obvious, classical conditioning has many practical uses. Commercial advertising has used classical conditioning for years to sell products. Advertisers often pair their products with male or female models who just happen to be celebrities or just happen to have gorgeous bodies. These models automatically trigger favorable responses in the people reading or viewing the ads. After repeated viewings, advertisers hope that the products alone will elicit those same favorable responses in the prospective consumers.

Conversely, many of the most troublesome behaviors that humans and animals exhibit result from unintentional classical conditioning. For example, our deepest fears may be classically conditioned. John B. Watson (Watson and Rayner, 1920) demonstrated the classical conditioning of fears with an 11-month-old infant named Albert. Using the fact that infants are generally very trusting and afraid of only a few things, like loud noises or falling from high places, Watson gave little Albert a small white rat to play with. After a few minutes, Watson deliberately made a loud noise that scared Albert and made him cry. He continued to pair the loud noise with the rat and, unfortunately for Albert, was immensely successful in classically conditioning the child to fear white rats.

Watson's research design is shown in Figure 6.3. First, Albert was presented with the white rat, the neutral stimulus. The neutral stimulus was then paired with the noise, the unconditioned stimulus (UCS), which elicited the crying, the unconditioned response (UCR). Later, after several pairings of the rat with the noise, the presence of the rat alone became the conditioned stimulus (CS), and crying at the sight of the rat alone was the conditioned response (CR).

Little Albert's fear of white rats is an example of a conditioned emotional response (CER). Many phobias, or severe and irrational fears of certain objects or situations, can

Conditioned Stimulus (CS): A previously neutral stimulus that, through conditioning, now causes a classically conditioned response.

Conditioned Response (CR): A learned response to a previously neutral stimulus that has been associated with the stimulus through repeated pairings.

Conditioned Emotional Response (CER): Any classically conditioned emotional response to a previously neutral stimulus.

Phobia: A severe irrational fear of an object or a situation.

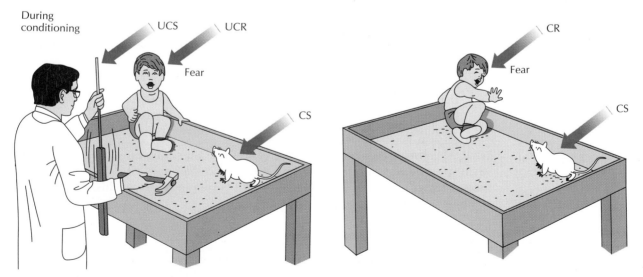

Figure 6.3 Little Albert and the white rat. Little Albert learned to fear rats through classical conditioning. Before conditioning, the rat was a neutral stimulus that caused no fear. During conditioning, John Watson made a loud noise (UCS) that frightened (UCR) Albert whenever the rat (NS) was near. After conditioning, the rat (CS) caused a fear response (CR) in Albert.

Advertisers have attempted to pair their products with models who automatically trigger favorable responses in people seeing the ads.

be thought of as CERs. Every time a phobic person is near or even thinks about the object causing the phobia, that person becomes extremely fearful and anxious. A student in one of our classes had a phobia about rats and mice. When she was younger, she had been bitten by a large rat and had been terrified of rats ever since. By the time she reached college, her phobia had become so severe that she refused to read her psychology textbook because it contained references to rats, and whenever rats were brought up in classroom discussions, she would leave the room. If you're interested in how this fear could have been "deconditioned," a more in-depth discussion of phobias, the problems they can cause, and methods of treatment is found in Chapters 15 and 16.

Not all conditioned emotional responses are as severe as phobias. Many of our everyday emotional responses have been classically conditioned. For example, Michael, a son of one of the authors, did not touch flowers growing in the yard for a long time because as a young boy he had picked a flower containing a bee and was stung. For Michael, the flower was the CS, the bee's sting was the UCS, the resulting pain and fear were the UCR, and the fear of touching the flower was the CR.

 Try This Yourself

We all have conditioned emotional responses to certain words, and those responses are unique because of our unique experiences. Read the following list of words:

honky	black	Nixon	Hannukah
Democrat	final exams	mother	Communist
father	Republican	Hitler	Santa Claus
vacations	Lincoln	sexist	atomic bomb

What did you *feel* as you read the words? Did you feel angry, depressed, or uncomfortable when you read some words and happy, warm, or comfortable with others? Your reactions, whether positive or negative, are a result of your own personal history of classical conditioning. ■

Higher Order Conditioning

Higher Order Conditioning: Classical conditioning in which a neutral stimulus is paired with a second stimulus that already causes a learned or conditioned response.

The type of conditioning in the above demonstration is known as higher order conditioning (as opposed to the conditioning Pavlov used with his dogs). Whereas in Pavlovian conditioning the neutral stimulus is paired with an unconditioned stimulus, in higher order conditioning a neutral stimulus is paired with a *conditioned* stimulus, another stimulus that already produces a learned response. If Pavlov had wanted to experiment with higher order conditioning in his dogs, he could have trained a dog to salivate to the *word* "bell." He could have done this by first conditioning the dog to salivate to the ringing of the bell and then pairing the word "bell" to the ringing of the bell. Eventually, the dog would salivate only to the word itself.

In a classic study of conditioned emotional responses, Arthur and Carolyn Staats (1958) conditioned subjects to experience emotional responses to the names "Tom" and "Bill." They paired a neutral word (such as the name "Tom") with a conditioned stimulus (such as the word "bad") that their subjects had already been conditioned to associate with negative stimuli. The pairing produced a new learned emotional response (a negative, unhappy feeling) to the neutral word. The distinction between Pavlovian and higher order conditioning can be very important. In the rest of this section, see if you can identify which kind of conditioning is involved in the examples we cite.

Can any other responses besides salivation and emotions be classically conditioned? Yes. For a response to be classically conditioned, it must be elicited by some kind of unconditioned stimulus. Thus, most classically conditioned responses involve either reflexive or autonomic responses (those produced by the autonomic nervous system) and are therefore either physical or emotional responses. One interesting example of a conditioned physical response is a *taste aversion.* Most people dislike some foods to some degree, but some people dislike a particular food so strongly that they get physically ill when they smell or even think about it. Many of these aversions to food are classically conditioned. For example, some people have acquired "beer aversions" from college drinking contests in which they drank until they got violently ill; from that time on, they have not been able to tolerate the taste or smell of beer.

Researchers have applied their knowledge of taste aversions to solving an economic problem of western ranchers: coyotes killing sheep. One "solution" to the problem would be to kill all the coyotes. Of course, this would be irresponsible and would cause serious ecological problems, since the coyotes also eat rabbits, ground squirrels, and other rodents that compete with sheep for the limited grass and edible plants in their particular region. A better solution would be to use classical conditioning to teach the coyotes not to eat sheep. Gustavson and Garcia (1974) were able to condition coyotes to develop a taste aversion to sheep by lacing freshly killed sheep with a chemical that causes coyotes to get sick when they eat the tainted meat. Their scheme worked so well that the mere sight and smell of sheep caused coyotes to run away from them on sight.

Coyotes find sheep a readily available source of food, but coyotes who have developed a conditioned taste aversion to sheep will avoid them and seek other food.

Extinction

Classical conditioning, like all learning, is "relatively" permanent. However, most things that are learned through classical conditioning can be unlearned. The process of unlearning a behavior or a response is called extinction. Extinction occurs when the unconditioned stimulus (the stimulus causing the unlearned, or reflex, behavior) is repeatedly withheld whenever the conditioned stimulus is presented. The previous association between the CS and the UCS is thereby broken. Pavlov (1927) demonstrated extinction in his dogs. After conditioning a dog to salivate to a tone by using meat powder as the unconditioned stimulus, he then withheld the meat powder. The salivary response to the tone decreased over several trials until it was finally extinguished (see Figure 6.4).

Suppose as a child you once had eight hot dogs at a picnic, got sick, and had difficulty eating hot dogs for several years. Why can you now eat them? First let's review what happened: The taste of the hot dogs was the CS, the overfull stomach was the UCS, and the resulting nausea and vomiting was the UCR. After the eating spree, either the sight of a hot dog or the attempt to eat one became the CS that elicited the CR, the sick feeling. For a conditioned response to be maintained, it is necessary to occasionally reintroduce the unconditioned stimulus; if it is never again presented, the strength of the conditioned response will weaken over time and will eventually cease altogether. Thus, if you don't get violently ill when you subsequently take a bite of a hot dog, you don't have another occurrence of that unconditioned stimulus producing an undesired response. Therefore, extinction occurs and hot dogs are again a neutral stimulus.

Extinction: The gradual unlearning of a behavior or a response that occurs when a CS is repeatedly presented without the UCS with which it had been previously associated.

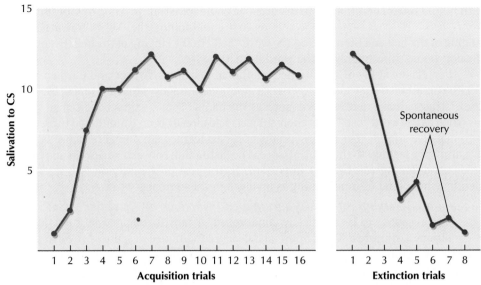

Figure 6.4 Acquisition and extinction in Pavlov's experiment. The graph on the left illustrates the acquisition phase of classical conditioning during which Pavlov counted the number of drops of saliva produced in response to the conditioned stimulus. He plotted the number of drops on the vertical axis and the number of trials on the horizontal axis. After 16 acquisition trials, extinction trials began. Extinction results are shown in the graph on the right. Note in this graph the sharp peaks in response rate that are characteristic of spontaneous recovery. (After Pavlov, 1927.)

Forgetting: The unlearning of a behavior due to continued withholding of the CS as well as the UCS.

Isn't extinction just a fancy name for forgetting? No, there is an important difference between extinction and forgetting. Extinction occurs only when the conditioned stimulus is presented alone, without the UCS, leading to a gradual weakening of the conditioned response over several trials. Forgetting, on the other hand, occurs most often when neither the conditioned stimulus nor the unconditioned stimulus is presented for a long period of time. This example will clarify the difference: Suppose that the first time you rode a horse it tripped and fell, the second time it tried to bite you, and the third time the horse threw you off. Given these experiences, you can bet you wouldn't be wild about riding horses—you might even have a conditioned emotional response of fear for horses. One solution to this problem would be to avoid horseback riding, whereby several years later, you might have *forgotten* the experience altogether. Another solution, which would be faster and would allow you to still enjoy horseback riding with your friends, would be to continue riding the horse, with the probability that the horse would get used to you and mishaps would stop occurring each time you rode. Your fear of horses would then have *extinguished* over time. (In forgetting, what are the CS and the UCS that are withheld? In extinction, what is the UCS that is withheld?)

Spontaneous Recovery

Spontaneous Recovery: The reappearance of a previously extinguished response.

Extinction of a classically conditioned response is often accompanied by a process called spontaneous recovery, in which a conditioned response that had been extinguished spontaneously reappears. If you go horseback riding without any mishaps, your fear of the horse at the end of the ride will probably have decreased considerably—extinction will have begun. On your next ride, however, some of the fear you lost the week before will have returned—it will have recovered. You will not fear the horse as much as you did at the beginning of the previous ride, but you will fear it more than you did at the end of the previous ride (see Figure 6.4). This cycle will continue through many trials, with your fear response spontaneously recovering, at lesser and lesser intensities, between trials.

Spontaneous recovery occurs when a significant amount of time has elapsed after an extinction trial. For this reason, it is not a simple matter to extinguish a classically conditioned response. To be effective, the extinction process must extend over several days or even weeks, depending on the response to be extinguished. Even when a response is completely extinguished, it can be relearned in fewer trials than it was originally learned.

Generalization and Discrimination

Remember Watson's experiment with Little Albert, in which he conditioned the infant to fear the white rat by using a loud noise as a UCS? After the conditioning experience, Albert feared not only rats but also furry white rabbits, cotton wool, and even a Santa Claus mask, with its white beard. This process, in which stimuli similar to the conditioned stimulus elicit the conditioned response, is called generalization. The more similar a stimulus is to the original stimulus, the greater the response. Thus, furry white rabbits frightened Albert more than Santa Claus masks because the rabbits were more similar to the white rat (Watson and Rayner, 1920).

Generalization: A tendency to respond in the same way to stimuli in the environment that have similar characteristics.

Would Little Albert still be afraid of Santa Claus as he grew older?   Probably not, since through the process of discrimination he would learn there is a difference between rats and people. Normally, generalization occurs initially in classical conditioning. However, as conditioning continues we begin to discriminate between stimuli when only one specific stimulus is paired with the UCS. A friend of the authors has lived for several years in Brawley, California, which is situated on a large earthquake fault. Being terrified of earthquakes, she at first panicked whenever she heard any low, rumbling noise, whether it signaled an earthquake, faraway thunder, or distant aircraft. However, after living through a severe earthquake and several serious aftershocks that were all preceded by a distinctive rumbling sound, she can now discriminate the sound of a quake from similar sounds. Now our friend no longer panics when the rumble she hears is due to thunder or a jet plane.

Discrimination: The process whereby a subject learns to differentiate one stimulus from others that are similar because that stimulus is the only CS that is paired with the UCS.

Discrimination learning takes place when the target stimulus is the *only* CS that is paired with the UCS. In Pavlov's experiment, each time a specific tone was sounded the dog was presented with the meat powder. Whenever a similar but different tone was sounded, no UCS was presented. Eventually, the dog learned to discriminate between tones and salivated only to the target tone. Discrimination can also be seen in the coyote study: Coyotes learned to associate sheep with sickness but did not stop eating other sources of food.

Review Questions

1. In classical conditioning, a(n) _____ is paired with a(n) _____ .

2. After conditioning, the _____ elicits the _____ .

3. Describe how John Watson produced a conditioned emotional response to white rats in little Albert.

4. Pairing a neutral stimulus with an existing conditioned stimulus is called _____ .

5. What is the difference between extinction and forgetting?

6. Suppose John Watson wanted to extinguish little Albert's fear of white rats, and he succeeded by the end of the first day of extinction trials. When Albert's CER reappeared at the beginning of the next day, _____ was occurring.

7. _____ occurs when stimuli similar to the conditioned stimulus evoke the conditioned response.

8. In effect, generalization and _____ are opposites.

Answers to Review Questions can be found in Appendix C.

Operant Conditioning: Learning from Consequences

* How do consequences lead to the type of learning known as operant conditioning? How do extinction, spontaneous recovery, generalization, and discrimination occur?

Through classical conditioning, we learn to associate a neutral stimulus with a stimulus that naturally produces an involuntary, reflexive response. Operant conditioning also involves learning through association, except that in operant conditioning, we associate a *voluntary* response with a particular *cue* in our environment. We make an intentional response to something—an object, a sound, a situation—and learn that our response produces an environmental change. We learn to repeat the response or not to repeat it depending on whether or not the change is favorable. For example, suppose you were playing a video game for the first time. When you pushed the white button, a little man jumped up and hit his head, resulting in 20 points. Naturally, you would try to make the same response the next time he walked under a similar structure. If making the man hit his head resulted in losing 20 points, you would learn *not* to make that response.

It is through operant conditioning that we learn to type, children learn to say "thank you," and students learn good study habits. It was through operant conditioning that Koko learned sign language. Koko voluntarily made a distinctive gesture for the word "food" and learned to repeat it because she was given a piece of fruit for doing so. In fact, operant conditioning is involved any time we learn a new motor skill or a new social behavior (Gordon, 1989). By *operating* in the environment and observing the effects of our behavior, we learn which behaviors lead to desired outcomes.

Operant versus Classical Conditioning

Note that three factors distinguish operant from classical conditioning: (1) In operant conditioning, the stimulus that leads to a voluntary response is really just a cue—it does not *evoke* the response in the same way an unconditioned stimulus evokes an unconditioned response; (2) an operant response is *voluntary*, not the reflex type of response in classical conditioning; and (3) the stimulus event that controls the learning—the unconditioned stimulus in classical conditioning or the reinforcement in operant conditioning—occurs at different times relative to the behavior: in classical conditioning, the UCS occurs before the behavior and in operant conditioning, the reinforcement occurs after.

A critical element in operant conditioning is feedback, in which learners are made aware of the results of their behavior. When an animal or a person makes a response, the feedback that occurs after that response determines whether it will be repeated. During her training sessions, Koko received immediate feedback from Patterson in the forms of praise and food when she made appropriate responses and by receiving a "no" sign and no reward when she made inappropriate responses.

The first psychologist to study operant conditioning was Edward Thorndike. His most famous experiment involved placing a cat inside a "puzzle box" (see Figure 6.5). Once inside the box, the only way the cat could escape was to pull on a rope or step on a

Feedback: Knowledge of the results of a particular response.

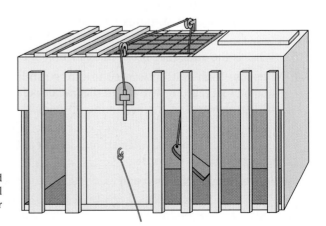

Figure 6.5 A Thorndike puzzle box. This is typical of the boxes Thorndike used in his trial-and-error experiments with cats. When a cat stepped on a pedal inside the box, the door bolt was released and the weight attached to the door pulled it open so the cat could escape. (From Thorndike, 1898.)

pedal, whereupon the door would open and the cat could exit and eat the food just outside. As you might imagine, the cat would spend some time wandering around inside the box, but eventually, by trial-and-error, would perform the necessary response to open the door. The amount of time the cat took to escape usually decreased with each trial until it would step on the pedal or pull the rope immediately upon being placed in the box. Thorndike concluded that the probability of a response being repeated is related to the effect that response has on the animal or the environment. This he called the *law of effect* (Thorndike, 1931).

Reinforcement and Punishment

The effects that Thorndike referred to result from reinforcement and punishment. Reinforcement is any operation or procedure that results in an increase in a response; conversely, punishment is any procedure that results in a decrease in a response. The distinction between reinforcement and punishment is critical to your understanding of this section and can significantly affect your relationships with others. For example, have you ever tried to punish someone and found that the person's behavior only got *worse?* As you will soon see, this could happen because you're actually *reinforcing* the person's undesirable behavior, rather than punishing it, or it could mean that the person is angry or resentful about being punished and the increase in undesirable behavior is a retaliatory act.

B. F. Skinner was the first to conduct systematic research on the effects of reinforcement. Although most of Skinner's original research was done with animals (rats and pigeons), the relationships he demonstrated between responses and reinforcement can easily be applied to human beings. A typical Skinner experiment required an animal, such as a rat, and an apparatus he designed that has come to be called a *Skinner box*. In one of his classic experiments, Skinner trained a rat to push a lever in order to receive a food reinforcer. The Skinner box automatically gave the rat a pellet of food each time it pushed the lever. At the same time, the number of responses made by the rat was recorded. Skinner used this basic experimental design to demonstrate a number of operant conditioning principles.

Types of Reinforcement

Skinner found that food was an effective reinforcer for responses in rats, but with humans, reinforcers include water, sex, money, attention, and material possessions, to name just a few. Reinforcers such as food, water, and sex are called primary reinforcers because they normally lead to the satisfaction of an *unlearned* biological need. Reinforcers such as money, praise, and material possessions that have no *intrinsic* value are called secondary reinforcers; the only power they have to reinforce behavior results from their *learned* value. A baby, for example, would find milk much more reinforcing than a hundred dollar bill. Needless to say, by the time this baby has grown to adolescence, he or she will have learned to prefer the money. In our adult culture, money is by far the most widely used secondary reinforcer because of its learned association with desirable commodities. During her training sessions with Koko, Patterson used a combination of primary (food) and secondary (praise) reinforcers to teach the gorilla sign language. She probably selected "food" as her first sign because Koko could thereby associate this sign with the primary reinforcer.

A behavior can be reinforced by the application or withholding of relevant stimuli. For instance, suppose you talk to a friend and she smiles at you. You are likely to talk to her again because she has, through her smiling, applied a reinforcer for your talking. On the other hand, suppose you are learning to drive a stick-shift car. Because of your inexperience, it continually bounces and jerks. Suddenly, you coordinate the pedals in such a way that the annoying jerkings cease. Their absence reinforces the coordinated motions you just made. In the first case, the smile is positive reinforcement. In the second case, the cessation of the jerking and bouncing is negative reinforcement.

Reinforcement: Any action or event that increases the probability that a response will be repeated.

Punishment: Any action or event that decreases the likelihood of a response being repeated.

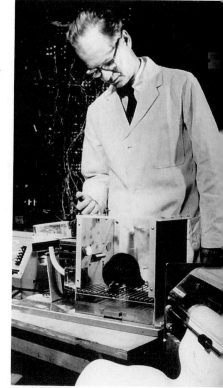

B. F. Skinner and a rat in a typical "Skinner box." The rat has been conditioned to press the bar to receive a reinforcement of food.

Primary Reinforcers: Stimuli that increase the probability of a response and whose value does not need to be learned, such as food, water, and sex.

Secondary Reinforcers: Stimuli that increase the probability of a response and whose reinforcing properties are learned, such as money and material possessions.

Positive Reinforcement: Reinforcement in which a stimulus is given or added that is desirable to the subject.

Negative Reinforcement: Reinforcement in which a painful or annoying stimulus is taken away.

Time out! I thought negative reinforcement was punishment. Right?   Wrong! Negative reinforcement is probably one of the most misunderstood terms in psychology. Negative reinforcement is *not* punishment. In thinking about the term, you must not dwell on the word "negative"; think more of the word "reinforcement." A reinforcer is anything that will cause a behavior to increase or a response to be repeated. When you think of the two different kinds of reinforcers, positive and negative, think of them in mathematical terms (+ and −), not in terms of good and bad. *Positive reinforcement* occurs when something desirable is given or *added*. If your boss compliments you on a job well done, you are receiving positive reinforcement, with the praise being a secondary reinforcer. If a mild foot shock ceases whenever a rat pushes a lever, the rat will probably continue to push it. The elimination of the shock provides negative reinforcement. (See Figure 6.6, a graphic summary of operant conditioning.)

In the praise and shock examples, the behavior or the response is *more* likely to be repeated after the reinforcement. You will try to continue producing good work and the rat will continue to push the lever. Of course, when you use either positive or negative reinforcement to increase individual response in others, be aware that their behavior may affect you as well. If you as a boss begin to praise your employees and production increases, the increase will serve as positive reinforcement and you will probably continue praising your workers.

The two-way nature of reinforcement explains why many bad situations often seem to escalate—two parties get locked into a vicious cycle where one is being negatively reinforced, the other is being positively reinforced, and both of their behaviors *increase!* Take the simple example of a child in a supermarket screaming for a lollipop. Her parents are embarrassed and frustrated, so they give in, the crying stops, and the parents are negatively reinforced. But what do you think is happening for the child? She is being positively reinforced for screaming. Do you see what everyone has learned in this exchange? The child may well scream louder and more readily the next time, thereby causing her parents to give in sooner. The lesson here is that if you find yourself in a situation where things are rapidly escalating, try to step back and analyze what's going on: What are the reinforcers? How can you remove them? How can you change them? Try to *use* your psychology.

I can see that negative reinforcement is not punishment. So what is *punishment?* Punishment occurs when some procedure or some type of event leads to a decrease in a response. There are two kinds of punishment, positive and negative (Gordon, 1989). As with reinforcement, remember to think in mathematical terms of adding and taking

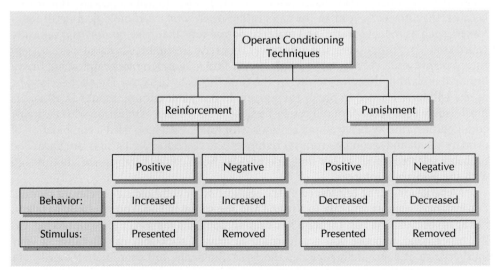

Figure 6.6 A summary of operant conditioning techniques. This figure illustrates the effects on a subject's behavior of either negative or positive reinforcement and negative or positive punishment. *Any* type of reinforcement causes an increase in behavior while *any* type of punishment causes a decrease in behavior.

This killer whale is receiving positive reinforcement.

away, rather than good and bad. Positive punishment is the application of an *aversive* (painful, disgusting, or otherwise undesirable) stimulus to decrease a response to a particular cue. If your dog digs a hole every time it sees a gopher mound and you swat him with a newspaper to decrease the digging, you are applying (literally!) positive punishment.

Opposed to positive punishment is negative punishment, which is the removal of a desired stimulus to decrease a response. If your puppy has an accident while being house-trained, you could use negative punishment by taking away its privilege of being in the house by putting it outside. (Again, see Figure 6.6 to help you understand operant conditioning techniques.)

Side Effects of Punishment

Punishment can help decrease unwanted behaviors, but it also has serious side effects and should therefore be avoided if possible. A major side effect of punishment is its tendency to lead to frustration in the person or animal being punished, which can lead to anger and eventually aggression. Although research has found a clear and direct connection between punishment and aggression in animals (Baenninger, 1974; Cairns, 1972; Hyman, 1981), the relationship is more complicated with humans. For example, most of us have learned from previous experience that retaliatory aggression toward a punisher (who is usually bigger and more powerful) is usually followed by more punishment. We therefore tend to control our impulse toward open aggression and instead resort to more subtle techniques, such as procrastination, pouting, stubbornness, or intentional inefficiency. Such behavior is known as passive aggressiveness (Coleman, Butcher, and Carson, 1984).

As well as leading to subversive behaviors on the part of the recipient, punishment may also lead to an escalation of aggression on the part of the punisher. Because the punishment generally produces a decrease in undesired behavior, at least for the moment, the punisher is in effect rewarded for applying punishment. Thus, a vicious cycle can be set up in which both people are actually being reinforced for inappropriate behavior—the punisher for punishing and the recipient for being submissive and subversive. Can you see how this cycle may partially explain the escalation of violence in spouse and child abuse cases, and the reluctance of the recipients to leave the situation?

Some researchers have pointed out that in China, Taiwan, Tahiti, and other cultures where physical punishment is far less common than it is in the United States, there is also far less child abuse. They suggest that by making physical punishment acceptable

Positive Punishment: Punishment in which an aversive or undesirable stimulus is applied to decrease a response.

Negative Punishment: Punishment in which a desired stimulus is removed to decrease a response.

Passive Aggressiveness: A subtle form of aggression characterized by pouting, procrastination, stubbornness, or intentional inefficiency.

as a normal disciplinary method, Americans may be inadvertently encouraging its abuse (Parke and Collmer, 1975).

Another side effect of punishment is avoidance behavior. People and animals do not like to be punished, so they try to avoid the punisher if they can. Suppose you come home from school and find that your dog just dug another hole in the yard. He has been repeatedly punished for this in the past and runs and hides with his tail between his legs as soon as he sees you, to avoid your anger. This also happens with people. If every time you came home your parents or your spouse started yelling at you, you would find another place to go. You would come to perceive home as a place for punishment. This aspect of punishment is one reason children lie to their parents. They don't want to be bawled out, spanked, or denied a privilege, so they fabricate any kind of explanation.

Learned Helplessness

Learned Helplessness: A state in which people or animals give up and quietly submit to punishment that they have previously been unable to escape.

It seems that people and animals *must* have a way to escape from punishment. If they don't, they often find themselves in a state of learned helplessness. Overmeier and Seligman (1967) investigated this condition of helplessness by conducting experiments using dogs as subjects. The first step was to expose each dog in the experimental condition to a series of inescapable shocks; dogs in the control condition were not shocked. The next step was to place each dog in a *shuttle box*—a box with two compartments separated by a low barrier—and electrify the floor of only one of the compartments. When the control dogs were shocked in the shuttle box, they ran around frantically, trying to escape, and eventually jumped the barrier into the nonelectrified compartment. However, when the experimental dogs received the shocks in the shuttle box, they ran around for only a few seconds, then lay down in a corner and whined without making any attempt to escape.

One thing is clear from such research. Constant and unavoidable punishment eventually causes people and animals to give up and quietly submit to the punishment. This learned helplessness has been offered as an explanation for many behaviors. Huesmann (1978) claims it is the source for such psychological problems as withdrawal, apathy, and severe depression. Gentile and Monaco (1986) have studied its role in low mathematical achievement. Feinberg, Miller, and Weiss (1983) have found a strong correlation between learned helplessness and depression in college-age subjects.

Greer and Wethered (1984) claim that the "burnout" experienced by many teachers of exceptional children (children who have severe mental or physical handicaps) is due to learned helplessness. *Burnout* is a state of physical and emotional exhaustion associated with a job or situation. The lack of control over the children's handicaps and the lack of reinforcement inherent in teaching children who make such slow progress lead to learned helplessness and, consequently, to burnout. Greer and Wethered suggest that to fight burnout teachers (1) set realistic and attainable goals, (2) recognize the control they do have, and (3) develop a realistic understanding of the cause for their failures. They also suggest that, because burnout results partially from a lack of positive reinforcement, there should be an increase in positive reinforcers—for example, monetary rewards or frequent praise from supervisors.

To recap: Punishment leads to such negative behaviors as aggression, avoidance, lying, and learned helplessness. An increase in these behaviors makes it more difficult for a person or animal to acquire new learning. What is ironic is that punishment does not really eliminate a response; it only temporarily suppresses it. Usually, the individual who is being punished stops or decreases the undesirable behavior only as long as the punisher is in sight. You have no doubt noticed, for example, the large number of people who drive well above the posted speed limit and slow down only when they see a police car.

Police officers are often placed in situations that can lead to emotional exhaustion and, finally, burnout.

Review Questions

1. When we learn to associate a voluntary response with a particular cue, we are learning through _____ .

2. You should use _____ if you want to *increase* the probability that a certain response will be repeated; you should use _____ if you want to *decrease* the probability that a response will be repeated.

3. What kinds of reinforcers are being used when an animal trainer gives food to an elephant whenever she does a behavior and the trainer gets paid money to train the elephant?

4. Explain how positive reinforcement and negative punishment might be used together to control an aggressive prisoner in a local jail.

5. Negative reinforcement occurs when something is _____ that the person or animal _____ .

6. When a teacher makes a child stay in the classroom at recess time in order to curtail his hitting on the playground, she is using _____ punishment.

7. When you spank your dog for wetting on your carpet, you are using _____ punishment.

8. A teenager who has been continually punished for not doing her chores displays passive aggressiveness. What kinds of things is she doing?

9. What is the cause of learned helplessness?

Answers to Review Questions can be found in Appendix C.

Extinction and Spontaneous Recovery

Extinction, the elimination of a response, occurs in operant conditioning as well as in classical conditioning. To extinguish a classically conditioned response, the unconditioned stimulus is withheld whenever the conditioned stimulus is presented. To extinguish an operantly conditioned response, the reinforcement is withheld whenever the learned behavior is performed. In the usual operant conditioning experiment, a rat is conditioned to press a bar for a pellet of food (bar pressing is the response and food is the positive reinforcement). To eliminate the bar-pressing behavior, the experimenter simply turns off the food dispenser. Since the bar-pressing response is no longer being reinforced, the response rate decreases until it ultimately ceases altogether (see Figure 6.7).

After extinction, does spontaneous recovery occur as it does in classical conditioning? Yes. If the rat that has undergone several successful extinction trials is taken out of the box for a few hours, it will show spontaneous recovery by pressing the bar on its return to the experimental box (see Figure 6.8). Similarly, if you had always kept your underwear in the top drawer of your dresser and then moved it to the bottom drawer, it may take several days for your "top drawer" habit to be extinguished. For a response to be com-

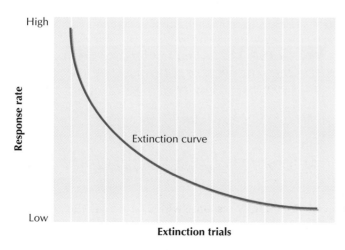

Figure 6.7 Extinction. A hypothetical graph from a typical experiment demonstrating extinction. Response rate decreases with more extinction trials.

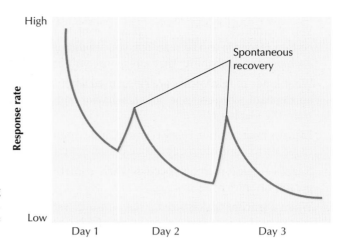

Figure 6.8 Spontaneous recovery. A hypothetical graph depicting spontaneous recovery of a response that is no longer being reinforced. At the beginning of each new day of extinction trials the response rate is greater than that at the end of the previous day.

pletely extinguished, the extinction process must be continued in several sessions extending over several days. The actual amount of time required to extinguish an operantly conditioned response is directly related to the schedule of reinforcement.

Schedules of Reinforcement

Schedule of Reinforcement: A schedule delineating when a response is to be reinforced.

Continuous Reinforcement: Reinforcement in which every response is reinforced.

Partial Reinforcement: Reinforcement in which some, but not all, responses are reinforced.

The term schedule of reinforcement refers to a program designating at what rate or at what intervals responses are reinforced. Although there are many different schedules of reinforcement, they can all be grouped into two types: continuous reinforcement and partial reinforcement. In continuous reinforcement, every response is reinforced. For example, every time a rat pushes a lever, it gets a pellet of food, and every time you make the correct response in a video game, you are rewarded with more points. In partial reinforcement, only *some,* but not all, responses are reinforced. For example, a cat may wait beside a mouse hole for hours. When a mouse finally does appear, the cat may not be quick enough and the mouse may escape. But once in a while, a mouse will see the cat too late and the cat will be reinforced.

Which schedule enables us to learn faster, continuous or partial reinforcement? Continuous reinforcement leads to more rapid learning. Imagine you are learning to play a video game in which you need to guide your starship with a joystick and press the firing button at the appropriate moment so that you can blast alien ships and win points. If you are rewarded for every hit (continuous reinforcement), you will learn how to play faster than if you are rewarded for every third or fourth hit (partial reinforcement).

Although a continuous schedule of reinforcement leads to faster initial learning, it is not an efficient system for maintaining long-term behaviors. You simply cannot reward someone constantly for every appropriate response. Can you imagine parents of teenagers having to reward their children every day for getting up, dressing, making their beds, brushing their teeth, and so on? It is therefore important to move to a partial schedule of reinforcement once a task is well learned. Under partial schedules behavior is

Video games provide continuous reinforcement, while slot machines provide partial reinforcement.

more resistant to extinction. To use the example of the slot machine, have you ever noticed how intense and serious people become as they're gambling, and how they will stand for hours pulling a lever in hopes of winning the elusive jackpot? (Sounds a bit like Skinner's rats, doesn't it?) This high response rate and the compulsion to keep on gambling in spite of significant losses are evidence of the maintenance power and the strong resistance to extinction that are characteristic of partial schedule reinforcement.

Types of Schedules

Partial schedules of reinforcement may be based on the number of responses between reinforcements *(ratio schedules)* or on the interval of time between reinforced responses *(interval schedules)*. In addition, either type of schedule may be fixed or variable. There are thus four main partial schedules of reinforcement: fixed ratio, variable ratio, fixed interval, and variable interval. The type of schedule selected by the experimenter depends on the type of behavior being studied and on the speed of extinction desired by the experimenter.

Suppose you want to teach your dog to sit. Initially you reinforce your dog for each occurrence of the behavior. Each time the dog sits, you give him a cookie. To save on your cookie bill, you eventually reinforce the animal only every other time he sits, or every third time, or every fifth time. This is a fixed ratio reinforcement schedule: The animal must make a *fixed* number of responses before it receives the reinforcement. A fixed ratio schedule can lead to a high response rate, especially if the ratio is very high, such as five or more responses to one reinforcement.

Fixed Ratio: A partial schedule of reinforcement in which a subject must make a certain number of responses before being reinforced.

Reinforcement schedules influence more than response rates; they also affect the rate of extinction when the reinforcement is withheld. Continuous reinforcement leads to rapid extinction when the reinforcement is withheld. Higher fixed ratios lead to slower extinction rates, but the subject eventually comes to realize that no more reinforcers are forthcoming.

Is it possible to set up a reinforcement schedule that will never allow extinction? Never is a long time. But it is possible to set up schedules of reinforcement that will make a behavior extremely resistant to extinction. Rather than being reinforced for a fixed number of responses, the subject is reinforced on a variable ratio schedule, in which reinforcers may be given for the first response, then the third response, then the twenty-third. *On the average,* the subject will be reinforced on a specific schedule (such as every fifth time), but the number of required responses on each trial will vary.

Variable Ratio: A schedule of reinforcement in which the subject is reinforced, on the average, for making a specific number of responses, but the number of required responses on each trial is varied.

Most slot machines are designed to reinforce gamblers on a variable ratio schedule. They might win on the first try or the thirteenth try—they never know whether the next try might be the jackpot. Whereas in a fixed ratio schedule the subject learns that a certain number of responses will lead to reinforcement, in a variable ratio it is impossible for the subject to know when he or she will receive the next reinforcer. This is why behavior reinforced on a variable ratio schedule is so resistant to extinction. There is always the chance that as soon as you walk away from the slot machine, the next person who pulls the handle will hit the big jackpot.

Partial reinforcement may also be given on a fixed interval schedule, in which the subject is reinforced for the first response *after* a fixed interval of time has elapsed. What are your study habits like when you know that you will have a psych quiz every Friday and you really care about your grade? Do you study at a moderate level at the beginning of the week and harder on Wednesday and Thursday so that you'll be reinforced with an "A" on Friday's quiz? If you do, you are like most animals (including humans) who, when put on a fixed interval schedule, respond at a low or moderate rate during most of the time interval and more rapidly toward the end of the interval.

Fixed Interval: A schedule of reinforcement in which a subject is reinforced for the first response after a definite period of time has elapsed.

It is relatively easy to extinguish a response that has been conditioned using a fixed interval schedule, since it is possible for a person or animal to predict approximately when a reinforcement will be given. If no reinforcement is forthcoming, there is no point in continuing the behavior.

On variable interval schedules, subjects are reinforced the first time they perform the target behavior after a variable, unpredictable interval of time. Imagine, for example,

Variable Interval: A schedule of reinforcement in which the subject is reinforced for the first response after a specified period of time has elapsed. This period of time varies from one reinforcement to the next.

that you are a hungry rat who is undergoing a learning session in which you are placed in a cage with a lever jutting out of one wall. After exploring the cage, you hit the lever a couple of times and then receive a bit of food. Having been reinforced for the behavior, you hit the lever several more times, with no result. You wait, then again hit the lever several times before you are again reinforced. After eating your food, you hit the lever and immediately receive more food. In this case, you have been rewarded after intervals of varying lengths.

Contrary to the response rates using fixed interval schedules, most animals trained on a variable interval schedule learn that the most efficient way to earn their reinforcers is to respond at a slow steady rate. This is so because the determining factor is not the actual number of responses but the length of time that has elapsed. Thus, if in your psych class you know that you will have occasional quizzes but you never know when they will be sprung on you, you are more likely to study at a constant rate and try to keep up with your reading assignments.

In discussing reinforcement schedules, we have dealt with continuous and partial reinforcement separately. Normally, however, learning occurs through a combination of the two. Initially, in learning a particular response we are continuously reinforced for that behavior; then, after the initial learning has taken place, we are only partially reinforced, enough so that the behavior will be continued. For example, when Patterson was teaching Koko her first sign, she noted that by the end of the session, in which she had used a continuous reinforcement schedule, Koko was "stuffed" and had no more interest in the food reinforcers. Such satiation also occurs when training people and other animals. A partial reinforcement schedule eliminates the problem of trying to train a subject who has lost interest in the reinforcer. Thus, most behavior is ultimately reinforced on a partial schedule, especially after it has been well established.

Superstitious Behavior

In 1948, B. F. Skinner conducted an experiment in which he altered the feeding mechanism on the cages for eight of his pigeons so that it would drop food pellets into the cages once every 15 seconds. No matter what the birds did, they were reinforced in intervals of 15 seconds. Of the eight pigeons, six acquired very noticeable types of behavior that they repeated over and over, even though the behaviors were not necessary to receive the food. For example, one pigeon kept turning in counterclockwise circles, and another kept making jerking movements with its head.

Why did the pigeons engage in such repetitive and unnecessary behavior? Recall that a reinforcer increases the probability that a response just performed will be repeated. Although Skinner was not using the food to reinforce any particular behavior, the pigeons associated the food with whatever behavior they were engaged in when the food was originally dropped into the cage. Thus, if the bird was circling counterclockwise when the food was dropped, it would repeat that motion to receive more food: It had formed a meaningless connection between the food and the behavior. This type of behavior is called superstitious behavior—behavior that is continually repeated because it is believed to be the cause of "something good," even though in reality it has no connection with the reinforcer.

Superstitious Behavior: Behavior that is continually repeated because it is thought to cause desired effects, though in reality the behavior and the effects are totally unrelated.

Calvin and Hobbes   by Bill Watterson

It is surprising how many people exhibit superstitious behavior. In a poll of junior high, senior high, college, and university athletes, 40 percent confessed to having superstitions (Buhrmann and Zaugg, 1981). Indeed, many professional and Olympic-level athletes carry lucky charms or engage in ritualistic behavior before every competition. Phil Esposito, a hockey player with the Boston Bruins and the New York Rangers for 18 years, performed the same superstitious actions before each game: He would always wear the same black turtleneck and drive through the same tollbooth on his way to the game. In the locker room, he would put on all his clothes in the same order and lay out his equipment in exactly the same way he had for every other game. All this because once when he had engaged in such behavior years before, he had been the team's high scorer.

Shaping

Suppose you wanted to teach your dog Charlie to bring you the newspaper. You would probably not use the operant conditioning principles presented thus far. They would require you to follow Charlie around until he happened to pick up your paper so that you could finally reinforce him. This could take a long, long time. To train Charlie in a relatively short time, you could use shaping, the process of rewarding successive approximations to the desired behavior. When shaping the behavior of animals or people, you initially reward the slightest look or movement toward the target object or response (you give Charlie a dog biscuit when he looks in the direction of the paper). Then you reinforce the subject when he or she makes a more distinct movement toward the desired response (Charlie walks toward the paper), and so on until—it may take awhile—the response you want to shape has been performed (Charlie picks up the paper and gives it to you).

Shaping: Teaching a desired response by reinforcing a series of successive steps leading to this final response.

Penny Patterson used shaping during one of her initial training sessions. When Koko approximated the food sign by placing only her index finger on her mouth, she was rewarded with tidbits of fruit. She was then rewarded for closer and closer approximations to the appropriate sign, until she finally made the correct sign, placing all the fingers of one hand on the mouth. After that, only the correct sign was reinforced.

Behavior is not always purposely shaped. It may be shaped by circumstances or the environment. One of the authors has a pony that roams around the yard, grazing on the grass. Lately, however, she has not been eating the grass; she has been eating apples off the apple tree. Picking apples is not an innate horse behavior; the pony's behavior was shaped. During her wanderings, the pony would sometimes graze under the apple tree, occasionally finding apples on the ground, which, since horses love apples, served as an excellent reinforcer for grazing in this area. After eating all the apples from the ground, the pony noticed the apples on the lower branches of the tree, ate those, and then learned that there were apples on the entire tree and that she could eat as many as she could reach. In this way, the pony's ability to pick apples off the apple tree was shaped by her environment.

Through the process of shaping, animals and people can learn to perform many complex behaviors as seen in animal shows at the zoo. In one popular trick the elephant lies on top of the trainer, shakes its head when the trainer points up, then finally gets up when the trainer tickles its ribs. Shaping is essentially a method of indicating to a person or animal those responses that lead to a desired behavior, which in turn is ultimately "controlled" by a particular cue or stimulus in the environment. When a certain stimulus is present, a shaped response sequence is likely to occur. For example, when the pony sees the apple tree (the stimulus), she responds by looking for apples on the ground and on the tree. Her shaped behavior (apple picking) is under the control of the stimulus (the apple tree) with which it is associated.

Generalization and Discrimination

Shaping is a lot like the discrimination training involved in classical conditioning. In fact, both generalization and discrimination occur in operant conditioning as well as in classical conditioning. A rat that is learning to push a lever to receive a pellet of food may at first push the lever with its paw, its nose, or any other part of its anatomy. This generalized behavior may be reduced to discriminative behavior only if a specific response is reinforced, such as pushing the bar with its paw.

The principles of generalization and discrimination can also be seen in the case of three-year-old Michael. His family was eating dinner at a local restaurant when a small man (a dwarf) walked in. Michael said in a voice loud enough for everyone in the restaurant to hear, "Look, Daddy, a hobbit." Michael had just seen the movie *The Hobbit* and had been reinforced for correctly identifying the hobbits in the film. To the embarrassment of his parents, he had *generalized* the term from cartoon characters to people. *Generalization* is, basically, a tendency to respond in the same way to cues in the environment that have similar characteristics. *Discrimination,* on the other hand, is the ability to distinguish relevant cues from irrelevant ones.

Discrimination occurs only when responses to specific stimuli are reinforced, so that responses to irrelevant stimuli are extinguished. You can imagine Michael's disappointment when he was told that the man in the restaurant was not a hobbit but a dwarf. This was the beginning of discrimination training, in that the boy was not reinforced for generalizing the term "hobbit" to all short people but *was* reinforced for using the correct word, "dwarf."

B. F. Skinner (1979) conducted a series of interesting experiments during World War II involving the discriminative abilities of pigeons: He taught pigeons to discriminate enemy ships from other variables in the surrounding environment. The object was to place the pigeons inside missiles and have them, though a previously trained pecking behavior, "guide" the missile into enemy ships. "Project Pigeon" was never approved by the U.S. Defense Department, so no pigeons were asked to give their lives for their country. The U.S. Coast Guard has, however, successfully used pigeons to help in search and rescue operations at sea by training the birds to respond only to the color orange, which is the color of life jackets.

At this point we encourage you to review Table 6.1, which summarizes the major differences and similarities between classical and operant conditioning.

 Try This Yourself

Having learned some basic principles governing operant conditioning, how can you effectively apply them in your own life?

The best rule to follow is to use a combination of the major techniques: *Reinforce* appropriate behavior, *extinguish* inappropriate behavior, and save *punishment* for the most extreme cases (such as a two-year-old's running into the street). Remember that you have grown up in a culture that often considers reinforcement to be "bribery" and slightly unethical and, ironically, stresses punishment. We encourage you to explore the technique of reinforcement—you'll find it very rewarding! Here are some further guidelines.

1. Feedback In using both reinforcement and punishment, be sure to provide immediate and clear feedback to the person or animal whose behavior you wish to change. When using punishment, it is particularly important to make clear the desired response, since punishment is merely an indication that the response is undesirable. In other words, give the subject an alternative response to the punished one.

2. Timing Reinforcers and punishers should be presented as close in time to the response as possible. The old policy of "waiting till Father gets home" is obviously inappropriate for many reasons. The chief one is that delayed punishment is no longer associated with the inappropriate response. The same is true for reinforcement. If you're trying to lose weight, don't say you'll buy yourself a new wardrobe when you lose 30 pounds; reward yourself with a small treat (like a new blouse or shirt) after every few pounds.

3. Consistency With both reinforcement and punishment, be consistent in your responses. Take our example of the parents who gave in to their child's screaming for a lollipop. Many such parents create a tremendous problem for themselves because they are firm one time, refusing to give in or even punishing the temper tantrum, but the

Table 6.1   **A Review of Conditioning**

	Classical Conditioning	Operant Conditioning
OTHER NAMES	Respondent conditioning Pavlovian conditioning	Instrumental conditioning Law of Effect (Thorndike) Skinnerian conditioning
PIONEERS	Ivan Pavlov John B. Watson	Edward Thorndike B. F. Skinner
EXAMPLE	Sound of bell (CS) begins to produce salivation	Baby cries and parent picks baby up
MAJOR TERMS	Unconditioned stimulus (UCS) Conditioned stimulus (CS) Unconditioned response (UCR) Conditioned response (CR) Conditioned emotional response (CER)	Reinforcers (primary and secondary) Reinforcement (positive and negative) Punishment (positive and negative) Shaping Reinforcement Schedules (continuous and partial)
SHARED TERMS	Extinction Spontaneous recovery Generalization Discrimination	Extinction Spontaneous recovery Generalization Discrimination
MAJOR DIFFERENCES	Involuntary (subject is passive)	Voluntary (subject is active)
BEHAVIOR ORDER	CS must come *before* the UCS	Reinforcement comes *after* the behavior

next time are so embarrassed or hassled that they go ahead and buy the lollipop. It would be much more productive to use extinction (by ignoring the tantrum) all the time. Since punishment requires such a high level of surveillance and consistency that few parents can effectively use it, what really occurs is a partial schedule of reinforcement, which maintains behaviors long-term.

4. Order of presentation   To use reinforcement or punishment effectively, be sure that it comes *after* the behavior, never before. Can you imagine how angry you would be if your instructor assumed that all students cheat on tests when given the chance and thus punished you ahead of time with restrictive rules during a testing situation? Undoubtedly you've managed to obtain a few unearned rewards by plying your parents with empty promises of washing the car or mowing the grass on Saturday if they would just let you use the car on Friday night. When you're teaching your own students or raising your own children, remember to use your psychology and only punish them *after* they've cheated and reward them *after* they've washed the car. ▪

Conditioning in Action: Using Learning Principles in Everyday Life

In the mid-1960s, Neal Miller and Leo DiCara (1967), among others, found that operant conditioning could be used to train rats to control their heart rates. Heart rate is regulated by the autonomic nervous system (see Chapter 2). Until this time, it had been thought that autonomic system function was totally automatic and not subject to conscious control. But Miller and DiCara demonstrated that autonomic functions *can* be regulated. By implanting an electrode in the pleasure center of a rat's brain, they trained the rat to increase its heart rate by stimulating the pleasure center every time the heartbeat increased. Very slowly, the rat began to increase its heart rate by itself. In the same way, Miller and DiCara trained rats to *lower* their heart rates.

Although Miller (Dworkin and Miller, 1986) has subsequently been unable to replicate his original 1967 research, he nonetheless opened the door to similar research with humans. Other researchers have documented that humans can be taught to control their heart rates, their blood pressure, their skin temperature, and even the electrical activity of their brains. The ability to do so is achieved through a procedure known as biofeedback.

During the process of biofeedback, short for "biological feedback," information about some biological function, such as heart rate, is fed back to the individual in some type of signal. Sit quietly for a moment and try to determine your heart rate without feeling your pulse. Is it high or low? Is it different from a few minutes ago? You can't tell, can you? Therefore, it is impossible for you to learn to control your heart rate consciously. But if you were hooked up to a device that displayed your heart rate to you, you would have the information (feedback) that you need to learn to control it.

Biofeedback is actually a type of secondary reinforcement, since it reinforces a desired physiological change that has beneficial results (the primary reinforcement). Several researchers have successfully used biofeedback techniques to treat problems such as epilepsy, by changing brain wave patterns (Psatta, 1983); hypertension, by lowering blood pressure (Erbeck, Elfner, and Driggs, 1983; McGrady, Fine, Woerner, and Yonker, 1983); and migraine headache, by redirecting blood flow (Labbe and Williamson, 1983).

When it was first discovered that humans could apply biofeedback, there was great optimism that it could be used to relieve a multitude of disorders, from high blood pressure to asthma. The enthusiasm has waned over the years because biofeedback techniques are difficult to learn. Even when they have been learned in a clinical setting, they are difficult to practice on returning to everyday life. However, biofeedback is still being used with considerable success in conjunction with other techniques, especially in pain control and stress management programs.

Biofeedback: A procedure in which people's biological functions are monitored and the results made known to them so they can learn to control these functions.

Biofeedback has been used in an attempt to control chronic pain.

Programmed Instruction: Personalized learning that makes use of operant conditioning techniques, whereby students read a section of text, then test themselves on the material. They continue on to the next section or review the previous one, depending on the results of the test.

Programmed Instruction

Programmed instruction, or personalized instruction, is another example of the practical use of operant conditioning techniques. In programmed instruction, you learn at your own pace. Typically, you read a chapter or section of a textbook and then test yourself on the section. If you pass the test, you are "rewarded" by being allowed to continue to the next section. If you fail the test, you are "punished" by being told not to advance to the following section until you have reread and mastered the previous section. In this way, you proceed at a pace that is right for you, not one that is dictated by a professor. Programmed instruction can be in the form of a workbook, a computer program, a record, a videotape, or any combination. The main idea behind programmed learning is to allow learning at an individual pace by rewarding appropriate study habits and punishing poor habits.

Review Questions

1. To extinguish an operant conditioned response, you should withhold the
   _____ .

2. Which type of reinforcement schedule is being described?
   a. every third response is being reinforced
   b. it leads to the slowest extinction
   c. subjects tend to respond with bursts of responses toward the end of the interval
   d. it leads to slow, steady response rates

3. Marshall wears the same necklace to every exam, even though in reality the necklace has nothing to do with the exam. Explain how his superstitious behavior might have developed.

4. How would you use shaping to teach a friend proper diving techniques?

5. For reinforcement or punishment to be effective, it must be administered _____ the target behavior.

Answers to Review Questions can be found in Appendix C.

COGNITIVE LEARNING

So far, we have examined learning processes that involve associations between a stimulus and an observable behavior. We have described how associations are formed between bells and salivation, between white rats and fear, between Koko's making a sign for food and her receiving a piece of fruit. Although most behaviorists argue that all learning can be explained in stimulus–response terms, many psychologists feel that there is more to learning than tangible, observable factors. *Cognitive psychologists* maintain that much, if not all, of learning involves internal mental processes that cannot be seen. Thus, they study thinking, or *cognitive,* processes. According to cognitive psychologists, we begin learning at the instant we pay attention to some stimulus, such as a winged creature alighting on the branch outside our window. We mentally compare it to similar creatures we already know and discover how it "fits" into our existing cognitive structure. In this way, we form a concept about the new creature and store it in memory according to how that concept fits with our preexisting ones.

Cognitive psychologists think of the learner as an information processing system. They are interested in how we acquire information about our world and process that information to store it in our memories. They study our perceptual processes of attention, selection, and organization. They examine our abilities to form mental images, to conceptualize, to reason, to solve problems. They probe how we remember information we've acquired by examining the stages and types of memory. Because these topics of study are discussed elsewhere in this book, particularly in the perception, memory, thinking, and development chapters, we will focus on the background of cognitive learning in this chapter.

Cognitive learning as a learning theory is relatively new—in fact, it did not gain full recognition until the 1960s. That is not to say there was no research investigating thinking processes before this time. Several researchers were active and set the stage for cognitive psychologists today. The most influential were Wolfgang Köhler and Edward C. Tolman.

The Study of Insight: Köhler's Work with Chimpanzees

Because thinking and reasoning are internal events and not directly observable, it is difficult to design experiments in which they can be directly observed and measured. This, along with the fact that most experiments had been conducted with animals that have less developed thinking abilities than humans, is a major reason conditioning theories were dominant for so long. However, in the earlier part of this century, Wolfgang Köhler successfully designed experiments to study the cognitive element in learning.

Köhler believed there was more to learning than isolated stimulus–response relationships—that learning to solve a complex problem, for instance, involves more than a series of responses to stimuli made in a trial-and-error fashion. He designed several experiments to study the role of insight in learning. Insight is a sudden flash of understanding that occurs when you are trying to solve a problem.

• How do we learn according to cognitive learning theory?

Insight: A sudden flash of understanding that occurs when you are trying to solve a problem.

Critical Thinking
PSYCHOLOGY IN ACTION
TRANSFERRING IDEAS TO NEW CONTEXTS
Operant Conditioning in the Real World

The major problem with "learning about learning" is that students don't integrate the new terminology and concepts into their everyday lives. They fail to appreciate the power of simple learning principles. Critical thinking requires the learner to rise above old, easy patterns of behavior and apply new knowledge to everyday situations. When you transfer an idea or concept from one situation to another your insight grows.

This exercise is designed to improve your basic understanding of operant conditioning while also developing your ability to apply new concepts to your everyday life.

Situation #1
Suppose a large number of students regularly arrive late to one of your classes. The professor is obviously disturbed. How would you advise your professor to reduce tardiness? Consider the following four questions in developing your course of action.

1. Would you recommend that the professor punish students for being late or reinforce students for being on time? Why?

2. If the professor decides to use punishment, what type of positive punishment could he or she employ? What type of negative punishment?

3. What type of positive reinforcement or negative reinforcement would be effective for reinforcing timely attendance?

4. Once the goal of reduced tardiness is met, what type of reinforcement schedule would be best to avoid either the extinction of the behavior of coming on time or eventual ineffectiveness of the reinforcement?

Situation #2
Because of the rising crime rate in your city, you have decided that you want to condition your St. Bernard, Otto, to run to the door and bark every time someone knocks or rings your doorbell. Since this is a relatively complicated behavior, you decide to shape this behavior using positive reinforcement. To arrive at a plan for shaping Otto's behavior, consider the following questions.

1. What will you use as the positive reinforcement for Otto?

2. What is a likely list of successive approximations to the desired behavior?

3. Once you have shaped Otto to bark when someone is at your door, how will you keep this barking behavior from extinguishing when you are the only person to come to your door for several weeks?

4. How will you extinguish Otto's behavior if your neighbors complain about his barking?

Grande, one of Köhler's chimps, has just solved a problem using insight.

In his experiments, Köhler posed several different types of problems to chimpanzees. In an experiment conducted in 1917, he placed a banana outside the reach of a caged chimpanzee. To reach the banana, the chimp would have to use a stick placed near the cage to extend its reach. The chimp did not solve this problem in the random trial-and-error fashion of Thorndike's cats or Skinner's rats and pigeons, but rather sat and seemed to think about the situation for a while. Then, in a flash of insight (as Köhler termed it), the chimp picked up the stick and maneuvered the banana within its grasp (Köhler, 1925).

Another of Köhler's chimps, an intelligent fellow named Sultan, was put in a similar situation. But this time there were two sticks available to him and the banana was placed even farther away, too far to reach with a single stick. Sultan played with the sticks and seemed to think about the problem for a period of weeks. One day, he got up and inserted one bamboo stick into the hollow end of another, producing a stick that was twice as long. With this longer stick he was able to reach the distant banana. Köhler designated this type of learning *insight learning*, because there was obviously some mental event that we can only describe as "insight" that went on between the presentation of the banana and using the stick to get it.

Latent Learning: Tolman's "Hidden Learning"

Most learning theorists, certainly the behaviorists, hold that for learning to occur, a response must be reinforced. Perhaps this is true for certain types of learning, but consider for a moment: Aren't you filled with "useless" knowledge that you have yet to demonstrate, simply because the right situation hasn't arisen? Children often ride their bikes around their neighborhoods for no particular purpose. In so doing, they learn names of streets, locations of mailboxes, which houses have RVs in their driveways, which streets end in cul-de-sacs, and so on. In effect, they form a map of the neighborhood in their minds, with no thought of ever having to retrieve the information for a reward.

Edward Tolman felt that a significant amount of learning consists of such latent learning, learning that occurs in the absence of any reward and remains hidden until some future time when it can be retrieved. If you were one of those aimlessly wandering bike riders, you probably learned a lot about your neighborhood, but this learning remained latent unless you needed to mail a letter or give directions to a newcomer to the neighborhood. (The information about the locations of the RVs, on the other hand, would probably never need to be retrieved.) Your learning was clearly cognitive in nature—you did not learn the locations of the mailboxes and RVs in exchange for a reward.

It's easy to see that we humans can learn without being immediately reinforced, but is that true of other animals as well? Tolman found that latent learning does indeed occur in other animals. He designed an experiment with two groups of rats. One group explored a maze in an aimless fashion and received no reinforcement for doing so, while the rats in another group were reinforced with food whenever they reached the end of the maze. The rats were allowed to explore their mazes for 10 days. On the eleventh day, food reinforcers were placed at the end of the maze for both the control and the experimental group. The previously unrewarded rats, after only one or two reinforced trials, reached the food as quickly as the rewarded rats (Tolman and Honzik, 1930). From this research, Tolman proposed that people and animals learn to navigate in their environment by creating cognitive maps of the area. In the case of his experimental rats, information in their cognitive maps remained latent until they discovered the food at the end of the maze. So it seems that rats, as well as people, learn information that remains latent until there is sufficient reason to retrieve it.

Latent Learning: Learning that occurs in the absence of a reward and remains hidden until some future time when it can be retrieved.

Cognitive Map: A mental image of an area that a person or animal has navigated.

OBSERVATIONAL LEARNING

Can you remember when you got into the driver's seat of a car for your first driving lesson? On your first time at the wheel, did you *randomly* push buttons, pull levers, and turn the steering wheel? Of course not. You had watched others drive cars countless times before. During the months immediately preceding your first chance at the wheel, you probably paid close attention to the driver every time you were in a car. You were learning how to drive through observation. Many things we do, from driving a car to brushing our teeth, have been learned by watching someone else, by reading a "how-to" book, or by being given direct instruction. This type of learning is called *observational learning.* Although early animal research with this type of learning met with little success (Thorndike, 1898, 1901), research gained recognition in the 1960s when Albert Bandura conducted a series of studies on social learning in children.

Bandura's research illustrates how children learn through observation. In one of his experiments he asked children to view a film of someone acting aggressively toward toys in a playroom (Bandura and Walters, 1963). Later, the children were given the opportunity to play in the same room with the same toys. The children who had seen the film were much more aggressive with the toys than children who had not seen it. They had learned how to act in a particular situation by observing another person in that situation. Bandura called this "social learning," which is essentially the same as observational learning. His social learning theory proposes that people learn various behaviors by observing others who serve as *models*.

• Can people learn merely by watching other people?

Social Learning Theory: A theory developed by Bandura proposing that people learn various behaviors by observing others who serve as models.

The Observational Learning Process

According to Bandura, there are four processes involved in learning through observation: (1) We must attend to the model (of course, if we aren't paying attention, we won't

The top series of photographs shows the woman model hitting the "Bobo" doll. The bottom series of photographs shows a girl imitating the model.

Many of the skills we have acquired have been learned through observing and imitating others or by listening to and carrying out their directions.

Modeling: Learning by imitating the behaviors of others.

Vicarious Conditioning: Learning by watching a model or reading about a task.

know what behavior is being exhibited); (2) we must use our cognitive abilities to organize and remember the modeled behavior; (3) we must be able to put into practice what was observed (for instance, we wouldn't be able to imitate someone riding a bike if we were paralyzed); and (4) we must decide whether we want to repeat the modeled behavior, based on whether the model was reinforced or punished and/or based on our esteem for the model.

We can see these processes at work when we apply them to the subjects in Bandura's experiment who learned to imitate the aggressive behavior they had observed in models. The children were paying attention to the aggressive behavior of the models. Their cognitive processes were organizing and remembering what they had seen, as confirmed by their subsequent actions. The children were able to physically perform the modeled behaviors. And many of the children made the decision to imitate the observed behaviors (Josephson, 1987).

Through modeling, we learn to imitate all kinds of behavior. Patterson and her associates served as models for Koko as she was learning to acquire new signs. Student teachers learn teaching and discipline techniques by observing their master teachers. Children, as Bandura's study showed, can learn aggression from watching aggressive models. Thus, if you as a parent were to spank your daughter for hitting her brother, you might temporarily suppress your daughter's hitting behavior, but you would also be serving as an aggressive model yourself. If you handle the situation in a calm, courteous manner, you model a behavior more consistent with how you would like your daughter to behave.

Vicarious Conditioning

We can be classically conditioned through observational learning. Patricia Barnett and David Benedetti (1960) have called this vicarious conditioning. In one experiment they asked subjects to observe a model who was being classically conditioned to react to a buzzer. The model heard a buzzer and a few seconds later received a shock. Each time the shock was administered, the model would quickly remove his or hand from the shock plate. When the observers were subsequently tested, they also reflexively removed their hands from the shock plate in response to the buzzer, even though they had never actually been shocked. Vicarious conditioning has also been demonstrated with operant conditioning (Bandura, 1971).

 Try This Yourself

Be aware of the power of modeling (Chance, 1979). If you are out with a friend or your child and observe some other person acting in a way that is against your standards or morals, be sure that you let the person you're with know how you feel about that act. If you don't, he or she may think you approve of the behavior. Parents, who are concerned about their children imitating good role models, must be doubly sure they make their opinions known. For example, if you take your child to see a movie with excessive violence and you say nothing—or worse yet, you cheer on the violence—your child will learn that violent behavior is acceptable. Make sure you let your children know by your words and actions which people you consider good models. Silence in the face of unacceptable behavior indicates approval. ■

In this chapter we have discussed a number of learning principles. Effective application of these principles can benefit all of us in our everyday learning situations. You can apply classical conditioning techniques to situations involving emotions and reflexes (e.g., extinguishing a fear of heights). Apply operant conditioning techniques to "training" situations and when you're trying to form new habits (e.g., giving candies as positive reinforcers when toilet training a toddler, or buying a new sweater when you've lost 5 pounds). Apply cognitive techniques to situations involving thinking, problem solving, and memory processes (e.g., learning and remembering information in a textbook). Finally, apply observational learning techniques when learning how to perform a new behavior through observation and modeling (e.g., learning how to tune up a car).

Keep in mind, however, that since human behavior is so very complex, most human learning is *not* a result of one specific learning method. Most behaviors such as human language are learned through a combination of conditioning, cognitive, and observational methods. Thus, although some learning theory purists really believe that all learning can be narrowed down to one type, most psychologists agree that our knowledge is acquired through a combination of methods.

Gender and Cultural Diversity

SCAFFOLDING AS A TEACHING TECHNIQUE IN DIFFERENT CULTURES

You probably have noticed that learning in the real world is often a combination of classical conditioning, operant conditioning, and observational learning. This is especially evident in informal learning situations where individual skills are acquired under the supervision of a master or mentor. The ideal process used by teachers in these situations is known as *scaffolding* (Wood, Bruner, and Ross, 1976). When using scaffolding, the teacher provides selective guidance to the student or apprentice that enables him or her to accomplish tasks that would be impossible without the greater skill and knowledge of the teacher. In most cases, scaffolding is a combination of shaping and modeling, where the teacher reinforces successes of the student and models more difficult parts of the task. Patricia Marks Greenfield (1984) describes two very different examples of scaffolding from two diverse cultures, language learning in Los Angeles and learning to weave in Zinacantan, Mexico. Although the cultures, tasks, and ages of the learners are quite different, the scaffolding process is quite similar.

The study of Los Angeles children focused on the process of how children learn the meaning of adult-initiated offers, such as "Do you want a cookie?" or "Do you want to go for a ride?" Greenfield defines a successful offer in terms of its organizational structure: The offer must be presented to the child; the child must acknowledge the offer; and some object, action, or information must be exchanged from the adult to the child. Therefore, in a successful offer of a piggy-back ride, the mother makes a verbal offer; the child acknowledges the offer in some way (by indicating he or she wants it), and the mother gives the child the ride. When the child's verbal skills are not developed to a point where the child can comprehend a verbal offer, the mother uses a scaffolding process. She uses nonverbal cues as the scaffold and models the correct verbal response. In this way, the mother shapes the response of the child capable of making a verbal response and models appropriate behavior for the child who has not yet acquired the necessary verbal skills. Thus, it is through the scaffolding process that mothers help children learn verbal and nonverbal language involved in accepting offers of things they want.

Weaving, of course, is not as universal as language, but the scaffolding process is similar. Weaving is an important part of the culture of the Zinacantecos who live in the highlands of southern Mexico. Greenfield taped 14 girls at different levels of learning to weave. The weaving skills of the girls varied considerably, but the researchers were unable to distinguish between the final products of the girls because of the widespread use of scaffolding. The inexperienced girls were constantly monitored by experienced teachers. Each girl was allowed to complete what she was able to do with ease, while a

This photo shows a younger Zina-canteco girl learning to weave through the scaffolding process.

more experienced teacher took over during the more difficult parts. However, no matter what the skill level of the novice weaver, she was able to produce a final product equal to the other weavers because of the scaffolding process. The experienced weaver created the scaffold by reinforcing correct weaving technique and modeling more difficult technique. For the first-time weavers, the teachers took over 53 percent of the time, during which the new weavers watched the teacher approximately 87 percent of the time.

Although both the tasks and the cultures are different, the scaffolding processes are similar. First, the scaffold is adapted to the skill level of the learner so that learners are able to accomplish tasks they cannot accomplish on their own. Second, the amount of scaffolding and intervention by the parent or teacher decreases as the skill level of the learner increases. Third, scaffolding always involves a combination of shaping and modeling. Finally, in both situations the teachers appear oblivious of their teaching methods or of the fact that they are teaching at all. Most of the Zinacanteco women believe that girls learn to weave by themselves, and it is a common belief in Western culture that children learn to talk by themselves. ■

Review Questions

1. Cognitive psychologists think of the learner as an information processing system. What does this mean?

2. You are experiencing _____ when all of a sudden you hit upon the solution to a problem that has been bothering you.

3. In order for learning to occur, must a response be reinforced? Explain.

4. Learning by watching others is called _____ learning.

5. If you taught a younger sibling to frost your mom's birthday cake by doing it yourself while he watched, you would be serving as a _____ .

Answers to Review Questions can be found in Appendix C.

REVIEW OF MAJOR CONCEPTS

LEARNING AND INNATE BEHAVIORS

1. Learning is a relatively permanent change in behavior or behavioral potential as a result of practice or experience. A learned behavior is opposed to an innate, or instinctual, behavior, which is affected by maturation only and not by practice. Both learned behaviors and innate behaviors are exhibited in animals, including humans.

2. Conditioning emphasizes the relationship between a stimulus and a response. There are both classical and operant conditioning theories.

3. Cognitive learning emphasizes thinking processes as they are related to learning.

4. Observational learning explains how people and animals learn by watching a model perform a task.

CLASSICAL CONDITIONING

5. Classical conditioning is the type of learning investigated by Ivan Pavlov in which an originally neutral stimulus is paired with another stimulus that causes a reflex response.

After several pairings, the neutral stimulus will cause the response to occur.

6. The terminology used in classical conditioning consists of the following:
   a. The neutral stimulus does not normally cause any particular reflex or emotional response. In classical conditioning, it is paired with a stimulus that does cause such a response.
   b. The stimulus that causes a reflex or emotional response is called the unconditioned stimulus (UCS).
   c. The reflex or emotional response is called the unconditioned response (UCR).
   d. When the neutral stimulus begins to cause the response, it is then called the conditioned stimulus (CS).
   e. When the response is caused by the conditioned stimulus, it is called the conditioned response (CR).

7. In higher order conditioning, the neutral stimulus is paired with a conditioned stimulus, one to which the subject has already been conditioned, rather than with an unconditioned stimulus as in primary conditioning.

8. In classical conditioning, extinction occurs when the unconditioned stimulus is repeatedly withheld and the previous association between the CS and the UCS is broken. Spontaneous recovery occurs when a CR that had been extinguished spontaneously reappears.

9. Generalization occurs when stimuli similar to the original CS elicit the CR. Discrimination occurs when only the CS elicits the CR.

OPERANT CONDITIONING

10. Operant conditioning is the type of learning originally investigated by B. F. Skinner in which people or animals learn by the consequences of their responses.

11. In operant conditioning, when a response is made it is either reinforced or punished. Reinforcement is anything that is likely to cause an increase in the response. Punishment is anything that is likely to cause a decrease in the response.

12. Positive reinforcement occurs when something desirable is given or added so that subjects will increase their response rates. Negative reinforcement occurs when something bad or aversive is removed to increase the response rate.

13. Positive punishment occurs when something bad or aversive is given to decrease the response rate. Negative punishment occurs when something good is removed to decrease the response rate.

14. In operant conditioning, extinction occurs when the reinforcement is withheld until the subject stops responding to the stimulus, and spontaneous recovery occurs just as it does after the classical conditioning extinction process.

The amount of time required for extinction is directly related to the schedule of reinforcement being used.

15. In operant conditioning, there are several schedules of reinforcement. Continuous schedules of reinforcement consist of subjects being reinforced for each response. Partial schedules of reinforcement consist of subjects being reinforced for some, but not all, responses.

16. Superstitious behaviors occur when people or animals make responses they think are connected to rewards when in reality their responses have nothing to do with the rewards.

17. Suggestions for the effective use of both reinforcement and punishment include the following:
    a. Provide clear and immediate feedback when the person or animal makes the desired response.
    b. Apply reinforcers or punishers as soon as possible after the response is made.
    c. Be consistent in applying both reinforcers and punishers.
    d. Be sure to reinforce or punish immediately after the behavior has been exhibited.

18. Shaping is the process of teaching a person or animal a complex task by reinforcing successive approximations to a desired response.

19. Biofeedback is the "feeding back" to subjects of biological information such as heart rate or blood pressure so they can use the information to control normally automatic functions of the body.

20. Programmed instruction is an application of operant conditioning techniques whereby people learn at their own pace.

COGNITIVE LEARNING

21. Cognitive psychologists are interested in investigating the mental or cognitive processes that lead to responses.

22. Wolfgang Köhler, in working with chimpanzees, demonstrated that learning could occur with a sudden flash of insight.

23. Edward Tolman demonstrated latent learning, learning that occurs in the absence of reinforcements and remains hidden until it is needed.

OBSERVATIONAL LEARNING

24. Observational learning is the process of learning how to do something by watching a behavior occur or reading about one, rather than learning through doing.

25. Social learning theory was proposed by Albert Bandura to explain how people learn by observing others who serve as models.

26. Scaffolding is a teaching technique used in many cultures; it is most often used in informal situations between a master or mentor and apprentice learner and always involves a combination of shaping and modeling.

SUGGESTED READINGS

BANDURA, A. (1977). *Social learning theory*. Englewood Cliffs, NJ: Prentice-Hall. A brief overview of social learning theory.

CHANCE, P. (1994). *Learning and behavior* (3rd ed.). Belmont, CA: Wadsworth. An introduction to the study of learning.

GORDON, W. C. (1989). *Learning and memory*. Pacific Grove, CA: Brooks/Cole. A readable introduction to both learning and memory, detailing the basics of both.

SKINNER, B. F. (1979). *The shaping of a behaviorist*. New York: Knopf. The autobiography of America's most influential behaviorist.

Memory

OUTLINE

In August 1979, Father Pagano, a polite and gentle Roman Catholic priest, was on trial for a string of armed robberies. He was accused of being the "Gentleman Bandit," a thief who impressed his victims with his mild-mannered behavior. Conviction seemed certain since seven witnesses positively identified Father Pagano as the man who had robbed them. It can be difficult to get one positive identification, so seven meant there was no risk of error; seven people couldn't be mistaken. The unwavering certainty of the crime victims was particularly surprising in light of Father Pagano's status as a priest—a champion of the poor—who maintained his innocence from the time of his arrest. Was he a modern-day Robin Hood who stole from the rich to help the downtrodden?

Father Pagano's trial was terminated when the real robber, Ronald Clouser, confessed. Clouser said he committed the robberies because his marriage was disintegrating and he was deeply in debt. Being a basically decent person, though, he did not want an innocent man to be punished for his crimes. This story could have gone down as a simple case of mistaken identity except that the two men were so unalike. At the time of the trial, Clouser was 39 and Father Pagano was 53 and balding (Loftus, 1980).

How could seven people have made such a mistake? Perhaps, through pure coincidence, all seven were born with bad memories. But is anyone really born with a good or bad memory? You would probably give anything for a memory like the winning contestants on TV's *Jeopardy* or those history buffs who can remember countless dates and facts. Are these people born with their abilities, or do they develop techniques that enable them to efficiently store and retrieve facts and figures?

Most early psychologists felt that some people have good memories whereas others have poor ones, and that not much could be done to change one's memory abilities. On the basis of these assumptions, they focused on devising tests to measure and diagnose individual differences in memory. Psychologists have discovered, however, that memory is not a "given" but rather an ever-changing ability strongly influenced by internal and situational factors. These factors can indeed account for memory errors such as Father Pagano's mistaken identity.

In this chapter, you will discover there are actually three types of memory that operate in different stages, the first holding information for a fleeting instant, the second for a short while, and the third for an indefinite time. You will learn about factors that determine how well we remember some things and why we forget others. You will find that our memories can be altered over time and that we remember things that never actually happened. You will also learn techniques to help you increase your memory capacity.

As you read Chapter 7, keep the following **Survey** questions in mind and answer them in your own words:

* What are the three stages of memory? What factors are involved in order for information to be sent on to the next stage, to be stored, and to be retrieved?

* Why do we forget, and what are some techniques to prevent forgetting?

* How can memory be explained in terms of biological processes? What are some factors leading to memory impairment?

* Can everyone improve his or her memory?

A THREE-STAGE MEMORY MODEL

Researchers have identified at least three distinct stages of memory: sensory memory, short-term memory, and long-term memory. Sensory memory is the initial storage of information within the senses, such as a visual or an auditory image. Short-term memory (STM) is the working memory where information is briefly stored and processed. Long-term memory (LTM) contains information and experiences that have been stored for future use (Atkinson and Schiffrin, 1968).

The flow of information from one type of memory to another is diagrammed in Figure 7.1. You can see that sensory memory is mainly an input into STM. Information can then move from STM into LTM. Since STM is the "working memory," information stored in LTM can also be moved back into STM. Note that forgetting can occur at any of the three stages in the model.

Sensory Memory: The First Stage of the Process

Hold your hand about 12 inches in front of you and look at it steadily for awhile. Now, close your eyes, and notice how long a clear image of your hand lasts. A clear visual image of an object will last in sensory memory about a half second after a stimulus is no longer received by the receptors. Any stimulus that is registered in sensory memory is available to be selected for attention and for processing into a more permanent type of memory.

Sperling's Research

George Sperling (1960) was the first to investigate sensory memory. Sperling found that his subjects had nearly unlimited access to information in visual images for a brief period of time. In one of his early experiments, he rapidly flashed a three-letter by three-letter matrix on a screen in front of his subjects. Then he asked the subjects to recall as many of the letters as they could. Even when the matrix was on the screen for only a few milliseconds, subjects were able to read several letters—just as many as if the entire matrix had been shown for a much longer time. Sperling's results suggest that *all* objects in the visual field are available in this first stage of memory if they can be attended to quickly. From this and other studies, early researchers assumed that sensory memory had an unlimited capacity. Later research has shown, however, that while the

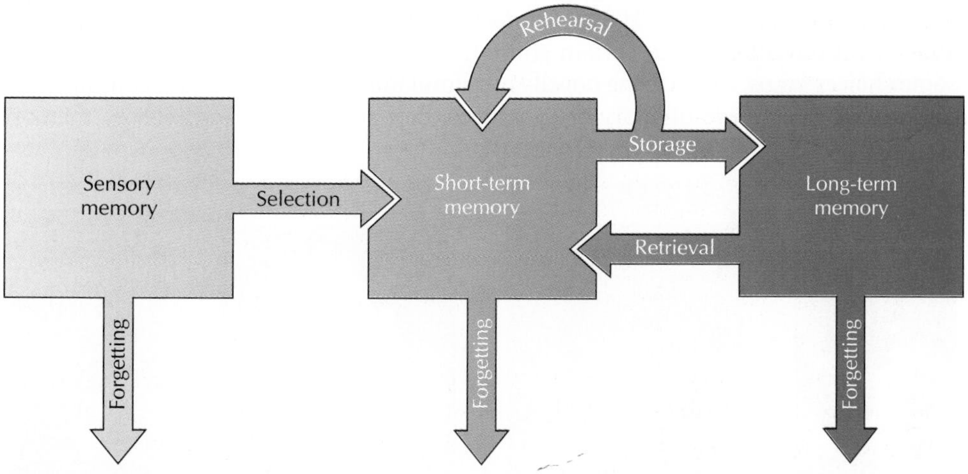

* *What are the three stages of memory? What factors are involved in order for information to be sent on to the next stage, to be stored, and to be retrieved?*

Sensory Memory: The type of memory that occurs within the senses while incoming messages are being transmitted to the brain.

Short-Term Memory (STM): Memory containing things a person is presently thinking about; its capacity is limited to about seven items and a duration of about 30 seconds.

Long-Term Memory (LTM): Relatively permanent memory in which information is stored for use at a later time.

Figure 7.1 The three-stage memory model. Information enters through sensory memory then passes into short-term memory. Maintenance rehearsal can keep information in short-term memory or the information can be transferred into long-term memory. Once information has been stored in long-term memory it must be transferred to short-term memory before it can be used again.

capacity of sensory memory is quite large, it is not unlimited, and the image stored in sensory memory is fuzzier than was once thought (Best, 1992, p. 144).

The information in sensory memory is temporary. As you just noticed, visual images last about ¼ to ½ second; sounds last a bit longer, up to four seconds (Neisser, 1967). Although these times seem very brief, four seconds of availability of auditory information is generally enough to reanalyze what we have heard and figure out what a person said before the sounds disappear completely. If you have ever said, "What?" to someone and then responded before the person had time to repeat the statement, you were able to refocus on the sound in auditory sensory memory and figure out what was said. When you refocus on a sound or visual image, it is entered into STM, the working space for current attention where sounds or sights can be interpreted. Only the information selected for passage into STM receives further processing and has a chance of being stored permanently.

Short-Term Memory: Selecting and Concentrating

Look up from this book for a moment and notice what occupies your visual attention. What do you see around you? Now try to identify the sounds and sensations you are currently experiencing and the thoughts that are occurring at this moment. What you have just identified is the contents of your short-term memory (STM).

Short-term memory, otherwise known as "working memory" (Baddeley, 1992), is actually the working area for the contents of our minds, much like the surface of a desk is the working area for material objects. We keep an item on our desktop long enough to work on it, then either dispose of it or store it for later use. So it is with short-term memory. Depending upon what we select for attention, the contents of STM can be dismissed, can be changed rapidly (Baddeley, 1981), or can be retained for a while. We hold information in STM long enough to evaluate it, organize it, and combine it with both new information and old information retrieved from storage (Norman, 1982). Short-term memory, then, works in two ways: to select and process ongoing information and to store memories for a short duration (Johnson and Hasher, 1987). As a working memory, STM is, in a sense, limited.

Selection

How do we decide what to allow into short-term memory? As you may remember from Chapter 4, we either pay attention to stimuli or do not pay attention through a process called *selective attention* (LaBerge, 1990). During the sensory memory stage, we select what should be sent on to STM either *automatically* or *deliberately*. If we don't deliberately direct our attention to certain stimuli, the nervous system automatically makes some choices for us. Because the novelty of stimuli was often an important consideration for survival during evolutionary development, new stimuli entering sensory memory

When you look up a telephone number, you can rehearse it to keep it in short-term memory; however, you might not remember the number after you dial unless you have stored it in long-term memory.

were given top priority for selection. Paying attention to new or unusual signals helped early humans avoid becoming meals for predators. That's why movements in the visual field or unfamiliar noises outside the room are likely to be selected for STM. In addition to novel stimuli, any input related to satisfying basic needs such as hunger or thirst is automatically selected. This is also a survival mechanism, but it can be quite unpleasant if you are on a diet and find yourself constantly noticing food stimuli.

A fortunate aspect of selecting contents for short-term memory is that it *can* be a deliberate process. It is possible to use the information stored in long-term memory to guide your attention at any particular time. For instance, if you are determined to do well in a course, you can direct your attention to the instructor's voice and make yourself think about what is happening in class rather than filling your short-term memory with distractions or daydreams.

Whenever your attention is diverted to something happening around you, it is possible to stop selecting that input and concentrate on whatever is more important to you. Goals and information stored in long-term memory can take priority over novel or drive-related stimuli like a person walking by or the smell of spaghetti.

Once something has been selected for attention in short-term memory, further processing is affected by two important characteristics of STM: its limited duration and its limited capacity. Both greatly affect our ability to remember things.

Duration of Short-Term Memory

A sound or visual image lasts for a maximum of 30 seconds in STM unless it is reentered (Craik and Lockhart, 1972). A stimulus can, however, be reentered for further processing in STM. Look back to the memory model in Figure 7.1. Note that there are two arrows indicating how STM contents can be reentered. The first method involves sensory memory: If the sensation (sound, smell, and so on) is still present, it is still available for selection into STM. The other method is maintenance rehearsal, indicated by the looping arrow in the figure. When you use maintenance rehearsal, you maintain information in STM by repeating or reviewing it mentally. You use maintenance rehearsal to keep a phone number in STM long enough to dial it. When you look up a number, you can repeat it to yourself to keep it in STM. If something interrupts you for as long as 30 seconds, you have to look up the number again to reenter it through sensory memory.

In laboratory research, rehearsal can be prevented by the use of an interference task. An interference task gives subjects something to do that takes their complete attention so that no other information can be reentered into STM. One frequently used interference task is to have subjects count backward by threes, starting with a number like 574, as soon as they have read a list of words to memorize (Peterson and Peterson, 1959). For most subjects, this type of interference task is difficult enough to prevent rehearsal of the words they are attempting to memorize. Within 18 seconds, the words are forgotten (see Figure 7.2).

Maintenance Rehearsal: The process of repeating the contents of short-term memory over and over to maintain it in STM.

Interference Task: Any task that prevents maintenance rehearsal or prevents memories from being transferred to LTM.

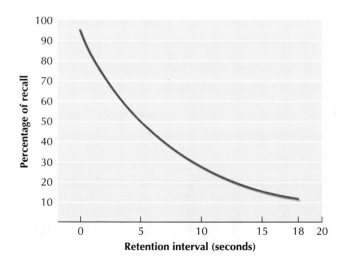

Figure 7.2 Rate of forgetting for information in short-term memory. This graph shows the rate of forgetting when an interference task prevents rehearsal of words in short-term memory.

Rehearsal is an important technique for coping with the limited duration of memory in this second stage, since information often needs to be revised and rearranged before it can be stored. The one drawback to maintenance rehearsal is that when information is continually reentered into STM, the amount of new information that can enter is curtailed because of STM's limited capacity.

Capacity of Short-Term Memory

Our capacity for holding information in STM is limited to about 7 items, compared to at least one million items (bytes) stored by microcomputers such as the IBM PC. The limited capacity of working memory can be a serious disadvantage unless you know how to use STM effectively.

For a long time, researchers were puzzled about exactly how much information could be contained in short-term memory. Psychologist George Miller described his grapplings with the problem in a famous 1956 journal article titled "The Magical Number Seven, Plus or Minus Two":

> My problem is that I have been persecuted by an integer. For seven years this number has followed me around, has intruded in my most private data, and has assaulted me from the pages of our most public journals. This number assumes a variety of disguises, being sometimes a little larger and sometimes a little smaller than usual, but never changing so much as to be unrecognizable. . . . Either there really is something unusual about the number or else I am suffering from delusions of persecution. (p. 81)

Miller noted that research study findings on the capacity of STM were not entirely consistent. For example, when subjects memorized nonsense syllables composed of three letters, like ZIQ or MUZ, they could usually keep only three syllables at a time in short-term memory. On the other hand, when subjects memorized words, they could usually remember up to seven words.

To explain this apparent inconsistency, Miller concluded that information in STM is grouped into units and that the capacity of STM is between five and nine *units* (the magical number 7, plus or minus two). Thus, the reason that only about three nonsense syllables are remembered at a time is that each of the letters of a nonsense syllable is processed in STM individually, so that three of the three-letter syllables comprise nine units. In contrast, a word is one unit regardless of the number of letters in it, so that up to nine complete words can be held in STM. Telephone numbers are easily held in short-term memory because they universally contain seven numbers. (Numbers are like the letters of nonsense syllables; they need to be processed individually.)

Doesn't this "magical number" severely limit our short-term memories? Yes, but under normal circumstances we need to retain only a few items in our short-term memories. Having too many items in STM is like having a horribly cluttered desk. If we wish to expand the number of items we can hold in STM, there are several ways. One technique is to group information into units, or chunks, a process known as chunking. Organizing letters into words and thinking of a telephone area code as a unit are examples of chunking. In reading-improvement courses, students are taught to chunk groups of words into phrases so that fewer eye movements are required and the brain can process the phrases as *units* rather than individual words.

Expert chess players use chunking to organize the information on a game board into meaningful patterns or units, as was discovered by researchers comparing expert players' memory skills to those of novice players (Chase and Simon, 1973). In these studies, a chess board was set up as it would appear during a game. Novice players who looked at the board for five seconds could remember the positions of only a few pieces, but expert chess players could frequently remember all the positions because they saw the pieces in typical groups that occur during a game. To the expert players, these groups formed meaningful patterns, just as readers see words instead of individual letters. When

Good chess players are able to remember groups of pieces by chunking them into meaningful patterns.

Chunking: The process of grouping information into units in order to store more information in short-term memory.

chess pieces were arranged randomly on the board in ways that would not occur during a game, the expert players did no better than novices in remembering the positions.

Using Short-Term Memory Effectively

Not everyone uses the maximum possible nine STM units. Some people regularly use only five units. Memory research shows that people who at first seem to have fewer spaces in STM actually have just as much STM capacity as anyone else, but they are not using this stage of memory efficiently. With attention to the limitations of STM, this stage of memory processing can be improved (Brown, Campione, and Barclay, 1978). For example, in one study, first-grade children were shown seven pictures. The teacher pointed to three of the pictures and then covered all of them. After 15 seconds, the children were asked to recall which of the pictures the teacher had pointed to and in what order. The children who had kept thinking about what had happened were able to remember the order, whereas the children who forgot the order had paid attention during the pointing but then thought about other things. When the latter children were taught how to keep the information in STM after the presentation, they were able to remember as well as the children who had spontaneously used this strategy. In a later test, only those children who went back to thinking about other things forgot the order again (Keeney, Cannizzo, and Flavell, 1967). This research points out the importance of paying attention to the things we are attempting to learn and organizing the information efficiently in STM in order to recall it later on.

If I have room for at least seven units, why do I have so much trouble remembering even three or four names during introductions?   The limited capacity and brief duration of STM both work against you in this situation. To be remembered, the name you have just heard must be selected as important enough for attention, and other things must not be selected as more important. If you want to remember a name long enough to carry on a conversation, you need to get it into your long-term memory. Because the name cannot be processed for transfer to LTM if other things occupy the STM spaces and cause interference, it helps to deliberately concentrate on the name and repeat it to improve its chances of being remembered.

When you are being introduced to people at a party, it may be that instead of concentrating on the names, you are using all the spaces in your short-term memory for wondering how you look and for rehearsing the brilliant things you will say. As you are being introduced to people, you might even notice that you have already forgotten some of the names, in which case you may fill your STM worrying about the fact that you haven't remembered them!

People who get anxious during introductions often occupy all their STM spaces with self-talk about how terrible it is not to be able to remember. People who are good at remembering names often repeat the name of each person out loud or to themselves to keep it entered in STM. They also make sure that other thoughts don't intrude until they have tested their ability to remember the name.

When being introduced, you will be more apt to remember a person's name if you can relate his or her name to something unique about the person.

Visual and Verbal Processing in STM

Visualization is a highly effective way of processing certain kinds of information but we also have a verbal "channel" for processing information contained in words and ideas. Allen Paivio (1982) refers to this two-part division of STM as a dual-coding system. Let's look at how dual coding works.

We use the visual transfer system when we look at an object such as a tree. Information about the tree is processed through STM as a visual image, and we later remember what the tree looks like in the form of a picture. Try to remember how many doors there are in the place where you live. If you visualize what the rooms look like, you can mentally walk through them to count the doors. This visual imagery system is vivid for many people. On the other hand, we use the verbal transfer system for processing words regardless of whether we hear them or see them. The word "tree" enters STM as a

Dual-Coding System: The process of coding information by both visual and verbal means.

word pattern rather than a picture of this object. The verbal channel appears to operate separately from the visual imagery system.

Since we have both visual and verbal pathways for STM information, use both systems rather than just one if you are trying to remember something. Research shows that subjects remember a word they have heard or read better when they also think of a visual image of the object that word represents (Paivio, 1969, 1971).

Levels of Processing

Another way of using STM effectively is to analyze the deeper meaning of information as opposed to simply focusing on superficial characteristics (Craik and Tulving, 1975; Morris, Bransford, and Franks, 1977). For example, if when meeting people at a party you just pay attention to their names, note whether they are male or female, and concentrate on their appearance, you are doing a superficial analysis. However, if you discuss their political or religious beliefs and find out what they like to do with their spare time, you are doing a deeper analysis and are more likely to remember them the next time you meet.

Levels of Processing: The depth to which STM contents are processed during consolidation to LTM.

According to this levels of processing approach, a deeper analysis of meaning enables us to remember information better because we store it in LTM more efficiently (Craik and Lockhart, 1972). In research on levels of processing, when subjects are instructed to look at each word on a list and think of a word that rhymes with it or notice whether the word is capitalized, they are performing a superficial analysis. When subjects are told to think of other words that have similar meanings, they are using a deeper level of processing that associates the information to be learned into the organization of LTM more effectively (Hyde and Jenkins, 1969). Thus, when you think about the meaning of the course materials you are studying, you are processing at a deeper level, which helps transfer the information more efficiently to LTM (Jacoby, 1974; Tulving and Thomson, 1973).

Review Questions

1. List and describe the three stages in the memory model.
2. How long does sensory memory last?
3. The type of memory used when remembering a telephone number just long enough to dial it is _____ .
4. What is maintenance rehearsal, and what is its purpose in short-term memory?
5. Why is it easier to memorize List A than List B (both have the same number of letters)?
    List A: art bee cat dog far get hot
    List B: ar tbe ec atd o gfa rg eth ot
6. We can process information both visually and verbally because STM has a _____ system.

Answers to Review Questions can be found in Appendix C.

Long-Term Memory: The Memory Storage System

Unlike the sensory memory and STM stages, LTM is not limited in capacity or duration. Information in LTM can last as long as we live and we never run out of places to store new information (Klatzky, 1984). However, for stored information to be useful, it must be organized so that it is available for future reference and can be updated by new information.

During the transfer of information from STM to LTM, incoming information is "tagged," or encoded, to be filed in the appropriate place. If it is not properly encoded and stored, it might not be accessible later. This storage process can require considerable time and effort. It is like organizing and filing away real items such as class notes, record albums, or tools so that they can be retrieved quickly and easily sometime in the future.

Some of the job of memory organization and filing apparently occurs during sleep. Some researchers believe that during REM sleep, our recent additions to long-term memory are reviewed, improved, and systematically catalogued (Crick and Mitchison, 1983).

Is it possible for me to learn something by listening to a tape while I'm asleep? Apparently not. Any learning from listening to a tape occurs just *before* falling asleep. Recordings of brain waves were used to determine when subjects listening to sleep learning machines were fully asleep. It was found that subjects who heard tapes while in a drowsy state could answer 50 percent of the questions they were asked about the information they heard. When they were in a transition state between drowsiness and light sleep, they could answer 5 percent of the questions. When they were fully asleep during the tape playing, they did not remember any of the information (Simon and Emmons, 1956). This research also suggests that you don't store information efficiently when you listen to lectures or study in a drowsy state. Proper encoding and storage of information require an alert mind.

The Accuracy of LTM

Have you ever been certain you're remembering something accurately but someone else has a different recollection and is just as certain he or she is correct? What causes these disagreements? Because of the nature of LTM, our memories can include additions to, omissions from, and revisions of the original event. It always seems amazing to us when we are shown that what we remember is not a perfect copy of the original event, especially if the memory seems vivid. The witnesses in Father Pagano's trial must have been startled to discover how little the real Gentleman Bandit resembled the man they had identified. Psychologists studying the memory process have identified how some stored memories are altered from the original versions while they are being encoded, filed, and stored (Kassin, Rigby, and Castillo, 1991; Loftus and Hoffman, 1989).

Sensory memory and short-term memory both tend to be like tape recordings or movies that replay information exactly, but transfer into long-term memory changes the form of the recording. For example, when subjects are given sentences to read, they can remember the exact wording if they are tested within 30 seconds. This information is coming from STM. However, when subjects are tested after 30 seconds and are prevented from using rehearsal to keep the information in STM, they often identify a sentence with the same meaning (but not the same wording) as the one they saw (Sachs, 1967). In the course of consolidating and storing the information in LTM, the exact wording has been lost.

Why isn't the original version stored in long-term memory? The answer seems to be that when information is encoded for filing in long-term storage, the meaning of the item is more important than its exact physical form. Before information is stored or catalogued, it is analyzed to determine how it can be added to what is already stored. During analysis, things can be added, left out, or rearranged. Most often, a rearranged memory is just as useful as the original version. We don't always need to remember something exactly, but we do need to know what it means. On the other hand, there are times when an exact duplicate is required of memory. When we memorize a poem or lines in a play, for example, we are making a special request of our memory processes to preserve the exact wording. It is difficult for most people to memorize exactly, since this isn't what long-term memory is designed to do.

Another reason we store an altered version of the original event is that during our analysis of incoming information, we make assumptions or inferences about the information. These assumptions occupy STM for a while and are filed along with the information being analyzed. Later, we can't accurately separate what we *assumed* from what we were given. For example, if your friend looks sad and tells you, "Fido was chasing a cat and was hit by a truck," you might assume that:

1. Fido is a dog, since this is a common name for dogs and dogs often chase cats.
2. Fido ran into the street.
3. Fido was injured or killed.

Later, what you remember your friend having said might be, "My dog Fido was killed by a truck when he ran into the street."

Another potential source of error that occurs during the storage phase of LTM is that the sources of information do not seem to be filed very carefully. That is, you may remember *what* you heard but not necessarily *where* you heard it. This can be a problem if you pay attention to both dependable and undependable sources of information. Suppose, for example, a famous movie star is interviewed on a television talk show and offers an opinion about a weight-loss diet. You might later recall that the information was presented by a dietary expert rather than a movie star with questionable credentials. A related phenomenon is known as the "sleeper effect." It occurs when a discounted previous message gains credibility or persuasiveness over time (Pratkanis et al., 1988). You've probably experienced this effect when a friend tells you about an innovative idea that is completely foreign to your way of thinking. At first, you reject the idea outright; but after a few weeks of consideration, the idea begins to seem quite plausible.

Semantic and Episodic Memory

Why do we have so much difficulty remembering where information comes from if we can analyze meaning so well? Psychologists studying memory have concluded that determining the meaning of something involves one type of memory and knowing where or when we learned about it involves a different type of memory. Why one type of memory is easier to use than the other is not known (Tulving, 1985).

The first type of long-term memory, knowledge of facts and how they relate to each other, is called semantic memory. It is like a dictionary or encyclopedia in which a large amount of factual information (such as the names of the months or mathematics skills) is stored. Once something is entered into semantic memory, it is durable and available for comparison to incoming information. The second type of long-term memory, called episodic memory, contains "autobiographical" information: when and where a specific

Semantic Memory: A type of LTM in which facts and relations between facts are stored.

Episodic Memory: A type of LTM in which memories of events are stored.

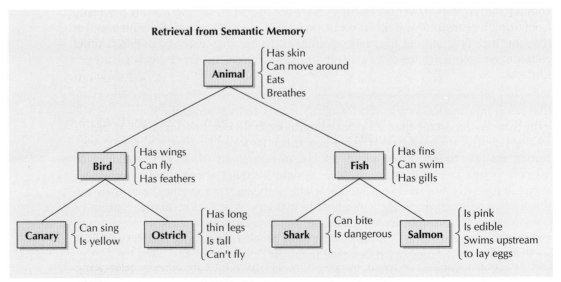

Figure 7.3 Semantic memory. Semantic long-term memory is thought to be organized as a hierarchy of concepts.

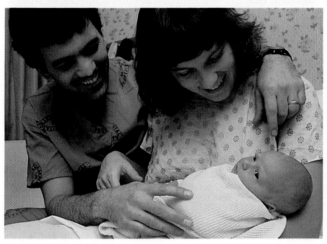

Graduation, marriage, the birth of a child, and buying a first house are examples of landmark events that enable us to locate other events in episodic memory.

event or episode happened (Tulving, 1972, 1985). For example, when you first learned to read the word "cat" years ago, it took some effort to relate that word to particular animals. By now, you have had numerous experiences with the word and it has many meanings stored in your semantic memory. These meanings are available to you any time you encounter the word. However, if you were asked to describe the exact time, date, and location of each of your experiences with the word, you would have to refer to your episodic memory and you would have a difficult time locating the information in LTM.

Several researchers have tried unsuccessfully to experimentally separate the two types of LTM (McKoon et al., 1986; Neely and Durgunoglu, 1985; Richards and Goldfarb, 1986). In explanation, Tulving (1985, 1986) has suggested that episodic memory may actually be a subsystem of semantic memory. Whether it is or not, the distinction between semantic and episodic memory is useful in studying human memory.

 Try This Yourself

Think about what you had for dinner the night of your high school senior prom or graduation. Now try to remember what you had for dinner three nights ago. The second task was probably a lot harder unless you were out on a hot date or were celebrating something. Events that are important to us—graduation, going into the Army, getting married, having a child—act as landmarks for our memory and in fact are known as

Landmark Events: Events that are important to us, such as high school graduation or getting married, that can be used as memory aids.

landmark events. We can use these events to search backward and forward in our memory to locate details about other events that occurred at about the same time. Without a landmark event, it is difficult to retrieve details from episodic memory about common everyday occurrences, such as meals (Lindsey and Norman, 1977). ■

Organization of Long-Term Memory

The diagram in Figure 7.3 illustrates one way concepts are thought to be arranged in LTM. Psychologists studying the organization of LTM believe information is filed in categories and subcategories as a network with several pathways to reach a piece of information (Collins and Quillian, 1969).

Tip-of-the-Tongue (TOT): The feeling that a word you are trying to remember is just barely inaccessible.

You can become aware of the associations and linkages by which your own LTM is organized whenever you experience the tip-of-the-tongue (TOT) phenomenon—the feeling that any second a word you are trying to remember will pop out from the tip of your tongue (Brown and McNeill, 1966; Read and Bruce, 1982). The gap in memory of a TOT state is an unusual case of forgetting because even though you can't say the word, you can often tell how many syllables it has, the beginning and ending letters, or what it rhymes with. When you try to remember a person's name or an unfamiliar word such as "sextant" or "ambergris" that is on the tip of your tongue, you can frequently eliminate words that are incorrect because they don't have the proper sound or length. Psychologists have studied the things that subjects know about a word while they are in the TOT state to identify the types of associations and linkages that form categories and hierarchies in LTM.

Redintegration: The type of remembering that occurs when something unlocks a rapid chain of memories.

Another common experience that provides clues about the organization of LTM is redintegration, a type of remembering that occurs when something unlocks a rapid chain of memories. For example, hearing a particular song or name can create a flood of memories and emotions, and rereading a diary or journal or looking at photographs of significant events will sometimes bring back groups of related memories. These thoughts and emotions seem to be connected through a chain of associations that illustrate the ways our long-term memories are organized in time and place and interconnected by meaning (Bower, 1976).

Retrieval Processes

Retrieval: The process of returning LTM contents to short-term memory for analysis or awareness.

Whatever system is used to organize stored information, the purpose of memory storage is to be able to use the information later on. The process of returning long-term memory contents to short-term memory for analysis or awareness is called retrieval. Being able to retrieve information stored in LTM is one important key to having a "good" memory.

The other day, I went from my bathroom to the kitchen to do something and when I got there, I couldn't remember what it was. I had to go back to the bathroom to remember. Why is that? In a situation like this, something in the bathroom acted as a cue or signal for you to remember something you wanted to do and that cue wasn't present in the kitchen to remind you. While you were walking to the kitchen, you were probably thinking of other things, which kept the idea generated in the bathroom from remaining in STM. A cue is a stimulus that can begin a retrieval process from LTM (Klatzky, 1984). Being asked a question is an example of a cue. Some cues are more subtle than direct questions and might not even be noticed as memory joggers. The smell of perfume or after-shave lotion or the look on someone's face can trigger a group of memories that seem to appear out of nowhere.

Cue: A stimulus that can begin a retrieval process from long-term memory.

The effect of environmental cues is illustrated in the research of anthropologist Margaret Mead (1964). When she lived with the aborigines of south Australia, she learned that some important aspects of their culture are transmitted through an oral tradition. Stories of culturally significant events are memorized to pass on to the next generation. These stories are sometimes long, with many important details. Mead found that in order to be able to tell a long story correctly, the storyteller had to walk through the places involved in the story. If the storytellers were tested in a laboratory without the retrieval cues of their physical environment, their memories were not so remarkable.

Recognition and Recall

When you can't recall someone's name but know you have seen his or her face before, you are using a retrieval strategy called recognition (Mandler, 1980). The operation you perform in recognition is to take the stimulus cue (the face) and check your long-term memory contents to see whether you have something there that matches the stimulus cue. When you use a recognition strategy, you are very accurate in judging whether you've seen something before. When you attempt to remember a name, you are using another type of retrieval process, recall, which is a more difficult task (Bransford, 1979). To recall information, you must use a more general cue than the exact information to be located and must find material in LTM *associated with* that cue. When you look at a face, for instance, it is a general cue for the person's name. This general cue often isn't enough to find the appropriate name among the many stored in long-term memory.

Recognition: Process of matching a specific stimulus cue to an appropriate item in LTM.

When you answer an essay question, you use a recall strategy to remember the information that is associated with the words of the question. For example, an essay question that asks you to compare recognition and recall strategies would require you to produce the pertinent information you have learned about these two terms. On the other hand, when you answer multiple choice items, you are given pieces of information to identify the ones that match the information you have already stored, which is a recognition task.

Recall: Process of using a very general stimulus cue to search the contents of LTM.

The ability to recognize faces and pictures of objects has been studied extensively. Humans seem to have a remarkable ability to recognize the things they have previously encountered (Shepard, 1967; Standing, Conezio, and Haber, 1970). In studies of recognition, subjects have looked at 10,000 slides (which takes five days) and later, when shown a pair of slides containing a new picture and an original, have been able to identify the original 98 percent of the time (Standing, 1973). In another study (see Figure 7.4), subjects were shown five pictures from yearbooks, one of which was a person from their high school graduating class. Fifteen years after graduation, subjects were accurate in identifying 90 percent of their classmates. Even subjects who had been out of high school for more than 40 years could identify 75 percent of their classmates (Bahrick, Bahrick, and Wittlinger, 1975).

Relearning

In addition to testing for recognition and recall, researchers have used measurements of relearning to study memory. One way of measuring relearning is to compare the amount of time it takes subjects to learn material again after they can no longer recognize or recall it. If relearning takes less time than the original learning, then some information must have been stored.

Relearning: Learning material a second time. Relearning usually takes less time than original learning.

The relearning method was introduced to experimental psychology in 1885 by Hermann Ebbinghaus, a pioneer memory researcher who often used himself as his only subject. To measure memory performance, he calculated the amount of time it took for him to first learn and then to relearn a list containing nonsense syllables such as SIM or

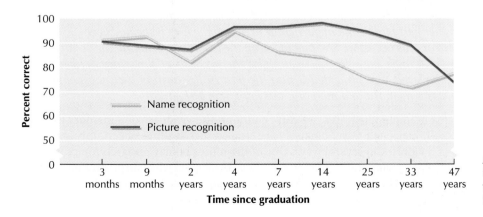

Figure 7.4 Recognition memory. Results from a study of recognition memory in which subjects were asked to identify pictures of their high school classmates.

RAL. Ebbinghaus chose three-letter nonsense syllables because he needed materials that were as equal to each other as possible so that he could calculate the amount of time it took to learn similar materials. Nonsense syllables were also useful because they do not have the previous meanings and associations that words do. He would thus avoid the complications of previous learning.

According to Ebbinghaus's research, we often have some memory for things we have learned, even when we seem to have forgotten them completely. This finding should be encouraging to you if you studied a foreign language many years ago but can no longer recall or recognize the vocabulary. If you need to pass a proficiency examination in the language someday, you could expect to learn the material more rapidly the second time.

Why do I sometimes remember something I thought I had forgotten, when I'm not even trying to remember it anymore?   Research has found that when thinking is left "unfinished," the brain will keep working on the problem unconsciously until an answer is obtained. Psychologists call this the Zeigarnik effect (Bonello, 1982; Zeigarnik, 1927). Apparently, an unfinished problem motivates us to find a solution. Our perceptual processes continue to select things that give us further information about the problem and we continue to search the categories of our memories until we find the information we need. If, for example, you had been trying to remember the names of the Seven Dwarfs, you might suddenly think of the name "Sleepy" as you sit in your chemistry class.

Zeigarnik Effect: Process of working unconsciously on a problem until it is solved.

The Alteration of Stored Memories

Until recently, psychologists thought short-term memory was like wet cement, still pliable, and long-term memory, like hardened cement, a permanent impression (Houston, Bee, and Rimm, 1983). Writing or drawing on cement can be erased or changed only while it is still wet. As we shall see later in the chapter, memories in STM are indeed fragile and can be erased (amnesia) or altered before a permanent memory is created. However, research has revealed a number of ways in which memory can be changed *after* the original is stored in LTM. Many memory researchers are convinced that long-term memories are easily modified after they are stored, rather than being permanent records that cannot be changed (Loftus and Hoffman, 1989; Loftus and Loftus, 1980).

As an example of the pliability of memory, consider this account offered by psychologist Jean Piaget (1951):

> One of my first memories would date, if it were true, from my second year. I can still see, most clearly, the following scene, in which I believed until I was about fifteen. I was sitting in my pram, which my nurse was pushing in the Champs Elysees, when a man tried to kidnap me. I was held in by the strap fastened round me while my nurse bravely tried to stand between me and the thief. She received various scratches, and I can still see vaguely those on her face. Then a crowd gathered, a policeman with a short cloak and a white baton came up, and the man took to his heels. I can still see the whole scene, and can even place it near the tube station. When I was about fifteen, my parents received a letter from my former nurse saying that she had been converted to the Salvation Army. She wanted to confess her past faults, and in particular to return the watch she had been given as a reward on this occasion. She had made up the whole story, faking the scratches. I, therefore, must have heard, as a child, the account of this story, which my parents believed, and projected it into the past in the form of a visual memory, which was a memory of a memory, but false. (pp. 187–188)

As this example illustrates, we can't count on the vividness of a memory as proof that it actually happened. Psychologists have studied such feelings of certainty about the accuracy of memories in several ways. One of the most popular research topics is flashbulb memories—vivid images of circumstances associated with surprising or strongly emotional events. These memories are like action pictures taken with a flash camera.

Flashbulb Memories: Vivid images of circumstances associated with surprising or strongly emotional events.

The death of President Kennedy and the Challenger disaster created vivid flashbulb memories for many people.

An event that created flashbulb memories for many people was the assassination of President John F. Kennedy in 1963. The news of his death was sudden and startling, and many people have vivid memories of where they were when they first heard it. Ten years after the assassination, for example, Billy Graham could remember having been on the golf course when he heard the news. Julia Child could visualize being in the kitchen and could remember what she was eating at the time (Loftus, 1980). Indeed, it is events such as sudden disasters and assassinations of important political or religious figures that have lasting effects on memory (Brown and Kulik, 1977). People relive such events in their minds over and over again. This increase in rehearsal affects the number and quality of associations with the event, making and keeping it vivid.

One psychologist studying flashbulb memories of Kennedy's assassination found evidence that some people were remembering inaccurately, even though, like Piaget, they were certain they remembered the event vividly. One person interviewed by psychologist Marigold Linton (1979) had a vivid memory of being interrupted by a friend while studying in the library and being told all about Kennedy's death. Yet the friend who supposedly described the events to her was actually attending a different school in a different state at the time of the assassination. In a study of flashbulb memories after the space shuttle Challenger explosion, Jeffrey Gutkin (1989) reports similar memory changes over a three-year period following the disaster.

How do memories get altered like this?   Several factors alter memories. As we discussed in the previous section, long-term memories (unlike sensory and short-term memories) are not exact duplicates of information. In our attempt to catalog and store memories in LTM, we often rearrange facts, leave out details, and add information to allow it to be stored with related topics. In addition, we have difficulty separating what was *assumed* from what was actually presented and with remembering whether the original source was reliable or not. Researchers have also discovered that information presented after the original event can have an important influence on our memory processes.

Eyewitness Research

In one eyewitness study, subjects were shown a film of a car driving through the countryside. Members of one group were then asked to estimate how fast the car was going when it passed *the barn*. Subjects in the other group who saw the same film were also asked to estimate the car's speed, but a *barn* was not mentioned. When all subjects were later asked if they saw a barn in the film, six times as many subjects in the group given the misinformation about the barn reported having seen it, even though it never appeared in the film (Loftus, 1982).

In a series of related experiments, subjects saw slides showing a red car drive down a street, approach an intersection, make a turn, and hit a pedestrian. The subjects in one group were asked the following question after viewing the slides: "Did another car pass the red car while it was stopped at the stop sign?" The sign at the corner was actually a "yield" sign, but 80 percent of the subjects were influenced by the misinformation they were given about the stop sign. They altered their long-term memories to include a memory of a stop sign that they never saw (Loftus, 1982).

Given these rather unsettling facts from research studies, how much weight do you think should be given to eyewitness testimony? If you were a juror for Father Pagano's trial, how much do you think you would be influenced by the testimony of eyewitnesses? Keeping in mind the results of eyewitness research, it is alarming to consider the influence of eyewitness testimony in court cases. The British government authorized a study of court cases in England and Wales involving police lineups. In the 347 cases where the *only* evidence presented against the defendant was the sworn statement of one or more eyewitnesses, the conviction rate was 74 percent (Loftus, 1980).

In laboratory experiments where variables can be controlled completely, the powerful influence of eyewitness testimony has been demonstrated repeatedly. In one mock trial experiment, the subjects acted as jurors in a robbery-murder case. Of the jurors who heard only circumstantial evidence, only 18 percent found the defendant guilty. Of subjects presented with exactly the same case except for the addition of the testimony of one eyewitness who identified the defendant as the guilty person, 72 percent found the defendant guilty (Loftus, 1980).

Even though eyewitnesses are often mistaken, Elizabeth Loftus (1980) has found that a discredited witness may be as effective as a nonchallenged witness. Bernard Whitley (1987) disagrees slightly with Loftus's findings. Still, he agrees that a discredited eyewitness can be more influential than no witness at all, and the unchallenged eyewitness is the most influential of all.

How often eyewitnesses are mistaken in their recollections of events is impossible to determine, but experimental evidence indicates that the inaccuracy rate might be disturbingly high. For example, in an experiment at the University of Nebraska, subjects watched people committing a staged crime. About an hour later, they looked at mugshots. A week later, they were asked to pick the suspects from a lineup. In this experiment, *none* of the participants in the staged crime appeared in the mugshots or lineups, yet subjects identified 20 percent of the innocent people in the mugshots as participants in the crime and 8 percent of the people in the lineup (Brown, Deffenbacher, and Sturgill, 1977).

How could the subjects have been so mistaken?   It would seem that at least two properties of memory could combine to create the type of mistaken identity that occurred at the lineup stage. First, according to research on recognition, seeing a face in the mugshots would give witnesses a sense of familiarity with the person's face when he or she was later seen in the lineup. Second, according to research on episodic memory, it would be difficult for witnesses to be certain about where they had seen the person before, which might lead to the assumption that they saw this person committing the crime.

Review Questions

1. What goes on during the transfer of information from short-term to long-term memory?
2. What is the difference between semantic and episodic memory?
3. What is a landmark event, and what are some of your own personal landmark events?

4. When we know the answer to a question, but can't quite get it out of our mouth, we are experiencing _____ .

5. The process of returning LTM contents to STM for analysis or awareness is called _____ .

6. In each instance, which retrieval strategy is being used, recognition or recall: (a) a multiple-choice test, (b) a fill-in-the-blank test with no choices presented, (c) an essay test, (d) a matching test?

7. Vivid images of circumstances associated with surprising or strongly emotional events are called _____ .

8. Why is eyewitness testimony not considered reliable in a court of law?

Answers to Review Questions can be found in Appendix C.

Critical Thinking
PSYCHOLOGY IN ACTION
PRACTICING REFLECTIVE THINKING
Exploring Your Memories

Reflective thinking, also known as recursive thinking, is the ability to review and analyze your own mental processes—to "think about thinking." Reflective thinking is an important component of critical thinking. It allows you to objectively examine your thoughts and cognitive strategies and evaluate their appropriateness and accuracy. In the context of this chapter, we could employ reflective thinking to evaluate the processes used in recalling old memories.

To practice reflective thinking:

1. Take out a clean sheet of paper and write down all you can remember about the first day of your Introductory Psychology course. What did you do from the minute you entered the room that day? What did the professor say or do? Write down only the things you can remember in vivid detail, not those you "think" you remember.

2. Now closely examine your memories by comparing them with those of classmates who also attended the first class period. Are your memories exactly the same? Are some personal and some shared? Do you remember only the ordinary first-day happenings, or do you remember any unusual occurrences? Do you remember any feelings or emotions? What do you remember that your classmates do not? Do additional memories come flooding back when triggered by others' recollections?

3. By exploring your memories and those of your classmates, you can see how memories are stored and organized in your brain. Most people do not remember things in vivid detail. Most often memories are more general, allowing you to fill in the details according to how you "think" the memory should have been rather than providing all the details for you.

4. Finally, try to recall an older memory, a vivid memory from your childhood. Write down as much detail as you can and then try to evaluate which part of that memory is likely to be factual and which part of that memory is reconstructed. You may find it necessary to ask your parents or old friends to verify the accuracy of these memories. But it is unlikely that even your most vivid childhood memories are a perfectly accurate representation of the past.

Gender and Cultural Diversity
CULTURAL DIFFERENCES IN MEMORY

We know that people in preliterate cultures are forced to rely solely on their memories to recall past information—information about history and commerce, for instance. Because they cannot depend on books, ledgers, maps, and computers to store information for them, they necessarily make more demands on their memories than people living in industrialized societies. Does this mean that people raised in preliterate societies have better memories? It seems the answer to this depends on what needs to be remembered.

Ross and Millson (1970) explored the question of whether people raised in preliterate societies with rich oral traditions remember orally presented stories better than those raised in literate societies. Subjects in their study consisted of college students in

In preliterate societies, tribal leaders pass down vital information through stories related orally. Because of this rich oral tradition, children living in these cultures have better memories for information related through stories. Children in literate societies, however, have better memories for information that is not necessarily related because of training received from formal schooling.

the United States and college students in Ghana. Testing memory for themes in stories presented aloud, they found that, in general, the Ghanaian students had better recall than the Americans. They attributed this difference to the Ghanaian students' extensive experience in hearing and telling oral stories.

Wagner (1982) studied recognition rates in different groups of subjects—urban schooled and rural unschooled Moroccan boys, adult Moroccan rug sellers, and University of Michigan students. He presented the subjects with photographs of rugs of various designs, some rug patterns being exact duplicates of others (woven rugs are culturally familiar stimuli for the Moroccans). As an interference task, groups of 1, 5, 10, and 25 photos were presented between each duplicate, and subjects were to tell whether they were seeing each picture for the first or second time. The rural Moroccans, the rug sellers, and the American students scored highest on the task. Although he attributed the high scores of the U.S. students to the fact that they were a select group of individuals, Wagner attributed the rural Moroccans' and the rug sellers' high memory performance to extended previous experience with rugs and weavings. So it seems that previous experience plays a part in facilitating memory recognition.

In still other studies, it has been found that formal schooling as well as experience contribute to the development of memory strategies. Cole, Gray, Glick, and Sharp (1971) reported that schooling teaches people clustering strategies to remember material that is not at first perceived as interrelated. Wagner (1982) describes another study conducted with both Moroccan and Mexican urban and rural children on serial position effect. Subjects were presented with seven cards placed face down in front of them one at a time. They were then shown a card and asked to point out which of the seven cards was its duplicate. The recency effect (recall of the most recent cards) seemed to be present in everyone, regardless of culture or amount of schooling. However, the amount of schooling had a significant effect in overall recall and in the primacy effect (recall of the earliest cards presented). Schooling seemed to provide the subjects with the memory strategy known as verbal rehearsal, which they used to mentally practice the locations of the cards that were first presented.

In summary, research indicates that there are fixed structures for short-term memory that are not affected by culture. Everyone has an innate short-term memory capacity. However, culture seems to affect retrieval from long-term memory. In cultures where communication relies on oral tradition, people develop good strategies for remembering orally presented stories. In cultures where people have much experience in weaving or selling woven rugs, they develop a good memory for various patterns in the rugs. In cultures where formal schooling is the rule, people learn memory strategies that help them remember lists of items. From these studies, we can conclude that a person's culture provides a background of experience and strategies for remembering factors specific to that culture. ■

THE PROBLEM OF FORGETTING

Some memory research has focused specifically on the circumstances involved in forgetting, a familiar process that can be either helpful or disturbing (Wixted and Effesen, 1991). Even though there are times when we would rather not remember something disturbing or embarrassing, most of the time forgetting is an inconvenience we would like to avoid. What causes forgetting and how can we prevent it when we want to?

• Why do we forget, and what are some techniques to prevent forgetting?

These questions have been important issues in psychology ever since Hermann Ebbinghaus explored the process of forgetting in memory studies over 100 years ago, as we discussed in the previous section. After Ebbinghaus memorized lists of nonsense syllables until he knew them perfectly, he retested his memory of the list at regular intervals. He found that one hour after he knew a list perfectly, he remembered only 44 percent of the syllables. A day later, he recalled 35 percent, and a week later only 21 percent. Figure 7.5 is his famous and depressing "forgetting curve."

Is everything forgotten this fast?   If you were to forget textbook materials and lecture notes this rapidly, you would be able to pass a test only if you took it immediately after memorizing the information. An hour later, you would fail the test because you would remember less than half of what you had studied. Keep in mind, however, that the forgetting curve in Figure 7.5 applies to meaningless nonsense syllables. Meaningful material is much less likely to be forgotten.

Research on Forgetting: Factors That Affect Remembering

How interference creates forgetting is demonstrated in studies on the serial position effect. When subjects are given lists of words to learn and are allowed to recall them in any order they choose, it has been found that the words at the beginning and end of the list are remembered better than those in the middle (see Figure 7.6). The middle words are quite often forgotten.

Serial Position Effect: The phenomenon of remembering the material at the beginning and the end of a list better than the material in the middle.

The first words on the list are better remembered because they are processed into LTM without as much interference as later words receive. Because most subjects want to do well on a memory task, they concentrate on and rehearse each word as it appears. Thus, the first words to be remembered are processed and transferred to LTM. But, when

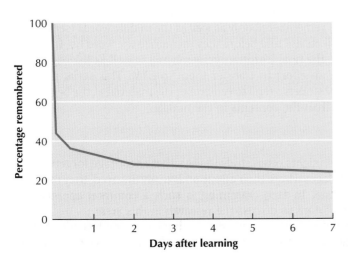

Figure 7.5 Ebbinghaus's forgetting curve. It is clear from this curve that nonsense syllables are forgotten rapidly during the first few hours after learning.

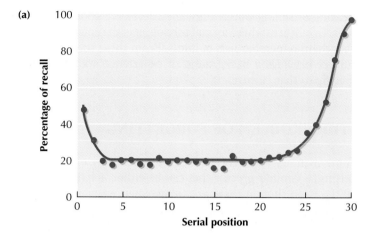

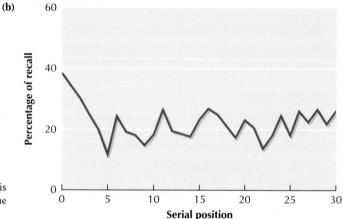

Figure 7.6 The serial position effect. (a) Results when the subject is tested immediately after learning a list of words. (b) Results when the subject is tested several hours after learning a list of words.

subjects get to about seven words, they can't continue to rehearse all of them. At this point, they will often take up some of their STM by trying to decide what they will do to try to remember more words than they have spaces for. During this time, the next words on the list do not get as much analysis and attention.

Why are the words at the end of the list remembered?   When subjects are allowed to recall the words they learned in any order they choose, they often use maintenance rehearsal to keep the words at the end of the list in STM until they are written down. Thus, in the long run, these words are not actually remembered as well as the words at the beginning of the list because they have not been stored. To find out how well these word lists are stored in LTM, subjects are retested on word recall at a later time. If subjects have not been told that it will be important to try to remember these words again later, they don't transfer all the final words on the list to LTM, and on the later surprise test the last words are remembered only as well as the middle words (see Figure 7.6). On the other hand, if subjects are told before they memorize the word list that they will be retested at a later time, the final words are remembered as well as the beginning words because subjects make an effort to transfer them to LTM. This serial position phenomenon also explains why students tend to remember the material at the beginning and end of the chapter better than the contents in the middle.

Strategies for Studying

Despite their best intentions, students often study in ways that encourage forgetting. In addition to studying in noisy places where their attention is easily diverted, they often try to learn too much at one time. In fact, cramming is such a common approach to studying that we feel it is important to discuss the research in this area.

Whether you are learning verbal materials such as the content of this textbook or motor skills such as typing, you are better off spacing your learning periods, with rest periods between practice sessions. Psychologists call this learning strategy distributed practice. "Cramming" is called massed practice because the time spent learning is massed into long, unbroken intervals. An early study of both strategies found that fewer nonsense syllables were forgotten when subjects were given a 126-second rest period between trials (distributed practice) compared to a 6-second rest period (massed practice)—see Figure 7.7 (Hovland, 1938). Similar benefits of distributed practice have been found for the learning of motor skills such as typing (Jones and Ellis, 1962).

Distributed Practice: A learning technique in which practice sessions are interspersed with rest periods.

Massed Practice: A learning technique in which time spent learning is massed into long, unbroken intervals; cramming.

State-Dependent Memory

Have you ever had trouble remembering material you studied and knew well when you were anxious during a test? When you are sad, do you tend to remember other things that made you sad in the past, or when you are angry, do you tend to remember past situations that made you angry? Such experiences are common because human memory systems are connected to our emotional arousal level and feelings. Memory research shows that the arousal level of the nervous system and the emotions that occur during learning have an important effect on remembering the learned material. This relationship is called state-dependent memory. We have all had experiences that we remember vividly because we were very aroused at the time and concentrated on what was happening. But research shows that people often have difficulty remembering something if they are experiencing a different arousal level or emotional state from the one they were in at the time they learned the information. This may be the reason why some of Father Pagano's accusers identified him inaccurately. If they were frightened during the robbery and relaxed when viewing the police lineup, their memory of the real robber might have been impaired.

State-Dependent Memory: Memory that is connected to a state of emotional arousal.

The *arousal level* of the nervous system—how serene or excited one is—has been studied as an important element in forgetting (Fischer, 1976). Arousal level can be altered by emotions like anxiety or by use of psychoactive drugs such as alcohol, caffeine, nicotine, or marijuana (see Chapter 5). Caffeine and nicotine raise arousal level, whereas alcohol and marijuana lower it. In one study, arousal level was altered through alcohol use. Subjects were asked to learn a list of words while either intoxicated or sober. It was found that subjects recalled the words best when they were in the same state as when they had learned the words, *either* intoxicated *or* sober (Weingartner et al., 1976). Marijuana has been shown to decrease reading comprehension, short-term memory processing, and ability to recall what was learned (Nicholi, 1983). Even though caffeine and nicotine are psychoactive drugs that make people feel more alert while they study or take tests, both of these drugs have been shown to decrease performance on complex memory tasks (Anderson, 1983; Mangan and Golding, 1983).

In addition to the effects of overall arousal level on memory, Gordon Bower (1981) has shown that *particular types* of emotions create state-dependent effects. In one of his

"Cramming" for an examination is an attempt to learn too much at one time and is therefore less effective than spacing out your studying over several days or weeks.

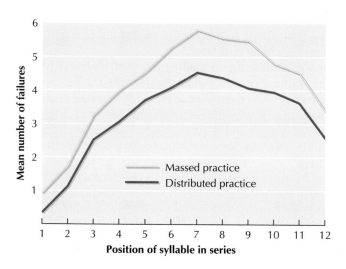

Figure 7.7 Massed practice versus distributed practice. This graph shows that massed practice causes more errors than distributed practice in the learning of a list of words.

studies, subjects learned lists of words while they were hypnotized to feel either happy or sad. When they attempted to recall the words, some subjects were hypnotized to be in the same emotional state as when they were learning, whereas others were put in the opposite state. Subjects who had been sad during learning remembered better when they were also sad during recall. Subjects who had been happy during learning remembered better when they were happy during recall. Learning was better when the acquisition and retrieval emotional states matched.

Does this mean that if I'm going to be anxious during a test, I should be anxious while I study? Absolutely not. According to Johnson and Hasher (1987), state-dependent effects on memory are almost always small. Therefore, conscientious studying is always more important than matching physiological and psychological states when trying to get a good grade on a test. However, if you want to match your arousal levels, try to reduce the differences in both directions rather than just changing your emotions during studying. If you know from past experience that you are anxious and aroused during tests, you could increase your arousal level during studying without having to resort to creating anxiety. You might try exercising during study breaks and checking frequently during study time to make sure you are not drowsy or bored. Perhaps you could figure out ways to make the information more interesting or personally relevant and thus increase your excitement level.

Also try to decrease your arousal level and anxiety during a test. You might set aside a few minutes before the examination for meditation or self-hypnosis to improve your relaxation and concentration abilities. In addition, avoid using stimulants such as coffee or caffeine-containing drinks just before the test that would add to your arousal level.

Theories of Forgetting: Why We Don't Remember Everything

Four major theories have been offered to explain why forgetting occurs. Each theory focuses on a different stage of the memory process or on a particular type of problem in processing information.

Interference Theory: The theory that claims we forget something because other information blocks its storage or retrieval.

According to interference theory, we forget something because other information blocks its retrieval (McGeoch, 1942). Just as interference from other contents disturbs the processing of information in STM, other information can interfere with our ability to remember information stored in LTM (Dempster, 1985). If you have studied two foreign languages, for instance, you might have found that you remember words from the first language instead of the second one when you attempt to communicate. Forgetting something because information *previously* learned interferes with it is called proactive interference. Forgetting something because information learned *afterward* interferes is called retroactive interference. (*Retro* means "behind," so in retroactive interference something learned behind, or after, something else causes forgetting of the material learned first.) If you've ever changed phone numbers, the new number might have caused retroactive interference for recall of the old one.

Proactive Interference: Forgetting because previously learned information interferes with new information.

Retroactive Interference: Forgetting because new information interferes with previously learned information.

Decay Theory: The theory that memory, like all biological processes, deteriorates with the passage of time.

Decay theory is based on the commonsense assumption that memory, like all biological processes, deteriorates as time passes. If memory is processed and stored in a physical form, the vitality of the representation could be expected to decrease over time. As appealing as this explanation seems, it appears not to be the case that long-term memories decay once they are stored (Waugh and Norman, 1965). Experimental support for decay theory has been difficult to obtain because it is hard to control for interference effects when trying to test for decay.

Motivated Forgetting Theory: The theory that people forget things that cause pain, threat, or embarrassment.

A third theory of forgetting focuses on our sometimes unconscious wish to forget something unpleasant. According to the motivated forgetting theory, people are blocked from remembering something that would cause pain, threat, or embarrassment. In such cases, the information is not "forgotten" because it is still in LTM and could be remembered if the protective mechanisms were overcome. Sigmund Freud claimed that people use protective defense mechanisms to keep painful memories from becoming conscious and creating anxiety. We will describe his theories of motivated forgetting in Chapter 14.

Anyone who has ever "blanked out" during an examination or a conversation only to remember the "forgotten" information later has had a first-hand experience with the retrieval failure theory of forgetting. According to this theory, memories stored in LTM are never really "forgotten" but rather are momentarily inaccessible as a result of such things as interference or emotional states.

Retrieval Failure Theory: The theory that forgetting is a problem with retrieval, not a problem with long-term storage of information.

How can I make information more accessible?   One way to avoid retrieval failure is to use the visual and verbal channels more effectively while learning so that the information can be more easily retrieved. Also, several memorizing strategies are described in the last section of the chapter.

Review Questions

1. Explain the serial position effect.
2. How would you study for a test using distributed practice? Using massed practice?
3. Memories associated with a particular level of emotional arousal are called
   _____ .
4. Proactive interference occurs when _____ learning interferes with _____ learning.
5. Retroactive interference occurs when _____ learning interferes with _____ learning.
6. Which theory of forgetting is being described in each example:
   (a) You are very nervous about having to introduce all the people at a party, and you forget a good friend's name.
   (b) You meet a friend you haven't seen for 25 years and you cannot remember his name.
   (c) You were molested as a child and have completely forgotten the incident.

Answers to Review Questions can be found in Appendix C.

THE BIOLOGY OF MEMORY

What happens in the nervous system when we learn something? Where are long-term memories physically stored? A great deal of research has been done to try to answer these questions, and psychologists have developed theories of memory based on their physiological findings.

• *How can memory be explained in terms of biological processes? What are some factors leading to memory impairment?*

Theories of Memory: Changes in the Brain

Physiological psychologists such as Donald Hebb have approached the biology of memory by studying the reactions of neurons to incoming stimuli. By measuring the electrical activity of the brain during learning, Hebb (1949, 1961) discovered that neurons fire in reverberating circuits—that is, a set of neurons fires over and over during the short-term memory process. Any disruption of this electrical event, such as by brain trauma or the passage of electrical current through the brain (electroconvulsive shock or ECS), interferes with memory storage processes. Hebb has shown that when a particular stimulus enters the brain, it causes a specific pattern of neurons to become active. If an

Reverberating Circuits: The firing of a set of neurons over and over again during memory processing.

Electroconvulsive Shock (ECS): Electrical shock applied to the brain such that it causes convulsions.

electrical current is passed through the brain at the same time, neurons throughout the brain will fire erratically and create a convulsion. As a result, the specific pattern created by the incoming stimulus cannot be consolidated and processed into a permanent memory. Hebb's theory accounts for the fragile nature of STM.

To transfer information into LTM, the temporary firing of neuron circuits initiates a permanent change in the nervous system. How this happens was described by Hebb in 1949:

> *When an axon of cell A is near enough to excite a cell B and repeatedly or persistently takes part in firing it, some growth process or metabolic change takes place in one or both cells such that A's efficiency, as one of the cells firing B, is increased.*

Thus, during the process of a short-term memory becoming a long-term memory, groups of neurons repeatedly fire in reverberating circuits, resulting in some chemical or physical modification of the neurons making up the circuits. One of the major theories used to explain this modification involves a process known as long-term potentiation (LTP) (Barnes and McNaughton, 1985; Brown et al., 1988; Lynch, Halpin, and Baudry, 1983).

Long-Term Potentiation (LTP): A process whereby short-term memories become long-term memories after repeated stimulation of a synapse leads to chemical and structural changes in the dendrites of the receiving neuron. This change results in increased sensitivity of the neuron to excitatory stimulation.

Long-Term Potentiation

LTP is a persistent increase in the efficacy of a synapse that can be induced relatively quickly. Quite simply, it is explained in this way: Repeated stimulation of a synapse causes a change in the dendrite of a neuron, which in turn causes an increase in the permeability of the cell to calcium ions. The movement of these calcium ions into the cell activates proteins that increase the sensitivity of the neuron to excitatory stimulation. This change in sensitivity is reasonably permanent (Barnes and McNaughton, 1980; Lynch, 1988; Lynch, Halpin, and Baudry, 1983).

Some researchers have found chemical and physical changes in the synapses (Deutsch, 1983; McGaugh, 1990). During the period of memory storage, the receiving dendrite membranes become more sensitive to the neurotransmitter acetylcholine. (Later, in the section on Alzheimer's disease, we will describe how this chemical is an important part of memory processing.) Other researchers have found evidence of physical changes occurring in the structure of the neurons themselves when something is learned (Crick, 1982; Lynch, 1984; Sokolov, 1977). These structural changes have been demonstrated dramatically in research on the effects of enriched and deprived environments on the brains of rats. Mark Rosenzweig et al. (1972) raised rats in enriched environments where they had many opportunities to learn. Later, the researchers found that neurons in the rats' brains had developed more sprouts on their dendrites compared to the neurons of rats raised without as many learning experiences. Such changes in the structure of neurons enable them to transmit impulses differently. Figure 7.8 shows some of the effects of learning on neurons.

Kinase Research

Recent research suggests that the changes in the dendrites associated with LTP involve the activation of kinases. *Kinases* are enzymes that trigger changes in cells through the simple act of adding phosphate to proteins. By changing the proteins that make up the membrane of the dendrites, the kinases change how the neuron responds to neurotransmitters and thus activates LTP. Most recently Alcino Silva, a postdoctoral student working in the laboratory of Susumu Tonegawa at the Massachusetts Institute of Technology, has been able to breed "knockout" mutant mice that are missing one of the kinases thought to be involved in producing LTP in the brain (Barinaga, 1992). These mice were grown from an embryo in which one gene, the one that makes the target kinase, is missing or knocked out. Therefore the knockout mutant mice are unable to make the

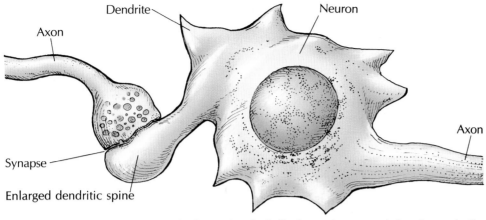

Figure 7.8 Long-term potentiation. A dendritic spine physically changes in response to long-term potentiation.

necessary kinase and subsequently less able than normal mice to produce LTP in the brain (Silva, Stevens, Tonegawa, and Wang, 1992). When the mutant mice were tested on a spatial memory task their performance was significantly worse than normal control mice (Silva, Paylor, Wehner, and Tonegawa, 1992). Although there are many problems still to be resolved, Silva's research with the knockout mutant mice is additional evidence that long-term potentiation is one of the major physiological components of memory.

Genetic Explanations of Memory

Another way memory may be preserved is through changes in the genetic mechanisms of neurons. That is, memories may be stored in the form of alterations in the DNA of the neuron nucleus or in the activity of RNA when it manufactures proteins.

The genetic approach to the biology of memory was popularized as a result of experiments conducted on planaria (a type of flatworm) in the 1960s by James McConnell (1962, 1968). He classically conditioned planaria to learn to fear a light. When a light was flashed, it was followed by a painful electric shock. Pain caused the planaria to scrunch their bodies, so observers could see when the animals had learned to associate the light with the shock. The animals that learned this response then became "donors." Their brain cells—containing the DNA, RNA, and proteins that might have been altered by the conditioning—were fed to planaria that had not been conditioned to fear a light. When these untrained worms were exposed to the light, they scrunched their bodies, indicating that the "memories" of the trained planaria had somehow been transferred to them. Improved performance with transfer of brain material from donors has also been demonstrated in rats and hamsters (Adam and Faiszt, 1967; Gay and Raphelson, 1967). This entire research area is controversial, however, since other research studies have not been able to obtain the same results (Bennett and Calvin, 1964; Chapouthier, 1973).

Is it possible to improve your memory by changing your diet or taking drugs?   At this moment the answer to that question is generally, no. It is not currently possible to use drugs to significantly improve memory or the ability to learn new material, although recent research has indicated that glucose taken before a memory test can enhance performance on some tasks for elderly humans (Hall and Gold, 1990). On the whole, memory enhancement through chemicals and drugs or through brain transplants remains in the realm of science fiction. But as the research into the neural basis of memory continues we may eventually have drugs that will enhance memory by, for instance, enhancing long-term synaptic potentiation and therefore allowing a person to more efficiently move information from short-term memory to long-term memory.

Amnesia: Trauma and Shock Effects

Amnesia: Forgetting that results from brain injury or from physical or psychological trauma.

Retrograde Amnesia: Difficulty in remembering previously learned material.

Anterograde Amnesia: The inability to form new memories.

Some of our knowledge of memory has come from studies of people who have suffered memory problems as the result of brain trauma or electroconvulsive shock. Forgetting as a result of such brain insults is called amnesia. In retrograde amnesia, the person has difficulty remembering events that occurred *before* the brain disruption. In anterograde amnesia, the person has difficulty processing memory of events occurring *after* the traumatic incident, because the memory processes are not working efficiently. Fortunately, amnesia is often temporary.

In the case of serious automobile accidents or other forms of head trauma, jarring the brain can cause a loss of memory for events before and after the impact. Sometimes whole days or months cannot be remembered, particularly if the person is unconscious for a period of time. Eventually, any permanent memory loss is usually confined only to the contents of STM during the time of the trauma since this information was never stored in LTM (Whitty and Zangwill, 1977). An example of short-term memory loss can be seen in the case of a stewardess who survived a fall from a Yugoslavian airplane that was exploded by a terrorist bomb. She suffered brain damage and spinal injuries and was paralyzed from the waist down after falling 30,000 feet. After regaining consciousness, she remembered getting on the airplane and waking up in the hospital, but had no memory of the events in between (Loftus, 1980).

Retrograde amnesia has been created in rats by administering electroconvulsive shock (ECS) during the time something to be learned is in short-term memory (Deutsch, 1969). For example, if rats are punished whenever they step off a platform, they learn to stay on the platform. However, if they receive ECS before the memory of the punishment has had time to be stored in long-term memory, they will continue to step off the platform and receive punishment. If ECS is administered *after* the memory of the punishment has had time to be stored, the rats remain on the platform to avoid punishment because they are able to remember that this happened in the past.

Memory Impairment: Brain Damage

Damage to certain parts of the brain by tumors, strokes, or surgery can produce various types of memory impairment. Consider the memory problems of patient H. M., who had portions of his temporal lobes surgically removed in an attempt to control severe epileptic seizures. After the surgery he had fewer seizures, but he had also lost the ability to transfer any new information into LTM (Scoville and Milner, 1957).

Because H. M. could no longer store permanent memories, it was difficult to test his mental abilities. For one thing, he forgot he was being tested as soon as this information was gone from his STM. H. M. could carry on a conversation with the psychologists who tested him and use their names as long as he was using maintenance rehearsal to keep this information in STM. However, if he looked away or didn't talk to them for a few minutes, he couldn't remember having seen them before or remember what he was doing. Despite such a serious memory problem, H. M. still had the same IQ scores after the surgery as before. Since his LTM was still intact and he could retrieve memories of things he had experienced before the surgery, he could perform LTM tasks as well as he ever did. Research with monkeys has demonstrated that H. M.'s inability to preserve memories must have been caused by removal of the hippocampus and amygdala in the subcortex when the temporal lobes were removed (Zola-Morgan, Squire, and Mishkin, 1982). More recent research has also implicated the hippocampus in the storage of short-term memories (Squire and Zola-Morgan, 1991).

Damage to structures involved in memory can be caused by brain tumors, strokes, alcoholism, or activities such as boxing that create brain trauma. Since a punch thrown by a heavyweight boxer can land at a force exceeding 1,000 pounds, nerve cells and blood vessels in the fragile brain tissue can be twisted, stretched, and ruptured, causing the "punch drunk" symptoms often seen in boxers. One study that examined the brain tissues of 15 boxers at autopsy found brain damage that could interfere with memory processes in all 15 (Corsellis, Bruton, and Freeman-Brown, 1973).

Public awareness of boxing's potential to cause brain damage was heightened in 1984 when Muhammad Ali developed impaired eye–hand coordination and often unintelligible speech. Ali's symptoms have decreased as a result of treatment with drugs ordinarily given to patients with Parkinson's disease, a disorder that occurs when the brain stops making adequate amounts of the neurotransmitter dopamine. Ali's doctors claim he does not have Parkinson's disease and that his symptoms are more likely the result of 30 years of brain trauma from boxing (Stoler, 1984). Instances such as these led the American Psychological Association to pass a resolution to work toward the eventual elimination of amateur and professional boxing (Mervis, 1985).

Alzheimer's Disease: Progressive Memory Loss

An extreme example of memory impairment occurs in Alzheimer's disease, a progressive mental deterioration that occurs most commonly in old age. The most noticeable early symptoms of Alzheimer's disease are disturbances in memory, beginning with typical incidents of "forgetfulness" that everyone experiences from time to time. With Alzheimer's, however, the forgetfulness progresses until, in the final stages, the afflicted person fails to recognize loved ones and needs total nursing care.

In the United States, over 1 million people (5 percent of the population over age 65) have this fatal brain disorder (Shodell, 1984). Although Alzheimer's disease does afflict people under 65, the incidence rises dramatically past middle age and affects an estimated 20 to 30 percent of the people who reach their mid-eighties (Heston and White, 1983). Since more people are living longer, it is estimated that by the year 2000, about 10 percent of the over 65 population of the United States (3 to 4 million people) will be victims. The current annual cost to Americans is estimated to be greater than $80 billion (Selkoe, 1991).

What is the difference between "normal" loss of memory as one gets older and Alzheimer's disease? Autopsies of persons with Alzheimer's disease reveal shrunken cerebral hemispheres and neuron damage in a part of the brain stem area called the *nucleus basalis* near the hippocampus. When the neurons in this area are functioning normally, they produce the neurotransmitter *acetylcholine,* which is used throughout the nervous system. In Alzheimer's disease, the damaged nucleus basalis lacks an important enzyme for making this acetylcholine. Without enough acetylcholine, a person's brain cannot function normally. So far, research on replacing acetylcholine has not proven successful.

Also of interest to psychologists is the pattern of memory loss in Alzheimer's patients. Not all types of memory are affected equally. One of the major differences between normal people and Alzheimer's patients is the latter's extreme decrease in episodic memory. Although nearly as good as normals at recalling information from

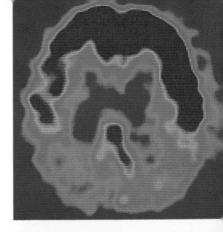

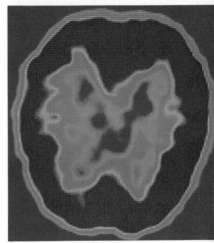

These PET scans show decreased blood flow in a brain with Alzheimer's disease (top photograph) compared to a normal brain (bottom photograph). Reduced blood flow in the temporal and parietal lobes in this Alzheimer's patient indicates decreased brain activity in the brain areas that are especially important in the storage of memories.

Alzheimer's Disease: A progressive mental deterioration that occurs most commonly in old age. It is characterized by severe memory loss.

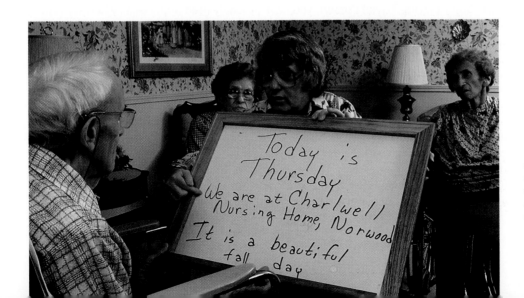

In the United States, over one million people suffer from Alzheimer's disease. The most noticeable early symptoms of Alzheimer's disease are disturbances in memory.

237

semantic memory, Alzheimer's patients are greatly inferior when tested on tasks that require retrieval of information from episodic memory (Nebes et al., 1984). This problem may be due to reduced control over their working memory (Morris and Baddeley, 1988). Because Alzheimer's patients are easily distracted, it may be harder for them to retrieve information from episodic memory, since episodic memories may be more complicated and take longer to retrieve.

Possible Causes of Alzheimer's

The cause of the brain changes in Alzheimer's disease is not known, although there are several theories as to why it occurs. Some experts claim the cause is genetic. Others blame it on a slow-acting virus. Because unusual amounts of aluminum have been found in the brains of some people who have died from Alzheimer's disease, theorists have suggested that the brain damage is caused by environmental pollution that builds up toxic mineral deposits in the brain tissue (Heston and White, 1983).

Since Alzheimer's disease relegates its victims to years of inability to remember what they have learned, it amounts to virtually a complete loss of personality. The most promising recent research for a cause and a cure has focused on the role of amyloid protein. Amyloid protein, which may be released by neurons, glial cells, or via the bloodstream, may accumulate in the nervous system as countless diffuse plaques. These plaques gradually cause nearby neurons to degenerate and thus result in the brain cell loss characteristic of Alzheimer's disease (Selkoe, 1991).

Review Questions

1. Circuits of neurons that fire over and over to process a memory are called
   _____ .
2. Describe the process of long-term potentiation (LTP).
3. How does the study of the "knockout mice" support long-term potentiation?
4. Forgetting that results from brain damage or trauma is called _____ .
5. What is Alzheimer's disease? Although the exact cause is not yet known, what are some proposed causes?

Answers to Review Questions can be found in Appendix C.

EXCEPTIONAL MEMORIES

• *Can everyone improve his or her memory?*

In striking contrast to victims of memory deficits are people with exceptional memories. If you enjoy playing Trivial Pursuit, you have probably been impressed by how well some people can remember seemingly insignificant details. Someone who always chooses the category "facts about the United States" is Michael Barone. Mr. Barone began memorizing facts such as census figures when he was eight years old. He knows the population for major cities during different years (he can tell you that St. Louis had 750,026 inhabitants in 1960, for example) and the boundaries of every congressional district in the United States.

Eidetic Imagery: The ability to recall memories—especially visual memories—that are so clear they can be viewed like a clear picture; photographic memory.

Some people are able to remember things so vividly they are said to have a "photographic memory." The scientific name for this ability is eidetic imagery. People with eidetic imagery can visualize an object so vividly that it is similar to a photograph (Klatzky, 1984; Neisser, 1982). They can tell you that a specific fact is located in the fourteenth line of the twentieth page of a book they've read and cite the exact wording of a paragraph. One example of a person with eidetic imagery is Elizabeth, a teacher at Harvard. Years after reading a poem in a foreign language, she can retrieve an image of

$$N \cdot \sqrt{d^2 \times \frac{85}{vx}} \cdot \sqrt[3]{\frac{276^2 \cdot 86x}{n^2 v^=} \cdot \pi 264} \, n^2 b = sv \frac{1624}{32^2} \cdot r^2 s$$

Figure 7.9 A difficult formula to remember. This is the formula that Luria's subject remembered 15 years after seeing it only for a short time.

the page it was printed on and copy the poem from the bottom line to the top line as fast as she can write. When she looks at a computer-generated pattern of 10,000 dots with her right eye, she is later able to combine this pattern with another one she viewed with her left eye. She can line up the remembered image so perfectly that she can see a three-dimensional image from the two patterns (Stromeyer, 1970).

Another person with a remarkable memory was a Russian newspaper reporter tested by psychologist Alexander Luria (1968). When the man looked at a chart of 50 numbers, he could remember the rows or columns perfectly after three minutes of study. He memorized a meaningless formula (see Figure 7.9) by using visual images that he linked together into a story. Even though he was not warned that he would be tested on his recall of this formula, he reproduced it perfectly 15 years later. If you are wishing you had this type of exceptional memory, think again. This man had great difficulty paying attention to important details. He even had trouble figuring out the meaning of what he was reading, since as he was reading his mind would be flooded with visual images of all his previous experiences.

Photographic memory is a rare ability that seems to disregard the limitations to remembering imposed by short-term memory. Instead of using a selection process that concentrates on the most important aspects of incoming information, the person with a photographic memory stores all the information.

Even though this type of exceptional memory cannot be acquired, most people can improve their memory skills dramatically when they study memory processes and apply what they have learned. One way to improve memory is to use a mnemonic strategy.

Improving Memory: Using Mnemonics

When you can't remember how many days there are in a particular month, and you don't have a calendar in front of you, do you resort to the "Thirty days hath September" rhyme? If so, you are using a mnemonic device. Mnemonic devices help you remember something by organizing or "tagging" information visually or verbally while you are learning it or by giving you a system for retrieving information (Glass and Holyoak, 1986). Three mnemonic devices that use visualization to improve memory are the method of loci, the peg-word system (Bellezza, 1982; Roediger, 1980), and the substitute word system. A fourth strategy, the method of word associations, uses verbal organization.

The method of loci was developed by early Greek and Roman orators to keep track of the parts of their long speeches. *Loci* is the Latin word for physical places. To use this method, the orators would imagine the parts of their speeches being attached to places inside a building or outside in a place like a courtyard. For example, if an opening point in a speech was the concept of "justice," they might visualize a courtroom placed in the first corner of their garden to remind them of this point. As they mentally walked around their garden during their speech, they would encounter each of the points to be made in their appropriate order.

Mnemonic Devices: Memory strategies in which information is organized or "tagged" visually or verbally.

Method of Loci: A mnemonic device in which an idea is associated with a place or a part of a building.

 Try This Yourself

To use the method of loci to help you remember things in a specific order you could use the places in your apartment or house as a sequence that you can visualize. Form a visual image for each of the items on your list and imagine them placed in order in specific areas as you mentally walk through the room. In one research study, college students associated lists of 40 nouns with 40 campus locations. When tested immediately, they

Reprinted with special permission of North America Syndicate.

remembered an average of 38 items. When tested a day later, they still remembered an average of 34 of them (Ross and Lawrence, 1968). ■

The Peg-Word System

Peg-Word Mnemonic System: A memory system in which peg words, or easy-to-visualize words in a specific order, are associated with difficult-to-remember words or numbers.

To use the second visualization strategy, the peg-word mnemonic system, you need to memorize a set of visual images for numbers 1 to 10. Then you can use these images as pegs or markers to "hang" ideas on. The easiest system of peg-words to learn is 10 objects that rhyme with the numbers they stand for. Form a specific graphic image for each of these objects.

one is a bun	six is sticks
two is a shoe	seven is heaven
three is a tree	eight is a gate
four is a door	nine is a line
five is a hive	ten is a hen

When you can produce the peg-word image for each number, you are ready to use the images as pegs to hold the items of any list. Try it with items you might want to buy on your next trip to the grocery store: milk, eggs, bread, razor blades. The first item (milk) should be visualized with the picture of a bun, the second (eggs) with a shoe, and so on. Imagine a bun lying all soggy in a bowl of milk. Imagine a giant shoe stepping on a carton of eggs, slices of bread hanging on a tree, and a giant razor blade as a door complete with doorknob. The peg-word device enables you to remember the whole list in order or to find any item according to its number. To remember the third item, for instance, you would recall the image that is attached to *tree* (Bransford, 1979).

The Substitute Word System

Substitute Word System: A memory system in which a word to be remembered is broken into parts and associated with easy-to-visualize words that sound like the word's parts.

But what if you need to remember words that can't be visualized (words such as *occipital* or *parietal*)? You can still use a mnemonic device. You can use substitute words that can be visualized or verbal associations for the words to be learned, the method of word associations.

To use the substitute word system (Lorayne, 1985; Lorayne and Lucas, 1974), break the word to be remembered into parts or use words that sound similar that can be visualized. For example, the word *occipital* can be converted into *ox, sip it, tall* or *exhibit hall*. Make a vivid image of either of these. You might see an ox on stilts sipping something through a straw or an exhibit hall displaying paintings (of brains with the occipital lobes emphasized). Try creating substitute words for *parietal* (*pear* or *pair, eye, it tall*). If you practice this substitute word technique, you will find yourself coming up with some very funny—but memorable—visual images for words you can't normally visualize.

Word Associations

Method of Word Associations: A memory method in which verbal associations are created for items to be learned.

The method of word associations is a mnemonic device that creates verbal associations for items to be learned. You use this method if you remember the order of colors in the rainbow or color spectrum by relating them to a man's name, "Roy G. Biv" (red, orange, yellow, green, blue, indigo, violet), or if you recall the names of the Great Lakes with the phrase "*homes* on a great lake" (Huron, Ontario, Michigan, Erie, Superior). Students of music use this verbal association technique to remember that the notes of the spaces of the treble clef spell FACE, and the notes of the lines create the sentence: "Every good boy does fine" (E, G, B, D, F).

To use the method of word associations, form words or sentences with the first letters of the items to be remembered, as in the preceding example, or make up a story that links the items together. If, for example, you wanted to remember the words ostrich, bus, wind, sidewalk, and coffee, you might create a story beginning at the zoo: "The *ostrich* was the first animal we saw from the *bus*. When the ride was over, the *wind* was so chilly that we hurried to the *sidewalk* cafe for *coffee* to warm us." In one research study, subjects who used this story-creation method remembered six times as much as subjects who learned by repeating the words to themselves (Loftus, 1980).

 Try This Yourself

Everyone can improve his or her memory. The way to do it is to expend some effort. Choose a strategy that appeals to you and work at it. The harder you work at it, the better your memory will become. You can learn to remember the names of people you meet or the contents of a textbook if you apply yourself and use some of the techniques discussed in this chapter. Below we have summarized key points from the chapter that you can put into practice to improve your own memory:

- When you learn something new, take the time to associate it with what you already know. By doing this, you'll be cataloguing the new information so that you can retrieve it easily.

- If you really want to remember something, you must pay attention to it. So when you're in class, sit away from people who might distract you and when you study, choose a place with a minimum of distractions.

- Remember that the duration of short-term memory is about 30 seconds, so to keep information in short-term memory you need to use maintenance rehearsal.

- Because the capacity of short-term memory is around 7 items, you can remember more if you chunk information into 7 groups.

- Put great effort into truly comprehending the meaning of things you need to remember.

- Get plenty of sleep, for two reasons: (1) We don't remember information acquired when we're in a drowsy state as well as when we're alert; and (2) it's when we're sleeping that new information is processed and stored.

- To avoid falling prey to the serial position effect, start at different places—sometimes at the second section, sometimes at the fourth—when reviewing material in a text; start in the middle when memorizing a list of items.

- Be sure to use distributed practice and avoid cramming when studying.

- Take advantage of your dual-coding system, both visualization as well as verbal association, in using the mnemonic devices described in the book. Following are some suggestions for their use, but you'll probably come up with some of your own. You can use:

  - the method of loci to remember points you want to make in a narrative or a speech.

  - the peg-word system to remember lists of items.

  - the substitute word system to remember unusual terms or people's names.

  - the method of word associations when you need to remember all the items on a list in order. ■

Review Questions

1. The scientific name for a photographic memory is _____ .

2. Strategies that help us remember by organizing information are called _____ .

3. Which memory device is being described?

(a) You remember things to bring to a meeting by visualizing them in association with a previously learned sequence of items.

(b) You remember a speech for your communications class by forming visual images of the parts of your speech and associating them with areas in the classroom.

(c) You remember errands you need to run by making up the rhyme: "First go to the store, then get books galore. Get my ring and then some gas, and the cleaners at the last."

(d) You remember a new acquaintance's name, Paul Barrington, by linking it to words that can be visualized: pall-bearing town.

Answers to Review Questions can be found in Appendix C.

REVIEW OF MAJOR CONCEPTS

A THREE-STAGE MEMORY MODEL

1. Humans have at least three different kinds of memory: sensory memory, short-term memory (STM), and long-term memory (LTM).

2. Sensory memory is the memory that occurs within our sensory apparatus while incoming messages are being transmitted to the brain.

3. Short-term memory involves memory for current thoughts. Short-term memory can hold about seven items and can store them for about 30 seconds; however, its capacity can be increased by chunking, and we can use maintenance rehearsal to retain information at this stage. Dual-coding refers to the visual and verbal input channels of STM. During the storage process between STM and LTM, the way information is processed affects its ability to be retrieved from LTM.

4. Long-term memory is a more permanent memory where information and ideas are stored for future use. The type of LTM in which facts and their relation to one another are stored is called semantic memory. Memories of specific events are stored in episodic memory. Information in LTM is organized into categories and subcategories that form a network. If it is necessary to retrieve a particular piece of information, there are several pathways within the network that will lead to that information, but stored memories are not always retrievable.

5. Retrieval is the process of getting information out of LTM. The two types of retrieval are recognition and recall. Studies of eyewitness testimony have shown that memory can be modified and that the retrieval process is not always accurate.

6. Cross-cultural research on memory indicates there are fixed structures for short-term memory that are not affected by culture. However, culture seems to affect retrieval from long-term memory because different cultures teach different strategies for remembering information important to the culture.

THE PROBLEM OF FORGETTING

7. One technique that can be used to minimize the effects of forgetting is distributed practice, in which short practice or study sessions are interspersed with rest periods. The worst way to study or try to remember information is to use massed practice, studying large amounts of information without rest.

8. Some memories are state-dependent and are affected by states of arousal. It is easier to remember these memories if you are in a state similar to that in which the learning took place.

9. The interference theory of forgetting states that memories are forgotten because of either proactive or retroactive interference. Proactive interference occurs when previously learned information interferes with newly learned information. Retroactive interference occurs when newly learned information interferes with previously learned information. One illustration of these two types of interference is the serial position effect, in which it is easiest to remember items at the beginning and at the end of a list.

10. The decay theory of forgetting simply states that memory, like all biological processes, deteriorates as time passes.

11. The motivated forgetting theory states that people forget things that are painful, threatening, or embarrassing.

12. The retrieval failure theory of forgetting claims that information stored in LTM is never forgotten but may at times be inaccessible.

BIOLOGY OF MEMORY

13. Researchers have shown that learning can cause physical changes within the brain neurons and their circuits. Re-

search on amnesia caused by electroshock, the learning and memory deficits found in brain-injured patients, and the deterioration of memory in Alzheimer's disease support several biological theories of memory. The case of H. M. illustrates that damage to specific parts of the brain can disrupt the formation of new memories.

EXCEPTIONAL MEMORIES

14. There are only a few cases of people who have eidetic imagery or photographic memory. These people are able to retrieve a detailed copy of the original visual image from LTM. For most people, retrieval can be greatly improved by more effective use of memory processes.

15. The most effective strategies to keep from forgetting are mnemonic devices, which organize or tag information visually or verbally. The method of loci, the peg-word system, and the method of word associations are examples of mnemonic memory systems.

SUGGESTED READINGS

BEST, J. B. (1992). *Cognitive psychology* (3rd ed.). St. Paul: West. Several chapters of this textbook on cognition cover memory processes.

BRANSFORD, J. D. (1979). *Human cognition: Learning, understanding, and remembering.* Belmont, CA: Wadsworth. A presentation of the research literature on memory processes (including Bransford's own research on levels of processing) and practical suggestions for benefiting from it.

KELLETT, M. (1983). *How to improve your memory and concentration.* New York: Monarch Press. Practical examples for improving concentration and organization of information in lectures and reading; analysis of how emotions and personality factors relate to memory.

LORAYNE, H., & LUCAS, J. (1974). *The memory book.* New York: Ballantine Books. Lorayne and Lucas present techniques from their memory course for remembering abstract information, with specific examples and exercises for converting difficult items into substitute words that can be visualized.

LOFTUS, E. (1980). *Memory.* Reading, MA: Addison-Wesley. Loftus describes the findings of her active research studies and illustrates the processes of forgetting and efficient memory.

Thinking and Intelligence

OUTLINE

Above Photo: Astronaut Dave Bowman and Hal.

"Er—Dave, I have a report for you."

"What's up?"

"We have another bad AE-35 unit. My fault predictor indicates failure within twenty-four hours."

Bowman put down his book and stared thoughtfully at the computer console. He knew, of course, that Hal was not really *there*, whatever that meant. If the computer's personality could be said to have any location in space, it was back in the sealed room that contained the labyrinth of interconnected memory units and processing grids, near the central axis of the carrousel. But there was a kind of psychological compulsion always to look toward the main console lens when one addressed Hal on the control deck, as if one were speaking to him face to face. Any other attitude smacked of discourtesy.

"I don't understand it, Hal. *Two* units can't blow in a couple of days."

"It does seem strange, Dave. But I assure you there is an impending failure. . . ."

"Have you any idea," he said, "what's causing the fault?"

It was unusual for Hal to pause so long. Then he answered:

"Not really, Dave. As I reported earlier, I can't localize the trouble."

"You're quite certain," said Bowman cautiously, "that you haven't made a mistake? . . . Anyone can make mistakes."

"I don't want to insist on it, Dave, but I am incapable of making an error."

"All right, Hal," he said, rather hastily. "I understand your point of view. We'll leave it at that."

He felt like adding "and please forget the whole matter." But that, of course, was the one thing that Hal could never do.

Arthur C. Clarke, 2001

In this excerpt from the novel *2001: A Space Odyssey* (based on the movie of the same name), Dave Bowman, astronaut on the spaceship *Discovery*, is talking to Hal, the ship's computer brain and guiding force on the mission. The excerpt is representative of the film, during which the audience has the overwhelming feeling that Hal the computer is quite humanlike, that "he" is an intelligent, thinking being. Even in this short segment, it sounds as if Bowman is talking to another person instead of a computer. What is it about Hal that makes Bowman, as well as us, feel that the computer is nearly human?

One of the first human qualities we notice about Hal is his ability to converse so naturally. He not only has the ability to use language but uses it in a way that is both spontaneous and accurate. He listens to Dave, processes what he hears, then responds accordingly. We notice other humanlike qualities about Hal. He takes time to analyze what is causing the failure of the AE-35 units. He patiently reasons with Dave. He even knows how to go about solving problems. Hal detects a malfunction within his computer unit and knows he will be disconnected if it is discovered. His solution? To subtly and systematically kill off the crew.

These humanlike qualities we observe in Hal—language usage, information processing, reasoning, problem solving—are known as cognitive abilities. Cognition refers to the process of "coming to know" and includes our abilities to sense, perceive, learn, remember, and think. In short, our cognitive abilities enable us to know our world and thereby function in it.

Most psychologists approach the study of cognition by taking one of two approaches (Best, 1992). The first is an information processing approach; the second is the

Cognition: The mental activities involved in acquiring, storing, retrieving, and using knowledge; it includes such mental processes as perceiving, learning, remembering, using language, and thinking.

connectionist approach. The information processing approach to cognition relies on abstract models of human cognition rather than trying to directly model how the brain works. A good example of an information processing model is the three-stage memory model described by Atkinson and Shiffrin in 1968. In this model, information enters through a sensory pathway and then is either processed in working memory or stored in long-term memory (we discussed this model in detail in Chapter 7). Most information processing models also hypothesize some kind of central processor or monitor that has executive control of the entire cognitive process. (The monitor, of course, would be part of the brain, but the specific area of the brain is not identified.) The connectionist approach, on the other hand, attempts to describe cognitive processes in terms of neural activity within the brain. Connectionists build mathematical models of human thinking that could possibly be carried out or computed with interconnected systems of nerve cells. The connectionist approach is also called the *distributed neural network approach*.

There are two major differences between these approaches. First, the information processing approach is abstract, while the connectionist approach is highly concrete, based on anatomical structures. The information processing model does not claim that there is a particular brain structure responsible for the working memory, only that the brain functions as if there were a working memory. The connectionists create models of cognition that work in the same way as the brain, attempting to show that the brain could do the calculations required by their models.

The second major difference between the two approaches involves how information is processed in the model. The information processing model basically assumes that most information is processed in a one-after-the-other or *serial* fashion. The connectionist model claims that in order for the brain to analyze and process the immense amount of information bombarding it every minute, it must do many different things at once, in a *parallel* fashion. The difference between serial and parallel processing can be demonstrated by a simple example. Suppose you must remove the 1000 most important works of art as fast as possible from a museum that is on fire. You could set up a single line of people and pass the art as quickly as possible from one person to the next and out through one museum exit. Alternately, you could set up ten lines of people and pass the art from person to person out through ten museum exits. In the first case, you are processing the art in a serial one-after-the-other fashion. In the other case, you have ten different lines working in a parallel fashion. Obviously, ten-at-a-time is faster than one-at-a-time. Connectionists claim that the slow rate at which action potentials move information in the brain, as discussed in Chapter 2, necessitates massive parallel processing. The brain, in order to solve a complex problem in a timely fashion, is forced to process many aspects of that problem at the same time.

Both of these models of cognition have their advantages and disadvantages. It will be some time before we can definitively say which better describes cognitive processes. Perhaps both are appropriate for modeling different types of thinking.

In this chapter, we will examine the cognitive abilities associated with thinking. You will learn that we think both in pictures and in words. You will discover how we form concepts and why concepts are so important. We will take you through the steps people normally use when faced with problems they need to solve. We will discuss the complexity of human language and the attempts to teach it to other animals. Finally, you will find that not only do psychologists disagree on how to measure intelligence, they cannot even agree on how intelligence should be defined.

As you read Chapter 8, keep the following **Survey** questions in mind and answer them in your own words:

- What is thinking, and how do we think and form concepts?
- How do we solve problems and think creatively?
- What is language? Is language limited to humans?
- What is intelligence, and how can it be measured?

Information Processing Approach: The approach to studying cognition that uses abstract models to depict how the brain, in a serial fashion, receives sensory information and processes, stores, and retrieves that information.

Connectionist Approach: The approach to studying cognition that uses mathematical models simulating the interconnected systems of neurons in the actual brain to show how the brain works in a parallel fashion to receive, process, store, and retrieve information.

THINKING

• *What is thinking, and how do we think and form concepts?*

Thinking: Using knowledge that has been gathered and processed; mentally manipulating concepts and images to perform such mental activities as reasoning, solving problems, producing and understanding language, and making decisions.

From the point of view of cognitive psychology, we come to know things by gathering, processing, and storing information. This is accomplished through sensation and perception, learning and memory, and thinking. Thinking involves mentally acting upon the information that we sense, perceive, learn, and store.

What do you mean when you say that we mentally act on information?   Suppose you are Dave Bowman and, upset by the death of your fellow astronauts, you cloister yourself and a colleague inside a cubicle, away (so you assume) from the discerning ear of Hal. (Unfortunately, unbeknownst to you, Hal also has a discerning eye that is adroit at lip-reading.) As you discuss the astronauts' deaths and other computer-related problems, you mentally picture Hal's computer console and the countless wires, computer chips, and other electronic hardware comprising Hal. You recall strange events and snatches of conversations you've heard in the past few days and start drawing connections between tham. You trace the problems to Hal. You discuss ways to remedy the problems and decide on one: disconnect the source of the problems.

What have you been doing? You have been thinking. You have been using information that was previously gathered and stored and have been mentally acting on it by forming ideas, reasoning, solving problems, drawing conclusions, making decisions, expressing your thoughts, and comprehending the thoughts of others. Thinking involves a variety of mental processes and operations. The ones we will examine here are mental imagery, concept formation, problem solving, creativity, and language. But before we get to these topics, we must address the larger issue of *how* we think. By what means do we encode incoming information so that we can think about it?

How Do We Think? Pictures and Words

Think about these two very different sentences:

1. The bulbous blue hippopotamus, reeking from the odor of stale fishy brine, waddled into the room and plopped onto the floor with a self-satisfied grin spreading over its face.

2. Our nation was conceived in a spirit of unity for all time, freedom from persecution, equality for the populace, and justice unequivocable.

After reading the first sentence, could you just "see" the hippo walking through the room? Were you almost disgusted at the fish odor? Could you "feel" the vibrations when the hippo plopped to the floor? How about the second sentence? Could you "see" unity? freedom? justice? How *do* we represent information in our minds? Do we think in pictures? As the sentence about the blue hippo illustrates, the answer seems to be yes. But most of us probably didn't call to mind any mental pictures when we read about the abstract concepts of justice and equality, yet we still understood what was being said.

There is some controversy over how information is represented in our minds. Some experts believe we encode information about real objects and events into mental representations of those objects and events. When we think, we mentally manipulate these mental images. Others believe that we encode information in terms of verbal descriptions called *propositions* and that mental images are sometimes added to the propositions after they are retrieved from memory (Pylyshyn, 1979).

Mental Images: Mental representations of objects and events that are not physically present; they are used in the thinking process to solve problems, express ideas, and so on.

A proposition is defined as the smallest unit of knowledge that can be validated as true or false. Even though propositions are really abstract cognitive events, most propositional theories depict them as short sentences, such as "Clinton is president." John Anderson (1978, 1983) has proposed a theory called adaptive control of thought (ACT) based on propositions. Anderson envisions propositions at the nodes of a net with all strands of the net leading to propositions. In this way, all thought processes are made up of propositions or combinations of propositions. Allan Paivio (1971, 1991) has combined mental images and verbal images (propositions) into a theory of cognitive processing known as the dual-coding hypothesis.

The Dual-Coding Hypothesis

According to the dual-coding hypothesis, information is encoded by means of both an imagery system and a verbal system, each working independently. We use the imagery system for processing real, concrete items and pictures, such as blue hippos and a painting of the Mona Lisa. We use the verbal system for more abstract items, such as spoken or written words and concepts such as liberty. So the imagery system is specialized for processing information about nonverbal objects and events, whereas the verbal system is specialized for processing linguistic information and generating speech (Paivio, 1991).

The two systems are interconnected to a degree, as shown by the fact that we can convert verbal information such as a description of a juicy hamburger sizzling on a grill into either a visual, tactile, olfactory, gustatory, or auditory mental image. Conversely, when we form a mental image of the juicy hamburger we can access our verbal system to find its name when we want to place an order at our favorite restaurant. A considerable amount of research in recent years has focused on mental imagery and is yielding a number of interesting findings, as we will see in the following section.

Dual-Coding Hypothesis: The theory proposing that information is encoded into two separate but interacting systems: an imagery system for concrete items and pictures and a verbal system for abstract ideas and spoken and written words.

Mental Imagery: Thinking in Pictures, Sounds, Smells . . .

One of the leading researchers in mental imagery, Stephen Kosslyn, wrote: "Having a visual mental image produces the conscious experience of 'seeing,' but with the 'mind's eye' rather than with real ones" (Kosslyn, 1987, p. 149). Similarly, we also hear with our "mind's ear," smell with our "mind's nose," and so on with our various other senses. In a survey of 500 adults, McKellar (1972) found that the overwhelming majority experienced not only visual and auditory imagery but also tactile, motor, gustatory, and olfactory imagery. (For instance, imagine sinking your hand into a sheep's woolly fleece or tasting a too-salty pretzel.)

Much of the research on imagery has demonstrated the similarity between actual physical objects and their mental representations. In one well-known study, Shepard and Metzler (1971) measured the amount of time subjects took to judge whether pairs of figures were the same or different.

 Try This Yourself

Some of Metzler and Shepard's figures are shown on the following page. Use a watch with a second hand and for each pair of figures, time how long it takes for you to tell whether they are the same or not. Which pair takes the longest to judge?

It should be (c). Here's why: Before you could judge whether both members of a pair were the same, you had to mentally rotate one of the objects, then compare the rotated image with the other object to see whether they match. Shepard and Metzler found that the angle of rotation—the amount the object had to be tilted or turned—had a strong influence on the decision time. Therefore, when we mentally rotate an object only 20 degrees, it takes less time to compare it with another object than if we rotate it, say, 150 degrees. This is also true with real objects. It takes less time to turn something part way around than to turn it all the way around.

Other studies have shown a correspondence between our actual perceptions and mental images. Just as a real elephant looks bigger than a real rabbit, a mental image of an elephant is bigger than the mental imge of a rabbit. Furthermore, the details of an elephant's anatomy are easier to see if its image is large than if it is small (Kosslyn, 1975). Not only are sizes of objects held constant in our mind's eye but so are their shapes, such as outlines of states (Shepard and Chipman, 1970).

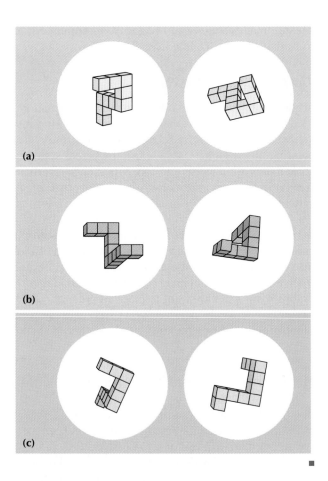

Mental images make thinking easier. For instance, if you think about a dog, you almost inevitably picture one in your mind. Much of our thinking is done with mental images. Often we solve problems by mentally manipulating images of the problem situation. Sometimes our most creative moments come when we're forming mind pictures of puzzling situations. In fact, Albert Einstein claimed that his first insight into relativity theory occurred when he pictured a beam of light and imagined himself chasing after it at its own speed.

Mental imagery has also been shown to be an invaluable aid to memory, as discussed in Chapter 7. In reviewing the literature, Paivio (1991) maintains that material high in imagery is remembered better than abstract material. In a study comparing various memory techniques, Richardson (1978) concluded that mental imagery was more effective than all other memory techniques studied. So if you take the time to

All (except one) of these animals fit the concept of "dog."

create mental images of material you are studying, you'll have a better chance of remembering it. Related to this is a fact that writers have discovered. By painting word pictures and thereby creating images in the reader's mind, they succeed not only in capturing interest but also in aiding comprehension of the written material. It has even been found that it is easier to learn new concepts when they are easy to image and particularly when people are instructed to use imagery when learning the concepts (Katz and Paivio, 1975). This is a noteworthy finding considering how much our thinking processes depend on our conceptual abilities.

Concepts: How We Organize Knowledge

Suppose you are suddenly transported to an exotic land somewhere in the Eastern Hemisphere. Although the people are friendly, you find it extremely hard to communicate because their language is totally unlike yours. You find yourself surrounded with unusual, sometimes bizarre objects and artifacts. How are you to manage in this unfamiliar environment? For a few days, you are completely disoriented, but after only a week you find that you have learned the names and uses for many of the common items and animals. How could this happen? How could you adapt so quickly?

The fundamental reason you could make such rapid progress in mastering this foreign culture is your ability to form and use concepts. When we see a new item or encounter a new situation, we relate it to our existing conceptual structure and categorize it according to where it fits. If in this alien land you see someone blow into an elongated pipelike object and produce a haunting melodious sound, you will probably categorize the pipe as something musical. It has characteristics that correspond to your concept of a musical instrument.

When we form concepts, we mentally group items or events into the same categories if they have similar characteristics, or attributes. The attributes of any particular concept are related to one another according to certain rules. One such rule is the *conjunctive* rule (Haygood and Bourne, 1965), in which attributes are combined with the word *and*. Thus, one person's conception of a children's book might be "It has easy-to-read words *and* it contains pictures." Slightly different is the *disjunctive* rule, in which attributes of a concept are related with the word *or*. Thus, someone else's concept of a children's book may be "It has easy-to-read words *or* it contains pictures." We tend to learn concepts employing the conjunctive rule more easily than those formed by other rules, because we more often use this rule in our everyday experiences (Bourne, 1974; Best, 1992).

How do we learn new concepts?   Because there is no way to directly observe people think or conceptualize, psychologists have had to be especially creative in designing experiments to study concept formation. Methods vary from one study to another, but typically subjects are asked to choose which of several items conforms to a particular concept. From the research, two main theories have emerged: the hypothesis-testing theory and the prototype theory.

According to the *hypothesis-testing theory,* people focus on some attribute or attributes and formulate a *hypothesis* (a tentative guess) about how the attribute contributes to the concept. They then test this hypothesis. If it is wrong, they change to a new hypothesis that may incorporate different attributes or the same attributes but with different rules. One of the most common strategies we use in hypothesis testing is systematically altering a hypothesis one attribute at a time until we find the combination of attributes that fits the concept (Bruner, Goodnow, and Austin, 1956). Marvin Levine (1975) proposed that people develop a pool of hypotheses. They select one of these and test it; if it is consistent with the feedback and with other feedback received in the past, they stick with it. If not, they choose another hypothesis from the pool that is consistent with the feedback.

Another current theory in concept formation, the *prototype theory,* was developed by Eleanor Rosch (1973). She proposed that in real life our concepts are organized in

Concept: A mental structure used to categorize things that share similar characteristics.

Attributes: Characteristics such as color, shape, and size that can change from one stimulus to another.

Prototype: A model or best example of items belonging to a particular category.

terms of prototypes, or best examples. Any one prototype is essentially a "summary representation" of all things fitting that concept (Medin, 1989). When we are confronted with a new item, we decide whether it is part of any particular concept by comparing it with a prototype of that concept. For example, suppose that while wandering along the sands of your exotic land, you stumble upon a small, round, metal disk with a symbol imprinted on each side. You will probably figure it is some type of money because it resembles your prototype of a coin.

 *Try This Yourself*

To experience your own concept formation, look at the figure below and try to figure out what a *glibbit* is. As you do so, pay attention to how you form the concept (do you use a certain strategy?). Try to notice any rules you use to combine attributes, which attributes seem to be the important ones, and so on. (Note how the yes/no feedback helps.)

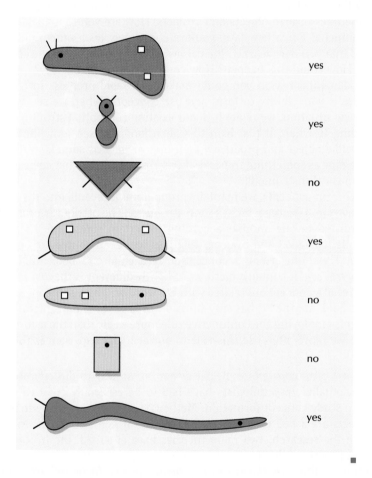

Did you discover that a glibbit is a creature with a curved contour *and* two antennae? These are the only *relevant* attributes; all other attributes—color, freckles, shape, and so on— are *irrelevant*. Using activities such as this, researchers have identified a number of other factors, in addition to relevance, that affect concept learning. Some of them are:

Number of attributes It is easier to learn a concept if there are only one or two relevant attributes or only a few irrelevant attributes than if there are several.

Salience It is easier to learn a concept if the relevant attributes are salient, or obvious.

Positive versus negative examples If we tell people what something *is,* they are more able to use that information than if we tell them what it *isn't*. Although it is sometimes helpful and even necessary to have some negative feedback, people tend to learn faster if they are given more positive examples. Thus, you would learn about a glibbit faster if you were told that a glibbit has a curved contour and two antennae than if you were told that a glibbit doesn't have horns and doesn't have legs.

Without our ability to form concepts, it would be impossible to think as we do. Every time we encountered something a little different from something else, we would have to learn about it just as if it were a totally new item. As a result, we would have to have a separate storage system for every bit of information, and none of it would be related to anything else. We would basically be able to function only on instinct because we wouldn't be able to relate prior learning to new situations. To manipulate mental information—to reason, to make decisions, to comprehend language, to communicate information to other people, to solve problems—would be virtually impossible without our conceptual abilities.

Review Questions

1. Define cognition.
2. There is a controversy over how we think, but research tends to support the _____, which proposes that information is coded via both an imagery system and a verbal system.
3. As you are learning new material in this book, you should take the time to form _____ of the material, because research indicates this is the most effective memory technique.
4. When forming concepts, we pay attention to the relevance, the salience, and the number of an item's characteristics, which are known as _____ .
5. Why is the ability to form concepts so important?

Answers to Review Questions can be found in Appendix C.

Problem Solving: Moving from a Given State to a Goal State

Several years ago in Los Angeles, a 12-foot-high tractor-trailer rig tried to pass under a bridge 11 feet, 6 inches high. As you might expect, the truck got stuck, unable to move forward or back up, causing a huge traffic jam. After hours of towing, tugging, and pushing the rig, police and transportation workers were stumped. About this time, a young boy happened upon the scene and said, "Why don't you let some air out of the tires?" It was a simple, creative, unique suggestion—and it worked.

Our everyday lives are filled with problems and dilemmas that may not be on as large a scale as this but that need solutions just the same. Deciding what to eat for dinner or which TV show to watch constitutes a problem. Some problems have solutions that are easily reached; others, like the tractor-trailer problem, are not so evident. Problem solving consists of moving from a given state, or problem, to a goal state, or solution.

Why was the boy able to find a solution to free the tractor-trailer rig when so many "experienced" workers couldn't? It seems that we all follow certain steps when we attempt to solve problems and at times we get stumped, as these workers did. The police officers and other workers probably tried to solve the problem by applying methods that had worked with other stuck trucks. The young boy, however, never having faced this problem before, went through the problem-solving steps with a fresh approach, not hindered by "tried-and-true" solutions. In this section we will explain the steps normally used in problem solving and then discuss barriers that sometimes prevent effective

* *How do we solve problems and think creatively?*

Problem Solving: A series of thinking processes we use to reach a goal that is not readily attainable.

problem solving. We will also discuss how incubating a problem—withdrawing from it for a time while engaging in another activity—can lead to sudden insights into a problem's solution.

Steps in Problem Solving

Psychologists have identified three stages of problem solving: preparation, production, and evaluation (Bourne, Dominowski, and Loftus, 1979). As we examine each stage, we will refer to the following problem:

> A woman has built a pond in her backyard. She goes to the local lily pad store to purchase lilies for her pond. There, the salesperson tells her that a special lily is on sale. Amazingly, each day it doubles in number. Frogs won't have to hop from pad to pad—they'll be able to walk. The salesperson tells the woman that if she purchases one lily, it will take only 30 days to fill her pond. Because the lilies are on sale, though, the woman buys two. How long will it take the two lily pads to fill the pond if it takes one pad 30 days?

Take a while to try to solve the problem. Write down your answer, and then continue reading. The answer appears in the next few pages.

Preparation

Preparation: The first stage in problem solving, in which the given facts are identified, relevant facts are distinguished from irrelevant facts, and the ultimate goal is identified.

The first stage in problem solving is preparation, in which all the groundwork is laid for a successful solution to the problem. During this stage, we identify the given facts, separate the relevant facts from the irrelevant, and define the ultimate goal. Solving a problem often depends on how carefully we scrutinize the critical facts and how broadly we define the goal. This latter point is illustrated by the stuck truck example. When the goal was thought of in terms of pulling the truck from under the bridge, attempts were unsuccessful. It was only when the boy thought of the goal in broader terms of *somehow* freeing the truck that a successful alternate solution became evident.

Let's apply the preparation step to the lily pad problem. First, we need to determine the given facts. Which facts are relevant, and which can be ignored? Relevant facts: (1) The pads double in number each day; (2) if the woman starts with one pad, it will take 30 days to fill the pond. Next, we need to identify the goal. Goal: To determine how long it will take to fill the pond if the woman starts with two pads. If you've had previous experience with this type of problem, this stage will probably be easy. If not, it may take some time and thought.

Production

Production: The problem-solving stage during which possible solutions to the problem are generated.

During the production process, the problem solver produces possible solutions, called *hypotheses,* to the problem. Under normal circumstances, the more hypotheses generated, the better chance of solving the problem, since a large number of hypotheses provide a wide choice of alternatives during the evaluation stage.

Algorithm: A problem-solving strategy that always eventually leads to a solution; it often involves trying out random solutions to a problem in a systematic manner.

There are two major ways of generating hypotheses—by using algorithms and by using heuristics. An algorithm is a procedure that, if appropriate to the problem, will *always* eventually lead to the solution. Math problems are ideal for demonstrating algorithms: An algorithm for solving the problem 2×10 is $2 + 2 + 2 + 2 + 2 + 2 + 2 + 2 + 2 + 2$. As you can see, algorithms will eventually lead to the correct answer, but they may take a long time. Can you develop an algorithm for the lily pad problem?

One approach would be first to calculate how many lilies there will be after 30 days if the woman starts with one pad (1, 2, 4, 8, 16, 32 . . . and so on, till we reach the thirtieth number, which is 536, 870, 912 lilies), then do the same thing starting with two lily pads (2, 4, 8, 16, 32 . . .) until we arrive at 536,870,912 and see how many days it took to get to that number. It may be obvious, after seeing the large numbers involved, that people don't generally rely too heavily on algorithms for problems other than simple mathematics. Because computers work at fantastic speeds and don't make arithmetic errors, however, working with algorithms presents no problem for them.

The other major approach to forming hypotheses is using heuristics, a much faster method—if it works. Heuristics are rules of thumb or educated guesses developed from experience with similar problems. The disadvantage of heuristics is that they do not guarantee a solution—they work most of the time, but not always. There are many different types of heuristics. We will describe the three most valuable: means–end analysis, working backward, and creating subgoals.

In *means–end analysis,* we determine what measure would reduce the difference between the given state and the goal. In other words, we try to figure out by what means we can arrive at our goal. When working a math problem, you identify the available information and figure out which mathematical procedures are needed to get the answer. If you want to move a new couch into your apartment and the door is too small, you use means–end analysis to figure out what measures you must take to get the couch into the apartment.

Working backward is the heuristic most often used in solving complex problems, such as mathematical proofs. This technique involves starting at the goal and working back toward the given state, rather than the more obvious method of working from the given state to the goal. Suppose you want to figure out how a magician pulls a rabbit out of a hat. This is a difficult problem to solve if you start from the given, an apparently empty hat. But if you start from the goal state, the emergence of the rabbit from the hat, it becomes more apparent that the rabbit must be placed in the hat either before or during the magician's act. Because it would be difficult for the magician to place it there during the show, the rabbit must be put there beforehand. If this is the case, then the hat must contain a compartment to hold the rabbit. As you can see, possible solutions become evident if you begin working on the problem from the end or the goal state.

Another way to solve complex problems is to *create subgoals* that lead to solving the main goal. In 1962, President John F. Kennedy stated that the goal of the U.S. Space Program was to have an American on the moon by the end of the decade. The National Aeronautics and Space Administration (NASA) didn't just build a big rocket and send a crew to the moon; it set up subgoals consisting of several smaller missions that increased in complexity. First NASA created the Mercury series for suborbital and orbital flights with one astronaut; then it set up the Gemini series, putting two astronauts in orbital flights; finally, it inaugurated the Apollo series, for three-person orbital flights, flights orbiting the moon, and ultimately landing an astronaut on the moon.

Heuristics: Problem-solving strategies developed from previous experience that involve selective searches for appropriate solutions to problems and generally, but not always, lead to a solution.

 Try This Yourself

See if you can use subgoals to solve the following problem developed by Bartlett (1958). Try to determine which of the numerals 0 through 9 are represented by the letters, with each letter representing a separate, distinct number. You get one hint before you start: D = 5. The answer is at the bottom of the page.

```
    D O N A L D
  + G E R A L D
    ---------
    R O B E R T
```

Can you see how this problem would be too difficult to solve in a reasonable amount of time using an algorithm? There are 362,880 possible combinations of letters and numbers. At the rate of 1 per minute, 8 hours per day, 5 days a week, 52 weeks a year, it would take nearly 3 years to try all the possible combinations. A heuristic approach is much easier and quicker. When you worked on the problem, you probably used your knowledge of arithmetic to set subgoals, such as determining what number "T" represents (if D = 5, then D + D = 10; so T = 0, with a carryover of 1 into the tens' column). ∎

Solution to the DONALD + GERALD = ROBERT problem:

```
    5 2 6 4 8 5
  + 1 9 7 4 8 5
    ---------
    7 2 3 9 7 0
```

Evaluation

Evaluation: The final stage in problem solving during which hypotheses are appraised to see whether they satisfy the conditions of the goal as it was defined in the preparation stage.

The evaluation stage begins when one or more possible solutions have been generated. These hypotheses are then evaluated to determine whether they meet the criteria defined in the preparation stage. If one of the hypotheses meets the criteria, then the problem is solved. If none of them fulfills the criteria, then you must return to the production stage and produce more possible solutions. In the lily pad problem, one hypothesis would be that if the woman begins with two lilies, it will take only half as long—that is, 15 days—to fill the pond. This is a logical assumption, but it is not correct, so other hypotheses must be generated. How do you know when your hypotheses are wrong? You try them out to see whether they work or not.

Barriers to Problem Solving

Do you find that you can solve some problems easily, yet seem to have a mental block when it comes to others? We all encounters barriers that prevent us from effectively solving problems. Two major barriers are *problem-solving set* and *functional fixedness*.

You've undoubtedly heard that as people grow older, they get "set in their ways." They tend to become more unbending in their opinions, to use the same familiar products, and to engage in activities they've enjoyed in the past. They also become "set" in the ways they go about solving problems. They rely on tried-and-true methods instead of searching for innovative and perhaps better solutions.

The first researchers to demonstrate that previous experience can affect problem-solving approaches were A. S. and E. H. Luchins (1950). They presented problems such as the following:

> If you have one jug that holds 25 liters of water, another jug that holds 5 liters, and a third that holds 2 liters, how can you obtain exactly 16 liters of water?

The answer? Fill the 25-liter jug, then fill the 5-liter jug from the 25-liter jug, leaving 20 liters in the large jug; then fill the 2-liter jug from the largest jug, pour out the 2 liters and fill it again, leaving 16 liters in the 25-liter jug.

 Try This Yourself

Before reading any further, try to solve the water jug problems presented below (after Luchins and Luchins, 1950). Work as quickly as possible.

Problem	Given Jars of the Following Sizes			Obtain the Amount
	A	**B**	**C**	
1.	29	55	3	20
2.	21	127	3	100
3.	14	163	25	99
4.	18	43	10	5
5.	9	42	6	21
6.	20	59	4	31
7.	23	49	3	20
8.	15	39	3	18
9.	28	76	3	25
10.	18	48	4	22
11.	14	36	8	6

Luchins (1942) found that over 70 percent of his subjects, whether children or adults, solved all the problems by using the same algorithm: B − A − 2C. They did not notice that problems 7, 9, and 11 can be solved simply by subtracting C from A, or that problems 8 and 10 can be solved merely by adding A and C. They failed to discover the shorter, easier solutions because their experience with the first five problems caused them (and probably you as well!) to develop a set problem-solving strategy.

Such a problem-solving set can be helpful if all the problems are of the same type. But it can also cause people to overlook other sometimes simpler solutions and prevent them from developing new strategies necessary for solving new types of problems. For example, one major difficulty people have in solving the DONALD + GERALD problem is the habit of working arithmetic problems from the right (ones) column to the left. If you were persistent in trying to solve the problem by using that set, you probably ran into a lot of trouble.

People can get stuck in their own rigid sets when trying to solve any kind of problem. For example, recently one of the authors wanted to paint something with a spray gun but couldn't find the little round quart can that fits onto the bottom. He searched endlessly for the can, with no luck, so was forced to borrow one from a friend. Later, he told his wife about the lost can and she said, "Do you mean the can in that box on your workbench?" There it was, on the workbench. He hadn't noticed it because he was looking for a can, not a box.

Now let's consider the other major barrier to problem solving. Suppose you were given the objects shown in Figure 8.1 and asked to mount the candle on the wall so that it could be easily lit in the normal fashion, with no danger of toppling (Duncker, 1945). How would you do this? The solution is to empty the box, use the tacks to attach it to the wall, light the candle and drop some wax on the bottom of the box, then set the candle in the dripped wax. Duncker found that his subjects had a much more difficult time solving the problem when the box was filled with matches than when it was presented with the matches separately. In the former situation the subjects saw the box as a container and thus had difficulty perceiving it as a useful item in itself. This tendency to see only familiar uses for well-known objects is known as functional fixedness.

Set and functional fixedness are only two of many obstacles to effective problem solving. Moreover, from experience, you know that the longer you're blocked from finding the correct solution to a problem, the more frustrated you become. One way to overcome obstacles to problem solving and alleviate the frustration is to take time out—put the problem aside for a while.

Incubation

Have you ever noticed that if you leave an especially difficult problem and return to it after doing something else, the solution suddenly pops into your head? It seems for some problems that a period of incubation, or time out, is necessary for the facts and possibilities to come into better focus. Köhler (1925) observed incubation in his chimpanzee Sultan. As described in Chapter 6, Sultan was presented with a banana that was out of

Problem-Solving Set: A mental barrier to problem solving that occurs when people apply only methods that have worked in the past rather than trying innovative ones.

Functional Fixedness: A barrier to problem solving that occurs when people are unable to recognize novel uses for an object because they are so familiar with its common use.

Incubation: A period of time during which active searching for a problem's solution is set aside; this is sometimes necessary for a successful solution of the problem.

Figure 8.1 The candle problem. How would you mount the candle on a wall so that it could be lit in a normal way?

The solution to the candle problem in Figure 8.1: Use the tacks to mount the matchbox tray to the wall. Stand the candle on the tray and light the candle.

reach with only two short sticks at his disposal. Initially, the chimp was stumped. After a few weeks' incubation period, however, the solution came to him in a flash of "insight." He fitted the two sticks together and successfully reached his banana.

If you had difficulty with the lily pad problem, perhaps you can come up with the solution after letting the problem incubate for a while. The correct answer is 29 days. The solution is simple, if you begin by thinking about what happens with one pad: On the second day, it divides and there are two pads. So, if the woman starts with two lilies, she is just one day ahead of starting with one lily and it will therefore take 29 days to fill the pond.

In solving the lily pad problem, you may have started with an algorithm (1, 2, 4, 8, . . . for starting with one pad, and 2, 4, 8, . . . for starting with two pads) and recognizing the duplications in the pattern, switched to the heuristic approach. People often begin solving a problem with one method and then switch to another when they realize it may be faster, or their original method is unsuccessful.

Flexibility in approaching problems is a valuable asset. Set and functional fixedness lead to rigidity in problem solving. To be effective problem solvers, people need to be creative in their problem-solving approaches and develop techniques that allow for flexibility, rather than rigidity, in their thinking.

Review Questions

1. List and describe the three stages of problem solving.
2. What is the difference between alogorithms and heuristics?
3. When we take measures to reduce the difference between the given state and the goal, we are using _____ .
4. If we solve a problem by working from the goal to the given state, we are _____ .
5. When working on an enormously complex problem such as how to halt further depletion of the ozone layer, we must create several _____ .
6. What are two barriers to problem solving, and what is one approach to use when faced with such a barrier?

Answers to Review Questions can be found in Appendix C.

Creativity: Finding Unique Solutions to Problems

Are you a creative person? We normally think of painters, dancers, and composers as creative, but don't we all have a certain amount of creativity? Even when doing something as mundane as taking notes, you probably use some amount of creativity. You certainly organize them in your own unique way, and you probably use some unusual and unique abbreviations for common words that are different from the person's next to you. To a greater or lesser degree, everyone exhibits a certain amount of creativity in some aspect of life (Richards et al., 1988).

What is creativity? Definitions of creativity vary greatly among cultures (Lubart, 1990), but it is generally agreed that creativity is a special way of solving problems that involves combining new or unusual elements in ways that are practical, useful, and meaningful to the culture (Gardner, 1988). Creative ability is not limited to humans. As just described, the chimpanzee Sultan found a creative solution to his banana problem. Moreover, just as Hal was able to come up with a creative plan to prevent his shutdown, today's computers have been designed to generate unique and useful solutions to problems they are not specifically programmed to solve (Waldrop, 1988).

Creativity: The ability to originate unique solutions to a problem that are also practical and useful.

 Try This Yourself

Below are examples of items typically found on creativity tests. Take a couple of minutes to work them, and see if you can determine which traits or abilities are being measured. (See Figure 8.2 for the solution to the coin problem.)

1. In five minutes, see how many words you can make out of the following word.	HIPPOPOTAMUS
2. In five minutes, list all the things you can do with a paper clip.	
3. Trace this figure onto a blank piece of paper and draw a picture incorporating the figure.	
4. Find 10 coins and arrange them in the configuration shown here. By moving only two coins, form two rows that each contain 6 coins.	

Brainstorming

One divergent thinking technique for creativity that most people have tried is brainstorming. A. F. Osborn (1963), the man responsible for the popularity of this technique, describes brainstorming as a group problem-solving situation in which four rules are followed:

Brainstorming: A group problem-solving technique in which participants are encouraged to generate as many solutions to a problem as possible by building upon others' ideas and disregarding whether solutions are practical.

Rule 1   No criticism. Postpone all judgments until after the brainstorming session.

Rule 2   Generate as many solutions to the problem as possible—the more, the better.

Rule 3   Encourage originality. The more unique and original the idea, the better. Do not consider whether the idea is practicable.

Rule 4   Try to build on previous ideas.

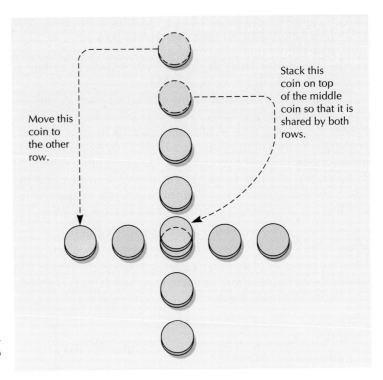

Figure 8.2 The solution to the coin problem. To solve this problem it is necessary to realize that you can stack one coin on top of the middle coin so it shares both the row and the column.

Osborn claims it is possible to generate double the normal amount of useful ideas in the same amount of time when brainstorming techniques are used (Vervalin, 1978).

There is some controversy, however, over the effectiveness of brainstorming compared with other creativity techniques. For example, several researchers have shown that people working independently develop a greater number of unique and creative ideas than people working together in a group (Diehl and Stroebe, 1987; Mullen, Johnson, and Salas, 1991; Taylor, Berry, and Block, 1958). One of the major reasons group brainstorming fails is that in large groups some individuals can socially loaf and let others do the work and generate the ideas (Mullen, Johnson, and Salas, 1991). Also it has been shown that people are more productive when instructions stress creating practical rather than unusual ideas (Weisskopf-Joelson and Eliseo, 1961).

According to J. P. Guilford (1959, 1967), a psychologist who has extensively studied thought processes, creative thinking is associated with the following abilities:

1. *Fluency.* The ability to generate large numbers of possible solutions to problems.

2. *Flexibility.* The ability to shift with ease from one type of problem-solving strategy to another.

3. *Originality.* The ability to see unique or different solutions to a problem.

Guilford has also suggested that there are two distinct types of thinking, convergent and divergent. In convergent thinking, we select, or *converge* on, a single correct answer or solution from among several alternatives. You used convergence in the DONALD + GERALD problem to find the one correct number represented by each letter. Divergent thinking is the opposite. In divergent thinking we generate as many different, or *divergent,* solutions as possible, such as listing all the possible uses for a paper clip. Divergent thinking is the type of thinking most often associated with creativity. Thus, most tests of creativity and most techniques for improving creative thinking focus on divergent thinking.

But what about all the books on training yourself to be more creative?   Many books and even courses at the university level claim to train people to be more creative. Most of the

Convergent Thinking: The type of thinking needed when there is only one correct answer or solution to a problem.

Divergent Thinking: The type of thinking needed when it is necessary to generate as many ideas as possible.

data on creativity point to the fact that the more a person knows about a particular type of problem, the more likely the person is to find a solution. So in this sense self-help books will likely help you by developing your range of problem-solving techniques. However, there is no substantive body of research indicating that a person can be trained or motivated to be more creative. In fact, Teresa Amabile (1983) has found that extrinsic rewards (toys or money) actually hinder the creative process. She found that groups motivated by a promised reward for creativity produced art that was significantly less creative than groups working for no reward (see Chapter 12 for further discussion of this phenomenon).

Another reason creativity programs fail is that creativity may not really exist at all. B. F. Skinner (1981) believed behavior that appears to be spontaneous is part of a "class" of responses that has been selected by past reinforcers. Therefore creative acts or creative thinking are merely the results of past reinforcers. If our behavior is the result of our lifelong experience, it would be very unlikely that a book or creativity course could significantly alter our behavior and therefore make us more creative.

Review Questions

1. What is creativity?
2. According to J. P. Guilford, creative thinking is associated with _____ , _____ , and _____ .
3. Which type of thinking is described in each example:
   a. A 16-year-old tries to think of as many excuses as she can to explain to her parents why she was out past curfew.
   b. On a test, a student must select the one correct answer for each question.
4. The problem-solving technique in which a group of people tries to generate as many solutions as possible to a problem is called _____ .
5. You are a music teacher. You would like your students to apply the music theory you have taught them by creating their own songs. To motivate them, should you offer a Nintendo game as an incentive for the most creative song? Why or why not?

Answers to Review Questions can be found in Appendix C.

Language and Thought: A Complex Interaction

• *What is language? Is language limited to humans?*

Our cognitive processes are intricately related with one another. When solving any problem, from the simplest to the most complicated, we bring to bear our previous knowledge, our conceptual framework, our mental imagery talents, and even our ability to use language. When trying to solve the lily pad problem, did you find that you were talking to yourself? To some extent or other, most of us talk to ourselves when we're thinking. In fact, if you recall, one way to encode information is by verbal description (see Chapter 7).

Some experts, led by Benjamin Whorf (1956), believe that language influences the way people think and approach problems. Whorf proposed that the structure of our everyday language determines the structure of our thought—our vocabulary determines how we perceive and categorize the world around us. For example, Eskimos have many words describing different kinds of snow—hard-packed snow, wet snow, and so on. According to Whorf's hypothesis, because Eskimo vocabulary contains these words, Eskimos are able to categorize and conceptualize the various types of snow better than people whose vocabulary consists of one word: *snow*. If language does indeed determine our thought structure, Whorf's hypothesis might partially explain why, when people who speak different languages come together, they find it hard to truly comprehend the other's ideas, even through an interpreter.

Critical Thinking
PSYCHOLOGY IN ACTION
USING A VARIETY OF APPROACHES IN PROBLEM SOLVING
Solving Everyday Problems

Critical thinking includes the ability to take different approaches to problem solving. This exercise presents you with an opportunity to try a number of approaches on some everyday problems.

The major problem-solving approaches discussed in this chapter were the *algorithmic* approach, which involves generating possible solutions using some systematic procedure, and the *heuristic* approach, which involves generating possible solutions based on previous knowledge and experience.

We discussed three specific heuristic approaches: *means–end analysis, working backward,* and *creating subgoals.*

Below you will find six real-world problems, some of which you may have encountered in your own life. For each problem, (1) write down your solution to the problem; (2) identify the approach you took as algorithmic or means–end analysis, working backward, or creating subgoals; and (3) see if you can generate a different solution to the problem by using one of the other approaches.

1. Your car has broken down and is in need of major repairs. You have a final exam tomorrow morning at 8:00, so you have to get to school, which unfortunately is 20 miles away. How will you get there?

2. Next weekend, you are having a party for 30 friends. What kind of food and drink will you serve?

3. You wake up early one morning to find a steady stream of rain water leaking through your bedroom ceiling. You must stop the leak as fast as possible. How will you do it?

4. The Internal Revenue Service has just notified you that, according to their records, you owe several hundred dollars in back taxes and interest. You need to find your tax records from three years ago and recheck the numbers to prove that you filed an accurate return.

5. It has been weeks since you've had a good night's sleep because of your new neighbors' barking dog. You need your sleep. How are you going to ensure that you get it?

6. You want to find a gentle, considerate way to tell your girlfriend or boyfriend that the relationship is over.

Intriguing though Whorf's hypothesis is, research does not support it. Among other studies is one conducted by Eleanor Rosch (1973) with the Dani tribe in New Guinea. Although the Dani language has two color names, one indicating cool, dark colors and the other warm, bright colors, Rosch found that the Dani people could discriminate among color hues just as well as people speaking languages full of multiple names for colors. This kind of research indicates that although it may be easier to *express* a particular idea in one language than in another, language does not determine how or what we think, but is merely a reflection of our thinking.

What is language?   Language is a specialized form of communication. It is different from the communications of beavers slapping their tails, birds singing their songs, and ants laying their trails. Communication by other forms of life is simple and ritualistic, based on instinct. It is bound by a limited repertoire of sounds or movements that are performed whenever a certain stimulus evokes them. On the other hand, human language is a *creative* form of expression whereby we put together sounds and symbols according to specified rules. Rather than being an instinctive behavior, human language is learned, passed on from parent to child, friend to friend, teacher to student. Once the rules of a language are learned, people use them in quite creative and complex ways to convey their thoughts and feelings to others. We use language to impart knowledge to others and to gain knowledge from them. We use it to persuade or convince others to do something or to see our point of view, and others use it to persuade or convince us.

The Elements of Language

All languages, from ancient Sanskrit to modern English, are composed of basic speech sounds combined in prescribed ways. The basic speech sounds are called phonemes. Each phoneme has a distinctive feature that distinguishes it from every other phoneme, such as an unvoiced versus voiced component in the sounds /s/ and /z/. (When we say /s/

Language: A creative form of expression in which sounds and symbols are combined according to specified rules.

Phoneme: The most basic unit of speech; an individual speech sound.

These girls are communicating in American Sign Language, which consists of hand formations and facial expressions put together according to a set of grammatical rules.

we merely hiss; /z/ is formed the same way, but we add the voice.) Our English language has some 40 to 50 phonemes. Here are some examples:

/p/   as in   *p*ansy   /oi/   as in   v*oi*ce
/ch/   as in   *ch*ariot   /ng/   as in   sti*ng*

Phonemes are combined to make up basic units of meaning, called morphemes. These are the smallest meaningful units of language. They include "root words" such as *think*, *play*, and *blanket*, as well as suffixes and prefixes such as *un, able, ed*, and *ing*. Thus, in the word *unthinkable* there are three morphemes, *un, think*, and *able;* in the word *playing* there are two morphemes, *play* and *ing*.

> **Morpheme:** The smallest meaningful unit of language, formed from a certain combination of phonemes.

Phonemes, morphemes, words, and phrases are put together by rules of grammar, which differ from one language to another. These rules govern combinations of phonemes into words, changes in the forms of words (from singular to plural, present tense to past tense, etc.), and the order of words and phrases in a sentence. For instance, the rules of English dictate that a descriptive adjective precedes the noun, as in *the big house*. On the other hand, in Spanish, the descriptive adjective *follows* the noun, as in *la casa grande*.

> **Grammar:** The rules of a language that specify how phonemes, morphemes, words, and phrases should be combined to express meaningful thoughts.

The branch of grammar that describes the order or arrangement of words and phrases in a sentence is syntax. The syntax of a sentence is important because changing the order of a few words or phrases can change the entire meaning of a sentence. See how the meaning of the following sentence is altered merely by changing the syntax:

> **Syntax:** The grammatical rules that specify in what order the words and phrases should be arranged in a sentence in order to convey meaning.

I just took a shower because I was dirty.

I was dirty because I just took a shower.

In this section we have described the basic building blocks and rules of language. But the essential element of language is that it enables people to communicate and comprehend ideas.

Language and Cognition

Psycholinguists study how the elements of a language (grammar and syntax) affect the way we produce and comprehend that language. They also study the cognitive processes involved in using language, both in producing our own language and in understanding the language of others. In trying to understand what others are saying, we hear the phonemes they produce and combine them so that what we hear makes sense. This may not seem so hard, but think about it. When we talk, we produce a continuous stream of sounds—phonemes get all jumbled together and are even modified to some degree by the other sounds around them (Liberman, 1970). This is particularly evident when we listen to people speaking a foreign language.

Then how do we ever make sense out of the jumbled sounds we hear?   We use a number of cognitive strategies. We use our previous knowledge to interpret phonemes, organize sounds into words, and make out individual words. We organize what we hear into *constituents,* phrases or basic units of a sentence, as in *we organize* and *what we hear.* We also use the context of the other words to figure out individual words (Cole and Jakimik, 1980). Warren (1970) demonstrated this in a well-known study. He played a recording of a sentence such as the following and substituted a cough for the *s* in *legislatures: The state governors met with their respective legi*latures convening in the capital city.* Only one of his 20 subjects detected that the *s* was missing.

Producing language is quite another thing. When we want to say something to someone else, we go through innumerable operations, both mental and physical. Before even opening our mouths or if using sign language, moving our hands, we first plan what we want to say. From our knowledge bank in long-term memory, we gather all the relevant information about our topic and organize it so that it will be meaningful to whoever is listening. We figure out what our audience already knows and decide what background information they need. We decide whether to use formal or colloquial speech, all the time forming a mental representation of what we want to say. Finally, we carry out the motor movements necessary to convey our message—when speaking, forcing air from our lungs through our vocal cords and moving our lips, tongue, and jaw, or when using sign language, moving the muscles in our arms, hands, and fingers.

Animals and Language

There is quite a heated controversy over whether animals are capable of using language. Certainly it has not been demonstrated that they are capable of the complicated forms of communication used by humans. But there has been considerable research in an attempt to see whether animals, particularly apes and dolphins, can learn a human-designed language.

The first attempts to teach animals to speak resulted in failure. Winthrop and Luella Kellogg (1933) brought up a baby chimpanzee named Gua with their own human baby, Donald. They raised their two "children" in much the same way, but although they tried for months to teach Gua to say the word "Papa," they never succeeded. Cathy and Keith Hayes (1951) undertook a similar project with a chimp named Viki, raising her in a stimulating environment and trying to teach her to speak human language. Although they spoke to her as much as they would had Viki been their own child, Viki never voluntarily tried to speak. After intense training the Hayeses eventually succeeded in teaching her to say "Mama," "Papa," "cup," and "up," but these words were uttered in a rasping voice and were produced only with much struggling and straining.

Washoe and Other Success Stories

Analyzing early animal language studies, researchers concluded that the reason they failed may have been simply because apes do not have the anatomical structure to vocalize that we do. Subsequent studies have focused on teaching apes nonvocal languages. One of the most successful and well-known is a study by Beatrice and Allen Gardner (1969), who recognized the manual dexterity of chimpanzees and their ability to imitate gestures. The Gardners used American Sign Language (ASL), a language used by many deaf people, with a chimp named Washoe. Their success story speaks for itself. By the time Washoe was four years old, she had learned 132 signs and was able to combine them into simple sentences such as "Hurry gimme toothbrush" and "Please tickle more."

Since the Gardners' success with Washoe, several other language projects have been conducted with apes (Itakura, 1992; Savage-Rumbaugh, 1990). David Premack (1976) taught a chimp named Sarah to "read" and "write" by placing plastic symbols on a magnetic board. She learned not only to use the symbols Premack had invented but also to follow certain grammatical rules in communicating with her trainers. Another well-known study was conducted with a chimp named Lana. She learned to depress symbols on a computer to receive things she wanted, such as food, a drink, a tickle from her trainers, or her curtains opened (Rumbaugh et al., 1974). And, of course, there is Koko, about whom you read in Chapter 6. Penny Patterson (1981) taught the gorilla over 600 signs in American Sign Language. (You will read more about Koko in Chapter 12.)

Dolphin Language Studies

In addition to language research with apes, a number of studies, particularly at the University of Hawaii, have focused on the acquisition of language by dolphins (see Herman, Morell, and Pack, 1990). In dolphin studies, communication is by means of hand signals and gestures or auditory commands. The commands may be spoken by trainers or generated by computers and transmitted through an underwater speaker system. In a typical study conducted by Herman, Richards, and Wolz (1984), dolphins were given commands made up of two- to five-word sentences. The dolphins were commanded to perform certain tasks with specific objects in their pool, such as "Big ball—square—return," which meant they should go get the big ball, put it in the floating square, and return to the trainer. The interesting part of the experiment was that the commands were varied in syntax and content, both of which altered the meaning of the sentence. For example, the next command might be "Square—big ball—return," which meant they should go to the square first, then get the big ball, then return to the trainer with the ball. Or the command might refer to one of the other objects floating in the pool, thereby changing its content: "Triangle—little ball—square," which means that the dolphin must discriminate among various shapes and various sizes of balls to carry out the command. Results of the study demonstrated that dolphins could carry out a great variety of commands that varied in meaning in both content and syntax.

Language studies are being conducted with dolphins in which researchers, by using particular hand signals and gestures as well as auditory commands, ask dolphins to perform various tasks. By varying not only the content of the commands but also the order of the tasks, researchers show that dolphins understand human communication that varies in meaning.

Evaluating Animal Language Studies

Though dolphin research and other recent animal language studies are impressive by any measure, the question still remains whether these animals are truly using language as humans do. Many psychologists criticize these studies on the grounds that human language consists of sentences put together creatively and meaningfully according to grammatical rules. Moreover, the average length of sentences produced or understood by humans is significantly more than the two- to five-word sentences used by animals. Critics claim that animals cannot possibly learn the countless rules of grammar, particularly syntactical rules, that humans use to convey subtle differences in meaning. They question whether animals can use language in ways that are considered creative or unique. Furthermore, they argue that animals do not have a conceptual understanding of the signs and symbols of language; they are merely imitating symbols in order to receive rewards. In short, they are not really trying to communicate but simply performing operantly conditioned responses (Savage-Rumbaugh et al., 1980; Terrace, 1979).

On the other hand, proponents of animal language are quick to point out that chimpanzees and gorillas do use language creatively and have even coined some words of their own. For example, Washoe called a refrigerator "open eat drink" and a swan a "water bird" (Gardner and Gardner, 1971). Koko signed "finger bracelet" to describe a ring and "eye hat" to describe a mask (Patterson and Linden, 1981). Proponents also argue that, as demonstrated by the dolphin studies, animals can be taught to understand basic rules of sentence structure and syntax.

Still, the fact remains that the gap between language as spoken and understood by humans and that generated and understood by other animals is considerable. Evidence of animals using language creatively is extremely sparse, whereas nearly every sentence humans write or speak is unique. Furthermore, the vocabulary of children as young as four years old far exceeds that of the most verbal ape. All the evidence seems to point to the fact that animals can learn language at a rudimentary level but that this language is a far cry from the complex, creative, rule-laden language used by humans.

Review Questions

1. Benjamin Whorf proposed that the structure of our language influences the way we _____ .
2. How is human language different from the communication of other animals?
3. The basic speech sounds /ch/ and /v/ are known as _____ ; the smallest meanful units of language such as "book," "pre," and "ing" are known as _____ .
4. What is the difference between grammar and syntax?
5. How do we make sense out of the jumble of sounds we call ordinary speech?
6. Why did early attempts to teach apes to speak human language fail, and what was the solution for this problem?
7. Studies have shown that dolphins can understand sentences that vary in _____ and _____ .

Answers to Review Questions can be found in Appendix C.

INTELLIGENCE AND INTELLIGENCE TESTING

• *What is intelligence, and how can it be measured?*

Finger on the buzzer, hot studio lights glaring down, the contestant stands poised to answer the question that will win the game. Faced with contradictory evidence, a forceful prosecution, and a powerful defense, the judge pronounces a decision that sets a precedent for future cases. Standing in front of hundreds of colleagues, the researcher describes the recombinant techniques by which he identified the cloning vectors that may finally lead to a cure for one of our most devastating diseases. Would you consider these people intelligent? If you live in a westernized country, you probably would. What is it about these people that makes us consider them intelligent? What is intelligence?

Intelligence Defined: More Difficult Than It Seems

Although most researchers agree that intelligence is a set of cognitive characteristics and abilities that cannot be directly observed, specific definitions of intelligence have changed over time and even today vary greatly. Basically, over the years psychologists have been divided into two camps, one feeling that intelligence is a single general ability and another feeling that there are actually several distinct kinds of intelligences. In the early years of intelligence testing, psychologists viewed intelligence as a broad mental ability that included all the cognitive functions. Charles Spearman was one of these. Based on his observations that scores on separate tests of mental abilities tend to correlate with each other, Spearman (1927) proposed that intelligence is a single factor, which he termed g. He maintained that g is a general cognitive ability that enables people to reason, solve problems, and perform well in all areas of cognition. Based on Spearman's work, standardized tests began to be widely used in such places as the military, schools, and businesses to measure this general intelligence.

About a decade later, L. L. Thurstone (1938) broke away from this view by proposing seven distinct primary mental abilities that he believed were independent of each other: verbal comprehension, word fluency, numerical fluency, spatial visualization,

Toni Morrison

Gabriel García Márquez

Sally Ride

Meryl Streep

Stevie Wonder

Bill Gates

Bonnie Blair

Some psychologists claim that there are many different kinds of intelligence and creativity. Award-winning authors Toni Morrison and Gabriel Garcia Marquez, for example, represent literary intelligence; Sally Ride, Stephen Hawking, and Bill Gates represent the intelligence and creativity associated with scientific inquiry; Meryl Streep and Stevie Wonder illustrate the intelligence and creativity associated with the performing arts; and Bonnie Blair represents the high level of motor intelligence required of world-class athletes.

Stephen Hawking

Fluid Intelligence: The capacity for acquiring new knowledge and solving new problems that is at least partially determined by biological and genetic factors and is relatively stable over short periods of time.

Crystallized Intelligence: Knowledge and learning that we have gained over the course of our lives through an interaction between fluid intelligence and environmental experience.

associative memory, perceptual speed, and reasoning. Many years later, J. P. Guilford (1967) expanded on this number and proposed that as many as 120 factors influence intelligence. At about the same time, however, after reanalyzing Thurstone's data, Raymond Cattell (1963, 1971) argued against the idea of multiple intelligences. He proposed that *g* does exist, but that there are two different types of *g*, which he called fluid intelligence and crystallized intelligence. Fluid intelligence refers to our ability to gain new knowledge and to attack and solve novel problems. Being both genetically and biologically determined, it consists more of our *capacity* for learning new things. Crystallized intelligence, on the other hand, refers to the actual accumulation of knowledge over our life span. The amount of knowledge gained depends on our level of fluid intelligence and on our culture, education, and past experiences. Research has found that crystallized intelligence tends to increase with age, while fluid intelligence tends to decrease after about age 40 (Horn, 1978).

Contemporary Cognitive Theory

Cognitive theorists working today argue that earlier theorists formulated definitions of intelligence in a cart-before-the-horse fashion—that they devised the intelligence tests, administered them, analyzed the data, and only then formulated their definitions of intelligence. Contemporary theorists believe there is more to intelligence than what is measured on traditional intelligence tests. They also tend to agree that, although there seems to be a relationship among diverse mental abilities, some people excel in specific areas of intelligence more than in other areas, so perhaps, as suggested by Thurstone and Guilford, mental abilities actually are distinct from one another. In 1983, Howard Gardner proposed a theory of multiple intelligences. He postulates at least six different types of intelligence—linguistic, musical, logical-mathematical, spatial, bodily-kinesthetic, and personal—and he feels that each person tends to excel in some areas more than in others. Consequently, he maintains, intelligence testing should consist of assessing a person's strengths rather than coming up with a single "IQ score" (Gardner, 1986). Educators have recognized the value of Gardner's theory and have implemented programs that build on children's various intellectual strengths. School systems both large and small throughout the country, from New York City to Vista, California, have created magnet schools in the sciences, in math and technology, and in visual and performing arts to provide learning environments tailored to students' unique strengths and learning styles.

Sternberg's Triarchic Theory

Based on findings from information processing research, Robert Sternberg (1985) developed what he calls a triarchic theory of human intelligence. Sternberg feels that even more important than the outward products of intelligence such as correct answers on an intelligence test or solutions to world problems are the thinking processes we use to arrive at answers to problems, and theories of intelligence should account for these processes. According to the triarchic theory, there are three aspects of intelligence that are separate but related: the internal components of intelligence, the use of these components to adapt to environmental changes, and the application of past experience to real-life situations (Frensch and Sternberg, 1990). Some people tend to have a stronger aptitude for using one or more of these aspects of intelligence. Below is a brief explanation of each.

1. The internal aspect of intelligence consists of our mental processes, which Sternberg breaks down into three megacomponents—those we use to acquire and store knowledge; those we use in perception, short- and long-term memory, and problem solving; and those we use to plan, monitor, and evaluate our thinking. Thus, when we complete an analogy such as "Den is to bear as hive is to ____," we call on knowledge stored in long-term memory, hold it in working memory, decide what strategy to use, and apply our reasoning and

problem-solving abilities to come up with the answer "bee." Sternberg believes that the component that sets intellectuals apart from the rest of us is their effective use of megacomponents to plan and evaluate problem-solving strategies.

2. The adaptive aspect of intelligence is evident when we use our internal components to adapt to or change our environment or select new environments that are more consistent with our goals. For instance, you would use adaptive intelligence to solve the barking dog problem described in the critical thinking exercise. You would use your thinking skills to decide how to either adapt to or change the situation.

3. Experiential aspects of intelligence refer to our ability to apply well-practiced automatic processes to familiar tasks and our ability to learn from past experience in solving new problems. Fire fighters excel in this aspect of intelligence. They repeatedly survive dangerous situations because they apply their honed skills and past experience to figure out what to do in emergencies.

The overwhelming value of Sternberg's theory of intelligence is that he emphasizes the *process* underlying thinking rather than just the end product, and the importance of the *application* of mental abilities to real-world situations rather than the testing of mental abilities in isolation.

We have examined several theories of intelligence, from Spearman's *g* to Gardner's multiple intelligences to Sternberg's triarchic view. We are ready to return to the question posed at the beginning of this section: What is intelligence? We offer this concise definition: Intelligence refers to the cognitive abilities employed in acquiring, remembering, and using knowledge of one's culture to solve everyday problems and to readily adapt to and function in both changing and stable environments.

Intelligence: The cognitive abilities employed in acquiring, remembering, and using knowledge of one's culture to solve everyday problems and to readily adapt to and function in both changing and stable environments.

Measuring Intelligence: What Constitutes a Good Test?

Even though there is more to intelligence than what is measured on an intelligence test, IQ tests have traditionally been used by educators and psychologists to estimate and rank the overall intelligence of individuals. An IQ score is a score on a test intended to measure verbal and quantitative abilities necessary to succeed in a normal public school system. IQ scores do not indicate overall intellectual abilities and do not necessarily predict success in the "real world."

We will examine intelligence tests in depth in the next section, but first we need to introduce some general principles of psychological testing: standardization, reliability, and validity.

Standardization

The term standardization has two meanings as it applies to testing. First, every test must have established norms. That is, it must be given to a large number of people to determine which scores are average scores, which scores are above average, and which are below average. This type of standardization is necessary to discover the statistical properties of the test and is especially important when the test is to be used in testing thousands of people. Most tests found in popular magazines are not standardized and are therefore not accurate for determining the "normalcy" of the behavior being tested.

Second, testing procedures must be standardized. The conditions under which a test is administered must be clearly and completely specified in a test manual. Everyone taking the test must be treated equally by receiving the same instructions and questions under identical conditions. This is so that any differences in scores can be attributed to differences in test-takers' abilities or characteristics rather than to the testing procedures. Scoring procedures should also be specifically detailed in the testing manual for similar reasons.

Standardization: The process of establishing the norms of a test in order to assess which skills, knowledge, or characteristics are representative of the general population. Also, the development of standard procedures for administering and scoring a test to ensure that the conditions are the same for everyone taking the test.

When administering standardized tests, every attempt is made to ensure that everyone takes the test under identical conditions and is given identical instructions.

You witnessed standardization in testing procedures if you took the nationwide college entrance exams, the Scholastic Aptitude Test (SAT) or the American College Test (ACT). Normally, these are given on the same day and at the same time of day to graduating high school seniors who take the same test under identical conditions. If conditions varied from one test center to another, the individual test scores might also vary as a result of the change in conditions rather than differences in students' abilities. For example, suppose the test center at High Tech High School permitted students to use electronic calculators for the math section of the test and the test center at Manual Arts High did not. The High Tech students with the calculators would have an unfair advantage over the Manual Arts students. Standardization, therefore, is a necessary requirement for a useful test. However, tests must also be reliable and valid.

Reliability

Reliability: A measure of the consistency and stability of test scores when the test is readministered over a period of time.

Reliability is a measure of the stability of test scores over time. The reliability of a test is usually determined by retesting subjects at a later date to determine whether their test scores have changed significantly. If a test were 100 percent reliable, any person taking it would get the same score every time he or she took it. In reality, this is never the case, but a good test must be relatively reliable over at least short periods of time. For example, if you took the SAT on one day and scored 475, then took the same test a week later and scored 250, it would definitely not be reliable and the test would be useless.

Validity

Validity: The ability of a test to actually measure what it is intended to measure.

Validity refers to whether a test actually measures what it is intended to measure. There are several types of validity. The most important is *criterion-related validity,* or the accuracy with which test scores can be used to predict another variable of interest, termed the criterion. Criterion-related validity is expressed as the correlation between the test score and the criterion. As we saw in Chapter 1, a *correlation* is a standard measure of how two variables are related. A high correlation indicates the two variables are closely related, and low or zero correlation indicates there is little or no relationship between them. If two variables are highly correlated, then one variable can be used to predict the other. Thus, if a test is valid, its scores will be useful in predicting people's behavior in some other specified situation. For example, a test given to prospective job applicants is valid if it predicts job performance, and the SAT is valid if it predicts grades in college.

Without being valid, a test is totally useless, even though it may be standardized and reliable. Suppose you are giving someone a test of skin sensitivity. Such a test may be easy to standardize (the instructions specify the exact points on the body to apply the test) and it may be reliable (similar results are obtained on each retest), but it would certainly not be valid for predicting grades in college, since the test results would be correlated with criteria other than success in college.

Most major psychological tests are carefully standardized, although they vary widely in their reliability and validity. Much of the controversy over testing in the United States and elsewhere concerns validity—what is actually being tested by psychological tests, especially IQ tests.

Review Questions

1. What is Spearman's view of intelligence, and what is at least one alternative to this view?
2. What is the difference between fluid and crystallized intelligence?
3. According to Sternberg's triarchic theory of intelligence, what are the three aspects of intelligence?
4. What is intelligence?
5. Tell which testing principle, standardization, reliability, or validity, is being described below:
    a. This assures that if the same person takes the same test two weeks after taking it the first time, her score will not significantly change.
    b. This assures that a test or other measurement device actually measures what it purports to measure.
    c. This assures that the test has been given to large numbers of people in order to determine which scores are average, above average, and below average—in short, which are representative of the general population.

Answers to Review Questions can be found in Appendix C.

IQ Tests: Predictors of School Performance

There are many different kinds of IQ tests, and each approaches the measurement of intelligence from a slightly different perspective. Most, however, attempt to measure abilities that allow the test to be a valid predictor of academic performance. In other words, most IQ tests are designed to predict grades in school. To see how that's done, let's take a look at the most commonly used IQ tests.

Individual IQ Tests

The first IQ test to be widely used in the United States was the Stanford–Binet Intelligence Scale. It was loosely based on the very first IQ tests developed in France around the turn of the century by Alfred Binet. Lewis Terman (1916) developed the Stanford–Binet (at Stanford University) to test the intellectual ability of U.S.-born children ages 3 to 16. The test is revised periodically—the latest revision was made in 1985. The test items are administered individually (one test-giver and one test-taker) and consist of such tasks as copying geometric designs, identifying similarities, and repeating a sequence of numbers. In the original version of the Stanford–Binet, results were expressed in terms of a *mental age*. For example, if a seven-year-old's score equaled that of an average eight-year-old, the child was considered to have a mental age of eight, as measured by the test.

Intelligence Quotient (IQ): A score on a test that is intended to measure verbal and quantitative abilities.

To determine the child's intelligence quotient (IQ), mental age was divided by the child's chronological age (actual age in years). The formula for an IQ was as follows:

$$IQ = \frac{MA}{CA} \times 100 = \frac{8}{7} \times 100 = 1.14 \times 100 = 114$$

(The ratio was multiplied by 100 to eliminate decimals or fractions.) Thus, a seven-year-old with a mental age of eight would have an IQ of 114. A "normal" child should have a mental age *equal* to his or her chronological age. ("Normal" in this case refers to the norms or statistics used to standardize the test. There is no child labeled "The Normal Child" locked in a vault at the National Bureau of Standards.)

Today, Stanford–Binet IQ test scores are expressed as a comparison of a single person's score to a national sample of similar-aged people. These *deviation IQs* are computed on the basis of how far the person's score on the test deviates from the national average. On a standardized IQ test such as the Stanford–Binet, the majority of people score within one standard deviation (16 points) above or one standard deviation below the national average, which is 100 points. Therefore, a child who scores two standard deviation units above the national average on the Stanford–Binet would get a deviation IQ equal to 132, and a child who scores one standard deviation unit below the national average would receive a deviation IQ equal to 84.

Figure 8.3 illustrates the typical distribution curve of scores on the Stanford–Binet: The majority (68 percent) of the children taking the test score within the normal range, whereas approximately 16 percent score above 116 and approximately 16 percent score below 84.

Because scores on the Stanford–Binet are meant to predict grades in school, a high IQ should be related to higher grades or to higher scores on achievement tests. In fact, the correlations between the Stanford–Binet and other tests of academic ability were found by Bossard et al. (1980) to be between .70 and .82, which indicates a relatively high relationship between IQ and academic ability. Thus, the Stanford–Binet can be said to be a valid predictor of school grades.

The Wechsler Tests

The other major IQ tests that are individually administered are the Wechsler tests. In 1939, David Wechsler, a clinical psychologist at Bellevue Hospital in New York, developed his own intelligence scale, taking a different approach than Terman. Terman's Stanford–Binet test consists of a set of various age-level items, and subjects must complete one age level before advancing to the next. Wechsler's scale consists of three *separate* tests: the Wechsler Preschool and Primary Scale of Intelligence (WPPSI), for ages 3 to 6; the Wechsler Intelligence Scale for Children–Third Edition (WISC-III), for ages 5 to 15; and the Adult Intelligence Scale–Revised (WAIS-R), for adults.

The other major difference between the Stanford–Binet and the Wechsler tests is the degree to which verbal abilities are measured. The Stanford–Binet (above age 6 or 7)

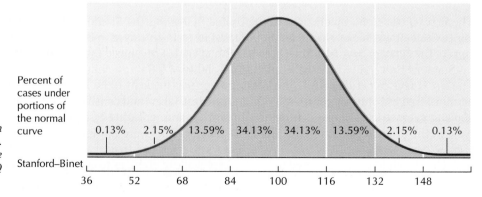

Figure 8.3 The distribution of scores on the Stanford–Binet Intelligence Test. Notice that over two-thirds of the people taking the test, 68.26 percent, have an IQ between 84 and 116.

The Weschler Intelligence Scale, unlike the Stanford-Binet, includes nonverbal performance measures such as the block design task being completed by this child.

is primarily designed to measure verbal abilities, while the Wechsler scales are half verbal and half nonverbal. The Wechsler approach has two advantages: The different abilities can be evaluated either separately or together, and people who are unable to speak or understand English can still be tested. The verbal portion of the tests doesn't have to be administered, since each subtest yields its own score. (See Table 8.1 for the various subtests of the WISC-III.)

In response to criticisms that individually administered tests are biased against certain cultural and ethnic groups, Alan and Nadeen Kaufman (1983) have constructed the Kaufman Assessment Battery for Children (K-ABC). The K-ABC is an individually administered test of achievement and aptitude that has been standardized to evaluate all students, including minority, hearing-impaired, speech- and language-disordered, and non–English-speaking children. In developing the test, the Kaufmans attempted to sample problem-solving ability as well as general knowledge. Some studies have found the reliability and predictive validity of the K-ABC to be high (Childers et al., 1985; Siegel and Piotrowski, 1985), but others find the test is less valid than the Stanford–Binet and the WISC-R (Bracken, 1985; Jensen, 1984). Much more research is necessary before we know whether or not the K-ABC makes a significant contribution to psychology and education.

Group IQ Tests

Most IQ tests given today are not individual tests; they are group tests. Individual IQ tests are useful in making diagnostic decisions because they are administered by psychologists who are trained to monitor not only right and wrong answers but also frustrations, points of difficulty, and so on. However, administering an individual IQ test is time-consuming (each test takes an average of one to two hours) and expensive (because of the amount of educational training and practice required of psychologists, they are paid a high fee). A faster and less expensive way to obtain an estimate of the intellectual abilities of a large group of individuals is to use a group IQ test.

The Army Alpha Test

Group IQ tests were first given to inductees in the U.S. Army during World War I. With nearly 2 million recruits to process in a short time, individual tests were out of the

Table 8.1   **Subtests of the WISC-III**

Verbal Subtests	Example*
Information	How many senators are elected from each state?
Similarities	How are computers and books alike?
Arithmetic	If one baseball card costs three cents, how much will five baseball cards cost?
Vocabulary	Define *lamp*.
Comprehension	What should you do if you accidently break a friend's toy?

Performance Subtests   Example*

Picture Completion
What is missing from this ambulance?

Coding
Write the appropriate number above each symbol.

Picture Arrangement
Arrange these pictures in chrono-logical order.

Block Design
Copy this design with blocks.

Object Assembly
Assemble this small jigsaw puzzle.

* These examples are similar to those used on the actual test.

question. So a team of psychologists headed by Robert Yerkes developed the first group test of intelligence, the Army Alpha. The first paper-and-pencil IQ test, it measured such cognitive abilities as mathematical reasoning, analogies, and practical judgment.

Since the Army Alpha, many types of group tests have been developed. Group achievement tests are designed to measure what a person has already learned. Group aptitude tests measure a person's aptitude, or capability, to learn a certain skill. If you grew up in the United States and attended a public school, you probably took a group achievement test once a year. And when you were in high school, you and your friends probably took the SAT or the ACT, mentioned earlier in this section. Both are group aptitude tests required by four-year colleges and universities to measure prospective students' academic aptitude. Although the scales of these two tests and the actual items differ, the SAT and the ACT are about equally valid in their ability to predict college grades (Aleamoni and Oboler, 1978; Halpin et al., 1981).

Although group aptitude tests such as the SAT and the ACT are used extensively by colleges and universities in their admissions procedures, high school grade point average is a better predictor of college grades.

Uses and Abuses of IQ Tests

Employers, educators, and clinicians routinely use individual and group IQ tests for many purposes. Employers use IQ tests as part of their hiring and promoting procedures. Schools use individual and group IQ tests to determine students' needs and abilities to place them into programs for the mentally gifted, for the educable mentally retarded, for the learning disabled, and so on. Clinicians use IQ tests for a number of reasons, including determining whether clients are functioning up to their intellectual potential. Yet, as critics point out, there is more to intelligence than what is measured on an IQ test, so relying solely on an IQ test to make critical decisions affecting individual lives is not warranted and possibly even unethical.

Gender and Cultural Diversity

CULTURAL DIFFERENCES IN SCHOOL SUCCESS

In the United States today there is a growing controversy that hinges on racial differences in average IQ scores. It is documented that African Americans and other minorities in the United States score an average of 15 points lower on IQ tests than whites (Graham and Lilly, 1984). Since the major contribution of IQ tests is their ability to predict success in school, it seems logical to predict that because African Americans score lower than whites on IQ tests, they will perform lower on measures of school success. Is this true? Actually, many African Americans do indeed fare worse in school than whites. What is the reason for this lowered school success?

John Ogbu (1988), himself an African-American psychologist, has studied the phenomenon extensively and has come up with some explanations. When children from white, middle-class families enter school, they enter ready—academically, socially, and emotionally—to learn in the school environment. Their parents have read to them since they were infants, so books are familiar friends. They know how to look at and decipher pictures (which, amazing as it sounds, is a learned skill). They know most letter names and many letter sounds. They have had experiences sharing toys with other children and been trained how to handle conflicts in a nonaggressive manner. They feel comfortable in the schoolroom because it looks a lot like their home, with chairs and tables in which they are expected to sit and blocks and other familiar toys arranged neatly in their own places on shelves. In short, their parents from their white, middle-class culture have prepared them for their first school experience.

Not so for many urban African-American children, who come from a different culture—the culture of the streets. Their parents are forced to prepare them to survive life on the streets of the city, rather than to read and write in a classroom. These children come to school overwhelmed by not only the kinds of materials they work with but also the expectations and demands placed on them. They may not ever have seen a picture book before, much less listened as someone read to them. They may never have even heard the alphabet song, much less had a chance to learn it. They may never have had a chance to learn how to work cooperatively with others or share—they may not have had many toys to share.

Low-Effort Syndrome

Another contributor to lowered school success is a phenomenon Ogbu refers to as *low-effort syndrome* (Ogbu, 1991, 1986). Stemming from their days as pre–Civil War slaves, African Americans have become reconciled to hearing others undermine their abilities —so much so that they fall into the delusion that they actually are incapable of succeeding in school. Some don't reach their full potential because of conflicts with and distrust of authority figures such as principals and teachers. Ironically, many fall prey to pressure from their peers *not* to succeed academically in order not to emulate the white people who have put them down for so many years. Others just don't try as hard as they might because they are disillusioned about job opportunities when their schooling is completed.

In addition, many African Americans, as well as other minorities such as Native American Indians (Phillips, 1983), have spent their lives speaking the language of their culture, the dialect of their neighborhood. When they enter school and hear standard American English, it sounds to them like a foreign language. When they learn to read, it is this standard, formal English they are expected to learn rather than the language with which they are fluent. It is no wonder they have more trouble than middle-class whites in learning the basics of education.

Despite the obstacles to quality schooling, there is hope in the future for disadvantaged African Americans and other minorities. Head Start's contribution to school readiness has been widely acclaimed, and during the 1992 campaign, President Bill Clinton made a commitment that by 1996, all eligible three- and four-year-olds will have an opportunity to enroll (Collins, 1993). But participation in Head Start only sets the stage for school success. To truly give children a boost toward success, they need to grow up in families that are free from poverty and drug abuse. They need to grow up with parents who know how to parent, who have satisfying, well-paying jobs, and who value education. Fortunately, help of this nature for low-income families is becoming increasingly available through government programs. The Job Opportunities and Basic Skills (JOBS) training program, the Parent and Child Centers (PCC) program, and programs created by the Administration on Children, Youth, and Families (ACYF), among others, promote self-sufficiency for low-income families by providing job training for parents, instruction for family literacy, high-quality child care, programs for parenting skills, family health services, and early childhood education (Collins, 1993). ■

Head Start programs throughout the country have been highly acclaimed in providing disadvantaged preschoolers a chance to acquire the readiness skills that are so crucial for school success.

Differences in Intelligence: How and Why We Are Different

Clearly, people vary in their intellectual abilities. Some of us can take apart a watch that's stopped ticking and reassemble it so that it keeps time better than ever. Others have trouble even winding a watch but can draw one that looks more real than the one on your wrist. In this section, we'll take a look at the ways people differ in intelligence. We'll examine the effect of age on intelligence and discuss the extremes of intelligence. We'll also investigate the controversy over which factor is more important in determining intellectual ability, heredity or environment.

Age and IQ

IQ test scores appear to vary with age (Birren and Schaie, 1985; Kausler, 1992). Botwinick (1977) describes the now-classic intellectual aging pattern, where intellectual performance remains the same across all ages when a person has unlimited time to complete a task, but scores decline with age when the task is timed for speed. Recently, Kaufman, Reynolds, and McLean (1989) demonstrated that this holds true on the WAIS. Scores on the verbal subtests, which are not timed, are not significantly related to age, while scores on the performance subtests, which are timed, tend to decrease with age. This pattern in turn correlates with the aging pattern of crystallized and fluid intelligence (Horn, 1978), where as people grow older, they tend to retain their ability to perform on tasks measuring crystallized intelligence but show a decline on tasks measuring fluid intelligence. All of these studies indicate there are age differences in intelligence, but that they are related not to the content of our minds but to the speed with which we can manipulate its contents and our ability to learn new material. So don't assume older individuals are "over the hill." They're just doing things, including thinking, a little more slowly, not less well.

Mental Retardation

Despite the criticisms of IQ tests, they are still used to assess mental ability if a person is suspected to have below-normal or above-normal intelligence and to then assign the person to a program specially designed to benefit him or her. No one would argue about mentally retarded persons needing special help from society in order to function. Similarly, any teacher of gifted students will readily attest that academically gifted children need—even demand—special opportunities to develop their talents.

The most obvious characteristic of mentally retarded individuals is that they are slower than normal people in intellectual functioning and their ability to cope with the problems of daily life is usually impaired (Grossman, 1983; Zigler and Hodapp, 1986). Clinicians tend to classify people scoring 70 and below on an IQ test as mentally retarded. Of course, people are retarded in varying degrees. Psychologists classify mentally retarded people by their degree of retardation, as shown in Table 8.2.

Keep in mind that, as in normal people, personality and motivational factors play a big part in the successes retarded people can achieve. Because retarded people tend to experience failure and often ridicule time and again, they become easily discouraged and afraid of trying new tasks. They become more dependent on parents or loved ones to do things for them that they could learn to do for themselves. Therefore, the mentally retarded need to be directed to activities that ensure some amount of success, such as the Special Olympics, to engender positive attitudes toward their capabilities. Furthermore, people can be retarded in most areas and be normal or even gifted in others. The most dramatic examples are *savants,* mentally deficient or disturbed people who excel in

Table 8.2 Degrees of Mental Retardation

Level of Retardation	IQ Scores	Percent of Population	Characteristics
Mild	50–70	80–85%	Usually able to become self-sufficient; may marry, have families, and secure full-time jobs in unskilled occupations.
Moderate	35–49	10–12%	Able to perform simple unskilled tasks; may contribute to a certain extent to their livelihood.
Severe	20–34	4–7%	Able to follow daily routines, but with continual supervision. With training, may learn basic communication skills.
Profound	below 20	1%	Able to perform only the most rudimentary behaviors, such as walking, feeding themselves, and saying a few phrases.

a specific area, such as rapid calculation, memory, or musical ability. You may have seen the movie *Rain Man*, in which Dustin Hoffman portrayed a savant with exceptional mathematical ability. Obviously, it would benefit mentally retarded people and the rest of us if they were to be given opportunities to use their talents.

What causes mental retardation?   Some forms of retardation stem from organic causes, whereas others have no known cause. *Down syndrome* is an example of organic retardation that results from an extra chromosome in the body's cells. It is characterized by a moderate level of retardation, protruding tongue, pudgy face, slurred speech, heart defects, and a pleasant, friendly personality. Most often, Down syndrome is found in babies borne by mothers under 20 and over 35, so it is associated with maternal age when the hormone estrogen is not being produced at peak levels. Other forms of retardation result from alcohol and other drug abuse during pregnancy, from extreme environmental deprivation in early life, and from genetic factors. However, in 70 to 75 percent of the cases, there is no known cause for the mental retardation. Generally, people in this unknown-cause group are only mildly retarded and come from families in the lower socioeconomic bracket. Often, too, there are several incidences of mental retardation in the family. This type of retardation is thus often referred to as *familial retardation*.

Mainstreaming versus Special Placement

The question of how to best help people with mental retardation depends on how they are viewed in comparison to normal people. Developmental theorists contend that mentally retarded people are merely delayed in their cognitive development, that they progress through the same cognitive stages of development as normal people, but at a slower rate. (See Chapter 9 for a description of the cognitive stages of development.) On the other hand, difference theorists contend there is an innate difference between mentally retarded and normal people because mental retardation is characterized by rigidity and deficiencies in verbal and other skills. Based on their views, then, the developmentalists believe mentally retarded children should receive the same instruction in school as normal children, but at a later age and with more time to learn skills. The difference theorists believe mentally retarded children should receive different instruction in the form of training to improve their existing skills. Most of the recent research has been based on the developmentalist point of view, and in fact, the term currently used to refer to mentally retarded children is *developmentally delayed*.

Throughout the United States today, developmentally delayed youngsters are currently being *mainstreamed* (integrated) into regular classrooms with predominantly nonhandicapped children to give them every opportunity to develop in as normal an environment as possible. Similarly, mentally retarded adults are being taken out of institutions and placed in small group homes. When their mental capabilities allow it, they are also helped to find jobs that match their ability levels. This is in contrast to isolating children in special classes and sequestering adults in institutions where they live away from the rest of society.

There are benefits as well as drawbacks to both special placement and mainstreaming. With special placement, mentally retarded individuals receive instruction in tasks tailored specifically to their needs and abilities. However, it also means that they are isolated from society at large and are thereby deprived of any interaction with people of normal intelligence. With mainstreaming, developmentally delayed individuals receive the extra stimulation of the same classroom environment and curriculum as people with normal intelligence, although teachers give them only the material they are capable of mastering. Although this idea is appealing in theory, it is less so in practice. Teachers with 30 to 32 children in the classroom must necessarily teach to the majority of the class and often just don't have the time to individualize for one child of less than normal intelligence. However, on the positive side, mainstreaming can lead to better academic achievement, increased social skills through contact with normal children and adults, and more racially integrated classrooms. Also, when developmentally delayed children are mainstreamed into a regular classroom, the other children learn to appreciate their many capabilities and contributions (Gottlieb, 1981).

Mental Giftedness

At the other end of the intellectual continuum are intellectually *gifted* people, those who score above 140 on IQ tests and who tend to exhibit the characteristics listed below. (Bear in mind that gifted people also possess other characteristics, and that all of them do not exhibit all of these traits.)

Are self-directed, self-motivated, and self-disciplined

Learn new information quickly

Have diverse interests and/or show intense interest in one specific area

Are curious, with an intense desire to know causes and effects

Think critically and analytically

Have well-developed communication skills with an extensive vocabulary

Are keenly observant

Generate creative ideas

Exhibit flexibility in thought and action

Learn to read early and continue to read at an advanced level

Are sensitive to others' feelings

Possess a good sense of humor

Have long attention spans

Demonstrate leadership skills

Relate well with peers and adults

Exhibit mature and responsible behavior

Do some of these traits surprise you? Often people tend to think of gifted people as socially maladjusted with their heads buried in books or glued to a computer screen. In 1921, Lewis Terman, who translated the Binet Intelligence Scale to form the Stanford–Binet, set out to study whether such a stereotype was well-founded. He conducted a long-term study of over 1500 children who scored 140 or better on IQ tests to see how intelligence relates to occupational and social success. By 1950, when their average age was 40, the number of these people "who became research scientists, engineers, physicians, lawyers, or college teachers, or who were highly successful in business and other fields, is in each case many times the number a random group would have provided" (Terman, 1954, p. 41). Today, Terman's subjects are in their eighties, and compared with average people of their age, they are happier, healthier, and richer, with far fewer suicides and divorces, and they have a lower incidence of alcoholism.

How are gifted people identified?   Usually, they are identified as children in the school setting. Parents or teachers notice that a child has many of the characteristics we described or they note a child who consistently scores high on school achievement tests, and they refer the child for testing. The child is identified as gifted after scoring above a certain score—usually around 135 or 140—on an individual or group IQ test. This method is reasonably accurate for children from a white upper- or middle-class culture. But it often misses identifying children, especially young children, from minority and/or economically deprived environments. Various methods are being tried to overcome the problem, including the Kent State University model, which uses computers to help analyze videotaped behaviors of children suspected of being gifted (Shaklee, 1992).

Just as there is controversy over how mentally retarded children should be educated, in institutions or mainstreamed into the regular classroom, there is controversy over how gifted children should be educated. On the one hand are those who feel gifted children should remain integrated in the regular classroom and receive the same instruction as other students, but with extra assignments and extra activities to do when they complete their regular schoolwork. On the other hand are those who feel that gifted children's abilities are stifled by being with average children and that they should be grouped homogeneously so they and their gifted peers can learn at their own rapid pace, work at more advanced levels, and receive higher-level instruction in the content areas (Feldhusen and Moon, 1992).

Why are some people gifted?   People's intellectual levels vary in all sorts of ways. Some people are mentally gifted, some are mentally retarded, and most are somewhere in between. To answer the question of why these differences exist, we must explore the influences of heredity and environment.

Heredity versus Environment: Which Determines Intelligence?

Today, most researchers believe both heredity and environment play a large part in determining people's intelligence (Bouchard et al., 1990; Plomin, 1989; Thompson, Detterman, and Plomin, 1991). But for years the debate went back and forth as different studies supported one or the other. Arthur Jensen (1969) was one of the major proponents who argued that IQ differences were due chiefly to genetic factors, while Leon Kamin (1974) and others argued that differences stemmed mainly from environmental factors. A classic study conducted by Skeels and Dye (1939) established environment as a significant factor in the determination of intelligence.

The Skeels and Dye study involved a group of orphans living in overcrowded, deprived conditions in an orphanage who, labeled mentally retarded and therefore unadoptable, were transferred to a women's ward in a state mental institution. Here each child was "adopted" by a mildly retarded woman who lavished her charge with love and attention in a stimulating environment full of toys and plenty of space for play—quite a contrast to the impoverished and neglectful conditions in which the children had previously lived. The IQ scores of these children showed a marked improvement. In fact, their retest scores placed them within the normal range of intelligence. Scores of a control group of children remaining in the orphanage showed a marked drop. Furthermore, a follow-up study conducted over 20 years later revealed that most of the children in the retarded women's care had finished high school and were leading normal, productive lives. Most of the children who had remained at the orphanage, however, had not gone beyond the third grade and were unable to fully support themselves (Skeels, 1966).

Twin/Sibling Studies

In recent years, research into whether heredity or environment dominates in determining intelligence has taken one of two approaches. One is the twin design, in which researchers compare similarities of identical twins (who developed from the same egg) with similarities of fraternal twins (who developed from different eggs). The second is the adoption design, in which researchers study twins separated at or soon after birth and reared apart, or they study genetically unrelated children adopted into a family and reared together. From these studies, it is found that IQs of adopted children correlate more closely with their biological parents than with their adoptive parents (Bouchard, 1984). It is also found that identical twins are significantly more similar than fraternal twins. Most remarkable, IQ correlations between identical twins are exceptionally high when they are raised together and only slightly less when they are reared apart (Plomin, 1989).

Whereas for many years, psychologists emphasized the importance of environment on the development of intelligence, these twin/sibling studies point to the heavy influence of heritibility on intelligence. In fact, these and other recent studies indicate that approximately half the individual differences in IQ stem from genetic factors, while the other half is due to the influence of the environment (Thompson, et al., 1991).

We have seen, then, that the genetic component in the development of intelligence is substantial. Heredity equips each person with innate intellectual capacities. But environment also has a significant amount of influence in determining whether a person will reach full potential. Regardless of which component has more influence, it is the environment that we as psychologists, parents, teachers, and citizens can change. We should therefore strive to improve the life experiences of our children in order to help them achieve the most they can with their inborn resources.

Review Questions

1. Is an IQ test an accurate measure of a person's true intellectual abilities?

2. What are the major differences between the Stanford–Binet and the Wechsler Intelligence Scales?

3. A newer test that was designed and standardized to evaluate all students, including, among others, minorities and hearing impaired, is the
_____ .

4. What do group IQ tests measure?

5. Is there a decline in intelligence as people grow older?

6. You own a business and need general help stocking shelves and keeping things clean and orderly. A friend is a counselor in a group home for mentally retarded people and asks you to hire one of her charges. Depending, of course, on their individual characteristics and personalities, would you be likely to hire someone who is moderately retarded? mildly retarded? severely retarded?

7. Suppose you have a child with an IQ of 55 who has been diagnosed as educable mentally retarded. Would you prefer your child be mainstreamed or placed in a special education classroom?

8. According to Terman's long-term study of 1500 gifted children, do gifted people tend to be socially maladjusted?

9. Which is more important in determining intelligence, heredity or environment?

Answers to Review Questions can be found in Appendix C.

REVIEW OF MAJOR CONCEPTS

THINKING

1. Cognition refers to the process of "coming to know." It is a process of gathering and processing information that includes sensation, perception, learning, memory, thinking, and problem solving.

2. Thinking is the mental manipulation of information that has been gathered and processed. It involves creating mental images, forming concepts, solving problems, and using language. There is some controversy regarding how we think, but the latest evidence supports a dual-coding theory with both an imagery system and a verbal system.

3. Mental images are mental representations of objects and events. Research in the areas of mental rotation and relative size and shape of objects demonstrates the similarity of real objects and our mental representations of them.

4. Concepts are ideas or notions about groups of objects or situations that share similar characteristics known as attributes. We form concepts by combining attributes according to various rules and by noting their relevance and their salience. Two theories of concept formation are the hypothesis-testing theory and the prototype theory.

5. There are three major steps in problem solving: preparation, production, and evaluation. During the preparation stage, the facts are identified, the relevant facts are sifted from the irrelevant, and the ultimate goal is determined.

6. During the production stage, possible situations, called hypotheses, are generated. There are two major procedures for generating hypotheses: using an algorithm, which is any procedure that guarantees a solution; or using heuristics, which are educated guesses that may or

may not lead to a solution but that are quicker and easier than algorithms. Three major types of heuristics are means–end analysis, working backward, and creating subgoals.

7. The evaluation stage begins when one or more hypotheses have been generated. These hypotheses are then evaluated, and if one of them meets the criteria set down in the preparation stage, the problem is solved.

8. Among the barriers to successful problem solving are problem-solving set and functional fixedness. Problem-solving set is trying to apply a previously successful but inappropriate solution to a new problem. Functional fixedness is the failure to see new or unique uses for common objects. To break through these barriers, it sometimes helps to take time out from a problem and let it incubate.

9. Creativity is the ability to originate new or unique solutions to a problem that are also practical and useful. Creative thinking is associated with fluency, flexibility, and originality. J. P. Guilford has identified two distinct types of thinking: convergent, in which the person works toward a single solution to a problem; and divergent, in which the person tries to generate as many solutions as possible. Brainstorming is an example of divergent thinking.

10. Language is a creative form of communication consisting of symbols put together according to a set of rules. Phonemes are the basic speech sounds; they are combined to form morphemes, the smallest meaningful units of language. Phonemes, morphemes, words, and phrases are put together by rules of grammar and syntax, or word order. Psycholinguists study both language structure and the cognitive processes involved in language comprehension and production.

11. Researchers have investigated animals' ability to learn human or humanlike language. The most successful of these studies have been done with apes using American Sign Language. In another successful study, dolphins were taught to comprehend sentences that varied in syntax and meaning. Although many psychologists believe that animals can truly learn a human language, skeptics suggest that the animals are being trained merely to respond for rewards.

INTELLIGENCE AND INTELLIGENCE TESTING

12. Ever since research into intelligence began, theorists have differed in their definitions of it: Charles Spearman viewed intelligence as *g*, a general cognitive ability; L. L. Thurstone viewed it as seven distinct mental abilities; J. P. Guilford viewed it as 120 or more separate abilities; and Raymond Cattell viewed intelligence as two types of *g* that he called fluid intelligence and crystallized intelligence.

13. Contemporary theorists feel that there is more to intelligence than what is measured on tests, and that there seems to be more than one type of intelligence. Howard Gardner proposed at least six different types of intelligence in which people can excel; he feels both teaching and assessing should take into account people's learning styles and cognitive strengths. Robert Sternberg developed what he calls a triarchic theory of intelligence, which emphasizes the thinking process rather than the end product

(the answer). According to the triarchic theory, there are three aspects of intelligence: internal components, use of these components to adapt to changes, and application of past experience to solve problems.

14. Our definition of intelligence is: Intelligence consists of the cognitive abilities employed in acquiring, remembering, and using knowledge of one's culture to solve everyday problems and to readily adapt to and function in both changing and stable environments.

15. For any test to be useful, it must be standardized, reliable, and valid. Standardization refers to (a) the process of giving a test to a large number of people in order for its norms to be developed; and (b) the use of identical procedures in administering a test so that everyone taking the test will do so under the same conditions. Reliability is a measure of the stability of test scores over time. Validity refers to how well the test measures what it is intended to measure.

16. IQ tests do not, and are not intended to, measure overall intelligence; rather, they are designed to measure verbal and quantitative abilities needed for school success. Several individual IQ tests are in common use. The Stanford–Binet measures primarily verbal abilities of children ages 3 to 16. The Wechsler tests, consisting of three separate tests for three distinct age levels, measure both verbal and nonverbal abilities. The K-ABC measures both problem-solving ability and general knowledge and was standardized to evaluate a large variety of students, including minority, hearing-impaired, and language-disordered children.

17. Group IQ tests can be given to large numbers of people at one time. The group test with which most college students are familiar is the Scholastic Aptitude Test.

18. Lowered school success for African Americans can be traced to lack of school readiness when first entering school, low-effort syndrome, and language barriers. Governmental programs such as Head Start and JOBS are designed to combat lowered success potential by providing early education for low-income children and helping their families become self-sufficient through family literacy, parenting training, health services, and job training.

19. As we age, there is no decline in our intellectual abilities except for the speed with which we perform them and acquire new knowledge. People with IQs of 70 and below are identified as mentally retarded, while people with IQs of 140 and above are identified as gifted. Causes of mental retardation include genetic factors, maternal drug abuse during pregnancy, and severe childhood deprivation, but in about 70 percent of the cases, there is no known cause. There is a continuing controversy over whether mentally retarded and gifted children should be mainstreamed into regular school classrooms or placed in classes specially designed to meet their individual needs.

20. For many years, there has been a controversy over whether heredity or the environment plays a more important part in determining intelligence. Recent twin and adoption studies indicate that about half the individual differences in intelligence can be attributed to heredity and the other half, to environment.

SUGGESTED READINGS

BEST, J. B. (1992). *Cognitive psychology.* St. Paul, MN: West. A recent introduction to the study of cognition.

EYSENCK, H. J., & KAMIN, L. (1981). *The intelligence controversy.* New York: Wiley. A debate between two well-known authorities on the nature of intelligence.

GARDNER, H. (1983). *Frames of mind.* New York: Basic Books. A book that outlines Gardner's theory of multiple intelligences.

GARDNER, M. (1982). *Aha! Gotcha: Paradoxes to puzzle and delight.* New York: Freeman. The title of this wonderful book says it all.

Life Span Development I

OUTLINE

I slip quietly into the back of the room, sit on the floor, lean back against the wall, and I watch the world's most important and most gentle revolution taking place. A beautiful little blond two-year-old girl is reading aloud. So absorbed is she in reading that she sometimes giggles as she reads a phrase that touches her sense of humor. The humor is lost on me because she is reading in Japanese.

When I arrived at the math class, Suzie and Janet were presenting math problems to the tiny kids faster than I could assimilate the problems. Their answers were correct—not nearly right but exactly right.

"What," Suzie asked, "is 16 times 19, subtract 151, multiply by 3, add 111, divide by 4 and subtract 51?" "How far is it from Philadelphia to Chicago?" asked Janet. "And if your car gets 5 miles to the gallon, how many gallons of gas will it take to drive to Chicago?"

Doman, 1979, pp. 25–29

You have just read Glen Doman proudly describing the accomplishments of very young children being educated by his revolutionary methods. If you think these are gifted children or prodigies, think again. Doman claims that almost any baby can master simple math at 7 months, read at 11 months, and appreciate fine art and music long before they walk or talk. Each child's genetic potential is assumed to be that of a da Vinci, Shakespeare, Mozart, Michelangelo, Edison, and Einstein (Langway et al., 1983).

In contrast to Doman, Robert Graham believes that child prodigies like Mozart or Einstein are largely the result of genetic contributions from the best and brightest parents (Lowry, 1987). To encourage selective breeding for such children, Graham established an exclusive sperm bank in 1980 and invited Nobel Prize winners, and others possessing exceptionally high IQs, to contribute their sperm.

What do you think? Should academic instruction begin in the first few months of life? Should parents be encouraged to use "exclusive" sperm to increase the IQ of their offspring? What about the recent trend of paying college women up to $2,000 for "harvesting" a few of their eggs? These are only a few of the fascinating questions that arise when we study human development.

Developmental Psychology: The branch of psychology that describes, explains, predicts, and sometimes aims to modify age-related behaviors from conception to death. This field emphasizes maturation, early experiences, and various stages in development.

The field of developmental psychology is concerned with age-related changes in behavior and abilities not just during conception and childhood but throughout the entire life span—from conception to death (see Table 9.1). Developmental psychologists study when certain skills appear, how they change with age, and whether they change in a sudden spurt or gradually. Developmental psychologists also look at how development in one area, such as physical growth, relates to changes in such other areas as language, cognition, and personality.

The field of developmental psychology, and its related interests, is very large. We will focus on key topics and group them into two chapters. In this chapter we will focus on physical development, language development, and cognition. In the next chapter we will explore age-related changes in the areas of moral development, social and personality development, as well as special issues related to development. As we discuss each developmental topic, we will look at how it affects an individual throughout his or her entire life span.

As you read Chapter 9, keep the following **Survey** questions in mind and answer them in your own words:

- How is research in developmental psychology different from research in other areas of psychology?

- What are the major physical changes that occur throughout the life span?

- How do children learn language?
- How does cognition, or the way we think about the world, change during the life cycle?

STUDYING DEVELOPMENT

What were you like as a child? Has your personality stayed the same or have you changed a great deal? Have you ever wondered why the returning housewife who sits at the front of your psychology class gets such high grades? Is it because she studies a lot or was she exceptionally bright in high school? What about the young Vietnamese student who only recently learned English? Will his inherited intelligence be more important in determining his college grades or is the current English-speaking environment more influential?

- *How is research in developmental psychology different from research in other areas of psychology?*

Research Issues: Three Major Questions

In all fields of psychology, certain theoretical issues seem to guide the basic direction of research. The three most important issues or questions in human development are (1) nature versus nurture, (2) continuity versus stages, and (3) stability versus change.

Nature or Nurture?

People who support the *nature* side of the nature versus nurture debate would say that human behavior and development are governed by automatic, genetically predetermined signals known as maturation. Just as a flower unfolds in accord with its genetic blueprint, we humans generally crawl before we walk and walk before we run. While severe environmental influences such as physical deprivation to the point of malnutrition or total isolation can retard development, naturists believe that growth tendencies are inborn.

Maturation: Changes in development that result from automatic, genetically determined signals.

On the other side of the debate, those who support the *nurture* perspective argue that the primary determinants of development are learning and interactions with the environment. Glen Doman's belief that with his special training any child can become a Mozart is an example of the extreme nurturist position. Similarly, Robert Graham's belief that high intelligence can be produced by selectively breeding "exclusive" sperm and eggs represents the extreme naturist perspective.

Which position is most correct? As you will see, some early psychologists, including John B. Watson, championed the nurture perspective, while others espoused the nature model. Today, however, most psychologists support an interactionist model, which sees both inborn, genetic processes *and* environmental factors contributing to human development (Plomin, 1989; Vasta, Haith, and Miller, 1992).

Interactionist Model: The perspective that human development results from both nature and nurture factors.

Table 9.1 Life-Span Development

Stage	Approximate Age
Prenatal	Conception to birth
Infancy	Birth to 18 months
Early childhood	18 months to 6 years
Middle childhood	6 to 12 years
Adolescence	12 to 20 years
Young adulthood	20 to 45 years
Middle adulthood	45 to 60 years
Later adulthood	60 years to death

Continuity or Stages?

The *continuity* proponents say development is continuous, with new abilities, skills, and knowledge gradually added at a relatively uniform pace. The continuity model, then, suggests adult thinking and intelligence differ *quantitatively* from those of a child. We simply have *more* math skills or verbal skills, for example. *Stage* theorists, on the other hand, believe development occurs at different rates, alternating between periods of little change and periods of abrupt, rapid change. Later in this chapter we will discuss Jean Piaget's elaborate stage theory of cognitive development that describes a child's thinking as *qualitatively* different from that of an adult. In Piaget's model, cognitive development remains relatively stable while the child is in a given stage, but movement to the next stage brings an abrupt shift in the child's abilities.

Like the nature versus nurture issue, the continuity versus stage question is not a matter of "either-or." Physical development and motor skills, for example, are believed to be primarily continuous in nature, while cognitive skills are usually described as the result of discrete stages.

Stability or Change?

Have you generally maintained your personal characteristics as you matured from infant to adult (*stability*)? Or does your current personality bear little resemblance to that which you displayed during infancy (*change*)? Psychologists who emphasize stability in development hold that measurements of personality taken during childhood are important predictors of adult personality. The discussion of infant and adult attachment in Chapter 10 is a good example of stability. On the other hand, in Chapter 14 we discuss research that demonstrates how other dimensions of personality vary greatly across the life span.

In sum, it seems that research has provided a qualified answer to each of the three major questions: Nature and nurture interact during human development, some aspects of development are continuous while others occur in stages, and some traits are stable while others change. We will return to these questions several times in this chapter and the next. Now we turn our attention to another aspect of studying development—how developmental psychologists collect their information.

Research Methods: Cross-Sectional versus Longitudinal Data

Cross-Sectional Method: A technique of data collection that measures individuals of various ages at one point in time and gives information about age differences.

Longitudinal Method: A data collection technique that measures a single individual or group of individuals over an extended period of time and gives information about age changes.

When studying development, psychologists first decide which technique they will use to gather the data (surveys, experiments, etc.) and then they choose either a *cross-sectional* or *longitudinal* method. The cross-sectional method examines individuals of various ages (20, 40, 60, and 80 years) at one point in time, and gives information about age *differences*. The longitudinal method follows a single individual or group of individuals (20-year-olds) over an extended period of time and gives information about age *changes* (see Figure 9.1).

Advantages and Disadvantages of the Two Methods

Pretend for the moment that you are a developmental psychologist interested in studying intelligence in adults. Which method would you choose—cross-sectional or longitudinal? For obvious reasons, your first choice might be the cross-sectional methods. (Who wants to wait many years for results?) But before you decide, study the graph in Figure 9.2. Note the difference between the two techniques. Cross-sectional studies have traditionally reported that intelligence reaches its peak in early adulthood and then gradually declines (Horn and Donaldson, 1980). Longitudinal research, on the other hand, tends to show an increase in intelligence until age 55 or 60 with a modest decline in the following years (Schaie, 1984). How would you explain the differences? Think critically; explore several possible answers.

CROSS-SECTIONAL RESEARCH

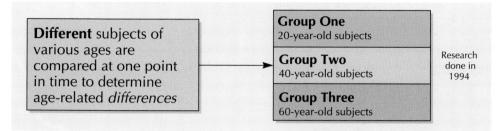

LONGITUDINAL RESEARCH

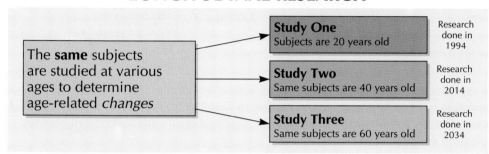

Figure 9.1 Cross-sectional versus longitudinal research. Cross-sectional research uses *different* subjects and is interested in age-related *differences*, whereas longitudinal research uses the *same* subjects to study age-related *changes*.

If you've given it some thought and would like an explanation, one of the best we've seen is that results from cross-sectional studies reflect group *averages* rather than individual developmental patterns. Cross-sectional results often confuse genuine age differences with cohort effects, differences that result from specific histories of the age group studied (Rosenfeld and Stark, 1987; Schaie, 1988). In the case of intelligence, cross-sectional studies overlook that older subjects have generally received less formal education than younger subjects, which would be correlated with lower test scores. In addition, older subjects tend to have different beliefs and values concerning the general idea of intelligence testing.

Cohort Effects: A problem sometimes found in cross-sectional research wherein subjects of a given age may be affected by factors unique to their generation.

If cross-sectional studies are subject to such misleading effects, why don't researchers design only longitudinal studies?   Longitudinal studies have their own set of problems. Not only are they expensive in terms of time and money, but their results are also restricted in generalizability. Since only a small number of subjects can realistically be tested, and since many of them drop out or move away during the extended test period,

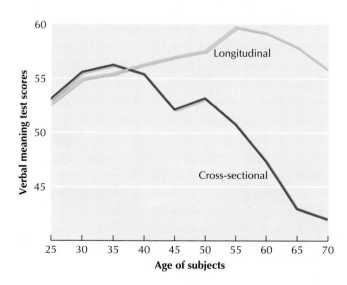

Figure 9.2 A test for verbal meaning. A comparison of the results of cross-sectional and longitudinal research on a typical measure of intelligence, the "verbal meaning" test.

Table 9.2   Advantages and Disadvantages For Cross-Sectional versus Longitudinal Research Designs

	Cross-Sectional	Longitudinal
Advantages	Gives information about age differences	Gives information about age changes
	Quick	Increased reliability
	Less expensive	
Disadvantages	Cohort effects	Typically smaller sample
	Restricted generalizability	Expensive
	Only measures behaviors at one point in time	Time consuming
		Restricted generalizability

the experimenter ends up with a self-selected sample that may differ from the general population in important ways. As you can see in Table 9.2, each method of research has its own strengths and weaknesses. Keep these differences in mind when you read the findings of developmental research.

Before leaving the topic of research, let's examine the contributions made by cultural psychologists.

Gender and Cultural Diversity

CULTURAL PSYCHOLOGY'S GUIDELINES FOR DEVELOPMENTAL RESEARCH

How would you answer the following question: "If you wanted to predict how a human child anywhere in the world was going to grow up and turn out, what his or her behavior was going to be like as an adult, and you could have only one fact about that child, what fact would you choose to have?"

According to cultural psychologists like Patricia Greenfield (1992), the answer to this question should be "culture." Yet, developmental psychology has traditionally stud-

Culture may be the most important determinant in development. An individual who grows up in a rural, agricultural culture is different from someone who grows up in a crowded, urban environment in many subtle as well as obvious ways.

ied its subjects (children, adolescents, and adults) with little attention to their sociocultural context (Berry et al., 1992; Brislin, 1993). In recent times, however, psychologists are paying increasing attention to the following points:

1. Culture May Be the Most Important Determinant of Development

Knowledge of a child's culture is critical to understanding how he or she will develop. For example, if a child grows up in an individualistic/independent culture (such as North America or most of Western Europe), we can predict this child will probably be competitive and questioning of authority as an adult. Were this same child reared in a collectivist/interdependent culture (common in Africa, Asia, and Latin America), she or he would most likely grow up to be cooperative and respectful of elders (Brislin, 1993; Delgado-Gaitan, in press; Segall et al., 1990).

2. Human Development, Like Most Areas of Psychology, Cannot Be Studied Outside Its Sociocultural Context

In parts of Korea, for example, a strict, authoritarian style of parenting is positively evaluated (even by Korean teenagers) as a sign of love and concern (Kim and Choi, in press). Korean-American and Korean-Canadian teenagers, however, see the same behavior as a sign of rejection. Rather than studying specific behaviors, such as "authoritarian parenting styles," researchers in child development suggest that children should be studied only within their *developmental niche* (Harkness and Super, 1983; Super and Harkness, 1986). A developmental niche has three components: the physical and social contexts in which the child lives, the culturally determined rearing and educational practices, and the psychological characteristics of the parents (Segall et al., 1990).

3. Culture Is Largely Invisible to Its Participants

By definition, culture consists of ideals, values, and assumptions about life that are widely shared among a given group and guide specific behaviors (Brislin, 1993). Because these ideals and values are "widely shared" they are seldom discussed or directly examined. We take our culture for granted, operating within it while being almost unaware of it.

 Try This Yourself

If you would like a personal demonstration of the "invisibility" of culture, try this simple experiment. The next time you walk into an elevator, don't turn around. Remain facing the rear wall. Watch how others respond when you don't turn around, or if you stand right next to them rather than walking to the other side of the elevator. Our North American culture has a long list of rules that prescribe the "proper" way to ride in an elevator, and people become very uncomfortable when these rules are violated. ■

4. Each Culture's Ethnotheories Are Important Determinants of Behavior

Within every culture, people have a prevailing set of ideas and beliefs (an *ethnotheory*) that attempts to explain the world around them. In the area of child development, for example, cultures have specific ethnotheories regarding how children should be trained. Our introductory incident that featured Glen Doman's method for teaching math and reading to babies is a good example of a North American ethnotheory. Can you see how Glen Doman is appealing to our general ethnotheory that recommends maximizing a child's individual potential in all areas of development?

As a critical thinker, you can anticipate that differing ethnotheories can lead to problems between cultures. Even the very idea of "critical thinking" is part of our North American ethnotheory regarding education. And it too can produce culture clashes. Concha Delgado-Gaitan (in press) has found that Mexican immigrants from a rural background have a difficult time adjusting to North American schools, which teach children to question authority and to think for themselves. In their culture of origin, these children are trained to respect their elders, be good listeners, and participate in conversation only when solicited. Children who argue with adults are reminded not to be "malcriados" (naughty or disrespectful). ■

Review Questions

1. Briefly define developmental psychology.
2. What are the three major questions that are studied in developmental psychology?
3. If a psychologist compared language skills of four-year-olds and eight-year-olds, she would be using the _____ method of research.
4. Differences in age groups that reflect factors unique to that generation are called _____ .
5. Compare the relative merits of the cross-sectional and longitudinal methods of research.
6. What can you learn about culture if you ride backward on an elevator?
7. Glen Doman's recommendation for maximizing early childhood education is a good example of a North American _____ .

Answers to Review Questions can be found in Appendix C.

PHYSICAL DEVELOPMENT

• *What are the major physical changes that occur throughout the life span?*

Perhaps the most obvious aspects of development are physical growth and alterations in body proportions and size. In this section we will look at four periods of life in which physical change has a major impact: the prenatal period (from conception to birth), early childhood, adolescence, and adulthood. We begin with the prenatal period.

Prenatal Development: From Conception to Birth

Conception: The fertilization of the female ovum or egg by the male sperm.

Human development begins at conception, when the mother's egg, or ovum, unites with the father's sperm cell. The product of this union is barely 1/175th of an inch in diameter—smaller than the period at the end of this sentence (see Figure 9.3). At the moment of conception, only *one* of the 200 to 400 million sperm in an average ejaculation actually fertilizes the ovum (each ejaculation contains enough sperm to more than repopulate the entire United States).

The union of sperm and ovum generally takes place in the woman's Fallopian tube. The new cell, called a *zygote,* then begins a process of rapid cell division that results in a multimillion-celled infant some nine months later. As you may remember from biology courses, all the other cells in the human body develop from the zygote. Within the nucleus of the zygote are the chromosomes and genes that carry important information from both parents. Because each of us receives a different combination of genes, each person is truly biologically unique. The only exception to this genetic uniqueness occurs with *identical (monozygotic) twins,* which result when a fertilized ovum divides and forms two identical separate cells. These cells go on to produce two complete individuals with identical genetic information. *Fraternal (dyzygotic) twins,* on the other hand, result from the fertilization of two separate eggs by different sperm. These two "womb mates" are genetically no more alike than brothers and sisters born at different times.

Thinking back to the nature versus nurture debate, can you see why the study of identical and fraternal twins is so important? Twins offer a unique and invaluable oppor-

Chromosomes: Threadlike strands of DNA (deoxyribonucleic acid) molecules that carry genetic information.

Genes: A segment of DNA that occupies a specific place on a particular chromosome.

tunity to evaluate the relative contributions of both genetic and environmental forces in development. Identical twins who are separated at birth and reared apart are particularly important because they allow a natural form of control for the relative contributions of nature and nurture.

Stages of Prenatal Development

Prenatal development is divided into three different stages or periods: the germinal stage, the embryonic stage, and the fetal stage. Each stage has its own unique characteristics.

1. During the germinal period (Figure 9.4*a*), which lasts from fertilization until about 14 days later, the original fertilized single cell undergoes repeated divisions at an astronomical rate of change. At the same time, the cells are beginning to form into distinct groups that will perform new and specialized functions. One major group of cells, for example, will become parts of the embryo, while others divide to become protective membranes and the placenta, which provides nourishment. The germinal period ends when the ball of cells implants in the wall of the uterus.

2. During the embryonic period (Figure 9.4*b*), which lasts from implantation to the eighth week of pregnancy, all the major organs develop and the basic plan of the body emerges. During embryonic development and later stages, growth at first proceeds from the head downward, in a sequence known as cephalocaudal development ("head-to-tail"). Among other things, this type of development results in the embryo having a head larger than its body. Subsequently, growth follows proximodistal development ("near-to-far"), meaning that it proceeds from the inside outward. Thus, the heart and lungs develop before the hands and fingers. The embryonic period is also a critical period — an optimal or sensitive time in development when the organism is most easily affected by environmental events. As we will see in the next section, any serious interference during this period may result in permanent and irreversible damage.

3. The final stage of development, the fetal period (Figure 9.4*c*), lasts from the end of the second month to birth. During this period, the fetus continues its rapid rate of growth and the organs and muscles begin to function. As the fetus develops, it becomes increasingly active inside the uterus. Although most women report sensations of fetal movement by the third or fourth month, during the last three months these movements become progressively stronger and more distinct. See Figure 9.4*d* for a photo of an infant moments after birth.

Hazards to Prenatal Development

Some problems in development occur as a result of defective genes. One example is Huntington's chorea, a progressive degeneration of the nervous system. Other problems result from abnormalities in the chromosomes, such as in Down syndrome, which produces various levels of mental and motor retardation, hearing defects, a protruding tongue, small head, and so on.

The age of the mother is also an important factor in birth defects. Most people are aware that older women are at greater risk for certain fetal abnormalities, in particular, Down syndrome. Yet, because of their overall higher birth rate, women under 35 actually bear 80 percent of Down infants (Kolata, 1988). Teenage mothers belong to the highest risk group *both* for birth complications and for fetal abnormalities (Brylawski, 1987; Schorr and Schorr, 1990). This is of increasing concern since the United States now leads all industrialized nations in the number of teenage mothers (see Chapter 10).

The environment can also exert a powerful influence on development before a child is born. As you can see in Figure 9.5, the specific effects of teratogens, or environ-

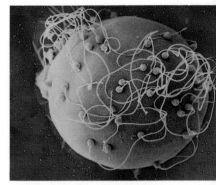

Figure 9.3 The moment of conception. When a sperm penetrates the outer wall of an ovum, conception occurs.

Germinal Period: The first stage of pregnancy (conception to 2 weeks), characterized by rapid cell division.

Embryonic Period: The second stage of pregnancy (from uterine implantation to the eighth week), characterized by development of major body organs and systems.

Cephalocaudal Development: A general pattern of physical growth in which development occurs first in the region of the head and later in lower regions.

Proximodistal Development: A general pattern of physical growth in which development starts at the center of the body and moves toward the extremities.

Critical Period: An optimal or sensitive time in development when the organism is most easily affected by environmental events.

Fetal Period: The third, and final, stage of prenatal development (8 weeks to birth), characterized by rapid weight gain in the fetus and the fine detailing of body organs and systems.

Teratogen: An external, environmental agent that may cross the placental barrier and disrupt development, causing minor or severe birth defects.

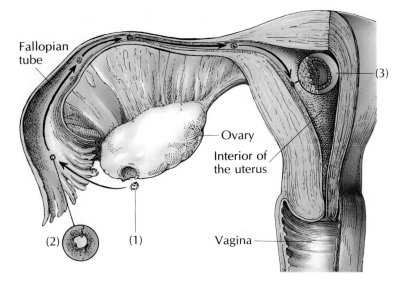

Fallopian tube

Ovary

Interior of the uterus

Vagina

(2)   (1)   (3)

Figure 9.4 (a) *From ovulation to implantation.* (1) After discharge from either the left or right ovary (ovulation), the ovum travels to the opening of the fallopian tube. If fertilization occurs (2), it normally takes place in the first third of the fallopian tube. The fertilized ovum is referred to as a *zygote*. When the zygote reaches the uterus, it implants itself in the wall of the uterus (3) and begins to grow tendril-like structures that intertwine with the rich supply of blood vessels located there. After implantation, the organism is known as an *embryo*.

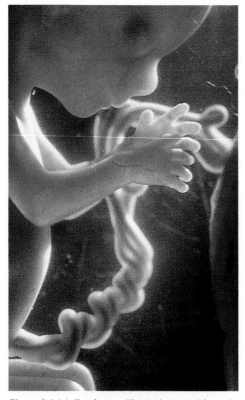

Figure 9.4 (c) *Fetal stage.* This is the period from the end of the second month to birth. At four months all the adult body parts and organs are established. The fetal stage is a time of increased growth and fine detailing.

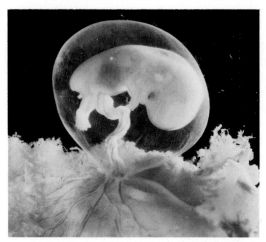

Figure 9.4 (b) *Embryonic period.* This stage occurs from implantation to eight weeks. At eight weeks the major organ systems have become well differentiated. At this stage, the head grows at a faster rate than other parts of the body.

Figure 9.4 (d) *Infant at birth.* This newborn is approximately 10 minutes of age.

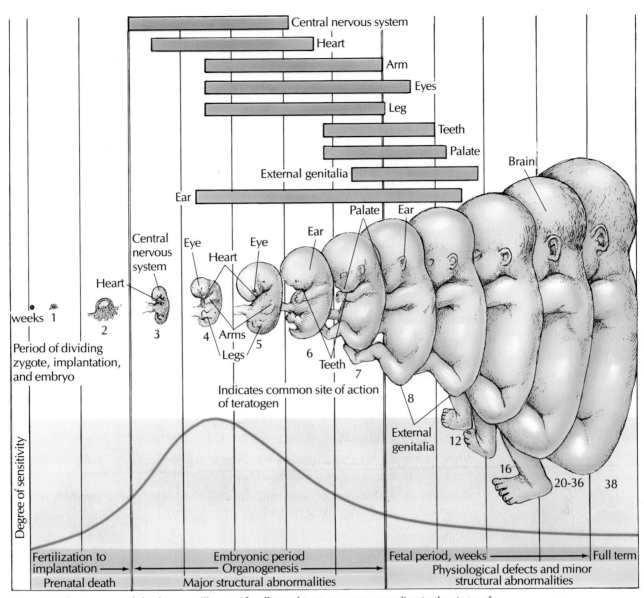

Figure 9.5 Teratogens and development. The specific effects of teratogens vary according to the stages of pregnancy. The fetus is at greatest risk of major birth defects when major body systems are forming during the first eight weeks.

mental substances that can cause birth defects, vary according to the time they're encountered during the prenatal period in development. During the critical period of the first eight weeks, the embryo is at its most vulnerable stage. If a mother contracts rubella (German measles) in the first four weeks of pregnancy, for example, the baby has a 50 percent chance of being born with one or more significant birth defects, but only a 17 percent chance if the disease is contracted in the third month of pregnancy (Rhodes, 1961).

The unborn child can also be affected by sexually transmitted diseases, including syphilis, chlamydia, genital herpes, and gonorrhea. One of the most serious sexually transmitted diseases is AIDS (acquired immune deficiency syndrome). The AIDS virus can be passed from mother to child before birth, during the birth process, and after the child is born (perhaps through breast milk) (Novick, 1990). The most likely route of transmission from mother to child is the blood. It is generally recommended that women considering pregnancy have blood tests to determine whether they have been exposed to the AIDS virus. Pregnant women who have AIDS or other sexually transmitted diseases (STDs) should discuss their disorders with their physicians. In most cases, measures can be taken to improve the mother's health and her chances for a healthy baby.

As you can see, there are innumerable environmental hazards to the unborn child; a partial list is provided in Table 9.3. In the following two sections we discuss the effects of nutrition and drugs on the unborn child.

Nutrition and Prenatal Development

Poor nutrition, both before and during pregnancy, can seriously affect the developing fetus. Inadequate maternal nutrition can lead to miscarriage, stillbirth, infant death, fewer neurons in the developing fetal brain, cerebral palsy, epilepsy, mental retardation, learning difficulties, premature birth, and low birth weight (Behnke and Eyler, 1991; Conger, 1988; Ricciuti, 1993). As you can see in Figure 9.6, the United States has a higher infant mortality rate than 21 other nations. Maternal malnutrition and the lack of universal access to prenatal and early pediatric care are two of the most important factors in the high number of infant deaths in our country.

Gender and Cultural Diversity

A CULTURAL COMPARISON OF PRENATAL AND INFANT HEALTH CARE

How can the United States have such a high rate of infant death? Living in one of the wealthiest and most advanced countries on earth, most Americans are unaware of our dismal record of child care. For example, did you know that in the United States:

* *Twenty-five percent of all children and more than half of all ethnic minority children are raised in poverty?*

* *Black infants are twice as likely as white infants to be born prematurely, to have low birth weight, and to die in the first year of life?*

* *Approximately 40 percent of black mothers and 20 percent of white mothers receive no prenatal care in the first three months of pregnancy?*

* *Every day 100,000 children are homeless?*

* *Every 67 seconds a teenager has a baby?*

* *Every 53 minutes a child dies because of poverty* (CDC, 1992; Edelman, 1991; Enthoven, 1992; Horowitz and O'Brien, 1989)?

Our national statistics are even more startling when we compare them with other nations:

* *Compared with seven other industrialized countries (Australia, Canada, England, Sweden, Switzerland, Norway, and West Germany), the United States has the highest poverty rate.*

* *The United States has the highest adolescent pregnancy rate of any industrialized Western nation.*

* *Fourteen other nations have a better immunization rate for polio than the United States* (Children's Defense Fund, 1990; Edelman, 1987, 1991; Wegman, 1986).

Why are these other countries so far ahead of the United States? Marian Wright Edelman (1991), president of the Children's Defense Fund and a tireless advocate of children's rights, believes part of the answer is that "70 nations provide medical care and financial assistance to all pregnant women—but ours is not one of them. Sixty-three nations provide a family allowance to workers and their children—but ours is not one of them. Seventeen industrialized nations have paid maternity/paternity leave programs—but ours is not one of them" (p. 76). ■

Table 9.3   Some Environmental Conditions That Endanger the Child

Maternal Behavior	Possible Effect on Embryo, Fetus, Newborn, or Young Child
Malnutrition	Low birth weight, malformations, less developed brain, greater vulnerability to disease
Stress exposure	Low birth weight, hyperactivity, irritability, feeding difficulties
Use of hormones:	
thalidomide	Hearing defects, deformed limbs, death
androgens	Masculinization of female fetus
diethylstilbestrol	Uterine and vaginal abnormalities in female fetus, possible carcinogenesis in male and female fetus, infertility
Excessive use of vitamin A	Cleft palate, congenital anomalies
Use of analgesics	Respiratory depression
Use of aspirin in large doses	Respiratory depression
Use of tetracycline	Inhibition of bone growth, discolored teeth
Use of streptomycin	Hearing loss
Narcotic addiction	Growth deficiency, withdrawal syndrome, central nervous system and respiratory depression, death
Heavy smoking	Low birth weight, increased fetal heart rate, prematurity, increased risk of spontaneous abortion, fetal death
Alcohol consumption	Fetal alcohol syndrome (growth deficiency, developmental lag, mental retardation); increased risk of spontaneous abortion, fetal death, attentional deficits in childhood
Cocaine consumption	Increased risk of spontaneous abortion, withdrawal syndrome, erratic emotions in infants
Marijuana consumption	Increased tremors and startles among newborns and poorer verbal and memory development at 4 years of age
Exposure to X rays	Malformations, cancer
German measles (rubella)	Blindness, deafness, mental retardation, heart malformations
Herpes, AIDS, other STDs	Brain infection, death, spontaneous abortion, premature birth, mental retardation

Source: Behnke and Eyler, 1991; Bower, 1989b; Day, 1991; Julien, 1992; Sehgal et al., 1993.

Death before age 1 per 1,000 births

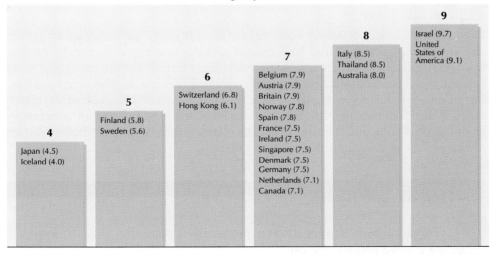

Figure 9.6 Infant mortality. Note that an infant born in the United States has less chance of surviving to its first birthday than infants born in most other industrialized nations. (Adapted from *Population & Vital Statistics,* Oct. 1992).

Drugs and Prenatal Development

In addition to poor nutrition and inadequate prenatal care, many drugs consumed before or during pregnancy are potential teratogens. Many drugs—both legal and illegal—can cross the placenta and harm the developing child (Sehgal et al., 1993; Coles et al., 1992). The most notorious example of drug-related birth defects occurred in the 1960s, when the drug thalidomide was prescribed for several hundred women to counteract morning sickness or as a mild tranquilizer. These women subsequently gave birth to infants with a variety of birth defects, including stunted limbs. Before this tragedy, it was widely believed that the only drugs that could harm the fetus were narcotics such as heroin. Thalidomide changed all this. Today doctors avoid prescribing all nonessential drugs and even warn their patients against taking common nonprescription drugs such as aspirin or antihistamines.

Nicotine and alcohol are also important teratogens. Mothers who smoke, for example, have significantly higher rates of premature births, low–birth-weight infants, and fetal deaths (Armstrong et al., 1992). Alcoholic mothers are likely to have infants suffering from fetal alcohol syndrome, which is characterized by deformities of the heart, face, and fingers, lags in motor development, and lowered intelligence or mental retardation (see Figure 9.7). Even moderate drinking—less than one drink per day—has been found to be related to attentional deficits in children at four years of age (Streissguth et al., 1984, 1991), decreased fetal growth, and increased risk of miscarriage (Roelevald et al., 1992). Results of animal studies also show serious problems resulting from single episodes of heavy alcohol consumption around the time of conception (Furey, 1984).

In view of these research findings, the Surgeon General has warned that pregnant women should avoid tobacco and alcohol entirely. Some areas, such as New York City, have passed ordinances that require all bars, restaurants, and liquor stores to post notices such as "Warning: Drinking alcoholic beverages during pregnancy can cause birth defects."

Is there anything that the father does that can affect the health of the fetus? The mother obviously plays the primary role, since her health influences that of the child she is carrying and since almost everything she ingests can cross the placental barrier between the mother and fetus. (Some have suggested that the term placental barrier be replaced with "placental sieve.") But the father can also affect the baby. Environmentally, the father's smoking may pollute the air the mother breathes. Genetically, problems can occur with the father's sperm. It has been discovered, for example, that irregularities in sperm cell division may account for 20 to 25 percent of the cases of Down syndrome, and the disorder is more common when the father is under 21 or over 55 years of age (Arehart-Treichel, 1979). In addition, recent research suggests sperm can be damaged by alcohol, opiates, cocaine, various gases, lead, pesticides, and industrial chemicals (Blakeslee, 1991).

What are my chances of having a normal baby? Although our discussion of genetic and environmental factors may have created a misleading impression of the dangers involved, the odds of having a child with a significant birth defect are only about seven percent. Our focus on the hazards is not intended to depress you or discourage you from having children. But if you do plan to have children, you should be aware of the importance of maternal nutrition and prenatal checkups, the need to avoid all unnecessary environmental risks, and the value of genetic counseling to determine whether you are at risk for having children with genetic disorders.

Fetal Alcohol Syndrome: A combination of birth defects, including organ deformities and mental, motor, and/or growth retardation, that results from maternal alcohol abuse.

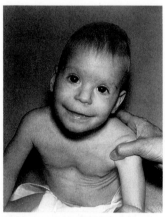

Figure 9.7 Fetal alcohol syndrome. This child was born with fetal alcohol syndrome (FAS). Note the wide-set eyes and thin upper lip. These facial abnormalities, as well as defective limbs and heart, result from the mother's heavy alcohol consumption during pregnancy. Many FAS children are also below average in intelligence and some are mentally retarded.

Review Questions

1. What are the three major stages of prenatal development?
2. What is the relationship between "genes" and "chromosomes"?

3. How do identical twins differ from fraternal twins?

4. Environmental substances that can cause birth defects are known as
   _____.

5. One of the major reasons for the high infant mortality in the United States
   is _____.

6. Alcoholic mothers may give birth to babies with _____.

Answers to Review Questions can be found in Appendix C.

Early Childhood Physical Development: Brain, Motor, and Sensory/Perceptual

Although Shakespeare described newborns as capable of only "mewling and puking in the nurse's arms," they are actually capable of much more. In this section we will explore the newborn's physical capabilities and how he or she grows and develops in the first few years of life.

Brain Development

The brain and other parts of the nervous system grow faster than any other part of the body during both prenatal development and the first two years of life. A newborn's brain is one-fourth its full adult size and will grow to about 75 percent of its adult weight and size by the age of two. At five years of age, the brain is nine-tenths its full adult weight (see Figure 9.8).

It is generally believed that the newborn's brain contains most of the neurons it will ever have (Chugani and Phelps, 1986). Further brain development and learning occur primarily because neurons grow in size, and the number of axons and dendrites as well as the extent of their connections increases (Shatz, 1992, p. 61). Although some axons of the brain continue adding myelin up to age 60 or beyond, 90 percent of myelination is complete by age three (Thatcher, Walker, and Guidice, 1987).

Understanding brain development can help us understand children's learning abilities. Myelination, for example, can account for unsuccessful toilet training. Few parents realize that a child's nervous system must achieve a certain level of myelination before he or she can recognize the signals of a full bladder—a necessary prerequisite to toilet training. Also, the parts of the brain involved in prolonged attention span and the ability to screen out distracting stimuli become increasingly myelinated between the

Myelination: The accumulation of myelin (a fatty tissue that coats the axons of nerve cells) in the nervous system, thereby increasing the speed of neural messages.

Figure 9.8 Body proportions. Notice how body proportions change as the individual grows older. At birth, the infant's head is one-fourth its full adult size.

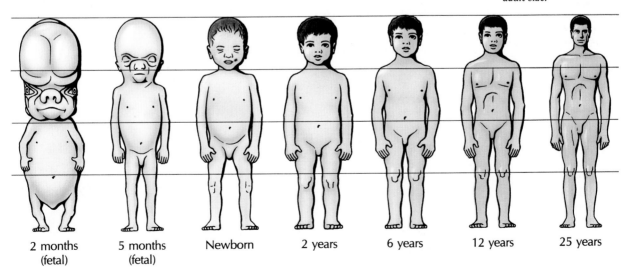

| 2 months (fetal) | 5 months (fetal) | Newborn | 2 years | 6 years | 12 years | 25 years |

ages of four and seven (Higgins and Turnure, 1984). As a consequence, most children first become ready to read and focus on schoolwork at some time between these ages (Rathus, 1992).

Doesn't this invalidate Glen Doman's claim about babies reading at 11 months? Wouldn't their nervous system be too immature at this age?   Although Doman generally ignores this type of question from his critics, many psychologists recognize these physiological limitations and do not advocate formal instruction for infants and young children. In terms of psychological damage, David Elkind (1981, 1988) warns that the current trend toward academic training in early childhood puts children at risk for short-term stress disorders and long-term personality problems. Signs of stress in two- and three-year-olds, such as pulling out their eyelashes or clumps of their hair, are frequently reported by pediatricians (Langway et al., 1983) and personality disturbances are becoming commonplace. An extreme example is the six-year-old who, while doing her homework, asked her mother, "If I don't get these right, will you kill me?" (Elkind, 1987).

Motor Development

Reflexes: Unlearned, involuntary responses of a part of the body to an external stimulus.

Compared to the hidden, internal changes in brain development, the orderly emergence of active movement skills, known as *motor development,* is easily observed and measured. The newborn's first motor abilities are limited to reflexes, involuntary responses to stimulation (see the photograph) but soon the infant begins to show voluntary control over movements of various body parts. In a few short months, a helpless newborn who can't even lift his or her head is transformed into an active toddler capable of crawling, walking, and climbing (see Figure 9.9). This transformation seems to be largely the result of maturation. For example, Hopi Indian infants spend a great portion of their first year of life being carried in a cradleboard, rather than crawling and walking freely on the ground. Yet, at the age of one their motor skills are very similar to infants who have not been restrained in this fashion (Dennis and Dennis, 1940).

Although babies in all known cultures tend to reach the major motor milestones within a few months of one another, the environment also has an effect (Berry et al., 1992). African infants, for example, generally sit, stand, and walk from one to several months earlier than North American infants (Geber and Dean, 1957; Super, 1981). (It is

Native-American babies often spend a great deal of time bound to cradleboards, yet they walk at about the same age as babies who have had extensive practice in crawling. Thus maturation can be even more important than practice in physical development.

Figure 9.9 Milestones in motor development. The "typical" progression of motor abilities range from "chin up" at age 2.2 months to walking up stairs at 17.1 months. However, no two children are alike; they follow their own individual timetable for physical development. (Adapted from Frankenburg and Dodds, 1967.)

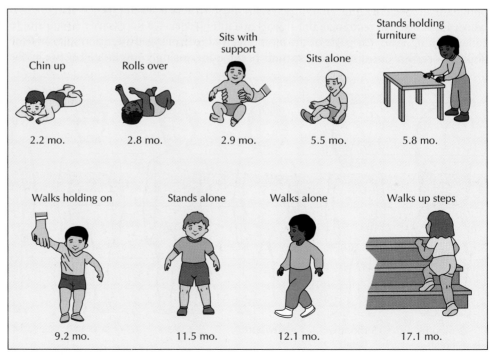

interesting to note that researchers have often referred to this as "African precocity." Could this be an example of the researchers' own Western ethnocentrism? Why are the African children "precocious," rather than the Western society babies being "delayed" or "retarded"? Apparently, the researchers are using Western babies as the standard by which other infants are compared.)

Why are the African infants further ahead in their motor skills? Differences between cultures in infant motor development may reflect particular child-rearing practices. For example, African infants spend more time in bodily and affective contact with their mothers and are frequently massaged by their mothers, which may promote motor development (Berry et al., 1992). Also, the parental ethnotheory in Africa strongly supports early motor development. Believing that infants need practice to sit, the Kipsigis in Western Kenya make a special hole in the ground and fill it with sand to help their infants practice sitting skills (Super, 1981). Similarly, the Congolese believe there is something wrong if an infant does not walk by eight months. And they seek a healer who manipulates the joints and applies an ointment made from the bones of ferocious animals and hot spices (Nkounkou-Hombessa, 1988).

Newborn infants will show the stepping reflex *if they are placed on a hard surface. They will also suck on any object that is placed in their mouth because of the* sucking reflex.

Sensory and Perceptual Development

William James (1890) believed that infants are so "assailed by eyes, ears, nose, skin, and entrails at once" that they view the world as "one great blooming, buzzing, confusion." Research, however, has shown that the newborn's senses are almost fully functional and the world is not nearly as confusing as James thought (Bower, 1990). At birth the newborn can smell most odors and can distinguish between sweet, salty, and bitter tastes (Ganchrow et al., 1983). Breastfed newborns also recognize and show preference for the odor and taste of their mother's milk over those of another mother's milk (Russell, 1976). The newborn's sense of touch and pain is also highly functional, as evidenced by reactions to heel pricks and circumcision (Chessare, 1992; Schoen and Fischell, 1991).

The sense of vision is one of the poorest developed. At birth a newborn's vision is estimated to be 20/200 to 20/600 (Haith, 1991). If you have normal 20/20 vision, you can imagine what the infant's visual life is like: The level of detail you see at 200 or 600 feet is what they see at 20 feet. Within the first few months, vision quickly improves. By six months of age, vision is 20/100 or better (Banks and Salapatek, 1983).

One of the most interesting findings regarding infant sensory and perceptual development is about hearing. Not only can the newborn hear at birth (Trehub et al., 1991), but during the last few months of pregnancy the fetus can apparently hear sounds outside the mother's body (Begley, 1991). This raises the interesting possibility of fetal learning. A popularized series of studies on this phenomenon found that infants easily recognize their own mother's voice over that of a stranger and show preferences for children's stories (such as "The Cat in the Hat" or "The King, the Mice, and the Cheese") that were read to them while they were still in the womb (DeCasper and Fifer, 1980; DeCasper and Spence, 1986; Lipsett, 1990; Trotter, 1987). Devices such as the "pregaphone" help interested parents talk to their babies before birth (see Figure 9.10).

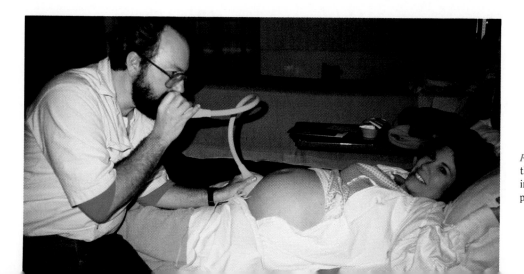

Figure 9.10 Fetal learning. This father is trying to increase fetal learning by talking to the baby on a pregaphone.

301

How can scientists measure the "preferences" and abilities of such young babies? Since newborns and infants obviously cannot talk or follow directions, researchers have devised ingenious experiments to evaluate perceptual skills in infants. One of the earliest experimenters, Robert Fantz (1956, 1963), designed a "looking chamber" in which infants lie on their backs and look at visual stimuli (see Figure 9.11). The researcher stands over the baby and measures the length of time the visual stimuli are reflected in the baby's cornea. With this technique Fantz discovered that infants prefer (as measured by their longer visual contact) complex rather than simple patterns, color rather than black and white, and pictures of faces rather than nonfaces.

Researchers also use the newborn's innate abilities, such as the sucking reflex and heart rate, to study how they learn and how their perceptual abilities develop. In the case of fetal learning, the researchers connected specially wired pacifiers to a tape recorder with stories the infants had heard while in the womb (either "The Cat in the Hat" or "The King, the Mice, and the Cheese"). If the infant sucked slowly, one story played, while sucking at a faster rate caused the other story to play.

To study the sense of smell, researchers can measure changes in the newborn's heart rate when different odors are presented. Presumably, if they can smell one, but not the other, their heart rate will change in the presence of the first but not the second. From research such as this, we now know that the senses develop very early in life.

As infants grow older their senses become even more fully developed, and their perceptual abilities improve through interactions with the environment. Young children, for example, often have difficulty learning to read because they cannot distinguish between the letters "p" and "q" and "b" and "d" or between the words "was" and "saw." This may be because a child's perception is generally more flexible and less bound by a left-to-right and vertical-horizontal orientation. In time the child gains perceptual experience and reading, like other tasks, becomes easier.

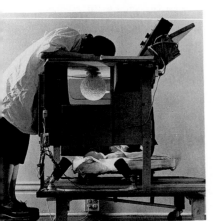

Figure 9.11 Fantz's "looking chamber." Using this specially designed testing apparatus, Fantz and his colleagues measured the length of time infants stared at various stimuli. They found that infants preferred certain stimuli, such as complex patterns rather than simple patterns.

Review Questions

1. The brain is nine-tenths its full adult weight by _____ years of age.
2. Why is infant toilet training so often unsuccessful?
3. The fact that Hopi Indian children spend much of their infancy on a cradleboard, yet show no impairment of motor skills, supports which side of the nature versus nurture debate?
4. How can the ethnotheory of African parents explain why their infants' motor skills are more advanced than those of infants in Western societies?
5. _____ is the poorest developed sense in the newborn infant.

Answers to Review Questions can be found in Appendix C.

Physical Changes in Adolescence: A Time of Rapid Change

Think back for a moment to your adolescence. Were you concerned about the physical changes you were going through? Did you worry about how you differed from your classmates? Differences in height and weight, the growth of breasts and menstruation for girls, and the deepening of voices and growth of beards for boys are all important milestones for adolescents. Puberty, the period of life when a person becomes capable of reproduction, is a major physical milestone for everyone. It is a clear biological signal of the end of childhood.

Although commonly associated with puberty, adolescence is the loosely defined psychological period of development between childhood and adulthood. In the United

Puberty: The period in life during which the sex organs mature to a point where sexual reproduction becomes possible. Puberty generally begins for girls around 8 to 12 years of age, and for boys about two years later.

Adolescence: The psychological period of development between childhood and adulthood, which in the United States roughly corresponds to the teenage years.

States, it roughly corresponds to the teenage years. It is important to recognize that adolescence, like childhood, is not a universal concept. Some nonindustrialized countries have no need for such a slow transition, and children simply assume adult responsibilities as soon as possible.

The clearest and most dramatic physical sign of both puberty and adolescence is the *growth spurt,* which is characterized by rapid increases in height, weight, and skeletal growth. Do you remember feelings of awkwardness, anxiety, and confusion at this time in your life? Growth during early stages of development is *proximodistal* (near to far), with the head and upper body developing before the lower body. Growth at puberty, however, is distalproximo (far to near), which results in faster development of hands, feet, nose, lips, and ears. This type of development, along with the characteristically unequal development of the two halves of the body (one foot, breast, or hand can be temporarily larger than the other), explains much of adolescent awkwardness.

Adolescence also is a time for rapid changes in reproductive structures and sexual characteristics. As a result of maturation and the secretion of hormones, the adolescent female body experiences rapid development of the ovaries, uterus, and vagina and undergoes the *menarche* (the onset of the menstrual cycle). At the same time the adolescent male experiences development of the testes, scrotum, and penis. The ovaries and testes in turn produce hormones that lead to the development of secondary sex characteristics, such as pubic hair, deepening of the voice, facial hair, breasts, and so on (see Figure 9.12).

Distalproximo Development: Physical development in an outer to inner direction, such that hands, feet, nose, etc. develop faster than internal organs.

Secondary Sex Characteristics: Hormonally generated sexual characteristics, secondary to the sex organs, that are not necessary for reproduction.

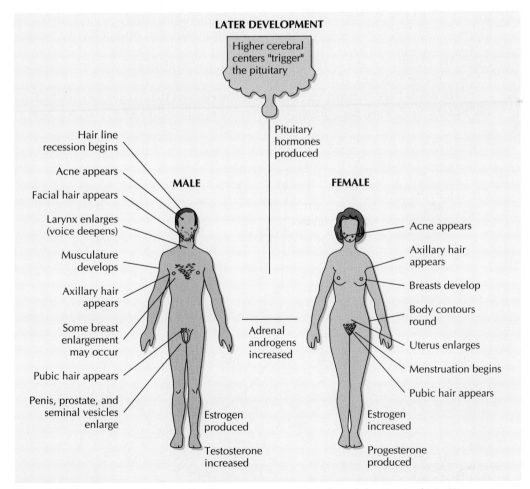

Figure 9.12 Secondary sex characteristics. Hormones cause complex physical changes at puberty. Hormones are secreted not only from the ovaries and testes but also from the pituitary gland in the brain and the adrenal glands near the kidneys.

Physical Changes and Psychological Adjustment

How these physical changes affect an individual's psychological adjustment may depend on how quickly he or she matures. Early maturation for boys correlates with higher school achievement, positive body image, positive moods, and higher regard from both peers and adults (Petersen, 1988; Tanner, 1982). In addition, most boys are about two years behind most girls in the pubertal growth spurt (see Figure 9.13). Thus, early-maturing males may also enjoy an important social advantage with the taller girls because of their increased height and physical abilities.

All is not entirely rosy for the early-maturing boy, however. He may enjoy his early height advantage and greater strength, but he lacks a comparison group to reassure him that some changes (such as acne and temporary enlargement of his breasts) are also normal and transitory. In addition, some studies have found that early-maturing boys show a disproportionate number of problem behaviors (Duncan et al., 1985).

The effects of early or late maturation for girls are also mixed. Although early-maturing females do seem to have higher school achievement and show more independence, they also tend to have lower self-esteem, poorer body image, and more conflicts with their parents (Blyth et al., 1981; Petersen, 1987). Anne Petersen and her colleagues have speculated that academic success may come at a high social cost for adolescent girls. They found that when early-maturing girls lowered their academic achievement, their popularity and self-image increased (Petersen et al., 1987). In addition, the poor body image of these girls may be due to their increased levels of estrogen. Since estrogen inhibits long bone growth and increases the percentage of fatty tissue, early-maturing females tend to be shorter and stockier than late-maturing females. In a society that values tallness and slimness in females, it is not surprising that early-maturing females tend to have a poorer body image. Finally, parents of early-maturing girls tend to increase their vigilance and restrictiveness, which may explain increased parent–child conflicts (Savin-Williams and Small, 1986).

The desire to be "normal" is perhaps the one element that is common to almost all adolescents. Even when early development results in culturally valued changes, such as

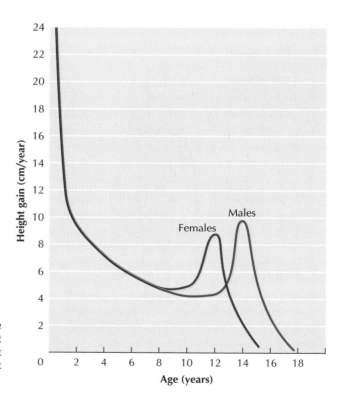

Figure 9.13 Adolescent growth spurt. The female growth spurt precedes the male's so that most girls tend to be taller than most boys from the ages of 10 to 14.

beards and deepened voices in males, the changes may lead to teasing or exclusion from the group that has not developed at the same rate.

Physical Changes in the Adult Years: A Time of Gradual Change

Once the large and obvious pubertal changes have occurred, further age-related physical changes are less dramatic. Beyond some continued increase in height and muscular development during the late teens and early twenties, most individuals experience only minor physical changes until middle age.

Middle Age

For the female, menopause, the cessation of the menstrual cycle, which occurs somewhere between the ages of 45 and 55, is the second most important life milestone in physical development. Although the decreased production of the female hormone estrogen leads to certain physical changes, the popular belief that menopause (or "the change of life") causes serious psychological mood swings, loss of sexual interest, and depression is not supported by current research (Hoyenga and Hoyenga, 1993; Siegal, 1990). Menopause, like most developmental changes, has both advantages and disadvantages and there is great variation in individual response.

Beginning in middle adulthood, males experience a gradual decline in the production of sperm and testosterone (the male hormone), although they may remain capable of reproduction well into their eighties or nineties. Physical changes such as unexpected weight gain, decline in sexual responsiveness, loss of muscle strength, and graying or loss of hair may lead some men (and women as well) to feel depressed and to question their life goals, since they see these changes as a biological signal of aging and mortality (Mulligan and Moss, 1991; Tavris, 1992). Such physical and psychological changes in males are known as the male climacteric. Whether all of these changes are an inevitable part of biological aging is called into question by the outstanding physical achievements of some older individuals, such as fitness guru Jack La Lanne. At the age of 45, La Lanne did 1000 push-ups and 1000 chin-ups in 82 minutes, at 60 he swam almost a mile in San Francisco Bay towing a 1000-pound boat while wearing handcuffs and leg shackles, and at the age of 70, again while shackled, swam a mile towing 70 manned rowboats (Dorman, 1986).

Late Adulthood

After middle age, most physical changes in development are related to gradual alterations in the heart and arteries, brain and nervous system, and the sensory receptors. Many of the supposedly inevitable age-related changes, such as reduced lung capacity, increased blood pressure, loss of muscle mass, and even some wrinkling of the skin, are primarily related to environmental factors and individual lifestyles (Evans and Rosenberg, 1992; Rodin and Salovey, 1989). Exposure to the sun and wind, for example, are environmental factors in skin damage. Personal factors such as nutrition, smoking, exercise, and degree of stress may also affect physical health (see Chapter 13). Thus, lifestyle changes, from using sunscreen to stopping smoking, increasing exercise, and eating healthily, allow older people to maintain most of their mental and physical abilities throughout their entire life span (Evans and Rosenberg, 1992; Horn and Meer, 1987).

Individual Differences and Aging

Not all body systems age at the same rate. Someone might have poor vision and hearing, but have a strong heart and exceptional mental acuity. Furthermore, there is consider-

Menopause: The gradual cessation of menstruation that occurs between the ages of 45 and 55; sometimes referred to as the climacteric or change of life.

Male Climacteric: A term used to describe the physical and psychological changes associated with the male's movement into midlife.

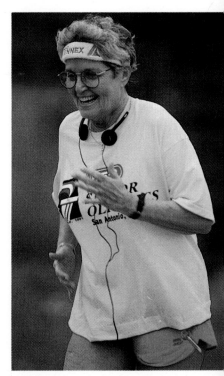

Exercise may be the most important factor in maintaining mental and physical abilities throughout the life span.

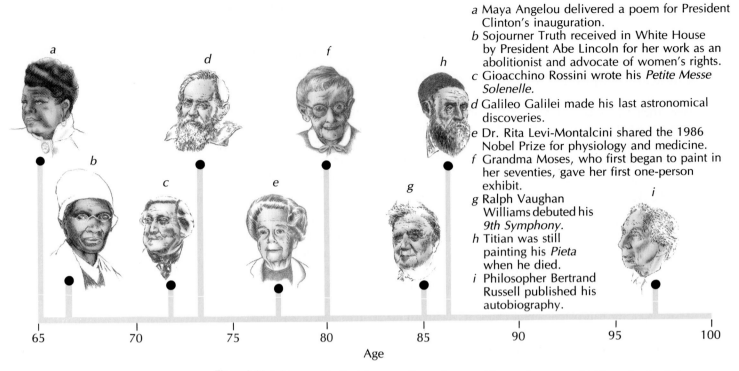

a Maya Angelou delivered a poem for President Clinton's inauguration.

b Sojourner Truth received in White House by President Abe Lincoln for her work as an abolitionist and advocate of women's rights.

c Gioacchino Rossini wrote his *Petite Messe Solenelle.*

d Galileo Galilei made his last astronomical discoveries.

e Dr. Rita Levi-Montalcini shared the 1986 Nobel Prize for physiology and medicine.

f Grandma Moses, who first began to paint in her seventies, gave her first one-person exhibit.

g Ralph Vaughan Williams debuted his *9th Symphony.*

h Titian was still painting his *Pieta* when he died.

i Philosopher Bertrand Russell published his autobiography.

Figure 9.14 Achievement in the later years. Some of our most famous figures were highly productive during the last few decades of life.

Parkinson's Disease: A neurological disorder characterized by rigidity, tremor, and uncontrollable movements, believed to be caused by a dopamine deficiency.

Secondary Aging: Acceleration in the normal physical changes associated with aging as a result of abuse, neglect, disuse, or disease.

Primary Aging: Gradual changes in physical and mental processes that inevitably occur with age.

able variation among individuals (Meaney et al., 1988). A small minority of older adults suffer from age-related disorders such as Alzheimer's disease and Parkinson's disease. Alzheimer's disease is a progressive deterioration of the brain characterized by loss of memory, confusion, and personality deterioration. Parkinson's disease is a neurological disorder characterized by rigidity, tremor, and uncontrollable movements. On the other hand, many individuals find the later years of life to be their happiest and most productive (see Figure 9.14).

What causes us to age and eventually die? If we set aside secondary aging, which results from disease, disuse, or abuse through certain lifestyles and environmental factors, we are left with the gradual changes that constitute primary aging. Although scientists do not really know what causes primary aging, there are two main theories. According to *programmed theories,* aging is genetically controlled (Cunningham and Brookbank, 1988; Ezzell, 1993). Once the ovum is fertilized, the program for aging and death is set and begins to run. Researcher Leonard Hayflick (1977, 1980) found that human cells seem to have a built-in life span. After about 50 doublings of laboratory-cultured cells, they cease to multiply—they have reached *the Hayflick limit.* Other theorists suggest that the programming is in the immunological system, which, with age, begins to lose its ability to recognize and fight off foreign substances and may begin to self-destruct (Walford, 1983).

The other explanation of primary aging is the *wear-and-tear theory,* which proposes that everyday life damages biological systems and limits their ability to repair themselves. Internal and external stressors gradually wear out the cells and they stop dividing. Whichever theory is correct, human beings appear to have a maximum life span of about 110 to 120 years. Although we can try to control secondary aging in an attempt to reach that maximum, so far we have no means to control the inevitability of primary aging.

Review Questions

1. The period of life when an individual first becomes capable of reproduction is known as _____ .

2. During the early stages of development, growth is _____ (from near to far), whereas growth during adolescence is _____ (from far to near).

3. _____ (such as deepening of the voice, pubic hair, and breasts) are primarily produced by hormones from the ovaries and testes.

4. The psychological equivalent to the female menopause for the male is the _____ .

5. What is the difference between primary and secondary aging?

6. Compare and contrast programmed theories of aging and the wear-and-tear theory.

Answers to Review Questions can be found in Appendix C.

LANGUAGE DEVELOPMENT

From birth the child has a multitude of ways to communicate. In addition to the obvious verbal communication (characterized at first by cries and later by speech), babies possess a "silent language" that is perhaps an even more powerful form of communication. Through such nonverbal means as facial expressions, eye contact, and body gestures, babies only hours old begin to "teach" their parents and caregivers when and how they want to be held, fed, and played with.

* *How do children learn language?*

Nonverbal Communication: The Earliest Form of Language

In the late 1800s Charles Darwin proposed that most emotional expressions, such as smiles, frowns, and looks of disgust, are universal and innate. As you can see in Figure 9.15, even young infants show distinct expressions such as anger, joy, disgust, and surprise (Field, 1987; Izard et al., 1980; Tronick, 1989). Darwin's contention is further supported by the fact that children who are born blind and deaf exhibit the same facial expressions for emotions as those of sighted and hearing children.

To experimentally document the child's early use of nonverbal communication, Carroll Izard and his associates (1980) exposed infants from one to nine months of age to a variety of situations (such as being separated from and reunited with their mothers, having balloons popped in their faces, and so on). They then spend thousands of hours carefully studying videotapes of the infants' reactions. They found the infants showed facial expressions very similar to those of adults in comparable circumstances. Nonetheless, most parents are unaware of the complexity of their baby's nonverbal communication.

In addition to facial expressions, children communicate through gestures, movements, and postures (Bower, 1989a). Lewis (1980) has shown that an infant uses its entire body to communicate. For example, the head is often tilted to invite friendship or turned to reject an approach, whereas uplifted arms are a gesture to encourage approach or request an adult's help. The trunk of the body is sometimes bent forward as a sign of domination or is held very straight during moments of nervous hesitation. Limp hands generally indicate fatigue while rapidly moving arms show frustration, rage, or joy.

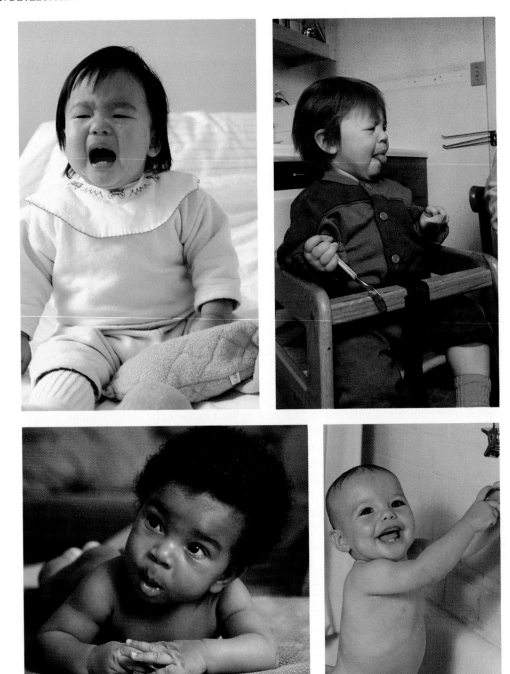

*Figure 9.15 **Early nonverbal communication.*** Young children often show distinct emotions. Can you label which child is showing anger, joy, disgust, and surprise?

Verbal Communication: The Development of Language

Most researchers agree that a baby's early cries, grunts, and "prompted" words are simple responses to the internal or external environment and do not qualify as true language. Therefore this stage is referred to as *prelinguistic*. The *linguistic stage* is said to begin when children are able to use novel or creative expressions that have meaning for them while attempting to communicate with others.

The Prelinguistic Stage

The prelinguistic stage begins with the newborn baby's first reflexive cry. Within a short time, crying becomes more purposeful. At least three distinct patterns have been identified: the basic hunger cry, the angry cry, and the pain cry (Wolff, 1969). Although many child-care texts suggest that each of these cries can be easily identified and responded to by the primary caregivers (Hostetler, 1988a), most parents find that they must learn through a process of trial-and-error what actions will satisfy their child.

After "mastering" crying, children at about two months of age begin to *coo* — to produce vowel sounds ("ooh," "aah," and "eee") — and at about six months they begin to *babble* — adding consonants to their vowels ("bababa" and "dadada"). Some parents mark babbling as the beginning of language and consider their child's vocalizations as "words" even though the child typically does not associate a "word" with a specific object or person, and despite the fact that all children the world over babble in the same fashion.

Babbling: An early stage of speech development in which infants emit virtually all known sounds of human speech.

The Linguistic Stage

The true linguistic stage begins toward the end of the first year of life, when babbling begins to sound more like the specific language of the child's home and when the child seems to understand that sound is related to meaning. At the beginning of this stage, the child is generally limited to a single-utterance vocabulary such as "mama," "go," "juice," or "up." Children manage to get a lot of mileage out of these singular utterances ("mama" can be used to say "I want you to come and get me," "I'm hurt," or "I don't like this stranger"). However, their vocabulary more than doubles once they begin to express themselves by joining words into two-word phrases such as "Go bye-bye," "Daddy milk," and "Dog bite."

At this age, children sometimes *overextend* the words they use. Overextension is using words to include objects that do not fit the word's meaning. For example, once a child has learned the word "doggie," he or she will overextend the word to include all small, furry animals (e.g., kittens, bunnies).

Overextension: A child's tendency to misuse words to include objects that do not fit the word's meaning.

By the time "average" children are two years of age, they are able to create short but intelligible sentences by linking two, three, four, or more words together. Just as adults tend to leave out nonessential words when sending a telegram, young children use telegraphic speech (two- or three-word sentences that contain only the most necessary words) — "No sit there," "Tommy want milk," "What doing?" and so on.

Telegraphic Speech: The two- or three-word sentences of young children that contain only the most necessary words.

While increasing their vocabulary at a phenomenal rate during these early years, children are also acquiring a wide variety of rules for grammar, such as adding "ed" to indicate the past tense and "s" to form plurals. They also make mistakes however, because they overgeneralize (extend the rules for past tense and plural to irregular forms) (Bates, O'Connell, and Shore, 1987). This results in novel sentences like "I goed to the zoo" and "My foots hurt." By the age of five, most children have mastered major rules of grammar and typically use about 2000 words — considered by many foreign language instructors to be adequate for getting by in any given culture. Past this point, vocabulary and grammar acquisition generally progress through gradual stages of improvement throughout the entire life span.

Overgeneralize: A common error in a child's language acquisition where the rules for past tense and plurals are extended to irregular forms.

Although vocabulary and grammar are certainly the foundations for language development, they represent only part of the requirements for verbal communication. Have you ever called someone and asked the child who answered the phone "Is your mommy at home?" and had the child answer "yes" and then hang up? This response demonstrates that children must also learn the *implied* messages of words. In addition, parents and caregivers must recognize that a child often has difficulty distinguishing between literal and figurative meanings. For example, one of the students in our classes who coached a young boys' baseball team was continually reminding a young batter to "keep his eye on the ball." Finally, the frustrated five-year-old dropped the bat, ran over to pick up the ball, and placed it against his eye! Given the child's tendency to interpret adult language in a literal sense, imagine what a small child might think when he or she hears adult comments like "Aunt Sally is really sharp," "There's a fork in the road," or "Daddy has gone away for a while to get his head together."

Theories of Language Development

Numerous theories have been proposed to explain how children acquire language. Some theorists believe the capability is innate, whereas others claim it is learned through imitation and reinforcement (the nature versus nurture controversy again). Although there are staunch supporters of both sides, most psychologists find neither of these extreme positions satisfactory. Most believe that language acquisition is a combination of both nature and nurture—the *interactionist* position (Damasio and Damasio, 1992; Rice, 1989).

According to the nativist position, the acquisition of language is primarily a matter of maturation. The most famous advocate of this viewpoint, Noam Chomsky (1968, 1980), suggests that children are born "prewired" to learn language. He believes they possess a type of language acquisition device (LAD) that needs only minimal exposure to adult speech to unlock its potential. The LAD enables the child to analyze language and unconsciously extract the basic rules of grammar. To support his viewpoint, Chomsky points to the fact that children all over the world go through similar stages in language development at about the same age and in a pattern that parallels that of motor development. He also cites the facts that babbling of babies is the same in all cultures and that deaf children babble just like hearing children.

Although the nativist position enjoys considerable support, it fails to adequately explain individual differences. Why does one child learn rules for English, for example, while another learns those for Spanish? The "nurturists" *can* explain individual differences and distinct languages. From their perspective children learn language through a complex system of rewards, punishments, and imitation. For example, any vocalization attempt from the young infant is quickly rewarded with smiles and other forms of encouragement. When the infant later babbles "mama" or "dada," proud parents are even more enthusiastic in their response.

Why do children say things like "My foots hurt" if they've never been rewarded for doing so and are not imitating others? Cognitive psychologist George Rebok (1987) suggests that imitative learning cannot explain these errors. While learning language, children apparently go through a regular and predictable sequence: (1) correct imitation, (2) rules of grammar acquisition, (3) errors in grammar, and (4) corrections in grammar. After first imitating the correct expression ("My feet hurt"), children then begin to observe and understand the basic rules of grammar and to overgeneralize, producing sentences such as "My foots hurt." Since these sentences are seldom used by adults, it is difficult to explain such errors from a simple learning perspective. In addition, parents often ignore imperfections in their children's grammar and even reward some mistakes for being "cute."

Isn't it wrong to encourage a child's mistakes? Although parents could carry this "cuteness" too far, the love and acceptance of such mistakes undoubtedly benefits a child. Research has shown that "baby talk" from the parents to the child encourages language development (Cross, 1977; Gelman et al., 1988). For example, simplifying "stomach" to "tummy" and "restroom" to "potty" seems to help the child grasp the language more easily. Can you imagine learning a foreign language if your instructors refused to shorten their sentences or slow their speech? The fact that baby talk (officially referred to as *caretaker speech* or *motherese*) is universal, and even shown by four-year-old children when talking to a younger child, suggests that it is important to the child's learning and perhaps an innate capacity of the teacher (Blewitt, 1983; Caporael, 1981).

In summary, it appears that language is both innate and learned, and the best way to foster its development is through gentle acceptance of the child and responsiveness to his or her individual needs.

Language Acquisition Device (LAD): In Noam Chomsky's view, the child's inborn brain capacity to analyze language and unconsciously understand essential grammatical rules.

Review Questions

1. Facial expressions, eye contact, and body gestures are all examples of _____ .

2. How is "cooing" different from "babbling"?

3. What is "telegraphic speech"?

4. Children make errors like "mouses" and "goed" versus "mice" and "went" because they _____ the rules of grammar.

5. Noam Chomsky believes we possess an inborn ability to learn language known as the _____ .

6. Should parents engage in "baby talk" with their infants?

Answers to Review Questions can be found in Appendix C.

COGNITIVE DEVELOPMENT

The following fan letter was written to Shari Lewis (1963), a children's television performer, about her puppet Lamb Chop:

> *Dear Shari:*
> *All my friends say Lamb Chop isn't really a little girl that talks. She is just a puppet you made out of a sock. I don't care even if it's true. I like the way Lamb Chop talks. If I send you one of my socks will you teach it how to talk and send it back?*
>
> *Randi*

• *How does cognition, or the way we think about the world, change during the life cycle?*

Randi's understanding of fantasy and reality is certainly different from an adult's. Just as a child's body and physical abilities change, his or her way of knowing and perceiving the world also grows and changes. This seems intuitively obvious, but early psychologists ignored children's cognitive development and focused instead on physical, emotional, language, or personality development. There was one major exception: Jean Piaget (pronounced Pee-ah-zhay).

Today Piaget is well known for his study of the development of thinking processes in children. One of his most significant contributions was demonstrating that the intellect of the child is fundamentally different from that of the adult (Flavell, 1993). He explained that a baby begins at a cognitively "primitive" level and that all subsequent intellectual growth progresses in distinct stages motivated by an innate *need to know.*

Why was Piaget interested in this topic when no one else was? Although initially trained as a biologist, Piaget in his early years worked at Alfred Binet's laboratory in Paris, helping develop the first intelligence tests. While performing the routine measurements required in developing Binet's tests, he noticed a pattern in the way children of certain ages routinely "passed" or "failed" various sections of tests. By asking them gentle, probing questions about their reasons for making certain responses and decisions, he uncovered some of the modes of thinking underlying their right and wrong test answers. (This method of verbal probing later became a hallmark of the Piagetian form of research.) By asking deeper questions, Piaget went beyond the simple measurement of a child's IQ and laid the foundation for his life's work, including a carefully constructed theory of cognitive development.

Piaget's comprehensive theory has proven so useful and insightful that it remains the major force in the cognitive area of developmental psychology today. In view of this fact, we will outline it in some detail.

Piaget's Approach: Major Terms and Concepts

Perhaps the best way to approach an understanding of Piaget is to recognize that his background was as a biologist. Thus, he saw human cognition as only one of the ongoing processes of biology. Piaget believed that we are all born with an innate *drive* toward knowledge as part of our overall need for survival. Just as food is taken in and then digested into forms that are useful for the organism's biological survival, information is taken in by the human brain and "digested" in ways that also help the individual to survive. The cognitive processes are the "digestive" mechanisms that help humans *adapt* to their environment, and "intelligence" is the ability to make adaptive choices (Cowan, 1978).

Schemata

Adaptation: Structural or functional changes that increase the organism's chances for survival.

Schemata: Cognitive structures or patterns consisting of a number of organized ideas that grow and differentiate with experience.

To understand the process of adaptation, we need to consider three major Piagetian concepts: schemata, assimilation, and accommodation. Schemata (plural form of *schema*, which is used interchangeably with *scheme*) are the most basic units of intellect. They act as patterns that organize our interactions with the environment. Like an architect's drawings or builder's blueprints, schemata are the guiding forces for the "construction" of the intellect. In the first few weeks of life, for example, the infant apparently has several schemata based on the innate reflexes of sucking, grasping, and so on. In these early days, the schemata are primarily motor and may be little more than stimulus and response mechanisms—the nipple is presented and the baby sucks. Soon, however, other schemata emerge. The infant develops a more detailed schema for the eating of solid food, a different schema for the concepts of "mother" and "father," and so on. These schemata, or tools for learning about the world, are enlarged and changed throughout our lives, thus enabling us to successfully interact with the environment.

Assimilation and Accommodation

Assimilation: The process of responding to a new situation in the same manner that is used in a familiar situation.

Accommodation: The process of adjusting existing ways of thinking (reworking schemata) to encompass new information, ideas, or objects.

Assimilation and accommodation are the two major processes that allow schemata to grow and change over time. Assimilation is the process of taking in new information that easily fits into an existing schema. For instance, infants use their sucking schema not only in sucking nipples but also in sucking blankets, fingers, and so on. They gain information about new objects in their environment by applying a reflexive response to them and *assimilating* this information into their existing schemata (Wadsworth, 1981).

Accommodation occurs when new information or stimuli cannot be assimilated and new schemata are developed or when old schemata are *changed* to adapt to the new features. An infant's first attempt to eat solid food with a spoon is a good example of accommodation. When the spoon first enters her mouth, the child attempts to assimilate it by using the previously successful "sucking schema"—shaping lips and tongue around the spoon as around a nipple. After repeated trials, with food all over her mouth, feeding tray, and anyone in close proximity, the infant will eventually try another strategy. She accommodates by adjusting her lips and tongue in a way that moves the food off the spoon and into her mouth.

Stages of Cognitive Development: Birth to Adolescence

As a result of assimilation, accommodation, and the corresponding changes in schemata, the child's cognitive abilities undergo an orderly series of increasingly complex changes. When enough changes have occurred, the individual undergoes a large developmental shift in his or her point of view (Cowan, 1978). Piaget called these developmental shifts cognitive *stages* in development (see Table 9.4).

According to Piaget, all children go through the same four stages at approximately the same age, regardless of the culture in which they live. No stage can be skipped, since

Table 9.4   Piaget's Stages of Cognitive Development

Age	Stage	Description
Birth to 2 years	Sensorimotor	Infant uses senses and motor skills to explore the world; object permanence develops
2 to 7	Preoperational	Child cannot think by operations but thinks in images and symbols; thinking is also egocentric and animistic
7 to 11	Concrete operational	Child understands conservation and applies logical operations to concrete, external objects
From 11 on	Formal operational	Adolescent or adult is able to think abstractly and about hypothetical concepts; adolescents often exhibit a special type of egocentrism

During the sensorimotor stage, the child explores the world through his or her senses and motor activities.

the skills acquired at the earlier stages are essential to the mastery of the later stages. Let's take a closer look at these four stages: sensorimotor, preoperational, concrete operational, and formal operational.

The Sensorimotor Stage

During the sensorimotor stage, which lasts from birth until the time of "significant" language acquisition (about age two), children explore the world and develop their schemata primarily through their senses and motor activities—hence the term *sensorimotor.* If you've ever spent time watching infants, you've probably noticed that they put everything into their mouths and sometimes bang pots and pans together for what may seem like hours. As Piaget explained, they do this because they are little experimenters eagerly searching the world for information.

One of the most important concepts acquired during this stage is object permanence. At birth and for the next three or four months, children lack object permanence. They seem to have no schemata for objects that disappear from their vision—out of sight is truly out of mind. You can check this out by letting an infant play with a toy and then covering it with your hand. The infant will act as if the toy never existed. If you interact with the same baby when he or she is four to eight months old, the infant may visually search for the toy if part of it is showing and will follow the path of your hand if you put the toy behind your back. Between the ages of eight and twelve months, the baby will physically search for the toy by lifting your fingers if you're covering it with your hand or by reaching behind your back if you've hidden it there. By the end of the sensorimotor stage, children's schema for object permanence is well developed and they will search a number of locations to find a hidden toy.

Preoperational Stage

Piaget's second period of cognitive development is called the preoperational stage (ages two to seven). At this stage children have acquired object permanence and can now understand that sounds can be used as symbols for objects (knowledge of objects *must* precede the use of language—you have to acknowledge an object before you can label it). As you may imagine, language has a powerful influence on all aspects of behavior, but in terms of cognitive development the acquisition of language is of critical importance. Once the child truly grasps that objects and events in the environment can be represented by words, a whole new world of learning opens up. In the story of Helen Keller (Chapter 4), who was both blind and deaf, the crucial turning point in her cognitive development was the moment she realized that the hand signals her loving teacher had so patiently repeated time after time were representational symbols. Following this

Sensorimotor Stage: The first of Piaget's stages (birth to age two), in which cognitive development is acquired through exploration of the world via sensory perceptions and motor skills.

Object Permanence: A Piagetian term for one of an infant's most important accomplishments: understanding that objects (or people) continue to exist even when they cannot directly be seen, heard, or touched.

Preoperational Stage: The second of Piaget's stages (ages two to seven), characterized by the child's ability to employ mental symbols, to engage in fantasy play, and to use words. Thinking is egocentric and animistic and the child cannot yet perform operations.

recognition, she immediately ran around asking the label for everything she could touch, not unlike the preoperational child's endless "What's that?" questions.

While the preoperational child has made significant advances in language and symbolic thinking, this stage is also characterized by several important limitations, two of which are egocentrism and animism.

Egocentrism: The inability to consider another's point of view, which Piaget considered a hallmark of the preoperational stage.

"Look what I can do, Grandma!"
Reprinted with special permission of King Features Syndicate, Inc.

Animism: According to Piaget, the preoperational child's belief that all things are living and capable of intentions, consciousness, and feelings.

1. Egocentrism refers to the preoperational child's limited ability to distinguish between his or her own perspective and that of someone else. Children at this stage have difficulty understanding that there are points of view other than their own. The preschooler who moves in front of you to get a better view of television or repeatedly asks questions while you're talking on the phone is demonstrating egocentrism. They assume that others see, hear, feel, and think exactly what they do. Consider the following telephone conversation between a three-year-old, who is at home, and her mother, who is at work:

Mother: Emma, is that you?
Emma: (Nods silently).
Mother: Emma, is Daddy there? Can I speak to him?
Emma: (Twice nods silently).

Egocentric preoperational children fail to understand that the phone caller cannot see their nodding head. They also feel that people and objects in the world exist only for their use and benefit. They typically believe that the sun follows them around and keeps them warm, that rivers are there for them to swim in, and that preschool teachers live in their classroom waiting for them to come to school.

2. Animism refers to the belief that all things are living (or animated). Preoperational children believe that objects such as the sun, trees, clouds, and bars of soap have motives, feelings, and intentions (for example, "dark clouds are angry" and "soap sinks to the bottom of the bathtub because it is tired"). A delightful example of animism came from a child of one of our students. To explain why stars come out at night, this preoperational child said "the sun is sleeping and is afraid. So the stars are the sun's night lights."

Concrete Operational Stage

Concrete Operational Stage: The third of Piaget's stages of cognitive development (ages 7 to 11), during which the child develops the ability to think logically, but not abstractly.

Operations: Piaget's term for the various internal transformations, manipulations, and reorganizations of mental structures that children use to solve problems.

During the period of ages 7 to 11, children are in the concrete operational stage. During this stage many important thinking skills emerge. One of the most important is the ability to perform operations—internal transformations, manipulations, and reorganizations of mental structures. (Piaget called the previous stage "preoperational" because children at that stage do not understand operations. Similarily, he named this stage *concrete* operations because children *can* perform operations but only on images of tangible, "concrete" objects.)

Pretend for the moment that you are observing Piaget at work testing one of his young preoperational subjects. He begins by placing the child in front of two equal-sized glasses, each filled with the same amount of water (see Figure 9.16). After the child agrees that the two glasses contain the same amount of water, Piaget pours the water from one of the glasses into a much taller and thinner glass. At this point, he asks the child if both glasses still contain the same amount of water.

What do you think the child says? Most preoperational children will reply that the taller glass now has more. When the same test is repeated with a concrete operational child, this child will recognize that the amount has remained the same.

Conservation: The ability to recognize that a given quantity, weight, or volume remains constant despite changes in shape, length, or position.

Why does the preoperational child make this kind of mistake?   According to Piaget, the preoperational child lacks conservation—an awareness that physical quantities remain constant in spite of changes in their shape or appearance. Because concrete operational children have the ability to perform operations, they also have the ability to understand the principles of conservation. They understand that certain physical attributes (such as

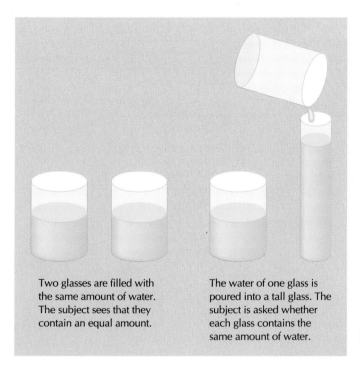

Two glasses are filled with the same amount of water. The subject sees that they contain an equal amount.

The water of one glass is poured into a tall glass. The subject is asked whether each glass contains the same amount of water.

Figure 9.16 Test for conservation. A preoperational child will say the taller glass on the far right has more than the other. This is because he or she lacks the cognitive ability known as "conservation."

volume) remain unchanged even though the outward appearance of the object is altered. One of the operations that youngsters master during the concrete operational stage is *reversibility.* Reversibility allows children to mentally "undo" something. For instance, when shown a ball of clay that is first rolled out to form a "snake" and then rolled back into a ball, the *preoperational* child will watch the transformation and say that the snake has more clay than the ball. The concrete operational child, on the other hand, can mentally reverse the action and recognize that the volume remains the same.

 Try This Yourself

If you know children in the preoperational and/or concrete operational stages, you may enjoy testing their grasp of conservation by trying some of the experiments shown in Figure 9.17. The equipment is easily obtained, and you will find their responses fascinating. ■

Why can't preoperational children be taught how to to use operations?   Although some researchers have reported success in accelerating the preoperational stage (e.g., Field, 1987), Piaget did not believe in pushing children ahead of their own developmental schedule. He believed children should be allowed to grow at their own pace, with minimal adult interference (Elkind, 1981). In view of the fact that Piaget also saw Americans as particularly guilty of pushing children (calling it the "Great American Kid Race"), you can imagine what his opinion would be of Doman's work with "superbabies" described at the beginning of this chapter.

Formal Operational Stage

The final period in Piaget's theory is the formal operational stage, which typically begins around age 11. In this stage children begin to apply their operations to *abstract* concepts, in addition to concrete objects. They also become capable of hypothetical thinking ("what if?"), deductive reasoning ("If . . . then"), and systematic formulation and testing of concepts. Using this advanced type of thinking, those who have achieved formal operations can easily solve this problem:

Formal Operational Stage: Piaget's fourth stage of cognitive development (age 11 and beyond) characterized by logical thinking, abstract reasoning, and conceptualization.

If Tom is taller than Jim, and Jim is taller than Bill, who is taller, Tom or Bill?

Type of Conservation	Step 1 of Experiment	Experimenter then . . .	Child is asked conservation question	Average age at which concept is grasped
Length	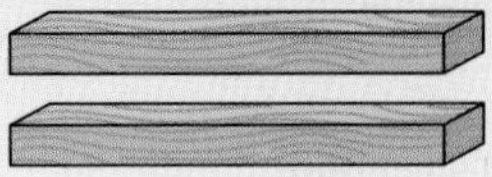 Center two sticks of equal length. Child agrees that they are of equal length.	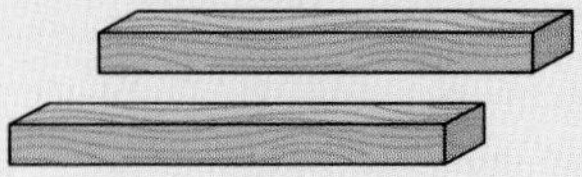 moves stick over.	*Which stick is longer?* Preconserving child will say that one of the sticks is longer. Conserving child will say that they are both the same length.	6–7
Substance amount	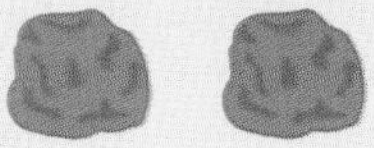 Center two identical clay balls. Child acknowledges that the two have equal amounts of clay.	 rolls out one of the balls.	*Do the two pieces have the same amount of clay?* Preconserving child will say that the long piece has more clay. Conserving child will say that the two pieces have the same amount of clay.	6–7
Area	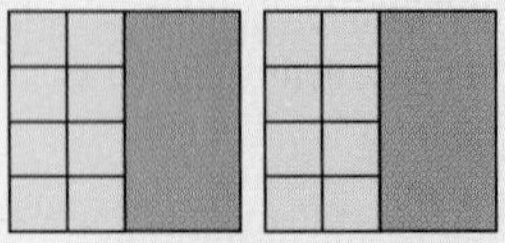 Center two identical sheets of cardboard with wooden blocks placed on them in identical positions. Child acknowledges that the same amount of space is left open on each piece of cardboard.	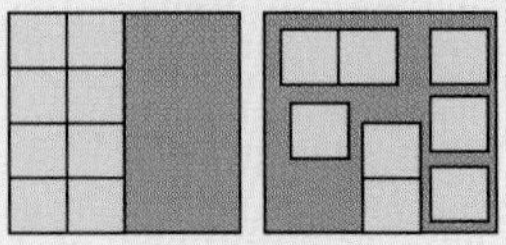 scatters the blocks on one piece of cardboard.	*Do the two pieces of cardboard have the same amount of open space?* Preconserving child will say that the cardboard with scattered blocks has less open space. Conserving child will say that both pieces have the same amount of open space.	8–10
Volume	 Center two balls of clay in two identical glasses with an equal amount of water. Child acknowledges that they displace equal amounts of water.	 changes the shape of one of the balls.	*Do the two pieces of clay displace the same amount of water?* Preconserving child will say that the longer piece displaces more water. Conserving child will say that both pieces displace the same amount of water.	10–12

Figure 9.17 Various tests for conservation. This is a sample of experiments used to test for Piaget's different types of conservation. You may want to try these tests on children of various ages.

Children in the earlier concrete operational stage often have significant difficulty with problems of this sort. They can only solve such problems when presented with concrete objects, such as three sticks of different sizes. Formal operational thinking also allows the adolescent to construct a well-reasoned argument based on hypothetical concepts, such as "What if dinosaurs were alive today?" Given the same task, the preoperational child would have difficulty separating fantasy and reality, and the concrete operational child might respond with a limited argument such as, "They can't; they died a long time ago."

Although some researchers have suggested that formal operational thought may never appear in many adults (Datan et al., 1987; Kohlberg and Gilligan, 1971), attaining this level of cognition has important benefits. For the first time in their cognitive developmental history, individuals can perform the abstract reasoning necessary to comprehend algebra and difficult grammar concepts (both of which involve manipulating symbols for symbols). Their ability to think about thinking allows formal operational thinkers to explore their own values and beliefs and compare them to those of their friends, teachers, and parents. And the fact that they can deal with the hypothetical means that they can reason from the real to the possible, which often results in intense *idealism*, thinking about what "should be" or "could be" rather than just "what is."

Along with the many benefits of this style of cognition come several problems. For example, just as two-year-olds hop everywhere when they first learn this new motor skill, newcomers to the formal operational style of thinking often become fascinated with their newly acquired cognitive skills. Have you ever heard parents complaining about their teenager who wants to argue with everything they say? If parents recognized that these debates are basically a form of "cognitive exercise" similar to the two-year-old's hopping, they could relax and maybe even enjoy the interaction.

Adolescent Egocentrism and the Personal Fable

During the formal operational period, adolescents begin to understand that others have unique thoughts and perspectives. However, they often fail to differentiate between what others are thinking and their own thoughts. This adolescent egocentrism helps explain what seems like extreme forms of self-consciousness and concern for physical appearance ("Everyone knows I don't know the answer," "They're noticing how fat I am and this awful haircut"). David Elkind (1981, 1984) believes that the adolescent's strong potential for embarrassment, affinity for mirrors, and preoccupation with grooming result from a characteristic cognitive error. Given the dramatic changes that are occurring both physically and cognitively, adolescents erroneously assume that everyone else is just as aware of their appearance, thoughts, and feelings as they are. They construct an *imaginary audience* whose eyes are all focused on their behaviors. Teenagers report times in high school when they would rather go thirsty than have the whole class watch them get up and leave the room. You can see how this style of thinking could also explain the passion for privacy that most adolescents have. If everyone is watching and evaluating you, then closed doors and time alone provide an important means of escape.

Adolescent egocentrism also leads to a closely related problem: the *personal fable*. The personal fable is the belief that what one is thinking and experiencing is original and special and that one is a unique individual and therefore an exception to the rule. One young student in our class remembered how upset she once was when her mother tried to comfort her over the loss of an important relationship. "I felt like she couldn't possibly know how it felt, no one could. I couldn't believe that anyone had ever suffered like this or that things would ever get better." Several forms of risk-taking, such as engaging in sexual intercourse without contraception, driving dangerously, or experimenting with drugs, also seem to arise from the personal fable (Kegeles, Adler, and Irwin, 1988). The adolescent has a sense of uniqueness, invulnerability, immortality, and other special abilities.

The personal fable and related forms of egocentric thinking tend to decrease in late adolescence, when the individual has made the full transition to the formal operational period—Piaget's final stage of cognitive development.

A Fifth Cognitive Stage?

Although Piaget never described postadolescent thinking in much detail, several neo-Piagetians have suggested that some adults may enter a fifth or later cognitive stage (Arlin, 1984; Commons et al., 1986). These researchers suggest that thinking during the formal operational period is primarily a passive, intellectual exercise whereas thinking in later years is active and employs logic to tackle problems in the real world. Thinking becomes a means to understanding the world, rather than just an end in itself. Information and insights from several sources are synthesized or combined with actual experience and applied to everyday problems in the individual's life or to problems in society. Although it seems intuitively obvious that cognitive changes continue throughout the

During Piaget's fourth stage of cognitive development (formal operational), a strong sense of justice and idealism often motivates young adults to participate in charitable drives and social protests.

Adolescent Egocentrism: The belief that one is the focus of others' thoughts and attention that is common in adolescence.

Although many people believe intelligence declines with age, research suggests that this is largely a myth.

life span and that the thinking of adults differs from that of adolescents, the exact nature of such changes and differences will remain a mystery without further research.

Assessing Piaget's Theory: Criticisms and Contributions

Piaget's account of cognitive development, originally developed in the 1920s and 1930s, continues to influence cognitive psychology today. Yet there are significant criticisms of his work. Let's look briefly at two major areas of concern: underestimation of abilities and underestimation of educational and cultural influences.

1. Underestimation of Abilities

Research has shown that Piaget may have underestimated young children's cognitive development. During the sensorimotor stage, for example, later research with more sophisticated equipment has shown that infants develop object permanence much earlier than Piaget suggested (Baillargeon, 1991; Spelke, 1988).

Research on the possibility of infant imitation of facial expression also raises questions about Piaget's estimates of early infant cognition. In a series of well-known studies, Meltzoff and Moore (1977, 1985, 1989) suggested that newborns can imitate such facial movements as tongue protrusion, mouth opening, and lip pursing. Meltzoff and Moore videotaped the infant's face as an adult model performed the target behavior (see Figure 9.18). The tapes were then scored by a rater who was unaware of the behavior being modeled.

Follow-up studies, however, have not always confirmed Meltzoff and Moore's results. Ethologists, for example, believe that infant responses such as tongue protrusion are simple, biological reactions to the eliciting stimuli provided by the adult model. This type of prewired, innate reaction is much simpler than the cognitive matching required in true imitation. At present, neonatal imitation remains a controversial topic in infant research (Anisfeld, 1991; Poulson et al., 1989). But the controversy is important to our understanding of Piaget's work. If the newborn is truly imitating the adult's facial expression, then Piaget once again underestimated infant intelligence. He believed that this type of imitation does not appear until at least seven or eight months (Piaget, 1951).

Studies of egocentrism in preoperational children have also found that preschool children *do* show an ability to take another's perspective when the testing situation is familiar and the research method simplified (Flavell, 1993; Klemchuk, Bond, and Howell, 1990; Sugarman, 1987). In the familiar surrounding of home, for example, children as young as two or three will (occasionally) show empathy for a younger sibling and will adjust their speech and vocabulary when communicating with another child as opposed to an adult. Similarly, when asked to show another person a picture, a two-year-old will

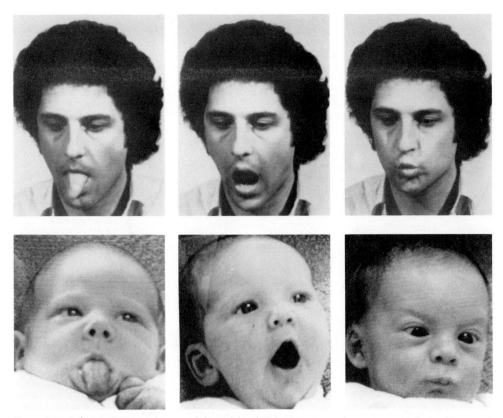

Figure 9.18 Infant imitation. When an adult models a facial expression, even very young infants will respond with similar gestures. Is this true imitation or a simple stimulus-response reflex?

hold the picture vertically so that its face is toward the viewer rather than toward the self (Lempers, Flavell, and Flavell, 1977). Although these examples represent relatively simple cognitive skills and behaviors, they do imply some ability to separate another's perspective from one's own — a quality Piaget thought lacking in the egocentric preoperational child.

2. Underestimation of Educational and Cultural Influences

Piaget's model, like other stage theories, has been criticized for its relative inattention to differences in educational and cultural experiences (Brislin, 1993; Berry et al., 1992; Chance and Fischman, 1987; Cole and Cole, 1989; Flavell, 1985). Formal education and specific cultural experiences can significantly affect cognitive development. Consider the following example of a researcher attempting to test the formal operational skills of a Kpelle farmer in Liberia (Scribner, 1977):

> *Researcher* All Kpelle men are rice farmers. Mr. Smith is not a rice farmer. Is he a Kpelle man?
>
> *Kpelle farmer* I don't know the man. I have not laid eyes on the man myself.

As you can see, the researcher was testing to see if the Kpelle farmer could reason in the traditional "logical" way. But this type of logic reflects specific educational training, and Piaget's theory may have underestimated the logic of those who are not formally educated.

Despite these criticisms, Piaget's theory is widely respected by educators (Cowan, 1978), by psychologists all over the world (Nyiti, 1982), and by parents who have gained invaluable insights into the qualitative differences between the cognitive abilities of children of different ages. Health practitioners also use Piaget's stages in dealing with children as patients (Maddux et al., 1986). Knowing a preoperational child's tendency toward egocentric thinking, for example, can help explain why some children perceive

Critical Thinking

PSYCHOLOGY IN ACTION

DEVELOPING INSIGHT INTO EGOCENTRICITY
Adult versus Childhood Egocentrism

Piaget asserted that preoperational children (ages two to seven) are *egocentric*. That is, they are unable to take the perspective of others because of their limited cognitive development. Although Piaget believed most adults naturally outgrow egocentric thinking, recent research suggests that a tendency toward egocentricity may persist throughout adulthood. It is difficult to outgrow our own egocentricity because we suppress facts that are inconsistent with our conclusions, and we fail to notice when our behavior contradicts our self-image.

The best antidote to egocentricity is self-awareness and critical self-analysis. To develop insight into your own egocentricity, use the following rating scale to first rate the personality traits of someone you find it hard to get along with. Then using the same scale, rate your best friend and then yourself.

1 = never behaves in this way
2 = seldom behaves in this way
3 = occasionally behaves in this way
4 = often behaves in this way
5 = always behaves in this way

	Disliked Person	Best Friend	Self
Is aggressive and irritable with others.	___	___	___
Is helpful and courteous to others.	___	___	___
Offers support and encouragement to others.	___	___	___
Takes advantage of others.	___	___	___
Is hardworking and reliable.	___	___	___
Is sociable and fun to be with.	___	___	___
Dominates conversations.	___	___	___
Values advice from others.	___	___	___
Is interested in trying new things.	___	___	___
Tries to be fair and just with others.	___	___	___

Now check back over the values you assigned in the first and third column. Compare the positive and negative items. Do you think the "disliked person" would agree with your evaluation? Why or why not? Can you see how your own egocentrism could explain the differences in perception?

Now compare the ratings you assigned to yourself and your best friend. If you are like most people, you will notice a strong similarity. An obvious, and somewhat egocentric, explanation for this is that similarity attracts—we like people who are like us. Further critical thinking, however, would explain this similarity as the result of *sociocentricity*—the extension of egocentrism to groups. The individual goes from thinking "I am right!" to "We are right!" When this egocentrism extends to ethnic groups, countries, and religions it is referred to as *ethnocentrism*. The best antidote to egocentrism, sociocentrism, and ethnocentrism is to listen carefully and with an open mind to those with whom we disagree and apply the full force of our critical thinking skills to our own behaviors.

their illness as a punishment for misbehavior (Sheridan, 1975), and how their animistic thinking blocks understanding of the finality of death (Spinetta et al., 1982).

The criticisms of Piaget's theory are generally not considered serious enough to offset his enormous contributions. In addition to stimulating a great deal of research from others, Piaget himself published more than 100 articles and 40 books on child psychology. Some psychologists consider him the most influential psychologist of this century, and perhaps of all time.

Information Processing: A Computer Model of Cognition

Information Processing Model: The process of taking in, remembering, or forgetting, and using information. This approach draws an analogy between the mind and the computer to explain cognitive development.

Piaget's theory continues to be highly influential, but a more contemporary approach to the study of cognitive development is the information processing model (McShane, 1991; Siegler, 1983, 1991). The information processing model compares the workings of the mind to a computer. Developmental psychologists who take this approach study how information is received, encoded, stored, organized, retrieved, and used by people of different ages. While Piagetian theories focus on *qualitative* changes in mental capacities, information processing theories emphasize *quantitative* changes that gradually occur over the life span. Researchers using the information processing model have provided important insights into two major areas of cognition: attention and memory.

Attention

Attention refers to focusing of awareness on a narrowed range of stimuli. Very young infants pay attention to their environment for only short periods of time. Although toddlers can pay attention for longer periods, they are easily distracted. In studies of children watching television, for example, two-year-olds talk more to other people, play more with toys, and look around the room more than four-year-olds (Anderson and Levin, 1976). As they get older, children's attention spans improve and they acquire more conscious control over what they pay attention to.

Memory

After children have attended to information and taken it into their information processing system, they must remember it. Attention determines what information enters the "computer," while memory determines what information is saved.

Like attention, memory skills also improve gradually throughout childhood. Preschoolers can hold only two or three pieces of information in their short-term memories, while most seven-year-olds can hold about seven pieces (Morrison, Holmes, and Haith, 1974). During the school years, children acquire several strategies that improve their storage and retrieval of information. For example, they learn to rehearse or repeat information over and over, to use mnemonics (like "i before e except after c"), and to organize their information in ways that facilitate retrieval. As people grow older, their use of information processing strategies and overall memory continues to improve.

What about older people? Aren't they more forgetful?   As you may recall from Chapter 7, memory can break down for a variety of reasons. Although many people tend to associate aging with senility and forgetfulness, psychologists have criticized earlier studies of memory deficits in the elderly and have concluded that much of memory ability is largely unaffected by the aging process (Crook and Larrabee, 1990; Schaie, 1988; Selkoe, 1992).

Memory deficits in older adults are largely confined to problems in *encoding* (putting information into long-term storage) and *retrieval* (getting information out of storage) (Erber, 1982). If memory is like a filing system, older people just have more filing cabinets and it takes them longer to initially file and later retrieve information. This increase in filing and retrieval time is often misinterpreted as a loss of intelligence. In our fast-paced technological society where computer advances are often measured in comparison to human memory capacity and speed of information processing, the elderly's need for greater time for encoding and retrieval takes on an unreasonably negative connotation. How these misconceptions and other problems associated with *ageism* (prejudice based on age) can be reduced will be discussed in the next chapter.

Review Questions

1. _____ was one of the first scientists to prove that a child's cognitive processes are fundamentally different from an adult's.

2. _____ occurs when existing schemata are used to interpret new information, whereas _____ involves changes and adaptations of the schemata.

3. Infants develop _____ when they realize that objects (or people) continue to exist even when they can no longer be seen.

4. A(n) _____ is a set of rules for transforming or maneuvering knowledge.

5. A preoperational child is often _____ , believing that he or she is the center of the world.

6. During the _____ stage of development, the child understands and applies logical operations to concrete, external objects.

7. List one major accomplishment in cognitive development for each of Piaget's four stages.

8. How does the information processing model explain why older adults sometimes seem to have memory problems?

Answers to Review Questions can be found in Appendix C.

REVIEW OF MAJOR CONCEPTS

STUDYING DEVELOPMENT

1. Developmental psychology is concerned with describing, explaining, predicting, and modifying age-related behaviors across the entire life span. Research performed by developmental psychologists is often directed toward three key questions: nature or nurture, continuity or stages, and stability or change.

2. Researchers in this field use basic scientific methods such as surveys, experiments, and so on. Two of the most widely used methods of data collection are cross-sectional and longitudinal studies. Each method has its own advantages and disadvantages.

3. Cultural psychologists have suggested several guidelines for developmental research. They propose that culture may be the most important determinant of development, human development cannot be studied outside its socio-cultural context, culture is largely invisible to its participants, and each culture's ethnotheories are important determinants of behavior.

PHYSICAL DEVELOPMENT

4. The prenatal period of development consists of three major stages: the germinal period, the embryonic period, and the period of the fetus. The embryonic period is a true critical period in development and the embryo is at particular risk for major birth defects.

5. Physical development is often affected by environmental influences. Poor prenatal nutrition is a leading cause of birth defects, and most drugs (both prescription and over-the-counter) are potentially teratogenic (capable of producing birth defects). Doctors advise pregnant women to avoid all unnecessary drugs, especially nicotine and alcohol. The father's behavior may also contribute to birth defects. Comparisons between the United States and other industrialized nations, shows that American infants are at much greater risk for death and disease.

6. During the prenatal period and the first year of life, the brain and nervous system grow faster than all other parts of the body. Early motor development (crawling, standing, and walking) is largely the result of maturation. Contrary to earlier beliefs, psychologists now know that the sensory and perceptual abilities of newborns are relatively well developed.

7. At puberty, the adolescent first becomes capable of reproduction and experiences a sharp increase in height, weight, and skeletal growth as a result of the pubertal growth spurt.

8. Both men and women experience bodily changes in middle age. Many female changes are related to the hormonal effects of menopause; similar psychological changes in men are called the male climacteric.

9. Although many of the changes associated with physical aging (such as decreases in cardiac output or visual acuity) are the result of primary aging, others are the result of abuse, disuse, and disease—secondary aging. Physical aging may be genetically built-in from the moment of conception (programmed theories) or it may result from the body's inability to repair damage (wear-and-tear theories).

LANGUAGE DEVELOPMENT

10. Language development involves both verbal and nonverbal channels. Through facial expressions, eye contact, and body gestures, infants communicate many things long before their first verbal skills appear.

11. Children go through two stages in their acquisition of language: prelinguistic (crying, cooing, babbling) and linguistic (which includes single utterances, telegraphic speech, and the acquisition of rules of grammar).

12. Nativists believe that language is an inborn capacity and develops primarily from maturation. Noam Chomsky suggests that humans are "prewired" for language and possess a language acquisition device (LAD) that needs only minimal environmental input.

13. Nurturists emphasize the role of the environment and suggest that language development results from rewards and punishments and imitation of models. Although this position does explain why a child learns a specific language, it fails to explain novel speech or the fact that chil-

dren around the world go through predictable stages at relatively the same age.

COGNITIVE DEVELOPMENT

14. Jean Piaget, perhaps more than any other researcher, has demonstrated the unique cognitive processes of children. He believed that children are driven toward knowledge because of their biological need for adaptation to the environment. During adaptation, the child uses schemata (mental patterns or blueprints) to interpret the world. Sometimes existing schemata can be used "as is" and information is assimilated, but on other occasions the situation requires modification of existing schemata, which calls for accommodation.

15. In Piaget's view, cognitive development occurs in an invariant sequence of four stages: sensorimotor (birth to 2 years), preoperational (from 2 to 7 years), concrete operational (from 7 to 11 years), and formal operational (from 11 on).

16. The sensorimotor stage is characterized by the acquisition of object permanence—the realization that objects (or people) continue to exist even when they are out of sight. During the preoperational stage, children are better equipped to use symbols, but their thinking is also egocentric and animistic. The concrete operational stage is characterized by the acquisition of operations and increased logic. During the formal operational stage, the adolescent is able to think abstractly and deal with the hypothetical.

17. Although Piaget has been criticized for underestimating abilities and educational and cultural influences, he remains one of the most respected psychologists in modern times.

18. Psychologists who explain cognitive development in terms of information processing have found this model especially useful in explaining attention and memory ability.

SUGGESTED READINGS

CLARKE-STEWART, A., PERLMUTTER, M., & FRIEDMAN, S. (1992). *Lifelong human development* (2nd ed.). New York: Wiley. A comprehensive, current, and engrossing general textbook that discusses the major developmental changes from conception through death.

DOMAN, G. (1979). *Teach your baby math.* New York: Pocket Books. Glen Doman's personal account of his daily learning program designed to teach math to very young children.

ELKIND, D. (1981). *The hurried child: Growing up too fast too soon.* Reading, MA: Addison–Wesley. In sharp contrast to the positive reports of Glen Doman, David Elkind warns that introducing children to formal education at too young an age may lead to physical, educational, and psychological damage.

GRANT, J. P. (1990). *The state of the world's children.* New York: UNICEF and Oxford University Press. This text provides a detailed analysis of children's illness, health, and death in more than 100 countries.

GREENFIELD, P. M., & COCKING, R. R. (In press). *The development of minority children: Culture in and out of context.* Hillsdale, NJ: Erlbaum. An excellent and up-to-date account of the effects of culture on childhood experiences and general development.

Life Span Development II

OUTLINE

At 17, Richard H. is ambivalent about his age. On some days he feels happy to be so young and just starting life, but at other times he complains that his age limits his access to alcohol, makes him pay too much for car insurance, and allows some adults to treat him with less respect than he believes he deserves. His 20-year-old sister, Kandis H., is also ambivalent about her age. Although she daydreams about all the exciting possibilities ahead of her ("Do I want to be a model, an actress, an obstetrician, or maybe governor?"), she also worries that she hasn't finalized her career plans. One of her strongest fears is that at middle age (which she believes begins around age 30 or 35) she will find herself locked into a career or marriage that she doesn't enjoy and she'll regret not choosing another alternative.

At 43, William B. (stepfather to Richard and Kandis) is concerned about his age. He appreciates the greater wisdom that has come with life experience, but he also worries about signs of aging. "I can't run as far as I did ten years ago," he says. "I also don't enjoy late night parties like I once did, and I wonder if I'll be able to work as long as I had planned."

At 80, Maggie Kuhn is proud of her age—"My wrinkles are a badge of distinction. I earned them" (*New York Times*, 1984). She notes that people spend a large portion of their life worrying about growing old and covering all signs of aging with hair coloring, "line

William B., Kandis H., and Richard H. during a family get together.

preventors," makeup, and so on. But once they reach retirement age and older, people are often pleasantly surprised at the many pleasures of this stage of life. As founder of one of the most active lobbyist groups in America, the Gray Panthers, Maggie Kuhn works long hours and travels all over the world to educate others about the real and imagined problems of growing old.

Of these four individuals, who are you most like? Like Richard or Kandis, are you just beginning your college education and worrying and dreaming about potential careers? Or are you more like William or Maggie Kuhn and perhaps taking this course in hopes of a career change, as part of continuing education, or just for personal enrichment? Although you are undoubtedly different from each of these individuals, you also share some important similarities with those who are in your own age group. The exact nature of these differences and similarities is of prime interest to developmental psychologists. As discussed in Chapter 9, developmental psychology is devoted to the study of age-related changes in behavior and abilities from conception to death. Chapter 9 explored life span changes in physical development, language development, and cognitive development. In this chapter, we continue our study by focusing on moral development, gender role development, social and personality development, and special issues in development.

As you read Chapter 10, keep the following **Survey** questions in mind and answer them in your own words:

• How does morality change over the life span?

• How do we develop our gender roles?

• What are the major influences on social and personality development?

• How do special issues such as attachment, parenting styles, families, and so on affect development?

MORAL DEVELOPMENT

What do you consider moral behavior? Is morality "in the eye of the beholder," and everyone simply argues for his or her own self-interest. Or are there universal truths and principles? Regardless of your answer, the very fact that you are able to think, reason, and eventually respond to this question demonstrates another type of development that is very important to psychology: moral development. How does an individual develop a sense of right and wrong and personal standards for behavior?

• *How does morality change over the life span?*

Some researchers argue that morality is composed of specific traits (such as empathy and sensitivity), and that these traits are a product of evolution and genetic inheritance (e.g., Eisenberg, 1986, 1989). They say humans are "prewired" through evolution to empathically and sensitively respond to distress signals from fellow humans (see Chapter 18). Other theorists argue that morality is learned by direct, personal experiences of being rewarded or punished for moral behavior and by watching others (e.g., Bandura, 1969, 1973, 1989).

Developmental psychologists have traditionally examined morality from a developmental, stage perspective. They study how moral thoughts, feelings, and behaviors change over the life span. In this section, we will look at two major theories of morality, Kohlberg's and Gilligan's.

Theories of Moral Development: Explaining Differences in Morality

The foremost theorist of moral develoment, Lawrence Kohlberg (1964, 1984), based his work on the foundation laid by Jean Piaget (1932). Kohlberg's theory has more recently been criticized and modified by Carol Gilligan.

Kohlberg's Stage Theory

Using the research techniques first developed by Piaget (see Chapter 9), Kohlberg presented subjects with descriptions of moral dilemmas and asked them what they would do in the same situation.

 Try This Yourself

Before we continue, take a moment to read one of Kohlberg's moral dilemma stories and jot down what you would do in the situation. ■

> *In Europe, a woman was near death from a special kind of cancer. There was one drug that the doctors thought might save her. It was a form of radium that a druggist in the same town had recently discovered. The drug was expensive to make, but the druggist was charging ten times what the drug cost him to make. He paid $200 for the radium and charged $2,000 for a small dose of the drug. The sick woman's husband, Heinz, went to everyone he knew to borrow the money, but he could only get together about $1,000, which is half of what it cost. He told the druggist that his wife was dying and asked him to sell it cheaper or let him pay later. But the druggist said, "No, I discovered the drug and I'm going to make money from it." So Heinz got desperate and broke into the man's store to steal the drug for his wife. Was Heinz morally right or wrong in stealing the drug? Why?*
> *Kohlberg (1964), pp. 18–19*

What is the right answer to this problem? Kohlberg was interested *not* in whether subjects judged Heinz as right or wrong but in the reasons they gave for their decision. On the basis of the responses of his original subjects, Kohlberg proposed three broad levels in the evolution of moral reasoning, as shown in Table 10.1. Each level consists of two stages, making six stages in all. (Can you find your own stage of development based on your response to the Heinz dilemma?)

Table 10.1   Kohlberg's Stages of Moral Development

Moral Reasoning	What Is Right	Heinz's Dilemma Responses	
		Pro	Con
Preconventional level			
Stage 1 "Punishment–obedience" orientation	Obedience to rules so as to avoid punishment	If you let your wife die, you will get in trouble. You'll be blamed for not spending the money to save her and there'll be an investigation of you and the druggist for your wife's death.	You shouldn't steal the drug because you'll be caught and sent to jail if you do. If you do get away, your conscience would bother you thinking how the police would catch up with you at any minute.
Stage 2 "Instrumental-exchange" orientation	Obedience to rules so that rewards or favors may be obtained	If you do happen to get caught, you could give the drug back and you wouldn't get much of a sentence. It wouldn't bother you much to serve a little jail term, if you have your wife when you get out.	You may not get much of a jail term if you steal the drug, but your wife will probably die before you get out so it won't do you much good. If your wife dies, you shouldn't blame yourself; it wasn't your fault she has cancer.
Conventional level			
Stage 3 "Good-child" orientation	Seeking and maintaining the approval of others	No one will think you're bad if you steal the drug, but your family will think you're an inhuman husband if you don't. If you let your wife die, you'll never be able to look anybody in the face again.	It isn't just the druggist who will think you're a criminal, everyone else will too. After you steal it, you'll feel bad thinking how you've brought dishonor on your family and yourself, and you won't be able to face anyone again.
Stage 4 "Law-and-order" orientation	Conforming to norms so as to avoid censure or reprimands by authority figures	If you have any sense of honor, you won't let your wife die just because you're afraid to do the only thing that will save her. You'll always feel guilty that you caused her death if you don't do your duty to her.	You're desperate and you may not know you're doing wrong when you steal the drug. But you'll know you did wrong after you're sent to jail. You'll always feel guilty for breaking the law.
Postconventional level			
Stage 5 "Social-contract" orientation	Obedience to democratically accepted laws and contracts	You'd lose other people's respect, not gain it, if you don't steal. If you let your wife die, it would be out of fear, not out of reasoning it out. So you'd just lose self-respect and probably the respect of others too.	You would lose your standing and respect in the community and violate the law. You'd lose respect for yourself if you're carried away by emotion and forget the long-range point of view.
Stage 6 "Universal ethics" orientation	Morality of individual conscience	If you don't steal the drug and let your wife die, you'll always condemn yourself for it afterward. You wouldn't be blamed and you would have lived up to the outside rule of the law, but you wouldn't have lived up to your own standards of conscience.	If you stole the drug, you wouldn't be blamed by other people but you'd condemn yourself because you wouldn't have lived up to your own conscience and standards of honesty.

Sources: Kohlberg (1966, 1969); Rest et al. (1969).

Like Piaget's stages of cognitive development, Kohlberg's stages of moral development are believed to be *universal* and *invariant.* That is, they supposedly exist in all cultures and everyone goes through each of the stages in a predictable fashion. But unlike Piaget's cognitive stages, there are no specific ages associated with particular levels of morality, and both children and adults can be at the same stage. The few age trends that *are* noticed tend to be rather broad:

Preconventional Level: Kohlberg's first level of moral development, characterized by moral judgments based on fear of punishment or desire for pleasure.

• *Birth to adolescence*—preconventional level.   At this level, moral judgment is *self-centered.* Stage 1 individuals are concerned with avoiding punishment. For example, one time as a child, Kandis, the young woman in our introductory vignette, was scolded by her father for misbehaving. When he concluded with "and never let me catch you doing that again," she replied, "I didn't mean to let you catch me this time." After this stage is mastered, the individual enters Stage 2 of the preconventional level. At this stage, moral reasoning is based on obedience to rules with the hope that good deeds will be repaid.

• *Adolescence and young adulthood*—conventional level. During this time, moral reasoning advances from being self-centered to *other-centered*. On entering this level, individuals are at Stage 3, and their primary moral concern is with being nice and gaining approval through obedience to authority—the "good child" morality. As this stage is mastered, a respect for authority and "doing one's duty" become more important and they enter Stage 4—a "law and order" morality.

Conventional Level: Kohlberg's second level of moral development, where moral judgments are based on compliance with the rules and values of society.

• *Adulthood*—postconventional level. Kohlberg believed that most adults remain at either Stage 3 or 4 in their moral development (see Figure 10.1). But for those few adults who do make it to this level, morality is based on *personal standards* or *universal principles* of justice, equality, and respect for human life. During Stage 5, reasoning is based on personal standards and the belief that it is best for society if people obey the law. During Stage 6, reasoning is based on personal standards, even if the standards conflict with the law. In his later writings, Kohlberg suggested that the sixth stage is actually more theoretical than real. But he went on to argue that there might also be a seventh stage that goes beyond moral reasoning and enters the arena of religious faith (Kohlberg, 1981). Kohlberg believed that the moral principles of Martin Luther King, Jr., Mother Teresa, and Mahatma Gandhi are characteristic of a Stage 7 orientation.

Postconventional Level: Kohlberg's highest level of moral development, which occurs when individuals develop personal standards for right and wrong.

Evaluating Kohlberg

Are the people who achieve higher stages on Kohlberg's scale really more moral than others, or do they just "talk a good game"? Although we might assume that moral reasoning would lead to moral *behavior,* there is considerable debate over whether Kohlberg's stages accurately predict an individual's actions. Some studies show a positive correlation between higher stages of reasoning and higher levels of moral behavior (Kohlberg, 1987; Langdale, 1986), but others have found that the pressures of the situation are better predictors of moral behavior (Bandura, 1986; Wynne, 1988).

Mother Theresa, with her selfless dedication to others, is an example of Kohlberg's highest stage of moral development.

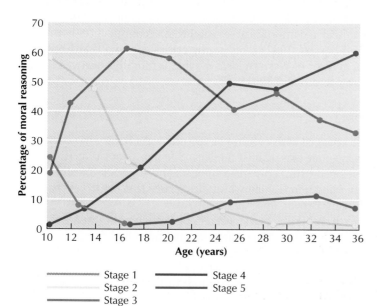

Figure 10.1 Variations in Kohlberg's stages. Note the varying percentages that reach Kohlberg's five stages of moral reasoning.

In a classic study of moral behavior and attitudes, Hugh Hartshorne and Mark May (1928–1930) observed the moral behavior of 11,000 children who were given the chance to lie, cheat, and steal in a variety of circumstances—ranging from homes to schools to churches. Despite the common belief that there are "good kids" and "bad kids," these researchers found almost no consistency across situations. The fact that a child stole in one situation, for example, was not useful in predicting whether he or she would cheat in another. The children were also interviewed about their attitudes toward dishonesty, and there was little correspondence between attitude and actual behavior. Hartshorne and May concluded that a child's morality was *situation-specific,* depending primarily on the circumstances, and not on an individual personality trait. While later analysis of this study suggested that some degree of consistency did exist (Burton, 1963, 1984), it remains clear that for the children in this study morality depended primarily on the situation.

In addition to the questionable relationship between moral reasoning and behavior, Kohlberg's model has also been criticized as politically biased (favoring liberals over conservatives), culturally biased (favoring Western ideals of what is morally "advanced"), and gender biased (favoring males over females). The last two points are the focus of our next section.

Gender and Cultural Diversity

INSIGHTS INTO MORALITY FROM CROSS-CULTURAL STUDIES AND GILLIGAN'S RESEARCH

As you may remember from Chapter 9, two of the basic questions that guide developmental research are "nature or nurture?" and "continuity or stages?" In the case of moral development, cross-cultural research confirms that children in different cultures do conform to Kohlberg's model and generally progress sequentially from his first stage, the preconventional, to his second, the conventional (Lei and Cheng, 1989; Snarey, 1985, 1987). Thus the *nature* and *stage* sides of these two basic questions are somewhat supported by cross-cultural studies.

At the same time, there are cultural *differences* that suggest *nurture,* or the culture, also determines morality. For example, Kohlberg's third stage, the *postconventional,* is more frequently found in the educated middle class of North America and Europe. This so-called highest level of morality seems to be limited to cultures that value individualism as opposed to community and interpersonal relationships. In Papua-New Guinea, India, China, and Israeli kibbutzim, rather than forcing a choice between the rights of the individual and the rights of society (as the top levels of Kohlberg's model require), the tendency is to seek a compromise solution that accommodates both interests (Dien, 1982; Miller and Bersoff, 1992). This is why critics contend that Kohlberg's theory is culturally biased in favor of Western ideas of what is morally advanced (Hogan and Schroeder, 1981; Snarey and Keljo, 1991).

Gilligan's Gender Theory

In addition to having been charged with cultural bias, Kohlberg's theory has been criticized by Carol Gilligan for gender bias against females. She points out that Kohlberg's stages were originally developed using only male subjects and suggests that this initial sampling bias explains why women in Kohlberg's studies tended to score lower than men (Gilligan, 1977, 1990; Gilligan, Brown, and Rogers, 1990).

According to Gilligan, Kohlberg's "higher" stages of development (Stages 5, 6, and 7) are based on traditional male values of independence and individual rights, so women naturally score lower because they have been socialized toward traditional female values of interdependence and responsibility for others (Stages 3 and 4). Gilligan thinks these values reflect two basic approaches to moral reasoning. In the justice perspective, the

Justice Perspective: Gilligan's term for an approach to moral reasoning that emphasizes individual rights and views people as differentiated and standing alone.

According to Gilligan, a woman's concern with family responsibilities makes her score "lower" on Kohlberg's levels of moral development.

person is seen as standing alone, and the focus is on the rights of the individual. In the care perspective, on the other hand, emphasis is on concern for others, and the person is viewed in terms of his or her relationship with others. Gilligan believes Kohlberg emphasized the justice perspective and underplayed the care perspective in the moral development of both females and males. For example, in the case of Heinz, a person who argues that Heinz should steal the drug because saving a life is more important than obeying laws is demonstrating a justice orientation according to Gilligan. On the other hand, arguing that Heinz should steal the drug because he has an obligation to help someone he loves reflects a care orientation. While Gilligan did find that women were much more likely to adopt the care perspective, she emphasized that female moral development was not lower than that of males. She believes that men and women have "separate-but-equal" paths of development.

At risk of leaving you with the mistaken idea that Gilligan is suggesting all women have only one standard for moral decision making, we should hasten to point out that Gilligan did find several differences among her subjects and that they fell into three separate levels (see Table 10.2). Using Kohlberg's three broad levels of morality as a point of comparison, she found that preconventional women tend to make decisions and judgments that reflect a self-interested and self-protective type of morality. But at the conventional stage women tend to give up their concern for themselves and focus primarily on the importance of their relationships and their responsibilities for others. At the highest, postconventional level, women tend to retain their concern for others and feelings of responsibility while also including themselves as worthy of their own care and protection.

Gilligan's criticism of Kohlberg has also produced criticism of her own work. Extensive follow-up research, using traditional Kohlbergian measures of moral development, has generally not supported Gilligan's claim of bias against females (Donenberg and Hoffman, 1988; Thoma, 1986; Walker, 1984, 1991). While studies have found that adult females may be more likely to use a care orientation in resolving moral issues, the gender differences are not absolute. Both sexes typically use both the care and justice orientation to some degree (Gilligan and Attanucci, 1988; Lyons, 1990). ■

Care Perspective: An approach to moral reasoning proposed by Gilligan that emphasizes interpersonal responsibility and views people in terms of their interconnectedness with others.

Table 10.2   Kohlberg's versus Gilligan's Theory of Moral Development

Kohlberg (male subjects)		Gilligan (female subjects)	
Level	Description	Level	Description
Preconventional	Morality focused on the consequences of the act —whether one is punished or whether it "feels good."	Orientation to individual survival	Early morality is practical and focused on individual survival. In later stages the focus is on responsibility and concern for others.
Conventional	Judgments of morality based on whether behavior is in compliance with the rules of society and on the need to "do one's duty."	Orientation to others	Morality focused on needs of others and responsibilities to relationships.
Postconventional	Standards for right and wrong based on the individual's conscience and personally derived principles and values.	Orientation to interdependence	During this stage the woman comes to see that "goodness" includes the responsibility to care for herself, which requires honest self-appraisal and self-assertion. Self-survival returns as a major concern.

Sources: Gilligan (1977, 1982); Kohlberg (1969).

Review Questions

1. Describe Kohlberg's three levels of moral development.
2. How is Kohlberg's theory culturally biased?
3. Why does Gilligan propose that Kohlberg's theory is gender biased?

Answers to Review Questions can be found in Appendix C.

GENDER ROLE DEVELOPMENT

• *How do we develop our gender roles?*

Imagine for a moment that your best friend just had a new baby. What would be your first question? Would you ask about the health of the mother or baby? Or would you ask "Is it a boy or a girl?" Research shows that 80 percent of the time, the first question is about the baby's sex (Intons-Peterson and Reddell, 1984). Why is the baby's sex so important?

Sex: The biological components of maleness and femaleness.

Gender: The social components of being male or female.

Gender Identity: How one psychologically perceives oneself as either male or female.

Gender Role: The societal expectations for proper female and male behavior.

In Western society, as well as in most other cultures around the world, gender is a very important part of an individual's life. What do we mean by *gender?* Generally, the term sex refers to the biological components of being male or female, while the term gender refers to the social components of being male or female. In addition, gender identity refers to the individual's personal sense of being male or female, and gender role is a set of cultural expectations that prescribes how males and females should think, act, and feel. Gender identity is generally acquired by the age of three—a three-year-old girl knows that she is a female and a three-year-old boy knows that he is a male. Gender role development, however, begins at birth when we are wrapped in either a pink or blue blanket and continues to grow and change throughout our life.

In this section we will explore four major theories of gender role development. The problem of gender role stereotypes is discussed in Chapter 11.

Psychoanalytic Theories: Is Anatomy Destiny?

As you will see in Chapter 14, gender is a central theme in Sigmund Freud's theories of personality development. He believed that between the ages of three and five children feel sexually attracted to their other-sex parent. They also feel guilt and anxiety over this attraction which they generally resolve by identifying with the same-sex parent around the ages of five or six (Freud, 1905, 1934).

Freud believed that the child's gender identification with the other-sex parent was crucial to long-term mental health and that human behavior is intricately linked to the reproductive processes. Erik Erikson (1968) extended Freud's theories to the area of psychological differences between men and women. He suggested that because of their differing genital structures, males are more intrusive and aggressive and females are more inclusive and passive. This has become known as the "anatomy is destiny" belief.

Both Freud and Erikson have been criticized, however, for their overemphasis on biology. Furthermore, today most psychologists do not believe that gender role development is based on identification, at least in terms of Freud's emphasis on childhood sexual attraction.

Social-Learning Theory: The Power of Rewards, Punishment, and Imitation

In contrast to the psychoanalytic theorists who emphasize inferred mental processes (such as guilt or anxiety), social-learning theorists emphasize the power of the immediate situation and observable behaviors. Social-learning theorists believe that girls learn how to be "feminine" and boys learn how to be "masculine" in two major ways: (1) They receive rewards or punishments for specific gender role behaviors, and (2) they watch and imitate the behavior of others (Bandura, 1989; Jacklin, 1989; Maccoby and Jacklin, 1974; Tavris, 1992).

Social-learning theorists agree with the psychoanalytic idea of imitation of the same-sex parent, but not because a child feels guilty or anxious over a supposed attraction to the other-sex parent. Instead, rewards and punishments guide behavior. A boy who puts on his father's tie or baseball cap wins big, indulgent smiles from his parents. But what do you suppose happens when he puts on his mother's nightgown or lipstick?

Critics of the social-learning model argue that gender development is not acquired as passively as the theory proposes. According to our next theory, children actively observe, interpret, and judge the world around them. And through this process, they develop their own unique explanations and adaptations to gender.

Cognitive-Developmental Theory: The Power of Thoughts

In this model, a child's own thought processes are primarily responsible for gender role development. Lawrence Kohlberg (1966) believes children learn about gender roles in the same way they learn about other concepts, such as morality. He suggests children identify with and imitate same-sex parents, and others of their same gender, because they recognize that these individuals belong to the same category they do (male or female).

According to Kohlberg, children's understanding of gender advances in concert with their general cognitive development. They first develop a concept of what sex category they belong to (gender identity) and only later come to realize that their gender and that of others does not change with age, dress, or behavior (gender constancy).

Would you give your son a baby doll as a toy? What might be some advantages if young boys were trained in nurturance and child care rather than aggression and competition? Are there disadvantages?

Although a three-year-old child can easily tell you, "I am a boy" or "I am a girl," it isn't until they are five or six that they understand they will always be male or female and that their sex will not change if they wear clothing of the opposite sex (Wehren and De Lisi, 1983). When three-year-old children label the gender of others, they appear to rely on external appearances such as hairstyles and clothing rather than on genital anatomy. For example, after watching a neighbor bathe her newborn, one preschool girl couldn't answer whether the child was male or female. "I don't know," she replied, "it's so hard to tell at that age, especially when it's not wearing clothes" (Stone and Church, 1973).

When their concept of gender constancy is firmly established, Kohlberg says children are then motivated to become "proper" boys or girls. They identify appropriate female or male activities and imitate this behavior. The external world then rewards them for their "choice."

Critics of the cognitive-developmental approach point out that according to this model children should not begin to show a preference for masculine or feminine behaviors until they have a well-developed sense of gender identity and gender constancy. Although some studies do support this contention (e.g., Ruble et al., 1981), others have found differences in social behavior and preferences in sex-appropriate toys within the first two years of life (Fagot, 1992; Weinraub et al., 1984). This would seem to indicate an earlier sense of gender identity than the cognitive-developmental theory would allow.

Does this mean that social-learning theory is a better explanation for gender role development?   Many researchers now believe the acquisition of gender roles is best explained by a combination of the social-learning and cognitive-developmental perspectives. This is the *gender-schema theory* (Bem, 1981, 1985; Jacklin, 1989; Murphy and Carter, 1991).

Gender-Schema Theory: An Integration of Two Major Theories

According to this theory, children use gender as a *schema* to organize and guide their view of the world. (Recall from Chapter 9's discussion of Piaget, a schema is a cognitive structure, a network of associations, that guides perception.) Gender-schema theory agrees that children acquire gender-specific behaviors through social learning, and it also stresses that children's own thought processes encourage gender development. It differs from the cognitive-developmental approach because it suggests that gender role behaviors occur much earlier than Kohlberg suggested. Accordingly, little Tommy plays with fire trucks and building blocks because he has been rewarded with smiles in the past and because he has seen more boys than girls playing with these same toys. However, he also chooses these toys because he realizes he is a boy, and boys should prefer fire trucks over dishes and dolls.

At present, the gender-schema theory is the dominant explanation for gender role development (Jacklin, 1989). A major advantage of this model is that it combines both the social-learning and cognitive-developmental approaches.

 Try This Yourself

Having concluded our brief introduction to the four major theories of gender role development, we encourage you to apply what you have learned. How did you develop your personal gender role behavior? What are your thoughts and feelings about gender roles in the United States today?

1. Which theory seems most applicable to your own life? If you spent some of your childhood with a single parent, did this affect your identification with the same-sex parent, or your imitation of "appropriate" gender roles?

2. Would you be willing to give your daughter a fire truck to encourage her toward nontraditional careers? How about giving your son a doll to encourage nurturance and fatherhood? Why is it easier to encourage masculine traits in females than vice versa?

3. What are the best and worst three things about being the gender you are? What are the best and worst three things about the other gender role?

4. Given that gender roles are primarily *learned* rather than biological, how could you maximize the positive aspects of gender roles and minimize the negatives? ■

Review Questions

1. What is the difference between *sex* and *gender?*

2. _____ refers to how one psychologically perceives oneself as being male or female, whereas _____ refers to the societal expectations for female and male behavior.

3. Psychoanalytic theories explain gender role development as a result of _____ .

4. Social-learning theory suggests gender role develops from _____ .

5. Cognitive-developmental theory explains gender role as a product of _____ .

6. Gender-schema theory combines which two major theories?

Answers to Review Questions can be found in Appendix C.

SOCIAL AND PERSONALITY DEVELOPMENT

What were you like as an infant? Do your parents say you were an "easy" or "difficult" baby? Are these early differences in personality related to later adult traits? In this section we explore two major explanations of social and personality development: Thomas and Chess's *temperament* theory and Erikson's *psychosocial* theory.

- *What are the major influences on social and personality development?*

Thomas and Chess's Temperament Theory: A Biological Look at Personality Development

From the moment you were born, you differed from other infants in characteristic ways. Some infants lie quietly and seem oblivious to loud noises, while others tend to kick and scream and respond immediately to every sound. Some babies respond warmly to people, while others fuss, fret, and withdraw. Each of these behavioral styles represents what developmental psychologists call temperament, the basic, natural disposition of an individual.

As you might imagine, there is considerable controversy over what the key dimensions of temperament are. One of the earliest and most influential theories came from the work of psychiatrists Stella Thomas and Alexander Chess (Thomas and Chess, 1977, 1987, 1991). Thomas and Chess found that approximately 65 percent of the babies they observed could be reliably separated into three categories:

Temperament: A basic, inborn dispositional quality that appears shortly after birth and characterizes an individual's style of approaching people and situations.

1. *Easy children* who were happy most of the time, were relaxed and agreeable, and adjusted easily to new situations (approximately 40 percent).

2. *Difficult children* who were moody, easily frustrated, tense, and overreactive to most situations (approximately 10 percent).

3. *Slow-to-warm-up children* who showed mild responses, were somewhat shy and withdrawn, and needed time to adjust to new experiences or people (approximately 15 percent).

Follow-up studies of these infants found that certain aspects of these basic temperamental styles tended to be consistent and enduring throughout early childhood and even adulthood (Campos et al., 1989; Stifter and Fox, 1990). For example, as you will see in Chapter 14, Jerome Kagan (1989, 1992) has shown that the trait termed *inhibition,* or *shyness,* seems to be present at birth and is relatively stable throughout life.

That is not to say every shy, cautious infant ends up a shy adult. Many events take place between infancy and adulthood that shape and direct an individual's development. One of the most influential factors is the *goodness of fit* between the child's nature and the social and environmental setting (Nitz and Lerner, 1991; Rothbart, 1992; Thomas and Chess, 1977). Imagine what would happen if you were a slow-to-warm-up baby and you were born to parents who were extremely social and emotionally expressive. Can you see how your parents might feel frustrated and rejected by your natural tendencies to withdraw from unfamiliar people or situations?

Erikson's Psychosocial Theory: The Eight Stages of Life

Think back to the material you read earlier in this chapter about Freud's theories of gender identification and how his follower, Erik Erikson, extended Freud's theories to

Table 10.3   Erikson's Eight Stages

Stage and Approximate Age	Psychosocial Crisis	Description
Infancy (0–1)	Trust versus mistrust	Infants learn to trust that their needs will be met by the world, especially by the mother; if not, mistrust develops.
Early Childhood (1–3)	Autonomy versus shame and doubt	Children learn to exercise will, to make choices, to control themselves; if not, they become uncertain and doubt that they can do things by themselves.
Play Age (3–6)	Initiative versus guilt	Children learn to initiate activities and enjoy their accomplishments, acquiring direction and purpose; if they are not allowed initiative, they feel guilty for their attempts at independence.
School Age (6–12)	Industry versus inferiority	Children develop a sense of industry and curiosity and are eager to learn; if not, they feel inferior and lose interest in the tasks before them.
Adolescence (12–20)	Identity versus role confusion	Adolescents come to see themselves as unique and integrated persons with an ideology; if not, they become confused about what they want out of life.
Young Adulthood (20–30)	Intimacy versus isolation	Young people become able to commit themselves to another person; if not, they develop a sense of isolation and feel they have no one in the world but themselves.
Adulthood (30–65)	Generativity versus stagnation	Adults are willing to have and care for children, to devote themselves to their work and the common good; if not, they become self-centered and inactive.
Mature (65+)	Ego integrity versus despair	Older people enter a period of reflection, becoming assured that their lives have been meaningful, and they grow ready to face death with acceptance and dignity; if not, they despair for their unaccomplished goals, failures, and ill-spent lives.

Sources: Adapted from Clarke-Stewart, A.; Friedman, S.; and Koch, J., 1985. *Child development: A topical approach.* Copyright © 1985 by John Wiley & Sons, Inc. Reprinted by permission of John Wiley & Sons, Inc.

Erikson's sixth stage—"intimacy versus isolation."

Erikson's first stage—"trust versus mistrust."

Erikson's second stage—"autonomy versus shame and doubt."

Erikson's final stage—"ego integrity versus despair."

encompass psychological differences between men and women. Erikson also used Freud's notion of inborn biological forces as the basis for his theory of personality. Erikson, like Freud, believed that human development unfolds in a series of stages. But unlike Freud, Erikson continued his stage theory beyond adolescence all the way to mature adulthood (65 and older). See Table 10.3. Erikson also believed that Freud underestimated the power of social and cultural influences on human behavior. For this reason Erikson called his theory psychosocial stages of development to contrast it with Freud's *psychosexual stages* (see Chapter 14).

Erikson's First Stage

Erikson's first stage, trust versus mistrust, begins at birth and lasts approximately one year. During this period of development, the infant is almost completely dependent on the external world for basic survival and satisfaction of needs. When and how these needs are met determines whether the infant decides the world is a good and satisfying place to live in or a source of pain, frustration, and uncertainty. If caregivers respond with warm affection and reasonable regularity, the infant will develop a feeling of trust toward the

Psychosocial Stages of Development: Erikson's theory that individuals undergo a series of eight developmental stages, and that adult personality reflects how the distinct challenges or crises at each stage are resolved.

Trust versus Mistrust: The first of Erikson's eight stages of psychosocial development (from birth to 12–18 months), in which the infant must determine whether the world and the people in it can be trusted.

world. But it the infant receives erratic care from an impatient, hostile, anxious, or tense adult, he or she may develop a lifetime sense of mistrust.

Stages 2 to 4

Autonomy versus Shame and Doubt: Erikson's second psychosocial stage (from 12 months to three years), in which the child's crisis or challenge is to develop independence and self-assertion.

The second of Erikson's stages, autonomy versus shame and doubt, covers the years from one to three. The infant moves away from babyhood and approaches childhood by developing a sense of self-awareness and a need for independence. In this search for autonomy, the child begins to gain control over bowels and bladder and show strong preferences for certain clothes, foods, and bedtime rituals. The toddler begins to insist on trying to dress himself or herself, to pick out clothes to wear, to push the stroller rather than ride in it, and to refuse parental offers to help or parental commands and requests. If the parents handle these beginning attempts at independence with patience and good-humored encouragement, the toddler will develop a sense of autonomy. Conversely, if the child encounters ridicule, impatience, or strong parental insistence on control, feelings of shame and doubt develop.

Initiative versus Guilt: The third stage in Erikson's psychosocial theory of development (ages three to six), in which the child must overcome feelings of guilt and doubt and develop feelings of power and initiative.

During the third stage, initiative versus guilt (ages three to five), the major conflict is between a child's desire to initiate activities and the guilt that comes from unwanted or unexpected consequences. Erikson believed that during this stage children begin to incorporate criticism and punishment into their self-images, learning to experience not only shame but also guilt. According to Erikson, children need to discover various activities and outlets for their frustrations that also provide opportunities for growth and accomplishment. If loving adults provide an environment that encourages the ever-increasing need for independence and provide opportunities for interaction with other children, the child will predominantly develop feelings of power and initiative rather than guilt and doubt.

Industry versus Inferiority: Erikson's fourth psychosocial stage of development (ages 6 to 11), in which the child faces the challenge of mastering the skills needed to succeed in his or her culture.

During the fourth stage, industry versus inferiority (six years through puberty), the child is primarily involved in an elaborate development of intellectual and physical skills. This development naturally includes lots of competition and skill comparisons. How the child's successes and failures are handled by the external world will determine whether she or he develops feelings of competency and industriousness or feelings of insecurity and inferiority.

Stages 5 and 6

Identity versus Role Confusion: Erikson's fifth stage of psychosocial development; the adolescent may become confident and purposeful through discovery of an identity, or confused and ill-defined.

Identity Crisis: According to Erikson, a period of inner conflict during which an individual examines his or her life and values and makes decisions about life roles.

Erikson's fifth stage is the period of identity versus role confusion. Erikson believes each individual's personal identity develops from a period of serious questioning and intense soul searching. During this identity crisis, adolescents attempt to discover who they are, what their skills are, and what kinds of roles they are best suited to play for the rest of their lives. The "Who am I?" question that characterizes this stage is most easily resolved by the selection of a career, but adolescents must also discover their own personal philosophy and individual values during this time in order to firmly establish a sense of who they are. While searching for their own values, most adolescents begin to emotionally separate and withdraw from their parents. Erikson believes this is a natural and desirable reaction. If adolescents are to function as adults, they must learn to make their own decisions based on their individual wants, needs, and aspirations. Failure to resolve the identity crisis can lead to a lack of a stable identity, delinquency, or difficulty in maintaining close personal relationships in later life (Kahn et al., 1985).

Intimacy versus Isolation: Erikson's sixth stage of psychosocial development; the young adult must develop a capacity for close interpersonal bonds or face isolation and loneliness.

Once a firm sense of identity is established, Erikson believes the individual (now in young adulthood) is ready to meet the challenges of intimacy versus isolation, Stage 6 of development. Establishing close interpersonal bonds is the major task of this stage. If bonds are made, a basic feeling of intimacy with others will result. If not, the individual may avoid interpersonal commitments and experience feelings of isolation. Erikson has commented that the current trend toward casual sex may lead to feelings of intense loneliness because it lacks mutuality—real intimacy. According to Erikson, "Real intimacy includes the capacity to commit yourself to relationships that may demand sacrifice and compromise. The basic strength of young adulthood is love—a mutual, mature devotion" (cited in Hall, 1983, p. 25).

Erikson's Last Two Stages

In the seventh stage, generativity versus stagnation, which characterizes middle adulthood, the individual expands feelings of love and concern beyond the immediate family group to include all of society. Generativity involves concern about the welfare of the next generation, and individuals who are successful at this stage work to make the world a better place to live. If this expansion and effort does not occur, an individual stagnates, becoming concerned with only material possessions and personal well-being.

In the final years of life, adults enter the period of ego integrity versus despair, Stage 8. The central developmental task of this stage is maintaining a sense of who you are and what you stand for (ego integrity) in the face of physical deterioration and impending death. During this stage, those who have been successful in resolving their earlier psychosocial crises will tend to look back upon their lives with feelings of accomplishment and satisfaction. Those who resolved their earlier crises in a negative way or who lived fruitless, self-centered lives may deeply regret lost opportunities. They may also become despondent since they realize it is too late to start over.

Evaluating Erikson's Theory

Do most researchers agree with Erikson's theory? Can I count on these ideas as predictive of my own future? Like most psychoanalytically based theories, Erikson's is subjective, coming from his own experiences, the recollections of his patients, and classic literature (Berger, 1988). This subjectivity, along with the vague terminology, makes objective evaluation difficult. The area that has received the most research attention—and support—is development of identity in adolescence (Waterman, 1982). In one study of psychological adjustment, for example, male and female adolescents who had established a clear identity also possessed a sense of trust and industry and good self-concepts, whereas adolescents who had not yet established firm identities showed greater maladjustment (La Voie, 1976). A study by Tesch and Gennelo (1985) also tentatively supports Erikson's stage of intimacy versus isolation.

While Erikson's theory has received some support, it has also been the subject of criticism. Like Kohlberg's stages of moral development, Erikson's theory has been criticized for being male biased and culturally biased. For example, it has been found that women tend to develop identity and intimacy simultaneously, rather than in the two stages suggested by Erikson (Marcia, 1980). And Carol Gilligan and her colleagues (1982, 1990) have found that a woman's individual identity is based more on interconnected relationships with others, unlike the male pattern in which identity is achieved through separation from others.

As a critical thinker, stop for a moment and think about what the cultural criticisms of Erikson's theory might be. Do you recall from Chapter 1 the distinction that was made between collectivist and individualistic cultures? In collectivist cultures, children are trained from infancy to cooperate, share, and subordinate their personal needs for the greater needs of the larger social group (Berry et al., 1992; Brislin, 1993). Yet, according to Erikson children "naturally" compete during the stage of industry versus inferiority, move away from their families to establish identity, and only during middle adulthood (the stage of generativity versus stagnation) are people expected to expand their love and concern beyond the immediate family to include other social groups. Can you see how Erikson's theory is most appropriate within an individualistic framework?

Despite the gender bias and individualistic cultural bias, Erikson's stages greatly contributed to the study of North American and European psychosocial development. Moreover, Erikson was among the first theorists to suggest that development continues past adolescence and his theory was an important stimulant to further research.

 Try This Yourself

Before we go on to the next section, it will help you master Erikson's theory if you apply it to your own personality. How would you answer the following questions?

1. What stage are you now in? Does the description of that stage seem valid to you?

Generativity versus Stagnation: The seventh stage in Erikson's theory of psychosocial development. To avoid stagnation, the adult must "generate" or give something back to the world beyond concern and care for the immediate family.

Ego Integrity versus Despair: During this eighth and final stage of psychosocial development, adults review their accomplishments and feel either satisfaction or regret.

2. How have you resolved the crises you have already gone through? Is your adult personality affected by a negative resolution at one of the earlier stages?

3. If you found it difficult to identify your current stage or that of your parents, is it because you are a woman? Or have you been raised in a collectivist culture? What do you think the comparable stages might be for women and for people in a collectivist culture? ■

Myths of Development

There are numerous beliefs about age-related crises that have not been supported by research. For example, the belief that adolescence is a period of extreme turmoil and rebellion is largely a myth. Movies and media reports of teenage drug use, runaways, prostitution, and pregnancy may grossly exaggerate the problems of adolescents. Until recently, most psychologists also characterized adolescence as a time of storm and stress, during which young people experience strong emotional turbulence and psychological strain. Research within the last 20 years, however, has found that adolescence is just one of many life transitions and no stormier than any other (Petersen, 1988; Powers, Hauser, and Kilner, 1989). And, contrary to Erikson's predicted need for psychological separation from parents in order to establish identity, most teenagers of both sexes remain close to and admiring of their parents (Apter, 1990; Offer and Sabshin, 1984).

The idea of a midlife crisis achieved a great deal of public attention largely as the result of Gail Sheehy's book *Passages* (1976). In this national best-seller, Sheehy drew upon the theories of Levinson (1977, 1990) and psychiatrist Roger Gould (1975), as well as her own interviews, and reported a "predictable crisis" at about age 35 for women and 40 for men. Although middle age *is* typically a time of reevaluation of one's values and lifetime goals, this phenomenally successful book has led many people to automatically expect a midlife *crisis* with drastic changes in personality and behavior. Other research has suggested that a severe reaction or crisis may actually be quite rare and not typical of what most people experience during middle age (McCrae and Costa, 1990; Schlossberg, 1987).

A third possible misconception is that when the last child leaves home, parents experience the empty nest syndrome—a painful separation and time of depression for the mother, the father, or both parents. Like the midlife crisis, however, research suggests that the empty nest syndrome may be an exaggeration of the pain experienced by a few individuals and a downplaying of the more common positive reactions (Rubin, 1992; Whyte, 1992). For example, one major benefit of the empty nest is an increase in marital satisfaction (see Figure 10.2). Furthermore, parent–child relationships do continue once the child leaves home. As one mother said, "The empty nest is surrounded by telephone wires" (Troll et al., 1979).

If these concepts are so questionable, what accounts for their continued popularity? Joseph Adelson (1979) believes one reason they persist is that research tends to focus on atypical factions of the population—addicts, delinquents, and so on—and people generalize from these minorities to the group as a whole. In addition, we tend to "see" and remember examples of behavior that fulfill our expectations. Our beliefs may also act as subtle encouragement for the expected behavior. As 17-year-old Richard (the young man in our introductory incident) puts it:

> *Most of my friends never tell their parents the truth about where they're going or what they're doing because they over-react. We're really pretty good. Parents would probably be bored by what we actually do on the weekends, but they worry all the time about drugs and pregnancies and stuff. They think we'll lie to them and we do, but not for the reasons they expect.*

One additional possibility for the prevalence of these myths, especially that of the adolescent rebellion, lies in the acceptance of the related myth of linear development. A great deal of developmental change is *cumulative*—the baby grows increasingly taller

---

Storm and Stress: The idea that emotional turmoil and rebellion are characteristic of all adolescents.

Midlife Crisis: A time of psychological and emotional turmoil that supposedly occurs around the age of 35 for women and 40 for men.

Empty Nest Syndrome: A painful separation and depression that parents supposedly feel when their last child leaves home.

Linear Development: The idea that development progresses in a fairly straight line, at a steady rate, and that each new development is built on the previous stages or abilities.

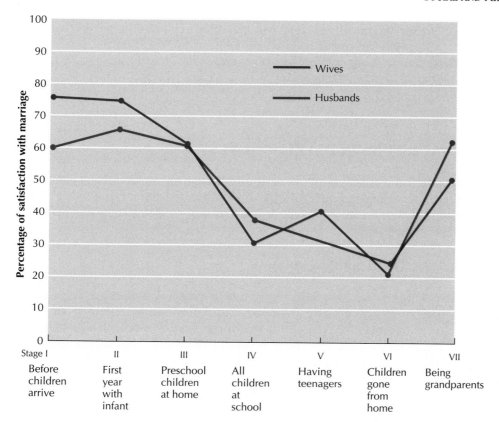

Figure 10.2 Life span marital satisfaction. Contrary to the popular belief that children make a marriage happy or that parents experience a depressing "empty nest" when children leave, this graph shows that reported marital satisfaction is higher before children are born and after they leave the home.

and larger, vocabulary increases, intelligence improves, and so on. We have little experience in dealing with plateaus, let alone reversals. Some problems experienced during adolescence arise because the teenager "flips" back and forth between adolescence and adulthood. As William (our middle-aged individual) notes in his teenagers, "Just when I get used to them being and acting like adults, they do a 180 on me and act like kids again. Won't they ever grow up?"

Although "growing up" may include some stabilizing of the personality, adults should remember that adult life is also not a simple plateau that continues to death. People grow and change and "flip" (the so-called midlife crisis?) many times in their lives.

Review Questions

1. An infant's inborn, dispositional qualities are known as _____ .
2. Briefly describe Thomas and Chess's temperament theory.
3. Erikson suggests that problems in adulthood are sometimes related to unsuccessful resolution of one of his eight stages. For each of the following individuals, identify the most likely "problem" stage:
   a. Marcos has trouble keeping friends and jobs because he continually asks for guarantees and reassurance of his worth. _____
   b. Ann has attended several colleges without picking a major, taken several vocational training programs, and has had numerous jobs over the last 10 years. _____
   c. Teresa is reluctant to apply for a promotion even though her co-workers have encouraged her to do so. She worries that she will be taking jobs from others and questions her worth. _____

d.   George continually obsesses over the value of his life. He regrets that he never married or had children and feels very lonely. _____
4.   Name four common myths of development.

Answers to Review Questions can be found in Appendix C.

SPECIAL ISSUES IN DEVELOPMENT

• *How do special issues such as attachment, parenting styles, families, and soon affect development?*

In addition to moral development, gender role development, and social and personality development, developmental psychologists are also interested in several special issues in development. In this section, we will explore four major topics: attachment, parenting styles, families, and work.

Attachment: The Beginnings of Love

Attachment: An active, intense, emotional relationship between two people that endures over time.

The infant arrives in the world with a multitude of behaviors that encourage a strong bond of attachment with primary caregivers. Attachment can be defined as an active, intense, enduring emotional relationship that is specific to two people. Although most research has focused on the attachment between mother and child, fathers, grandparents, and other caretakers may also form bonds with the infant.

In studying attachment behavior, researchers are often divided along the lines of the now familiar nature versus nurture debate. Those who advocate the innate or biological position cite John Bowlby's work (1969, 1989). He proposed that newborn infants are biologically equipped with verbal and nonverbal behaviors (such as crying, clinging, smiling) and with "following" behaviors (such as crawling and walking after the caregiver) that serve to elicit certain instinctive nurturing responses from the caregiver. The biological argument for attachment is also supported by Konrad Lorenz's (1937) studies of imprinting. Lorenz's studies demonstrated how baby geese attach to, and then follow, the first moving object they see during certain critical periods in their development.

Imprinting: The innate tendency of birds and some animals to follow and form attachment to the first moving object they see.

Further evidence for a biological basis to attachment is research suggesting that human mothers and their babies may form bonds on the basis of smell. By the third day of life a newborn infant will make special responses to pieces of gauze that have been worn against the neck and breasts of their mothers. Similarly, mothers can be blindfolded and still distinguish the scent of their baby's tee-shirt from those of other infants (McCarthy, 1986). However, like most arguments for either nature or nurture, attachment studies are complicated by the interaction of biology and environment. Since the mothers and infants were not isolated from each other immediately following birth (for

These ducklings are following scientist Konrad Lorenz because they instinctually form a strong attachment to the first moving object they see. Usually it is the mother, but in this case it was Lorenz.

obvious reasons), the results could certainly reflect that the mothers and infants *learned* to recognize their scents through previous interactions.

Surrogate Mother Research

One of the earliest experiments that attempted to distinguish the effects of nature from nurture in attachment is the classic research with baby rhesus monkeys conducted by Harry Harlow and Robert Zimmerman (1959). These researchers tried to limit the number of variables that might affect attachment by creating two types of wire-framed *surrogate* (substitute) "mother" monkeys: one covered by soft terrycloth and one left uncovered. The infant monkeys were fed by either the cloth or wire mother or had access to both mothers (see Figure 10.3). It was found that the monkeys who were "reared" by a cloth mother spent significant amounts of time clinging to the soft material of their surrogate mother. They also developed greater emotional security and curiosity than those assigned to the wire mother. The monkeys who were given both mothers also showed strong attachment behaviors toward the cloth mother, even when it was always the wire-framed mother that provided food. The researchers concluded that the most important variable in attachment was the *contact comfort* provided by the terrycloth covering on the cloth mother.

Figure 10.3 Contact comfort and attachment. Harlow and Zimmerman found that infant rhesus monkeys spent more time on the terry cloth covered "mother," even when it was the wire "mother" that provided food. They concluded that contact comfort, rather than feeding, was the most important determinant of a monkey's attachment to its caregiver.

However, that is not to say the infant monkeys who interacted with the cloth surrogates developed normally. Harlow found that monkeys raised with surrogate mothers rarely interacted well with other monkeys, had extreme difficulty in mating, and were unable to mother their own infants (Harlow and Suomi, 1971). On a more positive note, attempts at rehabilitation found that all signs of maladjustment could be removed by allowing the disturbed monkeys unlimited play with younger monkeys, who provided ample opportunity for nonthreatening interactions (Novack and Harlow, 1975; Suomi and Harlow, 1972, 1978).

Monkeys and humans differ in many ways, so caution is always advised in generalizing from animal experiments to the human experience. However, Harlow and Zimmerman's findings suggest that physical contact (holding, caressing, rocking) might be an important factor in human attachment. Researchers Klaus and Kennell (1976), in fact, believe skin contact and touching between human mother and child immediately after birth is an essential part of "bonding" (see Chapter 3). Although Klaus and Kennell may have overstated the importance of the first few hours of life on long-term attachment (see Chess and Thomas, 1986; Wheeler, 1993), children undoubtedly benefit from lots of cuddling and caressing, and attachment is an important part of normal psychosocial development.

What happens if a child doesn't form an attachment?   To investigate this question, researchers have looked at children or adults who spent their early years in institutions. Although many institutions provide excellent child care, some are so poorly funded and understaffed that they can only meet the physical needs of the children. Infants raised in such impersonal surroundings without significant touching and individualized mothering suffer from a number of problems. They tend to show intellectual, physical, and perceptual retardation, increased susceptibility to infection, neurotic "rocking" and isolation behaviors, and in some cases death (Bowlby, 1973, 1982; Gardner, 1992; Spitz and Wolf, 1946).

Levels of Attachment

While most children are never exposed to harsh institutional conditions, Mary Ainsworth and her colleagues (1967, 1978) have found significant differences in the *level* of attachment between infants and their mothers that can produce long-term differences in behavior. Using a method called the *strange situation procedure,* in which the researcher observes infants in the presence or absence of their mother and a stranger, these researchers found they could divide children into three groups:

1. *Securely attached.* The infant seeks closeness and contact with the mother, uses the mother as a safe base from which to explore, shows moderate distress

upon separation, and is enthusiastic when the mother returns. About 65 percent of babies tested reacted in this manner.

2. *Anxious-avoidant.* The infant does not seek proximity or contact with the mother, treats the mother much like a stranger, and rarely cries when the mother leaves the room. About 25 percent of infants follow this pattern.

3. *Anxious-ambivalent.* The infant becomes very upset as the mother leaves the room, and when she returns seeks close contact while at the same time squirming angrily to get away. Only about 10 percent of infants respond in this way.

In follow-up studies, securely attached children were found to be more sociable, enthusiastic, cooperative, persistent, curious, competent, and likely to have internal controls versus controls by external, authority figures (Frankel and Bates, 1990; Hartup, 1989; Pederson et al., 1990).

Researchers Cindy Hazen and Phillip Shaver (1987) have found that adult love styles are related to infant patterns of attachment. According to Hazen and Shaver, romantic love is an attachment process, and a person who had an anxious-ambivalent attachment in infancy tends to have adult romantic relationships characterized by anxiety and ambivalence. They report volatile, jealous relationships, preoccupation with love, and strong fears of rejection. Similarly, anxious-avoidant patterns in infancy were associated with difficulty in getting close to others and establishing intimacy during adulthood. Individuals who were securely attached as infants found it relatively easy to establish intimate, trusting relationships as adults.

Evaluating Attachment Theories

Although Hazen and Shaver's reported relationship between romantic love and early attachment has been supported by later studies (Feeney and Noller, 1990; Simpson, 1990), further research is necessary before we fully understand the link between infant attachment and intimate relations. Also, be aware that most research on attachment has been conducted with only North American subjects. Research with Western European, Japanese, and Israeli children, for example, found different proportions of securely attached, anxious-ambivalent, and anxious-avoidant infants (Van IJzendoorn and Kroonenberg, 1988). This could be the result of differing cultural expectations for independence or differing parenting styles—the topic of our next section. Finally, keep in mind that there is a great deal of general controversy over the importance of secure attachment, with many suggesting that it is given too much weight (Kagan, 1989; Thompson, 1991).

Parenting Styles: The Effects of Different Child-Rearing Methods

How much of our personality comes from the way our parents treat us as we are growing up? Researchers since the 1920s have studied the effects of different methods of child rearing on children's behavior, development, and mental health (Baldwin, 1949; Schaefer, 1960). More recent studies done by Diana Baumrind (1980, 1989) found that parenting styles could be reliably divided into three broad patterns:

1. *Authoritarian.* These parents value unquestioning obedience and mature responsibility from their children, while remaining aloof and detached. An authoritarian parent might say, "Don't ask questions. Just do it my way or else." Children of authoritarian parents are easily upset, moody, aggressive, and generally have poor communication skills.

2. *Permissive.* Permissive parents come in two styles—*permissive-indifferent*, the parent who sets few limits and provides little in the way of attention, interest, or emotional support, and *permissive-indulgent*, the parent who is highly involved but places few demands or controls on the child. Children of permissive-indifferent parents have poor self-control (becoming demanding

and disobedient) and poor social skills. Children of permissive-indulgent parents often fail to learn respect for others and are more impulsive, immature, and out of control.

3. *Authoritative.* These parents are caring and sensitive toward their children, but they also set firm limits and enforce them while encouraging increasing responsibility. As you might expect, children did best under the authoritative parents (Lewis, 1981). They became self-reliant, self-controlled, and high-achieving. They also seemed more content, friendly, and socially competent in their dealings with others.

Evaluating Baumrind's Research

Before you conclude that the authoritative pattern is the only way to raise successful children, you should know that many children raised in the other styles also become caring, cooperative adults (McClelland et al., 1978). Critics have also suggested that Baumrind's findings may reflect the child's temperament rather than the parenting style (Lewis, 1981). That is, the parents of mature and competent children may have developed the authoritative style because of the child's behavior rather than vice versa.

Cultural research also suggests that the child's *expectations* of how parents should behave plays an important role in parenting styles (Brislin, 1993). As we discovered in Chapter 9, adolescents in Korea and Japan expect strong parental control and interpret it as a sign of love and deep concern. Adolescents in North America, however, would interpret the same behaviors as a sign of parental hostility and rejection.

Cross-cultural studies suggest that the most important variable in parenting styles and child development might be the degree of warmth versus rejection parents feel toward their children. Based on analyses of over 100 societies, Rohner (1986) concluded that universally, parental rejection adversely affects a child. The neglect and indifference shown by rejecting parents tend to produce hostile, aggressive children who have a difficult time establishing and maintaining close relationships. These children are also more likely to develop psychological problems that require professional intervention (Brislin, 1993).

Do fathers differ from mothers in their parenting style?   Until recently, the father's role in discipline and child care was largely ignored. But as more fathers have begun to take an active role in child rearing, there has been a corresponding increase in research. From these studies we now know that fathers are absorbed, excited, and responsive to their newborns (Greenberg and Morris, 1974; Lamb, 1977) and that there are few differences in the way children form attachments to either parent (Hartup, 1989). After infancy, the father becomes increasingly involved with his children, yet he still spends less overall time in direct child care than the mother (Campos et al., 1983; Collins and Russell, 1988; Hartup, 1989). But they are just as responsive, nurturing, and competent as mothers when they do assume child care responsibilities (Parke et al., 1972).

Families: Their Effect on Development

For better or worse, our parents, siblings, and other family members exert an enormous influence on our development. Recent studies of sibling relationships, for example, have shown that a child's behavior is profoundly affected by the mother's interactions with other siblings. What do you think happens when one child receives relatively less affection and attention from the mother? Researchers have found that the relationship between these siblings is characterized by more hostility and conflict, and that the "unfavored" child tends to be more depressed, worried, and anxious than other children in general (Boer and Dunn, 1992).

Birth order is also associated with sibling relationships. Parents generally expect the oldest child to exercise self-control and care for younger siblings. Researchers have shown that older siblings are both more nurturant *and* more antagonistic toward their

Research shows that the family satisfies important social needs for all its members.

Around the world, older siblings are often expected to help with the care of younger brothers and sisters. Does this explain certain personality differences between first-born and later-born children?

younger siblings (Abramovitch et al., 1986). Their antagonism may result, in part, from receiving less maternal attention. In one study, mothers became more coercive, negative, and restraining and played less with the firstborn following the birth of a second child (Dunn and Kendrick, 1982).

Child Abuse

A too frequent tragedy of family life is parental abuse of their offspring—physical, emotional, or sexual. Abused children often have seriously impaired personalities and social development. They may be physically damaged (from the assault, poor nutrition, and neglect), or they may develop emotional disorders such as withdrawal, aggression, or suicidal tendencies (Edelman, 1991; Emery, 1989; Hart and Brassard, 1987). It is important to point out that child abuse is only partially caused by individual personality characteristics of the parents, and that its effects range from mild to severe.

Is there anything that can be done to help abused children and their parents?   Attempts to deal with family violence have taken two approaches. *Primary programs* attempt to identify "vulnerable" families and try to prevent abuse. *Secondary programs* attempt to rehabilitate the families after abuse has occurred (Finkelhor and Hotaling, 1988; Kaplan, 1986). Primary programs try to improve parenting and marital skills, teach people to recognize the signs of abuse, and encourage people to report suspected cases of abuse. Secondary programs involve improved social services, self-help groups such as Parents Anonymous and AMAC (Adults Molested as Children), and individual and group psychotherapy for both the victim and the abuser.

Teenage Parents

Abuse is just one of many family factors that may affect development. Another is becoming a parent and starting a family at too early an age. The United States currently has the highest rate of teen pregnancies among the major industrialized nations. Nearly one in six female adolescents becomes pregnant at least once before marriage (Conger, 1988). Pregnancy during adolescence carries with it considerable health risk for both the mother and child (see Chapter 9). In addition, teenage mothers—95 percent of whom currently keep their babies—face significant problems in other areas (Conger, 1988; Furstenberg, Brooks-Gunn, and Chase-Lansdale, 1989; White and De Blassie, 1992):

1. Lower educational achievement (pregnancy is the most common reason for dropping out of high school).

2. Reduced economic opportunities (teenage mothers are less likely to find employment, are more likely to become chronically dependent on welfare, and generally spend their lives below the official poverty level).

3. Impaired marital opportunities (teenage mothers are less likely to marry, and if they marry they are more likely to divorce).

In view of these statistics, is it any wonder that teen mothers also report one of the highest levels of depression (see Figure 10.4)?

What can be done to reduce the number of teen pregnancies?   Conger (1988) recommends the following steps:

1. *Sex education and family-life planning.* Adolescents need facts about sexuality and help in learning to integrate this information into their lives and future (Allen et al., 1990; Kent, 1992).

2. *Access to contraceptive methods.* Sexually active adolescents need easily accessible health services that provide comprehensive, high-quality care (Kent, 1992).

3. *The life options approach.* Motivation to avoid pregnancy is essential and can only be accomplished when young people feel good about themselves and have a "clear vision of a successful and self-sufficient future" (Edelman, 1987, p. 58).

4. *Broad community involvement and support.* Community support is the major reason why other industrialized nations have fewer pregnancies, abortions, and teenage mothers, despite comparable levels of sexual activity (Jones et al., · 1985).

The Impact of Divorce

Another aspect of family life that greatly influences development is divorce. Contrary to the belief that "time heals all wounds," 40 percent of divorced women and 30 percent of divorced men still feel rejected and angry at their former partners 10 years after breaking up (Fischman, 1986). In addition to the stress for the divorcing couple, their children suffer both short-term and long-lasting effects on their development (Chase-Landsdale and Hetherington, 1993; Grych and Fincham, 1992; Wallerstein and Kelly, 1992). De-

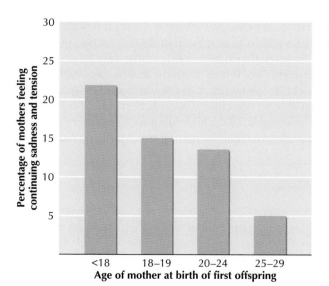

Figure 10.4 Maternal age and satisfaction. Note how the age of the mother directly relates to the percentage of reported feelings of sadness and tension.

Critical Thinking

PSYCHOLOGY IN ACTION

DEVELOPING THE ABILITY TO EMPATHIZE
Abortion, Adoption, or Keeping the Child?

In view of the increasing number of teen pregnancies in America, it becomes ever more important to fully understand and appreciate the questions and conflicts a pregnant teenager must face. Should she have an abortion, give the baby up for adoption, or keep her child? Should her boyfriend or parents have a say in what she decides?

This exercise is designed to improve your critical thinking skills through empathizing, the ability to consider others' points of view. Begin by reading the following scenario.

Anne is an average American high school student. She is a 17-year-old senior who gets top grades and has an excellent chance of getting an academic scholarship. In addition to school, Anne works 15 hours a week and is saving for college, which she hopes to attend the following fall. She is also pregnant.

Anne's father, who is morally opposed to abortion, warned her about premarital sex. He was very upset when he found out about her pregnancy and would never accept an abortion. He would like to see Anne keep the baby and try to get her boyfriend to marry her. Anne's mother, on the other hand, does not want anything to prevent Anne from getting a college degree and wants her to give the baby up for adoption. Anne's boyfriend does not want to marry her or be financially responsible. He plans to enter college in the fall and wants Anne to have an abortion.

Anne knows that, realistically, her pregnancy would prevent her from attending college in the fall, and that this delay would seriously jeopardize her scholarship opportunities. Without a substantial scholarship, she would need to work full-time. Anne's parents cannot afford to help her with college expenses or offer significant help with child care. Anne does not want to marry her boyfriend, nor does she assume that he will provide much support should she decide to keep the child. Anne must make a decision on her own. (Adapted from Bernards, 1988.)

With a group of friends or alone:

1. Make a list of several possible arguments from each character's perspective—Anne, her father, her mother, and her boyfriend.

2. Decide which of these arguments are the most compelling for keeping the child, putting it up for adoption, and for having an abortion.

3. Decide which argument is most persuasive against each option.

4. If you, your girlfriend, or your child were pregnant and in a similar situation, how would you decide? Are your reasons different from those listed above? If so, explain why.

spite widespread belief that divorce is a short-term crisis, recent research shows that divorce has a profound and lasting effect on all members of the family. Some children and parents exhibit remarkable adaptation and in the long term find the divorce experience life-enhancing, but for others it is a severe developmental disruption both initially and in the years that follow. Still others appear to adapt well in the early stages of divorce but show delayed effects at a later time (Hetherington, 1991; Wallerstein et al., 1988).

Whether children become "winners" or "losers" from the divorce process depends on the individual attributes of the child, the qualities of the custodial family, and the resources and support systems available to the child (Camara, Brennan, and Resnick, 1991; Emerson, 1993). As can be seen in Table 10.4, children's *initial* and *later* reactions to marital transitions also differ according to their age at the time of the divorce.

 Try This Yourself

If you are interested in estimating your personal chances for a *happy* marriage, consider the following points. Your chances for a successful marriage increase each time you answer "true."

1. _____	You and your partner are out of your teens and have known each other for at least six months.
2. _____	Both sets of parents do not oppose the marriage, and both sets of parents are not divorced.
3. _____	Neither you nor your partner is pregnant at the time of marriage.
4. _____	You and your partner finished college and have a good income.
5. _____	Both you and your partner think of one another as your best friend, and you both like one another as a person.
6. _____	You were engaged before getting married and did not cohabit.
7. _____	You agree on how to handle housework and child care.
8. _____	You and your partner are religious and believe that marriage is sacred.

Source: Adapted from Lauer, 1992; Stinnett, 1992.

■

Table 10.4 Typical Reactions to Parental Divorce by Children of Varying Ages

Age (at time of divorce)	Initial Reaction	Later Reaction (2–10 years later)
Preschool (2½ to 6 years)	Blames self for divorce; fears abandonment; confused; fantasizes reconciliation; difficulty in expressing feelings.	Few memories of either own or parents' earlier conflict; generally has developed close relations with custodial parent and competent step-parent; feels anger at unavailability of non-custodial parent.
Elementary School (7 to 12 years).	Expresses feelings of fear, sadness, anger; divided loyalties; better able to take advantage of extrafamilial support.	Least adaptable to step-parenting and remarriage; may challenge family rules and regulations; decreased academic performance; disturbed peer relations.
Adolescence (13 to 18 years)	Difficulty coping with anger, outrage, shame, and sadness; reexamines own values; may disengage from family.	Shares feelings of 7- to 12-year-olds, but may not be similarly expressed; fears long-term relations with others; more consciously troubled.

Sources: Bray (1988); Wallerstein et al. (1988); Wallerstein and Blakeslee (1989).

Occupational Choices: The Effect of Work and Careers

Most working adults spend more time on the job than they do with their families. Erikson emphasized the importance of "generativity" to adult development—the need to accomplish something with one's life. Most people channel their accomplishment needs into their work or occupation.

How can I find a rewarding career that best suits my personality and interests? Choosing an occupation is one of the most important decisions in our lives, and the task is becoming ever more complex as the number of career options increases as a result of specialization. The *Dictionary of Occupational Titles,* a government publication, currently lists more than 20,000 job categories. One way to learn more about job categories and potential careers is to visit your college career center. At such centers, career counselors will often suggest you take vocational interest tests.

Although disengagement theory suggests that older people naturally disengage and withdraw from life, activity theory *argues that everyone should remain active and involved throughout the entire life span.*

Once a career decision is made, careers, just like lives, can go through stages. In the initial phases there is often a great deal of "job hopping," especially among younger workers. Men between the ages of 16 and 19 have a 74 percent chance of a job change within five years, whereas men in their twenties have a 56 percent chance (Sommers and Eck, 1977). Most experts tend to agree that job satisfaction and stability peak during middle age. A 1991 Gallup poll found that 75 percent of American workers would continue to work even if it were not a financial necessity (Hugick and Leonard, 1991b).

But overestimating the importance of work is readily apparent when we look at the mythology that surrounds the final career stage: retirement. Like the midlife crisis and empty nest syndrome, the loss of self-esteem and depression that is commonly assumed to accompany retirement may be largely a myth. Many workers are glad to retire and are primarily depressed at the change in their standard of living (Schaie and Geiwitz, 1982). Although Maggie Kuhn was personally outraged at her forced retirement at age 65, she also recognized that many people do want to retire. Her group, the Gray Panthers, is opposed to mandatory retirement and hiring policies that discriminate on the basis of age (Kuhn, 1990). Like many researchers, Kuhn believes a fulfilling old age comes from remaining active and involved as long as possible—the activity theory of aging. This approach is in sharp contrast to the disengagement theory, which says that successful aging is a natural and graceful withdrawal from life roles the person can no longer fill because of lost physical capacity and ostracism by a youth-oriented society (Cumming and Henry, 1961). Although the disengagement theory has been strongly criticized and generally discredited, it has stimulated research into the causes of social withdrawal, which does occur among some elderly. But what may seem like natural and willing disengagement or "mellowness" may in fact reflect an older person's attempt to retreat to a smaller social world and avoid further alienation in an *ageist* society (Blau, 1973). A more positive approach to coping with ageism, as well as specific techniques for dealing with death, is offered in the next section.

Activity Theory: A theory of aging that suggests successful adjustment is fostered by a full and active commitment to life.

Disengagement Theory: A theory of aging that suggests successful aging involves a natural and mutual withdrawal, in which both the individual and society gradually pull away from each other as a preparation for death.

Gender and Cultural Diversity

CULTURAL DIFFERENCES IN AGEISM

As we discovered in Chapter 9, physical decline plays an important part in later life and causes emotional stress—although much less than most people think. A greater stress for the elderly in our society is the ageism they encounter. In a society where the old are seen as wise elders or keepers of valued traditions, the stress of aging is less than in a society where they are seen as mentally slow and socially useless. In cultures like ours where youth, speed, and progress are strongly emphasized, a loss or decline in any of these qualities is deeply feared and denied (Butler and Lewis, 1982; Gatz and Pearson, 1988; Linden, 1991).

Ageism: Negative attitudes toward the aged.

The Effects of Ageism

Like all forms of prejudice, ageism and the irrational fear of death punish both the victim and perpetrator. The victims in this case (the elderly and dying) are limited in their access to full support and respect from society, and the perpetrators are limited in their access to valuable information from "pilgrims" who journey on before them (Stoddard, 1978).

The Western world's emphasis on youth over elderly wisdom has created a dangerous problem for the entire planet. Over the ages, indigenous peoples have developed innumerable technologies that have allowed them to farm deserts without irrigation, to navigate vast ocean distances without compasses, and to successfully treat many illnesses with local plants. We are losing this knowledge by encroaching on tribal lands. And, when the young of remote cultures come in contact with the outside world, they too often conclude that traditional ways and elders' wisdom are illegitimate and irrelevant (Linden, 1991).

Linguist Ken Hale estimates that 3000 of the world's 6000 languages are doomed because no children speak them. And once a language disappears, traditional knowledge tends to vanish with it. Tribal women in parts of Africa have forgotten traditional methods of birth control and now typically bear 10 or more children, while their ancestors averaged five or six. Similarly, in Papua-New Guinea jobless people who return to the villages often lack the elders' knowledge of which trees are rot-resistant and can be used to build huts and which woods are poisonous and should be avoided when making a fire for cooking (Linden, 1991). Saem Majnep, a villager of New Guinea, notes that throughout his country the younger generation "feels shame rather than pride in what their ancestors knew" ("A Chronicler of Elders," 1991, p. 48).

While negative perceptions of aging are common among Anglo-Americans, some cultures highly revere their elderly for their wisdom and life experiences.

Aren't there some cultures that honor the elderly? Yes, there are some societies, notably Japan, China, and the Navajo in North America, in which the elderly are revered. Traditional families respect aging parents for their wisdom and experience, defer to them in family matters, and expect elderly parents to live with their children until they die (Beauvoir, 1972; Palmore and Maeda, 1985).

Ageism in the United States

Between the extremes of being held in high or low esteem, there is great diversity in the status and treatment of different subgroups of the elderly. A good example is found within the United States. Comparing women and men in our culture, studies have found that older men have more social status, income, and sexual partnerships than women. Elderly women, on the other hand, have more friends and are more involved in family relationships, but have lower status and income (Bell, 1989; Bengtson, Kasschau, and Ragan, 1977; Healey, 1986). Contrary to popular stereotypes of the "rich old woman," elderly females represent one of the lowest income levels in American society (Dressel, 1988).

It is also interesting to look at ethnic differences in aging in America. In a major study of 1269 African-American, Anglo-American, and Mexican-American persons between the ages of 45 and 74, minority groups were found to have more health problems, greater feelings of being old, and more negative views of aging (Bengtson et al., 1977). Yet, other research reported that blacks are more likely than whites to regard elderly persons with respect (Mui, 1992). Studies have also found that elderly blacks have a lower suicide rate than elderly whites and, after age 75, African-American, Pacific-Asian, and Native-American elderly actually have a greater life expectancy than Anglo-Americans (Cool, 1987). Gibson (1986) suggests that these survivors may have unusual biological vigor, psychological strength, or greater resources for coping. Compared with whites, ethnic groups often have a greater sense of community and may have stronger bonds of attachment due to their shared traits and experiences with prejudice. *Ethnicity* itself may, therefore, provide some benefits. "In addition to shielding them from majority attitudes, ethnicity provides the ethnic elderly with a source of esteem" (Fry, 1985, p. 233).

As we have seen, the elderly of all societies are a resource we cannot afford to lose. Just as the ethnic elderly in America may be able to teach Anglo-Americans better coping skills for aging in Western culture, the elderly of remote cultures around the world have wisdom that Western scientists are just beginning to acknowledge. Botanist Michael Balick, for example, currently travels the tropical forests of Latin America with shamans to discover the medicinal secrets of local plants. Balick and his colleagues hold ceremonies to honor the shamans, hoping that by showing respect for the "wisdom keepers" the young might "better weigh the value of their culture against blandishments of modernity" (Linden, 1991, p. 56). ■

Death and Dying: Another Stage in Development?

Confronting our own death and dying is the last major crisis we face in life. What is it like? Is there a "best" way to prepare to die? Is there such a thing as a "good death"? After spending hundreds of hours at the bedsides of the terminally ill, Elisabeth Kübler-Ross developed her stage theory of the psychological processes surrounding death (1983; 1989). Based on extensive interviews with these patients, Kübler-Ross proposed that most people go through five sequential stages when facing death: *denial* of the terminal condition ("This can't be true, it's a mistake!"), *anger* ("Why me? It isn't fair!"), *bargaining* ("God, if you let me live I'll dedicate my life to you!"), *depression* ("I'm losing everyone and everything I hold dear"), and finally *acceptance* ("I know that death is inevitable and my time is near").

Evaluating Kübler-Ross

Critics of the stage theory of dying stress that each person's death is a unique experience and that emotions and reactions depend on the individual's personality, life situation, age, and so on (Kastenbaum, 1982). Others worry that the popularization of her theory will cause further avoidance and stereotyping of the dying ("He's just in the anger stage right now"). In response, Kübler-Ross (1983, 1989) agrees that not all people go through the same stages in the same way and regrets that anyone would use her theory as a model for a "good death."

In spite of the potential abuses of her theory, it has given insights and spurred research into a long-neglected topic. Thanatology, the study of death and dying, has become a major topic in human development. We now recognize that dealing with death can help a person more fully enjoy everyday life. Thanks in part to thanatology research, the dying are also being helped to die with dignity by the *hospice* movement, which has created special facilities and has trained staff and volunteers to provide loving support for the terminally ill and their families (Brand, 1988). Just as the shame, fear, and superstition that once surrounded pregnancy and "birthing" have been replaced with open discussion and loving celebration, death awareness leaders hope that "deathing" can become a similarly natural and positive part of the life cycle (Foos-Graber, 1985).

Thanatology researchers also hope that through education, research, and exposure to death, ageism will decline. Once people recognize that their self-protective prejudices provide only short-term relief from their fears of an inevitable process, they may welcome coping with their own aging and death and that of their loved ones. Any form of discrimination or prejudice that limits the elderly from full participation is a cost to all of society. Maggie Kuhn speaks to the importance of rejecting stereotypes and valuing our elderly:

> *There are many stereotypes about growing old. We are not useless, toothless, and sexless. In fact, old people have a special place in society. My generation has been part of more changes than any other. We have to share that knowledge. We are the whistle blowers, the social critics. We are the ones who must be advocates for disarmament and safe, renewable sources of energy. (cited in Conniff, 1984, p. 273)*

Thanatology: The study of death and dying. The term comes from *thanatos*, the Greek name for a mythical personification of death, and was borrowed by Freud to represent the death instinct.

Gray panther activist Maggie Kuhn is an important role model in the battle against ageism.

Review Questions

1. What was the major finding of Harlow and Zimmerman's research with cloth and wire surrogate mothers?
2. List the three types of attachment reported by Mary Ainsworth.
3. Briefly summarize Baumrind's four parenting styles.

4. The _____ theory of aging suggests that you should remain active and involved until death, whereas the _____ theory suggests that you should naturally and gracefully withdraw from life.

5. Explain how ethnicity may help the elderly overcome some problems of aging.

6. Elisabeth Kübler-Ross's five stages of dying are _____ .

Answers to Review Questions can be found in Appendix C.

REVIEW OF MAJOR CONCEPTS

MORAL DEVELOPMENT

1. According to Kohlberg, morality progresses through three levels, with each level consisting of two subsets or stages. At the preconventional level, morality is based on the consequences of an act (either reward or punishment); at the conventional level, morality reflects the need for approval and the desire to avoid censure from authority figures; and at the postconventional level, moral reasoning comes from the individual's own principles and values.

2. One major criticism of Kohlberg's theory of moral development comes from Gilligan's research, which suggests that women have a "separate-but-equal" type of moral development. According to Gilligan, a woman goes through three stages of moral development, from a selfish, individual survival morality, to an all-giving, self-sacrificing style, to a final stage of caring for herself as well as others.

GENDER ROLE DEVELOPMENT

3. Psychoanalytic theorists emphasize identification with the same-sex parent in gender role development, whereas social-learning theory focuses on rewards, punishments, and imitation.

4. The cognitive-developmental theory of personality development emphasizes the active, thinking processes of the individual. Kohlberg explains gender roles as a result of the development of the concepts of gender identity and gender constancy. The gender-schema theory integrates the social-learning and cognitive-developmental theories.

SOCIAL AND PERSONALITY DEVELOPMENT

5. Thomas and Chess emphasize the genetic component of certain traits (such as sociability) and the fact that babies often exhibit differences in temperament shortly after birth.

6. Erik Erikson expanded on Freud's ideas to develop eight psychosocial stages that cover the entire life span. The four stages that occur during childhood are trust versus mistrust, autonomy versus shame and doubt, initiative versus guilt, and industry versus inferiority.

7. Erikson believes the major psychosocial crisis of adolescence is the search for identity versus role confusion. During young adulthood, the individual's task is to establish intimacy over isolation and during middle adulthood the person must deal with generativity versus stagnation. At the end of life, the older adult must establish ego integrity, which depends on the acceptance of the life that has been lived, or face overwhelming despair at the realization of lost opportunities.

8. Many researchers now suggest that the stage of adolescent storm and stress, the midlife crisis, and the empty nest syndrome may be exaggerated accounts of a few people's experiences and not the experience of most people.

SPECIAL ISSUES IN DEVELOPMENT

9. Nativists believe that attachment is innate, whereas nurturists believe it is learned. The Harlow and Zimmerman experiment with rhesus monkeys raised by cloth or wire surrogate mothers found that contact comfort may be the most important factor in attachment.

10. Infants who fail to form attachments may suffer serious effects. When attachments are formed, there may be differences in the level or degree. Research on securely attached, avoidant, and ambivalent children found significant differences in behaviors that often persist into adulthood.

11. Investigations of various styles of parenting found four major patterns: authoritarian, permissive-indifferent, permissive-indulgent, and authoritative. Each method had varying effects on the child's development.

12. Families play an important role in development. Child abuse, teenage pregnancies, and divorce can negatively influence all members of the family.

13. The kind of work people do and the occupational choices they make can play an important role in their lives. Before making a career decision, it is wise to research possible alternatives and take interest inventories. Careers tend to go through stages—from initial job-hopping to retirement. After retirement there are two major theories of successful aging. According to activity theory, people should remain active and involved throughout the entire life span. According to disengagement theory, the elderly naturally and gracefully withdraw from life because they welcome the relief from roles they can no longer fulfill.

14. Ageism is an important stressor for the elderly, but there are some cultures where aging is revered.

15. Elisabeth Kübler-Ross's theory of the five-stage process of dying (denial, anger, bargaining, depression, and acceptance) offers important insight and education concerning death. It is hoped that by confronting our fear of death, prejudice against the elderly will also decline.

SUGGESTED READINGS

GILLIGAN, C. (1982). *In a different voice: Psychological theory and women's development.* Cambridge, MA: Harvard University Press. An interesting and controversial discussion of a theory that contrasts the stages of moral development in women with traditional theories based largely on male subjects.

KIMMEL, D. C. (1990). *Adulthood and aging: An interdisciplinary, developmental view.* New York: Wiley. Written in an engaging, personal style, this book provides a comprehensive view of classic and recent research in the field of adulthood and aging.

KÜBLER-ROSS, E. (1989). *Death: The final stage of growth.* Englewood Cliffs, NJ: Prentice-Hall. The book that paved the way for the latest interest in the psychological experiences surrounding the "final stage" of development.

LICKONA, T. (1985). *Raising good children.* New York: Bantam Books. Using Kohlberg's basic theory of moral development, Thomas Lickona offers "how-to" advice on raising a child's level of morality.

WAGNER, V., & SWISHER, K. L. (EDS.) (1992). *The family in America: Opposing viewpoints.* San Diego: Greenhaven Press. This paperback presents up-to-date and thought-provoking opposing arguments regarding family issues such as divorce, family leave, and day care.

Human Sexuality

OUTLINE

It was an unusual circumcision. The identical twin boys were already seven months old when their parents took them to the doctor to be circumcised. For many years in the United States, most male babies have had the foreskin of their penis removed during their first week of life, when it is assumed they will experience less pain. The most common procedure is cutting or pinching off the foreskin tissue. In this case, however, the doctor used an electrocautery device, which applies an electrical current that is used to burn off moles or small skin growths. The electrical current used for one of the brothers was too powerful, and the entire penis was accidentally removed or ablated.

After this tragedy, the parents continued to raise their sons as identical twin boys while undergoing considerable personal anguish and repeated consultations with medical experts. Following discussions with John Money and other specialists at Johns Hopkins University, the parents and doctors made an unusual decision—the twin with the ablated penis would be raised as a girl.

The first step in the "reassignment" process occurred at 17 months of age, when the child's name was changed. "She" was then dressed in pink pants and frilly blouses and the parents let "her" hair grow long. At 21 months, plastic surgery was performed to create external female genital structures. Further plastic surgery to create a vagina was planned for the beginning of adolescence, when the child's physical growth would be nearly complete. At this time she would also begin to take female hormones to complete the boy-to-girl transformation.

By age three, the child wore nightgowns and dresses almost exclusively and was given bracelets and hair ribbons. She clearly preferred dresses over pants and took pride in her long hair. Her mother was surprised and pleased by the striking differences that were developing in her two children. By age four and one-half, the daughter was much neater than her brother and, in contrast to him, disliked being dirty. The mother reported, "She likes for me to wipe her face. She doesn't like to be dirty, and yet my son is quite different. I can't wash his face for anything. . . . She seems daintier. Maybe it's because I encourage it" (Money and Ehrhardt, 1972, p. 119).

During the preschool years, the girl preferred playing with "girl-type" toys and asked for a doll and carriage for Christmas. Her brother asked for a garage with cars, gas pumps, and tools. By age six, the brother was accustomed to defending his sister if he thought someone was threatening her. The daughter copied the mother in tidying and cleaning up the kitchen, whereas the boy did not. The mother agreed that she encouraged her daughter when she helped with the housework and expected the boy to be uninterested.

What do you think about the outcome of this surgery? Is it possible that the only thing that makes some children prefer "girl-type" toys and clothes is how parents or others treat them? Could surgery and opposite-sex hormones change your sexuality? How about dating and marriage? Would you still be attracted to the same type of person, or would this change if you took opposite-sex hormones? As you can see, the concepts of sex, attraction, and personal sense of maleness and femaleness are not so simple and obvious as we think. Human sexuality is a complex field, but researchers have made exciting discoveries that you will find useful in your interpersonal relationships.

In the first section of this chapter, we will survey early research into human sexuality and discuss various cultural differences in sexual practices and attitudes. The second section focuses on *gender*, the basic concept of maleness and femaleness and how it relates to specific issues in sexuality, such as transsexualism and homosexuality. We will also discuss how people come to identify themselves as men and women, and how males differ from females anatomically, hormonally, cognitively, and behaviorally. Next, we will describe sexual arousal and response, some common myths surrounding sexual behavior, and the role of sex therapy in the treatment of sexual problems or dysfunctions. We will also discuss AIDS and other sexually transmitted diseases. Finally, we will look at the general field of coercive sex, examining myths, effects, and prevention of child sexual abuse, sexual harassment, and rape.

As you read Chapter 11, keep the following **Survey** questions in mind and answer them in your own words:

- How do scientists study an emotional topic like sex?
- In what ways are males and females biologically and psychologically different?
- How do men and women differ in sexual arousal, sexual response, sexual problems, and sexually transmitted diseases?
- What factors influence child sexual abuse, sexual harassment, and rape?

THE STUDY OF HUMAN SEXUALITY

Sex is used and abused in many ways: as a major theme in literature, movies, and music; to satisfy sexual desires; to gain love and acceptance from partners and peer groups; as a way of expressing love or commitment in a relationship; as a way of ending relationships through affairs with others; to dominate or hurt others; and, perhaps most conspicuously, to sell products.

• How do scientists study an emotional topic like sex?

 Try This Yourself

Before we delve into what researchers have learned about human sexuality, you may be interested in sampling your level of sex knowledge. Try this quiz. The answers are at the bottom, and expanded explanations are found in the first three sections of this chapter.

Do you know which of the following statements are true and which are false?
1. The breakfast cereal Kellogg's Corn Flakes was originally developed to discourage masturbation.
2. Nocturnal emissions and masturbation are signs of abnormal sexual adjustment.
3. AIDS can be spread through swimming pools.
4. Transsexuals are basically homosexual.
5. If a developing male fetus fails to get sufficient testosterone during prenatal development, he may develop female genitals.
6. Women are less aroused by explicit sexual material than men.
7. There are documented physical differences between male and female brains.
8. Sexual skill and satisfaction are learned behaviors and can be increased through education and training.
9. Women fail to achieve vaginal orgasms due to psychological immaturity.
10. Only women are capable of multiple orgasms.

Answers: 1. T 2. F 3. F 4. F 5. T 6. F 7. T 8. T 9. F 10. F

Although people have probably always been interested in understanding their sexuality, strong cultural forces have suppressed and controlled this interest at times. During the nineteenth century, for example, polite society avoided mention of all parts of the body covered by clothing, the breast of chicken became known as "white meat", female patients were examined by male doctors in totally dark rooms, and some people even covered piano legs for the sake of propriety (Gay, 1983; Money, 1985a).

During this same Victorian period, medical experts warned that masturbation led to blindness, impotence, acne, and insanity. Believing that a bland diet helped suppress sexual desire, Dr. John Harvey Kellogg and Sylvester Graham, respectively, developed

Sexuality is an important part of everyone's life throughout the life cycle.

the original Kellogg's Corn Flakes and Graham crackers and marketed them as foods that would discourage masturbation (Money, Prakasam, and Joshi, 1991). One of the most serious concerns of many doctors was nocturnal emissions ("wet dreams"), which were believed to cause brain damage and death. Thus, special devices were marketed for men to wear at night to prevent sexual arousal (see Figure 11.1).

Havelock Ellis was one of the first sex researchers to celebrate eroticism and acknowledge female sexuality.

The Beginning of Modern Research: Havelock Ellis

In light of modern knowledge, it seems hard to understand these strange Victorian practices and outrageous myths about masturbation and nocturnal emissions. One of the first physicians to explore and question these practices was Havelock Ellis (1858– 1939). When he first heard of the dangers of nocturnal emissions, Ellis was extremely frightened, since he himself had personal experience with the problem. His fear led him to frantically search the medical literature, but instead of a cure, he found predictions of gruesome illness and eventual death. Initially he reacted to these predictions by contemplating suicide. On second thought, he decided he could give meaning to his life by keeping a detailed diary of his deterioration to dedicate to science when he died. After several months of careful observation, he began to realize that the books were wrong— he wasn't dying. He wasn't even sick. Angry that he had been so misinformed by the "experts," he dedicated his life to a search for reliable and accurate sex information. Today Havelock Ellis is acknowledged as one of the most important early pioneers in the field of sex research and as a leader in the advancement of the case study method.

Using the case study technique, Ellis studied the sexual experiences of hundreds of people. He found that nocturnal emissions and masturbation were normal, harmless, and commonly experienced. His case studies also led him to conclude that homosexuality did not always involve pathology and that the sexual capacities and needs of women were equal to those of men (Brecher, 1969). These latter beliefs failed to receive general acceptance during Ellis's own time, but he is respected today for his courageous and surprisingly modern views.

Baseline: A characteristic level of performance used to assess changes in behavior resulting from experimental conditions.

Research Milestones: Kinsey, Masters and Johnson

Although the case study approach is still widely used in sex research (as with the case of the twin boy who was reassigned as a female), interviews and surveys are probably the most popular research techniques today. Among the earliest and most extensive studies in sexuality were those conducted by Alfred Kinsey and his colleagues (1948, 1953). Kinsey and his coworkers personally interviewed over 18,000 subjects, asking detailed questions about their sexual activities and sexual preferences (Pomeroy, 1972). Despite criticisms concerning his methodology and sample of subjects (mostly young, single, urban, white, and middle class), Kinsey's work is still widely respected, and his data are frequently used as a baseline for modern research. In recent years, hundreds of sex surveys and interviews have been conducted on such topics as contraception, abortion, premarital sex, and rape (DeBruyn, 1992; DiClemente et al., 1992). By comparing Kinsey's data to the responses found in later surveys, we can see how sexual practices have changed over the years.

In addition to case studies, surveys, and interviews, some researchers have employed direct laboratory experimentation and observational methods. To document the physiological changes involved in sexual arousal and response, William Masters and Virginia Johnson (1966, 1970) and their research colleagues enlisted several hundred men and women volunteers. Using intricate physiological measuring devices, the researchers carefully monitored the subjects' bodily responses while masturbating or engaging in sexual intercourse. Masters and Johnson's research findings are hailed as a major contribution to our knowledge of sexual physiology. Some of their results are discussed in later sections.

William Masters and Virginia Johnson are probably the best known and most widely quoted sex researchers.

A CULTURAL LOOK AT SEXUAL BEHAVIORS

Some sex researchers conduct cultural studies by comparing the sexual practices, techniques, and attitudes of different societies (Beach, 1977; Brislin, 1993; Reiss, 1986). Since most people are exposed only to the sexual practices of their own culture, comparisons among cultures put sex in a broader perspective and help counteract the common tendency toward ethnocentrism, the tendency people have to judge their own cultural practices as "normal" and preferable to those of other groups (Brislin, 1993).

Before concluding that only *other* people are ethnocentric, have you examined your own beliefs and values? For example, do you find it strange that Apinaye women in Brazil often bite off pieces of their mate's eyebrows as a natural part of sexual foreplay (Goldstein, 1976)? Or does it make you uncomfortable to learn that in Mangaia, a small island in the South Pacific, adolescent boys routinely undergo *superincision,* a painful initiation rite in which the upper part of the penis is slit (Marshall, 1971)? (See Table 11.1 for other examples of cultural variation in sexuality.)

While other cultures' practices may seem unnatural and strange to us, we forget that our own sexual rituals may appear equally curious to other cultures. If the description of the Mangaian practice of superincision bothered you, what about our culture's routine circumcision of infant boys? How did you feel when you read about the damaging circumcision of the infant boy in the introduction to this chapter?

Male Genital Mutilation

Before you object that infant circumcision in the United States is "entirely different" and "medically safe and necessary," you might want to know that the complication rate for circumcision (including hemorrhage, gangrene, mutilation, infection, and surgical

Ethnocentrism: Viewing one's own *ethnic* group (or culture) as *central* and "correct" or "best," and then judging the rest of the world according to this standard.

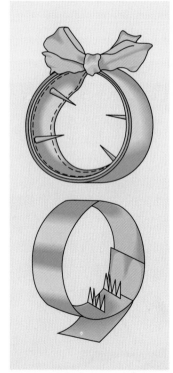

Figure 11.1 Victorian sexual practice. During the nineteenth century, men were encouraged to wear spiked rings around their penises at night to avoid nocturnal emissions ("wet dreams"). If the man had an erection, the spikes would cause pain and awaken him.

Table 11.1   Sexual Behaviors across Cultures

Childhood Sexuality	
Mangaia (Polynesian Island)	Children readily exposed to sex. Adolescents are given direct instruction in techniques for pleasuring their sexual partners, and both boys and girls are encouraged to have many partners.
Yolngu (Island near Australia)	Permissive attitude toward childhood sexuality. Parents soothe infants by stroking their genitals. Nudity accepted from infancy through old age.
Inis Beag (Irish Island)	Sexual expression is strongly discouraged. Children learn to abhor nudity and are given no information about sex. Young girls are often shocked by their first menstruation.
Adult Sexuality	
Mangaia (Polynesian Island)	After marriage, three orgasms per night are not uncommon for the male and he is encouraged to give three orgasms to his female partner for every one of his. Adults practice a wide range of sexual behaviors.
Yolngu (Island near Australia)	Males can have many wives and are generally happy with their sex life. Women are given no choice in marital partner and little power in the home. Women are apathetic about sex, seldom orgasmic, and generally unhappy.
Inis Beag (Irish Island)	Little sex play before intercourse. Female orgasm is unknown or considered deviant. Numerous misconceptions about sex (e.g., intercourse can be debilitating, menopause causes insanity).

Sources: Crooks and Baur (1993); Ford and Beach (1951); Money et al. (1970); Ortner and Whitehead (1981).

Although circumcision of infant boys is common in the United States, it is relatively rare in most parts of the world.

trauma) is about 4 percent (Andolsek, 1990). Moreover, in Canada circumcision is considered cosmetic surgery (Cadman, Gafini, and McNamee, 1984). In the United States, an increasing number of pediatricians are refusing to perform the surgery, and insurance companies and state Medicare agencies are refusing to cover routine circumcision.

Some parents have their male children circumcised because their religion prescribes it; other parents have it done for hygienic reasons or because they believe it reduces the risk of diseases like cancer and AIDS. However, the current medical evidence is inconclusive regarding the health risks of noncircumcision (Chessare, 1992; Poland, 1990; Schoen, 1990). The American Academy of Pediatrics (AAP) in 1989 concluded its review of the literature with the following recommendation (Schoen et al., 1989):

> *Newborn circumcision has potential medical benefits and advantages as well as disadvantages and risks. When circumcision is being considered, the benefits and risks should be explained to the parents and informed consent obtained. (p. 390)*

Female Genital Mutilation

If the controversy over infant male circumcision is new information to you, so too may be the practice of female genital mutilation. Throughout history, and as we're becoming increasingly aware, even today in parts of Africa, the Middle East, and Asia, young girls undergo several types of genital mutilation: circumcision (removal of the clitoral hood), clitoridectomy (removal of the clitoris), and genital infibulation (removal of the clitoris and labia and stitching together of the remaining tissue to allow only a small opening for urine and menstrual flow) (Assaad, 1980; Davies, 1992; Lightfoot-Klein and Shaw, 1990). In most countries the surgeries are performed on girls between the ages of 4 and 10 and often without anesthesia or antiseptic conditions. The young girls suffer numerous health problems as a result of these practices—the most serious from genital infibulation. Risks include severe pain, bleeding, chronic infection, and menstrual difficulties. As adults, these women frequently experience serious childbirth complications or infertility. In addition, most women with clitoridectomies or genital infibulation report little or no pleasure from sexual relations.

What is the purpose of these procedures? The main objective is to ensure virginity before marriage (Crooks and Baur, 1993). Without these procedures, young girls are considered unmarriageable and without status (Lightfoot-Klein, 1989). As you may imagine, these practices create serious culture clashes. For example, physicians in Western societies are being asked by parents who have emigrated from these cultures to perform these operations on their daughters. What should the doctor do? Should the parents be forbidden to subject their daughters to these operations? Or would this be another example of ethnocentrism?

As you can see, it is a complex issue. In the case of female genital mutilation, the United Nations has suspended its regular policy of nonintervention in the cultural practices of nations. The World Health Organization (WHO) and the United Nations International Children's Emergency Fund (UNICEF) have both issued statements opposing female genital mutilation and have developed programs to combat this and other harmful practices that affect the health and well-being of women and children (Ladjali and Toubia, 1990). ■

Review Questions

1. _____ used the case study method in his groundbreaking research into human sexuality.

2. Kinsey and his colleagues popularized the use of the _____ method in the study of human sexuality.

3. _____ pioneered the use of direct observation and physiological measurement of bodily responses during sexual activities.

4. What are the advantages of cultural studies in sex research?

5. What is the major reason for female genital mutilation?

Answers to Review Questions can be found in Appendix C.

GENDER DEVELOPMENT

• *In what ways are males and females biologically and psychologically different?*

Gender: The social classification as masculine or feminine.

Why is it that the first question most people ask after a baby is born is "Is it a girl or a boy?" What would life be like if there were no divisions according to maleness or femaleness? Would your career plans or friendship patterns change? These questions reflect the great importance of gender in our lives. This section begins with a look at the various ways in which gender can be defined, followed by a discussion of the major biological and psychological differences between men and women and potential causes of these differences.

Gender Dimensions: Defining "Maleness" and "Femaleness"

Before we can explore what is known about the differences between the sexes, we must clarify the terms "maleness" and "femaleness." In the case of the male twin who was reassigned as a female, do you still think of "her" as being basically male? Or do you think that her feminine dress and behavior patterns and her own personal identity as female are sufficient to label her female? As you can see, what exactly constitutes gender can be very confusing. To improve our understanding, Money and Ehrhardt (1972) define gender in terms of nine dimensions or categories:

1. *Chromosomal gender or genetic sex.* Females have a chromosome pattern of XX, whereas males have the XY pattern (see Chapter 9).

2. *Gonadal gender.* The gonads are the sex glands. The female gonads are the ovaries, which produce the ova, or egg cells. The male gonads are the testes, which produce sperm.

Estrogens: Hormones that stimulate maturation and functioning of the female reproductive system. Also found in lesser amounts in males.

Androgens: Hormones that stimulate maturation and functioning of the male reproductive system. Also found in lesser amounts in females.

3. *Hormonal gender.* Feminizing estrogens are hormones produced primarily in the ovaries; masculinizing androgens are produced primarily in the testes (testosterone is the most important androgen). The ovaries also produce small amounts of androgens; the testes produce small amounts of estrogens; and the adrenal glands of both sexes produce some androgens and estrogens. It is the relative proportion of these hormones that accounts for male–female differences in development.

4. *Genital sex.* The external sex organs of females include the vulva, clitoris, and vaginal opening. The external male genitals are the penis and scrotum (see Figure 11.2).

5. *Internal accessory organs.* The major internal organs for the female are the uterus, vagina, and fallopian tubes. The major internal structures for the male are the prostate gland, seminal vesicles, and vas deferens (see Figure 11.2).

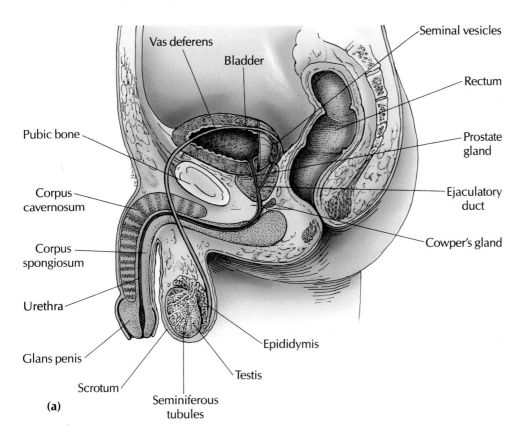

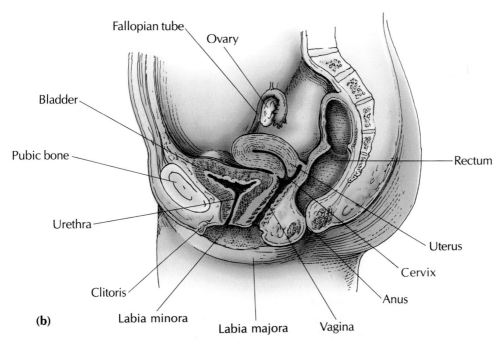

Figure 11.2 The male and female reproductive systems. (a) The basic internal and external sex organs of the male. (b) The basic internal and external sex organs of the female.

In addition to these biological dimensions of gender, there are also psychological and behavioral dimensions:

1. *Gender identity or psychosexual identity.* One's perception of oneself as being male or female.

2. *Gender role.* Gender role refers to the differing societal expectations for the proper male and female behavior. When these expectations are based on exaggerated and biased beliefs about differences between the sexes and are rigidly applied to all members of each sex, they are known as *gender role stereotypes.*

3. *Sexual orientation.* One's choice of same-sex (homosexual) or opposite-sex (heterosexual) persons as sexual partners.

4. *Sexual behavior.* Behavior related to sexual desire, including both arousal and gratification. Masturbation and intercourse are examples of sexual behaviors.

Gender role: The differing societal expectations for proper female and male behavior.

Using the summary of these nine dimensions of gender found in Table 11.2, you can see why the case of the reassigned twin is considered such a classic in the field of human sexuality. Although born a chromosomal male, the child's genital sex was first altered by the doctor who accidentally ablated the penis and later by the surgeons who created female genitals. The question now remains whether this surgery, along with the administration of female hormones and the gender role expectations of the parents, is enough to create a stable female gender identity for the child. Although numerous psychology and sociology texts have cited this sex reassignment case as evidence of the predominant role of the environment in creating gender identity, some research has proposed that the most important factor may be an inherent male or female nervous system bias that forms during prenatal development. This prenatal patterning is believed to set biological limits to the degree of sexual variation any person can comfortably display (Diamond, 1982, 1986; Imperato-McGinley et al., 1979). According to this per-

Table 11.2   **Dimensions of Gender**

Biological Dimensions	Male	Female
1 Chromosomes	XY	XX
2 Gonads	Testes	Ovaries
3 Hormones	Androgens	Estrogens
4 Genital sex	Penis, scrotum	Labia majora, labia minora, clitoris, vaginal opening
5 Internal accessory organs	Prostate gland, seminal vesicles, vas deferens, ejaculatory duct, Cowper's gland	Vagina, uterus, fallopian tubes, cervix

Psychological and Behavioral Dimensions		
1 Gender identity (self-definition)	"Male"	"Female"
2 Gender role (societal expectations)	Masculine ("boys like trucks and sports")	Feminine ("girls like dolls and clothes")
3 Sexual orientation	Heterosexual, homosexual, bisexual	Heterosexual, homosexual, bisexual
4 Sexual behavior	Masturbation, sexual intercourse	Masturbation, sexual intercourse

spective, certain gender problems such as transsexualism (feeling trapped in the body of the wrong gender) might result from a prenatal nervous system bias toward a gender identity that fails to match the external genitals.

Is a transsexual the same as a transvestite?   No, transvestites are individuals (almost exclusively men) who repeatedly and persistently become sexually aroused by wearing feminine clothing (cross-dressing) (Masters, Johnson, and Kolodny, 1992). Transvestites also sometimes become psychologically dependent on wearing feminine clothing as a form of tension release. On the other hand, transsexuals feel that they are *really* members of the opposite sex who have been imprisoned in the wrong body—their gender identity doesn't match their gonads, genitals, or internal accessory organs. Transsexuals may also cross-dress, but their motivation is to look like the *right* sex rather than to obtain sexual arousal. Transvestites can also be distinguished both from female impersonators (who are entertainers) and from gay men who occasionally "go in drag" (cross-dress). Although the labels *transvestite* or *transsexual* would not be appropriate in the case of the twin, it is unclear whether she has fully accepted the female gender role and gender identity or her female body.

What exactly is meant by the term homosexual?   When a person is described as homosexual, it is because of a sexual attraction toward the same sex. (The preferred terms today are *gay* and *lesbian* rather than *homosexual*.) Transsexuality, on the other hand, is unrelated to sexual orientation (Pauly, 1990). In fact, a transsexual can be heterosexual, gay or lesbian, or bisexual (being sexually attracted to both males and females). This can become very confusing. A male transsexual's preference for a male sex partner, for example, would seem to an observer to be a case of homosexuality. But after sex-change surgery this same sexual preference would logically be classified as heterosexual. There are also some male transsexuals who are married or sexually attracted to females before the sex-change operation and continue to prefer female partners after their bodies have been changed to females. The confusion between homosexuality and transsexuality can be avoided by remembering that sexual orientation and gender identity are two different things.

What causes someone to become transsexual, gay, or lesbian?   Scientists have many opinions and theories about this question, but few answers. Looking first at transsexuals, we know that they do have a gender identity conflict, yet we know very little about how their gender identity development differs from that of other children. One of the earliest theories suggested that transsexualism resulted from certain parental behavior or attitudes. The mother and father were either too warm or too cold, were either domineering or ineffectual, or encouraged inappropriate behaviors (Blanchard et al., 1987; Stoller, 1969). Despite the lack of later research support and other theories that suggest genetic or hormonal causes (Money, 1988), this "faulty parental role" theory is still widely accepted by the general public. At the present time no one really knows what causes transsexualism.

Biological Models of Homosexuality

When scientists attempt to explain homosexuality, the answers are generally either biological or psychosocial. The *biological model* suggests that homosexuality is caused by levels of circulating sex hormones, prenatal biasing of the brain (Ellis and Ames, 1987; Money, 1988; Zuger, 1989), structural differences in the brain, or genetic predisposition. There is little research support for hormonal explanations (Gladue, 1987; Money, 1988), and the data on prenatal biasing (a predisposing toward sexual orientation as a result of intrauterine hormonal influences) are conflicting (Ellis and Ames, 1987; Bailey et al., 1991).

The possibility of structural brain differences received some of its strongest support (and wide media attention) when Simon LeVay, a neuroscientist at the Salk institute in San Diego, reported measurable brain differences in heterosexual men and gay men and women. Anatomical dissections of 41 human brains (LeVay, 1991) showed that

Transsexualism: When an individual is physically one sex but psychologically the opposite and has a persistent desire to change his or her body to that of the other sex.

Transvestite: A male who gets sexual excitement and relief from tension by dressing in feminine clothing.

Homosexual: A person who has a primary sexual orientation toward members of his or her own sex.

Bisexual: An individual who engages in both heterosexual and homosexual relations.

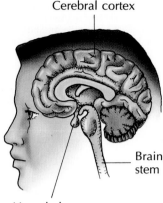

Cerebral cortex

Brain stem

Hypothalamus

Figure 11.3 The hypothalamus and sexual orientation. Researcher Simon LeVay found a significant size difference in an area of the hypothalamus between heterosexual men and gay men and women. Given that the hypothalamus exerts strong influences on sexual behavior, LeVay's findings of size difference may help explain differences in sexual orientation.

a specific area of the hypothalamus (an area of the brain that helps regulate sexual behavior) was twice as large in heterosexual men as compared to gay men and women. Figure 11.3 shows the location of the hypothalamus.

The position on genetic predisposition has also received recent support. Michael Bailey of Northwestern University and Boston psychiatrist Richard Pillard (1991) interviewed 161 gay men and surveyed their twins and/or adoptive brothers. Bailey and Pillard found 52 percent of the identical twins, 22 percent of the fraternal twins, and 11 percent of the adoptive brothers were also gay. Estimates of homosexuality in the general population run between 4 and 10 percent. Some researchers suggest that genes affect the hypothalamus, which LeVay studied (Holden, 1992).

Psychosocial Models of Homosexuality

Early psychoanalytic theory held that homosexuality resulted from disturbed patterns in the individual's family background. Sigmund Freud (1905) believed that men and women were innately bisexual and "normal" development resulted in a heterosexual orientation. Homosexuality was thought to result from certain kinds of early life experiences—especially if the male had a "close-binding intimate mother" and an emotionally detached, hostile father (Bieber et al., 1962). Although Freud originated most "disturbed family" theories, he also held a relatively benign view of homosexuality. Given the repressive nineteenth-century view of sexuality, Freud's advice to a mother who had written to him about her homosexual son can be seen as relatively sensitive and enlightened:

> *Dear Mrs. . . .*
> *I gather from your letter that your son is a homosexual. I am most interested by the fact that you do not mention this term yourself in your information about him. May I question you, why you avoid it? Homosexuality is assuredly no advantage, but it is nothing to be ashamed of, no vice, no degradation. It cannot be classified as an illness. . . . Many highly respectable individuals of ancient and modern times have been homosexuals, several of the greatest men among them (Plato, Michelangelo, Leonardo da Vinci, etc.). It is a great injustice to persecute homosexuality as a crime, and it is a cruelty too. . . .*
>
> *(Gay, 1988, p. 415)*

Modern research has found little support for the belief that childhood factors are the critical determinants of homosexuality. Gays and lesbians are just as likely as heterosexuals to have come from either a "disturbed family" or a well-adjusted family (Siegelman, 1987; Zuger, 1989).

While learning theorists might agree with Freud that early experiences play a role in the development of sexual orientation, they emphasize the importance of reinforcement rather than disturbed relationships with parents. They suggest that childhood experiences with homosexual activities may result in a homosexual orientation as an adult (Van Wyk, 1984). This argument, however, is contradicted by other research which finds that the overwhelming majority of homosexuals had a developing homosexual identity *before* they had homosexual experiences (Bell et al., 1981). Also, early research by Kinsey and his colleagues (1948) and Morton Hunt (1974) found that many people engage in some form of homosexual behavior in their lifetime, especially during adolescence, yet most do not report a homosexual orientation as adults.

In sum, research on the causes of homosexuality is inconclusive, but most psychologists believe that biological and psychosocial factors interact in the development of homosexuality. The possibility that sexual orientation might be at all biologically based has important implications. Some research has found that people who believe that gays and lesbians are "born that way" have a more positive and accepting attitude (Gelman et al, 1992). On the other hand, a biological explanation might encourage attempts to genetically alter homosexuality in utero or to abort "defective" fetuses.

These protesters are demonstrating support for gay fathers and working to overcome prejudice against gays and lesbians.

As evidenced by the public's reaction to President Clinton's proposal to allow gays and lesbians in the military, sexual orientation is a divisive issue in America. Many people in our society view homosexuality and gays and lesbians negatively. Some of these attitudes stem from what Martin Weinberg (1973) labeled homophobia, an irrational fear of homosexuality in oneself or others. Recent political efforts by gays and lesbians to fight discrimination, coupled with acknowledgment by the American Psychiatric and Psychological Associations that homosexuality is not a mental illness, may help overcome public misinformation and homophobia.

Homophobia: An irrational fear of homosexuality in others or oneself. (From the Greek roots meaning "fear" of members of the "same" gender.)

Review Questions

1. The chromosomal patterns of XX and XY determine one's _____ .
2. Males have a dominance of masculinizing hormones known as _____ , whereas females have a dominance of feminizing hormones known as _____ .
3. Societal explanations for behavior that differs for men and women are known as _____ .
4. Differentiate between a transsexual, a transvestite, and a gay or lesbian.
5. What evidence is there that sexual orientation is biologically determined?
6. Name the two models for explaining homosexuality.

Answers to Review Questions can be found in Appendix C.

Biological Differences: Anatomy and Hormones

Physical anatomy is the most obvious difference between males and females. Males have larger hearts and lungs, which help them recover more quickly from physical exertion; females have broader pelvises for childbearing. The average adult male is taller, heavier, and stronger than the average adult female, but he is also more likely to be bald and color-blind. There are major differences in sexual and reproductive organs, as we noted in the discussion of gender dimensions. In Chapter 10, we discussed how males and females differ in their secondary sex characteristics (facial hair, breasts, and so on), their signs of reproductive capability (the menarche for girls and the ejaculation of sperm for boys), and their physical reactions to middle age or the end of reproduction (the female menopause and male climacteric).

In view of these differences, it may be surprising to learn that in the first six weeks after conception all embryos are anatomically identical (see Figure 11.4). During this time, the gonads are *undifferentiated,* which means they have the potential to develop into either testes or ovaries. If the embryo is genetically male (XY chromosome pattern), the gonads differentiate into testes and begin to produce androgens. The most important androgen, testosterone, stimulates the further differentiation into internal and external male sex structures. If the embryo is female (XX chromosome pattern), ovarian tissue forms and begins to produce estrogen. It is important to recognize that it is the *presence* or *absence* of testosterone that determines anatomical sex. Without the Y chromosome

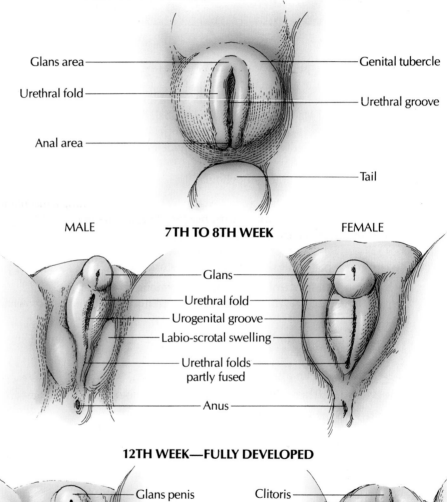

BEFORE THE 6TH WEEK—UNDIFFERENTIATED

Glans area — Genital tubercle
Urethral fold — Urethral groove
Anal area
— Tail

MALE   **7TH TO 8TH WEEK**   FEMALE

Glans
Urethral fold
Urogenital groove
Labio-scrotal swelling
Urethral folds partly fused
Anus

12TH WEEK—FULLY DEVELOPED

Glans penis   Clitoris
Urethra   Urethra
Shaft or body of penis   Labia minora
Labia majora
Scrotum   Vagina
Anus

Figure 11.4 Prenatal stages of external genital development. Notice that before the sixth week there is no visible difference between male and female genitals. As development continues, the embryonic tissue differentiates to become distinctly male or female.

and testosterone, *all* fetuses would develop female reproductive organs and genitals. It seems that nature's basic blueprint is for a female fetus (Hyde, 1994).

What happens if a male baby doesn't get enough testosterone or a female gets too much?   Although genital development almost always matches the genetic sex, there are rare exceptions. As a result of hormonal or genetic problems, some children are born with both male and female genital structures or with ambiguous genitals. In chromosomal females (the XX pattern), faulty genital development is generally due to an over-secretion of androgens by the adrenal glands (adrenogenital syndrome) or to masculinizing synthetic hormones that entered the fetus from the mother's bloodstream during pregnancy. (Such hormones were at one time given to pregnant mothers to prevent miscarriage.) In chromosomal males (the XY pattern), male genitals may fail to develop if testosterone is absent or low at the critical time of 6 to 12 weeks after conception. Even when testosterone is adequate and present, a genetic defect may prevent the cells of the body from responding to it (androgen-insensitivity syndrome). In this case, the male will develop normal-appearing external female genitals.

What happens with babies who are not clearly male or female at birth?   Most abnormalities can be corrected by surgery and the administration of extra hormones. The long-term physical and psychological adjustment of several such children has been closely followed, and the data have been used to support both sides of the ongoing nature–nurture controversy in gender identity studies.

In the case of the reassigned twin, for example, nurturists used "her" successful reassignment as evidence of the environment's primary importance in the development of gender identity. As the female twin entered adolescence, however, the "success" began to be questioned. The child's appearance and masculine gait led her classmates to taunt her, calling her "cavewoman." She also expressed thoughts of becoming a mechanic, and her fantasies showed some discomfort with her female role (Diamond, 1982). Although these conflicts may have reflected a need for an adjustment in her estrogen dose or even just the normal thoughts and problems of adolescence that could occur in any female, they do make it more difficult to use this case as support for the environmental position.

The nativist (nature) position has been strengthened by studies of female fetuses that received more masculine than feminine hormones during prenatal development because the mother took certain prescribed drugs during pregnancy. Although their hormone balance became more female at birth (when they were no longer exposed to masculinizing hormones) and they were raised as girls, these individuals were more frequently described as "tomboys." And during childhood, these girls seemed to prefer the company of boys, were more achievement oriented, and were more aggressive and athletic (Money, 1977). Researchers who wondered if the more masculine behavior could result from the parents' treatment of the child found that the parents were actually more concerned about encouraging feminine behaviors than the average parent (Ehrhardt and Meyer-Bahlburg, 1981). For all the studies that have been done, it remains impossible to truly separate the effects of biological and environmental or social influences on gender development.

Psychological Differences: Innate or Culturally Produced?

Do you think there are inborn psychological differences between women and men? Do you believe that women are more emotional and more concerned with aesthetics, whereas men are naturally more aggressive and competitive?

 Try This Yourself

To test your personal attitudes about possible psychological differences in men and women, stop for a moment and do the following exercise:

> *Imagine you have just entered a room full of strangers. To your right is a group of five females and to your left is a group of five males. Which group would you join?*

Adrenogenital Syndrome: A masculinization of a chromosomal female as a result of an excessive amount of androgens being produced during fetal development.

Androgen-Insensitivity Syndrome: A feminization of a chromosomal male as a result of a genetic defect in which androgens have no effect on the developing fetal tissues.

Jot down the first three reasons that come to mind for joining one group over the other.

Gender Role Stereotypes: Rigid, preconceived beliefs about the characteristics of males and females that are applied to all males and females without regard for individual differences.

Regardless of your choice of groups, either male or female, the reasons for your choice may reflect your personal gender role stereotypes, or fixed ways of thinking about men and women. Although your list probably contains general statements like "I feel more comfortable with . . ." or "I'm more attracted to . . . ," the underlying reasons for your comfort or attraction are often based on your assumptions (stereotypes) about the "average" male or female—"I feel more comfortable with women because they're not so competitive." ∎

What if I had positive reasons for joining the group? Aren't stereotypes negative?   Although the term "stereotype" *is* generally used in a negative manner, we also hold "positive" stereotypes, such as "women are warm and sensitive" and "men are independent and ambitious." The fact that men and women hold both positive and negative gender role stereotypes was demonstrated by Broverman and her colleagues (1970). First, subjects were asked to list the ways they thought men and women differed (characteristics, behavior). Then they were asked to indicate which traits were most desirable. As you can see in Table 11.3, the list of desirable traits is much longer for males than for females. Moreover, many of the "masculine" traits (e.g., independence, ambitiousness, self-confidence) are economically rewarded. This has serious implications for the financial future of "feminine" women. Finally, the so-called masculine traits of "hiding emotions" and "easily separating feelings from ideas" may conflict with the feminine trait of "easily expressing tender feelings," creating misunderstandings between men and women.

Aren't some gender role stereotypes true?   Yes. A stereotype can be true in the sense that it completely fits a specific individual (e.g., Paula Abdul is an excellent dancer, which supports the stereotype of women being better dancers than men). Also, a stereotype can contain a kernel of truth (e.g., there are more professional women dancers than male dancers). But the problem with stereotypes is that individual cases and kernels of truth are exaggerated and assumed to be true of all women and all men (e.g., all women are better than men in dancing). Individuals who do not fit the mold are then considered unnatural or "wrong." Males who are great dancers, for example, or women who never dance are considered unmasculine or unfeminine.

Table 11.3   **Male-Valued and Female-Valued Stereotypic Items**

Female-Valued Items	Male-Valued Items
Very talkative	Very aggressive
Very gentle	Very independent
Very aware of feelings of others	Almost always hides emotions
Very interested in own appearance	Likes math and science very much
Very strong need for security	Not at all excitable in a minor crisis
Easily expresses tender feelings	Very competitive
	Very logical
	Very adventurous
	Can make decisions easily
	Almost always acts as a leader
	Very self-confident
	Very ambitious
	Easily able to separate feelings from ideas

Sources: Adapted from Broverman et al. (1970). "Sex-role stereotypes and clinical judgments of mental health," *Journal of Consulting and Clinical Psychology, 34(1),* 3. Copyright © 1970 by the American Psychological Association. Used by permission of the author.

Stereotypes versus Generalizations

At this point, it is important to distinguish between stereotypes and generalizations. Although these terms are often used interchangeably by the general public, there are important differences between them. Both terms refer to a set of beliefs about the characteristics of members of a given group, and both terms include the idea of application to all group members. Stereotypes, however, are rigid preconceived ideas that are generally based on personal experience with a few people of a group or hearsay evidence. Generalizations, on the other hand, are beliefs about the characteristics of group members that are based on actual data that are collected scientifically. Stereotypes are also generally negative and untrue, while generalizations are usually neutral in value and true. The statement that "most men are taller than most women" is a generalization. It is neutral in value and it is true because it is scientifically researched. In comparison, the statement that "a man can't be as good a parent as a woman" is an example of a stereotype. It is negative toward men, and there is no scientific evidence that this is true. The research findings in Table 11.4 are examples of generalizations about males and females based on scientific research.

Stereotype: A rigid, preconceived set of beliefs about members of a group that are based on limited information and are generally untrue, but are applied to all members of that group without regard for individual differences.

Generalization: A set of beliefs about members of a group that are based on legitimate scientific findings and therefore considered to be true; they can be applied to most members of a group.

A Final Point about Generalizations

When psychologists offer their research findings about differences between groups of men and groups of women, in most cases the overall variance between the sexes is less than the variance within the sexes (Matlin, 1993). That is, the variation within each sex is almost always greater than the average difference between the sexes. This can be understood by drawing a comparison with the obvious male/female physical difference in height. As can be seen in Figure 11.5, there is approximately a six-inch difference in height between the average male and the average female (5′10″ minus 5′4″), but the range of heights within each sex is enormous. Just as knowing someone's gender doesn't allow us to predict how tall he or she is, we also cannot predict whether an individual will be good at math simply by knowing that the average male has slightly higher math scores than the average female. The famous English author Samuel Johnson once gave a very appropriate response to the question on whether males or females are more intelligent. He responded, "Which man? Which woman?"

What causes those differences that do exist between the sexes?   Explanations for gender differences again reflect the nature–nurture controversy. For example, the fact that males tend to be more aggressive and to have better spatial skills is considered by the nativists to be the result of inborn, genetic factors. The nativists point out that the female brain is apparently more symmetrically organized than the male brain (Halpern, 1992), and the relative size of the corpus callosum (the structure that connects the two cerebral hemispheres) in the female brain is larger than in the male (de Lacoste-Utamsing and Holloway, 1982). This finding of a structural sex difference in the corpus callosum is refuted by the work of Ruth Bleier (1987), a neuroanatomist at the University of Wisconsin. Whereas the earlier researchers based their report on 14 autopsied brains,

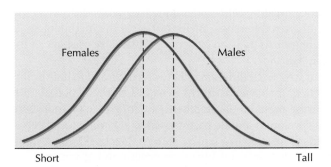

Approximate magnitude of sex differences in height

Figure 11.5 Variations in heights of males and females. Note the overlap between the sexes—some men are shorter than the average female and some women are taller than the average male. This is an example of how overall variance between the sexes is often less than the variance within the sexes.

Table 11.4   **Research-Supported Sex Differences**

Type of Behavior	More Often Shown by Men	More Often Shown by Women
Touching	Are touched, kissed, and cuddled less by parents	Are touched, kissed, and cuddled more by parents
	Exchange less physical contact with other men and respond more negatively to being touched	Exchange more physical contact with other women and respond more positively to being touched
	More likely to initiate both casual and intimate touch	Less likely to initiate either casual or intimate touch
Friendship	Have larger number of friends and express friendship by shared activities	Have smaller number of friends and express friendship by shared communication about self
Aggression	Are more aggressive from a very early age	Are less aggressive from a very early age
Personality	Are more self-confident of future success	Are less self-confident of future success
	Attribute success to internal factors and failures to external factors	Attribute success to external factors and failures to internal factors
	Achievement is task oriented; motives are mastery and competition	Achievement is socially directed with emphasis on self-improvement; have higher work motives
	Are more self-validating	Are more dependent on others for self-validation
	Have higher self-esteem	Have lower self-esteem
Intelligence	Are slightly superior in mathematics and visual–spatial skills	Are slightly superior in grammar, spelling, and perceptual speed
Sexual behavior	Begin masturbating sooner in life cycle and have higher overall occurrence rates	Begin masturbating later in life cycle and have lower overall occurrence rates
	Start sexual life earlier and have first orgasm through masturbation	Start sexual life later and have first orgasm from partner stimulation
	Are more likely to recognize their own arousal	Are less likely to recognize their own arousal
	Experience more orgasm consistency in their sexual relations	Experience less orgasm consistency in their sexual relations

Sources: Allgeier and Allgeier (1991); Crooks and Bauer (1993); Hoyenga and Hoyenga (1993); Hyde (1994).

Bleier used the magnetic resonance imaging (MRI) technique (see Chapter 2) on 39 live subjects and found no evidence of a sex difference. Bleier criticizes the methodology of the previous research and also suggests there is no evidence that the size or shape of the corpus callosum has an effect on behavior.

One of the best documented structural differences between male and female brains that does have measurable effects on behavior is in the synapses in the hypothalamus (Carlson, 1992; Marx, 1988). During prenatal development, a dominance of androgens stimulates the hypothalamus to develop in a male pattern, while a dominance of estrogens stimulates the hypothalamus to develop in a female pattern (MacLuskey and Naftolin, 1981). At the time of puberty, this prenatal hormone programming controls the relatively constant level of hormones in males and the cyclic sex hormone production and menstruation in females.

From an early age, children are socialized toward "appropriate" behaviors for either the male or female gender role.

Nurturist Explanations

In contrast to biological arguments, the nurturists believe male–female differences can be explained by environmental effects. One of the best arguments for this position, and against the biological model, is the recent finding that cognitive gender differences have dramatically declined over recent years (Jacklin, 1989). Using metaanalysis (a statistical technique for estimating the size of effects and comparing large numbers of studies), Hyde and her colleagues (1988, 1990) found a significant reduction in male–female differences in verbal-ability and math scores. The only exception to this trend of vanishing gender differences is in SAT math scores, where males still tend to perform better. However, females tend to receive higher grades in high school and college math classes (Kimball, 1989; Matlin, 1993).

Although cognitive gender differences seem to be disappearing, variations in personality factors like aggression seem relatively stable (Basow, 1986; Hoyenga and Hoyenga, 1993). Nurturists typically explain the consistency of these personality differences by referring to environmental pressures that encourage "sex-appropriate" behaviors and skills. Elementary school teachers, for example, often inadvertently encourage aggressive behavior in boys and passivity in girls. Research by Sadker and Sadker (1985) found that boys talked three times as often as girls. Whereas boys tended to call out their answers to teacher questions, girls usually raised their hands and waited to be called on. When a girl called out her answer, the teacher generally told her that such behavior was inappropriate. Sadker and Sadker concluded that "The message was subtle but powerful: Boys should be academically assertive . . . ; girls should act like ladies and keep quiet."

Socialization

Parents and peers are also important forces in gender role socialization—the process of imparting societal expectations (Fagot et al., 1992; Hyde, 1994; Mosher and Tomkins, 1988). During prenatal development, for example, mothers who have an active fetus that kicks and moves a great deal are more likely to assume it is a boy (Lewis, 1982). Within 24 hours after birth both parents often perceive strong sex-related differences in their newborn babies. Even when there is no physical difference in muscle tone, size, or reflexes, parents, especially fathers, perceive boy infants as stronger, more alert, larger, hardier, and better coordinated than girls (Rubin et al., 1974). Once children get older and go outside the home, the gender role training of the parents is generally reinforced by peer group pressure. Boys as young as three or four will often be ridiculed if they attempt to play "house" and "dolls" with the girls.

When we look at specific differences between the sexes that usually don't appear until adolescence, such as male superiority in visual and spatial tasks, we find that the

Socialization: The process of imparting the customs, habits, folkways, and mores of a given culture to a child or a newcomer to the society.

parents' "silent" expectations of these traits in males may foster their development. In a study where parents were interviewed about their child's mathematical skills, for example, it was found that when boys did well the parents attributed it to their natural ability, but when girls did well the parents downplayed natural abilities and assumed that they had had to work very hard (Eccles et al., 1984). In addition, many parents believe that math is more important for boys and are more likely to encourage additional math courses for boys (Basow, 1986; Lummis and Stevenson, 1990).

Subtle environmental forces may explain other male–female differences as well. For example, gifts of elaborate building blocks and erector sets for boys and encouraging active, rough-and-tumble play (wrestling, throwing, climbing) may provide differential growth experiences for boys that are important to the development of visual–spatial skills. Certainly the case of the reassigned twin shows how differential treatment by parents can lead to feminine rather than masculine traits. How else would you explain the preference for dolls and ribbons in one twin and the preference for cars and tools in the other?

Androgyny: The combining of some characteristics considered to be typically male (e.g., assertive, athletic) with those that are typically female (e.g., yielding, nurturant); from the Greek *andro* meaning "male" and *gyn* meaning "female."

It was very popular at one time to talk about encouraging androgyny (a combination of both male and female personality traits) as a possible "solution" to the problems created by male–female psychological differences (Bem, 1974, 1981; Spence, 1991). But further studies have suggested that it may not be the panacea that many anticipated (Hoyenga and Hoyenga, 1993). In addition to the basic problems of defining and measuring "masculinity" and "femininity," there is disagreement over which are the "best" traits of men and women that should be encouraged in both sexes. The major criticism of the concept of androgyny, however, is that it seems to advocate a specific combination of traits for "ideal" adjustment and such advocacy would be stepping beyond the bounds of scientific research.

Review Questions

1. In the prenatal determination of anatomical sex, the presence or absence of _____ is all-important.

2. Compare the adrenogenital syndrome and the androgen-insensitivity syndrome.

3. The beliefs that women are warm and sensitive and men are independent are examples of _____ .

4. How are stereotypes different from generalizations?

5. Gender role socialization by parents and peers is used by _____ to explain male–female differences.

6. Define androgyny.

Answers to Review Questions can be found in Appendix C.

SEXUAL BEHAVIOR

• *How do men and women differ in sexual arousal, sexual response, sexual problems, and sexually transmitted diseases?*

In this section we will explore what researchers have learned about sexual arousal and response patterns in American culture. As you read, keep in mind that there are individual differences within our culture and differences among cultures.

Sexual Arousal: The Role of Biology and Learning

All healthy men and women are biologically prepared to respond sexually to direct physical stimulation. Although the degree of sensitivity may vary among individuals, the various erogenous zones, such as the penis, the clitoris, the inside of the thighs, and so on, are particularly sensitive to touch because they have a higher concentration of skin receptors. The fact that these same biologically prepared individuals are *not* aroused by the stimulation of erogenous zones during a medical examination or while riding a bicycle demonstrates the powerful role of cultural learning and individual thoughts and expectations in sexual arousal. Many problems that are seen by sex therapists, such as erectile dysfunctions (the inability to get or maintain an erection firm enough for intercourse) and orgasmic dysfunctions (the inability to respond to sexual stimulation to the point of orgasm), are also clearly affected by the emotions and cognitions of the individual. Certain medical conditions such as diabetes, alcoholism, hormonal deficiencies, and circulatory problems also contribute to such problems. Most experts agree, however, that psychological causes (preoccupation with personal problems, fear of evaluation or consequences of the sexual activity, and early negative sexual experiences) are much more prevalent (Kaplan, 1987; "Sexual disorders," 1990). Our bodies are apparently biologically prepared to become aroused and respond to erotic stimulation, but learning is the over-riding factor in how we actually respond.

How do we learn to become sexually aroused?   From our earliest social interactions with others, according to John Gagnon (1977), we learn explicit sexual scripts that teach us "what to do, when, where, how, and with whom." In our culture, for example, traditional societal messages say the "best" sex is sexual intercourse at night, in a darkened room, with the male on top, and between attractive young people of the opposite sex. Yet, most sexual behaviors and people fail to fit within this narrow definition.

A less obvious difficulty with sexual scripts is that, though they do act as strong controls over sexual behavior, they are seldom discussed or examined. Many of our deepest fears and disappointments are a reflection of these unconscious scripts. Women who build their expectations for sexual interactions on the basis of romantic novels and men whose conceptions of the female body are based on photos in *Playboy* or *Penthouse* are often disappointed with real life. A major aim of sex therapy is to encourage individuals to examine their sexual scripts and then explore how these expectations may be interfering with their relationships.

Aren't some parts of arousal biological and unlearned?   Yes. Although many people may consider it unromantic, some parts of sexual arousal are clearly the result of biological processes. Most people consider an evening with a blazing fire and soft music, a romantic "recipe" for sexual arousal, but few people recognize the role of reflexes and the autonomic nervous system (ANS) in sexual desire.

As discussed in Chapter 2, several aspects of human behavior are reflexive—that is, unlearned, automatic, and occurring without conscious effort or motivation. Sexual arousal for both men and women is partially reflexive and somewhat analogous to simple reflexes like the eye blink response to a puff of air. Just as the puff of air produces an automatic response of closing the eye, certain stimuli, such as stroking of the genitals, *can* lead to automatic arousal. In both situations, nerve impulses from the receptor site travel to the spinal cord, which responds by sending messages to target organs or glands. In the case of sexual arousal, the spinal cord responds to stroking messages by telling valves in genital arteries to relax. When these valves relax, blood is allowed to flow into the area, and this increased blood volume results in the erection of the penis in the male and the engorgement of the clitoris and surrounding tissues in the female.

If this is so automatic, why do some people have difficulty getting aroused?   Unlike simple reflexes such as the eye blink, sexual arousal may be blocked by competing thoughts, expectations, and high emotional states. As you may remember from Chapter 2, the ANS is intricately involved in emotional (and sexual) responses. The ANS is composed of two subsystems: the *sympathetic,* which prepares the body for "fight or flight," and the *parasympathetic,* which maintains bodily processes at a steady and even balance. The parasympathetic branch of the nervous system is dominant during sexual arousal (the body must be relaxed to allow the blood flow to the genital area), and the sympathetic branch is dominant during *ejaculation* and *orgasm.*

Erogenous Zones: The areas of the body that elicit sexual arousal when stimulated.

Erectile Dysfunction: The inability to get or maintain an erection firm enough for intercourse.

Orgasmic Dysfunction: The inability to respond to sexual stimulation to the point of orgasm.

Sexual Scripts: Socially dictated descriptions of the sequences of behavior that are considered appropriate in sexual interactions.

Problems with arousal are sometimes explained by the fact that strong emotions, like fear or anxiety, place the individual in sympathetic dominance, which would block the initial arousal. Fear and anxiety also explain why young women often have difficulty with sexual arousal. The secretive and forbidden conditions of many early sexual experiences create strong anxieties and fear of discovery, loss of respect, and unwanted pregnancy. Many women discover that they need locked doors, committed relationships, and reliable birth control to enjoy sexual relations.

What about men? Males often have difficulty with arousal if they drink too much alcohol, are fatigued, or experience performance anxiety. These same factors have similar effects on female arousal, and many men also share the female's desires for privacy, commitment, and freedom from pregnancy concerns.

In spite of the similarities in male–female physiological response to arousal, men often seem more interested in sex and more easily aroused, at least during adolescence and early adulthood. Some sex therapists attribute this difference to the male's superior ability to fantasize (Barbach, 1975, 1982; LoPiccolo, 1992). Since men are encouraged more to think about sex, they are more easily aroused through their own cognitive activities—erotic thoughts send messages from the brain to the spinal cord. Also, the sexual scripts for men and women often reflect a double standard, which helps to explain some male–female differences in arousal. According to this standard, women are responsible for stopping male advances and are expected to refrain from sexual activity until marriage. Men, on the other hand, are often encouraged to explore their sexuality and bring a certain level of sexual knowledge into the marriage (Hyde, 1994). Overt examples of this double standard are less evident in modern times, but you can still see how covert or hidden traces of this belief may cause many problems (like differences in arousal) between men and women.

Sexual Response: The Physiology of Orgasm

Now that we have examined some of the many influences on sexual arousal, let us turn our attention to the bodily processes involved in the complete sexual response cycle identified by William Masters and Virginia Johnson. As mentioned at the beginning of this chapter, Masters and Johnson (1966) were among the first to study human sexual responses through systematic observation in a laboratory setting. Out of their work came a widely publicized model for describing the basic physiological processes that occur from initial arousal to orgasm and back to the unaroused state. Masters and Johnson's model divides the typical sexual response into four phases: excitement, plateau, orgasm, and resolution (see Figure 11.6).

In the excitement phase, which can last from a few minutes to several hours, arousal is initiated through physical factors, such as touching or being touched, or through psychological factors, such as fantasy or erotic stimuli. During this stage, heart rate and respiration increase, and blood flows to the pelvic region, causing engorgement of the penis and the comparable blood-storing spaces in the female. Both male and female nipples may become erect, and both may experience a *sex flush*, or reddening of the upper torso and face.

If stimulation continues, the individual enters the plateau phase, where there are further increases in heartbeat, respiration rate, and blood pressure. In the male, the penis becomes even more engorged and erect, while the testes swell and pull up closer to the body. In the female, the clitoris pulls up under the clitoral hood, and the entrance to the vagina contracts while the uterus rises slightly. This movement of the uterus causes the upper two-thirds of the vagina to "balloon" or expand. As excitement reaches its peak, some fluid, which may contain live sperm, may seep out of the opening of the penis and both sexes may experience a feeling that orgasm is imminent and inevitable.

During the orgasm phase, the individual experiences a highly intense and pleasurable release of tension. This sensation results from muscular contractions that force the

Performance Anxiety: A fear that one will be unable to meet the expectations for sexual "performance" of one's self or one's partner.

Double Standard: The belief that different rules for sexual behavior should be applied to men and women.

Sexual Response Cycle: Masters and Johnson's description of the bodily response to sexual arousal. The four stages are excitement, plateau, orgasm, and resolution.

Excitement Phase: The first phase of the sexual response cycle, characterized by increasing levels of muscle tension and contraction and increased amounts of blood concentration in the genitals.

Plateau Phase: The second phase of the sexual response cycle, characterized by intensification of sexual tensions.

Orgasm Phase: The third phase of the sexual response cycle, during which pleasurable sensations peak and the body suddenly discharges its accumulated sexual tension in the process of orgasm or climax.

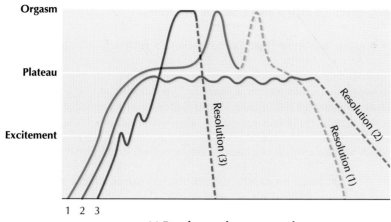

(a) Female sexual response cycles

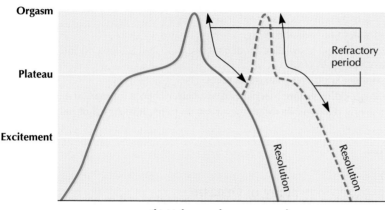

(b) Male sexual response cycle

Figure 11.6 Male and female sexual response patterns. (a) Three possible variations on the female pattern of arousal during the sexual response cycle. Line 1 shows a multiple orgasm pattern; line 2 shows a prolonged arousal at the plateau stage that does not end in orgasm (note the longer time in resolution associated with this lack of orgasm); and line 3 shows several minor drops in arousal during the excitement phase and a rapid resolution. (b) A typical male pattern of arousal from excitement through resolution is shown by the solid line. The dotted line represents the possibility of a second orgasm after the refractory period (the time immediately following ejaculation when a further orgasm is believed to be impossible). Males may also have cycles that resemble lines 2 and 3 in the female. Some researchers also believe that males have multiple orgasms, which would resemble the female's line 1.

blood that has been collecting in the genitals back into the bloodstream. In the female, muscles around the vagina push the vaginal walls in and out and the uterus pulsates. Muscles in and around the penis contract in the male, causing ejaculation, the discharge of semen or seminal fluid.

Both male and female bodies gradually return to their preexcitement state during the resolution phase. After one orgasm, most men enter a refractory period, during which further excitement to orgasm is considered to be impossible. Many women, however, are capable of multiple orgasms in fairly rapid succession.

Sexual Myths

Masters and Johnson's four-stage model of sexual response in the male and female has provided important insights into human sexuality. One of their major contributions was discounting the "vaginal versus clitoral" orgasm debate. Many couples seek therapy or help in acquiring the "right" kind of orgasm, which they interpret as a vaginal response to intercourse. This idea of a preferred type of orgasm can be traced to Freud and his followers. One of the major tenets of early psychoanalytic theory was that women who had orgasms only through direct clitoral stimulation were developmentally immature and rejecting their femininity. Vaginal orgasms through intercourse were considered the hallmark of sexually mature women. Masters and Johnson found, however, that the orgasms women achieved from breast, clitoral, or vaginal stimulation (or even fantasy alone) are not quantitatively different. A number of other myths about sex that researchers such as Masters and Johnson have been working to dispel are presented in Table 11.5.

Ejaculation: The discharge of semen and seminal fluid from the penis at orgasm.

Resolution Phase: The final stage of the sexual response cycle, characterized by continued relaxation as the body returns to its unaroused state.

Refractory Period: The period after orgasm during which further orgasm is considered physiologically impossible.

Table 11.5   Widely Accepted Myths about Sexual Behavior

1 Simultaneous orgasms are better than those experienced separately and should be worked for.
2 In a mutually satisfying sex life, there is no need for masturbation.
3 A male's effectiveness as a sexual partner is dependent upon penis size.
4 Men over 55 have an increased risk of heart attacks if they maintain an active sex life.
5 When a man and woman really love each other, they will intuitively know how to sexually please each other.
6 If a man is sexually aroused and fails to climax, he will experience strong pain for several hours.
7 Sexual activity the night before an athletic competition will reduce athletic performance.
8 If a man or woman lacks sexual interest at home, he or she must be getting sex somewhere else.
9 To have a satisfactory sex life, individuals should have sexual intercourse at least three times a week.
10 The absence of a hymen proves that a girl is not a virgin.
11 Alcohol is a stimulant for sexual activity.
12 General sex education and knowledge about contraception lead adolescents into premature experimentation with sex.
13 Blacks have stronger sex drives than other races.
14 Couples who live together before marriage have a better chance for marital happiness.
15 A partner in a loving relationship should never say no to requests by his or her partner for sex.

Recent Research

Although the work of Masters and Johnson is widely accepted and respected in the field of human sexuality, there has also been considerable criticism. Helen Singer Kaplan (1974, 1987) questions the existence of the separate plateau cycle and the need to describe a "nonstate" like the refractory period. She suggests that sexual response consists of only three phases: desire, excitement, and orgasm. Masters and Johnson also emphasize that only women have multiple orgasms and only men ejaculate, but this assertion has been disputed. Some researchers have found that some men experience multiple orgasms (Hartman and Fithian, 1984; Robbins and Jenson, 1978), and studies have presented highly controversial evidence of *female ejaculation* (an expulsion of fluid from the urinary opening during orgasm) (Darling et al., 1990; Perry and Whipple, 1982; Zaviacic et al., 1988). This ejaculation is said to occur in approximately 10 percent of the women who have experienced direct stimulation of the Grafenberg spot (or "G Spot") — a region in the front wall of the vagina that supposedly has a special sensitivity to erotic stimulation. Although most researchers question this "G Spot" and ejaculatory response (Alzate, 1985; Tavris, 1992), the idea of such a spot has received considerable media attention and public acceptance. Sex educators and therapists are also concerned that this type of public attention adds fuel to the "vaginal versus clitoral" orgasm debate and might also lead to one more goal for couples to achieve. As we will see in the next section, this type of goal setting is one of the primary causes of sex problems.

Sexual Problems: What Are They and How Can They Be Helped?

When sexual functioning is working well, we tend to ignore it and take it for granted. But what happens when things don't go smoothly? What causes normal functioning to stop for some people and never begin for others? Some problems in sexual responsiveness, as we have just seen, result from temporary, situational factors—the need for privacy, protection from pregnancy, too much alcohol, fatigue, and so on. Many sexual problems, however, are much more complex. As shown in Table 11.6, there are a wide variety of

Grafenberg Spot: A region in the front wall of the vagina that supposedly has a special sensitivity to erotic stimulation.

Table 11.6   The Major Male and Female Sexual Dysfunctions

Type of Dysfunction	Description	Causes
Male *Erectile dysfunction (impotence)*	Inability to have or maintain an erection firm enough for intercourse	*Physical*—diabetes, circulatory conditions, heart disease, drugs, extreme fatigue, alcohol consumption, hormone deficiencies *Psychological*—performance anxiety, guilt, difficulty in expressing desires to partner, severe antisexual upbringing
Primary erectile dysfunction	The male has never been able to have sexual intercourse	
Secondary erectile dysfunction	Erection problems occurring in at least 25 percent of sexual encounters	
Premature ejaculation	Rapid ejaculation that is beyond the male's control and his partner is non-orgasmic in at least 50 percent of their intercourse episodes	Almost always *psychological*—the male has learned to ejaculate quickly due to guilt, fear of discovery while masturbating, hurried experiences in cars or motels, and so on
Both male and female *Dyspareunia*	Painful intercourse, more frequent in females but also occurs in males	Primarily *physical*—irritations, infections, or disorders of the internal or external genitals
Inhibited sexual desire (sexual apathy)	Lack of willingness to participate in sexual relations due to disinterest	*Physical*—hormone deficiencies, alcoholism, drugs, chronic illness *Psychological*—depression, prior sex trauma, relationship problems, anxiety
Sexual aversion	Lack of participation in sex due to overwhelming fear or anxiety	*Psychological*—severe parental sex attitudes, prior sex trauma, partner pressure, gender identity confusion
Female *Orgasmic dysfunction (anorgasmia, frigidity)*	Inability or difficulty in reaching orgasm	*Physical*—chronic illness, diabetes, extreme fatigue, drugs, alcohol consumption, hormone deficiencies, pelvic disorders, lack of appropriate or adequate stimulation
Primary orgasmic dysfunction	The female has never had an orgasm	*Psychological*—fear of evaluation, poor body image, relationship problems, guilt, anxiety, severe antisexual upbringing, difficulty in expressing desires to partner, prior sex trauma, childhood sexual abuse
Secondary orgasmic dysfunction	The female was regularly orgasmic at one time, but no longer is	
Situational orgasmic dysfunction	Orgasms occur only under certain circumstances	
Vaginismus	The muscles around the outer one-third of the vagina have involuntary spasms and penile insertion is impossible or difficult and painful	Primarily *psychological*—the woman has learned to associate pain or fear with intercourse due to prior sexual trauma, severe antisexual upbringing, guilt

Sources: Adapted from Masters et al. (1992); Spector and Carey (1990).

sexual dysfunctions, or difficulties in sexual functioning, that may lead people to seek professional help from a sex therapist.

Of course, what is considered "dysfunctional" sexual behavior can vary from era to era, from culture to culture, and even from therapist to therapist. During the nineteenth century, for example, Western European married women who actively enjoyed sexual intercourse were considered abnormal and impure. The ideal woman "endured her husband's attentions" (Money, 1985a). Today the woman who simply endures intercourse is considered the one with the problem. Cultural differences in definitions of

Sexual Dysfunctions: Impairment of the normal physiological processes of arousal and orgasm.

Premature Ejaculation: Ejaculation that takes place too quickly for the pleasure of one or both partners.

"normal" sexual behavior can be seen in a comparison of Russian and American attitudes toward male ejaculation. In Russia it is believed that men should not delay their orgasms, and one Russian medical journal suggests that the ideal duration of the sexual act is two minutes (Stern, 1980). This same behavior would be classified as premature ejaculation by most Western sex therapists. Even Western therapists, however, vary in their definitions of premature ejaculation; many relate it to the partner's satisfaction (frequency of orgasm), which doesn't take into account possible female orgasmic difficulties.

In addition to historical, cultural, and intertherapist variations in defining sexual dysfunctions, there are also labeling and definitional considerations within specific sexual relationships. Not only is it difficult to separate "his" problem (premature ejaculation) from "hers" (orgasmic dysfunction), but many couples often disagree with each other and with therapists as to what constitutes a sexual dysfunction. Also, once the problem is labeled, some individuals experience a loss of self-esteem and perceive the label as a threat to their masculinity or femininity (Goldberg, 1983).

How do therapists work with sex problems?   For many years the major treatment for sexual dysfunctions was long-term psychoanalysis, based on the assumption that sexual problems result from deep-seated personality conflicts that originate in childhood experiences. During the 1950s and 1960s, behavior therapy, which focuses on learning through rewards and punishments as the cause of sexual dysfunctions, was also a method of treatment (see Chapter 15 for a more complete description of both psychoanalysis and behavior therapy). It wasn't until the early 1970s, and the publication of Masters and Johnson's *Human Sexual Inadequacy,* that sex therapy gained national recognition. Because the model of therapy that Masters and Johnson developed is still popular and used by many sex therapists, we will use it as our example of how sex therapy is conducted.

Masters and Johnson's Sex Therapy Program

Masters and Johnson's approach is founded on four major principles:

1. *A relationship focus.* Unlike forms of therapy that focus on the individual, Masters and Johnson's sex therapy focuses on the relationship between two people. To counteract any "blaming" tendencies, each partner is considered to be fully involved and affected by sexual problems.

2. *An integration of physiological and psychosocial factors.* Because medication and many physical disorders can cause or aggravate sexual dysfunctions, Masters and Johnson emphasize the importance of medical histories and exams. They also delve into such psychosocial factors as how the couple first learned about sex, what their current attitudes and values are, and so on.

3. *An emphasis on cognitive factors.* Recognizing that many problems result from fears of performance and *spectatoring* (a mental watching and evaluation of responses during sexual encounters), couples are discouraged from "goal setting" and from judging sex in terms of "success" or "failure."

4. *An emphasis on specific behavioral techniques.* Couples are seen in an intensive two-week program that consists mainly of discussions (to explore their values and misconceptions) and specific behavioral exercises or "homework assignments." In these exercises, couples often begin with the *sensate focus assignment* where each partner takes turns gently caressing the other, communicating what is pleasurable, but with *no* goal or performance demands. After this exercise, couples are given special assignments tailored to their particular sex problem.

Other Therapies

Important contributions to the field of sex therapy have also been made by Helen Kaplan (1974, 1987), who suggests that Masters and Johnson's program works mainly with milder sex problems and that some problems require extensive therapy at a deeper level of insight. In partial response to the expense of the Masters and Johnson's program (in 1992 the two-week program was $20,000), other therapists have offered group therapy to treat sexual dysfunctions (Zilbergeld, 1986). One of the most controversial treatments, once offered by Masters and Johnson and others, involves the use of a "surrogate partner"—a stranger who is paid to serve as a sexual partner during the course of therapy. There are obvious ethical and legal questions that surround this practice.

How effective is sex therapy?   Just as there are disagreements concerning what constitutes a sexual dysfunction, there are also disagreements over what constitutes success in therapy (Kolodny, 1981; "Sexual disorders," 1990). Although the high success rates reported by Masters and Johnson have been seriously questioned (LoPiccolo, 1992; Zilbergeld and Evans, 1980), a variety of studies show that sex therapy can be quite effective for many people. With further research, therapists may find ways to clearly document which elements of therapy are most successful with specific clients and specific disorders.

Improving Sexual Functioning

Work in sex therapy has provided several useful guidelines to improve general sexual functioning and avoid future sexual dysfunctions:

1. *Sex education should begin as early as possible.* Children should be given positive feelings about their bodies and an opportunity to discuss sexuality in an open, honest fashion.

2. *Goal- or performance-oriented approaches should be avoided.* Therapists often remind clients that there really is no "right" way to have sex. When couples or individuals attempt to judge or evaluate their sexual lives or to live up to others' expectations, they risk making sex work rather than pleasure.

3. *Couples need to learn clear communication skills.* Mind reading belongs on stage, not in the bedroom. Partners need to tell each other what feels good, and what doesn't. A sexual problem should be openly discussed without blaming, and if the problem does not improve with discussion and reading self-help books, professional therapy may be necessary.

The guidelines for choosing a therapist provided in Chapter 15 can also be used to select a responsible sex therapist.

Sexually Transmitted Diseases (STD): The Special Problem of AIDS

Early sex education and open communication between partners are not only important for full sexual functioning, they are the key to controlling some of our most serious social and medical problems—sexually transmitted diseases (STDs). Each year millions of Americans contract one or more STDs, and more than half of sexually transmitted disease victims are under the age of 25 (Turner and Robinson, 1993).

Although STDs such as genital warts and chlamydial infections have reached epidemic proportions on college campuses (Aral and Holmes, 1991; Stein, 1991), AIDS (acquired immune deficiency syndrome) has received the largest share of public attention. (See Table 11.7 for an overview of the signs and symptoms of the most common STDs, including AIDS.)

AIDS is now recognized as the most serious epidemic of our time (see Table 11.8). It is a tragic illness that destroys the body's natural defenses against disease and infection. People with AIDS are vulnerable to opportunistic infections that would not be a threat if their immune systems were functioning normally. The AIDS virus may also attack the brain and spinal cord, creating severe neurological deficits. These deficits (known as AIDS dementia) include impaired coordination, forgetfulness, difficulty in concentrating, personality changes, and even seizures and spasms (Stine, 1993).

AIDS is transmitted only through sexual contact or by exposure to infected blood. All known cases of AIDS have been contracted by one of five routes:

AIDS (Acquired Immune Deficiency Syndrome): A catastrophic illness in which a virus destroys the immune system's ability to fight disease. Although the term "AIDS" continues to be used, the President's Commission in 1988 recommended the use of the term *human immunodeficiency virus infection* (HIV infection). They believe that this term more correctly defines the problem and places proper emphasis on the entire spectrum of the epidemic.

Table 11.7 Common Sexually Transmitted Diseases (STDs)

Danger Signs	Could Be	Complications
COMMON MALE SIGNS: • Watery, white drip from penis • Clear discharge from penis • Soreness inside penis • Burning on urination • Swollen or red throat • Yellow discharge from penis	Gonorrhea Nongonococcal- Urethritis (NGU) Other genital infections that also need medical attention Chlamydia	Untreated gonorrhea can cause prostatitis, sterility, arthritis, and heart trouble. Repeated infections can cause partial or complete blockage of penis or cause abscesses in the genital area and elsewhere.
COMMON FEMALE SIGNS: • Burning on urination • Gray, offensive vaginal discharge • Thick and profuse vaginal discharge • Intense itching • Painful intercourse • Thick, cheesy discharge • Rectal irritation • Swollen or red throat • Out-of-cycle abdominal pain • Unusual vaginal or cervical bleeding	Gonorrhea Vaginitis Trichomoniasis Monilia (Yeast) Chlamydia	Untreated gonorrhea can cause pelvic inflammatory disease (PID), which can resemble appendicitis. PID causes severe pain, fever, and sterility. Untreated gonorrhea in the birth canal can cause blindness in the newborn.
COMMON SIGNS FOR BOTH SEXES: • Unexplained weight loss • Diarrhea • Painless sore on penis or vagina • Painful sore or blisters on or around genital area • Rash on hands and feet, or entire body • Loss of hair • Small cauliflower pink growths on or around sex organs • Intense itching • Flu-like feeling • Swollen glands in groin • Sore throat	Syphilis Herpes Virus Hepatitis Scabies Crabs Genital Warts AIDS	Untreated syphilis can cause brain and other organ damage; also paralysis, blindness, heart disease, or death. The most severe complication of herpes genitalis is infection of the newborn during birth. Can be fatal to the baby. Presently there is no demonstrated care for herpes. (Refer to this chapter for more information on AIDS).

You may have an "STD" without any of the danger signs, but still acquire the complications. Seek medical attention if you suspect that you have come in contact with any of the infections! Follow all medical recommendations. This may include returning for a check-up to make sure you are no longer infected. Take only medications prescribed by your doctor, and take all of them as directed. Don't share them.

Sources: Adapted from Kelly and Byrne (1992); Nevid and Gotfried (1993).

Table 11.8 Estimated Number of Cases of AIDS

Africa	6 million
Americas	1 million
Asia	>1 million
Europe	500,000
Oceania	20,000
Total	8–10 million

Sources: World Health Statistics, 1992/WHO.

1. *Sexual intercourse.* Having sex—oral, anal, or vaginal—with someone who is infected with the AIDS virus.

2. *Intravenous drug use.* Sharing needles or syringes with an infected drug user (Stine, 1993).

3. *Blood transfusions.* Receiving blood from an infected donor. The risk of infection from transfusions has been minimized as a result of rigorous screening. There is absolutely NO risk of contracting AIDS by donating blood. Since blood banks use sterile, throwaway needles and collection equipment, there is no way a donor can be exposed (Carson et al., 1992).

4. *Mother and child.* An infected mother can transmit AIDS to her child before birth, during the birth process, or after the child is born (perhaps through breast milk) (Stine, 1993). AIDS-infected infants have also transmitted the

virus to noninfected mothers while nursing (through cracks in the mother's nipple and tears in the nursing infant's mouth) (Lederman, 1992).

5. *Patients and medical personnel.* Inadvertently exposing medical personnel to the contaminated blood of infected patients and vice versa. Both, however, are extremely rare forms of transmission.

Protecting Yourself against AIDS

Since there is no AIDS vaccine, the best way to prevent HIV infection is to avoid risky behaviors. Some of the most important suggestions are:

1. If you use IV drugs, do not share needles or syringes. If you must share, use bleach to clean and sterilize your needles and syringes.

2. Avoid vaginal contact with blood or semen. The use of latex condoms and a spermicide containing nonoxydol-9 are the best methods to avoid contact.

3. Avoid unprotected oral sex ("unprotected" means without a condom or a latex dam).

4. Avoid anal intercourse. This is the riskiest of all sexual behaviors (DeBruyn, 1992; Voeller, 1991).

5. Avoid sex with persons who buy or sell sex. Prostitutes (male and female) have an unusually high rate of HIV infection (Dorfman et al., 1992; Sanders et al., 1991).

6. Do not use alcohol or other drugs to the point where your judgment is impaired (Denney and Quadagno, 1992).

Ads such as this help to combat prejudice and misinformation about AIDS.

Review Questions

1. Briefly explain the roles of the sympathetic and parasympathetic nervous systems in sexual response.

2. Society's different expectations for female and male sexual behavior are known as a _____ .

3. What are the four stages of Masters and Johnson's sexual response cycle?

4. Before the 1970s and the popularization of Masters and Johnson's program for sex therapy, _____ and _____ _____ were the primary methods for treating sexual dysfunctions.

5. _____ is a catastrophic illness that destroys the body's immune system.

6. What are the five ways that AIDS can be transmitted?

Answers to Review Questions can be found in Appendix C.

COERCIVE SEX

While sexuality is often a source of vitality and tender bonding in relationships, it can be severely traumatizing if directed against unwilling partners. Coercive, or forced, sex creates enormous problems for the victim and for our society. This section discusses three types of coercive sex—child sexual abuse, sexual harassment, and rape.

• *What factors influence child sexual abuse, sexual harassment, and rape?*

 Try This Yourself

Before going on, test your knowledge about sexual coercion with the following test. Answer *true* or *false* to the following:

1. Most child sexual abuse is perpetrated by strangers.

Critical Thinking

PSYCHOLOGY IN ACTION

DEVELOPING PERSPECTIVE
Clarifying Your Sexual Values

One of the most important ingredients of critical thinking is the ability to closely examine one's own *values* (ideals, mores, standards, and principles that guide behavior). Are the values you hold a simple reflection of the values of your family or peer group? Or are they the result of careful, deliberate choice? Have you listened carefully to opposing values and compared them to your own? Since values have such a powerful influence on thinking, you should critically evaluate them.

To help you explore your values regarding sex and love, we offer the following exercise. Read the four value statements. Then, in the space to the right, simply check whether you agree or disagree.

		Agree	Disagree
1.	Anyone who wants to prevent pregnancy should have easy access to reliable methods of contraception; it doesn't matter whether a person is married or single, young or old.	____	____
2.	Gay and lesbian couples should be allowed the same legal protections (property inheritance, shared pension plans, shared medical benefits) as heterosexual married couples.	____	____
3.	Abortion in the first four months of pregnancy should be a private deci-		

sion between the woman and her doctor.   ____ ____

4. Sex education belongs in the home, not in public schools.   ____ ____

Each person's sexual values come from a host of sources, some internal and others external to the individual. The second part of this exercise gives you an opportunity to examine some of these sources.

Using the table on the next page, review your agree or disagree responses to the previous four statements. Indicate the degree to which each of the sources listed in the left-hand column has influenced your beliefs by placing a check mark in the appropriate column.

Now reexamine the checks you made for each of your four sexual values and their source of influence. Do you notice any patterns in your check marks? Which source has been most influential in the development of your sexual values? Do you think this source is the most appropriate and most justifiable? Why or why not? Which source has been least influential in the development of your sexual values? How do you explain this? Do you notice any inconsistencies in your choice of sources? In what cases has personal experience played a more significant role than family patterns, peer standards, and so on?

To further clarify your sexual perspective and sharpen your critical thinking skills, share your responses with a close friend, dating partner, and/or spouse. ■

2. Children enjoy sexual relations with adults.

3. Some children are seductive and adults cannot stop themselves from responding.

4. The amount of sexual harassment is greatly exaggerated.

5. Sexual harassment is primarily an expression of sexual desire.

6. No woman can be raped against her will.

7. A man cannot be raped by a woman.

8. If you are going to be raped, you might as well relax and enjoy it.

9. All women secretly want to be raped.

10. Male sexuality is biologically overpowering and beyond a man's control.

Every one of these statements is false. But if you missed one or more of the answers, don't feel alone. These are common *myths* about coercive sex and they are believed by a surprising number of men and women. We will discuss each of these issues in the following pages. ■

Child Sexual Abuse: Pedophilia and Incest

Child Sexual Abuse: Sexual acts performed by an adult with a minor under 18 years of age.

Child sexual abuse is generally defined as an adult's engaging in sexual contact of any kind with a child, including indecent exposure, inappropriate touching, oral-genital

Sexual Values

Sources	Contraception			Homosexuality			Abortion			Sex Education		
	VS	SS	NS	VS	SS	NS	VS	SS	NS	VS	SS	NS
Personal experience												
Family patterns												
Peer standards												
Historical events												
Religious views												
Research findings												

VS = Very Significant Influence
SS = Somewhat Significant Influence
NS = Not a Significant Influence

stimulation, masturbation, anal and vaginal intercourse, and so forth. The law defines "child" as a minor under 18 years of age. These acts are made illegal since the child is not considered mature enough to give informed consent. In Chapter 1 we discussed the importance of informed consent with research participants. Before subjects can consent to participate, they must be fully informed of any possible harm they could suffer. Informed consent in sexuality implies "the possession of adequate intellectual and emotional maturity to understand fully both the meaning and possible consequences of a particular action" (Crooks and Bauer, 1993 p. 653). Informed consent regarding sexuality can be an important issue for the mentally ill and the mentally retarded, as well as the underaged, but in this section we will focus only on children.

Most researchers make a distinction between pedophilia (nonrelative sexual gratification from contact with children) and incest (sexual contact between two people who are related). But there are gray areas in both definitions. For instance, does sex between an 18-year-old male and a 17-year-old female constitute pedophilia? Does sex between cousins qualify as incest? While such examples are sometimes given by people who want to minimize the trauma of child sexual abuse, the legal system is rarely involved in anything other than extreme cases of serious abuse of young children. Moreover, child sexual abuse is underreported in our society.

Prevalence of Child Sexual Abuse

As you will see in an upcoming section, pedophilia and incest—like rape and sexual harassment—are common features of all cultures and throughout history. Similarly, all of these forms of coercive sex go unreported most of the time. This makes it difficult to accurately estimate the prevalence of these crimes. Victims of child sexual abuse, sexual harassment, and rape are reluctant to disclose the assaults for a variety of reasons (see Table 11.9).

Informed Consent: In sexuality, the possession of adequate intellectual and emotional maturity to understand fully and consent to sexual relations.

Pedophilia: Nonrelative sexual gratification from contacts with children.

Incest: Sexual contact between two people who are related.

Table 11.9   Reasons for Not Reporting Coercive Sex

Revictimization	Victims of child sexual abuse, sexual harassment, and rape are often victimized a second time in the reporting of the crime. Sex is an uncomfortable topic for discussion, and to report a sexual crime the victim must repeatedly provide humiliating and perhaps frightening details to parents, police, and medical personnel. These reports frequently leak out to friends, co-workers, and even the press. Furthermore, most sexual crime reports require extensive gynecological exams that can be embarrassing and painful.
Fear, confusion, guilt, and self-doubt	Perpetrators often threaten victims with further violence if they report the crime. Young children are also confused about sexual acts (What is okay and not okay?). Older children and adults are similarly unsure about what constitutes sexual harassment, date rape, and so on. Victims also typically blame and doubt themselves (for not fighting hard enough, not being more aware, etc.). Incest victims often feel guilty for going along with the assault out of fear of loss of love and attention. Sexual harassment victims sometimes submit to save their jobs, academic careers, reputations, letters of recommendation, etc.
Negative reactions from others	Victims are often not believed when they report the crime or they are blamed for the assault. They are also sometimes encouraged to keep silent to keep the family together, to protect the perpetrator from criminal charges, to protect their own or the family's reputation, and so on.

Sources: Allgeier and Allgeier (1991); Crooks and Baur (1993); Denton (1987); Finkelhor (1984, 1990); Waterman and Foss-Goodman (1984).

Estimates of child sexual abuse in America suggest that approximately one-quarter to two-thirds of all women, and one-tenth of all men, have been victims of sexual abuse as children (Finkelhor et al., 1990; Nelson, 1986; Trickett and Putnam, 1993). Although research has generally found that the perpetrators of child sexual abuse are male and the victims are typically female, recent research suggests that women as perpetrators and males as victims may have been underestimated (Bera et al., 1991; Elliott, 1992; Wolfers, 1992).

Is there more child sexual abuse today or is it just more often reported?   There has been a huge jump in the number of cases reported to national data-collection agencies that undoubtedly reflects greater media attention and enforcement of state laws requiring health professionals to report suspected cases. However, evidence from different age groups in a 1990 study by Finkelhor et al. suggests there has *not* been a recent epidemic of abuse. When asked to report on childhood instances of sexual abuse, women aged 50 to 59 were just as likely to report abuse as women aged 18 to 29. This indicates abuse was going on during the older women's childhoods, but it was not reported.

Myths about Child Sexual Abuse

Most people believe the common myth that child sexual abuse is usually perpetrated by strangers. Despite our picture of evil men lurking in alleys offering candy to children, the vast majority of perpetrators are friends and relatives. And, most sexual contact occurs in the child's home or in the friend's or relative's residence rather than in alleys or woods. Another common misperception is that most sexual abusers are gay men. Actually, most are heterosexual, and frequently they are married.

Perhaps the most damaging misconception is that children enjoy sex with adults. Children, like people of all ages, can experience pleasurable sensations from sexual stimulation, but the issue is not solely a physical matter. There are severe negative psychological consequences: inability to trust, feelings of powerlessness, fear of sexual relations. Pedophilia and incest victimize the child and children do not enjoy their victimization.

Many people also believe that small children are seductive and that the offender could not keep from responding (Groth and Burgess, 1980). For example, a judge in

Wisconsin called a five-year-old female victim of sexual assault by a 24-year-old man "an unusually sexually provocative young lady" ("Judge blames," 1982, p. 6). While small children sometimes mimic sexual behaviors of adults, and older children are sometimes deliberately seductive, we must not lose sight of the fact that it is always the responsibility of adults to control their own behavior.

Even when the child is not blamed for being seductive, one study found that a significant number of college students blamed the child "for letting it happen" or for not resisting (Waterman and Foss-Goodman, 1984). These college students, like many others, fail to appreciate the powerlessness of the victim and the nature of sexual abuse. Contrary to the myth of the "seductive child," in most cases of child sexual abuse the child is slowly seduced (with promises of love, special attention, and prizes), trapped (with threats of violence and rejection), and manipulated ("this is our special secret") by the adult over a period of time.

Perpetrator Characteristics

Most pedophiles and incest perpetrators share several psychological similarities. They generally are emotionally immature, very conservative, possess limited sexual knowledge, and tend to have poor interpersonal skills (Alford et al., 1984; Levin and Strava, 1987). While some highly publicized cases suggest that pedophiles desire to torture and punish their victims, most cases do not involve violence. The pedophile and incest perpetrator typically molest children not out of hate and aggression, but as a way of gaining sexual gratification in spite of his or her feelings of inadequacy and fear of rejection. A child is less threatening and more easily seduced than an adult partner.

The perpetrators also frequently have a distorted view of their actions. For example, incest perpetrators often believe that child sex is an effective way for children to learn about sex and that the child does not report contact because she/he enjoys it (Abel, 1984). Similarly, the pedophile often believes the problem is with a repressive society that doesn't allow children to express themselves sexually.

Effects of Child Sexual Abuse

There is considerable evidence that childhood sexual abuse can be severely traumatizing not only at the time of the abuse but throughout the victim's life (Boyer and Fine, 1992; Trickett and Putnam, 1993; Young, 1992). Some of the most lasting effects of child abuse are:

1. *Guilt and shame.* Victims often feel guilty because they didn't fight hard enough or because they may have enjoyed the physical stimulation or attention of the adult. These individuals also frequently believe there is something wrong with them or they wouldn't have been "chosen" (Frazier and Cohen, 1992; Harter et al., 1988).

2. *Difficulty forming intimate relations.* Female survivors frequently find it hard to trust men, and their relationships often are devoid of emotional or sexual fulfillment (Jackson et al., 1990). Also, many victims will choose inadequate mates—alcoholics, physical abusers, and so forth.

3. *Sexual dysfunctions.* History of childhood sexual abuse is a common feature of many women who seek sex therapy for orgasm difficulties and other forms of sexual dysfunction (Maltz, 1988).

4. *Psychological difficulties.* Drug and alcohol abuse, eating disorders (obesity, anorexia, and bulimia), elevated suicide rate, depression, low self-esteem, and a predisposition to being victimized are some of the serious long-term effects of sexual abuse in childhood (Felitti, 1991; Trickett and Putnam, 1993).

Many mental health professionals believe the severity of these effects can be reduced by proper reactions of adults at the time the assault is reported. Recall from Chapter 9 that young children are very egocentric and typically believe that the world revolves around them. When they are sexually assaulted, they frequently blame themselves. At the time of discovery or reporting of an assault, adults must be careful to place responsibility where it belongs, with the perpetrator, and to provide gentle, nonjudgmental support for the child.

Treatment for the adult survivor of child sexual abuse typically may involve individual or group therapy and support groups (Cahill et al., 1991; Patten et al., 1989). In Chapter 16, we discuss methods for selecting therapists that also apply to victims of sexual abuse.

Preventing Child Sexual Abuse

Programs to prevent sexual abuse focus on three major audiences: parents, children, and professionals. Parents must be alerted to the fact that most child sexual abusers are family members, friends, and acquaintances, not strangers. Helping parents identify warning signs of abuse (see Table 11.10) is one of the most important steps in preventing abuse.

Once parents are educated, they can teach their children the difference between "okay" and "not-okay" touches, and how to deal with an adult's attempt to coerce them into sexual contact. Children can be given specific examples of what to do when such situations arise—saying "Don't touch me!" or telling a responsible adult. Many perpetrators later interviewed say they would have been deterred by a child saying he or she would tell a specific adult (Daro, 1991).

Child sexual abuse prevention programs have also been developed to educate professionals, especially teachers, physicians, police officers, and mental health clinicians. If these groups are trained to be alert to the signs of abuse and to reinforce the messages of caution to children, the incidence of child sexual abuse can be reduced.

Sexual Harassment: An Exploitation of Power

Sexual Harassment: Unwelcome sexual advances, requests for sexual favors, and other unwelcome verbal or physical conduct of a sexual nature.

The legal definition of sexual harassment is unwelcome sexual advances, requests for sexual favors, and other unwelcome verbal or physical conduct of a sexual nature. A federal study defined three levels of sexual harassment: less severe (sexual teasing, jokes, sexual remarks, suggestive looks, gestures, etc.), severe (pressure for dates, touching, pinching, pressure for sexual favors, letters, phone calls, showing sexual pictures, stories, etc.), and criminal (rape, attempted rape, and sexual assault).

Myths about Sexual Harassment

Contrary to misperceptions that charges of sexual harassment are often made for the slightest provocation, a survey by The Working Women United Institute found that of the women who were harassed, 75 percent ignored the harassment and only 18 percent reported the harassment. Those who did not complain believed nothing would be done, worried they would be blamed, and felt they would suffer negative repercussions.

Also, people mistakenly believe that sexual harassment is primarily an expression of sexual desire, rather than generally being an assertion and abuse of power (Backhouse and Cohen, 1981). Because of this misperception of sexual desire, when older or less

Table 11.10   **Physical and Psychological Signs of Sexual Abuse**

Physical Signs	Difficulty in walking or sitting. Pain, bruises, bleeding, or itching in genital areas. Sexually transmitted diseases. Pregnancy.
Psychological Signs	Fear of being alone with a specific person. Changes in behavior (schoolwork, sleep disturbances, clinging to a parent, disturbed relationships with friends and siblings). Regression (behaving like a younger person—bedwetting, thumb sucking). Unexplained fears. Sexual sophistication (greater knowledge about sexual matters than age group).

Source: Adapted from Denney and Quadagno (1992).

attractive women complain of sexual harassment, they are often ignored or ridiculed ("Don't flatter yourself"). On the other hand, when the victim is young and attractive she is accused of "inviting" a sexual approach. Like other victims of sexual abuse, those who are harassed are often accused of "asking for it." During her testimony before a Senate subcommittee designed to establish guidelines for sexual harassment, antifeminist Phyllis Schlafly suggested that "Sexual harassment on the job is not a problem for the virtuous woman, except in the rarest of cases. . . . Men hardly ever ask sexual favors of women from whom the certain answer is no (Committee on Labor and Human Resources, 1981, p. 400). Schlafly provided no data to support her statement, and research studies document that sexual harassment is quite widespread.

Sexual Harassment on the Job

Law professor Anita Hill's charge that she was sexually harassed by Supreme Court Justice Clarence Thomas brought national attention to the issue of sexual harassment. But most people still underestimate the prevalence of occupational sexual harassment and consider it a minor issue (Crooks and Bauer, 1993). In the first large-scale study of over 20,000 men and women on active duty in the military, more than two out of three women said they had been sexually harassed (Schmitt, 1990). Similarly, a survey of almost 500 nurses revealed that 76 percent had been sexually harassed on the job (Grieco, 1987).

Sexual Harassment in Academia

Sexual harassment occurs in the academic setting as well as in the workplace. Power is misused to coerce students into sexual acts. Students comply with the perpetrator's demands out of fear of academic repercussions, a need for a letter of recommendation or a higher grade, or desire for a research or work opportunity (Riger, 1991).

Sexual harassment in educational settings is fairly common. Studies estimate that 13 to 40 percent of students, as well as 20 to 49 percent of female faculty are affected (Allen and Okawa, 1987; Paludi, 1992).

Effects of Sexual Harassment

Victims of sexual harassment on the job often face severe financial difficulties, such as unemployment, demotions, or loss of promotions, if they resist the harassment. Victims also suffer various physical and psychological effects, including nervousness, loss of motivation, sleeplessness, guilt, shame, anger, depression, and helplessness (Bullogh, 1990; Hamilton et al., 1987).

The effects of harassment in educational settings are less clear. Although students depend considerably on faculty for their academic success, they do have a few more options for escaping the harassment (Riger, 1991). They can take a different instructor and they are typically in school for a relatively brief period of time. On the other hand, students tend to be younger and more naive about harassment than employees. Some students may initially feel flattered by the attention of a professor, but many students do feel coerced. And one study found that women who were victims of academic sexual harassment viewed their experience as almost as stressful as attempted rape (DiVasto et al., 1984).

Preventing Sexual Harassment

In recent years, employers and university administrators have been taking increasingly strong stands against sexual harassment. Each group has a legal responsibility to train supervisors to recognize and avoid sexual harassment, to establish a grievance procedure, and to punish guilty parties when complaints are verified (Diamond et al., 1981).

What can the victim or target of sexual harassment do to stop the abuse?   Kelley and Byrne (1992) offer several suggestions:

1. If you are harassed by a professor or an employer, you should make your objections clear. A firm "no" is an important first step.

Anita Hill's testimony before the Senate Judiciary Committee brought national attention to the harassment of women in the workplace. Part of the public's confusion over this case resulted from the popular myth that sexual harassment is an expression of sexual desire, rather than a manifestation of power and domination of one person over another.

2. Discuss the problem with fellow students or employees. Identifying other victims bolsters your case and provides social and emotional support.

3. If the problem continues, keep a detailed record (noting times, dates, locations, possible witnesses, and precisely what was said or done). In addition, contact authorities on the campus or at work. You might begin by consulting another professor or supervisor whom you trust to help you determine the appropriate officials and channels for complaints.

4. If the harassment continues and your grievances are not acted upon, you may want to contact your state's civil rights commission and file a formal grievance. Current affirmative action regulations protect people who file harassment complaints from instructor retaliation and from job demotion or firing.

Review Questions

1. Define "child sexual abuse."
2. What is the difference between pedophilia and incest?
3. Most child sexual abuse is done by _____ not by _____ .
4. What are the four major long-term effects of child sexual abuse on the victim?
5. Unwelcome sexual advances, requests for sexual favors, and other unwelcome verbal or physical conduct of a sexual nature all represent what is known as _____ .
6. Sexual harassment is primarily _____ and not an expression of sexual desire.

Answers to Review Questions can be found in Appendix C.

Rape: An Increasingly Common Form of Coercive Sex

Rape: Oral, anal, or vaginal penetration that a person forces on an unconsenting or unwilling victim.

Rape can be defined in many ways. One of the most simple and inclusive definitions is "the oral, anal, or vaginal penetration that a person forces on an unconsenting or unwilling victim" (Denney and Quadagno, 1992, p. 593). Stranger rape refers to rape by an unknown assailant, while acquaintance rape or date rape is committed by someone who is known to the victim.

Surveys show that the percentage of women who have suffered from attempted rape or completed rape range from 15 to 30 percent (Koss 1992; Ward et al., 1991). For reasons such as those previously shown in Table 11.4, three out of four stranger rapes, and nearly all acquaintance rapes, are never reported (Kilpatrick et al., 1992).

Effects of Rape

The major physical effects of rape include nausea, headache, and sleep disorders, possible pregnancy, and infection with sexually transmitted diseases. In addition, most victims also suffer physical injuries such as bruises, abrasions, and vaginal or rectal tears (Beebe, 1991; Parrot and Bechhofer, 1991). Victims should seek immediate medical treatment for these injuries. Although the risk of pregnancy is low, contraceptive pills can be administered to prevent pregnancy. Also, if the woman decides to press charges against her attacker, she will need objective evidence of the rape. During her examination, samples of the rapist's blood, skin, pubic hair, and semen will be collected from the victim's body and clothing.

Rape Trauma Syndrome: The consequences suffered by a rape victim, including both physical and psychological effects.

The major psychological effects of rape have been labeled the rape trauma syndrome (Burgess and Holmstrom, 1974, 1988). In the *acute phase* of the syndrome, which begins right after the rape and may continue for hours or weeks, most women tend to react in either an expressive manner (crying and emotional turmoil) or an overly controlled manner (being subdued and unemotional).

Then the *long-term reorganization phase* takes place. This may last for several months or even years. The victim often fears that the rapist may return and she may frequently move her place of residence. She may also have fearful and negative feelings about sexual relationships, experience flashbacks, dislike being touched, and suffer from self-blame and depression (Parrot, 1990).

Rape victims often find that supportive counseling helps ease the trauma of rape (Burgess and Holmstrom, 1988; Duddle, 1991). The rape of their partner also causes many men serious emotional difficulties and they need help coping with their own feelings as well as their partner's (Cohen, 1988).

Myths about Rape

There are several myths about rape. One of the most prevalent is that no woman can be raped against her will. This is false for many reasons. First, most men are much stronger and faster than most women. And a woman's clothing and shoes typically hinder her ability to escape. Second, the female gender role encourages passivity. Few women have been taught to actively and aggressively defend themselves. Third, rapists generally have the benefit of advance planning and surprise. The man who rapes chooses the time and place. Finally, many rapists work in gangs and use weapons to control the victim.

A second myth is that women cannot rape men. Although most rapes are committed by men against women, surveys also find that some men have been forced into sexual activities that they did not want (Muehlenhard and Cook, 1988; Struckman and Johnson, 1988). Contrary to common belief, a man can have an erection despite negative emotions such as humiliation, fear, or anger. While many people might picture the male victim of female rape as enjoying it and suffering no aftereffects, males also suffer emotional trauma from being victimized, and sexual dysfunction is common (Myers, 1989).

Perhaps the most insulting myth about rape is the statement, "if you are going to be raped, you might as well relax and enjoy it." This myth is based on underlying misconceptions about the "enjoyable" nature of rape. A study of college men and women found that both sexes believe a substantial percentage of women would secretly enjoy being raped if no one knew (Malamuth, Haber, and Feshbach, 1980). It is important to

The widely publicized trial of William Kennedy Smith brought national attention to the issue of date rape.

note that when the women in this study were asked to state their own reaction to such a situation, very few (approximately 2 percent) believed they themselves would derive pleasure from such an experience.

How can this be explained? Women, like men, often fall victim to stereotypes and myths that are widely accepted in our culture. For example, novels and films typically portray a woman resisting her attacker, and then melting into passionate responsiveness. These portrayals ignore the fact that in real life physical violence is occurring and that almost all women fear for their lives during a rape (Brownmiller, 1975). Instead, these films and novels create an illusion that women are conflicted about their own sexuality and secretly want to be forced to submit (Aronson, 1992).

The myth of "enjoyment" is also perpetuated by the well-known fact that women often do report fantasies about being raped. This leads many people to believe that "all women secretly want to be raped." It is important to emphasize, however, that during fantasies the woman is in complete control, whereas in rape she is completely powerless. Also, fantasies contain no threat of physical harm, while rape does.

Finally, the most dangerous myth about rape is that male sexuality is biologically overpowering and beyond a man's control. This is the same myth used to justify adult reactions to a "seductive" child. In the case of rape, the woman is blamed for "enticing" the man. This myth is not only unfair and insulting to men, by suggesting that women and small children "manage" and control sexuality, but extremely dangerous to women and all of society because it justifies and perpetuates rape.

Motives for Rape

Studies have identified four major motives for rape. [The first three categories were developed by Groth and Hobson (1983) and the fourth is from Crooks and Bauer (1993).]

1. *Anger (or revenge) rape* is an impulsive, unpremeditated, savage assault by an angry, depressed, resentful man who feels he is getting even for wrongs done to him by a woman or women. The anger rapist frequently has difficulty obtaining an erection and generally does not find the rape to be sexually gratifying. The victim is often insulted, humiliated, and subjected to physical violence far in excess of what is needed to force sexual submission. The rape is seen as a chance to get even for the humiliation, rejection, or other "put downs" the anger rapist believes he has suffered from women.

2. *Power rape* is a premeditated attempt to gain power and control by an insecure, anxious man who feels overwhelmed and out-of-control in his personal life. While the power rapist does seek sexual gratification, his primary aim is to dominate and demonstrate that he has power over his victim. He normally uses only enough force to cause the woman to cooperate; he does not want to purposely injure her.

3. *Sadistic rape* is a premeditated, long-lasting, ritualistic assault and abduction by a violent, angry, sadistic man who becomes aroused by the victim's fear and suffering. The victim is degraded and humiliated and often forced to undergo bondage, torture, and mutilation. In this type of rape, aggression and power are both erotic experiences, and the victim is frequently physically tortured and/or murdered.

4. *Sexual gratification rape* is a sexual assault by a man who is willing to use varying degrees of force to obtain sexual gratification. If excessive force or violence is necessary to subdue the woman, the rapist may terminate his attack. The victim is often terrified and feels humiliated, but the rapist is likely to use no more force than necessary to obtain his sexual gratification.

Sexual gratification rape is the category most often associated with acquaintance rape. Acquaintance rape (date rape) is unfortunately a relatively common experience (Grauerholz and Koralewski, 1990; Koss, 1992). In one study 35 percent of female subjects reported having been victims of either attempted or completed acquaintance rape (Russell, 1984).

Causes of Acquaintance Rape

Unlike stranger rape, little force is typically used in acquaintance rape. The victim "cooperates" for a variety of reasons: being intoxicated, feeling obligated because of time and money expended by a partner, desire to be popular, peer pressure, threats to end the relationship, and so on. The perpetrator of acquaintance rape often feels pressured to make sexual advances, is intoxicated, and frequently misinterprets the female's behavior (a "no" is seen as token resistance so as not to appear too "easy") (Check and Malamuth, 1983; Muehlenhard et al., 1991).

As we discuss in the next section, acquaintance rape, like all forms of rape, reflects in various ways traditional societal views about the proper role for men and women. For example, hypermasculine, or "macho personality," men have been found to have callous attitudes toward women, to believe that violence is manly, and that danger is exciting (Mosher and Tomkins, 1988). On the other hand, hyperfeminine females tend to support the belief that attractiveness and sex should be used to get a man and keep him, and that relationships with men are of primary importance (Murnen and Byner, 1991). This research, then, suggests that traditional values may set the stage for date rape and other forms of rape both by encouraging men to exploit women for sexual purposes and by encouraging women to use sex to manipulate men.

Rape and Violent Pornography

One of the most highly researched possible causes of rape is violent pornography. In most forms of violent pornography, the woman is portrayed as initially fighting off her attacker, but eventually her resistance is overwhelmed and her passion is unleashed. According to research, this kind of violent pornography has two major effects:

1. Distorted attitudes about rape. Viewers of typical episodes of violent pornography have distorted perceptions of how women actually respond to sexual coercion. Both

In addition to the four psychological motives for rape discussed in the text, social factors such as hatred and revenge between warring nations can also lead to rape. These women in Bosnia suffered war-precipitated rape.

college men and noncollege men who are exposed to this type of pornography are more likely than other men to believe the previously mentioned myth that women enjoy rape (Check, 1984; Malamuth and Check, 1985). Furthermore, men who have been shown a sexually violent movie are less likely to sympathize with a rape victim when they serve as jury members in a simulated trial (Donnerstein and Linz, 1984; Linz, 1989).

2. Increased violence against women.   Viewing violent pornography has also been associated with increased aggression toward women, at least in laboratory settings. For example, Donnerstein and Berkowitz (1981) conducted a study in which male college students were angered by either a male or female research assistant who was posing as fellow student. The males were then shown either a violent pornographic film in which the woman responded positively to a rape; a violent pornographic film in which the woman responded negatively to a rape; a nonviolent pornographic film; or a neutral film. After viewing the films, the male subjects were allowed to administer shocks during a learning task to the research assistants who had previously angered them. What do you think happened? As predicted, viewing either form of violent pornography (with the woman responding negatively or positively) led to increased levels of aggression toward the female research assistant. It is important to note that in this study, as well as others, there was no increase in aggression toward the males, suggesting that the films do not increase generalized aggression but only increased aggression toward women (Zillman and Weaver, 1989).

Isn't it unethical to show films that encourage rape myths and to encourage male subjects toward aggression to women?   Excellent point. Researchers are extremely aware of the controversial nature of this type of research and take special precautions. First, the research assistants never receive an actual shock. Second, subjects are carefully selected, properly warned of the nature of the research, and extensively debriefed after the experiments.

During the debriefing, experimenters are careful to expose and debunk such rape myths as women secretly desire rape and women enjoy rape. A follow-up study showed that after debriefing, the subjects became less accepting of the "women enjoy rape" myth than students who did not see the films (Malamuth and Check, 1985).

Prevention of Rape

As the Malamuth and Check study just cited shows, alerting people to myths and then debunking them can be an important step in the prevention of rape. In addition, research offers several suggestions for reducing personal vulnerability to rape (Crooks and Baur, 1993; Denney and Quadagno, 1992).

To avoid stranger rape:

1. Follow commonsense advice for avoiding all forms of crime: lock your car, park in lighted areas, install dead-bolt locks on your doors, don't open your door to strangers, don't hitchhike, etc.

2. Make yourself as strong as possible. Take a self-defense course, carry a loud whistle with you, and demonstrate self-confidence with your body language. Research shows that rapists tend to select women who appear passive and weak (Richards et al., 1991).

3. During an attack, run away if you can, talk to the rapist as a way to stall, and/or attempt to alert others by screaming ("Help, rape, call the police") (Shotland and Stebbins, 1980). When all else fails, women should actively resist an attack, according to current research (Fischhoff, 1992; Furby and Fischhoff, 1992). Loud shouting, fighting back, and causing a scene may deter an attack.

To prevent acquaintance rape, women should:

1. Be careful on first dates—date in groups and in public places; avoid alcohol and other drugs (Muehlenhard and Schrag, 1991).

2. Be assertive and clear in your communication—say what you want, what you don't want, and don't say no when you mean yes.

3. If sexual coercion escalates, match his behavior with your own form of escalation—begin with firm refusals, get louder, threaten to call the police, begin shouting and use strong physical resistance. *Don't be afraid to make a scene!*

To prevent acquaintance rape, men should:

1. Avoid drugs and alcohol if you cannot control your behavior.

2. Reject such myths as sexy clothes mean she's asking for it or women enjoy rape. Debunk these myths in front of other men.

3. Accept a woman's refusal as genuine. Even in the rare case of a woman who doesn't really mean "no," accepting her first refusal is a good model for appropriate relating and effective communication.

Gender and Cultural Diversity

CULTURAL INFLUENCES ON COERCIVE SEX

Our discussion of coercive sex is based primarily on data collected from American subjects. To broaden our perspective, let's look at attitudes and practices in other cultures.

Prohibitions against incest are one of the clearest cultural universals. Every society has taboos against sexual relations and intermarriage with certain relatives. For that reason, it has been suggested that incest taboos are biologically based. The belief is that if closely related individuals mate, any shared defective genes are more likely to be passed on to the offspring. Therefore, incest taboos offer genetic advantages to our species.

This genetic argument for incest taboos helps explain some forms of prohibition, but Ford and Beach's (1951) large cultural study found considerable range in the number of people prohibited from mating. They found that in almost three-quarters of the non-Western societies the group of restricted partners was much more extensive than in modern Western societies. The fact that the Kwonia people of New Guinea and the Cheyenne Indians of North America extend their incest taboos to in-laws and in-laws of in-laws suggests that the taboos also serve a social and cultural function.

French anthropologist Claude Levi-Strauss (1969) believes less complex societies extend their incest taboos as a way of developing larger social units through kinship ties. If people marry outside their group, they increase access to other groups' resources and products. As technology develops, these types of alliances are less necessary and incest taboos are weakened.

When we look at rape throughout history and across cultures, we also discover several interesting facts. Until very recently, rape was considered a violation of male property rights. According to ancient Babylonian law (about 4000 years ago), a woman was not recognized as an independent being. As a girl she was owned by her father, and as an adult she belonged to her husband. Since virginity affected the dowry payment a father could expect for his daughter, raping a virgin was tantamount to stealing and punishable by death. While a virgin daughter was considered innocent, a married woman who was raped was considered guilty of adultery, as was the man. Both were tried and if found guilty, both were put to death. In the United States we see traces of this ancient heritage even today. In most states it is not a crime for a man to rape his wife. Also, rapes of nonmarried, young "virtuous" women are treated much more seriously in the legal system.

As important as historical influence is in predicting cultural attitudes toward rape, a number of researchers suggest that gender role socialization may be an even more important factor (Boeringer et al., 1991; Brownmiller, 1975; Fonow et al., 1992). This viewpoint is supported by Peggy Reeves Sanday's (1981) comparison of the incidence of rape in 95 societies. Sanday found that several cultural factors, including the nature of relations between the sexes, the status of women, and the attitudes and values fostered in boys during early development, could predict the level of rape in a society. In "rape prone" societies, men and boys are encouraged to be aggressive and competitive, and women generally have less power in the economic and political areas of life. On the other hand, in "rape free" societies women and men share power and authority. Also, children of both sexes are raised to value nurturance and cooperation and avoid aggression and violence.

It should come as no surprise that the United States is a "rape prone" society among those Sanday studied. The characterization of male and female roles in "rape prone" societies closely parallels those we see in our own. Perhaps, however, as American men and women move toward a more equal sharing of economic, social, and political power, we will see a decrease in all forms of coercive sex. ■

Review Questions

1. How is rape defined?
2. The major psychological effects of rape have been labeled the _____ .
3. What are the four major types of rape?
4. _____ and _____ are the two major negative effects of violent pornography.
5. What is the major social and cultural function of incest taboos?
6. Until very recently, rape of women was considered by law to be a violation of _____ .
7. How do "rape prone" societies differ from "rape free" societies?

Answers to Review Questions can be found in Appendix C.

REVIEW OF MAJOR CONCEPTS

THE STUDY OF HUMAN SEXUALITY

1. Although sex has always been an important part of human interest, motivation, and behavior, it received little scientific attention before the twentieth century. Using the case study technique, Havelock Ellis was among the first to study human sexuality despite the heavy repression and secrecy of nineteenth-century Victorian times.

2. Alfred Kinsey and his colleagues were the first to conduct large-scale, systematic surveys and interviews of the sexual practices and preferences of Americans during the 1940s and 1950s. The research team of Masters and Johnson pioneered the use of actual laboratory measurement and observation of human physiological response during sexual arousal. Cultural studies are also important sources of scientific information in human sexuality.

GENDER DEVELOPMENT

3. Maleness and femaleness (gender) can be differentiated along five biological dimensions: chromosomal gender, gonadal gender, hormonal gender, genital sex, and internal accessory organs. There are also four psychological and behavioral dimensions to gender: gender identity, gender role, sexual orientation, and sexual behavior.

4. These gender dimensions can be used to explain several misunderstandings. Transsexuals, for example, have a gender identity conflict (their anatomy fails to match their personal sense of being male or female), whereas transvestites cross-dress for the purpose of sexual arousal.

5. The causes of both transsexualism and homosexuality are seen by some to be environmental (parental modeling or treatment and learning through rewards and punishments), but others suggest their origins are biological (either genetically transmitted or due to hormonal imbalances). This is the nurture versus nature controversy.

6. Males and females have several obvious physical differences, such as height, body build, and reproductive organs, but during the first six weeks of prenatal development all embryos are anatomically identical. The presence of testosterone allows the male embryo to develop male genitals, and disruptions in this hormone can lead to problems in the development of both male and female genitals.

7. The belief in rigid, psychological differences in males and females is known as sex stereotyping. Although some actual differences have been documented (such as in aggression and verbal skills), the cause of these differences (either nature or nurture) is hotly debated.

SEXUAL BEHAVIOR

8. Several aspects of sexual arousal can be explained from a biological perspective. Erogenous zones contain increased sensory receptors, and ejaculation and orgasm are partially reflexive. Dominance of the parasympathetic nervous system allows for sexual arousal, but dominance of the sympathetic nervous system is necessary for orgasm to occur.

9. Arousal is also learned. Sexual scripts teach us what to consider the "best" sex, and these scripts may create problems if they are based on unrealistic expectations.

10. Arousal is increased through sexual fantasies and exploration. Since females are discouraged from both fantasy and exploration (part of the double standard), they may seem to have a slower arousal time.

11. Masters and Johnson identified a four-stage sexual response cycle during sexual activity—excitement, plateau, orgasm, and resolution. Although this model has received some criticism, it is still widely used and has helped to dispel several myths, such as that of the superiority of the vaginal orgasm.

12. Sexual problems or dysfunctions are sometimes treated by sex therapists. Although the labeling or defining of these problems can create difficulties, many people have been helped by sex therapy. Masters and Johnson's two-week intensive approach is the most popular therapy technique. Their program emphasizes the relationship, an integration of physiological and psychosocial factors, cognitions, and specific behavioral techniques (such as sensate focus exercises).

13. Professional sex therapists offer important guidelines for everyone: Sex education should be early and positive, a goal or performance orientation should be avoided, and communication should be improved and emphasized.

14. Sexual behavior is affected by the problem of AIDS and other sexually transmitted diseases (STDs). Although AIDS is known to be transmitted only through sexual con-

tact or exposure to infected blood, many people have irrational fears of contagion.

COERCIVE SEX

15. Child sexual abuse includes pedophilia (sexual gratification from contacts with children) and incest (sexual contact between two people who are related). Most child sexual abuse is committed by friends and relatives, not by strangers. The effects of child sexual abuse can last a lifetime.

16. Sexual harassment involves sexual advances, requests for sexual favors, and other unwelcome verbal or physical conduct of a sexual nature. Most sexual harassment is an assertion or abuse of power, not an expression of sexual desire. Victims of sexual harassment often suffer financial losses and psychological difficulties.

17. Rape is defined as the oral, anal, or vaginal penetration forced on an unconsenting victim. Surveys show that up to 30 percent of women have suffered from attempted or completed rape. The effects of being raped are serious and frequently long lasting. One of the most dangerous myths about rape is that male sexuality is overpowering and beyond a man's control. This myth requires women to control men.

18. The four major motives for rape are anger, power, sadism, and sexual gratification. Exposure to violent pornography creates distorted attitudes about rape and increases violence toward women. Studying other cultures' incest taboos and rape patterns may help us gain insight into the causes and prevention of coercive sex.

SUGGESTED READINGS

BLUME, E. S. (1990). *Secret survivors: Uncovering incest and its aftereffects in women.* New York: Wiley. The author sensitively addresses how incest affects its victims and provides an "incest survivor's aftereffects checklist" that helps identify survivors of incest who may have blocked memories of the abuse.

CROOKS, R., & BAUR, K. (1993). *Our sexuality* (5th ed.). Redwood City, CA: Benjamin Cummings. Students interested in an expanded discussion of the topics of this chapter, as well as related areas such as birth control and pregnancy, will find this introductory text highly readable and informative.

MILLER, H. G., TURNER, C. F., & MOSES, L. E. (EDS.). (1990). *AIDS: The second decade.* Washington, DC: National Academy Press. This text emphasizes trends in the HIV/AIDS epidemic expected to emerge in the 1990s, with special attention to such high-risk groups as women and adolescents.

O'CONNOR, D. (1989). *How to put the love back into making love.* New York: Doubleday. The author presents a balanced, down-to-earth guide to problems with intimacy and provides useful suggestions for increasing sensuality in intimate relationships.

PARROT, A., & BECHHOFER, L. (1991). *Acquaintance rape: The hidden crime.* New York: Wiley. This book provides up-to-date information about the problem of acquaintance rape and offers practical suggestions for educators, clinicians, and the general public.

ZILBERGELD, B. (1992). *The new male sexuality: A guide to sexual fulfillment.* New York: Bantam. Although there are many self-help books for women and their sexuality, few books exist for men and this is one of the best. It provides accurate, up-to-date, and insightful information about sexual functioning, self-awareness, and overcoming sexual difficulties.

Motivation and Emotion

In Chapter 6 you learned about Koko, the gorilla who "speaks" more than 800 words in American Sign Language (the hand language of the deaf). Koko's and other primates' ability to use sign language raises questions about whether language is unique to the human species. Koko has also raised interesting questions about behavior that many consider uniquely human: the need for companionship, feelings of love, and emotions of sadness and grief.

During her years of language training with Penny Patterson, Koko used signs in various ways—to converse with others, talk to herself, rhyme, joke, and even lie (Linden, 1993). Koko also communicated her personal preferences, including her strong attraction to cats. During training sessions, she often "talked" of cats, and "The Three Little Kittens" and "Puss in Boots" were two of her favorite stories. When Koko asked for a cat for Christmas in 1983 and was given a stuffed toy one, she "pouted" (Vessels, 1985).

In June 1984, a litter of three real kittens was brought to visit Koko. She selected one as her favorite and named him "All Ball" (based on his lack of a tail and her love of rhymes). After repeatedly requesting a cat for her birthday present, Koko finally got her wish—All Ball.

In their initial encounters, Koko treated the kitten as she might a baby gorilla—sniffing him, tucking him into her thigh, and trying to get him to nurse. She also behaved like a human child with a pet—dressing him in linen napkins and hats and playing chase games. Koko was also extremely gentle and patient with her pet. When All Ball demonstrated his natural kittenlike behavior by biting Koko, for example, she laughed and sometimes made the sign for "obnoxious" (Vessels, 1985).

If all of this seems too "humanlike," you will surely have trouble with Koko's reaction to the loss of her pet. According to media reports (Stone, 1988; Zimmerman, 1985), when Koko was told that her cat had wandered off one night and had been killed by a car, she showed typical signs of bereavement. When first told, she acted as if she hadn't heard, but later she "broke down" and wept the tearless hooting cry typical of lowland gorillas. When asked if she wanted to talk about her cat, she signed "cry" by running her finger from each eye down her cheeks.

Anthropomorphism: The act of attributing human characteristics to animals, gods, or inanimate objects. Also, interpreting the behavior of lower forms of animals in terms of human abilities or characteristics.

Motivation: The process of activating, maintaining, and directing behavior toward a particular goal.

Emotion: Feelings or affective responses that result from physiological arousal, thoughts and beliefs, subjective evaluation, and bodily expression.

Does Koko's behavior surprise you? Are you skeptical that a gorilla can become attached to a "pet" and feel grief at its loss? If so, you are not alone. Many people wonder whether animals can really experience emotions similar to those of humans. They question whether the reports on Koko aren't just an example of anthropomorphism—attributing human characteristics to animals, gods, or inanimate objects.

Although the motives and possible emotions of animals such as Koko are of interest to both scientists and the general public, in this chapter we will focus on the motives and emotions of human beings. Have you ever wondered, for example, why some people eat themselves into obesity whereas others starve themselves to death, or why some people seem addicted to dangerous sports like parachute jumping or to painful love relationships? These are the sorts of questions addressed in the research areas of motivation and emotion.

Motivation refers to factors within an individual (such as needs, desires, and interests) that activate, maintain, and direct behavior toward a goal. Emotion, on the other hand, refers to feelings or affective responses that result from physiological arousal, thoughts and beliefs, subjective evaluation, and bodily expression (frowns, smiles, gestures, and so on). In other words, motivation energizes and directs behavior, and emotion is the "feeling" response.

Motivation and emotion overlap. When you see your loved one in the arms of another, for example, you may react with a variety of emotions (jealousy, fear, sadness, disbelief), and a similar variety of motives may determine how you act in the situation. Your desire for safety and security may cause you to ignore the situation, while your need for love and belonging may motivate you to look for ways to excuse the behavior and protect your relationship. Although there is some inescapable overlap between motivation and emotion, and indeed with other areas of psychology, in this chapter we'll treat the topics separately and look at specific theories and problems related to each topic.

As you read Chapter 12, keep the following **Survey** questions in mind and answer them in your own words:

- Why do we feel hungry, search for stimulation, and need to achieve?
- Are we motivated primarily by biological or psychological forces?
- What major concepts do I need to know in order to understand emotion?
- What causes emotional arousal?

UNDERSTANDING MOTIVATION

Research in motivation attempts to answer the "why" questions about human and animal behavior. Why did Koko dress up her pet in hats and napkins? Why do you spend hours playing with a new computer game instead of studying for a major exam? Human behavior comes from many different motives, some of which have been discussed already. For example, the sleep motive and the need for alternate states of consciousness were covered in Chapter 5, and sexual motivation was discussed in Chapter 11. Affiliation, aggression, altruism, and interpersonal attraction will be discussed in Chapters 17 and 18. In this section of Chapter 12, we will focus on three basic categories of motives: *primary* (innate, unlearned motives that are basic to survival), *secondary* (biologically rooted motives that are less necessary for survival), and *learned/social* (acquired motives that result from experience and our need to be with others). For each category, we will discuss the representative motive that has been the most widely researched (hunger as a primary motive, stimulus-seeking as a secondary motive, and achievement as a learned/social motive). Finally, we will look at the major biological and psychological theories that best explain general motivation—or why we do what we do.

- *Why do we feel hungry, search for stimulation, and need to achieve?*

Hunger and Eating: An Example of a Primary Motive

How do you know when you are hungry? Is it your growling stomach that motivates you to eat? Or is it the sight of a juicy hamburger or the smell of a freshly baked cinnamon roll? Although hunger is obviously an internal, biological need (or primary motive), it is also heavily influenced by external, environmental forces. Let's examine both the internal and external factors.

Internal factors

One of the earliest experiments exploring the internal factors in hunger was conducted by Cannon and Washburn (1912). In this study, Washburn swallowed a balloon and then inflated it in his stomach. His stomach contractions and subjective reports of hunger feelings could then be simultaneously recorded (see Figure 12.1). Since each time Washburn reported having stomach pangs (or "growling") the balloon also contracted, the researchers naturally concluded that it was the stomach movements that caused the sensation of hunger.

What do you think is wrong with this conclusion? As you may remember from Chapter 1, researchers must always control for the possibility of *extraneous variables*, factors that contribute irrelevant data that confuse the results. In this particular case, it was later found that an empty stomach is relatively inactive and that the stomach

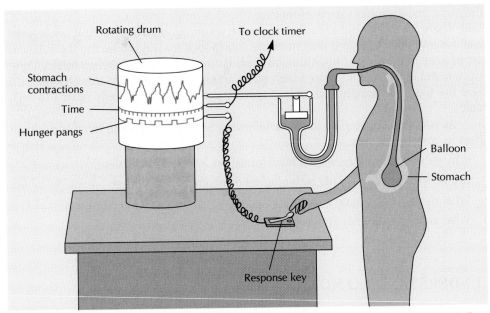

Figure 12.1 Cannon and Washburn's technique for measuring hunger. The subject first swallowed a balloon designed to detect stomach movements. The stomach movements were automatically recorded, and the recordings were compared to the voluntary key presses that the subject made each time he or she experienced a feeling of hunger. (Source: Cannon and Washburn, 1912.)

contractions experienced by Washburn were an experimental artifact resulting from the presence of the balloon. Washburn's stomach had been tricked into thinking it was full and was responding by trying to digest the balloon.

Further evidence for the lack of connection between stomach stimuli and feelings of hunger was provided in experiments in which rats had their stomachs removed or their nerve pathways to and from the stomach cut. The hunger behavior of these rats was essentially the same as that of the control rats (those with intact stomachs or nonsevered nerves) (Morgan and Morgan, 1940). Similarly, human patients who have had their stomachs removed in ulcer or cancer operations report normal feelings of hunger (Janowitz, 1967).

If stomach sensations aren't necessary, what does explain hunger? As explained in Chapter 2, a part of the brain known as the *hypothalamus* has centers that regulate eating, drinking, and body temperature. In specific reference to hunger, early research found that one area of the hypothalamus, the lateral hypothalamus (LH), seems to stimulate eating (Anand and Brobeck, 1951). Another area, the ventromedial hypothalamus (VMH), seems to create feelings of satiation or satisfaction and signal the organism to stop eating (Hetherington and Ranson, 1942). The LH has been called the "start eating," or *hunger* center, and the VMH, the "stop eating," or *fullness* center. So important is the VMH area that when it is destroyed in rats, they will overeat to the point of extreme obesity (see Figure 12.2). Similarly, when the LH area is destroyed, animals are not motivated to eat and may starve to death if they are not force-fed. With time, LH-damaged rats will resume eating but they maintain their weight well below normal. Humans with tumors in the LH or VMH area show similar weight reactions.

LH and VMH Function

Research into exactly how the LH and VMH function shows that these areas are not simple on–off switches for the control of eating. For example, lesions to the VMH make animals picky eaters—they reject food that doesn't taste good (Ferguson and Keesey, 1975; Weingarten, Chang, and McDonald, 1985). Lesions also increase their secretion of *insulin,* a hormone produced by the pancreas that converts blood *glucose* (a simple sugar nutrient that provides energy) into stored fat. Insulin therefore influences hunger

Lateral Hypothalamus (LH): Area of the hypothalamus responsible for stimulating eating behavior.

Ventromedial Hypothalamus (VMH): Area of the hypothalamus responsible for signaling the organism to stop eating. If destroyed, the organism will overeat and become obese.

Lateral
hypothalamus

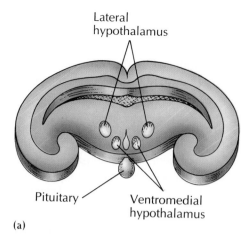

Pituitary   Ventromedial
hypothalamus

(a)

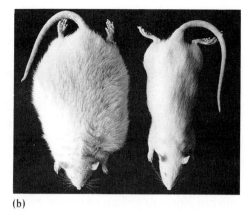

(b)

Figure 12.2 (a) Cross-sectional view of the rat brain. This diagram shows the rat's brain with the front half cut away. Note the positions of the ventromedial hypothalamus (VMH) and the lateral hypothalamus (LH). *(b) Lesioning the VMH.* The ventromedial area of the hypothalamus on the rat on the left was destroyed. Note its obesity compared to the normal rat on the right.

indirectly by decreasing glucose levels. When the VMH is lesioned, the increased level of insulin leads the animal to overeat, but when the LH is lesioned and insulin levels decrease, the animal eats less.

In addition to body chemistry factors such as insulin and glucose, researchers have suggested that the LH and VMH affect hunger because they regulate overall body weight. Most organisms have specific set points (or "weight thermostats") located in the hypothalamus. Damage to the VMH raises the set point, thus increasing hunger and making the animal eat more. In contrast, when the LH is lesioned the animal experiences an increase in hunger and a lowered metabolic rate that acts to restore the lost weight (Vilberg and Keesey, 1990).

In sum, internal factors such as structures in the hypothalamus (the LH and VMH) and related changes in body chemistry (insulin and glucose) do seem to play important roles in hunger and eating. Other internal factors have also been researched, including neural mechanisms in the brain stem (Mark and Scott, 1988; Norgren and Grill, 1982) and the presence or absence of certain neurotransmitters (Leibowitz et al., 1989; Stanley et al., 1989).

External Factors

Cultural conditioning is one of the most important external influences on when, what, where, and why we eat. North Americans, for example, tend to eat their evening meal around 6 P.M., while people in Spain and South America tend to eat around 10 P.M. When it comes to *what* we eat, have you ever considered eating rat, dog, or horse meat? If you are a typical North American, this might sound repulsive to you. But do you realize that most Hindus would have a similar revulsion to the thought of eating meat from cows?

In addition to cultural factors, other external factors such as visual stimuli also affect hunger and eating. Stanley Schachter (1971) and his colleagues conducted a series of experiments in which normal-weight and overweight individuals were given a range of external cues to eating (such as the presence of food or a clock that indicated "dinner time"). The researchers found that overweight subjects were more excited by the taste and sight of food and more attentive to the passage of time in determining when to eat than normal-weight subjects.

Internal-External Interaction

In a follow-up on this research, Judith Rodin (1981, 1992) found that people who respond to external eating cues (such as the presence of food) can be found in all weight categories. One reason some "externals" overeat may be that they experience a higher

Set Point: An organism's personal homeostatic level for a particular body weight that results from factors such as early feeding experiences and heredity.

insulin response to the sight of food. When Rodin (1984, 1985) invited subjects to her laboratory for lunch after they had gone 18 hours without food, she found that insulin levels in blood samples of the "external" subjects were stimulated by the mere sight and smell of a sizzling steak. If you've ever heard friends complain that they can "get fat" just by looking at or smelling food, you can now tell them that there may be some supportive experimental evidence for their observation—the increase in insulin encourages over-eating.

Rodin's research illustrates how internal and external factors may interact to motivate eating behavior. The internal, biological increase in insulin was triggered by the external sight and sound of the sizzling steak. This experiment also demonstrates classical conditioning (see Chapter 6). Like Pavlov's dogs who learned to salivate to the sound of the bell, "external" eaters learn to increase their insulin levels at the sight and smell of desirable food. Rodin's research on insulin and the set point theory gives some insight into our North American obsession with weight control.

Weight Control

Popular magazines and television commercials readily document the excessive amount of time and money we spend on weight management in our culture. Yet, most research finds that weight loss programs and restrictive diets lead to only temporary weight reduction (Marano, 1993; Meyer, 1984). One possible explanation may be that our natural, biological set point is higher than our artificial cultural standards. Recall that damage to the LH and VMH in rats may artifically disrupt the set point. As Figure 12.3 shows, in the natural state, the set point may act as the body's predetermined "weight thermostat" that adjusts to changes in food consumption by burning off more calories if weight

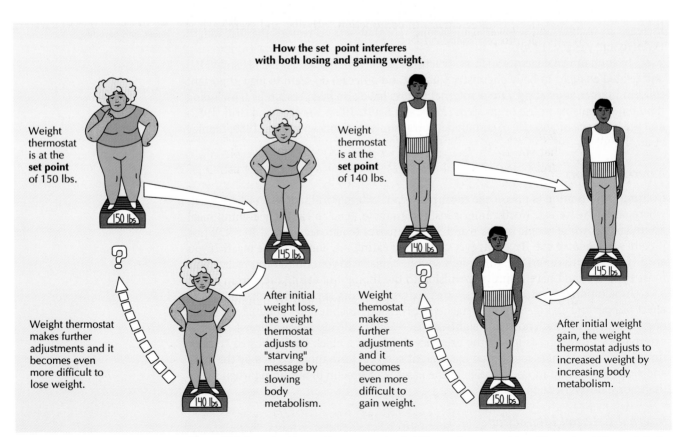

How the set point interferes with both losing and gaining weight.

Weight thermostat is at the **set point** of 150 lbs.

Weight thermostat makes further adjustments and it becomes even more difficult to lose weight.

After initial weight loss, the weight thermostat adjusts to "starving" message by slowing body metabolism.

Weight thermostat is at the **set point** of 140 lbs.

Weight thermostat makes further adjustments and it becomes even more difficult to gain weight.

After initial weight gain, the weight thermostat adjusts to increased weight by increasing body metabolism.

Figure 12.3 Set point theory. If your set point is 150 pounds, your weight will remain within a relatively narrow range—145 to 155 pounds. Your body responds to increased calorie intake with increased metabolism that burns off the calories. Decreased calorie intake leads to decreased metabolism and increased difficulty in losing weight.

goes above the set point and fewer if weight drops. The particular set point for any individual appears to be the result of a number of factors, including early feeding experiences and heredity. Many people believe obesity is a simple matter of consuming too many calories, but set point research says two people of the same height, age, activity level, *and* caloric consumption can be either fat or thin depending on their individual biological set point.

Although the theory of set points initially received a great deal of attention, critics question whether a set point actually exists or whether the concept has been overstated (Brownell and Venditti, 1982; Grinker, 1982). In addition, some researchers have criticized the overemphasis on biological factors, noting that psychological factors generally interact with biology to produce obesity (Hermann et al., 1989; Schwartz and Inbar-Saban, 1988). As we have seen, obese individuals may be more responsive to external cues for food (Schachter, 1971) and actually ignore internal, biological signals for eating (Evans and Rosenberg, 1992; Simmons, 1987). Research has also found that many people overeat when they are anxious (Schwartz, 1982) or binge when they are tense, lonely, or bored (Abraham and Beaumont, 1982; Marano, 1993; Wurtman, 1987).

Is there any way to counteract these effects and successfully lose weight?   Since most cases of obesity result from consuming more calories than the body can metabolize, or burn up, the safest and most reliable way to lose weight is to follow a *sensible* diet and exercise regularly (Polivy and Hermann, 1991). Daily, sustained exercise seems to lower the body's set point, making it easier to lose weight (Remington, Fisher, and Parent, 1984; Thompson et al., 1982). In addition, newly developed drugs, such as *dextrofenfluramine,* may help control obesity by controlling the cravings for carbohydrates. Other drugs are being tested to help correct metabolic defects that cause some obese people to burn fewer calories than normal-weight individuals.

There are problems, of course, with taking any drug for any length of time, and there are healthy and effective alternatives. In conjunction with diet and exercise, it is important to pay attention to psychological factors.

 *Try This Yourself*

If you would like to put psychology in action for your own weight management, there are three basic steps:

Step 1.   *Identify destructive thoughts, emotions, and behaviors.* Become aware of what you think, feel, and do each time you eat. Many people fail to recognize how many self-defeating thoughts they have about eating ("I can't control myself," "I'll go on a diet tomorrow," "Since I already went a little over my limit today, I might as well give up"). We also overlook how we use food and drink to change our mood. Coffee and doughnuts perk us up in the morning, lunch and break times allow us to escape boring work, and dinner and drinks provide us with entertainment and a chance to socialize.

Step 2.   *Identify and control food-related stimuli.* Because external cues can trigger eating behavior, arrange your environment to minimize such cues. Remove (or hide) tempting foods, throw out or freeze leftovers, stand away from the food tables at parties, and so on. You can also use an "eating habits" diary to identify and correct stimuli that induce overeating. If you find that you consume a large portion of your daily calories while reading, studying, or watching television, you may find it helpful to restrict your eating to one place (such as the kitchen or dining room table) and to not do anything else (such as watch television or read) while eating. The "mindless" eating that is associated with food-related stimuli ("I see peanuts and I want them") and the automatic associations you build around certain activities (television = snacks, movies = popcorn, baseball games = hotdogs) can undermine your desire for weight control. You need to avoid or control such stimuli.

Does the sight of these baked goods make your mouth water? Research indicates that controlling food-related cues helps in weight control.

Step 3. *Change destructive cognitions, emotions, and behaviors.* Instead of eating when you're depressed, bored, or tense and indulging in self-defeating thoughts, try substituting healthier activities for eating (such as jogging) and healthier thoughts ("I *can* control myself"). When you do eat, use behavioral techniques such as eating slowly, taking smaller bites, and using smaller serving plates. While changing your behavior, be sure to incorporate small nonfood rewards to reinforce yourself and reward yourself *after* the appropriate behavior, such as watching your favorite TV program after jogging two miles. ■

Before we leave this topic, it is important to recognize that there *are* other options to the whole problem of dieting and the national preoccupation with weight control. Although some people do need to reduce for physical health reasons, a large number of people in our society needlessly operate on a destructive cycle of diets and relapses, followed by guilt, depression, and new rounds of dieting. Given that each relapsed dieting episode makes future dieting more difficult, some people may be healthier and happier if they simply accept a certain level of "chubbiness" in themselves and others (Brownell, 1988; Levine, 1993).

Anorexia Nervosa and Bulimia

Anorexia Nervosa: An eating disorder, seen mostly in adolescent and young adult females, in which a severe loss of weight results from an obsessive fear of obesity and self-imposed starvation.

Bulimia: An eating disorder in which enormous quantities of food are consumed (binges), followed by purging by taking laxatives or vomiting.

Two serious disorders directly related to the fear of obesity are anorexia nervosa (self-starvation and extreme weight loss) and bulimia (intense, recurring episodes of binge eating followed by efforts to avoid weight gain, such as vomiting and taking laxatives).

Anorexia nervosa is a perplexing disorder characterized by prolonged refusals to eat, resulting in a loss of 20 to 25 percent of the original body weight. The anorexic's overwhelming fear of becoming obese does not diminish even with radical and obvious weight loss. The person's body image is so distorted that he or she still perceives a skeleton-like body as fat. The disorder primarily affects white, middle- and upper-class female adolescents and young adults. But there is growing evidence that the problem may begin as early as seven or eight years of age and that males may also be affected (Marano, 1993; Margo, 1987; Yates, 1990).

Anorexia nervosa is a serious disorder. Bone fractures and osteoporosis are common, menstruation often ceases, and brain CAT scans (X ray–like pictures) of anorexic patients show enlarged ventricles (cavities) and widened grooves. Such signs generally indicate loss of brain tissue (Hyde, 1991; Lankenau et al., 1985). Approximately 1 patient in 20 ultimately dies of the disorder (Hsu, 1986).

The anorexic's intense fear of obesity may also lead to extreme exercise regimens —hours of cycling or running, or constant walking and pacing. Occasionally the anorexic succumbs and gorges herself or himself with food, followed by vomiting or taking laxatives. This phenomenon is technically known as *bulimia*. When bulimia occurs by itself, it is referred to as *bulimia nervosa*. Bulimia causes eroded tooth enamel and tooth loss, digestive irritation, and serious digestive disease (Hyde, 1991; Levenkron, 1982). Some bulimics can ingest well over 6000 calories in a single sitting. Table 12.1 lists the foods that one bulimic individual consumed during a typical binge.

What causes anorexia nervosa or bulimia?   There are almost as many proposed causes as there are victims. Some theories focus on physical causes, such as hypothalamic disorders, lowered levels of various neurotransmitters, and genetic or hormonal disorders. Other theories emphasize psychological or social factors, such as perceived loss of control, depression, dysfunctional families, distorted body image, and societal pressures for thinness (Garner et al., 1990; Levine, 1993; Schweiger, 1991).

Even though there is no definitive theory to explain anorexia nervosa and bulimia, it is important to recognize the symptoms (see Table 12.2) and seek therapy if the symptoms apply personally to you. There is no question that both disorders are potentially life-threatening and require treatment.

Stimulus-Seeking: An Example of a Secondary Motive

Hunger is considered a *primary,* unlearned motive for behavior because it is necessary for basic survival. There is another group of motives that is also biological in origin but not as necessary for our survival. One of the best examples of a secondary motive is *stimulus-seeking.* When you see a box sitting on a table, do you peek to see what's in it? Do you like dangerous sports such as bungee jumping or hang gliding? Like the hunger motive, curiosity or the need for novel stimulation has an important influence on behavior.

Examples of stimulus-seeking behavior are easily found. Shortly after birth, infants show a marked preference for complex versus simple visual stimuli (see Chapter 9).

Several biographies of Princess Di suggest that she suffers from anorexia and/or bulimia.

Table 12.1   **One Bulimic's Typical Binge (lasting 3–5 hours)**

2 pounds of vanilla sandwich cookies with vanilla filling
1 pint of vanilla ice milk
1 pint of butter pecan ice cream
2 quarts of skim milk
4 waffles
1 loaf of white bread ⎫
½ pound of butter   ⎬ for French toast
6 eggs   ⎭
1 bottle of maple syrup
1 pound of Ritz crackers
½ pound of potato salad
½ pound of bakery cookies, assorted
a packaged crumb coffee cake (one pound)
2 ice cream sandwiches
2 yogurts
10 cream-filled chocolate cupcakes

Source: Levenkron, S. (1982). *Treating and overcoming anorexia nervosa.* New York: Scribner's.

Table 12.2   Symptoms of Anorexia Nervosa and Bulimia

Symptoms of Anorexia Nervosa
20–25% body weight loss
Hyperactivity
Distorted body image
Amenorrhea (in females) — loss of menstruation
Excessive constipation
Depression
Loss of hair (head)
Growth of fine body hair (called lanugo)
Extreme sensitivity to cold temperatures
Low pulse rate

Symptoms of Bulimia
Difficulty swallowing and retaining food
Swollen and/or infected salivary glands
Damage to esophagus, sometimes causing pain and/or internal bleeding.
Bursting blood vessels in the eyes
Excessive tooth decay, loss of tooth enamel (an irreversible condition)
Weakness, headaches, dizziness
Inconspicuous binge-eating
Frequent significant weight fluctuations due to alternating binges and fasts
Fear of inability to stop eating voluntarily

Source: B.A.S.H.^{SM}, Inc. St. Louis, MO.

Adults also pay more attention, and for a longer period of time, to complex and changing stimuli (see Chapter 4). Similarly, research with animals shows that monkeys will learn discrimination tasks for the simple "reward" of a brief look around the laboratory (Butler, 1954). As can be seen in Figure 12.4, they will also learn to open latches for the sheer pleasure of curiosity and manipulation (Harlow, Harlow, and Meyer, 1950).

In Koko's case, the need for physical and emotional stimulation was demonstrated in her excited preference for the game "Spin." In this game, Koko would lie on her back and Patterson would spin her around by the hand or foot—often at high speed because

Figure 12.4 Stimulus-seeking. Monkeys will work very hard at opening latches for the sheer pleasure of satisfying curiosity and the need for novel stimulation.

her fur made the ride frictionless. It was Koko's strong curiosity drive, a cognitive form of stimulus-seeking, that helped motivate her to learn sign language. This curiosity also occasionally got her into trouble. For example, when she was caught "exploring" (and destroying) a window screen with a chopstick, she compounded the damage by lying! Asked what she was doing, Koko tried to cover up by placing the chopstick in her mouth (simulating cigarette smoking) and signing "smoke mouth."

Although research shows that both animals and humans tend to prefer complex and changing stimuli, some research also suggests there is individual variation in the need for stimulation. Just as there are "homebodies" who prefer familiarity, stability, and a good book in front of a warm fire, there are people who actively seek out high adventure and risk. These two extremes represent differing levels of "sensation seeking" (Zuckerman, 1979, 1990).

    Try This Yourself

Are you a high or low sensation seeker? To discover your personal level of sensation seeking, score yourself on this shortened version of one of Marvin Zuckerman's tests. For each of the 13 items, circle the choice "A" or "B" that best describes your feelings.

1. A I would like a job that requires a lot of traveling.
   B I would prefer a job in one location.
2. A I am invigorated by a brisk, cold day.
   B I can't wait to get indoors on a cold day.
3. A I get bored seeing the same old faces.
   B I like the comfortable familiarity of everyday friends.
4. A I would prefer living in an ideal society in which everyone is safe, secure, and happy.
   B I would have preferred living in the unsettled days of our history.
5. A I sometimes like to do things that are a little frightening.
   B A sensible person avoids activities that are dangerous.
6. A I would not like to be hypnotized.
   B I would like to have the experience of being hypnotized.
7. A The most important goal of life is to live it to the fullest and experience as much as possible.
   B The most important goal of life is to find peace and happiness.
8. A I would like to try parachute-jumping.
   B I would never want to try jumping out of a plane, with or without a parachute.
9. A I enter cold water gradually, giving myself time to get used to it.
   B I like to dive or jump right into the ocean or a cold pool.
10. A When I go on a vacation, I prefer the comfort of a good room and bed.
    B When I go on a vacation, I prefer the change of camping out.
11. A I prefer people who are emotionally expressive even if they are a bit unstable.
    B I prefer people who are calm and even-tempered.
12. A A good painting should shock or jolt the senses.
    B A good painting should give one a feeling of peace and security.
13. A People who ride motorcycles must have some kind of unconscious need to hurt themselves.
    B I would like to drive or ride a motorcycle.

Scoring
Count one point for each of the following items that you have circled: 1A, 2A, 3A, 4B, 5A, 6B, 7A, 8A, 9B, 10B, 11A, 12A, 13B. Add up your total and compare it with the norms below.

    0–3   Very low
    4–5   Low
    6–9   Average
    10–11 High
    12–13 Very high

Research based on longer versions of this scale supports the idea that individuals differ in their desire for stimulation and varied experiences. High sensation seekers, on average, are more likely to experiment with drugs, to have more varied sexual experiences with a larger number of partners, to have been convicted of assaultive offenses, and to prefer higher risk sports and professions (Apter, 1992; Berman and Paisey, 1984; Montefiore, 1993; Zuckerman, 1979, 1990). Zuckerman suggests that large differences in desire for sensation seeking may lead to relationship problems between husband and wife, therapist and patient, and parent and child. Such differences might also create job difficulties for the person who is ill matched for either routine clerical or assembly-line work or a highly challenging and variable occupation.

Is there any way to change your sensation-seeking needs?   Considerable evidence indicates that one's optimal level of sensation seeking cannot be changed, since it is a basic part of personality that may be genetically determined through brain chemistry and gonadal hormones (Zuckerman, 1990). Instead, research using a related test for "thrill seeking" suggests that high sensation seekers should be identified early in life in order to funnel their energy toward constructive outlets (Farley, 1986). Psychologist Michael Apter (1992) argues that many acts of seemingly senseless vandalism, rape, "wilding," and even the Gulf War may result from the human need for excitement. By studying the psychological origins of this need, Apter believes we may be able to prevent, or at least reduce, the incidence of destructive forms of excitement seeking.

Achievement: An Example of a Learned/Social Motive

In addition to primary motives such as hunger, and secondary motives such as stimulus-seeking, we also have nonbiological, or learned/social, motives that are acquired through our interactions with the environment and our need to be with others. One of the best examples of a learned/social motive is our need for achievement.

Achievement Motivation: The need for success, for doing better than others, and for mastering challenging tasks.

Have you ever wondered why some people work so hard to achieve the highest grades in college, while others seem content to get by barely passing? Psychologist Henry Murray (1938) identified and defined achievement motivation as the need for success, for doing better than others, and for mastering challenging tasks.

How do you measure someone's need for achievement?   One of the most common methods is to use the assessment instrument known as the Thematic Apperception Test (TAT). Imagine for a moment that you are in a psychologist's office. You are about to take the TAT. The psychologist shows you a series of ambiguously drawn pictures (like Figure 12.5) and asks you to tell a brief story about what has just happened in this photo and what will happen in the future. When you look at the two women in Figure 12.5, what kind of story would you tell? If your tale for this photo included a strong theme of winning and attaining high standards, the psychologist might determine that you have a high achievement orientation. A response such as "The young woman is hoping that by the time she is an old woman she will be proud of the things she's accomplished in life" would reflect a clear need for achievement. (The TAT is discussed further in Chapter 14.)

Characteristics of Achievers

How do individuals with a high need for achievement differ from other people? To find out, researchers like McClelland (1958) and others often use a simple ring-toss game as one of their assessment tools. After first measuring their need for achievement with the TAT, subjects are asked to toss a ring at targets placed at various distances. The ring-toss game and other measures reveal several interesting differences between people with varying levels of need for achievement (nAch):

1. People high in nAch tend to prefer moderately difficult tasks. They avoid tasks that are too easy because they offer little challenge or satisfaction. They also avoid extremely difficult tasks because the probability of success is too low. In the ring-toss game, for instance, they often stand at an intermediate distance from the target.

Figure 12.5 A measurement of achievement. This is one of the cards from the Thematic Apperception Test (TAT). The strength of an individual's need for achievement is measured by the stories he or she tells about these photos.

2. High achievement oriented people tend to prefer tasks that have a clear outcome. They seek out situations where they can receive feedback on their performance. And they would rather receive criticism from a harsh, but competent evaluator than from one who is friendlier but less competent (McClelland, 1985).

3. People with high nAch prefer being personally responsible for a project. When they are directly responsible, they can feel satisfied when the task is well done.

4. High achievement oriented people are more likely to persist at a task when it becomes difficult (Cooper, 1983). When subjects were given a nonsolvable task, 47 percent of the high nAch individuals persisted until time was called. On the other hand, only 2 percent of those who were low on achievement motivation persisted (French and Thomas, 1958).

5. People who have high nAch scores *do* achieve more than others. They do better on exams, earn better grades in high school and college, and excel in their chosen professions.

What causes some people to be more achievement oriented than others?   Achievement orientation appears to be largely learned in early childhood, primarily through interactions with parents. Highly motivated children tend to have parents who encourage independence and frequently reward successes (Harold and Eccles, 1990). As you may remember from Chapter 10, first-born children often achieve more than later-born children, and in first-borns, independence is encouraged and more attention is paid to success.

Gender and Cultural Diversity

HOW CULTURE AND GENDER AFFECT ACHIEVEMENT

While individual differences account for some variation in achievement motivation, the culture that we are born and raised in and our identity as a male or female are also important factors. The events and themes in children's literature, for example, often contain subtle messages about what the culture values. In American and Western European cultures, many children's stories are about persistence and the value of hard work. A study by Richard de Charms and Gerald Moeller (1962) found a significant correlation between the achievement themes in children's literature and the actual industrial accomplishments of various countries. Conversely, can you see how television ads for the lottery and game shows based on luck or fate might lower a viewer's nAch?

 ### Try This Yourself

Stop for a moment and imagine you are asked to write a story about a fictional character, "Anne," that begins this way: "After first-term finals, Anne finds herself at the top of her medical school class." What would you write? (If you are a male, substitute the name "John" for "Anne" and "his" for "her.") Now read the following section on fear of success and Matina Horner's research. ∎

Fear of success

When Matina Horner (1968, 1972) analyzed the stories written by female and male college students to this same scenario, she found a large gender difference in the responses. While 62 percent of the women subjects described negative consequences for "Anne" as a result of her achievement, only 9 percent of the men characterized "John" in negative terms. Many female subjects wrote stories in which Anne was socially rejected or worried about her femininity. Male subjects wrote about how John's hard work resulted in great rewards and social approval. Horner's research generated over 200 other studies and received a great deal of attention from the American press (Paludi, 1992; Walsh, 1987).

Why was Horner's research so appealing? One reason might be that Horner did her research in the late 1960s, when women's rights and the women's movement were at their peak. The idea that women feared success was appealing because it called for women to change themselves, and not society. Horner's studies apparently explained why more women had not succeeded in high-status occupations—they simply feared success (Paludi, 1992).

However, more recent research finds fault with the early studies on a number of grounds (Mednick, 1989; Pfost and Fiore, 1990). For example, despite several attempts, researchers have failed to duplicate Horner's results (Heckhausen et al., 1985; Zuckerman and Wheeler, 1975). In addition, "Anne's" success was in medical school, a gender-inappropriate field at the time. Therefore, there may not be a generalized fear of success among women, but a fear of being successful at doing something perceived as gender inappropriate in the 1960s and 1970s. In fact, when the setting was changed from success in medical school to success in ballet or nursing, Horner's original findings were reversed. Male subjects reported more negative stories for "John" (Cherry and Deaux, 1978; Shapiro, 1979).

Do women fear success in high-status occupations? Despite the lack of research support, many people still use the "fear of success" notion to explain why women earn less than men and are underrepresented in positions of power.

Where does this leave us? Is there a fear of success for women or men? The answer is unclear (Paludi, 1992). While we are waiting for further research to clarify the issues, we need to keep in mind that fear of success *may* influence occupational choices and accomplishments of both women and men. Some women may be reluctant to major in physics or engineering and some men may shy away from poetry or nursing because they fear social disapproval. Parents, college counselors, and teachers need to be sensitive to this possibility. And as a college student, you need to critically think about whether such fears may be influencing your career plans and life options. ■

Review Questions

1. Attributing human characteristics to animals, gods, or inanimate objects is known as _____ .
2. Compare and contrast motivation and emotion.
3. How does the hypothalamus control eating behavior?
4. How have researchers explained overeating?
5. Compare and contrast anorexia nervosa and bulimia.
6. Why is stimulus-seeking a secondary and not a primary motive?
7. The need for success, for doing better than others, and for mastering challenging tasks is known as _____ .
8. Matina Horner's research suggested that women have a _____ that supposedly explained why women do not succeed in high-status occupations.

Answers to Review Questions can be found in Appendix C.

GENERAL THEORIES OF MOTIVATION

All sciences collect data through observation, experimentation, case studies, and so on. But simply collecting diverse information is not very productive—or interesting. Recall from Chapter 1 that one of the primary aims of any science is to develop *theories,* verifiable rules or underlying principles that explain certain observed phenomena. Although people typically use "theory" to mean "guess" in everyday conversation, a good scientific theory is based on carefully collected data that is then integrated into a general explanation. In Chapter 5, for example, we discussed facts and observations about sleep and dreaming and then looked at several theories scientists have developed to explain these phenomena. Similarly, in this chapter, we have just explored data related to three sample motives (hunger, achievement, and stimulus-seeking). Now we consider several theories of motivation. These theories fall into two general categories—biological or psychological.

* *Are we motivated primarily by biological or psychological forces?*

Biological Theories: Looking for Internal "Whys" of Behavior

Many theories of motivation take a biological approach—that is, they look for inborn processes that control and direct behavior. Among these biologically oriented theories are instinct and drive theories (discussed here) and psychoanalytic theory (discussed in Chapter 14).

Instinct Theories

A biological approach to the study of motivation would logically begin with a study of instincts. These are rigid and fixed motor response patterns that are not learned, are

Instincts: Behavioral patterns that are (1) unlearned, (2) uniform in expression, and (3) universal in a species.

Nest building and feeding of the young are instinctual behaviors for birds. Do humans have similar instincts that motivate behavior?

Ethology: The branch of biology that studies animal behavior under natural conditions.

characteristic of all members of a species, and have an inherited, genetic foundation established in the course of evolution. Instinctual behaviors are obvious in many animals: birds building nests, salmon swimming upstream to spawn, and so on. Such instinctive behaviors have been of prime interest to ethologists—biologists who specialize in the study of animals in their natural habitat. From their studies, ethologists have suggested that behaviors such as the fighting instinct have developed because they increase chances for survival (Dewsbury, 1989; Lorenz, 1966, 1974).

Do humans have instincts?   In the earliest days of psychology the definition of instinct was not as rigorous as the one we have just presented. At that time, researchers like William McDougall (1908) proposed that humans had numerous "instincts," including repulsion, curiosity, self-assertiveness, parenting, and so on. Other researchers added their favorite "instincts," and the list eventually became so long it was virtually meaningless. One account found listings for over 10,000 human instincts (Bernard, 1924). Some authors have jokingly referred to this as an example of the "instinct to believe in instincts" (Weiner, 1985).

In addition to the problem of a never-ending list, the label "instinct" produced circular explanations. Have you ever heard someone say that men are just naturally or instinctually aggressive, or that all women have a maternal instinct? When asked for evidence of these instincts, the person (like the researchers did in McDougall's time) will most likely point to examples of male aggression or female nurturing. Thus, the explanation *of* the behavior *is* the behavior: "They act that way because they naturally act that way." This type of circular reasoning, however, is not acceptable to scientific standards.

Sociobiology

Sociobiology: A branch of biology that emphasizes the genetic and evolutionary basis of social behaviors in all organisms, including humans.

In recent years, the case for instincts in McDougall's original broad sense has been strengthened by a branch of biology called sociobiology. Sociobiology proposes that genetics and evolution have shaped various social behaviors in both humans and animals. Sociobiologists such as Edward O. Wilson (1975, 1978) believe competition, war, aggression, male–female differences, altruism, and many other behaviors are genetically transmitted from one generation to another.

The basic idea in sociobiology is that social behavior evolves in ways that maximize fitness for survival. Any behavior that enhances both conception and survival of offspring to maturity tends to persist across generations. At the same time, behavior that interferes with reproduction and survival gradually disappears from the species. As you will see in Chapter 18, both aggressive and altruistic (helping) behaviors are seen by sociobiologists as particularly important human social behaviors because they supposedly give us a survival advantage.

Sociobiology's emphasis on *biological determinism* has generated a highly charged debate. Some critics argue that Wilson's theory overemphasizes biology. Other critics maintain that it is based on naive speculation and unjustified extrapolation from animal studies rather than solid human evidence (Gould, 1977, 1983; Kicher, 1985). Furthermore, some critics say these theories support the belief that human nature is fixed and therefore efforts to solve social problems are doomed to failure (Kriegman and Knight, 1988). According to sociobiology, sex, racial, and cultural differences might be viewed as unalterable biological differences. Such a belief could keep people from even attempting to change inequalities in male and female job opportunities, black and white educational options, or the economic progress of various nations.

In sum, sociobiology may have overstated the influence of biology on social behavior, and there are obvious dangers in any theory that suggests a biological determinant for social conditions. Nevertheless, most psychologists agree that biology and genetic contributions are very important to understanding human behavior. However, psychologists generally believe that instincts play less and less of a role as we move up the evolutionary ladder.

Drive-Reduction Theory

Beginning in the 1930s, the concepts of drive and drive reduction began to replace the theory of instincts. According to drive-reduction theory (Hull, 1952; Spence, 1951), motivation begins with a physiological *need* (a lack or deficiency). The need elicits a drive, a mobilization of psychological energy, directed toward satisfying the need (see Figure 12.6). Although "need" and "drive" are often used interchangeably, it is important to keep in mind that unmet needs seem to increase in intensity over time, whereas

Drive-Reduction Theory: The theory that motivation begins with a physiological need (a lack or deficiency) that elicits a psychological energy or drive directed toward behavior that will satisfy the original need.

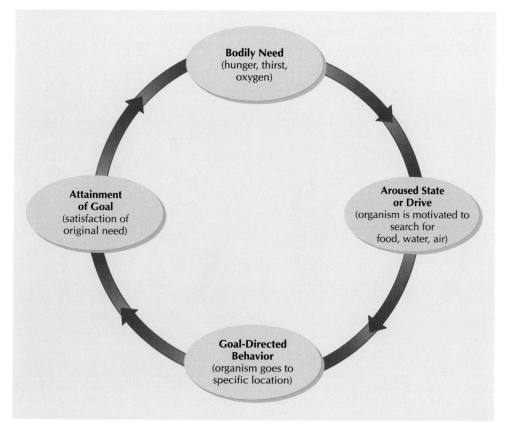

Figure 12.6 Drive reduction. According to drive-reduction theory, our basic bodily needs drive us to look for specific methods of satisfaction.

the drive to satisfy them can be psychologically ignored and even forgotten on some occasions. Your need for food, for example, may increase between breakfast and lunch, but if you run into a friend while walking toward the cafeteria, your hunger drive may be easily diverted by the chance to talk.

Both drive-reduction theory and instinct theory rely on innate, biological needs for the original impetus or "push." However, in drive-reduction theory the original arousal (drive) is nonspecific and the organism must *learn* which specific action to take to satisfy this need. Motivation is therefore a combination of biology and learning—your hunger "drives" you to search for food and you learn to go to the cafeteria.

Arousal and Homeostasis

Homeostasis: Balance or equilibrium of the internal environment, which is accomplished through constant adjustments of the nervous system.

While drives can be ignored, needs cannot. All animals must eat, drink, take in oxygen, maintain body temperature, and avoid painful injuries in order to survive. Strong feelings of biological "pushing" or tension are created by the body's demand for constancy or balance in the internal environment—a process known as homeostasis. When this balance is disrupted by deprivation of food or water or by changes in body temperature, the brain sends strong signals that direct activity designed to restore homeostasis (see Figure 12.7).

Arousal Theory: The idea that there is an ideal or optimal level of excitement that is maintained through the body's need for homeostasis in stimulus-seeking.

Arousal theory suggests that there is an ideal or *optimal* level of arousal that an organism is motivated to maintain (Berlyne, 1971; Hebb, 1955, 1966). Similar to the need for physiological homeostasis is a need for homeostasis in the stimulus-seeking we discussed earlier. When arousal is too low or too high, performance is negatively affected (see Figure 12.8). In the classroom, you may have noticed that both extremes of arousal, too relaxed or too anxious, can be detrimental to your test-taking abilities.

Psychological Theories: The Role of Incentives and Cognitions

There are also *nonhomeostatic* motives that influence behavior. Sex and reproductive desires, for example, do not contribute to individual balance or survival, but they *are* necessary to species survival. Each of us can freely choose whether to respond to these nonhomeostatic drives. Although in many animals the sex drive is a powerful determinant of behavior and parenting of offspring is paramount, among humans sex and nur-

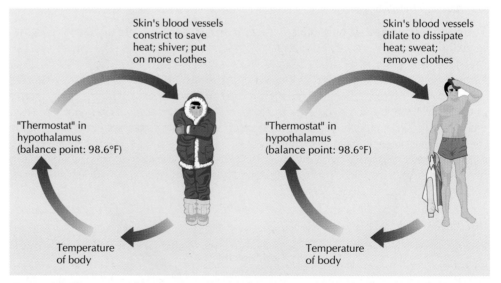

Figure 12.7 The concept of homeostasis. Like the thermostat in your home that adjusts the furnace to maintain a relatively stable room temperature, the "thermostat" in your hypothalamus sends messages that adjust your internal bodily heat (98.6 degrees Fahrenheit), one of the body's several homeostatic requirements for survival.

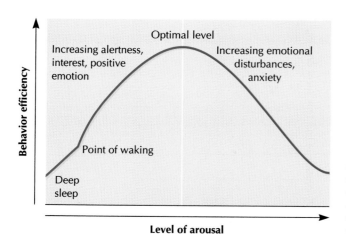

Figure 12.8 Optimal level of arousal. What is the best level of arousal for maximum efficiency? According to arousal theory, overall production is highest with moderate arousal.

Can you see how both incentive theory and cognitive theory could be used to explain the motivation behind buying a new sports car?

turing needs are less evident. As you discovered in Chapter 11, human sexual behaviors primarily reflect individual learning experiences.

The problem of explaining nonhomeostatic drives is one of the major limits of both drive-reduction and arousal theories. For example, how would these theories explain why we continue to eat even when our biological needs are completely satisfied? Or why someone continues to work overtime when his or her salary is sufficient to meet all basic biological needs? The answers to these questions can be better answered by theories that emphasize incentive or cognitive factors.

Incentive Theory

While drive theories say *internal* factors *push* people in certain directions, incentive theories say *external* stimuli *pull* people in certain directions (Bolles, 1970, 1975; Pfaffmann, 1982). Because of certain characteristics of the external stimuli, the individual is motivated to perform some action to obtain desirable goals or to act in ways that avoid or eliminate undesirable events.

People initially eat because their hunger "pushes" them. They continue to eat even when they no longer feel hungry, for example, because the sight of a piece of apple pie à la mode "pulls" them toward further food intake.

Incentive Theory: The theory that motivation results from environmental stimuli that "pull" the organism in certain directions, as opposed to internal needs that drive or "push" the organism in certain directions.

Cognitive Theories

The cognitive perspective on motivation emphasizes the importance of mental processes in goal-directed behavior. If you receive a high grade in your psychology course, you can interpret your grade in a variety of ways: You earned it because you really studied, you "lucked out," or the textbook was exceptionally interesting and helpful (our preferred interpretation!). Researchers who study such *attributions,* or explanations for the causes of behavior, have found that how we interpret our own behavior and that of others often has a strong effect on motivation (see Chapter 17). For example, people who attribute their successes to personal ability and effort tend to work harder toward their goals than people who attribute their successes to luck (Weiner, 1972, 1982). *Expectancies* are also important to motivation. Your anticipated grade on the test obviously affected your willingness to read and study the material.

Intrinsic versus Extrinsic Motivation

Psychologists have learned a great deal about the importance of attributions and expectancies on motivation from related work on intrinsic motivation (the desire to perform an activity for its own sake) and extrinsic motivation (the desire to perform an activity because of external rewards or the avoidance of punishment). Studies show that people who are paid or rewarded for doing a task that they had previously done for the sheer fun of it actually lose enjoyment and interest in the task (Amabile, 1985; Fabes, 1987).

Intrinsic Motivation: The desire to perform an activity for its own sake. The motivation is derived from the satisfaction arising out of the behavior itself.

Extrinsic Motivation: The desire to perform an activity because of external rewards or the avoidance of punishment. Motivation is not inherent in the behavior itself.

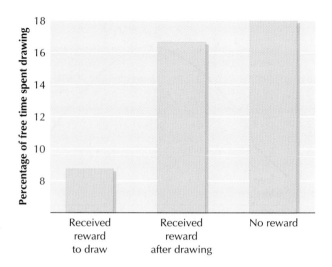

Figure 12.9 Intrinsic versus extrinsic motivation. When children were given free time to draw, those who had previously received a reward for drawing were less likely to later freely choose to draw. (Source: Lepper et al., 1973.)

In one study, preschool children who liked to draw were given artist's paper and felt-tipped pens (Lepper, Greene, and Nisbett, 1973). One group was promised a "Good Player" certificate with a gold seal and ribbon for their drawings. A second group was asked to draw and then received an unexpected reward when they were done. A third group received no promise of reward and was given none. A few weeks later, these same children were placed in a situation where they could draw if they wanted to, and the amount of time they spent drawing was recorded. As can be seen in Figure 12.9, having received rewards on the first occasion seemed to undermine the children's subsequent interest in drawing. In a similar study with college students, McNeill and Kimmel (1988) found that offering money for problem solving dramatically decreased the students' intrinsic motivation and detrimentally affected their performance. There's an old saying that seems appropriate: "When funds come in, fun goes out!"

How would you explain the test results? The critical factor in enjoyment of a task seems to be how we explain our motivation to ourselves. When we perform a task for no apparent reason, we seem to use internal, personal reasons ("I like it," "It's fun"). But when extrinsic rewards are added, the explanation seems to shift to external, impersonal

Children seem to have an intrinsic love of art, yet few adults find pleasure in the same behavior. Is this because we were given grades, praise, or other extrinsic rewards that destroyed our early intrinsic motivation?

reasons ("I did it for the money," "I did it to please the boss"). This shift generally causes a decrease in enjoyment and performance of the behavior.

But how does this theory explain situations where getting a raise, or receiving a gold medal, seems to increase enjoyment or productivity?   Researchers such as Deci and Ryan (1985) and Rosenfeld, Folger, and Adelman (1980) explain that rewards will not reduce intrinsic interest in an activity if the reward is based on competent or outstanding performance rather than on merely engaging in the behavior. Rewards for competency seem to produce a feeling of pride that may help to intensify the desire to do well again (Harackiewicz and Manderlink, 1984).

Applying the Theory

The concept of intrinsic and extrinsic motivation has important implications for business, education, and everyday interactions with others. Manufacturers who offer a substantial rebate for buying a product, for example, may find the gimmick works well for initial purchases but may also reduce "brand loyalty" (the tendency to repeat the purchase) once the rebate is withdrawn (Dodson, Tybout, and Steinthal, 1978). Similarly, educational institutions that use extrinsic rewards for school attendance may see an increase in overall absenteeism once the rewards are removed. As you learned in Chapter 6, for a reward to be motivating, it must come *after* the behavior is performed and must be given only as a way to provide feedback on achievement.

In sum, the inhibiting effects of rewards on motivation are extremely complex. Additional research in this area is necessary before we can make definitive recommendations. In the meantime, however, there are several *suggestions* that you might find useful for yourself and when working with others:

1. In general, it is almost always better to use the least possible extrinsic reward. This helps conceal the exact nature of the inducement, yet still opens the door for additional rewards if necessary.

2. Use rewards to provide feedback for competency or outstanding performance rather than just for engaging in the behavior.

3. Use rewards as a way of maintaining interest long enough for a task to become intrinsically interesting. When children are first learning to play a musical instrument, for example, it may help to provide small rewards until they gain a certain level of mastery. But once the child is working happily or practicing for the sheer joy of it, it may be best to leave him or her alone.

4. Emphasize intrinsic reasons for behaviors. For example, rather than thinking about other people you'll impress with good grades or all the great jobs you'll get when you finish college, focus instead on personally satisfying reasons. Think about how exciting it is to learn new things or the value of becoming an educated person and a critical thinker.

Learning and Opponent-Process Theory

As we discussed in Chapter 6, praise, money, pleasure, and the avoidance of pain all affect our learning of most behaviors. But how do people *learn* to enjoy terrifying sports such as bungee jumping or skydiving?

One possible explanation comes from opponent-process theory (not to be confused with the opponent-process theory of color vision discussed in Chapter 4). According to this theory, our bodies have a natural desire for homeostasis. Whenever an intense emotional experience upsets our psychological and physiological balance, a compensating force (the opponent-process) goes to work to restore equilibrium (Piliavin, Callero, and Evans, 1982; Solomon, 1980, 1982). In other words, if one set of activities (a process) goes too far in one direction, the brain responds with an opposite (opposing) emotional state that offsets the first emotion. During the initial experience, the individual apparently watches and learns a particular *range* of emotional response with the behavior.

Opponent-Process Theory: In motivation, the theory that one extreme emotional state will be offset by an opposing emotion. This opposite emotional state lasts long after the initial emotion has disappeared.

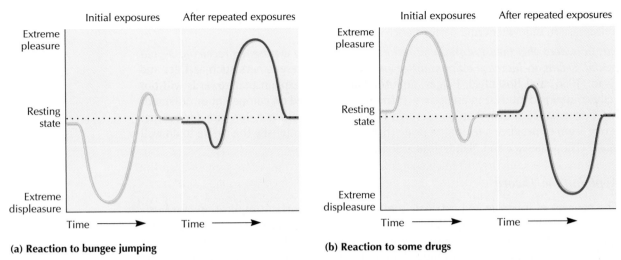

(a) **Reaction to bungee jumping**   (b) **Reaction to some drugs**

Figure 12.10 Opponent-process theory. How does someone become addicted to drugs or bungee jumping? According to the opponent-process theory of emotion, the individual's first emotional reaction is replaced with an opposing (opposite) emotion. As a result of the body's need for balance, combined with the psychological effects of learning, the person soon needs more of the drug to relieve the increasingly negative feelings, whereas the bungee jumper desires more (frequent) jumps to achieve the feelings of pleasure.

When this behavior is repeated many times, however, the initial emotional reaction diminishes in intensity because of simple habituation (see Chapter 6). Since the individual has learned a certain range of response, the intensity of the first emotion is shifted to the second, opposing emotion (see Figure 12.10).

In the example of bungee jumping, the first jump elicits an initial reaction of sheer terror in virtually everyone. After a few moments, however, the terror is replaced by a sense of relief and well-being (note the slight rise in positive feelings in the left-hand graph in Figure 12.10a). After repeated jumps, the bungee jumper gradually habituates to the initial emotional reaction and the terror diminishes (note the graph on the right side of Figure 12.10a). The previously learned contrast and range of emotions remain constant, however. As the terror decreases, the postjump elation increases. Thus, bungee jumpers may become addicted to the sport because of the intensely pleasurable aftereffects.

Addictive Behavior

The opponent process is also active in situations that start with positive emotional states. In the case of some drug taking (the two graphs in Figure 12.10b), the initial emotional experience is often one of euphoria, insight, and feelings of omnipotence (depending on the drug taken). But as time passes and the drug wears off, the opponent process of boredom, confusion, or worthlessness is experienced. After repeated drug-taking experiences, the drug user habituates to the initial stimulus (the drug) and the negative aftereffect gains strength. The drug taker soon learns that another joint or shot or snort will ease the bad feelings, even if it doesn't bring back the original good feelings. Thus, the drug addict takes the drug to combat the undesirable opponent process even after the drug no longer gives the positive benefits that provided the original motivation.

This same opponent-process theory helps to explain why some people stay in destructive love relationships long after the original pleasure has gone. Can you see how someone might become "addicted" to the high of the beginning stages of love and then find it painful to "withdraw"? Although complex behaviors such as bungee jumping, drug use, and love relationships obviously encompass more than just opponent processes, this theory does help explain some of the more puzzling aspects of addictive behaviors.

Opponent-process theory helps explain why some people become addicted to dangerous sports like bungee jumping. The initial feelings of sheer terror diminish over time and the jumper becomes addicted to the feelings of elation and excitement.

Maslow's Hierarchy of Needs: Combining Both Biological and Psychological Theories

One of the most ambitious attempts to explain motivation was Abraham Maslow's hierarchy of needs (1954, 1970). Maslow accounted for both biological and psychological needs and integrated many of the motivational concepts that we've discussed.

Maslow's theory is based on the belief that we all have numerous needs that compete for expression. At this moment, for example, your need for sleep may be competing with your need to finish reading this chapter before your next exam. Obviously, all needs are not equally important. According to Maslow, motives differ primarily on the basis of *prepotence,* or relative strength. The stronger needs (such as hunger and thirst) must be satisfied before one can move on to the higher needs, such as safety, belonging, and self-esteem. As shown in Figure 12.11, Maslow developed a five-level hierarchy of needs, with basic physiological needs at the bottom and self-actualization at the top. Although he saw "higher" motives as weaker than the more prepotent biological drives, Maslow believed that once freed from the "lower" needs, humans are drawn to satisfy needs that will help them grow and develop.

Hierarchy of Needs: Maslow's theory of motivation, that some motives (such as physiological and safety needs) have to be satisfied before advancing to higher needs (such as belonging and self-esteem).

Evaluating Maslow's Theory

Maslow's hierarchy of needs seems intuitively correct in many situations—a starving person would first look for food, then worry about safety, then seek love and friendship, and so on. Critics have argued, however, that portions of Maslow's theory were poorly researched. People sometimes seek to satisfy higher-level needs even when ones lower in the hierarchy have not been met (Geller, 1982; Neher, 1991; Williams and Page, 1989). In some nonindustrialized societies, for example, people may be extremely hungry, suffer severe illness and disease, and live in a wartorn area (the first two steps on Maslow's hierarchy), yet they still show strong social ties and a strong sense of self-esteem. During the famine and war in Somalia, there were numerous examples of par-

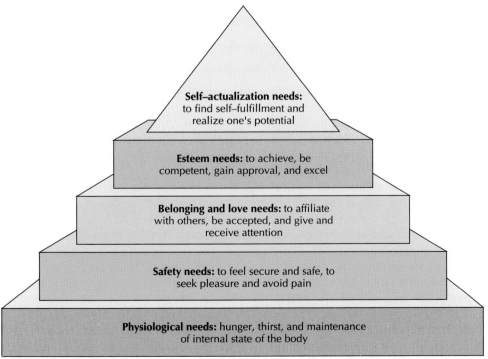

Figure 12.11 *Maslow's hierarchy of motives or needs.* According to Maslow, the basic, physical necessities must be satisfied before higher growth needs can be expressed.

ents who sacrificed their own lives carrying their starving children hundreds of miles to food distribution centers. And those parents who did make it to the centers often banded together to share the limited supplies. Since Maslow argued that each individual's own lower needs must be at least partially met before higher needs can influence behavior, cultural research and examples such as the parents in Somalia may "stand Maslow's need hierarchy on its head" (Neher, 1991, p. 97).

It seems, then, that Maslow may have overstated the importance of sequentially working one's way up the pyramid. Although basic needs *are* fulfilled first when possible, higher-level needs may be pursued even though total satisfaction of lower-level needs is made impossible by circumstances.

Review Questions

1. Compare and contrast ethology's and sociobiology's perspectives on instincts.
2. How does drive-reduction theory differ from incentive theory?
3. _____ theories emphasize the importance of thoughts, attributions, and expectancies in motivated behaviors.
4. _____ rewards have been found to decrease motivation because they shift the individual's internal explanations for their behavior to an external source.
5. The _____ theory suggests that one extreme emotional state will be offset by an opposing emotion that lasts long after the original emotion has disappeared.
6. According to _____ theory, basic survival and security needs must be satisfied before one can move on to such higher needs as self-actualization.

Answers to Review Questions can be found in Appendix C.

UNDERSTANDING EMOTION

• *What major concepts do I need to know in order to understand emotion?*

Have you ever used the expression, "I was so excited, I thought I would die"? Although this is a common use of words in casual conversation, for some people the expression is anything but casual. Consider the following: "Upon meeting his 88-year-old father after a 20-year separation, a 55-year-old man suddenly died. The father then dropped dead. A 75-year-old man, who hit the twin double for $1683 on a $2 bet, died as he was about to cash in his winning ticket" (Engel, 1977, p. 153).

The idea that sudden death can result from emotional trauma has been around for a long time, but only in the last few years have we been able to scientifically document the connection between emotions and physical health. A National Academy of Sciences panel in 1984 found that grief over the death of a family member may substantially raise the risk, especially among men, of contracting an infectious disease or of dying of a heart attack or stroke (Maranto, 1984). It has also been suggested that suppressing emotions (particularly anger and hostility) can lead to ulcers, high blood pressure, obesity, heart disease, and cancer (Eysenck, 1991).

The study of the interrelationship between psychological factors and physical health is an exciting new field known as health psychology or behavioral medicine (see Chapter 13). It has renewed interest in the basic study of emotions. Emotions play an important role in our lives. They color our dreams, memories, and perceptions, and when they are disturbed they contribute significantly to psychological disorders (see Chapter 15).

The Study of Emotions: How Scientists Study Feelings

As mentioned earlier, the term "emotion" refers to feelings or affective reactions. Every emotion has four basic components:

1. The *cognitive component,* the thoughts, beliefs, and expectations that determine the type and intensity of emotional response. For example, if you believe and expect your relationship will be monogamous and then find your partner in bed with someone else, you are much more angry and jealous than if you did not believe in or expect monogamy.

2. The *subjective component,* which includes elements of pleasure or displeasure, intensity of feeling, and complexity. What one person experiences as intensely pleasurable may be boring or aversive for another.

3. The *behavioral component,* the various forms of expression that emotions may take. Facial expressions, bodily postures and gestures, and tone of voice vary with anger, joy, sorrow, fear, and so on.

4. The *physiological component,* which involves physical changes in the body. When the body is emotionally aroused by fear or anger, for example, heart rate accelerates, pupils dilate, and respiration rate increases.

Self-Report Techniques

To study cognitive and subjective components of emotions, psychologists typically use self-report techniques such as paper-and-pencil tests, surveys, and interviews.

As you may imagine, there are numerous problems with the self-report technique. First, emotions are difficult to describe. People (and animals?) differ not only in their subjective experiences and expressions of emotions but also in their ability to accurately identify and describe their emotions. This is a particular problem when studying children or animals. How do Koko's emotional experiences described earlier, for example, compare with humans' experiences? Some people see Koko's use of sign language as a unique opportunity to obtain valid self-report data on animal emotions. But others believe that ape language capabilities are exaggerated and that trainers often interpret ape signs rather imaginatively (Savage-Rumbaugh, 1986; Terrace, 1979).

Second, some subjects may lie or hide their feelings because of social expectations or as an attempt to please the experimenter. Many people have learned, for example, that certain emotions are inappropriate to express ("Big boys don't cry" or "Ladies don't get angry").

Third, memories of past emotions may be inaccurate. Have you noticed that sometimes we remember only the good things about events ("That was the best camping trip ever")? And, other times we remember only the bad things ("That was the worst camping trip ever").

Finally, it is often impractical or unethical to artificially create conditions in a research setting that elicit strong emotions. Do you recall Milgram's obedience experiment described in Chapter 1? A major criticism of Milgram's research was that he created strong feelings of anxiety and guilt by asking subjects to deliver dangerous shocks to another supposed participant.

The Polygraph and Other Direct Measurements

One way to minimize the problems with self-report techniques is to directly monitor the external bodily expressions—the behavioral component of emotions. When subjects are angered, for example, systematic observations of their facial expressions (clenched teeth, furrowed eyebrows, etc.) provide important information to the researcher.

In addition to monitoring the behavioral component of emotion, we can also measure the physiological component. Researchers can study changes in the level of *internal* biological arousal by measuring variations in heart rate, electrodermal response

During the administration of a polygraph, or lie detector test, tapes around the subject's chest measure breathing rate, a cuff monitors blood pressure, and finger electrodes measure electrodermal response (sweating).

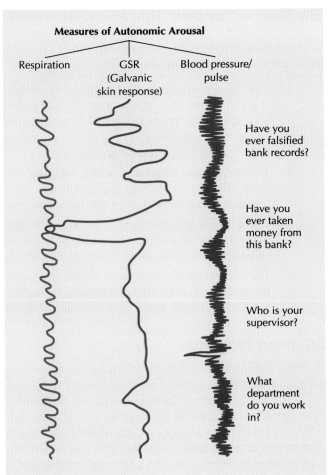

Figure 12.12 Polygraph testing. The polygraph measures autonomic arousal that some people experience when they tell a lie. The printout to the right shows how the subject's arousal level (particularly the GSR) changed when asked a threatening question.

Polygraph: Instrument that measures emotional arousal through various physiological reactions, such as heart rate, blood pressure, respiration rate, and electrodermal skin response.

(the resistance of the skin to passage of a weak electric current), respiratory rate, and blood pressure.

Perhaps the most widely known, and most controversial physiological measurement of emotion is the polygraph, or "lie detector" machine (see Figure 12.12). Polygraph readings of changes in heart rate, respiration rate, and so on have been used by police and courts to help determine whether someone is guilty or innocent of a specific crime. The claim is that people can verbally lie about their behavior, but they cannot control their internal physiological reactions which the polygraph measures. In recent years, the use of polygraph tests has been extended to security agencies, national government jobs, and general employers interested in screening applicants for jobs or in detecting employee theft (Ben-Shakhar and Furedy, 1990; Lykken, 1988).

Do lie detectors really work? Psychologists have serious doubts about the use of the polygraph for "lie detector" purposes (Elaad, 1991; Hyman, 1989). Although the polygraph does detect major changes in emotionality, it doesn't indicate whether subjects are aroused because they're lying, because they're afraid, or because they've taken certain drugs. For example, laboratory tests have demonstrated several ways in which polygraph tests can be "fooled" by people who are taking tranquilizers or who have consumed high levels of alcohol. In addition, *psychopathic* individuals (see Chapter 15) seem to experience little or no emotional reactions to their crimes and they often are not detected by polygraph tests (Bradley and Ainsworth, 1984; Waid and Orne, 1982). Finally, Waid and Orne found that test results could also be affected by the ethnic background of the examiner and respondent, by birth order (later-born children could lie more effectively), and by whether or not the respondent was depressed.

Although proponents often claim polygraph accuracy rates of 90 percent or higher (Lykken, 1988), actual tests show about 20 percent of the guilty people are misclassified as innocent, and up to 90 percent of the innocent are judged to be guilty (Kleinmuntz and Szucko, 1984; Lykken, 1984). Even though people say the innocent have nothing to fear from a polygraph test, the research would suggest otherwise.

Several proposals have been made for solving problems associated with the polygraph. One is to use "guilty knowledge" questions based on specific information that only a guilty person would know (such as the sex of the bank teller whom the defendant allegedly robbed or the time the robbery was committed). Lykken (1984) suggests a guilty person would recognize these specific cues and respond in a different way than a nonguilty person. Other psychologists have suggested using computers and statistical analyses to improve the reliability of the polygraph (Kleinmuntz and Szucko, 1984).

Integrity Tests

Even with improvements, many psychologists still strongly object to the use of polygraphs by untrained administrators or for the purpose of establishing guilt or innocence. In response to the growing concern over the use of lie detector tests, the U.S. Senate passed a bill in 1988 that limits their use in job screening to security guards and people with access to controlled substances ("Ask Me No Questions," 1988). However, restrictions on the polygraph have led to a new form of employment screening known as the *integrity test*. Some of these paper-and-pencil self-report tests supposedly measure a person's general attitude about dishonesty, whereas others are more broadly based and reportedly measure personality traits such as dependability, deviance, social conformity, and hostility to rules. Responding to the increasing number of these tests and their widespread use, the American Psychological Association has created a task force to review the use of integrity tests in employment decision making (Adler, 1989). Even if these tests are eventually shown to be scientifically sound, their use, like that of the polygraph, will be open to exploitation and abuse.

The Biology of Emotions: The Role of the Brain and Autonomic Nervous System

Pretend for the moment that you're walking alone on a dark street in a dangerous part of town. You suddenly see someone jump from behind a stack of boxes and start running toward you. How do you respond? Like most of us, you would undoubtedly interpret this situation as threatening and run to escape. Your accompanying emotion of fear would involve many of the following physiological experiences: increased heart rate and blood pressure, dilated pupils, perspiration, dry mouth, rapid or irregular breathing, increased blood sugar, trembling, decreased gastrointestinal motility, and piloerection ("goose bumps"). Such physiological reactions are triggered by the brain, particularly the frontal lobes of the cerebral cortex, the limbic system, and the autonomic branch of the nervous system.

Looking closely at the limbic system (see Figure 12.13), we note that it seems to play an important role in the more "primitive" types of emotion, such as fear, anger, and sexual desire. For example, electrical stimulation of separate areas in the limbic system (in particular the *hypothalamus*) can produce a "sham rage" that turns a cat into a hostile, hissing, and slashing animal. Stimulation of adjacent areas can cause the same animal to purr and lick your fingers. (The rage is considered "sham" since it occurs in the absence of provocation and disappears immediately.)

If you felt threatened on the dark street, your limbic system would undoubtedly be aroused. Your emotion of fear would also lead to a behavioral reaction of hiding, running, or preparing to fight. This motor response would be "programmed" by your frontal lobes, which organize and orchestrate responses to the hypothalamus.

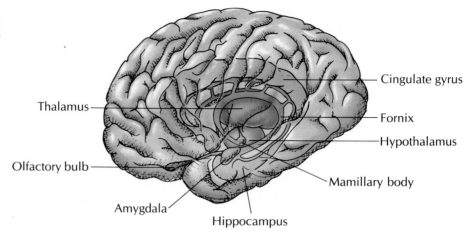

Figure 12.13 Brain areas involved in emotions. The limbic system consists of several subcortical structures that form a border (or *limbus*) around the brain stem. (Source: Kalat, 1992.)

Cingulate gyrus

Thalamus

Fornix

Hypothalamus

Olfactory bulb

Mamillary body

Amygdala

Hippocampus

The Autonomic Nervous System

Although the limbic system and frontal lobes play extremely important roles in creating emotion, the most obvious and easily recognized signs of arousal (increased heart rate, fast, shallow breathing, trembling, sweating, dry mouth) are produced by the autonomic nervous system (ANS). These largely automatic responses result from the interconnections of the ANS with various glands and muscles (it is these responses that the polygraph attempts to monitor and record). (See Figure 12.14.)

The ANS has two major subdivisions: the sympathetic nervous system and the parasympathetic nervous system. When you are emotionally aroused, the *sympathetic* branch works to increase heart rate, blood pressure, pupil dilation, salivation, and so on. When you are relaxed and resting, the *parasympathetic* branch tends to reverse these effects—heart rate decreases and blood pressure drops. The combined action of both systems allows you to respond appropriately to emotional arousal.

Where does adrenaline fit into this picture? Adrenaline, or more properly epinephrine, is a hormone secreted from the adrenal glands at the direction of the hypothalamus. Whereas the sympathetic nervous system is almost instantaneously "turned on" along with the limbic system and frontal lobes, epinephrine and another adrenal hormone, norepinephrine, keep the system in sympathetic control until the emergency is over. The damaging effects of too much sympathetic arousal as a result of stress are discussed in Chapter 13.

Sympathetic Nervous System: A subdivision of the autonomic nervous system that mobilizes the body's resources toward "fight or flight."

Parasympathetic Nervous System: A subdivision of the autonomic nervous system that restores the body to its "status quo" after sympathetic arousal.

Epinephrine: Hormone secreted by the adrenal glands in response to messages from the hypothalamus. Secretion is associated with emotional arousal, especially fear and anger.

Gender and Cultural Diversity

EVOLUTIONARY AND CULTURAL INFLUENCES ON EMOTIONS

Where do our emotions come from? Are they innate or do we learn them from personal experience and watching others? Are they a product of our evolutionary past? Do they differ from one culture to the next? As you might suspect, there are many answers to these questions.

Evolutionary Theories

Support for the idea that emotions are innate, and perhaps a product of evolution, comes from the following studies:

1. Infants only a few hours old show distinct expressions of emotions that closely match those of adults (Field et al., 1982). (See Chapter 9 for details.)

2. All infants, even those born deaf and blind, show similar facial expressions in similar situations (Eibl-Eibesfeldt, 1980b; Feldman, 1982).

3. Infants recognize facial expressions in others at a very young age (Nelson, 1987).

4. There is a striking similarity in the expression of emotions across a wide variety of cultures (Ekman, 1993).

Infant and cross-cultural similarities in emotional expression support the evolutionary theory of emotions first advanced by Charles Darwin in 1872. In his classic book, *The Expression of the Emotions in Man and Animals,* Darwin proposed that emotions evolved because of their value for survival and natural selection. Fear, for example, helps an organism avoid danger and therefore has survival value. Anger and aggression, on the other hand, prepare the organism to fight for a mate and necessary resources. Modern evolution theory further suggests that basic emotions (such as fear, anger, and sexual desire) originate in subcortical brain structures, known as the limbic system (see Figure 12.13). Given that higher brain areas (the cortex) developed later than the limbic system, evolution theory proposes that basic emotions evolved before thought.

Cultural Similarities

Several contemporary theorists, including Carroll Izard (1984), Paul Ekman and Wallace Friesen (1975), Robert Plutchik (1980), and Silvan Tomkins (1980) believe in the biological evidence of an evolution theory of emotions and offer cultural evidence in sup-

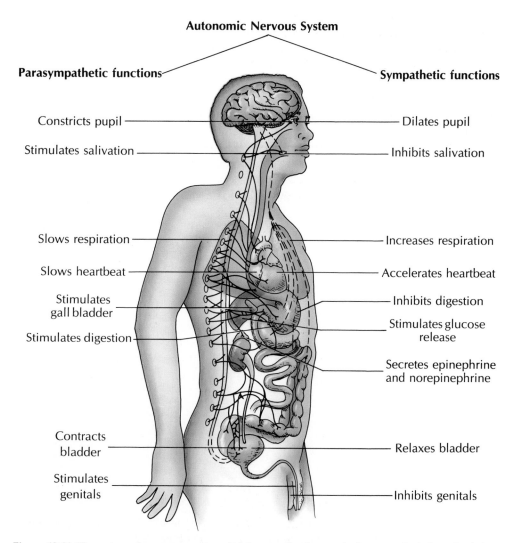

Autonomic Nervous System

Parasympathetic functions **Sympathetic functions**

Constricts pupil — — Dilates pupil
Stimulates salivation — — Inhibits salivation
Slows respiration — — Increases respiration
Slows heartbeat — — Accelerates heartbeat
Stimulates gall bladder — Inhibits digestion
Stimulates digestion — — Stimulates glucose release
— Secretes epinephrine and norepinephrine
Contracts bladder — — Relaxes bladder
Stimulates genitals — — Inhibits genitals

Figure 12.14 The autonomic nervous system. During emotional arousal, the sympathetic branch of the autonomic nervous system prepares the body for "fight or flight." Note how digestion and reproduction functions are inhibited since neither is important when you are preparing to fight or flee from an enemy.

Table 12.3 The Basic Human Emotions

Carroll Izard	Paul Ekman and Wallace Friesen	Robert Plutchik	Silvan Tomkins
Fear	Fear	Fear	Fear
Anger	Anger	Anger	Anger
Disgust	Disgust	Disgust	Disgust
Surprise	Surprise	Surprise	Surprise
Joy	Happiness	Joy	Enjoyment
Shame			Shame
Contempt	Contempt		Contempt
Sadness	Sadness	Sadness	
Interest		Anticipation	Interest
Guilt			
		Acceptance	
			Distress

port. As you can see in Table 12.3, each of these theorists proposes 7 to 10 primary or basic emotions that they have found to be *culturally universal*. That is, these emotions are expressed and recognized in essentially the same way in all cultures. Note the strong similarities among the lists.

How do these theorists explain emotions not on the list, such as love? They would say that love, like many other emotions, is simply a combination of primary emotions with variation in intensity. Plutchik suggests that primary emotions, such as fear, acceptance, and joy, are like colors on a color wheel that can combine to form secondary emotions, such as love, submission, awe, and optimism (Figure 12.15). Again like the color wheel, emotions that lie next to each other are considered more alike than those located farther away. For example, according to Plutchik fear is similar to acceptance, and both are very different from anger and disgust. Figure 12.16 is a variation of Plutchik's model that

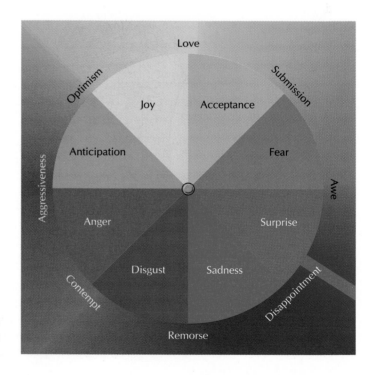

Figure 12.15 Plutchik's wheel of emotions. The inner circle represents the eight primary emotions. The outer circle demonstrates how primary emotions combine to form secondary emotions.

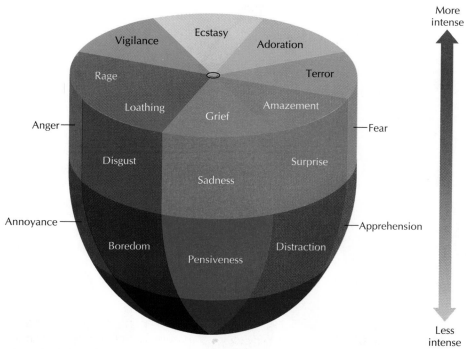

Figure 12.16 Plutchik's color solid. To explain more complex emotions than the primary and secondary ones described in his color wheel, Plutchik uses a three-dimensional form. Note that the intensity of the emotions varies vertically. Emotions at the top of the solid are the most intense, and those at the bottom, the least.

explains how basic emotions vary in their intensity, thereby accounting for the wide range of emotions.

Evolution theory is supported not only by the strong similarity among basic emotions in all cultures, but also by the fact that people around the world exhibit similar facial expressions when experiencing these basic emotions (Adelmann and Zajonc, 1989). As you can see by the photos in Figure 12.17, the facial expressions of the Western woman and the Fore tribesman from New Guinea are extremely similar for the same emotions.

Finally, not only are facial expressions of emotions similar in all cultures, but research also indicates that the interpretation of these expressions is universal. In other words, across cultures, a frown is recognized as a sign of displeasure and a smile as a sign of pleasure (Ekman, 1993). As the famous tune from *Casablanca* goes, "A kiss is still a kiss. . . ."

Cultural Differences

Once we go beyond the basic emotions and their expression, there are many cultural differences in expressions of emotion that can only be explained by learning theory and socialization. Researcher Theodore Kemper (1987) believes that many of our emotional experiences are the result of specific cultural norms and rules that teach us how, when, and where to express our emotions. Parents, for example, influence their children's emotions by responding angrily to some outbursts, by being sympathetic to others, and on occasion by simply ignoring them. In this way, children learn which emotions are considered appropriate in different situations, and which emotions they are expected to control.

A traditional Korean wife and husband, for example, almost never touch, hug, or kiss in public. And when they view these behaviors in American couples, they regard it as a sign of insecurity (Park, 1979). Similarly, while touching between men is generally avoided in the United States, it is common for two men to walk arm-in-arm, cradling the elbow, even holding hands in Korea, Greece, Italy, and the Middle East (Axtell, 1991).

There are significant cultural differences in the expression of emotions. It is common for Iranian men to greet one another with a kiss, for example, while men in North America generally shake hands or pat one another's shoulders.

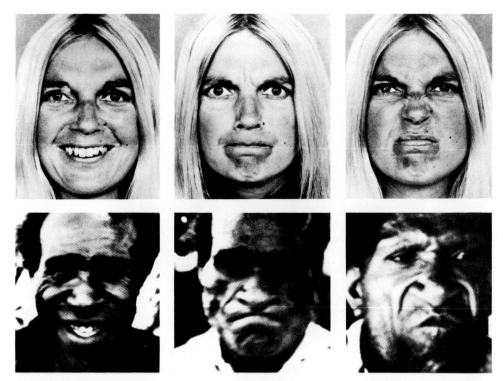

Figure 12.17 The cultural universals of emotion. To demonstrate that emotional facial expressions are universal rather than learned, Paul Ekman traveled to remote areas of New Guinea and found that members of the Fore tribe could easily identify the emotions on a Westerner's face (top line of photos). He also found that American college students had no difficulty identifying similar expressions in the Fore (bottom line of photos).

In sum, what these examples and studies suggest is that people of all cultures are born with similar capacities for emotion and with certain basic forms of expression. But how, when, and where we express different feelings depend in large part on learning and our socialization within a specific culture. ■

Review Questions

1. What are the four basic components of emotions?
2. Proponents of _____, or "lie detector," tests have claimed accuracy rates as high as 90 percent, but this is contradicted by other research.
3. How do the sympathetic and parasympathetic branches of the autonomic nervous system (ANS) work during emotional arousal?
4. How did Charles Darwin explain the evolution of emotions?
5. While researchers have found that basic emotions and their expression seem to be culturally universal, there are cultural differences in emotional expression that are generally explained by _____ .

Answers to Review Questions can be found in Appendix C.

GENERAL THEORIES OF EMOTION

• *What causes emotional arousal?*

Just as there are a number of theories that explain *what* influences emotion, there also are several theories that attempt to explain *how* we become emotional. Over the years three theories have dominated the field: the James-Lange theory, the Cannon-Bard theory, and the cognitive labeling theory. In this section, we will discuss each of these theories, as well as the facial feedback hypothesis. As you read, you will find it helpful to refer to Figure 12.18.

James-Lange Theory: The Reaction *Is* the Emotion

According to ideas originated by psychologist William James and later expanded by physiologist Carl Lange, emotions depend on feedback from the body (see Figure 12.18*a*). Contrary to popular opinion, which says we cry because we're sad, James wrote: "We feel sorry *because* we cry, angry *because* we strike, afraid *because* we tremble" (James, 1890).

Why would I tremble unless I first felt afraid?   According to the James-Lange theory, your bodily response of trembling is a reaction to a specific stimulus such as seeing a large bear in the wilderness. According to the James-Lange theory, you first perceive an event, your body reacts, and *then* you interpret the bodily changes as a specific emotion (see Figure 12.18*a*). William James suggested that your perception of autonomic arousal (palpitating heart, sinking stomach, flushed cheeks) as well as actions (running, hitting, yelling) and changes of facial expression (crying, smiling, frowning) produce what we refer to as "emotions." In short, bodily changes *cause* emotion. If there are no changes, there is no emotion.

James-Lange Theory: Theory that emotion is the *perception* of one's own bodily reactions and that each emotion is physiologically distinct.

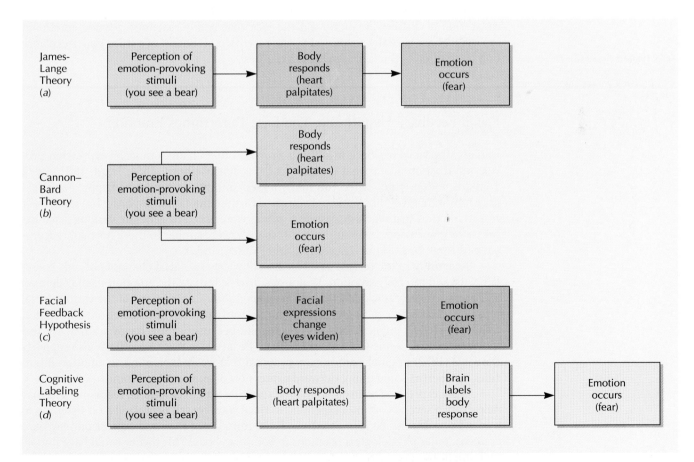

Figure 12.18 Comparing the four major theories of emotion. In the James-Lange theory *(a)*, the emotion occurs *after* the body is aroused. The Cannon-Bard theory *(b)* suggests that arousal and emotion occur *simultaneously.* The facial feedback hypothesis *(c)* proposes that changes in facial expression *produce* emotions. The cognitive labeling theory *(d)* suggests that autonomic arousal within the body causes the brain to search and find the reasons for the arousal; once the arousal is labeled, the emotion occurs.

Cannon-Bard Theory: Emotions and Reactions Are Simultaneous

Cannon-Bard Theory: Theory that the thalamus responds to emotion-arousing stimuli by sending messages simultaneously to the cerebral cortex and the autonomic nervous system. In this view, all emotions are physiologically similar.

Walter Cannon (1927) and Philip Bard (1934) disagreed with the James-Lange approach. They proposed that during perception of the emotion-provoking stimuli (seeing the bear) the thalamus sends *simultaneous* messages to both the general body and the cerebral cortex (see Figure 12.18*b*). Messages to the cortex produce the *experience* of emotion (fear), whereas other messages from the thalamus produce bodily changes (heart palpitations, running, widening eyes, and open mouth). A major point in the Cannon-Bard theory is that the body's response is not a necessary or even major factor in emotion. Cannon supported his position with several experiments in which animals were surgically prevented from experiencing physiological arousal. Yet, these surgically altered animals still showed observable behaviors (like growling and defensive postures) that might be labeled "emotional reactions" (Cannon, Lewis, and Britton, 1927).

Whereas the James-Lange theory argues that each emotion has its own distinct physiological reaction, the Cannon-Bard theory holds that all emotions are physiologically similar. Cannon also argued that emotions occur sooner than changes in the internal organs and that bodily changes are not enough to produce emotion.

Which theory is correct? The Cannon–Bard theory received a great deal of scientific support during the first part of the twentieth century. More recently, however, the pendulum of scientific opinion has begun to swing the other way. The James–Lange theory has substantial support on two major points. First of all, the James–Lange idea that different emotions are associated with different patterns of physiological activity has received research support (e.g., Davidson, 1984; Panskepp, 1982). Second, both the suggestion of distinct emotions and the idea that bodily reactions *precede* emotional experiences are partially supported by the recent development of a third major explanation of emotion—the facial feedback hypothesis.

Facial Feedback Hypothesis: Proposal that movements of the facial muscles *produce or intensify* emotional reactions.

Facial Feedback Hypothesis: The Face Determines Emotions

Initially, the facial feedback hypothesis proposed that changes in facial expression provide information about what emotion is being felt (Gelhorn, 1964; Izard, 1981, 1990; Tomkins, 1962). Thus, when you find yourself smiling, you must be happy. Facial expressions were involuntary and only directed further emotional response. However, later research found that when professional actors were asked to generate various facial expressions on demand, their autonomic responses were similar to those normally accompanying emotions (Ekman, Levenson, and Friesen, 1983).

According to the revised facial feedback hypothesis, facial changes not only correlate with and intensify emotions, but also *cause* or initiate the emotion itself (Adelman and Zajonc, 1989; Strack, Martin, and Stepper, 1988). Contractions of the various facial muscles send specific messages to the brain, identifying each basic emotion. Like James, these researchers suggest that we don't smile because we are happy; rather, we feel happy because we smile (see Figure 12.18*c*). The facial feedback hypothesis also supports Darwin's (1872) original evolutionary proposal that freely expressing an emotion intensifies it, whereas suppressing outward expression of an emotion diminishes it.

If the expression of an emotion *produces* subsequent emotional reactions, this may help explain several common experiences. Have you ever felt depressed after listening to a friend's problems? Your unconscious facial mimicry of their sad expression may have created similar physiological reactions in your own body. This theory could have important implications for therapists who constantly work with depressed clients and for actors who simulate emotions for their livelihood. If Darwin is right that expressing an emotion intensifies it, we also must question theorists who advocate the expression of anger and aggression as a way of *relieving* built-in tension (see Chapter 18).

Cognitive Labeling Theory: The Label Is the Emotion

Although each of the three previous theories provides some insight into the experience of emotions, they give little attention to the role of cognition and interpretation. According to Schachter and Singer's cognitive labeling theory (1962), an individual's interpretation or label for physiological arousal determines the emotion experienced. If we are crying at a wedding, for example, we often interpret our emotion as joy or happiness, but if we cry at a funeral we label it as sadness (see Figure 12.18*d*).

In Schachter and Singer's classic study, subjects were given shots of epinephrine and told it was a type of "vitamin," and their subsequent arousal and labeling were investigated (see Figure 12.19). One group of subjects was *correctly* informed about the expected effects (hand tremors, excitement, and heart palpitations), and a second group

Cognitive Labeling Theory: Theory that the cognitive (thinking), subjective (evaluating), and physiological arousal components are all necessary to emotional experiences.

Figure 12.19 Cognitive labeling theory. A comparison of informed, misinformed, and uninformed subjects in Schachter and Singer's classic experiment demonstrates the importance of cognitive labels in experiencing emotions.

was *misinformed* and told to expect itching, numbness, and headache. A third, *uninformed,* group was told nothing about the possible effects.

Following the injection, each subject was placed in a room with a *confederate* (a "stooge" who was part of the experiment but pretended to be a fellow volunteer). The confederate was told to act either happy and cheerful (throwing paper airplanes around the room and shooting wads of paper into the wastebasket) or unhappy and angry (complaining about the questionnaire and expressing general dissatisfaction with the entire experiment).

The results of the study confirmed the experimental hypothesis: Subjects who did not have an appropriate cognitive label for their emotional arousal (the misinformed group and the uninformed group) tended to look to the situation for an appropriate explanation. Thus, those placed with a happy confederate became happy, whereas those with an unhappy confederate were unhappy. Subjects in the correctly informed group, on the other hand, knew their physiological arousal was the result of the shot, so their emotions were generally unaffected by the confederate.

Misattribution

Misattribution: The incorrect attribution of internal arousal to false internal or external causes. More generally, any incorrect attribution of causality.

Although some researchers have been unable to replicate these specific findings (Marshall and Zimbardo, 1979; Reisenzein, 1983), indirect support can be found with studies of misattribution, when a person mistakenly believes the cause of an emotion is something other than it really is. For example, do you ever become unusually awkward and shy around attractive people whom you wish to impress? Using misattribution theory, we would predict that if you were provided a handy, alternative explanation for your anxiety, your shyness would be reduced. This is precisely what Susan Brodt and Philip Zimbardo (1981) found when they brought shy and not-shy women to the laboratory and had them interact with a handsome male who posed as a fellow subject. Prior to the interaction, both groups of women were placed in a small room and subjected to a loud noise. One-half of the women (the experimental group) were then told that the noise would leave them with a pounding heart, a common symptom of shyness. The other group of women (the control group) were given no instruction about the noise. When the informed group of shy women later talked to the handsome male, their shyness was significantly reduced. They apparently attributed their pounding hearts to the noise, rather than to shyness or social inadequacy.

Similar research has found that such emotional relabeling can also help alleviate the common problem of insomnia (Storms and Nisbett, 1970). Knowing that people suffering from insomnia experience a considerable amount of physiological arousal at bedtime (they fear not being able to fall asleep or stay asleep), researchers hypothesized that being able to attribute the arousal to a pill would help insomniacs fall asleep. Under the guise of a drug and fantasy experiment, insomniac subjects were given a placebo pill to take before going to bed. Subjects in the *relaxation* group were told that the pill would reduce their heart rates and relax them. Subjects in the *arousal* group were told that the pill would increase their tension and anxiety. (In using this explanation of the side effects of the pill, the experimenters allayed the subject's skepticism by saying that they needed more information about how insomniacs felt at bedtime.) Subjects in the control group were told that the pill would have no side effects.

All subjects were then asked to record how long it took them to fall asleep. As predicted, subjects in the arousal group fell asleep significantly faster than subjects in the control and relaxation groups. The arousal subjects apparently were able to relabel their insomniac arousal to the pill and not to their own sleeping problems. On the other hand, subjects in the relaxation group had *more,* not less, difficulty in falling asleep. It seems that when these subjects found their arousal existed in spite of the "relaxation" pill, they became even more aroused, thinking they had an even greater problem than they originally believed.

Critical Thinking

PSYCHOLOGY IN ACTION

RECOGNIZING EMOTIONAL APPEALS: ADS AND EVERYDAY ATTEMPTS TO PERSUADE

Advertisers spend billions of dollars each year to hire highly trained professionals who understand our deepest fears and desires and how to use them to motivate us to buy a car we can't really afford or put our purchases on a bank credit card. (Our closest friends and family members can be equally adept at using emotional appeals.) Sometimes emotional appeals are made in the service of a greater good, such as public safety warnings to wear seatbelts. But more often, this isn't the case and the appeal is an illegitimate exploitation of emotions. A critical thinker should be able to recognize and critically evaluate appeals to emotion as opposed to appeals to logic and good sense.

Below are some common examples of emotional appeals used to motivate us for someone else's benefit:

a. *Appeal to self-esteem*—an approach that manipulates our need to feel good about ourselves ("Fine wine drinkers prefer . . ." or "Mothers who care . . .").

b. *Appeal to social fears*—an approach that carries an implied threat of ostracism or social rejection ("Not even your best friend will tell you . . .").

c. *Appeal to authority or experts*—quoting or using authority figures to make a point. Although some authorities have legitimate expertise in the area in which they are advising (a qualified mechanic diagnosing a problem with a car), people often use "authorities" who are not qualified to give an expert opinion (a respected newscaster selling life insurance).

d. *Appeal to pity*—a person attempts to persuade you to do or buy something because he or she will be hurt if you don't agree.

e. *Appeal to force*—a person attempts to persuade you to do or buy something because he or she will hurt you if you don't agree.

f. *Plain folks*—an approach based on the similarity principle. If you think the persuader is "like you," "just one of the guys," or "regular folk," you will be persuaded more easily.

g. *Associations*—using a positive symbol to endorse whatever the persuader wants you to "buy." The idea is that

through classical conditioning (see Chapter 6) you will transfer the positive qualities of the endorser to the product.

The following activity will sharpen your skills in recognizing illegitimate emotional appeals. Beside each statement, mark the letter of the illegitimate appeal being used. More than one type of tactic may be applicable.

_____ 1. A Bell telephone ad shows a small, sweet grandmother sitting patiently by the phone waiting for her loved ones to call.

_____ 2. A teenager argues against the family's vacation plans, and the father responds by saying, "When you pay the bills, you can make the decisions."

_____ 3. Peanut butter ads suggest that "Choosy mothers choose Jif."

_____ 4. Scope mouthwash commercials show two people just waking up in the morning with the words "Yech! Morning breath, the worst breath of the day."

_____ 5. A college student asks his professor to accept a late paper: "I've worked all weekend on this report. I know that it's past your deadline, but I have to work full-time while also attending college."

_____ 6. While showing a very expensive home to a young couple, the realtor says "You owe it to yourself and your family to buy the very best."

_____ 7. Actor Robert Young, former star of "Father Knows Best" and "Marcus Welby, M.D.," "prescribes" Sanka coffee for people who are nervous, irritable, or in stressful situations.

_____ 8. A political ad shows the candidate wearing a hard hat at the steel workers' company picnic and pitching horseshoes in his backyard.

_____ 9. A Marlboro cigarette ad shows a strong, ruggedly handsome cowboy riding alone on the range.

_____ 10. After making it clear that he values employee "loyalty," a supervisor asks for "volunteers" to help a fellow supervisor move on the weekend.

Comparing answers helps to further your critical thinking skills. Although we are providing a list of possible answers, we encourage you to discuss your responses with your classmates.

ANSWERS: 1. D; 2. E; 3. A; 4. B; 5. D; 6. A; 7. C; 8. F; 9. G; 10. E.

As you can see, studies in misattribution can provide important insights into how each of us labels and interprets our emotions. They also suggest interesting questions about the role of placebos and a patient's cognitive processes. The relationship between such psychological factors and physical health and illness is the focus of our next chapter.

Review Questions

1. How is the James-Lange theory different from the Cannon-Bard theory of emotion?
2. The _____ hypothesis suggests that facial expressions produce emotional responses.
3. How does the cognitive-labeling theory explain emotions?
4. The incorrect attribution of internal arousal to false internal or external causes is known as _____ .
5. How has misattribution theory been used in research on insomniacs?

Answers to Review Questions can be found in Appendix C.

REVIEW OF MAJOR CONCEPTS

UNDERSTANDING MOTIVATION

1. Motivation is the study of the "whys" of behavior, whereas emotion is the study of feelings. Because motivated behaviors are often closely related to emotions, these two topics are frequently studied together.

2. A wide variety of motives are studied throughout this text. In this chapter, we focus on hunger, stimulus-seeking, and achievement as examples of the three basic categories of motives: primary (innate, unlearned motives that are basic to survival), secondary (biological motives less necessary for survival), and learned/social (acquired motives that result from experience and the need for others).

3. Eating is controlled by a complex interaction of both internal and external factors. In the brain the lateral and ventromedial areas of the hypothalamus (LH and VMH) appear to be involved in the control of hunger, but their exact role is unclear. Other areas of the brain, the level of sugar in the blood, and the sight of external cues for eating also seem to play a role in hunger.

4. A large number of people show evidence of one or more eating disorders. Obesity seems to result from biological factors, such as the individual's set point, which tends to maintain a given level of body fat, and from psychological factors, such as sensitivity to external cues. The most effective way to lose weight is a combination of exercise, diet, and behavioral principles (such as removing or managing food-related cues, changing the reinforcers, and so on).

5. Anorexia nervosa (extreme weight loss due to self-imposed starvation) and bulimia (excessive consumption of food followed by vomiting or taking laxatives) both seem to be related to an intense fear of obesity.

6. People and animals will apparently work very hard to satisfy their need for novel stimulation (a secondary motive). There are, however, individual differences in this need. According to Zuckerman, high sensation seekers are biologically "prewired" to need a higher level of stimulation, whereas the reverse is true for low sensation seekers.

7. Achievement involves the need for success, for doing better than others, and for mastering challenging tasks. This need is usually assessed through the interpretation of short stories generated in response to the Thematic Apperception Test (TAT), or through a subject's response to a competitive situation such as ring tossing.

8. Culture and gender have been studied as factors in achievement. While research supports the idea that culture has an important impact on achievement motivation, early studies suggesting that women have a "fear of failure" that limits their achievement have not been supported.

GENERAL THEORIES OF MOTIVATION

9. There are basically two approaches to the study of motivation: biological theories (which include instinct theory, drive-reduction theory and arousal theory), and psychological theories (which include incentive theory and cognitive theories).

10. Instinct theories suggest there is some inborn, genetic component to motivation. Although the original interest in this theory declined because of the unwieldy list of possible instincts, interest has been revived in recent years by the work of ethologists and sociobiologists. Drive-reduction theory suggests that internal tensions (produced by the body's demand for homeostasis) "push" the organism toward satisfaction of basic needs, and that the organism learns which specific behaviors will meet this goal. According to arousal theory, individuals seek optimal levels of arousal that help maximize their performance.

11. According to incentive theory, motivation results from the "pull" of external environmental stimuli. Cognitive theories emphasize the importance of thoughts, attributions, and expectations.

12. Research with intrinsic versus extrinsic motivation finds that when one receives extrinsic rewards interest and motivation decline.

13. According to opponent-process theory, when someone

first experiences dangerous sports such as bungee jumping he or she has a strong emotional reaction, which is then followed by an opposing (opposite) emotion. After several jumps, the initial terror is reduced and the opposing feelings of relief and joy are increased. Opponent-process theory can also be used to explain drug addiction.

14. Abraham Maslow proposed a hierarchy of needs or motives that incorporates both biological and psychological theories. He believed that the basic physiological and survival needs must be satisfied before a person can attempt to satisfy higher needs. The importance of sequentially working up through these steps has been questioned by critics.

UNDERSTANDING EMOTION

15. There are four basic components of all emotions: the physiological (increased heart rate, respiration rate, and so on); the cognitive (thoughts, beliefs, and expectations); the behavioral (facial expressions and bodily gestures); and the subjective (evaluations of intensity, pleasure versus displeasure, and so on).

16. The cognitive and subjective components are generally studied through self-report techniques, whereas the bodily expressions and physiological arousal components are measured more directly through observation of overt behavior or with a polygraph.

17. The polygraph is a mechanical measurement of changes in emotional arousal (increased heart rate, blood pressure, and so on). Although the polygraph is extensively used in police work and for employment purposes, psychologists generally object to this practice because they find the polygraph is a poor predictor of guilt or innocence or of truth or lies.

18. Biological studies have found that most emotions result from a general, nonspecific arousal of the nervous system. This arousal involves the cerebral cortex, the limbic system, and the frontal lobes of the brain. The most obvious signs of arousal (trembling, increased heart rate, sweating, and so on) result from activation of the sympathetic nervous system, a subdivision of the autonomic nervous system. The parasympathetic system restores the body to the "status quo."

19. Most psychologists believe that emotions result from a complex interplay between evolution and culture. Studies have identified 7 to 10 basic emotions that are universal —experienced and expressed in similar ways across almost all cultures.

GENERAL THEORIES OF EMOTION

20. There are four major explanations for the activation of emotions. The James–Lange theory suggests we interpret the way we feel on the basis of physical sensations such as increased heart rate, trembling, and so on. The Cannon–Bard theory suggests that feelings are created from independent and simultaneous stimulation of both the cortex and the autonomic nervous system.

21. The third general theory of emotion, the facial feedback hypothesis, asserts that facial movements elicit specific emotions. The cognitive labeling theory of Schachter and Singer maintains that emotions result from a combination of cognitive, subjective, and physiological components. People notice what is going on around them, as well as their own bodily responses, and then label the emotion accordingly.

SUGGESTED READINGS

AXTELL, R. E. (1991). *Gestures: The do's and taboos of body language around the world.* New York: Wiley. The author presents an entertaining and down-to-earth description of cross-cultural variations in body language.

BEN-SHAKHAR, G., & FUREDY, J. J. (1990). *Theories and applications in the detection of deception.* New York: Springer-Verlag. A good review of the methods of lie detection and research on its scientific reliability and validity.

CARLSON, J. G., & HATFIELD, E. (1989). *Psychology of emotion.* Belmont, CA: Wadsworth. A readable and informative description of the biology and psychology of emotion.

LEVENKRON, S. (1982). *Treating and overcoming anorexia ner-* *vosa.* New York: Scribner's. A fascinating account of the lives and treatment of six anorexic females.

PLUTCHIK, R., & KELLERMAN, H. (EDS.). (1990). *Emotion: Theory, research, and experience* (Vol. I). San Diego: Academic Press. This text offers up-to-date and comprehensive reviews of the scientific literature for the field of emotion.

REMINGTON, D., FISCHER, G., & PARENT, E. (1983). *How to lower your fat thermostat.* Provo, UT: Vitality House International. Intended for nonprofessional readers, this paperback offers a "scientific" explanation for the "set point theory" and a step-by-step method for weight reduction.

CHAPTER 13

Health Psychology

OUTLINE

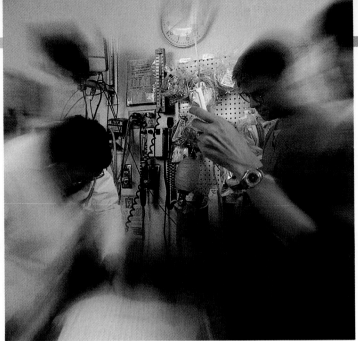

*T*hat noise—sounds like hundreds of explosions! I can't see—the light—too bright—hurts. Am I dead? I must be—can't breathe. I can't breathe! Gotta get this tube out of my throat. Can't —arms strapped down. What? Who's that? Nurse. Says my throat tube is hooked up to a respirator. Does my breathing for me. Okay. The noise is from life-support machines and monitors . . .

I must have dozed off. Where am I? Can't think —so groggy . . . I remember now. I had a heart attack. I had bypass surgery. It must be over now. Well, I seem to have come out of it all right. What an agonizing decision, to let them actually open up my chest and work on my heart. How scary. To think that my whole life depended on that heart–lung machine to keep me alive. Glad they called in that psychologist. The decision was a lot easier with him supporting us, answering Carol's and my questions, and showing those movies so we'd know what to expect.

Here's Carol. I have to tell her how much I—drat, I can't talk—the throat tube. How good it is to feel her hand in mine. We haven't held hands since our kids were babies. We'll have to do more of that when—if— I ever get out of here. What's that? Oh, the nurse says most people have their tubes out by now, but because of my heavy smoking I need the respirator for a longer time. Guess I should have tried harder to stop smoking. There are a lot of things the doctor told me to stop, but I didn't listen. She said that with my father dying of a heart attack at 55, I was a likely candidate for heart disease. She said that, besides stopping smoking, I should change my eating habits, lose weight, exercise, and try to reduce stress. Reduce stress? How could I?

There are always deadlines at work, meetings to attend, clients to court. How is the company going to get along while I'm in the hospital? And who's going to coach Elizabeth's soccer team? No one can coach those kids like I can—I coach them to win, and win I always do! And Jimmy's Boy Scout trip next weekend: Who's going to take them if I don't? And who'll run the Lion's Club meeting next week? . . . Wait a minute. The doctor told me to take it easy, but I didn't. That's why I'm here. Maybe I should stop worrying about who will take over for me and concentrate on changing my life. This heart attack thing sure is scary. Carol said I nearly died. Well, I'm gonna change. I'm never going to light up another cigarette. I'm going to bow out of these extra activities, just volunteer for one thing at a time. As for watching my diet and exercising—well, maybe it's time for those now, too.

Do you know someone like our heart attack victim? Your father? An aunt? A friend? Or maybe even yourself? Although the person we portrayed is fictitious, his personality is a composite of real, ordinary people. He illustrates some of the issues in health psychology. Because he was at risk for heart disease, our heart attack patient's doctor made several recommendations based on research findings from this relatively new field.

In this chapter, we will discuss many research findings that can have an important impact on your physical well-being. For example, did you know that according to some sources, smoking is the most preventable contributing factor in the development of serious disease, such as heart disease and lung cancer? That people with certain types of personalities are more prone to heart disease than others? That excess stress can lower your body's resistance not only to minor illnesses such as colds and the flu but also to major illnesses such as cancer and heart disease? That people who feel in control of themselves and their environment tend to handle stress better than those who feel helpless in most situations? And that today, causes of death stem more from our behavior patterns than from viral or bacterial disease? These and other health psychology findings will be examined in this chapter.

As you read Chapter 13, keep the following **Survey** questions in mind and answer them in your own words:

- What is health psychology? How do health psychologists help people handle chronic pain and stop smoking?
- What are the major causes and results of stress?
- How is stress related to cancer and coronary heart disease?
- What techniques and resources are available to help people cope with stress?

THE NATURE OF HEALTH PSYCHOLOGY

Health psychology is the study of the relationship between psychological behavior and physical health and illness, with an emphasis on "wellness" and the prevention of illness. Health psychologists study how people's lifestyles and activities, emotional reactions, ways of interpreting events, and personality characteristics influence their physical health. Some health psychologists are involved primarily in research, whereas others work directly with physicians and other health professionals to implement research findings.

The field of health psychology has grown exponentially in the last decade in terms of both research and practice. Throughout most of history, the relationship between mind and physical health had been a widely accepted fact. However, the discovery of physiological causes for infectious diseases such as typhoid and syphilis in the late 1800s led doctors to search for *only* physiological causes of disease. This in turn led to such marked advances in medicine and public health during the last century that our life expectancy has increased more than 50 percent, from 46.3 to 69.9 years for men and from 48.3 to 77.8 years for women (Matarazzo, 1984). Concurrently, the major causes of death have shifted from pneumonia, influenza, tuberculosis, and gastrointestinal infections to cancer, heart and cardiovascular disease, accidents, and chronic lung diseases (Matarazzo and Neckliter, 1988). Thus, causes of death have shifted from disease through infection to disease brought on by behavior and lifestyle. At the same time, we have returned to the realization that physical and mental health are related.

What Health Psychologists Do

Health psychologists work as practitioners and researchers, dealing with such problems as high cholesterol, hypertension, chronic pain, diabetes, cancer, and AIDS. As researchers, health psychologists work in a wide variety of areas. Following are only a few examples: Lewis, Thomas, and Worobey (1990) studied the relationship of infants' ability to cope with stress and their susceptibility to subsequent illness. They found that infants who reacted strongly to their two-month immunization shots were more likely to be susceptible to illness at 18 months of age than those who quieted more quickly. In another study, Margaret Chesney is examining how AIDS victims cope with their illness. She hopes to apply her findings to improve the quality of life and lengthen the lifespan of people with AIDS (DeAngelis, 1992).

Health psychologists who are practitioners work in the medical field, in such settings as hospitals and clinics. Astounding technological advances have been made in medicine in the last few years, including heart transplants and bypass surgery. When we hear of such advances, we can jump to the conclusion that people with severe medical problems need only have operations and their problems will disappear. But this is just not so. According to Jack Copeland, a cardiothoracic surgeon, patients almost uniformly have accompanying psychological problems—extreme guilt in the case of transplant patients, plus worry over changes in appearance, adjustment to dietary restrictions, changes in activity level, and so on (Rodgers, 1984). Health psychologists often work hand-in-hand with physicians, nurses, anesthesiologists, and others in helping patients with such problems. They help patients and their families make critical decisions. They help patients before and after surgery or other treatment by letting them know what to expect. For example, before recommending bypass surgery, cardiologists often order

What is health psychology? How do health psychologists help people handle chronic pain and stop smoking?

Health Psychology: The study of the relationship between psychological behavior and physical health and illness, with an emphasis on wellness and the prevention of illness.

several tests that can be frightening and painful. By discussing the purpose of the tests and suggesting ways to cope with them, psychologists can help patients through these stressful situations.

Where does the wellness part of health psychology come in?   Health psychologists also educate the general public about health maintenance. They provide information about the effects of stress, smoking, lack of exercise, and other health issues. They develop and administer programs to help people learn how to cope with chronic problems, such as pain and high blood pressure, as well as unhealthful behaviors, such as lack of assertiveness and aggression. In the next sections we will focus on two prevalent health problems, chronic pain and smoking, to illustrate how health psychologists work.

Chronic Pain: The Role of Psychologists in Helping Patients Cope

Chronic Pain: Continuous or recurrent pain over a period of six months or more.

If you've ever had your back "go out" or a headache that lasted for days, you have an idea of the suffering people experience with chronic pain from arthritis, cancer, migraine or tension headache, and neuralgia, for example. They experience the same kind of pain you feel from your bad back or your headache, except that their pain doesn't go away. Because their pain is always with them, they become irritable, anxious, depressed, and dependent on others, with a consequent loss of self-esteem. Their social lives and personal relationships are profoundly affected, their sporting and other activities are considerably curtailed, and some are forced to quit their jobs (Egan and Keaton, 1987; Olshan, 1980). They may be shuffled from one doctor to another and rebuffed with such statements as "I just don't know how to help you" or "It's all in your head" (which, of course, it is, since it's in our brain that we perceive pain). Doctors often prescribe pain medications to which the patient can become addicted and in some cases may perform surgery, which may not successfully relieve the pain.

Is chronic pain very common?   It has been estimated that as many as one-third of all Americans suffer from continuous or recurrent pain, and tens of millions are partially or completely disabled by their pain (Sanders, 1985; Turk, Meichenbaum, and Genest, 1983). In recent years, doctors have begun teaming up with or referring patients to health psychologists who can help them deal more effectively with pain. The psychologist may recommend increased activity and exercise or changes in diet, since chemicals such as monosodium glutamate and caffeine can contribute to pain, particularly headache. The psychologist may also use specific treatment methods, such as operant conditioning, biofeedback, relaxation, and hypnosis.

Operant Conditioning Techniques

Endorphins: Morphinelike chemicals occurring naturally in the brain that can lessen the perception of pain.

Working with chronic pain patients is no easy matter, for there are countless factors that may tend to reinforce the pain. For example, talking about the pain tends to focus attention on it, and anxiety tends to increase its perception, which further increases the anxiety. Often, the patient learns inappropriate behaviors, such as inactivity, that come to be associated with the pain. Contrary to the popular belief, an increase in activity and exercise can be beneficial. Exercise increases the release of endorphins, the chemicals that attach themselves to nerve cells in the brain and act to block the perception of pain. Pain patients, however, tend to *decrease* their activity levels and stop exercising altogether. Well-meaning friends and relatives reinforce this inactivity by doing things for the patients when they complain. In this way, patients can become operantly conditioned to inactivity and other disadvantageous behaviors, such as complaining about their pain, by being reinforced for them. In such cases, psychologists may initiate a behavior modification program not only for the patients but also for their families and friends.

Cairns and Pasino (1977) conducted the first controlled study on the effectiveness of operant conditioning techniques in the treatment of chronic pain. The researchers provided reinforcement by congratulating pain patients when they followed through with their pain treatment programs (daily exercise, use of relaxation techniques, and so on) and by charting their adherence to the program. The researchers found that both of these techniques were effective in reducing the subjective pain experienced by their patients. Thus, many pain control programs now incorporate an operant conditioning component, in which patients are reinforced for carrying through with changes in behavior.

Biofeedback

Biofeedback (see Chapter 6) with patients suffering from chronic pain has been done chiefly with the electromyograph (EMG). This is a device that measures muscle tension by recording the amount of electrical activity in an area of skin to which electrodes have been attached. Pain therapists use the EMG to help people whose pain has an exaggerated muscle tension component, such as tension headache and lower back pain. When the EMG is used, electrodes are attached to the site of the pain and the patient is instructed to relax. When sufficient relaxation is achieved, the machine gives a signal such as a tone or a light. This signal serves as feedback to the patient. Biofeedback is successful because it teaches patients to recognize patterns of emotional arousal and conflict that affect their physiological responses. They can then learn self-regulation skills to help them control their pain (McKee, 1991).

Electromyograph (EMG): Biofeedback device that can measure muscle tension by recording the amount of electrical activity in an area of skin to which electrodes are attached.

Proof of the effectiveness of biofeedback was demonstrated in a study with subjects suffering from tension headaches. Some received accurate EMG biofeedback while others were given pseudofeedback (inaccurate biofeedback). Patients receiving accurate biofeedback experienced greater reduction in headache intensity and needed medication less frequently than patients receiving the pseudofeedback (Philips, 1977). Although biofeedback does not reduce the number or frequency of tension headaches, it does reduce the severity, a great value in itself.

Also, in a follow-up study of subjects who had reported at least 50 percent improvement in pain relief from chronic headache from a combination of relaxation and biofeedback techniques, it was found that effects still endured after five years (Blanchard et al., 1987). This is good news to psychologists because relapse rates are often high for participants in treatment programs.

A study conducted by Nouwen and Solinger (1979) indicates that a major contribution of biofeedback is that it helps people feel they have some control over their pain. Subjects with lower back pain who received EMG biofeedback showed a significant decrease in their tension levels and in subjective reports of pain, as compared to controls. What is remarkable about this study is that when the same patients were studied three months later, their tension levels had returned to pretreatment levels, but they still reported lowered levels of pain. These results suggest that the EMG training was successful at teaching the patients that they need not accept the pain as uncontrollable. They could assume an internal locus of control over their pain and therefore cope more effectively with it.

Internal Locus of Control: The belief that one has significant control over the events in one's life.

Several researchers have attempted to use EEG (brain wave) biofeedback to alleviate pain (Gannon and Sternbach, 1971; Melzack and Perry, 1975; Pelletier and Peper, 1977; Sternbach, 1974). Subjects try to produce *alpha* brain waves, which tend to be associated with relaxed states. Although some success has been achieved with this type of biofeedback, results are mixed. EEG biofeedback has been shown effective in learning to cope with chronic headache pain, but not with other kinds of chronic pain.

Relaxation Techniques

Because the pain always seems to be there, chronic pain sufferers tend to talk and think about their pain whenever they're not thoroughly engrossed in other activities. When spouses or loved ones react to the pain behavior by giving extra attention and care, they seem to reinforce not only the behavior but also the patient's perception of the pain (Block, Kremer, and Gaynor, 1980; Flor, Kerns, and Turk, 1987). Thus, instead of doting over a chronic pain patient, loved ones might better spend their time trying to divert the person's attention. Watching TV shows or films, attending parties or exercising might all help to reduce their discomfort. Attention might also be diverted with relaxation techniques, which have the added advantage of easing the tension and anxiety components of pain.

Relaxation Techniques: Procedures used to relieve the anxiety and bodily tension accompanying such problems as stress and chronic pain.

Are these like the relaxation techniques used in natural childbirth?   Yes. Relaxation techniques are used in conjunction with breathing techniques as a way of reducing the anxiety and pain of childbirth. They work by focusing attention on the relaxation process rather than on the uncertainty and fear of the birthing process. They also help relieve the muscle tension that aggravates the pain perceived during childbirth. These same techniques can be used to try to relieve other kinds of pain. Again, these techniques do not eliminate the pain; they merely allow the person to ignore it for a time.

 Try This Yourself

Progressive relaxation is used not only for chronic pain, but for everyday stress. In fact, you can do it anytime and anywhere you feel stressed, sitting in a traffic jam or waiting for an exam to begin. Here's how to do it:

1. Sit in a comfortable position, with your head supported.
2. Start breathing slowly and deeply.
3. Let your entire body go limp—let go of all tension. Try to visualize your body getting more and more relaxed.
4. Systematically tense and release each part of your body, beginning with your toes. Focus your attention on your toes and try to visualize what they are doing. Curl them tightly while counting to 10, then release them and feel the difference between the tense state and the relaxed state. Next, tense your feet to the count of 5, then relax them and feel the difference between the two states. Continue with your calves, thighs, buttocks, abdomen, back muscles, shoulders, upper arms, forearms, hands and fingers, neck, jaws, facial muscles, and forehead.

This technique is most effective if you do the visualization, too. Also, try practicing progressive relaxation twice a day for about 15 minutes a session. You will be surprised at how much more relaxed you will be in general. ■

Hypnosis

Another approach used to alter people's focus on pain is hypnosis. As you read in Chapter 5, *hypnosis* is an alternate state of consciousness in which the brain is highly alert and more open to suggestion. The hypnotic state can be induced by focusing attention on the drone of a soft voice, the ticking of a watch, or the process of totally relaxing the body. Hypnosis can be either self-induced, in which case it is referred to as self-hypnosis, or it can be induced by a specially trained person. In the treatment of pain, the hypnotized individual can learn to ignore the pain or to experience it in a different way.

Self-Hypnosis: An alternate state of consciousness induced by oneself during which one is more relaxed, more alert, and more open to suggestion than in the normal state.

There is some controversy over whether hypnosis is effective in relieving pain or not, since research results are inconclusive. A few studies have shown definite benefits (Elton, Burrows, and Stanley, 1980). Paul Sacerdote (1978) found that hypnosis brought some degree of relief to 90 percent of pain patients, and in the 25 percent of those patients who had "high hypnotic talent" there was a highly significant degree of pain relief. In another study, Sachs, Feuerstein, and Vitale (1977) concluded that patients using self-hypnosis experienced reductions in pain intensity, life dissatisfaction and suffering, unpleasant personality characteristics associated with chronic pain (such as irritability), amount of pain medication used, and the amount that pain interfered with daily activities such as social life and sleep.

Whatever pain relief technique is used, one of the most important components for success is the patient's conviction that the pain *can* in fact be controlled. This brings us back to the importance of an internal locus of control. Weisenberg (1980) suggests that without this feeling of control, the effectiveness of any attempt at pain control would be

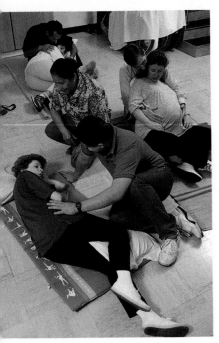

Relaxation techniques are often taught as part of natural-childbirth classes.

substantially reduced. Melzack and Perry (1975), in whose study over half of the patients achieved at least a 33 percent reduction in pain through biofeedback and hypnosis, attributed the success of their program to four factors: distraction of attention, suggestion, relaxation, and the sense of control over the pain.

Let's move along now to another major health problem health psychologists treat: smoking.

Review Questions

1. Health psychology is the study of the relationship between _____ and _____ .

2. What are the roles of health psychologists?

3. Long-term pain that continues for about six months or more is called _____ pain.

4. How can operant conditioning be used in the treatment of chronic pain?

5. Biofeedback teaches pain patients an _____ locus of control. Why is this so important?

6. Why do relaxation and hypnosis work in alleviating feelings of pain?

Answers to Review Questions can be found in Appendix C.

Smoking: Hazardous to Your Health

According to the U.S. Department of Health and Human Services, cigarette smoking is the single most preventable cause of death and disease in the United States. It will adversely affect the health of one out of every three people who smoke cigarettes. Like our heart attack patient, most people know that smoking is bad for their health and that the more they smoke, the more at risk they are. It is therefore not surprising that most professionals in the medical field are concerned with the prevention of smoking and with encouraging people who already smoke to stop.

Smoking Prevention

The first puff on a cigarette is rarely pleasant. Why, then, do people ever start smoking? The answer is complex, since the decision involves psychological, social, and biological factors. Although for some people smoking is an expression of rebellion against their parents or society (Krantz, Grunberg, and Baum, 1985), most people begin to smoke in response to social pressures from peers or in imitation of role models such as family members, movie stars, or athletes (Bowen and Peterson, 1988). Once a person begins to smoke, there is also a biological need to continue because of the addictive effects of nicotine. Therefore, one way to reduce the number of smokers is to prevent people from taking their first puff (Biglan et al., 1987).

Smoking prevention programs face a tough uphill battle against peer pressure and the advertising budgets of the large tobacco companies (see Chapter 18 on persuasion and the Joe Camel advertising campaign). Smoking provides adolescents with immediate short-term reinforcements from their peers, while the long-term health disadvantages seem totally irrelevant to them. Therefore, the most successful prevention techniques focus on the short-term detrimental effects of tobacco use, such as coughing, bad breath, difficulty in breathing, dependence on an addictive substance, and the effects on personal appearance and hygiene (Murray et al., 1984). Most young people do not realize that smoking makes them smell as well as taste like cigarette smoke until the facts are converted to such down-to-earth terms as, "Who wants to kiss a dirty ashtray?"

Many smokers begin as teens or preteens. Once a person begins to smoke there is a biological need to continue because of the addictive effects of nicotine. The best way to quit smoking is never to begin in the first place.

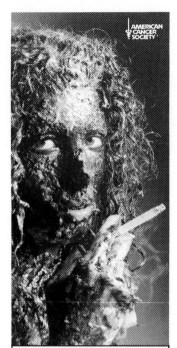

If what happened on your inside happened on your outside, would you still smoke?
JOIN THE GREAT AMERICAN SMOKEOUT.®

The single most preventable cause of death and disease in the United States is cigarette smoking. Posters like this one attempt to get young people to quit smoking by connecting the internal damage done to your body and the fact that smoking is also unattractive.

In addition, smoking prevention programs that focus on psychosocial factors have been developed. Through films and discussion groups, teens are educated to peer pressure and media influence on smoking; given opportunities to role play refusal skills, general social skills, and personal skills needed in decision making; and given strategies for coping with the stresses of adolescence and daily life (Botwin and Wills, 1985; Flay et al., 1985). Today, psychosocial programs are being implemented in many school districts, starting at the kindergarten level, on the rationale that if children have enough facts, refusal skills, self-esteem, and social skills, they will never feel the need to take that first puff on a cigarette. Not all programs are completely successful, especially with teens at high risk because they have already started smoking or have friends or parents who smoke, but the many successes indicate psychosocial programs should be implemented throughout the country to help prevent smoking (Best et al., 1988).

Stopping Smoking

Stopping smoking is very difficult because the same social pressures that help initiate the habit also help maintain it. These social pressures, combined with the facts that smoking is now part of everyday behavior and the smoker is now addicted to the nicotine, make smoking an especially hard habit to break. The maintenance of smoking behaviors is the result of both positive and negative reinforcement. Most smokers tend to associate smoking with pleasant things, such as good food, friends, and sex, as well as the "high" that nicotine gives them, so smoking is positively reinforced by these factors. When smokers are deprived of their cigarettes for a few hours, they start to go through an extremely unpleasant physical withdrawal. When they are finally able to smoke, the nicotine reduces these symptoms, and smoking is thereby negatively reinforced (Schachter, 1978). Any program to help smokers break their habit must therefore combat both the positive and the negative reinforcement obtained from smoking.

Several approaches are currently being used to help people quit smoking, including ad campaigns and cognitive and behavioral techniques.

One cognitive approach used to break the smoking habit is *covert sensitization,* a form of cognitive classical conditioning. With this technique, smokers are asked to mentally associate something extremely unpleasant with smoking. For example:

Imagine that your favorite brand of cigarettes is sitting on a table in front of you. Now imagine that a housefly lands on the cigarettes and lays her eggs inside the cigarettes. The eggs hatch and little maggots begin to crawl around inside each cigarette. You now pick up the cigarette and put it in your mouth. You light up and draw in your first breath with the maggots still inside. The heat of the cigarette forces the maggots to crawl into your mouth and down your throat and start to eat at your body from the inside out.

Calvin and Hobbes   by Bill Watterson

If smokers use this imagery every time they feel like having a cigarette, there is a good chance they can combat some of the positive associations of cigarette smoking.

Another approach used in eliminating the positive reinforcement of smoking is *coping response training.* Smokers are helped to identify stimuli or situations that make them feel like smoking so that they can cope with their urges in two ways, cognitively and behaviorally. A cognitive response would consist of refocusing attention on something other than smoking. The person might reappraise the stress-producing problem and decide it's not that bad after all. Or the person might keep reminding himself or herself of all the benefits of not smoking. Behavioral responses might include chewing gum, exercising, or chewing on a toothpick after a meal instead of lighting a cigarette. If the person used to smoke to put off solving problems, he or she could resolve to meet the problem head on and consider how to change it. Another alternative might be to simply avoid situations that bring on the urge to smoke (Marlatt, 1985).

Combined Strategies

Although covert sensitization and coping response training have been successful in reducing the number of cigarettes smoked each day or in short-term smoking cessation, they have not been very successful in helping people maintain abstinence (Leventhal et al., 1989). People seem to meet with more success by combining several methods. They might, therefore, also plan a reinforcement program for not smoking, practice aversion therapies, or use nicotine gum or nicotine skin patches.

If an appropriate reinforcer can be found, *reinforcement* for *not* smoking can be very effective. Basically, this technique involves choosing one or several alternative behaviors to smoking and trying to reinforce those behaviors. Ideally, these behaviors should be incompatible with smoking. Many forms of physical exercise fit this criterion —you certainly can't smoke when you're swimming. The most common reinforcer used is money. One successful approach asks the subject to make a large monetary deposit. The person is then paid for doing things other than smoking (Winett, 1973).

How does aversion therapy work?   Most commercial smoking clinics use *aversion therapy* (see Chapter 16) to help people stop smoking. In this approach, smoking behavior is paired with some kind of aversive stimulus, such as excessively heavy cigarette smoke. The most widely used technique is called "rapid smoking." The smoker takes a puff every 6 seconds (10 puffs per minute) while concentrating on the negative sensations produced by the rapid smoking. If the smoker gets sick, so much the better. Rapid smoking, accompanied by long-term support or therapy, has been a highly successful cessation technique (Suedfeld and Baker-Brown, 1986). Its success is attributed to two factors: One, it temporarily alleviates the nicotine withdrawal symptoms because smokers inhale high amounts of nicotine; and two, smokers come to associate smoking with highly negative aftereffects such as dizziness, nausea, burning mouth, and accelerated heartbeat (Tiffany et al., 1986). The one major drawback of rapid smoking aversion therapy is that it can produce a moderate amount of stress on the heart and lungs; it should therefore be used only under the supervision of a physician.

Another cessation strategy is to deal with the physical addiction to nicotine. *Nicotine gum* and *nicotine patches* have been successful in helping smokers withdraw slowly from nicotine dependency, especially when used with a behavioral therapy program designed to encourage long-term abstinence from smoking (Buckremer, Minneker, and Block, 1991; Gottlieb, Killen, Marlatt, and Taylor, 1987).

Of course, the best way to stop smoking is never to have started in the first place. It is extremely difficult for most people to stop. Successful cessation programs include techniques for physically kicking the habit and training in resisting the urge to start smoking again. No program works, though, without a tremendous amount of motivation to quit.

Rapid smoking, which involves smoking several cigarettes in a very short period of time, is one type of aversion therapy used to help people stop smoking.

Review Questions

1. The single most preventable cause of death and disease in the United States is _____ .

2. Describe a smoking prevention program you would organize for your local high school.

3. What smoking cessation program is being described?
   a. The smoker takes a puff every 6 seconds until he or she gets sick and then focuses on the negative feelings produced by the smoking.
   b. The smoker identifies stimuli and situations that lead to the desire to smoke and learns alternative cognitive and behavioral responses to curb the urge to smoke.
   c. The smoker imagines his or her cigarettes are infested with maggots.
   d. The smoker wears a skin patch or chews gum to gradually withdraw from the physical addition to the chemical found in tobacco.

Answers to Review Questions can be found in Appendix C.

STRESS AND ITS ROLE IN HEALTH

• *What are the major causes and results of stress?*

Stress: According to Selye, the non-specific response of the body to any demand made on it.

The study of stress and its effects on humans and animals has resulted in many different definitions of stress. We will use the definition proposed by Hans Selye (1974), a physiologist who has done a significant amount of research and writing in the area of stress since the 1930s. Selye defines stress as the nonspecific response of the body to any demand made on it. When you play two nonstop tennis matches in the middle of a heat wave, your body responds with a fast heartbeat, rapid breathing, and an outpouring of perspiration. When you find out 10 minutes before class starts that the term paper you had just started is due today rather than next Friday as you had mistakenly thought, your body might respond in precisely the same way, increasing its heart and breathing rates and breaking out in the sweats. Thus, "stress" is a bodily reaction that can occur in response to either internal, cognitive stimuli or external, environmental stimuli. A stimulus that causes stress is known as a stressor.

Stressor: Any stimulus that causes stress.

To clarify the terms *stress* and *stressor,* imagine you are taking a public speaking class and have just been asked to give an extemporaneous speech on a topic you know little about. The *stress* you experience consists of your bodily responses—increased heart rate and blood pressure, "butterflies" in your stomach, dry mouth, rapid breathing, and so forth. The *stressors* producing these responses are your own internal self-criticism, the stares and reactions of your classmates, and the comments and reactions of your instructor.

Eustress and Distress

Don't think from our public speaking example that stress is something you always want to—or can—avoid. If you think back, Selye's definition of stress states that anything placing a demand on the body can cause stress. That means that almost all external stimuli can cause some stress, and in fact, much of that stress is pleasant and beneficial. Exercise, for instance, is a beneficial stressor because it increases the efficiency of the cardiovascular system. Selye (1974) distinguishes between *eustress* (pleasant, desirable stress such as that produced by moderate exercise) and *distress* (unpleasant, objectionable stress such as that produced by prolonged illness). The body is nearly always in some state of stress, whether pleasant or unpleasant, mild or severe. The total absence of stress would mean the total absence of external stimulation, which would eventually lead to death. Because health psychology has been chiefly concerned with the negative effects of stress, we will adhere to convention and use the word "stress" to refer primarily to harmful or unpleasant stress (Selye's "distress") even though stress has its positive side.

Causes of Stress: From Major Life Changes to Minor Hassles

Although stress is pervasive in our lives, some things cause more stress than others. The major causes of stress include life changes, chronic stress, hassles, frustration, and conflicts.

Life Changes

Significant life events, such as marriage, death of a family member, or moving to a new home, tend to disrupt our lives and cause more stress than normal. Thomas Holmes and Richard Rahe (1967) postulated that exposure to numerous stressful life events within a short period of time may have a detrimental effect on health. Such events might be joyous as in the case of a marriage, grievous as in the case of a family member's death, or apparently neutral as in the case of a change in work hours; yet all cause extra stress, and an inordinate amount of such stress will exceed the body's ability to cope and may lead to moderate or serious illness.

Holmes and Rahe developed a scale of 43 life events and ranked them according to their relative importance in contributing to health problems. They assigned each event a value in terms of life change units (LCUs) and developed a *Social Readjustment Rating Scale.*

 Try This Yourself

Holmes and Rahe's scale is presented in Table 13.1. Read through the scale and add up the life change units for the events you have experienced in the last year. What is your total? A score of under 200 LCUs is considered low, 200–300 LCUs is moderate, and above 300 LCUs is high. According to Holmes and Rahe, people scoring high on the scale are more likely to experience problems such as heart disease, depression, and cancer than those scoring in the low to moderate range. Rahe and Arthur (1978) also believe increases in LCUs predict an increase in many types of accidents. ■

The most devastating and stressful life change occurs with the loss of a spouse or close family member.

Table 13.1   Social Readjustment Rating Scale

Rank	Life Event	Life Change Units (LCUs)
1	Death of spouse	100
2	Divorce	73
3	Marital separation	65
4	Jail term	63
5	Death of close family member	63
6 ✓	Personal injury or illness	53
7	Marriage	50
8	Fired at work	47
9	Marital reconciliation	45
10	Retirement	45
11	Change in health of family member	44
12	Pregnancy	40
13	Sex difficulties	39
14	Gain of new family member	39
15	Business readjustment	39
16 ✓	Change in financial state	38
17	Death of close friend	37
18	Change to different line of work	36
19	Change in number of arguments with spouse	35
20	Mortgage over $10,000	31
21	Foreclosure of mortgage or loan	30
22	Change in responsibilities at work	29
23	Son or daughter leaving home	29
24	Trouble with in-laws	29
25	Outstanding personal achievement	28
26	Wife begins or stops work	26
27	Begin or end school	26
28	Change in living conditions	25
29 /	Revision of personal habits	24
30 ✓	Trouble with boss	23
31	Change in work hours or conditions	20
32	Change in residence	20
33 ✓	Change in schools	20
34 ✓	Change in recreation	19
35	Change in church activities	19
36 ✓	Change in social activities	18
37 ✓	Mortgage or loan less than $10,000	17
38	Change in sleeping habits	16
39 ✓	Change in number of family get-togethers	15
40 ✓	Change in eating habits	15
41	Vacation	13
42	Christmas	12
43	Minor violations of the law	11

Source: Holmes and Rahe (1967).

Many events on the scale don't seem particularly stressful to me. How accurate is this scale?   Many people have criticized the Holmes–Rahe scale. Lazarus and Folkman (1984) pointed out three questionable assumptions underlying the life events approach to stress measurement. First, they question the assumption that change alone—any change—is stressful. They cite research on aging that suggests life events such as menopause and retirement do not pose serious problems for most people (Neugarten, 1970; Rosow, 1963).

Second, Lazarus and Folkman question that a life change must be major to create stress great enough to cause illness. They point out that individual perceptions of an event differ and that what may be highly stressful for one person may be minimally stressful for another. For example, one person may consider moving to another state a terrible sacrifice and experience a great amount of stress, while another person may see the move as a wonderful opportunity to explore a new region of the country and experience only a minimal amount of stress.

According to Lazarus (1990), an event is stressful if its demands exceed a person's resources to deal with it. Lazarus believes we appraise events to determine whether they involve harm or the threat of harm, or whether they present a challenge to be met with optimism and enthusiasm. The individual brings his or her own beliefs, abilities, and prior experience to the appraisal process, looks at the event itself, and gauges the interaction and outcome between all the components. Thus, any one event may be perceived either as a stressful ordeal or an exciting opportunity, depending upon the individual person's appraisal.

Third, Lazarus and Folkman challenge that significant life changes in themselves constitute a major factor in causing illness. It is true that *stress* is a major factor in many different types of illness, but the correlation between LCUs and illness is very small—around .12 (Rabkin and Struening, 1976; Tausig, 1982). Given this low relationship, it appears that the number of LCUs by itself is not especially valid in predicting potential illness.

People who are out of work or homeless face multiple stressors.

Chronic Stress

Not all stressful situations are single, short-term events such as a death or a birth. A bad marriage, poor working conditions, or an intolerable political climate can be *chronic* stressors. However, just as people react individually to significant life changes, so too do they react to chronic stressors in various ways. One person might spend years working under an abusive supervisor and ignore the situation, while a co-worker might suffer great stress and take it out on his or her family at home.

How we react to chronic stressors in our everyday lives depends on our cognitive appraisal of the situation. In our private lives, divorce, child abuse, spouse abuse, alcoholism, and money problems can place severe stress on all members of a family (Wallerstein and Kelly, 1980). Our social lives can also be very stressful, since making friends

Moving may be an adventure for some, but for most people it is a stressful event that may have a detrimental effect on their health.

and maintaining friendships can involve considerable thought and energy. This is especially true for people who tend to be shy or ill at ease with people they don't know well. Even old friendships can be hard to maintain when distance separates the friends or other involvements, such as marriage or career, limit one or both persons' amount of free time.

Much research on chronic life stressors has focused on work-related stress. People may experience stress associated with keeping or changing jobs, with job performance, or with interactions with coworkers (Gross, 1970). The most stressful jobs make great demands on performance and concentration while allowing little creativity or opportunity for advancement. Assembly-line work ranks very high in this category.

Chaya Piorkowske and Evan Stark (1985) documented that stress at work can also cause serious stress at home for other family members. Their research showed that if a father reported job stress, his son was more likely to report conflicts with the father, who tended to reject him. Also, the son was often depressed and expressed dissatisfaction about his relationships with his peers.

Hassles

In addition to chronic types of stress, much daily stress is in the form of little problems that themselves are not necessarily significant. These hassles, whether they are trying to find a parking place, running to the store for milk for breakfast cereal, or not being able to get a computer program to work, are a part of living. But when hassles pile up, they can become a major source of stress (deLongis et al., 1988).

Some authorities, including Pearlin (1980), believe that hassles can be more significant than major life events. In fact, the reason people are so affected by major life events may be because the number of hassles increases greatly at such times (deLongis et al., 1982). For example, a change in residence has a moderate LCU of 20, whereas a divorce has a high LCU of 73. Both of these life changes create an increase in hassles, but the divorce may mean a long-term increase in the number of hassles, including taking on extra chores and other hassles previously assumed by the spouse. It may also be true that preparing to move or having your house up for sale for an extended period of time can be more stressful than the actual move itself.

Frustration

Have you ever felt "stressed out" because you wanted to do something but couldn't? Whenever we set a goal and are prevented from attaining it, we feel frustrated, and this leads to stress. Frustration is a negative emotional state generally associated with a blocked goal, such as being refused a loan after having found just the right car, or not being accepted for admission to your first-choice college.

Frustration is closely associated with motivation. We wouldn't be frustrated if we had not been motivated to achieve a particular goal. Furthermore, the more motivated we are, the more frustration we experience when our goals are blocked. For example, suppose you get stuck in traffic on the way to school. If the delay causes you to be late for an important exam, you will be very frustrated. On the other hand, if it causes you to be five minutes late to a boring lecture, your frustration level will be practically nil.

Conflicts

A final major source of stress is conflict. Conflicts arise when people are forced to make a choice between at least two incompatible alternatives. The amount of stress produced by a conflict depends on the complexity of the conflict and the difficulty involved in resolving it. Three basic types of conflicts that can lead to varying levels of frustration and stress are approach–approach, avoidance–avoidance, and approach–avoidance.

In an approach–approach conflict, a person must choose between two or more favorable alternatives. Thus, no matter what choice is made, the result will be desirable. At first it might seem this type of conflict shouldn't create any stress, but consider this

Frustration: An unpleasant state of tension, anxiety, and heightened sympathetic activity resulting from the blocking or thwarting of a goal.

Conflict: A negative emotional state caused by an inability to choose between two or more incompatible goals or impulses.

Approach–Approach Conflict: Conflict in which a person must choose between two alternatives that will both lead to desirable results.

example. Suppose you have to choose between two summer jobs. One job is at a resort where you will meet interesting people and have a good time; the other job will provide you with valuable experience and be impressive on your resumé. No matter which job you choose, you will benefit in some way. In fact, you would like to take both jobs, but you can't, and herein lies the source of stress.

An avoidance–avoidance conflict involves making a choice between two or more unpleasant alternatives that will lead to negative results, no matter which choice is made. The film (and book) *Sophie's Choice* provides a good example of an avoidance–avoidance conflict. Sophie and her two children are sent to a German concentration camp. A soldier demands that she give up (apparently to be killed) either her daughter *or* her son, or they both will be killed. Obviously, neither alternative is acceptable; both will have tragic results. Although this is an extreme example, all avoidance–avoidance conflicts can lead to intense, and in Sophie's case long-lasting, stress.

Avoidance–Avoidance Conflict: Conflict in which a person must choose between two or more alternatives that will both lead to undesirable results.

An approach–avoidance conflict occurs when a person must choose whether to do something that will have both desirable *and* undesirable results. We have all been faced with such decisions as, "I want to spend more time in a close relationship, but that means I won't be able to see as much of my old friends." This conflict thus leads to a great deal of ambivalence. In an approach–avoidance conflict, we experience both good and bad results from any alternative we choose.

Approach–Avoidance Conflict: Conflict in which a person must make a choice that will lead to both desirable and undesirable results.

The longer any conflict exists or the more important the decision, the more stress a person will experience. Generally, the approach–approach conflict is the easiest to resolve because no matter what choice is made, we will benefit in some way. The avoidance–avoidance conflict, on the other hand, is usually the most difficult because all choices lead to unpleasant results. Approach–avoidance conflicts are somewhat less stressful than avoidance–avoidance conflicts, since they are usually moderately difficult to resolve.

Results of Stress: How the Body Responds

When you are stressed, whether from psychological or physiological causes, your body undergoes several major and minor physiological changes, some of which we have already mentioned. The most significant changes are controlled by the autonomic nervous system (see Chapter 2). These changes are particularly important because they can lower the body's resistance to disease.

Physiological Effects of Stress

Under normal, everyday low stress conditions, the parasympathetic part of the autonomic nervous system tends to lower heart rate and blood pressure while increasing muscle movement in the stomach and intestines. This allows the body to conserve energy, absorb nutrients, and maintain normal functioning. Under stressful conditions, the sympathetic part of the autonomic nervous system takes control. It increases heart rate, blood pressure, respiration, and muscle tension, decreases the movement of stomach muscles, constricts the blood vessels, and releases hormones such as epinephrine (adrenalin) and cortisol. These hormones in turn release fats into the bloodstream for energy.

Fight or Flight

There is a good reason for all this sympathetic activity. At the beginning of human evolutionary history, the autonomic nervous system served as the fight or flight system. Back then, when a person was under extreme stress—when she was confronted by a bear, or somebody bigger and stronger encroached on his territory—there were only two reasonable alternatives: fight or flee. Our ancestors, when faced with such stressors, needed the physiological boosts supplied to them by their sympathetic nervous system.

Critical Thinking

PSYCHOLOGY IN ACTION

MAKING SOUND DECISIONS
Recognizing the Role of Personal Values in Conflict Resolution

Most students can readily supply examples of approach–approach, avoidance–avoidance, and approach–avoidance conflicts in their lives and tell how they resolved the problem. Many report that when faced with a conflict, they turned to others for advice. Although others' opinions are valuable, critical thinkers recognize that ultimately, any decision must be guided by the decision maker's own personal values and goals. Good decision makers take full responsibility for their own future. They realize they are the only ones who can truly evaluate the merits of each alternative.

A critical thinker also recognizes that decisions are often stressful, but that they cannot be avoided. Avoiding a decision is, in fact, making one without the benefit of analyzing the problem.

To improve your decision-making skills, we offer the following chart to help you clarify some of your current conflicts (adapted from Seech, 1987):

1. At the top of the chart, identify your specific conflict as approach–approach, avoidance–avoidance, or approach–avoidance.

2. On the lines in the left-hand column, list all possible alternatives or courses of action. Although the wording of the "approach–approach" discussion may imply only two choices, most conflicts involve several options or alternatives. Identifying all your options will require a good deal of homework. Read up on your problem. Talk to as many people as you can.

3. Now list the logical outcome or consequence of each alternative, regardless of whether the consequence is significant or insignificant and regardless of whether it is a certain or a possible outcome.

4. Next, assess both the probability and significance of each outcome. Using a 0 to 5 rating scale (0 = won't occur and 5 = certain to occur), assign a numerical rating for the likelihood that each consequence will actually occur. Using a similar 0 to 5 rating scale (0 = no significance and 5 = high significance), assess the importance you place on each consequence.

5. Now review the chart. In some cases, you may find it helpful to multiply the probability and significance ratings and then compare those results for each alternative. In other cases, you will find it difficult to assign numerical values to complex issues and feelings. Even in the most difficult decisions, however, the thinking and evaluation elicited by this chart may provide useful insights to your conflict. Also note the feelings you associate with each alternative. Careful decision making involves integrated consideration of both feelings and cognitions.

6. Once you've reviewed each alternative, ask yourself which choice is most in line with your overall goals and values. Some alternatives may look more—or less—appealing when weighed against long-term relationship plans, career goals, and personal belief systems. You may also want to discuss your chart with a trusted friend before you make a final decision.

Once you make your decision, commit yourself and give it all you've got. Throw away your expectations. Many decisions don't turn out the way we imagine, and if we focus on the way it is supposed to be we miss enjoying the way it is. If the decision doesn't work out, don't stubbornly hang on for dear life. Change or correct your course.

TYPE OF CONFLICT _____

ALTERNATIVES	LOGICAL OUTCOME	PROBABILITY	SIGNIFICANCE
_____	_____		
	_____		
	_____		
	_____		
	_____		
_____	_____		
	_____		
	_____		
	_____		
_____	_____		
	_____		
	_____		

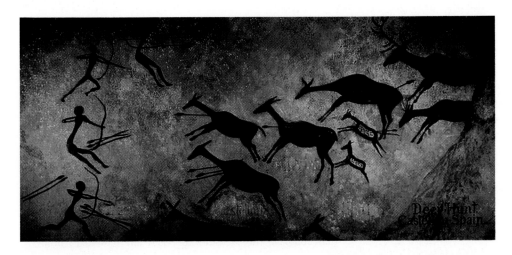

The fight/flight responses of the autonomic nervous system were necessary for a hunting and gathering society, but they may be less necessary for modern society.

Today we have the same autonomic responses of our ancient ancestors, but our world is quite different. When we encounter stressful situations, we rarely jump into action, so we have little need for increased heart rate, blood pressure, and hormone levels. We are taught not to fight or to flee but to stay calm and resolve stressful situations rationally. To comply with these cultural rules, we are left with no physical outlet for the physical changes caused by stressors. Thus, in our culture, the fight/flight response of the autonomic nervous system might even be *mal*adaptive (Gill, 1983). It causes physiological changes that in the long run can be detrimental to health, contributing to such serious illnesses as heart disease and cancer (as we will see later in this chapter).

In 1936, Hans Selye described a generalized physiological reaction to severe stressors that he called the general adaptation syndrome (see Figure 13.1). It consists of three phases. In the initial phase, called the *alarm reaction,* the body reacts to the stressor by activating the sympathetic nervous system (with increases in heart rate, blood pressure, secretion of hormones, and so on). The body has abundant energy and is highly alert and ready to deal with the stressor but is in a lowered state of resistance to illness. If the stressor remains, the body enters the *resistance phase.* In this phase, the alarm reaction subsides and the body adapts to the stressor, with resistance to illness increasing above normal levels. However, this adaptation and resistance is very taxing, and long-term exposure to the stressor will eventually lead to the *exhaustion phase.* During this final stage, the signs of the alarm reaction reappear, resistance to illness decreases, all adaptation energy becomes depleted, and the eventual result is death. Thus, Selye characterized long-term exposure to stressors as life-threatening.

General Adaptation Syndrome: As described by Selye, a generalized physiological reaction to severe stressors consisting of three phases: the alarm reaction, the resistance phase, and the exhaustion phase.

Stress and the Immune System

The physiological changes caused by stress can suppress immune system functioning (Baum et al., 1982). Normal functioning of the immune system includes detecting and defending against disease. Therefore, suppression of the immune system can render the body susceptible to any number of diseases. Several studies show that significant stress, such as from bereavement, surgery, or sleep deprivation, is related to changes in the immune system (Jemmott and Locke, 1984; Schleifer et al., 1980). These changes have been linked to high levels of such stress-related hormones as epinephrine, norepineph-

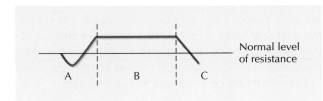

Figure 13.1 The general adaptation syndrome. According to Hans Selye, when the body is exposed to severe, prolonged stressors, it goes through three phases. During the initial phase, the alarm reaction (A), the body is in a lowered state of resistance to illness. If the stress continues, the body enters the resistance phase (B), when it is in a heightened state of resistance. After prolonged exposure to stress, the body enters into the exhaustion phase (C), when resistance to illness decreases, eventually ending in death.

rine, and cortisol in the bloodstream. Apparently, increases in these hormones often precede suppressed immune system function (Stein, 1983) and the appearance of infectious diseases (Jemmott and Locke, 1984).

So you're telling me that I might get a cold or the flu just because I've been under a lot of stress?   You would be *more likely* to get a cold or the flu when under a lot of stress. Recently, Sheldon Cohen and colleagues (1991) conducted a conclusive study showing that stress does indeed have a small to moderate effect both on becoming infected with the cold virus and on exhibiting full-blown cold symptoms. It seems that stress knocks down the body's first line of defense that prevents the virus from entering the bloodstream. Annoying as the common cold is, in most cases it is not life-threatening. However, excess stress may also set the stage for the development of more serious illnesses such as cancer or heart disease, as you will see next.

Review Questions

1. _____ is defined as the nonspecific response of the body to any demand made on it.

2. According to Holmes and Rahe's Social Readjustment Rating Scale, what would it mean if during the past year you got married, your father died, you bought a house and took on a $150,000 mortgage, and then were fired from your job?

3. Stressful problems that are just part of daily living are called _____.

4. What is the difference between frustration and conflict?

5. The three-phase bodily response to chronic stress that includes the alarm reaction, the phase of resistance, and the stage of exhaustion is the _____.

6. Why do students tend to get sick with a cold or flu at the end of the term, right after they finish their final exams and turn in their term papers?

Answers to Review Questions can be found in Appendix C.

STRESS AND SERIOUS ILLNESS

• *How is stress related to cancer and coronary heart disease?*

Psychological factors play a role in the development of a number of physical disorders, including heart disease, cancer, rheumatoid arthritis, bursitis, migraine headache, asthma, and gastrointestinal problems such as ulcers and colitis. We will discuss how stress caused by such psychological factors leads to physical ailments, but we will limit discussion to our society's two major killers: cancer and heart disease.

Cancer: A Variety of Causes—Even Stress

The word "cancer" is frightening to nearly everyone, and for good reason: Cancer is now the leading cause of death for women in the United States and may become the number one overall cause of death by the year 2000 (Henderson, Ross, and Pike, 1991).

Cancer occurs when a body cell begins to replicate out of control, producing many more of this type of cell than there should be. These cells then begin to invade areas of healthy cells and, unless destroyed or removed, eventually cause damage to tissues and organs, resulting in death. To date, over 100 types of cancers have been identified. They appear to be caused by an interaction between hereditary predispositions, environmental factors, and changes in the body's immune system. Although we can do nothing about heredity, we can reduce the risk of cancer by making changes in our behavior.

How can our behavior cause cancer? Sometimes it seems as if nearly everything causes cancer. Substances found in our environment, such as cigarette smoke and harmful chemicals, can cause cancer. Other major causes are internal biochemical (body chemistry) changes that may affect how cells replicate. What many people don't realize is that their behavior can affect both these factors. Your overt behavior can certainly put you in contact with environmental carcinogens. If you smoke you expose yourself to the cancer-causing substances in tobacco. If you work in an old building you may be exposed to asbestos fibers, and so on. To reduce environmental risk factors, avoid known carcinogens, which may not be simple if you have to change your way of life by quitting smoking or finding a new job, but you do have control over these factors. How your behavior affects internal biochemistry is much more complex, however, and not so easily changed.

Moving away from cancer-causing environments is a behavioral change that can lessen your likelihood of getting cancer.

Stress and Body Chemistry

To understand the relationship between behavior and body chemistry, it helps to understand what normally happens to cancerous cells. Whenever cancer cells start to multiply, the immune system acts to check the uncontrolled growth by attacking the cancerous cells and bringing the growth under control (see the photograph on this page). This type of fight goes on constantly within the body, and in a normal, healthy person, the immune system manages to keep cancer cells in check.

Something different happens when the body is stressed. As you read earlier, the stress response involves release of adrenal hormones that suppress immune system functioning. This suppression reduces the body's ability to resist not only disease organisms but cancer cell growth as well. Specifically, Riley (1981) has found that stress in animals can inhibit immune system defenses against cancer and can enhance tumor growth. This may indicate that, once a person has cancer, additional stress may further the growth of the tumor. Solomon, Amkraut, and Kasper (1974) have presented evidence suggesting that stress can also directly affect lymphocytes, the main immune system cells that control cancer.

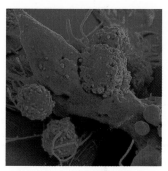

This photomicrograph depicts a T-lymphocyte, the round structure in the center of the photo, which has just killed a cancer cell, the "sweet potato-shaped" structure with the T-lymphocyte sticking out of it.

Stress is not the only way psychological factors influence immune function and possible cancer development. Ader and Cohen (1984) have shown in a classical conditioning experiment that suppression of immune function can be learned. They paired a neutral stimulus (saccharin) with drugs that suppress the normal functioning of the immune system. (The drug was the UCS and the suppressed immune function was the UCR.) Later, when the subjects were exposed to saccharin alone, they showed decreases in antibody response, an indication that the saccharin had become a conditioned stimulus and that there was a *learned* decrease in the immune system response. It is possible, then, that people somehow inadvertently learn to lower their immunity to certain environmental carcinogens and therefore to be more susceptible to cancer.

Cardiovascular Disorders: The Leading Cause of Death in the United States

Cardiovascular disorders—specifically, hypertension and heart disease—are the major causes of over half of *all* deaths in the United States (Krantz et al., 1985). Understandably, then, health psychologists are especially concerned with the effects of stress and other risk factors that have been identified as major contributors to these disorders.

Hypertension

Hypertension is a state of chronically elevated blood pressure. In a small percentage of the cases of hypertension, the increased blood pressure is caused by some physical ailment, such as kidney disease, but in the vast majority of cases—about 85 percent—there is no medical cause (Sarafino, 1990). In these latter cases, the disorder is called essential hypertension.

Hypertension: Excessive muscular tension and high blood pressure.

Essential Hypertension: State of chronically elevated blood pressure that has no detectable medical cause.

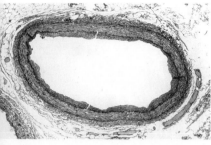

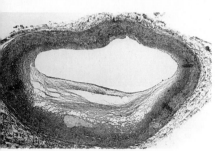

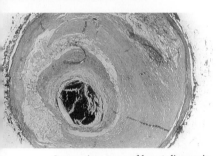

One major cause of heart disease is the blockage of arteries that supply blood to the heart. The artery on the top is normal, the one in the center is partially blocked by fatty deposits, and the one on the bottom is completely blocked. The reduction of stress and a change in exercise and diet can help prevent the buildup of fatty deposits in the arteries.

Heart Disease: General term used to include all disorders that in some way affect the heart muscle and can ultimately result in heart failure.

Type A Personality: Set of behavior characteristics that includes intense ambition, competition, drive, constant preoccupation with responsibilities, a sense of time urgency, and a cynical, hostile outlook.

Type B Personality: Set of behavior characteristics consistent with a calm, patient, relaxed attitude toward life.

It is not clear whether stress can actually cause essential hypertension, but it is clear that people with essential hypertension tend to react to stressful situations with more exaggerated and prolonged blood pressure increases (Goldstein, 1981). These exaggerated reactions have been demonstrated in response to cold (Hines and Brown, 1936), to breath holding (Ayman and Goldshine, 1939), to exercise (Alam and Smirk, 1938; Groen et al., 1977), and to mental stressors such as doing arithmetic problems (Brod, 1970; Faulkner et al., 1979).

Why should people with high blood pressure be concerned? Because their blood pressure reactions are more intense and last longer, hypertensive people are good candidates for stroke, since the extra pressure in brain blood vessels could cause weakened or clogged vessels to burst. In addition, high blood pressure places undue stress on the heart, causing it to work harder, which could ultimately lead to heart attack. Therefore, it is a good idea to follow a doctor's advice if he or she tells you, as our heart attack patient's doctor told him, to reduce your salt intake or lose weight. Excess sodium increases the amount of water in the blood, making the heart pump faster to supply the body with enough oxygen. Excess weight means excess tissue that needs to be oxygenated.

Heart Disease

Heart disease is a general term for all disorders that eventually affect the heart muscle and lead to heart failure. Coronary heart disease results from atherosclerosis, a thickening of the walls of the coronary arteries that reduces or blocks the blood supply to the heart. Atherosclerosis causes angina (chest pain due to insufficient blood supply to the heart) or heart attack (death of heart muscle tissue) (Rhode, Watt, and Smith, 1989).

Researchers have identified factors that contribute to heart disease: smoking, stress, certain personality characteristics, obesity, a high-fat diet, and lack of exercise.

I understand how stress can contribute to cancer, but how does it contribute to heart disease? Remember that one of the major autonomic nervous system fight/flight reactions is the release of the hormones epinephrine and cortisol into the bloodstream. Epinephrine and cortisol together increase heart rate and remove fat from the body's stores to give muscles a quickly available source of energy. If some physical action is taken, such as fight or flight, the fat is used as an energy source and there are no ill effects. If, on the other hand, no physical action is taken (and this is most likely the case in our modern lives), the fat that is released into the bloodstream may become fatty deposits on the walls of blood vessels (see the photograph in the margin). These fatty deposits are often the major blood supply blockages that cause heart attacks (Lee, 1983). In fact, the heart attack of the patient in our opening example could very well have been caused in this way, since he was a person continually under a lot of stress.

Type A Personalities

The effects of stress may be amplified if an individual tends to be hard-driving, competitive, ambitious, impatient, and hostile. People with such Type A personalities are chronically on edge, tend to talk rapidly, feel an intense time urgency, and like our heart attack patient, are preoccupied with responsibilities. The antithesis of the Type A personality is Type B. People with a Type B personality have a laid-back, calm, relaxed attitude toward life.

The Type A personality was first described by two cardiologists, Meyer Friedman and Ray Rosenman (1959). The idea for the Type A personality may have been planted in the mid-1950s, when an upholsterer who was recovering the waiting room chairs in Friedman's office noticed an odd wear pattern. He mentioned to Friedman that all the chairs looked like new except for the front edges, which were badly worn, as if all the patients sat only on the edges of the chairs. Initially, this didn't seem too important to Friedman, but he since changed his mind. He and Rosenman formulated a theory that the Type A personality may be a contributing factor to heart disease and essential hypertension.

"*Wow! What a day to be a workaholic!*"

How can I tell if I'm a Type A?   Psychologists assess personality types by using a questionnaire in an interview. You can get an idea of whether you are Type A, Type B, or some combination of the two by looking over Table 13.2, which profiles Type A and Type B personalities.

Initial research into Type A behavior suggested it was a prominent risk factor in both heart disease and hypertension. However, more recent research has not found such a strong relationship (Mathews, 1984; Williams, 1984). Apparently not all the Type A personality characteristics contribute to heart disease; perhaps only certain characteristics—hostility, anger, and vigorous speech—are contributors (Dembroski and Costa, 1988). This is supported by findings that Type A's exhibit more heightened physiological responses than Type B's when confronted with situations that require active, effortful coping or that arouse anger (Contrada and Krantz, 1988).

Redford Williams (1984) isolated hostility and cynicism as contributing factors to heart disease. He believes Type A's with a cynical, hostile outlook on life are at an *increased* risk for heart disease, whereas Type A's with a positive outlook on life are actually at *lowered* risk.

How can cynicism be related to heart disease?   Having a negative attitude toward the world in general means cynical people always expect problems, so they are constantly on the alert to foresee problems and try to avert them. This attitude produces a nearly constant state of stress. In addition, Type A people also tend to have a more pronounced and longer-lasting reaction to stressful situations (Williams, 1984).

Is it possible to change a Type A into a Type B?   Type A's with a positive outlook on life may not need to change their behavior, but cynical Type A's would be well advised to slow down and smell the roses. Health psychologists have developed two approaches to Type A behavior modification, the shotgun approach and the target behavior approach.

The shotgun approach aims to change all the behaviors that relate to the Type A personality. Meyer Friedman and colleagues (1986) use the shotgun approach in their Recurrent Coronary Prevention Program. Their program consists of counseling in the diagnosis and treatment of coronary heart disease; advice on diet, exercise, and drugs; and group therapy to eliminate or modify Type A behaviors. Type A's are encouraged to slow down and perform tasks incompatible with their personalities. For example, they might try to *listen* to other people without interrupting or stand in the longest supermarket line on purpose. The major criticism of the shotgun approach is that it eliminates desirable as well as undesirable Type A traits.

The alternative approach is called the target behavior approach. It focuses on only those Type A behaviors that are likely to cause heart disease, especially those that lead to a cynical and hostile outlook on life. By modifying these targeted behaviors, the person will more than likely reduce his or her risk of heart disease.

Shotgun Approach: The technique used in behavioral change whereby there is an attempt to change all the behaviors constituting the Type A personality.

Target Behavior Approach: The technique used in behavioral change whereby there is an attempt to change only Type A behaviors that have specifically been found to lead to heart disease, particularly a hostile and cynical attitude.

Table 13.2   Profiles of the Type A and Type B Behavior Patterns

Characteristics	Type A	Type B
Speech		
Rate	Rapid	Slow
Word production	Single-word answers; acceleration at the end of sentences	Measured; frequent pauses or breaks
Volume	Loud	Soft
Quality	Vigorous, terse, harsh	"Walter Mitty" monotone
Intonation/inflection	Abrupt, explosive speech, key word emphasis	
Response latency	Immediate answers	Pauses before answering
Length of responses	Short and to the point	Long, rambling
Other	Word clipping, word omission, word repetition	
Behaviors		
Sighing	Frequent	Rare
Posture	Tense, on the edge of the chair	Relaxed, comfortable
General demeanor	Alert, intense	Calm; quiet attentiveness
Facial expression	Tense, hostile; grimace	Relaxed, friendly
Smile	Lateral	Broad
Laughter	Harsh	Gentle chuckle
Wrist clenching	Frequent	Rare
Responses to the interview		
Interrupts interviewer	Often	Rarely
Returns to previous subject when interrupted	Often	Rarely
Attempts to finish interviewer's questions	Often	Rarely
Uses humor	Rarely	Often
Hurries the interviewer ("yes, yes," "m-m," head nodding)	Often	Rarely
Competes for control of the interview	Wide variety of techniques—interruptions, verbal duets, extraneous comments, lengthy or evasive answers, questioning or correcting the interviewer	Rarely
Hostility	Often demonstrated during the interview through mechanisms such as boredom, condescension, authoritarianism, challenge	None
Typical content		
Satisfied with job	No, wants to move up	Yes
Hard-driving, ambitious	Yes, by own and others' judgments	Not particularly
Feels a sense of time urgency	Yes	No
Impatient	Dislikes waiting in lines, will not wait at a restaurant, annoyed when caught behind a slow-moving vehicle	Takes delays of all kinds in stride and does not become frustrated or annoyed
Competitive	Enjoys competition on the job, plays all games (even with children) to win	Does not thrive on competition and rarely engages in competitive activities
Admits to polyphasic thinking and activities	Often does or thinks two (or more) things at the same time	Rarely does or thinks two things at once
Hostility	In content and stylistics—argumentative responses, excessive qualifications, harsh generalizations, challenges, emotion-laden words, obscenity	Rarely present in any content

Source: Chesney, Eagleston, and Rosenman (1981).

Stress and Type A behavior are not the only risk factors associated with heart disease, of course. Obesity can place direct stress on the heart itself because excess weight causes the heart to pump more blood to the excess body tissue. A high-fat diet, especially one high in cholesterol, can contribute to the fatty deposits that clog blood vessels. Lack of exercise contributes to weight gain and prevents the body from obtaining important exercise benefits, including strengthening heart muscles, increasing heart efficiency, and releasing hormones such as serotonin that alleviate stress and promote well-being.

Gender and Cultural Diversity

THE EFFECTS OF LIFESTYLE ON HEALTH

To fully appreciate the important part our Western lifestyle plays in the development of cardiovascular ailments and cancer, let's look at some cultural studies. The Ni-Hon-San (Nipon-Honolulu-San Francisco) is an ongoing study of coronary heart disease (CHD) in 12,000 Japanese men that began in 1964. Japanese men living in Japan who were involved in the study had the lowest rates of CHD. Japanese men who migrated to Hawaii had intermediate rates, and those who migrated to California had the highest rates. Ni-Hon-San researchers traced the differences to acculturation, the process by which people from one culture adopt the behaviors and practices of another culture. The Japanese men who remained in Japan and thereby held on to their traditional lifestyle exhibited fewer risk factors for CHD. They had lower serum cholesterol, smoked fewer cigarettes, were less obese, ate 40 percent less fat in their diets, and were physically more active than their Westernized counterparts (Kagan, Marmot, and Kato, 1980; Kato et al., 1973; Lichton, Bullard, and Sherrell, 1983). Researchers also determined that in both traditional Japanese and the Western cultures, blood pressure was the most reliable risk factor predicting CHD. Other significant risk factors were age, cholesterol level, cigarette smoking, and serum glucose levels. Interestingly, alcohol consumption and physical activity were negatively correlated with CHD, indicating that they acted as buffers against the development of the disease (Yano et al., 1988).

Before you get the idea that drinking is the answer to good health, read on: Japan, with high alcohol consumption rates, has one of the highest mortality rates due to stroke worldwide, and it has been found that stroke is positively correlated to alcohol consumption. Moderate to heavy drinkers are three to four times more at risk for stroke than nondrinkers.

To end this section on an optimistic note, let's take a look at the Adventist Health Study, a cross-cultural study of Seventh-day Adventists (SDAs), a Christian religious denomination. Studies of SDAs living in many different countries show they are healthier and live longer than other residents in every country studied. This is attributed to their lifestyle, which is similar worldwide (Ilola, 1990). As a whole, SDAs eat well-

Japanese men living in Japan who eat traditional Japanese food tend to have fewer heart attacks than Japanese men living in the United States who eat traditional American food.

balanced diets of unrefined foods, grains, vegetable protein, fruits, and vegetables. About 84 percent drink less than one cup of coffee a day; 99 percent don't smoke; and 90 percent don't drink alcohol (Phillips, Kuzma, Beeson, and Lotz, 1980). As a result, they are less likely than others living in their cultures to develop coronary heart disease, stroke, or other circulatory diseases or to develop any kind of cancer, including lung, breast, pancreatic, and colorectal. Moreover, Seventh-day Adventists who do develop cancer are more likely to survive because they immediately seek medical attention for physical symptoms (Zollinger, Phillips, and Kuzma, 1984).

The virtue of both the Adventist Health Study and the Ni-Hon-San Study is that they illuminate the risk factors for the development of cancer and cardiovascular disease. Western societies can learn from cultural studies like these how to decrease the incidence of serious illness by adopting healthful behaviors. ■

Review Questions

1. How can stress contribute to the development of cancer?
2. What is hypertension and why is it dangerous to our health?
3. Stress can contribute to heart disease by releasing the hormones _____ and _____, which increase the level of fat in the blood.
4. What is the difference between a Type A and a Type B personality?
5. The factor within the Type A personality that is most related to heart disease is _____.
6. The two major approaches to modifying Type A behavior are the _____ approach and the _____ approach. Which one do you think would work best for you, and why?

Answers to Review Questions can be found in Appendix C.

COPING WITH STRESS

• *What techniques and resources are available to help people cope with stress?*

Coping: Managing stress in some effective way.

It would be helpful if we could avoid all stressful situations, but this is virtually impossible. Everyone encounters pressure at work, daily hassles, the death of a family member, and so on. Since we can't escape stress, we need to learn how to effectively deal with our stressors.

Lazarus and Folkman (1984) define coping as "constantly changing cognitive and behavioral efforts to manage specific external and/or internal demands that are appraised as taxing or exceeding the resource of the person." In simpler terms, *coping* is an attempt to manage stress in some effective way. It consists not of one single act but is a process that allows us to deal with various stressors. This process can focus on the emotional effects of the stressor, or it can focus on solving the problem causing the stress.

Emotion-Focused Forms of Coping: Reappraising the Situation

Emotion-Focused Forms of Coping: Coping strategies that lead to changes in one's perceptions of stressful situations.

Emotion-focused forms of coping are emotional or cognitive strategies that change how we view or appraise stressful situations. For example, suppose you are turned down for a job you wanted very much. You might reappraise the situation and decide that the job must not have been for you in the first place. You may conclude that the employer didn't feel you had the qualifications to succeed, so it's just as well you didn't get in over your head and fail.

Often, as a means of coping, people use psychological *defense mechanisms,* strategies that are unconsciously employed to protect the ego and avoid anxiety by distorting reality (see Chapter 14). Although defense mechanisms may alleviate feelings of anxiety or guilt, they may not be beneficial in the long run. For instance, people often use *rationalization,* fabricating excuses when frustrated in attaining particular goals. For example, they might decide they didn't get a job because they didn't have the right "connections." Defense mechanisms, as well as other emotion-focused forms of coping, can sometimes even lead to dangerous results. For example, in *denial,* a person refuses to acknowledge that a problem exists. When our heart attack patient was diagnosed with essential hypertension, he denied the seriousness of his situation (it was too anxiety-provoking) and refused to take the doctor's recommendations, which led to a life-threatening situation.

Although emotion-focused forms of coping can at times distort reality, they can be used successfully as positive coping strategies when they are accurate reappraisals of stressful situations. Many times, however, it is necessary and more effective to confront the stressor directly.

Problem-Focused Forms of Coping: Putting Problem-Solving Skills to Work

Problem-focused forms of coping are strategies that deal directly with the situation or the stressor in ways that will eventually decrease or eliminate it. Generally, these approaches are the same as problem-solving strategies (see Chapter 8). Thus, the better a person is at solving problems, the more likely he or she will develop effective coping strategies. These strategies consist of identifying the stressful problem, generating possible solutions, selecting the appropriate solution, and applying the solution to the problem, thereby eliminating the stress.

To illustrate the difference between the two forms of coping, let's suppose that your professor loses your term paper and, thinking you never turned it in, says you will get an "F" for the semester. You could cognitively reappraise the situation and decide that one "F" won't hurt you (emotion-focused approach). Or you could generate ideas and decide on a course of action that would prove you did the work and submitted it on time (problem-focused approach).

It sounds as if emotion-focused forms of coping are really just "copping out." Is this right?   Many people think of problem-focused coping as true coping and of emotion-focused coping as copping out. However, it is not necessary to master a problem or stressor to relieve stress, and at times emotion-focused coping may be the only way to deal with a problem. For example, humor is an emotion-focused coping strategy that is

Problem-Focused Forms of Coping: Coping strategies in which one views stressful situations as problems and uses problem-solving strategies to decrease or eliminate the source of stress.

highly effective in altering negative moods, eliminating depression, and decreasing anger and tension (Berkowitz, 1970; Mannell and McMahon, 1982; Martin, Labott, and Stote, 1987).

Also, in many situations, dealing with emotions can even lead to mastery of the problem. Imagine that you are about to take your first exam in a difficult course. You are very anxious: You don't know whether you studied enough, you don't know what kind of test the professor gives, and you worry that you'll forget everything you've learned when the test is in front of you. Exams can be extremely stressful for many students. If you take an emotion-focused approach to this situation, you will first try to calm your fears. You might say to yourself, "Relax and take a deep breath; it can't be as bad as I imagine." If this strategy proves effective at reducing your anxiety, you can then use problem-focused coping techniques and focus on answering the questions on the test, thereby dispelling both your stress and your problem. As this example illustrates, both types of coping can be used in certain situations.

Resources for Effective Coping: From Good Health to Money

A person's ability to cope effectively depends on the stressor itself—its complexity, intensity, and length of duration—and on the type of coping strategy used. It also depends on what resources are available to provide support for the individual. Lazarus and Folkman (1984) list several major types of coping resources: health and energy, positive beliefs, problem-solving skills (which were already discussed), an internal locus of control, social skills, social support, and material resources.

Health and Energy

All stressors cause some type of physiological changes. Therefore, an individual's health significantly affects his or her ability to cope. If you refer to Figure 13.1 on the general adaptation syndrome, you will see that the resistance stage is a coping stage. The stronger and healthier people are, the longer they can cope without entering the stage of exhaustion.

Positive Beliefs

A positive self-image and a positive attitude can be especially significant coping resources. Research shows that even temporarily raising self-esteem reduces the amount of anxiety caused by stressful events (Greenberg et al., 1989). Also, hope can sustain a person in the face of severe odds, as is often documented in news reports of people who have triumphed over seemingly unbeatable circumstances. According to Lazarus and Folkman, hope can come from a belief in oneself, which can enable us to devise our own coping strategies; a belief in others, such as medical doctors who we feel can effect positive outcomes; or a belief in a just and helpful God. In his book *Anatomy of an Illness* (1979) Norman Cousins attributes his recovery from a usually fatal disease to an overall positive outlook and to such positive emotions as laughter, hope, confidence, and the will to live. Having read Hans Selye's (1956) account of how negative emotions can lead to negative effects on body chemistry, Cousins pondered the effects of positive emotions. This led him to initiate, in partnership with his physician, a self-prescribed recovery program that, he claims, proves true the saying "Laughter is the best medicine." Cousins had a determined will to live and he refused many traditional treatments for similar illnesses. Perhaps most important, however, he took liberal doses of comedies, including *Candid Camera* and Marx Brothers films, and read humorous books. Martin and Lefcourt (1983) and Nezu et al. (1988) provide research support for Cousins's approach.

Internal Locus of Control

When people have an internal locus of control, a feeling that they have significant control over the events in their lives, they cope more successfully than people who feel they have no control or are incapable of dealing with events in their lives (Strickland, 1978). People with an external locus of control feel that they are helpless and powerless to change their circumstances. For example, when faced with severe illness, people with an internal locus of control are more likely to collect information about their disease and stay on a program of health maintenance than people who have an external locus of control (Wallston, Maides, and Wallston, 1976). In fact, Cohen and Edwards (1989) found that an internal locus of control is one of the very few stress buffers with any reliability.

Social Skills

Social situations—meetings, discussion groups, dates, parties, and so on—are often a source of pleasure, but they can also be a source of considerable stress. Merely meeting someone new, trying to find something to talk about with a recent acquaintance, or sometimes even talking with a friend can be stressful. People who have acquired the social skills of knowing appropriate behaviors for certain situations, having conversation-starters "up their sleeves," and expressing themselves in an interesting way suffer less anxiety than those who haven't. In fact, people lacking social skills are more at risk for developing illness (Cohen and Williamson, 1991). Effective social skills help us not only interact effectively with others but also communicate our needs and desires, enlist help when we need it, and decrease hostility in tense situations. Thus, people with weak social skills may find it worth the effort to learn how to act in a variety of social situations. They can observe others and ask advice of people with good social skills. When they are aware of appropriate social behaviors, they can practice those behaviors in role-playing situations before applying them in real-life social encounters.

These recently widowed women have realized that an important resource for coping with stresses such as the death of a spouse is social support from friends, families, and social organizations.

Social Support

Social support for coping comes from friends, families, and social organizations such as fraternal organizations and churches (deLongis et al., 1988). Social support can buffer the stressful effects of divorce, loss of a loved one, chronic illness, pregnancy, job loss, and work overload (Winnubst, Buunk, and Marcelissen, 1988). When we are faced with stressful circumstances, our friends and family help us by making sure we take care of our health (such as getting plenty of rest and eating right), listening to us and "holding our hand," making us feel that we are important to them, helping us see the folly of doing something we would later regret, and providing stability to offset the changes in our lives.

In recent years, the range of support groups for people with specific problems has grown. There are hospices for terminally ill people and their families, Alcoholics Anonymous and related groups for families of alcoholics, support groups for former drug addicts and for families of drug addicts, support groups for divorced people and for single parents, and so on. Support groups help people cope not only because they provide other people to lean on but also because people can learn techniques for coping from others with similar problems. The idea of community support maintenance organizations providing psychological and social support has been suggested by Leff and Bradley (1986). Support groups can be invaluable for people faced with long-term stressful situations such as illness or poverty (House, Landis, and Umberson, 1988).

Material Resources

We've all heard the saying, "Money isn't everything." But when it comes to coping with stress, money and the things that money can buy can be very real resources. Money increases the number of options available to eliminate sources of stress or to reduce the effects of stress. When people have sufficient income, they can afford to eat a balanced and healthful diet, seek needed medical or psychological help, or quit a job that is detrimental to their health and reeducate themselves for another. They can afford to enroll in exercise programs, live in a relatively crime-free neighborhood, buy a house that was built according to current fire, earthquake, and other safety standards, and so on. Whether they are faced with the minor hassles of everyday living, with chronic stressors, or with major catastrophes, people with money who have the skills to effectively use that money generally fare much better and experience much less stress than people without money (Lazarus and Folkman, 1984).

Specific Coping Strategies: How You Can Reduce Stress

Many ways to successfully cope with stress have already been discussed: appraising situations rationally and realistically, believing that you are in control of your life and have control over how you deal with your stress, focusing on the positive rather than on the negative aspects of stressful situations, and learning as much as you can about how to solve problems and resolve conflicts.

In addition to these cognitive coping methods, there are a number of other active methods. Active coping methods "provide more direct and deliberate means of controlling and reducing the impact of stress . . . [and] prepare us to deal with unexpected stress and keep us in stress-ready condition" (Gill, 1983, p. 84). We will discuss relaxation, exercise, and several specific self-care strategies.

Relaxation

One of the most effective means of dealing with physical stress reactions is to relax during the stressful situation. There are a variety of relaxation techniques. We have already introduced you to biofeedback, hypnosis, and progressive relaxation. Here we will discuss the technique of meditation.

Throughout the ages people, particularly in the East, have been practicing the art of meditation. This practice establishes parasympathetic control of the body in decreasing oxygen consumption, respiratory rate, heart rate, and blood pressure. Herbert Benson (1975) provided scientific support for the beneficial effects of meditation and has modified it into a program he calls "the relaxation response," which incorporates four basic components of meditation. These components are

1. A quiet, calm environment.
2. A mental device: some type of constant stimulus, either an object at which you can constantly gaze or a sound, word, or phrase you can repeat to yourself, either aloud or silently.
3. A passive attitude: probably the most important component, this is a disregard for distracting thoughts. If you find yourself thinking about problems, return to concentrating on the mental device.
4. A comfortable position: to promote relaxation and avoid any undue muscle tension.

Benson claims that by practicing the relaxation response for 10 to 20 minutes twice a day, you can call on your body's resources to counter the harmful effects of stress—namely, high blood pressure, heart attack, and stroke.

Exercise

If you exercise and keep yourself physically fit, you will more likely experience less anxiety, depression, and tension than people who do not exercise or who are less fit (Blumenthal and McCubbin, 1987). Moreover, researchers comparing adults participating in strenuous versus moderate exercise programs have found that people engaging in strenuous exercise experienced greater reductions in anxiety than those in the moderate program (Blumenthal, Williams, Needles, and Wallace, 1982; Goldwater and Collis, 1985).

Exercise plays several roles in reducing the negative effects of stress. First, it uses up the hormones secreted into the bloodstream during stress, thereby reducing the chances of their inhibiting immune system functioning. Second, exercise can help work

Even mild forms of exercise, such as walking, can help reduce the negative effects of stress.

out tension that has built up in muscles. Third, exercise increases strength, flexibility, and stamina for encountering future stressors and increases the efficiency of the cardiovascular system. The best exercise for these purposes is *aerobic exercise*—regular strenuous activity that heightens cardiovascular functioning, such as brisk walking, jogging, bicycling, swimming, dancing, and so on.

Self-Care

There are several small but very important ways you can relieve the stress in your life. We list them here:

1. *Share your stress.* Talk over your worries and problems with family members or friends. Sometimes others can help you put problems in a new perspective or suggest alternatives you hadn't thought of. For more serious problems, you might seek help from a mental health professional (see Chapter 16).

2. *Appraise your situation.* Take time to appraise your stressful situation. Could you use problem-solving coping skills (maybe your overloaded calendar needs some trimming)? Would emotion-focused skills be more appropriate (if your mother dies, you must deal with the reality of her death)?

3. *Do one thing at a time.* When you feel overwhelmed by work, school, family matters, and commitments to friends, list your priorities and then do them one at a time. Don't try to do everything.

One way to reduce stress in your life is to take time to enjoy it. Make time for fun.

4. *Eat right and get enough rest.* Stressful situations are much easier to cope with when you eat healthful foods and get plenty of rest.

5. *Take time to enjoy life.* Make time for fun. Establishing a balance between work and play contributes to your well-being and helps you be more efficient at work.

You are the one who is ultimately responsible for your own health and well-being. While doctors, nurses, and other health professionals are there for you if you do become ill, it is best to do all you can to *prevent* disease from developing in the first place. By minimizing the amount of stress in our lives, we help our bodies stay well and fight off disease.

Review Questions

1. The attempt to manage stress in some effective way is known as _____ .

2. Which form of coping is being used in the following reactions to forgetting your best friend's birthday?
   a. "I can't be expected to remember everyone's birthday."
   b. "I'd better put Cindy's birthday on my calendar so this won't happen again."

3. What are some defense mechanisms, and why should people try to avoid using them?

4. People are better able to cope with stress if they have an _____ locus of control.

5. What are some resources that help us cope with stress?

6. What are three ways to relieve stress once we are feeling its effects?

Answers to Review Questions can be found in Appendix C.

REVIEW OF MAJOR CONCEPTS

THE NATURE OF HEALTH PSYCHOLOGY

1. Health psychology is the study of the relationship between psychological behavior and physical health and illness, with an emphasis on "wellness" and the prevention of illness.

2. Health psychologists work with patients who are about to undergo complex surgical procedures by teaching them what to anticipate during and after the operation and by giving them and their families suggestions for dealing with psychological problems that may develop following surgery.

3. Health psychologists help chronic pain patients by teaching them to cope with their pain through operant conditioning, biofeedback, and altered attention techniques such as relaxation and self-hypnosis.

4. Because smoking is the single most preventable cause of death and disease in the United States, prevention and cessation of smoking are of primary importance to all health practitioners, including health psychologists.

5. Smoking prevention programs involve educating the public about short- and long-term consequences of smoking, trying to make smoking less socially acceptable, and helping nonsmokers resist social pressures to smoke.

6. Approaches to help people quit smoking include behavior modification techniques such as covert sensitization, stimulus control, and aversion therapy; techniques to aid smokers in their withdrawal from nicotine; and techniques for dealing with social pressures.

STRESS AND ITS ROLE IN HEALTH

7. Stress is the nonspecific response of the body to any demand made on it. Any stimulus that causes stress is called a stressor. There are both beneficial and nonbeneficial types of stress.

8. Among the many causes of stress are life changes, chronic stress, hassles, frustration, and conflicts. Frustrations have to do with blocked goals. Conflicts may be of three types: approach–approach, avoidance–avoidance, and approach–avoidance.

9. When stressed, the body undergoes several physiological changes. The sympathetic part of the autonomic nervous system is activated, increasing heart rate and blood pres-

sure. This sympathetic activation is beneficial if people need to fight or flee, but it can have negative consequences if they do not.

10. Hans Selye described a generalized physiological reaction to severe stressors, which he called the general adaptation syndrome. The general adaptation syndrome has three phases: the alarm reaction, the resistance phase, and the exhaustion phase.

11. Prolonged stress can cause suppression of the immune system, which can render the body susceptible to any number of diseases, including colds, flu, and even such serious diseases as cancer and heart disease.

STRESS AND SERIOUS ILLNESS

12. Cancer can be caused by environmental factors, such as cigarette smoke or asbestos, or by changes in body chemistry that affect how certain cells within the body replicate. During times of stress, the body may be less able to check cancerous tissue growth because of suppression of the immune system.

13. The leading cause of death in the United States is cardiovascular disease. The two major cardiovascular diseases are essential hypertension and heart disease. Essential hypertension is an increase in blood pressure that does not have a medical cause. Hypertension can cause the heart to work harder, making the individual more prone to stroke and heart attack. Heart disease includes all illnesses that eventually affect the heart muscle and lead to heart failure.

14. Risk factors in heart disease include smoking, stress, obesity, a high-fat diet, lack of exercise, and Type A personality traits. The two main approaches to modifying Type A be-

havior are the shotgun approach and the target behavior approach.

15. The Ni-Hon-San study and the Adventist Health Study point out the significant role of the Western lifestyle in the development of serious illnesses such as coronary heart disease and cancer. In the Ni-Hon-San study, Japanese men maintaining a traditional Japanese lifestyle have had lower rates of coronary heart disease than those who migrated and adopted a Western lifestyle. Similarly, people throughout the world who follow the Seventh-day Adventist lifestyle promoting a healthful diet and avoidance of caffeine, alcohol, and smoking are less likely than others in their country to develop coronary heart disease, stroke, or cancer.

COPING WITH STRESS

16. The two major forms of coping with stress are emotion-focused and problem-focused. Emotion-focused forms of coping are strategies that lead to changes in how we view or appraise stressful situations, rather than strategies for changing the situations themselves. Problem-focused forms of coping involve strategies that deal directly with the situation or the factor causing the stress in ways that will eventually decrease or eliminate it.

17. The ability to cope with a stressor also depends on the resources available to help people cope with the stress. Such resources include health and energy, positive beliefs, an internal locus of control, social skills, social support, and material resources.

18. Relaxation, exercise, and self-care strategies are specific behaviors that can help people cope effectively with stress.

SUGGESTED READINGS

BENSON, H., & KLIPPER, M. (1975). *The relaxation response.* New York: William Morrow. A handbook detailing the reasons we must counter the effects of stress and showing how to do this through a type of meditation called the relaxation response.

FISHER, S., & REASON, J. (EDS.). (1988). *Handbook of life stress, cognition, and health.* New York: Wiley. A comprehensive, readable review of current issues in health psychology.

GREENBERG, J. S. (1983). *Comprehensive stress management.* Dubuque, IA: Wm. C. Brown. Written in a personal, informal style, this book provides a comprehensive view of stress and stress management.

LAZARUS, R. S., & FOLKMAN, S. (1984). *Stress, appraisal, and coping.* New York: Springer. A detailed theory of the psychology of stress.

MATARAZZO, J. D., WEISS, S. M., HERD, J. A., MILLER, N. E., & WEISS, S. M. (EDS.). (1984). *Behavioral health.* New York:

Wiley. A collection of some of the most significant findings in health psychology.

SARAFINO, E. P. (1990). *Health psychology: Biopsychosocial interactions.* New York: Wiley. A good introductory health psychology book that provides an overview of the field with an engrossing, narrative writing style.

SELYE, H. (1974). *Stress without distress.* New York: Signet. A short book outlining how to use stress as a positive force in your life.

For a free leaflet on how to handle stress, entitled "Plain talk about . . . handling stress," write to:
U.S. Department of Health and Human Services
Public Health Service
Alcohol, Drug Abuse, and Mental Health Administration
5600 Fishers Lane
Rockville, Maryland 20857

Personality

OUTLINE

Freud's office.

$\mathcal{S}$igmund Freud was born in 1856 and died in 1939. Historians believe that Freud's life and personality development were significantly influenced by the fact that he was a Jew living in Austria, a country where Jews were not only discriminated against but persecuted. The Vienna that was to teach Adolf Hitler his passionate hatred of Jews was Freud's social environment. His family's poverty may have left indelible impressions on him as well.

Despite these conditions, Freud did well in school and entered the University of Vienna as a medical student at the age of 17. He enjoyed laboratory research and wanted to become a professor. But when one of his favorite professors told him that he would have little chance of advancing in that profession because he was poor and Jewish, he studied neurology and entered private practice. As a neurologist, treating nervous system problems, he became interested in patients whose physical problems (such as paralysis or blindness) seemed to be psychologically caused and were not curable by the usual medical treatments. In Freud's day, this kind of problem was called **hysterical neurosis,** and he found that the symptoms could often be treated through the use of hypnosis. Eventually, Freud limited his practice to patients whose problems were assumed to be psychological. He spent his days listening to patients relate their childhood experiences, often reliving with them their memories of sexual assault and betrayal.

Sharing the unpleasant experiences of his patients may have deepened Freud's own cynicism about human nature. From his letters to friends and his descriptions of himself, we have a picture of a man wrestling with pain, one who suffered from periodic depressions, apathy, and fatigue. He sometimes had attacks of anxiety and dwelt on fears of dying. He was moody and alternated between periods of excitement when he felt confident and periods of depression when he doubted himself and could neither write nor concentrate. When he was 29, he wrote in a letter, "I never felt so fresh in my life," and then the following day wrote of his despondency: "I can't stand it much longer" (Jones, 1961, p. 112). Freud suffered migraine headaches, indigestion, and constipation, and he was afraid of traveling by railroad. He also used cocaine to alleviate his depression and became dependent on cigars.

Arising from a modest family background and an anti-Semitic culture, Freud founded an entire school of psychology and became such an eminent therapist that Hollywood's Samuel Goldwyn offered $100,000 for his consulting services (Sheppard, 1988). Freud refused to capitalize on his fame, however, and remained in Austria until the Nazis and World War I threatened his safety. He emigrated to England in 1938 and died the following year from mouth cancer. Sigmund Freud is one of the most famous (and controversial) figures in modern psychology. His personality theories remain the subject of great debate even today —over 50 years after his death.

Hysterical Neurosis: A disorder with physical symptoms created by psychological factors. Today we use the term "conversion disorder."

✱ **Personality:** An individual's relatively stable and enduring pattern of thoughts, feelings, and behavior.

What is personality? In everyday conversation, people use *personality* to mean "charm," "charisma," or "likability." We talk about someone having "lots of personality." But to a psychologist, it makes little sense to talk about personality in terms of likability or relative amount. Psychologists attempt to define personality in a systematic, nonjudgmental, scientific way. Like the terms "perception" and "intelligence," however, personality is difficult to define. As far back as 1937 Gordon Allport identified more than 50 different definitions for the word "personality."

Today there is still considerable controversy over the *best* way to describe personality, but one of the most widely accepted models defines personality as an individual's unique and relatively stable pattern of thoughts, feelings, and behavior. In other words, your personality defines you as a person: how you are different from other people and what patterns of behavior are typical of you. You might qualify as an "extrovert," for example, if you are more talkative and outgoing than most people, and if you are this way most of the time and in most situations. Or, you might be described as "practical" because you are typically more concerned with the usefulness or results of an action (you'd rather get a pair of warm gloves for your birthday than flowers or a sentimental card).

Psychologists who specialize in the study of personality are interested in two things: scientifically *describing* individual differences in personality and *explaining* how those differences came about. To meet these goals, we will discuss six major theories, one of which, of course, is Freud's psychoanalytic theory. The others are learning, humanistic, cognitive, biological, and interactionism. The final section of the chapter explores various methods psychologists use to assess or measure personality.

As you read Chapter 14, keep the following **Survey** questions in mind and answer them in your own words:

- What are the dispositional theories of personality?
- What is Freud's psychoanalytic theory, and how did his followers build on Freudian theory?
- What do learning theorists believe about personality?
- What characterizes the humanistic theories of personality?
- What are the cognitive and biological perspectives on personality? How does the interactionist approach pull it all together?
- How do psychologists measure personality?

DISPOSITIONAL THEORIES

When you say, "He's not my type," or "She has all the traits of a successful business person," you are using one of the oldest and simplest methods for describing personality—the dispositional approach. Psychologists who use this approach are primarily interested in describing the core characteristics of an individual and how these characteristics differ from one person to the next—*not* in explaining these differences. Two of the most influential dispositional approaches are *type theories* and *trait theories*.

• What are the dispositional theories of personality?

Type Theories: The "Discrete Categories" View of Personality

One way to describe personality differences is to categorize people into discrete *types* on the basis of a major characteristic (Coan, 1984). This approach goes back at least as far as Hippocrates, a fifth-century B.C. physician in ancient Greece. Hippocrates said that *temperament,* or basic behavioral tendencies, were associated with the body's four basic fluids, or *humors:* blood, phlegm, yellow bile, and black bile. An excess of one of the humors was associated with specific personality characteristics. Table 14.1 details these temperamental characteristics. This *humoral theory* of personality was further popular-

Table 14.1　The Four Humoral Personality Types

Personality Type	An Excess of	Personality Description
Sanguine	Blood	Warm, passionate, cheerful, confident, optimistic, hopeful
Melancholic	Black bile	Gloomy, irritable, depressed, pensive, sad
Phlegmatic	Phlegm	Hard to rouse to action, sluggish, dull, calm, cool, imperturbable, not easily disconcerted or aroused
Choleric	Yellow bile	Easily angered, quick tempered, volatile

ized in the second century A.D. by another Greek physician, Claudius Galen. Even today, despite the lack of empirical support for this theory, the terms for these personality types survive and we call cheerful people, for example, sanguine.

Another example of terminology persisting despite lack of supporting evidence comes from *somatotype theory*. After personally viewing photographs of 4000 men, William Sheldon proposed three basic body shapes, or somatotypes, that he believed correlated with specific personality traits (Sheldon and Stevens, 1942). These traits and their corresponding body types are shown in Figure 14.1. Using Sheldon's theory, how would you classify your body type and those of your friends? Do the associated personality descriptions match your own observations?

Sheldon's somatotype theory has been strongly criticized as both biased and inaccurate. Recall from Chapter 1, that a cardinal rule of scientific research is that experimenters should never rely on their own judgments and ratings. Given that Sheldon himself rated both the somatotypes and personality traits of the men in the 4000 photos, his research has been criticized for possible *experimenter bias*. Nevertheless, terms from Sheldon's theory (endomorph, mesomorph, and ectomorph) can still be found in some college texts and occasionally in the popular press.

Why do terms and theories like these persist?   The desire to categorize people into a few basic personality types has great appeal. In our daily interactions we are bombarded with information, and it is often convenient and helpful to make quick decisions about the characteristics and dispositions of others. Simple personality descriptions ("He's the quiet type" or "She's the hardworking type") often help us to live and work together peaceably, but they also sometimes lead to faulty judgments.

 Try This Yourself

One of the five individuals pictured on the next page once tried to assassinate a U.S. president, one is a convicted rapist and serial killer, and three are authors of this text. Can you tell which is which? If you're in your critical thinking mode right now, you might be resisting this obvious "setup" and would argue that you can't make such judgments solely on the basis of appearance. However, research shows that we often do make such snap decisions about people. And that when we do, we rely on individualized *typing* systems that reflect our specific life experiences and personal stereotypes (Deaux

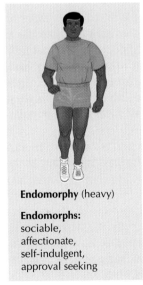

Endomorphy (heavy)

Endomorphs:
sociable,
affectionate,
self-indulgent,
approval seeking

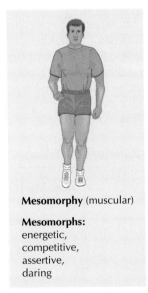

Mesomorphy (muscular)

Mesomorphs:
energetic,
competitive,
assertive,
daring

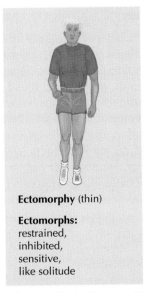

Ectomorphy (thin)

Ectomorphs:
restrained,
inhibited,
sensitive,
like solitude

Figure 14.1 Sheldon's somatotype theory. According to Sheldon, you can predict an individual's personality type by their body shape. This theory has been soundly criticized, but many people continue to believe such stereotypes as "Fat people are always jolly."

(1)   (2)   (3)   (4)   (5)

Are you a good judge of character and personality? Which of these five individuals is a vicious serial killer, which is an attempted assassin of a United States President, and which are authors of this text? The answers appear at the bottom of this page.

and Wrightsman, 1988). (If you want to check your "guesses" regarding the five photos, the answers are provided at the bottom of this page.) ▪

Trait Theories: The "Continuum" Approach to Personality

A major complaint about type theories is that human personality is so varied it won't fit into a few discrete categories. For example, you saw in Chapter 12's discussion of Type A's and Type B's that most people are actually a *blend* of types—not clearly one type or another. An approach to personality that addresses this issue and recognizes a range or combination of possibilities is the *trait* approach. Whereas typologies classify people as *either* Type A or Type B, trait theorists believe personality characteristics exist along a continuum. Individuals are perceived as having varying degrees of traits, or predispositions to respond in certain ways.

> **Trait:** An enduring predisposition to respond in a particular way, distinguishing one individual from another. People can vary in their personality traits along a wide range of values.

An easy way to understand the difference between types and traits is to think about the physical characteristic of height. Using type theories, we would have two groups—tall people and short people. With trait theory, however, we recognize that height varies along a continuum from very short to very tall, so we can describe each person according to his or her specific height. Trait theorists reject the notion of discrete categories of personality. They are interested in first discovering *how* people differ (which key traits best describe them), and then in measuring *how much* they differ (the degree of variation in traits within the individual and between individuals).

Allport's Trait Theories

As you may imagine, identifying and measuring key traits sounds much easier than it actually is. Every individual differs from every other in a great number of different ways. An early study of dictionary terms found almost 18,000 words that could be used to describe personality (Allport and Odbert, 1936). Faced with this enormous list of potential traits, Gordon Allport (1937) believed the best way to understand personality was to study an individual and then arrange his or her unique personality traits into a hierarchy, with the most important and pervasive traits at top and the least important at the bottom. He also divided this hierarchy into three groups of traits: cardinal, central, and secondary.

At the very top of Allport's hierarchy are cardinal traits. Allport believed some rare individuals' personalities are organized around only one or two fundamental (cardinal) characteristics and that these traits influence all or nearly all areas of their lives. Abraham Lincoln's honesty, Adolf Hitler's hatred, and Albert Schweitzer's and Mother Ter-

> **Cardinal Traits:** In Allport's theory, a pervasive, all-encompassing personality characteristic that seems to influence most areas of a person's life. Cardinal traits are relatively uncommon and are observed in only a few people.

Answers to "personality quiz" in the photographs above: Photo 1 *Ken Bianchi (convicted rapist and serial killer)*, Photo 2 *Mark Vernoy (an author of this text)*, Photo 3 *Judy Vernoy (another author of this text)*, Photo 4 *"Squeaky" Fromme (an attempted assassin)*, Photo 5 *Karen Huffman (a third author of this text)*.

esa's humanitarianism are examples of cardinal traits. But few people possess such dominant and pervasive traits.

In contrast to the small number of individuals exhibiting cardinal traits, Allport believed that *everyone* possessed central traits—specific behavioral tendencies that are highly characteristic of an individual. If you asked several friends to list five or so words that describe your personality (outgoing, intelligent, ambitious, etc.), these would be your central traits. According to Allport, each of us possesses only a few central traits and these are easily identified by others.

All other traits of an individual are called secondary traits in Allport's scheme. Secondary traits are far less enduring and general than cardinal or central traits, and less important as descriptions of personality. Examples of secondary traits might be liking the outdoors or enjoying foreign films.

Allport believed that no two people have exactly the same traits. Indeed, one hallmark of Allport's trait theory was his emphasis on the uniqueness of the individual. In contrast, two other prominent trait theorists emphasize the universality of basic traits.

Cattell's and Eysenck's Theories

Two well-known advocates of the universality of traits are Raymond Cattell and Hans Eysenck. Using a mathematical technique called factor analysis, each of these researchers developed a cluster of traits believed to represent the *core personality*. Cattell (1965, 1990) identified 16 basic personality dimensions, which he calls source traits. They are outlined in Figure 14.2. Eysenck (1967, 1982, 1990), on the other hand, found that two dimensions (introversion–extroversion and stability–instability) could explain most personality differences. Figure 14.3 summarizes Eysenck's theory. Eysenck later proposed a third major personality category, a normality–psychotism dimension, that interacts with introversion–extroversion and stability–instability. A person who scores

Central Traits: For Allport, a small number of traits that are highly characteristic of a given individual and easy to infer.

Secondary Traits: In Allport's theory, these traits are not as important as central traits for describing personality since they influence few situations or behaviors.

Factor Analysis: A mathematical procedure used to determine the basic units or factors that constitute personality or intelligence.

Source Traits: Cattell's term for the basic personality traits he believed are shared by most individuals.

Figure 14.2 Cattell's Sixteen Personality Traits. Using responses from individuals, or groups of individuals (creative artists, writers, and pilots are shown here), personality profiles are plotted on a scale from one to ten. Note the profile for airline pilots. It may reassure you to know that pilots, as a group, tend to be emotionally stable, toughminded, practical, self-assured, controlled, and relaxed.

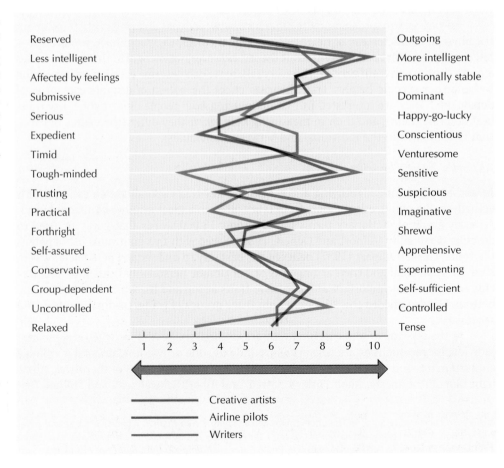

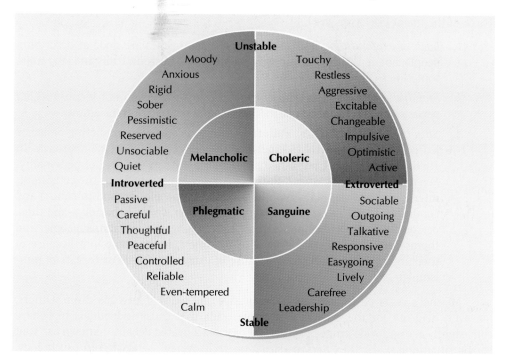

Figure 14.3 Eysenck's Dimensions of Personality. Eysenck believes most personality types can be divided along two major dimensions —introversion versus extroversion and stable versus unstable. The personality traits that lie along the outer ring are related to the two dimensions (e.g., a moody person would be high on the dimension of unstableness and somewhat introverted). Note how these personality characteristics are related to Hippocrates' four major personality types, shown in the inner circle.

high on *psychotism* tends to be hostile, egocentric, and antisocial and is generally considered "peculiar" by others.

The "Big 5" Model

At this point, you are probably feeling overwhelmed by the variety of models and large number of traits that can be used to describe personality. You are not alone. Many researchers over the years also felt trait theories were not clearly defined and persisted in the search for the *basic* factors or traits that could describe human personality. After nearly 50 years of sophisticated factor analysis research, there is something of a consensus on what these basic factors are (Digman, 1990; Goldberg, 1993; McCrae and Costa, 1986, 1990). The key factors in this so-called "Big 5" model are presented in Figure 14.4 and described below.

1. *Extroversion.* This dimension is the same as Eysenck's introversion–extroversion scale illustrated in Figure 14.3.

2. *Agreeableness.* This dimension describes whether a person is goodnatured, gentle, cooperative, trusting, and helpful at one end of the continuum or irritable, ruthless, suspicious, uncooperative, and headstrong at the other.

3. *Conscientiousness.* This dimension ranges from responsible, self-disciplined, and achieving at one end to irresponsible, careless, and undependable at the other.

4. *Neuroticism.* This dimension is the same as Eysenck's stability–instability component depicted in Figure 14.3.

5. *Openness to experience.* People who rate high in this dimension are intelligent, open to new ideas, and interested in cultural pursuits. Low scorers tend to be conventional, down-to-earth, narrower in their interests, and unartistic.

Evaluating Type and Trait Theories: Three Major Criticisms

Although there may be some consensus on these five major dimensions of personality, there are still several problems and weaknesses associated with type and trait theories.

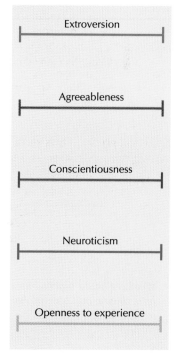

Figure 14.4 "Big 5" Model of Personality. Researchers generally agree that most personality traits exist along a continuum and can be condensed to these five major factors: extroversion, agreeableness, conscientiousness, neuroticism, and openness to experience.

Researchers have found that shyness is one of the most enduring and stable personality traits. Shy children generally grow up to be shy adults.

Three of the major criticisms are

1. *Lack of explanation.* Both type and trait approaches are good at describing people, but do little to explain why people develop certain traits and why traits sometimes change.

2. *Stability versus change.* Most type and trait theories do not identify which personality characteristics last a lifetime and which are transient.

3. *Situational determinants.* Failure to find consistency in predicting behavior led personality theorists to challenge the entire trait and type approach. In 1968, Walter Mischel published a landmark book in the field of personality, *Personality and Assessment.* Rather than seeing personality as the consistent, internal traits of an individual, he argued that people respond to factors and conditions in the external environment. In other words, behavior—and thus, personality—is determined almost entirely by the situations people find themselves in. People are honest or dishonest, for example, not because of their internal personality but because of external rewards or threats of punishment.

Mischel's research findings were persuasive and many joined his camp. Others, however, held out for the existence of stable traits that cause individuals to behave consistently across a wide range of settings. For years a heated debate—known as "trait versus situationism" or the "person–situation controversy"—existed in psychology. After nearly two decades of continuing debate and research, the consensus seems to be that relatively stable traits do exist but they are affected by situational pressures (Kenrick and Funder, 1988). This *interactionist* position is becoming increasingly common in many areas of psychology, and we will return to it later in this chapter.

Review Questions

1. An individual's relatively stable and enduring patterns of behavior are known as _____ .

2. What approach to personality is taken by the dispositional theorists?

3. How do type theorists differ from trait theorists?

4. Cattell and Eysenck both used the method called _____ to determine a cluster of personality traits they believe are universally shared.

5. What are the "big five" factors of personality?

Answers to Review Questions can be found in Appendix C.

PSYCHOANALYTIC THEORIES

• *What is Freud's psychoanalytic theory, and how did his followers build on Freudian theory?*

In contrast to type and trait theories, which *describe* personality as it currently exists, *psychoanalytic* (or psychodynamic) *theories* of personality attempt to *explain* individual differences by examining how unconscious mental forces interplay with thoughts, feelings, and behavior. The founding father of psychoanalytic theory is Sigmund Freud, about whom you read at the beginning of this chapter. Here we will examine his theories in some detail. Then we will briefly discuss three of Freud's most influential followers, Alfred Adler, Carl Jung, and Karen Horney.

Freud's Psychoanalytic Theory: The Power of the Unconscious

Who is the most well-known figure in all of psychology? Most people immediately name Sigmund Freud. Even before you studied psychology, you probably came across his

"*Good morning, beheaded—uh, I mean beloved.*"
Is this an example of a Freudian slip or a mere "slip of the tongue?"

Drawing by Fradon © 1983 the New Yorker Magazine, Inc.

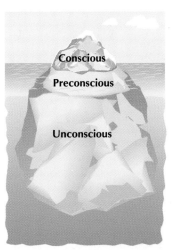

Figure 14.5 Freud's Three Levels of Consciousness. The parts of the mind can be compared to an iceberg in the ocean. The tip of the iceberg is like the *conscious* mind—open to easy inspection. Directly below the conscious mind is the *preconscious,* whose contents can be viewed with a little extra effort. The large base of the iceberg is like the *unconscious* mind, completely hidden from personal inspection.

name in other courses. Freud's theories have been discussed in the fields of anthropology, sociology, religion, medicine, art, and literature. Working from about 1890 until he died in 1939, Freud developed a theory of personality that has been one of the most influential and, at the same time, most controversial in all of science (Torrey, 1992b).

In discussing Freud's theory, we will focus on four of his most basic and debatable concepts: levels of consciousness, the structure of personality, defense mechanisms, and psychosexual stages of development.

Levels of Consciousness

What would you think if you heard a flight attendant say, "It's been a real *job* serving you . . . I mean *joy!*"? From a Freudian perspective, this little slip of the tongue (known as a *Freudian slip*) might reflect the attendant's true, unconscious feelings. Freud believed that the unconscious is hidden from our personal awareness, but that it has an enormous impact on our behavior—and reveals itself despite our intentions.

What exactly is the unconscious?   Freud called the mind the *psyche* and saw the unconscious as one of three levels of awareness or consciousness (see Figure 14.5). Using Freud's analogy of an iceberg, the first level of awareness, the conscious, is the only part of the iceberg above water and therefore available to our mental inspection. This conscious part of the mind consists of all thoughts, feelings, and actions of which we are actively aware at the moment. Just below the conscious realm, and the water's surface, is the somewhat larger preconscious, which includes mental activities not part of our current thoughts but which can readily be brought to mind if needed. The third level, the unconscious, lies beneath the preconscious and forms the bulk of the human mind. According to Freud, the unconscious stores our primitive, instinctual motives, plus anxiety-laden memories and emotions that are prevented from entering the conscious mind.

Freud's concept of the unconscious is one of his most intriguing and influential ideas. Just as the captain of the ocean liner *Titanic* belatedly discovered that it was the enormous mass of iceberg below the surface that destroyed his ship, so too can the unconscious, unknown part of our minds undermine our intentions and result in destructive behavior. The thoughts, memories, impulses, and desires that, like the base of the iceberg, remain hidden can play havoc with our lives. However, according to Freud, we can gain insight into this secret realm through *psychoanalysis,* a specific form of therapy Freud developed. (See Chapter 16 for a full discussion of psychoanalysis.)

Conscious: In Freudian terms, thoughts or information one is currently aware of or is remembering.

Preconscious: Freud's term for thoughts or information one can become aware of easily.

Unconscious: Freud's term for thoughts, motives, impulses, or desires that lie beyond a person's normal awareness, but which can be made available through psychoanalysis.

As you may imagine, Freud's emphasis on the conscious, preconscious, and unconscious mind, and his subsequent attempts to interpret hidden, unconscious motives, would be difficult to study scientifically. They have therefore been the subject of great debate in psychology. Before we discuss this debate though, let's continue our exploration of Freud's theory with a look at a second major element—the structure of personality.

Personality Structure

Freud viewed personality as a dynamic interplay between three mental structures: the *id,* the *ego,* and the *superego.* Each of these structures is believed to reside, fully or partially, in the unconscious (see Figure 14.6). And each structure accounts for a different aspect of personality. (Keep in mind that the id, ego, and superego are mental concepts—or hypothetical constructs. They are not physical structures you could see if you dissected a human brain.)

The id is the original part of the psyche believed to be present at birth. Like a newborn child, the id is immature, impulsive, and irrational. The id is the reservoir of mental energy. When the forcefulness of its primitive drives builds up, the id seeks immediate gratification in order to relieve the tension. Thus, the id functions according to what Freud called the pleasure principle, which is the immediate and uninhibited seeking of pleasure and avoidance of discomfort.

Because it is such a primitive and completely unconscious part of the psyche, the id operates without any consideration for logic or reality. The id *can,* however, obtain partial gratification for its instinctual energy by forming mental images of desired objects. Freud called this *wish-fulfillment.* These mental images are the basis of many daydreams, fantasies, and dreams according to Freud.

If the id were the only part of the psyche, we might seek pleasure and avoid pain in immediate and dangerously impulsive ways, since this is what the id often urges us to do. However, Freud also postulated two other parts of the psyche that control and channel the id's potentially destructive energy. These parts, the ego and the superego, protect us from the id's desire for immediate gratification.

The ego is the second part of the psyche to develop. It is capable of planning, problem solving, reasoning, and controlling the id. In Freud's system, the ego corresponds to the "self"—our conscious identity of ourselves as persons. Unlike the id, which lies entirely in the unconscious, the ego resides in both the conscious and preconscious.

One of the ego's tasks is to channel and release the id's energy in ways that are consistent with the external environment. Thus, the ego is responsible for delaying gratification when necessary. Contrary to the id's pleasure principle, the ego operates on

---

Id: According to Freud, the source of instinctual energy, which works on the pleasure principle and is concerned with immediate gratification.

Pleasure Principle: In Freud's theory, the principle on which the id operates—that immediate pleasure is the sole motivation for behavior.

Ego: In Freud's theory, the rational part of the psyche that deals with reality and attempts to control the impulses of the id while also satisfying the social approval and self-esteem needs of the superego.

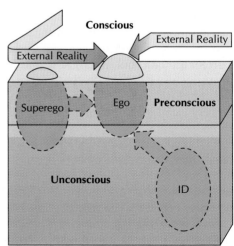

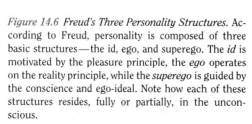

Figure 14.6 Freud's Three Personality Structures. According to Freud, personality is composed of three basic structures—the id, ego, and superego. The *id* is motivated by the pleasure principle, the *ego* operates on the reality principle, while the *superego* is guided by the conscience and ego-ideal. Note how each of these structures resides, fully or partially, in the unconscious.

the reality principle, since it has the ability to understand and deal with objects and circumstances in the external environment.

Freud used the example of a rider and his horse to illustrate the relationship of the ego and id:

> *In its relation to the id [the ego] is like a man on horseback, who has to hold in check the superior strength of the horse. . . . Often a rider, if he is not to be parted from his horse, is obliged to guide it where it wants to go; so in the same way the ego is in the habit of transforming the id's will into action as if it were its own.*

> *Freud (1923/1961), p. 25*

The final part of the psyche to develop is the superego. It originates as part of the ego but separates from it to become an overseer or moral censor for the psyche. The separation of the superego occurs when the child learns the rules and values of the parents and society. The superego is a set of ethical standards or rules for behavior. It has two parts, the conscience and the ego-ideal. The *conscience* is a group of social prohibitions, similar to a penal code or legal statutes. It lists the things we should *not* do. The *ego-ideal* is a list of things we *should* do to feel proud of ourselves. The superego might be thought of as operating on the *morality principle,* since violating the rules of either the conscience or ego-ideal both result in feelings of guilt.

The superego constantly strives for perfection and is, therefore, as unrealistic as the id. So now, the job of the ego becomes much more complicated. Not only must the ego find objects and events that satisfy the id, but these same objects and events must not violate the standards of the superego. For this reason, the ego is often referred to as the *executive* of the personality (Hergenhahn, 1990).

Defense Mechanisms

When the ego fails to find ways to satisfy both the id and the superego, anxiety slips into conscious awareness. Anxiety is uncomfortable, so people try to rid themselves of it any way they can. One common way to ward off anxiety is through the use of defense mechanisms. Defense mechanisms are strategies the ego unconsciously uses to reduce anxiety by distorting our perceptions of reality. Although Freud described many kinds of defense mechanisms, he believed repression was the most important. Repression is the mechanism by which the ego prevents the most anxiety-provoking thoughts (in other words, the most unacceptable thoughts) from entering the conscious level. It is the first and most basic form of anxiety reduction. Repression and several other Freudian defense mechanisms (all of which are unconscious) are listed in Table 14.2.

I see people using these different defense mechanisms all the time. Is this bad? Although defense mechanisms do twist the truth and distort reality, research supports Freud's belief that some misrepresentation seems to be necessary for our psychological well-being (Pervin, 1993; Snyder, 1988; Taylor et al., 1988). During a gruesome surgery, for example, physicians and nurses may *intellectualize* the procedures as an unconscious way of dealing with their personal anxieties. By focusing on abstract thoughts, words, or ideas, they do not become emotionally overwhelmed by the potentially tragic situations they sometimes encounter. Most psychologists agree that the use of defense mechanisms is healthy as long as it does not become extreme.

Psychosexual Stages of Development

Freud proposed that experiences during early childhood were important predictors of later adult personality. He believed each of us passes through five psychosexual stages during the first twelve or so years of life. The term "psychosexual" reflects Freud's major emphasis on the importance of *infantile sexuality*—his belief that children experience sexual feelings from birth (although in different forms from those of adolescents or adults). Four of his stages are named for the area of the body (or *erogenous zone*) that

Reality Principle: According to Freud, the principle on which the conscious ego operates as it tries to meet the demands of the unconscious id and the realities of the environment.

Superego: In psychoanalytic theory, the part of the personality that incorporates parental and societal standards for morality.

Defense Mechanisms: In psychoanalytic theory, unconconscious strategies used by the ego to avoid anxiety and resolve conflict. Everyone uses defense mechanisms. They only cause serious problems when they are excessively used.

Repression: Freud's most important defense mechanism that involves unconscious blocking of unacceptable impulses to keep them from awareness.

Psychosexual Stages: In psychoanalytic theory, a developmental period in which individual pleasures must be gratified if personality development is to proceed normally.

Table 14.2   Eight Sample Psychological Defense Mechanisms

Defense Mechanism	Description	Example
Repression	Preventing painful or dangerous thoughts from entering consciousness.	Forgetting early childhood sexual abuse.
Sublimation	Working off unmet desires, or unacceptable impulses, in activities that are constructive.	Rechanneling sexual desires into art or music.
Denial	Protecting oneself from an unpleasant reality by refusing to perceive it.	Alcoholics refusing to admit their addiction.
Rationalization	Socially acceptable reasons are substituted for thoughts or actions based on unacceptable motives.	Justifying cheating on an exam by saying "everyone else does it."
Intellectualization	Ignoring the emotional aspects of a painful experience by focusing on abstract thoughts, words, or ideas.	Ignoring your emotional pain while academically discussing the reasons for your divorce.
Projection	Unacceptable motives or impulses are transferred to others.	Not acknowledging even to yourself your own temptations, while becoming unreasonably jealous of your mate.
Reaction formation	Refusing to acknowledge unacceptable urges, thoughts, or feelings by exaggerating the opposite state.	Being domineering, loud, and boastful when you feel inferior and low in self-esteem.
Regression	Responding to a threatening situation in a way appropriate to an earlier age or level of development.	Throwing a temper tantrum when a friend refuses to meet your demands.

corresponds to the primary source of pleasure at these stages—the mouth, anus, phallus, and genitals (see Table 14.3).

Freud believed that movement through all five stages is motivated by strong biological drives, but he also suggested that if a child's needs are not met or are overindulged at one particular stage the child may *fixate* and a part of the personality will remain stuck at that stage. Even if they make it through all five stages, some people may

Toilet training is a central source of conflict during the anal stage, according to Freud.

Table 14.3   Freud's Five Stages of Psychosexual Development

Stage	Approximate Age	Erogenous Zone	Key Conflict or Developmental Task
Oral	0–1	Mouth	Weaning (from breast or bottle)
Anal	1–3	Anus	Toilet training
Phallic	3–6	Genitals	Overcoming the Oedipal or Electra complex (by identifying with same-sex parent)
Latency	6–12	None	Expanding interests and social contacts
Genital	12–adult	Genitals	Establishing intimate relationships

return (or *regress*) to a stage at which earlier needs were badly frustrated or overgratified.

During the oral stage (birth to 12–18 months), the erogenous zone is the mouth and the infant receives satisfaction through sucking, eating, biting, and so on. Because the infant is highly dependent on parents and caregivers to provide opportunities for oral gratification, fixation at this stage can easily occur. According to Freud, if the mother overindulges her infant's oral needs, the child may fixate and as an adult become gullible ("swallowing" anything), dependent, and passive. The underindulged child, however, will develop into an aggressive, sadistic person who exploits others. Orally fixated adults may also orient their life around their mouth—overeating, drinking, smoking, talking a great deal, and so on.

During the anal stage (from 12–18 months to 3 years), the erogenous zone shifts to the anus and the child receives satisfaction by having and retaining bowel movements. Since this is also the time when most parents begin toilet training, the child's desire to control his or her own bowel movements often leads to strong conflict. Adults who have fixated at this stage may display an *anal-retentive* personality and be compulsively neat, stingy, orderly, and obstinate. Or they may become disorderly, rebellious, and destructive—the *anal-expulsive* personality. (It may help you to remember these two personalities types by thinking of *The Odd Couple*—Felix would be the anal-retentive and Oscar the anal-expulsive.)

During the phallic stage (from 3 to 6 years), the major center of pleasure becomes the phallus (penis) for the boy and the clitoris for the girl. Children develop a desire for the opposite-sex parent and a wish to displace the same-sex parent. This attraction creates a conflict (the Oedipus complex for boys and Electra complex for girls) that must be resolved. Freud based his name for these complexes on characters in Greek plays: King Oedipus, who killed his father and married his mother, and Electra, a character from the Greek play *Agamemnon,* who induces her brother to kill their mother. In Freud's view, young boys desire their mother and unconsciously want to replace their father, but, recognizing the father's power, they fear he will punish them by castration. This *castration anxiety* and the Oedipus conflict are resolved when the boy represses his sexual feelings for his mother, gives up his rivalry with his father, and begins to *identify* with him. If the resolution of this stage is not complete or positive, the boy will grow up resenting his father and generalize this feeling to all authority figures (Nye, 1975).

In the case of young girls, Freud believed young girls desire their father and unconsciously want to replace their mother. Unlike the young boy who develops castration anxiety, however, the young girl discovers that she lacks a penis which causes her to develop *penis envy*. The Electra conflict is resolved when the girl suppresses her desire for her father, gives up her rivalry with her mother, and identifies with her. Freud believed that most young girls never really overcome penis envy and fully identify with their mothers. This belief led him to suggest that women generally have a lower level of morality than men. (You are undoubtedly surprised or outraged by this statement, but remember that Freud's theories are very controversial—some more than others.)

Following the phallic period is the latency stage (from 6 years to puberty). Freud believed that the individual's personality is generally completed by this stage, a time of relative sexual calm. During this period sexual energy is directed toward schoolwork, hobbies, and same-sex friendships.

With the beginning of adolescence comes the genital stage. The genitals are once again erogenous zones and individuals receive satisfaction through heterosexual matings outside the family.

Why was Freud so "hung up" on sex? His whole theory seems to revolve around it. Freud has been criticized for his overemphasis on sex, perhaps for the wrong reasons. It is important to recognize that Freud was a product of his times. He was writing and seeing patients during the Victorian age, probably the most sexually repressive period in all of history. Thus, Freud's emphasis on sex may simply reflect the reported experiences of his patients who lived in an extremely restrictive society (Gay, 1988).

Oral Stage: Freud's psychosexual stage (from birth to 12–18 months) during which the mouth is the center of pleasure and feeding is the primary source of conflict.

Anal Stage: Freud's psychosexual stage (from 12–18 months to 3 years) during which the anal area is the center of pleasure and toilet training is the primary source of conflict.

Phallic Stage: Freud's psychosexual stage (ages 3 to 6) during which the child experiences either the Oedipus or Electra complex, which can only be resolved through identification with the same-sex parent.

Oedipus Complex: The Freudian term for the sexual attachment of a boy to his mother and his desire to replace his father.

Electra Complex: The Freudian term for the sexual attachment of a girl to her father and her desire to replace her mother.

Latency Stage: Freud's fourth psychosexual stage (age 6 to puberty), characterized by the relative lack of sexual interests.

Genital Stage: The stage of psychosexual development that begins in puberty and represents mature adult sexuality and personality development.

Perhaps one of the most valid criticisms of Freud comes from research suggesting that he rejected his patients' tales of sexual trauma because he lacked personal courage (Masson, 1984, 1992). Initially Freud believed his patients' stories of sexual assault and rape by parents and other trusted adults were factually true and he discussed these assaults in his early lectures. But, Freud's early lectures were ridiculed. In his later writings, Freud deemphasized the importance of *actual* sexual trauma, claiming that his patients were only describing things *as if* they were true. They were really expressing unconscious fantasies and wishes. Given our knowledge today of the high frequency of rape and incest throughout history, Masson and others think Freud was probably right in initially trusting his patients, and wrong to retreat from his original position.

But as we will see in the next section, many of Freud's early followers found fault with his theories for other reasons, too, and broke away to form branches of psychoanalytic theory.

Neo-Freudian Theories: Revising Freud's Ideas

Neo-Freudians: Contemporaries of Freud who both supported and criticized his theory.

In time, Freud's theories gained a following, but as might be expected in any new movement, frequent and intense disagreements led to dramatic severing of friendships and allegiances. Some of these psychoanalysts left Freud and proposed theories of their own; they became known as neo-Freudians. While many neo-Freudians accepted Freud's emphasis on the unconscious, they disagreed that personality is fully formed during the first five years of life and they felt he paid inadequate attention to social and cultural forces. Three of Freud's most influential followers were Alfred Adler, Carl Jung, and Karen Horney.

Adler's Individual Psychology

Alfred Adler was the first to leave Freud's inner circle of followers. He developed a theory he called *individual psychology* (Mosak, 1989). Instead of seeing behavior as motivated by unconscious forces, he claimed that behavior is purposeful and goal-directed. Unlike Freud, he felt that *consciousness* is the center of personality. He believed that each of us has the capacity to choose and to create. According to Adler (1964), our goals in life provide the source of our motivation—especially those goals that aim to obtain security and overcome feelings of inferiority. Adler believed that almost everyone suffers from feelings of inferiority, or the inferiority complex.

Inferiority Complex: Adler's idea that feelings of inferiority develop from early childhood experiences of helplessness and incompetence.

Why are inferiority feelings so common?   In Adler's view, we have inferiority feelings because we begin life as completely helpless infants. Every young child feels small, incompetent, and helpless when dealing with skilled adults. These early feelings of inadequacy result in a *will-to-power* that causes children to strive to develop superiority over others or, more positively, to develop their full potential and to gain mastery and control in their lives. Thus, the childhood inferiority complex can lead to negative adult traits of dominance, aggression, or envy of others, or positive traits such as self-mastery and creativity (Adler, 1964). Adler also suggested that the will-to-power could be positively expressed through *social interest*—identifying with others and cooperating with them for the social good. In stressing social interest and the positive outcomes of inferiority feelings, Adlerian theory is more optimistic than Freudian theory.

Jung's Analytic Psychology

Another early dissenter, Carl Jung (pronounced "yoong"), developed *analytical psychology*, which emphasized the unconscious mind and its influence on dream processes (Haynie, 1984). Jung believed the unconscious mind contains positive and spiritual motives as well as sexual and aggressive forces. He also believed we have two forms of unconscious mind, the personal unconscious and the collective unconscious. The *personal unconscious* is created from our experiences, whereas the collective unconscious is identical in each person and is inherited (Jung, 1936/1969). The collective uncon-

Collective Unconscious: Jung's concept of an inherited portion of the unconscious that all humans share.

Figure 14.7 A Sample Jungian Archetype. This Tibetan *mandala* (Sanskrit for "circle") is a symbol for the *self* archetype described by Jung. The circle symbolizes oneness, or wholeness, and completion within the personality. The mandala is used in numerous religions around the world, as well as in other cultural and historical contexts.

scious consists of primitive images and patterns for thought, feeling, and behavior that Jung called archetypes. He considered the collective unconscious the ancestral memory of the human race that gives people of different cultures their similarities in religion, art, symbolism, and dream imagery (see Figure 14.7). The archetype patterns contained in the collective unconscious cause us to perceive and react in certain predictable ways. One set of archetypes refers to gender roles. Jung claimed that both males and females have patterns for feminine aspects of personality *(anima)* and masculine aspects *(animus)*. The anima and animus within allow each of us to express both masculine and feminine personality traits and to understand and relate to the other sex.

Archetypes: The images or patterns for thought, feelings, and behavior that reside in the collective unconscious, according to Jung.

Gender and Cultural Diversity

HORNEY, FREUD, AND PENIS ENVY

Karen Horney (pronounced "horn-eye") was trained as a Freudian psychoanalyst in Germany and came to the United States in 1934. One of her major contributions was a creative blending of Freudian, Adlerian, and Jungian theory (Hergenhahn, 1990). She altered or rejected certain ideas of each theorist and added important concepts of her own (Horney, 1939, 1945).

One of Horney's strongest disagreements with Freud was over his belief in the biological determinants of differences between men and women. Horney wrote many articles showing that much of what Freud said about female personality reflected male biases and misunderstanding. She rejected psychoanalytic claims that "biology is destiny," contending that male/female differences were largely the result of social and cultural factors. She argued that Freud's concept of penis envy, for example, reflected women's feelings of cultural inferiority, not biological inferiority. Horney said:

> *The wish to be a man . . . may be the expression of a wish for all those qualities or privileges which in our culture are regarded as masculine, such as strength, courage, independence, success, sexual freedom, and right to choose a partner. (1926/1967, p. 108)*

Horney suggested the term *penis envy* be replaced by *power envy*. She also countered that some men develop *womb envy*—the desire to bear and nurse children. Horney emphasized that each sex has attributes and powers that are admired by the other, and that neither should be seen as inferior or superior. Though Freud's theories have since been criticized by a number of researchers for their male bias, Horney was one of the first to do so (e.g., Chodorow, 1978, 1989; Masson, 1992; Paludi, 1992).

In addition to her criticism of penis envy and biological determinants of gender differences, Horney is known for her contributions to theories of personality development. While Freud believed that fixation at any stage of psychosexual development (oral, anal, etc.) was the strongest influence on adult personality, Horney believed it was the child's relationship to the parents that most influenced adult personality.

Stop for a moment and try to recapture your earliest childhood feelings and experiences. If as a child you felt alone and isolated in a hostile environment, and your needs were not met with proper parental nurturance, Horney believed you would experience extreme feelings of basic anxiety. How people respond to this basic anxiety—a major concept in Horney's theory—greatly determines emotional health.

According to Horney, we all search for security in one of three basic and distinct ways: We can *move toward* people (by seeking affection and acceptance from others), we can *move away* (by striving for independence, privacy, and self-reliance), or we can *move against* people (by trying to gain control and power over others). In Horney's theory, emotional health requires a balance among these three styles. Exaggerating or overusing one constitutes a *neurotic*, or emotionally unhealthy, response. ■

Basic Anxiety: According to Horney, people develop feelings of helplessness and insecurity (basic anxiety) when as children they felt alone and isolated in a hostile environment.

Evaluating Psychoanalytic Theories: Four Areas of Criticism

Freud and his psychoanalytic theories have been enormously influential, but as we said at the onset, his theories have also been the subject of great debate. Four of the most important criticisms are presented here.

1. *Poor testability.* From a scientific point of view, a major problem with psychoanalytic theory is that most of its concepts cannot be empirically tested (Torrey, 1992b). How do you conduct an experiment on the id? Or on unconscious conflicts? Scientific standards require testable hypotheses and operational definitions.

2. *Overemphasis on biology and unconscious forces.* Like many of the neo-Freudians, modern psychologists believe that Freud overemphasized biological determinants and did not give sufficient attention to the influence of society and learning in shaping behavior. In particular, the psychoanalytic belief that "anatomy is destiny" completely ignores the power of culture and the environment to create differences between men and women.

3. *Biased sampling.* Freud derived his ideas almost exclusively from patients who were primarily upper-class Viennese women with serious problems. Thus his sampling techniques are open to criticism, and his theory may describe only disturbed personality development in upper-class Viennese women.

4. *Nonsupportive and inadequate evidence.* Scientific investigations, by both supporters and nonsupporters, have generally found little or no support for

Freudian theories (Torrey, 1992b). Moreover, modern research often finds Freudian explanations inadequate in light of recent findings. Chapter 5's discussion of why we dream, for example, reported better scientific support for the mental housecleaning theory than for Freud's notion of "wish-fulfillment."

Similarly, the Freudian concepts that ought to be most easily supported empirically—the biological determinants of personality—are generally not borne out by cross-cultural studies. The Oedipus complex, for example, was proposed as a cultural universal by Freud, yet Malinowski (1929) found no evidence for it in the Trobiand Islands—at least in the form Freud described.

In this culture the mother's brother, rather than the father, is the primary authority. According to the Oedipus complex, this familial arrangement should make no difference—the little boy should still have sexual feelings for his mother and see his father as the hated rival. Malinowski, however, found no indication of conflict between fathers and sons among the Trobrianders. The fact that he did observe the boys directing some negative feelings toward their maternal uncle suggests that power, not sexual relations, may play the primary role in resentment and rivalry between fathers and sons. Similarly, Bettelheim (1962) found little cross-cultural support for Freud's concept of "penis envy," but did find support for Horney's idea of male "womb envy."

Review Questions

1. How does psychoanalytic theory explain personality?

2. Using the analogy of an iceberg, explain Freud's three levels of awareness.

3. The _____ operates on the pleasure principle, seeking immediate gratification. The _____ operates on the reality principle, and the _____ contains the conscience and ego-ideal, which provide moral guidance for the ego.

4. What are the five psychosexual stages described by Freud, and what role do they play in the development of personality?

5. Match the following concepts with the appropriate theorist, Adler, Jung, or Horney:
   a. _____ inferiority complex
   b. _____ power envy
   c. _____ collective unconscious
   d. _____ basic anxiety

6. What are the four major criticisms of Freudian theory?

Answers to Review Questions can be found in Appendix C.

LEARNING THEORIES

In the type, trait, and psychoanalytic approaches discussed so far, personality is seen as an abstract, *internal* part of each individual that may or may not be related to external behavior. An introverted, shy person, for example, may become a movie star or politician and spend most of each day giving speeches and interacting with others, yet according to these theories still remain a "true" introvert on the inside.

From the learning perspective, however, the term "personality" is used as a concrete, *external* label for the sum total of an individual's behavior. Personality is assessed from the outside by measuring observable behaviors, such as public speaking or attending parties. The label "introverted personality" would be applied only if an individual

• What do learning theorists believe about personality?

behaved in an introverted, shy manner in *most* circumstances. For the learning theorist, personality and behavior are basically the same thing.

Why would someone behave in a shy way if it isn't part of an internal personality trait? Learning theorists believe motivation comes from an individual's history of learning. Personality, like other learned behaviors, is acquired through classical and operant conditioning, modeling, and so forth (see Chapter 6). Behavior (or personality) is considered *situationally specific*. That is, a person is capable of many behaviors, and the rewards, punishments, or modeling by others within the immediate situation are the best predictors of an individual's behavior at any given moment.

But how do learning theorists explain the obvious consistencies in behavior among people? Someone who is always *shy and introverted, for example?* From the learning perspective, this apparent stability merely reflects that we all experience distinctive life—and learning—experiences. From our individual histories of repeated reinforcements or punishments, we learn to respond in a *habitual* pattern that is labeled "personality." In this section, we'll briefly review two important areas of learning theory—behavior and social learning perspectives—as they apply to personality.

Behavioral Perspectives: Watson's and Skinner's Contributions

One of the earliest behaviorists was John B. Watson. Using research on classical conditioning, Watson claimed that *all* human behavior or personality is determined by learning. Like many behaviorists of his day, Watson believed that an infant is born as a *tabula rasa,* or "blank slate," waiting to be written on by learning experiences. On one occasion he even went so far as to say:

> *Give me a dozen, healthy infants, well-formed, and my own specified world to bring them up in, and I'll guarantee to take any one at random and train him to become any type of specialist I might select—doctor, lawyer, artist, merchant-chief, and, yes, even beggar-man and thief, regardless of his talents, penchants, tendencies, activities, vocations, and race of his ancestors.*
>
> *Watson (1930), p. 65*

Following in Watson's footsteps, modern-day behaviorist B. F. Skinner believed we do not need to resort to biological or internal aspects of the person to explain personality, we need only look at stimuli and responses. If you are shy and are afraid to approach others for dates or friendship, Skinner would say you *learned* to behave in this fashion as a result of previous interactions with family members, friends, teachers, and others (Skinner, 1990).

Social Learning Theory: The Power of Observation and Imitation

Social learning theorists agree with behaviorists that personality is learned and influenced by environmental experiences, but they also think less observable phenomena, such as thinking and observation of others, play an important role.

How does observing others influence personality? When you observe another person doing something, you evaluate and interpret his or her behavior. You not only see the consequences of that person's actions, you also think about whether that particular behavior would be appropriate for you. For example, children observe the behavior of both male and female adults, but they tend to imitate the adults who are judged to be most "like themselves." Thus, little girls most often choose to imitate their mother's behavior because they have been told they too are female and will grow up to be women.

Because of their emphasis on imitation, social learning theorists are particularly concerned about children having appropriate role models. They strongly criticize the prevalence of models for aggression in movies and on television. Research tends to support this criticism. As you saw in Chapter 6, experiments show that children who

Children frequently imitate the behaviors they observe in adults.

watch aggressive behaviors on film behave more aggressively compared to children who have not seen aggressive acts modeled (Bandura, 1969, 1973; Huesmann and Eron, 1986; Wood et al., 1991).

Evaluating Learning Theories: Admirers versus Critics

The behavioral and social learning perspectives hold several attractions. As you might imagine, most psychologists admire the learning approach to personality because it meets most standards for scientific research. It offers testable, objective hypotheses and operationally defined terms and relies on empirical data for its basic principles. In addition, it has been successfully used to change many maladaptive or abnormal behaviors (see Chapter 16).

Critics of learning theory, however, believe behavioral and social learning theories are too narrow, focusing only on observable behaviors and ignoring genetic, physiological, and cognitive factors in personality. Learning theorists have been criticized for considering people merely the sum of what they have learned, nothing more. Behaviorists, in particular, have been accused of taking the *person* out of personality and viewing the organism as "empty" (Phares, 1984). The individual personality, critics argue, also reflects unique perceptions, values, beliefs, and free-will intentions. Critics who stress these aspects of the personality usually take a humanistic approach, the topic of our next section.

Review Questions

1. Learning theorists believe personality is situationally specific. What does this mean?
2. How do learning theorists account for consistent responses and personality traits?
3. How does a behaviorist explain shyness?
4. _____ theories emphasize the effects of observing others on personality development.
5. What are the major attractions and criticisms of learning theories of personality?

Answers to Review Questions can be found in Appendix C.

HUMANISTIC THEORIES

The humanistic orientation is known as the "third force" in psychology because it developed as a reaction to both psychoanalytic and learning theories. The humanistic perspective on personality offers a distinctly different approach from the pessimism of psychoanalysts such as Freud and the "mindless" approach of behaviorism (Rogers, 1980). Humanistic theories approach the study of personality from the "inside out," emphasizing internal experiences—feelings and thoughts—and the basic worth of the individual human being.

From a humanistic perspective people are basically good (or, at worst, neutral), and they possess a positive drive toward self-fulfillment. Humanistic approaches to personality are sometimes referred to collectively as the phenomenological perspective. This means that each individual's personality is created out of his or her unique way of perceiving and interpreting the world. Behavior is controlled by the individual's perception of reality, not by traits, unconscious impulses, or rewards and punishments. Since

• *What characterizes the humanistic theories of personality?*

Phenomenological Perspective: The view that understanding another person requires knowing how he or she perceives the world. The term comes from philosophy, where the mental experiencing of the environment is called a phenomenon, and the study of how each person experiences reality is *phenomenology.*

there is no external, objective *reality,* to fully understand another human being you must know how he or she perceives the world. Humanistic psychology was developed largely through the writings and efforts of Carl Rogers and Abraham Maslow.

Carl Rogers: The Self-Concept Theory of Personality

To humanistic psychologist Carl Rogers (1902–1987), the most important component of personality is the *self,* that part of experience that a person comes to identify early in life as "I" or "me." This concept is known today as the self-concept, and it refers to all the information and beliefs you have as an individual regarding your own nature, unique qualities, and typical behaviors. Rogers was very concerned with the match between a person's self-concept and his or her actual experiences with life. He believed poor mental health and maladjustment developed from an *incongruence* or disparity between the self-concept and actual life experiences (see Figure 14.8).

Self-Concept: In Rogers's theory, all the information and beliefs individuals have about their own nature, qualities, and behavior.

Mental Health, Congruence, and Self-Esteem

According to Rogers, there is an intimate connection between mental health, congruence, and self-esteem—how we feel about ourselves. If our self-concept is congruent with our life experiences, we have high self-esteem and generally good mental health and adjustment. These three states (mental health, congruence, and self-esteem) are also part of our innate, biological capacities. Each of us is born into the world with an innate need to survive, grow, and enhance ourselves (Hergenhahn, 1990). We naturally approach and value people and experiences that enhance our growth and fulfillment and avoid those that don't. Therefore, Rogers believed we can—and *should*—trust our own internal feelings to guide us toward mental health and happiness.

Self-Esteem: According to Rogers, the feelings each of us has about ourselves, either good or bad.

If everyone has an inborn, positive drive toward self-fulfillment, why do some people have low self-esteem and poor mental health? Rogers believed these states generally result from early childhood experiences with parents and other adults who make their love *conditional.* That is, children learn that their acceptance is contingent upon behaving in certain ways and expressing only certain feelings. When affection and love seem conditional, children will block out the existence of negative impulses and feelings (which others label as "bad"), and their self-concepts and self-esteem become distorted. If a child is angry and hits his younger brother, for example, some parents might punish the older child or deny his anger, saying "Nice children don't hit their brothers, they love them!" To gain parental approval, the child has to block out his true feelings of anger, which damages his self-esteem. He is obviously not "nice" since he *did* hit his sibling and he felt anger toward his brother instead of love.

Carl Rogers, on the right, is one of the major figures in humanistic theories of personality.

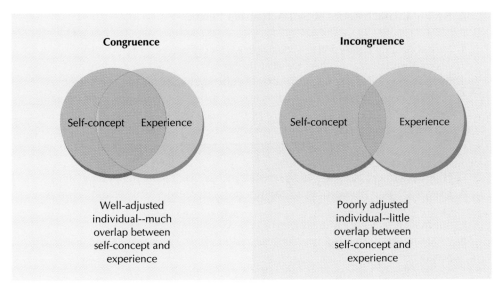

Congruence   Incongruence

Self-concept   Experience   Self-concept   Experience

Well-adjusted   Poorly adjusted
individual--much   individual--little
overlap between   overlap between
self-concept and   self-concept and
experience   experience

Figure 14.8 Self-Concept and Adjustment. According to Rogers, your mental health is directly related to the degree of congruence between your self-concept and life experiences. If your self-concept is reasonably consistent and overlaps with actual life experiences, the self is said to be congruent and the person is "well-adjusted." The reverse is true when there is little overlap and incongruity.

Unconditional Positive Regard

To help a child develop to fullest potential, adults need to create an atmosphere of unconditional positive regard—a setting in which children realize that they will be accepted no matter what they say or do. According to child expert Thomas Gordon:

> *Acceptance is like the fertile soil that permits a tiny seed to develop into the lovely flower it is capable of becoming. The soil only* enables *the seed to become the flower. It* releases *the capacity of the seed to grow, but the capacity is entirely within the seed. As with the seed, a child contains entirely within this organism the capacity to develop. Acceptance is like the soil—it merely enables the child to actualize his potential.*
>
> Gordon (1975), p. 31

Does unconditional positive regard and acceptance mean that we should allow people to do whatever they please? Humanists are often misinterpreted as being advocates of wholesale acceptance of all behaviors, good and bad. Actually, however, humanists separate the value of the person from his or her behaviors. They still accept the person's positive nature while believing that specific self-destructive or hostile behaviors of the person should be limited, not encouraged. Hitting a playmate or grabbing a friend's toy is contrary to the child's positive nature as well as offensive to others. Such actions reveal that the child has not learned effective ways to behave. Children need appropriate guidance in controlling their behavior, which will enable them to develop a healthy self-concept as well as healthy relationships with others. One way to provide such guidance is to allow individuals, at whatever age, to communicate their feelings to someone who takes time to listen and appreciate their experiences. This can be provided by parents and friends, as well as by professional therapists. In Chapter 16, we will describe the humanistic therapy approach based on this premise.

Abraham Maslow: The Search for Self-Actualization

Like Rogers, Abraham Maslow believed there is a basic goodness to human nature and a natural tendency toward self-actualization. He saw personality as the expression of this tendency.

What exactly is "self-actualization"? According to Maslow, self-actualization is the inborn drive to develop all one's talents and capacities. It involves understanding one's own potential, accepting oneself and others as unique individuals, and using a problem-centered approach to situations (Maslow, 1970). Self-actualization is an ongoing process

Unconditional Positive Regard: Rogers's term for how we should behave toward someone to increase his or her self-esteem; positive behavior shown toward a person with no contingencies attached.

Self-Actualization: According to Maslow, an innate tendency toward growth that motivates all human behavior and results in the full realization of a person's highest potential.

Table 14.4   Characteristics of Self-Actualized People

1. Perceive reality clearly and are comfortable with uncertainty.
2. Accept themselves and others for what they are.
3. Spontaneous in behavior, motivated by the attempt to develop their own style.
4. Problem-centered rather than self-centered, focusing on accomplishing unselfish tasks.
5. Enjoy solitude and make decisions privately.
6. Maintain an inner serenity in unpleasant circumstances and when dealing with social pressures.
7. Have a continued freshness of appreciation rather than taking things for granted.
8. Experience peak experiences, or feelings of transcendence and intense joy in basic experiences of life.
9. Affectionately identify with other people.
10. Establish deep, satisfying interpersonal relationships with a few, rather than many, people.
11. Are democratic and unprejudiced in dealing with others.
12. Are strongly ethical in behavior as well as attitudes.
13. Have a spontaneous, unhostile sense of humor.
14. Are creative.
15. Resist enculturation, although not purposely unconventional.

Source: Maslow (1970).

of growth rather than an end-product or accomplishment—such as winning a trophy or graduating from college. Table 14.4 summarizes the characteristics of self-actualized people.

Although Maslow believed that only a few, rare individuals, such as Abraham Lincoln, Albert Einstein, and Eleanor Roosevelt, ever fully achieve self-actualization, he saw it as part of every person's basic hierarchy of needs. As we discussed in the chapter on motivation and emotion, self-actualization is seen by Maslow as more of a journey or a way of life than as a final goal.

Evaluating Humanistic Theories: Three Major Criticisms

Humanistic psychology was extremely popular during the 1960s and 1970s. Following the negative determinism of the psychoanalytic approach and the mechanistic flavor of learning theories, the humanistic/phenomenological approach offered a refreshing new perspective on personality. While this early popularity has declined, interest in the *self* as a central concept in personality persists today (Hergenhahn, 1990; Markus and Nurius, 1986).

Despite its positive contributions, the humanistic theories have also been subject to intense criticism. Three of the most important criticisms are:

1. *Naive assumptions.* Critics have suggested that the humanists have been unrealistic, romantic, and even naive about human nature. Are all people as inherently good as this approach suggests? Our continuing history of murders, warfare, and other acts of aggression suggests otherwise.

2. *Poor testability and inadequate evidence.* Like many psychoanalytic terms and concepts, humanistic ideas such as unconditional positive regard and self-actualization are difficult to operationally define and scientifically test.

3. *Narrowness.* Similar to the complaints about dispositional theories, humanistic theories have been criticized for merely describing personality—rather than explaining it. For example, where does the motivation for self-

actualization come from? To say that it is an "inborn drive" doesn't satisfy those who favor experimental research and hard data as the way to learn about personality.

Review Questions

1. The _____ approach is known as the "third force" in psychology.
2. What is Carl Rogers's idea of a "self-concept"?
3. Abraham Maslow's belief that all people are motivated toward personal growth and development is known as _____ .
4. What are the three major criticisms of humanistic theories?

Answers to Review Questions can be found in Appendix C.

OTHER APPROACHES TO PERSONALITY

Two of the most important advances in personality research have been in the areas of cognition and biology. In this section, we will take a brief look at the personality theories generated from the *cognitive* and *biological perspectives* and conclude with the approach called *interactionism*.

• What are the cognitive and biological perspectives on personality? How does the interactionist approach pull it all together?

Cognitive Perspectives: Bandura's and Rotter's Contributions

According to the cognitive perspective, each of us has a unique personality because we *think* about the world and interpret things that happen to us in distinctive and unique ways. Two of the most influential psychologists who have contributed to our understanding of the role of cognition in personality are Albert Bandura and Julian Rotter.

Bandura's Social Cognitive Theory

Although Albert Bandura is perhaps best known for his work on observational learning or social learning, he has also played a major role in reintroducing thought processes into personality theory. The importance of cognition is central to his concept of self-efficacy, which refers to a person's learned expectation of success (Bandura, 1977, 1982). How do you generally perceive your personal chances of being able to select, influence, and control the circumstances of your life? According to Bandura, if you have a strong sense of self-efficacy, you believe you can generally succeed, regardless of past failures and current obstacles. This belief will in turn affect the challenges you accept and the effort you expend in reaching goals.

Self-Efficacy: According to Bandura, a person's belief about whether he or she can successfully engage in behaviors related to personal goals.

Doesn't such a belief also affect how others respond to you and thereby your chances for success? Precisely! This type of mutual interaction and influence is a core part of another major concept of Bandura's—reciprocal determinism. According to Bandura, our cognitions (or thoughts), behaviors, and the environment are all interdependent and interactive (see Figure 14.9). Thus, a cognition ("I can succeed") will affect behaviors ("I will ask for a promotion"), which in turn will affect the environment (I become an executive), which then affects cognitions ("I am a success"), and so on.

Reciprocal Determinism: Bandura's observation that the individual's cognitions and behaviors and the learning environment interact and continually influence one another.

Rotter's Locus of Control

Julian Rotter's theory is similar to Bandura's in suggesting that learning creates cognitive *expectancies* that guide behavior and influence the environment (Rotter, 1954, 1990). According to Rotter, your behavior or personality is determined by (1) what you

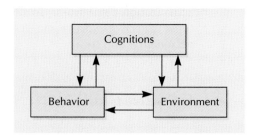

Figure 14.9 *Bandura's Theory of Reciprocal Determinism.* According to Bandura, thoughts (or cognitions), behavior, and the environment all interact to produce personality.

Locus of Control: According to Rotter, a person's belief and expectancy regarding the control of events. A person with an *internal* locus of control believes he or she is in charge, whereas a person with an *external* locus of control believes the environment, chance, or fate determines outcomes.

expect to happen following a specific action, and (2) the *reinforcement value* attached to specific outcomes—the degree to which you prefer one reinforcer over another.

To understand your personality and behavior, Rotter would want to determine your expectancies, and what you see as the source of life's rewards and punishments. To do this, Rotter would use the personality test he developed which consists of a series of statements that measure a respondent's internal or external locus of control.

 Try This Yourself

Before we further discuss locus of control, answer "yes" or "no" to the following questions:

1. Do you believe that people get ahead in this world primarily by luck and connections rather than their own hard work and perseverance?

2. Do you feel that when someone doesn't like you there is little you can do about it?

3. Do you believe that no matter how hard you study you will not be able to get high grades in most classes?

4. Have you ever kept a rabbit's foot or special object as a good-luck charm?

5. Have you refused to vote because you believe that little can be done to control what politicians do in office? ∎

How did you do? These few questions are better predictors of locus of control than you might think. On several occasions we have asked students in our classes to answer these questions and we have administered Rotter's complete 32-item locus of control personality test. Students who answer "yes" to four or more of these questions tend to score as "externals" on Rotter's scale and those who answer "no" to four or more tend to score as "internals." As you may suspect, externals think environment and external forces have primary control over their lives, whereas internals think they can control events in their lives through their own efforts.

Both Bandura's and Rotter's theories emphasize cognition and social learning, but they are a long way from a strict behavior theory, which suggests that only environmental forces control behavior. They are also a long way from the biological theories, which say inborn, innate qualities determine behavior and personality.

Biological Theories: A Genetic Approach to Personality

Have you ever wondered why some people are extremely shy and withdrawn? What makes someone so afraid of being with others? While learning and cognitive theorists might explain shyness on the basis of past reinforcements, punishments, and current thinking patterns, biological theories propose several exciting alternative answers. Some studies have shown, for example, that shy children show intense physiological responses to unexpected changes in the environment (Adler, 1993; Kagan, Reznick, and Snidman, 1988). These responses are believed to be due to an inherited variation in the response to social and physical stimulation, with shy people having a lower threshold of arousal than people who aren't shy.

The idea that psychological characteristics such as shyness may be inherited has gained considerable attention as a result of research being done at the Minnesota Center for Twin and Adoption Research. Since 1979 literally hundreds of sets of twins have been tested at this center. The most recent findings of Tellegren and his colleagues (1988) suggest that the old nature versus nurture debate may have taken a decisive turn. Using a test of 11 traits, the researchers found that about 50 percent of the variation in personality was attributable to heredity, whereas nurture or the environment accounted for only about 20 to 35 percent (the remaining percentage could not be accounted for experimentally). Heritability was the primary predictor of the personality traits of aggressiveness, need for achievement, vulnerability to stress, and proneness to imaginative activities. It was particularly surprising to find that *traditionalism,* or commitment to traditional moral and family values, did not show the expected familial or environmental effect. Instead, it was primarily related to genetics.

Researchers are cautious about overemphasizing the genetic basis of personality (Hoffman, 1991; Plomin, 1990; Rose et al., 1988). For example, some fear that this latest research on "genetic determinism" could be misused to "prove" that some races are inferior, that male dominance is natural, and that social progress is impossible (Wellborn, 1987). There is no doubt that genetic discussions have produced some of the most exciting and controversial results, but it is also clear that more high-quality research is necessary before we will have a cohesive biological theory of personality.

Interactionism: Pulling the Perspectives Together

When it comes to personality, no one theory has been shown to be more accurate or correct than the others. Each provides a different perspective and offers different insights into how a person develops the distinctive set of characteristics we call "personality." In fact, instead of adhering to any one theory, many psychologists take an approach called *interactionism.* Even some psychologists who have done major research in one area of personality theory lean toward interactionism.

Eysenck (1990), for example, considered one of the leaders of the dispositional or trait theory of personality, thinks certain traits may have a biological basis. He tied differences in introversion and extroversion to inherited characteristic variations in cortical arousal. In addition, Eysenck suggests that learning and experience also shape personality. Someone with an introverted personality, and therefore a higher level of cortical arousal, might try to avoid excessive stimulation by seeking friends and jobs with low stimulation levels.

Eysenck is a good example of how dispositional, biological, and learning theories can be combined to provide a better insight into personality. The trend toward integrating diverse approaches is reflected in a growing number of books and articles, and in decreased polarization on certain issues. For example, the "either/or" debate between trait theorists and situational determinists that we discussed earlier in the chapter seems to be resolving itself toward an interactionist position. That is not to say the interactionist position is a compromise. Rather, it is a blending of views based on research findings. Scientific progress often results from intense, ongoing critical debate because it provokes research and the more research we do, the more we learn (Houts, Cook, and Shadish, 1986).

Review Questions

1. How does cognitive theory explain personality?
2. Albert Bandura used the term _____ to refer to a person's learned expectation of success.
3. How does Julian Rotter explain personality?

4. In Rotter's locus of control concept, _____ expect the environment and external forces to control events, while _____ believe in personal control.

5. What concerns people about biological explanations for personality?

6. The _____ approach represents a blending of all the major theories of personality.

Answers to Review Questions can be found in Appendix C.

PERSONALITY ASSESSMENT

• *How do psychologists measure personality?*

Phrenology: Pseudoscience that measures the skull to determine personality characteristics.

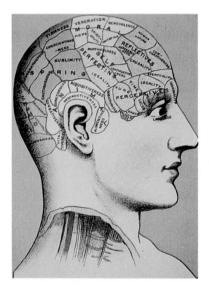

Franz Gall, founder of phrenology, believed that personality could be measured by "reading" the bumps on different areas of the skull. Note that "destructiveness" was believed to be located above the right ear, while "conscientiousness" was near the top of the skull.

Back in the 1800s, if you wanted to have your personality assessed, your best bet was to go to a phrenologist. This highly respected person would carefully measure your skull, examine the bumps on your head, and then give you a psychological profile of your unique qualities and characteristics (Reuder, 1984). Phrenologists used a phrenology chart to determine which personality traits were associated with bumps on different areas of the skull. Today personality differences are assessed more scientifically. Personality assessment involves interviews, observation, self-report, and projective tests.

How do we know these modern methods are any better than phrenology? You might very well be suspicious of the accuracy of current testing methods in light of the fact that there are so many differing theories of personality. You have no doubt also been bombarded with so-called personality tests in popular magazines and supermarket tabloids. You may even have taken official personality tests as part of a job or school selection process. Fortunately, there are scientific standards to judge the value of any psychological test, including personality tests.

The two main standards for evaluating tests are reliability and validity. As explained in Chapter 8, *reliability* is a measure of the stability of test scores over time. Reliability measures the extent to which a test gives similar scores with retesting. If an individual's score on a given personality test varies significantly from one testing to another, the test is considered *un*reliable. *Validity*, on the other hand, is the extent to which a test measures what it was designed to measure rather than some other dimension. If we develop a test for extroversion, for instance, we have to provide some evidence that it really measures outgoingness and sociability rather than assertiveness or aggressiveness. Every item on every standardized psychological personality test has been measured by teams of psychologists for reliability and validity. That's how we know it is better today to take a personality test than to have the bumps on your head read.

Interviews and Observational Methods: Listening and Watching

When you want to know more about people's personalities, you talk to them or watch them in action. Psychologists use these same methods, but on a more sophisticated level. These methods are known as interviews and observations.

Psychological interviews may be either structured or unstructured. Unstructured interviews are often used for job and college selections and for diagnosing psychological problems. In an unstructured format, interviewers get impressions and pursue hunches or let a person expand on information that promises to disclose personality characteristics. The interviewee has a chance to explain unique qualifications in his or her own words. Structured interviews, on the other hand, ask specific questions and follow a set procedure so that the person being evaluated can be compared more objectively. The results of a structured interview are often charted on a rating scale to standardize the evaluations for comparison purposes.

In addition to structured or unstructured interviews, psychologists also use direct behavioral observations to assess personality. Most of us enjoy "people watching" on college campuses, at airports, and in other public places. When used as an official assessment procedure, however, the psychologist is looking for examples of specific behaviors and following a careful set of evaluation guidelines. For instance, a psychologist might arrange to observe a troubled client's interactions with his or her family. Does the client become agitated by the presence of certain family members and not others? Does he or she become passive and withdrawn when asked a direct question? Through careful observation, the psychologist gains valuable insights into the client's personality characteristics.

Objective Tests: Paper-and-Pencil Self-Reports

By far the most widely used method for assessing personality is the objective test. Objective tests are paper-and-pencil questionnaires or inventories that ask people to describe themselves—or self-report. These tests are called *objective* because they have a limited range of possible responses to items and empirical standards for constructing test items and scoring.

You have been introduced to several self-report personality tests in this textbook. There was the locus of control scale in this chapter and the sensation-seeking scale in Chapter 12. The complete versions of these tests measure one specific personality trait and are used primarily in research. Psychologists in clinical, counseling, and industrial settings, however, are interested in assessing a range of personality traits all at once. To do this they generally use *multitrait* (or multiphasic) inventories.

Many multitrait tests have been developed, including the Millon Clinical Multiaxial Inventory (MCMI), the Sixteen Personality Factors Questionnaire (16PF), and the California Psychological Inventory (CPI). Perhaps the most widely used multitrait test is the Minnesota Multiphasic Personality Inventory (MMPI).

The MMPI was first developed during the 1930s at the University of Minnesota by Starke Hathaway and J. C. McKinley. The test consists of over five hundred statements that subjects respond to with "True," "False," or "Cannot say." The following are examples of the kinds of statements found on the MMPI:

> My stomach frequently bothers me.
> I have enemies that really wish to harm me.
> I sometimes hear things that other people can't hear.
> I would like to be a mechanic.
> I have never indulged in any unusual sex practices.

Why are most of the questions about abnormal behavior?   Although there *are* many so-called "normal" questions on the full MMPI, it is primarily designed for clinical and counseling psychologists to diagnose psychological disorders. As you can see in Table 14.5, MMPI test items are grouped into ten *clinical scales,* each measuring a different disorder. Depressed people, for example, tend to score higher on one group of questions, while people with schizophrenia score higher on a different group. These groups of items are called *scales.* There are also four *validity scales* designed to reflect the extent to which respondents distort their answers, do not understand the items, or are being uncooperative.

The MMPI has recently undergone a major revision and modernization, known as the MMPI-2 (Butcher et al., 1989; Graham, 1990). Although more than 250 items have been added, deleted, or changed, the 10 clinical scales are essentially unchanged. Early reports from clinicians who have used the MMPI-2 have been generally positive (Buie, 1989).

Vocational Interest Tests

In addition to the various personality tests, you may be interested in self-report tests called *vocational interest tests.*

Table 14.5   Subscales of the MMPI-2

Name of Subscale	Typical Interpretations of High Scores
Clinical scales	
Hypochondriasis	Numerous physical complaints
Depression	Seriously depressed
Hysteria	Suggestible, immature, self-centered, demanding
Psychopathic deviancy	Rebellious, nonconformist
Masculinity/Femininity	Artistic interests, effeminate
Paranoia	Suspicious and resentful of others
Psychasthenia	Fearful, agitated, brooding
Schizophrenia	Withdrawn, seclusive, bizarre thinking
Mania	Distractable, impulsive, dramatic
Social introversion	Shy, introverted, self-effacing
Validity scales	
L (lie)	Denial of common problems, "saintliness," presenting a false picture
F (confusion)	Validity of profile is doubtful
K (defensiveness)	Minimizes social and emotional complaints
? (cannot say)	Number of items left unanswered

Are these the tests that ask you what sorts of things you like to do?   Yes, that is one type of vocational interest test. For example, the Strong Vocational Interest Blank (Darley, 1984), asks whether you would rather write, illustrate, print, or sell a book. This is a self-report test that compares the things you like to do to the responses of people in various occupational groups.

Given your vocational interest test profile along with your scores on *aptitude tests* (which measure potential abilities) and *achievement tests* (which measure what you have already learned), a counselor can help you identify the types of jobs that best suit you. Most colleges have vocational interests tests in their career centers that you may use in guiding your career decisions.

Projective Techniques: Ambiguous Stimuli and Personality Assessment

Projective Tests: Techniques for assessing personality in which the individual is asked to talk about a relatively ambiguous or neutral stimulus (such as an inkblot). It is believed that inner thoughts, feelings, and conflicts will be projected onto the stimulus.

Unlike objective tests, projective tests use ambiguous, unstructured stimuli, such as inkblots, which can be perceived in many ways. For example, if you look at the card the woman is holding in Figure 14.10, what do you see? The idea behind projective tests is

Figure 14.10 The Rorschach (or "Ink blot") Test. The Rorschach is a major type of projective test. Subjects are asked to tell what the blot might mean and to explain why. Their responses are believed to reflect unconscious aspects of their personality.

Figure 14.11 The Thematic Apperception Test (TAT). Like the Rorschach, the TAT is a projective test that reportedly uncovers unconscious parts of the personality. Subjects are asked to explain what led up to the pictured situation, what is happening now, and how the story will end.

that different people exposed to the same ambiguous stimuli report something different. Each person supposedly "projects" himself or herself into the ambiguous stimulus, thus revealing important parts of his or her personality. Two of the most widely used projective tests are the Rorschach and the TAT.

The Rorschach Test

Hermann Rorschach (1884–1922) was a Swiss psychiatrist who got the idea for his now-famous Rorschach inkblot test while riding in the countryside with his two children. He was struck by the fact that what his children saw in the cloud patterns revealed their personality differences. As a result, he created a series of 10 cards with black and gray or colored inkblots on them as a projective test for his patients.

Rorschach Inkblot Test: A projective personality test using ambiguous "inkblots." The individual tells the examiner what he or she sees in the blots and, it is hoped, reveals hidden aspects of his or her personality.

A person taking the Rorschach test is instructed to tell what each blot looks like or might be. On the average, subjects give about 30 to 40 responses to the card series. These responses are then evaluated on several dimensions, including content, areas of the cards described, and appropriateness. Because subjects can reply in any way they wish, their responses are often difficult to interpret, so the reliability and validity of the Rorschach are low (Anastasi, 1982). Despite these problems, some therapists, especially Freudians, continue to use the inkblots on the assumption that they reveal unconscious processes unable to be evaluated in other ways.

The Thematic Apperception Test

The Thematic Apperception Test (TAT) was created by personality researcher Henry Murray in 1938 and is still one of the most widely used projective tests worldwide (Piotrowski and Keller, 1989). It consists of a series of cards like the one in Figure 14.11, an ambiguous scene, usually with people.

Thematic Apperception Test (TAT): A projective personality test requiring subjects to tell stories about pictures shown on cards. Presumably, the subjects will "project" themselves into the story, and their narrative will reflect their hidden needs.

 Try This Yourself

If you are interested in experiencing what it might be like to take the TAT test, imagine you have just been shown the following drawing:

Try to tell as complete a story as possible as you answer the following questions:

1. What led up to the event in the picture?
2. What is happening now?
3. What is each of these people thinking and feeling?
4. What will happen next?

Now compare your responses with this student's:

> *The guy and the girl just had a fight, and she's getting ready to walk away. The guy is worried that she won't come back this time because she seems really mad and different from previous times. They often have fights about his lack of attention and insensitivity, but he genuinely doesn't know what she wants. He has dated lots of girls, but he can never find someone who will stay with him. He'll probably decide to break up with her so she can't do it first.*

It's interesting to compare your story with the other student's and wonder what the differences tell about your respective personalities. But it is important to remember that extensive education and training are required to accurately interpret projective tests. Today, the Rorschach and TAT are primarily used by psychoanalytically trained therapists. They believe, in the case of the TAT, that respondents identify with the main character and project their psychological needs and conflicts into the story they tell. Psychologist David McClelland (1958, 1985) has also used the TAT to measure motives, such as the need for achievement and power (see Chapter 12). ▪

Evaluating Personality Tests: Objective versus Projective Techniques

All tests, whether objective or projective, have certain strengths and weaknesses. Objective tests like the MMPI-2, for example, provide precise, objective information about a broad range of personality traits in a relatively short period of time. The accuracy of these tests, however, is based on the assumption that the respondent is cooperative and answers truthfully. Although the MMPI does have *validity scales* specifically designed to detect "faking" and uncooperativeness, it remains, like other objective, self-report inventories, subject to three major criticisms:

1. *Deliberate deception and social desirability bias.* Some items on self-report inventories are easy to "see through" and respondents may intentionally, or unintentionally, fake particular personality traits. In addition, some respondents want to "look good" and will answer questions in ways that they perceive as *socially desirable*.

2. *Diagnostic difficulties.* When self-report inventories are used for diagnosis, overlapping items sometimes make it difficult to pinpoint a diagnosis (Graham, 1991). In addition, clients with severe disorders sometimes score within the normal range and normals may score within the elevated range (Cronbach, 1990).

3. *Inappropriate use.* Perhaps the major problem with self-report inventories is their increasing use in business and government for such purposes as job screening, promotions, determining honesty, and so on. While psychologists are well aware of the limitations of these tests, nonprofessional test administrators often are not and errors and abuses do occur.

In contrast to objective tests, proponents of projective tests say that because their tests have no right or wrong answers, respondents are less able to deliberately deceive or fake their responses. In addition, since these tests are unstructured, respondents may be more willing to talk about sensitive, anxiety-laden topics. Some psychologists, primarily psychoanalysts, also believe that these tests offer unique methods for accessing the unconscious, hidden aspects of personality.

Critics point out, however, that the reliability and validity of projective tests is among the lowest of all tests of personality. One problem with the Rorschach, in particular, is that interpreting the clients' responses depends in large part on the subjective judgment of the examiner and some examiners are simply more experienced or skilled than others. Also there are problems with *interrater* reliability. Two examiners may interpret the same response in very different ways. However, attempts to develop a comprehensive, standardized scoring system for the Rorschach are meeting with some success (Exner and Weiner, 1982).

In summary, just as there are many theories about the causes and correlates of personality, there are also many methods for assessment. Rather than being clearly in

Table 14.6   A Comparison of Major Personality Theories and Assessment Techniques

Theory	Major Proponents	Determinants of Personality	Major Concepts	Methods of Assessment
Dispositional *Type*	Hippocrates, Galen, Sheldon	Individual characteristics or dispositions	Bodily humors, somatotypes	Interviews, observation
Trait	Allport, Cattell, Eysenck	Individual characteristics or dispositions	Cardinal, central, and secondary traits	Interviews, observation, objective (self-report) tests
Psychoanalytic	Freud	Unconscious drives, intrapsychic conflicts, and psychosexual development	Conscious, preconscious, unconscious, id, ego, superego, defense mechanisms	Interviews, projective tests, observation
	Adler, Jung, Horney	Similar to Freud, but more emphasis on social and cultural factors	Inferiority complex, will-to-power, collective unconscious, archetypes, basic anxiety, power envy	Interviews, projective tests, observation, objective (self-report) tests
Learning	Watson, Skinner	Learning from direct experiences and watching others	Rewards, punishments, modeling	Observation, objective (self-report) tests, interviews
Humanistic	Rogers, Maslow	Subjective perception of reality	Self-concept, conditions of worth, unconditional positive regard, self-esteem, self-actualization	Interviews, objective (self-report) tests
Cognitive	Bandura, Rotter	Cognitive interpretation of events	Reciprocal determinism, self-efficacy, locus of control	Interviews, objective (self-report) tests
Biological	Kagan et al., Tellegren et al.	Body chemistry, genetic inheritance	Genetic inheritance	Observation, surveys for genetic inheritance, objective (self-report) tests

one camp or another, most psychologists and clinicians consider themselves *eclectic*—borrowing or choosing from several sources. Skilled clinicians generally use a *battery* (or group) of tests and interviews, as well as observation, to create a detailed and comprehensive picture of a client's unique personality.

That professionals prefer an eclectic approach can serve as a good model for you as a student of psychology and a critical thinker. Rather than trying to decide which theory or method is the "best," recognize the contributions each has made to our understanding of personality (see Table 14.6).

Gender and Cultural Diversity

CULTURAL CONCEPTS OF "SELF"

The concept of "self" is central to the field of personality: All of the major theorists describe a unique self, or individual, and all of the methods for assessing personality are designed to measure a unique self, or individual. But as a critical thinker and appreciator of diversity, do you see the Western bias in these theorists and their assessment tools? Do you see how the concepts of *conscious, preconscious, unconscious, id, ego, superego, inferiority complex, basic anxiety, self-concept, self-esteem, self-actualization* and so on all assume a "self" that is composed of discrete traits, types, motives, abilities, and so forth? Our Western perspective is an individualistic perspective: Personality is composed of individual *parts* (traits and motives), and the self is a bounded individual who is separate and autonomous from others (Berry et al., 1992).

But when we examine other cultures, we find that concepts of person and self are cultural constructions. For example, collectivist cultures in Asia do not see the self as a discrete entity, but as inherently linked to others. Relatedness, connectedness, and interdependence are valued, and people are described not by a set of enduring traits, but in terms of social relationships (Markus and Kitayama, 1991). The person is defined and understood primarily by looking at his or her place in the social unit.

If you are a member of an individualistic culture, such as the American or Western European, you may find the concept of a self defined in terms of others almost contradictory. If so, you are at one end of the spectrum—and very possibly a white male—because even within individualistic cultures women and minorities are likely to see themselves as intricately connected with others (Triandis, 1989).

In sum, most current theories and methods of assessing personality are heavily biased toward Western, individualistic cultures and their perception of the independent "self." Although this limits our understanding of personality in other cultures, recognizing that the field of personality is biased not only explains why some theories may not apply to all groups, it also encourages research across cultures. ■

Review Questions

1. Interviews can be _____ or _____ in format, enabling the interviewer to obtain informal impressions or specific, comparative ratings on interviewees.

2. Perhaps the most widely used objective self-report personality test is the _____ .

3. The use of ambiguous stimuli is most characteristic of which method of personality assessment?

4. How are the Rorschach and TAT used by clinicians?

5. What are the three major criticisms of objective personality assessment?

6. What is the major criticism of projective tests?

Answers to Review Questions can be found in Appendix C.

Critical Thinking

PSYCHOLOGY IN ACTION

RECOGNIZING PERSONAL BIASES
Popularized Personality Tests

Newspapers and magazines often present personality tests that claim to measure your sexual attractiveness, your chances for business success, or your marriageability quotient. Why are so many people attracted to these tests? One answer is that they aren't thinking critically about the concept of personality and the problems with its assessment.

Consider the following personality description. How well does it describe your own personality?

You have a strong need for other people to like you and admire you. You have a tendency to be critical of yourself. You have a great deal of unused capacity that you have not turned to your advantage. Although you have some personality weaknesses, you are generally able to compensate for them. You pride yourself on being an independent thinker and do not accept other opinions without satisfactory proof. Disciplined and self-controlled outside, you tend to be worrisome and insecure inside. At times you have serious doubts whether you have made the right decision or done the right thing. (Adapted from Ulrich, Stachnik, and Stainton, 1963.)

If you are like most college students, you probably found this description to be a fairly accurate portrayal of your personality. When students are told that the description is written specifically for them on the basis of previous psychological tests or astrological data, a high percentage rate the description *very* accurate. In fact, when given a choice between this fake assessment and a bona fide personality description based on scientifically designed tests, most people prefer the phony assessment (Hyman, 1981).

Why are people so gullible? There are four major reasons: the *Barnum effect*, the *fallacy of positive instances*, the *self-serving bias*, and *ad hoc explanations*.

The Barnum Effect

The Barnum effect is named after P. T. Barnum, the legendary circus promoter who said "Always have a little something for everybody" and "There's a sucker born every minute." Reread the personality description and you will see that it includes several ambiguous and general statements that fit almost everyone. Given the human tendency to overestimate one's own uniqueness, such general statements are easily accepted as pertaining especially to oneself.

The Fallacy of Positive Instances

Now reread the description and notice the number of times it contains both sides of a personality dimension ("You have a

strong need for other people to like you. . . . You pride yourself on being an independent thinker . . ."). As we discussed in Chapter 4, the "fallacy of positive instances" allows people to remember or notice instances that confirm their expectations and ignore the rest. People who believe in horoscopes can always find "Gemini" characteristics in a Gemini, but they fail to notice the times when the Gemini predictions "miss" or when the same Gemini traits appear in Scorpios or Leos.

The Self-Serving Bias

Read the personality description once again and compare it with any daily newspaper's horoscope predictions. Do you notice an overall flattering tone? Most nonscientific personality tests are also composed primarily of flattering personality traits. The "self-serving bias" (see Chapter 17) refers to the human tendency to prefer information that maintains our positive self-image. Research shows that the more favorable a personality description is, the more people believe it, and the more likely they are to perceive it as unique to themselves (Shavit and Shouval, 1980).

Ad Hoc Explanations

Finally, the use of "ad hoc explanations" works to maintain the belief in pseudosciences like astrology. "Ad hoc" is Latin for "special purpose." When horoscope descriptions don't seem to fit, it's easy to make up a special purpose explanation. Suppose you objected that you did *not* "have a strong need for other people to like and admire" you? A "talented" interpreter of horoscopes might offer this ad hoc explanation: "Given your exceptional talents and people skills, you automatically receive liking and admiration from others. Therefore, you just don't recognize how much you need and appreciate their approval." Ad hoc explanations make it impossible to logically refute astrological claims because even when they're wrong, they're right!

Taken together, you can see how these four fallacies help perpetuate a belief in "pop psych" personality tests. The tests offer "something for everyone" (the Barnum effect); we remember only those descriptions that confirm our expectations (the fallacy of positive instances); we like flattering descriptions (the self-serving bias); and any inconsistencies can be readily explained (ad hoc explanations). Be alert to these deceptive appeals. And remember that the best antidote to any form of nonscientific personality assessment is the active application of critical thinking.

REVIEW OF MAJOR CONCEPTS

1. Personality is defined as an individual's relatively stable and enduring pattern of thoughts, emotions, and behavior. Psychologists describe and explain personality differences according to different theoretical orientations.

DISPOSITIONAL THEORIES

2. For centuries, people have attempted to categorize personality into a few, discrete types. This approach has been largely unsuccessful.

3. Trait theorists believe personality can be identified by unique characteristics that fall along a continuum—rather than discrete, "either-or" type categories. Although the list of possible traits has historically been very long, recent research has found five major traits that can be used to describe most individuals.

PSYCHOANALYTIC THEORIES

4. The psychoanalytic, or psychodynamic, approach to personality was founded by Freud. Freud emphasized the power of the unconscious and believed that the mind (or psyche) functioned on three levels, the conscious, the preconscious, and the unconscious.

5. In Freud's theory, personality has three distinct parts, the id, ego, and superego. The ego struggles to meet the demands of the id and superego, and when these demands are in conflict the ego may resort to defense mechanisms to relieve the resultant anxiety.

6. According to Freud, all human beings pass through five psychosexual stages: the oral, anal, phallic, latency and genital. How the conflicts at each of these stages are resolved is important to personality development.

7. Followers of Freud, who later revised his theory, are known as neo-Freudians. Three of the most influential were Adler, Jung, and Horney. While they generally agreed with many of Freud's theories, they broke away because they emphasized different issues. Adler emphasized the "inferiority complex" and the compensating "will-to-power." Jung introduced the "collective unconscious" and "archetypes." Horney stressed the importance of "basic anxiety" and refuted Freud's idea of "penis envy," replacing it with "power envy."

8. Critics of the psychoanalytic approach, especially Freud's theories, argue that it cannot be scientifically tested, overemphasizes biology and unconscious forces, is based on a biased sampling, and has inadequate empirical support.

LEARNING THEORIES

9. Learning theories of personality take behaviorist and social learning approaches. They assume human nature is neutral and that personality patterns develop because of unique learning experiences.

10. Behaviorists such as Watson and Skinner emphasize the importance of observable behaviors and the consequences, whereas the social learning theorists emphasize observation and imitation of others.

11. Learning theories are criticized for their narrow focus on observable behaviors and their lack of attention to cognitive and biological factors in personality.

HUMANISTIC THEORIES

12. Humanistic theories emphasize internal experiences, thoughts and feelings that create the individual's self-concept. Humanists such as Carl Rogers and Abraham Maslow emphasize the potential for self-actualization when people receive acceptance or unconditional positive regard.

13. Critics of the humanistic approach argue that these theories are based on naive assumptions, and have poor scientific testability and inadequate empirical evidence. In addition, their focus on description, rather than explanation, makes them narrow.

OTHER APPROACHES TO PERSONALITY

14. Cognitive approaches, such as Bandura's social-cognitive theory and Rotter's locus of control theory, emphasize the importance of thoughts (expectancies, beliefs, values) on personality.

15. Biological theories emphasize inherited genetic components of personality. Research on twins and studies of specific traits such as shyness strongly support the biological approach.

16. The interactionist approach suggests that the major theories overlap and each contributes to our understanding of personality.

PERSONALITY ASSESSMENT

17. Psychologists use several methods to measure or assess personality, including interviews, observations, self-report inventories, and projective techniques. Reliability and validity are the two major criteria for assessing personality assessment techniques.

18. Personality is most commonly measured through objective tests (such as the MMPI-2), which ask test-takers to respond to paper-and-pencil questionnaires or inventories. These tests provide objective standardized information about a large number of personality traits. But they have been criticized for the possibility of deliberate deception and social desirability bias, diagnostic difficulties, and inappropriate use.

19. Projective tests are the second major category of personality assessment. They ask test-takers to respond to ambiguous stimuli (such as the Rorschach or "inkblot"). These tests are said to provide insight into unconscious elements of personality. Critics contend that these tests have unacceptably low levels of reliability and validity.

20. Most theories and methods of assessing personality are biased toward Western, individualistic cultures and their perception of the "self." Recognizing and understanding this bias helps keep our study of personality in perspective.

SUGGESTED READINGS

FREEMAN, A., & DEWOLF, R. (1992). *The ten dumbest mistakes smart people make and how to avoid them.* New York: HarperCollins. An engaging and informative book offering insight into the cognitive view of personality. It also provides self-help techniques for those who suffer from mistakes in thinking such as "perfectionism" or "catastrophizing."

FREUD, S. (1965). *The interpretation of dreams.* New York: Avon/Discus. (First German edition, 1900.) One of Freud's most popular books, it presents his analysis of common dream elements and offers readers a first-hand look at one of the pioneers in personality theory.

HERGENHAHN, B. R. (1990). *An introduction to theories of personality.* Englewood Cliffs, NJ: Prentice Hall. Hergenhahn presents an in-depth look at all the major personality theorists with interesting insights and details about the lives (and personalities) of famous psychologists.

PERVIN, L. A. (1993). *Personality: Theory and research (6th ed.).* New York: Wiley. A comprehensive, but highly readable, presentation of the basics of personality theory and the latest in personality research.

ROGERS, C. R. (1961). *On becoming a person.* Boston: Houghton Mifflin. One of Carl Rogers's earliest books; an interesting and clear presentation of the humanistic orientation.

TORREY, E. F. (1992). *Freudian fraud: The malignant effect of Freud's theory on American thought and culture.* New York: HarperCollins. A noted researcher and clinical psychologist examines the powerful, and destructive, impact Freud's theories have had on twentieth-century American thought and culture.

CHAPTER
15

Abnormal Behavior

OUTLINE

*M*aria, a 25-year-old legal secretary, was about to leave her office one evening when she was suddenly overwhelmed by intense feelings of anxiety. Believing that something dreadful and frightening was going to happen to her, she became flushed and found it difficult to breathe—almost as though she were choking. She stumbled outside for some fresh air and the feelings gradually subsided. As Maria later described her terror, "It could not be worse if I were hanging by my fingertips from the wing of a plane in flight. The feeling of impending doom was just as real and frightening."

Fishman and Sheehan (1985), p. 26

Jim is . . . a third year medical student. Over the last few weeks he has been noticing that older men appear to be frightened of him when he passes them on the street. Recently, he has become convinced that he is actually the director of the Central Intelligence Agency and that these men are secret agents of a hostile nation. Jim has found confirmatory evidence for his idea in the fact that a helicopter flies over his house every day at 8:00 a.m. and at 4:30 p.m. Surely, this surveillance is part of the plot to assassinate him.

Bernheim and Lewine (1979), p. 4

Ken Bianchi, the "Hillside Strangler," terrorized the Los Angeles area for more than a year. Working with his cousin, Angelo Buono, Bianchi used phony police badges to lure victims into his car or home where they were later raped, systematically tortured, and then murdered. Bianchi and Buono killed 10 females aged 12 to 28. Bianchi killed two more after moving to Washington state. After the longest trial in Los Angeles history, Bianchi was sentenced to life in prison. Presiding Judge Ronald M. George stated: "If ever there was a case where the death penalty was appropriate, this is that case. Angelo Buono and Kenneth Bianchi . . . abducted children and young women, torturing, raping and, finally, depriving their family and friends of them forever as they slowly squeezed out of their victims their last breath of air and their promise of a future life. And for what? The momentary, sadistic thrill of enjoying a brief perverted sexual satisfaction and the venting of their hatred of women."

Magid and McKelvey (1987), pp. 15–18

Paranoia: A mental disorder characterized by delusions, or mistaken beliefs, of persecution or grandeur.

Each of these individuals has a severe psychological problem, and each case raises interesting questions. What caused Maria's anxiety, Jim's paranoia, and Ken's cold-blooded murders? Was there something in their early backgrounds that could explain their later behaviors? Is there something medically wrong with each of them?

What about less severe forms of abnormal behavior? Is a person who dreams of airplane crashes and refuses to fly mentally ill? Does a compulsively neat student who types all his lecture notes and refuses to write in any textbook qualify for psychiatric examination? What is the difference between being eccentric and disordered? In short, how do we draw the line between normal and abnormal?

Of course, none of these questions can be answered simply. The best we can do is address the issues they raise. This chapter discusses the diverse definitions of abnormal behavior, examines historical perspectives on abnormal behavior, and provides an overview of the various categories of abnormal behavior. Using the classification system mental health specialists use, we present 7 representative psychological disorders found in our culture (anxiety, schizophrenia, mood disorders, dissociative disorders, somatoform disorders, personality disorders, and substance related disorders).

We conclude with a discussion of problems in classifying abnormal behavior and examine discrimination against the mentally disturbed. Chapter 16 is devoted to how various psychological disorders are professionally treated.

A cautionary note is in order before you read on. Talking about the symptoms for mental disorders and studying the details of specific categories of abnormal behavior sometimes create a psychological version of *medical student's disease* (the tendency of medical students to notice in themselves whatever symptoms they are studying at the time). As psychology students learn about abnormal behaviors, they typically begin to notice these very same abnormal characteristics in themselves and other people. When you read about depression, for example, you may wonder whether your occasional feelings of depression are abnormal. While it's easy to overreact, if you do become seriously concerned about any of the thoughts or feelings you have while studying this chapter, we suggest you seek the advice of your instructor or a counselor. On the other hand, studying about abnormal psychology also gives you an opportunity to evaluate the healthiness of your lifestyle and to adjust or change it when appropriate. As you will see here and in the next chapter, there are many effective ways to change problem behaviors.

As you read Chapter 15, keep the following **Survey** questions in mind and answer them in your own words:

- How do psychologists define abnormal behavior?
- What causes anxiety disorders?
- What are the major symptoms and causes of schizophrenia?
- When do disturbances in mood become abnormal?
- What causes dissociative disorders and other forms of abnormal behavior?
- What are the major problems with diagnosis and labeling?

STUDYING ABNORMAL BEHAVIOR

As the introductory cases show, abnormal behavior varies from person to person and in its severity. Arriving at a definition that covers such a range is difficult, and psychologists disagree on what exactly constitutes abnormal behavior, or psychopathology. We will define it as patterns of behavior (thoughts, feelings, or actions) that are maladaptive, disruptive, and/or harmful either for the person affected or for others.

Such a broad definition solves our first problem, but raises another: Where do you draw the line between normal and abnormal? While it is tempting to want to place people in tidy, discrete categories (crazy versus sane), abnormal behavior, like most behaviors, exists along a continuum. Normality and abnormality are located on a continuum of mental functioning, with one often shading into the other.

• How do psychologists define abnormal behavior?

Abnormal Behavior: Patterns of behavior that are maladaptive, disruptive, and/or harmful for the individual and/or society.

Would this behavior be considered abnormal? Although it is not statistically "normal"—few people collect this many buttons—the term abnormal behavior *is generally restricted to behavior that is maladaptive, disruptive, and/or harmful either to the person affected or others.*

Identifying Abnormal Behavior: Three Standards

When psychologists need to determine whether specific behaviors have moved from the normal end of the continuum into the abnormal, they rely upon three basic standards: statistical, subjective discomfort, and maladaptive functioning. Each of these standards can also be seen as existing along a continuum (see Figure 15.1).

Statistical Standard

Statistical Standard: Evaluates behavior as abnormal when it deviates from average behavior in that particular culture.

One way to judge whether a person's behavior is abnormal is to compare it to the ways other people in that culture behave. Although standards for normality vary from one culture to another, all cultures have expectations or norms for what is considered appropriate behavior. Individuals who do not adhere to these standards may be labeled mentally ill. When we use the model of "average" behavior in a given culture as our standard for deciding whether a behavior is abnormal, we are using a statistical standard. In our culture, for instance, it is considered abnormal for a man to wear a dress, bra, and nylons. Women, on the other hand, are allowed, and even encouraged by the "Dress for Success" standard, to dress in men's style clothing. According to the statistical standard, the same overt behavior (cross-sex dressing) is deemed acceptable for women and deviant for men.

Subjective Discomfort Standard

Subjective Discomfort Standard: Evaluates behavior as abnormal when the individual is discontented with his or her own psychological functioning.

Given the cultural relativity found in the statistical approach, some mental health professionals prefer to concentrate on the individual's own judgment of his or her current level of functioning and feelings. This subjective discomfort standard allows people to define for themselves what they individually accept as abnormal or normal. A moderate fear of snakes is statistically normal, for example, but a herpetologist might find this level of fear to be an obstacle to career advancement and might seek therapy to remove the fear. Since many people with alcohol-dependence disorders and most psychopaths don't see themselves as having psychological problems, however, the subjective discomfort standard, by itself, is not a sufficient basis for determining abnormality.

Maladaptive Functioning Standard

Maladaptive Functioning Standard: Evaluates behavior as abnormal when it interferes with an individual's functioning within his or her own life and within society.

A third alternative to the statistical and subjective discomfort approaches is the maladaptive functioning standard. According to this view, people are judged abnormal if their thoughts, feelings, or actions interfere with their ability to function in their own lives and within society. This approach is the primary standard for substance use (drug) disorders. Given the high use of recreational drugs in many cultures, the *statistical standard* could not be used for identifying many drug abusers. The *subjective discomfort standard* would not be appropriate for drug abusers who do not recognize their behaviors as problematic. According to the *maladaptive functioning* model, when the use of a

Figure 15.1 Normal and abnormal behavior. Normal and abnormal behaviors are not discrete categories but points along a continuum. Behavior is judged abnormal to the degree that it deviates from statistical norms, is personally distressing, or is maladaptive.

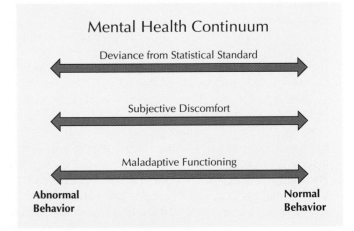

drug interferes with a person's normal social or occupational functioning, a substance use disorder exists. In this model, it is the maladaptive quality of the behavior that makes it disordered.

Each of the three approaches to defining abnormal behavior has its own advantages and disadvantages. Most mental health professionals alternate between these models in their approach to psychological disorders. The key points to remember about abnormal behavior are:

1. Normal and abnormal behavior are not discrete categories. They exist on a continuum. On occasion, we all step outside our cultural norms, experience subjective discomfort, and exhibit maladaptive behaviors. People are judged to have psychological disorders only when they engage in *extreme* behaviors on a fairly regular basis.

2. Diagnoses of abnormal behavior involve *value judgments.* As the following section on culture and mental health shows, whether behavior is judged normal or abnormal, appropriate or inappropriate, depends on the prevailing cultural values and social trends, as well as scientific knowledge.

Gender and Culture Diversity

CULTURE AND MENTAL HEALTH

Among the Chippewa, Cree, and Montagnais-Naskapi Indians in Canada, there is a malady called *windigo,* or *wiitiko, psychosis,* which is characterized by cannibalistic impulses and delusions. Affected individuals become severely depressed and believe they have been possessed by the spirit of a *windigo,* or cannibal giant with heart or entrails of ice (Barnouw, 1985). As the malady begins, the individual with windigo psychosis typically experiences a loss of appetite, diarrhea, vomiting, and insomnia and may see the people around him or her turning into beavers or other edible animals.

In later stages of the disorder, the affected individual becomes obsessed with cannibalistic thoughts, and family members often seek help from a shaman. This folk healer has the power to rid victims of their possession with special incantations and ceremonies that overpower the spell of the windigo spirit. If help is not sought in time, the victim may reach a frenzied state and attack and kill loved ones in order to devour their flesh (Berreman, 1971).

As you can see in Table 15.1, windigo psychosis is only one of many unique forms of mental disorders that have been reported around the world. These disorders are considered *culturally relative* because they are unique to specific cultures and understandable only in terms of that culture. In the case of windigo psychosis, for example, it has been suggested that the disorder developed particularly after fur trade competition depleted game that the Canadian tribes used for food, leading to widespread famine (Bishop, 1974). Facing starvation could have led to cannibalism and the subsequent "creation" of a windigo spirit. The belief in spirit possession is a common feature of many cultures, and in this case the people may have extended the belief to explain a socially and psychologically abhorrent behavior, cannibalism.

While some researchers question the famine explanation, there is little doubt that mental disorders do show some degree of cultural relativism. On the other hand, there are also indications that some mental disorders are *universal* (present in some form in all societies, but subject to cultural influence) (Berry et al., 1992).

Robert Nishimoto (1988), for example, has found several culture-general and culture-specific symptoms that are useful in diagnosing mental health difficulties. Using the Langer (1962) index of psychiatric symptoms, Nishimoto gathered data from three diverse groups, Anglo-Americans in Nebraska, Vietnamese-Chinese in Hong Kong, and Mexicans living in Texas and Mexico. (The Langer index is a screening instrument widely used to identify people who are not institutionalized but have psychological disorders that disrupt their everyday functioning.) When asked to think about their lives, respon-

Table 15.1 Examples of Culturally Relative Abnormal Behaviors

Culture	Disorder	Symptoms
Puerto Rican and other Latin cultures	*Ataque de nervios*	Trembling, heart palpitations, and seizure-like episodes often associated with the death of a loved one, accidents, or family conflict.
Southeast Asian, Malaysian, Indonesian, Thai	*Running Amok*	Wild, out-of-control, aggressive behaviors and attempts to injure or kill others.
South Chinese and Vietnamese	*Koro*	Belief that the penis is retracting into the abdomen, and when fully retracted death will result. Attempts to prevent the supposed retraction may lead to severe physical damage.
Westerners	*Anorexia Nervosa*	Eating disorder occurring primarily among young women in which a preoccupation with thinness produces a refusal to eat. This condition may result in death.

Source: Berry et al. (1992); Brislin (1993); Carson, Butcher and Coleman (1992); Guarnaccia, Good, and Kleinman (1990); Pfeiffer (1982); Simon and Hughes (1985).

dents in need of mental health services all named one or more of the same 12 symptoms (see Table 15.2).

In addition to the culture-general symptoms (such as "nervousness" or "trouble sleeping"), Nishimoto also found culture-specific symptoms. For example, the Vietnamese-Chinese reported "fullness in head," the Mexican respondents had "problems with my memory," and the Anglo-Americans reported "shortness of breath" and "headaches."

Why would there be culturally specific symptoms of mental disorders? People *learn* to express their problems in ways acceptable to others in the same culture (Brislin, 1993). For example, most Americans learn that headaches are a common response to stress, while Mexicans learn that complaints about memory will be understood by others in their culture. As you may imagine, it is very important that mental health professionals who work with culturally diverse populations understand that culturally general and culturally specific symptoms exist and what these are for any population.

Not only is there cultural variation in what constitutes abnormality, our concept of what is abnormal changes over time. Our next section examines historical views of abnormality. ■

Explaining Abnormality: From Superstition to Science

Over the ages, popular views of the causes of abnormal behavior have changed. In prehistoric times, people believed in the existence of good and evil spirits that made them see strange things and behave in unusual ways. During the Stone Age, for example, it was believed that demons could *possess* a person's body and soul, and the only recognized treatment was trephining. In this operation, stone instruments were used to chip away an area of the skull, presumably to allow the troublesome evil spirit to escape.

The *demonological model* of abnormality persisted until the fourth century B.C., when the Greek physician Hippocrates suggested a physical basis for behavior disorders. According to this early medical model, common problems such as epilepsy and depression were not seen as punishments from angry spirits but results of disease of the brain or body.

Trephining: In modern usage, any surgical procedure in which a hole is bored into the skull. In ancient times, a type of therapy that involved deliberate chipping of holes into the skull to allow evil spirits to escape.

Medical Model: Perspective that assumes abnormal behaviors reflect a type of mental or physical illness.

Table 15.2   Twelve Culture-General Symptoms of Mental Health Difficulties

Nervous	Trouble sleeping	Low spirits
Weak all over	Personal worries	Restless
Feel apart, alone	Can't get along	Hot all over
Worry all the time	Can't do anything worthwhile	Nothing turns out right

Source: Adapted from Brislin (1993).

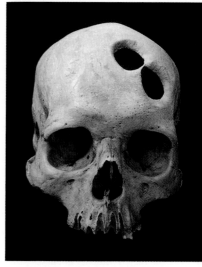

One of the earliest treatments for abnormal behavior was trephining. Holes were bored into the person's skull presumably to allow evil spirits to escape.

The Middle Ages

During the Middle Ages (from about the fifth to the fifteenth century A.D.), supernatural explanations for abnormal behavior once again dominated. This time the devil was the major evil spirit believed to possess people, and the afflicted person was treated with religious practices known as *exorcism*. Exorcism involved prayers, fasting, noisemaking, beatings, and drinking terrible-tasting brews. The idea was to make the body uncomfortable or uninhabitable by the devil (Davison and Neale, 1994).

During the fifteenth century, people became even more obsessed with the devil. Now, not only could you be possessed, you could also *choose* to consort with the devil. These "willing people" (usually women) were called witches and were tortured, imprisoned for life, or executed. A church manual published in 1484 called *Malleus Maleficarum* ("the witches hammer") described the characteristics of witches, which included sudden loss of reason, delusions, and hallucinations. Given these symptoms, many of the accused witches were probably mentally disturbed, but a large percentage were sane (Davison and Neale, 1994).

During "dunking tests" in the Middle Ages, individuals who behaved abnormally were dunked into local rivers or ponds. Due to the prevailing belief that abnormal behavior was caused by possession by demons, individuals who did not drown were believed to be possessed by the devil. Those who did drown were judged to be innocent.

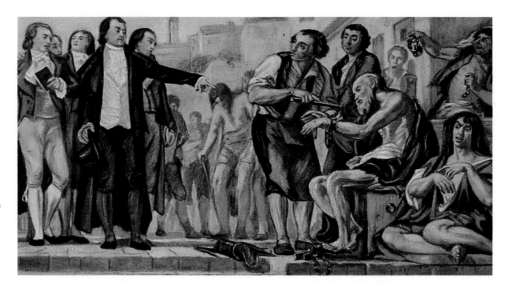

Phillipe Pinel was one of the first to believe that mental disorders have an underlying physical cause. Here he is shown, demanding the removal of chains from the insane at the Bicetre Hospital in Paris.

The Eighteenth-Century Asylum

As the Middle Ages came to a close, some advances were made in the treatment of mental disorders. By the eighteenth century, specialized hospitals, or *asylums,* began to appear in Europe. Initially designed to provide quiet retreats from the world, the asylums quickly became overcrowded and noisy. A turning point came in 1792 when Philippe Pinel, a French physician, was put in charge of a Parisian asylum where the inmates were shackled to the walls of unlighted and unheated cells. Pinel removed some of the inmates from their dungeons and insisted they be treated humanely. Many inmates improved so dramatically they were able to be released. Pinel's belief that abnormal behavior was caused by "sick" minds soon became the accepted way of viewing people who had previously been feared and punished for their abnormality. His idea that disturbed individuals had an underlying physical *illness* also served to resurrect the medical model first conceptualized by Hippocrates.

Modern Times

Psychiatry: The specialized branch of medicine dealing with the diagnosis, treatment, and prevention of mental disorders.

Pinel's medical model eventually gave rise to the modern specialty of psychiatry and to the founding of mental hospitals specifically designed to treat mental patients. In these hospitals, disorders are diagnosed as physical illnesses and treatments are prescribed.

Unfortunately, when we assume that a mental "disease" exists and label people "mentally ill," we can increase rather than alleviate their problems. One of the most outspoken critics of the medical model is psychiatrist Thomas Szasz (1960, 1987). Szasz believes the medical model encourages people to believe they have no responsibility for their actions, and that solutions are to be found in drugs, hospitalization, or surgery. He contends that mental illness is a "myth" used to label people who are peculiar or who are offensive to others. The medical model does not acknowledge that these labels are made within a particular social and cultural context. Furthermore, as we will see, labels can become self-perpetuating, that is, the person begins behaving according to the diagnosed disorder.

Despite these criticisms, the medical model remains a founding principle of psychiatry, and diagnosis and treatment of mental disorders continue to be based on the concept of mental *illness.* In contrast, psychology offers a multifaceted approach to explaining abnormal behavior. Each of the five major perspectives in psychology—psychoanalytic, learning, humanistic, cognitive, and biological—offers unique explanations. Table 15.3 summarizes these perspectives.

Table 15.3   Five Major Psychological Perspectives on Abnormal Behavior

> **Psychoanalytic Perspective.** Based on Sigmund Freud's theories of personality (see Chapter 14), psychoanalytic theory suggests that abnormal behavior is the result of a person's *intrapsychic conflicts.* When anxiety and conflict become too great for even the defense mechanisms to handle, abnormal behavior results.
>
> **Humanistic Perspective.** The humanistic view suggests that when people develop feelings of powerlessness and frustration instead of responsibility and self-esteem, they engage in maladaptive behaviors (see Chapter 14).
>
> **Learning Perspective.** According to the learning approach, *maladaptive behaviors* result from learning inappropriate role expectations through the processes of conditioning and modeling (see Chapter 6).
>
> **Cognitive Perspective.** The cognitive orientation focuses on the role of faulty thinking and problem solving as the causes of abnormal behaviors (see Chapter 14).
>
> **Biological Perspective.** According to this perspective, abnormal behavior results from organic causes, such as structural differences in the brain, genetic predisposition, injury to the nervous system, and imbalances in neurotransmitters.

Classifying Abnormal Behaviors: The Diagnostic and Statistical Manual IV

Intellectually we welcome many viewpoints, and without scientific evidence, who is to say which explanation for a psychological disorder is correct. Still, if we want to communicate clearly, we need a clear and reliable *system* for identifying the wide range of disorders. Just as physicians need to differentiate between cancer and heart disease, psychologists and psychiatrists must make a distinction between the anxiety attacks described by Maria in our introductory vignette and the feelings of paranoia experienced by Jim. Without a uniform system for classifying and describing psychological disorders, scientific research on them would be almost impossible and communication among mental health professionals would be seriously impaired.

Fortunately, most mental health specialists do share a common set of terms for labeling abnormal behaviors. This shared system for classification is published as a professional reference book, the Diagnostic and Statistical Manual of Mental Disorders (DSM-IV), by the American Psychiatric Association.

The DSM-IV categorizes abnormal behaviors according to major similarities and differences in the way disturbed people behave. For example, the category of *mood disorders* includes disorders for which the predominant problem is an emotional disturbance (such as depression) rather than a sexual or a drug problem. The DSM-IV contains descriptions of hundreds of disorders. Each description includes typical patterns of behavior, thought, and emotion, so that therapists can make a diagnosis. This manual does not attempt to explain the causes of disorders, however. It is strictly descriptive.

The first edition of the *Diagnostic and Statistical Manual,* now known as DSM-I, was published in 1952, the second edition in 1968, and the third edition, DSM-III, in 1980. A revised version of DSM-III (DSM-III-R) was published in 1987. A fourth edition, DSM-IV, is scheduled to be published in 1994. (Information in this chapter, related to the DSM-IV, is based on a preliminary draft. Problems associated with the use of the DSM-IV for labeling and diagnosing behavior will be discussed at the end of this chapter.)

Why do they need to keep changing the manual?   Each revision has expanded the list of disorders and changed the specific descriptions and categories. Revisions are made in response to new information from scientific research and also to reflect changes in the way abnormal behaviors are viewed within our own social context. Revisions in the terms neurosis and psychosis are examples of two important changes. In previous editions of the DSM, the term *neurosis* was used to describe individuals suffering from anxiety. The anxiety could be felt and expressed directly (through phobias, obsessions, compulsions), or the unconscious could convert it into bodily complaints (somatoform disorders). All neurotic conditions were believed to reflect underlying problems with repressed anxiety. However, mental health professionals found this psychoanalytic ap-

Diagnostic and Statistical Manual of Mental Disorders (DSM-IV): A classification system, developed by a task force of the American Psychiatric Association, used to describe abnormal behaviors.

Neurosis: A term used in early versions of the DSM to describe mental disorders related to anxiety.

Psychosis: Serious mental disorders characterized by loss of contact with reality and extreme mental disruption. Since daily functioning is often impaired, psychotic individuals are more likely to need hospitalization.

proach too limiting and the category too large to be maximally useful. In the DSM-IV, conditions previously grouped under neurosis have been redistributed as anxiety disorders, somatoform disorders, and dissociative disorders. Despite these changes, the term *neurosis* continues as a part of everyday language, and some professionals continue to use the term to refer generally to excessive anxiety.

Psychosis is another commonly used term that has been revised in the latest versions of the DSM. Individuals with a psychosis suffer extreme mental disruption and loss of contact with reality (Davison and Neale, 1994). Psychotic individuals often have trouble meeting ordinary demands of life, making hospitalization necessary. As you will see, schizophrenia, some mood disorders, and some disorders due to medical conditions are recognized as psychoses. While these disorders are not grouped under a single category of psychosis, the term remains in the DSM-IV because it is useful in distinguishing between the most severe mental disorders, where the individual loses contact with reality, and the less disruptive disorders.

What about the term "insanity"? Where does it fit in?   Insanity is a legal term indicating that a person cannot be held responsible for his or her actions because of mental

Insanity: A legal term for those with a mental disorder that implies a lack of responsibility for their behavior and an inability to manage their affairs in a competent manner.

Table 15.4   **Main Categories of Mental Disorders and Their Descriptions in DSM-IV**

1. *Disorders usually first diagnosed in infancy, childhood, or early adolescence:* mental retardation, bedwetting, etc.
2. *Delirium, dementia, amnestic and other cognitive disorders:* problems caused by Alzheimer's, HIV (AIDS), Parkinson's, etc.
3. *Mental disorders due to a general medical condition not elsewhere classified:* problems caused by physical deterioration of the brain due to disease, drugs, etc.
* 4. *Substance-related disorders:* problems caused by dependence on alcohol, cocaine, tobacco, and so forth.
* 5. *Schizophrenia and other psychotic disorders:* A group of disorders characterized by major disturbances in perception, language and thought, emotion, and behavior.
* 6. *Mood disorders:* problems associated with severe disturbances of mood, such as depression, mania, or alternating episodes of both.
* 7. *Anxiety disorders:* problems associated with severe anxiety, such as phobias, obsessive–compulsive disorder, and posttraumatic stress disorder.
* 8. *Somatoform disorders:* problems related to unusual preoccupation with physical health or from physical symptoms with no physical cause.
9. *Factitious disorders:* disorders that the individual adopts to satisfy some economic or psychological need.
*10. *Dissociative disorders:* disorders in which the normal integration of consciousness, memory, or identity is suddenly and temporarily altered, such as amnesia and multiple personality disorder.
11. *Sexual and gender identity disorders:* problems related to unsatisfactory sexual activity, finding unusual objects or situations arousing, gender identity problems, and so forth.
12. *Eating disorders:* problems related to food, such as anorexia nervosa, bulimia nervosa, and so forth.
13. *Sleep disorders:* serious disturbances of sleep, such as insomnia, sleep terrors, or hypersomnia.
14. *Impulse control disorders not elsewhere classified:* problems related to kleptomania, pathological gambling, pyromania, and so forth.
15. *Adjustment disorders:* problems related to specific stressors such as divorce, family discord, economic concerns, and so forth.
*16. *Personality disorders:* problems related to lifelong behavior patterns such as self-centeredness, overdependency, and antisocial behaviors.
17. *Other conditions that may be a focus of clinical attention:* problems related to physical or sexual abuse, relational problems, occupational problems, and so forth.

*Disorders discussed in this chapter.
Source: DSM-IV (1994).

illness. When a judge or jury finds a defendant insane he or she is considered innocent of wrongdoing and incapable of conducting his or her affairs in a competent manner and may therefore be involuntarily committed to treatment facilities. The standards and problems of forced treatment and commitment are discussed at the end of Chapter 16.

In the following sections, we focus on the three most common psychological disorders: anxiety, substance related disorders, and mood disorders. We also will discuss the four less common categories of schizophrenia, personality disorders, somatoform, and dissociative disorders. Because of space limitations we are focusing on only seven of the 17 major DSM-IV categories listed in Table 15.4.

Before we examine these disorders, we want to remind you the DSM-IV classifies disorders that people have, *not* the people themselves. To reflect this important distinction, this text (like the DSM-IV) avoids the use of terms such as "schizophrenic." Instead, we use the more awkward (but accurate) term, "a person with schizophrenia." An additional reminder is in order regarding cultural differences. Although the DSM-IV provides a culture-specific section and a glossary of culture-bound syndromes, the classification of most disorders still reflects a Western European and American perspective.

 Try This Yourself

As mentioned earlier, students who begin studying abnormal behavior sometimes have unnecessary worries about their own mental health. Many students also have unwarranted fears about the entire area of abnormal behavior. To test your own misconceptions, answer "True" or "False" to the following statements.

_____ #1	People with psychological disorders act in bizarre ways and are very different from normal people.
_____ #2	Mental disorders are a sign of personal weakness.
_____ #3	Mentally ill people are often violent and dangerous.
_____ #4	A person who has been mentally ill can never be normal.
_____ #5	Most mentally ill individuals can only work successfully at low-level jobs.

Each of these five statements is a myth. The facts are provided below and discussed further in this chapter.

#1 Fact: This is true for only a small minority of individuals and during a relatively small portion of their lives. In fact, sometimes even mental health professionals find it difficult to distinguish normal from abnormal individuals without formal screening.

#2 Fact: Psychological disorders are a function of many factors, such as exposure to stress, genetic disposition, family background, and so on. Mentally disturbed individuals can't be blamed for their problems any more than people who develop heart disease or other physical illnesses.

#3 Fact: Only a few disorders, such as some paranoid and antisocial personalities, are associated with violence toward others. If anything, many mentally disturbed individuals are most dangerous to themselves. The stereotype that connects mental illness and violence persists because of prejudice and selective media attention.

#4 Fact: The vast majority of people who are diagnosed as mentally ill eventually improve and lead normal productive lives. In addition, mental disorders are generally only temporary. A person may have an episode that lasts for days, weeks, or months and then go for years—even a lifetime—without further difficulty.

#5 Fact: Mentally disturbed persons are individuals. As such, their career potentials depend on their particular talents, abilities, experience, and motivation, as well as their current state of physical and mental health. Some of the most creative and distinguished people have suffered serious mental disorders (e.g., Virginia Woolf, Robert Schumann, and Winston Churchill).

Source: Adapted from "Fourteen Worst Myths" (1985).   ■

Review Questions

1. What is abnormal behavior?
2. The three standards for judging abnormal behavior are _____ .
3. The _____ replaced a belief in demons or witchcraft with the assumption that abnormal behaviors were "mental illnesses."
4. What is the DSM-IV?
5. What is the major difference between the labels "neurosis" and "psychosis"?
6. _____ is a legal term for psychological disorders implying a lack of legal responsibility for behavior.

Answers to Review Questions can be found in Appendix C.

ANXIETY DISORDERS

- *What causes anxiety disorders?*

A 38-year-old business executive experienced overwhelming anxiety whenever he was in an unfamiliar place or had to be involved in extended business meetings. On two occasions, his anxiety produced symptoms similar to a heart attack, and he had to be rushed to a hospital. His episodes of panic occurred whenever he couldn't immediately get to a bathroom when he had an urge to urinate. He was deathly afraid he would wet his pants in public.

Leon (1977)

Anxiety Disorders: Type of abnormal behavior characterized by unrealistic, irrational fear.

Like this man and Maria in our introduction, people with an anxiety disorder have a persistent feeling of threat in facing everyday problems. They feel anxious, ineffective, unhappy, and insecure in a world that seems dangerous and hostile. According to a recent National Institute of Mental Health (NIMH) study, anxiety disorders are the most widespread of all major mental disorders and are found about twice as often in women as in men (Regier et al., 1993).

Unreasonable Anxiety: Five Major Anxiety Disorders

Symptoms of anxiety, such as rapid breathing, dry mouth, and increased heart rate, plague all of us during major exams, first dates, and visits to the dentist. But some people experience unreasonable anxiety that is so intense and chronic it seriously disrupts their lives. We will consider five major types of anxiety disorders: generalized anxiety disorder, panic disorder, phobia, obsessive-compulsive disorder, and posttraumatic stress disorder.

Generalized Anxiety Disorder

Generalized Anxiety Disorder: Type of long-term anxiety that is not focused on any particular object or situation.

As the name implies, generalized anxiety disorder is characterized by long-lasting anxiety that is not focused on any particular object or situation *(free-floating anxiety)*. The individual feels afraid of *something,* but he or she is generally unable to articulate the specific fear. Because of persistent muscle tension and autonomic fear reactions, individuals may develop headaches, heart palpitations, dizziness, and insomnia. These physical complaints, combined with the intense, long-term anxiety, make it difficult for the individual to cope with normal daily activities.

Panic Disorder

Panic Disorders: Type of anxiety disorder characterized by severe attacks of exaggerated anxiety.

In panic disorders, anxiety is concentrated into specific episodes, or panic attacks, during which the person may have heart palpitations, breathing difficulties, dizziness, and fears of going crazy or doing something uncontrollable. A panic attack usually lasts several

"WHAT A RELIEF. NOW I CAN FOCUS MY FREE-FLOATING ANXIETY ON TO SOMETHING SPECIFIC."

Drawing by Sidney Harris

Although abnormal behavior has provided considerable material for cartoonists, the afflicted individual's pain and discomfort are no laughing matter.

minutes but may last for hours. Maria's sudden feelings of fear and breathing difficulties described at the beginning of this chapter are symptomatic of most panic attacks. Worried about having these unpredictable attacks, Maria began to curtail her business and social activities to the point that she went on to develop *agoraphobia,* an exaggerated fear of open spaces. This pattern of initial panic attacks followed by later development of agoraphobia is very common (DSM-IV, 1994; Eaton and Keyl, 1990).

Phobia

Agoraphobia, like other phobias, involves a strong, irrational fear of an object or situation that should not cause such a reaction. Phobic disorders differ from generalized anxiety disorders and panic disorders because there is a specific stimulus that elicits the strong fear response. Imagine how it would feel to be so frightened by a spider that you would attempt to jump out of a speeding car to get away from it. This is how a person suffering from phobia may feel. These individuals recognize that their fears are excessive and unreasonable but don't seem to be able to control their anxiety. People with phobias have especially powerful imaginations and can vividly anticipate severe consequences from encountering such feared objects as knives, bridges, blood, enclosed places, or certain animals. (See Table 15.5 for examples of phobias and their official names).

So far we have been discussing only those fears that would qualify as specific or *simple* phobias in the DSM-IV classification system. *Social* phobias, the other major category, usually center on the fear of being negatively evaluated by others, or on the prospect of being publicly embarrassed because of impulsive acts. One of the most common social phobias is "stage fright." Although each of us experiences some anxiety when speaking or performing in front of a group, people with social phobias become so anxious that performance is out of the question. Their fears of public scrutiny and potential humiliation become so pervasive that normal life becomes impossible (Robins and Regier, 1991; Yudolfsky and Silver, 1987).

Phobia: Mental disorder characterized by exaggerated fears of an object or situation.

Table 15.5 Phobias

Type of Phobia	Object or Situation Feared
Acrophobia	High places
Agoraphobia	Open spaces
Claustrophobia	Small or enclosed places
Cynophobia	Dogs
Cypridophobia	Sexually transmitted disease
Electrophobia	Electricity
Genophobia	Sex
Gynophobia	Women
Hydrophobia	Water
Kakorrhaphiophobia	Failure
Mysophobia	Dirt
Nyctophobia	Darkness
Social phobia	Observation or evaluation by others
Thanatophobia	Death
Zoophobia	Animals

Obsessive-Compulsive Disorder

Obsessive-Compulsive Disorder (OCD): Type of anxiety disorder characterized by intrusive thoughts (obsessions) and urges to perform repetitive, ritualistic behaviors (compulsions).

Unlike phobias, in which the anxiety is focused on specific objects or situations, obsessive-compulsive disorders (OCD) are characterized by diffuse anxiety created by obsessive thoughts or compulsive behaviors. An *obsession* is a persistent preoccupation with something, most often an idea or feeling. A *compulsion* is an irresistible impulse to perform ritualistic behaviors, such as handwashing, counting, or putting things in order. In OCD, individuals feel driven to think about certain things or to carry out some action against their will. They generally recognize that the behavior is irrational but cannot seem to control it. When OCD sufferers resist performing compulsive behaviors, they generally experience a feeling of mounting tension that can only be relieved by yielding to the compulsion.

I sometimes find myself checking the stove burners before I leave my home. Would this be considered an obsessive-compulsive disorder? The difference between an OCD and milder forms of compulsion is that OCD behaviors are much more extreme, appear irrational to almost everyone, and interfere considerably with everyday life. Individuals with OCD sometimes wash their hands hundreds of times a day or spend hours performing senseless rituals of organizing and cleaning. Billionaire Howard Hughes provides an example of obsessive-compulsive behavior.

> *Due to his unreasonable fear of germs, he made people who worked with him wear white gloves, sometimes several pairs, when handling documents he would later touch. When newspapers were brought to him, they had to be in stacks of three so he could slide the middle one out by grasping it with Kleenex. To escape contamination by dust, he ordered that masking tape be put around the doors and windows of his cars and houses.*
>
> *Fowler (1986)*

Posttraumatic Stress Disorder

Posttraumatic Stress Disorder (PTSD): Type of anxiety disorder that follows an overwhelming, traumatic event.

The essential feature of posttraumatic stress disorder (PTSD) is that the symptom of anxiety develops after a traumatic event, such as rape, war combat, or sudden disaster. Other symptoms include intense terror, fear, and helplessness during the trauma and recurrent flashbacks, nightmares, impaired concentration, and/or emotional numbing afterward (Davison and Neale, 1994). Although PTSD has received much attention, there

Survivors of natural disasters sometimes experience long-lasting emotional disturbances known as posttraumatic stress disorders (PTSD).

is considerable controversy concerning its prevalence and diagnosis (Jones and Barlow, 1990; Smith et al., 1990). For individuals who do suffer from PTSD, the symptoms may continue for years after the initial traumatic incident. Rape victims and combat veterans in particular may experience unpleasant emotional consequences the rest of their lives (Buie, 1989b). Some experts believe the largest single group of PTSD sufferers are female sexual assault and abuse victims (Foa, Olasov, and Steketee, 1987; Kelley and Byrne, 1992).

Causes of Anxiety Disorders: Learning or Biology?

The exact cause of anxiety disorders is a matter of considerable debate, but recent research has focused primarily on the roles of learning and biology.

Learning

The learning perspective on anxiety disorders suggests that phobias and other reactions are the result of *classical* and *operant* conditioning (see Chapter 6). The original neutral stimulus (e.g., the office building in Maria's case) may be paired with a frightening event (the sudden panic attack) so that it becomes a conditioned stimulus which elicits anxiety. After this type of classical conditioning, the phobia is typically maintained through the process of operant conditioning. Maria continues to avoid the anxiety-producing stimulus (her office) because avoiding the stimulus leads to a reduction in the unpleasant feelings of anxiety (a process known as negative reinforcement). (See Figure 15.2). Maria's later development of *agoraphobia* could be explained by the process of stimulus generalization—her fear of having a panic attack spread from her office to all open places (Martin and Pear, 1992).

Social learning theorists propose that some phobias are the result of modeling and imitation. Overprotective, fearful parents may make their children more prone to developing phobias and other anxiety disorders. Howard Hughes, for instance, was raised by an extremely overprotective mother who worried constantly about his physical health (Fowler, 1986).

Biology

How biology contributes to anxiety disorders seems to depend on the specific disorder. With phobias, generalized anxiety, and posttraumatic stress disorders, biology plays a minor role. Phobias seem to result primarily from classical and operant conditioning, while generalized anxiety disorders apparently reflect the individual's hypervigilant personality. Research shows that individuals who suffer from generalized anxiety disorder

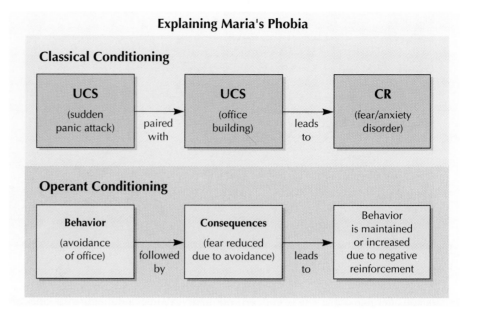

Figure 15.2 Explaining Maria's phobia. According to the learning perspective, Maria's phobia (which was described in our introductory vignette) developed as a result of classical and operant conditioning. In classical conditioning terms, the initial panic attack was paired with the office building where she worked, and a conditioned response of fear and anxiety developed. Maria's phobia was maintained through operant conditioning—avoiding the office led to a reduction in fear, which in turn reinforces her phobia.

seem to go around the world actively searching and screening for threatening stimuli (Eysenck et al., 1991). Posttraumatic stress disorders result primarily from the stress of extreme environmental events.

Biological factors seem much clearer for the other two major anxiety disorders—obsessive-compulsive disorders and panic disorders. Obsessive-compulsive disorders seem to be related to a disrupted biochemistry, damage to the brain, and/or a genetic predisposition (Andreasen and Black, 1991; Rapaport, 1989). Also, studies show that the brain pathways that link the frontal lobes of the cerebral cortex to the basal ganglia and cingulate gyrus appear to be disrupted in individuals with OCD. This means that the motor-related activity that leads to compulsive behaviors (such as washing and checking) may originate in the basal ganglia and the frontal lobes are unable to control the compulsion due to the disrupted pathways. The good news is that sufferers of OCD have been helped with a combination of drug therapy (which increases levels of serotonin) and behavior therapy (Gelman, 1989).

There is also good evidence that panic disorders have a strong biological component. Research has found that certain individuals with this disorder seem to have a genetic predisposition toward an overreaction of the autonomic nervous system (Foa and Kozak, 1986). These people apparently respond more quickly and intensely to stressful stimuli. Panic attacks can be induced in people who experience them by asking them to hyperventilate—to breathe deeper and faster than usual. In addition, the fact that drugs, such as caffeine, and even lactic acid, can trigger an attack also suggests a biochemical disturbance (Bower, 1989; Yudolfsky and Silver, 1987).

Review Questions

1. What are the five major types of anxiety disorders?

2. Which type of anxiety disorder does each of the following examples describe?

    _____ Mary was raped and is experiencing recurring nightmares and flashbacks of the rape.

    _____ Terry is overwhelmed with feelings of terror that cause him to have difficulty breathing.

    _____ John is excessively concerned with cleanliness and sometimes washes his hands hundreds of times a day.

3. How do learning theorists and social learning theorists explain anxiety disorders?

4. Of the five forms of anxiety disorders, _____ are thought to be due primarily to biological causes.

Answers to Review Questions can be found in Appendix C.

SCHIZOPHRENIA

Imagine for the moment that your daugher just left for college and you hear voices inside your head shouting "You'll never see her again, you have been a bad mother, she'll die." How would you react if you saw dinosaurs on the street and live animals in your refrigerator? These are the actual experiences that have plagued Mrs. T for almost three decades (Gershon and Rieder, 1992).

Mrs. T suffered the disorder known as schizophrenia. Literally, *schizophrenia* means "split mind." When Eugene Bleuler coined the term in 1911 he was referring to the fragmenting of thought processes and emotions found in schizophrenic disorders (Neale, Oltmanns, and Winters, 1983). Unfortunately, "split mind" and "split personality" are often confused by the general public. One study of college freshmen found that 64 percent believed that multiple personality was a common symptom of schizophrenia (Torrey, 1988). As you will discover later, *multiple personality disorder* is the rare condition of having more than one distinct personality. Schizophrenia is a much more common, and altogether different, type of psychological disorder. What are the nature and symptoms of schizophrenia? What different forms does it take? What are its causes? These are the questions we will now address.

* *What are the major symptoms and causes of schizophrenia?*

Schizophrenia: Group of psychotic disorders involving distortions in language and thinking, perception, emotion, and behavior.

Symptoms of Schizophrenia: Disturbances in Perception, Language and Thought, Affect, and Behavior

Schizophrenia is generally considered the most serious and severe form of mental disturbance. According to statistics, one out of every 100 people will develop schizophrenia and approximately half of all people admitted to mental hospitals are diagnosed with schizophrenia (Gottesman, 1991; Regier et al., 1993). Schizophrenic disorders usually emerge during adolescence or young adulthood and only rarely after age 45.

Schizophrenia is also a form of *psychosis,* a term describing general lack of contact with reality. All the disorders we have considered so far are serious. They involve considerable pain and distress to the afflicted individual, but most sufferers can still function in their daily lives. But people with schizophrenia, due to their lack of contact with reality, are often unable to meet the demands of ordinary life and may require institutional or custodial care.

What are the signs and symptoms of schizophrenia?   Schizophrenia is characterized by psychological disturbances or disruptions in four major areas: perception, language and thought, affect (or emotions), and behavior.

Perceptual Symptoms

The senses of people with schizophrenia may be either enhanced (as in the case of Mrs. T) or blunted. The filtering and selection processes that allow most people to concentrate on whatever they choose are impaired, and sensory stimulation is jumbled and distorted. One patient reported:

> *When people are talking, I just get scraps of it. If it is just one person who is speaking, that's not so bad, but if others join in then I can't pick it up at all. I just can't get in tune with the conversation. It makes me feel all open — as if things are closing in on me and I have lost control.*

(McGhie and Chapman, 1961, p. 106).

Disorganized thoughts, emotions, and perceptions are often reflected in the artwork of people with schizophrenia.

Hallucinations: Sensory perceptions that occur in the absence of a real external stimulus.

People with schizophrenia also experience hallucinations—they perceive things for which there are no appropriate external stimuli. Hallucinations can occur in any of the senses (visual, tactile, olfactory), but auditory hallucinations are most common in schizophrenia. As Mrs. T's case demonstrates, people with schizophrenia often hear voices speaking their thoughts aloud, commenting on their behavior, or telling them what to do. The voices seem to come from inside their own heads or from an external source such as an animal, telephone wires, or a television set.

On rare occasions people with schizophrenia will hurt themselves or others in response to their distorted internal experiences or the voices they hear. These cases get media attention and create exaggerated fears of "mental patients." In reality, the seriously mentally ill make a trivial contribution to crime statistics; "you are safer visiting a patient in a mental hospital than you are on the streets of any major American city after dark" (Gottesman, 1991, p. 191).

Language and Thought Disturbances

For people with schizophrenia, words lose their usual meanings and associations, logic is impaired, and thoughts are disorganized and bizarre. For example, a patient with schizophrenia gave this explanation for the meaning of the proverb "People who live in glass houses shouldn't throw stones":

> People who live in glass houses shouldn't forget people who live in stone houses and shouldn't throw glass.

© 1992, Ziggy and Friends, Inc. Distributed by Universal Press Syndicate.

When language and thought disturbances are mild, speech is tangential, switching from one idea to another. In more severe disturbances, phrases and words are jumbled together (referred to as *word salad*) and the person creates artificial words (*neologisms*). Table 15.6 presents some examples of these language variations.

The most common thought disturbances experienced by people with schizophrenia are distorted beliefs called delusions. Contrary to common mistaken beliefs that we all experience from time to time, such as thoughts that a friend is trying to avoid us or that our parents' divorce was our fault, delusions are mistaken beliefs maintained in spite of strong evidence to the contrary. Mrs. T held the delusion that others were speaking about her. In *delusions of grandeur,* people believe they are someone very important, perhaps Jesus Christ or the Queen of England. In *delusions of persecution,* individuals believe they are the target of a plot to harm them, as was the case with Jim in our introduction who believed that secret agents were trying to assassinate him. In *delusions of reference,* unrelated events are given special significance, as when a person believes a radio program or newspaper article is giving him or her a special message.

Delusions: Mistaken beliefs maintained in spite of strong evidence to the contrary.

Affect Disturbances

Changes in affect, or emotions, are common in schizophrenia. In some cases, emotions can be exaggerated and may fluctuate rapidly in inappropriate ways. For example, a person may become extremely fearful, guilty, or euphoric for no reason. In other cases, emotions may become blunted or decrease in intensity. In some instances, people with schizophrenia have *flattened affect*—almost no emotional response of any kind.

Table 15.6   Language Variations in Schizophrenia

Language Variation	Examples
Word salad	"The same children are sent of a rose, sweet-smelling perfume that gives us peace and parts and whole."
	"The sad kind and peaceful valleys of the mind come beckoning under rivers."
Neologisms	"splisters" (combination of splinters and blisters)
	"smever" (combination of smart and clever)

Behavioral Disturbances

The abnormal behaviors of individuals with schizophrenia are often related to disturbances in their perceptions, thoughts, and feelings. For example, experiencing a flood of sensory stimuli or overwhelming confusion, a person with schizophrenia will often withdraw from social contacts and refuse to communicate.

Disturbances in behavior may also include abnormal mannerisms, grimacing, and pacing the floor. Although they may appear bizarre to others, a schizophrenic's unusual actions sometimes have special meanings for them. One patient shook his head rhythmically from side to side to try to shake the excess thoughts out of his mind. Another massaged his head repeatedly "to help clear it" of unwanted thoughts.

People with schizophrenia also may become cataleptic and assume an uncomfortable, nearly immobile stance for an extended period of time. A few people with schizophrenia also have a symptom called waxy flexibility, a tendency to maintain whatever posture is imposed upon them.

Catalepsy: A symptom of schizophrenia in which the individual assumes an uncomfortable, nearly immobile posture for an extended period of time.

Waxy Flexibility: A symptom of schizophrenia in which the individual maintains whatever posture is imposed upon him or her.

Subtypes of Schizophrenia: Recent Methods of Classification

For many years, researchers divided schizophrenia into *paranoid, catatonic, disorganized,* and *undifferentiated* subtypes. Although these terms are still used in the DSM (and sometimes by the general public), recent research casts doubt on their value. Critics note that these subtypes do not differentiate in terms of prognosis, etiology (cause), or response to treatment, and that the undifferentiated subtype is a catchall for difficult diagnostic cases.

For all these reasons, Nancy Andreasen and others (Andreasen, 1982; Andreasen et al., 1990; Crow, 1980, 1985) propose an alternative classification system, two groups, instead of four:

1. *Positive symptoms* involving distorted or excessive activity (e.g., bizarre delusions, hallucinations, inappropriate laughter and tears, and erratic behaviors).

2. *Negative symptoms* involving behavioral deficits or loss of activity (e.g., toneless voice, flattened emotions, social withdrawal and poverty of speech).

Researchers have demonstrated a number of important relationships that support this two-type classification (Carpenter et al., 1988; Gottesman, 1991). For example, people with schizophrenia and negative symptoms seem to be more impaired (greater cognitive deficits, lower intelligence, poorer social functioning) than those with positive symptoms. Positive symptoms of schizophrenia tend to occur during acute episodes and then disappear, whereas negative symptoms are more enduring and persistent. In addition, negative symptoms respond less well to medication, and patients presenting these symptoms function less effectively after hospitalization. Finally, as we will discuss later, the overall usefulness of this new classification may be that it provides a better model for explaining possible causes and treatments for schizophrenia.

Causes of Schizophrenia: Nature and Nurture Theories

There are several theories that attempt to explain schizophrenia. Biological theories emphasize physical changes in the nervous system based on abnormal brain functioning or inherited predispositions. Other theories emphasize psychosocial factors such as disturbed family interactions or stressful experiences.

Biological Theories

An enormous amount of scientific research has been done concerning possible biological factors in schizophrenia. Most of this research has been in three areas: neurotransmitters, brain damage, and genetics.

1. *Neurotransmitters,* primarily dopamine, have long been suspected of playing a major role in schizophrenia (Lucins, 1975; Miklowitz et al., 1986; Torrey,

Dopamine Hypothesis: A theory suggesting that schizophrenia is caused by an overactivity of dopamine neurons in a specific region of the brain.

1988). The dopamine hypothesis suggests that an overactivity of certain dopamine neurons in the brain causes schizophrenia. This hypothesis is based on two important observations:

- Large doses of amphetamines are capable of producing the positive symptoms of schizophrenia (such as delusions of persecution) in people with no history of psychological disorders. Furthermore, low doses of amphetamines worsen these symptoms in people who are schizophrenic. (Recall from Chapter 5 that amphetamines increase the amounts of both dopamine and norepinephrine that are present at the synapse.)

- Drugs effective in treating schizophrenia, such as chlorpromazine, block the effects of dopamine in the brain.

2. *Brain damage.* The second major biological theory for schizophrenia centers on the possibility of brain damage. Researchers have found larger cerebral ventricles (cavities that contain cerebrospinal fluid) in some people with schizophrenia (Raz and Raz, 1990). As you can see in Figure 15.3*a*, the enlarged ventricles of one patient with schizophrenia are clearly shown through the technique of magnetic imaging (MI). Another technique, positron emission tomography (PET), shows that some people with chronic schizophrenia tend to have a lower level of activity in the frontal and temporal lobes of their brains (see Figure 15.3*b*).

3. *Genetics.* The third biological theory is that certain people inherit a predisposing vulnerability to schizophrenia. Family studies show that the probability of developing schizophrenia increases with genetic similarity (see Figure 15.4). For example, if one identical twin develops schizophrenia, the other twin has a 48 percent chance of also developing schizophrenia (Gottesman, 1991). But if one sibling develops schizophrenia, the chances of the other sibling developing it are only 10 percent. If you compare these percentages with the risk for the general population (which is 1 percent) genetics clearly seem to play a role in the development of schizophrenia (Gershon and Rieder, 1992).

In sum, there is strong evidence linking schizophrenia to biological factors—neurotransmitters, brain damage, and genetics. However, there also is evidence that nonbiological, psychosocial factors contribute to schizophrenia.

Figure 15.3 Two views of schizophrenia. (a) A three-dimensional magnetic imaging reconstruction shows the structural changes in the shrunken hippocampus (yellow) and enlarged, fluid-filled ventricles (gray) of the brain of the patient with schizophrenia (far left), as compared with a normal volunteer (center). (b) These PET scans show variations in the brain activity of normal individuals, people with major depressive disorder, and individuals with schizophrenia. Note how the levels of activity correspond to the colors and numbers at the far right of the photo. Higher numbers and warmer colors indicate increased brain activity.

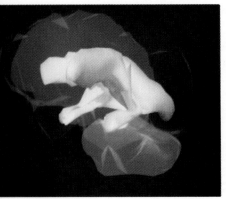 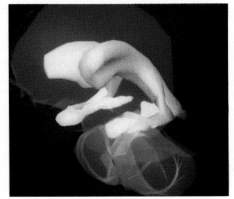 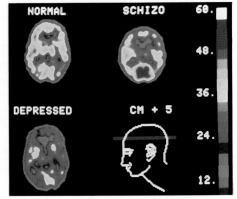

(a)   (b)

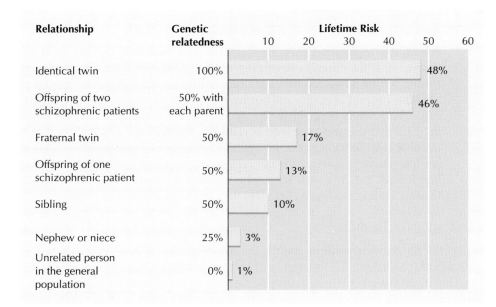

Figure 15.4 Genetics and schizophrenia. Your lifetime risk of developing schizophrenia depends on how closely you are genetically related to a person with schizophrenia. Although environmental factors also play a role in the development of schizophrenia, these statistics demonstrate the importance of genetic predisposition. (Source: Berheim and Levine, 1979; Gottesman and Shields, 1982; Gottesman, 1991.)

Psychosocial Theories

One of the best ways to understand to what degree psychosocial factors contribute to the development of schizophrenia is to look at genetic statistics for identical twins. Remembering that these two children share *identical* genes, what would be the percentage chance that both twins would develop schizophrenia if the disorder were totally hereditary? If you guessed 100 percent, you're doing great. Since the rate is actually only 48 percent, nongenetic factors must contribute the remaining 52 percent. Other biological factors (such as neurotransmitters and brain structure) may take up part of the "leftover" percentage, but most psychologists believe there are at least three possible nonbiological contributors: stress, communication deviance, and family pathology.

1. *Stress.* Most theories of schizophrenia support the position that stress plays a key role in *triggering* schizophrenic disorders (Gottesman and Bertelsen, 1989; Zubin, 1986). Recent research also suggests that stress may be associated with patient relapse (Ventura et al., 1989). Still further evidence for the role of stress in schizophrenia comes from Hollingshead and Redlich's (1958) classic study on social class. These researchers found that individuals who suffer from schizophrenia are nine times more likely to come from the lowest socioeconomic class than from the two highest social classes combined. This suggests that the stress of living in impoverished conditions may contribute to schizophrenia. Other researchers have countered by suggesting that people with schizophrenia may socially drift downward because they lack the social skills and cognitive functioning necessary to hold down higher paying jobs (Turner and Wagonfield, 1967).

2. *Communication deviance.* Some investigators suggest that communication disorders in parents and family members may be a predisposing factor for schizophrenia (Goldstein, 1984). Such disorders include unintelligible speech; vague, fragmented communications; and contradictory messages. In these families, the child might find it easy to withdraw into a private world and thereby set the stage for later schizophrenia.

   Differences between men and women who suffer from schizophrenia support the communication deviance model. Research shows that women tend to cope better with schizophrenia. They are generally diagnosed later in life, are hospitalized for shorter periods, and are more likely to make a full recovery (Goldstein, 1988). Women patients with schizophrenia also tend to have higher social and communication skills, and it may be that it is these skills that allow them to cope better (Mueser et al., 1990).

3.   *Family environment.* Other investigators have looked at the family as the source of schizophrenia. According to the disturbed family environment theory, a child subjected to rejection or mistreatment will fail to develop an adequate concept of reality and normal emotional responses (Roff and Knight, 1981). This theory is supported by studies that evaluate *expressed emotionality* (EE). By measuring the level of criticism and hostility aimed at the family member with schizophrenia, as well as emotional overinvolvement in his or her life, researchers found greater relapse and worsening of symptoms among hospitalized patients with schizophrenia who go home to high-EE families (Brown, Birley, and Wing, 1972; Hooley, 1988; Vaughn et al., 1984).

An Evaluation of Theories

Critics of the dopamine hypothesis and the brain damage theory argue that they only fit some cases of schizophrenia. Moreover, with both it is difficult to determine cause and effect. That is, does overactivity in dopamine neurons *cause* schizophrenia, does schizophrenia *cause* overactivity of dopamine neurons, and brain damage, or are they merely *correlated* and both caused by a third, as yet unknown, factor.

The disturbed family theory also is hotly debated, and research is equally inconclusive. One reason for the high level of inconclusiveness of all theories might be that schizophrenia is really two or more separate disorders with correspondingly different causes and treatments. This two-syndrome hypothesis gets support partly because it reconciles differences in the biological theories. Research into the two-syndrome hypothesis has found that a malfunction of neurotransmitters (especially dopamine) seems to produce the positive symptoms of schizophrenia (delusions, hallucinations, etc.), and genetic influences and brain damage correlate with the negative symptoms (flat affect, social withdrawal, etc.). According to this view, schizophrenia is actually two separate syndromes: Type 1, which is related to increased sensitivity to dopamine and produces positive symptoms, and Type 2, which is related to genetics and brain abnormalities and produces negative symptoms (Crow, 1982, 1985).

The primary importance of the two-syndrome hypothesis is that it suggests schizophrenia is not a single condition with one underlying cause, a position that has been suspect for a long time. A combination of interacting (known and unknown) factors is probably involved in schizophrenia (see Figure 15.5).

Two-Syndrome Hypothesis: A theory that suggests that schizophrenia is composed of two separate syndromes: Type 1, which is related to dopamine sensitivity and produces positive symptoms (such as delusions and hallucinations), and Type 2, which is related to genetics and brain abnormalities and produces negative symptoms (such as flat affect and social withdrawal).

Gender and Cultural Diversity

CULTURE AND SCHIZOPHRENIA

At the beginning of this chapter, we discussed how some researchers believe that certain mental disorders may be culturally universal, and schizophrenia is a prime example (Berry et al., 1992). Culturally general symptoms of schizophrenia include delusions, thinking aloud, incoherent speech, difficulty forming emotional ties with others, poor rapport with others, and poor self-insight (Draguns, 1990; Lin and Kleinman, 1988; World Health Organization, 1979).

In contrast to these cultural commonalities, there are at least four major ways schizophrenia differs across cultures:

1.   *Prevalence.* Although schizophrenia is one of the more common disorders in the world, the reported incidence *within any given culture* varies. It is unclear whether differences between cultures results from an actual difference in prevalence of the disorder or from differences in definition, diagnosis, or reporting (Berry et al., 1992; Draguns, 1990). Comparisons of cross-national mental health statistics after World War II, for example, showed that U.S. psychiatrists diagnosed four times as many people with schizophrenia as British psychiatrists (Gottesman, 1991).

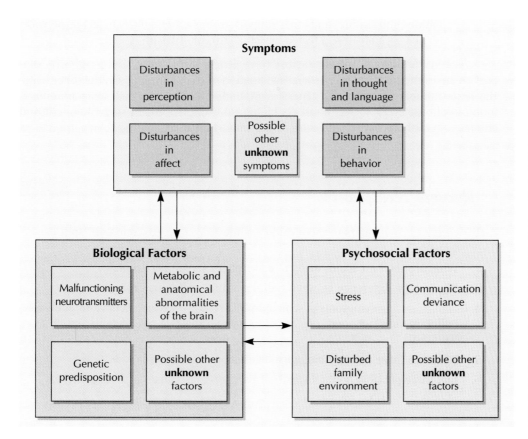

Figure 15.5 Interacting factors in schizophrenia. Research in schizophrenia has produced a wide variety of possible explanations. Today most researchers believe that biological factors (malfunctioning neurotransmitters, metabolic and anatomical abnormalities in the brain, genetic predispositions, and possible other unknown factors) interact with psychosocial factors (stress, communication deviance, disturbed family environment, and possible other unknown factors). These biological and psychosocial factors combine to produce the symptoms of schizophrenia: disturbances in perception, in thought and language, in affect, in behavior, and possible other unknown symptoms.

2. *Form.* The form or major mode of expression of schizophrenia also varies across cultures. In Nigeria, for example, the major symptom of schizophrenia is usually intense suspicion of others, accompanied by bizarre fears and thoughts of personal danger (Katz, et al., 1988). Given that in Nigeria it is commonly believed evil beings cause illness, you can see how cultural forces would influence people with schizophrenia to develop this particular set of symptoms.

   It is also interesting to look at how technology has affected the form of schizophrenia in North America and Europe. In these cultures, auditory hallucinations are the most common symptoms of schizophrenia. In the 1920s the voices that people heard came from the radio; in the 1950s they came from television; in the 1960s it was satellites in outer space; and in the 1970s and 1980s they often came from microwave ovens (Brislin, 1993).

3. *Onset.* As we discussed, some theories suggest that stress may trigger the onset of schizophrenia. Research by Day and colleagues (1987) in nine different sites in Asia, Europe, South America, and the United States supports the relationship between stress and schizophrenia. While some stressors were shared by many cultures, such as the unexpected death of a spouse or loss of a job, others were culturally specific, such as feeling possessed by evil forces or the victim of witchcraft.

4. *Prognosis.* The prognosis, or prediction for recovery, from schizophrenia also varies between cultures. Given the advanced treatment facilities and wider availability of trained professionals and drugs in industrialized nations, it may surprise you to learn that the prognosis for people with schizophrenia is better in *nonindustrialized* societies (Lin and Kleinman, 1988). This may be because the core symptoms of schizophrenia (poor rapport with others, incoherent speech, etc.) make it more difficult to survive in highly industrialized countries. In addition, individualism is highly encouraged in most industrialized

nations and families and other support groups are less likely to feel responsible for the care of those affected by schizophrenia (Brislin, 1993).

The four culturally specific factors (prevalence, form, onset, and prognosis) support an environmental or psychosocial explanation of schizophrenia. On the other hand, the large number of culturally general symptoms and the fact that schizophrenia is found in almost every society supports biological explanations. In sum, then, cultural studies suggest both nature and nurture are important in explaining schizophrenia. ■

Review Questions

1. _____ refers to "split mind," while _____ refers to "split personality."
2. What are the four major areas of disturbance in schizophrenia?
3. What is the difference between hallucinations and delusions?
4. _____ symptoms of schizophrenia refer to "excess" behaviors, such as hallucinations, whereas _____ symptoms refer to "deficits," such as flat affect.
5. What are three possible biological causes of schizophrenia?
6. List three possible nonbiological, or psychosocial, causes of schizophrenia.

Answers to Review Questions can be found in Appendix C.

MOOD DISORDERS

• *When do disturbances in mood become abnormal?*

Ann had been divorced for eight months when she called a psychologist for an emergency appointment. Although her husband had verbally and physically abused her for years, she had had mixed feelings about staying in the marriage. She had anticipated feeling good after the divorce, but she became increasingly depressed. She had trouble sleeping, had little appetite, felt very fatigued, and showed no interest in her usual activities. She stayed home from work for two days because she "just didn't feel like going in." Late one afternoon she went straight to bed, leaving her two small children to fend for themselves. Then, the night before calling for an appointment, she took five sleeping tablets and a couple of stiff drinks. As she said, "I don't think I wanted to kill myself; I just wanted to forget everything for a while."

Meyer and Salmon (1988), p. 312

Ann's case is a good example of a *mood disorder* (also known as an affective disorder). This category encompasses not only excessive sadness like Ann's but also unreasonable elation and hyperactivity.

Understanding Mood Disorders: Major Depressive Disorder and Bipolar Disorder

It may sound strange that it is possible to be too happy, but the key words in classifying a person's happy feelings as disordered are *excessive* and *unreasonable*. Both depression and elation are problem reactions when they are extreme or when the person is not in touch with reality. There are two main types of mood disorders—major depressive disorder and bipolar disorder.

Major Depressive Disorder

Everyone occasionally feels depressed, but people suffering from major depressive disorder experience a lasting and continuously depressed mood that interferes with the ability to function, feel pleasure, or maintain interest in life. These feelings may be without apparent cause and may be so severe that the individual loses contact with reality. As you saw in the case of Ann, depressed individuals have a hard time thinking clearly or recognizing their own problems. But they can be helped by family or friends who recognize the symptoms.

 Try This Yourself

There are several emotional, cognitive, and behavioral signs of major depressive disorder. The following questions can help you decide if a friend is seriously depressed and may need help.

Does the person express feelings of
_____ Sadness or "emptiness"?
_____ Hopelessness, pessimism, or guilt?
_____ Helplessness or worthlessness?
Does the person seem
_____ Unable to make decisions?
_____ Unable to concentrate or remember?
_____ To have lost interest or pleasure in ordinary activities—like sports or talking on the phone?
_____ To have more problems with school, work, and/or family?
Does the person complain of
_____ Loss of energy and drive?
_____ Trouble falling asleep, staying asleep, or getting up?
_____ Appetite problems; is he or she losing or gaining weight?
_____ Headaches, stomachaches, or backaches?
_____ Chronic aches and pains in joints and muscles?
Has his or her behavior changed suddenly so that he or she
_____ Is restless or irritable?
_____ Wants to be alone most of the time?
_____ May be drinking heavily or taking drugs?
Has the person talked about
_____ Death?
_____ Suicide—or has he or she attempted suicide?

Source: National Institute of Mental Health (1985). ■

Bipolar Disorder

When depression ends, most people return to a "normal" emotional level. Some people, however, rebound to the opposite state, known as "mania." In bipolar disorder, the person experiences depression, mania (an excessive and unreasonable state of overexcitement and impulsive behavior), and normal periods (see Figure 15.6).

During a manic episode, the person is overly excited and elated, with an inflated and unrealistic sense of his or her own importance. The person with a manic episode often makes elaborate plans for becoming rich and famous and may have delusions of grandeur. These individuals are hyperactive and may not sleep for days at a time without becoming fatigued. Thinking is speeded up and can change abruptly to new topics, showing "rapid flight of ideas." These individuals also generally speak rapidly ("pressured speech"), and it is difficult to get a word in edgewise. Poor judgment is common. In a manic phase, a person may give away valuable possessions or go on wild spending sprees.

Major Depressive Disorder: A DSM-IV diagnostic term for individuals experiencing a long-lasting depressed mood which interferes with the ability to function, feel pleasure, or maintain interest in life. The feelings are without apparent cause, or excessive to the given situation, and the individual may experience loss of contact with reality.

Bipolar Disorder: A diagnostic term in DSM-IV for individuals who experience both episodes of depression and mania—an excessive and unreasonable state of elation and hyperactivity.

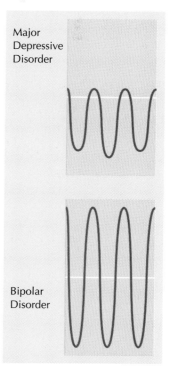

Figure 15.6 Mood disorders. If major depressive disorders and bipolar disorders were depicted on a graph, the changes in mood might look something like this.

Manic episodes generally last a few days to a few months and often end abruptly. Irritability sometimes occurs suddenly, causing a shift back to depression and anger. During the depressive episode, the person's previous manic mood, rapid thinking and speaking style, and hyperactivity are reversed. A depressive episode generally lasts three times as long as the manic episode.

Causes of Mood Disorders: Biological versus Psychological Factors

Numerous studies and theories have attempted to explain major depressive disorder and bipolar disorder. These explanations can be categorized as either biological or psychological.

Biological Factors

Early biological research suggested that depression was due to depletion of the neurotransmitters norepinephrine and serotonin, and mania was due to an excess of these same chemicals (Goodwin and Potter, 1979). Later research, however, failed to support such a straightforward mechanism. Today the theories are complex. Several lines of evidence suggest that depression is caused by abnormalities in the metabolism, release, and/or transmission of norepinephrine or serotonin. *Tricyclic antidepressant* drugs (such as Prozac and imipramine) alleviate the symptoms of depression and have a direct effect on synapses that utilize norepinephrine and serotonin. The drug *lithium carbonate* relieves the symptoms of bipolar disorders, but, as yet, no one knows why.

There also is evidence that major depressive disorders, as well as bipolar disorders, may be inherited (Gershon and Reider, 1992; Offer and Sabshin, 1993). Twenty-five percent of patients with major depressive disorder and up to 50 percent of patients with bipolar disorder have a relative with some form of mood disorder. It is important to remember, however, that relatives generally have similar environments, as well as similar genes.

Psychological Theories

Psychological theories of depression focus on disturbances in the person's interpersonal relationships, thought processes, self-concept, and learning history (Nolen-Hoeksema and Morrow, 1991; Seligman, 1991; Wood et al., 1990). The psychoanalytic explanation of depression sees it as anger turned inward against oneself when an important relationship or attachment is lost. Anger is assumed to come from feelings of rejection or withdrawal of affection, especially when a loved one dies. The humanistic school says depression is created when a person's self-concept is overly demanding or when positive growth is blocked.

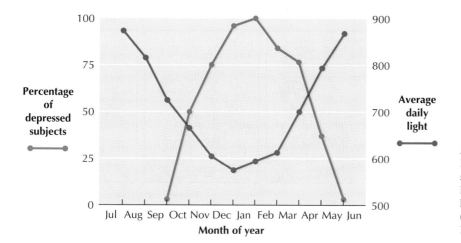

Figure 15.7 Seasonal affective disorder (SAD). Research has shown that some forms of depression strongly correlate with the amount of daily light. This graph indicates that the months of lowest light are the highest for depression. (Source: Adapted from Wurtman and Wurtman, 1989).

The learned helplessness theory of depression, developed by Martin Seligman (1975, 1991), is an outgrowth of research on avoidance learning in animals (see Chapter 6). Seligman has demonstrated that when animals or humans are subjected to pain they cannot escape, they develop a sense of helplessness or resignation and thereafter do not attempt to escape painful experiences. The perception of an inability to change things for the better leads to depression. Seligman also suggests that our general societal emphasis on individualism and diminished involvement with others makes us particularly vulnerable to depression.

The learned helplessness theory may also involve a cognitive element, known as attribution or the explanations people assign to their own and others' behavior (Abramson, Alloy, and Metalsky, 1990; Peterson and Seligman, 1984). Once someone perceives that his or her behaviors are unrelated to outcomes (learned helplessness), depression is likely to occur if the person attributes failure to causes which are *internal* ("my own weakness"), *stable* ("this weakness is a longstanding and unchanging one"), and *global* ("this weakness is a problem in lots of settings") (Suinn, 1987). This type of reasoning is further discussed under the topics of attribution theory in Chapter 17.

Is depression affected by the seasons? I've heard of people being treated by simply sitting under bright lights. Some individuals do suffer from seasonal depression, also known as *seasonal affective disorder* (SAD). Although some researchers have found people whose depression occurred during the summer months, most SAD sufferers report winter depression followed by normal mood or even elevation in the spring and early summer (Bower, 1988a; Terman and Link, 1989; Wehr et al., 1986, 1987). Figure 15.7 shows the winter depression pattern of SAD is closely correlated with average daily light from month to month. Studies with controlled periods of exposure to artificial lights for winter depression produced dramatic improvement in mood, and when treatment was discontinued relapses occurred (Rosenthal et al., 1984; Sack et al., 1990).

Learned Helplessness: In Seligman's theory a state of helplessness or resignation in which people or animals learn that escape is impossible and depression results.

Gender and Cultural Diversity
GENDER, CULTURE, AND DEPRESSION

Research shows that depression is best explained by a combination of both biological and psychological theories, and cultural studies bear this out. Although the evidence for a culture-general set of symptoms is not as strong as it is for schizophrenia, five major symptoms have been found to exist across cultures: frequent and intense sad affect, loss of enjoyment, anxiety, difficulty in concentrating, and lack of energy (Escobar, Gomez, and Tuason, 1983; World Health Organization, 1983). There also is evidence of culture-specific symptoms. For example, feelings of guilt are found more often in North America and Europe (Draguns, 1990; Marsella, 1980). In China, somatization (converting depression into bodily complaints) is more frequent than in other parts of the world (Draguns, 1990; Kleinman, 1982).

DOONESBURY   by Garry Trudeau

Women are two to three times more likely than men to suffer serious depression. Some research suggests this gender difference may be the result of prejudice and discrimination or womens' higher levels of poverty.

Universal Press Syndicate © 1976 G. Trudeau.

Not only does culture have an impact on depression, so does gender. One of the most widely accepted conclusions in the analysis of mental illness is that women are more likely than men to suffer depressive symptoms (Brislin, 1993). In America, the rate of clinical (or severe) depression for women is two to three times that of men, and this ratio holds true in several other Western, industrialized nations (McGrath et al., 1990; Nolen-Hoeksema, 1990; Strickland, 1992).

Why are women more depressed?   Recall that some cases of severe depression are linked to biochemical imbalances in serotonin and norepinephrine. Noting that reproductive-related events, such as menstruation, pregnancy, childbirth, and menopause, may cause changes in certain hormones that also affect serotonin levels, some researchers suggest that this covariance between hormones and serotonin may explain gender differences in depression (Hamilton and Gallant, 1990; Hoyenga and Hoyenga, 1993).

On the other hand, a recent three-year study conducted by the American Psychological Association (APA) found that the higher rate of female depression was best explained by cultural factors, such as poverty, discrimination, unhappy marriages, and sexual or physical abuse (McGrath et al., 1990). Brislin (1993) suggested that the powerlessness of women in almost all societies and the subsequent frustrations better explain their higher rate of depression than biological factors.

Other researchers suggest that socialization patterns for males and females reinforce certain behaviors that predispose women toward depression (Cox and Radloff, 1984; Nolen-Hoeksema, 1990). Females are encouraged toward passivity, dependence, and emotional sensitivity, whereas males are socialized toward activity, independence, and suppression of emotions. Because depression is related to lack of activity, low energy, and feelings of helplessness, it is not surprising that women may be more depressed than men. In addition, the greater degree of aggression found in males may mean that they act out their frustrations rather than do nothing or blame themselves. ■

Suicide: Ending Your Own Life

Whatever the causes of depression, one of the major dangers associated with it is the increased risk of suicide. Severely depressed people often become suicidal as a result of their feelings of hopelessness and helplessness. Ironically, they may be unable to act on their suicidal feelings while deeply depressed, but in the period following the deepest depression, when others see them getting better, they may muster sufficient energy to carry out their wish to die.

At the present time, suicide ranks among the top 10 causes of death in most Western countries (Carson, Butcher, and Coleman, 1992). In the United States, there are over 25,000 suicides a year and as many as 200,000 suicide attempts. Statistics, however accurate, can never describe the full horror of suicide. If we look at the typical suicide victim, we find a depressed, lonely individual who is often undergoing a *temporary* crisis in his or her life. During this temporary, albeit severe psychological distress, the person makes the *permanent* decision to end his or her life. Studies show that the vast majority of people who take their own lives are actually very ambivalent (Shneidman, 1987). They don't necessarily want to die, they're just unsure about how to go on living. They cannot see their problems objectively enough to see an alternative course of action.

A second major tragedy associated with suicide is the lifelong sadness experienced by the friends and relatives of the suicide victim. Children of parents who kill themselves are at particularly high risk of severe personality disturbances and of committing suicide themselves (Ojanlatua et al., 1987). As Shneidman (1969) puts it, "The person who commits suicide puts his psychological skeleton in the survivor's emotional closet" (p. 22).

How can you tell if someone is suicidal?   A list of high-risk factors is presented in Table 15.7, but as a general rule signs of depression and dramatic changes in behavior are good clues. People who attempt suicide often give suicidal threats or warnings, such as "I wish I were dead" or "I have nothing to live for." If you believe someone is contemplating suicide, act on your beliefs. Stay with the person if there is any immediate danger, and encourage him or her to talk to you rather than withdraw. Show the person that you care, but don't give false reassurances that "everything will be O.K." This type of response makes the suicidal person feel more alienated. Instead, openly ask if the person is feeling hopeless. Do not be afraid to discuss suicide with persons who feel depressed or hopeless, fearing that you will just put ideas into their heads. The reality is that people who are left alone or who are told they can't be serious about suicide often attempt it. If you suspect someone is suicidal, it is vitally important that you help the person obtain counseling or surveillance in a treatment center and share your suspicions with parents, friends, or others who can help in a suicidal crisis. In order to save a life you may have to betray a secret when someone confides in you (Orbach, 1988). There is an American Association of Suicidology (1-303-692-0985) for anyone who needs or wants help or further information.

Table 15.7   **Risk Factors for Suicide**

Factors	Findings
History	People who have previously attempted suicide, have family members who committed suicide, have high levels of anxiety or hopelessness, or threaten suicide are more likely to commit suicide.
Ethnicity	Whites and Native-Americans are more likely to commit suicide than Black-Americans and Mexican-Americans.
Social isolation	People who have few significant social contacts and who keep to themselves and communicate poorly with others are at higher risk of suicide.
Substance abuse	Drug abuse is the major problem in about half the suicide cases under 30 years old. In half of the cases in this age range, the drug abuse preceded other problems such as depression.
Psychiatric disorders	About 78% of all persons who commit suicide suffer from mood disorders. At least 20% of schizophrenic individuals make suicide attempts and about 10% eventually take their lives.
Gender	Males are more likely to commit suicide, but more females attempt suicide. (This occurs because men tend to use more lethal weapons such as guns.)
Marital status	The suicide rate for unmarried individuals is over twice as high as the rate for married people.
Stresses	25% of all suicide victims have suffered a broken love affair or marriage in the year before their death. In most other cases, the stresses are less catastrophic but lead to a sense of hopelessness.
Profession	Certain occupations, such as physicians, dentists, lawyers, and clinical psychologists, have a higher risk of suicide.

Source: Davis and Kosky (1991); Jamison (1993); Murphy and Wetzel (1990); Sarason and Sarason (1993).

Review Questions

1. How are mood disorders different from everyday changes in feelings?
2. What are the two major types of mood disorders?
3. What is Seligman's learned helplessness theory of depression?
4. People who experience depression primarily during certain seasons may be suffering from _____ .
5. One of the major dangers of severe depression is the increased risk of _____ .

Answers to Review Questions can be found in Appendix C.

OTHER DISORDERS

- *What causes dissociative disorders and other forms of abnormal behavior?*

We have just discussed anxiety, schizophrenia, and mood disorders. In this section, we will briefly describe four additional disorders—dissociative, somatoform, personality, and substance-related disorders.

Dissociative Disorders: When the Personality Splits Apart

Dissociative Disorder: Stress-related disorder characterized by amnesia, fugue, or multiple personality.

The most dramatic and popularized cases of psychological disorders are the dissociative disorders. There are several types of dissociative disorders, but all involve a splitting apart (dissociation) of critical elements of the personality. Individuals separate themselves from the core of their personality by failing to recall or identify past experience *(dissociative amnesia),* by leaving home and wandering off *(dissociative fugue),* or by developing completely separate personalities *(dissociative identity disorder,* also known as *multiple personality disorder).*

Why would someone want to separate from their basic personality? The major problem underlying all dissociative disorders is the need to escape from stress. By developing amnesia, running away, or creating separate personalities, the individual is able to cope (though in a maladaptive way) with the stressors and deny responsibility for unacceptable behavior. Children who are victims of incest, for example, may develop amnesia for the actual sexual episodes (Berkowitz, 1987). In cases of violent or sadistic incest, the victim may block out all memories for long segments of time. Some researchers have also found that about 98 percent of people with multiple personalities were abused as children (Chance, 1986).

Dissociative Amnesia

Dissociative Amnesia: Inability to recall the personal past as a result of psychological stress.

Dissociative amnesia is a partial or total inability to recall past experience. Although memory loss also occurs with brain damage, psychosis, and substance abuse, dissociative amnesia involves a failure to *recall* specific information. The "forgotten" information is still there, but it is beneath the level of consciousness. People with this disorder tend to forget personal information such as their name and address and are unable to recognize parents and friends. But they rarely forget impersonal facts such as the name of their country or skills such as driving a car and reading a book (Carson et al., 1992).

During the period of amnesia, the person is often indifferent about the memory disturbance but may seem perplexed and disoriented and may wander purposelessly. In movies, a return of memory often occurs when the person is hit over the head. In real life, however, memories generally return spontaneously with no physical stimulus. Complete recovery with no return of amnesia is usual.

Dissociative Fugue

Dissociative fugue is a more unusual form of amnesia in which the person retreats further from stress by developing what is called a *fugue* (Latin for "to flee") state. Individuals wander away from home and often assume a new identity. Although all personal memories from the former life are blocked, other abilities are unimpaired and the individual appears normal to others. After a period of time—days, months, or sometimes years—they suddenly "wake up" and find themselves in a strange place, not knowing how they got there and with complete amnesia for the period of the fugue. Recovery is usually complete, but people seldom recall experiences that happened during the fugue state.

Dissociative Fugue: A type of amnesia in which people suddenly leave where they live and assume a new identity.

Multiple Personality (MPD) or Dissociative Identity Disorder

A person with multiple personality disorder (MPD), or dissociative identity disorder, has two or more distinct personality systems that become dominant at different times. Each personality has unique memories, behaviors, and social relationships. Transition from one personality to another occurs suddenly and is often associated with psychological stress. Usually the original personality has no knowledge or awareness of the existence of the alternate subpersonalities, but all of "them" may be aware of lost periods of time. Often, the alternate personalities are very different from the original personality and may be of the opposite sex or a different race or age.

Multiple Personality Disorder (MPD): Dissociative identity disorder characterized by the presence of two or more distinct personality systems within the same individual.

Although MPD is believed by many psychologists to be rare, a few well-publicized cases have drawn attention to it. The book and movie *The Three Faces of Eve* presented the story of Chris Sizemore, a young homemaker who discovered that she had three separate personalities: "Eve White," a mild, meek, and virtuous wife and mother; "Eve Black," an extroverted, seductive, adventurous woman who rejected her marriage and family; and a nameless third personality who seemed to blend the traits of the other two. The book and movie *Sybil* portrayed the case of Sybil Dorsett, a midwestern schoolteacher who experienced 16 personalities that would take turns controlling her body. Instead of thinking of herself as one person who behaved differently at times Sybil had lapses of memory when she became "another person." When she was "Peggy Lou," she was aggressive and capable of anger. As "Vickie," she was a confident and sophisticated woman who knew of the other personalities.

What caused Sybil to develop these other personalities?   As a child, Sybil would escape from the cruel reality of physical and emotional abuse at the hands of her sadistic mother by imagining that what she was experiencing was happening to another imaginary person. She apparently resorted to this method of dealing with trauma and stress again and again. The dissociation from ordinary consciousness to the imagined personality became so complete that she would often find herself regaining consciousness without any memories of the previous days or years. Eventually, she sought the help of a psychiatrist, who treated her for 11 years before she became *just* Sybil (Schreiber, 1973).

Multiple personality disorder is a very controversial psychological disorder. Some researchers and mental health professionals even question whether the disorder actually exists. They suggest that many cases of multiple personality are faked and that other cases result from unconscious efforts by the persons involved to please the therapist ("Dissociation and Dissociative Disorders," 1992; Loftus, 1993; Spanos, Weekes, and Bertrand, 1985). Such skeptics believe that therapists may be unintentionally encouraging and thereby overreporting multiple personalities. On the other side of the debate are psychologists who not only accept the validity of multiple personality but believe the condition is underdiagnosed (Kluft, 1991). They point out that people who suffer this disorder often have histories of child abuse or sexual abuse ("Dissociation and Dissociative Disorders," 1992; Herman and Harvey, 1993; Ross et al., 1989). They believe the child was so traumatized during early childhood abuse that the only escape was to retreat into an alternate personality.

In the television drama Sybil, actress Sally Field won an Emmy Award for her sensitive portrayal of a woman suffering from multiple personality disorder (MPD). Joanne Woodward portrayed the psychiatrist who spent long hours helping Sybil recover.

Somatoform Disorders: Psychological Disorders and the Body

Somatoform Disorder: Psychological disorders in which the symptoms take a somatic (bodily) form without apparent physical cause.

In somatoform disorders people experience physical symptoms such as blindness, paralysis, or pain without a physical cause (Chelune, 1984). *Soma* is the Latin word for body, hence somatoform disorders are thought to be psychological disorders that take the form of bodily ailments. There are several different somatoform disorders. We will discuss one of the most dramatic, conversion disorder.

Conversion Disorder: A somatoform disorder in which a person "converts" an emotional conflict into a physical symptom such as paralysis.

In a conversion disorder the person "converts" severe emotional conflict into a physical symptom such as paralysis, inability to speak, seizures, or blindness. The conversion generally serves to excuse the person from a threatening situation (e.g., a soldier may become blind or paralyzed just before a battle). In some cases of conversion disorder, there are telltale clues about the psychological origins of the illness. For example, the person may show little concern over his or her symptoms—a pattern known as *la belle indifference,* or beautiful indifference. Or, the person may have physical symptoms inconsistent with the known facts about anatomy and physiology. Also, conversion symptoms typically disappear when the victim is asleep, hypnotized, or anesthetized.

Hypochondriasis: A somatoform disorder in which a person has an extreme fear of illness and disease.

Is conversion disorder a type of hypochondria? No, hypochondriasis is a separate type of somatoform disorder in which people have a powerful and exaggerated fear of disease. They are convinced they either presently have, or will soon develop, serious physical disorders. They spend hours examining medical books and their bodies, searching for signs of serious illness. Even when thorough medical examinations reveal no physical disorder, a person with hypochondriasis remains fearful.

What causes a conversion disorder? During the nineteenth century, as a young physician, Sigmund Freud was among the first to note that hysterical symptoms could be removed through hypnosis. As you may recall from Chapter 14, Freud's treatment of hysterical neurosis was a turning point in his career and the foundation for the therapy that he developed, known as psychoanalysis. Freud believed hysterical neurosis was a *conversion* of repressed sexual instincts. That is, anxiety over unacceptable sexual urges was converted into a somatic or bodily complaint. On the other hand, learning theorists suggest that the *sick role* associated with conversion disorders has important rewards and payoffs. The person gets attention and often avoids unpleasant situations (both positive and negative reinforcement) through the "illness."

Gender and Cultural Diversity

HYSTERIA AND THE "WANDERING UTERUS"

Have you ever wondered why the surgical removal of the uterus is called a "hysterectomy?" Why not "uterusectomy" or "uterectomy?" Today few people realize that conversion disorder was originally called hysteria or hysterical neurosis. The word *hysteria* comes from the Greek word for uterus, and it was once believed that symptoms of *hysterical neurosis* could be relieved through the surgical removal of the uterus—hence the term "hysterectomy."

At the time of the early Greeks, who coined the term *hysteria,* it was believed that childless women and women without sexual partners suffered from various physical disorders that could be traced to their "wandering" uterus. Some physicians believed the uterus dried out from lack of use and tended to float or wander around the female's body, presumably symbolizing the woman's longing for procreation. Depending on where the wandering uterus settled, it produced particular physical symptoms. Lodging in the throat, for example, resulted in sensations of choking. While treatments for hysteria included leaching, cauterizing, and removal of the uterus, the best remedy was believed to be pregnancy, since it supposedly anchored the uterus. ■

Personality Disorders: The Antisocial Personality

Personality Disorders: A DSM-IV category that describes individuals with inflexible, maladaptive personality traits. The best known type is the antisocial personality.

People are diagnosed as having a personality disorder if they have inflexible and maladaptive personality traits that cause significant social and/or occupational problems.

There are several types of personality disorders included in this category in DSM-IV, but here we will focus on the best-known type, antisocial personality disorder.

The term antisocial personality is used interchangeably with the terms "sociopath" and "psychopath." These labels describe behavior so far outside of the usual ethical or legal standards that it seems to represent a particular type of abnormal personality development. From the perspective of public safety and societal harm, antisocial personality disorder is the most serious of all mental disorders. Like Ken Bianchi, who was introduced at the beginning of this chapter, people with antisocial personality disorder typically display persistent patterns of impulsive, selfish, immoral, and even criminal behavior. They are often unable to sustain consistent work behavior, maintain enduring attachments, or function as a responsible parent.

Symptoms

The four hallmarks of an antisocial personality disorder are egocentrism, lack of conscience, impulsive behavior, and superficial charm (DSM-IV, 1994). Egocentrism refers to a preoccupation with one's own concerns and insensitivity to the needs of others. An individual with an antisocial personality "continues to move through the world wrapped in his separateness as though in an insulator, touched rarely and never moved by his fellow man" (Horton, Louy, and Cappolillo, 1974). These individuals often suspect they are different from other people and seem not to know what it feels like to care for *anyone*.

People with antisocial personality disorder do not experience anxiety, guilt, or feelings of remorse, even when they have caused great distress or suffering in other people (Magid and McKelvey, 1987). They often remain serene and poised when confronted with their destructive behaviors and feel contempt for anyone they are able to manipulate.

Unlike most adults who have learned to sacrifice immediate gratification for the sake of long-range goals, these individuals act on their impulses, without giving thought to the consequences. They change jobs and relationships suddenly and can be assaultive or reckless. They often have a history of truancy from school and may have been expelled repeatedly for destructive behavior or violation of school rules. Even when they have been consistently punished for their behaviors, they seem to lack insight into the connection between their behavior and its consequences.

Interestingly enough, people with antisocial personalities can be quite charming and persuasive, and they have remarkably good insight into the needs and weaknesses of other people. Even while exploiting the rights of others, they can inspire feelings of trust and confidence. Kenneth Bianchi was so good at charming and manipulating others that he convinced a woman to fabricate an alibi for him to cover the time of some of the killings. Bianchi knew this woman only casually before his arrest, and it wasn't until he was behind bars that he persuaded her to help him (Magid and McKelvey, 1987).

Causes

Although the causes of antisocial personality disorder are not completely understood, research supports both nature and nurture explanations, and a combination of the two is very possible.

Evidence for biological causes comes from studies that find abnormal brain waves in people with antisocial personalities (Volavka, 1990). They have also been found to have a lowered basal metabolism and level of physiological arousal (Carson et al., 1988; Newman and Kosson, 1986). Twin and adoptive studies suggest a possible genetic predisposition to this disorder (Gunderson, 1988).

Evidence for environmental or psychological causes comes from studies that have found a high correlation between styles of parenting and inappropriate modeling and the production of antisocial personalities (Doren, 1987; Eisenberg and Miller, 1989). People with antisocial personality often come from homes characterized by emotional deprivation, harsh and inconsistent disciplinary practices, and antisocial behaviors on the part of parents (Patterson et al., 1989; Pollock et al., 1990).

Antisocial Personality: Personality disorder characterized by egocentrism, lack of conscience, impulsive behavior, and charisma.

Egocentrism: In terms of mental disorders, preoccupation with one's own concerns and insensitivity to the needs of others.

Jeffrey Dahmer and his cannibalism of his murdered victims was a highly publicized example of an antisocial or "sociopathic" personality.

How common is this personality disorder?   The incidence of antisocial personality disorder is about 2 to 3 percent of the population—4 percent for men and about 1 percent for women (Cadoret, 1986; Robbins et al., 1984). Although it would seem that such people would most likely become criminals and wind up in jail, many sociopaths avoid problems with the law and harm people in less dramatic ways as con artists, ruthless business people, and "crooked" politicians.

Substance Related Disorder: When Does Drug Use Become Abnormal?

Substance Related Disorders: Problem use of drugs, such as alcohol, barbiturates, and amphetamines that affect mental functioning.

In DSM-IV, substance related disorders encompass the problem use of many types of drugs. Some of these substances are legal and are used in "normal" ways by the majority of people. For example, in our society drinking alcoholic and caffeine-containing beverages is considered a normal and appropriate way to modify mood or behavior. Having a few beers after work or wine with dinner is commonplace, and many Americans would have a hard time starting their day without a cup of coffee. Many people also use illegal substances occasionally, smoking pot at a party, for example, or taking amphetamines to stay up to study for a test. Drug use becomes a psychological disorder when the individual becomes physically or psychologically dependent on a substance. In DSM-IV, the category of *substance related disorder* is subdivided into two general groups: substance *abuse* and substance *dependence*.

Substance Abuse: Use of a psychoactive drug in ways that interfere with social or occupational functioning.

Substance abuse occurs when drug use interferes with the person's social or occupational functioning. A person would be considered an alcohol abuser if he or she were intoxicated throughout the day or unable to cut down or stop drinking, or if the pattern of use caused erratic, impulsive, or aggressive behavior.

Substance Dependence: Abuse of a psychoactive drug that includes the physical reactions of drug tolerance or withdrawal symptoms.

Drug use becomes substance dependence when it not only interferes with social and occupational functioning but also causes the physical reactions of either drug tolerance (requiring more of the substance to get the same effect) or withdrawal symptoms (physical reactions that occur when a drug is discontinued). These reactions and the problems associated with the use and abuse of psychoactive drugs were described in Chapter 5.

Although recent attention has focused on the problem of use of illegal drugs such as marijuana and cocaine, abuse of alcohol continues to be our major drug problem, creating massive social and personal difficulties. Alcohol causes, or is associated with, over 100,000 deaths each year; it contributes to domestic violence and child abuse; it is the leading known cause of mental retardation; and, after tobacco, it is the leading cause of premature death in America ("Alcohol's toll," 1993). Table 15.8 presents the World Health Organization's guidelines for identifying alcohol dependence.

Table 15.8   Signs of Alcohol Dependence Syndrome

Drinking increases, sometimes to the point of almost continuous daily consumption.
Drinking is given higher priority than other activities, in spite of its negative consequences.
More and more alcohol is required to produce behavioral, subjective, and metabolic changes; large amounts of alcohol can be tolerated.
Even short periods of abstinence bring on withdrawal symptoms, such as sweatiness, trembling, and nausea.
Withdrawal symptoms are relieved or avoided by further drinking, especially in the morning.
The individual is subjectively aware of a craving for alcohol and has little control over the quantity and frequency of intake.
If the person begins drinking again after a period of abstinence, he or she rapidly returns to the previous high level of consumption and other behavioral patterns.

Source: DSM-IV (1994); Edwards et al. (1977); Julien (1992).

What causes alcoholism? Learning theorists generally suggest that alcohol is a powerful reinforcer. It reduces stress, lessens tension and anxiety, and its use is socially conditioned by our culture (Nicoli, 1988; Rodin and Salovey, 1989).

In contrast to learning views, other researchers attribute alcoholism to genetic factors, citing as evidence the fact that the problem tends to run in biological families. Alcoholism in a first-degree relative is considered to be the single best predictor of alcoholism (Mednick, Moffitt, and Stack, 1987). Some studies have shown that 20–25 percent of the sons and 5 percent of the daughters of alcoholics become alcoholics themselves (Goodwin, 1988). These rates are about four or five times greater than those for the general population (Cloninger et al., 1986). Even when children are separated from their biological parents and raised by nonalcoholic parents they remain at higher risk of becoming alcoholic.

Review Questions

1. The major, underlying problem for *all* dissociative disorders is the psychological need to escape from _____ .

2. How is dissociative amnesia different from dissociative fugue?

3. What are somatoform disorders?

4. Another term for sociopathic or psychopathic personality is _____ .

5. When does drug use become substance abuse or substance dependence?

Answers to Review Questions can be found in Appendix C.

PROBLEMS WITH DIAGNOSIS AND LABELING

Now that we have discussed seven major forms of abnormal behavior, let's step back to consider two important questions: Can mental health professionals truly distinguish between the mentally ill and the mentally healthy? What are the consequences of being labeled and treated for mental illness?

In an attempt to answer these questions, David Rosenhan (1973) recruited seven colleagues and friends to help him test whether normal people posing as patients could

• *What are the major problems of diagnosis and labeling?*

Children of alcoholic parents are at much greater risk of also becoming alcoholics. Is this because of a genetic predisposition, modeling by the parents, or the emotional devastation of growing up with an alcoholic parent?

Critical Thinking

PSYCHOLOGY IN ACTION

EVALUATING ARGUMENTS
Do Diagnostic Labels of Mental Disorders Help or Hinder Effective Treatment?

Some researchers, including David Rosenhan, argue that diagnostic labels create a dangerous self-fulfilling prophecy, but others believe that diagnostic classification is necessary and valuable. As a reader, what do you think about this debate? Which argument do you believe is strongest?

Evaluating arguments is one of the most important critical thinking skills. Critical thinkers do not simply endorse the popular position, or choose any side just to avoid saying "I don't know." Critical thinkers analyze the relative strengths and weaknesses of each position in an argument. They are especially sensitive to arguments with which they personally disagree because they recognize the natural human tendency to ignore or oversimplify opposing information. The critical thinker keeps an open mind, objectively evaluates the reasons both sides give, and then develops his or her own independent position.

To sharpen your skills in critically evaluating arguments, we offer the following guidelines.

1. Begin by listing the points and counterpoints of each argument. When all points and counterpoints are not explicitly stated, you will need to read between the lines and make your best guess of what each side might say. Here is an example of this process using the Rosenhan labeling debate:

Point	Counterpoint
Diagnostic labels are sometimes incorrectly applied.	Errors are a natural part of all human endeavors.
Labels can become a self-fulfilling prophecy for the doctor or patient.	This can be minimized by careful attention to correct diagnoses.

(Can you add your own additional points and counterpoints?)

_____   _____

_____   _____

2. After clarifying all the points and counterpoints, use the following analytical tools to evaluate both sides:
(a) *Differentiating between fact and opinion.* As discussed in the critical thinking exercise for Chapter 5, the ability to recognize statements of fact versus statements of opinion is an important first step to successfully analyzing arguments. Reread the arguments regarding diagnostic labels, and label at least two facts and two opinions on each side.
(b) *Recognizing logical fallacies and faulty reasoning.* Several critical thinking exercises in this text are about recognizing faulty logic. For example, incorrect assumption of cause/effect relationships is discussed in Chapter 1, deceptive appeals are presented in Chapters 12 and 14, and incorrect or distorted use of statistics is discussed in the Appendix.
(c) *Exploring the implications of conclusions.* Questions such as the following can help expand your analysis of arguments. "What are the conclusions drawn by proponents of each side of the issue?" "Are there other logical alternative conclusions?"
(d) *Recognizing and evaluating author bias and source credibility.* Ask yourself questions such as, "What does the author want me to think or do?" "What qualifications does the author have for writing on this subject?" "Is the author a reliable source for information?"

Although each of these steps requires additional mental time and energy, the payoff is substantial. You will make better decisions and your opinions will be more valuable because you will have arrived at them through careful reasoning.

gain admission to a psychiatric hospital. Each of these "pseudopatients" followed the same procedure: They called for an appointment at the hospital, and on arrival they complained of hearing voices that said "empty," "hollow," and "thud." Other than this single complaint and giving false names and occupations, each pseudopatient gave totally truthful information to the interviewer and acted normally.

Can you guess what happened? *All* subjects were admitted to various hospitals, and all but one were diagnosed with schizophrenia. Once inside the hospital, the pseudopatients acted normally and never mentioned hearing voices. They spoke normally with hospital personnel, interacted naturally with other patients, and kept extensive notes on their observations. Nevertheless, the hospital staff continued to think of them as patients and treated them as such, never challenging the diagnostic label of schizophrenia even though it did not match their daily behaviors. That they spent a lot of time note taking was described in their charts as "paranoid" behavior.

Despite their normal behavior and full cooperation with the staff, the average length of stay was 19 days. During this time several real patients voiced suspicions that the pseudopatients were not really mentally ill, but no staff member ever detected the deception. On release, the subjects' charts noted their condition as "schizophrenia in remission."

How could this have happened?   Rosenhan suggests that diagnosing mental illness is difficult under the best conditions, and once inside the hospital the psychiatric setting influenced the staff's perceptions. However, critics of Rosenhan's study have pointed out that therapists tend not to suspect patients will lie about experiencing symptoms such as hearing voices (Davis, 1976; Spitzer, 1988). As one of the psychiatrists pointed out, if eight pseudopatients swallowed blood and then reported to an emergency room with blood coming from their mouths, we would never fault the staff for admitting them.

But the fact that eight normal people were misdiagnosed is not the major point of Rosenhan's study. More important is what Rosenhan refers to as the "stickiness of the diagnostic label." Once a diagnostic label is assigned, it can become central and *self-perpetuating.* That is, when a patient is labeled "schizophrenic," the label becomes the central defining characteristic of the person. Individuality is lost. One pseudopatient reported a nurse unbuttoned her uniform to adjust her bra in front of several male patients. She was not attempting to be seductive, she simply did not see the patients as men and real people (Hock, 1992). Diagnostic labels can also become self-perpetuating for the individual. After being treated a certain way consistently over time, he or she may begin to behave in ways that confirm the preconceptions.

Rosenhan's study, a classic in psychology, has significantly benefited the field by leading to greater care in diagnosis and increased awareness of the dangers of diagnostic labels (Hock, 1992). But once a person leaves a mental hospital, the problem of labels and discrimination against the mentally ill continues. The history of once having been a "mental patient" can lead to difficulty in obtaining employment and housing. Even seeking help from a counselor or therapist has been a liability for some candidates for public office (Buie, 1988b).

As we conclude this chapter, you may be feeling overwhelmed by the problems of diagnosing mental disorders and with the many ways of being disturbed. It is important, therefore, that we emphasize the advantages of diagnosis and classification. The DSM is useful for describing the symptoms of various disorders, it standardizes diagnosis and treatment, and it facilitates communication between professionals (McReynolds, 1989). Also, keep in mind that effective treatments exist for most of the disorders discussed in this chapter. These treatments are the topic of our next chapter.

Review Questions

1. Rosenhan and his colleagues were admitted to mental hospitals and all but one were diagnosed with _____ .

2. How are labels of mental disorder central and self-perpetuating?

3. What are the two benefits of Rosenhan's study?

4. What are the advantages of the DSM method of classifying mental disorders?

Answers to Review Questions can be found in Appendix C.

REVIEW OF MAJOR CONCEPTS

STUDYING ABNORMAL BEHAVIOR

1. The statistical standard defines abnormality according to social practices in a culture. The subjective discomfort approach evaluates behavior as abnormal when the individual is discontented. The maladaptive functioning model considers behavior abnormal when it interferes with an individual's functioning within his or her own life and within society.

2. Windigo *psychosis* is an example of a culturally relative mental disorder. Research has also found several culturally general symptoms of mental disorders.

3. Belief that demons cause abnormal behavior was common in ancient times. The medical model, which emphasizes diseases and illness, replaced this demonological model. During the Middle Ages, demonology returned and exorcisms were used to treat abnormal behavior. Asylums began to appear toward the close of the Middle Ages.

4. Critics of the medical model often use psychological perspectives, which emphasize unconscious conflicts, inappropriate learning, faulty cognitive processes, and negative self-concepts in the development of abnormal behavior. Modern biological theories emphasize physiological causes for problem behaviors.

5. The *Diagnostic and Statistical Manual of Mental Disorders* (DSM-IV) categorizes disorders and provides detailed descriptions useful for communication.

ANXIETY DISORDERS

6. People with anxiety disorders have persistent feelings of threat in facing everyday problems. Phobias are exaggerated fears of specific objects or situations, such as agoraphobia, a fear of being in open spaces. In generalized anxiety disorders, there is a persistent free-floating anxiety. In panic disorder, anxiety is concentrated into brief or lengthy episodes of panic attacks. In obsessive-compulsive disorder, persistent anxiety-arousing thoughts (obsessions) are relieved by ritualistic actions (compulsions) such as handwashing.

7. In posttraumatic stress disorder, a person who has experienced an overwhelming trauma, such as rape, experiences recurrent maladaptive emotional reactions, such as exaggerated startle responses, sleep disturbances, and flashbacks.

8. Two common explanations for anxiety disorders are learning and biology. Learning theorists suggest anxiety disorders result from classical and operant conditioning, as well as modeling and imitation. The biological perspective suggests that genetic predispositions, brain abnormalities, and heredity influence the development of anxiety disorders.

SCHIZOPHRENIA

9. Schizophrenia is a serious psychotic mental disorder that afflicts approximately one out of every 100 people. The four major symptoms are disturbances in perception (impaired filtering and selection, and hallucinations); language and thought disturbances (impaired logic, word salads, neologisms, and delusions); affect (emotional disturbances—either exaggerated or blunted); and behavioral disturbances (social withdrawal, bizarre mannerisms, catalepsy, waxy flexibility).

10. In reaction to problems with previous categories of schizophrenia (paranoid, catatonic, disorganized, and undifferentiated), an alternative classification system has been proposed. Schizophrenic symptoms involving distorted or excessive mental activity (e.g., delusions and hallucinations) would be classified as *positive symptoms,* whereas symptoms involving behavioral deficits (e.g., toneless voice, flattened emotions) would be classified as *negative symptoms.*

11. Biological theories of the causes of schizophrenia emphasize disruptions in neurotransmitters (primarily dopamine), brain damage (such as enlarged ventricles and lower levels of activity in the frontal and temporal lobes), and genetics (people inherit a predisposition).

12. Psychosocial theories of schizophrenia focus on stress as a trigger for initial episodes and for relapse. Communication deviance also has been suggested. That females traditionally have better communication skills may help explain why females cope better with schizophrenia. Studies of family environments suggest that high expressed emotionality may be linked to a worsening and relapse of schizophrenic symptoms.

13. Explanations for schizophrenia get mixed research support. One proposed solution is the two-syndrome hypothesis, which proposes that schizophrenia is really two separate syndromes with different causes and prognoses.

14. Schizophrenia is the most culturally universal mental disorder in the world. There are numerous culturally general symptoms (such as delusions), but also four major differences across cultures: prevalence, form, onset, and prognosis.

MOOD DISORDERS

15. Mood disorders are disturbances of affect (emotion) that may include psychotic distortions of reality. In major depressive disorder, individuals experience a long-lasting depressed mood, feelings of worthlessness, and loss of interest in most activities. The feelings are without apparent cause and the individual may lose contact with reality. In bipolar disorder, episodes of mania and depression alternate with normal periods. During the manic episode, speech and thinking are rapid, and the person may experience delusions of grandeur and engage in impulsive behaviors.

16. Biological theories of mood disorders emphasize disruptions in neurotransmitters (especially dopamine and serotonin). Tricyclic antidepressants are often effective in relieving major depression. Bipolar disorders are generally treated with lithium carbonate. There is also evidence for a genetic predisposition for both major depression and bipolar disorder.

17. Psychological theories of mood disorders emphasize disturbed interpersonal relationships, faulty thinking, poor self-concept, and maladaptive learning. Learned helplessness theory suggests that depression results from repeated failures at attempted escape from the source of stress.

18. Depression also has been shown to be related to the season of the year. Most seasonal affective disorder (SAD) sufferers report problems with depression in the winter. Studies with controlled periods of light have been effective in relieving this type of depression.

19. Depression seems to involve several culture-general symptoms (such as frequent and sad affect and loss of enjoyment). Women are more likely than men to suffer depressive symptoms in many countries. Some researchers explain this in terms of hormonal differences, but a large-scale study found cultural factors (such as poverty and discrimination) were better predictors. Other researchers

suggest women are socialized toward certain behaviors (such as passivity and dependence) that predispose them toward depression.

_20._ Suicide is a serious problem associated with depression. By becoming involved and showing concern, individuals can help reduce the risk of suicide.

OTHER DISORDERS

_21._ In dissociative disorders, critical elements of personality split apart. This split is manifested in failing to recall or identify past experiences (dissociative amnesia), by leaving home and wandering off (dissociative fugue), or by developing completely separate personalities (multiple personality disorder or dissociative identity disorder).

_22._ In somatoform disorders, there are physical symptoms without physical causes. In the somatoform disorder called conversion disorder, the person converts an emotional conflict into a physical symptom such as blindness or paralysis. In hypochondriasis, another somatoform disorder, a person is preoccupied with an extreme fear of illness and disease.

_23._ Conversion disorders were once known as hysteria or hysterical neurosis. In ancient times hysteria was believed to be caused by a female's "wandering uterus" and the long-

ing for procreation. Freud thought sufferers of hysteria were converting their sexual urges into bodily complaints.

_24._ Personality disorders involve inflexible, maladaptive personality traits. The best known type is the antisocial personality, characterized by egocentrism, lack of guilt, impulsivity, and superficial charm. Some research has suggested this disorder may be related to defects in brain waves and arousal patterns, genetic inheritance, and disturbed family relationships.

_25._ Substance-related disorder is diagnosed when use of a psychoactive drug interferes with social or occupational functioning and drug tolerance or withdrawal symptoms occur. Learning theories point to maladaptive reinforcement in substance-related disorder. Genetic inheritance patterns occur for abuse of alcohol.

PROBLEMS WITH DIAGNOSIS AND LABELING

_26._ DSM classification has both advantages and disadvantages. The advantages are description of symptoms, standardization of diagnosis and treatment, and improved communication between professionals. However, misdiagnosis is possible, and once someone is labeled "mentally ill" the label often becomes self-perpetuating. Also, individuals diagnosed with mental disorders often suffer social and economic discrimination.

SUGGESTED READINGS

DAVISON, G. C., & NEALE, J. M. (1994). _Abnormal psychology_ (6th ed.). New York: Wiley. A thorough, yet highly readable, presentation of diagnostic categories for abnormal behaviors, their diagnosis, and current treatment.

MALLINGER, A. E., & DEWYZE, J. (1993). _Too perfect: When being in control gets out of control._ New York: Random House. The authors present a fascinating look inside the world of obsessive-compulsive personality disorder. They offer extensive case histories, as well as specific treatment suggestions.

OFFER, D., & SABSHIN, M. (Eds.). (1993). _The diversity of normal behavior: Further contributions to normatology._ New York: HarperCollins. As discussed in this chapter, the concepts of normality versus abnormality are difficult to grasp. The authors offer important insights and clarification of this issue.

SZASZ, T. (1974). _The myth of mental illness._ New York: Perennial Library, Harper & Row. A classic critique of the existing views toward statistically infrequent behaviors, which Szasz describes as "problems in living."

TORREY, E. F. (1988). _Surviving schizophrenia: A family manual._ New York: Harper & Row. Describes the nature, causes, symptoms, treatment, and course of schizophrenia, with special attention to living with schizophrenia from both the sufferer's and the family's point of view.

WOLMAN, B. (Ed.). (1991). _The family guide to mental health._ Englewood Cliffs, NJ: Prentice Hall. This easy-to-read text offers brief descriptions of the various mental disorders and discusses the wide range of possible treatments, all in lay terms.

When she was in college, Frances Farmer decided to become an actress. She eventually became a movie star, but in her efforts to succeed she alienated many people. She argued, screamed, and belittled everyone who disagreed with her. Like many other actresses consumed by their passion for acting, she had volatile confrontations with her directors and often worked herself into a state of exhaustion. As one of her directors said, "The nicest thing I can say about Frances Farmer is that she is utterly unbearable." Her assertiveness and independence also deepened conflicts she had always had with her mother, who eventually became her worst enemy. Frances retreated from the stresses of her career and the loneliness of her life by drinking excessively. Unfortunately, she often became assaultive and verbally abusive during drinking bouts. When she became abusive toward a police officer and a judge, she was committed to a sanitarium. When her conflicts with her mother became violent, she was repeatedly committed against her will to an asylum. Her final stay lasted eight years and terminated only when her parents requested that Frances come home to care for them in their old age.

While in the asylum, Frances was given a number of treatments designed to calm her. One of these was hydrotherapy. She was bound with canvas straps that held her motionless in a cold bath for hours at a time until she became semiconscious. After a few hydrotherapy treatments, she decided to be compliant and passive in order to avoid being subjected to this "therapy." However, she could not avoid outbursts entirely, and her fits of violence led doctors to give her the ultimate "calming" treatment: a frontal lobotomy.

After her release, Frances described her institutional-ization in an autobiography. Here are some of her words:

> For eight years I was an inmate in a state asylum for the insane. During those years I passed through such unbearable terror that I deteriorated into a wild, frightened creature intent only on survival.
> And I survived.
> I was raped by orderlies, gnawed on by rats, and poisoned by tainted food.
> And I survived.
> The asylum itself was a steel trap, and I was not released from its jaws alive and victorious. I crawled out mutilated, whimpering and terribly alone.
> But I did survive.
> The three thousand and forty days I spent as an inmate inflicted wounds to my spirit that could never heal. They remain, raw-edged and festering, for I learned there is no victory in survival—only grief.
>
> *Farmer (1972), p. 9*

Does Frances Farmer's therapy remind you of the early treatments for abnormal behavior described in Chapter 15? While her hospitalization may seem only slightly less barbaric than trephining (boring a hole in the skull) or witch burning, it is important to note that treatments such as hydrotherapy and frontal lobotomy were honestly believed to be helpful. These techniques were not devised for punishment, even though they may have occasionally been used in that way. It is also important to recognize that treatments change and improve over time and can be judged only within their historical framework. Just as we legitimately criticize some of these early therapies, future psychologists will criticize and improve our current methods of treatment.

Today only people with the most severe and intractable disturbances are institutionalized, and abuses such as those described by Frances Farmer are rare. Most people with psychological disorders can be helped with drugs, psychotherapy, or a combination of the two. Psychotherapy is a general term for the various therapeutic techniques employed to improve psychological functioning and promote adjustment to life.

In its strictest sense, psychotherapy includes only therapies used by professionals, for example, behavior modification, client-centered therapy, family systems therapy, and psychoanalysis. The professionals who do psychotherapy include not only psychologists

Psychotherapy: A general term for the various methods of therapy that aim to improve psychological functioning and promote adjustment to life.

who specialize in mental disorders, but also psychiatrists, psychiatric nurses, social workers, counselors, and members of the clergy with special training in pastoral counseling. More loosely, *psychotherapy* can refer to informal talks with friends, teachers, and parents.

In this chapter, we will be talking about *psychotherapy* in the strict, professional sense, and we will focus on the therapies used primarily by psychologists. One exception to this is our discussion of *biomedical therapies* (drug treatments, electroconvulsive shock [ECT], and psychosurgery). Only psychiatrists and other medical doctors can prescribe biomedical techniques, but the biomedical approach is an important adjunct to the type of therapy done by psychologists. This chapter begins with a discussion of the major psychologically based forms of treatment—psychoanalysis, cognitive, humanistic, behavioral, and group therapies. Following this, we discuss biomedical therapies. The chapter concludes by exploring several issues in psychotherapy: the ethics of forced institutionalization, women and minorities as clients, and selecting an appropriate therapy and type of therapist.

As you read Chapter 16, keep the following **Survey** questions in mind and answer them in your own words:

- What do all psychotherapies have in common?
- What is Freudian psychoanalysis? Are there more modern forms of this therapy?
- What are the major cognitive therapies?
- What is different about humanistic therapies?
- How are learning principles used in behavior therapy?
- How is psychotherapy done in groups?
- What are the major biomedical therapies?
- When is therapy necessary and how do you choose a therapist?

ESSENTIALS OF PSYCHOTHERAPY

There are numerous types of psychotherapy, yet all share some common ground. Depending on the individual therapist's specific training and the client's needs, psychotherapy focuses on one or more of the following areas (see Figure 16.1):

• *What do all psychotherapies have in common?*

1. *Disturbed Thoughts.* Troubled individuals typically suffer some degree of confusion, destructive thought patterns, or blocked understanding of their problems. Therapists work to change these thoughts, provide new ideas or

Figure 16.1 The five goals of psychotherapy. Most therapies focus on one or more of these goals with clients.

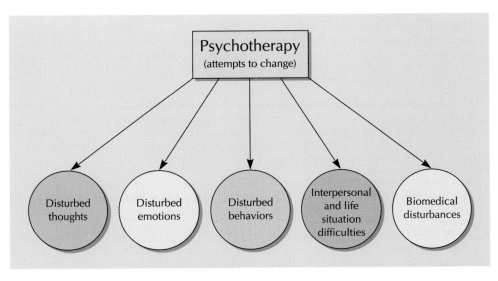

information, or guide the individual toward finding his or her own solutions to problems.

2. *Disturbed Emotions.* People who seek therapy generally suffer from extreme emotional discomfort. By encouraging free expression of feelings and by providing a warm, supportive environment, therapists help their clients replace feelings such as despair or incompetence with feelings of hope and self-confidence.

3. *Disturbed Behaviors.* Troubled individuals usually exhibit problem behaviors. Therapists help their clients eliminate troublesome behaviors and guide them toward more effective living.

4. *Interpersonal and life situation difficulties.* Therapists help clients improve their interpersonal relationships with family, friends, and co-workers. They also help them avoid or minimize sources of stress in their lives, such as job demands or home and family conflicts.

5. *Biomedical disturbances.* Troubled individuals sometimes suffer biological disruptions that directly cause or contribute to psychological difficulties. Therapists help relieve these problems primarily through drugs, and occasionally with electroconvulsive therapy and/or psychosurgery.

Although most therapists work on several problem areas with each client, the emphasis may vary according to the training of the therapist. Psychoanalysts, for example, generally emphasize unconscious thoughts and emotions. Cognitive therapists focus on their client's faulty thinking and belief patterns, whereas humanistic therapists attempt to alter the client's negative emotional responses. Behaviorists, as the name implies, focus on changing maladaptive behaviors. Therapists who use biomedical techniques attempt to change biological disorders.

 Try This Yourself

Psychotherapy is often misunderstood by the general public and many popular myths surround it (Buie, 1988a). Before we begin our discussion of the various therapies, let us examine some of these myths:

MYTH: There is one best therapy.
Fact: As we will discuss at the close of this chapter, many problems can be treated equally well with all major forms of psychotherapy.

MYTH: Therapists can "read minds."
Fact: Good therapists often seem to have an uncanny ability to understand how their clients are feeling and to know when someone is trying to avoid certain topics. This is not due to any special mind-reading ability, but is a reflection of their specialized training and daily experience working with troubled people.

MYTH: People who go to therapists are crazy or just weak individuals.
Fact: Most people seek counseling because they are experiencing some current stress in their life or because they realize that therapy can enrich their current level of functioning. Since most people find it difficult to be objective about their own problems, seeking therapy is not only a sign of wisdom but also one of personal strength.

MYTH: Only the rich can afford therapy.
Fact: Although therapy *is* expensive, there are many clinics and therapists who charge on a sliding scale based on the client's income. Some insurance plans also cover psychological services.

Review Questions

1. The application of various therapeutic techniques to improve psychological difficulties and promote everyday adjustment is known as _____ .

2. How do psychologically based psychotherapies differ from biomedical therapies?

3. Psychotherapy and biomedical therapies focus on five major areas of difficulty. What are they?

4. Match the following therapists with their primary emphasis:

_____ psychoanalysts   (a) faulty thinking and belief patterns

_____ behaviorists   (b) unconscious thoughts and emotions

_____ humanistic therapists   (c) biological disorders

_____ biomedical therapists   (d) negative emotions

_____ cognitive therapists   (e) maladaptive behaviors

Answers to Review Questions can be found in Appendix C.

PSYCHOANALYSIS

What do you think of when you hear the word "therapy"? When we ask this question in class, our students most frequently describe a small, cluttered office with a sofa where patients recline while they tell their secrets to a therapist with a dark beard. Does this description match the one in your own mind?

Actually, this popular, stereotypical image has little to do with the realities of modern therapy. It is probably based on popular photos of Sigmund Freud's office (see the opening photo for Chapter 14) and the film industry's common portrayal of therapy. As you can see in the photos in Figure 16.2, the film industry has a long history of presenting psychotherapy Freudian-style, with a therapeutic couch somewhere in the scene.

Didn't Freud use a couch in his therapy?   Yes, but most modern forms of therapy do not. Freud believed that the unconscious was more accessible when the patient reclined on a couch with only the ceiling to look at. He also felt the therapist should sit out of sight behind the patient. Freud wanted his patients to feel relaxed and nondefensive, almost as if they were talking to themselves rather than revealing information to another person.

But the use of a couch is only one aspect of Freud's specific type of therapy. Let's put the couch in perspective by looking at the general goals and methods of psychoanalysis.

Goals and Methods of Freudian Psychoanalysis: Exploring the Unconscious

Psychoanalysis means just what the name implies: A person's psyche (or mind) is analyzed. During psychoanalysis, the therapist (or "psychoanalyst") works to bring unconscious conflicts, which are believed to date back to early childhood experiences into consciousness. This traditional psychoanalysis is based on Sigmund Freud's central belief that abnormal behavior is caused by unconscious conflicts between the three parts of the psyche—the *id, ego,* and *superego.* Recall from Chapter 14 that Freud believed primitive urges from the id, or overwhelming feelings of guilt from the superego, caused the ego to develop extensive defense mechanisms and compulsive or self-defeating be-

• What is Freudian psychoanalysis? Are there more modern forms of this therapy?

Psychoanalysis: A system of therapy developed by Freud that seeks to bring unconscious conflicts, which usually date back to early childhood experiences, into consciousness. Psychoanalysis is also Freud's theoretical school of thought, which emphasizes the study of unconscious processes.

(a)

(b)

Figure 16.2 The Media's Portrayal of Therapy. Note how Hollywood movies generally portray therapy as being conducted on sofas, and how frequently the therapist falls in love with the patient/client—a highly unethical practice. *(a)* During the movie *Sex and the Single Girl*, journalist Tony Curtis plans to expose his therapist Helen Gurley Brown (played by actress Natalie Wood), but he falls in love with her. *(b)* In the *Prince of Tides*, Barbra Streisand plays a therapist who falls in love with her client (portrayed by Nick Nolte).

haviors. During psychoanalysis these unconscious conflicts are brought to consciousness. The patient comes to understand the reasons for his or her behavior and realizes that the childhood conditions under which the conflicts developed no longer exist. Once this realization (or *insight*) occurs, the conflicts can be resolved and the patient is free to develop more adaptive behavior patterns.

How can it change your behavior just to become aware of a conflict in your unconscious mind? Freud explained that becoming aware of a painful conflict permits a release of tensions and anxieties. He observed that when his patients relived a traumatic incident, complete with disturbing emotions, the conflict seemed to lose its power to control the person's behavior. This process of emotional release, known as catharsis, frees up psychic energy previously devoted to id, ego, and superego conflicts. Healthier, less anxious living now becomes possible.

Catharsis: In psychoanalytic theory, the release of tensions and anxieties through the reliving of a traumatic incident.

Gaining insight into unconscious conflicts is not as simple as it sounds. The ego has strong defense mechanisms that block unconscious thoughts from coming to light. In order to gain insight into the unconscious, the ego must be tricked into relaxing its guard. The four major techniques for "unlocking the unconscious" are free association, dream interpretation, resistance, and transference.

Free Association

Have you ever let your mind wander without attempting to monitor or control the direction of your thoughts? If so, you've probably discovered that some rather unexpected thoughts pop up. In the process of temporarily removing the conscious censorship over thoughts—called free association—interesting and even bizarre connections seem to spring into awareness. In psychoanalysis, the patient is told to say whatever comes to mind. Analysts use free association to overcome the ego's usual style of *repression*—keeping unconscious those thoughts that are embarrassing, irrational, or painful. To encourage free association rather than conversation, the patient reclines on a couch or sits in a comfortable chair while the analyst sits out of sight, often saying little or nothing during the sessions.

Free Association: In psychoanalysis, reporting whatever comes to mind, regardless of how painful, embarrassing, or irrelevant it may seem. Freud believed that the first thing to come to a patient's mind was often an important clue to what the unconscious mind wants to conceal.

The analyst speaks only to offer an interpretation or explanation of what the patients says or does. The rest of the time, the analyst listens closely in order to observe patterns and hidden meanings in the patient's seemingly disconnected ramblings. For example, if a patient's references to his or her father are often interspersed with expressions of anger or with descriptions of frustrating experiences involving various authority figures, the analyst might offer the interpretation that repressed feelings about the father are causing present-day symptoms.

Interpretation: A psychoanalyst's explanation of the significance of a patient's free associations and dreams.

Dream Interpretation

Freud called dreams "the royal road to the unconscious." Because the ego is not as efficient in defending itself against unconscious conflicts during sleep, these conflicts may be expressed in the form of dreams. As we saw back in Chapter 5, Freud felt that dreams could be interpreted on two levels. On a superficial level, interpretation can be based on the *manifest content* of the dream, or the dream's actual events. On a deeper level, dreams may be interpreted in terms of their *latent content,* or the hidden meaning that is expressed in dream symbols. Thus, according to Freudian dream theory, a therapist might interpret a dream of riding a horse or driving a car (the manifest content) as a desire or concern about sexual intercourse (the latent content).

Resistance

When observing the patient's behaviors and verbalizations, the analyst looks for examples of resistance, the tendency to block or prevent the free expression of unconscious material. For example, if the patient is late or cancels an appointment, the analyst assumes that the patient's ego defenses are attempting to keep unconscious conflicts from being revealed. Similarly, if the patient pauses in conversation or changes topics suddenly, the analyst will try to find out what is causing the resistance by pursuing the topic that preceded the block. Resistance is a very specialized form of therapy. It is not the same as a friend suddenly changing the subject or becoming evasive in discussing something with you. To help you remember the concept of resistance, think of this classic joke about psychoanalysis: "If patients arrive on time for their appointment, they're compulsive, if they're early, they're dependent, and if late, they're resistant."

Resistance: A stage in psychoanalysis where the patient avoids (resists) the analyst's attempts to bring unconscious material to conscious awareness.

Transference

Transference: In psychoanalysis, the patient may displace (or transfer) onto his or her relationship with the therapist emotions experienced in the past—especially relationships with the mother or father or other important figures.

During psychoanalysis, the patient may begin to displace (or "transfer") onto his or her relationship with the therapist feelings that were experienced at an earlier stage in life, generally with the mother, father, or other important figures. This process is known as transference. Transference is assumed to have occurred if the patient becomes overly dependent on the analyst or falls in love and seeks to establish an intimate relationship. Rather than taking these reactions and emotions at face value, the analyst interprets them as evidence of unresolved attachments or conflicts in childhood or previous relationships. Transference is considered a valuable technique in psychoanalysis because exposing repressed feelings offers the patient a chance to "work through" unconscious conflicts and gain insight into past and current relationships.

What happens if the patient really does fall in love with the therapist? Or vice versa? Just as the film industry inaccurately portrays therapy as always being conducted on a couch, movies also frequently portray love affairs between patient and therapist. While romance may enliven a movie, it is extremely destructive in a therapeutic setting (Strasburger, 1993). As we discussed in Chapter 1, therapists must have their clients' trust, and they must uphold the highest standards of ethical behavior. A love affair between patient and therapist is a serious breach of professional ethics, and in eight states, psychotherapist–patient sex is a criminal offense (Strasburger, 1993).

Countertransference: The displacement (or transference) by the therapist of feelings derived from his or her past onto his or her relationship with the patient.

If a patient expresses feelings of love in a therapy session, the psychoanalyst would recognize it as transference, and the feelings would be explored for insight into previous pathological or unresolved relationships. Feelings of love or attraction from the therapist to the client are termed countertransference. During their professional training, psychoanalysts are taught to identify and overcome their own tendencies to displace (or "countertransfer") emotional reactions from their past onto their relationship with their clients (Jacobson and McKinney, 1982).

Evaluating Psychoanalysis: Two Major Criticisms

As we discussed in Chapter 14, Freud's theories of personality have been enormously influential, yet also the subject of great debate. The same can be said of his method of therapy. Criticisms of psychoanalysis focus on two major points:

1. *Limited applicability.* Freud's methods were developed in the early 1900s for a particular clientele—upper-class Viennese people (primarily women). While psychoanalysis has been refined and improved by Freud's colleagues (Adler, Jung, Horney, etc.) and modern-day practitioners, it still seems to suit only a select group of individuals. Traditional psychoanalysis is time consuming (often lasting several years with four to five sessions a week) and expensive (sometimes over $100,000). Thus it is unavailable to the general public.

    In addition, psychoanalysis does not work well with severe mental disorders, such as schizophrenia. This is logical since psychoanalysis is based on verbalization and rationality—the very abilities most significantly affected by serious disorders. Success appears to be best with less severe disorders, such as anxiety disorders, and with highly motivated, articulate patients. Critics jokingly suggested the "YAVIS" acronym to describe the perfect psychoanalysis patient: young, attractive, verbal, intelligent, and successful (Schofield, 1964).

2. *Lack of scientific credibility.* The goals of psychoanalysis are explicitly stated —bringing unconscious conflicts to conscious awareness. But how do you know when this goal has been achieved? If the patient accepts the analyst's interpretation of his or her conflicts, his or her "insight" may be nothing more than cooperation with the therapist's belief system (Bandura, 1969). On the other hand, if the patient refuses to accept the analyst's interpretation he or she may be exhibiting resistance. Moreover, the therapist can always explain away a failure. If the patient gets better, it's because insight was obtained. If he

or she doesn't, then the insight was not real—it was only intellectually accepted. This type of ad hoc reasoning is not acceptable by scientific standards (see Chapter 14's section on critical thinking).

How seriously should these criticisms be taken?   While psychoanalysts acknowledge that it is impossible to scientifically document certain aspects of their therapy, they insist that most patients benefit. Partially in response to criticism, however, more streamlined forms of psychoanalysis have been developed. In modern psychoanalytic therapies (which are called *psychodynamic)*, treatment is briefer (usually only one to two times a week), the patient is typically seen face-to-face (rather than reclining on a couch), and the therapist takes a more active and directive approach (rather than waiting for the patient's personal insight). Such refinements have helped make psychoanalysis available to a larger number of people and more immediately effective (Gelman, 1988; Weiss, 1990).

Review Questions

1. What is the basic goal of psychoanalysis?
2. Reliving a traumatic incident to release the associated emotions is called _____ .
3. Which psychoanalytic technique best explains the following situations:
   a. Mary is extremely angry with her therapist. He seems unresponsive and uncaring about her personal needs.
   b. John is normally very punctual, but he has trouble being on time for his therapy appointment.
4. Why is dream interpretation an important part of psychoanalysis?
5. What are the two major criticisms of psychoanalysis?

Answers to Review Questions can be found in Appendix C.

COGNITIVE THERAPIES

Cognitive therapy assumes that problem behaviors and emotions are created by faulty thought processes and beliefs. For example, a cognitive therapist would say that feelings of depression are created by such beliefs as "If I don't do everything perfectly, I am worthless" or "I'm helpless to change my life so that I could feel satisfied." When people have beliefs that are irrational, that are overly demanding, or that fail to match reality, their emotions and behaviors become disturbed (Beck, 1991; Elks, 1987; Freeman and DeWolf, 1992).

Cognitive therapy is similar to psychoanalysis in that the therapist analyzes a person's thought processes, believing that altering destructive thoughts enables the person to live more effectively. Like psychoanalysts, cognitive therapists assume that many of the beliefs that create problem behaviors operate at an unexamined level. Cognitive therapists also agree that exploring an unexamined belief system can produce insight into the reasons for disturbed behaviors. However, instead of believing that a change in behavior occurs because of catharsis, cognitive therapists believe that insight into the unrealistic things a person has been telling himself or herself allows the individual to directly change how he or she interprets events and, in turn, change maladaptive behaviors. That is, self-talk can be changed to sane statements like, "I can accept my faults" or "I can make constructive changes in my behavior." Cognitive restructuring is the name for this process of changing destructive thoughts or inappropriate interpretations.

• *What are the major cognitive therapies?*

Cognitive Therapy: Therapy that focuses on faulty thought processes and beliefs to treat problem behaviors.

Cognitive Restructuring: The process in cognitive therapy by which the therapist and client work to change destructive ways of thinking.

While psychoanalysts focus primarily on childhood relationships within the patient's family, cognitive therapists emphasize the way events and people both inside and outside the family influence beliefs. Going to college or boot camp, falling in love, or becoming a parent can change attitudes and beliefs in significant ways, and interactions with teachers, bosses, and friends can create disturbed as well as realistic ways of thinking.

Rational-Emotive Therapy: Changing Irrational Beliefs

Rational-Emotive Therapy (RET): Cognitive therapy system developed by Albert Ellis that attempts to change the troubled person's belief system.

One of the best-known cognitive therapists is Albert Ellis, a former psychoanalytic therapist who developed his approach, rational-emotive therapy (RET), during the 1950s. Ellis calls RET an A-B-C approach, referring to the three steps involved in creating disturbed responses: (A) an activating event, which is some type of stimulus such as criticism from a boss or a failing grade on an examination; (B) the belief system, which is the person's interpretation of the activating experience; and (C) the emotional consequence the person experiences (see Figure 16.3). Ellis claims that unless we stop to think about our interpretation of events, we will erroneously believe that we go automatically from A (the activating event) to C (the emotional consequence). We fail to see that Step B (the belief system) actually creates the subsequent emotion. Receiving a failing grade on an exam doesn't *cause* the emotion of depression. It is Step B (the belief that "I must be perfect or I'm worthless") that is the culprit.

Ellis's A-B-C model is based on the premise that every person has a fundamental drive for success, love, and security. When these goals are blocked (the activating event), one of two kinds of beliefs results:

1. *Rational beliefs,* such as "I don't like criticism or a failing grade, but it's not the end of the world" or "I have other ways to reach my goals."

2. *Irrational beliefs,* such as "I can't stand any criticism and failure" or "I absolutely *must* perform well at all times."

Ellis believes these irrational beliefs not only produce negative emotions, they also create neurotic behaviors. Convinced that they must achieve impossible goals and unable to cope with the normal frustrations of life, people become anxious, angry, and/or depressed. Ironically, once these negative feelings develop, they tend to perpetuate the faulty, irrational beliefs that caused them in the first place (part B of the model). For example, the depression that commonly results from an irrational belief in perfectionism is often manifested in low energy and low motivation. So the person may turn in work late and it may be of lower quality. The inferior or late work elicits deserved criticism (Part A—the activating event), which supports the irrational belief in the need for perfection (Part B—the belief system), which in turn makes the person more depressed (Part C—the emotional consequence). The inner dialogue goes along these lines: "This poor work and low grade just prove how inadequate I am. I must try harder. Only

Figure 16.3 The development of irrational misconceptions. According to Ellis, people often experience frustrations from blocked goals (A). They then go on to interpret this event in an irrational way (B). Such beliefs lead to negative emotional responses, and these responses then sustain the irrational belief (C).

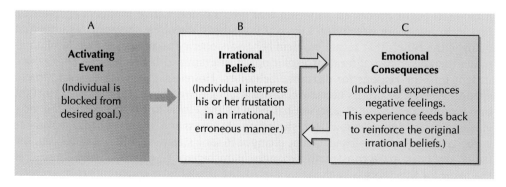

perfection will do." Unfortunately, perfection is not an attainable goal and the thought of having to work harder for something that's impossible is very depressing. Ellis calls this vicious cycle "the Catch-22 of human neurosis" (Ellis, 1987, p. 367).

 Try This Yourself

Before going on, examine your own belief system. Mark "TRUE" or "FALSE" in the space to the left of each item:

_____	1. I must have love or approval from all the people I find significant.
_____	2. I must be thoroughly competent, adequate, and achieving.
_____	3. When people act obnoxiously or unfairly, they should be blamed for being bad, wicked, or rotten individuals.
_____	4. When I am seriously frustrated, treated unfairly, or rejected, I must view the situation as awful, terrible, horrible, and catastrophic.
_____	5. Emotional misery comes from external pressures and I have little ability to control or change my feelings.
_____	6. If something seems dangerous or fearsome, I must preoccupy myself with it and make myself anxious about it.
_____	7. It is better to avoid facing my difficulties and responsibilities than it is to use self-discipline to obtain rewarding things.
_____	8. My past experiences remain all-important. Since something once strongly influenced my life, it has to keep determining my feelings and behavior today.
_____	9. It is awful and horrible if I do not find good solutions to life's grim realities.
_____	10. I can achieve maximum human happiness by inertia and inaction or by passively and uncommittedly "enjoying myself."

Source: Ellis, A., & Harper, R. A. (1975. *A new guide to rational living.* Wilshire Book Co.: Hollywood, CA).

After winning prizes or awards for top performances, some individuals may tell themselves "Now I must perform well at all times." This is the type of irrational thinking that would interest a cognitive therapist.

How can we change our irrational beliefs?   Although Ellis believes that most people require the help of a therapist to see through their defenses and force them to challenge their self-defeating responses, some are able to change their own behaviors. If you marked any of the 10 items in the exercise "true," you may want to try rational-emotive therapy techniques to improve your belief system. Ellis recommends the following steps:

1. *Evaluate the consequences.* Emotions such as anger, anxiety, and depression often seem "natural," but they don't have to happen. Instead of perpetuating these negative consequences by assuming that they *must* be experienced, focus on whether such reactions help you live effectively and enable you to solve your problems.

2. *Identify your belief system.* Find out what your beliefs are by asking yourself *why* you feel the particular emotions you do. By confronting your beliefs, Ellis believes you can discover the irrational assumptions that are creating the problem consequences.

3. *Dispute the self-defeating beliefs.* Once you have identified an overly demanding or irrational belief, argue against it. For example, it is gratifying when people you cherish love you in return, but if they do not, continuing to insist that they must give you what you want will only be self-defeating.

4. *Practice effective ways of thinking.* Continue to examine your reactions to events and situations to create opportunities to dispute irrational beliefs and substitute realistic perceptions. Practice more effective behaviors by acting them out at home and imagining more successful outcomes.

Critical Thinking

PSYCHOLOGY IN ACTION

RECOGNIZING FAULTY REASONING
Logic and Ellis's Rational-Emotive Therapy

Albert Ellis's approach to psychotherapy is based on his belief that illogical thinking is the basis for most human suffering. To improve your logical, critical thinking skills, we will briefly discuss the two basic tests for sound reasoning, and then give you a chance to apply these principles to some irrational misconceptions.

Part I
Consider the following syllogism:

Premise 1	All dogs are animals.
Premise 2	All animals are blue.
Conclusion	Therefore, all dogs are blue.

Is this sound and logical reasoning? To determine whether an argument is sound and whether the conclusions should be accepted, critical thinkers ask two basic questions: "Is the argument valid?" and "Are all premises true?" An argument is considered valid *if* the conclusion logically follows from the premises. The previous syllogism, for example, would be considered valid because *if* all dogs are animals, and all animals are blue, then *logically* all dogs *must* be blue.

Although the test for validity does not rest on the truth or falsity of the premises, the second step in evaluating the soundness of arguments *does* require an examination of the content of the argument. For an argument to be sound, each premise must also be true. This is where the previous syllogism falls apart. All dogs are obviously not blue.

Part II
The same faulty reasoning that underlies the blue-dog syllogism underlies the irrational beliefs that Ellis's form of cognitive therapy seeks to dispel. See if you can identify the problems with the following misconception.

Premise 1	I must have love or approval from all the people I find significant [in order to be happy].

Premise 2	I don't have approval from my mother.
Conclusion	Therefore, I am unhappy.

Is this argument valid? If not, why not? _____
_____

Are the premises of this argument true? If not, which ones are false and why? _____
_____

Think carefully now about your own personal irrational misconceptions (e.g., "I must make everyone happy," "Life must be fair," etc.). In the following spaces, analyze the self-talk surrounding your misconception and try to put it in syllogism form by identifying your two basic premises and your conclusion.

Premise 1	_____
Premise 2	_____
Conclusion	_____

Now answer the following questions:

Is my argument valid? If not, why not? _____
_____

Are the premises of my argument true? If not, which one is false and why? _____
_____

To further practice your reasoning skills, follow this same procedure and logically examine each of your irrational misconceptions. Actively applying your logical skills to your own thought processes will not only improve your basic critical thinking skills, but according to Ellis you will also be in a better position to change self-destructive thought patterns which will, in turn, lead to changes in behavior.

Cognitive-Behavior Therapy: Treating Depression

Another well-known cognitive therapist is Aaron Beck (1967, 1987, 1991). Like Ellis, Beck believes that psychological problems result from illogical thinking and from destructive forms of self-talk. But, unlike Ellis and psychoanalysts who encourage the client to express thoughts and feelings in order to gain insight into the origins of maladaptive behaviors, Beck is more in line with the behavior therapists we will meet in an upcoming section. Beck, and other *cognitive-behavior* therapists, do not consider it essential that the client understands the underlying process that creates illogical thoughts and negative self-talk. Beck takes a much more active approach with his clients and seeks to directly confront and change the behaviors associated with destructive cognitions—hence the term cognitive-behavior therapy.

Cognitive-Behavior Therapy: A therapy that works to change not only destructive thoughts and beliefs, but the associated behaviors as well.

Drawings by Charles Schulz; © 1956 United Feature Syndicate, Inc. Reprinted by permission of UFS, Inc.

Is Charlie Brown engaging in selective perception, overgeneralization, magnification, or all-or-nothing thinking?

One of the most successful applications of Beck's theory has been in the treatment of depression. Beck has identified several thinking patterns that he believes are associated with depression. Among the most important are:

1. *Selective perception.* Depression-prone people tend to focus selectively on negative events while ignoring positive events.

2. *Overgeneralization.* On the basis of limited information, the depressed person will overgeneralize and draw negative conclusions about his or her worth as a person. An example would be considering yourself *totally* worthless because you lost a promotion or failed a class.

3. *Magnification.* A tendency to exaggerate the importance of undesirable events or personal shortcomings and see them as catastrophic and unchangeable.

4. *All-or-nothing thinking.* The depressed person sees things in black-or-white categories. Everything is either totally good or bad, right or wrong, a success or a failure.

Beck's cognitive-behavior therapy works like this: To begin, clients are taught to recognize and keep track of their thoughts. Examples might be, "How come I'm the only one alone at this party" (selective perception), or "If I don't get straight A's, I'll never get the kind of job I need" (all-or-nothing thinking). Next, clients are trained to subject these automatic thoughts to reality testing. Together, the client and therapist devise ways to test these beliefs. For example, if the client believes that he or she must have "straight A's" for a certain job, the therapist needs to find only one instance of this not being the case in order to refute the belief. Obviously, the therapist maintains enough control over these "tests" so they do not confirm the client's negative beliefs, but lead instead to positive outcomes.

This approach, identifying dysfunctional thoughts, followed by active testing, helps depressed people discover that negative attitudes are largely inappropriate. This form of cognitive restructuring is usually combined with Beck's second major technique, persuading the client to actively pursue pleasurable activities in life. Depressed individuals often lose the motivation to seek out experiences they used to find enjoyable. Simultaneously taking an active rather than passive role and reconnecting with enjoyable experiences help in recovering from depression.

Evaluating Cognitive Therapy: What Are the Keys to Its Success?

Considerable evidence suggests that Beck's procedures are highly effective in overcoming not only depression, but also other disorders, such as agoragphobia, eating disorders, anxiety, and even some symptoms of schizophrenia (Beck, 1991; Freeman and DeWolf, 1992). Ellis's rational-emotive therapy has had similar successes with a wide variety of disorders (Dryden and DiGiuseppe, 1990; Ellis, 1987).

Both Beck and Ellis have been criticized, however, for ignoring or denying the client's unconscious dynamics and minimizing the importance of the client's past (Corey, 1993). In addition, Ellis has been criticized for "preaching an ethical system" (Davison and Neale, 1990, p. 541). By labeling his patient's beliefs "irrational" and insisting that they be replaced with "rational" thoughts, he is imposing his own set of standards.

Other critics of cognitive therapies argue that behavioral techniques, not cognitive restructuring, are the key ingredients to success in cognitive therapy (Bandura, 1977, 1986; Wolpe, 1976, 1989). Whether cognitive therapies are successful because they employ behavior techniques or because they change the underlying cognitive structure will undoubtedly continue to be a matter of debate. Many theorists, however, agree that cognitive therapy belongs within the province of behavior therapy. On the other hand, others have noted considerable overlap between cognitive therapy and humanistic therapies. Cognitive therapists emphasize the importance of paying attention to the client's interpretation of the world. This, as you will see in the next section, is the central thesis of the humanists (Davison and Neale, 1994).

Review Questions

1. How do cognitive therapists explain disturbed behavior?
2. Cognitive therapy alters _____ , the things people say to themselves when they interpret events.
3. What are the three steps (the A-B-C) of Ellis's rational-emotive therapy (RET)?
4. What are Ellis's four ways to change irrational beliefs?
5. How does Beck's form of cognitive therapy differ from Ellis's?
6. Aaron Beck identified four types of destructive thought patterns associated with depression (selective perception, overgeneralization, magnification, and all-or-nothing thinking). Using these terms, label the following thoughts:
   _____ (a) Manuel left me, and I'll never fall in love again, I'll always be alone.
   _____ (b) My ex-spouse is an evil monster and our entire marriage was a sham.

Answers to Review Questions can be found in Appendix C.

HUMANISTIC THERAPIES

* *What is different about humanistic therapies?*

Humanistic Therapy: Therapy approaches that assist individuals to become creative and unique persons through affective restructuring (or emotional readjustment) processes.

As you know from Chapter 14, humanists believe human potential includes the freedom to become what one wants to be as well as the responsibility to make choices. Humanistic therapy assumes that people with problems are suffering from a blockage or disruption of their normal growth potential. This blockage creates a defective self-concept. When obstacles are removed, the individual is free to become the self-accepting and genuine person everyone is capable of being.

Imagine for a minute how you feel when you are with someone who believes you are a good person with unlimited potential, a person whose "real self" is unique and valuable. These are the feelings that are nurtured in humanistic therapy approaches.

Client-Centered Therapy: Carl Rogers's Approach

Client-Centered Therapy: A type of psychotherapy developed by Carl Rogers that emphasizes the client's natural tendency to become healthy and productive; specific techniques include empathy, unconditional positive regard, and genuineness.

One of the best-known humanistic therapists, Carl Rogers (1961, 1980), developed a therapy approach that encourages people to actualize their potentials and relate to others in genuine ways. His approach is referred to as client-centered therapy. Using the term "client" instead of "patient" was very significant to Rogers. He believed the label "patient" implied being "sick" or "mentally ill," rather than responsible and competent. Treating people as "clients" emphasizes the fact that *they* are the ones in charge of the therapy and focuses on the equality of the therapist–client relationship.

Empathy and unconditional positive regard are important techniques in humanistic therapies.

Client-centered therapy, like psychoanalysis and cognitive therapies, encourages exploration of thoughts and feelings in order to obtain insight into the causes for behaviors. For Rogerian therapists, however, the focus is on encouraging healthy emotional experiences. Clients are responsible for discovering their own maladaptive patterns and connections, while the therapist provides an accepting atmosphere in which the client is able to freely explore important thoughts and feelings.

How does the therapist create such an atmosphere?   Rogerian therapists learn to create a therapeutic relationship by focusing on three important qualities of communication: empathy, unconditional positive regard, and genuineness (Hergenhahn, 1990).

Empathy

Empathy is a sensitive understanding and sharing of another person's inner experience. When we put ourselves in other people's shoes, we enter their inner world, or *phenomenological experience,* with them. To express empathy, therapists watch body language and listen for subtle cues that will help them understand the emotional experiences of clients. When clients express feelings verbally, they are encouraged to explore them further. The therapist uses open-ended statements such as "You found that upsetting . . ." or "You haven't been able to decide what to do about this . . ." rather than asking questions or offering explanations.

Empathy: In Rogerian terms, an insightful awareness and ability to share another person's inner experience.

Unconditional Positive Regard

Unconditional positive regard is genuine caring for people based on their innate value as individuals. Since humanists assume that human nature is positive and each person is unique, clients can be respected and cherished without having to prove themselves worthy of the therapist's esteem. Unconditional positive regard allows the therapist to trust that clients have the best answers for their own lives. To maintain a climate of unconditional positive regard, the therapist avoids making evaluative statements such as "That's good" or "You did the right thing," which give the idea that clients need to receive approval. When people receive unconditional caring from others, they become better able to value themselves in a similar way.

Unconditional Positive Regard: According to Carl Rogers, the nonjudgmental attitude and genuine caring that the therapist should express toward the client.

Genuineness

Genuineness, or authenticity, is being aware of one's true inner thoughts and feelings and being able to share them honestly with others. When people are genuine, they are not artificial, defensive, or "playing a role." Rogerian therapy is based on the belief that when a therapist is authentic, clients develop a feeling of trust in themselves and are then able to know and express themselves honestly, too.

Genuineness: In Rogerian terms, authenticity or congruence; the awareness of one's true inner thoughts and feelings and being able to share them honestly with others.

Gestalt Therapy: Becoming "Whole"

Gestalt Therapy: A form of therapy originated by Fritz Perls that emphasizes awareness and personal responsibility and adopts a wholistic approach, giving equal emphasis to mind and body.

Gestalt therapy was developed by Fritz Perls (1969), an early leader of the human potential movement. Although Perls was trained as a Freudian psychoanalyst, his therapy techniques are more similar to the humanistic approach. Like client-centered therapists, Gestalt therapists enable clients to find their own meanings for behaviors rather than offering interpretations. The emphasis is on integrating present experiences into a "whole" (or *gestalt*) through a continuing awareness of one's current thoughts, feelings, and body sensations.

But isn't my past a part of the whole? Gestaltists believe that focusing on the past distracts people from the quality of their current reality (Polster and Polster, 1973). Past experiences are disregarded except when they reappear as memories, at which time they can have an effect on the current situation. Instead of focusing on the past, other people, or the environment as the source for current problems, Gestalt clients are taught to understand and assume full responsibility for their present lives (Perls, 1969).

One technique in Gestalt therapy is the *awareness exercise*. In an awareness exercise, the therapist asks "what" questions ("What are you aware of right now?") instead of "why" questions that evaluate the past. During such exercises, clients are taught to pay attention to their body cues, such as muscle tension, facial expressions, and gestures. They are told to repeat and exaggerate facial expressions and gestures to discover their full function and significance. Clenched hands, for instance, might be increased to a strangling motion when the gesture is exaggerated.

Although Perls's Gestalt therapy is in many ways similar to Rogers's client-centered approach, it differs in important ways. Rogerians seek to create a warm and accepting environment in the therapy situation. But Gestaltists believe it is important to challenge and confront clients when they are inconsistent or insincere in their statements. For example, if a client is speaking of a painful event yet smiling at the same time, the Gestalt therapist would call attention to the lack of consistency between the smile and the stated feelings. Gestaltists believe that in the safe environment of therapy, confrontation with the therapist is invaluable. Each client must reclaim those parts of themselves they have disowned if they are to become whole.

Evaluating Humanistic Therapy: Does It Help?

Critics argue that the basic tenets of humanistic therapy, such as self-actualization and self-awareness, are difficult to test scientifically. Most of the research on the outcomes of humanistic therapy relies on client self-reports. Given that people are motivated to justify their time and expense in therapy, self-reports are not given much credence. In addition, research on specific therapeutic techniques, such as Rogerian "empathy" or the Gestalt "awareness exercise" has had mixed results (Beutler et al., 1986; Simkin and Yontef, 1984).

Nevertheless, humanistic therapy can help unhappy people, if not the severely disturbed, to understand themselves better (Davison and Neale, 1990). Who wouldn't enjoy and profit from talking about their problems with a warm and accepting therapist like Carl Rogers? And who couldn't benefit from working with a good Gestalt therapist to increase awareness of their behavior and take responsibility for it?

Review Questions

1. Humanistic therapy assumes problem behavior results from _____ .
2. Label each of the following Rogerian therapy techniques:
   _____ (a) A sensitive understanding and sharing of another's inner or phenomenological experience.

_____ (b) The honest sharing of inner thoughts and feelings.

_____ (c) A nonjudgmental and caring attitude toward another that does not have to be earned.

3. In an _____ exercise, a Gestalt therapist asks "what" questions instead of "why."

4. What is the major difference between Rogerian therapy and Gestalt therapy?

Answers to Review Questions can be found in Appendix C.

BEHAVIOR THERAPIES

Have you ever understood why you were doing something you would rather not do but continued to do it anyway? Sometimes having insight into a problem does not automatically solve it. Take the example of Mrs. D, an agoraphobic woman who had not left her house for 3½ years except with her husband. She had undergone 1½ years of insight therapy and had become well aware of the causes of her problem, but she did not change her behavior. She finally sought the help of a behavior therapist who, instead of working on her understanding of her problems or attempting to restructure her feelings, systematically trained her to behave differently. Mrs. D's behavior therapist worked with her to *extinguish* the anxiety she felt about leaving her house. For several therapy sessions, she was guided by her therapist to visualize herself traveling alone to the clinic where she was treated. During these visualization exercises, she concentrated on keeping her body relaxed. Whenever she experienced anxiety, she thought the words "calm, no panic" to relax herself. After less than two months of behavior therapy, she was able to leave her house and travel alone to appointments (Lazarus, 1971).

As this example shows, behavior therapy (also known as behavior modification) uses learning principles to change behaviors (see Chapter 6). Behavior therapists believe it is generally unnecessary to obtain insight or restructure feelings before changes in behavior can occur. The focus in this approach is on the problem behavior itself rather than on any underlying causes or "disease" states. But the person's feelings and interpretations are not disregarded. Behavior therapists believe that abnormal or maladaptive behaviors are learned in the same way that adaptive behaviors are learned. Thus, abnormal behaviors can also be "unlearned" if treated systematically.

In behavior therapy, the therapist diagnoses the problem by listing the maladaptive behaviors that occur and the adaptive behaviors that are absent. The therapist then attempts to *decrease* the frequency of maladaptive behaviors and *increase* the frequency of adaptive behaviors. To accomplish this type of change, a behavior therapist draws on principles of classical conditioning, operant conditioning, and modeling.

Classical Conditioning Techniques: Changing Associations

Principles of classical conditioning, derived from Pavlov's model for associating two stimulus events, are used to decrease maladaptive behavior by creating new associations to replace the faulty ones (Chapter 6). Behavior therapy techniques based on classical conditioning principles include systematic desensitization and aversion therapy.

Systematic Desensitization

Mrs. D's behavior therapist used systematic desensitization to extinguish her agoraphobia, which behavior therapists consider a classically conditioned anxiety response. Systematic desensitization is a gradual process of associating a hierarchy of fear-evoking stimuli with deep relaxation. It is based on the opposite actions of the sympathetic and parasympathetic branches of the autonomic nervous system (see Chapter 2). Since the

• How are learning principles used in behavior therapy?

Behavior Therapy: A group of techniques based on learning principles that are used to change maladaptive behaviors.

Systematic Desensitization: In behavior therapy, a gradual process of associating a hierarchy of fear-evoking stimuli with deep relaxation.

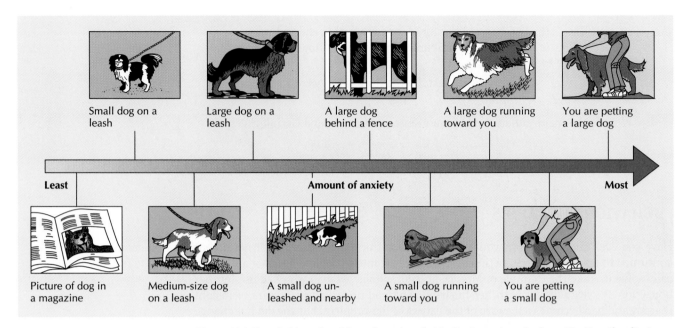

Figure 16.4 *Sample hierarchy of items for a dog phobia*. During systematic desensitization, the client constructs a hierarchy, or ranked listing of anxiety-arousing images, from those that produce very little anxiety to those that arouse extreme anxiety. Note how the images in this figure begin with a picture of a dog in a magazine and end with images of petting a large dog. Each image is graphically visualized in conjunction with relaxation techniques until it no longer arouses anxiety.

parasympathetic nerves control autonomic functions when we are relaxed and the sympathetic nerves are dominant when we are anxious, it is physiologically impossible to be both relaxed and anxious at the same time. The goal, then, is to replace an anxiety response with a relaxation response when confronting the feared stimulus.

Desensitization, is a three-step process. First, a hierarchy, or ranked listing of anxiety-arousing images, is constructed. The therapist and client list about 10 scenes ranging from those that produce very little anxiety to those that arouse extreme anxiety (see Figure 16.4). In the second step, the client is taught how to maintain a state of deep relaxation that is physiologically incompatible with an anxiety response. As the final step, the client visualizes items of the hierarchy, beginning with the least anxiety-arousing image, while maintaining the relaxation state. If any image begins to create an anxious feeling, the client stops visualizing it and returns to a state of complete relaxation. The

Hierarchy: Ranked listing of something; used in the behavior therapy process of systematic desensitization.

During the final stages of desensitization, the phobic individual directly confronts the originally feared stimulus.

THE FAR SIDE   By GARY LARSON

Professor Gallagher and his controversial technique of simultaneously confronting the fear of heights, snakes and the dark.

items are introduced in ascending order until all of them can be visualized without anxiety. Research shows that this imagery technique helps reduce anxiety in actual situations outside the therapist's office (Martin and Pear, 1992; Wolpe, 1990).

In some cases, actual behaviors, such as climbing a ladder for fear of heights or approaching a feared animal such as a dog or snake, are performed instead of imagining the behaviors. In treating Mrs. D's agoraphobia, for example, she first visualized herself traveling unaccompanied to and from the clinic where she was treated and then gradually practiced leaving her home by herself.

Systematic desensitization has many practical applications. If there is something that creates excessive anxiety for you, such as taking examinations or being in small spaces, try the three-step process described above to decrease the anxiety response and develop more realistic and effective behaviors.

Aversion Therapy

In sharp contrast to systematic desensitization, aversion therapy uses principles of classical conditioning to *create* anxiety rather than extinguish it.

Why would a therapist want to make someone feel anxious?   Aversion therapy techniques create anxiety to stop maladaptive behaviors, such as smoking and excessive drinking, that have built up a number of pleasurable associations, such as relaxation or relief of tension. Since these pleasurable associations cannot always be prevented, aversion therapy provides *negative* associations to compete with the pleasurable ones.

If a person wants to stop smoking, for example, he or she is given a brief electric shock (an aversive stimulus) on holding or lighting a cigarette. Similarly, someone who chose aversion therapy for alcohol abuse would take a drug called Antabuse that causes vomiting whenever alcohol enters the system. When the new connection between smoking and pain or alcohol and nausea has been classically conditioned, engaging in the once desirable habit will cause an immediate negative response.

Aversion Therapy: Behavior therapy technique that pairs an aversive stimulus with a maladaptive behavior.

Isn't this also an example of operant conditioning, which uses punishment to decrease a response? Yes. In addition to the classically conditioned associations that are learned in aversion therapy, voluntary behaviors such as smoking and drinking are also influenced by operant conditioning principles.

Operant Conditioning Techniques: Changing the Consequences of Behaviors

Operant conditioning techniques use punishments and extinction to decrease maladaptive behaviors and shaping and reinforcement to increase adaptive ones.

Punishment and Extinction

Punishment can take the form of *positive punishment,* in which an aversive stimulus is applied to an operant behavior to decrease its frequency, or *negative punishment,* in which a rewarding stimulus is removed whenever a maladaptive behavior occurs. In both cases, the result is a decrease in the problem behavior.

One of the most successful applications of positive punishment has been to reduce maladaptive behaviors in autistic children. Autistic children do not respond normally to other people, fail to develop effective speech, and frequently engage in self-mutilating behaviors, such as biting and head banging. In the past, such children often had to be restrained in beds or chairs at all times to prevent injuries. However, use of positive punishment in the form of mild electric shocks whenever the children begin to injure themselves has been successful in eliminating the self-mutilating behaviors (Lovaas, 1987; Martin and Pear, 1992).

One use of negative punishment in behavior therapy is called time out. In time out, the person is physically removed from sources of rewards whenever he or she behaves inappropriately. In one hospital, for example, an overweight schizophrenic patient had

Autism: A condition originating in infancy in which an individual becomes immersed in fantasy to avoid stimulation and communicating with others.

Time Out: Use of negative punishment through removal of people from sources of rewards whenever they behave inappropriately.

In the movie Rainman, *actor Dustin Hoffman offered a sensitive portrayal of autism, while actor Tom Cruise depicted some of the effects of autism on family interactions.*

resisted all attempts to keep her from stealing food from other patients (Ayllon, 1963). Finally, it was decided to remove the woman from the cafeteria whenever she attempted to take more food. The negative punishment of time out removed her from a reward (access to food), and within two weeks her food-stealing behavior was extinguished and she eventually attained a more normal weight.

The technique of *extinction,* or removing all rewards, can also be used to eliminate maladaptive behavior. In the case of the overweight patient, the nurses had been inadvertently rewarding her with attention whenever she misbehaved. Even without the time out procedure, if the staff had completely ignored her misbehavior on the ward floor, it's possible she would not have misbehaved in the cafeteria, since that was just another way to get attention. When diagnosing problem behaviors, behavior therapists try to identify instances such as this in which inappropriate rewards should be discontinued.

Of course, getting rid of problem behaviors is only part of behavior therapy. It is also important to make sure that *appropriate* behaviors are learned in place of inappropriate ones. Behavior therapists use several approaches to increase adaptive behaviors.

Shaping and Reinforcement

In behavior therapy, a behavior to be acquired is known as a *target behavior.* By being rewarded for successive approximations of the target behavior, the person is able eventually to perform the desired response. In one research study, for example, a schizophrenic patient who had not talked for 19 years was given gum as a reward to reacquire language (Isaacs, Thomas, and Goldiamond, 1960). At first the patient was rewarded for any sounds and then later only for words and sentences. In situations such as this, in which the target behavior is not likely to appear on its own, *shaping* techniques can help patients acquire desirable behaviors.

Shaping is also used in behavior therapy to help people acquire social skills, such as making a presentation to a group or asking for a date. In *behavior rehearsal,* clients practice different types of behaviors and are given reinforcement in the form of feedback about how well each works (Lazarus, 1991; Rimm and Masters, 1979). Behavior rehearsal is the technique behind *assertiveness training,* which teaches people to express genuine feelings, improve their social skills, and obtain fair treatment from others. Clients practice using effective verbal and nonverbal responses, beginning with simple situations and progressing to more complex circumstances where they must make an active response. In treating Mrs. D.'s agoraphobia, for example, her therapist used role playing to shape assertive behaviors such as standing up to her domineering father.

Adaptive behaviors can also be taught or increased with techniques that provide immediate reinforcement. One such technique that has proved successful in group situations or institutional settings is the token economy (Martin and Pear, 1992). Tokens are secondary (conditioned) reinforcers such as poker chips, "credit" cards, or other tangible objects that can be exchanged for primary rewards such as food, treats, watching television, a private room, or outings. In a token economy at a treatment facility, patients are rewarded with tokens and gradually shaped toward desirable activities such as taking medication, attending group therapy sessions, or engaging in recreational programs. Patients can also be "fined" for inappropriate or symptomatic behaviors by having tokens taken away.

Doesn't this approach depend too much on the tokens to have any lasting effect? Advocates of the token approach point out that tokens help people acquire beneficial behaviors that become rewarding in themselves. A full-fledged token economy has a series of levels so that increasingly complex adaptive behaviors are required to earn tokens. For example, patients would at first be given tokens for merely attending group therapy sessions. Once this behavior is established, they would be rewarded only for actually participating in the sessions. Eventually, the tokens could be discontinued when the patient receives the reinforcement of being helped by participation in the therapy sessions.

Token Economy: Therapeutic use of tokens in a prescribed way to reward and shape appropriate behaviors.

Token: Tangible secondary (conditioned) reinforcer that can be exchanged for primary rewards.

Modeling: Changing Behavior by Watching Others

Modeling Therapy: A branch of behavior therapy that involves watching and imitating appropriate models who demonstrate desirable behaviors.

In addition to being treated by classical and operant conditioning techniques, clients can learn to overcome maladaptive behaviors by observing others, termed modeling therapy. Both children and adults learn "good" and "bad" behaviors by watching and imitating others. A child's table manners or an adult's taste in clothing are generally a result of observation and imitation. Seeing other people act in various ways can also weaken or strengthen our preexisting tendencies. For example, if you are a fast driver but are observing the 55 miles per hour speed limit, you may be tempted to increase your speed when other cars pass you.

How is modeling done in a therapeutic situation? By watching *appropriate* people perform desired behaviors, the client learns new behaviors. For example, Bandura and his colleagues (1969) asked clients with snake phobias to watch other (nonphobic) people handle snakes. After only two hours of exposure, over 92 percent of the previously phobic observers would allow a snake to crawl freely over their hands, arms, and neck. When live modeling is combined with direct and gradual practice on the part of the client it is called *participant modeling.*

Modeling is also part of social skills training and assertiveness training. Clients learn such social skills as interviewing for a job by first watching the therapist role play the part of the job interviewee. The therapist models the appropriate language (assertively asking for a job), body posture, and so forth, and then asks the client to imitate the behavior and play the same role. Over the course of several sessions, the client becomes gradually desensitized to the anxiety of interviews and learns the appropriate interviewing skills.

Evaluating Behavior Therapy: Successes and Problems

Behavior therapy techniques based on classical and operant conditioning and modeling have been shown effective in treating a wide variety of behaviors (Bandura et al., 1969; Lazarus, 1990; Rice et al., 1991; Rosenthal and Steffek, 1991). For example, token economies have vastly improved the morale and adjustment of seriously mentally ill, retarded, and delinquent individuals (Martin and Pear, 1992; Paul and Lentz, 1977; Schneider and Byrne, 1987). Some patients have been returned to their homes and communities after years of institutionalization.

Critics of behavior therapy, however, raise important questions about its overall effectiveness. These questions are in three major areas:

1. *Generalizability.* What happens after the treatment stops? Can the results be generalized? Critics argue that in the "real world" patients will not be consistently reinforced, and their newly acquired appropriate behaviors may disappear. To deal with this possibility, behavior therapists work to gradually shape clients toward rewards typical of life outside the clinical setting.

2. *Symptom substitution.* Advocates of the psychoanalytic approach argue that behavior therapies simply substitute one symptom for another rather than resolving the underlying psychological problems. A person with a phobia about spiders, for example, may develop a new phobia. However, there is little evidence that symptom substitution actually occurs.

3. *Ethics.* Is it ethical for one person to control another's behavior? Are there some situations in which behavior therapy should not be used? In the movie *Clockwork Orange,* people in positions of power used behavior modification principles to control the general population. Behaviorists reply that our behaviors are already controlled by rewards and punishments, and behavior therapy actually increases the public's freedom by making these controls overt. Also, say the behaviorists, behavior therapy increases self-control by teaching people how to change their own behavior and to maintain these changes when they leave the clinical setting.

Review Questions

1. A group of techniques based on learning principles that are used to change maladaptive behaviors is known as _____ .

2. What is systematic desensitization?

3. When alcoholics take Antabuse, a drug that causes vomiting when alcohol is ingested, they are using _____ therapy.

4. Rewarding successive approximations of the target behavior is known as _____ .

5. How does a token economy work?

6. _____ involves watching and imitating appropriate models who demonstrate desirable behaviors.

7. What are the three major areas of concern regarding behavior therapy?

Answers to Review Questions can be found in Appendix C.

GROUP THERAPIES

Most of the therapies we have discussed can be adapted for use in groups. Group therapies began as a response to the need for more therapists than were available and for a more economical form of therapy. What began as a practical and economic necessity, however, has now become an institution. In addition to being less expensive and more available, group therapy provides other advantages not found in individual therapy:

• How is psychotherapy done in groups?

1. *Group support.* During times of stress and emotional trouble, it is easy to imagine we are alone and our problems unique. Knowing that others have problems similar to ours can be very reassuring. In addition, seeing others improve can be an important source of hope and motivation.

2. *Feedback and information.* When a group member receives similar comments about his or her behavior from all the members of a group, the message may be more convincing than that coming from a single therapist. Furthermore, since group members typically have similar problems, they can learn from each other's mistakes and share insights.

3. *Behavioral rehearsal.* In group therapy, members can role play one another's employers, spouses, parents, children, or prospective dates. By playing the different roles in relationships, people gain insight into their problems and practice new social skills.

These significant advantages have made group therapies very popular. In this section we will focus on three of the most common forms—family therapy, encounter groups, and support groups.

Group therapy provides support from other people and the opportunity to assist one another with shared problems.

In family systems therapy, each member of the family learns ways to improve his or her communication style and faulty interaction patterns.

Family Therapy: Helping Families Cope

Family Therapy: Group therapy that treats the family as a unit, and members work together to resolve problems.

Mental health professionals have long known that dealing with an individual's problem is not enough. To help an unhappy person, therapists often find they must heal relationships within the family structure. Because a family is a system of interdependent parts, the problems of any one of the members unavoidably affect all the others (Beck, 1989; Szapocznik and Kurtines, 1993). A teen's delinquency or a parent's drug problem affects everyone. Family intervention therapy has become very common in recent years (Corey, 1993; Sayette and Mayne, 1990).

The central theme of family therapy is treatment of the family as a whole unit. The problems are seen as affecting everyone, and members work as a group to resolve problems. All members of the family attend therapy sessions, though at times the therapist may also see family members individually or in twos or threes. There are several forms of family therapy, but the most common is family systems therapy.

In *family systems therapy,* the family is seen as an interrelated system in which each member has a major role. Thus, the therapist treats each member of the family while at the same time emphasizing relationships between family members. (The therapist, incidentally, make take any orientation—behavioral, cognitive, etc.) Many families initially come into therapy believing that one member is *the* cause of all their problems ("Johnny's delinquency" or "Mom's drinking"). However, family systems therapists generally find that this "identified patient" is the scapegoat for disturbances within the entire family. For example, instead of confronting their own problems with intimacy, the parents may focus all their attention and frustration on the delinquent child. According to Virginia Satir (1976), it is usually necessary to change ways of interacting within the family system to promote the growth of family members and the family as a whole.

Encounter Groups: Promoting Personal Growth

Encounter Groups: A form of group therapy for people who are not seriously disturbed that focuses on personal growth and interpersonal communication.

Encounter groups are a form of group therapy dedicated to personal growth and interpersonal communication; they are not designed for people who are seriously disturbed. Generally speaking, members work to improve awareness of their own needs and feelings and those of others. To accomplish their goal, they engage in intense confrontations, or *encounters,* with other group members. At group meetings, individuals are encouraged to be open and unguarded—to tear down one another's defenses, openly share emotions, and "talk straight" with one another.

Can these sessions be dangerous? As a result of these confrontations, a few people have gotten worse during treatment. But most studies find "casualty" rates of less than 3 percent (Davison and Neale, 1990). Encounter groups are safest when members are carefully screened and trained leaders guide the interactions.

Support Groups: Helping One Another

People suffering from drug abuse, obesity, and depression have traditionally been seen by private therapists. But they can also be helped by participating in *support groups*. Well-known examples of these groups, such as Alcoholics Anonymous, Weight Watchers, and Gamblers Anonymous, are now established throughout the world. Residential programs such as Daytop Village and Phoenix House are also based on the support group approach. There are also support groups for assertiveness training, parent training, and couple communication, as well as groups to help people cope with life crises such as breast cancer, suicide, and so on.

Therapeutic communities, such as halfway houses, are important resources for people with mental disorders. As you will learn in the next section, only rarely is hospitalization the treatment of choice for the mentally ill. In residential therapeutic communities people share the work of running the home and meet regularly to discuss group and individual problems. Though halfway houses can greatly facilitate mental patients' return to the community, neighbors often resist the use of homes in their area for this purpose.

Evaluating Group Therapy: The Special Problem of "Pop Therapies"

Group therapies offer significant advantages to participants, including lower cost and group support and feedback. Family therapy can improve the interactions and personal well-being of each family member (Markus, Lange, and Pettigrew, 1990; Todd and Stanton, 1983). Encounter and support groups provide unique opportunities for people to get information and practice new behaviors in a supportive environment (Galanter, 1989; Valliant and Valliant, 1990).

Despite the overwhelmingly positive aspects of most group therapy, there is a special problem that must be addressed. In recent years a large number of therapies that are commonly practiced in groups and that may qualify for the title "pop therapy" have arisen. One of these unconventional therapies is called *past lives therapy*. It emphasizes the importance of previous lives on our present functioning. Another is called *rebirthing* therapy. In rebirthing, participants are helped to reexperience trauma attending their birth. These fringe therapies are often get-rich-quick schemes of unscrupulous group leaders. Still, the list grows—jogging therapy, soap opera therapy, and so on.

Media attention to these pop therapies and the public's misperceptions of legitimate therapy are both concerns among psychologists. Pop therapies not only mislead people about the true nature of psychology, but they also can be dangerous and expensive for the unwary consumer. Before you join any therapy group, check out the credentials and academic training of the leader, and investigate the group's history.

Review Questions

1. In addition to decreased cost and increased availability, the three major advantages of group therapy are _____ .
2. What is family therapy?
3. Why is it worthwhile to seek family therapy if it appears that only one member of the family has a problem?
4. Encounter groups focus on _____ and _____ .
5. What is the problem with "pop therapies"?

Answers to Review Questions can be found in Appendix C.

BIOMEDICAL THERAPIES

- *What are the major biomedical therapies?*

Biomedical Therapy: Therapy involving physiological interventions (such as drugs or psychosurgery) to reduce symptoms associated with psychological disorders.

Drug Therapy: Use of chemicals (drugs) to treat physical and psychological disorders.

As you read in Chapter 15, drug therapy has been extremely helpful in treating the symptoms of schizophrenia and mood disorders. Hundreds of thousands of severely disturbed patients, who would otherwise spend their entire lives in institutions, can lead productive lives because of antipsychotic, antianxiety, and antidepressant drugs.

Biomedical therapies, such as drug treatment, psychosurgery, and electroshock therapy, must be prescribed by a physician rather than a psychologist. These therapies are based on the premise that problem behaviors are caused, at least in part, by chemical imbalances or by disturbed nervous system functioning. Psychologists work with patients receiving biological therapies and are frequently involved in research programs to evaluate their effectiveness. We will begin our discussion with the most common form of biological therapy—drug treatment.

Drug Therapy: The Pharmacological Revolution

Since the 1950s, drug companies have developed an amazing variety of chemicals to treat abnormal behaviors. In some cases, drug therapy corrects a chemical imbalance in the nervous system. In these instances, using a drug is similar to administering insulin to diabetics, whose own bodies fail to manufacture enough. In other cases, the drugs create effects that relieve or suppress the symptoms of psychological disturbances even if the underlying cause is not thought to be biological.

There are problems in drug therapy such as maintaining the proper dosage level and controlling *side effects,* unwanted reactions. In addition, like other medical treatments, effective drug therapy depends on cooperation of the patient (taking the medication as prescribed) and proper evaluation of the consequences of the treatment.

Psychiatric drugs are classified into four major categories: antianxiety, antipsychotic, antidepressant, and mood stabilizer drugs. Table 16.1 gives examples of drugs in each category.

Table 16.1 Drug Therapy

Type of Drug	Psychological Disorder (see Chapter 15)	Chemical Group	Generic Name	Brand Name
Antianxiety drugs	Anxiety disorders	Benzodiazepines	Chlordiazepoxide Diazepam	Librium Valium
		Glycerol derivatives	Meprobamate	Miltown Equanil
Antipsychotic drugs	Schizophrenia	Phenothiazines	Chlorpromazine Fluphenazine Thioridazine	Thorazine Prolixin Mellaril
		Butyrophenones	Haloperidol	Haldol
		Dibenzodiazepine	Clozapine	Clozaril
Antidepressant drugs	Severe depression (with suicidal tendencies)	Tricyclic antidepressants	Imipramine Amitriptyline	Tofranil Elavil
		MAO inhibitors	Phenelzine	Nardil
		Second generation antidepressants	Tranylcypromine Fluoxetine	Parnate Prozac
Mood stabilizer drugs	Bipolar disorder	Antimanic drugs	Lithium carbonate	Lithonate Lithane Eskalith

Antianxiety Drugs

Antianxiety drugs (also known as "minor tranquilizers") create feelings of tranquility and calmness in addition to relief of muscle tension. These drugs have replaced sedatives (which had side effects of drowsiness and sleepiness) in the treatment of anxiety disorders. Antianxiety drugs, such as Valium and Librium, lower the sympathetic activity of the brain—the crisis mode of operation—so that anxiety responses are diminished or prevented.

Why are there so many warnings about the dangers of drugs like Valium? Unfortunately, people can easily develop tolerance to anxiety drugs, requiring increasing dosages to get the same effects (Gillin, 1991). Also, people become physically dependent on these drugs, and withdrawal symptoms such as convulsions and hallucinations can occur when they stop taking the drugs. Overdosing with these drugs intentionally (to get a stronger effect) or unintentionally (by combining them with other drugs, such as alcohol) can be fatal.

Antianxiety Drugs: Medications used to treat anxiety disorders.

Antipsychotic Drugs

The antipsychotic drugs developed to treat psychotic disorders such as schizophrenia are often referred to as "major tranquilizers," creating the impression they invariably have a strong calming or sedating effect. Some antipsychotic drugs, such as Thorazine, do dampen the positive symptoms of schizophrenia, such as hallucinations and delusions. But other antipsychotic drugs, such as Clozaril, energize and animate patients who suffer the negative symptoms of withdrawal and apathy. The main effect of antipsychotic drugs is to diminish or eliminate psychotic symptoms, including hallucinations, delusions, withdrawal, and apathy. They are not designed to sedate the patient (Baldessarini, 1990a).

Antipsychotic Drugs: Chemicals administered to dimish or terminate hallucinations, delusions, withdrawal, and other symptoms of psychosis.

Do these drugs correct a chemical imbalance or just cover up symptoms? As we discussed in the previous chapter, the symptoms of schizophrenia have been related to an increase in activity of the neurotransmitter dopamine in parts of the brain. The antipsychotic drugs are thought to block the activity of dopamine receptors and therefore restore a more normal chemical balance in schizophrenics (Julien, 1992).

Studies of the effectiveness of antipsychotic drugs have shown that when they work, it is apparently because they change brain chemistry. We know this because nonchemical methods, psychotherapy, and placebos are almost never effective in alleviating the same symptoms (Baldessarini, 1990; May, Tuma, and Dixon, 1981).

Not all patients, however, are helped by these drugs. Between 10 and 20 percent of people with schizophrenia do not respond to medication and 20 to 30 percent who initially respond later relapse (Kane et al., 1988). Antipsychotic drugs also produce a wide range of side effects, from reduced alertness and drowsiness to symptoms similar to Parkinson's disease—muscle rigidity, tremors, and an unusual shuffling gate (Julien, 1992). Recall from Chapter 5 that Parkinson's disease is related to a *deficit* in dopamine, and that the drug L-DOPA increases dopamine and reduces the symptoms of Parkinson's. Since antipsychotic drugs work by reducing excess dopamine, you can see how prolonged use could eventually produce Parkinson-like symptoms. Anti-Parkinsonian medications can reduce the side effects, but they have their own side effects and their use is controversial (Wilson, O'Leary, and Nathan, 1992).

One of the most serious side effects of antipsychotic drugs is Tardive dyskinesia, which develops in 15 to 20 percent of the patients. The symptoms generally appear after prolonged use (hence the term "tardive," from the Latin root for "slow"). They include involuntary movements of the trunk and limbs that can be severely disabling (Julien, 1992). Perhaps more characteristic are the facial and tongue motor disturbances. When students see films about schizophrenia, they often confuse the patient's sucking and smacking of their lips or lateral jaw movements as signs of the disorder rather than the side effects of the drug treatment.

Tardive Dyskinesia: A serious movement disorder associated with prolonged use of antipsychotic drugs.

Because of the large number of nonresponders, the serious side effects, and the possibility of permanent damage from use of dopamine-based antipsychotic drugs, there has long been a search for alternatives. The drug Clozapine was hailed as a wonder drug because it seemed to work with some nonresponders and it did not seem to have serious side effects. Following a number of deaths in Finland, however, Clozapine was removed from the market, though today it is used if accompanied by weekly blood monitoring, a procedure that increases the cost of this drug treatment by up to $9,000 a year (Weitz, 1991).

Despite the problems associated with antipsychotic drugs, they have led to revolutionary changes in mental health. Professionals have moved toward low-dose and intermittent medication strategies, and most schizophrenic patients can now be treated in open wards or in general hospitals. Before the use of drugs, patients were destined for a lifetime in psychiatric institutions. With medication, most improve enough to return to their homes.

Antidepressants and Mood Stabilizer Drugs

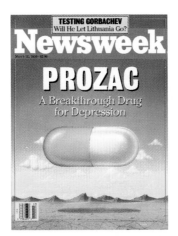

Figure 16.5 Is Prozac a "wonder drug"? Prozac was called the wonder drug of mental health in 1990 because it led to relief from serious depression with relatively few side effects. Public sentiment later turned against this "wonder drug" due to highly publicized reports of a few cases of violence and suicide among its users.

Drug treatments are available to reduce the symptoms of both severe depression and bipolar disorders. For many years, the two major types of antidepressant drugs were the tricyclics (named because of their chemical structure containing three rings) and the monoamine oxidase (MAO) inhibitors. Tricyclic antidepressants, such as Elavil, and MAO inhibitors, such as Nardil, work by different mechanisms. But both seem to alleviate depression by increasing the action of two important neurotransmitters—norepinephrine and serotonin (Julien, 1992).

For persons suffering from bipolar disorders, mood stabilizer drugs such as lithium are used to treat manic episodes and break the manic-depressive cycle. Lithium alters the levels of norepinephrine and prevents the characteristic swings from extreme highs to extreme lows (Baldessarini and Cole, 1988).

Just as do antipsychotic medications, antidepressants have both major and minor side effects. Antidepressants may cause dry mouth, fatigue, weight gain, and memory difficulties (Klerman, 1988). Mood stabilizer drugs such as lithium can also impair memory and cause weight gain. In excessive dosages, lithium can be fatal. Thus, as with other drug therapies, it is important to carefully monitor dosage level and patient reactions (Baldessarini, 1990b).

It is interesting to note that, as happened with Clozapine, the antidepressant Prozac was initially heralded as a "wonder drug" (see Figure 16.5) and it too lost credibility. There appeared to be evidence that Prozac increased risk of suicide (Teicher et al., 1990). As a critical thinker, can you see what is wrong with the public's extreme swing from "wonder drug" to "danger drug"? Partly the reaction comes from not understanding that all forms of drug therapy have costs as well as benefits. Partly, too, the reaction is due to not understanding psychological disorders. For example, people tend to forget that suicidal thoughts are common in depressed patients. In the case of Prozac, it is not clear whether the drug increased suicidal impulses or whether it improved the patient's mood, but only enough to allow action on previous suicidal ideation. Moreover, with all antidepressants it takes one to three weeks for neurotransmitter levels to change and depression to lift. During this time, seriously depressed patients are often hospitalized to prevent them from committing suicide.

Does a depressed person have to keep taking the drugs indefinitely? When the antidepressant medication has restored the person's chemical balance, he or she may think more clearly and deal more effectively with problems, in addition to feeling less depressed. By making constructive changes in their lives, some previously depressed people can discontinue the antidepressant medication without a return of symptoms. But others need to continue the medication to prevent the return of serious depression.

Electroconvulsive Therapy: Promising or Perilous Treatment?

Electroconvulsive Therapy (ECT): Passage of electrical current through the brain as a therapy technique. It is used almost exclusively to treat serious depression.

Electroconvulsive therapy (ECT) is also known as electroshock therapy (EST) or simply as "shock therapy." In an ECT treatment, a current of moderate intensity is passed through the brain tissue between two electrodes placed on the outside of the head (see

Figure 16.6). The electrical current is applied for less than a second, but it triggers a widespread firing of brain neurons that is similar to an epileptic seizure. When consciousness returns several minutes later, the patient has amnesia for the period immediately before the shock (retrograde amnesia) and is usually somewhat confused for the next hour or so (anterograde amnesia). If treatments are continued, usually three to five times a week, the patient becomes more generally disoriented, a state that usually begins to improve soon after termination of treatments (see Chapter 7 for a discussion of the effects of ECT on memory). Most ECT patients are given an anesthetic such as sodium pentothal, so they have no memory of the experience. It is also routine to administer a muscle relaxant drug to reduce muscle contractions during the seizure (Wilson et al., 1992). Unlike the portrayal in the movies *One Flew Over the Cuckoo's Nest* and *The Snake Pit,* patients show few, if any, visible reactions to the treatment.

Prior to the use of ECT, convulsions or comas were induced by administering nitrogen or carbon dioxide gas or by injecting chemicals such as camphor (Metrazol) or insulin. Frances Farmer received daily insulin shock therapy, a popular form of therapy during the 1940s, for 30 days.

During the early years of ECT, some patients received hundreds of treatments (Fink, 1985; Valenstein, 1987). In recent years, it is most common to give 12 or fewer ECT treatments. Sometimes the electrical current is applied only to the right hemisphere (unilateral ECT), which causes less interference with verbal memories and left hemisphere functioning.

In the 1940s and 1950s, ECT was used to treat all types of disorders, including schizophrenia. As the result of research studies that compared changes in patients in carefully controlled experiments, ECT is now primarily administered to seriously depressed patients who have not responded to antidepressant medication and who are suicidal (Isaac and Armat, 1990; Thompson and Blaine, 1987).

How does creating a convulsion relieve depression?   Convulsions produce many changes in the central and peripheral nervous systems. Convulsions activate the autonomic nervous system, increase secretion of various hormones and neurotransmitters, and change the blood-brain barrier (Fink, 1985; Sackheim, 1988). Still, after nearly half a century of use, we do not understand why an ECT-induced convulsion alleviates depression (Kalat, 1992).

Partly because we can't explain how it works, but also because it seems barbaric and it causes memory loss, ECT is a controversial treatment. In 1982, the voters in Berkeley, California, passed a referendum to ban the use of ECT in their city. The prohibition was subsequently overturned in the courts. Despite opposition, many clinicians support the careful use of ECT, especially when other treatments have been ineffective (American Psychiatric Association, 1990; Frankel, 1988).

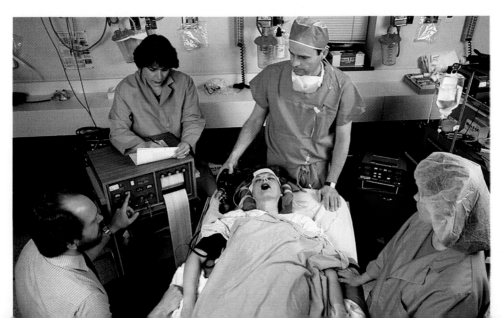

Figure 16.6 Electroconvulsive therapy (ECT). During (ECT), electrodes are placed on the forehead to apply electric currents to the brain and create a convulsion. ECT is used mainly to treat major depressive disorder.

Psychosurgery: Altering the Brain

Lobotomy: A brain operation in which the nerve pathways between the frontal lobes and the thalamus and hypothalamus are cut in hopes of treating psychological disorders.

Psychosurgery: Operative procedures on the brain designed to relieve severe mental symptoms that have not responded to other forms of treatment.

Attempts to change disturbed thinking and behavior by altering the brain have a long history. In Roman times, for example, it was believed that insanity could be relieved by a sword wound to the head. In 1936, Egaz Moniz, a Portuguese neurologist, began treating uncontrollable psychotics by cutting the nerve fibers between areas of the frontal lobes (where association areas for monitoring and planning behavior are found) and the thalamus and hypothalamus. Severing these connections decreases emotional response and the patient accepts frustrating circumstances with a "philosophical calm." Moniz was awarded the Nobel Prize in medicine in 1949 for developing this technique, called a lobotomy (Rodgers, 1992; Valenstein, 1987).

In the years since the introduction of the lobotomy, this and other variations of psychosurgery have been used to treat depression, agitation, and psychotic symptoms such as hallucinations (Rodgers, 1992). In 1943, when hospitals were crowded with veterans discharged from military service for psychiatric problems, the Veterans Administration issued a communication that encouraged consulting and staff neurosurgeons to obtain training in lobotomy operations. They were urged to select cases for surgery "in which apprehension, anxiety, and depression are present, also cases with compulsions and obsessions, with marked emotional tension" when other forms of therapy including shock therapy had failed (Valenstein, 1973, p. 390).

During the 1940s, about 50,000 patients received lobotomies. One American neurosurgeon claimed that he performed over 4000 operations, using a gold-plated ice pick that he carried in a velvet-lined case. Since the procedure required only a local anesthetic and a small incision at the edge of the eye socket, he often performed the surgery in his office or in the patient's home (Rodgers, 1992).

But wouldn't there be serious side effects from damaging the brain? Despite our understandable revulsion over past abuses and the high risks of any form of brain surgery, psychosurgery is still considered useful in some cases (Gregory, 1988; Rodgers, 1992). Some lobotomy patients, for example, are calmed with no dramatic detrimental effect on their behavior. After her lobotomy, Frances Farmer was able to care for herself outside the institution and communicate well enough to write a book describing her experiences. But brain surgery is always risky and its side effects and complications may be irreversible. Patients sometimes suffer personality changes, becoming bland, colorless, and unemotional. In other cases, patients become aggressive and unable to control their impulses. Despite the problems, psychosurgery is still considered useful in extreme cases (Gregory, 1988; Rodgers, 1992).

Review Questions

1. The dramatic reduction in numbers of hospitalized patients is primarily attributable to _____ .
2. What are the four major categories of psychiatric drugs?
3. What type of drug is Valium and why is it dangerous?
4. Schizophrenia is often treated with _____ drugs.
5. The public's reaction to a new psychiatric drug is often characterized by a swing from "wonder drug" to "danger drug." Can you explain this response?
6. ECT is used today primarily to treat _____ .
7. A lobotomy is a _____ procedure that attempts to relieve abnormal symptoms.

Answers to Review Questions can be found in Appendix C.

ISSUES IN THERAPY

When is it appropriate to institutionalize people against their will? How do you choose a therapist? Is therapy effective? These are all major issues in psychotherapy.

• *When is therapy necessary and how do you choose a therapist?*

Institutionalization: Treating Chronic and Serious Mental Disorders

We all believe in the right to freedom, but are there instances when people should be protected from their own mental disorders? What about people who threaten suicide or are potentially violent? Forced institutionalization of the mentally ill posed serious ethical problems in Frances Farmer's day and it still does today.

Involuntary Commitment

The legal grounds for involuntary commitment vary from state to state. But, generally, people can be sent to psychiatric hospitals if they are assumed to be (1) dangerous to themselves (usually suicidal) or dangerous to others (potentially violent), (2) in need of treatment (indicated by bizarre behavior and loss of contact with reality), and (3) there is no reasonable, less restrictive alternative (Ruzovsky, 1984). In emergency situations, psychologists and other professionals can authorize temporary commitment for 24 to 72 hours. During this observation period, laboratory tests can be performed to rule out medical illnesses that could be causing the symptoms. The patient can also receive psychological testing, medication, and short-term therapy (Torrey, 1988).

Deinstitutionalization

Although the courts have established stringent requirements for involuntary commitment, abuses do occur. In response to the potential for abuse, the problems that come with long-term chronic institutionalization, and the expense of properly housing and treating the mentally ill, many states have initiated a policy of deinstitutionalization, discharging as many patients from mental hospitals as possible and also discouraging admissions (Davison and Neale, 1994).

Deinstitutionalization: The policy of discharging as many people as possible from state hospitals and discouraging admissions.

While proponents hail deinstitutionalization as a humane and positive step (Lerman, 1981; Okin, 1987), critics argue that thousands of ex-patients have been discharged without continuing provision for their protection (Burt, 1992; Torrey, 1988). Many of these people end up living on the street with no shelter or means of support. Studies

Although critics deplore the crowded conditions of many state hospitals, many former mental patients have been released onto metropolitan streets through deinstitutionalization with no facilities to care for them.

show that about one-third of the homeless suffer disabling psychological disorders (Cohen, 1992; Levine and Rog, 1990). In response to these problems, some communities have attempted to reinstitutionalize the mentally ill. This reinstitutionalization has also been widely criticized (Stengel, 1987).

What else can be done? Rather than returning patients to state hospitals, most clinicians suggest an extension and improvement of community care. They recommend that general hospitals be equipped with special psychiatric units where acutely ill patients could receive inpatient care. For less disturbed individuals and chronically ill patients, they recommend walk-in clinics, crisis intervention services, improved residential treatment facilities, and psychosocial and vocational rehabilitation. State hospitals would be reserved for the most unmanageable patients.

Community Mental Health Centers (CMH)

Community mental health centers (CMH) are a prime example of alternative treatment to institutionalization. CMH centers provide outpatient services such as individual and group therapy and prevention programs. They also coordinate short-term inpatient care and programs for discharged mental patients, such as halfway houses and aftercare services. CMH centers are staffed by psychiatrists, social workers, nurses, and volunteers who live in the neighborhood.

As you can imagine, CMH centers and their support programs are enormously expensive. Individual psychotherapy currently costs $70 to $120 an hour, and hospital costs are well over $300 a day. The total cost for one patient whose illness persisted for almost 20 years was estimated to be $636,000 (Sarason and Sarason, 1993). These costs could be substantially reduced by investments in *primary prevention* programs. Instead of waiting until someone loses his or her job, home, and family, we could develop more intervention programs for high-risk individuals and offer short-term immediate services during crisis situations. People would also need to be educated about the pros and cons of the different therapies and how to select an appropriate therapist.

Choosing the Right Therapy and Therapist: Tips for the Consumer

Some psychological disorders are best treated with certain forms of psychotherapy. Systematic desensitization and other behavioral techniques work best for phobias. Group therapy works well for drug dependence. Recognizing that some theoretical approaches work better for some problems than others, most clinicians use a combination of techniques depending on the particular individual and the specific problem. Using a combination of techniques is known as an eclectic approach. One study of 400 counseling and clinical psychologists found that 41 percent of the therapists surveyed identified themselves with the eclectic approach (see Table 16.2). The remainder practice a particular type of therapy.

Eclectic Approach: An approach to psychotherapy in which the therapist freely borrows from various theories to find the appropriate treatment for the client.

Differences Among Therapists

There are four basic kinds of therapists, distinguished by their training:

Clinical Psychologist: A psychologist with an advanced graduate degree who specializes in treating psychological and behavioral disturbances or who does research on such disturbances.

1. Clinical psychologists are therapists who have an advanced degree such as a Ph.D. (Doctor of Philosophy), a Psy.D. (Doctor of Psychology), or Ed.D. (Doctor of Education). They have usually had four or more years of graduate education, including a supervised internship, and have often conducted research studies.

Psychiatrist: A medical doctor who has additional training in the diagnosis and treatment of mental illness.

2. Psychiatrists are physicians who specialize in psychiatry after graduation from medical school and completing a year of internship. The three-year residency program in psychiatry includes supervised practice in therapy techniques and training in the biological treatment of disorders. Since only psychiatrists are physicians, they are the only therapists who can prescribe drugs for patients.

Table 16.2   Percentages of Therapists by Type

Therapist's Orientation	Number	Percentage
Eclectic	171	41
Psychoanalytic	57	14
Humanistic	45	11
Cognitive behavioral	43	10
Behavioral	28	7
Family	11	3
Gestalt	7	2
Rational-emotive	7	2
Transactional analysis	4	1
Other	42	9
Total in Survey	415	100

Source: Smith, D. (1982). Trends in counseling and psychotherapy. *American Psychologist, 37* (3), 802–809.

3. Psychoanalysts are almost always psychiatrists with additional specialized training in the techniques of psychoanalysis. (The exceptions are persons trained in analysis after completing other graduate education, such as social work.) During the specialized training period, students must themselves undergo psychoanalysis.

4. Social workers have obtained at least a master's degree in social work (M.S.W.). During their year or two of graduate education, they are supervised in the treatment of clients in hospitals and outpatient settings. Social workers can also obtain a doctorate degree or specialize further in specific types of therapy, becoming certified to conduct private practice as licensed marriage, family, and child counselors or as licensed clinical social workers.

Psychoanalyst: A mental health professional (usually a physician) who is trained to practice psychoanalysis.

Social Worker: A therapist who has obtained at least a master's degree in social work, and who typically works with patients and their families to ease their community relations.

Does Therapy Work?

Scientifically evaluating the effectiveness of psychotherapy can be tricky. How can you trust the perception and self-report of clients or clinicians? Both have biases and a need to justify the time, effort, and expense of therapy.

To avoid these problems, psychologists use controlled research studies. Clients are randomly assigned to different forms of therapy or to control groups that receive no treatment. After therapy, subjects are independently evaluated and reports from friends and families of all clients are collected. The results of these studies, and other forms of outcome research, are then averaged together in a statistical procedure known as *meta-analysis.*

The results of these studies suggest that between 50 to 80 percent of those who receive treatment are better off than those who do not receive treatment (Lazarus, 1990; Robinson et al., 1990; Smith and Glass, 1977; Stiles et al., 1986). Unfortunately, a large number of people who could benefit from therapy do not receive it. A recent National Institute of Mental Health survey found that of the 44.7 million Americans who currently suffer from one or more of the mental and addictive disorders, less than one-third receive treatment from our medical or mental health care facilities (Regier et al., 1993). This is due in part to the high cost of treatment, but people also need help in finding the right therapist.

Finding a Therapist

Considering the expense, and the many forms of therapy and types of therapists to choose from, you could spend months—or years—evaluating therapies and gathering information on therapists and their methods. If you have time (and the money) to explore options, do "shop around" for a therapist best suited to your specific goals.

However, if you are in a crisis—if you have suicidal thoughts, are failing your college classes, or you are in an abusive relationship, get help fast. Most communities have telephone "hotlines" that provide counseling on a 24-hour basis. You might consult your psychology instructor, your college's counseling center, or a local community mental health center. These are also good places to get referrals if you are not in a crisis situation.

If you are encouraging therapy for someone who refuses to seek help, you might offer to assist in locating a therapist or even accompany that person to therapy. If he or she refuses help and the problem affects you, it is often a good idea for you to get help on your own. If the other person won't change, your therapy will offer important insights and skills that will help you deal with the situation more effectively.

Gender and Cultural Diversity

CULTURAL VARIATIONS AND THE SPECIAL NEEDS OF WOMEN IN THERAPY

All the therapies we have described in this chapter are based on Western European and American culture. Does this mean they are unique? Or do our psychotherapists do some of the same things that, say, a native healer or witch doctor does? That is, are there cultural universals in therapy? Conversely, are there fundamental cultural differences between therapies? Finally, there is the matter of women in therapy: Do women have special needs? Let's take up these issues one at a time.

Cultural Universals

When we look at therapies in all cultures, we find certain key features are *culturally universal* (Draguns, 1975, 1990; Ponterotto and Benesch, 1988; Torrey, 1986). These features have been summarized by Richard Brislin (1993):

The magic rituals of the Siamese Shaman serve an important therapeutic function for the people of Thailand.

1. *Naming the problem.* One important step toward improvement in psychological disorders is labeling the problem. People often feel better just by knowing their problem is experienced by others, and that the therapist has had experience with their particular problem. This relief due to labeling has sometimes been referred to as the "Rumpelstiltskin principle" (Torrey, 1992b).

2. *Qualities of the therapist.* Clients must feel the therapist is caring, competent, approachable, and concerned with finding solutions to the problem.

3. *Establishing credibility.* Word of mouth testimonials and status symbols (such as diplomas on the wall) establish the therapist's credibility. Among native healers, in lieu of diplomas, credibility may be established by serving as an apprentice for many years to a revered healer.

4. *Placing the problem in a familiar framework.* If the client believes evil spirits cause psychological disorders, the therapist will direct treatment toward these spirits. Similarly, if the client believes in the importance of early childhood experiences and the unconscious mind, psychoanalysis will be the likely treatment of choice.

5. *Applying techniques to bring relief.* In all cultures, therapy involves action. Either the client or the therapist must do something, and what they do must fit the client's expectations. For example, the person who believes he or she is possessed by evil spirits expects the witch doctor to perform a ceremony to expel the demons. In the Western European and American models, clients expect to reveal their thoughts and feelings and provide background information. This "talk therapy" may also have biological or behavioral components, but the person who seeks therapy generally expects to *talk* about his or her problem.

6. *A special time and place.* The fact that therapy occurs outside the client's everyday experiences seems to be an important feature of all therapies. People apparently need to set aside a special time and go to a special place to concentrate on their problems.

Cultural Differences

While there are basic similarities in therapies across cultures, there are also important differences. In the traditional Western European and American models, clients are encouraged toward self-awareness, self-fulfillment, self-actualization, and modification of self-behavior. The emphasis is on the "self" and on independence and control over one's life—qualities that are highly valued in individualistic cultures. When we look at therapies in collectivist cultures, however, the focus is on interdependence and acceptance of the realities of one's life.

Japanese Naikan therapy is a good example of a collectivist culture's approach to psychological disorders. In Naikan therapy the patient sits quietly from 5:30 A.M. to 9:00 P.M. for seven days, being visited by an interviewer every 90 minutes. During this time the patient is instructed to look at his or her relationships with others from three perspectives: *Care received* (recollect and examine the care and kindness you have received from others); *repayment* (recall what you have done to repay the care and kindness of others); and *troubles caused* (think about the troubles and worries you have caused others) (Berry et al., 1992).

The goals of Naikan therapy are to discover personal guilt for having been ungrateful and troublesome to others, and to develop gratitude toward those who have helped you. When these goals are attained, the person will have a better self-image and interpersonal attitude (Murase, 1982).

As you can see, there are pronounced differences between these goals and methods and those we have described in this chapter. Recognizing cultural differences is very important for building trust between therapists and clients and for effecting behavioral change. Clinicians who work with clients from different cultural backgrounds should learn about their clients' cultures, as well as become more aware of their own cultural and ethnic-based values and beliefs (Pinderhughes, 1992).

Naikan Therapy: A Japanese form of therapy that aims to help a person discover personal guilt and develop gratitude to others.

Women and Therapy

Not only do therapists need to develop sensitivity to their clients' cultural backgrounds, they need training to deal with gender differences. Within the individualistic Western culture, men and women present different needs and problems to therapists. How to best serve the special needs of women in therapy, however, has been intensely debated in the psychological community (Matlin, 1993; Tavris, 1992). Research conducted by the National Institute of Mental Health has identified five major areas of concern:

1. *Rates of diagnosis and treatment of mental disorders.* In a review of the literature, it was found that women are diagnosed and treated for mental illness at a much higher rate than men (Landrine, 1988). Is this because women are "sicker" than men as a group, more willing to admit their problems, or are the categories for illness biased against women? More research is needed to fully answer this question.

2. *Stresses of poverty.* Poverty is an important contributor to stress, and stress is directly related to many psychological disorders. Therefore, women bring special challenges to the therapy situation because of their overrepresentation among the lowest economic groups (Unger and Crawford, 1992).

3. *Stresses of Multiple Roles.* Women today are mothers, wives, homemakers, wage earners, students, and so on. The conflicting demands of their multiple roles often create special stresses for women (Etaugh, 1990).

4. *Stresses of aging.* Aging brings special concerns for women. They not only live longer than men, but they also tend to be poorer, less educated, and have more serious health problems (Hyde, 1991; Mercer et al., 1989). Elderly women also account for over 70 percent of the chronically mentally ill who live in nursing homes in America.

5. *Violence against women.* Rape, violent assault, incest, and sexual harassment all take a harsh toll on women's mental health. With the exception of violent

assault, each of these forms of violence is much more likely to happen to women than to men. These violent acts may lead to depression, insomnia, posttraumatic stress disorders, eating disorders, and other problems (Foa, Olasov, and Steketee, 1987; Leidig, 1992; Unger and Crawford, 1992).

Each of these five areas of concern is important to therapists who treat women. Therapists must be sensitive to possible connections between clients' problems and their gender and/or culture. Rather than prescribing drugs to relieve depression in women, for example, it may be more appropriate for the therapist to explore ways to relieve the stresses of poverty, violence, and so on. ■

Review Questions

1. Under what conditions can someone be involuntarily committed?
2. What is the eclectic approach to therapy?
3. _____ are therapists who have advanced degrees such as a Ph.D., whereas _____ are physicians who can prescribe drugs for patients.
4. Name the six features of therapy that are culturally universal features of therapy.
5. What are the five major concerns for women in therapy?

Answers to Review Questions can be found in Appendix C.

REVIEW OF MAJOR CONCEPTS

ESSENTIALS OF PSYCHOTHERAPY

1. Psychotherapy is a general term for the various methods designed to improve psychological functioning and/or promote adjustment to life. There are numerous forms of psychotherapy, but they all focus treatment on five basic areas of disturbance—thoughts, emotions, behaviors, interpersonal and life situations, and biomedical.

PSYCHOANALYSIS

2. The psychoanalytic method of therapy was developed by Sigmund Freud to uncover unconscious conflicts, which usually date back to childhood experiences, and bring them into conscious awareness. The four major techniques of psychoanalysis are free association, dream interpretation, resistance, and transference.

3. Like psychoanalytic theories of personality, psychoanalysis has been the subject of great debate. Two major areas of criticism are its limited availability (it is time-consuming, expensive, and restricted to a small group of people), and its lack of scientific credibility.

COGNITIVE THERAPIES

4. Cognitive therapy emphasizes the importance of faulty thought processes and beliefs in the creation of problem behaviors. Albert Ellis's rational-emotive therapy works to replace a client's irrational beliefs with rational beliefs and accurate perceptions of the world. Aaron Beck, a cognitive-behavior therapist, takes a more active approach with clients—emphasizing changes in thought processes along with changes in behavior.

5. Evaluations of cognitive therapies find Beck's procedures particularly effective for relieving depression, and Ellis has had similar success with a wide variety of disorders. Both Beck and Ellis, however, have been criticized for ignoring the importance of unconscious processes and the client's history. Some critics suggest that when cognitive therapies are successful it is because they have also changed behavior.

HUMANISTIC THERAPIES

6. Humanistic therapies are based on the premise that problems result from blocking or disruption of an individual's normal growth potential. In Rogers's client-centered approach, the therapist offers empathy, unconditional positive regard, and genuineness as means of facilitating personal growth. Perls's Gestalt therapy emphasizes awareness and personal responsibility to help the client integrate present experiences into a "whole" or gestalt.

7. Humanistic therapies are difficult to evaluate scientifically, and research on specific therapeutic techniques has had mixed results. Nevertheless, the therapy seems to help unhappy people, but not the severely disturbed.

BEHAVIOR THERAPIES

8. Behavior therapies use learning principles to change maladaptive behaviors. They use classical conditioning principles to change associations. In systematic desensitization, the client replaces anxiety with relaxation, and in aversion therapy, an aversive stimulus is paired with maladaptive behaviors. Punishment, extinction, shaping, and reinforcement are also used, and they are based on operant conditioning principles. Modeling principles are employed by having clients watch and imitate positive role models.

9. Behavior therapies have been successful with a number of psychological disorders. But they have also been criticized for lack of generalizability, the chance of symptom substitution, and the questionable ethics of controlling behavior.

GROUP THERAPIES

10. In addition to being less expensive and more available, group therapies have three other advantages over individual therapies—group support, feedback and information, and behavioral rehearsal. Family therapy, encounter groups, and support groups are types of group therapies.

11. Although group therapies offer significant advantages to their members, some forms of therapy commonly practiced in groups can be destructive. "Pop therapies" such as past-lives therapy and rebirthing can give a false impression of legitimate therapies and may pose dangers to the participants.

BIOMEDICAL THERAPIES

12. Biomedical therapies use biological techniques to relieve psychological disorders. Three major forms of biomedical therapy are drug therapy, electroconvulsive therapy (ECT), and psychosurgery.

13. Drug therapy is the most common form of biomedical therapy. Antianxiety drugs, such as Valium, have been used in the treatment of anxiety disorders; antipsychotic drugs, such as Thorazine, are used to relieve the symptoms of schizophrenia; antidepressants, such as Elavil, are used to treat depression; and mood stabilizers, such as lithium, are used to stabilize bipolar disorders. While drug therapy has been responsible for major improvements in many disorders, there are also problems with dosage levels, side effects, and patient cooperation.

14. Electroconvulsive therapy (ECT) has been criticized for being "barbaric" and causing memory loss, and because no one really knows how it works. Today it is used primarily to relieve serious depression, on which other methods have been ineffective. Psychosurgeries, such as lobotomies, have been successful in treating certain disorders, but they are highly risky.

ISSUES IN THERAPY

15. People believed to be mentally ill and dangerous to themselves or others can be involuntarily committed to mental hospitals for diagnosis and treatment. Due to abuses of involuntary commitments and other problems associated with state mental hospitals, many states practice a policy of deinstitutionalization—discharging as many patients as possible and discouraging admissions. In place of institutionalization, community services such as Community Mental Health (CMH) centers have been recommended.

16. Most therapists adopt an eclectic approach, borrowing freely from a variety of psychotherapeutic techniques. Mental health professionals include clinical psychologists, psychiatrists, psychoanalysts, and social workers.

17. Research on the effectiveness of psychotherapy has found that 50 to 80 percent of those who receive treatment are better off than those who do not receive treatment.

18. Studies of cultural variations in therapy have found six major features that are culturally universal: naming a problem, qualities of the therapist, establishing credibility, placing the problems in a familiar framework, applying techniques to bring relief, and a special time and place.

19. There are also important cultural differences in therapies. While therapies in individualistic cultures emphasize the "self" and independence and control over one's life, collectivist culture's therapies emphasize interdependence and acceptance of the realities of one's life. Japan's Naikan therapy is a good example of a collectivist culture's therapy.

20. There are five areas of special concern therapists need to take into account when treating women clients: higher rate of diagnosis and treatment of mental disorders, stresses of poverty, stresses of multiple roles, stresses of aging, and violence against women.

SUGGESTED READINGS

BECK, A. T. (1989). *Love is never enough*. New York: Harper & Row. A clearly written presentation of the cognitive therapy approach with extensive illustrations of its effectiveness in treatment of marital problems.

COREY, G. (1993). *Theory and practice of counseling and psychotherapy* (5th ed.). Monterey, CA: Brooks/Cole. A practical guide to the major approaches to therapy, including therapy processes and applications.

BERGIN, A. E., & GARFIELD, S. L. (EDS). (1994). *Handbook of psychotherapy and behavior change* (4th ed.). New York: Wiley. This widely used text emphasizes the similarities and differences in research methods and current therapeutic practices for various disorders.

HILLMAN, J., & VENTURA, M. (1993). *We've had 100 years of psychotherapy and the world's getting worse*. New York: HarperCollins. The authors present a scathing critique of psychology and psychotherapy as ideologies that perpetuate individualism—a position they believe is untenable in a collectivist world.

RODGERS, J. (1992). *Damaging the brain to save the mind*. New York: HarperCollins. A powerful look at the history of psychosurgery from the crude lobotomies popular in the 1930s and 1940s to modern procedures practiced under surprisingly few ethical or legal guidelines.

TORREY, E. F. (1988). *Surviving schizophrenia: A family manual*. New York: Harper & Row. Helpful for understanding the implications of short- and long-term therapy for psychotic disorders. Includes discussion of legal and ethical issues and describes resources.

CHAPTER

17

Social Behavior and Cognition

OUTLINE

On Monday, April 19, 1993, a 51-day siege by federal agents of the Branch Davidian Compound in Waco, Texas ended in an all-consuming inferno. At least seventy-four people, including many children and cult leader David Koresh, died in the blaze. According to federal authorities, the fire began simultaneously in three locations, indicating that it was set purposely by at least some of the victims. This was disputed by several cult member survivors who claim that the fire was started when government armored vehicles rammed the building (Davidson and Harlan, 1993).

How did this happen? What kind of man was cult leader David Koresh? Did his followers willingly commit suicide or were they forcibly restrained and murdered? Some blame David Koresh for the disaster. They say he was charming and persuasive as he espoused his version of the Holy scriptures and proclaimed himself "God's chosen one." He not only convinced his followers that he was the messiah, but also that his seed was divine and that only he had the right to procreate (Lacayo, 1993, p. 35). While he enjoyed sex with the women and children (some as young as 11), the men in the compound lived in celibacy and in stark dormitory conditions.

How could the cult members buy into this? It is known that Koresh employed more than his persuasive personality to manipulate his followers. By separating husbands and wives and parents and children, he broke down social ties within families. In addition, he gradually took control over each member's financial assets and personal property, thus removing an important source of personal independence. In addition, he controlled every resource essential for survival. Although the cult had stockpiled enough food to last for months, Koresh controlled the dispensing of food, using it as a weapon to insure obedience (Gibbs, 1993).

In considering the Waco tragedy, we cannot help but remember a similar situation in Jonestown, Guyana on November 18, 1978, where Jim Jones and 900 of his followers in the People's Temple died in a mass murder/suicide. In this instance there was no assault by outside forces, but only the threat of intervention and extreme paranoia on the part of some cult members. In both situations, however, a tragedy occurred that involved a highly charismatic leader and numerous followers who were led (or pushed) to accept death and the promise of glory in the life to come.

Was it David Koresh and Jim Jones who were most to blame for what happened in Waco and Guyana? Were the followers duped by skillful, paranoid manipulators? Or did the cult members follow their leader willingly because he offered a sense of belonging—a relief from feelings of alienation and worthlessness? Or can it be, as some have suggested, that our fragmented, industrial society is most to blame (Cialdini, 1993; Galanter, 1989, 1990; Lifton, 1979)?

Social Psychology: The branch of psychology that studies how an individual's behavior (thoughts, feelings, and actions) is influenced by other people.

How would you answer these questions? If you are like most people, you find the tragedies in Waco and Guyana both confusing and fascinating. This combination of confusion and fascination about social behaviors is what draws many students to the field of social psychology. Social psychologists study how an individual's behavior (thoughts, feelings, and actions) is influenced by other people. Social psychologists study both the bizarre and the ordinary, obedience and murder in cults, as well as and what makes friends turn into lovers. They use the same basic tools of science that other psychologists use (experiments, surveys, case studies, self-report, and so on) because like other psychologists, they want *scientific* answers to their questions.

The topics in social psychology are extremely broad and complex. For this reason, we will present social psychology in two chapters. In this chapter we will look at different kinds of social influence (conformity, compliance, and obedience). Then we will explore how group processes affect behavior (affiliation, membership, and decision making). Next, we will examine attribution (how we explain the causes of behavior) and social cognition (how we process social information). Finally, we will discuss interpersonal attraction (how we come to like and love others).

As you read Chapter 17, keep the following **Survey** questions in mind and answer them in your own words:

- What is the difference between conformity, compliance, and obedience?
- What are the most influential factors in group behavior?
- How are internal and external factors involved in attribution?
- How do heuristics function in social cognition?
- How can liking and loving be explained?

SOCIAL INFLUENCE

The society and culture into which we are born directly influence us from the moment of birth until the moment of death. Our culture teaches us to believe certain things, feel certain ways, and act in accordance with these beliefs and feelings. These influences are so strong, and so much a part of who we are, that we find it difficult to recognize them. Just as a fish doesn't know it's in water, we are largely unaware of the strong impact cultural and social factors have on all our behaviors. Social psychology is essentially a study of "the influences that people have upon the beliefs or behaviors of others" (Aronson, 1992, p. 6). There are three kinds of *social influence:* conformity, compliance, and obedience.

 Try This Yourself

Before we begin our discussion of social influence, you may want to test your understanding of social psychology and how it operates in everyday life by answering "true" or "false" to the following statements. The answers are at the bottom, and expanded explanations are found throughout the next two chapters.

_____ 1. Groups will generally make more conservative decisions than a single individual.

_____ 2. Most people tend to judge others more harshly than they judge themselves.

_____ 3. "Looks" are the primary factor in our initial feelings of attraction, liking, and romantic love.

_____ 4. Opposites attract.

_____ 5. Romantic love rarely lasts longer than 6 to 30 months.

_____ 6. The most effective way to change behavior is to first change attitude.

_____ 7. Prejudice is the same as discrimination.

_____ 8. There are positive as well as negative forms of prejudice.

_____ 9. Watching a violent sports match or punching a pillow is a good way to release steam and reduce aggression.

_____ 10. People are more likely to help another individual when they are alone than when they are in a group.

Answers 1. F 2. T 3. T 4. F 5. T 6. F 7. F 8. T 9. F 10. T

> • What is the difference between conformity, compliance, and obedience?

Conformity: Going Along with Others

Imagine for a moment that you have volunteered for a psychology experiment on perception. You find yourself seated around a table with six other students. You are all

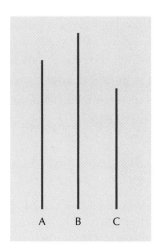
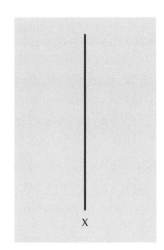

Figure 17.1 Asch's study of conformity. Subjects were shown four lines such as these and then asked which line (A, B, or C) was most similar to the one on the right (X).

shown a card containing three lines labeled A, B, and C, as in Figure 17.1, and are asked to select the line that is closest in length to a fourth line, X. Each of you is asked to state your choices out loud, in order, around the table. At first, everyone agrees on the correct line, and the experiment seems pretty boring. On the third trial, however, the first subject gives what is obviously a wrong answer. You know that line B is correct but he says line A. When the second, third, fourth, and fifth subjects also say line A, you really start to wonder: "What's going on here? Are they blind? Or am I?"

What do you think you would do at this point in the experiment? Would you stick with your convictions and say line B, regardless of what the others have answered? Or would you go along with the group? In the original version of this experiment, conducted by Solomon Asch (1951), the six other subjects were actually confederates of the experimenter, and seating was arranged so that the real subject was always in the next-to-last position. The five confederates had been instructed to respond incorrectly on the third trial and selected later trials as a way of testing the actual subject's degree of conformity, or changing one's behavior as a result of real or imagined group pressure.

Conformity: A type of social influence in which individuals change their behavior as a result of real or imagined group pressure.

How did Asch's subjects respond? More than one-third conformed and agreed with the group's obviously incorrect choice. This level of conformity is particularly intriguing when it is compared with responses in the control group, which experienced no group pressure and chose correctly virtually 100 percent of the time.

Why would so many people conform?   To the onlooker, conformity is often difficult to understand, and even the conformer sometimes has a hard time explaining his or her behavior. We can better understand cult members' behavior, Asch's subjects, and our own forms of conformity if we look at three factors: (1) *normative* social influence (the

In Asch's study of conformity, the true subject (#6) was seated with six other subjects who had been secretly trained ahead of time to give incorrect responses to an obvious line discrimination task.

desire to be liked), (2) *informational* social influence (the desire to be right), and (3) the role of *reference groups* (the desire to be similar to people we admire).

Normative Social Influence

The first factor, normative social influence, refers to conformity to group pressure out of a need for approval and/or acceptance by the group. A norm is an expected behavior that is adhered to by members of the group. Norms are society's definition of how we "should" behave. They are sometimes explicit; clubs may write rules for membership and nations may pass laws that determine citizenship. Most often, however, norms are more subtle and implicit; they can only be inferred by closely observing the behavior of others. Have you ever asked what others are wearing to the party or watched the table manners of others at a dinner party to be sure you pick up the right fork? Such behavior reflects your desire to conform and the power of normative social influence.

Our strong need for approval and group acceptance was evident in Asch's subjects. Many reported conforming out of fear of being ridiculed or excluded from the group (Asch, 1956). This type of conformity was also found in Jim Jones's followers. Deborah Blakely, a long-time member and later defector from The People's Temple, testified: "Any disagreement with Jim Jones's dictates came to be regarded as 'treason.' . . . Although I felt terrible about what was happening, I was afraid to say anything because I knew that anyone with a differing opinion gained the wrath of Jones and other members" (cited in Osherow, 1988, p. 75).

Normative Social Influence: Conforming to group pressure out of a need for acceptance and/or approval.

Norm: Cultural rule of behavior that prescribes what is acceptable or approved of in a given situation.

Informational Social Influence

Conforming to group pressure out of a need for direction and information is considered the result of informational social influence. Have you ever bought a specific brand of ski equipment or automobile simply because of a friend's recommendation? You conform not to gain their approval (normative social influence), but because you assume they have more information than you. Subjects in Asch's experiment might also have conformed for similar reasons. Recognizing the importance of information in social influence, totalitarian governments generally maintain strict control over books and news reports within their country.

Informational Social Influence: Conforming to group pressure out of a need for direction and information.

Reference Groups

The third major factor in conformity is the power of reference groups—those people we most admire, like, and want to resemble. Attractive actors and popular sports stars are paid millions of dollars to endorse certain products because advertisers know that we want to be as cool as Michael Jackson or as beautiful as Cindy Crawford. Of course, we also have more important reference groups in our lives—parents, friends, family, teachers, religious leaders, and so on. By breaking down family ties and isolating the members of his congregation in remote areas, both David Koresh and Jim Jones made themselves the primary referents for their followers.

Reference Groups: People who we conform (or go along with) because we like and admire them and want to be like them.

Do Asch's study and cult members' devotion to their leader mean that all conformity is bad and even dangerous? Not at all. In fact, most people conform most of the time because it is in their best interests and everyone else's to do so. You stand in line at the bookstore instead of pushing ahead of everyone and you expect others to wait their turn, too. Conformity allows social life to proceed with order and predictability.

Conformity is adaptive, and its adaptiveness is best illustrated by the fact that *every* culture socializes its young to conform to important social norms (Berry et al., 1992; Brislin, 1993). The degree and specific nature of conformity obviously vary among cultures. For example, studies using Asch's model have found that subjects in Brazil, Hong Kong, and Lebanon showed conformity rates very similar to those in the United States, but among the Bantu of Zimbabwe conformity rates are higher (Whittaker and Meade, 1967). Although overall conformity rates have shown a modest decline in Canada, Britain, and the United States since Asch's original studies in the 1950s (Larsen, 1974, 1990;

Perin and Spencer, 1981), conformity remains an expectation in all societies, otherwise "social cohesiveness would be so minimal that the group could not continue to function" (Berry et al., 1992, p. 46).

Compliance: Going Along with a Request

Compliance: A form of social influence in which individuals change their behavior in response to direct requests from others.

In addition to conforming to group expectations or pressures, people often *comply* (or yield) to direct requests from others. The practice of compliance often explains why we contribute to charities, return phone calls, and sometimes buy things we don't need simply because someone asks us to. What makes us so willing to go along with such requests? Research has identified three major techniques that increase the odds for compliance—ingratiation, multiple requests, and guilt.

Ingratiation

Ingratiation: Using favors, flattery, and statements of shared similarities as a method of getting someone to like you. Ingratiation is sometimes used as a first step toward gaining compliance.

We use ingratiation to gain compliance when we try to make people like us before we hit them with a request. We can increase their liking for us, and thereby obtain greater compliance, by convincing them that we are similar to them (Byrne, 1971), by doing favors for them (Isen and Levine, 1972), and by flattering them (Drachman et al., 1978). Both Koresh and Jones used ingratiation techniques when they spoke of their similarly "humble beginnings" and shared feelings of powerlessness. They also provided food and shelter, and flattered their followers by telling them they were "the chosen people."

Multiple Requests

Multiple Requests: Compliance technique in which a first request is used as a "setup" for later requests. The foot-in-the-door and door-in-the-face are two types of multiple requests.

Making multiple requests is also highly effective in eliciting compliance because the first appeal is used as a "setup" for the second or later appeals (Beaman et al., 1983; Cialdini, Kalgren, and Reno, 1991). The requester may, for example, begin by asking for a small favor and then gradually increase the level of request. This is called the *foot-in-the-door* technique. The panhandler who first asks for a quarter for a cup of coffee and then works up to asking for $5 for a full meal is using this approach. In contrast, the *door-in-the-face* technique works by starting off with a large request and then backing down. "If you can't give me $5, can you at least give me a quarter?"

How can such opposite techniques both work?   The foot-in-the-door technique seems to result from subtle cognitive shifts in the individual being asked to comply. By agreeing to the smaller request, the person apparently comes to see himself or herself as a helper. The shift in self-perception then transfers over to the later, larger request. In contrast, the door-in-the-face technique seems to work as a result of subtle rules (or

Is this an example of conformity, compliance, or obedience? Or is it a combination of all three?

Is this an example of the foot-in-the-door technique of persuasion or the door-in-the-face?

norms) for interpersonal interactions. During socialization, we all learn that when another person backs down or makes a concession, we are expected to make a similar response—the rule of *reciprocal concessions*. People may worry that they will appear unfriendly or hostile if they fail to comply with the smaller request after refusing the larger one (Cialdini, 1993).

Guilt Induction

A third very effective and popular compliance technique is guilt induction. We've all been subjected to this tactic by friends and parents ("After all I've done for you, the least you could do is . . ."), by commercials (phone company ads that imply "if you're not going to visit your friends or family often enough, the least you could do is phone"), and by charity organizations (photos of children with heartrending expressions asking for help). Although these techniques remind us of our social obligations, they also have a built-in cost that should be kept in mind. As you will discover in the liking and loving section at the end of this chapter, we tend to like people who make us feel good about ourselves and avoid those who make us feel bad. Thus, we may comply because we feel guilty, but afterward we might resent and avoid the person or organization that made us feel bad.

Guilt Induction: Method of gaining compliance based on the tendency for people to comply when they feel remorse for wrong behavior.

Obedience: Going Along with a Command

Pretend for a moment that it is 1968, the peak of the Vietnam War, and you are a front-line soldier in the U.S. Army. You have seen many friends killed or maimed, and each day you wonder whether it will be your last. You are a highly trained fighting machine, conditioned to take the rough life in the jungle and above all to trust and follow the orders of your commanding officer. On one particular day, your company collects some Vietnamese villagers suspected of hiding weapons and harboring the enemy. The men, women, and children huddle together, silent and frightened, when your lieutenant, William Calley, yells "Shoot!" What would you do? The soldiers who were at My Lai that day obeyed their leader's orders. The third form of social influence, obedience, involves going along with a direct command, usually from someone in a position of authority. One participant's report: "[Lieutenant Calley] told me to start shooting. So I started shooting. I poured about four clips into the group. . . . They was begging and saying, 'No, no.' And the mothers was hugging their children, and . . . Well, we kept right on firing. They was waving their arms and begging . . ." (Wallace, 1969).

Obedience: A type of social influence in which an individual follows direct commands, usually from someone in a position of authority.

Although almost everyone can sympathize with the soldiers given such a ghastly order, many believe they would have defied Lt. Calley's orders. But would they have? This is the question social psychologist Stanley Milgram studied in a series of experiments at Yale University. You read about Milgram's study in Chapter 1. Milgram told his subjects he was testing the effects of punishment on learning. Under increasing demands and orders by the experimenter, most subjects gave dangerously high levels of shock to another research participant. Although the experiment was rigged and no shocks were ever administered, the subjects *believed* that the prearranged screams and groans were real and that they were inflicting severe pain (Milgram, 1963, 1974).

Using Milgram's original research model, cultural studies have found that the high rate of obedience in the United States is matched by those in Australia, Austria, Spain, Italy, Jordan, Germany, and South Africa (Meeus and Raaijmakers, 1986; Milgram, 1974).

Factors in Obedience

What can be concluded from Milgram's experiments? One obvious conclusion is that people in positions of *authority* have a powerful ability to elicit obedience, and that this power is often underestimated. We can also conclude that the placement of *responsibility* plays an important part in the degree of obedience. Subjects in Milgram's experiment were assured early in the session that the experimenter was responsible for the well-being of the learner, which may have encouraged their high level of obedience. Finally, the *gradual* nature of many obedience situations may explain the extremes to which people finally go. The mild level of shocks at the beginning of the session may have worked like the foot-in-the-door technique. Once a subject complied with the initial request from the experimenter, he or she may have felt trapped by his or her own behavior and the nature of the situation (Sabini and Silver, 1993). The subjects in Milgram's experiment, like Koresh's and Jones's followers, may have been seduced by the gradual nature of the increasing demands. Just as Milgram's subjects were asked to give higher and higher levels of shock, cult members were first asked for small monetary donations, then for larger amounts of money and valuable possessions, and ultimately for their lives.

Is there any way to reduce destructive obedience?   One of Milgram's strongest beliefs was that once people understand the factors involved in obedience they can use their understanding to decide when obedience is appropriate and ethical and when it isn't (Milgram, 1974). Just being aware of the power of authority figures and the gradual nature of most obedience situations is a big step toward reducing destructive obedience. Research has also found that when subjects are reminded that they will be held responsible for any harm to the victim, obedience is sharply reduced (Hamilton, 1978). Finally, recent world events offer testimony to the impact of *disobedient models*. Lech Walesa, the Polish leader of Solidarity, is an example. Another is the lone student standing in front of the tanks in Tiananmen Square in China. Their acts of courage inspire the rest of us to question when it is and when it is not good to obey authority.

Gender and Cultural Diversity

WHAT HAPPENS WHEN CULTURES CLASH?

One of the most important concepts in cultural psychology is that an individual's behavior can be understood only in a social context (Brislin, 1993). A behavior that is perfectly acceptable in one situation or in one culture can be totally inappropriate in another situation or culture. The problems associated with conformity, compliance, and obedience within a person's own culture are magnified in interactions between cultures.

Business people traveling abroad and tourists sometimes find themselves in embarrassing or awkward situations when they unknowingly violate the norms or rules for behavior in the host country. Worse, they may lose important business or find themselves in serious legal trouble.

Given our multicultural society and our expanding interactions with other nations, it becomes increasingly important not only to understand and appreciate diversity, but also to prevent *culture clashes*. Consider this story from Richard Brislin (1993):

Kiyoshi, a Japanese executive, was visiting an automobile plant in the American Midwest and was exploring the possibility of a joint venture involving the manufacturing of a new model of car. Hank, an executive at the plant, wanted to show Kiyoshi (who was traveling with his wife) some American hospitality. So he invited Kiyoshi and his wife to dinner at his house. After a prompt arrival at the agreed upon time of 6:00 P.M. and after some pleasant conversation over soft

Men and women are socialized toward separate gender role behaviors. Differences between their two cultures may explain why males and females spend a great deal of time trying to understand one another.

drinks ("No one drinks hard liquor any more!" Hank thought), dinner was served at 7:00 P.M. After cake was served for dessert at about 8:15 P.M., Kiyoshi and his wife thanked Hank for his thoughtfulness and walked slowly toward the door. Hank thought something was wrong, either with himself or with Kiyoshi's manners, because he left right after dessert was served. What went wrong? (p. 98)

What were Hank's norms for a successful dinner party? What must Kiyoshi's have been? Do you see how differing cultural expectations led to an awkward and confusing situation? In Kiyoshi's culture, remaining after dinner is a sign that you are still hungry and the host would be expected to offer more food. The norms in Hank's culture require guests to engage in pleasant conversation after dessert, and if people leave early it is considered an insult.

An additional area of possible culture clash has to do with appropriate distance between people. Research shows that people treat the physical space immediately around them as if it were a part of themselves—an area known as personal space (Sommer, 1969). Edward T. Hall (1966, 1983), an anthropologist, suggests that the preferred interpersonal distance differs according to the situation (see Table 17.1).

Personal Space: Physical space around each individual that is treated as if it were an extension of the self.

 Try This Yourself

Before we go any further, try this experiment to see for yourself how the rules regarding personal space work. Approach a fellow student on campus and ask for directions to the bookstore, library, or some other landmark. As you are talking, move toward the person until you invade his or her personal space. You should be close enough to almost touch toes. How does the person respond? How do you feel? Although most people think this will be a fun assignment, they often find it extremely difficult to willingly break our culture's unwritten norms for personal space. ∎

Why do some people like to stand closer than others?   There are a number of possible explanations. First, culture and socialization have a lot to do with personal space. People from Mediterranean, Moslem, and Latin American countries tend to maintain smaller interpersonal distances than North Americans and Northern Europeans (Axtell, 1991; Steinhart, 1986). Children also tend to stand very close to others until they are socialized to recognize and maintain a larger personal distance (Shea, 1981). Second, certain relationships, situations, and personalities affect interpersonal distances. Friends stand closer than strangers (Ashton and Shaw, 1980), women tend to stand closer than men to whomever they are with (Harnett et al., 1970), and violent prisoners require approximately three times the personal space of nonviolent prisoners (Gilmour and Walkey, 1981).

The importance of these seemingly innocuous differences in human behavior becomes apparent when cultures, ages, or sexes are mixed. People might easily misinter-

Table 17.1   Appropriate Distances for Various Interpersonal Relationships and Activities

Appropriate Space	Relationship or Activity
Intimate distance (0 to 18 inches)	Lovemaking, wrestling, cuddling, fighting
Personal distance (18 inches to 4 feet)	Commonly used by friends for casual conversation
Social distance (4 to 12 feet)	Impersonal and business transactions
Public distance (more than 12 feet)	Formal contacts between an individual and the public (e.g., a speaker or actor and the audience)

Source: E. T. Hall (1966).

Critical Thinking
PSYCHOLOGY IN ACTION
FOSTERING INDEPENDENT THINKING
Would You Have Followed Koresh or Jones?

Have you always thought of yourself as an independent thinker? Perhaps even a bit of a nonconformist? Do the research studies and real-life stories of Waco and Jonestown make you wonder just how well you know this side of yourself? Experts in the field of critical thinking believe some destructive behavior results from not knowing how social forces influence behavior and from a lack of practice in confronting authority figures (see Chaffee, 1992).

To encourage your own independent thinking and increase your resistance to unethical manipulation by others, we have developed the following exercise.

Part I

Rank the following three situations by placing a 1 next to the situation you believe is the most unacceptable form of social influence and a 3 next to the least objectionable.

_____ Jane is 19 and wants very much to become a commercial artist. She has been offered a scholarship to a good art school, but her parents strongly object to her choice of career. After considerable pressure, she enrolls at the same engineering school her father attended.

_____ Bill is 21 and is having serious doubts about his decision to marry Sue. After discussing his concerns with Sue, he realizes how brokenhearted she would be if he canceled the wedding. He decides to marry her.

_____ Mary is 20 and a senior in college. She desperately wants to get into a graduate program at a very prestigious school, but she is failing an important class. The instructor has made it clear that she could have an A in his course if she would sexually "cooperate." She agrees.

Part II

To overcome destructive obedience, John Sabini and Maury Silver (1993) believe individuals should actively practice con-

fronting authority, understand the kinds of social forces that operate on them, and work to eliminate intellectual illusions that foster nonintellectual obedience. These three suggestions can be usefully applied to the three situations you just rank ordered.

1. Mentally review the situation you ranked as most unethical and rehearse how you could effectively combat a similar form of coercion. What would you say? What could you do?

2. This chapter's discussion on social influence should help to educate you about why people conform, comply, and obey, as well as how to resist such manipulation. For example, can you see how normative social influence, reference groups, and guilt induction played a role in the three situations described above? Can you use the text material to help develop an effective rebuttal in each situation?

3. One of the most common intellectual illusions that hinders critical thinking is the belief that "only evil people do evil things" or that "evil announces itself." In Milgram's research, the experimenter who ordered the subjects to continue looked and acted like a reasonable person who was simply carrying out a research project. Because he was not seen as personally corrupt and evil, the subject's normal moral guards were not alerted. But if we are to think critically about destructive obedience, we must avoid looking at personality and focus instead on the morality of our own and others' *acts*. In each of the three situations, can you identify the unethical acts without looking at individual personalities?

Now that you have analyzed Jane's, Bill's, and Mary's situations, think of a current or past situation in your own life where you were unethically persuaded. Applying Sabini and Silver's three suggestions to your own situation can further develop your own autonomous thinking and help you to resist future manipulation.

pret each other's intentions if they are unaware of cultural norms. An Arab, who generally prefers a smaller interpersonal distance, for example, might try to move in closer to an American, who would most likely move back to reestablish his or her preferred distance. Clashes between cultures are inevitable, but the following suggestions may improve your chances for successful interactions (adapted from Brislin, 1993):

1. *Examine your thought processes.* Consider again the Arab and American trying to adjust their personal space. The Arab might misinterpret the American's desire for more personal space and assume he or she is cold and unfriendly. On the other hand, the American might misinterpret the Arab's attempts to get physically closer as aggressive or pushy. Similarly, many Native Americans prefer more silence in their communications than Anglo-Americans who usually interpret silence as a sign that interactions are not going well. Recognizing cultural differences helps us avoid misinterpretations.

2. *Recognize that culture clashes are emotionally stressful.* When people cannot meet their everyday needs as they would in their own culture, stress is inevitable. It *is* frustrating not to be able to communicate with others and to find that familiar ways of behaving do not work in other cultures. Simply acknowledging these feelings will help alleviate the stress.

3. *Adjust your behaviors to match the other's culture.* Adjusting your behavior demonstrates that you recognize diversity and respect the other person's culture. The American could adjust to a smaller personal space as a way of improving interactions with the Arab. The Anglo-American interacting with a Native-American could refrain from rushing to fill any silence with idle talk. ■

Review Questions

1. What are the three major forms of social influence?
2. What is the difference between normative and informational social influence?
3. When we point out our similarities, flatter, and do favors for others in an attempt to gain their compliance, we are using the _____ technique.
4. Asking first for a quarter and then for $5 is known as the _____ technique, whereas first asking for the $5 and backing down to accept a quarter is called the _____ technique.
5. The assignment of _____ is one of the best ways to decrease destructive forms of obedience.
6. What are some ways to prevent culture clashes?

Answers to Review Questions can be found in Appendix C.

GROUP PROCESSES

Psychologists define a group as "two or more persons interacting with one another in such a manner that each person influences and is influenced by each other person" (Shaw, 1981, p. 8). In other words, a group consists of any collection of people who have some mutually recognized relationship with one another. A couple on their first date, a family, a class in psychology, and a tennis club are all considered groups. On the other hand, people riding together in an elevator would not be a group.

* *What are the most influential factors in group behavior?*

Group: In social psychology, two or more people interacting and influencing one another's behavior.

Affiliation: The Need to Be with Others

Why do people group together? There are a number of reasons. We are automatically a member of some groups, for example, our families. Other groups we voluntarily join out of some shared goal or interest. And sometimes we join with others out of the simple desire to be with others—the need for affiliation. If you've ever heard some really wonderful news and had to search desperately to find someone to share it with, or if you've been really frightened and wanted someone to comfort you, you understand what Aristotle meant when he called us "social animals."

Affiliation: Need for friendly association with others.

What about people who are lone wolves, rather than social animals? Is there something wrong with this? Not at all. People differ in their need for affiliation. Although some seem to prefer a great deal of time alone and find solitude stimulating, others seem to like having others with them at all times and find being alone deeply disturbing.

In addition to differences between individuals, each of us also feels more affiliative in some circumstances than in others. As can be seen in Table 17.2, research finds that we most want to be with others during good times or frightening times. In a now classic experiment, Stanley Schachter (1959) first demonstrated the relation between fear and affiliation by leading subjects to believe that they would be undergoing a series of electrical shocks. He then allowed them to choose whether they wanted to wait by themselves or with others while the experiment was being set up. Half the subjects were told the shocks would be extremely painful but that there would be "no permanent damage" (high-fear condition). The other half of the subjects were led to expect virtually painless shocks that would feel, at worst, like a tickle (low-fear condition).

As you might imagine, those in the high-fear group were much more likely to choose to wait with others than were those in the low-fear group. Fully two-thirds of the high-level subjects chose to be with others, compared to only one-third of the low-fear subjects. As was the case with the obedience study by Stanley Milgram, no shocks were actually administered. The experiment was terminated after subjects made their choice, and the experimenter fully debriefed each subject by explaining the reason for the deception and describing the details of the experiment—what was done, why it was done, and what it meant.

Social Comparison Theory

There are many possible explanations why high stress or fear makes us want to be with someone else. People may think others will provide important information, or perhaps

Table 17.2 Student Preferences for Being Alone or with Others in 13 Different Situations

Situations in Which	Percentage of Students Who		
	Wished to be with Others	Wished to be Alone	Had No Preference
Most want to be with others			
When very happy	88	2	10
When in a good mood	89	0	11
On Saturday night	85	1	14
In a strange situation or doing something you've never done before	77	13	10
Most want to be alone			
When physically tired	6	85	9
When embarrassed	16	76	8
When you want to cry	8	88	4
When busy	12	70	18
After an extensive period of social contact (after being with others for a long time)	12	75	13
There is no consensus			
When depressed	42	48	10
When worried about a serious personal problem	52	44	4
When mildly ill (e.g., with a cold)	32	49	19
When feeling very guilty about something you have done	45	43	12

Source: Middlebrook, P. N. (1992). *Social psychology and modern life* (4th ed., p. 284). Copyright © 1980 Alfred A. Knopf, Inc. Reprinted by permission.

they hope that the presence of others will serve as a distraction. Or, as social comparison theory proposes, people in this situation may be unsure of their own feelings and reactions and seek out others as a source of comparison. Leon Festinger (1954) developed this theory to explain our need to look to others as a sort of yardstick for evaluating our own attitudes and abilities. We want to know whether what we feel is similar to what others feel ("Is this normal?" "Am I better or worse than others in important abilities?"). The need for social comparison is particularly acute when there is no clear physical or objective standard against which to assess ourselves. This was the case for subjects who believed they were waiting for a painful shock procedure. Can you also see how this theory would apply to the followers of Koresh and Jones, who were both physically and psychologically isolated from their families and friends? Without access to conflicting opinions, many followers looked to their leader for their social comparison data.

Social Comparison Theory: Festinger's view that we seek out others as a way to interpret and compare our own abilities, attitudes, and reactions.

Group Membership: How It Affects the Individual

Whatever the type or function of a group, membership has a variety of effects. Have you ever been with friends and found yourself doing something that you might not have done alone? Or have you noticed that you behave differently with your friends than with your parents or with your employer or roommates? In each situation, your behavior is largely the result of your group membership. Although we seldom recognize the power of such membership, social psychologists have identified at least two important ways that groups affect us: (1) through the roles we play, and (2) through the group's ability to induce a feeling of anonymity and reduced self-monitoring (deindividuation).

Roles in Groups

Every person in a group is expected to play one or more roles—a set of behavioral patterns connected with particular social positions. Some roles are very specifically spelled out and regulated (police officer), whereas others are assumed through informal learning and inference (father). Have you ever wondered how these roles might affect behavior? This was the question that fascinated social psychologist Philip Zimbardo. In his famous study at Stanford University, 20 carefully screened, well-adjusted young college men were paid $15 a day for participating in a simulation of prison life (Haney, Banks, and Zimbardo, 1978; Zimbardo, 1993).

Role: A category of people and the set of normative expectations for people in that category.

 *Try This Yourself*

As a way of appreciating Zimbardo's study, pretend for a moment that you are one of the 20 college students selected and you have been randomly assigned to be a prisoner. You are watching TV at home, and you hear a loud knock on your front door. You open the door to face several uniformed police officers who take you outside and spread-eagle you against the police car. As they frisk you, they tell you you are being arrested. As you drive away with the siren screaming, do you wonder what you've gotten yourself into? At the police station, you are photographed, fingerprinted, and booked. You are then blindfolded and driven to your final destination. Here you are stripped, deloused, and given a shapeless gown to wear, a tight nylon cap to conceal your hair, and no underwear. You are given an ID number in place of your name and locked in a cell. From this point on, you are part of the "Stanford Prison." All prisoners are in their prisoner clothes, and the guards, with their official-looking uniforms, billy clubs, and whistles, have complete control. What do you think happened? ■

Not even Zimbardo foresaw how the experiment would turn out. Within a short time, the guards became aggressive, abusive, and brutal. They insisted that prisoners obey unhesitatingly not only the prison rules but also rules they made up. The slightest disobedience was punished with degrading tasks (such as cleaning the toilet with bare hands) or the loss of "privileges" (such as eating, sleeping, and washing). Although some guards were "good guys" who did little favors for the prisoners and others were "tough

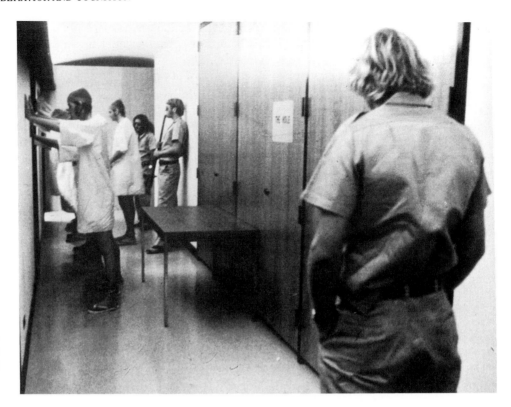

Subjects in Zimbardo's simulation were searched before being assigned to their cells. How do you think these sacklike uniforms affected the "prisoners'" behavior?

but fair," they *all* became authoritarian and engaged in some abuse of power. Most prisoners initially responded to the bossing and arbitrary rules with good-humored acceptance. But as the rules increased and the abuses began, one prisoner went on a hunger strike (which was quickly punished), and a few became model prisoners who obeyed every rule. The majority became passive and depressed.

Four prisoners had to be released within the first four days because of severe reactions, such as uncontrollable sobbing, fits of rage, severe depression, and, in one case, a psychosomatic rash over his entire body. Although the study was planned to last two weeks, it was stopped after only six days because of the alarming psychological changes in the student participants. The guards were seriously abusing their power, and the traumatized prisoners were becoming more and more depressed and dehumanized.

How could this have happened?   According to interviews conducted after the study, the students apparently became so absorbed in their roles they forgot they were volunteers in a university experiment (Zimbardo et al., 1977). This new *social reality* was so powerful it even trapped Zimbardo: "In the end, I called off the experiment not because of the horror I saw out there in the prison yard, but because of the horror of realizing that I could have easily traded places with the most brutal guard or have become the weakest prisoner full of hatred at being so powerless . . ." (1977, p. 9).

Although this was not a true experiment, in that it lacked control groups and clear measurements of the dependent variable, it does offer insights into the potential power of roles on individual behavior. If this type of personality disintegration and abuse of power could be generated in a mere six days in a mock prison with *volunteers,* what actually happens during life imprisonment, six-year sentences, or even overnight jail stays?

Zimbardo's study should also inspire us to question everyday roles between parents and children or between teachers and students. For example, should parents have the legal right to use corporal punishment on their children? Should students have more control over course content and faculty selection and retention?

Deindividuation

Have you ever participated in ripping down goal posts after a big football game? As a child, do you remember being with friends on Halloween and feeling freer to engage in socially unacceptable actions while wearing your halloween masks? If so, you have experienced deindividuation. When people become *deindividuated* they temporarily suspend their own private self-identity and adopt instead the identity of the group. The individual becomes less aware of his or her own values and personal responsibilities, has a lessened fear of evaluation by others, and gets caught up in the group identity (Diener, 1980). Although this lack of self-awareness and heightened sensitivity to the group may lead to dangerous mob actions, it may also encourage acts of altruism (see Chapter 18) and even heroism (Spivey and Prentice-Dunn, 1990).

Deindividuation: Being so caught up in a group identity that individual self-awareness and evaluation apprehension are temporarily suspended.

What causes deindividuation?   As can be seen in Figure 17.2, certain environmental conditions predispose people to reduced self-awareness, which then leads to deindividuation and its consequences. The riots in Los Angeles after the first trial related to the Rodney King beating may have been an example of deindividuation (see Chapter 18).

In one of the earliest experiments to test deindividuation, Zimbardo (1970) created conditions of anonymity by asking New York University female students to wear identical white coats and hoods, making them resemble members of the Ku Klux Klan. In addition, they sat in darkened rooms and were never referred to by name. When given the

Figure 17.2 Deindividuation. When people are caught up in group identity and lose their sense of self-awareness, they experience deindividuation. This state of mind can be positive if you're dancing or at a family gathering, but it also has the potential for dangerous decision making and destructive behaviors.

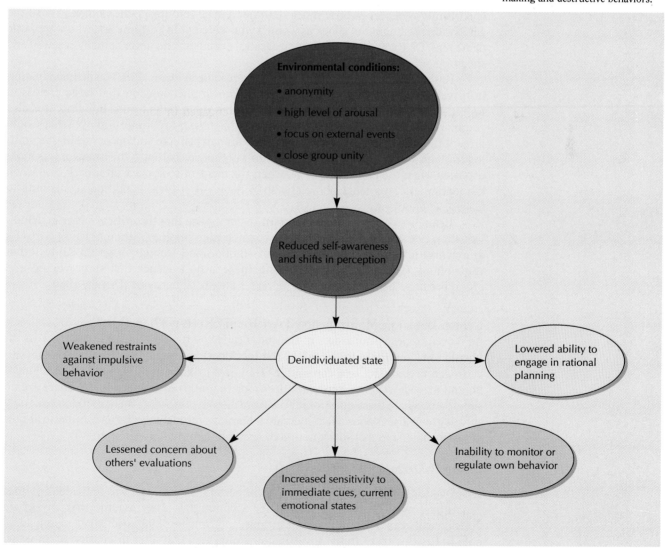

When college women were covered with hoods and white coats, their anonymity encouraged stronger acts of aggression.

opportunity to deliver electric shocks to other female volunteers, the women in costume gave twice the amount of shock as women who were not in costume and who wore large name tags. (The volunteers were confederates, of course, and never actually received any shock.)

It is also interesting (and depressing) to read Leon Mann (1981) on deindividuation in threatened or actual suicide. It is a well-known phenomenon that large crowds of people gather to watch a suicidal person threatening to jump from a building. It is also common to hear the crowd cheer and taunt the person to "Jump! Jump!" What would prompt these people to encourage a distraut human being to end his or her life? According to Mann's analysis of newspaper accounts of "suicide baiting," the behavior was more common when the crowd was large, when the incident took place after dark, and when the victim was on a ledge above the sixth floor. All of these conditions contribute to feelings of anonymity.

Before we conclude, it is important to emphasize that the critical factor in deindividuation is this *anonymity,* not simple group membership. Although being part of a group may lead to an intensification of emotion and feelings of group unity (other contributing factors in deindividuation), there is no evidence that simply being in a group produces deindividuation or increases antisocial behavior (Diener, 1980).

Group Decision Making: Are Two Heads Better Than One?

Should only one individual (such as the president) be responsible for decisions on nuclear war, or should it be a committee? Do juries make better judgments than a judge? Should managers assign important decisions to groups or to individuals? There are no simple answers to these questions. To formulate some response, we need to look not only at how group discussions affect individual opinions (group polarization), but also at how group membership may affect access to accurate information (groupthink).

Group Polarization

When considering whether to trust an important decision to one individual or to a committee, most people tend to opt for a committee. They assume that any group decision will be more conservative, cautious, and "middle of the road" than an individual one. But is this true? Initial investigations indicated that after discussion of an issue, groups would actually support *riskier* decisions than ones they made as individuals before the discussion (Stoner, 1961). Partly because it contradicted the common belief about group caution and moderation, this *risky shift* concept sparked a great deal of research.

Subsequent research shows that the risky shift phenomenon is only part of the picture in group decision making. Although some groups do, in fact, make riskier decisions, others become extremely *conservative* (MacCoun and Kerr, 1988; Whyte, 1992). Whether the final decision is risky or conservative depends primarily on the dominant preexisting tendencies of the group. That is, as individuals interact and discuss their opinions, their initial positions become more exaggerated. This movement toward one "polar" extreme or the other is known as group polarization.

Group Polarization: The exaggeration of a group's initial tendencies as a result of group discussion.

Why does this happen?   The tendency toward group polarization generally results from increased exposure to *persuasive arguments*. When people hear arguments from other people, they are exposed to new information. However, since most informal, political, or business groups consist of like-minded individuals, members will most often hear additional arguments that reinforce their original opinion. Thus, the groups preexisting tendencies are strengthened by the group discussion. As you can see, the process of group polarization has important implications in decision making. If you are excited about investing in a risky business and you discuss it with other like-minded investors, for example, you are more likely to make the risky investment. On the other hand, if you are overly cautious and discuss the same investment with others who are cautious, you may make an unnecessarily conservative decision.

Groupthink

Group decision making may not only be affected by the tendency toward group polarization, there is the other equally dangerous tendency toward groupthink. Irving Janis (1972, 1989) defines groupthink as "a mode of thinking that people engage in when they are deeply involved in a cohesive in-group, and when the members' strivings for unanimity override their motivation to realistically appraise alternative courses of action" (p. 9). That is, when groups are strongly cohesive (a family, a panel of military advisers, an athletic team) they generally share a strong desire for agreement (to see themselves as "one"). This desire may lead them to ignore important information or points of view held by outsiders or critics (Kruglanski and Webster, 1991).

Groupthink: Condition in which a highly cohesive group with a strong desire for agreement leads to an avoidance of inconsistent information and faulty decision making.

After analyzing several governmental decisions, such as the U.S. invasion of Cuba (the "Bay of Pigs") in 1962, Janis concluded that many disastrous decisions were largely the result of groupthink. As outlined in Figure 17.3, the process of groupthink begins with group members feeling a strong sense of cohesiveness and relative isolation from

In the film Twelve Angry Men, *both group polarization and groupthink played a role in the jury's deliberation.*

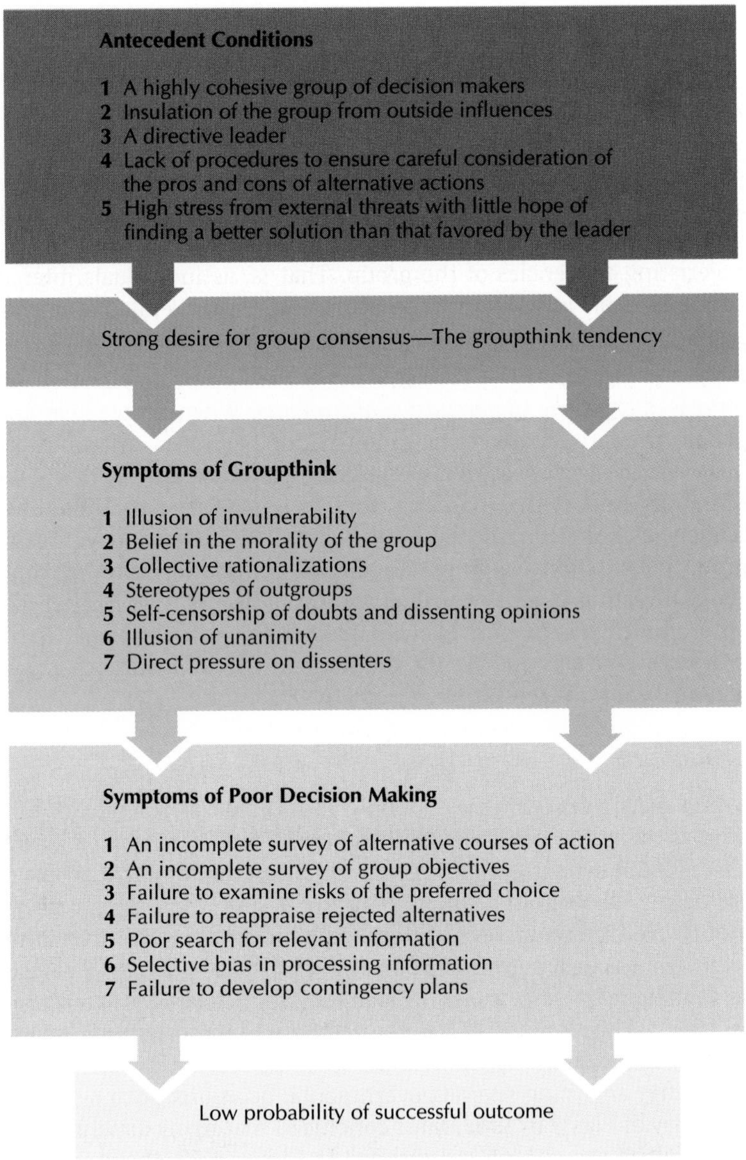

Antecedent Conditions

1 A highly cohesive group of decision makers
2 Insulation of the group from outside influences
3 A directive leader
4 Lack of procedures to ensure careful consideration of
    the pros and cons of alternative actions
5 High stress from external threats with little hope of
    finding a better solution than that favored by the leader

Strong desire for group consensus—The groupthink tendency

Symptoms of Groupthink

1 Illusion of invulnerability
2 Belief in the morality of the group
3 Collective rationalizations
4 Stereotypes of outgroups
5 Self-censorship of doubts and dissenting opinions
6 Illusion of unanimity
7 Direct pressure on dissenters

Symptoms of Poor Decision Making

1 An incomplete survey of alternative courses of action
2 An incomplete survey of group objectives
3 Failure to examine risks of the preferred choice
4 Failure to reappraise rejected alternatives
5 Poor search for relevant information
6 Selective bias in processing information
7 Failure to develop contingency plans

Low probability of successful outcome

Figure 17.3 How groupthink *works.* Note how appropriate antecedent conditions (such as being in a highly cohesive group, isolation from others, and so on) can set the stage for groupthink. You can prevent groupthink by watching for symptoms, such as the illusion of invulnerability. If groupthink takes over, it will likely lead to poor decision making.

the judgments of qualified outsiders. Add a directive leader and little chance for debate, and you have the recipe for a potentially dangerous decision. During the actual discussion process, the members also come to believe they are invulnerable, tend to share rationalizations and stereotypes of the outgroup, and exert considerable pressure on anyone who dares to offer a dissenting opinion. Some members actually start to play the role of group "mindguards," working rather like bodyguards to isolate and protect the group from all differences in opinion. During the meetings that resulted in the decision to invade Cuba, for example, Robert Kennedy protected his brother, the president, and other members of the group by discouraging any direct or indirect criticism of the initial plan and even the slightest evidence of nonsupport (Janis, 1972, 1989).

Groupthink and Marriage

One of the most immediate and personal applications of groupthink is the group decision to marry (remember that groups are composed of two or more). When dating couples begin to think about marriage, they often show several of the *antecedent conditions* for groupthink. (1) They have a strong need for cohesiveness ("we agree on almost everything"). (2) They are often insulated from others' opinions ("we do almost everything as a couple"). (3) They lack the resources or desire to methodically evaluate the

Table 17.3   How to Avoid Groupthink

1. Group members should be told about groupthink and its causes and consequences.
2. The leader should be impartial and not endorse any position.
3. The leader should instruct everyone to critically evaluate options and should encourage objections and doubts.
4. One or more members should be assigned the role of "devil's advocate."
5. From time to time, the group should be subdivided, with subgroups meeting separately and then coming together to air differences.
6. When the issue concerns relations with a rival group, time should be taken to survey all warning signals and identify various possible actions by the rival.
7. After reaching a preliminary decision, a "second-chance" meeting should be called at which each member is asked to express remaining doubts.
8. Outside experts should attend meetings on a staggered basis and be asked to express concerns.
9. Each group member should air the group's deliberations to trusted associates and report their reactions.
10. Several independent groups should work simultaneously on the same question.

Source: Adapted from Janis (1982).

correctness or advisability of their decision to marry. When discussing a pending marriage, they also show many *symptoms* of groupthink: the illusion of invulnerability ("we're different, we won't ever get divorced"); collective rationalization ("two can live more cheaply than one"); and shared stereotypes of the outgroup ("couples with problems just don't know how to communicate"). Couples may also self-censor their own doubts and avoid any "dissenter" who tries to discourage them.

Is there any way to avoid groupthink?   As can be seen in Table 17.3, Janis and Mann (1977) developed several prescriptions for preventing groupthink. Some suggestions on this list obviously do not apply to a couple's decision concerning marriage, but each point has something of value that can be used in decision-making situations you will encounter in your lifetime—which product to introduce into your business, where to take your family vacation, or even whether or not to have children.

Review Questions

1. The need to _____, or the need to belong, is a primary reason for joining groups.
2. Why do people often compare their abilities with others'?
3. Zimbardo's simulation of prison life provided a dramatic demonstration of the power of _____ on behavior.
4. What is deindividuation?
5. _____ refers to the fact that after group discussion members' preexisting and dominant tendencies or opinions will be reinforced and intensified.
6. What is groupthink?

Answers to Review Questions can be found in Appendix C.

ATTRIBUTION

As we try to understand the world around us, we look for reasons for people's behavior. What are the reasons or causes for the tragedies in Waco and Guyana, for example? When we offer an explanation for behavior, we *attribute* it to something—"the people were

• How are internal and external factors involved in attribution?

Attribution: The principles people follow in making judgments about the causes of events, others' behavior, and their own behavior.

isolated," "the people were weak," "Koresh and Jones were overpowering," and so on. Psychologists use the term attribution to describe statements explaining why people do what they do. In this section, we'll first look at the major criteria for attribution and then at several potential attributional errors.

Criteria for Attribution: Internal versus External Factors

How do you go about deciding why someone did something? After extensive analysis, Harold Kelley (1967, 1973) found that most people begin with a basic question: Does the behavior stem mainly from *internal* or *external* causes? Did someone act as a result of his or her own characteristics, motives, or intentions, or from some situational demands or environmental pressures? Kelley went on to suggest that we answer the internal-external question by applying three criteria: *consistency, consensus,* and *distinctiveness.*

1. *Consistency.* Does the person react to the same stimulus in a similar way on other occasions? If the person responds in a similar fashion at different times, his or her behavior is predictable, and consistency is *high.* When the person's behavior is irregular, consistency is *low.*

2. *Consensus.* How do other people react to the same stimulus? If other people behave in a similar fashion, then consensus is *high.* When the reverse is true, consensus is *low.*

3. *Distinctiveness.* How does the person react to other, different stimuli? Is the person's behavior unusual or distinctive? If an individual has an unusual response to this one, particular stimulus, then distinctiveness is *high.* But if the person reacts in a similar manner to different stimuli, then the behavior is not unusual and distinctiveness is *low.*

When consistency, consensus, and distinctiveness are *all* high, Kelley says we tend to make *external* attributions. But when consistency and consensus are low, and distinctiveness is high, we tend to make *internal* attributions (see Figure 17.4).

Consistency and distinctiveness sound similar. What is the difference? Consistency refers to how the individual reacts to the *same* stimulus at different times, whereas distinctiveness refers to how the individual reacts to *different* stimuli. One way to un-

Figure 17.4 Attribution. When we try to understand someone's behavior, we rely on three criteria—consistency, consensus, and distinctiveness. This figure shows how we might explain a coworker's "pushy and obnoxious" behavior at work. Under conditions of high consistency, low consensus, and low distinctiveness, we would be likely to make an *internal attribution*—we would blame the person. On the other hand, if there is high consistency, high consensus, and high distinctiveness, most people would make an *external attribution*—they would blame the situation.

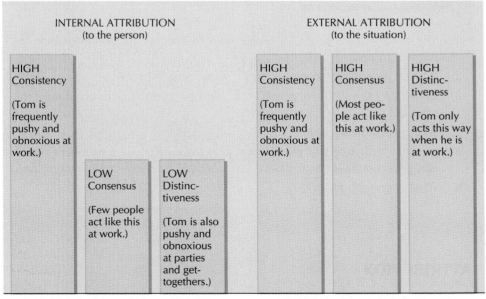

INTERNAL ATTRIBUTION (to the person)   EXTERNAL ATTRIBUTION (to the situation)

HIGH Consistency

(Tom is frequently pushy and obnoxious at work.)

LOW Consensus

(Few people act like this at work.)

LOW Distinctiveness

(Tom is also pushy and obnoxious at parties and get-togethers.)

HIGH Consistency

(Tom is frequently pushy and obnoxious at work.)

HIGH Consensus

(Most people act like this at work.)

HIGH Distinctiveness

(Tom only acts this way when he is at work.)

Tom's behavior would be attributed to his "pushy and obnoxious" personality.   Tom's behavior would be attributed to the work situation.

derstand this is to think about our introductory incident. We would say that the cult members were consistent in their behavior because they had also followed orders on several occasions. We would also say that their behavior was distinctive because they only displayed this type of obedience when David Koresh or Jim Jones ordered it. The fact that over 70 people in Waco and 900 in Guyana also followed the same orders would suggest that there was strong consensus for this behavior. Given that consistency, consensus, and distinctiveness were all high, according to Kelley we should logically attribute the cult members' obedience to *external* influences (the situation) and not to internal (personality) factors. But most people attribute blame in both instances to personality factors in either the leaders (Koresh or Jones) or the cult members. How do we account for this discrepancy?

Attributional Errors: Failures in Perception

The kind of careful analysis described by Kelley is difficult. How do you determine whether someone is *consistent, distinctive,* and whether there is a *consensus* when you have limited time, energy, and information? Given that we are bombarded with hundreds of social interactions everyday, we frequently rely on cognitive shortcuts that help us cope with this large amount of information. Sometimes, however, these shortcuts distort our views of behavior and we make mistakes.

Fundamental Attribution Error

One error, or shortcut, is so common and basic that it is known as the fundamental attribution error. People simply tend to prefer an internal, personality explanation for behavior rather than an external, situational one (Baron and Byrne, 1992). This explains why we blame people and personality rather than the external situation for the Waco and Guyana tragedies. This also happens in our everyday life. When we see someone trip while walking across campus, for example, we're likely to attribute it to that person's carelessness or lack of coordination rather than uneven ground or ill-fitting shoes.

Fundamental Attribution Error: A mistake in judging the causes of others' behavior that comes from the tendency to overestimate internal, personal factors and underestimate external, situational influences.

Explaining the Fundamental Attribution Error

There are several possible explanations for our tendency to make internal rather than external attributions. But the most important is that human personalities and behaviors are more salient (or noticeable) than situational factors (Wilder and Thompson, 1988). This saliency bias helps explain why people so often blame welfare recipients for their joblessness. The large situational factors that lead to poverty and joblessness are not concrete and conspicuous. On the other hand, there are examples of a few people who seemingly exploit the system by buying liquor or cigarettes with food stamps. Politicians frequently use these salient examples of so-called "welfare cheaters" to explain increasing taxes.

Saliency Bias: The tendency to focus attention on vivid (salient) factors when explaining the causes of behavior.

Would this be an example of "blaming the victim"?   Yes. One of the most dangerous problems associated with saliency bias is this common tendency to blame the victim. When people are victimized by poverty, robbery, or rape, they are often interrogated about *why* they got themselves into such a situation. Blaming the victim for his or her misfortune helps us to maintain our belief that we live in a *just world,* where bad things only happen to bad people (Frazier, 1990; Lerner, 1980).

Blaming the Victim: The act of placing blame on an individual who suffers from an injustice. It involves the belief that bad things happen to people because they deserve it.

Self-Serving Bias

When we judge others' behavior we tend to emphasize internal, personality factors over external, situational causes. But when we explain our own behavior we favor internal, personal attributions for our successes and external, environmental attributions for our failures. If we do well on an exam, for instance, we generally take personal credit ("I really studied" or "I'm pretty smart"). If we fail the test, however, we tend to blame the

Assuming responsibility for failures (internal attributions) can help us to improve our performance, but if carried to extremes it can also lead to depression.

Self-Serving Bias: Way of maintaining a positive self-image by taking credit for one's successes and emphasizing external causes for one's failures.

instructor, the textbook, or the "tricky" questions. This self-serving bias is motivated by a desire to maintain our self-esteem, as well as a desire to look good to others. (Mutter and Bryson, 1993).

Wouldn't this type of distortion be unhealthy? Shouldn't people admit their failures? Although blaming external factors can obviously limit our personal motivation to change inappropriate behavior, it is also interesting that mildly depressed college students and clinically depressed patients generally *lack* the self-serving bias (Peterson and Seligman, 1984; Robins, 1988). People who are depressed or have low self-esteem tend to attribute unfavorable outcomes in their lives to their own stable personal characteristics and attribute positive outcomes to external, unstable causes such as luck. Successful coping, therefore, seems to be a mixture of: (1) taking credit for our successes [don't attribute positive outcomes to external, unstable causes (e.g., luck)]; and (2) changing personal behaviors that contribute to failures (don't assume negative behaviors are unchangeable personality characteristics). Taking a dual approach allows us to feel good about ourselves while encouraging us to change our inappropriate behaviors.

Review Questions

1. What is "attribution"?
2. When deciding whether behavior is due to internal or external causes, what are the three criteria we apply?
3. What is the fundamental attribution error?
4. Why are people likely to "blame the victim"?
5. In judging the causes of our own behavior, we tend to take personal credit for our successes and externalize our failures; this is known as _____ .

Answers to Review Questions can be found in Appendix C.

SOCIAL COGNITION

• *How do heuristics function in social cognition?*

Social Cognition: Processes through which we interpret, analyze, remember, and use information about the social world.

In our interactions, we not only try to figure out the causes of others' behavior, we also form opinions about other people. We decide whether we like or dislike them, whether they would be good for a certain job, and so on. How we go about making these decisions is studied under the heading social cognition (Miller, Turnbull, and McFarland, 1990). Social cognition is concerned with understanding the processes through which we interpret, analyze, remember, and use information about the social world.

In our discussion of attribution, we made the point that we encounter a huge amount of social information about other people and to process this information we often take mental shortcuts. Such shortcuts are *generally* fairly accurate, but there is always the chance of a mistake. In this section we will first look at two major shortcuts (known as heuristics) that help us process information and make decisions about others. Then we will discuss four common errors in social cognition.

How We Make Decisions about Others: The Use of Heuristics

In Chapter 8, we discussed *heuristics,* mental rules based on experience that we use to solve problems more quickly. We noted that heuristics are generally accurate and offer us an efficient way to process a large amount of information. For example, when you're playing soccer, you can't stop to consider all the possible outcomes each time you make a move. Instead, you rely on heuristics such as "control the center of the field" and "defend the goal."

Just as we have heuristics for problems, we also have them for people, hence the term *social* cognition. Just as heuristics can help us make decisions in a soccer game, they also help us understand other people and make predictions about their behavior.

The Availability Heuristic

When we encounter new people or new social situations, we predict an outcome based on our memories of similar situations. If many memories come easily to mind, we have greater confidence in our predictions. For example, if we have many memories of people divorcing, we will conclude that our friends who are fighting are likely to get a divorce. This illustrates what is referred to as the availability heuristic, a mental shortcut based on the availability of information in our memories. When instances are readily available, we judge them to be more likely to happen (Tversky and Kahneman, 1974).

Availability Heuristic: A mental shortcut in social cognition used to predict how likely something is to happen based on how quickly examples come to mind.

The Representative Heuristic

In addition to how readily instances comes to mind, we consider whether these instances match the present situation. If the new person or situation closely resembles our memories, we are more certain of our predictions. In judging the likelihood of our friends' divorce, we also consider how closely their behavior matches the behavior of other people we have known who have divorced. If our memories include similar fights among other divorced people, our confidence in predicting our friends' divorce increases. This is an example of the representative heuristic, a mental shortcut based on how well a new situation matches our memory of similar situations. When the new situation closely matches our memory, we judge it more likely to happen (Tversky and Kahneman, 1974, 1981).

Representative Heuristic: A mental shortcut used in social cognition to judge the probability of certain events based on how well a newly encountered situation matches our memory of similar situations. When it closely matches, we judge it as being likely to have a similar outcome.

In sum, when we encounter new people or new situations, we tend to rely on two mental shortcuts: how easily other examples come to mind (the availability heuristic), and how closely these examples match the present situation (the representative heuristic). If the examples are readily available and a close match, we are more certain of our predictions.

How We Make Mistakes Judging Others: Errors in Social Cognition

Although heuristics are generally helpful, research on decision making has found that they sometimes lead to certain types of errors and consequently to poor decisions. Fortunately, evidence also shows that if we know what these errors are, we can avoid them and make better decisions. There are four major social cognition errors or biases: overestimating the improbable, priming, base-rate fallacy, and the false consensus bias.

1. *Overestimating the improbable.* In our discussion of attribution, we covered the saliency bias, which suggests that we tend to pay more attention to vivid, easy-to-imagine events and anecdotes when explaining the causes of behavior. Similarly, in social cognition vividness affects the availability of information. News coverage of plane crashes creates vivid memories that are readily brought to mind, and this vividness causes us to overestimate the danger of flying and underestimate dangers such as riding in an automobile. (According to the 1991 National Safety Council, you are 26 times more likely to die in a car crash than in a commercial flight covering the same distance.)

2. *Priming.* Certain events and procedures can heighten the availability of information so that it can be more easily brought to mind—the *priming effect* (Forgas, 1992; Wyer and Srull, 1980). Do you remember reading in Chapter 15 about the various forms of abnormal behavior? We reminded you then of the *medical student syndrome:* You begin to suspect you or your family may have one of the disorders. Just reading about these disorders *primes* you to look for symptoms in yourself and others. Similarly, can you see how televised coverage of such events as the Rodney King beating and the Los Angeles riots in

1992 can prime viewers to see police officers as brutal and African-Americans as either victims or rioters? Or how our description of the murder/suicide in Guyana can inadvertently prime you to consider Jones's followers gullible victims?

3. *Base-rate fallacy.* When people judge themselves and others they often ignore or underuse *base-rate* information—information that describes most people. Instead, we tend to focus on distinctive, individual cases. For example, if you are trying to decide which washing machine to buy, will you be more influenced by your friend's belief that one particular brand has a horrible repair record, or would you rely instead on the base-rate information offered by surveys of thousands of customers in *Consumer Reports?* Research shows that we frequently fall into the base-rate fallacy and rely too heavily on the singular report (Krosnic et al., 1990; Nisbett et al., 1976).

4. *False-consensus bias.* We often overestimate the number of people we believe agree with us and support us. Research shows that when people are asked to estimate the proportion of others who agree with their beliefs about drugs, abortion, and toxic waste, they significantly overestimate the degree of agreement (Gilovich, 1990). The false consensus bias serves the same function in social cognition that the self-serving bias serves in attribution: By overestimating the "correctness" or popularity of our views, we protect our self-image.

At this point you may be wondering how we ever manage to make a good decision, if attribution and social cognition are so riddled with faulty thinking and biases. Actually, these errors are exceptions to our normal information processing, not the rule. We study errors in thinking primarily as a way of understanding the normal processes and as a way of improving social interactions because awareness of potential biases can improve decision making. Also, being aware of biases in attribution and social cognition can prevent the *self-fulfilling prophecy,* a problem discussed in the next section.

Review Questions

1. What is social cognition?
2. What are the two major heuristics we use in social cognition?
3. Due to _____ , many people consider it more dangerous to fly than to ride in an automobile.
4. How does "priming" explain why you're likely to be frightened while walking home alone after watching a horror film?
5. Overestimating the degree that others agree with us is known as the _____ .
6. Why do social psychologists study errors in social cognition?

Answers to Review Questions can be found in Appendix C.

INTERPERSONAL ATTRACTION

• *How can liking and loving be explained?*

Interpersonal Attraction: The degree of positive or negative feelings toward another.

Stop for a moment and think about someone you like very much. Now picture someone you really dislike. Can you explain your feelings? Social psychologists use the term interpersonal attraction to refer to the degree of positive or negative feelings toward another. Attraction accounts for a variety of social experiences—admiration, liking, friendship, intimacy, lust, and love. In this section, we will discuss several factors and theories that explain interpersonal attraction.

Key Factors in Attraction: Physical Attractiveness, Proximity, and Similarity

Social psychologists have found there are three compelling factors in interpersonal attraction—physical attractiveness, proximity, and similarity. While physical attractiveness and proximity are more influential in the beginning stages of relationships, similarity is the single most important factor in maintaining a long-term relationship.

Physical Attractiveness

Can you remember what first attracted you to your best friend or romantic partner? Was it his or her warm personality, sharp intelligence, or great sense of humor? Or was it looks? Research has consistently shown that physical attractiveness (size, shape, facial characteristics, and manner of dress) is one of the most important factors in our initial liking or loving of others (Hendrick and Hendrick, 1993).

Physical Attractiveness: Having the physical properties (size, shape, facial characteristics, and so on) that elicit favorable evaluations from others.

Gender and Cultural Diversity

PHYSICAL ATTRACTIVENESS ACROSS CULTURES

Standards of attractiveness vary considerably from era to era and from culture to culture. In the fairly recent past it was considered desirable in American culture for both men and women to have fair skin, rounded bodies, and no evidence of muscles, whereas today the emphasis is on tans, thinness, and well-defined muscles. The Chinese once practiced foot binding because small feet were considered very attractive in women. All the toes except the big one were bent under a young girl's foot and into the sole. The physical distortion made it almost impossible for her to walk, and she suffered excruciating pain, chronic bleeding, and frequent infections (Dworkin, 1974). Compare this to America today where each year almost 100,000 women undergo surgery to increase the size of their breasts, and millions of women engage in dangerous forms of dieting to conform to cultural demands for thinness (Wolf, 1991).

The importance of physical attractiveness for women as opposed to men differs dramatically across cultures. In most patriarchal cultures (societies dominated by men), physical beauty is the most important attribute in a potential wife. And in 37 cultures around the world, women are judged more beautiful if they are youthful in appearance (Buss, 1989). (Given the social value assigned to beauty and youth, can you see why women in America seem overly concerned with their appearance and sometimes reluctant to reveal their age?) For men, on the other hand, maturity and financial resources are more important than appearance in attracting a mate.

How would you explain such different standards? One of the most intriguing—and controversial—explanations comes from *sociobiology.* According to sociobiologists, the male's preference for youthful, fertile-appearing mates has survival value since mating with such a woman increases the odds of passing on one's genes. Similarly, the female's preference for an older, economically secure mate insures that her offspring will be well fed and protected and therefore more likely to survive to pass along her genes (Kenrick and Keefe, 1992; Wilson, 1975). As you read in Chapter 12, there are numerous critics of the sociobiologists' perspective.

In spite of historical and cultural variations, there is generally agreement on the ideals of beauty within a culture at any one time (Wolf, 1991). In our society, for example, "babyish" characteristics (large eyes and head, small nose, rounded features, and soft skin) are considered attractive for women (Keating, 1985), whereas strong, jutting chins and facial hair (mustaches, beards) are desirable in men. Men with "baby faces" are seen as naive but also unusually warm and kind (Berry and McArthur, 1985). ■

Which of these women do you find most attractive? Your judgment is a reflection of your specific cultural conditioning, and what may be attractive in one culture may be judged as strange or unattractive in another.

Physical Attractiveness and the Self-Fulfilling Prophecy

Physical attractiveness plays an incredibly important role in our perceptions of others throughout the entire life span. As early as nursery school, for example, beautiful children are more popular with their classmates and are judged to be more intelligent and well adjusted by their teachers (Felson, 1980). By the time they reach adulthood, attractive individuals are seen by both men and women as more poised, interesting, sociable, independent, exciting, and sexually warm (Eagly et al., 1991).

Aren't these beliefs similar to stereotypes?   Yes. Just as we often form impressions and stereotypes of others on the basis of their sex or race, we also form stereotypes on the basis of physical attractiveness. One problem with stereotypes is that they may lead us to interact with others in such a way that they eventually *exhibit* those characteristics. People we stereotype as "poised, interesting, and sociable" become "poised, interesting, and sociable" in response to being treated as such. This process is referred to as a self-fulfilling prophecy. An interesting study that documents the self-fulfilling prophecy

Self-Fulfilling Prophecy: A sequence in which a perceiver's expectations about a person causes that person to behave in ways that confirm those expectations.

was done by Snyder, Tanke, and Berscheid (1977). In this experiment, a male student engaged in microphone and headphone conversations with a female student after being shown a photo of her as either very attractive or somewhat unattractive. When the males thought they were talking to an attractive female, they were judged by student observers to be friendlier, more outgoing, and overall more sociable. The female students, who were actually equal in their physical attractiveness and did not know of the impression the males had been given, tended to respond in a manner that *fulfilled* the expectations of the caller. That is, those women who talked with men who believed them to be attractive were also judged by observers to be more poised, humorous, and sociable.

Although such studies can serve as a useful caution against an excessive emphasis on physical attractiveness, they also can depress anyone who happens to fall outside the rather narrow range of our culture's current standard of beauty. It is therefore comforting to know that research has also shown that physical attractiveness loses its importance once a relationship goes beyond its initial stages. According to Hendrick and Hendrick (1993), perceived attractiveness increases with repeated exposure—we generally find familiar people more attractive than strangers. Attractiveness is also related to shared values and interests. If you're a surfer, you'll find other surfers more attractive.

Proximity

Attraction largely depends on people being in the same place at the same time, making proximity or physical nearness another major factor in attraction. The nearer you live or work with someone, the more likely it is you will like that person. One of the classic studies of the proximity effect showed that simple distance between apartments seemed to determine who became friends with whom (Festinger et al., 1950). Similarly, a study of friendship in college dormitories found that the person next door was more often liked than the person two doors away, the person two doors away was liked more than someone three doors away, and so on (Priest and Sawyer, 1967). This closeness effect can also be found in the classroom—when students are assigned seating according to alphabetical order, their friendships reflect the alphabetical listing (Segal, 1974). Those of us who remember begging our grade school teachers to let us sit by attractive strangers probably had an early intuitive understanding of this principle of proximity.

Proximity: A key factor in attraction involving geographic, residential, and other forms of physical closeness.

How does proximity promote attraction? One of the major reasons seems to be *mere exposure.* Repeated exposure to all sorts of stimuli apparently increases liking (Bornstein, 1989; White and Shapiro, 1987). You've no doubt observed that you gradually come to accept and eventually like outrageous changes in fashions or hairstyles. Research has also shown that liking for presidents and actors or actresses is strongly correlated to the number of times they appear in the mass media (Harrison, 1977).

Similarity

Once we've had the repeated opportunity to get to know someone through simple physical proximity, and assuming we find him or her attractive, we then need something to hold the relationship together over time. This major cementing factor for long-term relationships, whether liking or loving, is similarity. We tend to prefer, and stay with, those people who are most like us—those who share our ethnic background, social

Similarity: A sharing of common interests, values, and beliefs—an important factor in long-term attraction.

Reprinted with special permission of King Features Syndicate.

Research shows that similarity is the single, best predictor for long-term relationships. Yet, many people ignore dissimilarities and hope that their partners will change over time.

class, interests, and attitudes (Caspi and Herbener, 1990; Hendrick and Hendrick, 1993). In other words, "Birds of a feather flock together."

What about the old saying, "Opposites attract"? Although it does seem that these two pieces of common folklore are contradictory, the term "opposites" here probably refers to personality traits rather than to social backgrounds or values. An attraction to a seemingly opposite person is more often based on the recognition that in one or two important areas that person offers us something we lack. If you are a talkative and outgoing person, for example, your friendship with a quiet and reserved individual may endure because each of you provides important resources for the other. Psychologists refer to this as need complementarity, as compared to the need compatibility represented by similarity.

Need Complementarity: The tendency to seek out and be attracted to people whose qualities we admire but personally lack.

Need Compatibility: A sharing of similar needs.

Theories of Attraction: Explaining Our Feelings Toward Others

At this point in our discussion you may be wondering how these different, and sometimes disparate, factors in attraction are related. Once scientists have established that several variables seem to be operating in a specific field, they generally attempt to integrate these findings into comprehensive theories—to go beyond the "whats" to the "whys" and "hows." Four of the most important theories of attraction that tie together the concepts we've been discussing are reinforcement theory, equity theory, social exchange theory, and gain–loss theory.

Reinforcement Theory

Reinforcement Theory of Attraction: The theory that attraction results from a positive emotional arousal. We like those who make us feel good and dislike those who make us feel bad.

According to the reinforcement theory of attraction we come to like or dislike others as a result of learning (Byrne, 1971). Through a system of rewards and punishments, attractiveness, proximity, and similarity work individually and in combination to create our preferences for certain people. That is, we tend to obtain the greatest rewards from those who are near us and who share similar backgrounds and values. One interesting combination effect is seen in the fact that repeated exposure through proximity makes some people become more physically attractive to us. It has also been found that we tend to judge attractive people as more similar to us than nonattractive persons (Beaman and Klentz, 1983).

Equity Theory

Equity Theory: The theory that people are highly motivated to seek a fair ratio between benefits and contributions for both members in a relationship.

If rewards were the only reason for liking, we would logically prefer those who did the most for us. But since we have also learned that it is important to be fair with others, we tend to feel most comfortable and satisfied with relationships that are *equitable*. According to equity theory, we like people and relationships in which the output is proportional to the input (Van Yperen and Buunk, 1990). Research shows that the partner who feels the relationship is out of balance will become distressed and try to restore equity. He or she attempts to rebalance the relationship by altering inputs and outcomes or by psychologically altering his or her perception of the gains and costs.

One of the interesting predictions of equity theory is that people become dissatisfied whether the imbalance is negative or positive, that is, whether they are over- or underbenefiting in comparison with their partner. There are some gender differences in this dissatisfaction. When men feel overbenefited they are more likely to express anger, whereas women report feelings of guilt. In the case of underbenefits, women report feeling depressed whereas men feel angry (Sprecher, 1986). Regardless of the male–female emotional responses to imbalances, relationships that are considered equitable are most likely to endure.

Social Exchange Theory

Social Exchange Theory: The theory that people prefer to maximize their benefits and minimize their costs in their relationships with others.

According to social exchange theory, friendships must not only be fair and equitable but must also show a net profit to both parties. Attraction is said to result from a type of "interpersonal marketplace" where the traders exchange certain "commodities." If the relationship becomes too costly it is terminated. Have you ever heard someone explain the end of a relationship because he or she "just wasn't getting anything out of it anymore" or because "the cost were outweighing the benefits"? Such comments show exchange theory at work.

Gain–Loss Theory

If the reinforcement, equity, and social exchange theories are correct, how do you explain a husband running off with his secretary? This is an interesting exception (and this is where the gain–loss theory comes in, as you will see). Although it *should* be more reinforcing, fairer, and less costly for the husband to stay in his marriage, it is also true that human beings tend to *habituate* to unchanging stimuli — to become less responsive with repeated exposure. After spending many years together, people sometimes tend to take each other for granted and become more responsive to the attention of new friends.

Experimental evidence of this effect in even short-term relationships is offered by a study in which college students were allowed to "accidentally" overhear another student discussing his or her "honest opinion" of the student subject. These conversations were actually staged by the experimenter and arranged so that the subject heard someone give a consistently positive personal evaluation, a consistently negative evaluation, a negative turning to positive evaluation, or a positive turning to negative evaluation (Aronson and Linder, 1965).

Which evaluation do you think you would prefer? Although it seems we ought to most like the person who made consistently positive comments, researchers found that the subjects responded most favorably to the person who initially expressed negative attitudes and then changed to positive ones. They responded least favorably to the person who first made positive comments and then became negative. According to the fourth principle of attraction, gain–loss theory, unexpected gains in liking or approval are more rewarding than constant liking; conversely, sudden losses are more punishing than constant dislike.

Ironically, in long-term relationships we operate in a *double-bind* or no-win situation. That is, since our attention and approval no longer offer a gain to our friends or partners, we have little rewarding power. But if we withdraw our affections we have an increased potential to hurt (lending some truth to the old saying, "you always hurt the one you love"). In contrast, a stranger's attention is powerfully reinforcing, since it represents an unexpected gain, and his or her withdrawal is less punishing, since little was expected.

Isn't there any way to counteract this double-bind?   Fortunately, there is. Although we *are* attracted to changing stimuli, we also have memories for the benefits of old relationships and apprehension about the costs of replacement. Simply being aware of the dangers of habituation and the limited nature of the "gain" from a stranger's flattery makes us less vulnerable to the lure of a stranger's attentions. Awareness of the gain–loss theory can also help us when it is our partner or friend who is losing interest in us. Just as detour signs and red traffic lights alert us to possible hazards, so too does the anxious feeling we experience when others show a reduced interest. Pay attention to the warning signs. At the same time, don't become overly anxious about your relationships. Long-term relationships (husband–wife, parent–child, friend–friend, and so on) go through cycles of more or less interest, loving, liking, and even disliking at times. Also, remember that most relationships do survive because of the overriding factors in reinforcement, equity, and social exchange theory.

Gain–Loss Theory: The theory that increased attraction will result when we receive unexpected approval from others and that attraction will decrease if initial liking is lost.

Loving: The Many Faces of Love

Is love an appropriate area for research? Not everyone thinks so. One of the strongest critics of love research has been William Proxmire. When Proxmire was in the United States Senate, he discovered the National Science Foundation had awarded a grant to psychologists interested in studying romantic love; he called it a big waste of taxpayer's money. He went on to say, "I believe that 200 million Americans want to leave some things in life a mystery, and right at the top of things we don't want to know about is why a man falls in love with a woman and vice versa" (Walster and Walster, 1978, p. 8).

Given the high percentage of marriages that end in divorce and the strong emphasis on love as a basis for marriage in our society, Proxmire's negative response is surprising. The reason for his response, as well as the relative lack of research in this area, may be because love is so difficult to define and measure. Some attempts to study love have concluded that we label certain feelings as love when we experience the appropriate combination of strong physiological arousal (from sexual attraction, excitement, fear, and so on) and an available and appropriate love object (see Chapter 12). For most of us, however, love seems more than just an "aroused label." Since love relationships often develop from friendships and initial feelings of liking for another, many people define love as an intense form of liking. Theorists have also looked at the similarities between love and attachment relationships in infancy (see Chapter 10).

To complete our discussion of interpersonal attraction, we will explore three perspectives on the mystery of love: liking versus loving, romantic love, and companionate love.

Liking versus Loving

Since love relationships often develop from friendships and initial feelings of liking for another, Zick Rubin (1970, 1992) developed two paper-and-pencil tests to explore the relationship between liking and loving.

 Try This Yourself

Just for fun, why not try a few items from Rubin's liking–loving scales? Fill in the blanks with the name of your current date or lover, or your spouse. Then, for each of the six items, write a number from 1 ("disagree completely") through 9 ("agree completely") rating your feelings about that person.

Love Scale	Rating
1. I feel that I can confide in _____ about virtually everything.	_____
2. I would do almost anything for _____ .	_____
3. If I could never be with _____ , I would feel miserable.	_____

Liking Scale	
1. I think that _____ is unusually well adjusted.	_____
2. I would highly recommend _____ for a responsible job.	_____
3. In my opinion, _____ is an exceptionally mature person.	_____

Source: Rubin, Z. (1970). "Measurement of romantic love," *Journal of Personality and Social Psychology, 16,* 265–273. Copyright © 1970 by the American Psychological Association. Reprinted by permission of the author.

How did you do? Do these items accurately reflect whether you are more "in like" or "in love" with your partner? (Rubin's original scales had 13 items each. In his study, for comparison, subjects were asked to take the test a second time, using someone different from their partner.) ■

In spite of the apparent simplicity of Rubin's scales, they have proven to be useful indicators of both liking and loving. For example, Rubin hypothesized that "strong love" couples would spend more time gazing into one another's eyes than would "weak love" couples. To test his hypothesis, while the couples were waiting for the experiment to begin, Rubin and his assistants secretly recorded the actual amount of eye contact between all couples. As predicted, the couples who scored highest on the love scale also spent more time looking into one another's eyes. In addition, Rubin found that while both partners tended to match each other on their love scores, women *liked* their dating partners significantly more than they were liked in return.

How does love differ from liking on Rubin's scales?   Rubin found that liking involves a favorable evaluation of another, as reflected in greater feelings of admiration and respect. He found love to be not only more intense than liking, but composed of three basic elements: *caring,* the desire to help the other person, particularly when help is needed; *attachment,* the need to be with the other person; and *intimacy,* a sense of empathy and trust that comes from close communication and self-disclosure from another.

Problems in Love Relationships

Each of the three elements Rubin identified as present in love relationships—caring, attachment, and intimacy—can cause problems. When there are differences in each partner's definition of these elements, or if one feels that he or she is more caring, more attached, or more desiring of intimacy than the other, the relationship is in jeopardy (Hendrick, Hendrick, and Adler, 1988). Caring, for example, is an area where women are often assumed to give more and do more than men, but research has often failed to support this assumption (Hoyenga and Hoyenga, 1993; Matlin, 1993). Perceived differences may be a reflection of how males and females are trained to express caring. For example, a woman might be socialized to assume primary responsibility for caring for her partner's feeling and for the well-being of the relationship itself. If she marries, she might be expected to assume the major responsibility for the primary care of the children. A man, on the other hand, is more likely to be socialized toward caring about the safety of his love partner. If he marries, he might assume primary responsibility for the family's economic well-being. Though these gender role expectations are less rigid today, they often remain part of our unconscious scripts and definitions of love. Males may welcome a sharing of financial responsibilities while also experiencing some anxiety over a partner's independence ("Does she still love me if she doesn't need me?"). Females, on the other hand, may value the shared independence of the newer relationships

Women tend to disclose more intimate information than men, which may explain some frustrations associated with male/female relationships.

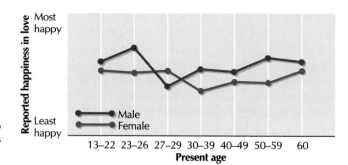

Figure 17.5 Happiness in love throughout the life cycle. Contrary to popular opinion, men generally report higher levels of love happiness than women.

but still have some unfulfilled scripts for protection ("Why doesn't he offer to go investigate the strange noise in the basement?").

Attachment and intimacy also present problems for relationships. Attachment can be so powerful that people often stay in, or go back to, destructive relationships because they desperately "need" the other person. In the search for intimacy, many people look to sex for fulfillment and are confused and disappointed when physical intimacy leaves them empty and sad. Each of us apparently has a deep need for the trust and shared communication in an intimate love relationship. The fact that women tend to have overall lower scores in love happiness (see Figure 17.5) is sometimes attributed to their unfulfilled needs for intimacy from men (Rubenstein, 1983).

Why do women seem to value intimacy more than men?   Women tend to disclose more intimate information than men and do so earlier in the relationship, but men may simply define intimacy differently than women (Hays, 1985; Rubin, 1992). Men's need for intimacy appears to be largely satisfied through physical presence, whereas women tend to need close talk. Fear of intimacy, however, seems to be shared by both males and females, and Hatfield and Rapson (1993) suggest that this fear may be justified. They argue that many people have suffered when disclosure of personal information has led to rejection by the other person. Their trust may also have been exploited and the information used against them. Such violations of trust make people fearful of again opening themselves to others.

Findings about intimacy have important implications for our individual lives. Not only should we honor the trust and disclosures of others, but we should also protect ourselves. Since research shows that liking seems to be maximized in situations where there is an equal and shared amount of disclosure (Cunningham and Strassberg, 1981), we can protect ourselves and others by giving relationships time to develop. By waiting for shared trust to evolve and matching our disclosures to those of our partner, we may avoid the pitfalls of unequal intimacy and also help minimize the male–female differences. The time factor should also be kept in mind if we want to use physical intimacy or sex as a way to feel closer and more bonded to another.

Romantic Love

Romantic Love: An intense feeling of attraction to another person that is characterized by high passion, obsessive thinking, and emotional fluctuation.

When you think of romantic love, do you think of falling in love, a magical experience that puts you on cloud nine? Romantic love, also called passionate love or limerence (Tennov, 1979), "is a wildly emotional state: tender and sexual feelings, elation and pain, anxiety and relief, altruism and jealousy coexist in a confusion of feelings" (Berscheid and Walster, 1978, p. 177). It is the stuff of which most novels, plays, films, and popular songs are made, and is probably the type of love Proxmire objected to studying, since it also relies on mystery and uncertainty. If romantic love were only used as a basis of entertainment, as was true in the Middle Ages, it might *not* be a worthy subject for study. But since both women and men overwhelmingly regard this form of love as very important to their relationships, it is important that we understand it.

To Americans and Western Europeans, romantic love often seems so natural and desirable that they are shocked to learn it is a relatively new concept in human history.

Romantic love first developed early in the Middle Ages among the nobility. It was an expression of the feudal ideal by which knights pledged themselves in service to noble-women whom they revered from a distance but were ineligible to marry (Gregersen, 1983). Such love was never meant to develop into intimate personal relationships. Although romantic love has now become the ideal basis for marriage in most Western European countries and the United States, arranged marriages are still the norm in most countries of the world. India, where arranged marriages have long been the rule, seems to be a country in transition. American movies depicting passionate love and love that defies parental wishes have become very popular in India. Also, young people in the middle class are increasingly moving toward marriages based on love, primarily as a result of Western influences.

Problems with Romantic Love

Although most Western Europeans and Americans find the idea of arranged marriages personally distasteful, let's look more closely at a few of the problems associated with romantic love. First of all, romantic love is typically shortlived. Even in the most devoted couples, the intense attraction and excitement generally begin to fade after 6 to 30 months (Walster and Walster, 1978). Although this research finding may disappoint you, as a critical thinker do you really think any emotion of this intensity could last forever? What would happen if other intense emotions, such as anger or joy, were eternal? And, given the time-consuming nature of romantic love, what would happen to other parts of our lives, such as school, career, and family?

A second major problem with romantic love that research has identified is that it is largely based on mystery and fantasy. People fall in love with others not necessarily as they are, but as they want them to be (Hatfield and Rapson, 1993). What happens to these illusions when we are faced with everyday interactions and long-term exposure? Our "beautiful princess" isn't supposed to snore, and our "knight-in-shining armor" doesn't look very "knightly" flossing his teeth. And, of course, no princess or knight would ever notice our shortcomings, let alone comment on them.

Is there any way to keep love alive?   If you mean romantic love, one of the best ways to fan the flames is through *interference,* or some form of frustration that keeps you from fulfilling your desire for the presence of your love. Researchers have found that interference (for example, the parents in Shakespeare's *Romeo and Juliet*) apparently increases the feelings of love (Driscoll et al., 1972). The married man who runs off with his secretary may be experiencing the "Romeo and Juliet effect." His marriage may act as an interference, intensifying his feelings of attraction toward the secretary.

Because romantic love depends on uncertainty and fantasy, it can also be kept alive by situations in which we never really get to know the other person. This may explain the old saying "Absence makes the heart grow fonder," and why old high school romances and unrequited loves have such a tug on our emotions. Since we never really get to test these relationships, we can always fantasize about what might have been.

One of the most constructive ways of keeping romantic love alive is to recognize its fragile nature and nurture it with carefully planned "surprises," flirting and flattery, and special dinners and celebrations. In the long run, however, romantic love's most important function might be to keep us attached long enough to move on to companionate love.

Companionate Love

Companionate love is based on admiration and respect (liking) combined with deep feelings of caring and commitment to the relationship. Studies of close friendships show that satisfaction grows with time as we come to recognize the value of companionship and of having an intimate confidante (Kobak and Hazen, 1991). Companionate love, unlike romantic love, which is very short lived, seems to grow stronger with time and often lasts a lifetime.

Companionate Love: A strong feeling of attraction to another person characterized by trust, caring, tolerance, and friendship. It is believed to provide an enduring basis for long-term relationships.

Childhood stories and modern movies often perpetuate romantic myths. One of the most common themes has Prince Charming rescuing the damsel in distress, followed by love, marriage, and living "happily ever after."

Companionate love is what we feel for our best friends and it can be the basis for a strong and lasting marriage. If you avoid the pitfalls of romantic love, you have a chance to move on to companionate love. This is no easy task. Since many of our expectations for love are based on romantic fantasies and unconscious programming from fairy tales and television shows in which everyone lives happily ever after, we are often ill-equipped to deal with the hassles and boredom that come with any long-term relationship.

Resolving Love's Problems

In the final analysis, many problem areas in love as well as human sexuality (see Chapter 11)—intimacy, romantic love, unwanted pregnancies, and sexual dysfunctions—may be the result of "faulty programming." After a lifetime of socialization into a world of "pinks and blues" in which parents, teachers, and general society expect different behaviors on the simple basis of gender and into marriages and relationships built on the shaky foundation of romantic love, is it any wonder that people have problems? Some researchers suggest that a greater acceptance of the "masculine" and "feminine" parts in each individual might eliminate some problems (men could be more self-disclosing and intimate, and women could be more sexually assertive and communicative about their desires). In addition, male–female and individual differences in friendships and love may be improved by developing a wider variety of friends and social resources. Romantic lovers need to be reminded that no single relationship can provide all their social needs. Some needs are better fulfilled through significant relationships with relatives, through casual acquaintances and coworkers, and through both same-sex and opposite-sex friendships. Good psychological adjustment seems to depend on having a wide network of overlapping social relations.

Unlike romantic love, which rarely lasts longer than 6 to 30 months, companionate love often lasts a lifetime.

Review Questions

1. _____ is one of the most important factors in the initial stages of liking and loving.

2. How does sociobiology explain male and female differences in what each sex finds attractive about the other?

3. When we interact with others in such a way that our expectations of them actually turn out to influence their behavior, we have created a _____ .

4. What are the three key factors in loving according to Rubin?

5. An intense feeling of attraction to another person that is characterized by high passion, obsessive thinking, and emotional fluctuation is known as _____ .

6. What are the two major problems associated with romantic love?

7. What is companionate love?

Answers to Review Questions can be found in Appendix C.

REVIEW OF MAJOR CONCEPTS

SOCIAL INFLUENCE

1. Through the process of social influence, we are taught important cultural values and behaviors that are essential to successful social living. Three of the most important forms of social influence are conformity, compliance, and obedience.

2. Conformity refers to changes in behavior in response to real or imagined pressure from others. Asch's classic study of conformity demonstrated that people will often conform to group opinion even when the group is clearly wrong. People conform in order to be approved and accepted by others (normative social influence), out of a need for more information (informational social influence), and in order to match the behavior of those they admire and feel similar to (their reference group). People also conform because it is often adaptive to do so.

3. Compliance refers to giving in to the requests of others. Requestors often attempt to ingratiate themselves to us, to make multiple requests (the foot-in-the-door and door-in-the-face techniques) that "oblige" us to give in and make us feel guilty.

4. Obedience involves giving in to a command from others. Milgram's experiment with obedience to authority demonstrated that a large number of people will follow orders even when another human being is physically threatened.

5. Culture clashes occur when norms are violated or when individuals fail to conform, comply, or obey different cul-

tural rules for behavior. To cope with culture clashes, Brislin recommends examining your thought processes, recognizing that culture clashes are emotionally stressful, and adjusting your behavior to match the other person's culture.

GROUP PROCESSES

6. Groups differ from mere collections of people if members share a mutually recognized relationship with one another. People join groups for a variety of reasons, one of which is the need to affiliate, to simply be with others.

7. Schachter's classic study of affiliation demonstrated that one of the strongest factors in our desire to be with others comes from our need for social comparison. People need to compare their abilities and reactions to those of others, particularly during times of stress and fear.

8. Groups affect us through the roles we play. The importance of these roles in determining and controlling behavior was dramatically demonstrated in Philip Zimbardo's Stanford Prison Study. College students who were assigned to play the role of either a prisoner or guard in a simulated prison became so completely and dangerously immersed in acting out their roles that the experiment was prematurely ended.

9. Groups also affect us because they increase the chances for deindividuation among members. Deindividuation refers to the temporary suspension of self-awareness and personal restraints on behavior. The fact that people are more willing to shock others when they are in costumes, and will "bait" or encourage a potential suicide victim under the cover of darkness and distance from the victim, demonstrates the strong role of anonymity in deindividuation.

10. Groups are often trusted with decisions because we believe their response will be more conservative and "middle of the road" than the potentially extreme decisions of individuals. Research shows, however, that groups are actually more extreme in their decisions. Sharing ideas with "like-minded" others often reinforces the group's preexisting and dominant tendencies.

11. Groupthink is a dangerous type of thinking that occurs when the group's desire for agreement overrules its tendency to critically evaluate information. President Kennedy's Bay of Pigs decision is often given as evidence of groupthink. Couples who are planning to marry also demonstrate many symptoms of groupthink.

ATTRIBUTION

12. In attempting to find answers or reasons for others' behavior (making attributions), we often seek to determine whether their actions are internally caused (from their own traits and motives) or externally caused (from the environment or situation). To answer this question, we rely on three criteria—consistency, consensus, and distinctiveness.

13. Attribution is subject to several forms of error and bias. The most basic of these is the fundamental attribution error, our tendency to overestimate internal, personality influences and underestimate external, situational influences when judging the behavior of others. When we attempt to find reasons for our own behavior, we tend to take credit for positive outcomes and attribute negative outcomes to external causes (the self-serving bias).

SOCIAL COGNITION

14. When we make social judgments about others, we must process a vast quantity of information. To help us, we rely on heuristics—mental shortcuts or rules based on experience. The availability heuristic (which bases predictions on how quickly examples come to mind) and the representative heuristic (which bases predictions on how well a new situation matches our memory of similar situations) are two of the most common mental shortcuts.

15. The use of heuristics also sometimes leads to biases in social cognition. Overestimating the improbable, the priming effect, the base-rate fallacy, and the false-consensus bias are four causes of faulty thinking and poor decision making.

INTERPERSONAL ATTRACTION

16. Physical attractiveness is very important to initial attraction. Physically attractive people are often perceived as being more intelligent, sociable, and interesting than less attractive people.

17. Standards for physical attractiveness vary across cultures and historically. Physical attractiveness is generally more important for women than men.

18. Physical proximity increases one's attractiveness. The nearer you live or work with someone, the more likely it is you will like that person. Although people commonly believe that "opposites attract," research shows that similarity is a much more important factor in attraction.

19. The four major theories of liking are: reinforcement theory, which sees attraction resulting from learning through rewards and punishments; equity theory, which says people prefer a balanced relationship, with outputs matching inputs; social exchange theory, which holds that each partner must show a "net profit" for a relationship to succeed; and the gain–loss theory, which says unexpected increases in approval from others are particularly rewarding and losses of approval are particularly punishing.

20. Rubin's research on liking and loving found that love can be defined in terms of caring, attachment, and intimacy. Each of these three dimensions may present problems if there are real or perceived imbalances.

21. Romantic love is highly valued in our society, but because it is based on mystery and fantasy it is hard to sustain in long-term relationships. Companionate love relies on mutual trust, respect, and friendship and seems to grow stronger with time.

SUGGESTED READINGS

ARONSON, E. (1992). *The social animal* (6th ed.). New York: Freeman. An award-winning book that offers a witty and enjoyable overview of social psychology.

CIALDINI, R. B. (1993). *Influence: Science and practice* (3rd ed.). New York: HarperCollins. A small paperback that provides an engaging overview of the topic of social influence.

FISKE, S. T., & TAYLOR, S. E. (1991). *Social cognition* (2nd ed.). New York: McGraw-Hill. A basic introduction to social cognition that is well written and should be enjoyed by those who desire more information on this topic.

HATFIELD, E., & RAPSON, R. L. (1993). *Love, sex, and intimacy: Their psychology, biology, and history.* New York: HarperCollins. An up-to-date review of the major research on love, sex, and intimacy written in an engaging, readable style.

JANIS, I. L. (1989). *Crucial decisions: Leadership in policymaking and crisis management.* New York: Free Press. A leading researcher on *groupthink* discusses how decisions are made and the sometimes-disastrous role of group influences.

JONES, E. E. (1991). *Interpersonal perception.* New York: Freeman. A leading researcher in social psychology describes how we perceive and explain our own and other's behavior.

SOLOMON, R.C. (1989). *About love: Reinventing romance for our times.* New York: Touchstone. Philosopher Robert Solomon looks at love and loving in a modern version of Erich Fromm's *The Art of Loving.*

Social Interactions

OUTLINE

For more than a year, television stations across America repeatedly broadcast a home video showing Los Angeles police officers beating an African-American man. Was this standard procedure for subduing a suspect? Or was this prejudice and police brutality? During the subsequent trial of the police officers, racial tension ran high, and when the jury acquitted the officers on the afternoon of April 29, 1992, violence erupted. Buildings were set on fire, motorists were pulled from their cars and beaten, journalists were attacked, and thousands of demonstrators clashed with police (Hammer, 1992).

L.A.'s mayor, the police chief, and community leaders pleaded with residents to remain calm as the nation's second-largest city suffered the worst violence since the Watts Riots in 1965. The staggering toll on the city finally came to 54 people dead, 2,383 injured, over 17,000 riot-related arrests, and losses exceeding $1 billion (Salholz, Wright, and Crandall, 1992). The violence ended only after more than 10,000 National Guard troops arrived in tanks and full battle attire. Perhaps the most poignant moment in this whole tragedy was a news conference in which the beating victim, Rodney King, tearfully begged, "Can we get along? . . . It's not right. . . . It's just not right because these people will never go home to their families again" (Meyer, 1992).

The 1965 and 1992 riots in Los Angeles are not unique. A short look at the history of humankind, with its revolutions, lynchings, wars, murders, rapes, terrorism, and so on, shows that aggression has always been a part of human existence. But history also shows that people will help their fellow human beings even when this places them at great personal risk. How do we explain these differences? Are there certain personality traits that predispose some people toward aggression and others toward helping? Or are situational factors and social forces the primary determinants of how people will behave? Such questions are the focus of social psychologists who study attitudes, prejudice and discrimination, aggression, and altruism, the topics we will study in this chapter.

As you read Chapter 18, keep the following **Survey** questions in mind and answer them in your own words:

- How are attitudes formed and changed?
- What causes prejudice and discrimination?
- Is aggression primarily biological or environmental?
- What causes people to help (or not help) others?

ATTITUDES

* *How are attitudes formed and changed?*

Attitude: A learned predisposition to respond cognitively, affectively, and behaviorally to a particular object.

An attitude is a *learned* predisposition to respond cognitively, affectively, and behaviorally to a particular object in a particular way (Rajecki, 1990). The object can be anything from pizza to people, from diseases to drugs, and abortion to psychology.

 Try This Yourself

Stop for a moment and write your reactions to the following words—just jot down whatever comes to mind:

Rodney King	Abortion	Bill Clinton	Psychology
Marijuana	AIDS	Pizza	Jackie Joyner Kersey

What are your responses? How do you feel about the Rodney King case? Are you concerned about the spread of AIDS? What do you think about the job Bill Clinton is doing as president of the United States? Do you plan to take another psychology class after this introductory course? The thoughts and feelings you wrote down, and the actions they would lead to, are all part of your attitudes.

You are not born with your attitudes—they are learned. From earliest childhood you began forming your attitudes through direct experience (eating pizza) and through indirect observation (listening to your parents discuss politics). The principles we discussed in Chapter 6, on learning, all play a role in the formation of attitudes. Through social learning, you acquired some attitudes by watching and imitating your parents, teachers, and friends. Your attitudes were also developed through operant conditioning. Adults probably rewarded you for expressing the "correct" views—the ones held by your parents, teachers, and friends. And, through classical conditioning you learned to make associations between certain people or objects—Walter Cronkite and the news, popcorn and movies.

Although attitudes begin in early childhood, they are not permanent. Politicians spend millions of dollars on campaigns because they know attitudes can be shaped and manipulated throughout the entire life span. In this section, we begin with a brief discussion of the general components of attitudes, and then we explore how we sometimes change our attitudes in response to cognitive dissonance. Finally, we examine techniques for persuading others to change their attitudes.

Components of Attitudes: Cognitive, Affective, and Behavioral

Most social psychologists agree that an attitude has three components (see Figure 18.1): cognitive, affective, and behavioral. The *cognitive* component consists of thoughts and beliefs, such as "Rodney King should not have resisted the police officers" or "The police officers should have been convicted." The *affective,* or emotional, component involves feelings, such as frustration with the legal system or anger toward the rioters. The *behavioral* component consists of *predispositions* to act in certain ways toward an attitude object. For example, someone who held a positive attitude toward the police officers' behavior would believe the videotape was edited and might write to TV stations criticizing the media for manipulating public feeling.

Attitudes and Behavior

Have you ever been uncomfortable because of a racist or sexist remark made by a friend, yet failed to speak up? If so, you can see that the three components of behavior do not

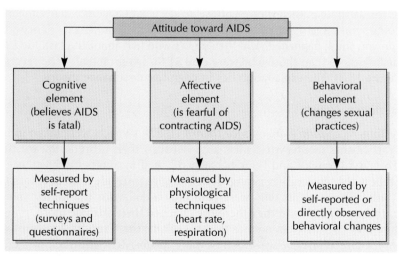

Figure 18.1 The three components of attitudes. Every attitude has three separate components—cognitive, affective, behavioral. Each component is measured in a different way.

always match. Sometimes we have thoughts and feelings on which we do not act. One of the earliest research demonstrations of this discrepancy came from a psychologist named Richard LaPiere (1934), who traveled across the United States with a Chinese couple, eating in restaurants and staying overnight in hotels. Although prejudice against Asians was fairly common in the United States during the early 1930s, only one of the many restaurants refused to serve them. About six months after his trip, LaPiere wrote to these same restaurants and asked whether the owners would provide restaurant and hotel services to Asian people. Over 90 percent said they would *not* seat Chinese patrons.

What if the person who answered the letter wasn't the same person who waited on LaPiere and the Chinese couple? Excellent question. Although this *is* a serious problem with this early study, numerous follow-up studies confirmed the original point, that attitudes have less influence on behavior than we might expect (Greenwald, 1990; McGuire, 1989; Wicker, 1969). Such a discrepancy between attitudes and behavior could reflect problems in measurement of the true, underlying attitude. But it could also mean that people sometimes actively suppress or distort their true attitudes, perhaps to make a good impression or to serve other needs.

Remember that the behavioral component of an attitude consists only of tendencies, or *predispositions* toward certain actions. Whether you activate your behavioral tendencies or not often depends on situational constraints. Just as you may have hesitated to speak up when someone told a racist or sexist joke, the servers who waited on LaPiere and his companions may have feared making a scene in front of other customers. When the behavioral constraints are changed, behaviors frequently change. Today, in the 1990s, restaurant owners in America would no doubt reply that they would seat customers from any ethnic or religious group. And, in ironic contrast to LaPiere's study, some servers might find subtle ways of refusing actual service.

Cognitive Dissonance: How We Sometimes Change Our Own Attitude

Now picture yourself in another situation. You, the same person who objects to racist and sexist remarks, must give a speech in favor of the Ku Klux Klan. How do you think this would affect your attitudes? Do you think you would feel more or less favorable toward this group afterwards?

This is the type of question that led to a classic experiment conducted by Leon Festinger and J. Merrill Carlsmith (1959). Subjects were given excruciatingly boring tasks to do — turning pegs and wooden knobs over and over again. After about an hour of such tedium, the subject was told the experiment was over. The subject was then asked to do the experimenter a favor and tell the incoming subject that the task was interesting. Sometimes the subject (who no longer thought he was a subject) was offered a dollar for helping and sometimes $20. After the subject lied to the incoming subject and was paid, he was led to another room and asked about his true feelings toward the experiment tasks. The real purpose of the experiment was to see what happens when someone is coaxed into doing something (lying) that is inconsistent with his or her experience and attitude. What do you think happened? Did the subject who lied about the task for $20 report liking the task more than those who were paid $1 for lying? Actually, the reverse was true (see Figure 18.2). The explanation lies in cognitive dissonance theory.

Cognitive Dissonance Theory

Cognitive Dissonance Theory: Festinger's theory that tension results whenever people discover inconsistencies between their attitudes, or between their attitudes and their behaviors. This tension drives people to make attitudinal changes that will restore harmony or consistency.

According to Festinger's *cognitive dissonance theory* (1957), subjects were taken in by their own lie. Participants faced with a mismatch between their attitude toward the experiment ("That was boring") and their behavior ("I lied to another subject") felt discomfort. To relieve the tension they changed their original attitude from boredom to "I enjoyed the task." The students who were paid only a dollar for the lie felt more discomfort than those paid $20, and they therefore changed their attitude more.

Let's explore how cognitive dissonance theory explains these results. In cognitive dissonance theory, a discrepancy between two or more inconsistent attitudes, or a discrepancy between attitudes and behaviors, leads to psychological discomfort. People

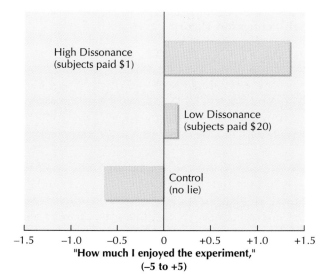

Figure 18.2 Cognitive dissonance theory. In Festinger and Carlsmith's study, subjects who were paid $1 to lie experienced the greatest amount of dissonance. To resolve this dissonance, they changed their attitude about the research and rated it as fairly enjoyable. The group paid $20 had less dissonance and less reason to change their attitude. The control group (which had no reason to change their true attitudes) rated the experiment not enjoyable.

have a strong need to feel that their attitudes are in sync with one another and their attitudes and behavior are in harmony or *consistent*. When this harmony is disrupted, people feel distress and are motivated to change *something* to restore the balance. In other words, the need for cognitive consistency leads to tension or anxiety (cognitive dissonance) and it is this tension that motivates us to change our initial attitudes to match our subsequent behavior.

Festinger and his colleagues (1956) noticed a classic example of cognitive dissonance when they studied a group that had prophesied the end of the world. The leader, Mrs. Keech, predicted that the world would be destroyed on December 21, but that those who followed her to a prearranged spot would be rescued by a spaceship from the planet Clarion. When December 21 came and went and the expectations were not met, dissonance was obviously high since many people had left college, jobs, and spouses to join the group. Although you might think these people would quietly slink away in embarrassment, they apparently reduced their dissonance by loudly proclaiming that their prayers had actually saved the world—at least for the time being. Whether we change our original attitudes ("The world is ending on December 21") or whether we maintain or adjust our current attitudes ("Our prayers saved the world") depends on which change is the least costly. Attitude formation and change seem to follow the *path of least resistance*. Since the world obviously didn't end, and the group needed to justify their losses, they chose the easiest route—that of believing they saved the world.

How does this differ from rationalization?   *Rationalization,* one of the defense mechanisms discussed in Chapter 14, is often confused with cognitive dissonance, but there are at least two major differences. First, the function of rationalization is to save face or protect the ego from *unconscious* threats to self-esteem, whereas the function of cognitive dissonance is to reduce *conscious* inconsistencies. Second, rationalization doesn't necessarily bring a change in the underlying attitudes, whereas cognitive dissonance does.

Self-Perception Theory

Festinger's cognitive dissonance theory has generated more than 1000 research articles with mixed but largely favorable results (Aronson, 1992; Cooper and Scher, 1993). There are, however, also competing theories. Daryl Bem (1972), for example, believes that self-perception, rather than dissonance, explains why people get taken in by their own lies. According to Bem's self-perception theory, people often *infer* their attitudes from watching their own behavior. Thus, self-perception theory says that in Festinger and Carlsmith's experiment, it wasn't tension or dissonance being created that led to the change in attitude, but subjects simply looking at their behavior and then developing

Self-Perception Theory: Bem's theory that people form attitudes by observing their own behavior.

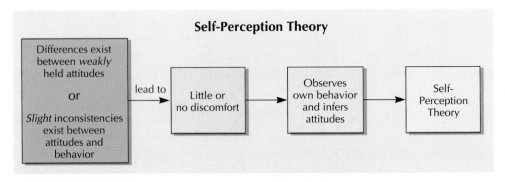

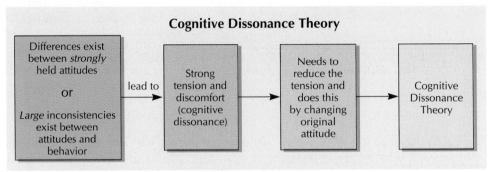

Figure 18.3 Comparing self-perception theory and cognitive dissonance theory. The top row of boxes shows that when differences exist between weakly held attitudes or when there are slight inconsistencies between attitudes and behavior, self-perception theory offers the best explanation for attitude change. On the other hand, when differences exist between strongly held attitudes or when there are large inconsistencies between attitudes and behavior, cognitive dissonance is a better explanation, as shown in the bottom row of boxes.

their attitude. Subjects paid $20 thought to themselves, "I lied for $20 because it was worth it," whereas subjects paid $1 thought "A dollar isn't enough money to make me lie, so I must have enjoyed the task."

Which theory is correct? Research continues on this question. But a possible resolution to the controversy is that cognitive dissonance explains attitude changes related to firmly established, *strong* attitudes and large inconsistencies between attitudes and behavior, whereas self-perception theory works primarily with *weakly* held attitudes and *slight* inconsistencies between attitudes and behaviors (Chaiken and Baldwin, 1981; Tesser and Shaffer, 1990). For example, a woman strongly opposed to divorce who later gets a divorce would probably experience a great deal of tension and dissonance and be motivated to change her opinion about divorce. On the other hand, a woman who is slightly against divorce and later gets divorced might think, "I got a divorce, therefore I must believe in it." Self-perception theory and cognitive dissonance theory are compared in Figure 18.3.

Whichever theory is correct, the phenomena they attempt to explain are real. One of our students volunteered a personal insight after studying these theories. This young man said he now realized why women seemed to fall more in love after they had sex with someone: Either they had to justify their behavior to match their belief that sex is meaningful only in the context of a love relationship (cognitive dissonance theory), or they observed their intimate behavior and concluded that they must be in love (self-perception theory). What do you think? Could cognitive dissonance or self-perception mislead someone into believing they were in love as a way to justify their sexual behaviors?

Persuasion: Direct Attempts at Attitude Change

Although the need to avoid dissonance can produce adjustments or total reversals in attitudes, there *are* more direct methods. What technique would you recommend in the

Table 18.1   Factors in Persuasion

Source Characteristics:	Message Characteristics:	Audience Characteristics:
Credibility (trust, expertise, fast-talking)	Cognitive appeals (logic, reason)	Personality traits (self-esteem)
Likability	Emotional appeals (fear)	Age and vulnerability (young, lonely, depressed, etc.)
Similarity		Involvement (degree of participation)
Physical attractiveness		Reactance (perceived freedom to choose)
"Who Says?"	"What?"	"To Whom?"

Voters often respond favorably to this style of political campaigning. Can you explain why?

following situations? Joe wants to talk his parents into helping him finance an expensive car while he's still in college; Mary wants to switch colleges next year and hopes to talk her roommate into going with her; and Juan wants to convince his five-year-old that candy is not good for him. Each person wants to change an attitude of someone else, but should each use the same techniques? And what technique works best?

If you are like most people, your initial suggestions for Joe, Mary, and Juan would be based on communication techniques—"Tell them . . ." "Have someone else tell them . . ." or "Make sure they're listening when you . . ." Such communication techniques, when applied in a direct attempt to influence the attitude of another, are known as methods of persuasion. The effectiveness of persuasion depends on the *source* of the communication, the *message* itself, and on the *audience*—in other words, on *who says what to whom* (see Table 18.1).

Persuasion: Direct attempts to influence the attitude of another through communication techniques.

Characteristics of the Source

If the object is to change the attitudes of others on relatively trivial matters, the source should be someone they like, are similar to, and find physically attractive (Chaiken and Eagly, 1983; Wilder, 1990). Beautiful models, for example, are paid a great deal merely to smile and stand next to a product.

When the attitude is not trivial but part of someone's deeply held values and convictions, the credibility of the source becomes the most important factor in persuasion. The two major components of credibility are trustworthiness and expertise. We seem to trust sources more when they have no apparent association with the product and have little to gain (Wood and Eagly, 1981). And we judge expertise by personal qualifications and associations with prestigious organizations. The importance of expertise has been documented in numerous studies (such as Hennigan et al., 1982).

Credibility: Degree of trustworthiness or expertise that is associated with a particular source of persuasion.

If the communicator is knowledgeable and trustworthy, the audience is obviously more likely to be convinced. But it is also interesting to note that the *illusion* of honesty can be created simply by looking a person in the eye and by speaking confidently and fast.

Don't we usually distrust "fast talkers"?   Although we are often warned about the dangers of such people, it actually appears that an audience's perceptions of knowledge and trust, and thus their degree of persuasion, is positively influenced by communicators who speak at a relatively rapid rate (Apple, Streeter, and Krauss, 1979; Smith and Shaffer, 1991). John F. Kennedy has often been considered one of the most powerful communicators in modern times, which may in part be due to the fact that he often approached a speaking rate of over 300 words per minute (the average rate is somewhere around 140–150 words per minute). Since most people can listen and comprehend at a much faster rate than they can talk, a faster pace may attract more interest and allow less time for the audience's thoughts to drift away or build counterarguments.

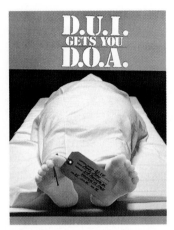

Fear induction is one of the most effective persuasion techniques, and it is commonly used in advertisements and public service announcements.

Characteristics of the Message

Of course, there is more to persuasion than likeable, credible, and fast-talking sources. The message itself—the content and the way it is presented—is of key importance. Some researchers have found that messages that appeal to cognitive processes, such as logic and reason, are the most persuasive (Verplanken, 1991; Wood, 1982). Others have found that appeals to emotion are more powerful (Edwards, 1990; Mullis and Lippa, 1990). Madison Avenue advertisers apparently agree with the latter researchers, judging by the preponderance of emotional appeals in advertising.

One common emotional appeal is *fear induction:* Politicians warn us of higher taxes and more crime if we don't vote for them; doctors show us horrible photos of diseased lungs to make us stop smoking; and advertisers warn us of the social rejection we face if we don't use their mouthwash, dandruff shampoo, or acne medication. For fear tactics to work (1) the appeal must engender a lot of fear, (2) the audience must believe the message, and (3) specific instructions for avoiding the danger must be presented (Bandura et al., 1982; Mullis and Lippa, 1990; Zimbardo and Leippe, 1991).

Characteristics of the Audience

Are some people easier to persuade than others? In this section we will look at four major audience factors that have been studied in relation to persuasion: personality traits, vulnerability, involvement, and reactance (resistance to persuasion).

1. *Personality traits.* As you discovered in Chapter 17, the relationship between personality traits and social influence (conformity, compliance, and obedience) is complex. The same is true for persuasion. Consider as an example self-esteem. Research has shown mixed findings between low, moderate, and high feelings of self-esteem and vulnerability to persuasion. People with low self-esteem may be less confident of their opinions, but they also tend to be less attentive to persuasive arguments and are therefore harder to persuade. On the other hand, people with high self-esteem tend to be more confident of their opinions and are therefore harder to persuade. Interestingly, people with moderate self-esteem tend to be the easiest to influence. Because they pay attention to the message and they are somewhat unsure of their opinions, they tend to change their attitudes the most (Baumeister and Covington, 1985; Rhodes and Wood, 1992; Zellner, 1970).

2. *Vulnerability.* Young children and adolescents are particularly vulnerable to certain appeals. Parents and health officials are thus understandably concerned about cigarette advertisements that apparently target these groups. Despite market studies that consistently show most adult smokers developed their habits before age 18, cigarette manufacturers deny having any interest in this "startup" group. Recent research by the American Medical Association (AMA) suggests otherwise.

    Suspecting that young people are the true targets of many cigarette ads, the AMA designed three studies to explore the effects of a hip-looking cartoon character, Joe Camel, and the increased use of Camel cigarettes. These studies found that teenagers were more likely than adults to recognize Joe, to know what brand he represents, and to find his ads appealing. It was also found that 91 percent of six-year-olds could match Joe with a Camel cigarette (Bower, 1991; Cowley, 1991). Although manufacturers such as R. J. Reynolds insist they advertise only to promote brand loyalty, Camel sales to the under-18 market have risen from $6 million a year prior to Joe's arrival in 1988 to $476 million in 1991 (Cowley, 1991).

    Young people are not the only age group vulnerable to persuasion. Adults are particularly susceptible if they are lonely, depressed, inexperienced, poorly educated, or physically isolated. Studies of cult recruitment techniques, for example, have found that many groups target middle-class youths

Critics have suggested that Joe Camel, a hip-looking cartoon character used to advertise Camel cigarettes, may encourage young children to smoke.

Calvin and Hobbes

by Bill Watterson

Figure 18.4 Psychological reactance. Can you see how the father in this cartoon is using the principle of psychological reactance to get Calvin to eat his vegetables?

who have just left home for the first time and are without good support systems (Galanter, 1989, 1990; Kapitza, 1991). Groups such as the "Moonies" and "Hare Krishnas" typically offer simplistic answers to difficult questions and immediate love and acceptance.

3. *Involvement.* Audience involvement or degree of participation is an important element of persuasion. The more actively an individual becomes involved in an idea or product, the more likely he or she is to be persuaded. If you can get someone to sign a petition, write a letter to a candidate, or solicit door-to-door, they are likely to become committed to your cause or product. (Do you recognize how this increased commitment might result from cognitive dissonance? In their need to justify their actions and work, people convince themselves that they really approve of the cause or like the product.)

4. *Reactance.* Regardless of individual differences in personality, vulnerability, and involvement, most recipients of persuasive messages share a common need to believe they are free to choose and free to disagree. As the parents of Romeo and Juliet discovered, when people feel pressured, they often increase their resistance to persuasion—a phenomenon known as reactance (Brehm, 1989). Studies of reactance show that people not only increase their resistance to persuasion, they may also rebel and do just the opposite. In one experiment, children were allowed to choose any brand of candy on display, except Brand X (Hammock and Brehm, 1966). Can you guess what the children did? Those who were told *not* to choose Brand X chose it significantly more often than those who were given a free choice. Parents of two-year-olds are acutely aware of this phenomenon and often employ "reverse psychology" to counteract its effect (see Figure 18.4).

Reactance: Increased resistance to persuasion that is experienced when the recipient feels that his or her freedom to choose is threatened.

Review Questions

1. What is an "attitude"?
2. What are the three components of all attitudes?
3. According to _____ theory, people are motivated to change their attitudes due to tension created by a mismatch between two or more competing attitudes or between their attitudes and behavior.
4. The belief that people sometimes form their attitudes by observing their own behavior is known as _____ theory.
5. The effectiveness of persuasion techniques depends on the _____ of the communication, the _____ itself, and on _____ characteristics.

6. If people feel they are not free to choose or disagree with the persuader, they often increase their resistance to persuasion, a phenomenon known as _____ .

Answers to Review Questions can be found in Appendix C.

PREJUDICE AND DISCRIMINATION

• *What causes prejudice and discrimination?*

Prejudice: A generally negative attitude directed toward others because of their membership in a specific group. Like all attitudes, prejudice involves three components: cognitions (or thoughts), affect (or feelings), and behavioral tendencies.

Stereotype: (1) A set of beliefs about the characteristics of people in a group that is generalized to all group members, or (2) the cognitive component of prejudice.

Discrimination: Negative behaviors directed at members of a group.

Having explored the factors in attitude formation and attitude change, we now turn our attention to one of the most damaging of all attitudes—prejudice. Prejudice is a generally negative attitude directed toward specific people solely because of their membership in an identified group. *Positive* forms of prejudice do exist, such as "all women love babies" or "African-Americans are natural athletes." And like negative forms, positive forms of prejudice also harm the victims. For example, women might believe there must be something wrong with them if they don't like being around babies, or African-Americans might see athletics as their only way to achieve success. Research and definitions of prejudice, however, almost always focus on the negative forms.

Prejudice is *prejudgment* of others based on limited knowledge and limited contact (Brislin, 1993). It biases us against others and limits our ability to accurately process information. The term "prejudice" is commonly used to refer to negative stereotypes about group members. But prejudice, like all attitudes, is actually composed of three separate elements: (1) the *cognitive component* (or stereotype), consisting of negative thoughts and beliefs, (2) the *affective component*, consisting of feelings and emotions associated with objects of prejudice, and (3) the *behavioral component*, consisting of predispositions to act in certain ways toward members of the group.

Prejudice versus Discrimination

Although the terms *prejudice* and *discrimination* are often used interchangeably, there is an important difference between them. Prejudice is an attitude, whereas discrimination refers to negative behavior directed at members of a group. Discrimination is usually based on prejudice, but not always (see Figure 18.5). As LaPiere's (1934) study of discrimination in restaurant seating showed, people do not always act on their prejudices. As with all attitudes, the behavioral component of prejudice only indicates predispositions or tendencies toward action. Prejudiced people may or may not act upon their attitudes and discriminate against others.

Despite repeated attempts to reduce prejudice, groups such as the White Supremacists and the Ku Klux Klan still exist.

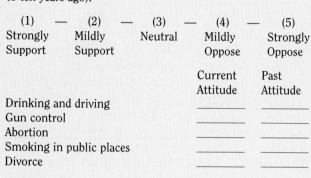

Critical Thinking

PSYCHOLOGY IN ACTION

DEVELOPING SELF-UNDERSTANDING
Exploring the Processes of Attitude Formation

Critical thinking requires self-understanding and an awareness that our most important attitudes are developed from specific learning experiences and the influence of important people in our lives. Critical thinkers know what their attitudes are and know how and why they acquired them. Understanding oneself is the first step toward self-control and self-improvement.

To help you explore your attitudes, we offer the following exercise.

In the space next to each issue, place a number (1 to 5) that indicates your CURRENT attitude and your PAST attitude (five to ten years ago).

(1)	(2)	(3)	(4)	(5)
Strongly	Mildly	Neutral	Mildly	Strongly
Support	Support		Oppose	Oppose

	Current Attitude	Past Attitude
Drinking and driving	_____	_____
Gun control	_____	_____
Abortion	_____	_____
Smoking in public places	_____	_____
Divorce	_____	_____

1. Circle the three issues you currently feel most strongly about. Briefly state your attitudes toward each of these issues. How did your attitudes develop (classical conditioning, operant conditioning, social learning, self-perception theory, cognitive dissonance, etc.)? What important experiences or significant individuals influenced these attitudes? Can you identify the three components of each of your three attitudes (cognitive, affective, and behavioral)?

2. Now compare your CURRENT and PAST attitudes. On which issues were your attitudes most subject to change? Why? On which issues were you most resistant to change? How do you explain this?

3. How might you use the persuasion principles discussed in this chapter to change someone's attitude on one of these issues? (Consider the characteristics of the communicator, the message, and the audience.) Can you apply the same principles to changing your own attitude?

4. Cognitive dissonance theory asserts that "changing behavior changes attitudes." Using this theory, how would you design a program to change an undesirable attitude in yourself or others?

Prejudice and discrimination have been found in all groups and in all eras of recorded history, and they are remarkably resistant to change (Adler, 1991; Brislin, 1993; Miller and Brewer, 1984). Part of the reason people cling to prejudices and discriminate against others is that certain functions are served. In this section we will discuss the sources and functions of prejudice, and the costs of being a victim. Then we will look at strategies for reducing prejudice. Before we begin, however, let's examine a special issue—prejudice and discrimination against the physically disabled.

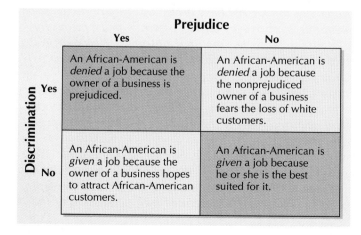

		Prejudice	
		Yes	**No**
Discrimination	**Yes**	An African-American is *denied* a job because the owner of a business is prejudiced.	An African-American is *denied* a job because the nonprejudiced owner of a business fears the loss of white customers.
	No	An African-American is *given* a job because the owner of a business hopes to attract African-American customers.	An African-American is *given* a job because he or she is the best suited for it.

Figure 18.5 Prejudice and discrimination. Note how prejudice can exist without discrimination and vice versa. The only condition under which neither prejudice nor discrimination exists is when someone is given a job simply because he or she is the best suited for it.

For Better or For Worse®   **by Lynn Johnston**

*Why would teasing someone demonstrate liking? Is the **lack** of teasing a well-intentioned, but damaging, form of prejudice against the physically disabled?*

Gender and Cultural Diversity

PREJUDICE AND DISCRIMINATION AGAINST THE PHYSICALLY DISABLED

Do you remember the 1992 controversy surrounding Jerry Lewis's fund raising for muscular dystrophy? While some people praised him for his humanitarian efforts, others objected that he increased prejudice toward the physically disabled. We wouldn't show African-Americans living in horrible poverty to raise money for "their cause," so why parade "victims" in wheelchairs across the stage, while begging for donations? Lewis's fund-raising techniques were criticized for being demeaning and dehumanizing to the physically disabled and for perpetuating common stereotypes of the "helpless cripple always needing money and pity from others." As you discovered in Chapter 15, once someone is labeled "schizophrenic," we no longer see the person as an individual. Similarly, once people see a person in a wheelchair, they often forget that "everyone is a person first, and some are disabled second" (Denney and Quadagno, 1992, p. 467).

Another problem with Jerry Lewis's fund-raising activities, according to critics, is the constant referral to both children and adults as "Jerry's kids." When people have illnesses or disabilities that make them dependent on others for care, they are often seen as childlike and generally incapable and uninterested in normal, adult activities (Asch and Ruousso, 1985). When these "children" expect to be treated as adults, the world is often uncomfortable and surprised. The following letter was written by Dr. Kathleen Navarre, a professor of psychology in Michigan who had polio as a child. Her words remind us that we all have the same basic needs and wants, rights, opportunities, and responsibilities.

Professor Kathleen Navarre lecturing to her introductory psychology course.

We were the darlings of the 50s. Like a basket of newborn kittens, there is nothing more appealing than a dewy-eyed poster child with crutches, braces, and a brave and ready smile. Now in the 90s, the kittens have grown up. We are no longer polio victims but rather polio survivors. We are strong, assertive, and a medically expensive challenge. The kitten's soft mew has matured into an assertive roar. We now demand quality service from insurance companies, state and federal government agencies, and from the physicians who serve us.

Quality care is a major issue for we polio survivors. As most of us are well aware, we find ourselves in a position of needing to educate doctors, insurance companies, and government agencies. None of these groups are known for openness to input from those they serve.

We only have one shot at this thing called life, Shirley MacLaine aside. We survived the humiliating poster child era of the 50s. We can handle the post-polio crisis of the 90s with knowledge, courage, support, unity, and advocacy. None of these challenges are new to us "old polios." (Reprinted with permission of the author.) ■

Sources of Prejudice and Discrimination: Five Major Factors

How do prejudice and discrimination originate? Why do they persist? As we explore this topic, you may find your values and beliefs challenged. Use this opportunity to apply your highest critical thinking skills to evaluate your attitudes. We begin with a look at the five most commonly cited sources of prejudice: learning, cognitive processes, individual personality needs, economic and political competition, and displaced aggression.

Learning

Just as people learn their attitudes about divorce or pizza, they learn prejudice through classical and operant conditioning and social learning. Children hear their parents, friends, and teachers expressing prejudice and they imitate them. Children watch television and movies and read books and magazines in which minorities and women are still portrayed in demeaning and stereotypical roles, and they learn this must be acceptable. Exposure of this kind initiates and reinforces the learning of prejudice (Huston, Watkins, and Kunkel, 1989; Matlin, 1993).

People also learn their prejudices through direct experience. They receive attention and sometimes approval for expressing racist or sexist remarks. Also, they may have a single, negative experience with a specific member of a group that they then generalize and apply to all members of the group.

Cognitive Processes

A second way people develop prejudice is through cognitive processes. According to this view, prejudice develops as a result of normal cognitive processes and the everyday attempt to explain a complex social world (Bodenhausen and Wyer, 1985; Fiske, 1989). Grouping people into men and women, blacks and whites, Protestants and Jews, gays and lesbians and heterosexuals simplifies and quickly organizes a large amount of information. Along these same lines, people also create *ingroups* and *outgroups*. An ingroup is any category in which people see themselves as a member, while an outgroup consists of all others.

This "quick and dirty" type of categorizing may simplify things, but it also creates problems. For example, people tend to see ingroup members as more attractive, as having more desirable personality characteristics, and as engaging in more socially accepted forms of behavior. In other words, cognitively, they practice ingroup favoritism and outgroup negativity (Meindl and Lerner, 1984; Turner, 1987).

A second type of cognitive bias in prejudice is the tendency to see more diversity among members of one's ingroup and less among the outgroup (Judd and Park, 1988; Park and Rothbart, 1982). Young people, for example, think old people are "all alike," while the elderly think the same about the young. This "they-all-look-alike-to-me" tendency is termed the outgroup homogeneity effect. This is a very dangerous kind of cognitive bias. When members of minority groups are not perceived as varied and complex individuals who have the same needs and feelings as the dominant group, it is easier to perceive them as faceless objects and to treat them in discriminatory ways. During the Vietnam War, for example, Asians were labeled "gooks" to whom "life is cheap." This made it easier to kill large numbers of Vietnamese civilians (Johnson, 1992). The Ku Klux Klan operates similarly, negatively labeling African-Americans and Jews to justify their aggressive philosophy.

A third cognitive process by which we develop prejudice is the tendency to *blame the victim.* Blaming the victim is a type of attribution bias (Chapter 17). Out of our need to believe in a *just world* we tend to blame victims of prejudice for their own misfortune. Just as women are often blamed for being raped ("They shouldn't dress like that"), minorities are often blamed for their poverty and lower-class standing ("They don't work hard enough" or "They should have gone to college"). Americans like to believe in equal opportunity for all. Evidence of discrimination, therefore, creates *cognitive dissonance,* which can be resolved by blaming the victim.

Ingroup Favoritism: A cognitive process in prejudice whereby members of an ingroup are viewed in more favorable terms than members of the outgroup.

Outgroup Negativity: A cognitive process in prejudice whereby members of the outgroup are evaluated more negatively than members of the ingroup.

Outgroup Homogeneity Effect: A cognitive process in prejudice whereby members of the outgroup are judged as less individual, or diverse, than members of the ingroup.

Individual Personality Needs

A third way prejudice develops is out of an individual's personality needs. One of the earliest studies of specific personality traits associated with prejudice was done by Theodore Adorno and his associates (1950). Their initial research into the social climate and anti-Semitism (prejudice against Jews) during World War II led them to construct a paper-and-pencil test for prejudice. The F Scale ("F" for fascism) portion of the test was designed to identify individuals with traits (rigidity, conventionality, and sadism) that predisposed them toward prejudice. People who scored high on the F Scale came to be known as the authoritarian personality.

Authoritarian Personality: Personality type that includes traits of rigidity, conventionality, and sadism. These traits are said to predispose the individual toward prejudice.

 Try This Yourself

Would you like to test your own level of authoritarianism? The more statements you agree with or strongly endorse, the higher your score would be and the more authoritarian your personality type.

---

1. America is getting so far from the true American way of life that force may be necessary to restore it.
2. Familiarity breeds contempt.
3. One of the main values of progressive education is that it gives the child great freedom in expressing those natural impulses and desires so often frowned upon by conventional middle-class society.
4. Contemptible, indeed, is the person who does not feel undying love, gratitude, and respect for his or her parents.
5. Reports of atrocities in Europe have been greatly exaggerated for propaganda purposes.
6. Homosexuality is a particularly abhorrent form of delinquency and ought to be severely punished.
7. It is essential for learning or effective work that our teachers and supervisors outline in detail what is to be done and exactly how to go about it.
8. There are some activities so flagrantly un-American that, when responsible officials won't take the proper steps, wide-awake citizens should take the law into their own hands.
9. All people should have a deep faith in some supernatural force higher than themselves to which they give allegiance and whose decisions they do not question.
10. Obedience and respect for authority are the most important virtues children should learn.
11. Nowadays when so many different kinds of people move around so much and mix together so freely, a person has to be especially careful to protect himself or herself against infection and disease.
12. No sane, normal, decent person could ever think of hurting a close friend or relative.

Source: Adapted from Adorno et al. (1950). Reprinted by permission.   ■

What makes someone develop an authoritarian personality?   Since Adorno and his colleagues were strongly influenced by Freudian personality theory, they saw authoritarianism and prejudice as an expression of unconscious needs, conflicts, and defense mechanisms. They believed that early rearing by domineering fathers and punitive mothers, who both use harsh discipline to enforce strict standards of obedience, led to insecure, dependent, hostile children. When these children grew up and were in "the driver's seat," anyone who was deviant, disobedient, or a member of a minority ethnic group became a target for their unconscious anger and hatred of their parents.

Both Adorno's test and his theory have generated considerable controversy. Critics argue that the items on the F Scale are slanted toward right-wing political conservatives even though authoritarian personalities can be found at both ends of the political spectrum (Rokeach et al., 1960). Other critics suggest that unconscious defense mechanisms are not the primary cause of prejudice, and that children learn their prejudices directly from their parents (Brown, 1992). Still, the theory of authoritarianism has received some support (Altemeyer, 1992; McCann and Stewin, 1987). Moreover, studies on college campuses show a dramatic increase in authoritarianism in recent years. In the 1970s, 54 percent of college students showed authoritarian tendencies, but by 1987 over 80 percent scored in that range (Altemeyer, 1992).

Economic and Political Competition

Some researchers believe a fourth way prejudice develops is out of competition for limited resources, and it is maintained because it offers significant economic and political advantages to the dominant group. For years, manufacturing in many countries in Western Europe has depended heavily on foreign workers. Now, as economic conditions have worsened and there is competition for jobs, there is growing discrimination against Turks in Germany, for example, and Algerians in France. The fact that in the United States lower-class whites have been found to hold more racist attitudes than higher-class whites also supports the economic conflict explanation for prejudice. The upper class can *afford* to look unprejudiced and liberal because their employment, status, and income are not threatened by the lower class (Johnson, 1992). Whites in the lower class, however, are vulnerable to unemployment because minorities compete with them for scarce resources.

Displaced Aggression

Have you ever wondered why lower-class groups tend to blame each other, rather than blaming the upper class or the class system itself? Or why African-Americans in Los Angeles lashed out at Korean shopkeepers during the 1992 riots and not the police? As you will see in the next section on aggression, frustration often leads people to attack the source of frustration. But when the source is bigger and capable of retaliating, or when the cause of the frustration is ambiguous, people often displace their aggression. That is, they take out their frustration on an alternative, nonthreatening target. The innocent victim of displaced aggression is known as a *scapegoat*. Because lower-class people depend on the upper class for their jobs, they are more likely to become prejudiced against less powerful minority groups, rather than vent their frustrations on their employers.

There is strong historical evidence for the power of scapegoating. During the Great Depression of the 1930s, Hitler used Jews and Communists as scapegoats on which Germans could blame their economic troubles. In nineteenth-century America, the Chinese in California and blacks in the South served the same scapegoat function. In modern America, Hispanics, African-Americans, and the welfare system are scapegoats for increasing crime, unemployment, homelessness, and higher taxes.

Gender and Cultural Diversity

THE PRICE OF PREJUDICE AND DISCRIMINATION

If it's true that a picture is worth a thousand words, then the photos in Figure 18.6 may serve as a small reminder of the atrocities that have come from prejudice and discrimination. Although there are many kinds of "costs" associated with prejudice and many groups affected (the elderly, gays and lesbians, physically disabled, and so on), we only have space to discuss two issues, economic penalties and power inequalities, and how they apply to African-Americans and women.

Economic Penalties

Wealth in America is sharply divided along ethnic and gender lines. As Table 18.2 shows, U.S. white households have almost 10 times the net wealth of black households. Similarly, as shown in Table 18.3, in every year since 1946, women have earned less than 70 percent of what men earn.

(a)

Figure 18.6 Extreme costs of prejudice. Here are only a few examples of the atrocities associated with prejudice in world history: (a) the Holocaust, when millions of Jews were exterminated by the Nazis; (b) slavery in America, when millions of African-Americans were deprived of their basic rights; (c) starvation in Somalia, with thousands dying from hunger because of prejudice between warring groups; (d) the relocation of Native Americans to reservations, which almost led to their extermination. Can you think of other examples?

(b)

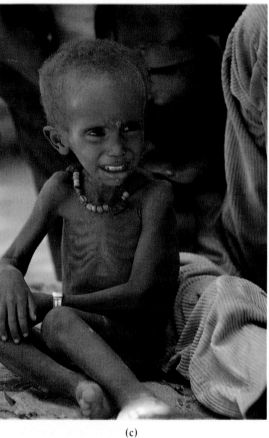

(c)

(d)

Table 18.2   Distribution of Wealth in the United States

Wealth	Whites	Blacks
Median net worth[a] of households	$43,300	$4,200
Percent with		
zero or negative net worth	9%	29%
$100,000 or more	29%	5%
Percent who own homes	68%	44%

[a]Net worth is the sum of assets minus debts and other liabilities.
Source: Adapted from Johnson, 1992; the United States Census Bureau, 1991.

Why do whites and men make so much more money?   Education is a common response, but it isn't the only factor. For example, women tend to make less than men even when they have the same level of education (see Table 18.4). If we look deeper than education for the discrepancies in wage and wealth, we find two possible answers: Unemployment is more likely among nonwhites and women, regardless of education, and nonwhites and women tend to occupy lower-level and lower-paying jobs (United States Census Bureau, 1990). If we look only at women, we see that divorce is one of the most important factors in female poverty. In California, for example, women and children typically experience an average drop of 73 percent in their standard of living following a divorce. Men, however, tend to experience a 42 percent increase in their average standard of living after divorce (Weitzman, 1985).

Table 18.3   Comparison of Median Earnings of Year-Round Full-Time Workers, by Gender, Selected Years

Year	Median Earnings Women	Men	Women's Earnings as a Percent of Men's	Year	Median Earnings Women	Men	Women's Earnings as a Percent of Men's
1990	$20,556	$29,989	68.6	1973	$6,335	$11,186	56.6
1989	18,780	27,430	68.5	1972	5,903	10,202	57.9
1988	17,606	26,656	66.0	1971	5,593	9,399	59.5
1987	16,909	26,008	65.0	1970	5,323	8,966	59.4
1986	16,232	25,256	64.3	1969	4,977	8,227	60.5
1985	15,624	24,195	64.5	1966	3,973	6,848	58.0
1984	14,780	23,218	63.7	1965	3,823	6,375	60.0
1983	13,915	21,881	63.6	1964	3,690	6,195	59.6
1982	13,014	21,077	61.7	1963	3,561	5,978	59.6
1981	12,001	20,260	59.2	1962	3,446	5,974	59.5
1980	11,197	18,612	60.2	1961	3,351	5,644	59.4
1979	10,151	17,014	59.7	1960	3,293	5,317	60.8
1978	9,350	15,730	59.4	1959	3,193	5,209	61.3
1977	8,618	14,626	58.9	1958	3,102	4,927	63.0
1976	8,099	13,455	60.2	1957	3,008	4,713	63.8
1975	7,504	12,758	58.8	1956	2,827	4,466	63.3
1974	6,772	11,835	57.2	1955	2,719	4,252	63.9

Source: Income, poverty, and wealth in the United States: A chart book, 1992; Johnson, 1992.

Table 18.4   Mean Income by Years of Education and Gender for Year-Round, Full-Time Workers (United States)

| Years of School Completed | Mean Income | | For Each Dollar Men Earn, Women Earn: |
	Women	Men	
Elementary			
8 Years	$13,322	$19,188	69¢
High School			
1 to 3 Years	$15,381	$22,564	68¢
4 Years	$18,954	$28,043	68¢
College			
1 to 3 Years	$22,654	$34,188	66¢
4 Years	$28,911	$44,354	65¢
5 Years or More	$35,827	$55,831	64¢

Source: Johnson, 1992; Statistical Abstract of the United States, 1992; United States Census Bureau, 1990.

Power Inequalities

The most immediate cause of the 1992 Los Angeles riots was the jury's "not guilty" verdict for the four police officers. The lack of racial balance (an all-white jury) and perceived prejudice among the jury members was the last straw of frustration for many African-Americans. The justice system in America is often cited as a prime example of the unequal distribution of power between whites and blacks (Rothenberg, 1992). For example, nonwhites are far less likely to serve on juries or use bail to stay out of jail. When convicted of crimes, nonwhites tend to receive harsher sentences (Baldus, 1987).

Both women and minorities also suffer unequal access to power within the legislative and executive branches of the American government. Power is disproportionately concentrated in the hands of white males. Blacks comprise 12 percent of the population, for example, but only 1 percent of all public offices (Johnson, 1992). Women make up 52 percent of the population, but only 7 percent of the U.S. Congress. Despite these statistics, there are encouraging signs. During the 1980s Americans had a woman as a vice-presidential candidate for a major party, and 1992 was frequently cited by politicians and newspapers as the "Year of the Woman." Both political parties have also started to appoint more nonwhites as a result of their increasing political clout. ■

Reducing Prejudice and Discrimination: Four Major Methods

Having some perspective on how prejudice develops and the cost to its victims, you are now prepared to consider what can be done to combat it. We will look at four methods to reduce prejudice: cooperation, superordinate goals, increased contact, and empathy.

Cooperation

Research shows that one of the best ways to combat prejudice is to encourage *cooperation* rather than *competition* (Kohn, 1986; Rabow, 1988). Muzafer Sherif and his colleagues (1953, 1966) conducted an ingenious experiment to show the role of competition in promoting prejudice. The researchers created strong feelings of ingroup and outgroup identification in a group of 11- and 12-year-old boys at a summer camp by physically separating the boys in different cabins and assigning different projects to each group, such as building a diving board or cooking out in the woods. Once each group developed strong feelings of group identity and allegiance, the experimenters set up a series of competitive games, including tug-of-war and touch football, and awarded desirable prizes to the winning teams. As a result of this treatment, the groups began to pick fights, call each other names, and raid each other's camps—behaviors the researchers pointed to as evidence of experimentally created prejudice.

Isn't this type of research unethical? Shouldn't we be trying to reduce prejudice instead of creating it? Although the experiment so far does seem questionable, what happened next may offset these concerns. After using competition to create the prejudice between the two groups, the researchers demonstrated how cooperation can be successfully used to eliminate it. The experimenters created "mini-crises" and tasks that required expertise, labor, and cooperation from both groups, and prizes were awarded to all. The hostilities and prejudice between groups slowly began to dissipate, and by the end of the camp the boys voted to return home in the same bus and the self-chosen seating did not reflect the earlier camp divisions.

Superordinate Goals

Sherif's study showed not only the importance of cooperation as opposed to competition, but also the importance of superordinate goals (the "mini-crises") in reducing prejudice (Johnson et al., 1984; Shofield, 1982). It is interesting to speculate that international prejudice might also be reduced by this principle as people unite to overcome our shared environmental crises. "The planet's problems could become so paramount they would force a new spirit of international partnership, one that could serve as a model for cooperation on political, economic, and military matters" (Thompson, 1988, p. 22).

Superordinate Goal: Way of reducing prejudice that involves creating a goal that is "higher" than individual goals and is of benefit to both parties.

Increased Contact

A third approach to reducing prejudice is *increasing contact between groups.* According to both cognitive dissonance theory and self-perception theory, to require people of differing ethnic groups to live next to one another, share the same buses and public facilities, and go to integrated schools should reduce prejudice. Cognitive dissonance theory might act like this: "I live next to blacks (or whites) and I said I didn't like them (dissonance), so I guess I didn't really mean it" (it's easier to change opinions than move). Self-perception theory might work in this way: "I live next to blacks (or whites) so I must like them."

Research on increased contact and prejudice reduction, however, is mixed (Brewer and Kramer, 1985). For contact to be successful in reducing prejudice it must involve (1) close interaction (if minority students are "tracked" into vocational educational courses and whites in the same school are primarily in college prep courses, they seldom interact with one another, and prejudice is increased); (2) interdependence (both groups must be involved in superordinate goals that require cooperation); and (3) equal status (a black janitor working for a Jewish shopkeeper obviously perpetuates stereotypes).

Empathy

A dramatic illustration of the role empathy (identifying with another) can play in combating prejudice was provided by a third-grade teacher in Iowa named Jane Elliot. After the assassination of Dr. Martin Luther King, Ms. Elliot wanted to help her class of all white children better understand prejudice and discrimination. She knew that one of the best ways to reduce prejudice was to teach empathy. She divided the class on the basis of eye color—one group of blue eyes and one group of brown eyes. On the first day, the blue-eyed children were assigned a higher status than the brown-eyed children. They were told they were better than the brown-eyes and given special privileges (extra recess time, seconds on food in the cafeteria, and so on). Ms. Elliot also told the class that the brown-eyes were duller, lazier, and sloppier than the blue-eyes. As evidence of their lower status, the brown-eyes had to wear special cloth collars to identify them as members of the inferior group.

What do you think happened? Even Ms. Elliot was surprised by the shocking reactions of her students. After only one day of being the victim of prejudice, the brown-

One way to reduce prejudice is to portray minorities in roles that contradict popular stereotypes.

eyed children showed signs of being depressed and unhappy, and they were slower in their academic performances. On the other hand, the blue-eyed children retained their self-esteem and some enjoyed and exploited their position of power and prestige. During recess time, the brown-eyed children were teased and excluded and fights broke out between the two groups.

On the second day, Ms. Elliot reversed the roles—allowing the brown-eyes to be the "superior" group. At the end of the second day, Ms. Elliot debriefed both groups and talked about what they had learned. The two-day simulation had apparently worked. The children seemed to understand some of the costs of prejudice and to have developed empathy for the victims.

Most important, the experimental effects were long lasting. When Ms. Elliot brought the class back 15 years later, one of the most frequent comments was that the experience had literally changed lives. Even a brief experience as a victim of prejudice sensitized these individuals to the everyday world of most minorities. (The original classroom study was recreated many times and later documented in a classic film entitled *Eye of the Storm*.)

Review Questions

1. _____ is a generally negative attitude directed toward people because of their membership in a specific group.
2. The cognitive component of prejudice is also known as _____ .
3. How does "prejudice" differ from "discrimination"?
4. What are the five major sources of prejudice?
5. _____ and _____ are two of the many "costs" of prejudice and discrimination.
6. How can prejudice and discrimination be reduced?

Answers to Review Questions can be found in Appendix C.

AGGRESSION

* *Is aggression primarily biological or environmental?*

Aggression: Any behavior that is intended to harm someone.

Aggression is any form of behavior directed toward harming or injuring another living being who is motivated to avoid such treatment (Baron and Byrne, 1992). The beating of Rodney King and the rioters' attacks on motorists and shopkeepers are obvious examples of aggressive behavior. Why do people, whether police officers or rioters, act aggressively? We will explore a number of internal and external explanations for aggression. Then we will look at theories on how aggression can be controlled or reduced.

Internal Factors: Instinct and Biology

Two of the major internal explanations for aggression are instinct and biology.

Instinct

Because aggression has a long history and is found among all cultures, many theorists believe humans are instinctively aggressive. After personally witnessing the massive death and destruction that occurred during World War I, Sigmund Freud stated that aggressive impulses are inborn. He argued that the drive for violence arises from a basic instinct to aggress. Therefore, human aggression cannot be eliminated (Gay, 1988).

Depending on the specific area of the brain that is electrically stimulated, cats will show either unusual inhibition of aggression or extreme rage.

Another instinct theory is proposed by *ethologists,* scientists who study animal behavior. They believe that aggression evolved over the generations because it contributes to survival of the fittest. Whereas Freud saw aggression as destructive and disruptive, the ethologists believe aggression prevents overcrowding and allows the strongest animals to win mates and reproduce the species (Allman, 1992; Lorenz, 1981; Eibl-Eibesfeldt, 1980a). Most social psychologists, however, today reject Freud's and the ethologists' view of instinct as the source of aggression.

Biology

Other psychologists who suspect a biological basis for aggression have studied the brain and nervous system in an effort to discover physiological causes of aggressive behavior. They have found that electrical stimulation or severing of specific parts of an animal's brain has a direct effect on aggression (Delgado, 1960; Kalat, 1992). Research with brain injuries and organic disorders has also identified specific aggression "centers" in the brain—in particular the hypothalamus, amygdala, and other parts of the limbic system (Blanchard and Blanchard, 1988; Siegel and Brutus, 1990). But brain research does not identify the conditions that activate these aggression centers in the natural state. Just as knowing that the carburetor and battery are important to understanding how a car motor works, we also need to recognize that this isn't the whole story. A car and the human nervous system are both complex, interrelated systems.

A second line of biological research has focused on the role of hormones and neurotransmitters in aggression. For example, many studies have linked the male gonadal hormone *testosterone* to aggressive behavior (Archer, 1991; Dabbs and Morris, 1990; Freeman-Longo and Wall, 1986). However, the relationship between human aggression and testosterone is complex and research results are inconclusive.

Research with neurotransmitter function and aggression has found an interesting correlation between serotonin and aggressive behavior. People who have committed suicide or attempted it by violent means have low levels of serotonin (Edman et al., 1986; Mann, Arango, and Underwood, 1990). In addition, people convicted of arson and other violent crimes have been found to have lower than normal serotonin turnover (Virkkunen et al., 1987). Given that lowered serotonin is also related to alcohol abuse, overeating, depression, and obsessive–compulsive disorders (Delgado et al., 1990; Goodman et al., 1990; Schwartz et al., 1989), it may be that serotonin has something to do with suppressing impulsive behaviors (Charney et al., 1990).

The complex interplay between biological factors is further supported by the fact that alcohol consumption is also related to physical aggression (Bushman and Cooper, 1990; Newcomb and Bentler, 1989). A case in point: Over one-fourth of the criminals in a large survey of state prisoners admitted to heavy consumption of alcohol prior to committing their crimes (Rosewicz, 1983). The fact that alcohol is so widely available and so widely used in our culture makes it particularly important in studies on aggression.

External Factors: Frustration, Social Learning, and Group Influence

In addition to internal factors, there are numerous external factors related to aggression. In this section we will discuss the role of frustration (and its relation to displaced aggression), social learning, and group influence.

Frustration

Have you ever been in a hurry to mail a package at a crowded post office and had the clerk close the window just as it was your turn? Did you feel angry and tempted to force someone to reopen the window? The relationship between frustration and aggression was noted more than half a century ago by John Dollard and his colleagues (1939). From their research they concluded that "aggression is always a consequence of frustration" and "frustration always leads to some form of aggression."

Does frustration always lead to aggression? How does this account for the differences in the amount of aggression I feel in different situations? People do vary in the intensity of their responses to frustration and in the way they express aggression. But what the frustration–aggression hypothesis says is that everyone has the motive to aggress as a result of frustration and some form of aggression will result. This does not mean if you get mad at your boss, you necessarily punch him or her in the nose. You may displace your aggression and take out your anger on your family when you get home. Or, you may turn your aggression toward yourself, becoming self-destructive or withdrawing, giving up, and getting depressed. According to Dollard's hypothesis, in every case frustration creates tension and the desire to release that tension through aggression.

Experimental tests of the frustration–aggression hypothesis have produced conflicting results. Although frustration is undoubtedly related to aggression, it is obvious now that the case was overstated. Frustration does not *always* lead to aggression, and not all aggression is the result of frustration. For example, when someone accidentally frustrates us, or when there is a good explanation for the "blocked goal," we often do not become aggressive. Furthermore, aggression is also a common reaction to pain, heat (as in riots on hot summer nights), and general emotional arousal (as in the case of the riots in Los Angeles) (Bell, 1992; Berkowitz, 1990; Reifman et al., 1991).

Frustration–Aggression Hypothesis: Idea that the motive to aggress is always a consequence of frustration and that frustration always leads to some form of aggression.

Social Learning

Social learning theorists believe we *learn* to be aggressive by observing models who are rewarded for aggression. If we see people we admire act aggressively and violently, or if we see people rewarded for aggressive behavior, we may be inclined to imitate them.

One of the most controversial sources of the modeling of aggression is the mass media. Despite protestations that violence in movies and on television is only "entertainment," there is considerable evidence that the media can be a contributing factor in aggression (Gerbner et al., 1993; Huston et al., 1989). Research on the media's influence has focused primarily on television, and results indicate that the more violent the content of a child's TV viewing, the more aggressive the child (Eron and Huesmann, 1984). A report by the National Institute of Mental Health (1982) decisively stated that children *do* imitate what they see on television and also seem to internalize the general value that violence is acceptable behavior.

Could it be that aggressive children just tend to prefer violent television programs? Research suggests it is a two-way street. Cross-cultural studies among children in 5 different countries (Australia, Finland, Israel, Poland, and the U.S.) found that exposure to TV violence did increase aggressiveness *and* that aggressive children tend to seek out violent programs (Huesman and Eron, 1986). However, the link remains between TV violence and aggression. For example, when television is introduced to new areas of the

THE FAR SIDE   By GARY LARSON

In the days before television

world the homicide rate shows an abrupt and dramatic increase (Centerwall, 1989; Hennigan et al., 1982). Experimental studies also support the argument that exposure to media violence is a contributing factor in aggression. Recall from Chapter 6 that when children were shown films of an adult hitting an inflated toy clown (known as a Bobo doll) they behaved more aggressively than children shown a nonaggressive film (Bandura and Walters, 1963). Also, in Chapter 11 we discussed the well-established relationship between crimes against women and viewing violent pornography (Brownmiller, 1984; Donnerstein, 1980; Malamuth, 1989).

Group Influence

As you discovered in Chapter 17, group membership has a strong influence on all our behaviors. In relation to aggression, role behaviors may be a particularly important influence. Consider how roles might explain the beating of Rodney King. Just as *some* college students became aggressive and abusive of their power as guards in Philip Zimbardo's prison study (see Chapter 17), *some* police officers *may* have abused their role and power during the Rodney King beating.

Deindividuation (loss of self-awareness and responsibility) is another group influence in aggression, and could well have been a factor in the Rodney King incident. Being part of a group of fellow police officers may have led to an intensification of emotion and strong feelings of group unity. These factors in turn contribute to a lessening awareness of individual values and responsibilities, an increased sensitivity to the group and the immediate situation, and ultimately to actions associated with deindividuation. Deindividuation also helps explain the actions of the rioters. Can you see how the high emotionality following the jury's decision and the shared group identity of African-Americans may have contributed to a deindividuated state among the rioters?

Controlling or Eliminating Aggression: Can We Do It?

Based on Freud's belief that the biological drive toward aggression builds up a lot of pressure that must be periodically released to prevent an "explosion," some therapists advise people to release our aggressive impulses by engaging in harmless forms of aggression, such as vigorous exercise, punching a pillow, and watching competitive sports. According to the Freudian approach, these and other socially acceptable behaviors can provide direct or symbolic substitutes for overt aggression, thus producing catharsis. However, the fact that many sports events actually tend to *increase* the incidence of violence would seem to disprove this idea. Experimental studies also suggest that "draining the aggression reservoir" doesn't really help. Punching pillows, watching the violence of others, and even verbally expressing anger apparently do little to reduce the chances for violence (Geen, 1978; McKenzie-Mohr and Zanna, 1990; Tavris, 1989). In fact, as we pointed out in Chapter 12, the expression of an emotion, anger or otherwise, tends to intensify the feeling rather than reduce it.

Catharsis: Freudian belief that pent-up aggressive impulses can be released through violent acts; some theorists believe it can occur vicariously, as when people watch violent sports matches.

A second approach, which *does* seem to effectively reduce or control aggression, is to introduce incompatible responses. Because certain emotional responses, such as empathy and humor, are incompatible with aggression, Baron (1983) suggests purposely inducing them in the presence of anger and frustration as a preventive measure. In your own experiences, you may have noticed that it is hard to keep fighting when something happens that makes you laugh or allows you to empathize with the other person's position.

A third approach to controlling aggression is to improve social and communication skills. Studies have found that people with the most deficient communication skills account for a disproportionate share of the violence in society (Baron, 1988; Toch, 1980). Unfortunately, little effort is made in our schools or families to teach basic communication skills or techniques of conflict resolution.

One final way to curb aggression is to address it on the societal level. To reduce the incidence of child abuse, for example, we need to reduce stress in families (Emery, 1989;

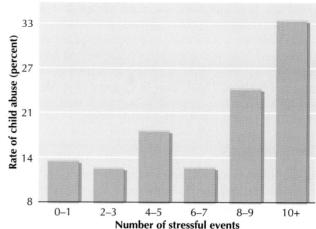

Figure 18.7 Family stress and child abuse. As the number of stressful events (such as unemployment, illness, alcoholism) rises, child abuse also increases.

McLoyd, 1989). One study of 2,143 abusive families found that the highest incidence of abuse occurred during times of economic and personal distress, as Figure 18.7 shows (Straus, Gelles, and Steinmetz, 1980). We must also find ways to reduce the amount of violence in the mass media and discourage alcohol use in potentially violent situations (Bushman and Cooper, 1990). Finally, in reference to the LA riots we need to take large societal measures toward improving relations between minorities and police officers and solving the social problems that underlie riot behaviors.

Gender and Cultural Diversity

IS AGGRESSION A CULTURAL UNIVERSAL?

Research has found that males around the world tend to commit more aggressive acts than females, and that this may, in fact, be a *cultural universal* (Segall et al., 1990). But is aggression itself culturally universal? The evidence is less clear. While warfare and violence occur throughout recorded history, there are some cultures that have not engaged in war for centuries, and others that have only intermittently gone to war (Groebel and Hinde, 1989). Also, there are small, isolated societies in which aggression is severely condemned and virtually nonexistent (Nanda, 1991). The Semai of Malaysia, for example, consider anger a very bad thing, and observers note that the Semai rarely get angry. They are so gentle that they won't kill animals they have raised for food. Instead, they exchange with someone from another village. Nonaggressiveness is an internalized ideal and an important component of the individual's self-image (Robarcheck and Dentan, 1987). When conflict arises, it is settled peacefully. No murder has ever been recorded in their culture (Nanda, 1991).

Evidence that aggression is not universal also comes from nonbiological factors. Landau (1984) examined criminal acts of violence in 13 major industrialized nations (Austria, Denmark, Finland, India, Israel, Japan, the Netherlands, New Zealand, Norway, Sweden, Switzerland, the United States, and West Germany) from the mid-1960s through the late 1970s. He found that violent crime was directly correlated to increased social stressors and failing social-support systems in 12 of the 13 countries. Japan was the sole exception. Rather than showing an increase in violent crime, Japan experienced an increase in suicide (which some might interpret as a form of inward-directed violence).

Many people tend to prefer a biological explanation for aggression. They point to the long history of warfare as evidence of the instinctually aggressive side of human nature (e.g., Ardry, 1966; Lorenz, 1966, 1986). As Nanda (1991) points out, however, wars are fought between countries, not between individuals. Societies that highly value warfare teach their citizens (particularly males) to be more aggressive. Thus, society can set the stage for the human *potential* for aggression to be expressed. Frustration, learning, group influences, and social factors all play important roles in determining when, and if, aggression will be displayed. ■

On this street in Queens, New York, Kitty Genovesee was stabbed to death while 38 of her neighbors failed to heed her cries for help. How can we explain their lack of response?

Review Questions

1. Any form of behavior directed toward harming or injuring another living being who is motivated to avoid such treatment is known as _____ .

2. How do instinct theories explain aggression?

3. Name three major factors that contribute to aggression.

4. According to the _____ hypothesis, people experience a motive toward aggression after experiencing frustration.

5. _____ theorists believe that you learn to be aggressive by observing models who are rewarded for aggression.

6. Humor tends to _____ aggression, while watching violent sports tends to _____ aggression.

Answers to Review Questions can be found in Appendix C.

ALTRUISM

After reading about prejudice, discrimination, and aggression, you will no doubt be relieved to discover that human beings demonstrate positive social behavior as well. People help and support one another by donating blood, giving time and money to charities, helping stranded motorists, and so on. There are also times when people don't help. Consider the following: In 1965, on Austin Street in Queens, New York, a woman named Kitty Genovese was stabbed to death as she returned to her apartment. Thirty-eight of her neighbors heard her screams and pleas for help: "Oh my God, he stabbed me! Please help me! Please help me!" and watched as she struggled to fight off her assailant. The lights in the windows of the observers' apartments apparently scared off the attacker, who left Kitty lying in the street, wounded but still alive. But when the neighbors turned off their lights and went back to bed, the attacker returned and stabbed her again. He was once more scared off by the returning lights and attention, but the neighbors went back to bed a second time. He then returned for a third and fatal attack.

Why did the neighbors keep going back to bed, and why didn't the police come? Throughout the entire series of attacks (which lasted for over 35 minutes), not one of the 38 neighbors called either the police or an ambulance, which explains the lack of police aid. But why didn't the neighbors help? What caused their apparent indifference? More generally, under what conditions do people sometimes help and sometimes ignore others' pleas for help? These are the questions about altruism that psychologists try to answer.

• *What causes people to help (or not help) others?*

Why Do We Help? Biological and Psychological Explanations

Altruism (or prosocial behavior) refers to actions designed to help others with no obvious benefit to oneself. In attempting to explain altruism, psychologists have taken two major approaches, biological and psychological.

Altruism: Actions designed to help others with no obvious benefit to the individual.

Biological Explanations

From discussions in Chapter 12, you know that evolutionary theory and sociobiology suggest that the survival of one's genes is the major motivation for behavior. From this perspective altruism is an instinctual behavior that has evolved because it favors survival of one's genes (Rushton, 1989, 1991; Wilson, 1975). Altruistic acts among lower species (e.g., worker bees living for their mother, the queen) and the fact that altruism in humans is strongest toward one's own children and other relatives have been cited as support for this position.

How could risking your life, even for your own child, be genetically advantageous? The key word here is *genetically*. Altruism protects not the individual, but the individual's genes. By helping or even dying for your child or sibling, you increase the odds that your genes will be passed on to future generations. Each individual is motivated not only to pass on his or her individual genes, but also to enhance the reproductive odds for those who share some of those same genes. Some evolutionary psychologists even suggest that our preference for helping our "kin" also extends to ethnic groups and geographic neighbors (Rushton, 1991). Given that historically we are more genetically related to people who belong to our same ethnic group and who live near us, our biology supposedly drives us to help these groups over "foreigners."

Critics of the evolutionary/sociobiological approach to altruism say it is based on overgeneralizations from animal studies and on naive speculation (Kitcher, 1985). Perhaps an even more important criticism (and danger) is the suggestion of biological favoritism toward ethnic ingroups and neighbors. In a global economy that demands increasing interaction and interdependence among nations, a biological limit on our willingness to help others could be a serious impediment to peace and progress.

Psychological Explanations

An additional problem with the evolutionary approach is that it has only been applied to large groups and not to individual behaviors (Tooby and Cosmides, 1989). Psychological explanations for altruism show great variation among individuals in their willingness to help (Clary and Thieman, 1988). Interviews with people who had intervened in dangerous crime situations, for example, found that these individuals were exceptionally self-assured and felt certain they could handle the potential problems (Huston et al., 1981; Kohn, 1989). They were also more likely to have had specialized training in life saving, first aid, or police work.

The Egoistic Model

While individual differences in personality and training may explain some forms of altruism, the psychological perspective also suggests that helping may be a simple form of egoism or disguised self-interest. According to this *egoistic* model, helping is always motivated by some degree of anticipated gain. We help others because we hope for later reciprocation, because it makes us feel good about ourselves, or because it helps us avoid feelings of distress and guilt if we don't help (Cialdini, 1991; Piliavin et al., 1982; Weiss et al., 1973).

Negative State Relief: The proposal that altruistic behavior is motivated by the desire to reduce negative feelings through helping others.

Support for the egoistic position comes from other research that finds helping others reduces negative moods and unpleasant feelings—a process known as negative state relief. According to this perspective, seeing others in distress is unpleasant and disturbing, and the best way to rid ourselves of these feelings is by helping. Also, we learn from childhood that helping is expected in many circumstances, and if we don't help we experience strong feelings of guilt and shame.

The Empathy–Altruism Hypothesis

Empathy–Altruism Hypothesis: The proposal that altruistic behavior is motivated by empathy for the distressed person in need of help.

Opposing the egoistic model and negative state relief perspective is the empathy–altruism hypothesis proposed by Batson and his colleagues (Batson, 1991; Batson et al., 1991). As Figure 18.8 shows, Batson sees some altruism motivated by simple, selfish concerns (the top part of the diagram), *but* he also argues that in some situations helping is truly selfless and motivated by concern for others (the bottom part of the diagram). According to the empathy–altruism hypothesis, simply seeing another per-

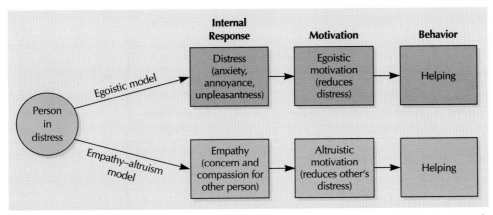

Figure 18.8 Two major approaches to helping. According to Batson and his colleagues, helping is motivated by *both* egoistic, self-serving motives and altruistic, selfless motives.

son's suffering or hearing of their need can create *empathy,* a subjective grasp of that person's feelings or experiences. When we feel empathic toward another we focus on their distress, not our own, and are motivated to help the person for his or her own sake (Eisenberg, 1991). The ability to empathize may even be innate. Research with infants in the first few hours of life shows that they become distressed and cry at the sound of another infant's cries (Hoffman, 1981; Sagi and Hoffman, 1976).

In sum, there seems to be general agreement that egoism is an important component of altruism. Whether we help because of a "selfish gene" that evolved as a means of insuring genetic survival, or because it relieves our distress and makes us feel good, our motive is selfish. The question remains whether anyone is *truly* altruistic—aiming simply to relieve the distress of another. Some researchers believe there are forms of true altruism (Batson, 1991; Dovidio, 1991), while others remain convinced that egoism still plays a role (Cialdini, 1993).

Why Don't We Help?: Diffusion of Responsibility

Many theories have been proposed to explain why people help, but few explain why we don't. How do we explain the Kitty Genovese incident? Some suggest that large cities like New York breed dehumanization and apathy; people stop caring. Although research has found that there is less helping in areas of larger population (Amato, 1983; Korte, 1980), the reasons for this are debated.

One of the most comprehensive explanations for helping or not helping comes from the research of Bibb Latané and John Darley (1970). They found that whether or not someone helps depends on a series of interconnected events and decisions. The potential helper must first *notice* what is happening, must then *interpret* the event as an emergency, must accept personal *responsibility* for helping, and then must *decide* how to help and actually initiate the helping behavior (see Figure 18.9).

Where did the sequence break down for Kitty Genovese?   Since Kitty's neighbors obviously noticed what was happening and interpreted it as an emergency, the first break in the sequence was in their willingness to accept personal responsibility. But contrary to the popular portrayal of New Yorkers as uncaring and apathetic, Kitty's neighbors were *not* indifferent to her attack. Later newspaper interviews with each of the neighbors showed a great deal of anguish among the observers, but each of them "naturally" assumed that someone else had already called the police. This is an example of what has come to be known as the diffusion of responsibility phenomenon—the tendency when part of a group to assume that someone else will respond and take action. It is ironic that if only one of Kitty's neighbors had watched her attack, and known that he or she was alone, Kitty might still be alive today.

Diffusion of Responsibility: When people are in groups of two or more, there is a tendency toward less individual responsiveness due to the assumption that someone else will take action (or responsibility).

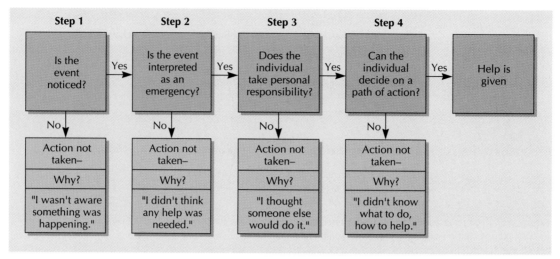

Figure 18.9 Steps that determine whether helping occurs. Potential helpers will not come to a person's aid if they answer no to any question in the top boxes. Only after they notice the situation, define it as an emergency, take personal responsibility, and decide on a course of action will they help.

Increasing Altruism: How Can We Promote Helping?

The most obvious way to improve the chances for altruistic behavior is to counteract ambiguous, inhibitory factors and reward factors that promote the chances for altruism. For example, the ambiguity of situations could be reduced by speaking up and clarifying what is going on. If you notice a situation where it seems unclear whether someone needs help, you can simply ask. On the other hand, if you are the one in need of help, look directly at anyone who may be watching and give specific directions, such as "Call the police."

Societal rewards for a broader range of helping behaviors could also be improved. Some researchers suggest that states need to enact more laws that protect the helper from potential suits or recrimination and punish those who fail to respond. Certain existing police programs, such as Crime Stoppers, actively recruit public compliance in reporting crime, give monetary rewards, and assure anonymity. Such programs have apparently been highly effective in reducing crime (Rosenbaum and Lurigio, 1985).

Because people are more likely to help when they feel competent and self-assured, others suggest we train people in helping skills so they do not feel embarrassed in offering help, but can recognize emergencies and feel equipped to assume responsibility. Classes in first aid and cardiopulmonary resuscitation (CPR) are two examples of such training.

A Final Note

Sometimes our students ask if these techniques for promoting altruism could really work for large-scale problems. It depends. If we adopt the view that people are rational and behavior can be described, explained, predicted, and changed, then no problem is insurmountable. As you may remember, these are the four basic goals of psychology that we discussed at the very beginning of this text.

Now that we are closing this final chapter, we sincerely hope that this introduction to psychology has encouraged you to see psychology as not only a science and academic discipline but also as a method for positive social influence. We encourage you to apply the information you've gained from this text and course to both personal and societal problems. We also invite you to continue your study and exploration of the subject through a career in psychology or simply as a part of your lifelong learning and personal growth.

Review Questions

1. _____ refers to actions designed to help others with no obvious benefit to the respondent.

2. How do evolutionary theory and sociobiology explain altruism?

3. How do the egoistic model of altruism and the process of negative state relief explain aggression?

4. According to the _____ hypothesis, another person's suffering creates empathy, which motivates helping behaviors.

5. The major reason Kitty Genovese's neighbors failed to respond to her cries for help was the _____ phenomenon.

Answers to Review Questions can be found in Appendix C.

REVIEW OF MAJOR CONCEPTS

ATTITUDES

1. Attitudes are learned predispositions to respond cognitively, affectively, and behaviorally to a particular object. The three components of all attitudes are the cognitive response (thoughts and beliefs), affective response (feelings), and behavioral tendencies (predispositions to actions).

2. We sometimes change our attitudes because of cognitive dissonance, which is the state of tension or anxiety we feel when there is a difference between two or more attitudes or when our attitudes do not match our behaviors. This mismatch and tension motivate us to change our attitude to restore balance. Self-perception theory, which suggests that people infer their attitudes from watching their behavior, developed in response to cognitive dissonance theory.

3. Attitudes can also be changed through direct persuasion. The effectiveness of persuasion depends on characteristics of the source (likability, credibility, and speed of speech), the message (appeals to logic and reason versus emotional appeals), and the audience (personality traits, vulnerability, involvement, and reactance—the resistance to change).

PREJUDICE AND DISCRIMINATION

4. Prejudice is a generally negative attitude directed toward specific people solely on the basis of membership in a specific group. It contains all three components of attitudes (cognitive, affective, and behavioral tendencies). Discrimination is not the same as prejudice. It refers to the actual negative behavior directed at members of a group. Even nonprejudiced people may discriminate. The physically disabled also suffer both prejudice and discrimination, and some methods of fund raising may perpetuate stereotypes about them.

5. The five major sources of prejudice are learning (classical and operant conditioning and social learning), cognitive processes (ingroup favoritism, outgroup negativity, outgroup homogeneity effect, and blaming-the-victim), individual personality needs (authoritarian personalities), economic and political competition, and displaced aggression (scapegoating).

6. Two of the most important "costs" associated with discrimination and prejudice are economic penalties and power inequalities. Women and African-Americans, among other groups, suffer serious losses in both areas.

7. Cooperation, superordinate goals, increased contact, and empathy are four major methods for reducing prejudice and discrimination.

AGGRESSION

8. Aggression is any deliberate attempt to harm or injure another living being who is motivated to avoid such treatment. In looking for internal factors for aggression, some researchers have focused on inborn instinctual factors, whereas others have done research on the brain (primarily on the hypothalamus and other parts of the limbic system). Biological investigations have also explored the role of hormones (primarily testosterone) and neurotransmitters (primarily serotonin).

9. External factors also play a role in aggression. Frustration (and displaced aggression), social learning (observation of models who are rewarded for aggression), and group influence (role behaviors and deindividuation) are two of the most important external factors.

10. Releasing aggressive feelings through violent acts or watching violence (catharsis) has not been shown to be an effective way to reduce aggression. Three more effective ways are to produce incompatible responses (such as humor), improve social and communication skills, and change the social system. While aggression may, or may not, be a cultural universal, variations among groups and throughout history suggest that warfare is not inevitable.

ALTRUISM

11. Altruism refers to actions designed to help others with no obvious benefit to oneself. Evolutionary theorists and so-

ciobiologists believe altruism is innate and has survival value.

12. Psychological explanations for altruism emphasize the egoistic model, which suggests that helping is motivated by anticipated gain, or the empathy–altruism hypothesis, which proposes that helping is activated when the helper feels empathy for the victim.

13. Whether or not someone helps depends on a series of interconnected events, starting with noticing the problem and ending with a decision to help. Altruism is also inhibited by the fact that many emergency situations are ambiguous and the potential respondent is unsure of what to do. Inhibition also comes from not taking personal responsibility and assuming someone else will respond (the diffusion of responsibility phenomenon).

14. To increase the chances of altruism, we should increase the rewards and decrease the costs. We can also reduce ambiguity by giving clear directions to those who may be watching. It also helps if people are trained in specific helping skills.

SUGGESTED READINGS

CLARK, M. S. (Ed.) (1991). *Prosocial behavior.* Newbury Park, CA: Sage. A collection of important research in the field of altruism—its causes and effects.

DONALD, J., & RATTANSI, A. (Eds.) (1992). *Race, culture, and difference.* Newbury Park, CA: Sage. This book presents important debates on race and how concepts of "us" and "them" create current social problems.

DONOHUE, W. A., AND KOLT, R. (1992). *Managing interpersonal conflict.* Newbury Park, CA: Sage. The authors provide specific insights and sensible suggestions to help readers manage routine interpersonal conflicts.

ROTHENBERG, P. S. (1992). *Race, class, and gender in the United States* (2nd ed.). New York: St. Martin's Press. A collection of readings dedicated to exposing the nature of racism and sexism within the class society found in the United States.

ZIMBARDO, P. G., & LEIPPE, M. R. (1991). *The psychology of attitude change and social influence.* New York: McGraw-Hill. Two leading social psychologists discuss attitude formation and persuasion techniques with a special emphasis on practical applications.

PRATKANIS, A. R., & ARONSON, E. (1992). *Age of propaganda: The everyday use and abuse of persuasion.* New York: Freeman. An alarming and educational look at how persuasion techniques can be used for positive outcomes and abused for personal gain and exploitation of others.

Statistics and Psychology

We are constantly bombarded by numbers: "On sale for 30 percent off," "70 percent chance of rain," "9 out of 10 doctors recommend. . . ." The president uses numbers to try to convince us that the economy is healthy. Advertisers use numbers to convince us of the effectiveness of their products. Psychologists use statistics to support or refute psychological theories and demonstrate that certain behaviors are indeed results of specific causal factors.

When people use numbers in these ways, they are using statistics. **Statistics** is a branch of applied mathematics that uses numbers to describe and analyze information on a subject.

Statistics make it possible for psychologists to quantify the information they obtain in their studies. They can then critically analyze and evaluate this information. Statistical analysis is imperative for researchers to describe, predict, or explain behavior. For instance, Albert Bandura (1973) proposed that watching violence on television causes aggressive behavior in children. In carefully controlled experiments, he gathered numerical information and analyzed it according to specific statistical methods. The statistical analysis helped him substantiate that the aggression of his subjects and the aggressive acts they had seen on television were related, and that the relationship was not mere coincidence.

Although statistics is a branch of applied mathematics, you don't have to be a math whiz to use statistics. Simple arithmetic is all you need to do most of the calculations. For more complex statistics involving more complicated mathematics, computer programs are available for virtually every type of computer.

THE STAT FAMILY

Drawing by M. Stevens; © 1989 the New Yorker Magazine, Inc.

What is more important than learning the mathematical computations, however, is developing an understanding of when and why each type of statistic is used. The purpose of this appendix is to help you understand the significance of the statistics most commonly used.

GATHERING AND ORGANIZING DATA

Psychologists design their studies to facilitate gathering information about the factors they want to study. The information they obtain is known as **data** (**data** is plural; its singular is **datum**). When the data are gathered, they are generally in the form of numbers; if they aren't, they are converted to numbers. After they are gathered, the data must be organized in such a way that statistical analysis is possible. In the following section, we will examine the methods used to gather and organize information.

Variables

When studying a behavior, psychologists normally focus on one particular factor to determine whether it has an effect on the behavior. This factor is known as a **variable**, which is in effect anything that can assume more than one value (see Chapter 1). Height, weight, sex, eye color, and scores on an IQ test or a video game are all factors that can assume more than one value and are therefore variables. Some will vary between people, such as sex (you are either male *or* female but not both at the same time). Some may even vary within one person, such as scores on a video game (the same person might get 10,000 points on one try and only 800 on another). Opposed to a variable, anything that remains the same and does not vary is called a **constant**. If researchers use only females in their research, then sex is a constant, not a variable.

In nonexperimental studies, variables can be factors that are merely observed through naturalistic observation or case studies, or they can be factors about which people are questioned in a test or survey. In experimental studies, the two major types of variables are independent and dependent variables.

Independent variables are those that are manipulated by the experimenter. For example, suppose we were to conduct a study to determine whether the sex of the debater influences the outcome of a debate. In this study, one group of subjects watches a videotape of a debate between a male arguing the "pro" side and a female arguing the "con"; another group watches the same debate, but with the pro and con roles reversed. In such a study, the form of the presentation viewed by each group (whether "pro" is argued by a male or a female) is the independent variable because the experimenter manipulates the form of presentation seen by each group. Another example might be a study to determine whether a particular drug has any effect on a manual dexterity task. To study this question, we would administer the drug to one group and no drug to another. The independent variable would be the amount of drug given (some or none). The independent variable is particularly important when using inferential statistics, which we will discuss later.

The dependent variable is a factor that results from, or depends on, the independent variable. It is a measure of some outcome or, most commonly, a measure of the subjects' behavior. In the debate example, each subject's choice of the winner of the debate would be the dependent variable. In the drug experiment, the dependent variable would be each subject's score on the manual dexterity task.

Frequency Distributions

After conducting a study and obtaining measures of the variable(s) being studied, psychologists need to organize the data in a meaningful way. Table A.1 presents test scores from a statistics aptitude test collected from 50 college students. This information is called raw data because there is no order to the numbers. They are presented as they were collected and are therefore "raw."

The lack of order in raw data makes them difficult to study. Thus, the first step in understanding the results of an experiment is to impose some order on the raw data. There are several ways to do this. One of the simplest is to create a frequency distribution, which shows the number of times a score or event occurs. Although frequency distributions are helpful in several ways, the major advantages are that they allow us to see the data in an organized manner and they make it easier to represent the data on a graph.

The simplest way to make a frequency distribution is to list all the possible test scores, then tally the number of people (N) who received those scores. Table A.2 presents a frequency distribution using the raw data from Table A.1. As you can see, the data are now easier to read. From looking at the frequency dis-

Table A.1   Statistics Aptitude Test Scores for 50 College Students

73	57	63	59	50
72	66	50	67	51
63	59	65	62	65
62	72	64	73	66
61	68	62	68	63
59	61	72	63	52
59	58	57	68	57
64	56	65	59	60
50	62	68	54	63
52	62	70	60	68

Table A.2   Frequency Distribution of 50 Students on Statistics Aptitude Test

Score	Frequency
73	2
72	3
71	0
70	1
69	0
68	5
67	1
66	2
65	3
64	2
63	5
62	5
61	2
60	2
59	5
58	1
57	3
56	1
55	0
54	1
53	0
52	2
51	1
50	3
Total	50

tribution, you can see that most of the test scores lie in the middle with only a few at the very high or very low end. This was not at all evident from looking at the raw data.

This type of frequency distribution is practical when the number of possible scores is 20 or fewer. However, when there are more than 20 possible scores it can be even harder to make sense out of the frequency distribution than the raw data. This can be seen in Table A.3, which presents the life change units for 50 students. Even though there are only 50 actual scores in this table, the number of possible scores ranges from a high of 400 to a low of 150. If we included zero frequencies there would be 251 entries in a frequency distribution of this data, making the frequency distribution much more difficult to understand than the raw data. If there are more than 20 possible scores, therefore, a group frequency distribution is normally used.

In a group frequency distribution, individual scores are represented as members of a group of scores or as a range of scores (see Table A.4). These groups are called class intervals. Grouping these scores makes it much easier to make sense out of the distribution, as you can see from the relative ease in understanding Table A.4 as compared to Table A.3. Group frequency distributions are easier to represent on a graph.

When graphing data from frequency distributions, the class intervals are represented along the abscissa (the horizontal or x

Table A.3 Life Change Units for 50 College Students

150	175	375	210	400
216	300	175	374	163
263	152	176	185	192
197	233	216	241	221
232	316	233	357	321
368	300	277	298	254
274	216	285	219	276
222	245	264	233	361
242	304	251	176	221
165	212	222	196	196

axis), whereas the frequency is represented along the ordinate (the vertical or *y* axis). Information can be graphed in the form of a bar graph, called a **histogram,** or in the form of a point or line graph, called a **polygon.** Figure A.1 shows a histogram presenting the data from Table A.4. Note that the class intervals are represented along the bottom line of the graph (the *x* axis) and the height of the bars indicates the frequency in each class interval. Now look at Figure A.2. The information presented here is exactly the same as that in Figure A.1 but is represented in the form of a polygon rather than a histogram. Can you see how both graphs illustrate the same information? Even though reading information from a graph is simple, we have found that many students have never learned to read graphs. In the next section we will explain how to read a graph.

How to Read a Graph

Every graph has several major parts. The most important are the labels, the axes (the vertical and horizontal lines), and the points, lines, or bars. Find these parts in Figure A.1.

Table A.4 Group Frequency Distribution of Life Change Unit Scores for 50 College Students

Life Change Units	
Class Interval	Frequency
400–424	1
375–399	1
350–374	4
325–349	0
300–324	5
275–299	4
250–274	5
225–249	7
200–224	10
175–199	9
150–174	4
Total	50

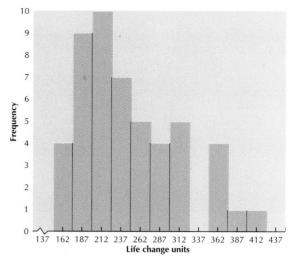

Figure A.1 A histogram illustrating the information found in Table A.4.

The first thing you should notice when reading a graph are the labels because they tell what data are portrayed. Usually the data consist of the descriptive statistics, or the numbers used to measure the dependent variables. For example, in Figure A.1 the horizontal axis is labeled "Life Change Units," which is the dependent variable measure; the vertical axis is labeled "Frequency," which means the number of occurrences. If a graph is not labeled, as we sometimes see in TV commercials or magazine ads, it is useless and should be ignored. Even when a graph *is* labeled, the labels can be misleading. For example, if graph designers want to distort the information, they can elongate one of the axes. Thus, it is important to pay careful attention to the numbers as well as the words in graph labels.

Next, you should focus your attention on the bars, points, or lines on the graph. In the case of histograms like the one in Figure A.1, each bar represents the mean (average) in a class interval. The width of the bar stands for the width of the class interval, whereas the height of the bar stands for the frequency in that interval. Look at the third bar from the left in Figure A.1. This bar represents the interval "200–224 life change units," which has a frequency of 10. You can see that this directly corresponds to the same class interval in Table A.4, since graphs and tables are both merely alternate ways of illustrating information.

Reading point or line graphs is the same as reading a histogram. In a point graph, each point represents two numbers, one found along the horizontal axis and the other found along the vertical axis. A polygon is identical to a point graph except that it has lines connecting the points. Figure A.2 is an example of a polygon, where each point represents a class interval and is placed at the center of the interval and at the height corresponding to the frequency of that interval. To make the graph easier to read, the points are connected by straight lines.

Displaying the data in a frequency distribution or in a graph is much more useful than merely presenting raw data and can be especially helpful when researchers are trying to find relations between certain factors. However, as we explained earlier, if psychologists want to make predictions or explanations about behavior, they need to perform mathematical computations on the data.

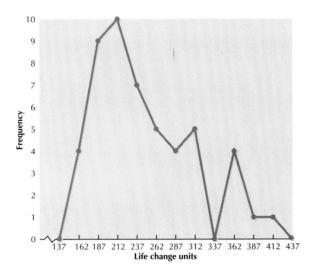

Figure A.2 A polygon illustrating the information found in Table A.4.

USES OF THE VARIOUS STATISTICS

The statistics psychologists use in a study depend on whether they are trying to describe and predict behavior or explain it. When they use statistics to describe behavior, as in reporting the average score on the Scholastic Aptitude Test, they are using **descriptive statistics**. When they use them to explain behavior, as Bandura did in his study of children modeling aggressive behavior seen on TV, they are using **inferential statistics**.

Descriptive Statistics

Descriptive statistics are the numbers used to describe the dependent variable. They can be used to describe characteristics of a **population** (an entire group, such as all people living in the United States) or a **sample** (a part of a group, such as a randomly selected group of 25 students from Cornell University). The major descriptive statistics include measures of central tendency (mean, median, and mode), measures of variation (variance and standard deviation), and correlation.

Measures of Central Tendency

Statistics indicating the center of the distribution are called **measures of central tendency** and include the mean, median, and mode. They are all scores that are typical of the center of the distribution. The **mean** is what most of us think of when we hear the word "average." The **median** is the middle score. The **mode** is the score that occurs most often.

Mean. What is your average golf score? What is the average yearly rainfall in your part of the country? What is the average reading test score in your city? When these questions ask for the average, they are really asking for the "mean." The arithmetic **mean** is the weighted average of all the raw scores, which is computed by totaling all the raw scores and then dividing that total by the number of scores added together. In statistical computation, the mean is represented by an "X" with a bar above it ($\overline{X}$, pronounced "X bar"), each individual raw score by an "X," and the total number of scores by an "N." For example, if we

wanted to compute the $\overline{X}$ of the raw statistics test scores in Table A.1, we would sum all the X's (ΣX, with Σ meaning sum) and divide by N (number of scores). In Table A.1, the sum of all the scores is equal to 3,100 and there are 50 scores. Therefore, the mean of these scores is

$$\overline{X} = \frac{3,100}{50} = 62$$

Table A.5 illustrates how to calculate the mean for 10 IQ scores.

Table A.5   **Computation of the Mean for 10 IQ Scores**

IQ Scores X
143
127
116
98
85
107
106
98
104
116
$\Sigma X = 1{,}100$

$$\text{Mean} = \overline{X} = \frac{\Sigma X}{N} = \frac{1{,}100}{10} = 110$$

Table A.6   **Computation of Median for Odd and Even Numbers of IQ Scores**

IQ	IQ
139	137
130	135
121	121
116	116
107	108 ← middle score
101	106 ← middle score
98	105
96 ← middle score	101
84	98
83	97
82	$N = 10$
75	N is even
75	
65	$\text{Median} = \dfrac{106 + 108}{2} = 107$
62	

$N = 15$
N is odd
Median = 96

Table A.7 Finding the Mode for Two Different Distributions

IQ	IQ
139	139
138	138
125	125
116 ←	116 ←
116 ←	116 ←
116 ←	116 ←
107	107
100	98 ←
98	98 ←
98	98 ←
Mode = most frequent score	Mode = 116 and 98
Mode = 116	

Median. The **median** is the middle score in the distribution once all the scores have been arranged in rank order. If N (the number of scores) is odd, then there actually is a middle score and that middle score is the median. When N is even, there are two middle scores and the median is the mean of those two scores. Table A.6 shows the computation of the median for two different sets of scores, one set with 15 scores and one with 10.

Mode. Of all the measures of central tendency, the easiest to compute is the **mode**, which is merely the most frequent score. It is computed by finding the score that occurs most often. Whereas there is always only one mean and only one median for each distribution, there can be more than one mode. Table A.7 shows how to find the mode in a distribution with one mode (unimodal) and in a distribution with two modes (bimodal).

There are several advantages to each of these measures of central tendency, but in psychological research the mean is used most often. A book solely covering psychological statistics will provide a more thorough discussion of the relative values of these measures. (See the Suggested Readings at the end of Appendix A.)

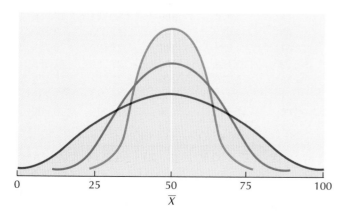

Figure A.3 Three distributions having the same mean but a different variability.

Measures of Variation

When describing a distribution, it is not sufficient merely to give the central tendency; it is also necessary to give a **measure of variation**, which is a measure of the spread of the scores. By examining the spread, we can determine whether the scores are bunched around the middle or tend to extend away from the middle. Figure A.3 shows three different distributions, all with the same mean but with different spreads of scores. You can see from this figure that, in order to describe these different distributions accurately, there must be some measures of the variation in their spread. The most widely used measure of variation is the standard deviation, which is represented by a lowercase s. The standard deviation is a standard measurement of how much the scores in a distribution deviate from the mean. The formula for the standard deviation is

$$s = \sqrt{\frac{\Sigma(X - \overline{X})^2}{N}}$$

Table A.8 illustrates how to compute the standard deviation.

Most distributions of psychological data are bell-shaped. That is, most of the scores are grouped around the mean, and the farther the scores are from the mean in either direction, the fewer the scores. Notice the bell shape of the distribution in Figure A.4. Distributions such as this are called **normal** distributions. In normal distributions, as shown in Figure A.4, approximately two-thirds of the scores fall within a range that is one standard deviation below the mean to one standard deviation above the mean. For example, the Wechsler IQ tests (see Chapter 8) have a mean of 100 and a standard deviation of 15. This means that approximately two-thirds of the people taking these tests will have scores above 85 and below 115.

Correlation

Suppose for a moment that you are sitting in the student union with a friend. To pass the time, you and your friend decide to

Table A.8 Computation of the Standard Deviation for 10 IQ Scores

IQ Scores X	$X - \overline{X}$	$(X - \overline{X})^2$
143	33	1089
127	17	289
116	6	36
98	−12	144
85	−25	625
107	−3	9
106	−4	16
98	−12	144
104	−6	36
116	6	36
$\Sigma X = 1100$		$\Sigma(X - \overline{X})^2 = 2424$

$$\text{Standard Deviation} = s = \sqrt{\frac{\Sigma(X - \overline{X})^2}{N}} = \sqrt{\frac{224}{10}}$$

$$= \sqrt{22.4} = 15.569$$

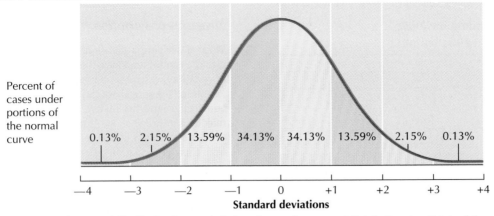

Figure A.4 The normal distribution forms a bell-shaped curve. In a normal distribution, two-thirds of the scores lie between one standard deviation above and one standard deviation below the mean.

play a game in which you try to guess the height of the next male who enters the union. The winner, the one whose guess is closest to the person's actual height, gets a free piece of pie paid for by the loser. When it is your turn, what do you guess? If you are like most people, you will probably try to estimate the mean of all the males in the union and use that as your guess. The mean is always your best guess if you have no other information.

Now let's change the game a little and add a friend who stands outside the union and weighs the next male to enter the union. Before the male enters the union, your friend says "125 pounds." Given this new information, will you still guess the mean height? Probably not—you will probably predict *below* the mean. Why? Because there is a **correlation**, a relationship, between height and weight, with tall people usually weighing more than short people. Since 125 pounds is less than the average weight for males, you will probably guess a less-than-average height. The statistic used to measure this type of relationship between two variables is called a correlation coefficient.

Correlation Coefficient. A correlation coefficient measures the relationship between two variables, such as height and weight or IQ and SAT scores. Given any two variables, there are three possible relationships between them: **positive, negative,** and **zero** (no relationship). A positive relationship exists when the two variables vary in the same direction (e.g., as height increases, weight normally also increases). A negative relationship occurs when the two variables vary in opposite directions (e.g., as temperatures go up, hot chocolate sales go down). There is no relationship when the two variables vary totally independently of one another (e.g., there is no relationship between peoples' height and the color of their toothbrushes). Figure A.5 illustrates these three types of correlations.

The computation and the formula for a correlation coefficient (correlation coefficient is delineated by the letter "*r*") are shown in Table A.9. The correlation coefficient (*r*) always has a value between + 1 and − 1 (it is never greater than + 1 and it is never smaller than − 1). When *r* is close to + 1, it signifies a high positive relationship between the two variables (as one variable goes up, the other variable also goes up). When *r* is close to − 1, it signifies a high negative relationship between the two variables (as one variable goes up, the other variable goes down). When *r* is 0, there is no linear relationship between the two variables being measured.

Correlation coefficients can be quite helpful in making pre-

dictions. Bear in mind, however, that predictions are just that: *predictions.* They will have some error as long as the correlation coefficients on which they are based are not perfect (+ 1 or − 1). Also, correlations cannot reveal any information regarding causation. Merely because two factors are correlated, it does not mean that one factor causes the other. Consider, for example, ice cream consumption and swimming pool use. These two variables are positively correlated with one another, in that as ice cream consumption increases, so does swimming pool use. But nobody would suggest that eating ice cream *causes* swimming, or vice versa. Similarly, just because Michael Jordan eats Wheaties and can do a slam dunk it does not mean that you will be able to do one if you eat the same breakfast. The only way to determine the cause of behavior is to conduct an experiment and analyze the results by using inferential statistics.

Table A.9 Computation of Correlation Coefficient between Height and Weight for 10 Male Subjects

Height (inches) X	X²	Weight (pounds) Y	Y²	XY
73	5,329	210	44,100	15,330
64	4,096	133	17,689	8,512
65	4,225	128	16,384	8,320
70	4,900	156	24,336	10,920
74	5,476	189	35,721	13,986
68	4,624	145	21,025	9,860
67	4,489	145	21,025	9,715
72	5,184	166	27,556	11,952
76	5,776	199	37,601	15,124
71	5,041	159	25,281	11,289
700	41,140	1,630	272,718	115,008

$$r = \frac{N \cdot \Sigma XY - \Sigma X \cdot \Sigma Y}{\sqrt{[N \cdot \Sigma X^2 - (\Sigma X)^2]} \sqrt{[N \cdot \Sigma Y^2 - (\Sigma Y)^2]}}$$

$$r = \frac{10 \cdot 115,008 - 700 \cdot 1,630}{\sqrt{[10 \cdot 49,140 - 700^2]} \sqrt{[10 \cdot 272,718 - 1,630^2]}}$$

$$r = 0.92$$

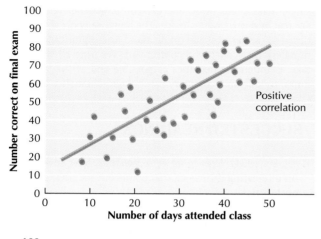

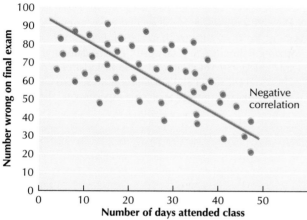

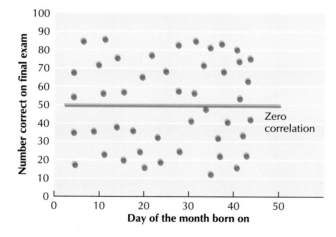

Figure A.5 Three types of correlation. Positive correlation (top): As the number of days of class attendance increases, so does the number of exam items correct. Negative correlation (middle): As the number of days of class attendance increases, the number of incorrect exam items decreases. Zero correlation (bottom): The day of the month on which one is born has no relationship to the number of exam items correct.

Inferential Statistics

Knowing the descriptive statistics associated with different distributions, such as the mean and standard deviation, can enable us to make comparisons between various distributions. By making these comparisons, we may be able to observe whether

one variable is related to another or whether one variable has a causal effect on another. When we design an experiment specifically to measure causal effects between two or more variables, we use **inferential statistics** to analyze the data collected. Although there are many inferential statistics, the one we will discuss is the *t*-test, since it is the simplest.

t-Test

Suppose we believe that drinking alcohol causes a person's reaction time to slow down. To test this hypothesis, we recruit 20 subjects and separate them into two groups. We ask the subjects in one group to drink a large glass of orange juice with one ounce of alcohol for every 100 pounds of body weight (e.g., a person weighing 150 pounds would get 1.5 ounces of alcohol). We ask the control group to drink an equivalent amount of orange juice with no alcohol added. Fifteen minutes after the drinks, we have each subject perform a reaction time test that consists of pushing a button as soon as a light is flashed. (The reaction time is the time between the onset of the light and the pressing of the button.) Table A.10 shows the data from this hypothetical experiment. It is clear from the data that there is definitely a difference in the reaction times of the two groups: There is an obvious difference between the means. However, it is possible that this difference is due merely to chance. To determine whether the difference is real or due to chance, we can conduct a *t*-test. We have run a sample *t*-test in Table A.10.

Table A.10 **Reaction Times in Milliseconds (msec) for Subjects in Alcohol and No Alcohol Conditions and Computation of *t***

RT (msec) Alcohol X_1	RT (msec) No Alcohol X_2
200	143
210	137
140	179
160	184
180	156
187	132
196	176
198	148
140	125
159	120
$\Sigma X_1 = 1{,}770$	$\Sigma X_2 = 1{,}500$
$N_1 = 10$	$N_2 = 10$
$\overline{X}_1 = 177$	$\overline{X}_2 = 150$
$s_1 = 24.25$	$s_2 = 21.86$

$$S_{\overline{X}_1} = \frac{s}{\sqrt{N_1 - 1}} = 8.08 \qquad S_{\overline{X}_2} = \frac{s}{\sqrt{N_2 - 1}} = 7.29$$

$$S_{\overline{X}_1 - \overline{X}_2} = \sqrt{S_{\overline{X}_1}{}^2 + S_{\overline{X}_2}{}^2} = \sqrt{8.08^2 + 7.29^2} = 10.88$$

$$t = \frac{\overline{X}_1 - \overline{X}_2}{S_{\overline{X}_1 - \overline{X}_2}} = \frac{177 - 150}{10.88} = 2.48$$

$$t = 2.48, p < .05$$

The logic behind a *t*-test is relatively simple. In our experiment we have two samples. If each of these samples is from the *same* population (e.g., the population of all people, whether drunk or sober), then any difference between the samples will be due to chance. On the other hand, if the two samples are from *different* populations (e.g., the population of drunk people *and* the population of sober people), then the difference is a significant difference and not due to chance.

If there is a significant difference between the two samples, then the independent variable must have caused that difference. In our example, there is a significant difference between the alcohol and the no alcohol groups. We can tell this because *p* (the probability that this *t* value will occur by chance) is less than .05. To obtain the *p*, we need only look up the *t* value in a statistical table, which is found in any statistics book. In our example, because there is a significant difference between the groups, we can reasonably conclude that the alcohol did cause a slower reaction time.

As research designs grow more and more complicated, the statistics needed to analyze them grow more and more complex. However, as this appendix has demonstrated, even simple research can benefit from statistics. By using statistics we can make observations about distributions of data, observe relationships, make predictions, and determine whether relationships are real or due to mere chance. The more we know about statistics, the better we will understand the significance of the numbers that constantly confront us. We urge all students to take as much mathematics as possible and at the very minimum, to take an elementary psychological statistics course.

SUGGESTED READINGS

HUFF, D. (1954). *How to lie with statistics.* New York: Norton. An interesting little book that points out the uses and abuses of statistics.

STANOVICH, K. E. (1991). *How to think straight about psychology* (3rd ed.). New York: HarperCollins College. This book offers sound advice on how to evaluate psychological and pseudopsychological research.

VERNOY, M. W., & VERNOY, J. A. (1991). *Behavioral statistics in action.* Belmont, CA: Wadsworth. This readable and appealing introduction to the study of the use of statistics in psychology covers all the major statistical procedures, from creating frequency distributions to analyzing experimental data.

Applied Psychology

Do you have trouble operating your VCR? Have you ever wondered why a pot of water wasn't boiling and then discovered that you had turned on the wrong burner? Do you sometimes wonder how noise pollution affects your behavior? What about urban crime? Do you think it's caused by overpopulation and crowding? The field of *applied psychology* tackles questions such as these.

Applied psychology uses psychological principles and methods to investigate and help solve human problems. There are many areas of applied psychology, some of which we discussed in the text. Clinical and counseling psychologists, for example, apply the principles and methods of psychology to help clients with mental disorders and academic or vocational problems (see Chapter 16). Health psychologists apply psychological principles to prevent and treat stress and disease (see Chapter 13). In this appendix, we will focus on two additional areas of applied psychology—industrial/organizational psychology and environmental psychology.

INDUSTRIAL/ORGANIZATIONAL PSYCHOLOGY

We Americans take justifiable pride in our technological advancements, but we rank fifth in productivity compared with other industrialized nations (Hatfield, 1990). Production problems, foreign debt, and trade deficits have all brought increasing attention to the field of **industrial/organizational (I/O) psychology**. I/O psychology studies how individual behavior is affected by the work environment, organizations, and coworkers. Psychologists who work in this field are frequently employed by business, industry, and the government, and they focus on three major areas: (1) human factors engineering (improving the design and function of machines and the work environment); (2) personnel psychology (recruitment, testing, training, placement, and evaluation of workers); and (3) interpersonal relations in the work setting (worker motivation and productivity, managerial styles, and job satisfaction).

Human Factors Engineering

The goal of human factors engineering is to make appliance and machinery design compatible with normal human sensory and motor capacities. While you may blame yourself because you can't program your VCR or work your electric range on the first try, a human factors engineer would say the fault more likely lies in poorly designed machines (Heron, 1991; Norman, 1988). Human factors research not only reduces our daily frustrations, but it also helps prevent accidents involving machinery (stove tops, computers, nuclear power plants) and vehicles (automobiles, airplanes, trains). For example, the knob arrangement on the right of Figure B.1a not only makes it easy to turn on the correct stove burner, but it makes it easy to turn off the right knob in an emergency. Similarly, placing fuel and oil gauges and the speedometer above the steering wheel for easy visibility means drivers only need to take their eyes off the road for a split second (see Figure B.1b). In addition to designing for spatial correspondence and visibility, human factors engineering tries to correlate shape and function. As you can see in Figure B.1c, the shape of the landing gear knob and landing flap controls mimic those parts of the plane. This design takes advantage of the pilot's sense of touch and allows him or her to operate these controls while simultaneously monitoring gauges.

Donald A. Norman (1988), a prominent human factors psychologist, emphasizes the importance of *natural design*. Good design, says Norman, makes use of logical arrangements and signals that are intuitively understood by people. Just as the controls for a stove top should be arranged in a pattern that reflects the placement of the burners (see Figure B.1a), knobs and buttons should operate only one function. (This explains why most people have difficulty with single-knob shower faucets that control both the hot and cold water.) Also, well-designed appliances and machinery should provide clear and immediate feedback. The audible click of the keys on a typewriter and the tones you hear as you press numbers for a phone call are examples of effective feedback design.

Human factors psychologists consult not only on machinery design, but also when employees suffer from work-related illnesses and injuries. They design equipment and analyze working conditions to minimize worker stress and physical damage to tendons, ligaments, and joints (Sanders and McCormick, 1993).

Personnel Psychology

Do you realize that work consumes the largest percentage of hours in your lifetime? Or that the quality of your life is closely related to the satisfaction you receive from your work? Just as you need a job that maximizes your happiness and satisfaction, business and industry need employees who have the skills and ability to maximize their productivity. I/O psychologists play an important role in locating the "right person for the right job."

Figure B.1 *Psychology of everyday things.* Well-designed appliances and machinery are easily understood and operated. (a) The controls for stove tops should be arranged in a pattern that corresponds to the placement of burners. (b) In an automobile, gauges for fuel, oil, and speed should be easily visible to the driver. (c) Controls and knobs are easier to use if their shape corresponds to their function. For example, a pilot could rely on a sense of touch to let down wheels for landing and adjust wing flaps.

(a) Spatial Correspondence

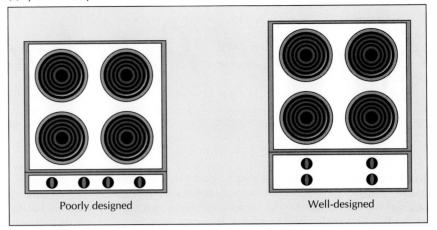

Poorly designed   Well-designed

(b) Visibility

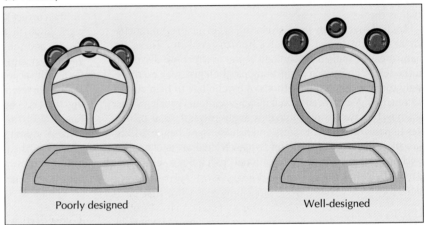

Poorly designed   Well-designed

(c) Shape Indicates Function

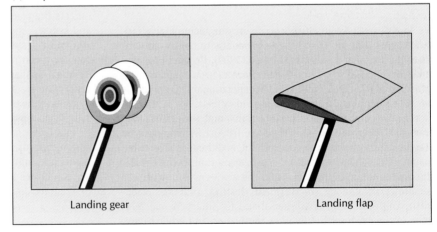

Landing gear   Landing flap

They are also responsible for training new employees in an organization, upgrading employee skills, and developing objective criteria to evaluate employee performance.

Personnel selection typically begins with a *job analysis*. For example, the job of a college instructor is to teach classes, assist students during office hours, prepare and grade exams and papers, attend departmental meetings, serve on college committees, and so on. In addition, many colleges and universities expect a high level of academic research and publication. By identifying the duties and responsibilities for a position such as "college instructor," the I/O psychologist can improve the match between employer and employee.

Once the job analysis is complete and the field of candidates has been narrowed, the next step is selecting the best person for the job. The measures most often used include interviews, standardized psychological tests, performance tests, and evaluation of *biodata* (detailed biographical information). Because of their training, I/O psychologists are certified to use intelligence tests (see Chapter 8), vocational interest tests, and personality tests (see Chapter 14). These tests help determine the suitability of a candidate for a given job.

After applicants are tested and interviewed and the best candidate is hired, the I/O psychologist helps in training, placement, and evaluation. Research shows that training not only provides workers with appropriate skills for the assigned job, but it also reduces worker frustration and stress (Saal and Knight, 1988). In addition, research shows that employees fare better when their work is evaluated, when reinforcers are closely related to job performance, and when criticism is delivered constructively (Baron, 1990; Locke and Latham, 1990).

Interpersonal Relations in the Work Setting

In addition to recruitment, hiring, training, placement, and evaluation, I/O psychologists work to improve employee motivation, productivity, and job satisfaction. One of the most important aspects of worker efficiency and satisfaction is an employer's *managerial style.*

Douglas McGregor (1960) has identified two basic types of managers whose approaches reflect different assumptions about human nature. *Theory X* managers believe that employees must be prodded or manipulated into being productive. As a result, they use close supervision, work quotas, bonuses, and commissions to motivate their workers. *Theory Y* managers, however, believe that employees enjoy autonomy and work that challenges their potential and allows for some creativity. In other words, Theory X assumes workers are lazy and motivated by extrinsic rewards such as money, whereas Theory Y believes workers are industrious and motivated by intrinsic rewards such as challenging work.

As businesses and industry come to recognize that workers' self-esteem and satisfaction are important to job efficiency, Theory Y is becoming increasingly popular. Two key Theory Y methods are *participatory management* and *management by objectives.* "Quality circles" are one form of participatory management. Workers, managers, and employers all meet and discuss ways to promote efficiency and employee satisfaction (Jewell, 1990; Matsui and Onglatco, 1990). In management by objectives, employees are assigned specific goals to meet, but allowed some freedom in choosing how they will achieve their goals. When workers are able to tell when they are doing a good job and given a greater voice in how their work will be accomplished, both efficiency and job satisfaction are improved (Katzell and Thompson, 1990; Levi, 1990; Rodgers and Hunter, 1991).

Industrial/organizational psychologists play many roles in the world of work. Their training and background in psychological principles and methods enable them to help employee and employer make a good match. On the job, I/O psychologists help increase personal job satisfaction and overall efficiency. After this brief survey of the ways psychology has been applied to business and industry, we now turn our attention to a second area of applied psychology—the environment.

ENVIRONMENTAL PSYCHOLOGY

Environmental psychology focuses on the relationship between psychological processes and the physical environment. We will explore three areas in environmental psychology: territoriality, crowding, and social traps.

Territoriality

In Chapter 18 you learned that people like to maintain a certain distance between themselves and other people. This *personal space* varies among individuals, between cultures, and in different settings (intimate distances, casual conversation, and so on). People also have a need to stake out and mark certain areas as their own. This behavior, known as **territoriality**, can take such forms as building fences around homes or leaving a coat or books to mark "your" spot in a classroom.

Territorial marking appears to serve many functions. It distinguishes "insiders" (those who are allowed access to the area) from "outsiders," it decreases conflict (the first in line get the first tickets), and it establishes zones of privacy (a stack of books on an adjacent chair provides "protection" from unwanted intrusion). The importance of territoriality was demonstrated at a *Who* concert in Cleveland in 1979. Because of a break in security, almost 7000 fans with unreserved (general admission) tickets rushed to get as close as possible to the stage. Eleven people were trampled to death in the confusion. Recognizing that the norms associated with territoriality provide social control, most concert organizers today require reserved seating.

Crowding

Every day the earth adds about 200,000 new people (births minus deaths). At this rate, world population will double within the next 35 years. What will your life be like with twice as many people on our finite planet? How will colleges and the workplace deal with twice the number of students, workers, and commuters? Not only will there be more congestion, there will be increased competition for jobs and housing, and for leisure time activities such as skiing, camping at national parks, and concerts and sporting events.

Given the implications of our ever-increasing population, a great deal of research has been conducted concerning the effects of crowding and overpopulation. One of the earliest and most influential studies of environmental issues was done by John Calhoun (1962). To study the effects of increased population, Calhoun created a rat "utopia" with unlimited food, water, and nesting material (see Figure B.2). Since this study has been widely quoted in the popular press as evidence for the general problems of overpopulation, you may already be aware of the findings: The rats became hypersexual, aggressive, cannibalistic, and hyperactive or extremely lethargic.

After Calhoun's study was published, there were also several research studies that documented a strong correlation between human population density and mental illness, crime, and delinquency (Altman, 1975; Freedman, 1975). Using these data, many people concluded that the pathological behaviors found in some ghetto areas in modern cities were *caused* by overpopulation. As noted in Chapter 1, however, correlational studies can never prove causation. In this case, closer examination revealed that the negative effects of crowding were confounded by the fact that socioeconomic factors are also related to crowding (Steinhart, 1986). Since it is usually the poor who live in the most crowded environments, it may be that poverty, not crowding per se, is the most important factor in the negative behaviors associated with high-density city living.

Crowding versus Density

Experiments and correlational studies that *have* controlled for economic factors found a wide variety of responses to crowding, ranging from no ill effects to serious, long-term negative reactions (Fisher et al., 1984; Rattner, 1990). Such variations led researchers to distinguish between **density**, the actual number of people in a given space, and **crowding**, the negative psychological experience of being exposed to a larger number of people than you prefer. People can obviously enjoy high-density conditions during rock concerts, football games, and parties, but they would find the same concentration of people to be stressful or intolerable under other conditions. Crowding is a subjective judgment that we make when (1) *density* interferes with our goals, (2) we feel a lack of control, and (3) we experience **information overload**—having to deal with more information than we can process (Bell, Fisher, and Baum, 1990; Cohen, 1978).

Is it crowding or poverty that best explains the high level of crime, delinquency, and mental illness in certain areas of large cities?

Figure B.2 Calhoun and his "rat utopia." John Calhoun found that rats who were allowed unlimited access to food, water, and nesting material overpopulated and developed several maladaptive behaviors, such as cannibalism and increased aggression. How does overpopulation and crowding affect human behavior?

Environmental Design

Environmental psychologists have found that the design of residential and office spaces can have a dramatic effect on perceptions of crowding and individual satisfaction and productivity (Carter, 1992; Nassar, 1988). For instance, one study found that when three students were assigned to a dorm room rather than two, residents reported feeling crowded and more dissatisfied with college life, and they liked their roommates less. They also obtained lower grade point averages (Gormley and Aiello, 1982). Similarly, traditional dorm architecture (a single long row of rooms) is less desired by college students than the more modern suite arrangement (see Figure B.3). Studies show that students who live in suites spend more time in their dorms, express greater desire to interact with other residents, and feel that they have more control over what happens in the dorms than residents of traditional style dorms (Baum and Valins, 1977). It may be that the traditional dorm arrangement is too isolating, while the suite design allows both a controlled level of social interaction and room to "escape."

Environmental design can influence the general perception of crowding, but personality differences are also important. For example, the urban dweller who loves the exciting night life would feel less crowded and stressed by a high-density area than would a small-town resident who loves a quiet, star-lit evening. Similarly, international comparisons demonstrate wide cultural variations in the effects of crowding and density on human behavior. The density of Japan's population is 12 times greater than that of the United States, yet their homicide rate is 9 times

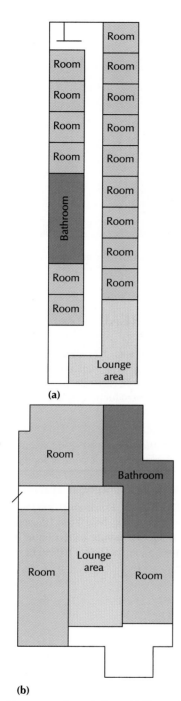

(a)

(b)

Figure B.3 Architecture and psychology. (a) Most college dorms are arranged in a single corridor, with bedrooms aligned down a long hallway and one large lounge and bathroom shared by all. (b) In a suite-style dorm, the number of students per square foot is about the same, but students complain less about crowding and lack of privacy and control. (Source: Baum & Valins, 1977.)

lower (Statistical Abstracts, 1990; United States Census Bureau, 1990).

As you can see, crowding and density are complex issues. What makes the city dweller love a higher density atmosphere more than the rural resident? How can the Japanese maintain such a low crime rate despite their high density? The challenge for environmental psychologists is to explain these differences and to help develop strategies to maximize the satisfaction and feelings of control for people of all cultures.

Social Traps

Attempts to change people's behavior concerning the environment, whether the issue is overpopulation, pollution, or depletion of the earth's resources, are too often beset by **social traps**, or social dilemmas. These traps arise because individuals pursue their own immediate self-interests at the expense of long-term individual benefits or the collective best interests of the group. Early American cattle owners who overgrazed shared pastureland are often cited as a prime example of social traps. Because each owner attempted to obtain as much milk and meat as possible, the pastures were destroyed—resulting in less milk and meat for everyone. Social traps are also referred to as "the tragedy of the commons" (Hardin, 1968).

Modern examples of social traps are easily found: Wilderness campers who toss their trash in the bushes ("What difference does this one piece of trash make in all this space?"); automobile drivers who resist using mass transit systems or car pools ("What difference does my one car make?"); and governments that continue to stockpile weapons ("What difference does one more gun make?"). Thanks, in part, to the "logic" of each of these positions we have polluted wilderness areas, dangerous smog levels and horrendous traffic jams, and enough nuclear weapons to destroy the planet 30 times over.

Solutions

Environmental psychologists offer several suggestions to sidestepping social traps:

1. *Change the payoff.* When laboratory experiments with social traps made cooperation toward mutual goals more rewarding than individualistic competition, subjects quickly recognized the difference and adjusted their behavior (McDaniel and Sistrunk, 1991). Power companies change the payoff when they give rebates or lower rates for use during off-peak hours, highway planners use this technique by installing carpool lanes on freeways, and you do it when you vote in favor of laws that punish those who pollute.

2. *Increase communication.* People who are locked into social traps must be able to communicate directly with one another (Dawes, 1987; Mannix and White, 1992). Through improved education, people can also be encouraged to examine the long- versus short-term consequences of their behavior (Messick and Mackie, 1989).

3. *Set a good example.* In one study of littering, a "Drive Carefully" handbill was placed under the windshield wipers of cars in a parking garage (Cialdini et al., 1990). On the way to their cars, people passed through either a litter-free garage or a garage sprinkled with other "Drive Carefully" handbills. In addition, some subjects were exposed to a model who either littered or didn't litter the garage. As Figure B.4 shows, littering was greatest when it was directly modeled by someone else and when it was indirectly modeled by the sight of the previously littered garage. In sum, when you

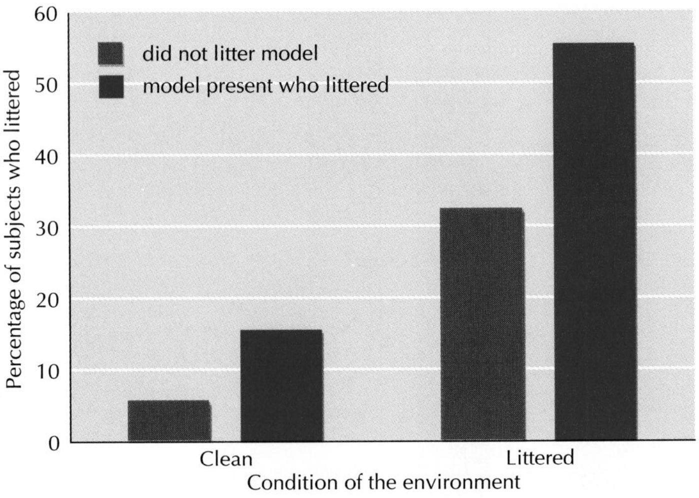

Figure B.4 Environmental influences on littering. Subjects were significantly more likely to fall into the social trap of littering if they were in a littered environment and saw someone littering. Conversely, the opposite was also true. What does this study tell you about the importance of an individual's impact on the environment? (Source: Cialdini, Reno, & Kallgren, 1990.)

model desirable behavior, you show others how to break out of a social trap.

Just as our coverage of industrial/organizational psychology was necessarily brief, so too has been our discussion of environmental psychology. One of the biggest frustrations for authors of an introductory psychology text, or instructors of introductory psychology classes, is that space and time allow us to only briefly expose our readers and students to the entire field of psychology. Our fondest wish is that after reading our text you will be excited about psychology and will continue your exploration into the field by taking additional courses. If you would like to write to us with comments on the text or about psychology in general, please do so. You can address your letter to any one of us at: *Palomar College, 1140 W. Mission Rd., San Marcos, CA 92069.* We would like to hear from you—psychologists need feedback, too!

SUGGESTED READINGS

BARON, R. A., & GREENBERG, J. (1990). *Behavior in organizations: Understanding and managing the human side of work* (3rd ed.). Boston: Allyn Bacon. This up-to-date text provides a broad introduction to the field of industrial/organizational psychology.

SANDERS, M. S., & McCORMICK, E. J. (1993). *Human factors in engineering and design* (7th ed.). New York: McGraw-Hill. This text surveys major contemporary theories and applications in the area of human factors, with a special focus on how design influences human performance.

WHITE, R. K. (Ed.). (1986). *Psychology and the prevention of nuclear war.* New York: New York University Press. An interesting and enlightening collection of 35 essays that discuss the psychological factors related to war and peace.

Answers to Review Questions

CHAPTER ONE

Page 14
1. Psychology is the *scientific* study of behavior.   2. Overt behaviors are easily observed, whereas covert behaviors are not observable.   3. describe, explain, predict, change;   4. Basic research is conducted to study a theoretical question with no regard for immediate real-world applications, whereas applied research is conducted specifically to solve an existing problem or answer a particular question.   5. pseudopsychologies.

Page 19
1. In an experiment, researchers isolate one single factor and examine the effect of it alone on a behavior.   2. hypothesis;   3. variables;   4. independent, dependent;   5. control;   6. to avoid experimenter bias.

Page 24
1. naturalistic observation;   2. population;   3. Case studies are used when a topic of study is so rare that it is impossible to gather enough subjects to conduct an experiment.   4. Absolutely not—the only technique that definitively determines cause is an experiment.   5. statistics;   6. Researchers replicate a study to substantiate it.

Page 28
1. confederate;   2. debriefed;   3. it is impossible to use humans and when the research has been approved by animal care committees.

Page 34
1. structuralist;   2. Functionalists;   3. Instead of using experimental research methods, Freud used the case-study method and developed his theory using his disturbed patients as subjects, with no "normal" controls.   4. gestalt;   5. humanistic;   6. cognitive psychology;   7. psychobiology;   8. Answers will vary, but perhaps you would take an eclectic approach.

CHAPTER TWO

Page 42
1. central, the brain and the spinal cord, peripheral, the remaining nerves outside the CNS;   2. Check your diagram against Figure 2.2.   3. action potential;   4. A neuron is a single nerve cell with three parts: the soma, the dendrites, and the axon, whereas a nerve is a bundle of axons having a similar function.   5. sodium, potassium;   6. The sodium-potassium pump removes excess sodium left in the cell following an action potential.   7. Because myelinization is not complete until

about age 12, the six-year-old's action potentials travel slower than her older sister's.

Page 48
1. synapse;   2. excitatory, inhibitory;   3. The endocrine system consists of glands that secrete hormones into the bloodstream.   4. the body's steady state of normal functioning.

Page 50
1. The somatic system conveys incoming sensory information and outgoing motor information; the autonomic maintains homeostasis.   2. to, from;   3. parasympathetic before, sympathetic after.

Page 63
1. A reflex occurs when information passes from a sensory receptor to the spinal cord and then to a muscle, bypassing the brain. A reflex increases the speed at which you can respond to a potentially harmful stimulus.   2. cerebral cortex;   3. frontal, occipital, temporal + parietal + frontal, parietal;   4. corpus callosum;   5. thalamus;   6. homeostasis;   7. pons, medulla, reticular formation.

Page 69
1. anatomical;   2. Permanent damage is inflicted to a living animal and once damaged, the researcher is no longer observing a normal brain.   3. electrodes;   4. Electrodes deliver small electrical currents to a particular part of the brain and the subject reports the response, which can be seeing flashes of lights, a memory, an odor, etc.   5. split;   6. left, right;   7. CAT, PET, MRI; MRI

CHAPTER THREE

Page 78
1. sensation;   2. Nerve receptors convert a stimulus into neural impulses that travel via neurons to the brain.   3. reticular activating system;   4. absolute threshold;   5. sensory adaptation.

Page 86
1. The wavelength is the distance between the crests of a light wave, whereas the amplitude is the height of the wave. Wavelength determines color; amplitude determines brightness.   2. cornea, pupil, lens, retina;   3. flattening, bulging, accommodation;   4. cones, because they function in bright light to enable us to see fine detail; rods, because they are more sensitive in dim light;   5. dark adaptation;   6. a-e-h, b-d-f, c-d-g.

Page 92

1. sound waves; 2. high, low; 3. amplitude; 4. horn, air, pinna, auditory canal, eardrum, malleus, incus, stapes, oval window, cochlea, basilar membrane, hair cells, auditory nerve, brain; 5. hair cells, cochlea; 6. high, low; 7. Answers will vary, but in general, try to avoid continuous exposure to loud noises or, if this is impossible, wear earplugs.

Page 96

1. smell, taste, olfaction, gustation; 2. We are able to smell a particular odor because the shape and size of its molecules enable it to fit into a certain type of receptor cell. 3. pheromones; 4. salty, sweet, sour, bitter; 5. The juice runs over the papillae and then down into the pores to the taste buds.

Page 103

1. The skin senses protect internal organs and indicate pressure, temperature, and pain; the vestibular sense is our sense of balance; the kinesthetic sense is our sense of bodily orientation and movement. 2. pressure, warmth, cold, pain; 3. gate-control; 4. Pain serves as a warning that something is wrong with our body and as a signal to do something about it. 5. close, opens; 6. semicircular canals.

Page 106

1. boredom, irritability, hallucinations, relaxation; 2. autism; 3. The body compensates for loss of one sense with heightened sensitivity in the others.

CHAPTER FOUR

Page 116

1. Perception is the process of selecting, organizing, and interpreting raw sensory data. 2. An illusion is a false impression of the environment caused by the physical distortion of a stimulus or by an error in the perceptual process. 3. interpretation, selection, organization; 4. selective attention; 5. feature detectors; 6. habituation.

Page 121

1. It states that our perceptions consist of two aspects: the figure, which stands out and has a definite contour or shape and the ground, which is more indistinct. 2. proximity, continuity, closure; 3. size constancy; 4. brightness constancy.

Page 131

1. two, one; 2. Both are binocular cues to judging distance. Retinal disparity works because each eye receives a different image which the brain fuses into one image. Convergence works because our brain analyzes the amount of muscle strain our eyes undergo when turning inward to see an object. 3. linear perspective, aerial perspective, texture gradient, interposition, light and shadow, relative size, accommodation, motion parallax; 4. trichromatic; 5. opponent-process; 6. Both: trichromatic operates at the level of the retina, and opponent-process operates at the level of the optic nerve and the brain. 7. strobo-scopic.

Page 138

1. It demonstrates the importance of early experiences in learning how to perceive the world. 2. Perceptual expectancy; 3. No, because as they grew up in their different cultures they had very different experiences that would lead them to perceive visual illusions in different ways. 4. There is no controlled scientific research that supports a belief in extra sensory perception.

CHAPTER FIVE

Page 147

1. They considered it too unscientific and not the proper focus of psychology. 2. the general state of being aware and responsive to stimuli and events in both the external and internal environments; 3. selective attention; 4. awareness, control; 5. There may be an innate need to experience nonordinary reality. 6. as a part of sacred rituals, for social and political functions, and for individual rewards.

Page 154

1. yearly or seasonal, monthly or 28-day, 24-hour daily, 90-minute cycle; 2. circadian; 3. electroencephalograph (EEG); 4. beta, alpha; 5. REM; 6. Repair/restoration theory suggests we sleep to physically restore our body, whereas evolutionary/circadian theory says that sleep evolved because it helped conserve energy and provided protection from predators.

Page 157

1. unconscious mind; 2. Manifest content is the disguised, symbolic meaning, and latent content is the true meaning. 3. activation–synthesis hypothesis; 4. sleep apnea, night terrors, narcolepsy.

Page 165

1. psychoactive; 2. Psychoactive drugs can alter the production of neurotransmitters, affect storage or release, alter the reception, and block the reuptake or destruction of excess neurotransmitters. 3. drug abuse; 4. Physical dependence refers to changes in the bodily processes that require continued use of the drug for functioning, whereas psychological dependence refers to the mental desire or craving to achieve the effects produced by the drug. 5. set, setting; 6. synergistic effect.

Page 169

1. Depressant drugs depress the central nervous system; stimulant drugs activate the central nervous system; narcotics relieve pain; and hallucinogens alter perceptions. 2. amphetamines, cocaine; 3. LSD; 4. designer drug.

Page 175

1. The brain responds to an unchanging external environment by creating more interesting internal thoughts and images. 2. hypnosis; 3. dissociation; 4. Hypnosis requires the subject to make a conscious decision to relinquish personal control. 5. meditation.

CHAPTER SIX

Page 183

1. Both are innate, rigid, automatic responses, triggered by some type of environmental stimuli; however, a reflex is a single response, whereas an instinct is a complex sequence of responses. 2. learning; 3. No, our human behaviors are so complex that most are learned by a combination of many types of learning.

Page 189
1. neutral stimulus, unconditioned stimulus;   2. conditioned stimulus, conditioned response;   3. He presented the neutral stimulus (white rat), paired it with UCS (noise), which elicited the UCR (crying). After several pairings the rat became the CS which elicited the CER (crying and fear).   4. higher order conditioning;   5. In extinction, the conditioned stimulus continues to be presented but the unconditioned stimulus is withheld; in forgetting, neither the conditioned stimulus nor the unconditioned stimulus is presented.   6. spontaneous recovery;   7. generalization;   8. discrimination.

Page 194
1. operant conditioning;   2. reinforcement, punishment;   3. The food is a primary positive reinforcer whereas the money is a secondary positive reinforcer.   4. You would first use negative punishment by taking away any privileges to decrease the aggressive behavior, then once the aggressive behavior had decreased you would begin using positive reinforcement by giving back the privileges for nonaggressive behavior.   5. taken away (subtracted), dislikes;   6. negative;   7. positive;   8. She does chores sloppily or ineffectively, puts them off till the last minute, pouts and grumbles.   9. constant and unavoidable punishment.

Page 202
1. reinforcement;   2. (a) fixed ratio, (b) variable ratio, (c) fixed interval, (d) variable interval;   3. It probably developed when Marshall got a high grade on the first exam he took when wearing the necklace.   4. At first, praise every dive that approximates a proper dive, then successively praise closer and closer approximations to a perfect dive.   5. immediately after.

Page 208
1. We input information through the perceptual processes of attention, selection, and organization, process that information through such means as forming mental images and conceptualizing, and store our information in memory.   2. insight;   3. Not according to Tolman, who says that much of learning is latent and occurs in the absence of any reward.   4. observational;   5. model.

and how they relate to one another, whereas episodic memory involves remembering where and when an event happened.   3. Landmark events are personally important events that we use to remember less memorable events; personal landmark events vary, but your own list might include graduations, weddings, holidays, traumatic events, etc.   4. tip-of-the-tongue phenomenon; 5. retrieval;   6. (a) recognition, (b) recall, (c) recall, (d) recognition;   7. flashbulb memories;   8. Research shows that memories can be altered when subjects are presented with misinformation after the event being remembered.

Page 233
1. We experience the serial position effect when we remember things at the beginning and the end of a list but forget things in the middle.   2. Using distributed practice, you would space your study time into many learning periods with rest periods in between; using massed practice, you would "cram" all your learning into long, unbroken periods.   3. state-dependent memories;   4. old, new;   5. new, old;   6. (a) retrieval failure theory, (b) decay theory, (c) motivated forgetting theory.

Page 238
1. reverberating circuits;   2. LTP begins with repeated stimulation at a synapse, which leads to a change in the dendrite, which causes increased calcium ion flow into the neuron. This in turn activates proteins that increase the neuron's sensitivity to any subsequent stimulation. LTP explains the brain changes that occur when short-term memory is processed into long-term memory.   3. Without the gene that stimulates production of a particular kinase, which in turn activates LTP, the mice performed worse on a memory task than mice that had the gene.   4. amnesia;   5. Alzheimer's disease is a progressive mental deterioration of the brain that normally affects people over 65. Its cause may be genetic, a slow-acting virus, or environmental.

Page 242
1. eidetic imagery;   2. mnemonic devices;   3. (a) peg-word system, (b) method of loci, (c) method of word associations, (d) substitute word system.

CHAPTER SEVEN

Page 218
1. Sensory memory, which is the brief storage of sensory input; short-term memory, the working memory in which we process information; and long-term memory, which contains stored information and experiences.   2. ¼ to ½ second for visual information and up to 4 seconds for auditory information; 3. short-term memory;   4. Maintenance rehearsal is the continual mental repetition of information that maintains it in short-term memory for further processing. Without maintenance rehearsal the information would not be retained more than 30 seconds.   5. The letters in List A are chunked into words and there are 7 words, seven plus or minus two being the number of items most people are able to remember.   6. dual-coding system.

Page 226
1. Incoming information is encoded and stored for later retrieval.   2. Semantic memory involves remembering facts

CHAPTER EIGHT

Page 253
1. Cognition is the process of coming to know about our world through the mental activities of acquiring, storing, retrieving, and using knowledge.   2. dual-coding hypothesis;   3. mental images;   4. attributes;   5. Concept formation makes it possible for us to categorize new knowledge and relate it to previous knowledge, and hence to think as we do.

Page 258
1. Preparation, in which we identify the facts, determine which ones are relevant, and define the goal; production, in which we propose possible solutions, or hypotheses; and evaluation, in which we determine whether the solutions meet the goal.   2. Algorithms may take a very long time, but they always eventually lead to a problem's solution; heuristics are much faster, but do not guarantee a solution.   3. means–end analysis;   4. working backwards;   5. subgoals;   6. problem-solving set, functional fixedness, incubation.

Page 261

1. Creativity is the ability to originate new or unique successful solutions to a problem. 2. fluency, flexibility, originality; 3. (a) divergent, (b) convergent; 4. brainstorming; 5. No, because people tend to be less creative when they are working for extrinsic rewards.

Page 266

1. think; 2. Other animals communicate in a ritualistic fashion that is dictated by instinct, whereas human language is a creative, complex form of communication that is learned. 3. phonemes, morphemes; 4. Grammar is an entire system of rules dictating the makeup of a language, whereas syntax is merely the branch of grammar that dictates correct word order. 5. We use previous knowledge and the context to interpret words and phrases and organize what we hear. 6. Apes are physically unable to produce human speech, so researchers have used other means of communication, including sign language, magnetic symbols, and computer symbols. 7. content, syntax.

Page 271

1. Spearman felt the intelligence consists of a single general cognitive ability that he called *g*; alternative views held by Thurstone, Guilford, Gardner, and others hold that intelligence cannot be defined as one single ability but as many distinct abilities. 2. Fluid intelligence is our innate capability to acquire new knowledge and solve new problems, whereas crystallized intelligence is our store of knowledge acquired through an interaction of our fluid intelligence and our environment. 3. internal components, adaptation to change through use of our internal components, and application of past experience to problem solving; 4. Intelligence consists of the cognitive abilities employed in acquiring, remembering, and using knowledge of one's culture to solve everyday problems and to readily adapt to and function in both changing and stable environments. 5. reliability, validity, standardization.

Page 281

1. No, an IQ test merely measures verbal and quantitative abilities and predicts school success. 2. The Stanford–Binet is a single test consisting of several sets of various age-level items, whereas the Wechsler consists of three separate tests; also the Stanford–Binet primarily measures verbal abilities, while the Wechsler measures both verbal and performance abilities. 3. K-ABC; 4. Group IQ tests measure people's achievement —what they already know. 5. No; there is a decline in speed but not in actual knowledge. 6. You could hire someone moderately or mildly retarded but not severely retarded. 7. Answers will vary. If you choose mainstreaming, it is probably because you would like as normal an environment as possible for your child; if you choose special placement, it is probably because you would like a program specially designed for your child. 8. No, they are happier and healthier than the normal population. 9. Both heredity and environment are important, in a ratio of about 50/50.

CHAPTER NINE

Page 292

1. Developmental psychology studies age-related changes in behaviors and abilities from conception to death. 2. nature or nurture, continuity or stage, stability or change; 3. cross-sectional; 4. cohort effects; 5. Cross-sectional studies are faster and less expensive than longitudinal studies but suffer from the cohort effect, which confuses different histories with genuine age differences. Because of their typically small sample, longitudinal studies have limited generalizability. 6. When you ride backward, you are demonstrating how *invisible* cultural rules affect human behavior. 7. ethnotheory.

Page 298

1. The three major stages are the germinal period, the embryonic period, and the fetal period. 2. A gene is a particular segment of DNA occupying a specific place on the chromosome. 3. Identical twins develop from a single fertilized egg, while fraternal twins develop from two separate fertilized eggs. 4. teratogens; 5. Maternal malnutrition and lack of universal access to medical care are both correct answers. 6. fetal alcohol syndrome.

Page 302

1. five; 2. Myelination is not yet complete. 3. nature; 4. Because the African parents' ethnotheory supports early motor development, they make special efforts to encourage their infants' motor skills. 5. vision.

Page 307

1. puberty; 2. proximo distal, distal proximo; 3. secondary sex characteristics; 4. male climacteric; 5. Primary aging is the age-related biological changes in physical and mental processes, whereas secondary aging results from abuse, neglect, disuse, or disease. 6. Both theories relate strictly to primary aging. Programmed theories say aging is controlled by our genes, whereas the wear-and-tear theory argues that life wears down our ability to repair.

Page 311

1. nonverbal communication; 2. Cooing is when the baby produces only vowel sounds ("eee"), while babbling is when consonants are added ("dadada"). 3. Telegraphic speech is a child's two-or three-word sentences that contain only the most necessary words. 4. overgeneralize; 5. language acquisition device (LAD); 6. Research shows that caretaker speech ("babytalk") may be an essential part of a child's language development.

Page 321

1. Piaget; 2. assimilation, accommodation; 3. object permanence; 4. operation; 5. egocentric; 6. concrete operational; 7. object permanence for the sensoriomotor stage, representing things with words and images during the preoperational stage, conservation or operations during the concrete operational stage, abstract reasoning for the formal operational stage; 8. Memory problems for older adults are primarily problems of encoding, taking more time to store the information, and retrieval, taking more time to find the information.

CHAPTER TEN

Page 332

1. At the preconventional level, individuals tend to judge right and wrong on the basis of the consequences (reward or punishment); those at the conventional level tend to comply with the rules of society in an attempt to please others or "do one's duty";

and those at the postconventional level have developed their own standards for right and wrong.   2. Kohlberg's highest level of morality is limited to individualistic cultures.   3. According to Gilligan, women tend to score lower on Kohlberg's scale because his theory emphasizes the male's justice perspective over the female's care perspective.

Page 335
1. Sex refers to the biological components of being male or female, while gender refers to the social components.   2. gender identity, gender role;   3. identification with the same-sex parent;   4. rewards, punishments, and imitation of others;   5. the child's thought processes;   6. social-learning and cognitive-developmental.

Page 341
1. temperament;   2. Thomas and Chess describe three categories of temperament—easy, difficult, and slow-to-warm-up—that seem to correlate with stable personality differences.   3. trust versus mistrust, identity versus role confusion, initiative versus guilt, ego integrity versus despair;   4. midlife crisis, empty nest syndrome, adolescent storm and stress, and linear development.

Page 353
1. These researchers found that contact comfort may be the most important variable in attachment.   2. securely attached, anxious-avoidant, anxious-ambivalent;   3. Authoritarian parents require obedience and responsibility from their children; permissive-indifferent parents set few limits and offer minimal support; permissive-indulgent parents set few limits but are highly involved; and authoritative parents set firm limits but are also caring and sensitive.   4. activity; disengagement.   5. Ethnic group membership may provide a greater sense of community, a shield from majority group prejudice, and increased esteem.   6. denial, anger, bargaining, depression, acceptance.

CHAPTER ELEVEN

Page 364
1. Havelock Ellis;   2. survey;   3. Masters and Johnson;   4. Cultural comparisons put sex in a broader perspective and help counteract ethnocentrism.   5. It insures female virginity before marriage, thus increasing the young woman's status and making her more marriagable.

Page 369
1. chromosomal gender;   2. androgens, estrogens;   3. gender roles;   4. A transsexual is someone who feels trapped in the body of the wrong gender; a transvestite dresses in the opposite sex's clothing primarily for the purpose of sexual excitement; and a gay or lesbian is an individual who is sexually attracted to the same sex.   5. LeVay reported measurable differences in the hypothalamus between heterosexual men and gay men, and Bailey and Pillard found that heritability for homosexuality might be as high as 50 percent.   6. biological, psychosocial.

Page 376
1. testosterone;   2. An oversecretion of androgens in the developing female fetus produces the adrenogenital syndrome, whereas the androgen-insensitivity syndrome is produced when the developing male fetus's body fails to respond to testosterone.   3. gender role stereotypes;   4. Stereotypes are rigid, preconceived notions about members of a group that are based on limited information and are usually untrue. Generalizations are a set of beliefs about members of a group that are based on legitimate scientific findings and therefore are considered true.   5. nurturists;   6. Androgyny is a combination of both male and female personality traits in the same individual.

Page 385
1. The parasympathetic branch of the autonomic nervous system dominates during sexual arousal, whereas the sympathetic branch dominates during ejaculation and orgasm.   2. double standard;   3. excitement, plateau, orgasm, and resolution phases;   4. psychoanalysis, behavior therapy;   5. AIDS;   6. sexual intercourse, intravenous drug use, blood transfusions, mother and child, patient and medical personnel.

Page 392
1. Sexual acts performed by an adult with a minor under 18 years of age.   2. Pedophilia involves sexual gratification from contacts with children who are not relatives, whereas incest refers to sexual contact between two people who are related.   3. friends and relatives, strangers;   4. guilt and shame, difficulty forming intimate relations, sexual dysfunctions, and psychological difficulties;   5. sexual harassment;   6. an assertion and abuse of power.

Page 398
1. The oral, anal, or vaginal penetration forced on an unconsenting or unwilling victim.   2. rape trauma syndrome;   3. anger rape, power rape, sadistic rape, and sexual gratification rape;   4. distorted attitudes about rape, increased violence against women;   5. It serves as a way of increasing alliances with other groups.   6. male property rights;   7. In "rape prone" societies men and boys are encouraged to be aggressive and competitive, and women generally have less power in economic and political arenas. In "rape free" societies women and men share power equally, and both sexes are raised to value nurturance and cooperation.

CHAPTER TWELVE

Page 415
1. anthropomorphism;   2. While these two terms often overlap and interact to influence behavior, motivation refers to internal factors that energize and direct behavior, whereas emotion refers to feelings or affective responses.   3. The lateral hypothalamus (LH) stimulates eating behaviors, and the ventromedial hypothalamus (VMH) signals the organism to stop eating.   4. According to Schachter, overweight individuals are more responsive to external cues, whereas Rodin suggests that overeating can be explained by a higher insulin level in the blood that results from the sight of food.   5. Both anorexia nervosa and bulimia are motivated by an extreme fear of obesity, but anorexia nervosa is characterized by self-starvation and bulimia refers to binges of eating followed by purging.   6. Stimulus seeking is an unlearned (biological) motive, but it is not as necessary to our basic survival as, for example, hunger, which is a primary motive.   7. achievement motivation;   8. fear of success.

Page 424

1. Both fields are based on the existence of instincts, but while ethologists believe instincts evolve because they increase chances for survival, sociobiologists believe much of human social behavior is due to natural selection and "genetic selfishness." 2. Drive-reduction theory says internal biological needs push the organism to look for satisfaction and that the specific action taken results from learning, whereas incentive theory proposes that external, environmental stimuli pull the organism toward certain goal-directed behaviors. 3. cognitive; 4. extrinsic; 5. opponent-process; 6. Maslow's hierarchy of needs.

Page 432

1. physiological, cognitive, behavioral, and subjective experience; 2. polygraph; 3. The sympathetic nervous system prepares the body for "fight or flight," while the parasympathetic nervous system restores the body to its "status quo" after sympathetic arousal. 4. Darwin believed that emotions evolved because of their value in survival and natural selection. 5. learning and socialization.

Page 438

1. According to the James–Lange theory, physiological arousal precedes the experience of the emotion, whereas the Cannon–Bard theory says emotions result from simultaneous stimulation of the cortex and the autonomic nervous system. 2. facial feedback; 3. Cognitive-labeling theory says emotions result from a combination of the subjective, cognitive, and physiological components of emotion. 4. misattribution; 5. Insomniacs were told that a placebo pill would increase their arousal. This caused the subjects to misattribute their emotional arousal and thus more readily fall asleep.

CHAPTER THIRTEEN

Page 447

1. psychological behavior, physical health; 2. They work as researchers, practitioners in health care settings, and educators promoting healthful lifestyles. 3. chronic; 4. Operant conditioning reinforces behavior (exercise, relaxation, etc.) that alleviates pain perception. 5. internal; it gives them the feeling that they can control their pain. 6. Both focus attention on something else besides the pain.

Page 450

1. cigarette smoking; 2. A successful high school program would focus on teaching short- rather than long-term effects of smoking; discuss the influence of peers and the media; teach refusal skills, social skills, and coping skills; and build self-esteem. 3. (a) aversion therapy—specifically, rapid smoking; (b) coping response training; (c) covert sensitization; (d) nicotine patch or nicotine gum.

Page 458

1. stress; 2. You would be experiencing a lot of stress and would be a likely candidate for serious illness. 3. hassles; 4. Both are negative emotional states, but frustration results from a goal's being blocked and conflict results when you must choose between two goals or alternatives. 5. general adaptation syndrome; 6. They have probably experienced a lot of stress, and stress can suppress the immune system, making them vulnerable to cold and flu viruses.

Page 464

1. Stress suppresses the immune system, which normally works to check the growth of cancerous cells. 2. Hypertension is a state of chronic high blood pressure. Hypertensives tend to overreact physically to stress, which leads to stroke and heart disease. 3. cortisol, epinephrine; 4. Type A personalities are always on edge, preoccupied with their responsibilities, competitive, always in a hurry, and they talk rapidly. Type B's are calm and have a laid-back attitude toward life. 5. hostility; 6. shotgun, target behavior. Answers will vary, but alternatives include a shotgun approach, because it will change my whole Type A personality, or a target behavior approach, because it will change only the behaviors that lead to a hostile attitude.

Page 470

1. coping; 2. (a) emotion-focused, (b) problem-focused; 3. Rationalization and denial. Defense mechanisms alleviate anxiety but distort reality. 4. internal; 5. good health, self-esteem, a positive attitude, a good sense of humor, internal locus of control, good social skills, a supportive social network, a comfortable income; 6. relaxation, exercise, and self-care.

CHAPTER FOURTEEN

Page 480

1. personality; 2. Dispositional theorists are interested in describing the core characteristics and how they differ from one person to the next, not in explaining how characteristics develop or change. 3. Type theorists describe personality differences in terms of discrete categories on the basis of a major characteristic. Trait theorists say personality characteristics exist along a continuum. 4. factor analysis; 5. extroversion, agreeableness, conscientiousness, neuroticism, and openness to experience.

Page 489

1. Personality is seen as the result of unconscious mental forces. 2. The conscious is the tip of the iceberg and the highest level of awareness; the preconscious is just below the surface but can readily be brought to awareness; the unconscious is the large base of the iceberg and operates below the level of awareness. 3. id, ego, superego; 4. oral, anal, phallic, latency, genital; Freud believed that an individual's adult personality resulted from his or her resolution of the crisis each psychosexual stage presented. 5. (a) Adler, (b) Horney, (c) Jung, (d) Horney; 6. poor testability, overemphasis on biology and unconscious forces, biased sampling, nonsupportive or inadequate evidence.

Page 491

1. The response a person makes in any situation is specific to the expected rewards or punishment. 2. Repeated learning experiences develop habitual patterns of response. 3. Behaviorists say shyness is learned from interactions with others. 4. social learning; 5. Learning theories of personality are admired for being scientifically grounded, but criticized for being too narrow in focus and taking the "person" out of personality.

Page 495

1. humanistic; 2. The "self-concept" refers to all the information and beliefs individuals have about their own nature, qualities, and behavior. 3. self-actualization; 4. Humanistic theories are criticized for their naive assumptions, poor testabi-

lity and inadequate evidence, and narrowness in merely describing, not explaining, behavior.

Page 497

1. Personality results from how each individual thinks about the world and interprets experiences.   2. self-efficacy;   3. Rotter thinks personality is determined by individual expectations and the reinforcement value attached to specific outcomes.   4. externals, internals;   5. People worry about possible misuses of biologically based research to justify racism, sexism, and social apathy.   6. interactionist.

Page 504

1. structured, unstructured;   2. MMPI-2;   3. projective;   4. Subject's responses are interpreted as a reflection of unconscious motives and feelings.   5. Objective tests can allow deliberate deception and social desirability bias, make diagnosis difficult, and be used inappropriately.   6. They have low reliability and validity.

CHAPTER FIFTEEN

Page 520

1. Patterns of behavior that are maladaptive, disruptive, or harmful for the affected person or others.   2. statistical, subjective discomfort, and maladaptive functioning;   3. medical model;   4. The DSM-IV is the manual developed by psychiatrists to describe the many categories of mental disorders.   5. With a neurosis, an individual can still function moderately in daily life, but in psychosis there is a major loss of contact with reality.   6. insanity.

Page 524

1. generalized, panic, phobia, obsessive-compulsive, and posttraumatic stress;   2. posttraumatic stress disorder, panic disorder, obsessive-compulsive disorder;   3. General learning theorists believe anxiety disorders result from classical and operant conditioning, while social learning theorists argue that imitation and modeling are the cause.   4. panic attacks and obsessive-compulsive disorders.

Page 532

1. schizophrenia, multiple personality;   2. Schizophrenia is characterized by disturbances in perception, thought and language, affect, and behavior.   3. Hallucinations involve perceptual distortions in any of the senses (e.g., hearing voices), whereas delusions are mistaken beliefs that persist even when there is strong evidence to the contrary.   4. positive, negative;   5. Three possible biological causes of schizophrenia may be an overactivity of certain neurons (especially dopamine), brain damage, and genetics.   6. Three possible psychosocial causes of schizophrenia may be stress, communication deviance, and disturbed family environment.

Page 538

1. Individuals with mood disorders have *excessive* and *unreasonable* changes in feelings.   2. The two major types of mood disorders are major depressive disorder and bipolar disorder.   3. Seligman believes the individual becomes resigned to pain and sadness and feels unable to change his or her situation for the better.   4. seasonal affective disorder (SAD);   5. suicide.

Page 543

1. stress;   2. Dissociative amnesia is a partial or total inability to recall the past, whereas dissociative fugue is running away from the previous residence and creating a new identity.   3. disorders with physical symptoms such as blindness, paralysis, or pain that are without a physical cause;   4. antisocial personality;   5. Drug use becomes substance abuse when it interferes with social and occupational functioning; when drug use also involves tolerance and withdrawal symptoms, it becomes substance dependence.

Page 545

1. schizophrenia;   2. Once labels are assigned and the label becomes the central characteristic, individuality is lost. Also, the patient may begin to behave in ways that confirm preconceptions.   3. Greater care in diagnosis and increased awareness of the dangers of labels.   4. It describes the symptoms, standardizes diagnosis and treatment, and facilitates communication between mental health professionals.

CHAPTER SIXTEEN

Page 553

1. psychotherapy;   2. Psychotherapies are practiced by psychologists, social workers, and other similarly trained professionals, whereas biomedical therapies can be used only by physicians.   3. disturbed thoughts, disturbed emotions, disturbed behaviors, interpersonal and life situation difficulties, and biomedical disturbances;   4. b, e, d, c, a.

Page 557

1. The basic goal is to bring unconscious conflicts to conscious awareness.   2. catharsis;   3. Mary is exhibiting transference, reacting to her therapist as she apparently did to someone earlier in her life. John is exhibiting resistance, arriving late because he fears what his unconscious might reveal.   4. Dreams reveal unconscious conflicts because the ego is not good at defending itself during sleep.   5. limited applicability, lack of scientific credibility.

Page 562

1. Cognitive therapists believe disturbed behavior results from faulty thought processes and beliefs.   2. self-talk;   3. activating event, belief system, and emotional consequence.   4. evaluate the consequences, identify your belief system, dispute the self-defeating beliefs, and practice effective ways of thinking;   5. Beck's therapy is not based on insight; it attempts to directly change behavior, whereas Ellis thinks insight into underlying thought processes must precede an effective change in behavior.   6. (a) magnification, (b) all-or-nothing thinking.

Page 564

1. blocked growth;   2. empathy, genuineness, unconditional positive regard;   3. awareness;   4. Gestalt therapy believes it is important to confront and challenge clients, whereas Rogerian therapy emphasizes a warm and accepting approach.

Page 571

1. behavior therapy;   2. A behavior therapy process of associating fear-evoking stimuli with deep relaxation.   3. aversion;   4. shaping;   5. Tokens (tangible objects such as poker chips) are used in a prescribed way to reinforce and shape appropriate behaviors.   6. modeling;   7. Behavior therapy is criticized for lack of generalizability, symptom substitution, and questionable ethics.

Page 573
1. group support, feedback and information, behavioral rehearsal; 2. Family therapy is a form of group therapy that treats the family as a unit and members work together to resolve problems. 3. A family is a system of interdependent parts, so the problems of any one member unavoidably affect the other family members. 4. personal growth, interpersonal communication; 5. Pop therapies create a false impression of legitimate therapies and they can be dangerous and expensive.

Page 578
1. drug therapy; 2. antianxiety, antipsychotic, antidepressant, mood stabilizer; 3. Valium is an antianxiety drug. It is dangerous because continued use can lead to tolerance and withdrawal symptoms, and overdosing can be fatal. 4. antipsychotic; 5. The public does not understand that all drugs have both costs and benefits, and they generally lack information about psychological disorders. 6. major depressive disorder; 7. psychosurgery.

Page 584
1. People can be involuntarily committed when they are believed to be dangerous to themselves or others, in need of treatment, or there is no other reasonable alternative. 2. In an eclectic approach to therapy, the therapist freely borrows from all of the five major types to find the most appropriate treatment. 3. clinical psychologists, psychiatrists; 4. naming the problem, qualities of the therapist, establishment of credibility, placing the problem in a familiar framework, applying techniques to bring relief, a special time and place; 5. rates of diagnosis and treatment of mental disorders, stresses of poverty, stresses of multiple roles, stresses of aging, violence against women.

CHAPTER SEVENTEEN

Page 597
1. conformity, compliance, obedience; 2. Normative social influence acts on a person's need for belonging and group acceptance, whereas informational social influence acts on the need for direction and information. 3. ingratiation; 4. foot-in-the-door, door-in-the-face; 5. responsibility; 6. Examine your thought processes, recognize that culture clashes are emotionally stressful, and adjust your behavior to match the other person's culture.

Page 605
1. affiliate; 2. According to social comparison theory, when people are unsure of their own feelings, reactions, or abilities they seek out others as a social "yardstick" to decide whether they're normal or to rank themselves. 3. roles; 4. Deindividuation is when an individual becomes so caught up in group identity that his or her individual self-awareness and evaluation apprehension are temporarily suspended. 5. group polarization; 6. A condition in which a highly cohesive group with a strong desire for agreement leads to an uncritical consensus and faulty decision making.

Page 608
1. Attribution refers to the principles people follow in making judgments about the causes of events, others' behavior, and their own behavior. 2. consistency, consensus, distinctiveness; 3. When judging the causes of others' behaviors, we tend to overestimate personality factors and underestimate social or situational factors. 4. Blaming the victim allows people to believe that the world is just and fair and to feel safe because bad things only happen to bad people. 5. a self-serving bias.

Page 610
1. Social cognition refers to processes through which we interpret, analyze, remember, and use information about the social world. 2. availability, representativeness; 3. Overestimating the improbable and the availability heuristic are both correct answers. 4. Priming involves procedures that heighten the availability of certain categories of information so that they can be readily brought to mind. 5. false-consensus bias; 6. Studying errors helps us understand normal information processing and awareness of errors helps improve personal decision making.

Page 621
1. physical attractiveness; 2. Sociobiologists say that men are attracted to young, fertile-appearing women and that women are attracted to mature, economically secure men because these preferences help insure the survival of the male's and female's genes. 3. self-fulfilling prophecy; 4. caring, attachment, intimacy; 5. romantic love; 6. It is shortlived, and it is based largely on mystery and fantasy. 7. Companionate love is based on admiration and respect, combined with deep feelings of caring and commitment to a relationship.

CHAPTER EIGHTEEN

Page 633
1. An attitude is a learned predisposition to respond cognitively, emotionally, and behaviorally to a particular object. 2. cognitive, affective, behavioral; 3. cognitive dissonance; 4. self-perception; 5. source, message, audience; 6. reactance.

Page 644
1. Prejudice; 2. stereotypes; 3. Prejudice is an attitude with behavioral tendencies that may or may not be activated, whereas discrimination is actual negative behavior directed at members of a group. 4. learning, cognitive processes, individual personality needs, economic and political competition, displaced aggression; 5. economic penalties, power inequalities; 6. We can reduce prejudice and discrimination by encouraging cooperation over competition, creating superordinate goals on which all people can work together, increasing contact (especially equal-status contact), and providing experiences that develop empathy for the victims of prejudice.

Page 649
1. aggression; 2. According to Freud, we have an innate drive for violence and instinct for aggression, and the ethologists believe aggression contributes to survival of the fittest. 3. frustration, social learning, group influences; 4. frustration–aggression; 5. social learning; 6. decrease, increase.

Page 653
1. Altruism; 2. According to these theories, altruism evolved because it favored overall genetic survival. 3. The egoistic model says helping is motivated by anticipated gain for the helper, and helping others produces negative state relief by reducing negative moods and unpleasant feelings. 4. empathy–altruism; 5. diffusion of responsibility.

Glossary

Abnormal Behavior Patterns of behavior that are maladaptive, disruptive, and/or harmful for the individual and/or society.

Absolute Threshold The smallest magnitude of a certain stimulus energy that can be detected.

Accommodation 1. The bulging and flattening of the lens in order to focus an image on the retina. 2. The process of adjusting existing ways of thinking (reworking schemata) to encompass new information, ideas, or objects.

Achievement Motivation The need for success, for doing better than others, and for mastering challenging tasks.

Action Potential An electrochemical impulse that travels down an axon to the axon terminal buttons.

Activation–Synthesis Hypothesis The idea that dreams have no real significance, but in fact are simply unimportant by-products of random stimulation of brain cells.

Activity Theory A theory of aging that suggests successful adjustment is fostered by a full and active commitment to life.

Adaptation Structural or functional changes that increase the organism's chances for survival.

Adolescence The psychological period of development between childhood and adulthood, which in the United States roughly corresponds to the teenage years.

Adolescent Egocentrism The belief that one is the focus of others' thoughts and attention that is common in adolescence.

Adrenogenital Syndrome A masculinization of a chromosomal female as a result of an excessive amount of androgens being produced during fetal development.

Aerial Perspective A monocular depth cue based on the fact that more distant objects appear less distinct than closer objects because of dust or haze in the air.

Afferent Incoming sensory information.

Affiliation Need for friendly association with others; formation of friendships; joining of groups and cooperation.

Ageism Negative attitudes toward the aged.

Aggression Any behavior that is intended to harm someone.

Agonist A chemical (or drug) that mimics the action of a specific neurotransmitter.

AIDS (Acquired Immune Deficiency Syndrome) A catastrophic illness in which a virus destroys the immune system's ability to fight disease. Although the term "AIDS" continues to be used, the President's Commission in 1988 recommended the use of the term *human immunodeficiency virus infection (HIV infection)*. They believe that this term more correctly defines the problem and places proper emphasis on the entire spectrum of the epidemic.

Algorithm A problem-solving strategy that always eventually leads to a solution; it often involves trying out random solutions to a problem in a systematic manner.

All-or-Nothing Principle The principle whereby an axon either fires an action potential or does not—there are no graduations; if one is fired, it is of the same intensity as any other.

Alternate States of Consciousness (ASC) Any state of consciousness other than normal waking consciousness.

Altruism Actions designed to help others with no obvious benefit to the individual.

Alzheimer's Disease An irreversible, progressive deterioration of the brain characterized by severe memory loss that occurs most commonly in old age.

Amnesia Forgetting that results from brain injury or from physical or psychological trauma.

Amplitude The height of a light or sound wave; pertaining to light, it refers to brightness; pertaining to sound, it refers to loudness.

Anal Stage Freud's psychosexual stage (from 12–18 months to 3 years) during which the anal area is the center of pleasure and toilet training is the primary source of conflict.

Androgens Hormones that stimulate maturation and functioning of the male reproductive system.

Androgen-Insensitivity Syndrome A feminization of a chromosomal male as a result of a genetic defect in which androgens have no effect on the developing fetus.

Androgyny The combining of some characteristics considered to be typically male (e.g., assertive, athletic) with those that are typically female (e.g., yielding, nurturant); from the Greek *andro* meaning "male" and *gyn* meaning "female."

Animism According to Piaget, the preoperational child's belief that all things are living and capable of intentions, consciousness, and feelings.

Anorexia Nervosa An eating disorder, seen mostly in adolescent and young adult females, in which a severe loss of weight results from an obsessive fear of obesity and self-imposed starvation.

Antagonist A chemical (or drug) that opposes or blocks the action of a neurotransmitter.

Anterograde Amnesia The inability to form new memories.

Anthropomorphism The act of attributing human characteristics to animals, gods, or inanimate objects. Also, interpreting the behavior of lower forms of animals in terms of human abilities or characteristics.

Antianxiety Drugs Tranquilizers used in the treatment of anxiety disorders.

Antipsychotic Drugs Chemicals administered to diminish or terminate psychotic symptoms such as hallucinations, delusions, withdrawal, and apathy.

Antisocial Personality Personality disorder characterized by egocentrism, lack of conscience, impulsive behavior, and charisma.

Anxiety Disorders Type of abnormal behavior characterized by unrealistic, irrational fear.

Aphrodisiacs Substances that supposedly increase sexual desire.

Applied Psychology The area of psychology that uses psychological principles and methods to investigate and solve human problems.

Applied Research Research that utilizes the principles and discoveries of psychology for practical purposes, to solve real-world problems.

Approach–Approach Conflict Conflict in which a person must choose between two alternatives that will both lead to desirable and undesirable results.

Approach–Avoidance Conflict Conflict in which a person must make a choice that will lead to both desirable and undesirable results.

Aqueous Humor The clear fluid that fills the front chamber of the eye.

Archetypes The images or patterns for thought, feelings, and behavior that reside in the collective unconscious according to Jung.

Arousal Theory The idea that there is an ideal or optimal level of excitement that is maintained through the body's need for homeostasis in stimulus seeking.

Assimilation The process of responding to a new situation in the same manner that is used in a familiar situation.

Association Areas The areas in the cerebral cortex that are involved in such mental operations as thinking, memory, learning, and problem solving.

Attachment An active, intense, emotional relationship between two people that endures over time.

Attitude A learned predisposition to respond cognitively, affectively, and behaviorally to a particular object.

Attitude-Discrepant Behavior The tension (or dissonance) that is experienced when one becomes aware that one's behavior does not match one's attitudes, and the corresponding need to justify the behavior by rearranging the original attitude to match the behavior.

Attributes Characteristics such as color, shape, and size that can change from one stimulus to another.

Attribution The principles people follow in making judgments about the causes of events, others' behavior, and their own behavior.

Audition The sense of hearing.

Auditory Canal A tubelike structure into which sound is channeled by the pinna.

Auditory Nerve The cranial nerve that carries auditory information from the hair cells to the brain.

Authoritarian Personality Personality type that includes traits of rigidity, conventionality, and sadism; these traits are said to predispose the individual toward prejudice.

Autism An abnormal condition in which an individual becomes immersed in fantasy to avoid communicating with others.

Autokinetic Effect The perceived motion of a single stationary light in the dark.

Autonomic Nervous System (ANS) A subdivision of the peripheral nervous system that maintains normal functioning of glands, heart muscles, and the smooth muscles of the blood vessels and internal organs.

Autonomy Versus Shame and Doubt Erikson's second psychosocial stage (from 12 months to 3 years), in which the child's crisis or challenge is to develop independence and self-assertion.

Aversion Therapy Behavior therapy that pairs an aversive stimulus with a maladaptive behavior.

Availability Heuristic A mental shortcut in social cognition used to predict how likely something is to happen based on how quickly examples come to mind.

Avoidance–Avoidance Conflict Conflict in which a person must choose between two or more alternatives that will both lead to undesirable results.

Axon A long tubelike structure attached to the neuron cell body that conveys impulses away from the cell body toward other neurons.

Axon Terminal Buttons Small structures at the ends of axons that release neurotransmitter chemicals.

Babbling An early stage of speech development in which infants emit virtually all known sounds of human speech.

Baseline A characteristic level of performance used to assess changes in behavior resulting from experimental conditions.

Basic Anxiety According to Horney, people develop feelings of helplessness and insecurity (basic anxiety) when as children they felt alone and isolated in a hostile environment.

Basic Research Research conducted to study theoretical questions without trying to solve a specific problem.

Basilar Membrane The membrane in the cochlea that contains the hearing receptors.

Behavior Anything a person or animal does, feels, thinks, or experiences.

Behavior Therapy A group of techniques based on learning principles that are used to change maladaptive behaviors.

Behaviorism The school of psychology that focuses on objective or observable behaviors.

Biofeedback A procedure in which people's biological functions are monitored and the results made known to them so they can learn to control these functions.

Biomedical Therapy Therapy involving physiological interventions (such as drugs or psychosurgery) to reduce symptoms associated with psychological disorders.

Bipolar Disorder A diagnostic term in DSM III-R describing individuals who experience both episodes of depression and mania, an excessive and unreasonable state of elation and hyperactivity.

Bisexual An individual who engages in both heterosexual and homosexual relations.

Blaming the Victim The act of placing blame on an individual who suffers from an injustice. It involves the belief that bad things happen to people because they deserve it.

Blind Spot A part of the retina containing no receptors; the area where the optic nerve exits the eye.

Body Senses These include the skin senses of pressure, warmth and cold, and pain; the vestibular sense of balance; and the kinesthetic sense of body position and movement.

Brain An extremely complex mass of nerve tissue organized into structures that control all voluntary and much involuntary behavior.

Brain Stem An area of the brain below the subcortex and in front of the cerebellum that includes the pons, the medulla, and the reticular formation.

Brainstorming A group problem-solving technique in which participants are encouraged to generate as many solutions to a problem as possible by building upon other's ideas and disregarding whether solutions are practical.

Brightness Constancy The phenomenon in which objects tend to maintain their appropriate brightness even when illumination varies.

Broca's Area A brain area found in the left frontal lobe that controls the muscles used to produce speech.

Bulimia An eating disorder in which enormous quantities of food are consumed (binges), followed by purging, which involves taking laxatives or vomiting.

Bystander Effect The finding that a person is less likely to respond when others are present.

Cannon–Bard Theory The theory that the thalamus responds to emotion-arousing stimuli by sending messages simultaneously to the cerebral cortex and the autonomic system. In this view, all emotions are physiologically similar.

Cardinal Traits In Allport's theory, a pervasive, all-encompassing personality characteristic that seems to influence most areas of a person's life. Cardinal traits are relatively uncommon and are observed in only a few people.

Care Perspective An approach to moral reasoning proposed by Carol Gilligan that emphasizes interpersonal responsibility and views people in terms of their interconnectedness with others.

Case Study An in-depth study of a single research subject.

CAT (Computerized Axial Tomography) Scan X-ray pictures of internal organs that are clearer and more accurate than normal X-rays.

Catalepsy A symptom of schizophrenia in which the individual assumes an uncomfortable, nearly immobile posture for an extended period of time.

Catharsis Freudian belief that pent-up aggressive impulses can be released through violent acts; some theorists believe it can occur vicariously, as when people watch violent sports matches.

Central Nervous System (CNS) The part of the nervous system that consists of the brain and the spinal cord.

Central Traits For Allport, a small number of traits that are highly characteristic of a given individual and easy to infer.

Cephalocaudal Development A general pattern of physical growth in which the greatest growth occurs first in the region of the head and later in lower regions.

Cerebellum The brain area responsible for the maintenance of smooth movement and for coordinated motor activity.

Cerebral Cortex The bumpy, convoluted area on the outside surface of the brain that contains primary sensory centers, motor control centers, and areas responsible for higher mental processes.

Child Sexual Abuse Sexual acts performed by an adult with a minor under 18 years of age.

Chromosomes Threadlike strands of DNA (deoxyribonucleic acid) molecules that carry genetic information.

Chronic Pain Long-lasting pain that often is recurring.

Chronobiology The study of biological rhythms.

Chunking The process of grouping information

into units in order to store more information in short-term memory.

Ciliary Muscles Muscles attached to the lens that stretch and relax it in order to focus images on the retina.

Circadian Rhythms Biological changes that occur on a 24-hour cycle.

Clairvoyance The ability to perceive objects or events that are inaccessible to the normal senses.

Classical Conditioning Learning a response to a neutral stimulus when that neutral stimulus is paired with a stimulus that causes a reflex response.

Client-Centered Therapy A type of psychotherapy developed by Carl Rogers that emphasizes the client's natural tendency to become healthy and productive; specific techniques include empathy, unconditional positive regard, and genuineness.

Clinical Psychologist A psychologist with an advanced graduate degree who specializes in treating psychological and behavioral disturbances or who does research on such disturbances.

Closure The Gestalt principle proposing that people have a tendency to perceive a finished unit even if there are gaps in it.

Cochlea The inner ear structure that contains the receptors for hearing.

Coding The three-part process that converts a particular sensory input into a specific sensation.

Cognition The mental activities involved in acquiring, storing, retrieving, and using knowledge; it includes such mental processes as perceiving, learning, remembering, using language, and thinking.

Cognitive Behavior Therapy A therapy that works to change not only destructive thoughts and beliefs but also the associated behaviors as well.

Cognitive Dissonance Theory Festinger's theory that tension results whenever people discover inconsistencies between their attitudes, or between their attitudes and their behaviors. This tension drives people to make attitudinal changes that will restore harmony or consistency.

Cognitive Labeling Theory Theory that the cognitive (thinking), subjective (evaluating), and physiological arousal components are all necessary to emotional experiences.

Cognitive Learning Theory The idea that learning involves more than an observable response, that it often involves thought processes that may not be directly observed or objectively measured.

Cognitive Map A mental image of an area that a person or animal has navigated.

Cognitive Psychology A school of psychology that focuses on reasoning and the mental processing of information.

Cognitive Restructuring The process in cognitive therapy by which the therapist and client work to change destructive ways of thinking.

Cognitive Therapy Therapy that focuses on faulty thought processes and beliefs to treat problem behaviors.

Cohort Effects A problem sometimes found in cross-sectional research wherein subjects of a given age may be affected by factors unique to their generation.

Collective Unconscious Jung's concept of an inherited portion of the unconscious that all humans share.

Color Aftereffects Color images that are seen after staring at a particular colored pattern for a long time.

Color Constancy The tendency for the color of objects to be perceived as remaining the same even when illumination varies.

Companionate Love A strong feeling of attraction to another person characterized by trust, caring, tolerance, and friendship. It is believed to provide an enduring basis for long-term relationships.

Compliance A form of social influence in which individuals change their behavior in response to direct requests from others.

Concept A mental structure used to categorize things that share similar characteristics.

Conception The fertilization of the female ovum or egg by the male sperm.

Concrete Operational Stage The third of Piaget's stages of cognitive development (ages 7 to 11), during which the child develops the ability to think logically but not abstractly.

Conditioned Emotional Response (CER) Any classically conditioned emotional response to a previously neutral stimulus.

Conditioned Response (CR) A learned response to a previously neutral stimulus that has been associated with the stimulus through repeated pairings.

Conditioned Stimulus (CS) A previously neutral stimulus that, through conditioning, now causes a classically conditioned response.

Conditioning The type of learning involving stimulus–response connections, in which the response is conditional on the stimulus.

Cones Receptors in the retina that respond to color and fine detail.

Conflict A negative emotional state caused by an inability to choose between two or more incompatible goals or impulses.

Conformity A type of social influence in which individuals change their attitudes or behavior to adhere to the expectations of others or the norms of groups to which they belong or wish to belong.

Connectionist Approach The approach to studying cognition that uses mathematical models simulating the interconnected systems of neurons in the actual brain to show how the brain works in a parallel fashion to receive, process, store, and retrieve information.

Conscious In Freudian terms, thoughts or information one is currently aware of or is remembering.

Consciousness The general state of being aware and responsive to stimuli in the internal and external environments.

Conservation The ability to recognize that a given quality, weight, or volume remains constant despite changes in shape, length, or position.

Constancy The tendency for the environment to be perceived as remaining the same even with changes in sensory input.

Contiguity The Gestalt principle stating that when two events happen at a time and place near to each other, one is perceived as causing the other.

Continuity The Gestalt principle proposing that patterns or objects that continue in one direction, even if interrupted by another pattern, tend to be perceived as being grouped together.

Continuous Reinforcement Reinforcement in which every response is reinforced.

Control Condition The part of an experiment in which subjects are treated identically to subjects in the experimental condition, except that the independent variable is not applied to them.

Conventional Level Kohlberg's second level of moral development, where moral judgments are based on compliance with the rules and values of society.

Convergence A binocular depth cue in which the closer the object, the more the eyes converge, or turn inward.

Convergent Thinking The type of thinking needed when there is only one correct answer or solution to a problem.

Conversion Disorder A somatoform disorder in which a person "converts" an emotional conflict into a physical symptom such as paralysis.

Coping Managing stress in some effective way.

Cornea The transparent bulge at the front of the eye where light enters.

Corpus Callosum A connecting bridge of nerve fibers between the left and right hemispheres of the cerebral cortex.

Correlation The relationship between variables.

Countertransference In psychoanalysis, the displacement, or transference, by the therapist of feelings derived from his or her past onto the relationship with the patient.

Covert Hidden or unobservable.

Creativity The ability to originate solutions to a problem that are also practical and useful.

Credibility Degree of trustworthiness or expertise that is associated with a particular source of persuasion.

Critical Period An optimal or sensitive time in development when the organism is most easily affected by environmental events.

Cross-Sectional Method A technique of data collection that measures individuals of various ages at one point in time and gives information about age differences.

Crowding Negative psychological experience of being overstimulated by a larger number of people than you prefer.

Crystallized Intelligence Knowledge and learning that we have gained over the course of our lives through an interaction between fluid intelligence and environmental experience.

Cue A stimulus that can begin a retrieval process from long-term memory.

Culture Values and assumptions about life and patterns of behavior that develop as a response to social and environmental factors and are passed on from generation to generation.

Dark Adaptation Visual adjustment that increases the sensitivity of the rods and cones and allows us to see better in dim light.

Data Facts, statistics, pieces of information.

Daydreaming An alternate state of consciousness characterized by internal reverie or inwardly focused thought.

Debriefing Explaining the research process to subjects who participated.

Decay Theory The theory that memory, like all biological processes, deteriorates with the passage of time.

Defense Mechanisms In psychoanalytic theory, unconscious strategies used by the ego to avoid anxiety and resolve conflict. Everyone uses defense mechanisms. They only cause serious problems when they are excessively used.

Deindividuation Being so caught up in a group identity that individual self-awareness and evaluation apprehension are temporarily suspended.

Deinstitutionalization The policy of discharging as many people as possible from state mental hospitals and discouraging admissions.

Delusions Mistaken beliefs maintained in spite of strong evidence to the contrary.

Dendrites Branching neuron structures that receive neural impulses from other neurons and convey impulses toward the cell body.

Density Actual number of people in a given physical space.

Dependent Variable A measurable behavior that is exhibited by a subject and is affected by the independent variable.

Depressants Psychoactive drugs that act on the central nervous system to suppress or slow down bodily processes and reduce overall responsiveness.

Depth Perception The ability to perceive distance and therefore perceive space in three dimensions.

Designer Drugs Drugs produced by slightly altering the molecular structure of psychoactive drugs, thereby creating a new drug that has similar effects.

Detached Retina A disconnection of the retina from the back of the eye, which causes total or partial blindness of that eye.

Developmental Psychology The branch of psychology that describes, explains, predicts, and sometimes aims to modify age-related behaviors from conception to death. This field emphasizes maturation, early experiences, and various stages in development.

Diagnostic and Statistical Manual of Mental Disorders (DSM III-R) A classification system, developed by a task force of the American Psychiatric Association, used to describe abnormal behaviors.

Dichromat A person having the type of color weakness in which only two types of cones are present, rather than the normal three.

Difference Threshold The smallest magnitude of difference in stimulus energy that a person can detect.

Diffusion of Responsibility When people are in groups of two or more, there is a tendency toward less individual responsiveness due to the assumption that someone else will take action (or responsibility).

Disconfirmed Expectancy The tension (dissonance) that is felt when one's expectations are not fulfilled, and the corresponding tendency to justify one's losses by rearranging original attitudes to match the outcome.

Discrimination 1. The process whereby a subject learns to differentiate one stimulus from others that are similar because that stimulus is the only CS that is paired with the UCS. 2. Negative behaviors directed at members of an outgroup.

Disengagement Theory A theory of aging that suggests successful aging involves a natural and mutual withdrawal, in which both the individual and society gradually pull away from each other as a preparation for death.

Dissociation A splitting or separating of consciousness. Under hypnosis, one part of consciousness seems to be aware and observing hypnotic suggestions, while another part is responding to the suggestion.

Dissociative Disorder Stress-related disorder characterized by amnesia, fugue, or multiple personality.

Distal-Proximo Development Physical development in an outer to inner direction, such that hands, feet, nose, etc. develop faster than internal organs.

Distributed Practice A learning technique in which practice sessions are interspersed with rest periods.

Divergent Thinking The type of thinking needed when it is necessary to generate as many ideas as possible.

Dopamine Hypothesis A theory suggesting that schizophrenia is caused by an overactivity of dopamine neurons in a specific region of the brain.

Double-Blind Experiment An experiment in which neither the subject nor the experimenter knows which treatment is being given to the subject or to which group the subject has been assigned.

Double Standard The belief that different rules for sexual behavior should be applied to men and women.

Drive-Reduction Theory The theory that motivation begins with a physiological need (a lack or deficiency) that elicits a psychological energy or drive directed toward behavior that will satisfy the original need.

Drug Therapy Use of chemicals to treat physical and psychological disorders.

Dual-Coding Hypothesis The theory proposing that information is encoded into two separate but interacting systems: an imagery system for concrete items and pictures and a verbal system for abstract ideas and spoken and written words.

Dual-Coding System The process of coding information by both visual and verbal means.

Dyslexia An inability or difficulty in reading.

Eardrum (Tympanic Membrane) The membrane located between the auditory canal and the middle ear that vibrates in response to sound waves.

Eclectic Approach An approach to psychology that considers the whole person and utilizes techniques appropriate for the specific circumstance.

Efferent Outgoing motor information.

Ego In psychoanalytic theory, the rational part of the psyche that deals with reality and attempts to control the impulses of the id while also satisfying the social approval and self-esteem needs of the superego.

Ego Integrity Versus Despair During this eighth and final stage in Erikson's theory of psychosocial development, adults review their accomplishments and feel either satisfaction or regret.

Egocentrism The inability to consider another's point of view, which Piaget considered a hallmark of the preoperational stage. In terms of mental disorders, preoccupation with one's own concerns and insensitivity to the needs of others.

Eidetic Imagery The ability to recall memories —especially visual memories—that are so clear they can be viewed like a clear picture; photographic memory.

Ejaculation The discharge of semen from the penis at orgasm.

Electra Complex The Freudian term for the sexual attachment of a girl to her father and her desire to replace her mother.

Electroconvulsive Shock (ECS) Electrical shock applied to the brain such that it causes convulsions.

Electroconvulsive Therapy (ECT) Passage of electrical current through the brain as a therapy technique.

Electrodes Small devices (normally wires) used to conduct electricity to or from brain tissue.

Electroencephalograph (EEG) A machine that monitors large changes in brain activity with electrodes attached to a person's scalp. Recordings of these changes on sheets of paper are known as electroencephalograms.

Electromagnetic Spectrum The band of radiant energy generated by the sun; visible light is only a small part of this spectrum.

Electromyograph (EMG) Biofeedback device that can measure muscle tension by recording the amount of electrical activity in an area of skin to which electrodes are attached.

Embryonic Period The second stage of pregnancy (from uterine implantation to the eighth week), characterized by development of major body organs and systems.

Emergent Norm Theory A theory of crowd behavior suggesting that new norms emerge in situations lacking firm guidelines for coping.

Emotion Feelings or affective responses that result from physiological arousal, thoughts and beliefs, subjective evaluation, and bodily expression.

Emotion-Focused Forms of Coping Coping strategies that lead to changes in one's perceptions of stressful situations.

Empathy In Rogerian terms, an insightful awareness and ability to share another person's inner experience.

Empathy–Altruism Hypothesis The proposal that altruistic behavior is motivated by empathy for the distressed person in need of help.

Empty Nest Syndrome A painful separation and depression that parents supposedly feel when their last child leaves home.

Encounter Groups A form of group therapy for people who are not seriously disturbed that focuses on personal growth and interpersonal communication.

Endocrine System A system of glands that, by releasing bodily chemicals into the bloodstream, is responsible for distributing chemical information throughout the body to effect behavioral change or to maintain normal bodily functions.

Endorphins Morphinelike chemicals occurring naturally in the brain that can lessen pain responses.

Environmental Psychology Branch of applied psychology that focuses on the relationship between psychological processes and the physical environment.

Epinephrine Hormone secreted by the adrenal glands in response to messages from the hypothalamus. Secretion is associated with emotional arousal, especially fear and anger.

Episodic Memory A type of long-term memory in which memories of events are stored.

Equity Theory The theory that people are highly motivated to seek a fair share of the rewards and that they prefer a balanced relationship.

Erectile Dysfunction The inability to get or maintain an erection firm enough for intercourse.

Erogenous Zones The areas of the body that elicit sexual arousal when stimulated.

Essential Hypertension State of chronically elevated blood pressure that has no detectable medical cause.

Estrogens Hormones that stimulate maturation and functioning of the female reproductive system.

Ethnocentrism The feeling that one's own cultural group is superior to others and its customs and ways of life are the standards by which other cultures should be judged.

Ethology The branch of biology that studies animal behavior under natural conditions.

Eugenics The biosocial movement endorsing the selection of certain human traits of the species.

Evaluation The final stage in problem solving during which hypotheses are appraised to see whether they satisfy the conditions of the goal as it was defined in the preparation stage.

Evolutionary/circadian theory A theory suggesting that sleep is a part of circadian rhythms and evolved as a means of conserving energy and protecting individuals from predators.

Excitement Phase The first phase of the sexual response cycle, characterized by increasing levels of muscle tension and contraction and increased amounts of blood concentration in the genitals.

Experiment A carefully controlled scientific procedure conducted to determine whether certain variables manipulated by the experimenter have an effect on other variables.

Experimental Condition The part of an experiment in which the independent variable is applied to the subjects.

Experimenter Bias The tendency of experimenters to influence the results of a research study in the expected direction.

Extinction During operant conditioning, the elimination of maladaptive behaviors by removing the rewards that were previously connected with them. During classical conditioning, the gradual unlearning of a behavior or a response that occurs when a CS is repeatedly presented without the UCS with which it had been previously associated.

Extrasensory Perception (ESP) Perceptual, or "psychic," abilities that go beyond the "known" sense, including telepathy, clairvoyance, procognition, and telekinesis.

Extrinsic Motivation The desire to perform an activity because of external rewards or the avoidance of punishment. Motivation is not inherent in the behavior itself.

Facial Feedback Hypothesis Proposal that movements of the facial muscles produce emotional reactions.

Factor Analysis A mathematical procedure used to determine the basic units or factors that constitute personality or intelligence.

Family Therapy Group therapy that treats the family as a unit, and members work together to resolve problems.

Feature Detectors Specialized cells in the brain that respond only to certain sensory information.

Feedback Knowledge of the results of a particular response.

Fetal Alcohol Syndrome A combination of birth defects, including organ deformities and mental, motor, and/or growth retardation, that results from maternal alcohol abuse.

Fetal Period The third, and final, stage of prenatal development (8 weeks to birth), characterized by rapid weight gain in the fetus and the fine detailing of body organs and systems.

Figure and Ground A Gestalt law of perceptual organization stating that our perceptions consist of two aspects: the figure, which stands out and has a definite contour or shape, and the ground, which is more indistinct.

Fixed Interval A schedule of reinforcement in which a subject is reinforced for the first response after a definite period of time has elapsed.

Fixed Ratio A partial schedule of reinforcement in which a subject must make a certain number of responses before being reinforced.

Flashbulb Memories Vivid images of circumstances associated with surprising or strongly emotional events.

Fluid Intelligence The capacity for acquiring new knowledge and solving new problems that is at least partially determined by biological and genetic factors and is relatively stable over short periods of time.

Forgetting The unlearning of a behavior due to continued withholding of the CS as well as the UCS.

Formal Operational Stage Piaget's fourth and final stage of cognitive development (age 11 and beyond), characterized by logical thinking, abstract reasoning, and conceptualization.

Fovea The point on the retina containing only cones, where light from the center of the visual field is focused; the point responsible for our clearest vision.

Frame Cognitive pattern that describes which behaviors are appropriate in a given social context. Frames include both role expectations and scripts for interaction.

Free Association In psychoanalysis, reporting whatever comes to mind, regardless of how painful, embarrassing, or irrelevant it may seem. Freud believed that the first thing to come to a patient's mind was often an important clue to what the unconscious mind wants to conceal.

Frequency The number of sound pressure waves per second, perceived as the pitch of a sound.

Frontal Lobes The cortical lobes located at the front of the brain whose functions include motor and speech control, the ability to plan ahead, initiative, and self-awareness.

Frustration An unpleasant state of tension, anxiety, and heightened sympathetic activity resulting from the blocking or thwarting of a goal.

Frustration-Aggression Hypothesis Idea that the motive to aggress is always a consequence of frustration and that frustration always leads to some form of aggression.

Functional Disorders Abnormal symptoms

with psychological causes or for which no physical cause is known.

Functional Fixedness A barrier to problem solving that occurs when people are unable to recognize novel uses for an object because they are so familiar with its common use.

Functionalism The psychological school that investigates the function of mental processes in adapting the individual to the environment.

Fundamental Attribution Error A mistake in judging the causes of others' behavior that comes from the tendency to overestimate internal, personal factors and underestimate external, situational influences.

Gain–Loss Theory Increased attraction will result when we receive unexpected approval from others and attraction will decrease if initial liking is lost.

Gate-Control Theory of Pain The idea that pain sensations are processed and altered by mechanisms within the spinal cord.

Gender The social components of being male or female.

Gender Identity How one psychologically perceives oneself as either male or female.

Gender Role The societal expectations for proper female and male behavior.

Gender Role Stereotypes Rigid, preconceived beliefs about the characteristics of males and females that are applied to all males and females without regard for individual differences.

General Adaptation Syndrome As described by Selye, a generalized physiological reaction to severe stressors consisting of three phases: the alarm reaction, the resistance phase, and the exhaustive phase.

Generalization 1. A tendency to respond in the same way to stimuli in the environment that have similar characteristics. 2. A set of beliefs about members of a group that are based on legitimate scientific findings and therefore considered to be true; they can be applied to most members of a group.

Generalized Anxiety Disorder Type of long-term anxiety that is not focused on any particular object or situation.

Generativity Versus Stagnation The seventh stage in Erikson's theory of psychosocial development. To avoid stagnation, the adult must "generate" or give something back to the world beyond concern and care for the immediate family.

Gene A segment of DNA that occupies a specific place on a particular chromosome.

Genital Stage The stage of psychosexual development that begins in puberty and represents mature adult sexuality and personality development.

Genuineness In Rogerian terms, authenticity or congruence; the awareness of one's true inner thoughts and feelings and being able to share them honestly with others.

Germinal Period The first stage of pregnancy (conception to 2 weeks), characterized by rapid cell division.

Gestalt An organized whole or pattern of perception.

Gestalt Psychology A school of psychology that focuses on principles of perception and believes the whole experience is qualitatively different from the sum of the distinct elements of that experience.

Gestalt Therapy A form of therapy originated by Fritz Perls that emphasizes awareness and personal responsibility and adopts a holistic approach, giving equal emphasis to mind and body.

Grafenberg Spot A region in the front wall of the vagina that supposedly has a special sensitivity to erotic stimulation.

Grammar The rules of a language that specify how phonemes, morphemes, words, and phrases should be combined to express meaningful thoughts.

Group In social psychology, two or more people interacting with one another and influencing one another's behavior.

Group Polarization Tendency for a group decision to become either more cautious or more risky than an individual decision, depending on the preexisting dominant tendencies of the group.

Groupthink Condition in which a highly cohesive group with a strong desire for agreement leads to uncritical consensus and faulty decision making.

Guilt Induction Method of gaining compliance based on the tendency for people to comply when they feel remorse for wrong behavior.

Gustation The sense of taste.

Habituation The tendency of the brain to ignore environmental factors that remain constant.

Hair Cells Auditory receptors in the cochlea.

Hallucinations Sensory perceptions that occur in the absence of a real external stimulus.

Hallucinogens Drugs that produce visual, auditory, or other sensory hallucinations.

Health Psychology The study of the relationship between psychological behavior and physical health and illness, with an emphasis on wellness and the prevention of illness.

Heart Disease General term used to include all disorders that in some way affect the heart muscle and can ultimately result in heart failure.

Heuristics Problem-solving strategies developed from previous experience that involve selective searches for appropriate solutions to problems and generally, but not always, lead to a solution.

Hierarchy Ranked listing of something; used in the behavior therapy systematic desensitization process.

Hierarchy of Needs Maslow's view of motivation; that some motives (such as physiological and safety needs) have to be satisfied before advancing to higher needs (such as belonging and self-esteem).

Higher Order Conditioning Classical conditioning in which a neutral stimulus is paired with a second stimulus that already causes a learned or conditioned response.

Homeostasis The body's steady state of normal functioning.

Homophobia Irrational fears of homosexuality; the fear of the possibility of homosexuality in oneself, or self-loathing toward one's own homosexuality. (From the Greek roots meaning "fear" of members of the "same" gender.)

Homosexual A person who has a primary sexual orientation toward members of his or her own sex.

Hormones Chemicals manufactured within the body that are circulated in the bloodstream to produce bodily changes or to maintain normal bodily functions.

Hue The visual dimension seen as a particular color; determined by the length of a light wave.

Humanistic Psychology A school of psychology that emphasizes the importance of the inner, subjective self and stresses the positive side of human nature.

Humanistic Therapy Therapy approaches that assist individuals to become creative and unique persons through affective restructuring processes.

Hyperopia Farsightedness; the eye is shorter than normal and the image falls behind its ideal position on the retina.

Hypertension Excessive muscular tension and high blood pressure.

Hypnogogic State A state of consciousness at the beginning of sleep in which many people experience visual, auditory, and kinesthetic sensations.

Hypnosis An alternate state of heightened suggestibility characterized by relaxation and intense focus.

Hypochondriasis A somatoform disorder in which a person has an extreme fear of illness and disease.

Hypothalamus A group of neuron cell bodies that ultimately controls the endocrine system and regulates drives such as hunger, thirst, sex, and aggression.

Hypothesis A possible explanation for a behavior being studied that can be answered or affirmed by an experiment or a series of observations.

Hysterical Neurosis A disorder with physical symptoms created by psychological factors. Today we use the term "conversion disorder."

Id According to Freud, the source of instinctual energy, which works on the pleasure principle and is concerned with immediate gratification.

Identity Crisis According to Erikson, a period of inner conflict during which an individual examines his or her life and values and makes decisions about life roles.

Identity Versus Role Confusion Erikson's fifth stage of psychosocial development; the adolescent may become confident and purposeful through discovery of an identity, or confused and ill-defined.

Illusion A false impression of the environment.

Imprinting The innate tendency of birds and some animals to follow and form attachment to the first moving object they see.

Incentive Theory The theory that motivation results from environmental stimuli that "pull" the organism in certain directions, as opposed to internal needs that drive or "push" the organism in certain directions.

Incest Sexual contact between two people who are related.

Incubation A period of time during which active searching for a problem's solution is set aside; this is sometimes necessary for a successful solution of the problem.

Incus The middle ossicle, attached to the malleus and the stapes.

Independent Variable A variable that is controlled by the experimenter and is applied to the subject to determine its effect.

Industrial/Organizational (I/O) Psychology The area of psychology that focuses on how individual behavior is affected by the work environment, organizations, and co-workers.

Industry Versus Inferiority Erikson's fourth psychosocial stage of development (ages 6 to 11), in which the child faces the challenge of mastering the skills needed to succeed in his or her culture.

Inferiority Complex Adler's idea that feelings of inferiority develop from early childhood experiences of helplessness and incompetence.

Information Overload Receiving more information than can be comfortably handled in a given period of time.

Information Processing Approach The approach to studying cognition that uses abstract models to depict how the brain, in a serial fashion, receives sensory information and processes, stores, and retrieves that information.

Informational Social Influence Conforming to group pressure out of the need for direction and information.

Informed Consent In sexuality, the possession of adequate intellectual and emotional maturity to understand fully and consent to sexual relations.

Ingratiation Use of favors, flattery, and statements of shared similarities as a method of getting someone to like you and increasing their compliance.

Ingroup Favoritism A cognitive process in prejudice whereby members of an ingroup are viewed in more favorable terms than members of the outgroup.

Initiative Versus Guilt The third stage in Erikson's psychosocial theory of development (ages 3 to 6), in which the child must overcome feelings of guilt and doubt and develop feelings of power and initiative.

Innate Referring to any inborn behavior that emerges during a predetermined period of an organism's life as a result of maturation only and not as a result of practice.

Insanity A legal term for those with a mental disorder that implies a lack of responsibility for their behavior and an inability to manage their affairs in a competent manner.

Insight 1. In psychoanalysis, a bringing in of awareness of motives, relationships, feelings, or impulses that had previously been poorly understood or of which the subject was totally unaware. 2. A sudden flash of understanding that occurs when you are trying to solve a problem.

Insomnia A sleep disorder in which a person has repeated difficulty in falling asleep, or staying asleep, or awakens too early.

Instincts Behavioral patterns that are (1) unlearned, (2) uniform in expression, and (3) universal in a species.

Intelligence The cognitive abilities employed in acquiring, remembering, and using knowledge of one's culture to solve everyday problems and to readily adapt to and function in both changing and stable environments.

Intelligence Quotient (IQ) A score on a test that is intended to measure verbal and quantitative abilities. On the Standard–Binet Intelligence Test, the IQ is the ratio of mental age to chronological age, times 100.

Interactionist Model The perspective that human development results from both nature and nurture factors.

Interference Task Any task that prevents maintenance rehearsal or prevents memories from being transferred to long-term memory.

Interference Theory The theory that claims we forget something because other information blocks its storage or retrieval.

Internal Locus of Control The belief that one has significant control over the events in one's life.

Interpersonal Attraction The degree of positive or negative feelings toward another.

Interposition A monocular depth cue in which an object that partially obscures another object is seen as being closer.

Interpretation A psychoanalyst's explanation of the significance of a patient's free associations and dreams.

Intimacy Versus Isolation Erikson's sixth stage in his theory of social development; the young adult must develop a capacity for close interpersonal bonds or face isolation and loneliness.

Intrinsic Motivation The desire to perform an activity for its own sake. The motivation is derived from the satisfaction arising out of the behavior itself.

Introspection A research method popular during the late nineteenth century in which trained subjects reported their current conscious experience.

Ions Molecules that carry positive or negative electrical charges.

Iris The colored part of the eye consisting of muscles that control the size of the pupil.

James–Lange Theory The theory that emotion is the perception of one's own bodily reactions and that each emotion is physiologically distinct.

Justice Perspective Gilligan's term for an approach to moral reasoning that emphasizes individuals' rights and views people as differentiated and standing alone.

Kinesthesis The sensory system that provides information on body posture and orientation.

Landmark Events Events that are important to us, such as high school graduation or getting married, that can be used as memory aids.

Language A creative form of expression in which sounds and symbols are combined according to specified rules.

Language Acquisition device (LAD) In Noam Chomsky's view, the child's inborn brain capacity to analyze language and unconsciously understand essential grammatical rules.

Latency Stage Freud's fourth psychosexual stage (age 6 to puberty), characterized by the relative lack of sexual interests.

Latent Content The true, unconscious meaning of a dream, according to Freudian dream theory.

Latent Learning Learning that occurs in the absence of a reward and remains hidden until some future time when it can be retrieved.

Lateral Hypothalamus (LH) Area of the hypothalamus responsible for stimulating eating behavior.

Learned Helplessness In Seligman's theory, a state of helplessness or resignation in which people or animals give up and quietly submit to punishment that they have previously been unable to escape. This may result to various levels of depression.

Learning A relatively permanent change in behavior or behavioral potential as a result of practice or experience.

Lens The transparent elastic structure in the eye that focuses light on the retina by changing shape.

Lesion Technique Any brain research technique that systematically destroys brain tissue to observe the effect of the destruction on behavior.

Levels of Processing The depth to which short-term memory contents are processed during consolidation to long-term memory.

Light Adaptation The visual adjustment of the rods and cones that reduces sensitivity to bright light.

Light and Shadow A monocular depth cue in which brighter objects are perceived as closer, whereas darker, dimmer objects are perceived as farther away.

Limbic System An interconnected system of subcortical structures involved with many types of emotional behavior, particularly aggression.

Linear Development The idea that development progresses in a fairly straight line, at a steady rate, and that each new development is built on the previous stages or abilities.

Linear Perspective The principle that as parallel lines recede, they appear to come together at the horizon.

Lobotomy A brain operation in which the nerve pathways between the frontal lobes and the thalamus and hypothalamus are cut in hopes of treating psychological disorders.

Lock-and-Key Theory The idea that each odor molecule will fit into only one type of smell receptor cell according to shape.

Locus of Control According to Rotter, a person's belief and expectancy regarding the control of events. A person with an *internal* locus of control believes he or she is in charge, whereas a person with an *external* locus of control believes the environment, chance, or fate determines outcomes.

Long-Term Memory (LTM) Relatively permanent memory in which information is stored for use at a later time.

Long-Term Potentiation (LTP) A process whereby short-term memories become long-term memories after repeated stimulation of a synapse leads to chemical and structural changes in the dendrites of the receiving neuron. This change results in increased sensitivity of the neuron to excitatory stimulation.

Longitudinal Method A data collection technique that measures a single individual or group of individuals over an extended period of time and gives information about age changes.

Maintenance Rehearsal The process of repeating the contents of short-term memory over and over to maintain it in STM.

Major Depression A DSM III-R diagnostic term for individuals experiencing a longlasting depressed mood that interferes with the ability to function, feel pleasure, or maintain interest in life. The feelings are without apparent cause or excessive for the given situation, and the individual may experience loss of contact with reality.

Maladaptive Functioning Standard An approach that evaluates behavior as abnormal when it interferes with an individual's functioning within his or her own life and within society.

Male Climacteric A term used to describe the physical and psychological changes associated with the male's movement into midlife.

Malleus The first of the ossicles, attached to the eardrum and the incus.

Manifest Content The surface content of a dream, containing dream symbols that distort and disguise the true meaning of the dream according to Freudian dream theory.

Massed Practice A learning technique in which time spent learning is massed into long, unbroken intervals; cramming.

Maturation Changes in development that result from automatic, genetically determined signals.

Medical Model Perspective that assumes abnormal behaviors reflect a type of mental or physical illness.

Meditation A relaxed state of consciousness that is characterized either by detachment from the external world or by directed focus on the external world.

Medulla A structure in the brain stem responsible for automatic body functions, such as respiration.

Menopause The gradual cessation of menstruation that occurs between the ages of 45 and 55; sometimes referred to as the climacteric or change of life.

Mental Housecleaning Hypothesis A theory that the function of dreaming is to rid the brain of useless, bizarre, or redundant information.

Mental Images Mental representations of objects and events that are not physically present; they are used in the thinking process to solve problems, express ideas, and so on.

Method of Loci A mnemonic device in which an idea is associated with a place or a part of a building.

Method of Word Associations A memory method in which verbal associations are created for items to be learned.

Midlife Crisis A time of psychological and emotional turmoil that supposedly occurs around the age of 35 for women and 40 for men.

Misattribution The incorrect attribution of internal arousal to false internal or external causes. More generally, any incorrect attribution of causality.

Mnemonic Devices Memory strategies in which information is organized or "tagged" visually or verbally.

Modeling Learning by imitating the behaviors of others.

Modeling Therapy A branch of behavior therapy that involves watching and imitating appropriate models who demonstrate desirable behaviors.

Monochromat A person who is truly colorblind because he or she has only rods and no cones.

Morpheme The smallest meaningful unit of language, formed from a certain combination of phonemes.

Motion Parallax A monocular depth cue that occurs when a moving observer perceives that objects at various distances move at different speeds across the retinal field.

Motivated Forgetting Theory The theory that people forget things that cause pain, threat, or embarrassment.

Motivation The process of activating, maintaining, and directing behavior toward a particular goal.

Motor Control Area The area located at the back of the frontal lobes of the cortex that is responsible for instigating voluntary movements.

MRI (Magnetic Resonance Imaging) A research technique utilizing radio waves instead of X rays to allow researchers to see structures within the brain.

Multiple Personality Dissociative disorder characterized by the presence of two or more distinct personality systems within the same individual.

Multiple Requests Compliance technique in which a first request is used as a "setup" for later requests.

Myelin Fatty insulation that serves to greatly increase the speed at which an action potential moves down an axon.

Myelination The accumulation of myelin (a fatty tissue that coats the axons of nerve cells) in the nervous system, thereby increasing the speed of neural messages.

Myopia Nearsightedness; the eye is longer than normal and the image falls in front of the ideal position on the retina.

Naikan Therapy A Japanese form of therapy that aims to help a person discover personal guilt and develop gratitude to others.

Narcolepsy A disease marked by sudden and irresistible onsets of sleep during normal waking hours.

Narcotics Drugs that are derived from opium and function as an analgesic or pain reliever.

Naturalistic Observation The systematic recording of behavior in the subject's natural state or habitat.

Need Compatibility A sharing of similar needs.

Need Complementarity The tendency to seek out and be attracted to people whose qualities we admire but personally lack.

Negative Punishment Punishment in which a rewarding stimulus is removed to decrease a response.

Negative Reinforcement Reinforcement in which a painful or annoying stimulus is taken away.

Negative State Relief The proposal that altruistic behavior is motivated by the desire to reduce negative feelings through helping others.

Neo-Freudians Contemporaries of Freud who both supported and criticized his theory.

Nerve A bundle of axons that have a similar function.

Neuron Individual nerve cells responsible for transmitting information throughout the body.

Neurosis A term used in early versions of the DSM to describe mental disorders related to anxiety.

Neurotransmitters Special chemicals released from axon terminal buttons that cross the synaptic gap and bind to receptor sites on the membrane of another neuron.

Neutral Stimulus An external stimulus that

does not ordinarily cause a reflex response or an emotional response.

Night Terrors Abrupt awakenings from NREM sleep accompanied by intense physiological arousal and feelings of panic.

Nightmares Anxiety-arousing dreams that generally occur near the end of the sleep cycle, during REM sleep.

Non-Rapid Eye Movement (NREM) Sleep Sleep stages 1 through 4, which are marked by an absence of rapid eye movements, relatively little dreaming, and variations in EEG activity.

Norm Cultural rule of behavior that prescribes what is acceptable or approved in a given situation.

Normative Social Influence Group pressure based on threats to reject group members who do not accept the positions of the group.

Obedience A type of social influence in which an individual follows direct commands, usually from someone in a position of authority.

Object Permanence A Piagetian term for one of an infant's most important accomplishments: understanding that objects (or people) continue to exist even when they cannot directly be seen, heard, or touched.

Observational Learning Theory The idea that we learn certain behaviors merely by watching someone else perform them.

Obsessive-Compulsive Disorder (OCD) Type of anxiety disorder characterized by intrusive thoughts (obsessions) and urges to perform repetitive, ritualistic behaviors (compulsions).

Occipital Lobes The cortical lobes located at the back of the brain that are dedicated entirely to vision and visual perception.

Oedipus Complex The Freudian term for the sexual attachment of a boy to his mother and his desire to replace his father.

Olfaction The sense of smell.

Olfactory Epithelium The mucus-coated membrane lining the top of the nasal cavity and containing the receptors for smell.

Operant Conditioning Learning that occurs when a response to an environmental cue is reinforced.

Operations Piaget's term for the various internal transformations, manipulations, and reorganizations of mental structures that children use to solve problems.

Opponent-Process Theory The theory of color vision first proposed by Ewald Hering that claims that there are three color systems—blue-yellow, red-green, and black-white.

Opponent-Process Theory of Emotions Idea that an intense emotional experience elicits an opposite (opposing) emotion. With repeated experiences, the second emotion becomes stronger than the first.

Optic Nerve The cranial nerve that carries visual information from the retina to the brain.

Oral Stage Freud's psychosexual stage (from birth to 12–18 months) during which the mouth is the center of pleasure and feeding is the primary source of conflict.

Organic Mental Disorders A DSM III-R disorder believed to be caused by temporary or permanent physical assaults on the nervous system, for example, alcohol-induced disorders or Alzheimer's disease.

Orgasm Phase The third phase of the sexual response cycle, during which pleasurable sensations peak and the body suddenly discharges its accumulated sexual tension in the process of orgasm or climax.

Orgasmic Dysfunction The inability to respond to sexual stimulation to the point of orgasm.

Ossicles Three small bones in the middle ear: the malleus, the incus, and the stapes.

Outgroup Homogeneity Effect A cognitive process in prejudice whereby members of the outgroup are judged as less individual, or diverse, than members of the ingroup.

Outgroup Negativity A cognitive process in prejudice whereby members of the outgroup are evaluated more negatively than members of the ingroup.

Oval Window The membrane of the cochlea that is moved by the stapes.

Overextension A child's tendency to misuse words to include objects that do not fit the word's meaning.

Overgeneralize A common error in a child's language acquisition where the rules for past tense and plurals are extended to irregular forms.

Overt Observable; not concealed.

Panic Disorder Type of anxiety disorder characterized by severe attacks of exaggerated anxiety.

Papillae Small bumps on the surface of the tongue that contain the taste receptors.

Paranoia A mental disorder characterized by delusions, or mistaken beliefs, of persecution or grandeur.

Parasympathetic Nervous System The part of the autonomic nervous system that is normally dominant when a person is in a relaxed, nonstressful physical and mental state, and that restores the body to its "status quo" after sympathetic arousal.

Parietal Lobes The cortical lobes located at the top of the brain that are the seat of body sensations and memory of the environment.

Parkinson's Disease A neurological disorder characterized by rigidity, tremor, and uncontrollable movements, believed to be caused by a dopamine deficiency.

Partial Reinforcement Reinforcement in which some, but not all, responses are reinforced.

Passive Aggressiveness A subtle form of aggression characterized by pouting, procrastination, stubbornness, or intentional inefficiency.

Pedophilia Nonrelative sexual gratification from contacts with children.

Peg-Word Mnemonic System A memory system in which peg words, or easy-to-visualize words in a specific order, are associated with difficult-to-remember words or numbers.

Perception The process of selecting, organizing, and interpreting sensory data into usable mental representations of the world.

Performance Anxiety A fear that one will be unable to meet the expectations for sexual "performance" of one's self or one's partner.

Peripheral Nervous System (PNS) The part of the nervous system outside the central nervous system that consists of the nerves going to and from the brain and spinal cord.

Personal Space Immediate physical space that surrounds each individual and is treated as if it were an extension of the self.

Personality An individual's characteristic pattern of thought, emotions, and behaviors, which make him or her unique.

Personality Disorders A DSM-III category that describes individuals with inflexible maladaptive personality traits. The best known type is the antisocial personality.

Persuasion Direct attempts to influence the attitudes of another through communication techniques.

PET (Positron Emission Tomography) Scan A type of brain scan in which radioactive glucose is injected into the bloodstream in order to see brain activity in an intact, living brain.

Phallic Stage Freud's psychosexual stage (ages 3 to 6) during which the child experiences either the Oedipus or Electra complex, which can only be resolved through identification with the same-sex parent.

Phenomenological Perspective The view that understanding another person requires knowing how he or she perceives the world. The term comes from philosophy, where the mental experiencing of the environment is called a phenomenon, and the study of how each person experiences reality is *phenomenology*.

Pheromones Bodily chemicals that affect others' behavior.

Phobia A severe irrational fear of an object or situation.

Phoneme The most basic unit of speech; an individual speech sound.

Photo Receptors Receptors for vision; the rods and cones.

Phrenology Pseudoscience that measures the skull to determine personality characteristics.

Physical Attractiveness Having the physical properties (size, shape, facial characteristics, and so on) that elicit favorable evaluations from others.

Physical Dependence A condition in which bodily processes have been so modified by repeated use of a drug that continued use is required to prevent withdrawal symptoms.

Pinna The fleshy part of the outer ear that we think of as "the ear."

Pitch The highness or lowness of tones or sounds, depending on their frequency.

Placebo A substance that would normally produce no physiological effect that is used as a control technique, usually in drug research.

Placebo Effect A change in subjects' behavior brought about because the subjects believe they have received a drug that elicits that change when in reality they have received a placebo, an inert substance.

Plateau Phase The second phase of the sexual response cycle, characterized by intensification of sexual tensions.

Pleasure Principle According to Freud, the id's strategy of seeking immediate and uninhibited pleasure and avoiding discomfort.

Polydrug Use Combining several drugs, which results in unknown and potentially serious side effects.

Polygraph Instrument that measures emotional arousal through various physiological reactions, such as heart rate, blood pressure, respiration rate, and electrodermal skin response.

Pons A brain structure located at the top of the brain stem that is involved with functions such as respiration, movement, and sleep.

Population The total of all possible cases from which a sample is selected.

Positive Punishment Punishment in which an aversive or undesirable stimulus is applied to decrease a response.

Positive Reinforcement Reinforcement in which a stimulus is given that is desirable to the subject.

Post-Decision Dissonance The tension (dissonance) that is felt once a decision is made, and the corresponding need to look for confirming evidence and avoid contradictory information.

Post-Traumatic Stress Disorder (PTSD) Type of anxiety disorder that follows an overwhelming, traumatic event.

Postconventional Level Kohlberg's highest level of moral development, which occurs when individuals develop personal standards for right and wrong.

Precognition The ability to predict the future.

Preconscious Freud's term for thoughts or information one can become aware of easily.

Preconventional Level Kohlberg's first level of moral development, characterized by moral judgments based on fear of punishment or desire for pleasure.

Prejudice A generally negative attitude directed toward others because of their membership in a specific group. Like all attitudes, prejudice involves three components: cognitions (or thoughts), affect (or feelings), and behavioral tendencies.

Premature Ejaculation Ejaculation that takes place too quickly for the pleasure of one or both partners.

Preoperational Stage The second of Piaget's stages (ages 2 to 7), characterized by the child's ability to employ mental symbols, to engage in fantasy play, and to use words. Thinking is egocentric and animistic and the child cannot yet perform operations.

Preparation The first stage in problem solving, in which the given facts are identified, rele-

vant facts are distinguished from irrelevant facts, and the ultimate goal is identified.

Presbyopia Farsightedness due to age.

Primary Aging Gradual changes in physical and mental processes that inevitably occur with age.

Primary Reinforcers Stimuli that increase the probability of a response and whose value does not need to be learned, such as food, water, and sex.

Proactive Interference Forgetting because previously learned information interferes with new information.

Problem-Focused Forms of Coping Coping strategies in which one views stressful situations as problems and uses problem-solving strategies to decrease or eliminate the source of stress.

Problem Solving A series of thinking processes we use to reach a goal that is not readily attainable.

Problem-Solving Set A mental barrier to problem solving that occurs when people apply only methods that have worked in the past rather than trying innovative ones.

Production The problem-solving stage during which possible solutions to the problem are generated.

Programmed Instruction Personalized learning that makes use of operant conditioning techniques, whereby students read a section of text, then test themselves on the material. They continue on to the next section or review the previous one, depending on the results of the test.

Projection Areas Parietal areas of the brain that receive incoming sensory information.

Projective Tests Techniques for assessing personality in which the individual is asked to talk about a relatively ambiguous or neutral stimulus (such as an inkblot). It is believed that inner thoughts, feelings, and conflicts will be projected onto the stimulus.

Prototype A model or best example of items belonging to a particular category.

Proximity 1. The Gestalt principle proposing that elements that are physically close together will be grouped together and perceived as a single unit. 2. A key factor in attraction involving geographic, residential, and other forms of physical closeness.

Proximodistal Development A general pattern of physical growth in which development starts at the center of the body and moves toward the extremities.

Pseudopsychologies "False psychologies;" popular systems that pretend to discover psychological information through nonscientific or deliberately fraudulent methods.

Psychiatrist A medical doctor who has additional training in the diagnosis and treatment of mental illness.

Psychiatry The specialized branch of medicine dealing with the diagnosis, treatment, and prevention of mental disorders.

Psychoactive Drugs Chemicals that affect the

nervous system and cause a change in behavior, mental processes, and conscious experience.

Psychoactive Substance Use Disorders Problem use of drugs such as alcohol, barbiturates, and amphetamines that affect mental functioning

Psychoanalysis 1. Sigmund Freud's theoretical school of thought, which emphasizes the study of unconscious processes. 2. A type of psychotherapy originated by Sigmund Freud that seeks to bring unconscious conflicts, which usually date back to early childhood experiences, into consciousness.

Psychoanalyst A mental health professional (usually a physician) who is trained to practice psychoanalysis.

Psychoanalytic Theory Freud's theory of personality that emphasizes the influence of the unconscious mind.

Psychobiology The study of the biology of behavior.

Psychogenic Amnesia Inability to recall the personal past as a result of psychological stress.

Psychogenic Fugue A type of amnesia in which people suddenly leave where they live and assume a new identity.

Psychokinesis The ability to move or affect objects without touching them.

Psychological Dependence A desire or craving to achieve the effects produced by a drug.

Psychology The scientific study of behavior.

Psychophysics The study of the relationships between physical stimulation and the sensations evoked by such stimulation.

Psychosexual Stages In psychoanalytic theory, a developmental period in which individual pleasures must be gratified if personality development is to proceed normally.

Psychosis Serious mental disorder characterized by loss of contact with reality and extreme mental disruption. Since daily functioning is often impaired, psychotic individuals are more likely to need hospitalization.

Psychosocial Stages of Development Erikson's theory that individuals undergo a series of eight developmental stages and that adult personality reflects how the distinct challenges or crises at each stage are resolved.

Psychosurgery Operative procedures on the brain designed to relieve severe mental symptoms that have not responded to other forms of treatment.

Psychotherapy A general term for the various methods of therapy used to treat psychological disorders. All psychotherapies involve the application of psychological principles and techniques to the treatment of mental disorders or to the problems of everyday adjustment.

Puberty The period in life during which the sex organs mature to a point where sexual reproduction becomes possible. Puberty generally begins for girls around 8 to 12 years of age, and for boys about two years later.

Punishment Any action or event that decreases the likelihood of a response being repeated.

Pupil An opening surrounded by the iris through which light passes into the eye.

Rape Oral, anal, or vaginal penetration that a person forces on an unconsenting or unwilling victim.

Rape Trauma Syndrome The consequences suffered by a rape victim, including both physical and psychological effects.

Rapid Eye Movement (REM) Sleep A stage of sleep marked by rapid eye movements, high-frequency brain waves, and dreaming.

Rational-Emotive Therapy (RET) Cognitive therapy system developed by Albert Ellis to attempt to change the troubled person's belief system.

Reactance Increased resistance to persuasion that is experienced when the recipient feels that his or her freedom to choose is threatened.

Reality Principle According to Freud, the principle on which the conscious ego operates as it tries to meet the demands of the unconscious id and the realities of the environment.

Recall Process of using a very general stimulus cue to search the contents of long-term memory.

Receptors Body cells specialized to detect and respond to stimulus energy.

Reciprocal Determinism Bandura's observation that the individual's cognitions, behaviors, and the learning environment interact and continually influence one another.

Recognition Process of matching a specific stimulus cue to an appropriate item in long-term memory.

Redintegration The type of remembering that occurs when something unlocks a chain of memories.

Reference Groups Groups that we like and feel similar to and are therefore more likely to conform to.

Reflex Arc The path that the neural impulse travels to initiate a reflex.

Reflexes Unlearned, involuntary responses of a part of the body to an external stimulus that do not require input from the brain.

Refractory Period The period after orgasm during which further orgasm is considered physiologically impossible.

Reinforcement Any action or event that increases the probability that a response will be repeated.

Reinforcement Theory of Attraction The theory that attraction results from a positive emotional arousal. We like those who make us feel good and dislike those who make us feel bad.

Relative Size A monocular cue to distance in which smaller objects appear more distant than larger objects.

Relaxation Techniques Procedures used to relieve the anxiety and bodily tension accompanying such problems as stress and chronic pain.

Relearning Learning material a second time. Relearning usually takes less time than original learning.

Reliability A measure of the consistency and stability of test scores when the test is readministered over a period of time.

Repair/Restoration Theory A theory suggesting that sleep serves a restorative function, allowing organisms to recuperate from physical, emotional, and intellectual demands.

Replicate To conduct a research study again, following the same procedure.

Representative Heuristic A mental shortcut used in social cognition to judge the probability of certain events based on how well a newly encountered situation matches our memory of similar situations. When it closely matches, we judge it as being likely to have a similar outcome.

Repression Freud's most important defense mechanism that involves unconscious blocking of unacceptable impulses to keep them from awareness.

Research Methodologies Standardized scientific procedures for conducting investigations.

Resistance A stage in psychoanalysis where the patient avoids (resists) the analyst's attempts to bring unconscious material to conscious awareness.

Resolution Phase The final stage of the sexual response cycle, characterized by continued relaxation as the body returns to its unaroused state.

Resting Potential The resting state of the axon membrane, which consists of a high concentration of sodium molecules outside the axon and a high concentration of potassium and protein molecules inside the axon.

Reticular Activating System (RAS) A diffuse set of cells in the medulla, pons, hypothalamus, and thalmus that serves as a filter for incoming sensory information.

Retina An area at the back of the eye containing light receptors in the shape of rods and cones.

Retinal Disparity A binocular cue to distance in which the separation of the eyes causes different images to fall on each retina.

Retrieval The process of returning long-term memory contents to short-term memory for analysis or awareness.

Retrieval Failure Theory The theory that forgetting is a problem with retrieval, not a problem with long-term storage of information.

Retroactive Interference Forgetting because new information interferes with previously learned information.

Retrograde Amnesia Difficulty in remembering previously learned material.

Reverberating Circuits The firing of a set of neurons over and over again during memory processing.

Reversible Figure An ambiguous figure that has more than one possible figure and ground organization.

Reward Centers Areas in the brain that, when stimulated, invoke a highly satisfying feeling.

Rods Receptors in the retina that are most sensitive in dim light; they do not respond to color.

Role A category of people and the set of normative expectations for people in that category.

Romantic Love An intense feeling of attraction to another person that is characterized by high passion, obsessive thinking, and emotional fluctuation.

Rorschach Inkblot Test A projective personality test using ambiguous "inkblots." The individual tells the examiner what he or she sees in the blots and, it is hoped, reveals hidden aspects of his or her personality.

Saliency Bias The tendency to focus attention on vivid, salient factors when explaining the causes of behavior.

Sample A selected group of subjects that is representative of a larger population.

Sample Bias The tendency for the sample of subjects in a research study to be atypical of a larger population.

Schedule of Reinforcement A schedule delineating when a response is to be reinforced.

Schemata Cognitive structures or patterns consisting of a number of organized ideas that grow and differentiate with experience.

Schizophrenia Group of psychotic disorders involving distortions in thinking, perception, emotion, and behavior.

Sclera The white, opaque outer wall of the eye.

Secondary Aging Acceleration in the normal physical changes associated with aging as a result of abuse, neglect, disuse, or disease.

Secondary Reinforcers Stimuli that increase the probability of a response and whose reinforcing properties are learned, such as money and material possessions.

Secondary Sex Characteristics Hormonally generated sexual characteristics, secondary to the sex organs, that are not necessary for reproduction.

Secondary Traits In Allport's theory, these traits are not as important as central traits for describing personality since they influence few situations or behaviors.

Selective Attention The process whereby the brain manages to sort out and attend only to the important messages from the senses.

Self-Actualization According to Maslow, an innate tendency toward growth that motivates all human behavior and results in the full realization of a person's highest potential.

Self-Concept In Roger's theory, all the information and beliefs individuals have about their own nature, qualities, and behavior.

Self-Efficacy According to Bandura, a person's belief about whether he or she can successfully engage in behaviors related to personal goals.

Self-Esteem According to Rogers, the feelings each of us has about ourselves, either good or bad.

Self-Fulfilling Prophecy A sequence in which an individual's or others' expectations lead to behaviors that cause the expected events to occur.

Self-Hypnosis An alternate state of consciousness induced by oneself during which one is more relaxed, more alert, and more open to suggestion than in the normal state.

Self-Perception Theory Bem's theory that people form attitudes by observing their own behavior.

Self-Serving Bias Way of maintaining a positive self-image by taking credit for one's successes and emphasizing external causes for one's failures.

Semantic Memory A type of long-term memory in which facts and relations between facts are stored.

Semicircular Canals Three arching structures in the inner ear containing the hair receptors that provide balance information from head movements.

Sensation The process of receiving, translating, and transmitting information to the brain from the external and internal environments.

Sensorimotor Stage The first of Piaget's stages (birth to age 2), in which cognitive development is acquired through exploration of the world via sensory perceptions and motor skills.

Sensory Adaptation A decrease in response of a sensory system to continuous stimulation.

Sensory Deprivation A state in which all sensory stimulation is diminished as much as possible.

Sensory Memory The type of memory that occurs within the senses while incoming messages are being transmitted to the brain.

Serial Position Effect The phenomenon of remembering the material at the beginning and the end of a list better than the material in the middle.

Set The internal state (beliefs and expectations) of a drug user that influences the overall effects of any drug.

Set Point An organism's personal homeostatic level for a particular body weight that results from factors such as early feeding experiences and heredity.

Setting The physical and interpersonal environment that surrounds a drug user and influences the effects of the drug.

Sex The biological components of maleness and femaleness.

Sexual Dysfunction Impairment of the normal physiological processes of arousal and orgasm.

Sexual Harassment Unwelcome sexual advances, requests for sexual favors, and other unwelcome verbal or physical conduct of a sexual nature.

Sexual Response Cycle Masters and Johnson's description of the bodily response to sexual arousal. The four stages are excitement, plateau, orgasm, and resolution.

Sexual Scripts Socially dictated descriptions of the sequences of behavior that are considered appropriate in sexual interactions.

Shape Constancy The process in which the perceived shape of an object remains the same, even though the retinal image of that object changes.

Shaping Teaching a desired response by reinforcing a series of successive steps leading to this final response.

Short-Term Memory (STM) Memory containing things a person is presently thinking about; its capacity is limited to about seven items and a duration of about 30 seconds.

Shotgun Approach The technique used in behavioral change whereby there is an attempt to change all the behaviors constituting the Type A personality.

Similarity 1. The Gestalt principle proposing that things that appear similar or act in a similar fashion are perceived as being the same. 2. A sharing of common interests, values, and beliefs—an important factor in long-term attraction.

Size Constancy The process in which the perceived size of an object remains the same, even though the size of the retinal image changes.

Skin Senses The sensory system for detecting pressure, temperature, and pain.

Sleep Apnea A temporary cessation of breathing during sleep; one of the causes of snoring and a suspected cause of sudden infant death syndrome.

Social Cognition Processes through which we interpret, analyze, remember, and use information about the social world.

Social Comparison Theory Festinger's view that we seek out others as a way to interpret and compare our own abilities, attitudes, and reactions.

Social Exchange Theory The theory that interpersonal interactions are governed by the costs and benefits each person gives and receives.

Social Learning Theory A theory developed by Bandura proposing that people learn various behaviors by observing others who serve as models.

Social Psychology The branch of psychology that studies how the thoughts, feelings, and actions of individuals are influenced by the actual, imagined, or implied presence of others.

Social Trap Dilemma created when individual short-term best interests conflict with long-term goals or group interests.

Social Worker A therapist who has obtained at least a master's degree in social work, and who typically works with patients and their families to ease their community relations.

Socialization The process of imparting the customs, habits, folkways, and mores of a given

culture to a child or a newcomer to the society.

Sociobiology A branch of biology that emphasizes the genetic and evolutionary basis of social behaviors in all organisms, including humans.

Sodium–Potassium Pump An ongoing process whereby sodium ions are continually moved out and potassium ions are continually moved into the axon to restore and preserve the resting period.

Soma The cell body of the neuron; it integrates incoming information from the dendrites, absorbs nutrients, and produces the majority the protein molecules needed by the neuron.

Somatic Nervous System A subdivision of the peripheral nervous system that consists of nerves carrying afferent sensory information and efferent motor information to and from the central nervous system, the sense organs, and the skeletal muscles.

Somatoform Disorder Psychological disorders in which the symptoms take a somatic (bodily) form without apparent physical cause.

Sound Waves The movement of air molecules produced by a vibrating object.

Source Traits Cattell's term for the basic personality traits he believed are shared by most individuals.

Spinal Cord The part of the nervous system found within the spinal column that is involved in reflexes and the relay of neural information to and from the brain.

Spontaneous Recovery The reappearance of a previously extinguished response.

Standardization The process of establishing the norms of a test in order to assess which skills, knowledge, or characteristics are representative of the general population. Also, the development of standard procedures for administering and scoring a test to ensure that the conditions are the same for everyone taking the test.

Stapes The last of the ossicles, attached to the incus and to the oval window.

State-Dependent Memory Memory that is connected to a state of emotional arousal.

Statistical Standard A standard that evaluates behavior as abnormal when it deviates from average behavior in that particular culture.

Statistically Significant A relationship believed not to be caused by chance.

Statistics Data collected in a research study and the mathematical procedures used to analyze the data.

Stereoscopic Vision Three-dimensional vision that results from the brain fusing the two different images received from the eyes into one image.

Stereotype 1. A set of beliefs about the characteristics of people in a group that is generalized to all group members. 2. The cognitive component of prejudice.

Stimulants Drugs that act on the brain and nervous system to increase their overall activity and general responsiveness.

Stimulus An object or event that causes an organism to respond.

Storm and Stress The idea that emotional turmoil and rebellion are characteristics of all adolescents.

Stress According to Selye, the nonspecific response of the body to any demand made on it.

Stressor Any stimulus that causes stress.

Stroboscopic Motion The illusion of motion in which alternating lights are seen as one moving light.

Structuralism An early psychological school that focused on the sensations and feelings of perceptual experience.

Subject A participant in a research study.

Subjective Discomfort Standard An approach that evaluates behavior as abnormal when the individual is discontent with his or her own psychological functioning.

Subliminal Pertaining to any stimulus presented below the threshold of conscious awareness.

Substance Abuse Use of a psychoactive drug in ways that interfere with social or occupational functioning.

Substance Dependence Abuse of a psychoactive drug that includes the physical reactions of drug tolerance or withdrawal symptoms.

Substitute Word System A memory system in which a word to be remembered is broken into parts and associated with easy-to-visualize words that sound like the word's parts.

Superego In psychoanalytic theory, the part of the personality that incorporates parental and societal standards for morality.

Superordinate Goal Way of reducing prejudice that involves creating a goal that is "higher" than individual goals and is of benefit to both parties.

Superstitious Behavior Behavior that is continually repeated because it is thought to cause desired effects, though in reality the behavior and the effects are totally unrelated.

Surveys Nonexperimental research techniques that sample behaviors and attitudes of a population.

Sympathetic Nervous System The part of the autonomic nervous system that dominates when a person is under mental or physical stress, and that mobilizes the body's resources toward "fight or flight."

Synapse The junction between two neurons where neurotransmitter passes from the axon of one neuron to the dendrite or soma of another.

Synergistic Effect The interaction of two or more drugs such that the combined effects are much stronger than a simple summation of their individual doses.

Syntax The grammatical rules that specify in what order the words and phrases should be arranged in a sentence in order to convey meaning.

Systematic Desensitization In behavior therapy, a gradual process of associating a hierarchy of fear-evoking stimuli with deep relaxation.

Tardive Dyskinesia Potential side effect of antipsychotic drugs; it includes effects on voluntary muscles.

Target Behavior Approach The technique used in behavioral change where there is an attempt to change only Type A behaviors that have specifically been found to lead to heart disease, particularly a hostile and cynical attitude.

Telegraphic Speech The two- or three-word sentences of young children that contain only the most necessary words.

Telepathy The ability to read other people's minds.

Temperament A basic, inborn dispositional quality that appears shortly after birth and characterizes an individual's style of approaching people and situations.

Temporal Lobes The cortical lobes whose functions include auditory perception, language memory, and some emotional control.

Teratogen An external, environmental agent that may cross the placental barrier and disrupt development, causing minor or severe birth defects.

Territoriality Tendency to mark, maintain, or defend certain areas as one's own.

Texture Gradients Monocular cue to distance based on the fact that texture changes from coarse to fine as the distance of an object increases.

Thalamus A subcortical area located below the corpus callosum that serves as the major relay area for incoming sensory information.

Thanatology The study of death and dying. The term comes from *thanatos,* the Greek name for a mythical personification of death, and was borrowed by Freud to represent the death instinct.

Thematic Apperception Test (TAT) A projective personality test requiring subjects to tell stories about pictures shown on cards. Presumably, the subjects will "project" themselves into the story, and their narrative will reflect their hidden needs.

Theory An interrelated set of concepts that is developed in an attempt to explain a body of data and generate testable hypotheses.

Thinking Using knowledge that has been gathered and processed; mentally manipulating concepts and images to perform such mental activities as reasoning, solving problems, producing and understanding language, and making decisions.

Time Out Use of negative punishment through removal of people from sources of rewards whenever they behave inappropriately.

Tip-of-the-Tongue (TOT) The feeling that a word you are trying to remember is just barely inaccessible.

Token Tangible secondary (conditioned) reinforcer that can be exchanged for primary rewards.

Token Economy Therapeutic use of tokens in a prescribed way to reward and shape appropriate behavior.

Tolerance A decreased sensitivity to a drug that requires larger and more frequent doses to produce the desired effect.

Trait An enduring predisposition to respond in a particular way, often distinguishing one individual from another. People can vary in their personality traits over a wide range of values.

Transduction The process by which energy stimulating a receptor is converted into neural impulses.

Transference In psychoanalysis, the tendency of a patient to displace, or transfer, onto his/her relationship with the therapist emotions experienced in the past in relationships with the mother, father, or other important figures.

Transsexual An individual who is physically one sex but psychologically the opposite and has a persistent desire to change his or her body to that of the other sex.

Transvestite An individual who gains sexual satisfaction and relief from anxiety by dressing in the clothing of the other sex.

Trephining In modern usage, any surgical procedure in which a hole is bored into the skull. In ancient times, a type of therapy that involved deliberate chipping of holes into the skull to allow evil spirits to escape.

Trichromatic Theory The theory of color vision first proposed by Thomas Young stating that there are three color systems—red, green, and blue.

Trust Versus Mistrust The first of Erikson's eight stages of psychosocial development (from birth to 12–18 months), in which the infant must determine whether the world and the people in it can be trusted.

Two-Syndrome Hypothesis A theory that suggests that schizophrenia is composed of two separate syndromes: Type 1, which is related to dopamine sensitivity and produces positive symptoms (such as delusions and hallucinations), and Type 2, which is related to genetics and brain abnormalities and produces negative symptoms (such as flat affect and social withdrawal).

Type A Personality Set of behavior characteristics that includes intense ambition, competition, drive, constant preoccupation with responsibilities, a sense of time urgency, and a cynical, hostile outlook.

Type B Personality Set of behavior characteristics consistent with a calm, patient, relaxed attitude toward life.

Unconditional Positive Regard According to Carl Rogers, the nonjudgmental attitude and genuine caring that the therapist should express toward the client.

Unconditioned Response (UCR) The reflex response evoked by a stimulus without the necessity of learning.

Unconditioned Stimulus (UCS) Any stimulus that causes a reflex or emotional response without the necessity of learning or conditioning.

Unconscious Freud's term for the part of the mind whose contents, which consist of thoughts, motives, impulses, and desires, lie beyond a person's normal awareness, but which can be made available through psychoanalysis.

Validity The ability of a test to actually measure what it is intended to measure.

Variable Interval A schedule of reinforcement in which the subject is reinforced for the first response after a specified period of time has elapsed. This period of time varies from one reinforcement to the next.

Variable Ratio A schedule of reinforcement in which the subject is reinforced, on the average, for making a specific number of responses, but the number of required responses on each trial is varied.

Variables Factors that can be varied and can assume more than one value.

Ventromedial Hypothalamus (VMH) Area of the hypothalamus responsible for signaling the organism to stop eating. If destroyed, the organism will overeat and become obese.

Vestibular Sacs Inner ear structures containing hair receptors that respond to the specific angle of the head, to provide balance information.

Vestibular Sense The sense of how the body is oriented in relation to the pull of gravity; the sense of balance.

Vicarious Conditioning Learning by watching a model or reading about a task.

Vitreous Humor A semiliquid gel that nourishes the inside of the eye and is responsible for maintaining the eye's shape.

Wavelength The length of a sound or light wave, measured from the crest of one wave to the crest of the next.

Waxy Flexibility A symptom of schizophrenia in which individuals maintain whatever posture is imposed upon them.

Wernicke's Area An area of the cerebral cortex responsible for the thinking and interpreting aspect of language production.

Wish-Fulfillment Theory Freud's theory of dream interpretation that emphasizes the roles of manifest and latent content.

Withdrawal Unpleasant, painful, or agonizing physical reactions resulting from discontinued use of a drug.

Zeigarnik Effect Process of working unconsciously on a problem until it is solved.

References

A chronicler of elders' wisdom. (1991, September 23). *Time*, p. 48.

AAMODT, M. G. (1991). *Applied industrial/organizational psychology*. Belmont, CA: Wadsworth.

AARONS, L. (1976). Evoked sleep-talking. *Perceptual and Motor Skills, 31,* 27–40.

ABEL, E. (1984). Opiates and sex. *Journal of Psychoactive Drugs, 16,* 205–216.

ABELSON, R. P., KINDER, D. R., PETERS, M. D., & FISKE, S. T. (1982). Affective and semantic components in political person perception. *Journal of Personality and Social Psychology, 42,* 619–630.

ABRAHAM, S. F., & BEAUMONT, P. J. V. (1982). How patients describe bulimia or binge eating. *Psychological Medicine, 12,* 625–635.

ABRAMOVITCH, R., CORTER, C., PEPLER, D. J., & STANHOPE, L. (1986). Sibling and peer interaction: A final follow-up and comparison. *Child Development, 47,* 217–229.

ABRAMSON, L. Y., ALLOY, L. B., & METALSKY, G. I. (1990). The cognitive diathesis-stress theories of depression: Toward an adequate evaluation of the theories' validities. In L. B. Alloy (Ed.), *Cognitive processes in depression*. New York: Guilford Press.

ADAM, G., & FAISZT, J. (1967). Conditions for successful transfer effects. *Nature, 216,* 198–200.

ADAM, K. (1980). Sleep as a restorative process and a theory to explain why. *Progress in Brain Research, 53,* 289–305.

ADELMAN, P. K., & ZAJONC, R. B. (1989). Facial efference and the experience of emotion. In M. R. Rosenzweig & L. W. Porter (Eds.), *Annual review of psychology* (pp. 249–280). Palo Alto, CA: Annual Reviews Inc.

ADELSON, J. (1979, September). Adolescence and the generation gap. *Psychology Today*, pp. 33–37.

ADER, R., & COHEN, N. (1984). Behavior and the immune system. In W. D. Gentry (Ed.). *Handbook of behavioral medicine.* New York: Guilford Press.

ADLER, A. (1964). The individual psychology of Alfred Adler. In H. L. Ansbacher & R. R. Ansbacher (Eds.), *The individual psychology of Alfred Adler.* New York: Harper & Row (Torchbooks).

ADLER, A. (1979). *Superiority and social interest: A collection of later writings* (3rd rev. ed.). Evanston, IL: Northwestern University Press.

ADLER, N. A. (1991). *International dimension of organization behavior* (2nd ed.). Boston: PWS-Kent.

ADLER, T. (1989, December). Integrity test popularity prompts close scrutiny. *APA Monitor*, p. 7.

ADLER, T. (1991). Hypothalamus study stirs social questions. *APA Monitor, 22* (11), 8–9.

ADLER, T. (1993, January). Shy, bold temperament? It's mostly in the genes. *APA Monitor*, p. 7.

ADORNO, T. W., FRENKEL-BRUNSWICK, E., LEVINSON, D. J., & SANFORD, R. N. (1950). *The authoritarian personality.* New York: Harper & Row.

AINSWORTH, M. D. S. (1967). *Infancy in Uganda: Infant care and the growth of love.* Baltimore: The Johns Hopkins University Press.

AINSWORTH, M. D. S., BLEHAR, M., WATERS, E., & WALL, S. (1978). Patterns of attachment: Observations in the strange situation and at home. Hillsdale, NJ: Erlbaum.

AKABAS, M. H., DODD, J., & AL-AWQATI, Q. (1988). A bitter substance induces a rise in intracellular calcium in a subpopulation of rat taste cells. *Science 242,* 1047–1050.

ALAM, N., & SMIRK, F. H. (1938). Blood pressure raising reflexes in health, essential hypertension, and renal hypertension. *Clinical Science, 3,* 259–266.

Alcohol's toll: Alcohol in perspective. (1993). *University of California at Berkeley Wellness Letter, 9*(5), 4–6.

ALEAMONI, L. M., & OBOLER, L. (1978). ACT versus SAT in predicting first semester GPA. *Educational and Pyschological Measurement, 38,* 393–399.

ALEXANDER, C. N., LANGER, E. L., NEWMAN, R. I., CHANDLER, H. M., & DAVIES, J. L. (1989). Transcendental meditation, mindfulness, and longevity: An experimental study with the elderly. *Journal of Personality and Social Psychology, 37,* 950–964.

ALFORD, J., KASPER, C., & BAUMANN, P. (1984). Diagnostic classification of child sexual offenders. *Corrective and Social Psychiatry, 30,* 40–46.

ALLEN, C. (1989). *The hold life has: Coco and cultural identity in an Andean community.* Washington, DC: Smithsonian Institute.

ALLEN, D., & OKAWA, J. B. (1987). A counseling center looks at sexual harassment. *Journal of NAWDAC, 50,* 9–15.

ALLEN, J., PHILLIBER, S., & HOGGSON, N. (1990). School-based prevention of teenage pregnancy and school dropout: Process evaluation of the national replication of Teen Outreach Program. *American Journal of Community Psychology, 18,* 505–524.

ALLEN, L. S., HINES, M., SHRYNE, J. E., & GORSKI, R. A. (1989). Two sexually dimorphic cell groups in the human brain. *Journal of Neuroscience, 9,* 497–506.

ALLEN, L. S., RICHEY, M. F., CHAI, Y. M., & GORSKI, R. A. (1991). Sex differences in the corpus collosum of the living human being. *Journal of Neuroscience, 11*(4), 933–942.

ALLGEIER, A. R., & ALLGEIER, E. R. (1991). *Sexual interactions.* (3rd ed.). Lexington, MA: Heath.

ALLISON, T., & CICCHETTI, D. V. (1976). Sleep in mammals: Ecological and constitutional correlates. *Science, 194,* 732–734.

ALLMAN, W. F. (1992, May 11). The evolution of aggression. *U. S. News and World Report*, pp. 58–60.

ALLPORT, G. (1937). *Personality: A psychological interpretation.* New York: Holt, Rinehart and Winston.

ALLPORT, G. W., & ODBERT, H. S. (1936). Trait-names: A psycho-lexical study. *Psychological Monographs: General and Applied, 47,* 1–21.

ALTEMEYER, B. (1992). *Six studies of right-wing authoritarianism among American state legislators.* Unpublished manuscript, University of Manitoba.

ALTEMEYER, R. (1989). *Enemies of freedom: Understanding right wing authoritarianism.* San Francisco: Jossey-Bass.

ALTMAN, I. (1975). *The environment and social behavior.* Monterey, CA: Brooks/Cole.

ALZATE, H. (1985). Vaginal eroticism: A replication study. *Archives of Sexual Behavior, 14,* 529–537.

AMABILE, T. M. (1985). Motivation and creativity: Effects of motivational orientation on creative writers. *Journal of Personality and Social Psychology, 48,* 393–399.

AMATO, P. R. (1983). Helping behavior in urban and rural environments: Field studies based on a taxonomic organization of helping episodes. *Journal of Personality and Social Psychology, 45,* 571–586.

American Psychiatric Association. (1994). *Diagnostic and statistical manual of mental disorders* (4th ed). Washington, DC: Author.

American Psychiatric Association (1990) *The practice of ECT: Recommendations for treatment, training, and privileging.* Washington, DC: American Psychiatric Press.

American Psychological Association. (1984). *Behavioral research with animals.* Washington, DC: Author.

American Psychological Association. (1990). Ethical principles of psychologists. *American Psychologist, 45,* 390–395.

AMOORE, J. E. (1977). Specific anosmia and the concept of primary odors. *Chemical Senses and Flavor, 2,* 267–281.

AMOORE, J. E., JOHNSTON, W., JR., & RUBIN, M. (1964). The stereochemical theory of odor. *Scientific American, 210*(2), 42–49.

ANAND, B. K., & BROBECK, B. R. (1951). Localization of the feeding center in the hypothalamus of the rat. *Proceedings for the Society of Experimental Biology and Medicine, 77,* 323–324.

ANASTASI, A. (1982), *Psychological testing* (5th ed.). New York: Macmillan.

ANDERSON, C. A. (1989). Temperature and aggression: Ubiquitous effects of heat on occurrence of human violence. *Psychological Bulletin, 106,* 74–96.

ANDERSON, D. R., & LEVIN, S. R. (1976). Young children's attention to Sesame Street. *Child Development, 47,* 806–811.

ANDERSON, J. R. (1978). Arguments concerning representations for mental imagery. *Psychological Review, 85,* 249–277.

ANDERSON, J. R. (1983). *The architecture of cognition.* Cambridge, MA: Harvard University Press.

ANDERSON, K. J. (1983). The interactive effects of caffeine, impulsivity and task demands on a visual search task. *Personality and Individual Differences, 4*(2), 127–134.

ANDOLSEK, K. (1990). *Obstetric care: Standards of prenatal intrapartum, and postpartum management.* Philadelphia: Lea & Febiger.

ANDREASEN, N. C. (1982). Negative versus positive

schizophrenia: Definition and validation. *Archives of General Psychiatry, 39,* 789–794.

ANDREASEN, N. C. (1988). Brain imaging: Applications in psychiatry. *Science, 239,* 1381–1388.

ANDREASEN, N. C., & BLACK, D. W. (1991). *Introductory textbook of psychiatry.* Washington, DC: American Psychiatric Press.

ANDREASEN, N. C., FLAUM, M. SWAYZE, V. W., TYRRELL, G., & ARNDT, S. (1990). Positive and negative symptoms in schizophrenia. *Archives of General Psychiatry, 47,* 615–621.

ANISFELD, M. (1991). Neonatal imitation. *Developmental Review, 11,* 60–97.

ANTROBUS, J. S., FEIN, G., JORDAN, L., ELLMAN, S. J., & ARKIN, A. M. (1991). Measurement and design in research on sleep reports. In S. A. Ellman & J. S. Antrobus (Eds.). *The mind in sleep: Psychology and psychophysiology* (2nd ed., pp. 83–122). New York: Wiley.

APPLE, W., STREETER, L. A., & KRAUSS, R. B. (1979). Effects of pitch and speech rate on personal attributions. *Journal of Personality and Social Psychology, 37,* 715–727.

APTER, M. J. (1992). *The dangerous edge: The psychology of excitement.* New York: Free Press.

APTER, T. (1990). *Altered loves: Mothers and daughters during adolescence.* New York: St. Martin's Press.

ARAL, S. O., & HOLMES, K. K. (1991). Sexually transmitted diseases in the AIDS era. *Scientific American, 264,* 62–69.

ARCHER, J. (1991). The influence of testosterone on human aggression. *British Journal of Psychology, 82,* 1–28.

ARDRY, R. (1966). *The territorial imperative.* New York: Atheneum.

AREHART-TREICHEL, J. (1979, December 1). Down's syndrome: The father's role. *Science News,* pp. 381–382.

ARIES, P. (1962). *Centuries of childhood: A social history of family life.* New York: Random House.

ARKIN, A. A. (1991). Sleeptalking. In S. A. Ellman & J. S. Antrobus (Eds.), *The mind in sleep: Psychology and psychophysiology* (2nd ed., pp. 415–436). New York: Wiley.

ARLIN, P. K. (1984). Adolescent and adult thought: A structural interpretation. In M. L. Commons, F. A. Richards, & C. Armon (Eds.), *Beyond formal operations: Late adolescent and adult cognitive development* (pp. 239–252). New York: Praeger.

ARMSTRONG, B. G., McDONALD, A. D., & SLOAN, M. (1992). Cigarette, alcohol, and coffee consumption and spontaneous abortion. *American Journal of Public Health, 82,* 85–87.

ARONSON, E. (1992). *The social animal* (6th ed.). New York: Freeman.

ARONSON, E., & LINDER, D. (1965). Gain and loss of esteem as determinants of interpersonal attractiveness. *Journal of Experimental Social Psychology, 1,* 156–171.

ARTMANN, H., GRAU, H., ADELMAN, M., & SCHLEIFFER, R. (1985). Reversible and non-reversible enlargement of cerebrospinal fluid spaces in anorexia nervosa. *Neuroradiology, 27,* 103–112.

ASCH, A., & ROUSSO, H. (1985). Therapists with disabilities. Theoretical and clinical issues. *Psychiatry, 48,* 1–12.

ASCH, S. E. (1951). Effects of group pressure upon the modification and distortion of judgment. In H. Guetzkow (Ed.), *Groups, leadership, and men.* Pittsburgh: Carnegie Press.

ASCH, S. E. (1956) Studies of independence and conformity: A minority of one against a unanimous majority. *Psychological Monographs, 70*(9, Whole No. 416).

ASERINSKY, E., & KLEITMAN, N. (1953). Regularly occurring periods of eye motility and concomitant phenomena during sleep. *Science, 118,* 273–274.

ASHER J. (1987, April). Born to be shy? *Psychology Today,* pp. 56–64.

ASHTON, N. L., & SHAW, M. E. (1980). Empirical investigations of a reconceptualized personal space. *Bulletin of the Psychonomic Society, 15,* 309–312.

Ask me no questions. (1988, June 20). *Time,* p. 31.

ASSAAD, M. B. (1980). Female circumcision in Egypt: Social implications, current research, and prospects for change. *Studies in Family Planning, 11,* 3–16.

ATKINSON, R. C., & SHIFFRIN, R. M. (1968). Human memory: A proposed system and its control processes. In K. W. Spence & J. T. Spence (Eds.), *The psychology of learning and motivation* (Vol. 2). New York: Academic Press.

AVERILL, J. R. (1969). Autonomic response patterns during sadness and mirth. *Psychophysiology, 5*(4), 399–414.

AXTELL, R. E. (1991). *Gestures: The do's and taboos of body language around the world.* New York: Wiley.

AYLLON, T. (1963). Intensive treatment of psychotic behavior by stimulus satiation and food reinforcement. *Behavior Research and Therapy, 1,* 33–61.

AYMAN, D., & GOLDSHINE, A. D. (1939). The breath holding test: A simple standard stimulus of blood pressure. *Archives of Internal Medicine, 63,* 899–906.

BAARS, B. J., & BANKS, W. P. (1992). On returning to consciousness. *Consciousness and Cognition, 1,* 1–2.

BACH, J. S. (1988). *Drug abuse: Opposing viewpoints.* St. Paul, MN: Greenhaven Press.

BACKHOUSE, C., & COHEN, L. (1981). *Sexual harassment on the job.* Englewood Cliffs, NJ: Prentice-Hall.

BADDELEY, A. (1981). The concept of working memory: A view of its current state and probable future development. *Cognition, 10,* 17–23.

BADDELEY, A. (1992). Working memory. *Science, 255,* 556–559.

BAENNINGER, R. (1974). Some consequences of aggressive behavior. A selective review of the literature on other animals. *Aggressive Behavior, 1*(1), 17–37.

BAHRICK, H. P., BAHRICK, P. O., & WITTLINGER, R. P. (1975). Fifty years of memories of names and faces: A cross-sectional approach. *Journal of Experimental Psychology, 104,* 54–75.

BAILEY, J. M., & PILLARD, R. (1991). A genetic study of male sexual orientation. *Archives of General Psychiatry, 48,* 1089–1096.

BAILEY, J. M., WILLERMAN, L., & PARKS, C. (1991). A test of the maternal stress theory of human male homosexuality. *Archives of Sexual Behavior, 20,* 277–293.

BAILLARGEON, R. (1991, April). *Infants' reasoning about collision events.* Paper presented at the Society for Research in Child Development, Seattle.

BAIRD, J. C. (1982). The moon illusion. II. A reference theory. *Journal of Experimental Psychology: General, 111,* 304–315.

BAIRD, J. C., & WAGNER, M. (1982). The moon illusion. I. How high is the sky? *Journal of Experimental Psychology: General, 111,* 296–303.

BALDESSARINI, R. J. (1988). Update on antipsychotic agents. *Harvard Medical School Mental Health Letter, 4*(10), 4–6.

BALDESSARINI, R. J. (1990a). Drugs and the treatment of psychiatric disorders. In A. G. Gilman, T. W. Rall,

A. S. Nies, & P. Taylor (Eds.), *Goodman and Gilman's The pharmacological basis of therapeutics* (8th ed., pp. 395–400). Elmsford, NY: Pergamon.

BALDESSARINI, R. J. (1990b). Update on antidepressants. *Harvard Medical School Mental Health Letter, 6*(7), 4–6.

BALDESSARINI, R. J., & COLE, J. O. (1988). Chemotherapy. In A. M. Nicholi (Ed.), *The new Harvard guide to psychiatry* (pp. 481–533). Cambridge, MA: Harvard University Press.

BALDUS, D. (1987, March 23). Death penalty. *New York Times,* pp. B2–7.

BALDWIN, A. L. (1949). The effect of home environment on nursery school behavior. *Child Development, 20,* 49–61.

BALES, J. (1988, July). Bill reigning in polygraphs takes legislative fast track. *APA Monitor,* p. 17.

BANDURA, A. (1969). *Principles of behavior modification.* New York: Holt, Rinehart and Winston.

BANDURA, A. (1973). *Aggression: A social learning analysis.* Englewood Cliffs, NJ: Prentice Hall.

BANDURA, A. (1977). *Social learning theory.* Englewood Cliffs, NJ: Prentice Hall.

BANDURA, A. (1982). Self-efficacy mechanism in human agency. *American Psychologist, 37,* 122–147.·

BANDURA, A. (1986). *Social foundations of thought and action: A social cognitive theory.* Englewood Cliffs, NJ: Prentice Hall.

BANDURA, A. (1989). Social cognitive theory. In R. Vasta (Ed.), *Annals of child development* (Vol. 6). Greenwich, CT: JAI Press.

BANDURA, A., BLANCHARD, E. B., & RITTER, B. J. (1969). The relative efficacy of desensitization and modeling therapeutic approaches for inducing behavioral, affective, and attitudinal changes. *Journal of Personality and Social Psychology, 13,* 173–199.

BANDURA, A., REESE, L., & ADAMS, N. (1982). Microanalysis of action and fear arousal as a function of differential levels of perceived self-efficacy. *Journal of Personality and Social Psychology, 43*(1), 5–21.

BANDURA, A., & WALTERS, R. H. (1963). *Social learning and personality development.* New York: Holt, Rinehart and Winston.

BANKS, M. S., & SALAPATEK, P. (1983). Infant visual perception. In M. M. Haith & J. J. Campos (Eds.), *Handbook of child psychology* (Vol. 2). New York: Wiley.

BANKS, W. P., & KRAJICEK, D. (1991). Perception. *Annual Review of Psychology, 42,* 305–331.

BARBACH, L. G. (1975). *For yourself: The fulfillment of female sexuality.* New York: Doubleday.

BARBACH, L. G. (1982). *For each other: Sharing sexual intimacy.* Garden City, NY: Anchor Press.

BARBER, T. X. (1969). *Hypnosis: A scientific approach.* New York: Van Nostrand.

BARBER T. X. (Ed.). (1976). *Advances in sheltered states of consciousness and human potentialities.* (Vol. 1). New York: Psychological Dimensions.

BARBER, T. X. (1986). Realities of stage hypnosis. In B. Zilbergeld, M. G., Edelstein, & D. L. Araoz (Eds.), *Hypnosis: Questions and answers* (pp. 22–27). New York: Norton.

BARD, C. (1934). On emotional expression after decortication with some remarks on certain theoretical views. *Psychological Review, 41,* 309–329.

BARINAGA, M. (1991). Is homosexuality biological? *Science, 253,* 956–957.

BARINAGA, M. (1992). Knockouts shed light on learning. *Science, 257,* 162–163.

BARNES, C. A., & McNAUGHTON, B. L. (1985). An age comparison of the rates of acquisition and forgetting of spatial information in relation to long-term enhancement of hippocampal synapses. *Behavioral Neuroscience, 99,* 1040–1048.

BARNES, D. M. (1986). The biological tangle of drug addiction. *Science, 241,* 415–417.

BARNETT, P. E., & BENEDETTI, D. T. (1960, May). *A study in "vicarious conditioning."* Paper presented at the annual meeting of the Rocky Mountain Psychological Association, Glenwood Springs, CO.

BARNOUW, V. (1985). *Culture and personality* (4th ed.). Homewood, IL: Dorsey Press.

BARON, R. A. (1983). The reduction of human aggression: An incompatible response strategy. In R. G. Geen & Donnerstein (Eds.), *Aggression: Theoretical and empirical reviews.* New York: Academic Press.

BARON, R. A. (1988). Negative effects of destructive criticism: Impact on conflict, self-efficacy, and task performance. *Journal of Applied Psychology, 73,* 199–207.

BARON, R. A. (1990). Countering the effect of destructive criticism: The relative efficacy of four interventions. *Journal of Applied Psychology, 75,* 235–245.

BARON, R. A., & BYRNE, D. (1992). *Social psychology: Understanding human interaction* (6th ed.). Boston, MA: Allyn & Bacon.

BARTLETT, F. C. (1958). *Thinking.* London: Allen & Unwin.

BASOW, S. A. (1986). *Gender stereotypes: Traditions and alternatives* (2nd ed.). Monterey, CA: Brooks/Cole.

BATES, E., O'CONNELL, B., & SHORE, C. (1987). Language and communication in infancy. In J. D. Osofsky (Ed.), *Handbook of infant development* (2nd ed.). New York: Wiley.

BATSON, C. D. (1991). *The altruism question: Toward a social-psychological answer.* Hillsdale, NJ: Erlbaum.

BATSON, C. D., BATSON, J. G., SLINGSBY, J. K., HARRELL, K. L., PEEKNA, H. M., & TODD, R. M. (1991). Empathic joy and the empathy-altruism hypothesis. *Journal of Personality and Social Psychology, 61,* 413–426.

BAUM, A., GRUNBERG, N. E., & SINGER, J. E. (1982). The use of psychological and neuroendocrinological measurements in the study of stress. *Health Psychology, 1,* 217–236.

BAUM, A., & VALINS, S. (1977). *Architecture and social behavior: Psychological studies of social density.* Hillsdale, NJ: Erlbaum.

BAUMEISTER, R. F., & COVINGTON, M. V. (1985). Self-esteem, persuasion, and retrospective distortion of initial attitudes. *Electronic Social Psychology, 1,* 1–22.

BAUMRIND, D. (1980). New directions in socialization research. *American Psychologist, 35,* 639–652.

BAUMRIND, D. (1985). Research using intentional deception: Ethical issues revisited. *American Psychologist, 40,* 165–174.

BAUMRIND, D. (1989). Rearing competent children. In W. Damon (Ed.), *Child development today and tomorrow.* San Francisco: Jossey-Bass.

BEACH, F. A. (1977). *Human sexuality in four perspectives.* Baltimore: The Johns Hopkins University Press.

BEAMAN, A. L., COLE, C. M., PRESTON, M., KLENTZ, B., & STEBLAY, N. M. (1983). Fifteen years of foot-in-the-door research: A meta-analysis. *Personality and Social Psychology Bulletin, 9,* 181–196.

BEAMAN, A. L., & KLENTZ, B. (1983). The supposed physical attractiveness bias against supporters of the women's movement: A meta-analysis. *Personality and Social Psychology Bulletin, 9*(4), 544–550.

BEAVOIR, S. D. (1972). *The coming of age.* (Translated by P. O'Brian.) New York: Putnam.

BECK, A. T. (1967). *Depression.* New York: Harper & Row.

BECK, A. T. (1987). Cognitive models of depression. *Journal of Cognitive Psychotherapy, 1,* 2–27.

BECK, A. T. (1989). *Love is never enough.* New York: Harper & Row.

BECK, A. T. (1991). Cognitive therapy: A 30-year retrospective. *American Psychologist, 46,* 368–375.

BEEBE, D. (1991). Emergency management of the adult female rape victim. *American Family Physician, 43,* 2041–2046.

BEGLEY, S. (1991, Summer). Do you hear what I hear? *Newsweek* (Special Edition), pp. 12–14.

BEHNKE, M., & EYLER, F. D. (1991). *Issues in perinatal cocaine abuse research: The interface between medicine and child development.* Paper presented at the Society for Research in Child Development, Seattle.

BELL, A. P., WEINBERG, M. S., & HAMMERSMITH, S. K. (1981). *Sexual preference: Its development in men and women.* Bloomington: Indiana University Press.

BELL, I. P. (1989). The double standard: Age. In J. Freeman (Ed.), *Women: A feminist perspective* (4th ed., pp. 236–244). Mountain View, CA: Mayfield.

BELL, P. A., FISHER, J. D., & BAUM, A. (1990). *Environmental psychology* (3rd ed.). New York: Holt, Rinehart and Winston.

BELL, P. A. (1992). In defense of the negative affect escape model of heat and aggression. *Psychological Bulletin, 111,* 342–346.

BELLEZZA, F. S. (1982). Updating memory using mnemonic devices. *Cognitive Psychology, 14,* 301–327.

BEM, S. L. (1974). The measurement of psychological androgyny. *Journal of Consulting and Clinical Psychology, 42*(2), 155–162.

BEM, S. L. (1981). Gender schema theory: A cognitive account of sex typing. *Psychological Review, 88,* 354–364.

BEM, S. L. (1985). Androgyny and gender schema theory: A conceptual and empirical integration. *Nebraska Symposium on Motivation, 32,* 179–226.

BENGTSON, V. L., KASSCHAU, P. L., & RAGAN, P. K. (1977). The impact of social structure on aging individuals. In J. E. Birren & K. W. Schaie (Eds.), *Handbook of the psychology of aging* (pp. 327–353). New York: Van Nostrand Reinhold.

BENNETT, E. L., & CALVIN, M. (1964). Failure to train planarians reliably. *Neurosciences Research Program Bulletin, 2,* 3–24.

BENNETT, W., & GURIN, J. (1982). *The dieter's dilemma: Eating less and weighing more.* New York: Basic Books.

BEN-SHAKHAR, G., & FUREDY, J. J. (1990). *Theories and applications in the detection of deception.* New York: Springer-Verlag.

BENSON, H. (1975). *The relaxation response.* New York: Morrow.

BENSON, H. (1977). Systematic hypertension and the relaxation response. *New England Journal of Medicine, 296,* 1152–1156.

BENSON, H. (1987). *Your maximum mind.* New York: Morrow.

BENSON, H. (1988). The relaxation response: A bridge between medicine and religion. *Harvard Medical School Mental Health Letter, 4*(9), 4–6.

BERA, W., GONSIOREK, J., & LETOURNEAU, D. (1991). *Male adolescent sexual abuse.* Newbury Park, CA: Sage.

BERGER, K. S. (1988). *The developing person through the life-span.* New York: Worth.

BERKHOUT, J. (1979). Information transfer characteristics of moving light signals. *Human Factors, 21,* 445–455.

BERKOWITZ, L. (1970). Aggressive humor as a stimulus to aggressive responses. *Journal of Personality and Social Psychology, 16,* 710–717.

BERKOWITZ, L. (1984). Human aggression. In N. S. Endler & J. McV. Hunt (Eds.), *Personality and the behavioral disorders* (2nd ed., Vol. 1). New York: Wiley.

BERKOWITZ, L. (1989). Frustration-aggression hypothesis: Examination and reformulation. *Psychological Bulletin, 106,* 59–73.

BERKOWITZ, L. (1990). On the formation and regulation of anger and aggression. *American Psychologist, 45,* 494–503.

BERKOWITZ, N. (1987). Balancing the statute of limitations and the discovery rule: Some victims of incestuous abuse are denied access to Washington courts—Tyson versus Tyson. *University of Puget Sound Law Review, 10,* 721.

BERLYNE, D. E. (1971). *Aesthetics and psychobiology.* New York: Appleton-Century-Crofts.

BERMAN, T., & PAISEY, T. (1984). Personality in assaultive and non-assaultive juvenile male offenders. *Psychological Reports, 54*(2), 527–530.

BERMAN, W. H. (1988). The role of attachment in the post-divorce experience. *Journal of Personality and Social Psychology, 54*(3), 496–503.

BERNARD, L. L. (1924). *Instinct.* New York: Holt.

BERNARDS, N. (1988). *Teenage sexuality: Opposing viewpoints.* St. Paul, MN: Greenhaven Press.

BERNE, E. (1964). *Games people play: The psychology of human relationships.* New York: Grove Press.

BERNHEIM, K. F., & LEWINE, R. R. J. (1979). *Schizophrenia: Symptoms, causes, and treatments.* New York: Norton.

BERREMAN, G. (1971). *Anthropology today.* Del Mar, CA: CRM Books.

BERRY, D. S., & MCARTHUR, L. Z. (1985). Some components and consequences of a babyface. *Journal of Personality and Social Psychology, 48*(2), 312–323.

BERRY, J. W., POORTINGA, Y. A., SEGALL, M. H., & DASEN, P. R. (1992). *Cross-cultural psychology: Research and applications.* New York: Cambridge University Press.

BERSCHEID, E., & WALSTER, E. H. (1978). *Interpersonal attraction* (2nd ed.). Reading, MA: Addison-Wesley.

BEST, J. A., THOMSON, S. J., SANTI, S. M., SMITH, E. A., & BROWN, K. S. (1988). Preventing cigarette smoking among school children. In L. Breslow, J. E. Fielding, & L. B. Lave (Eds.), *Annual review of psychology* (Vol. 9). Palo Alto, CA: Annual Reviews Inc.

BEST, J. B. (1992). *Cognitive psychology.* St. Paul, MN: West.

BETTELHEIM, B. (1962). *Symbolic wounds.* New York: Collier Books.

BEUTLER, L. E., CARGO, M., & ARIZMENDI, T. G. (1986). Therapist variables in psychotherapy process and outcome. In S. L. Garfield & A. E. Bergin (Eds.), *Handbook of psychotherapy and behavior change* (3rd ed.). New York: Wiley.

BEXTON, W. H., HERON, W., & SCOTT, T. H. (1954). Effects of increased variation in the sensory environment. *Canadian Journal of Psychology, 8,* 70–76.

BIEBER, I., DAIN, H. J., DINCE, P. R., DRELLICH, M. G., GRAND H. G., GUNDLACH, R. H., KREMER, M. W., RIFKIN, A. H., WILBUR, C. G., & BIEBER, T. B. (1962). *Homosexuality: A psychoanalytic study of male homosexuals.* New York: Basic Books.

BIGLAN, A., SEVERSON, H., ARAY, D. V., FALLER, C. ET AL. (1987). Do smoking prevention programs really work? Attrition and the internal and external validity of an evaluation of a refusal skills training program. *Journal of Behavioral Medicine, 10*(2), 159–171.

BIRREN, J. E., & SCHAIE, K. W. (Eds.). (1985). *Handbook of the psychology of aging* (2nd ed.). New York: Van Nostrand Reinhold.

BISHOP, C. A. (1974). *The northern Objibwa and the fur trade.* Toronto: Holt, Rinehart, and Winston.

BLAKEMORE, C., & COOPER, G. F. (1970). Development of the brain depends on the visual environment. *Nature, 228,* 477–478.

BLAKESLEE, S. (1991, January). Research on birth defects turns to flaws in sperm. *New York Times Medical Science, 1,* 36.

BLANCHARD, D. R., & BLANCHARD, R. J. (1988). Ethoexperimental approaches to the biology of emotions. In M. R. Rosenzweig & L. W. Porter (Eds.), *Annual review of psychology* (pp. 43–68). Palo Alto, CA: Annual Reviews Inc.

BLANCHARD, E. B., APPELBAUM, K. A., GUARNIERI, P., MORRILL, B., & DENTINGER, M. P. (1987). Five-year prospective follow-up on the treatment of chronic headache with biofeedback and/or relaxation. *Headache, 27,* 580–583.

BLAU, Z. S. (1973). *Old age in a changing society.* New York: New Viewpoints.

BLEICK, C. R., & ABRAMS, A. I. (1987). The Transcendental Meditation program and criminal recidivism in California. *Journal of Criminal Justice,* 211–230.

BLEIER, R. (1987, October). *Sex differences research in the neurosciences.* Paper presented at the annual meeting of the American Association for the Advancement of Science, Chicago.

BLEWITT, P. (1983). Dog versus collie: Vocabulary in speech to young children. *Developmental Psychology, 19,* 602–609.

BLOCK, A. R., KREMER, E., & GAYLOR, M. (1980). Behavioral treatment of chronic pain: The spouse as a discriminative cue for pain behavior. *Pain, 8,* 367–375.

BLOOM, F. E. (1983). The endorphins: A growing family of pharmacologically pertinent peptides. *Annual Review of Pharmacology and Toxicology, 23,* 151–170.

BLOOM, F. E., LAZERSON, A., & HOFSTADTER, L. (1985). *Brain, mind, and behavior.* New York: Freeman.

BLUME, S. B. (1992). Compulsive gambling: Addiction without drugs. *Harvard Mental Health Letter, 8*(8), 4–5.

BLUMENTHAL, J. A., & McCUBBIN, J. A. (1987). Physical exercise as stress management. In A. Baum & J. E. Singer (Eds.), *Handbook of psychology and health* (Vol. 5). Hillsdale, NJ: Erlbaum.

BLUMENTHAL, J. A., WILLIAMS, R. S., NEEDLES, T. L., & WALLACE, A. G. (1982). Psychological changes accompany aerobic exercise in healthy middle-aged adults. *Psychosomatic Medicine, 44,* 529–536.

BLYTH, D. A., BULCROFT, R., & SIMMONS, R. G. (1981, August). *The impact of puberty on adolescents: A longitudinal study.* Paper presented at the annual meeting of the American Psychological Association, Los Angeles.

BODENHAUSEN, G., & WYER, R. (1985). Effects of stereotypes on decision making and information-processing strategies. *Journal of Personality and Social Psychology, 48,* 267–282.

BOERINGER, S., SHEHAN, C., & AKERS, R. (1991). Social contexts and social learning in sexual coercion and aggression. Assessing the contribution of fraternity membership. *Family Relations, 40,* 58–64.

BOLLES, R. C. (1970). Species-specific defense reactions and avoidance learning. *Psychological Review, 77,* 32–48.

BOLLES, R. C. (1975). *Theory of motivation* (2nd ed.). New York: Harper & Row.

BONELLO, P. H. (1982, June). The Zeigarnik effect and the recall of geometric forms. *Dissertation Abstracts International, 42* (12-A), 5060.

BORBELY, A. A. (1982). Circadian and sleep-dependent processes in sleep regulation. In J. Aschoff, S. Daan, & G. A. Groos (Eds.), *Vertebrate circadian rhythms* (pp. 237–242). Berlin: Springer/Verlag.

BORBELY, A. A. (1984). Sleep regulation: Outline of a model and its implications for depression. In A. A. Borbely & J. L. Valatx (Eds.), *Sleep mechanisms* (pp. 272–284). Berlin: Springer/Verlag.

BORBELY, A. A. (1986). *Secrets of sleep.* New York: Basic Books.

BORNSTEIN, R. F. (1989). Exposure and affect: Overview and meta-analysis of research, 1968–1987. *Psychological Bulletin, 106,* 265–289.

BORNSTEIN, R. F., KALE, A. R., & CORNELL, K. R. (1990). Boredom as a limiting condition on the mere exposure effect. *Journal of Personality and Social Psychology, 58,* 791–800.

BOSSARD, M. D., REYNOLDS, C. R., & GUTKIN, T. B. (1980). A regression analysis of test bias on the Stanford-Binet Intelligence Scale for black and white children referred for psychological services. *Journal of Clinical and Child Psychology, 9,* 52–54.

BOTVIN, G. T., & WILLS, T. A. (1985). Personal and social skills training: Cognitive-behavioral approaches to substance abuse prevention. In C. S. Bell & R. Battjes (Eds.), *Prevention research: Deterring drug abuse among children and adolescents* (NIDA Research Monograph 63). Washington, DC: U. S. government Printing Office.

BOTWINICK, J. (1977). Intellectual abilities. In J. E. Birren & K. W. Schaie (Eds.), *Handbook of the psychology of aging* (2nd ed.). New York: Van Nostrand Reinhold.

BOUCHARD, T. J. (1984). Twins reared together and apart: What they tell us about human diversity. In S. W. Fox (Ed.), *Individuality and determinism* (pp. 147–148). New York: Plenum Press.

BOUCHARD, T. J., JR., LYKKEN, D. T., McGUE, M., SEGAN, N. L., & TELLEGEN, A. (1990). Sources of human psychological differences: The Minnesota study of twins reared apart. *Science, 250,* 223–228.

BOURGUIGNON, E. (1973). Introduction: A framework for the comparative study of altered states of consciousness. In E. Bourguignon (Ed.), *Religion, altered states of consciousness and social change.* Columbus: Ohio State University Press.

BOURNE, L. E. (1974). An inference model of conceptual role learning. In R. Solso (Ed.), *Theories of cognitive psychology.* Hillsdale, NJ: Erlbaum.

BOURNE, L. E., DOMINOWSKI, R. L., & LOFTUS, E. F. (1979). *Cognitive processes.* Englewood Cliffs, NJ: Prentice Hall.

BOWEN, D. J., & PETERSON A. V. (1988, August). *Comparisons of the smoking onset process for girls and boys.* Paper presented at the annual meeting of the American Psychological Association, Atlanta.

BOWER, B. (1985, November 16). "Day after" effects of pot smoking. *Science News,* p. 310.

BOWER, B. (1988a). Let there be more light. *Science News, 133,* 331.

BOWER, B. (1988b). Low-dose advantage for schizophrenics. *Science News, 134,* 196.

BOWER, B. (1989a). Deceptive successes in young children. *Science News, 135,* 343.

BOWER, B. (1991). Psychiatric smoke signals. *Science News, 139,* 15.

BOWER, B. (1992a). Babies add up basic arithmetic skills. *Science News, 142,* 132.

BOWER, B. (1992b). No go for fetal tissue transplantation. *Science News, 142,* 15.

BOWER, G. H. (1976). Experiments on story understanding and recall. *Quarterly Journal of Experimental Psychology, 28,* 211–234.

BOWER, G. H. (1981). Mood and memory. *American Psychologist, 36*(2), 129–148.

BOWER, T. G. R. (1989). *The rational infant.* San Francisco: W. H. Freeman.

BOWLBY, J. (1969). *Attachment and loss, Vol. I: Attachment.* New York: Basic Books.

BOWLBY, J (1973). *Attachment and loss, Vol. II: Separation and anxiety.* New York: Basic Books.

BOWLBY, J. (1982). Attachment and loss: Retrospect and prospect. *American Journal of Orthopsychiatry, 52,* 664–678.

BOWLBY, J. (1988). *A secure base: Parent-child attachment and healthy human development.* New York: Basic Books.

BOWLBY, J. (1989). *Secure attachment.* New York: Basic Books.

BOYER, D., & FINE, D. (1992). Sexual abuse as a factor in adolescent pregnancy and child maltreatment. *Family Planning Perspectives, 24,* 4–19.

BOYNTON, R. M. (1988). Color vision. In M. R. Rosenzweig & L. W. Porter (Eds.), *Annual review of psychology* (pp. 69–100). Palo Alto, CA: Annual Reviews Inc.

BRACKEN, B. A. (1985). A critical review of the Kaufman Assessment Battery for Children (K-ABC). *School Psychology Review, 14*(1), 21–36.

BRADLEY, M. T., & AINSWORTH, D. (1984). Alcohol and the psychophysiological detection of deception. *Psychophysiology, 21*(1), 63–71.

BRAND, D. (1988, September 5). Dying with dignity. *Time,* pp. 56–58.

BRANSFORD, J. D. (1979). *Human cognition.* Belmont, CA: Wadsworth.

BRAY, J. H. (1988). Children's development during early remarriage. In E. M. Hetherington & J. D. Arasteh (Eds.), *Impact of divorce, single-parenting, and step-parenting on children* (pp. 279–298). Hillsdale, NJ: Erlbaum.

BRAY, R. M., & NOBLE, A. M. (1978). Authoritarianism and decisions of mock juries: Evidence of jury bias and group polarization. *Journal of Personality and Social Psychology, 36,* 1424–1430.

BRECHER, E. (1969). *The sex researchers.* Boston: Little, Brown.

BREGER, L. (1967). Function of dreams. *Journal of Abnormal Psychological Monographs, 72*(5), 1–28.

BREHM, J. W. (1989). Psychological reactance: Theory and applications. *Advances in Consumer Research, 16,* 72–75.

BRETT, A. S., PHILLIPS, M., & BEARY, J. F. (1986). Predictive power of the polygraph: Can the "lie dector" really detect liars? *Lancet, 1,* 544–547.

BREWER, M. B., & KRAMER, R. M. (1985). The psychology of intergroup attitudes and behavior. *Annual Review of Psychology, 36,* 219–243.

BRISLIN, R. W. (Ed.). (1990). *Applied cross-cultural psychology: Cross-cultural research and methodology series* (Vol. 14). Newbury Park, CA: Sage.

BRISLIN, R. W. (1993). *Understanding culture's influence on behavior.* Orlando, FL: Harcourt Brace Jovanovich.

BROCA, P. (1861). Remarques sur le siege de la faculte du language article. *Bulletin de la Societe Anatomique de Paris, 6,* 330–357.

BROD, J. (1970). Haemodynamics and emotional stress. In M. Koster, H. Musaph, & P. Visser (Eds.), *Psy-*

chosomatics in essential hypertension. New York: Karger.

BRODT, B. B., & ZIMBARDO, P. G. (1981). Modifying shyness-related social behavior through symptom misattribution. *Journal of Personality and Social Psychology, 41*(3), 437–449.

BROSS, M., HARPER, D., & SICZ, G. (1980). Visual effects of auditory deprivation: Common intermodal and intramodal factors. *Science, 207,* 667–668.

BROVERMAN, I. K., BROVERMAN, D. M., CLARKSON, F. E., ROSENFRANTZ, P., & VOGEL, S. R. (1970). Sex-role stereotypes and clinical judgments of mental health. *Journal of Consulting and Clinical Psychology, 34*(1), 3.

BROWMAN, C. P., & CARTWRIGHT, R. D. (1980). The first-night effect on sleep and dreams. *Biological Psychiatry, 15,* 809–812.

BROWN, A. L., CAMPIONE, J. C., & BARCLAY, C. R. (1978). *Training self-checking routines for estimating test readiness: Generalization from list learning to prose recall.* Unpublished manuscript. University of Illinois.

BROWN, E. DEFFENBACHER, K., & STURGILL, K. (1977). Memory for faces and the circumstances of encounter. *Journal of Applied Psychology, 62,* 311–318.

BROWN, G., BIRLEY, J., & WING, J. (1972). Influence of family life on the course of schizophrenic disorders: A replication. *British Journal of Psychiatry, 121,* 241–258.

BROWN, R. (1986). *Social psychology* (2nd ed.). New York: Free Press.

BROWN, R. (1992). *Social psychology* (2nd ed.) New York: Free Press.

BROWN, R., & KULIK, J. (1977). *flashbulb memories.* Cognition, 5, 73–99.

BROWN, R., & McNEILL, D. (1966). The "tip of the tongue" phenomenon. *Journal of Verbal Learning and Verbal Behavior, 5,* 325–337.

BROWN, T. H., CHAPMAN, P. R., KAIRISS, E. W., & KEENAN, C. L. (1988). Long-term synaptic potentiation. *Science, 242,* 724–728.

BROWNE, M. W. (1989, October 24). Problems loom in effort to control use of chemicals for illicit drugs. *New York Times, pp. B1, B9.*

BROWNELL, K. D. (1988, January). Yo-Yo dieting: Repeated attempts to lose weight can give you a hefty problem. *Psychology Today,* pp. 20–23.

BROWNELL, K. D., & VENDITTI, E. M. (1982). The etiology and treatment of obesity. In W. E. Fann, I. Karacan, A. D. Pokorny, & R. L. Williams (Eds.), *Phenomenology and treatment of psychophysiological disorders.* New York: Spectrum.

BROWNMILLER, S. (1975). *Against our will: men, women, and rape.* New York: Simon & Schuster.

BROWNMILLER, S. (1984, November). Comments in debate on "The place of poronography," *Harper's,* pp. 31–45.

BRUNER, J. S., GOODNOW, J. J., & AUSTIN, G. A. (1956). *A study of thinking.* New York: Wiley.

BRUNNER, D. P., KIJK, D. J., TOBLER, I., & BORBELY, A. A. (1990). Effect of partial sleep stages and EEG power spectra: Evidence for non-REM and REM sleep homeostasis. *Electroencephalography and Clinical Neurophysiology, 75,* 492–499.

BRYLAWSKI, R. (1987, November). Prenatal tests: Screening for Down's syndrome. *American Health,* pp. 18–19.

BUCHKREMER, B., MINNEKER, E., & BLOCK, M. (1991). Smoking-cessation treatment combining transdermal nicotine substitution with behavioral therapy. *Pharmacopsychiatry, 24*(3), 96–103.

BUHRMANN, H., & ZAUGG, M. (1981). Superstitions among basketball players: An investigation of various forms of superstitious beliefs and behavior among competitive basketballers at the junior

high school to university level. *Journal of Sport Behavior, 4* (4), 163–174.

BUIE, J. (1988a, November). Ad campaign spotlights psychology. *APA Monitor,* p. 18.

BUIE, J. (1988b, November). Messaage catches publicity wave. *APA Monitor,* p. 20.

BUIE, J. (1989a, December). Age, race, gender all influence PTSD. *APA Monitor,* p. 32.

BUIE, J. (1989b, December). MMPI-2 earns praise as improved instrument. *APA Monitor,* p. 22.

BULLOGH, V. (1990). Nightingale, nursing, and harassment. *Image: Journal of Nursing Scholarship, 22,* 4–7.

BURGESS, A., & HOLMSTROM, L. (1974). Rape trauma syndrome. *American Journal of Psychiatry, 131,* 981–986.

BURGESS, A., & HOLMSTROM, L. (1988, January). Treating the adult rape victim. *Medical Aspects of Human Sexuality,* pp. 36–43.

BURT, M. (1992). *Over the edge: The growth of homelessness in the 1980's.* New York: Russell Sage Foundation.

BURTON, R. V. (1963). The generality of honesty reconsidered. *Psychological Review, 70,* 481–499.

BURTON, R. V. (1984). A paradox in theories and research in moral development. In W. M. Kurtines & J. L. Gewirtz (Eds.), *Morality, moral behavior, and moral development.* New York: Wiley.

BUSHMAN, B. J., & COOPER, H. M. (1990). Effects of alcohol on human aggression: an integrative research review. *Psychological Review, 107,* 341–354.

BUSHMAN, B. J. & GREEN, R. G. (1990). Role of cognitive-emotional mediators and individual differences in the effects of media violence on aggression. Journal of Personality and Social Psychology, 58, 156–163.

BUSS, D. M. (1989). Sex differences in human mate preferences: Evolutionary hypotheses tested in 37 cultures. *Behavioral and Brain Sciences, 12,* 1–49.

BUTCHER, J. N., DAHLSTROM, W. G., GRAHAM, J. R., TELLEGEN, A. & KAEMMER, B. (1989). *MMPI-2: Manual for administration and scoring.* Minneapolis: University of Minnesota Press.

BUTLER, R. A. (1954, February). Curiosity in monkeys. *Scientific American, 190,* 70–75.

BUTLER, R. N., & LEWIS, M. I. (1982). *Aging and mental health* (3rd ed.). St. Louis: Mosby.

BYRNE, D. (1971). *The attraction paradigm.* New York: Academic Press.

CADMAN, D., GAFNI, A., & McNAMEE, J. (1984). Newborn circumcision: An economic perspective. *Canadian Medical Association Journal, 131,* 1353–1355.

CADORET, R. J. (1986). Epidemiology of antisocial personality. In W. H. Reid, D. Dorr, J. I. Walker, & J. W. Bonner III (Eds.), *Unmasking the psychopath: Antisocial personality and related syndromes.* New York: Norton.

CAHILL, C., LLEWELYN, S., & PEARSON, C. (1991). Treatment of sexual abuse which occurred in childhood: A review. *British Journal of Clinical Psychology, 30,* 1–12.

CAIRNS, D., & PASINO, J. A. (1977). Comparison of verbal reinforcement and feedback in the operant treatment of disability due to chronic back pain. *Behavior Therapy, 8*(4), 621–630.

CAIRNS, R. B. (1972). fighting and punishment from a developmental perspective. *Nebraska Symposium on Motivation, 20,* 59–124.

CALHOUN, J. B. (1962). Population density and social pathology. *Scientific American, 206*(3), 139–148.

CAMARA, K. A., BRENNAN, K., & RESNICK, G. (1991). *Emerging family cultures in single-and two-parent households: Relationships to the social and academic functioning of children.* Paper presented

at the Society for Research in Child Development, Seattle.

CAMPOS, J. J., CAMPOS, R. G., & BARRETT, K. C. (1989). Emergent themes in the study of emotional development and emotion regulation. *Developmental psychology, 25,* 394–402.

CAMPOS, J. J., HIATT, S., RAMSAY, D., HENDERSON, C., & SVEJDA, M. (1978). The emergence of fear on the visual cliff. In M. Lewis & L. A. Rosenblum (Eds.), *The development of affect.* New York: Plenum.

CAMPOS, J., LAMB, M. E., GOLDSMITH, H. H., & STENBERG, C. (1983). Socio-emotional development. In J. Campos & M. M. Haith (Eds.), *Handbook of child psychology: Infancy and developmental psychobiology* (Vol. 2, pp. 783–916). New York: Wiley.

CANNON, W. B. (1927). The James-Lange theory of emotions: A critical examination and an alternative theory. *American Journal of Psychology, 39,* 106–124.

CANNON, W. B., LEWIS, J. T., & BRITTON, S. W. (1927). The dispensability of the sympathetic division of the autonomic nervous system. *Boston Medical Surgery Journal, 197,* 514.

CANNON, W. B., & WASHBURN, A. (1912). An explanation of hunger. *American Journal of Physiology, 29* 441–454.

CAPORAEL, L. R. (1981). The paralanguage of caregiving: Baby talk to the institutionalized aged. *Journal of Personality and Social Psychology, 40,* 876–884.

CARLSON, N. R. (1992). *Foundations of physiological psychology* (2nd ed.) Needham Heights, MA: Allyn & Bacon.

CARPENTER, W. T., JR., HEINRICHS, W., & WAGMEN, E. N. (1988). Deficit and nondeficit forms of schizophrenia: The concept. *American Journal of Psychiatry, 145,* 578–584.

CARSON, R. C. (1989). Personality. In M. R. Rosenzweig & L. W. Porter (Eds.). *Annual review of psychology* (pp. 227–248). Palo Alto, CA: Annual Reviews Inc.

CARSON, R. C., BUTCHER, J. N., & COLEMAN, J. C. (1988). *Abnormal psychology and modern life* (8th ed.). Glenview, IL: Scott, Foresman.

CARSON, R. C., BUTCHER, J. N., & COLEMAN, J. C. (1992). *Abnormal psychology and modern life* (9th ed.). Glenview, IL: Scott, Foresman.

CARTER, A. G. (1992). *Human arrangements* (3rd. ed.). San Diego: Harcourt Brace Jovanovich.

CARTWRIGHT, R. D. (1978). Sleep and dreams, Part II. *Annual Review of Psychology, 29,* 223–252.

CASPI, A., & HERBENER, E. S. (1990). Continuity and change: Assortative marriage and the consistency of personality in adulthood. *Journal of Personality and Social Psychology, 58,* 250–258.

CATTELL, R. B. (1963). Theory of fluid and crystallized intelligence: A critical experiment. *Journal of Educational Psychology, 54,* 1–22.

CATTELL, R. B. (1965). *The scientific analysis of personality.* Baltimore: Penguin.

CATTELL, R. B. *Abilities: Their structure, growth, and action.* Boston, MA: Houghton Mifflin.

CATTELL, R. B. (1990). Advances in Cattellian personality theory. In L. A. Pervin (Ed.), *Handbook of personality: Theory and research.* New York: Guilford Press.

Centers for Disease Control. (1992a). Infant mortality —United States, 1989. *Morbidity and Mortality Weekly Report, 41,* 81–85.

Centers for Disease Control. (1992b). The second 100,000 cases of acquired immunodeficiency syndrome—United States, June 1981–December 1991. *Morbidity and Mortality Weekly Report, 41,* 28–29.

CENTERWALL, B. S. (1989). Exposure to television as a

risk factor for violence. *American Journal of Epidemiology, 129,* 643–652.

CHAFFEE, J. (1992). *Thinking critically* (3rd ed.). Boston, MA: Houghton Mifflin.

CHAIKEN, S., & BALDWIN, M. W. (1981). Affective-cognitive consistency and the effect of salient behavioral information on the self-perception of attitudes. *Journal of Personality and Social Psychology, 41,* 1–12.

CHAIKEN, S., & EAGLY, A. H. (1983). Communication modality as a determinant of persuasion: The role of communicator salience. *Journal of Personality and Social Psychology, 45,* 241–256.

CHAN, T. C., & TURVEY, M. T. (1991). Perceiving the vertical distance of surfaces by means of a handheld probe. *Journal of Experimental Psychology: Human Perception and Performance, 17,* 347–358.

CHANCE, P. (1979). *Learning and behavior.* Belmont, CA: Wadsworth.

CHANCE, P. (1986, September). The divided self. *Psychology Today,* p. 72.

CHANCE, P., & FISCHMAN, J. (1987, May). The magic of childhood. *Psychology Today,* pp. 48–58.

CHAPOUTHIER, G. (1973). Behavioral studies of the molecular basis of memory. In J. A. Deutsch (Ed.), *The physiological basis of memory* (pp. 1–25). New York: Academic Press.

CHARNEY, D. S., WOODS, S. W., KRYSTAL, J. H., & HENINGER, G. R. (1990). Serotonin function and human anxiety disorders. *Annals of the New York Academy of Sciences, 600,* 558–573.

CHASE, W. G., & SIMON, H. A. (1973). The mind's eye in chess. In W. Chase (Ed.), *Visual information processing.* New York: Academic Press.

CHASE-LANSDALE, P. L., & HETHERINGTON, E. M. (1993). The impact of divorce on life-span development: Short and long-term effects. In P. B. Baltes, D. L. Featherman, & R. M. Lerner (Eds.), *Life-span development and behavior.* Hillsdale, NJ: Erlbaum.

CHECK, J. (1984). Can there be positive effects of participation in pornography experiments? *Journal of Sex Research, 20,* 14–31.

CHECK, J., & MALAMUTH, N. (1983). Sex role stereotyping and reactions to depictions of stranger versus acquaintance rape. *Journal of Personality and Social Psychology, 45,* 344–356.

CHELUNE, G. J. (1984). Conversion disorders. In R. J. Corsini (Ed.), *Encyclopedia of psychology* (Vol. 1, pp. 291–292). New York: Wiley.

CHENEY, D., & FOSS, G. (1984). An examination of the social behavior of mentally retarded workers. *Education and Training of the Mentally Retarded, 19*(3), 216–221.

CHERRY, F., & DEAUX, K. (1978). Fear of success versus fear of gender-inappropriate behavior. *Sex Roles, 4,* 97–102.

CHESNEY, M. A., EAGLESTON, J. R. (1981). Type A behavior: Assessment and intervention. In C. K. Prokop & L. A. Bradley (Eds.), *Medical psychology: Contributions to behavioral medicine* (pp. 21–22). New York: Academic Press.

CHESS, S., & THOMAS, A. (1986). *Annual progress in child psychiatry and child development.* New York: Brunner/Mazel.

CHESSARE, J. (1992). Circumcision: Is the risk of urinary tract infection really the pivotal issue? *Clinical Pediatrics, 4,* 100–104.

CHILDERS, J. S., DURHAM, T. W., BOLEN, L. M., & TAYLOR, L. H. (1985). A predictive validity study of the Kaufman Assessment Battery for Children with the California Achievement Test. *Psychology in the Schools, 22*(1), 29–33.

CHODOROW, N. (1978). *The reproduction of mothering.* Berkeley: University of California Press.

CHODOROW, N. (1989). *Feminism and psychoanalytic theory.* New Haven, CT: Yale University Press.

CHOLLAR, S. (1989, November). Body-wise: Safe solutions for night work. *Psychology Today,* p. 26.

CHOMSKY, N. (1968). *Language and mind.* New York: Harcourt, Brace, World.

CHOMSKY, N. (1980). *Rules and representations.* New York: Columbia University Press.

CHUGANI, H. T., & PHELPS, M. E. (1986). Maturational changes in cerebral function in infants determined by FGG positron emission tomography. *Science, 231,* 840–843.

CIALDINI, R. B. (1993). *Influence: Science and practice* (3rd ed.). New York: Harper Collins.

CIALDINI, R. B. (1991). Altruism or egoism: That is (still) the question. *Psychological Inquiry, 2,* 124–126.

CIALDINI, R. B., KALLGREN, C. A., & RENO, R. R. (1991). A focus theory of normative conduct: A theoretical refinement and reevaluation of the role of norms in human behavior. *Advances in Experimental Social Psychology, 24,* 201–234.

CIALDINI, R. B., RENO, R. R., & KALLGREN, C. A. (1990). A focus theory of normative conduct: Recycling the concept of norms to reduce littering in public places. *Journal of Personality and Social Psychology, 58,* 1015–1026.

CIALDINI, R. B., SCHALLER, M., HOULIHAN, D., ARPS, K., FULTZ, J., & BEAMAN, A. L. (1987). Empathy-based helping: Is it selflessly or selfishly motivated? *Journal of Personality and Social Psychology, 52,* 749–758.

CIALDINI, R. B., VINCENT, J. E., LEWIS, S. K., CATALAN, J., WHEELER, D., & DARBY, B. L. (1975). Reciprocal concessions procedure for inducing compliance: The door-in-the-face technique. *Journal of Personality and Social Psychology, 31,* 206–215.

CICCHETTI, D. (1991, April). *Developmental theory: Lessons from the study of risk and psychopathology.* Invited address presented at the Society for Research in Child Development, Seattle.

CLARKE, A. C. (1968). *2001: A space odyssey.* New York: New American Library.

CLARKSON, M. G., & BERG, W. K. (1983). Cardiac orienting and vowel discrimination in newborns: Crucial stimulus parameters. *Child Development, 54,* 162–171.

CLARY, E. G., & THIEMAN, T. J. (1988, August). *Self perceptions of helpfulness: Different meanings for different people?* Paper presented at the annual meeting of the American Psychological Association, Atlanta.

CLONINGER, G. B., DINWIDDIE, S. H., & REICH, T. (1989). Epidemiology and genetics of alcoholism. *Annual reviews of psychiatry, 8,* 331–336.

COAN, R. W. (1984). Personality types. In R. J. Corsini (Ed.), *Encyclopedia of psychology* (Vol. 3, pp. 23–26). New York: Wiley.

COHEN, B. M., GILLER, E., & LYNN, E. (1991). *Multiple personality disorder from the inside out.* San Francisco: Sudran Press.

COHEN, J. B., & CHAKRAVARTI, D. (1990). Consumer psychology. *Annual Review of Psychology, 41,* 243–288.

COHEN, L. (1988). Providing treatment and support for partners of sexual-assault survivors. *Psychotherapy, 25,* 94–98.

COHEN, L. D., KIPNES, D., KUNKLE, E. G., & KUBZANSKY, P. E. (1955). Observations of a person with insensitivity to pain. *Journal of Abnormal and Social Psychology, 55,* 33–38.

COHEN, N. L. (1992). Taking psychiatry to the streets. *Harvard Mental Health Letter, 9*(6), 5–6.

COHEN, S. (1978). Environmental load and the allocation of attention. In A. Baum, J. E. Singer, & S. Valins (Eds.), *Advances in environmental psychology* (Vol. 1). Hillsdale, NJ: Erlbaum.

COHEN, S. (1981). Sensory changes in the elderly. *American Journal of Nursing, 81,* 1851–1880.

COHEN, S., & EDWARDS, J. R. (1989). Personality characteristics as moderators of the relationship between stress and disorder. In R. W. Neufeld (Ed.), *Advances in the investigation of psychological stress.* New York: Wiley.

COHEN, S., TYRELL, D. A., & SMITH, A. P. (1991). Psychological stress and susceptibility to the common cold. *New England Journal of Medicine, 325,* 606–612.

COHEN, S., & WILLIAMSON, G. M. (1991). Stress and infectious disease in humans. *Psychological Bulletin, 109,* 5–24.

COLE, D. L. (1982). Psychology as a liberating art. *Teaching of Psychology, 9,* 23–26.

COLE, M., & COLE, S. R. (1989). *The development of children.* New York: Scientific American.

COLE, M., GRAY, J., GLICK, J. A., & SHARP, D. W. (1971). *The cultural context of learning and thinking.* New York: Basic Books.

COLE, R. A., & JAKIMIK, J. (1980). A model of speech perception. In R. A. Cole (Ed.), *Perception and production of fluent speech.* Hillsdale, NJ: Erlbaum.

COLE, S. (1980, September). Send our children to work? *Psychology Today,* p. 44.

COLEMAN, J. C., BUTCHER, J. N., & CARSON, R. C. (1984). *Abnormal psychology and modern life* (7th ed.). Glenview, IL: Scott, Foresman.

COLEMAN, R. M. (1986). *Wide awake at 3:00 A.M.: By choice or by chance?* New York: Freeman.

COLES, C. D., PLATZMAL, K. A., SMITH, I., JAMES, M. E., & FALCK, A. (1992). Effects of cocaine and alcohol abuse in pregnancy on neonatal growth and neurobehavioral status. *Neurotoxicology and Tetratology, 14,* 23–33.

COLGROVE, M., BLOOMFIELD, H. H., & McWILLIAMS, P. (1976). *How to survive the loss of a love.* New York: Bantam.

COLLINS, A. M., & QUILLIAN, M. R. (1969). Retrieval time from semantic memory. *Journal of Verbal Learning and Verbal Behavior, 8,* 240–248.

COLLINS, C. C. (1970). Tactile television: Mechanical and electrical image projection. *IEEE Transactions on Man-Machine Systems, 11*(1), 65–71.

COLLINS, R. C. (1993). Head start: Steps toward a two-generation program strategy. *Young Children, 48*(2), 25–33, 72–73.

COLLINS, W. A., & RUSSELL, G. (1988). *Mother–child and father–child relationships in middle childhood and adolescence.* Minneapolis: University of Minnesota Press.

Committee on Labor and Human Resources. (1981). *Sex discrimination in the workplace.* Hearings before the Committee on Labor and Human Resources, United States Senate, Ninety-seventh Congress. Washington, DC: U. S. Government Printing Office.

COMMONS, M. L., SINNOTT, J., RICHARDS, F. A., & ARMON, C. (Eds.). (1986). *Beyond formal operations: Comparisons and applications of adolescent and adult development models* New York: Praeger.

CONGER, J. J. (1988). Hostages to fortune: Youth, values, and the public interest. *American Psychologist, 43,* 291–300.

CONNIFF, R. (1984). Living longer. In H. E. Fitzgerald & M. G. Walraven (Eds.), *Human development 84/85* (pp. 268–273). Guilford, CT: Dushkin.

CONTRADA, R. J., & KRANTZ, D. S. (1988). Stress, reactivity, and Type A behavior: Current status and future directions. *Annals of Behavioral Medicine, 10,* 64–70.

COOL, L. E. (1987). The effects of social class and ethnicity on the aging process. In P. Silverman (Ed.), *The elderly as modern pioneers* (pp. 263–282). Bloomington, IN: University Press.

COOPER, J., & SCHER, S. J. (1993). Actions and attitudes: The role of responsibility and aversive consequences in persuasion. In T. Brock & S. Shavitt (Eds.), *The psychology of persuasion*. San Francisco: Freeman.

COOPER, W. H. (1983). An achievement motivation nomological network. *Journal of Personality and Social Psychology, 44,* 841–861.

CORCORAN, K. J. (1988). Relapse and obesity: A comment. *American Psychologist, 43,* 825–826.

COREY, G. (1993). *Theory and practice of counseling and psychotherapy* (5th ed.). Monterey, CA: Brooks/Cole.

CORNELL, J. (1984, March). Science versus the paranormal. *Psychology Today,* pp. 28–34.

CORSELLIS, J. A., BRUTON, C. J., & FREEMAN-BROWNE, D. (1973). The aftermath of boxing. *Psychological Medicine, 3*(3), 270–303.

COSTA, P. T., JR., & McCRAE, R. R. (1980). Still stable after all these years: Personality as a key to some issues in adulthood and old age. In P. B. Baltes & O. G. Brim, Jr. (Eds.), *Life-span development and behavior* (Vol. III). New York: Academic Press.

COSTA, P. T., JR., & McCRAE, R. R. (1988). Personality in adulthood: A six-year longitudinal survey of self-reports and spouse ratings on the NEO Personality Inventory. *Journal of Personality and Social Psychology, 54,* 853–863.

COSTA, P. T., JR., & McCRAE, R. R. (1989). Personality, stress, and coping: Some lessons from a decade of research. In K. S. Markides & C. L. Cooper (Eds.), *Aging, stress, social support, and health*. New York: Wiley.

COUNCIL, J. R. (1993). Context effects in personality research. *Current Directions in Psychological Science, 2,* 31–34.

COUSINS, N. (1979). *Anatomy of an illness*. New York: Norton.

COWAN, P. A. (1978). *Piaget with feeling: Cognitive, social, and emotional dimensions*. New York: Holt, Rinehart and Winston.

COWLEY, G. (1991, December 23). I'd toddle a mile for a Camel. *Newsweek,* p. 70.

COX, S., & RADLOFF, L. S. (1984). Depression in relation to sex roles: Differences in learned susceptibility and precipitating factors. In C. Widom (Ed.), *Sex roles and psychopathology* (pp. 123–144). New York: Plenum.

COZBY, P. C. (1985). *Methods in behavioral research* (3rd ed.). Palo Alto, CA: Mayfield.

COZBY, P. C. (1989). *Methods in behavioral research* (4th ed.). Palo Alto, CA: Mayfield.

CRAIK, F. I. M., & LOCKHART, R. S. (1972). Levels of processing: A framework for memory research. *Journal of Verbal Learning and Verbal Behavior, 11,* 671–684.

CRAIK, F. I. M., & TULVING, E. (1975). Depth of processing and the retention of words in episodic memory. *Journal of Experimental Psychology: General, 104,* 268–294.

CRASKE, B. (1977). Perception of impossible limb positions induced by tendon vibrations. *Science, 196,* 71–73.

CRICK, F. (1982, February). Do dendritic spines twitch? *Trends in Neuroscience,* pp. 44–46.

CRICK, F., & KOCH, C. (1992). The problem of consciousness. *Scientific American, 267*(3), 152–159.

CRICK, F., & MITCHISON, G. (1983). The function of dream sleep. *Nature, 304,* 111–114.

CRONBACH, L. (1990). *Essentials of psychological testing*. New York; Harper & Row.

CROOK, T. H., III, & LARRABEE, G. J. (1990). A self-rating scale for evaluating memory in everyday life. *Psychology and Aging, 5,* 48–57.

CROOKS, R., & BAUR, K. (1993). *Our sexuality* (5th ed.). Redwood City, CA: Benjamin/Cummings.

CROSS, T. G. (1977). Mother's speech adjustments. In O. Ferguson & C. Snow (Eds.), *Talking to children*. Cambridge, England: Cambridge University Press.

CROW, T. J. (1980). Positive and negative schizophrenia symptoms and the role of dopamine. *British Journal of Psychiatry, 137,* 383–386.

CROW, T. J. (1982). Two dimensions of pathology in schizophrenia: Dopaminergic and non-dopaminergic. *Psychopharmacology Bulletin, 18,* 22–29.

CROW, T. J. (1985). The two syndrome concept: Origins and current status. *Schizophrenia Bulletin, 11,* 471–486.

CUMMING, E., & HENRY, W. E. (1961). *Growing old: The process of disengagement*. New York: Basic Books.

CUNNINGHAM, J. D., & STRASSBERG D. S. (1981). Neuroticism and disclosure reciprocity. *Journal of Counseling Psychology, 28,* 455–458.

CUNNINGHAM, W. R., & BROOKBANK, J. W. (1989). *Gerontology: The psychology, biology, and sociology of aging*. New York: Harper & Row.

DABBS, J. M., & MORRIS, R. (1990). Testosterone, social class, and antisocial behavior in a sample of 4,462 men. *Psychological Science, 1,* 209–211.

DAMASIO, A. (1979). The frontal lobes. In K. M. Heilman & E. Valenstein (Eds.), *Clinical neuropsychology*. New York: Oxford University Press.

DAMASIO, A. R., & DAMASIO, H. (1992). Brain and language. *Scientific American, 267*(3), 88–109.

DARLEY, J. G. (1984). Vocational interest measurement. In R. J. Corsini (Ed.), *Encyclopedia of psychology* (Vol. 3, pp. 459–462). New York: Wiley.

DARLEY, J. M., & BATSON, C. D. (1973). "From Jerusalem to Jericho": A study of situational and dispositional variables in helping behavior. *Journal of Personality and Social Psychology, 27,* 100–108.

DARLING, C. A., DAVIDSON, J. K., SR., & CONWAY-WELCH, C. (1990). Female ejaculation: Perceived origins, the Grafenberg spot/area, and sexual responsiveness. *Archives of Sexual Behavior, 19,* 29–47.

DARO, D. (1991). Child sexual abuse prevention: Separating fact from fiction. *Child Abuse and Neglect, 15,* 1–4.

DARWIN, C. R. (1872). *The expression of the emotions in man and animals*. London: John Murray.

DATAN, N., RODEHAEAVER, D., & HUGHES, F. (1987). Adult development and aging. In M. R. Rosenzweig & L. W. Porter (Eds.), *Annual review of psychology* (pp. 153–180). Palo Alto, CA: Annual Reviews Inc.

DAVIDSON, B. (1984). A test of equity theory for marital adjustment. *Social Psychology Quarterly, 47,* 36–42.

DAVIDSON, J., & HARLAN, C. (1993, April 20). As Waco ends, Clinton's leadership comes under scrutiny. *The Wall Street Journal,* pp. A1, A6.

DAVIDSON, K., & HOFFMAN, L. (1986). Sexual fantasies and sexual satisfaction: An empirical analysis of erotic thought. *Journal of Sex Research, 22,* 184–205.

DAVIES, J. (1992, February). Female genital mutilation—a practice that should have vanished. *Midwives Chronicle and Nursing Notes,* p. 33.

DAVIS, A. T., & KOSKY, R. J. (1991). Attempted suicide in Aelaide and Perth: Changing rates for males and females, 1971–1987. *Medical Journal of Australia, 154,* 666–670.

DAVIS, D. (1976). On being detectably sane in insane places: Base rates and psychodiagnosis. *Journal of Abnormal Psychology, 85,* 416–422.

DAVIS L. (1990). Why do people take drugs? *In Health, 4*(6), 52.

DAVISON, G. C., & NEALE, J. M. (1990). *Abnormal psychology* (5th ed.). New York: Wiley.

DAVISON, G. C., & NEALE, J. M. (1994). *Abnormal psychology* (6th ed.). New York: Wiley.

DAWES, R. M. (1987, August). *Not me or thee but we*. Paper presented at the 11th. SPUDM Conference, Cambridge, England.

DAY, R., NIELSEN, J., KORTEN, A., ERNBERG, G., ET AL. (1987). Stressful life events preceding the onset of schizophrenia: A cross-national study from the World Health Organization. *Culture, Medicine, and Psychiatry, 11,* 123–205.

DE ANGELIS, T. (1992). Health psychology grows both in stature, influence. *APA Monitor, 23*(4), 10–11.

DEAUX, K., & WRIGHTSMAN, L. S. (1988). *Social psychology* (5th ed.). Pacific Grove, CA: Brooks/Cole.

DEBRUYN, M. (1992). Women and AIDS in developing countries. *Social Sciences and Medicine, 34,* 249–262.

DECASPER, A. J., & FIFER, W. D. (1980). Of human bonding: Newborn's prefer their mother's voices. *Science, 208,* 1174–1176.

DECASPER, A. J., & SPENCE, M. J. (1986). Prenatal maternal speech influences newborn's perception of speech sounds. *Infant Behavior and Development, 9,* 133–150.

DE CHARMS, R., & MOELLER, G. H. (1962). Values expressed in American children's readers: 1800–1950. *Journal of Abnormal and Social Psychology, 64,* 136–142.

DECI, E. L., & RYAN, R. M. (1985). *Intrinsic motivation and self-determination in human behavior*. New York: Plenum.

DE LACOSTE-UTAMSING, C., & HOLLOWAY, R. L. (1982). Sexual dimorphism in the human corpus callosum. *Science, 216,* 1431–1432.

DELGADO, J. M. R. (1960). Emotional behavior in animals and humans. *Psychiatric Research Report, 12,* 259–271.

DELGADO, P. L., CHARNEY, D. S., PRICE, L. H., AGHAJANIAN, G. K., LANDIS, H., & HENINGER, G. R. (1990). Serotonin function and the mechanism of antidepressant action. *Archives of General Psychiatry, 47,* 411–418.

DELGADO-GAITAN, C. (in press). Parenting in two generations of Mexican-American families. In P. M. Greenfield & R. R. Cocking (Eds.), *International roots of minority child development*. Special section of *International Journal of Behavioral Development*.

DELONGIS, A., COYNE, J. C., DAKOF, G., FOLKMAN, S., & LAZARUS, R. S. (1982). Relationship of daily hassles, uplifts, and major life events to health status. *Health Psychology, 1,* 119–136.

DELONGIS, A., FOLKMAN, S., & LAZARUS, R. S. (1988). The impact of daily stress on health and mood: Psychological and social resources as mediators. *Journal of Personality and Social Psychology, 54,* 486–495.

DEMBROSKI, T. M., & COSTA, P. (1988). Assessment of coronary-prone behavior: A current overview. *Annals of Behavioral Medicine, 10,* 60–63.

DEMENT, W. C. (1983). A life in sleep research. In M. H. Chase & E. D. Weitzman (Eds.), *Sleep disorders: Basic and clinical research*. New York: Spectrum.

DEMENT, W. C., & KLEITMAN, N. (1957). Cyclic variations in EEG and their relation to eye movements, bodily motility, and dreaming. *Electroencephalography Clinical Neurophysiology, 9,* 673–690.

DEMENT, W. C., & WOLPERT, E. (1958). The relation of eye movements, bodily motility, and external stimuli to dream content. *Journal of Experimental Psychology, 53,* 543–553.

DEMPSTER, F. N. (1985). Proactive interference in sentence recall: Topic-similarity effects and individual differences. *Memory and Cognition, 13,* 81–89.

DENNEY, N. W., & QUADAGNO, D. (1992). *Human sexuality* (2nd ed.). St. Louis, MS: Mosby.

DENNIS, W. (1973). *Children of the creche.* New York: Appleton-Century-Crofts.

DENNIS, W., & DENNIS, M. G. (1940). Cradles and cradling customs of the Pueblo Indians. *American Anthropologist, 42,* 107–115.

DENTON, L. (1987). Child abuse reporting laws: Are they a barrier to helping troubled families? *The APA Monitor, 18*(6), 1, 22–23.

DEUTSCH, J. A. (1983). *The physiological basis of memory.* New York: Academic Press.

DEVALOIS, R. L. (1965). Behavioral and electrophysiological studies of primate vision. In W. D. Neff (Ed.), *Contributions to sensory physiology* (Vol. 1). New York: Academic Press.

DEMENT, W. C. (1992, March). The sleepwatchers. *Stanford,* pp. 55–59.

DEMENT, W. C. (1974). *Some must watch while some must sleep.* San Francisco: Freeman.

DEWAN, E. (1970). The programming (P) hypothesis for REM sleep. In E. Hartmann (Ed.), *Sleep and dreaming.* Boston: Little, Brown.

DEWSBURY, D. A. (1989). Comparative psychology, ethology, and animal behavior. In M. R. Rosenzweig & L. W. Porter (Eds.), *Annual review of psychology* (pp. 581–602). Palo Alto CA: Annual Reviews Inc.

DIAMOND M. (1977). Human sexual development. In F. Beach (Ed.), *Human sexuality in four perspectives* (pp. 22–61). Baltimore: The Johns Hopkins University Press.

DIAMOND, M. (1982). Sexual identity, monozygotic twins reared in discordant sex roles and a BBC follow-up. *Archives of Sexual Behavior, 11,* 181–186.

DIAMOND, M. (1986). *The world of sexual behavior: Sexwatching.* New York: W. H. Smith.

DIAMOND, R., FELLER, L., & RUSSO, N. F. (1981). *Sexual harassment action kit.* Washington, DC: Federation of Organizations for Professional Women.

DICLEMENTE, R., DURBIN, M., SIEGEL, D., KRASNOVSKY, F., LAZARUS, N., & COMACHO, T. (1992). Determinants of condom use among junior high school students in a minority, inner-city school district. *Pediatrics, 89,* 197–202.

DIEHL, M., & STROEBE, W. (1987). Productivity loss in brainstorming groups: Toward the solution of a riddle. *Journal of Personality and Social Psychology, 53,* 497–509.

DIEN, D. S. F. (1982). A Chinese perspective on Kohlberg's theory of moral development. *Developmental Review, 2,* 331–341.

DIENER, E. (1980). Deindividuation: The absence of self-awareness and self-regulation in group members. In P. B. Paulus (Ed.), *The psychology of group influence.* Hillside, NJ: Erlbaum.

DIVASTO, P. V., KAUFMAN, A., ROSNER, L., JACKSON, R. CHRISTY, J., PEARSON, S., & BURGETT, T. (1984). The prevalence of sexually stressful events among females in the general population. *Archives of Sexual Behavior, 13,* 59–67.

DIGMAN, J. M. (1990). Personality structure: Emergence of the five-factor model. *Annual Review of Psychology, 41,* 417–440.

Dissociation and dissociative disorders. (1992, March). *Harvard Mental Health Letter, 8,* (9), 1–4.

DOBLIN, R., & KLEIMAN, M. A. R. (1991). Medical use of marijuana. *Annals of Internal Medicine, 114,* 809–810.

DODSON, J. A., TYBOUT, A. M., & STEINTHAL, E. (1978). Impact of deals and deal retraction on brand switching. *Journal of Marketing Research, 15*(1), 72–81.

DOLLARD, J., DOOB, L., MILLER, N., MOWRER, O. H., & SEARS, R. R. (1939). *Frustration and aggression.* New Haven, CT: Yale University Press.

DOMAN, G. (1979). *Teach your baby math.* New York: Simon & Schuster.

DONENBERG, G. R., & HOFFMAN, L. W. (1988). Gender differences in moral development. *Sex Roles, 18,* 701–717.

DONNERSTEIN, E. (1980). Aggressive erotica and violence against women. *Journal of Personality and Social Psychology, 39,* 269–277.

DONNERSTEIN, E., & BERKOWITZ, L. (1981). Victim reactions in aggressive erotic films as a factor in violence against women. *Journal of Personality and Social Psychology, 41,* 710–724.

DONNERSTEIN, E., & LINZ, D. (1984, January). Sexual violence in the media: A warning. *Psychology Today,* pp. 14–15.

DOREN, D. (1987). *Understanding and treating the psychopath.* New York: Wiley.

DORFMAN, L., DERISH, P., & COHEN, J. (1992). Hey girlfriend: An evaluation of AIDS prevention among women in the sex industry. *Health Education Quarterly, 19,* 25–40.

DORMAN, M. (1986, January 3). Jack La Lanne: We're just now catching up with fitness pioneer. *San Diego Tribune,* p. D-1.

DOVIDIO, J. F. (1991). The empathy-altruism hypothesis: Paradigm and promise. *Psychological Inquiry, 2,* 126–128.

DRACHMAN, D., DE CARUFEL, A., & INSKO, C. A. (1978). The extra credit effect in interpersonal attraction. *Journal of Experimental Social Psychology, 14,* 458–465.

DRAGUNS, J. (1975). Resocialization into culture: The complexities of taking a worldwide view of psychotherapy. In R. Brislin, S. Bochner, & W. Lonner (Eds.), *Cross-cultural perspective on learning* (pp. 273–289). Beverly Hills, CA: Sage.

DRAGUNS, J. (1990). Applications of cross-cultural psychology in the field of mental health. In R. Brislin (Ed.), *Applied cross-cultural psychology* (pp. 302–324). Newbury Park, CA: Sage.

DRESSEL, P. L. (1988). Gender, race, and class: Beyond the feminization of poverty in later life. *The Gerontologist, 28,* 177–180.

DRISCOLL, R., DAVIS, K. E., & LIPETZ, M. E. (1972). Parental interference and romantic love: The Romeo and Juliet effect. *Journal of Personality and Social Psychology, 24,* 1–10.

DRYDEN, W., & DIGIUSEPPE, R. (1990). *A primer on rational-emotive therapy.* Champaign, IL: Research Press.

DUDDLE, M. (1991). Emotional sequelae of sexual assault. *Journal of the Royal Society of Medicine, 84,* 26–28.

DUNCAN, D., & GOLD, R. (1982). *Drugs and the whole person.* New York: Wiley.

DUNCAN, P., RITTER, P., DORNBUSH, S., GROSS, P., & CARLSMITH, J. (1985). The effects of pubertal timing on body image, school behavior, and deviance. *Journal of Youth and Adolescence, 14,* 227–236.

DUNCKER, K. (1945). On problem solving. *Psychological Monographs, 58*(5, Whole No. 270).

DUNN, J., & KENDRICK, C. (1982). The speech of two- and three-year-olds to infant siblings: "Baby talk" and the context of communication. *Journal of Child Language, 9,* 579–595.

DUSEK, J. B., & FLAHERTY, F. (1981). The development of the self-concept during the adolescent years. *Monographs of the Society for Research in Child Development, 46*(4), 191.

DWORKIN, A. (1974). *Woman hating.* New York: E. P. Dutton.

DWORKIN, B. R., & MILLER, N. E. (1986). Failure to replicate visceral learning in the acute curarized rat preparation. *Behavioral Neuroscience, 100,* 299–314.

DYWAN, J. (1984). Hyperamnesia, hypnosis, and memory: Implications for forensic investigation. *Dissertation Abstracts International, 44*(10-B), 3190.

DYWAN, J., & BOWERS, K. A. (1983). The use of hypnosis to enhance recall. *Science, 222*(4620), 184–185.

EAGLY, A. H., & HIMMELFARB, S. (1978). Attitudes and opinions. In M. R. Rosenzweig & L. W. Porter (Eds.), *Annual review of psychology* (Vol. 29). Palo Alto, CA: Annual Reviews Inc.

EAGLY, A. H., ASHMORE, R. D., MAKHIJANI, M. G., & LONGO, L. C. (1991). What is beautiful is good, but . . . A meta-analytic review of research on the physical attractiveness stereotype. *Psychological Bulletin, 110,* 109–128.

EATON, W. W., & KEYL, P. M. (1990). Risk factors for the onset of Diagnostic interview Schedule/DSM-III: Agoraphobia in a prospective, population-based study. *Archives of General Psychiatry, 47,* 819–824.

EBBINGHAUS, H. (1913). *Memory: A contribution to experimental psychology* (H. A. Ruger and C. E. Bussenius, Trans.). New York: Teacher's College. (Original work published 1885.)

ECCLES P., J., ADLER, T., & MEECE, J. L. (1984). Sex differences in achievement: A test of alternate theories. *Journal of Personality and Social Psychology, 46,* 26–43.

EDELMAN, M. W. (1987). *Families in peril: An agenda for social change.* New York: Alan Guttmacher Institute.

EDMAN, G., ASBERG, M., LEVANDER, S., & SCHALLING, D. (1986). Skin conductance habituation and cerebrospinal fluid 5-hydroxyindoleacetic acid in suicidal patients. *Archives of General Psychiatry, 43,* 586–592.

EDWARDS, G., GROSS, M. M., KELLER, J., MOSER, J., & ROOM, R. (1977). *Alcohol related disabilities.* Geneva, Switzerland: World Health Organization.

EDWARDS, K. (1990). The interplay of affect and cognition in attitude formation and change. *Journal of Personality and Social Psychology, 59,* 202–216.

EGAN, K. J., & KEATON, W. J. (1987). Responses to illness and health in chronic pain patients and healthy adults. *Psychosomatic Medicine, 49,* 470–481.

EGGER, M. D., & FLYNN, J. P. (1967). Further studies on the effects on amygdaloid stimulation and ablation of hypothalamically elicited attack behavior in cats. In W. R. Adey & T. Tokizane (Eds.), *Progress in brain research: Vol. 27. Structure and function of the limbic system.* Amsterdam: Elsevier.

EHRHARDT, A., & MEYER-BAHLBURG, H. (1981). Effects of prenatal sex hormones on gender-related behavior. *Science, 211,* 1312–1318.

EIBL-EIBESFELDT, I. (1980a). *The biology of peace and war.* New York: Viking.

EIBL-EIBESFELDT, I. (1980b). Strategies of social interaction. In R. Plutchik & H. Kelerman (Eds.), *Emotion: Theory, research, and experience.* New York: Academic Press.

EISENBERG, N. (1986). *Altruistic emotion, cognition, and behavior.* Hillsdale, NJ: Erlbaum.

EISENBERG, N. (1989). Empathy and sympathy. In W. Damon (Ed.), *Child development today and tomorrow.* San Francisco: Jossey-Bass.

EISENBERG, N. (1991). Meta-analytic contributions to the literature on prosocial behavior. *Personality and Social Psychology Bulletin, 17*, 273–282.

EISENBERG, N., & MILLER, P. (1989). The relation of empathy to prosocial and related behaviors. *Psychological Bulletin, 101*, 91–119.

EKMAN, P. (1972). Universals and cultural differences in facial expressions of emotion. In J. Cole (Ed.), *Nebraska symposium on motivation* (Vol. 19). Lincoln: University of Nebraska Press.

EKMAN, P. (1993). Facial expression and emotion. *American Psychologist, 48*, 384–392.

EKMAN, P., & FRIESEN, W. V. (1975). *Unmasking the face*. Englewood Cliffs, NJ: Prentice Hall.

EKMAN, P., FRIESEN, W., O'SULLIVAN, C. A., DIACOYANNII-TARIATZIS, H. K., HEIDER, K., KRAUSE, R., LE-COMPTE, W., PITCARIN, T., RICCI-BITI, P. E., SCHENER, K., TOMITA, M., & TZAVARAS, A. (1987). Universals and cultural differences in the judgment of facial expressions of emotion. *Journal of Personality and Social Psychology, 53*, 712–717.

EKMAN, P., LEVENSON, R. W., & FRIESEN, W. V. (1983). Autonomic nervous system activity distinguishes among emotions. *Science, 221*, 1208–1210.

ELAAD, E. (1990). Detection of guilty knowledge in real-life criminal investigations. *Journal of Applied Psychology, 75*, 521–529.

ELKIND, D. (1981). *The hurried child*. Reading, MA: Addison-Wesley.

ELKIND, D. (1984). *All grown up and no place to go*. Reading, MA: Addison-Wesley.

ELKIND, D. (1987, May). Superkids and super problems. *Psychology Today*, pp. 60–61.

ELKIND, D. (1988). An essential difference. In J. Rubinstein & B. Slife (Eds.), *Taking sides: Clashing views on controversial psychological issues* (5th ed., pp. 163–173). Guilford, CT: Dushkin.

ELLIOTT, M. (1992, March). Tip of the iceberg? *Social Work Today*, pp. 12–13.

ELLIS, A. (1987). The impossibility of achieving consistently good mental health. *American Psychologist, 42*, 364–375.

ELLIS, A., & HARPER, R. A. (1975). *A new guide to rational living*. Hollywood, CA: Wilshire.

ELLIS, B., & SYMONS, D. (1990). Sex differences in sexual fantasy: An evolutionary psychological approach. *Journal of Sex Research, 27*, 527–555.

ELLIS, L., & AMES, M. (1987). Neurohormonal functioning and sexual orientation: A theory of homosexuality–heterosexuality. *Psychological Bulletin, 101*, 233–258.

ELLMAN, S. J., & ANTROBUS, J. S. (Eds.). The mind in sleep: Psychology and psychophysiology (2nd ed.). New York: Wiley.

ELLMAN, S. J., SPIELMAN, A. J., LUCK, D., STEINER, S. S., & HALPERIN, R. (1991). REM deprivation: A review. In S. A. Ellman & J. S. Antrobus (Eds.), *The mind in sleep: Psychology and psychophysiology* (2nd ed., pp. 329–368). New York: Wiley.

ELTON, D., BURROWS, G. D., & STANLEY, G. V. (1980). Hypnosis and chronic pain. *Australian Journal of Clinical & Experimental Hypnosis, 8*, 83–90.

EMERSON, D. (1993, April). *Factors moderating children's adjustment to parental divorce: A review of current research*. Paper presented at the meeting of the Western Psychological Association, Phoenix, AZ.

EMERY, R. E. (1989). Family violence. *American Psychologist, 44*, 321–328.

ENGEL, G. (1977, November). Emotional stress and sudden death. *Psychology Today, 11*(11), 144.

ENTHOVEN, A. C. (1992, September). Health care: A prescription for change. *Stanford*, pp. 28–33.

EPSTEIN, Y. M. (1981). Crowding stress and human behavior. *Journal of Social Issues, 37*(1), 126–144.

ERBECK, J., ELFNER, L., & DRIGGS, D. (1983). Reduction of blood pressure by indirect biofeedback. *Biofeedback and Self Regulation, 8*(1), 63–72.

ERBER, J. T. (1982). Memory and age. In T. M. Field, A. Huston, H. C. Quay, L. Troll, & G. E. Finler (Eds.), *Review of human development*. New York: Wiley.

ERIKSON, E. H. (1968). *Identity: Youth and crisis*. New York: W. W. Norton.

ERIKSON, E. H. (1987). *A way of looking at things: Selected papers from 1930 to 1980* (S. Schlein, Ed.). New York: Norton.

ERICKSON, M. T. (1993). Rethinking Oedipus: An evolutionary perspective of incest avoidance. *American Journal of Psychiatry, 150*(3), 411–416.

ERON, L. D., & HUESMANN, L. R. (1984). The control of aggressive behavior by changes in attitudes, values, and the conditions of learning. In R. J. Blanchard & C. Blanchard (Eds.), *Advances in the study of aggression* (Vol. 1). Orlando, FL: Academic Press.

ESCOBAR, J., GOMEZ, J., & TUASON, V. (1983). Depressive phenomenology in North and South American patients. *American Journal of Psychiatry, 140*, 47–51.

ESTES, W. K. (1991). Cognitive architectures from the standpoint of an experimental psychologist. *Annual Review of Psychology, 42*, 1–28.

ESTRICH, S. (1993, April 25). The Waco legacy. *Los Angeles Times*, pp. M1, M6.

ETAUGH, C. (1990). Women's lives: Images and realities. In M. A. Paludi & G. A. Steuernagel (Eds.), *Foundations for a feminist restructuring of the academic disciplines*. Binghamton, NY: Haworth.

EVANS, C. (1984). *Landscapes of the night: How and why we dream*. New York: Viking.

EVANS, W., & ROSENBERG, I. H. (1992). *Biomarkers: The 10 keys to prolonging vitality*. New York: Simon & Schuster.

EXNER, J. E., & WEINER, I. B. (1982). *The Rorschach: A comprehensive system* (Vol. 3). New York: Wiley.

EYSENCK, H. J. (1967). *The biological basis of personality*. Springfield, IL: Charles C Thomas.

EYSENCK, H. J. (1991). *Smoking, personality, and stress: Psychosocial factors in the prevention of cancer and coronary heart disease*. New York: Springer-Verlag.

EYSENCK, H. J. (1982). *Personality, genetics, and behavior: Selected papers*. New York: Prager.

EYSENCK, H. J. (1990). Biological dimensions of personality. In L. A. Pervin (Ed.), *Handbook of personality: Theory and research*. New York: Guilford Press.

EYSENCK, M. W., MOGG, K., MAY, J., RICHARDS, A., & MATTHEWS, A. (1991). Bias in interpretation of ambiguous sentences related to threat in anxiety. *Journal of Abnormal Psychology, 100*, 144–150.

EZZELL, C. (1992). A time to live, a time to die. *Science News, 142*, 344–345.

FABES, R. A. (1987). Effects of reward contexts on young children's task interest. *Journal of Psychology, 121*, 5–19.

FACKELMANN, K. A. (1989, April 1). Cocaine mothers imperil babies brains. *Science News, 135*, 198.

FACKELMANN, K. A. (1992). Pacific cocktail: The history, chemistry, and botany of the mind-altering kava plant. *Science News, 141*, 424–425.

FAGOT, B. I., LEINBACH, M. D., & O'BOYLE, C. (1992). Gender labeling, gender stereotyping, and parenting behaviors. *Developmental Psychology, 28*, 225–230.

FANTZ, R. L. (1956). A method for studying early visual development. *Perceptual and Motor Skills, 6*, 13–15.

FANTZ, R. L. (1963). Pattern vision in newborn infants. *Science, 140*, 296–297.

FARLEY, F. (1986, August). *The Type T personality*. Invited address at the meeting of the American Psychological Association, Washington, DC.

FARMER, F. (1972). *Will there really be a morning?* New York: Dell.

FARTHING, W. G. (1992). *The psychology of consciousness*. Englewood Cliffs, NJ: Prentice Hall.

FAULKNER, B., ONESTI, G., ANGELAKOS, E. T., FERNANDES, M., & LANGMAN, C. (1979). Cardiovascular response to mental stress in normal adolescents with hypertensive parents. Hemodynamics and mental stress in adolescents. *Hypertension, 1*, 23–30.

FEENEY, J. A., & NOLLER, P. (1990). Attachment style as a predictor of adult romantic relationships. *Journal of Personality and Social Psychology, 58*, 281–291.

FEINBERG, R., MILLER, F., & WEISS, R. (1983). Verbal learned helplessness. *Representative Research in Social Psychology, 13*(1), 34–45.

FELDHUSEN, J. F., & MOON, S. M. (1992). Grouping gifted students: Issues and concerns. *Gifted Child Quarterly, 36*(2), 63–67.

FELDMAN, R. S. (Ed.). (1982). *Development of nonverbal behavior in children*. Seacaucus, NJ: Springer-Verlag.

FELITTI, V. (1991). Long-term medical consequences of incest, rape, and molestation. *Southern Medical Journal, 84*, 328–331.

FELSON, R. B. (1980). Physical attractiveness, grades, and teachers' attributions of ability. *Representative Research in Social Psychology, 11*, 64–71.

FERGUSON, N. B. L., & KEESEY, R. E. (1975). Effect of a quinine-adulterated diet upon body weight maintenance in male rats with ventromedial hypothalamic lesions. *Journal of Comparative and Physiological Psychology, 89*, 478–488.

FESTINGER, L. A. (1954). A theory of social comparison processes. *Human Relations, 7*, 117–140.

FESTINGER, L. A. (1957). *A theory of cognitive dissonance*. Evanston, IL: Row, Peterson.

FESTINGER, L. A., & CARLSMITH, L. M. (1959). Cognitive consequences of forced compliance. *Journal of Abnormal and Social Psychology, 58*, 203–210.

FESTINGER, L. A., RIECKEN, H. W., & SCHACHTER, S. (1956). *When prophesy fails*. Minneapolis: University of Minnesota Press.

FESTINGER, L., RIECKEN, H. W., & SCHACHTER, S. (1956). *When prophecy fails*. New York: Harper and Row.

FIELD, D. (1981). Can preschool children really learn to conserve? *Child Development, 52*, 326–334.

FIELD, K. M., WOODSON, R., GREENBERG, R., & COHEN, D. (1982). Discrimination and imitation of facial expressions by neonates. *Science, 218*, 179–181.

FIELD, T. (1987, May). Baby research comes of age. *Psychology Today*, pp. 46–47.

FINK, M. (1985). Convulsive therapy: Fifty years of progress. *Convulsive Therapy, 1*, 204–216.

FINKELHOR, D. (1984). *Child sexual abuse: Theory and research*. New York: Free Press.

FINKELHOR, D., & HOTALING, G. (1988). *Stopping family violence: An agenda of research priorities for the coming decade*. Newbury Park, CA: Sage.

FINKELHOR, D., HOTALING, G., LEWIS, I., & SMITH, C. (1990). Sexual abuse in a national sample of adult men and women: Prevalence, characteristics, and risk factors. *Child Abuse and Neglect, 14*, 19–28.

FISCHBACH, G. D. (1992). Mind and brain. *Scientific American, 267*(3), 48–57.

FISCHER, R. (1976, May). On the remembrance of things present: The statebound and stage-bound nature of consciousness. *Man-Environment Systems, 6*(3), 131–136.

FISCHHOFF, B. (1992). Giving advice: Decision theory perspective on sexual assault. *American Psychologist, 47,* 577–588.

FISCHMAN, J. (1986, January). Women and divorce: Ten years later. *Psychology Today,* p. 14.

FISHER, J. D., BELL, P. A., & BAUM, A. S. (1984). *Environmental psychology* (2nd ed.). New York: Holt, Rinehart & Winston.

FISHMAN, S. M., & SHEEHAN, D. V. (1985, April). Anxiety and panic: Their cause and treatment. *Psychology Today,* pp. 26–32.

FISKE, S. T. (1989). Examining the role of intent: Toward understanding its role in stereotyping and prejudice. In J. S. Uleman & J. A. Bargh (Eds.), *Unintended thought.* New York: Guilford Press.

FLAVELL, J. H. (1985). *Cognitive development* (2nd ed.). Englewood Cliffs, NJ: Prentice Hall.

FLAVELL, J. H. (1993). Young children's understanding of thinking and consciousness. *Current Directions in Psychological Science, 2,* 40–43.

FLAY, B. R. (1985). Psychosocial approaches to smoking prevention: A review of findings. *Health Psychology, 4,* 449–488.

FLOR, H., KERNS, R. D., & TURK, D. C. (1987). The role of spouse reinforcement, perceived pain, and activity levels of chronic pain patients. *Journal of Psychosomatic Research, 31,* 251–259.

FOA, E., & KOZAK, M. (1986). Emotional processing of fear: Exposure to corrective information. *Psychological Bulletin, 99,* 20–35.

FOA, E. B., OLASOV, B., & STEKETEE, G. S. (1987). *Treatment of rape victims.* Paper presented at the conference of the State of the Art in Sexual Assault, Charleston, SC.

FODERARO, L. W. (1989, October 18). Teenagers find drink stronger lure than crack. *New York Times,* p. C1.

FOLKS, D. G., FORD, C. V., & REGAN, W. M. (1984). Conversion symptoms in a general hospital. *Psychosomatics, 25,* 285–295.

FONOW, M., RICHARDSON, L., & WEMMERUS, V. (1992). Feminist rape education: Does it work? *Gender and Society, 6,* 108–121.

FOOS-GRABER, A. (1985). *Deathing: An intelligent alternative for the final moments of life.* Reading, MA: Addison-Wesley.

FORD, C. S., & BEACH, F. A. (1951). *Patterns of sexual behavior.* New York: Harper & Brothers.

FORGAS, J. P. (1992). Mood and the perception of atypical people: Affect and prototypicality in person memory and impressions. *Journal of Personality and Social Psychology, 62,* 115–125.

FOULKES, D., & FLEISHER, S. (1975). Mental activity in relaxed wakefulness. *Journal of Abnormal Psychology, 84,* 66–75.

Fourteen worst myths about recovered mental patients. (1985). Department of Health and Human Services (DHHS Publication No. ADM 35-1391). Washington, DC: U. S. Government Printing Office.

FOWLER, R. D. (1986, May). Howard Hughes: A psychological autopsy. *Psychology Today,* pp. 22–33.

FRANKEL, F. H. (1988). Electro-convulsive therapy. In A. M. Nicholi, Jr. (Ed.), *New Harvard guide to psychiatry* (pp. 580–588). Cambridge, MA: Harvard University Press.

FRANKEL, K. A., & BATES, J. E. (1990). Mother-toddler problem solving: Antecedents of attachment, home behavior, and temperament. *Child Development, 61,* 810–819.

FRANKENBURG, W. K., & DODDS, J. B. (1967). The Denver Developmental Screening Test. *Journal of Pediatrics, 71,* 181–191.

FRAZIER, P. A. (1990). Victim attributions and post-rape trauma. *Journal of Personality and Social Psychology, 59,* 293–311.

FRAZIER, P., & COHEN, B. (1992). Research on the sexual victimization of women. *The Counseling Psychologist, 20,* 141–158.

FREEDMAN, J. (1975). *Crowding and behavior.* San Francisco: Freeman.

FREEMAN, A., & DEWOLF, R. (1992). *The 10 dumbest mistakes smart people make and how to avoid them.* New York: HarperCollins.

FREEMAN, W. (1959) Psychosurgery. In S. Arieti (Ed.), *American handbook of psychiatry* (Vol. 2, pp. 1521–1540). New York: Basic Books.

FREEMAN-LONGO, R. E., & WALL, R. V. (1986, March). Changing a lifetime of sexual crime. *Psychology Today,* pp. 59–64.

FREMGEN, A., & FAY, D. (1980). Overextensions in production and comprehension: A methodological clarification. *Journal of Child Language, 7,* 205–211.

FRENCH, E. G., & THOMAS, F. H. (1958). The relationship of achievement motivation to problem-solving effectiveness. *Journal of Abnormal and Social Psychology, 56,* 45–48.

FRENSCH, P. A., & STERNBERG, R. J. (1990). Intelligence and cognition. In M. W. Eysenck (Ed.), *Cognitive psychology: An international review.* (pp. 57–103). New York: Wiley.

FREUD, S. (1953). The interpretation of dreams. In J. Stratchey (Ed. and Trans.), *The standard edition of the complete psychological works of Sigmund Freud* (Vols. 4 and 5). London: Hogarth Press. (Original work published 1900)

FREUD, S. (1905). Three essays on the theory of sexuality. In J. Stratchey (Ed. and Trans.), *The standard edition of the complete psychological work of Sigmund Freud* (Vol. 11). London: Hogarth Press. (Original work published 1900)

FREUD, S. (1963). On the history of the psycho-analytic movement. In J. Stratchey (Ed. and Trans.), *The standard edition of the complete psychological works of Sigmund Freud* (Vol. 14). London: Hogarth Press. (Original work published 1914)

FREUD, S. (1961). The ego and the id. In J. Stratchey (Ed. and Trans.), *The standard edition of the complete psychological works of Sigmund Freud* (Vol. 19). London: Hogarth Press. (Original work published 1923)

FREUD S. (1934). *Collected papers.* London: Hogarth.

FREY, C. L. (1985). Culture, behavior, and aging in the comparative perspective. In J. E. Birren & K. W. Schaie (Eds.), *Handbook of the psychology of aging* (2nd ed., pp. 216–244). New York: Van Nostrand Reinhold.

FREY, D. (1981). Postdecisional preference for decision-relevant information as a function of the competence of its source and the degree of familiarity with this information. *Journal of Experimental Social Psychology, 17,* 51–67.

FREY D. (1982). Different levels of cognitive dissonance, information seeking, and information avoidance. *Journal of Personality and Social Psychology, 43,* 1175–1183.

FREZZA, M., DI PADOVA, C., POZZATO, G., TERPIN, M., BARAONA, E., & LIEBER, C. S. (1990). High blood alcohol levels in women: The role of decreased gastric alcohol dehydrogenase activity and first-pass metabolism. *New England Journal of Medicine, 322,* 95–99.

FRIEDMAN, M., & ROSENMAN, R. H. (1959). Association of specific overt behavior pattern with blood and cardiovascular findings—Blood cholesterol level, blood clotting time, incidence of arcus senilis, and clinical coronary artery disease. *Journal of the American Medical Association, 162,* 1286–1296.

FRIEDMAN, M., THORESEN, C. E., GILL, J. J., ULMER, D., POWELL, L. H. PRICE, V. A., BROWN, B., THOMPSON, L., RABIN, D. D., BREALL, W. S., BOURG, E., LEVY, R., & DIXON, T. (1986). Alteration of Type A behavior and its effect on cardiac recurrences in past myocardial infarction patients: Summary results of the Recurrent Coronary Prevention Project. *American Heart Journal, 112,* 653–665.

FROMER, M. J. (1983, January). Motion sickness: All in your head? *Psychology Today,* p. 65.

FROMM, E. (1992). Dissociation, repression, cognition, and voluntarism. *Consciousness and cognition, 1*(1), 40–46.

FURBY, L., & FISCHHOFF, B. (1992). Rape self-defense strategies: A review of their effectiveness. *Victimology, 50,* 299–313.

FUREY, E. M. (1984). The effects of alcohol on the fetus. In H. E. Fitzgerald & M. G. Walraven (Eds.). *Human development 84/85.* Guilford, CT: Dushkin.

FURSTENBERG, F. F., BROOKS-GUNN, J., & CHASE-LANSDALE, L. (1989). Teenaged pregnancy and childbearing. *American Psychologist, 44,* 313–320.

GAGNON, J. H. (1977). *Human sexualities.* Glenview, IL: Scott, Foresman.

GALABURDA, A. M., & KEMPER, T. L. (1979). Cytoarchitectonic abnormalities in development dyslexia: A case study. *Annals of Neurology, 6,* 94–100.

GALANTER, M. (1989). *Cults: Faith, healing, and coercion.* Fairlawn, NJ: Oxford University Press.

GALANTER, M. (1990). Cults and zealous self-help movements: A psychiatric perspective. *American Journal of Psychiatry, 147,* 543–551.

GALANTER, E. (1962). Contemporary psychophysics. In R. Brown (Ed.), *New directions in psychology* (Vol. 1, pp. 87–156). New York: Holt, Rinehart and Winston.

GALLUP, G. G., & SUAREZ, S. D. (1985). Alternatives to the use of animals in psychological research. *American Psychologist, 40,* 1104–1111.

GANCHROW, J. R., STEINER, J. E., & DAHER, M. (1983). Neonatal facial expressions in response to different qualities and intensities of gustatory stimuli. *Infant Behavior and Development, 6,* 189–200.

GANNON, L., & STERNBACH, R. A. (1971). Alpha enhancement as a treatment for pain: A case study. *Journal of Behavior Therapy and Experimental Psychiatry, 2,* 209–213.

GARCIA-ARRARAS, J. E., & PAPPENHEIMER, J. R. (1983). Site of action of sleep-inducing muramyl peptide isolated from human urine: Microinjection studies in rabbit brains. *Journal of Neurophysiology, 49,* 528–533.

GARDNER, B. T., & GARDNER, R. A. (1971). Two-way communication with an infant chimpanzee. In A. M. Schrier & F. Stollnitz (Eds.), *Behavior of nonhuman primates* (Vol. 4). New York: Academic Press.

GARDNER, H. (1983). *Frames of mind.* New York: Basic Books.

GARDNER, H. (1986). From testing intelligence to assessing competencies. A pluralistic view of intellect. *Roeper Review, 8*(3), 147–150.

GARDNER, H. (1988). Creativity: An interdisciplinary perspective. *Creativity Research Journal, 1,* 8–26.

GARDNER, M. (1977, November/December). A skeptic's view of parapsychology. *The Humanist,* pp. 76–94.

GARDNER, R. A., & GARDNER, B. T. (1969). Teaching sign language to a chimpanzee. *Science, 165,* 664–672.

GARNER, D. M., OLMSTED, M. P., DAVIS, R., ROCKERT, W., GOLDBLOOM, D., & EAGLE, M. (1990). The association between bulimic symptoms and reported psychopathology. *International Journal of Eating Disorders, 9,* 1–15.

GARVIN, V., KALTER, N., & HANSELL, J. (1988, August). *Divorced women: A study in stress and coping.*

Paper presented at the annual meeting of the American Psychological Association, Atlanta.

GARWAD, S. G., PHILLIPS, D., HARTMAN, A., & ZIGLER, E. F. (1989). As the pendulum swings: Federal agency programs for children. *American Psychologist, 44,* 434–440.

GATZ, M., & PEARSON, C. G. (1988). Ageism revised and the provision of psychological services. *American Psychologist, 43,* 184–188.

GAWIN, F. H. (1991), Cocaine addiction: Psychology and neurophysiology. *Science, 251,* 1580–1586.

GAWIN, F., & KLEBER, H. (1984). Cocaine abuse treatment. *Archives of General Psychiatry, 47*(2), 370–376.

GAY, P. (1983). *The bourgeois experience: Victoria to Freud. Vol. 1: Education of the senses.* New York: Oxford University Press.

GAY, P. (1988). *Freud: A life for our time.* New York: Norton.

GAY, R., & RAPHELSON, A. (1967). "Transfer of learning" by injection of brain RNA: A replication. *Psychonomic Science, 8,* 369–370.

GAYLORD, C., ORME-JOHNSON, D., & TRAVIS, F. (1989). The effects of the Transcendental Meditation technique and progressive muscle relaxation on EEG coherence, stress reactivity, and mental health in black adults. *International Journal of Neuroscience, 46,* 77–86.

GAZZANIGA, M. S. (1970). *The bisected brain.* New York: Appleton-Century-Crofts.

GAZZANIGA, M. S. (1989). Organization of the human brain. *Science, 245,* 947–952.

GEBER, M., & DEAN, R. F. A. (1957). Gesell tests on African children. *Pediatrics, 202,* 1055–1065.

GREEN, R. G. (1978). Some effects of observing violence upon the behavior of the observer. In B. A. Maher (Ed.), *Progress in experimental personality research* (Vol. 8). New York: Academic Press.

GEEZE, D. S., & PIERSON, W. P. (1986). Airsickness in B-52 crew members. *Military Medicine, 151,* 628–629.

GELDERLOOS, P., WALTON, K. G., ORME-JOHNSON, D. W., & ALEXANDER, C. N. (1991). Effectiveness of the Transcendental Meditation program in preventing and treating substance abuse: A review. *The International Journal of the Addictions, 25*(3), 293–325.

GELLER, L. (1982). The failure of self-actualization theory: A critique of Carl Rogers and Abraham Maslow. *Journal of Humanistic Psychology, 22,* 56–73.

GELHORN, E. (1964). Motion and emotion: The role of proprioception in the physiology and pathology of the emotions. *Psychological Review, 71,* 457–472.

GELMAN, D. (1988, June 27). Where are the patients? *Newsweek,* pp. 62–66.

GELMAN, D. (1989), March 27). Haunted by their habits. *Newsweek,* pp. 71–75.

GELMAN, D., DOHERTY, S., JOSEPH N., & CARROLL, G. (1988). How infants learn to talk. *Newsweek on Health,* pp. 32–34.

GELMAN, D., FOOTE, D., BARRETT, T., & TALBOT, M. (1992), February). Born or bred? *Newsweek,* pp. 46–53.

GENTILE, J. R., & MONACO, N. M. (1986). Learned helplessness in mathematics: What educators should know. *Journal of Mathematical Behavior, 5,* 159–178.

GEORGOTAS, A., & CANCRO, R. (1988). *Depression and mania.* New York: Elsevier.

GERBNER, G., GROSS, L., MORGAN, M., & SIGNORIELLI, N. (1993). Growing up with television: The cultivation perspective. In J. Bryant & D. Zillman (Eds.), *Media effects: Advances in theory and research.* Hillsdale, NJ: Erlbaum.

GERSHON, E. S., & RIEDER, R. O. (1992). Major disorders of mind and brain. *Scientific American, 267*(3), 126–133.

GIBBONS, A. (1991). The brain as "Sexual Organ." *Science, 253,* 957–969.

GIBBS, N. (1993, May 3). Fire storm in Waco. *Time,* pp. 26–43.

GIBSON, E. J., & WALK, R. D. (1960). The visual cliff. *Scientific American, 202*(2), 67–71.

GIBSON, R. C. (1986). Outlook for the black family. In A. Pifer & L. Bronte (Eds.), *Our aging society: Paradox and promise* (pp. 181–197). New York: Norton.

GIBSON, W. (1975). *The miracle worker.* New York: Bantam.

GILL, J. L. (1983). *Personalized stress management.* San Jose, CA: Counseling & Counseling Services Publications.

GILLIGAN, C. (1977). In a different voice: Women's conseption of morality. *Harvard Educational Review, 47*(4), 481–517.

GILLIGAN, C. (1982). *In a different voice.* Cambridge, MA: Harvard University Press.

GILLIGAN, C. (1990). Teaching Shakespeare's sister. In C. Gilligan, N. Lyons, & T. Hanmer (Eds.), *Mapping the moral domain* (pp. 73–86). Cambridge, MA: Harvard University Press.

GILLIGAN, C., & ATTANUCCI, J. (1988). Two moral orientations. In C. Gilligan, J. V. Ward, J. M. Taylor, & B. Bardige (Eds.), *Mapping the moral domain* (pp. 73–86). Cambridge, MA: Harvard University Press.

GILLIGAN, C., BROWN, L. M., & ROGERS, A. G. (1990). Psyche embedded: A place for body, relationships, and culture in personality theory. In A. I. Rabin, R. A. Zucker, R. Emmons, & S. Frank (Eds.), *Studying lives and persons.* New York: Springer.

GILLIN, J. C. (1991). The long and short of sleeping pills. *New England Journal of Medicine, 324,* 1735–1736.

GILLUND, G., & SHIFFRIN, R. M. (1984). A retrieval model for both recognition and recall. *Psychological Review, 91*(1), 1–67.

GILMOUR, D. R., & WALKEY, F. H. (1981). Identifying violent offenders using a video measure of interpersonal distance. *Journal of Consulting and Clinical Psychology, 49,* 287–291.

GILOVICH, T. (1990). Differential construal and the false consensus effect. *Journal of Personality and Social Psychology, 59,* 623–634.

GLADUE, B. A. (1987). Psychobiological contributions. In L. Diamant (Ed.), *Male and female homosexuality: Psychological approaches* (pp. 129–153). Washington, DC: Hemisphere.

GLASS, A. L., & HOLYOAK, K. J. (1986). *Cognition.* New York: Random House.

GOLD, M. S., GALLANTER, M., & STIMMEL, B. (1987). *Cocaine.* Binghamton, NY: Haworth Press.

GOLDBERG, H. (1983). *The new male–female relationship,* New York: Morrow.

GOLDBERG, L. R. (1993). The structure of phenotypic personality traits. *American Psychologist, 48,* 26–34.

GOLDBLATT, P. B., MOORE, M. E., & STUNKARD, A. J. (1965). Social factors in obesity. *Journal of the American Medical Association, 192,* 1039–1044.

GOLDMAN, B. D. (1978). Developmental influences of hormones on neuroendocrine mechanisms of sexual behavior: Comparisons with other sexually dimorphic behaviors. In J. B. Hutchinson (Ed.), *Biological determinants of sexual behavior* (pp. 127–152). New York: Wiley.

GOLDMAN, R., JAFFA, M., & SCHACHTER, S. (1968). Yom Kippur, Air France, dormitory food and eating behavior of obese and normal persons. *Journal of Personality and Social Psychology, 10,* 65–72.

GOLDMAN-RAKIC, P. S. (1992). Working memory and the mind. *Scientific American, 267*(3), 111–117.

GOLDSTEIN, B. (1976). *Introduction to human sexuality.* New York: McGraw-Hill.

GOLDSTEIN, E. B. (1984). *Sensation and perception.* Belmont, CA: Wadsworth.

GOLDSTEIN, I. B. (1981). Assessment of hypertension. In C. K. Prokop & L. A. Bradley (Eds.), *Medical psychology.* New York: Academic Press.

GOLDSTEIN, T. (1988, February 12). Women in the law aren't yet equal partners. *New York Times,* p. B7.

GOLDWATER, B. C., & COLLIS, M. L. (1985). Psychologic effects of cardiovascular conditioning: A controlled experiment. *Psychosomatic Medicine, 47,* 174–181.

GOODENOUGH, D. R. (1991). Dream recall: History and current status of the field. In S. A. Ellman & J. S. Antrobus (Eds.), *The mind in sleep: Psychology and psychophysiology* (2nd ed., pp. 143–171). New York: Wiley.

GOODMAN, W. K., PRICE, L. H., DELGADO, P. L., PALUMBO, J., KRYSTAL, J. H., NAGY, L. M., RASMUSSEN, S. A., HENINGER, G. R., & CHARNEY, D. S. (1990). Specificity of serotonin reuptake inhibitors in the treatment of obsessive-compulsive disorder. *Archives of General Psychiatry, 47,* 577–585.

GOODWIN, D. *Is alcoholism inherited?* New York: Random House.

GOODWIN, F., & POTTER, W. (1979). Catecholamines. In E. Usdin, I. Kopen, & J. Barchas (Eds.), *Catecholamines: Basic and clinical frontiers.* Elmsford, NY: Pergamon.

GORDON, T. (1975). *Parent effectiveness training.* New York: Plume.

GORDON, W. C. (1989). *Learning and memory.* Pacific Grove, CA: Brooks/Cole.

GORMLEY, E. G., & AIELLO, J. R. (1982). Social density, interpersonal relationships, and residential crowding stress. *Journal of Applied Social Psychology, 12,* 22–36.

GOTTESMAN, I. I. (1991). *Schizophrenia genesis: The origins of madness.* New York: Freeman.

GOTTESMAN, I. I., & BERTELSEN, A. (1989). Confirming unexpressed genotypes for schizophrenia. *Archives of General Psychiatry, 46,* 867–872.

GOTTESMAN, I. I., McGUFFIN, P., FARMER, A., McGUE, M., VOGLER, G., BERTELSEN, A., & RAO, D. (1988). Genetics and schizophrenia: Current state of negotiations. In F. Vogler & K. Sperling (Eds.), *Human genetics* (pp. 50–58). New York: Springer-Verlag.

GOTTESMAN, I. I., & SHIELDS, J. (1982). *Schizophrenia: The epigenetic puzzle.* New York: Cambridge University Press.

GOTTLIEB, A. M., KILLEN, J. D., MARLATT, G. A., & TAYLOR, C. B. (1987). Psychological and pharmacological influences in cigarette smoking withdrawal: Effects of nicotine gum and expectancy on smoking withdrawal symptoms and relapse. *Journal of Consulting and Clinical Psychology, 55,* 606–608.

GOTTLIEB, J. (1981). Mainstreaming: Fulfilling the promise: *American Journal of Mental Deficiency, 56,* 115–126.

GOULD, R. L. (1975, August). Adult life stages: Growth toward self-tolerance. *Psychology Today,* pp. 74–78.

GOULD, R., MILLER, B. L., GOLDBERG, M. A., & BENSON, D. F. (1986). The validity of hysterical signs and symptoms. *The Journal of Nervous and Mental Disease, 174,* 593–597.

GOULD, S. J. (1977). *Ever since Darwin.* New York: Norton.

GOULD, S. J. (1983, June 30). Genes of the brain. *New York Review of Books,* pp. 5–10.

GRADY, D. (1988, March 7). Is losing weight a losing battle? *Time,* p. 59.

GRAHAM, J. R. (1990). *MMPI-2: Assessing personality and psychopathology.* New York: Oxford University Press.

GRAHAM, J. R. (1991). Comments on Duckworth's review of the Minnesota Multiphasic Personality Inventory-2. *Journal of Counseling and Development, 69,* 570–571.

GRAHAM, J. R., & LILLY, R. S. (1984). *Psychological testing.* Englewood Cliffs, NJ: Prentice-Hall.

GRAUERHOLZ, E., & KORALEWSKI, M. (Eds.) (1990). *Sexual coercion: A sourcebook on its nature, causes, and prevention.* Lexington, MASS: Lexington Books.

GRAY, C., KOOPMAN, E., & HUNT, J. (1991). The emotional phases of marital separation: An empirical investigation. *American Journal of Orthopsychiatry, 61,* 138–143.

GREEN, B. G. (1977). The effect of skin temperature on vibrotactile sensitivity. *Perception and Psychophysics, 21,* 243–248.

GREENBERG, M., & MORRIS, M. (1974). Engrossment: The newborn's impact upon the father. *American Journal of Orthopsychiatry, 44,* 520–531.

GREENBERGER, E., & STEINBERG, L. D. (1981). *Project for the study of adolescent work: Final report.* Report prepared for the National Institute of Education, U.S. Department of Education, Washington, DC.

GREENFIELD, P. (1992, June). *Making Basic Texts in Psychology more Culture-Inclusive and Culture-Sensitive.* Paper presented at the workshop on making basic texts in psychology more culture-inclusive and culture-sensitive, Bellingham, WA.

GREENFIELD, P. M. (1984). A theory of the teacher in the learning activities of everyday life. In B. Rogoff & J. Lave (Eds.), *Everyday Cognition* (pp. 117–138). Cambridge, MA: Harvard University Press.

GREENFIELD, P. M. (in press). International roots of minority child development: Introduction to the special issue. In P. M. Greenfield & R. R. Cocking (Eds.), *International roots of minority child development.* Special section of *International Journal of Behavioral Development.*

GREENWALD, A. G., SPANGENBERG, E. R., PRATKANIS, A. R., & ESKENAZI, J. (1991). Double-blind tests of subliminal self-help audiotapes. *Psychological Science, 2,* 119–122.

GREER, J., & WETHERED, C. (1984). Learned helplessness: A piece of the burnout puzzle. *Exceptional Children, 50*(6), 524–530.

GREENWALD, A. G. (1990). What cognitive representations underlie social attitudes? *Bulletin of the Psychonomic Society, 28,* 254–260.

GREGERSEN, E. (1983). *Sexual practices: The story of human sexuality.* New York: Franklin Watts.

GREGORY, R. L. (1966). *Eye and brain.* New York: McGraw-Hill.

GREGORY, R. L. (1969). Apparatus for investigating visual perception. *American Psychologist, 24*(3), 219–225.

GREGORY, R. L. (1977). *Eye and brain* (3rd Ed.). New York: McGraw-Hill.

GREGORY, R. L. (1988). *The Oxford companion to the mind.* New York: Oxford University Press.

GRIECO, A. (1987). Scope and nature of sexual harassment in nursing. *Journal of Sex Research, 23,* 261–266.

GRINKER, J. A. (1982). Physiological and behavioral basis of human obesity. In D. W. Pfaff (Ed.), *The physiological mechanisms of motivation.* New York: Springer-Verlag.

GROEBEL, J., & HINDE, R. A. (1989). *Aggression and war: Their biological and social bases.* Cambridge, England: Cambridge University Press.

GROEN, J. J., HANSEN, B., HERMANN, J. M., SCHAFER, N., SCHMIDT, T. H., SELBMANN, K. H., VEXKULL, T. V., & WECKMAN, P. (1977). Haemodynamic responses during experimental emotional stress and physical exercise in hypertensive and normotensive patients. *Progress in Brain Research, 47,* 301–308.

GROSS, E. (1970). Work; organization, and stress. In S. Levine & N. A. Scotch (Eds.), *Social stress.* Chicago: Aldine.

GROSSMAN, H. J. (Ed.). (1983). *Manual on terminology and classification in mental retardation* (3rd. rev.). Washington, DC: American Association on Mental Deficiency.

GROTH, A. N., & BURGESS, A. (1980). Male rape: Offenders and victims. *American Journal of Psychiatry, 137,* 806–810.

GROTH, N., & HOBSON, W. (1983.). The dynamics of sexual assult. In L. Schlesinger and E. Revitch (Eds.), *Sexual dynamics of antisocial behavior* (pp. 241–256). Springfield, IL: Thomas.

GROVES, P. M., & REBEC, G. V. (1988). *Introduction to biological psychology* (3rd ed.) Dubuque, IA: Wm. C. Brown.

GRUSH, J. E. (1980). Impact of candidate expenditure, regionality, and prior outcomes on the 1976 Democratic presidential primaries. *Journal of Personality and Social Psychology, 38,* 337–347.

GRYCH, J. H., & FINCHAM, F. D. (1992). Interventions for children of divorce: Toward greater integration of research and action. *Psychological Bulletin, 111,* 434–454.

GUARNACCIA, P., GOOD, B., & KLEINMAN, A. (1990). A critical review of epidemiological studies of Puerto Rican mental health. *American Journal of Psychiatry, 147,* 1449–1456.

GUERRERRO, A. G. (1992). *Human arrangements* (3rd ed). San Diego: Harcourt Brace Jovanovich.

GUILFORD, J. P. (1959). The three faces of intellect. *American Psychologist, 14,* 469–479.

GUILFORD, J. P. (1967). *The nature of human intelligence.* New York: McGraw-Hill.

GUILLEMINAULT, C. (1979, June). The sleep apnea syndrome. *Medical Times,* pp. 59–67.

GUNDERSON, J. G. (1988). Personality disorders. In A. A. Nicholi, Jr. (Ed.), *The Harvard guide to modern psychiatry.* Cambridge, MA: Harvard University Press.

GUSTAVSON, A. R., DAWSON, M. E., & BONETT, D. G. (1987). Androstenol, a putative human pheromone, affects human *(Homo sapiens)* male choice performance. *Journal of Comparative Psychology, 101,* 210–212.

GUSTAVSON, C. R., & GARCIA, J. (1974, August). Pulling a gag on the wily coyote. *Psychology Today,* pp. 68–72.

GUTKIN, J. (1989). *A study of "flashbulb" memories for the moment of the explosion of the space shuttle Challenger.* Unpublished manuscript, Emory University, Atlanta.

HALL, C. S. (1966). *The meaning of dreams.* New York: McGraw-Hill.

HALL, C. S., & NORDBY, V. J. (1972). *The individual and his dreams.* New York: Mentor.

HALL, C., & VAN DE CASTLE, R. I. (1966). *The content analysis of dreams.* New York: Appleton-Century-Crofts.

HALL. E. T. (1983, June). A conversation with Erik Erikson. *Psychology Today,* pp. 22–30.

HALL, E. T. (1966). *The hidden dimension.* New York: Doubleday.

HALL, G. S. (1904). *Adolescence.* New York: Appleton.

HALMI, K. A., FALK, J. R., & SCHWARTZ, E. (1981). Binge eating and vomiting: A survey of a college population. *Psychological Medicine, 11,* 697–706.

HALPERN, D. F. (1992). *Sex differences in cognitive abilities.* Hillsdale, NJ: Erlbaum.

HALPIN, G., HALPIN, G., & SCHAER, B. B. (1981). Relative effectiveness of the California Achievement Tests in comparison with the ACT Assessment, College Board Scholastic Aptitude Test, and high school grade point average in predicting college grade point average. *Educational and Psychological Measurement, 41,* 821–827.

HAMID, A. (1990). The political economy of crack-related violence. *Contemporary Drug Problems, 6,* 90–95.

HAMILTON, V. L. (1978). Obedience and responsibility: A jury simulation. *Journal of Personality and Social Psychology, 36,* 126–146.

HAMILTON, J., ALAGNA, S., KING, L., & LLOYD, C. (1987). The emotional consequences of gender-based abuse in the workplace: New counseling programs for sex discrimination. *Women and Therapy, 6,* 155–182.

HAMILTON, J. A., & GALLANT, S. J. (1990). Problematic aspects of diagnosing premenstrual phase dysphoria: Recommendations for psychological research and practice. *Professional Psychology Research and Practice, 2*(1), 60–68.

HAMMER, J. (1992, May 18). L.A. What's next: Back on the block. *Newsweek,* pp. 40–44.

HAMMOCK, T., & BREHM, J. W. (1966). The attractiveness of choice alternatives when freedom to choose is eliminated by a social agent. *Journal of Personality, 34,* 546–554.

HAMPSON, E. (1990). Estrogen-related variations in human spatial and articulatory-motor skills. *Psychoneuroendocrinology, 15*(2), 97–111.

HANEY, C., BANKS, C., & ZIMBARDO, P. (1978). Interpersonal dynamics in a stimulated prison. *International Journal of Criminology and Penology, 1,* 69–97.

HANSEL, C. E. M. (1980). *ESP and parapsychology: A critical reevaluation.* Buffalo, NY: Prometheus.

HARACKIEWICZ, J. M., & MANDERLINK, G. A. (1984). A process analysis of the effects of performance. Contingent rewards on intrinsic motivation. *Journal of Experimental Social Psychology, 20,* 531–551.

HARDIN, G. R. (1968). The tragedy of the commons. *Science, 162,* 1243–1248.

HARKNESS, S., & SUPER, C. M. (1983). The cultural construction of child development. *Ethos, 11,* 221–231.

HARLOW, H. F., & HARLOW, M. K. (1966). Learning to love. *American Scientist, 54,* 244–272.

HARLOW, H. F., HARLOW, M. K., & MEYER, D. R. (1950). Learning motivated by a manipulation drive. *Journal of Experimental Psychology, 40,* 228–234.

HARLOW, H. F., HARLOW, M. K., & MEYER, D. R. (1985). Learning motivated by a manipulation drive. *Journal of Experimental Psychology, 40,* 228–234.

HARLOW, H. F., & SUOMI, S. J. (1971). Social recovery by isolation-reared monkeys. *Proceedings of the National Academy of Science, 68,* 1534–1538.

HARLOW, H. F., & ZIMMERMAN, R. R. (1959). Affectional responses in the infant monkey. *Science, 130,* 421–432.

HARNETT, J. J., BAILEY, K. G., & GIBSON, F. W., JR. (1970). Personal space as influenced by sex and type of movement. *Journal of Psychology, 76,* 139–144.

HAROLD, R. D., & ECCLES, J. S. (1990). *Maternal expectations, advice, and provision of opportunities; Their relationships to boys' and girls' occupational aspirations.* Paper presented at the meeting of the Society for Research in Adolescence, Atlanta.

HARPER, R. M. (1983). Cardiorespiratory and state control in infants at risk for the sudden death syndrome. In M. H. Chase & E. D. Weitzman (Eds.), *Sleep disorders: Basic and clinical research.* (pp. 315–328). New York: Spectrum.

HARRISON, A. A. (1977). Mere exposure. In L. Berkowitz

(Ed.), *Advances in experimental social psychology* (Vol. 10, pp. 39–83). New York: Academic Press.

HART, D. (1988). A longitudinal study of adolescents' socialization and identification as predictors of adult moral judgment development. *Merrill-Palmer Quarterly, 34,* 245–260.

HART, S. N., & BRASSARD, M. R. (1987). A major threat to children's mental health: Psychological maltreatment. *American Psychologist, 42,* 160–165.

HARTE, D. B. (1975). Estimates of the length of highway guidelines and spaces. *Human Factors, 17,* 455–460.

HARTER, S., ALEXANDER, P., & NEIMEYER, R. (1988). Long-term effects of incestuous child abuse in college women: Social adjustment, social cognition, and family characteritics. *Journal of Consulting and Clinical Psychology, 56,* 5–8.

HARTMAN, W. E., & FITHIAN, M. A. (1984). *Any man can.* New York: St. Martin's Press.

HARTMANN, E. (1983). Two case reports: Night terrors with sleepwalking: A potentially lethal disorder. *Journal of Nervous and Mental Disease, 171*(8), 503–505.

HARTMANN, E. (1985). *The nightmare: The psychology and biology of terrifying dreams.* New York: Basic Books.

HARTSHORNE, H., & MAY, M. A. (1928). *Studies in the nature of character. Vol. I: Studies in deceit.* New York: Macmillan.

HARTUP, W. W. (1989). Social relationships and their developmental significance. *American Psychologist, 44,* 120–126.

HASSETT, J. (1978, March). Sex and smell. *Psychology Today,* pp. 40–45.

HATFIELD, E. (1988). Passionate and companionate love. In R. J. Sternberg & M. L. Barnes (Eds.), *The psychology of love* (pp. 311–324). New Haven, CT: Yale University Press.

HATFIELD, E., & RAPSON, R. L. (1993). *Love, sex, and intimacy.* New York: HarperCollins.

HATFIELD, M. O. (1990). Stress and the American worker. *American Psychologist, 45,* 1162–1164.

HAYES, C. (1951). *The ape in our house.* New York: Harper.

HAYFLICK, L. (1977). The cellular basis for biological aging. In C. E. Finch & L. Hayflick (Eds.), *Handbook of the biology of aging* (pp. 159–186). New York: Van Nostrand Reinhold.

HAYFLICK, L. (1980). The cell biology of human aging. *Scientific American, 242*(1), 58–65.

HAYGOOD, R. C., & BOURNE, L. E. (1965). Attribute and rule learning aspects of conceptual behavior. *Psychological Review, 72,* 175–195.

HAYNIE, N. A. (1984). Sigmund Freud. In R. J. Corsini (Ed.), *Encyclopedia of psychology* (Vol. 2, pp. 37–38). New York: Wiley.

HAYS, R. B. (1985). A longitudinal study of friendship development. *Journal of Personality and Social Psychology, 48*(4), 909–924.

HAZEN, C., & SHAVER, P. (1987). Romantic love conceptualized as an attachment process. *Journal of Personality and Social Psychology, 52,* 511–524.

Health care: Billion-dollar Rx for infant mortality. (1988, August 8). *U.S. News and World Report,* p. 10.

HEBB, D. O. (1949). *The organization of behavior.* New York: Wiley.

HEBB, D. O. (1955). Drive and the CNS (central nervous system). *Psychological Review, 62,* 243–254.

HEBB, D. O. (1966). *A textbook of psychology* (2nd ed.) Philadelphia: Saunders.

HECHINGER, N., & LEWIN, R. (1981). Seeing without eyes. *Science, 165,* 38–43.

HECHT, S., HAIG, C., & WALD, G. (1935). The dark adaptation of retinal fields of different size and loca-

tion. *Journal of General Physiology, 19,* 321–337.

HECKHAUSEN, H., SCHMALT, H. D., & SCHNEIDER, K. (1985). *Achievement motivation in perspective.* Orlando, FL: Academic Press.

HELD, R., & HEIN, A. (1963). Movement-produced stimulation in the development of visually-guided behavior. *Journal of Comparative and Physiological Psychology, 56,* 872–876.

HELLIGE, J. B. (1990). Hemispheric asymmetry. *Annual Review of Psychology, 41,* 55–80.

HENDERSON, B. E., ROSS, R. K., & PIKE, M. C. Toward the primary, prevention of cancer. *Science, 254,* 1131–1138.

HENDRICK, C. (1989). *Close relationships.* Newbury Park, CA: Sage.

HENDRICK, C., & HENDRICK, S. S. (1993). *Romantic love.* Newbury Park, CA: Sage.

HENDRICK, S. S., & HENDRICK, C. (1992). *Liking, loving, and relating.* Pacific Grove, CA: Brooks/Cole.

HENDRICK, S. S., HENDRICK, C., & ADLER, N. L. (1988). Romantic relationships: Love, satisfaction, and staying together. *Journal of Personality and Social Psychology, 54,* 980–988.

HENNINGAN, K. M., COOK, T. D., & GRUDER, C. L. (1982). Cognitive tuning set, source credibility, and the temporal persistence of attitude change. *Journal of Personality and Social Psychology, 42,* 412–425.

HERBERT, W. (1988, December). Getting people to give. *Psychology Today,* p. 66.

HERGENHAHN, B. R. (1990). *An introduction to theories of personality* (3rd ed.). Englewood Cliffs, NJ: Prentice Hall.

HERMAN, J. L., & HARVEY, M. R. (1993). The false memory debate: Social science or social backlash? *Harvard Mental Health Letter, 9*(10), 4–6.

HERMAN, L. M., MORREL, S. P., & PACK, A. A. (1990). Bottlenosed dolphin and human recognition of veridical and degraded video displays of an artificial gestural language. *Journal of Experimental Psychology: General, 199,* 215–230.

HERMAN, L. M., RICHARDS, D. G., & WOLTZ, J. P. (1984). Comprehension of sentences by bottlenosed dolphins. *Cognition, 16,* 129–139.

HERMANN, C. P., & POLIVY, J. (1984). A boundary model for the regulation of eating. In A. J. Stunkard & E. Stellar (Eds.), *Eating and its disorders* (pp. 141–156). New York: Raven Press.

HERON, R. M. (1991). The ergonomist. In R Gifford (Ed.), *Applied psychology: Variety and opportunity* (pp. 301–325). Boston: Allyn Bacon.

HERZOG, H. A., JR. (1988). The moral status of mice. *American Psychologist, 43,* 473–474.

HESTON, L. L., & WHITE, J. A. (1983). *Dementia.* New York: Freeman.

HETHERINGTON, A. W., & RANSON, S. W. (1942). The spontaneous activity and food intake of rats with hypothalamic lesion. *American Journal of Physiology, 136,* 609–617.

HETHERINGTON, E. M (1991). The role of individual differences and family relationships in coping with divorce and remarriage. In P. A. Cowan & E. M. Hetherington (Eds.), *Family transitions.* Hillsdale, NJ: Erlbaum.

HETHERINGTON, E. M., COX, M., & COX, R. (1985). Long term effects of divorce and remarriage on the adjustment of children. *Journal of American Academy of Pediatrics, 24,* 518–530.

HETHERINGTON, E. M., STANLEY-HAGAN, M., & ANDERSON, E. R. (1989). Martial transitions: A child's perspective. *American Psychologist, 44,* 303–312.

HIGGINS, A. T., & TURNURE, J. E. (1984). Distractibility and concentration of attention in children's development. *Child Development, 55,* 1799–1810.

HILGARD, E. R. (1978). Hypnosis and consciousness. *Human Nature, 1,* 42–51.

HILGARD, E. R. (1986). *Divided consciousness: Multiple controls in human thought and action* (expanded ed.). New York: Wiley-Interscience.

HILGARD, E. R. (1992). Divided consciousness and dissociation. *Consciousness and Cognition, 1,* 16–31.

HILGARD, J. R., & LEBARON, S. (1984). *Hypnotherapy of pain in children with cancer.* Los Altos, CA: Kaufmann.

HILTS, L. (1984, September). Clocks that make us run. *Omni,* pp. 49–55, 100.

HIMES, E. A., & BROWN, G. E. (1936). The cold pressor test for measuring the reactability of blood pressure: Data concerning 571 normal and hypertensive subjects. *American Heart Journal, 11,* 1–9.

HINTON, G. E. (1992). How neural networks learn from experience. *Scientific American, 267*(3), 144–152.

HINTZMAN, D. L. (1990). Human learning and memory: Connections and dissociations. *Annual Review of Psychology, 41,* 109–139.

HOBSON, J. A. (1989). *Sleep.* New York: Freeman.

HOBSON, J. A., & McCARLEY, R. W. (1977). the brain as a dream state generator: An activation-synthesis hypothesis of the dream process. *American Journal of Psychiatry, 134,* 1335–1348.

HOCK, R. R. (1992). *Forty studies that changed psychology.* Englewood Cliffs, NJ: Prentice-Hall.

HOEK, D., INGRAM, D., & GIBSON, D. (1986). Some possible causes of children's early word overextensions. *Journal of Child Language, 13,* 477–494.

HOFFMAN, L. W. (1991). The influence of the family environment on personality: Accounting for sibling differences. *Psychological Bulletin, 110,* 197–203.

HOFFMAN, M. L. (1981). Is altruism part of human nature? *Journal of Personality and Social Psychology, 40,* 121–137.

HOFFMAN, M. L. (1984). Empathy, its limitations, and its role in a comprehensive moral theory. In W. M. Kurtines & J. L. Gewirtz (Eds.), *Morality, moral behavior, and moral development* (pp. 341–357). New York: Wiley.

HOFMAN, A. (1968). Psychotomimetic agents. In A. Burger (Ed.), *Drugs affecting the central nervous system* (Vol. 2). New York: Dekker.

HOFSTEDE, G. (1980). *Culture's consequences: International differences in work-related values.* Beverly Hills, CA: Sage.

HOGAN, R., & SCHROEDER, D. (1981, August). Seven biases in psychology. *Psychology Today,* pp. 8–14.

HOLDEN, C. (1992, January). Twin study links genes to homosexuality. *Research News,* p. 33.

HOLLINGSHEAD, A. B., & REDLICH, F. C. (1958). *Social class and mental illness: A community study.* New York: Wiley.

HOLMES, D. S. (1984). Meditation and somatic arousal reduction: A review of the experimental evidence. *American Psychologist, 39,* 1–10.

HOLMES, T. H., & RAHE, R. H. (1967). The social readjustment rating scale. *Journal of Psychosomatic Research, 11,* 213–218.

HOOLEY, J. (1988). How do family attitudes affect relapse in schizophrenia? *Harvard Medical School Mental Health Letter, 5*(4), 8.

HOPSON, J. L. (1984, November). A love affair with the brain: A conversation with Marian Diamond. *Psychology Today,* pp. 62–73.

HORN, J. C., & MEER. J. (1987, May). The vintage years. *Psychology Today,* pp. 76–90.

HORN, J. L. (1978). Human ability systems. In P. B. Baltes (Ed.), *Life-span developmental psychology* (Vol. I). New York: Academic Press.

HORN, J. L., & DONALDSON, G. (1980). Cognitive development in adulthood. In O. G. Brimm, Jr. & J. Kagan (Eds.), *Constancy and change in human development.* Cambridge, MA: Harvard University Press.

HORNE, J. A. (1983). Mammalian sleep function with particular reference to man. In A. R. Mayers (Ed.), *Sleep mechanisms and functions in humans and animals* (pp. 262–312). Workingham, England: Van Nostrand Reinhold.

HORNE, J. A. (1989). Sleep loss and "divergent" thinking ability. *Sleep, 11,* 528–536.

HORNER, M. S. (1968). *Sex differences in achievement motivation and performance in competitive and non-competitive situations.* Unpublished doctoral dissertation, University of Michigan.

HORNER, M. S. (1972). Toward an understanding of achievement-related conflicts in women. *Journal of Social Issues, 28,* 157–175.

HORNEY, K. (1923/1967). *Feminine psychology.* New York: Norton.

HORNEY, K. (1939). *New ways in psychoanalysis.* New York: International Universities Press.

HORNEY, K. (1945). *Our inner conflicts: A constructive theory of neurosis.* New York: Norton.

HOROWITZ, F. D., & O'BRIEN, M. (1989). In the interest of the nation: A reflective essay on the state of knowledge and the challenges before us. *American Psychologist, 44,* 441–445.

HORTON, P. C., LOUY, J. W., & CAPPOLILLO, H. P. (1974). Personality disorder and transitional relatedness. *Archives of General Psychiatry, 30*(5), 618–622.

HOSTETLER, A. J. (1988, July). Why baby cries: Data may shush skeptics. *APA Monitor,* p. 14.

HOUSE, J. S., LANDIS, K. R. & UMBERSON, D. (1988). Social relationships and health. *Science, 241,* 540–545.

HOUSTON, J., BEE, H., & RIMM, D. (1983). *Essential of psychology.* Orlando, FL: Academic Press.

HOUTS, A. C., COOK, T. D., & SHADISH, W. R. (1986). The person-situation debate: a critical multiplist perspective. *Journal of Personality, 54,* 52–105.

HOVLAND, C. I. (1938). Experimental studies in rote-learning theory. 1. Reminiscence following learning by massed and by distributed practice. *Journal of Experimental Psychology, 22,* 201–244.

HOYENGA, K. G., & HOYENGA, K. T. (1993). *Gender-related differences: Origins and outcomes.* Boston, MA: Allyn & Bacon.

HSU, L. K. G. (1986). The treatment of anorexia nervosa. *American Journal of Psychiatry, 143,* 573–581.

HUBEL, D. H. (1963). The visual cortex of the brain. *Scientific American, 209,* 54–62.

HUBEL, D. H. (1984). The brain. In Editors of *Scientific American, The brain.* San Francisco: Freeman.

HUBEL, D. H., & WIESEL, T. N. (1962). Receptive fields, binocular interaction and functional architecture in the cat's visual cortex. *Journal of Physiology, 160,* 106–154.

HUBEL, D. H., & WIESEL, T. N. (1965). Receptive fields and the functional architecture in two nonstriate visual areas (18 and 19) of the cat. *Journal of Neurophysiology, 28,* 229–289.

HUBEL, D. H., & WIESEL, T. N. (1968). Receptive fields and the functional architecture of the monkey striate cortex. *Journal of Physiology, 195,* 215–243.

HUESMANN, L. R. (Ed.). (1978). Learned helplessness as a model of depression [Special issue]. *Journal of Abnormal Psychology, 87*(1).

HUESMANN, L. R., & ERON, L. D. (1986). Television and the aggressive child: A cross-national comparison. Hillsdale, NJ: Erlbaum.

HUGICK, L., & LEONARD, J. (1991a). Despite increasing hostility, one in four Americans still smokes. *Gallup Poll Monthly,* No. 315, 2–10.

HUGICK, L., & LEONARD, J. (1991b). Job dissatisfaction grows: "Moonlighting" on the rise. *Gallup Poll Monthly,* No. 312, 2–15.

HUGICK, L., & LEONARD, J. (1991c). Sex in America. *Gallup Poll Monthly,* No. 313, 60–73.

HUI, Y. H. (1985). *Principles and issues in nutrition.* Belmont, CA: Wadsworth.

HULL, C. (1952). *A behavior system.* New Haven, CT: Yale University Press.

HUNT, M. (1974). *Sexual behavior in the 1970's.* Chicago: Playboy Press.

HUNT, H. T. (1989). *The multiplicity of dreams.* New Haven, CT: Yale University Press.

HUSTON, A. C., WATKINS, B. A., & KUNKEL, D. (1989). Public policy and children's television. *American Psychologist, 44,* 424–433.

HUSTON, T. L., RUGGIERO, M., CONNER, R., & GEIS, G. (1981). Bystander intervention into crime: A Study based on naturally occurring episodes. *Social Psychology Quarterly, 44,* 14–23.

HUXLEY, A. (1954). *Doors of perception.* New York: Harper & Row.

HYDE, J. S. (1984). How large are gender differences in aggression? A developmental meta-analysis. *Developmental Psychology, 20,* 722–736.

HYDE, J. S. (1994). *Understanding human sexuality* (5th ed.). New York: McGraw-Hill.

HYDE, J. S. (1991). *Half the human experience* (4th. ed.). Lexington, MA: D. C. Health.

HYDE, J., FENNEMAN, E., & LAMON, S. (1990). Gender differences in mathematics performance: A meta-analysis. *Psychological Bulletin, 107,* 139–155.

HYDE, J. S., & LINN, M. C. (1988). *The psychology of gender: Advances through meta-analysis.* Baltimore: The Johns Hopkins University Press.

HYDE, T. S., & JENKINS, J. J. (1969). Differential effects of incidental tasks on the organization of recall of a list of highly associated words. *Journal of Experimental Psychology, 82,* 472–481.

HYMAN, R. (1981). Cold reading: How to convince strangers that you know all about them. In K. Fraizer (Ed.), *Paranormal borderlands of science* (pp. 232–244). Buffalo, NY: Prometheus.

HYMAN, R. (1989). The psychology of deception. In M. R. Rosenzweig & L. W. Porter (Eds.), *Annual review of psychology* (pp. 133–154). Palo Alto, CA: Annual Reviews Inc.

IMPERATO-MCGINLEY, J., PETERSON, R. E., GAUTIER, T., & STURLA, E. (1979). Androgens and the evolution of male-gender identity among male pseudohermaphrodites with 5-reductase deficiency. *New England Journal of Medicine, 300,* 1233–1237.

INDOW, T. (1991). Spherical model of colors and brightness discrimination by Izmailov and Sokolov. *Psychological Science, 2,* 260–262.

INTONS-PETERSON, M. J., & REDDEL, M. (1984). What do people ask about a neonate? *Developmental Psychology, 20,* 358–359.

INTRAUB, H. (1979). The role of implicit naming in pictorial encoding. *Journal of Experimental Psychology: Human Learning and Memory, 5*(2), 78–87.

IOLA, L. M. (1990). Culture and health In R. W. Brislin (Ed), *Applied Cross-Cultural Psychology,* (pp. 278–301). Newbury Park, CA: Sage.

ISAAC, R. J., & ARMAT, V. C. (1990). *Madness in the streets: How psychiatry and the law abandoned the mentally ill.* New York: Free Press.

ISAACS, W., THOMAS, J., & GOLDIAMOND, I. (1960). Application of operant conditioning to reinstate verbal behavior in psychotics. *Journal of Speech and Hearing Disorders, 25,* 8–12.

ISEN, A. M., & LEVINE, P. F. (1972). Effect of feeling good on helping: Cookies and kindness. *Journal of Personality and Social Psychology, 21,* 384–388.

ITAKURA, S. (1992). Symbolic association between individuals and objects by a chimpanzee as an initiation of ownership. *Psychological Reports, 70,* 539–544.

IYER, P. (1988, January 18). Of weirdos and eccentrics. *Time,* p. 76.

IZARD, C. E. (1984). Emotion-cognition relationships and human development. In C. E. Izard, J. Kagan, & R. B. Zajonc (Eds.), *Emotion, cognitions, and behavior.* New York: Cambridge University Press.

IZARD, C. E. (1990). Facial expressions and the regulation of emotions. *Journal of Personality and Social Psychology, 58,* 487–498.

IZARD, C. E., HUEBNER, R. R., RISSER, D., McGINNES, G. C., & DOUGHERTY, L. M. (1980). The young infant's ability to produce discrete emotion expressions. *Development Psychology, 16,* 132–141.

JACK, R. (1992). *Women and attempted suicide.* Hillsdale, NJ: Erlbaum.

JACKIN, C. N. (1989). Female and male: Issues of gender. *American Psychologist, 44,* 127–133.

JACKSON, J., CALHOUN, K., AMICK, A., MADDEVER, H., & HABIF, V. (1990). Young adult women who report childhood intrafamilial sexual abuse: Subsequent adjustment. *Archives of Sexual Behavior, 19,* 211–221.

JACOBSON, A., & MCKINNEY, W. T. (1982). Affective disorders. In J. H. Greist, J. W. Jefferson, & R. L. Spitzer (Eds.), *Treatment of mental disorders.* New York: Oxford University Press.

JACOBY, L. L. (1974). The role of mental contiguity in memory: Registration and retrieval effects. *Journal of Verbal Learning and Verbal Behavior, 13,* 483–496.

JAMES, W. (1890). *The principles of psycholog* (Vol. 2). New York: Holt.

JAMES, W. (1936). *The varieties of religious experience: A study in human nature.* New York: Longmans, Green. (Original work published 1902)

JAMISON, K. R. (1993). *Touched with fire: Manic-depressive illness and the artistic temperament.* New York: Free Press.

JANIS, I. L. (1972). *Victims of groupthink: A psychological study of foreign-policy decisions and fiascoes.* Boston: Houghton Mifflin.

JANIS, I. L. (1982). Counteracting the adverse effects of concurrence-seeking in policy-planning groups. In H. Brandstatter, J. H. Davis, & G. Stocker-Kreichgauer (Eds.), *Group decision making.* New York: Academic Press.

JANIS, I. L. (1989). *Crucial decisions: Leadership in policymaking and crisis management.* New York: Free Press.

JANIS, I. & MANN, L. (1977). *Decision making: A psychological analysis of conflict, choice, and commitment.* New York: Free Press.

JANOWITZ, J. F. (1967). There's no hiding place down there. *American Journal of Orthopsychiatry, 37*(2), 296.

JEMMOTT, J. B., & LOCKE, S. E. (1984). Psychosocial factors, immunologic mediation, and human susceptibility to infectious diseases: How much do we know? *Psychological Bulletin, 95,* 52–77.

JENSEN, A. R. (1969). How much can we boost IQ and scholastic achievement? *Harvard Educational Review, 39,* 1–23.

JENSEN, A. R. (1984). The black-white difference on the K-ABC: Implications for future tests. *Journal of Special Education, 18*(3), 377–408.

JEWELL, L. N. (1990). *Contemporary industrial/organizational psychology.* St. Paul, MN: West.

JOHNSON, A. G. (1992). *Human arrangements* (3rd ed.). San Diego: Harcourt Brace Jovanovich.

JOHNSON, D. (1991). Animal rights and human lives: Time for scientists to right the balance. *Psychological Science, 1,* 213–214.

JOHNSON, D. W., JOHNSON, R. T., & MARUYAMA, G.

(1984). Goal interdependence and interpersonal attraction in heterogeneous classrooms: A meta-analysis. In N. Miller & M. B. Brewer (Eds.), *Groups in contact: The psychology of desegregation*. San Diego: Academic Press.

JOHNSON, M. K., & HASHER, L. (1987). Human learning and memory. In M. R. Rosenzweig & L. W. Porter (Eds.), *Annual review of psychology* (pp. 631–688). Palo Alto, CA: Annual Reviews Inc.

JOHNSTON, L. D., BACHMAN, J. G., & O'MALLEY, P. M. (1986). *Monitoring the future: Questionnaire responses from the nation's high school seniors, 1985*. Ann Arbor: University of Michigan, Institute of Social Research.

JONES, E. R., FORREST, J. D., GOLDMAN, N., HENSHAW, S. K., LINCOLN, R., ROSOFF, J. I., WESTOFF, C. F., & WULF, D. (1985). Teenage pregnancy in developed countries: Determinants and policy implications. *Family Planning Perspectives, 17*, 53–63.

JONES, E. (1961). *The life and work of Sigmund Freud* (L. Trilling & S. Marcus, Eds.). Garden City, NY: Anchor.

JONES, J. C., & BARLOW, D. H. (1990). The etiology of posttraumatic stress disorder. *Clinical Psychology Review, 10*, 299–328.

JONES, W. R., & ELLIS, N. R. (1962). Inhibitory potential in rotary pursuit acquisition. *Journal of Experimental Psychology, 63*, 534–537.

JOSEPHSON, W. L. (1987). Television violence and children's aggression: Testing the priming, social script, and disinhibition predictions. *Journal of Personality and Social Psychology, 53*, 882–890.

JUDD, C. M., & PARK, B. (1988). Out-group homogeneity: Judgments of variability at the individual and group levels. *Journal of Personality and Social Psychology, 54*, 778–788.

Judge blames sex assult on 5-year-old victim. (1982, January/February). *National NOW Times*, p. 6.

JULIEN, R. M. (1992). *A primer of drug action* (6th ed.) New York: Freeman.

JUNG, C. (1969). The concept of the collective unconscious. In *Collected works* (Vol. 9, Part 1). Princeton, NJ: Princeton University Press. (Original work published 1936).

JUNG, C. G. (1933). *Modern man in search of a soul.* New York: Harcourt, Brace, World.

KAGEN, J. (1989). *Unstable ideas: Temperament, cognition, and self.* Cambridge, MA: Harvard University Press.

KAGEN, J., REZNICK, J. S., & SNIDMAN, N. (1988). Biological bases of childhood shyness. *Science, 240*, 167–171.

KAHN, E., FISHER, C., & EDWARDS, A. (1991). Night terrors and anxiety dreams. In S. A. Ellman & J. S. Antrobus (Eds.), *The mind in sleep: Psychology and psychophysiology* (2nd ed., pp. 437–448). New York: Wiley.

KAHN, S., ZIMMERMAN, G., CSIKSZENTMIHALYI, M., & GETZELS, J. W. (1985). Relations between identifying in young adulthood and intimacy at midlife. *Journal of Personality and Social Psychology, 49*, 1316–1322.

KALAT, J. W. (1992). *Biological psychology* (4th ed.). Belmont, CA: Wadsworth.

KALES, A., & KALES, J. (1973). Recent advances in the diagnosis and treatment of sleep disorders. In G. Usdin (Ed.), *Sleep research and clinical practice.* (pp. 72–85). New York: Brunner/Mazel.

KAPLAN, H. (1987). *The illustrated manual of sex therapy.* New York: Brunner/Mazel.

KAMIN, L. J. (1974). *The science and politics of I. Q.* Hillsdale, NJ: Erlbaum.

KANE, J., HONIGFELD, G., SINGER, J., MELTZER, H., & the Clozaril Collaborative Study Group. (1988). Clozapine for the treatment-resistant schizophrenic. *Archives of General Psychiatry, 45*, 789–796.

KAPITZA, S. (1991). Antiscience trends in the U.S.S.R. *Scientific American, 134*, 32–38.

KAPLAN, H. S. (1974). *The new sex therapy.* New York: Brunner/Mazel.

KAPLAN, H. (1987). *The illustrated manual of sex therapy.* New York: Brunner/Mazel.

KAPLAN, P. S. (1986). *A child's odyssey: Child and adolescent development.* St. Paul, MN: West.

KASAMATSU, T. (1976). Visual cortical neurons influenced by the oculomotor input: Characterization of their receptive field properties. *Brain Research, 113*, 271–292.

KASSIN, S. M., RIGBY, S., & CASTILLO, S. R. (1991). *Journal of Personality and Social Psychology, 61*, 698–707.

KASTENBAUM, R. (1982). New fantasies in the American death system. *Death Education, 6*(2), 155–166.

KATCHADOURIAN, H. A. (1989). *Fundamentals of human sexuality* (5th ed.). Fort Worth, TX: Holt, Rinehart and Winston.

KATZ, H. N., & PAIVIO, A. (1975). Imagery variables in concept identification. *Journal of Verbal Learning and Verbal Behavior, 14*, 284–293.

KATZ, M., MARSELLA, A., DUBE, K., OLATAWURA, M. ET AL. (1988). On the expression of psychosis in different cultures: Schizophrenia in an Indian and in a Nigerian community. *Culture, Medicine, and Psychiatry, 12*, 331–355.

KAUFMAN, A. S., & KAUFMAN, N. L. (1983). *Kaufman Assessment Battery for Children Administration and Scoring Manual.* Circle Pines, MN: American Guidance Service.

KAUFMAN, A. S., REYNOLDS, C. R., & McLEAN, J. E. (1989). Age and WAIS-R intelligence in a national sample of adults in the 20- to 74-year age range: A cross-sectional analysis with educational level controlled. *Intelligence, 13*, 235–253.

KAUFMAN, L. (1974). *Sight and mind.* New York: Oxford University Press.

KAUSLER, D. H. (1992). *Experimental psychology and human aging.* New York: Wiley.

KEATING, C. F. (1985). Gender and the physiognomy of dominance and attractiveness. *Social Psychology Quarterly, 48*, 61–70.

KEENEY, T. J., CANNIZZO, S. R., & FLAVELL, J. H. (1967). Spontaneous and induced verbal rehearsal in a recall task. *Child Development, 38*, 953–966.

KEESEY, R. E., & POWLEY, T. L. (1975). Hypothalamic regulation of body weight. *American Scientist, 63*, 558–565.

KEESEY, R. E., & POWLEY, T. L. (1986). The regulation of body weight. *Annual Review of Psychology, 37*, 109–134.

KEGELES, S. M., ADLER, N. E., & IRWIN, C. E. (1988). Sexually active adolescents and condoms: Changes over one year in knowledge, attitudes, and use. *American Journal of Public Health, 78*, 460–461.

KELLER, H. (1902). *The story of my life.* New York: Doubleday.

KELLER, H. (1910). *The world I lived in.* New York: Century.

KELLER, H. (1962). Quoted in R. Harrity & R. G. Martin, *The three lives of Helen Keller* (p. 23). Garden City, NY: Doubleday.

KELLEY, H. H. (1967). Attribution theory in social psychology. In D. Levine (Ed.), *Nebraska Symposium on Motivation* (Vol. 15, pp. 192–241). Lincoln: University of Nebraska Press.

KELLEY, H. H. (1973). The process of causal attribution. *American Psychologist, 28*, 107–128.

KELLEY, K., & BYRNE, D. (1992). *Exploring human sexuality.* Englewood Cliffs, NJ: Prentice Hall.

KELLOGG, W. N., & KELLOGG, L. A. (1933). *The ape and the child.* New York: McGraw-Hill.

KEMPER, T. D. (1987). How many emotions are there? Wedding the social and the automatic compo-

nents. *American Journal of Sociology, 93*, 263–289.

KENNELL, J. H., & KLAUS, M. H. (1984). Mother-infant bonding: Weighing the evidence. *Developmental Review, 4*, 275–282.

KENRICK, D. T., & FUNDER, D. C. (1988). Profiting from controversy: Lessons from the person situation debate. *American Psychologist, 43*, 23–34.

KENRICK, D. T., KEEFE, R. C. (1992). Age preference in mates reflect sex differences in reproductive strategies. *Behavioral and Brain Sciences, 15*, 75–133.

KENT, C. (1992, January). Health care goes to school. *Medicine and Health Perspectives*, pp. 3–6.

KENT, D. (1991). Subliminal advertising, messages, and conspiracy. *APS Observer, 4*(5), 18–20.

KICHER, P. (1985). *Vaulting ambition: Sociobiology and the quest for human nature.* Cambridge, MA: MIT Press.

KIESTER, E., JR. (1984, July). The playing fields of the mind. *Psychology Today*, pp. 18–24.

KILHAM, W., & MANN, L. (1974). Level of destructive obedience as a function of transmitter and executant roles in the Milgram obedience paradigm. *Journal of Personality and Social Psychology, 29*(5), 696–702.

KILPATRICK, D. G., EDMUNDS, C. N., & SEYMOUR, A. (1992). *Rape in America.* Arlington, VA: National Victim Center.

KIM, U., & CHOI, S. (in press). Individualism, collectivism, and child development: A Korean perspective. In P. M. Greenfield & R. R. Cocking (Eds.), *The development of minority children: Culture in and out of context.* Hillsdale, NJ: Erlbaum.

KIMBALL, M. M. (1989). A new perspective on women's math achievement. *Psychological Bulletin, 105*, 198–214.

KIMURA, D. (1992). Sex differences in the brain. *Scientific American, 267*(3), 118–125.

KINSEY, A. C., POMEROY, W. B., & MARTIN, C. E. (1948). *Sexual behavior in the human male.* Philadelphia: Saunders.

KINSEY, A. C., POMEROY, W. B., MARTIN, C. E., & GEBHARD, P. H. (1953).*Sexual behavior in the human female.* Philadelphia: Saunders.

KLATZKY, R. L. (1984). *Memory and awareness.* New York: Freeman.

KLAUS, M. H., & KENNELL, J. H. (1976).*Maternal-infant bonding: The impact of early separation or loss on family development.* St. Louis: Mosby.

KLEINMAN, A. (1982). Neurasthenia and depression: A study of somatization and culture in China. *Culture, Medicine, and Psychiatry, 6*, 117–190.

KLEINMUNTZ, B., & SZUCKO, J. J. (1984). A field study of the fallibility of polygraph lie detection. *Nature, 308*, 449–450.

KLEITMAN, N. (1963). *Sleep and wakefullness* (2nd ed.). Chicago: University of Chicago Press.

KLEMCHUK, H. P., BOND, L. A., & HOWELL, D. C. (1990). Coherence and correlates of level 1 perspective taking in young children. *Merrill-Palmer Quarterly, 36*, 369–387.

KLERMAN, G. L. (1988). Depression and related disorders of mood (affective disorders). In A. M. Nicholi, Jr. (Ed.), *The Harvard guide to psychiatry.* Cambridge, MA: Harvard University Press.

KLINGER, E. (1987, October). The power of daydreams. *Psychology Today*, pp. 37–44.

KLINGER, E. (1990). *Daydreaming: Using waking fantasies and imagery for self-knowledge and creativity.* New York: Jeremy Tarcher, Inc.

KLUFT, R. P. (1991). Multiple personality disorder. In A. Tasman & S. M. Goldfinger (Eds.), *Review of psychiatry* (Vol. 10). Washington, DC: American Psychiatric Press.

KLUVER, H., & BUCY, P. C. (1939). Preliminary analysis

of the functions of the temporal lobes in monkeys. *Archives of Neurology and Psychiatry, 42,* 979–1000.

KOBAK, R. R., & HAZAN, C. (1991). Attachment in marriage: Effects of security and accuracy of working models. *Journal of Personality and Social Psychology, 60,* 861–869.

KOELLA, W. P. (1985). Serotonin and sleep. In W. P. Koella, E. Ruther, & H. Schulz (Eds.), *Sleep '84* (pp. 6–10). Stuttgart: Gustav Fischer Verlag.

KOHL, R. L. (1987). Mechanisms of selective attention and space motion sickness. *Aviation, Space, & Environmental Medicine, 58,* 1130–1132.

KOHLBERG, L. (1964). Development of moral character and moral behavior. In L. W. Hoffman & M. L. Hoffman (Eds.), *Review of child development research* (Vol. 1). New York: Sage.

KOHLBERG, L. (1966). A cognitive-developmental analysis of children's sex-role concepts and attitudes. In E. E. Maccoby (Ed.), *The development of sex differences.* Stanford, CA: Stanford University Press.

KOHLBERG, L. (1969). Stage and sequence: The cognitive-developmental approach to socialization. In D. A. Goslin (Ed.), *Handbook of socialization theory and research.* Chicago: Rand McNally.

KOHLBERG, L. (1981). *The philosophy of moral development: Essays on moral development* (Vol. I). San Francisco: Harper & Row.

KOHLBERG, L. (1984). *The psychology of moral development: Essays on moral development* (Vol. II). San Francisco: Harper & Row.

KOHLBERG, L. (1987). The development of moral judgment and moral action. In L. Kohlberg (Ed.), *Child psychology and childhood education: A cognitive-developmental view.* New York: Longman.

KOHLBERG, L. (1988). Moral growth stages. In J. Rubinstein & B. Slife (Eds.), *Taking sides: Clashing views on controversial psychological issues* (pp. 136–144). Guilford, CT: Dushkin.

KOHLBERG, K., & GILLIGAN, C. (1971). The adolescent as a philosopher: The discovery of the self in a postconventional world. *Daedalus, 100,* 1051–1086.

KÖHLER, W. (1925). *The mentality of apes.* New York: Harcourt, Brace.

KOHN, A. (1986). *No contest: The case against competition.* Boston: Houghton Mifflin.

KOHN, A. (1989), February). Evidence for a moral tradition. *Psychology Today,* pp. 72–73.

KOLATA, G. (1988, October 13). New Down's syndrome blood test could ease risk of miscarriage. *San Diego Union,* p. C-40.

KOLODNY, R. C. (1981). Evaluating sex therapy: Process and outcome at the Masters and Johnson Institute. *Journal of Sex Research, 17,* 301–318.

KOOB, G. F., & BLOOM, F. E. (1988). Cellular and molecular mechanisms of drug dependence. *Science, 242,* 715–723.

KOPP, C. B., & KALER, S. R. (1989). Risk in infancy: Origins and implications. *American Psychologist, 44,* 224–230.

KORTE, C. (1980). Urban-nonurban differences in social behavior and social psychological models of urban inpact. *Journal of Social Issues, 36,* 29–51.

KOSS, M. (1992). The underdetection of rape: Methodological choices influence incidence estimates. *Journal of Social Issues, 48,* 61–75.

KOSSLYN, S. M. (1975). Information representation in visual images. *Cognitive Psychology, 7,* 341–370.

KOSSLYN, S. M. (1987). Seeing and imagining in the cerebral hemispheres: A computational approach. *Psychological Review, 94,* 148–175.

KRANTZ, D. S., GRUNBERG, N. E., & BAUM, A. (1985). Health psychology. *Annual Review of Psychology, 36,* 349–383.

KRISHNA, G. (1971). *Kundalini: The evolutionary energy in man.* Berkeley, CA: Shambala.

KROSNIC, J. A., LI, F., & LEHMAN, D. R. (1990). Conversational conventions, order of information acquisition, and the effect of base rates and individuating information on social judgments. *Journal of Personality and Social Psychology, 59,* 1140–1152.

KRUGLANSKI, A. W., & WEBSTER, D. M. (1991). Group members' reactions to opinion deviates and conformists at varying degrees of proximity to decision deadline and of environmental noise. *Journal of Personality and Social Psychology, 61,* 212–225.

KÜBLER-ROSS, E. (1983). *On children and death.* New York: Macmillan.

KÜBLER-ROSS, E. (1989). *Death: The final stage of growth.* Englewood Cliffs, NJ: Prentice Hall.

KUHN, M. E. (1990). The Gray Panthers. In J. M. Henslin (Ed.), *Social problems* (pp. 56–57). Englewood Cliffs, NJ: Prentice Hall.

LABBE, E., & WILLIAMSON, D. (1983). Temperature biofeedback in the treatment of children with migraine headaches. *Journal of Pediatric Psychology, 8*(4), 317–326.

LABERGE, D. (1990). Attention. *Psychological Science, 1,* 156–162.

LABERGE, S. P. (1992). *Physiological studies of lucid dreaming.* Hillsdale, NJ: Erlbaum.

LACAYO, R. (1993, May 3). In the grip of a psychopath. *Time,* pp. 34–35.

LADJALI, M., & TOUBIA, N. (1990). Female circumcision: Desperately seeking a space for women. *International Planned Parenthood Federation Medical Bulletin, 24,* 1–2.

LAMB, M. E. (1977). Father-infant and mother-infant interaction in the first year of life. *Child Development, 48,* 167–181.

LAMB, M. E. (1982). Second thoughts on first touch. *Psychology Today, 16*(4), 9–11.

LANDAU, S. F. (1984). Trends in violence and aggression: A cross-cultural analysis. *International Journal of Comparative Sociology, 24,* 133–158.

LANDRINE, H. (1988). Revising the framework of abnormal psychology. In P. Bronstein & K. Quina (Eds.), *Teaching a psychology of people: Resources for gender and sociocultural awareness.* Washington, DC: American Psychological Association.

LANGDALE, C. J. (1986). a revision of structural-developmental theory. In G. L. Sapp (Ed.), *Handbook of moral development: Models, processes, techniques, and research* (pp. 15–54). Birmingham, AL: Religious Education Press.

LANGER, T. (1962). A twenty-two item screening score of psychiatric symptoms indicating impairment. *Journal of Health and Human Behavior, 3,* 269–276.

LANGWAY, L., JACKSON, T. A., ZABARSKY, M., SHIRLEY, D., & WHITMORE, J. (1983, March 28). Bringing up superbaby. *Newsweek,* pp. 62–68.

LANKENAU, H., SWIGAR, M. E., BHIMANI, S. LUCHINS, S., & QUINLON, D. M. (1985). Cranial CT scans in eating disorder patients and controls. *Comprehensive Psychiatry, 26,* 136–147.

LAPIERE, R. T. (1934). Attitudes and actions. *Social Forces, 13,* 230–237.

LARGENT, D. R. (1989, September). *"Ice": Crystal methamphetamine.* Oceanside, CA: McAlister Institute.

LARSEN, K. (1974). Conformity in the Asch experiment. *Journal of Social Psychology, 94,* 303–304.

LARSEN, K. (1990). The Asch conformity experiment: Replication and transhistorical comparisons. *Journal of Social Behavior and Personality, 5,* 163–168.

LATANÉ, B., & DARLEY, J. M. (1968). Group inhibition of bystander intervention in emergencies. *Journal of Personality and Social Psychology, 10,* 215–221.

LATANÉ, B., & DARLEY, J. M. (1970). *The unresponsive bystander: Why doesn't he help?* New York: Appleton-Century-Crofts.

LATANÉ, B., & NIDA, S. (1981). Ten years of research on group size and helping. *Psychological Bulletin, 89,* 308–324.

LAUER, J., & LAUER, R. (1992). Marriages made to last. In J. M. Henslin (Ed.), *Marriage and family in a changing society* (4th ed., pp. 481–486). New York: Free Press.

LAVOIE, J. (1976). Ego identity formation in middle adolescence. *Journal of Youth and Adolescence, 5,* 371–385.

LAZARUS, A. A. (1971). *Behavior therapy and beyond.* New York: McGraw-Hill.

LAZARUS, R. S. (1990). Theory-based stress measurement. *Psychological Inquiry, 1,* 3–13.

LAZARUS, R. S. (1991). Progress on a cognitive-motivational-relational theory of emotion. *American Psychologist, 46,* 819–834.

LAZARUS, R. S., & FOLKMAN, S. (1984). *Stress appraisal and coping.* New York: Springer.

LEARY, W. E. (1988, January 14). Young adults show drop in cocaine use. *New York Times,* p. C1.

LEAVITT, F. (1982). *Drugs and behavior* (2nd ed.). New York: Wiley.

LEDERMAN, S. (1992). Estimating infant mortality from human immunodeficiency virus and other causes in breast-feeding and bottle-feeding populations. *Pediatrics, 89,* 290–296.

LEE, J. A. (1983). The role of the sympathetic nervous system in ischaemic heart disease: A review of epidemiological features and risk factors, integration with clinical and experimental evidence and hypothesis. *Activitas Nervosa Superior, 25*(2), 110–121.

LEFF, H. S., & BRADLEY, V. J. (1986). DRGs are not enough. *American Psychologist, 41*(1), 73–78.

LEI, T., & CHENG, S. (1989). A little but special light on the universality of moral judgment development. In L. Kohlberg, D. Candee, & A. Colby (Eds.), *Rethinking moral development.* Cambridge, MA: Harvard University Press.

LEIBOWITZ, H. W. (1985). Grade crossing accidents and human factors engineering. *American Scientist, 73,* 558–562.

LEIBOWITZ, S. F., WEISS, G. F., WALSH, U. A., & VISWANATH, D. (1989). Medial hypothalamic serotonin: Role in circadian patterns of feeding and macronutrient selection. *Brain Research, 503,* 132–140.

LEIDIG, M. L. (1992). The continuum of violence against women: Psychological and physical implications. *American Journal of College Health, 40,* 149–155.

LEMPERS, J. D., FLAVELL, E. R., & FLAVELL, J. H. (1977). The development in very young children of tacit knowledge concerning visual perception. *Genetic Psychology Monographs, 95,* 3–53.

LEO, J. (1986, July 7). How cocaine killed Leonard Bias. *Time,* p. 52.

LEON, G. R. (1977). *Anxiety neurosis: The case of Richard Benson: Case histories in deviant behavior* (2nd ed.). Boston: Holbrook Press.

LEPPER, M. R., GREENE, D., & NISBETT, R. E. (1973). Undermining children's intrinsic interest with extrinsic rewards: A test of the overjustification hypothesis. *Journal of Personality and Social Psychology, 28,* 129–137.

LERNER, R. M. (1978). Nature, nurture, and dynamic interactionism. *Human Development, 21,* 1–20.

LERNER, M. J. (1980). *The belief in a just world: A fundamental delusion.* New York: Plenum.

LETTVIN, J. Y., MATURANA, H. R., McCULLOCH, W. S., & PITTS, W. H. (1959). What the frog's eye tells the frog's brain. *Proceedings of the Institute of Radio Engineers, 47,* 1940–1951.

LEVAY, S. (1991). A difference in hypothalimic structure between heterosexual and homosexual men. *Science, 253,* 1034–1038.

LEVENKRON, S. (1982). *Treating and overcoming anorexia nervosa.* New York: Scribner's.

LEVENTHAL, H., BAKER, T., BRANDON, T., & FLEMING, R. (1989). Intervening and preventing cigarette smoking. In T. Ney & A. Gale (Eds.), *Smoking and human behavior.* New York: Wiley.

LEVI, L. (1990). Occupational stress: Spice of life or kiss of death? *American Psychologist, 45,* 1142–1145.

LEVI-STRAUSS, C. (1969). *The elementary structures of kinship.* Boston: Beacon Press.

LEVIN, S., & STRAVA, L. (1987). Personality characteristics of sex offenders. *Archives of Sexual Behavior, 16,* 57–79.

LEVINE, I. S., & ROG, D. J. (1990). Mental health services for homeless mentally ill: Federal initiatives and current service trends. *American Psychologist, 45,* 963–968.

LEVINE, M. A. (1975). *A cognitive theory of learning.* Hillsdale, NJ: Erlbaum.

LEVINSON, D. J. (1977). The mid-life transition, *Psychiatry, 40,* 99–112.

LEWINE, R. J., FOGG, L., & MELTZER, H. Y. (1983). Assessment of negative and positive symptoms in schizophrenia. *Schizophrenia Bulletin, 9,* 968–976.

LEWIS, C. C. (1981). The effects of parental firm control: A reinterpretation of findings. *Psychological Bulletin, 90,* 547–563.

LEWIS, D. (1980). *The secret language of your child.* New York: St. Martin's Press.

LEWIS, M. (1982). State as an infant–environment interaction: An analysis of mother-infant behavior as a function of sex. *Merrill-Palmer Quarterly, 18,* 95–211.

LEWIS, M., THOMAS, D. A., & WOROBEY, J. (1990). Developmental organization, stress and illness. *Psychological Science, 1,* 316–318.

LEWIS, S. (1963). *Dear Shari.* New York: Stein & Day.

LI, C. (1975). *Path analysis: A primer.* Pacific Grove, CA: Boxwood Press.

LI, X., & SHEN, Z. (1985). Positive electron emission layer scanning technique and its application in psychological research. *Information on Psychological Sciences, 3,* 54–58.

LIBERMAN, A. M. (1970). The grammars of language and speech. *Cognitive Psychology, 1,* 301–323.

LIBERMAN, R. P., CARDIN, V., McGILL, C. W., FALLOON, I. R. H., & EVANS, C. (1987). Behavioral family management of schizophrenia: Clinical outcome and costs. *Psychiatric Annals, 17,* 610–619.

LICHTON, I. J., BULLARD, L. R., & SHERRELL, B. U. (1983). A conspectus of research on nutritional status in Hawaii and western Samoa—1960–1980 with references to diseases in which diet has been implicated. *World Review of Nutrition and Dietetics, 41,* 40–75.

LICKONA, T. (1985). *Raising good children.* New York: Bantam.

LIFTON, R. J. (1979, January 7). Appeal of the deth trip. *New York Times Magazine,* pp. 26–27.

LIGHTFOOT-KLEIN, H. (1989b). The sexual experience and marital adjustment of genitally circumcised and infibulated females in the Sudan. *The Journal of Sex Research, 26,* 375–392.

LIGHTFOOT-KLEIN, H., & SHAW, E. (1991). Special needs of ritually circumcised women patients. *Journal of*

Obstetrics, Gynecology, and Neonatal Nursing, 20, 102–107.

LIN, E., & KLEINMAN, A. (1988). Psychopathology and clinical course of schizophrenia: A cross-cultural perspective. *Schizophrenia Bulletin, 14,* 555–567.

LINDEN, E. (1991, September 23). Lost tribes, lost knowledge. *Time Magazine,* pp. 46–56.

LINDEN, E. (1993, March 22). Can animals think? *Time,* pp. 54–61.

LINDSEY, P. H., & NORMAN, D. A. (1977). *Human information processing.* New York: Academic Press.

LINTON, M. (1979, July). I remember it well. *Psychology Today,* pp. 81–86.

LINZ, D. (1989). Exposure to sexually explicit materials and attitudes toward rape: A comparison of study results. *Journal of Sex Research, 26,* 50–84.

LIPSITT, L. P. (1990). Learning processes in the human newborn: Sensitization, habituation, and classical conditioning. *Annals of the New York Academy of Sciences, 608,* 113–123.

LOCKE, E. A., & LATHAM, G. P. (1990). Work motivation and satisfaction: Light at the end of the tunnel. *American Psychological Society, 1,* 240–246.

LOFTUS, E. F. (1980). *Memory.* Reading, MA: Addison-Wesley.

Loftus, E. F. (1982). Memory and its distortions. In A. G. Kraut (Ed.), *The G. Stanley Hall Lecture Series* (Vol. 2, pp. 123–154). Washington, DC: American Psychological Association.

LOFTUS, E. F. (1992). When a lie becomes memory's truth: Memory distortion after exposure to misinformation. *Current directions in Psychological Science, 1*(4), 121–123.

LOFTUS, E. F. (1993). Repressed memories of childhood trauma: Are they genuine? *Harvard Mental Health Letter, 9*(9), 4–6.

LOFTUS, E. F., & HOFFMAN, H. G. (1989). Misinformation and memory: Creation of new memories. *Journal of Experimental Psychology: General, 118,* 100–104.

LOFTUS, E. F., & LOFTUS, G. R. (1980). On the permanence of stored information in the human brain. *American Psychologist, 35*(5), 409–420.

LOGAN, G. D. (1988). Toward an instance theory of automaticity. *Psychological Review, 95,* 492–527.

LONG, J. W. (1989). *The essential guide to prescription drugs.* New York: Harper & Row.

LONG, P. (1986, January). Medical mesmerism. *Psychology Today,* pp. 28–29.

LoPICCOLO, J. (1992). Postmodern sex therapy for erectile failure. In R. C. Rosen & S. R. Leiblum (Eds.), *Erectile disorders: Assessment and treatment* (pp. 107–144). New York: Guilford Press.

LORAYNE, H. (1985). *Harry Lorayne's page-a-minute memory book.* New York: Holt, Rinehart and Winston.

LORAYNE, H., & LUCAS, J. (1974). *The memory book.* New York: Ballantine.

LORD, L. J., GOODE, E. E., GEST, T., McAULIFFE, K., MOORE, L. J., BLACK, R. F., & LINNON, N. (1987, November 30). Coming to grips with alcoholism. *U.S. News and World Report,* pp. 56–62.

LORENZ, K. (1937). The companion in the bird's world. *Auk, 54,* 245–273.

LORENZ, K. (1966). *On aggression.* London: Methuen.

LORENZ, K. (1974). *The eight deadly sins of civilized man* (M. Kerr-Wilson, Trans.). New York: Harcourt Brace Jovanovich.

LORENZ, K. Z. (1981). *The foundations of ethology.* New York: Springer-Verlag.

LORENZ, K. (1981). *Foundations of ethology.* New York: Springer-Verlag.

LOVAAS, O. I. (1987). Behavioral treatment and normal educational and intellectual functioning in young

autistic children. *Journal of Consulting and Clinical Psychology, 55,* 3–9.

LOWRY, K. (1987, November 1). The designer babies are growing up. *Los Angles Times Magazine,* pp. 12–32.

LOZOFF, B. (1989). Nutrition and behavior. *American Psychologist, 44,* 231–236.

LUBART, T. I. (1990). Creativity and cross-cultural variation. *International Journal of Psychology, 25,* 39–59.

LUCE, G. (1971). *Body time.* New York: Pantheon.

LUCE, G., & SEGAL, J. (1966). *Sleep.* New York: Lancet.

LUCHINS, A. S. (1942). Mechanization in problem solving. *Psychological Monographs, 54*(6, Whole No. 248).

LUCHINS, A. S., & LUCHINS, E. H. (1950). New experimental attempts at preventing mechanization in problem solving. *Journal of General Psychology, 42,* 279–297.

LUCINS, D. (1975). The dopamine hypothesis of schizophrenia: A critical analysis. *Neuropsychobiology, 1,* 365–378.

LUDWIG, A. M. (1966). Altered states of consciousness. *Archives of General Psychiatry, 15,* 255–233.

LUMMIS, M., & STEVENSON, H. W. (1990). Gender differences in beliefs and achievement: A cross-cultural study. *Developmental Psychology, 26,* 254–263.

LURIA, A. R. (1968). *The mind of a mnemonist.* New York: Basic Books.

LURIA, A. R. (1973). *The working brain.* New York: Basic Books.

LURIA, A. R. (1976). *Cognitive development: Its cultural and social foundations.* Cambridge, MA: Harvard University Press.

LURIA, A. R. (1980). *Higher cortical functions in man.* New York: Basic Books.

LYKKEN, D. T. (1984). Polygraphic interrogation. *Nature, 307,* 681–684.

LYKKEN, D. T. (1988). The case against polygraph testing. In A. Gale (Ed.), *The polygraph test: Lies, truth, and science.* London: Sage.

LYNCH, G. (1984, April). A magical memory tour. *Psychology Today,* pp. 29–39.

LYNCH, G. (1988). *Identification of a memory mechanism.* Paper presented at the Cognitive Sciences Colloquium, University of California, Irvine, CA.

LYNCH, G., HALPIN, S., & BAUDRY, M. (1983). Structural and biochemical effects of high frequency stimulation in the hippocampus. In W. Seifert (Ed.), *Neurobiology of the hippocampus* (pp. 253–264). London: Academic Press.

LYNN, S. J., & RHUE, J. W. (1988). Fantasy proneness: Hypnosis, developmental antecedents, and psychopathology. *American Psychologist, 43,* 35–44.

LYONS, N. P. (1990). Listening to voices we have not heard. In C. Gilligan, N. P. Lyons, & T. J. Hammer (Eds.), *Making connections.* Cambridge, MA: Harvard University Press.

MACCOBY, E. E., & JACKLIN, C. N. (1974). *The psychology of sex differences.* Stanford, CA: Stanford University Press.

MACCOBY, E. E., & MARTIN, J. A. (1983). Socialization in the context of the family: Parent-child interaction. In E. M. Hetherington (Ed.), *Handbook of child psychology: Vol. 4. Socialization, personality, and social development.* New York: Wiley.

MacCOUN, R. J., & KERR, N. L. (1988). Asymmetric influence in mock jury deliberation: Jurors' bias for leniency. *Journal of Personality and Social Psychology, 54,* 21–33.

MacLUSKY, N., & NAFTOLIN, F. (1981). Sexual differentiation of the central nervous system. *Science, 211,* 1294–1303.

MADDUX, J. E., ROBERTS, M. C., SLEDDEN, E. A., & WRIGHT, L. (1986). Developmental issues in child health psychology. *American Psychologist, 1,* 25–34.

MAGID, K., & MCKELVEY, C. A. (1987). *High risk: Children without a conscience.* New York: Bantam.

MALAMUTH, N. M. (1989). The attraction to sexual aggression scale: Part one. *Journal of Sex Research, 26,* 26–49.

MALAMUTH, N. M., & CHECK, J. V. P. (1985). Debriefing effectiveness following exposure to pornographic rape depictions. *The Journal of Sex Research, 20,* 1–13.

MALAMUTH, N., HABER, S., & FESHBACK, S. (1980). Testing hypotheses regarding rape: Exposure to sexual violence, sex differences, and the "normality" of rapists. *Journal of Research in Personality, 14,* 121–137.

MALINOWSKI, B. (1929). *The sexual life of savages.* New York: Harcourt, Brace, World.

MALTZ, W. (1988). Identifying and treating the sexual repercussions of incest: A couples therapy approach. *Journal of Sex and Marital Therapy, 14,* 142–170.

MANDLER, G. (1980). Recognizing: The judgment of previous occurrence. *Psychological Review, 87,* 252–272.

MANGAN, G. L., & GOLDING, J. F. (1983). The effects of smoking on memory consolidation. *Journal of Psychology, 115,* 65–77.

MANN, J. J., ARANGO, V., & UNDERWOOD, M. D. (1990). Serotonin and suicidal behavior. *Annals of the New York Academy of Sciences, 600,* 476–485.

MANN, L. (1981). The baiting crowed in episodes of threatened suicide. *Journal of Personality and Social Psychology, 41,* 703–709.

MANNELL, R. C., & MCMAHON, L. (1982). Humor as play: Its relationship to psychological well-being during the course of a day. *Leisure Sciences, 5,* 143–155.

MANNIX, E. A., & WHITE, S. B. (1992). The impact of distributive uncertainty on coalition formation in organizations. *Organizational, Behavioral, and Human Decision Processes, 51,* 198–219.

MARANO, H. (1993, January/February). Cravings and chemistry. *Psychology Today, 26,* 30–37.

MARANTO, G. (1984, November). Emotions: How they affect your body. *Discover,* pp. 35–38.

MARCIA, J. E. (1980). Identify in adolescence. In J. Adelson (Ed.), *Handbook of adolescent psychology* (pp. 12–43). New York: Wiley.

MARGO, J. L. (1987). Anorexia nervosa in males: A comparison with female patients. *British Journal of Psychiatry, 151,* 80–83.

MARK, G. P., & SCOTT, T. R. (1988). Conditioned taste aversions affect gustatory activity in the NTS of chronic decerbrate rats. *Neuroscience Abstracts, 14,* 1185.

MARKS, M. T. (1986, March). The question of quality circles. *Psychology Today,* pp. 36–46.

MARKUS, E., LANGE, A., & PETTIGREW, T. F. (1990). Effectiveness of family therapy: A meta-analysis. *Journal of Family Therapy, 12,* 205–211.

MARKUS, H. R., & KITAYAMA, S. (1991). Culture and the self: Implications for cognition, emotion, and motivation. *Psychological Review, 98,* 224–253.

MARKUS, H. R., & NURIUS, P. (1986). Possible selves. *American Psychologist, 41,* 954–969.

MARLATT, G. A. (1985). Lifestyle modification. In G. A. Marlatt & J. R. Gordon (Eds.), *Relapse prevention* (pp. 71–127). New York: Guilford Press.

MARLER, P., & MUNDINGER, P. (1971). Vocal learning in birds. In H. Moltz (Ed.), *The ontogeny of vertebrate behavior.* New York: Academic Press.

MARLOWE, W. B., MANCALL, E. L., & THOMAS, J. J. (1975). Complete Kluver-Bucy syndrome in man. *Cortex, 11,* 53–59.

MARSELLA, A. J. (1980). Depressive experience and disorder across cultures. In H. Triandis & J. Draguns (Eds.), *Handbook of cross-cultural psychology. Vol. 6: Psychopathology.* Boston: Allyn & Bacon.

MARSHALL, D. S. (1971). Sexual behavior in Mangaia. In D. S. Marshall & R. C. Suggs (Eds.), *Human sexual behavior* (pp. 103–162). Englewood Cliffs, NJ: Prentice Hall.

MARSHALL, G. P., & ZIMBARDO, P. G. (1979). Affective consequences of inadequately explained physiological arousal. *Journal of Personality and Social Psychology, 37,* 970–988.

MARTIN, C. L., & LITTLE, J. K. (1990). The relation of gender understanding to children's sex-typed preferences and gender stereotypes. *Child Development, 61,* 1427–1439.

MARTIN, G., & PEAR, J. (1992). *Behavior modification: What it is and how to do it* (4th ed.). Englewood Cliffs, NJ: Prentice Hall.

MARTIN, R. A., & LEFCOURT, H. M. (1983). Sense of humor as a moderator of the relation between stressors and moods. *Journal of Personality and Social Psychology, 45,* 1313–1324.

MARTIN R. B., LABOTT, S. M., & STOTE, J. (1987). Emotional crying and exposure to humor as factors in the recovery from depressed mood. Paper presented at the Eastern Psychological Association Convention, Arlington, VA.

MARX, J. L. (1988). Sexual responses are almost all in the brain. *Science, 241,* 903–904.

MASLOW, A. H. (1954). *Motivation and personality.* New York: Harper & Row.

MASLOW, A. H. (1970). *Motivation and personality* (2nd ed.). New York: Harper & Row.

MASSON, J. M. (1984a). *The assault on truth: Freud's suppression of the seduction theory.* New York: Farrar, Straus, & Giroux.

MASSON, J. M. (1992). *The assault on truth: Freud's suppression of the seduction theory.* New York: Harper Perennial.

MASTERS, W. H., & JOHNSON, V. E. (1966). *Human sexual response.* Boston: Little, Brown.

MASTERS, W. H., & JOHNSON, V. E. (1970). *Human sexual inadequacy.* Boston: Little, Brown.

MASTERS, W. H., JOHNSON, V. E., & KOLODNY, R. C. (1992). *Human sexuality* (4th ed.). Boston: Little, Brown.

MATARAZZO, J. D. (1984). Behavioral health: A 1990 challenge for the health sciences professions. In J. D. Matarazzo, S. M. Weiss, J. A. Herd, N. E. Miller, & S. M. Weiss (Eds.), *Behavioral health: A handbook of health enhancement and disease prevention.* New York: Wiley.

MATARAZZO, J. D., & NECKLITER, I. N. (1988). Behavioral health: The role of good and bad habits in health and illness. In S. Maes, C. D. Spielberger, P. B. Defares, & I. G. Sarason (Eds.), *Topics in health psychology.* New York: Wiley.

MATHEWS, K. A. (1984). Assessment of type A, anger, and hostility in epidemiological studies of cardiovascular disease. In A. Ostfeld & E. Eaker (Eds.), *Measuring psychosocial variables in epidemiologic studies of cardiovascular disease.* Bethesda, MD: National Institute for Health.

MATLIN, M. W. (1993). *The psychology of women* (2nd ed.). Orlando, FL: Harcourt Brace Jovanovich.

MATSUI, T., & ONGLATCO, M. L. U. (1990). Relationships between employee quality circle involvement and need fulfillment in work as moderated by work type: A compensatory or a spillover model? In U. Kleinbeck, H. Quast, H. Thierry, & H. Hacker (Eds.), *Work motivation.* Hillsdale, NJ: Erlbaum.

MAY, P. R. A., TUMA, H., & DIXON, W. J. (1981). Schizophrenia: A follow-up study of the results of five forms of treatment. *Archives of General Psychiatry, 38,* 776–784.

MCALLISTER, W. R., MCALLISTER, D. E., SCOLES, M. T., & HAMPTON, S. R. (1986). Persistence of fear-reducing behavior: Relevance for the conditioning theory of neurosis. *Journal of Abnormal Psychology, 95,* 365–372.

MCCANN, S. J., & STEWIN, L. L. (1987). Threat, authoritarianism, and the power of U.S. presidents. *Journal of Psychology, 121,* 149–157.

MCCARTHY, P. (1986, July). Scent: The tie that binds. *Psychology Today,* pp. 6–10.

MCCLELLAND, D. C. (1958). Risk-taking in children with high and low need for achievement. In J. W. Atkinson (Ed.), *Motives in fantasy, action, and society.* Princeton, NJ: Van Nostrand.

MCCLELLAND, D. C., CONSTANTIN, C. A., REGALADO, D., & STONE, C. (1978). Making it to maturity. *Psychology Today,* pp. 42–53, 114.

MCCONNELL, J. V. (1962). Memory transfer through cannibalism in planarians. *Journal of Neuropsychiatry, 3,* Suppl. 1, 542–548.

MCCONNELL, J. V. (1968). The modern search for the engram. In W. C. Corning & M. Balaban (Eds.), *The mind: Biological approaches to its functions.* New York: Interscience.

MCCRAE, R. R., & COSTA, P. T. (1986). Clinical assessment can benefit from recent advances in personality psychology. *American Psychologist, 41,* 1001–1002.

MCCRAE, R. R., & COSTA, P. T. (1987). Validation of the five-factor model of personality across instruments and observers. *Journal of Personality and Social Psychology, 52,* 81–90.

MCCRAE, R. R., & COSTA, P. T., JR. (1990). *Personality in adulthood.* New York: Guilford.

MCDONALD, A. D., ARMSTRONG, B. G., & SLOAN, M. (1992). Cigarette, alcohol, and coffee consumption and prematurity. *American Journal of Public Health, 82,* 87–90.

MCDOUGALL, W. (1908). *Social psychology.* New York: Putnam's Sons.

MCGAUGH, J. L. (1990). Significance and remembrance: The role of neuromodulatory systems. *Psychological Science, 1,* 15–25.

MCGEOCH, J. A. (1942). *The psychology of human learning.* New York: Longmans, Green.

MCGHIE, A., & CHAPMAN, H. (1961). Disorders of attention and perception in early schizophrenia. *British Journal of Medical Psychology, 34,* 103–116.

MCGILL, M. B. (1985). *The McGill Report on male intimacy.* New York: Holt, Rinehart and Winston.

MCGRADY, A., FINE, T., WOERNER, M., & YONKER, R. (1983). Maintenance of treatment effects of biofeedback-assisted relaxation on patients with essential hypertension. *American Journal of Clinical Biofeedback, 6*(1), 34–39.

MCGRATH, E., KIETH, G. P., STRICKLAND, B. R., & RUSSO, N. F. (1990). *Women and depression.* Washington, DC: American Psychological Association.

MCGREGOR, D. (1960). *The human side of enterprise.* New York: McGraw-Hill.

MCGUER, M. (1982). When assessing twin concordances, use the probandwiser, not the pairwise rate. *Schizophrenia Bulletin, 18*(2), 171–176.

MCGUIRE, W. J. (1985). Attitudes and attitude change. In G. Lindzey & E. Aronson (Eds.), *Handbook of social psychology* (Vol. II, 3rd ed.). New York: Random House.

MCGUIRE, W. J. (1989). The structure of individual attitudes and attitude systems. In A. R. Pratkanis, S. J. Breckler, & A. G. Greenwald (Eds.), *Attitude structure and function.* Hillsdale, NJ: Erlbaum.

MCINTOSH, I. D. (1984). Smoking and pregnancy: Attributable risks and public health implications.

Canadian Journal of Public Health, 75, 141–148.

McKee, M. G. (1991). Contributions of psychophysiologic monitoring to diagnosis and treatment of headache pain: A case study. *Headache Quarterly, 2,* 327–330.

McKellar, P. (1972). Imagery from the standpoint of introspection. In P. W. Sheehan (Ed.), *The function and nature of imagery.* New York: Academic Press.

McKenzie-Mohr, D., & Zanna, M. P. (1990). Treating women as sexual objects. Look at the (gender schematic) male who has viewed pornography. *Personality and Social Psychology Bulletin, 16,* 296–308.

McKoon, G., Ratcliff, R., & Dell, G. S. (1986). A critical evaluation of the semantic-episodic distinction. *Journal of Experimental Psychology: Learning, Memory and Cognition, 12,* 295–306.

McLoyd, V. C. (1989). Socialization and development in a changing economy. *American Psychologist, 44,* 293–302.

McMurray, G. A. (1950). Experimental study of a case of insensitivity to pain. *Archives of Neurological Psychiatry, 64,* 650–667.

Meill, D. (1966). Developmental psycholinguistics. In F. Smith & G. A. Miller (Eds.), *The genesis of language: A psycholinguistic approach* (pp. 15–84). Cambridge, MA: MIT Press.

Meill, S. F., & Kimmel, E. B. (1988). *Effects of extrinsic incentives on problem solving: Motivation, performance, and recall.* Paper presented at the annual meeting of the American Psychological Association, Atlanta.

McReynolds, P. (1989). Diagnosis and clinical assessment: Current status and major issues. In M. R. Rosenzweig & L. W. Porter (Eds.), *Annual review of psychology* (pp. 83–108). Palo Alto, CA: Annual Reviews Inc.

McShane, J. (1991). *Cognitive development: An information processing approach.* Oxford: Basil Blackwell.

Mead, M. (1964). *Continuities of cultural evolution.* New Haven, CT: Yale University Press.

Meaney, M. J., Aitken, D. H., Van Berkel, C., Bhatnager, S., & Sapolsky, R. M. (1988). Effect of neonatal handling on age-related impairments associated with the hippocampus. *Science, 239,* 766–768.

Meddis, R., Pearson, A. J. D., & Langford, G. N. (1973). An extreme case of healthy insomnia. *EEG in Clinical Neurophysiology, 35,* 213–224.

Medin, D. L. (1989). Concepts and conceptual structure. *American Psychologist, 44,* 1469–1481.

Mednick, M. T. S. (1989). On the politics of psychological constructs: Stop the bandwagon, I want to get off. *American Psychologist, 44,* 1118–1123.

Mednick, S. A., Moffitt, T. E., & Stack, S. (1987). *The causes of crime: New biological approaches.* New York: Cambridge University Press.

Meer, J. (1986b, June). The reason of age. *Psychology Today,* pp. 60–64.

Meeus, W. H. J., & Raaijmakers, Q. A. W. (1986). Administrative obedience: Carrying out orders to use psychological-administrative violence. *European Journal of Social Psychology, 16,* 311–324.

Meindly, J. R., & Lerner, M. J. (1984). Exacerbation of extreme responses to an out-group. *Journal of Personality and Social Psychology, 47,* 71–84.

Melton, G. B., & Garrison, E. G. (1987). Fear, prejudice, and neglect: Discrimination against mentally disabled persons. *American Psychologist, 42,* 1007–1026.

Meltzoff, A. N., & Moore, M. K. (1977). Imitation of facial and manual gestures by human neonates. *Science, 198,* 75–78.

Meltzoff, A. N., & Moore, M. K. (1985). Cognitive foundations and social functions of imitation and intermodal representation in infancy. In J. Mehler & R. Fox (Eds.), *Neonate cognition: Beyond the blooming buzzing confusion.* Hillsdale, NJ: Erlbaum.

Meltzoff, A. N., & Moore, M. K. (1989). Imitation in newborn infants: Exploring the range of gestures imitated and the underlying mechanisms. *Developmental Psychology, 25,* 954–962.

Meltzoff, A. N., & Moore, M. K. (1990). Imitation in newborn infants: Exploring the range of gestures imitated and the underlying mechanisms. *Developmental Psychology, 25,* 954–962.

Melzack, R., & Perry, C. (1975). Self-regulation of pain: The use of alpha-feedback and hypnotic training for the control of chronic pain. *Experimental Neurology, 46,* 452–464.

Melzack, R., & Wall, P. D. (1965). Pain mechanisms: A new theory. *Science, 150,* 971–979.

Menyuk, P. (1983). Language development and reading. In T. M. Gallagher & C. A. Prutting (Eds.), *Pragmatic assessment and intervention issues in language.* San Diego: College-Hill Press.

Mercer, R. T., Nichols, E. G., & Doyle, G. C. (1989). *Transitions in a woman's life* (Vol. 12). New York: Spring Publishing Company.

Merikle, P. M., & Reingold, E. M. (1990). Recognition and lexical decision without detection: Unconscious perception? *Journal of Experimental Psychology: Human Perception and Performance, 16,* 574–583.

Merlin, M., Lebot, V., & Lindstrom, L. (1992). *Kava: The Pacific drug.* New Haven, CT: Yale University Press.

Mervis, J. (1985). Council pledges greater support for state efforts. *APA Monitor, 16*(10), 2.

Mesirow, K. (1984, August). *Animal research survey.* Paper presented at the annual meeting of the American Psychological Association, Toronto, Ontario.

Messick, D. M., & Mackie, D. M. (1989). Intergroup relations. In M. R. Rosenzweig & L. W. Porter (Eds.), *Annual review of psychology* (pp. 45–82). Palto Alto, CA: Annual Reviews Inc.

Meyer, A. (1984, October 8). Latest diet craze—Not for everyone. *U. S. News and World Report, 97,* 57–60.

Meyer, M. (1992, May 18). Los Angeles will save itself. *Newsweek,* p. 46.

Meyer, R. G., & Salmon, P. (1988). *Abnormal psychology* (2nd ed.). Boston: Allyn & Bacon.

Michael, R. P., & Keverne, E. B. (1970). Primate sex pheromones of vaginal origin. *Nature, 224,* 84–85.

Miklowitz, D. J., Strachan, A. M., Goldstein, M. J., Doane, J. A., Snyder, K. S., Hogarty, G. E., & Falloon, I. R. (1986). Expressed emotion and communication deviance in the families of schizophrenics. *Journal of Abnormal Psychology, 95,* 60–66.

Milgram, S. (1963). Behavioral study of obedience. *Journal of Abnormal and Social Psychology, 67,* 371–378.

Milgram, S. (1974). *Obedience to authority: An experimental view.* New York: Harper & Row.

Miller, D. T., Turnbull, W., & McFarland C. (1990). Counterfactual thinking and social perception: Thinking about what might have been. In M. P. Zanna (Ed.), *Advances in experimental social psychology* (Vol. 23). Orlando, FL: Academic Press.

Miller, G. A. (1956). The magical number seven, plus or minus two: Some limits on our capacity for processing information. *Psychological Review, 63,* 81–97.

Miller, J. G., & Bersoff, D. M. (1992). Culture and moral judgment: How are conflicts between justice and interpersonal responsibilities resolved? *Journal of Personality and Social Psychology, 62,* 541–554.

Miller, N. E. (1991). Commentary on Ulrich: Need to check truthfulness of statements by opponents of animal research. *Psychological Science, 2,* 422–424.

Miller, N. E., & DiCara, L. (1967). Instrumental learning of heart rate changes in curarized rats: Shaping and specificity to discriminative stimulus. *Journal of Comparative and Physiological Psychology, 63,* 12–19.

Miller, N. M. (1982). Hypnoaversion treatment in alcoholism, nicotinism, and weight control. *Journal of the National Medical Association, 68,* 129–130.

Miller, N., & Brewer, M. (Eds.). (1984). *Groups in contact: The psychology of desegregation.* Orlando, FL: Academic Press.

Mills, J. (1979). *Six years with God.* New York: A & W Publishers.

Mills, J. L., Braubard, B. I., Harley, E. E., Rhoads, G. G., & Berendes, H. W. (1984). Maternal alcohol consumption and birth weight: How much drinking during pregnancy is safe? *Journal of the American Medical Association, 252,* 1857–1879.

Milner, B. (1959). The memory defect in bilateral hippocampal lesions. *Psychiatric Research Reports, 11,* 43–52.

Minde, K. (1986). Bonding and attachment: Its relevance for the present-day clinician. *Developmental Medicine and Child Neurology, 28,* 803–806.

Mishkin, M., & Pribram, K. H. (1954). Visual discrimination performance following partial ablation of the temporal lobe. I. Ventral vs. lateral. *Journal of Comparative and Physiological Psychology, 47,* 14–20.

Money, J. (1977). Determinants of human gender identity/role. In J. Money & H. Musaph (Eds.), *Handbook of sexology* (pp. 57–79). Amsterdam: Elsevier/North-Holland/Biomedical Press.

Money, J. (1985a). Sexual reformation and counter-reformation in law and medicine. *Medicine and Law, 4,* 479–488.

Money, J. (1986). *Lovemaps: Clinical concepts of sexual/erotic health and pathology, paraphilia, and gender transposition in childhood, adolescence, and maturity.* New York: Irvington.

Money, J. (1988a). *Gay, straight, and in-between: The sexology of erotic orientation.* New York: Oxford University Press.

Money, J., & Ehrhardt, A. A. (1972). *Man and woman, boy and girl.* Baltimore: The Johns Hopkins University Press.

Money, J., Prakasam, K. S., & Joshi, V. N. (1991). Semen-conservation doctrine from ancient Ayurvedic to modern sexological theory. *American Journal of Psychotherapy, 45,* 9–13.

Montagu, A. (1971). *Touching: The human significance of the skin.* New York: Columbia University Press.

Montefiore, S. S. (1993, January/February). The thrill of the kill. *Psychology Today, 26,* pp. 42–45.

Moorcroft, W. H. (1989). *Sleep, dreaming, and sleep disorders.* New York: University Press.

Moore, T. E. (1982). Subliminal advertising: What you see is what you get. *Journal of Marketing, 46*(2), 38–47.

Morgan, C. T., & Morgan, J. D. (1940). Studies in hunger. II: The relation of gastric denervation and dietary sugar to the effects of insulin upon food intake in the rat. *Journal of General Psychology, 57,* 153–163.

MORRIS, C. D., BRANSFORD, J. D., & FRANKS, J. J. (1977). Levels of processing versus transfer appropriate processing. *Journal of Verbal Learning and Verbal Behavior, 16,* 519–533.

MORRIS, N. M., & UDRY, J. R. (1978). Pheromonal influences on human sexual behavior: An experimental search. *Journal of Biosocial Science, 10,* 147–157.

MORRIS, R. G., & BADDELEY, A. D. (1988). Primary and working memory functioning in Alzheimer-type dementia. *Journal of Clinical and Experimental Neuropsychology, 10,* 279–296.

MORRIS, S. (1980, April). Interview with James Randi. *Omni,* pp. 46–54.

MORRISON, F., HOLMES, D. L., & HAITH, M. M. (1974). A developmental study of the effects of familiarity on short term visual memory. *Journal of Experimental Child Psychology, 18,* 412–425.

MOSAK, H. H. (1989). Adlerian psychotherapy. In R. Corsini & D. Wedding (Eds.), *Current psychotherapies.* Itasca, IL: Peacock Publishers.

MOSES-ZIRKES, S. (1993, March). Outcomes research: Everybody wants it. *APA Monitor,* pp. 22–23.

MOSHER, D., & TOMKINS, S. (1988). Scripting the macho man: Hypermasculine socialization and enculturation. *Journal of Sex Research, 25,* 60–84.

MOSKOWITZ, H. (1973). *Alcohol and drug impairment of the driver.* New York: Society of Automotive Engineers.

MOSS, S., & BUTLER, D. C. (1978). The scientific credibility of ESP. *Perceptual & Motor Skills, 46*(3), 992.

MUEHLENHARD, C., & COOK, S. (1988). Men's self-reports of unwanted sexual activity. *Journal of Sex Research, 24,* 58–72.

MUEHLENHARD, C., GOGGINS, M., JONES, J., & SATTERFIELD, A. (1991). Sexual violence and coercion in close relationships. In K. McKinney & S. Sprecher (Eds.), *Sexuality in close relationships* (pp. 56–73). Hillsdale, NJ: Erlbaum.

MUEHLENHARD, C., SCHRAG, J. (1991). Nonviolent sexual coercion. In A. Parrot & L. Bechhofer (Eds.), *Acquaintance rape: The hidden crime* (pp. 115–128). New York: Wiley.

MUESER, K. T., BELLACK, A. S., MORRISON, R. L., & WADE, J. H. (1990). Gender, social competence, and symptomatology in schizophrenia: A longitudinal analysis. *Journal of Abnormal Psychology, 99,* 138–147.

MUI, A. C. (1992). Caregiver strain among black and white daughter caregivers: A role theory perspective. *The Gerontologist, 32,* 203–212.

MULLEN, B., JOHNSON, C., & SALAS, E. (1991). Productivity loss in brainstorming groups: A meta-analytic integration. *Basic and Applied Psychology, 12,* 3–23.

MULLIGAN, T., & MOSS, C. R. (1991). Sexuality and aging in male veterans: A cross-sectional study of interest, ability, and activity. *Archives of Sexual Behavior, 20,* 17–25.

MULLIS, J. P., & LIPPA, R. (1990). Behavioral change in earthquake preparedness due to negative threat appeals: A test of protective motivation theory. *Journal of Applied Social Psychology, 20,* 619–638.

MURASE, T. (1982). Sunao: A central value in Japanese psychotherapy. In A. J. Marsella & G. White (Eds.), *Cultural conceptions of mental health and therapy.* (pp. 317–329). Dordrecht: Reidel.

MURNEN, S. K., & BYRNE, D. (1991). Hyperfemininity: Measurement and initial validation of the construct. *Journal of Sex Research, 26,* 85–106.

MURPHY, G. E., & WETZEL, R. D. (1990). The lifetime risk of suicide in alcoholism. *Archives of General Psychiatry, 47,* 383–392.

MURPHY, J. M., & HELZER, J. E. (1986). Epidemiology of schizophrenia in adulthood. In G. L. Klerman, M. M. Weissman, P. S. Appelbaum, & L. H. Roth (Eds.), *Psychiatry. Vol. 5: Social, epidemiologic, and legal psychiatry* (pp. 234–251). New York: Basic Books.

MURPHY, M. P., & CARTER, D. B. (1991). *Familial characteristics and the development of gender schemas.* Paper presented at the Society for Research in Child Development, Seattle.

MURPHY, S. M. (1990). Models of imagery in sport psychology: A review. *Journal of Mental Imagery, 14,* 153–172.

MURRAY, D. M., JOHNSON, C. A., LUEPKER, R. V., & MITTELMARK, M. B. (1984). The prevention of cigarette smoking in children: A comparison of four strategies. *Journal of Applied Social Psychology, 14*(3), 274–288.

MURRAY, H. A. (1938). *Explorations in personality.* New York: Oxford University Press.

MUSSEN, P. H., CONGER, J. J., KAGAN, J., & GEIWITZ, J. (1979). *Psychological development: A life-span approach.* New York: Harper & Row.

MUTTER, K., & BRYSON, J. (1993, April). *The questioner superiority effect revisited: A self-serving bias explanation.* Poster presented at the meeting of the Western Psychological Association, Phoenix, AZ.

MYERS, M. F. (1989). Men sexually assaulted as adults and sexually abused as boys. *Archives of Sexual Behavior, 18,* 203–215.

NADON, R., HOYT, I. P., REGISTER, P. A., & KIHLSTROM, J. F. (1991). Absorption and hypnotizability: Context effects reexamined. *Journal of Personality and Social Psychology, 60,* 144–153.

NAEYE, R. L. (1980). Sudden infant death. *Scientific American, 4*(242), 56–62.

NAGELMAN, D. B., HALE, S. L., & WARE, S. L. (1983). *Prevalence of eating disorders in college women.* Paper presented at the meeting of the American Psychological Association, Anaheim, CA.

NANDA, S. (1991). *Cultural anthropology* (4th ed.). Belmont, CA: Wadsworth.

NASSAR, J. L. (ED.). (1988). *Environmental aesthetics: Theory research, and applications.* New York: Cambridge University Press.

NASH, M., & BAKER, E. (1984, February). Trance encounters: Susceptibility to hypnosis. *Psychology Today,* pp. 72–73.

NATHAN, P. W. (1976). The gate control theory of pain: A cultural review. *Brain, 99*(4), 123–158.

NATHANS, J. (1989). The genes for color vision. *Scientific American, 260*(2), 42–49.

NATHANS, J., PIANTANIDA, T. P., EDDY, R. L., SHOWS, T. B., & HOGNESS, D. S. (1986). Molecular genetics of inherited variation in human color vision. *Science, 232,* 203–232.

NATHANS, J., THOMAS, D., & HOGNESS, D. S. (1986). Molecular genetics of human color vision: The genes encoding blue, green, and red pigments. *Science, 232,* 193–202.

National Institute of Mental Health. (1982). *Television and behavior: Ten years of scientific progress and implications for the eighties* (Vol. I). Washington, DC: U. S. Government Printing Office.

National Institute of Mental Health. (1985). *What to do when a friend is depressed: A guide for teenagers.* Washington, DC: U. S. Government Printing Office.

Nature and causes of depression—Part I. (1988). *Harvard Medical School Mental Health Letter, 4*(7), 1–4.

NAUTA, W. J. H. (1972). Neural associations of the frontal cortex. *Acta Neurobiologiae Experimentalis, 32,* 125–140.

NEALE, J. M., OLTMANNS, T. F., & WINTERS, K. C. (1983). Recent developments in the assessment and conceptualization of schizophrenia. *Behavioral Assessment, 5,* 33–54.

NEBES, R. D., MARTIN, D. C., & HORN, L. C. (1984). Sparing of semantic memory in Alzheimer's disease. *Journal of Abnormal Psychology, 93,* 321–330.

NEELY, J. H., & DURGUNOGLU, A. Y. (1985). Dissociative episodic and semantic priming effects in episodic recognition and lexical decision tasks. *Journal of Memory and Language, 24,* 466–489.

NEHER, A. (1991). Maslow's theory of motivation: A critique. *Journal of Humanistic Psychology, 31,* 89–112.

NEISSER, U. (1967). *Cognitive psychology.* New York: Appleton-Century-Crofts.

NEISSER, U. (1982). *Memory observed.* San Francisco: Freeman.

NELSON, C. A. (1987). The recognition of facial expression in the first two years of life: Mechanisms of development. *Child Development, 58,* 880–909.

NEUGARTEN, B. L. (1970). Dynamics of transition of middle age to old age: Adaptation and the life cycle. *Journal of Geriatric Psychiatry, 4,* 71–87.

NEVID, J. S., & GOTFRIED, F. (1993). *A student's guide to AIDS and other sexually transmitted diseases.* Boston, MA: Allyn and Bacon.

NEWCOMB, M. D., & BENTLER, P. M. (1989). Substance use and abuse among children and teenagers. *American Psychologist, 44,* 242–248.

NEWMAN, J. P., & KOSSON, D. S. (1986). Passive avoidance learning in psychopathic and nonpsychotic offenders. *Journal of Abnormal Psychology, 95,* 252–256.

NEZU, A. M., NEZU, C. M., & BLISSETT, S. E. (1988). Sense of humor as a moderator of the relation between stressful events and psychological distress: A prospective analysis. *Journal of Personality and Social Psychology, 54,* 520–525.

NICHOLI, A. M. (1983, October). The college student and marijuana: Research findings concerning adverse biological and psychological effects. *Journal of American College Health, 32*(2), 73–77.

NICOLI, A. (1988). *New Harvard guide to psychiatry.* Cambridge, MA: Harvard University Press.

NIDEFFER, R. M. (1976). Altered states of consciousness. In T. X. Barber (Ed.), *Advances in altered states of consciousness and human potentialities.* New York: Psychological Dimensions.

NISHIMOTO, R. (1988). A cross-cultural analysis of psychiatric symptom expression using Langer's twenty-two item index. *Journal of Sociology and Social Welfare, 15,* 45–62.

NITZ, V., & LERNER, J. V. (1991). Temperament during adolescence. In R. M. Lerner, A. C. Petersen, & J. Brooks-Gunn (Eds.), *Encyclopedia of adolescence* (Vol. 2). New York: Garland.

NKOUNKOU-HOMBESSA, E. (1988). *The psychomotor development of Kongo-Lari infants: Environment, culture, and cognitive aspects.* Thesis, University Rene Descartes, Paris, V.

NOLEN-HOEKSEMA, S. (1990). *Sex differences in depression.* Stanford, CA: Stanford University Press.

NOLEN-HOEKSEMA, S., & MORROW, J. (1991). A prospective study of depression and post-traumatic stress symptoms following a natural disaster: The 1989 Loma Prieta earthquake: *Journal of Personality and Social Psychology, 61,* 115–121.

NORGREN, R., & GRILL, H. (1982). Brainstem control of

ingestive behavior. In D. W. Pfaff (Ed.), *The physiological mechanisms of motivation* (pp. 544–567). New York: Springer-Verlag.

NORMAN, D. A. (1982). *Learning and memory.* New York: Freeman.

NORMAN, S. A. (1988). *The psychology of everyday things.* New York: Basic Books.

NOUWEN, A., & SOLINGER, J. W. (1979). The effectiveness of EMG biofeedback training in low back pain. *Biofeedback and Self Regulation, 4,* 103–111.

NOVAK, M. A., & HARLOW, H. F. (1975). Social recovery of monkeys isolated for the first year of life: Rehabilitation and therapy. *Developmental Psychology, 11,* 453–465.

NOVICK, B. (1990). Pediatric AIDS: A medical overview. In J. M. Seibert & R. A. Olson (Eds.), *Children, adolescents, and AIDS* (pp. 765–777). Lincoln: University of Nebraska Press.

NYE, R. D. (1975). *Three views of man.* Monterey, CA: Brooks/Cole.

NYITI, R. M. (1982). The validity of "cultural differences explanations" of cross-cultural variation in the rate of Piagetian cognitive development. In D. A. Wagner & H. W. Stevenson (Eds.), *Cultural perspectives on child development* (pp. 146–166). San Francisco: Freeman.

OFFER, D., & SABSHIN, M. (1984). Adolescence: Empirical perspectives. In D. Offer & M. Sabshin (Eds.), *Normality and the life cycle.* New York: Basic Books.

OFFER, D., & SABSHIN, M. (1993). *The diversity of normal behavior: Further contributions to normatology.* New York: HarperCollins.

OGBU, J. U. (1986). Black students' school success: Coping with the "burden of acting white." *Urban Review, 18*(3), 176–206.

OGBU, J. U. (1988). Cultural diversity and human development. In D. T. Slaughter (Ed.), *Black children and poverty: A developmental perspective.* San Francisco: Jossey-Bass.

OGBU, J. U. (1991). Minority coping responses and school experience. *Journal of Psychohistory, 18*(4), 433–456.

OGILVIE, R. D., WILKINSON, R. T., & ALLISON, S. (1989). The detection of sleep onset: Behavioral, physiological, and subjective convergence. *Sleep, 12*(5), 458–474.

OJANLATUA, A., HAMMER, A. M., & MOHR, M. G. (1987). The ultimate rejection: Helping the survivors of teen suicide victims. *Journal of School Health, 57,* 181–182.

OKIN, R. L. (1987). The case for deinstitutionalization. *Harvard Medical School Mental Health Letter, 4*(4), 5–7.

OLDS, J., & MILNER, P. (1954). Positive reinforcement produced by electrical stimulation of septal area and other regions of rat brain. *Journal of Comparative and Physiological Psychology, 47,* 419–427.

OLSHAN, N. (1980). *Power over your pain without drugs.* New York: Rawson Wade.

ORBACH, I. (1988). *Children who don't want to live.* San Francisco: Jossey-Bass.

ORFORD, J. (1985). *Excessive appetites.* New York: Wiley.

ORNE, M. T., & EVANS, F. J. (1965). Social control in the psychological experiment: Antisocial behavior and hypnosis. *Journal of Personality and Social Psychology, 1,* 189–200.

ORNSTEIN, R. E. (ED.). (1973). *Nature of human consciousness.* San Francisco: Freeman.

ORTNER, S. B., & WHITEHEAD, H. (Eds.). (1981). *Sexual meanings: The cultural construction of gender and sexuality.* New York: Cambridge University Press.

OSBORN, A. F. (1963). *Applied imagination.* New York: Scribner's.

OSHEROW, N. (1988). Making sense of the nonsensical: An analysis of Jonestown. In E. Aronson (Ed.), *Readings about the social animal* (4th ed., pp. 68–86). New York: Freeman.

OST, L. (1987, March 26). Marijuana may trigger dormant AIDS virus. *Orlando (Florida) Sentinel,* p. 51:E3.

OSTERWEIS, M., SOLOMON, F., & GREEN M. (1984). *Bereavement: Reactions, consequences, and care.* Washington, DC: National Academy Press.

OVERMEIER, J., & SELIGMAN, M. (1967). Effects of inescapable shock upon subsequent escape and avoidance learning. *Journal of Comparative and Physiological Psychology, 63,* 23–33.

PAGANO, R. R., & WARRENBURG, S. (1983). Meditation. In R. J. Davidson, G. E. Schwartz, & D. Shapiro (Eds.), *Consciousness and self-regulation* (pp. 153–210). New York: Plenum.

PAIVIO, A. (1969). Mental imagery in associative learning and memory. *Psychological Review, 76,* 241–263.

PAIVIO, A. (1971). *Imagery and verbal processes.* New York: Holt, Rinehart and Winston.

PAIVIO, A. (1982). The empirical case for dual coding. In J. Yuille (Ed.), *Imagery, cognition and memory.* Hillsdale, NJ: Erlbaum.

PAIVIO, A. (1991). Dual coding theory: Retrospect and current status. *Canadian Journal of Psychology, 45,* 255–287.

PALMORE, E. B., & MAEDA, D. (1985). *The honorable elders revisited: A revised cross-cultural analysis of aging in Japan.* Durham, NC: Duke University Press.

PALUDI, M. A. (1990). *Ivory power: Sexual harrasment on campus.* Albany: State University of New York Press.

PALUDI, M. A. (1992). *The psychology of women.* Dubuque, IA: Wm. C. Brown.

PANSKEPP, J. (1982). Toward a general psychobiological theory of emotions. *Behavioral and Brain Sciences, 5,* 447–467.

PARK, B., & ROTHBART, M. (1982). Perception of out-group homogeneity and levels of social categorization: Memory for the subordinate attributes of in-group and out-group members. *Journal of Personality and Social Psychology, 42,* 1051–1068.

PARK, M. (1979). *Communication styles in two different cultures: Korean and American.* Seoul: Han Shin.

PARKE, R., & COLLMER, C. (1975). Child abuse: An interdisciplinary analysis. In E. M. Hetherington (Ed.), *Review of child development research* (pp. 509–590). Chicago: University of Chicago Press.

PARKE, R. D., O'LEARY, S. E., & WEST, S. (1972). Mother–father–newborn interaction: Effects of maternal medication, labor and sex of infant. *Proceedings of the American Psychological Association, 7,* 85–86.

PARKES, C. M. (1972). *Bereavement: Studies of grief in adult life.* New York: International Universities Press.

PARKES, C. M., & WEISS, R. S. (1983). *Recovery from bereavement.* New York: Basic Books.

PARROT, A. (1990). Date rape. *Medical Aspects of Human Sexuality, 24,* 28–31.

PARROT, A., & BECHHOFER, L. (EDS.). (1991). *Acquaintance rape: The hidden crime.* New York: Wiley.

PATTEN, S., GATZ, Y., JONES, B., & THOMAS, D. (1989). Posttraumatic stress disorders and the treatment of sexual abuse. *Social Work, 34,* 197–203.

PATTERSON, F., & GOODREAU, M. (1987). Speech sound discrimination in a gorilla. *Journal of the Gorilla Foundation, 11*(1), 2–4.

PATTERSON, F., & LINDEN, E. (1981). *The education of Koko.* New York: Holt, Rinehart and Winston.

PATTERSON, G. R., DE BARYSHE, B. D., & RAMSEY, E. (1989). A developmental perspective on antisocial behavior. *American Psychologist, 44,* 329–335.

PAUL, G. L., & LENTZ, R. J. (1977). *Psychosocial treatment of chronic mental patients: Milieu versus social-learning programs.* Cambridge, MA: Harvard University Press.

PAULY, I. B. (1990). Gender identity disorders: Evaluation and treatment. *Journal of Sex Education and Therapy, 16,* 2–24.

PAVLOV, I. (1927). *Conditioned reflexes* (G. V. Anrep, Ed. and Trans.). London: Oxford University Press.

PEARLIN, L. I. (1980). The life cycle and life strains. In H. M. Blalock (Ed.), *Sociological theory and research: A critical approach.* New York: Free Press.

PEDERSON, D. R., MORAN, G., SITKO, C., CAMPBELL, K. GHESQUIRE, K., & ACTON, H. (1990). Maternal sensitivity and the security of infant-mother attachment: A Q-Sort study. *Child Development, 61,* 1974–1983.

PELLETIER, K. R., & PEPER, E. (1977). Developing a biofeedback model: Alpha EEG feedback as a means for pain control. *International Journal of Clinical and Experimental Hypnosis, 25,* 361–371.

PENDLETON, M. G., & BATSON, C. D. (1979). Self-presentation and the door-in-the-face technique for inducing compliance. *Personality and Social Psychology Bulletin, 5,* 77–81.

PENFIELD, W. (1975). *The mystery of the mind: A critical study of consciousness and the human brain.* Princeton, NJ: Princeton University Press.

PERLS, F. S. (1969). *Gestalt therapy verbatim.* Layfayette, CA: Real People Press.

PERRIN, S., & SPENCER, C. (1981). Independence or conformity in the Asch experiment as a reflection of cultural or situational factors. *British Journal of Social Psychology, 20,* 205–209.

PERRY, J. D., & WHIPPLE, B. (1982). Multiple components of female orgasm. In B. Graber (Ed.), *Circumvaginal musculature and sexual function.* New York: Karger.

PERRY, N. J. (1982, November 28). Industrial time clocks—Often at odds with those inside a worker's body. *New York Times,* pp. F8–F9.

PERVIN, L. A. (1993). *Personality: Theory and research* (6th ed.). New York: Wiley.

PETERSEN, A. C. (1987, September). Those gangly years. *Psychology Today,* pp. 28–34.

PETERSEN, A. C. (1988). Adolescent development. In M. R. Rosenzweig & L. W. Porter (Eds.), *Annual review of psychology* (pp. 583–607). Palo Alto, CA: Annual Reviews Inc.

PETERSEN, A. C., EBATA, A. T., & GRABER, J. A. (1987). *Coping with adolescence: The functions and dysfunctions of poor achievement.* Paper presented at biennial meeting of the Social Research Development, Baltimore, MD.

PETERSON, C., & SELIGMAN, M. E. P. (1984). Causal explanations as a risk factor for depression: Theory and evidence. *Psychological Review, 91,* 347–374.

PETERSON, J. L., & ZILL, N. (1981). Television viewing in the United States and children's intellectual, social, and emotional development. *Television and Children, 2*(2), 21–28.

PETERSON, L. R., & PETERSON, M. J. (1959). Short-term retention of individual verbal items. *Journal of Experimental Psychology, 58,* 193–198.

PEVSNER, J., REED, R., FEINSTEIN, G., & SNYDER, S. (1988). Molecular cloning of ordorant-binding protein: Member of a ligand carrier family. *Science, 241*, 336–339.

PFAFFMANN, C. (1982). Taste: A model of incentive motivation. In D. W. Pfaff (Ed.), *The physiological mechanisms of motivation.* New York: Springer-Verlag.

PFEIFFER, W. (1982). Culture-bound syndromes. In I. Al-Issa (Ed.), *Culture and psychopathology.* Baltimore, MD: University Park Press.

PFOST, K. S., & FIORE, M. (1990). Pursuit of nontraditional occupations: Fear of success or fear of not being chosen? *Sex Roles, 23*, 15–24.

PHARES, E. J. (1984). *Personality.* Columbus, OH: Merrill.

PHELPS, M. E., & MAZZIOTTA, J. C. (1985). Positron emission tomography: Human brain function and biochemistry. *Science, 228*, 799–809.

PHILIPS, C. (1977). Modification of tension headache pain using E.M.G. biofeedback. *Behavior Research and Therapy, 15*, 119–129.

PHILLIPS, R. L., KUZMA, J. W., BEESON, W. L., & LOTZ, T. (1980). Influence of selection versus lifestyle on risk of fatal cancer and cardiovascular disease among Seventh-day Adventists. *American Journal of Epidemiology, 112*, 296–314.

PHILLIPS, S. U. (1983). *The invisible culture: Communication in classroom and community on the Warm Springs Indian Reservation.* New York: Longman.

PIAGET, J. (1932). *The moral judgment of the child.* New York: Harcourt, Brace.

PIAGET, J. (1951). *Play, dreams, and imitation in childhood.* New York: Norton.

PILIAVIN, J. A., CALLERO, P. L., & EVANS, D. E. (1982). Addiction to altruism? Opponent-process theory and blood donation. *Journal of Personality and Social Psychology, 43*, 1200–1213.

PILIAVIN, J. A., DIVIDIO, J. F., GAERTNER, S. L., & CLARK, R. D., III. (1982). *Emergency intervention.* New York: Academic Press.

PINDERHUGHES, E. (1992). Does work with culturally different patients require special training? *Harvard Mental Health Letter, 8*(10), 8.

PIORKOWSKE, C., & STARK, E. (1985, June). Blue-collar stress worse for boys. *Psychology Today,* p. 15.

PINES, A. M., & ARONSON, E. (1983). Combatting burnout. *Children & Youth Services Review, 5*(3), 263–275.

PIOTROWSKI, C., & KELLER, J. W. (1989). Psychological testing in outpatient mental health facilities. *Professional Psychology Research and Practice, 20*, 423–425.

PIVIK, R. T. (1991). Tonic states and phasic events in relation to sleep mentation. In S. A. Ellman & J. S. Antrobus (Eds.), *The mind in sleep: Psychology and psychophysiology* (2nd ed., pp. 214–248). New York: Wiley.

PLATT, J. J. (1986). *Heroin addiction* (2nd ed.). Malabar, FL: Kreiger.

PLOMIN, R. (1989). Environment and genes: Determinants of behavior. *American Psychologist, 44*, 105–111.

PLOMIN, R. (1990). The role of inheritance in behavior. *Science, 248*, 183–188.

PLOTNICK, A. B., PAYNE, P. A., & O'GRADY, D. J. (1991). Correlates of hynotizability in children: Absorption, vividness of imagery, fantasy play, and social desirability. *American Journal of Clinical Hypnosis, 34*, 51–58.

PLOUS, S. (1991). An attitude survey of animal rights activists. *Psychological Science, 2*, 194–196.

PLUTCHIK, R. (1980). *Emotion: A psycho-evolutionary synthesis.* New York: Harper & Row.

POLAND, R. L. (1990). The question of routine neonatal circumcision. *New England Journal of Medicine, 322*, 1312–1315.

POLIVY, J., & HERMAN, C. P. (1991). Good and bad dieters: Self-perception and reaction to a dietary challenge. *International Journal of Eating Disorders, 10*, 91–99.

POLLOCK, V. E., BRIERE, J., SCHNEIDER, L., KNOP, J. ET AL. (1990). Childhood antecedents of antisocial behavior. *American Journal of Psychiatry, 147*, 1290–1293.

POLSTER, E., & POLSTER, M. (1973). *Gestalt therapy integrated: Contours of theory and practice.* New York: Brunner/Mazel.

POMEROY, W. B. (1972). *Dr. Kinsey and the Institute for Sex Research.* New York: Nelson.

PONTEROTTO, J., & BENESCH, K. (1988). An organizational framework for understanding the role of culture in counseling. *Journal of Counseling and Development, 66*, 237–241.

POSNER, M. I., & SNYDER, C. R. R. (1975). Attention and cognitive control. In R. L. Solso (Ed.), *Information processing and cognition: The Loyola Symposium.* Hillsdale, NJ: Erlbaum.

POULOS, C. X., & CAPPELL, H. (1991). Homeostatic theory of drug tolerance: A general model of physiological adaptation. *Psychological Review, 98*, 390–408.

POULSON, C. L., NUNES, L. R., & WARREN, S. F. (1989). Imitation in infancy: A critical review. In H. W. Reese (Ed.), *Advances in child development and behavior* (Vol. 22). San Diego: Academic Press.

POWERS, S. I., HAUSER, S. T., & KILNER, L. A. (1989). Adolescent mental health. *American Psychologist, 44*, 200–208.

PRATKANIS, A. R., GREENWALD, A. G., LEIPPE, M. R., & BAUMGARDNER, M. H. (1988). In search of persuasion effects. III. The sleeper effect is dead. Long live the sleeper effect. *Journal of Personality and Social Psychology, 54*, 203–218.

PREMACK, D. (1976). Language and intelligence in ape and man. *American Scientist, 64*(6), 674–683.

PRIEST, R. F., & SAWYER, J. (1967). Proximity and peership: Bases of balance in interpersonal attraction. *American Journal of Sociology, 72*, 633–649.

PSATTA, D. (1983). EEG and clinical survey during biofeedback treatment of epileptics. *Neurologie et Psychiatrie, 21*(2), 63–75.

Psychedelic drugs. (1990). *Harvard Medical School Mental Health Letter, 6*(8), 1–4.

PUTNAM, F. W., GUROFF, J. J., SILBERMAN, E. K., BARBAN, L., & POST, R. M. (1986). The clinical phenomenology of multiple personality disorder: Review of 100 recent cases. *Journal of Clinical Psychiatry, 47*, 285–293.

PYKETT, I. L. (1982). NMR imaging in medicine. *Scientific American, 246*(5), 78–88.

PYLYSHYN, Z. W. (1979). The rate of mental rotation of images: A test of a holistic analogue hypothesis. *Memory and Cognition, 7*, 19–28.

RABKIN, J. G., & STRUENING, E. L. (1976). Life events, stress, and illness. *Science, 194*, 1013–1020.

RABOW, G. (1988, January). The competitive edge. *Psychology Today,* pp. 54–58.

RAHE, R. H., & ARTHUR, R. J. (1978). Life changes and illness studies: Past history and future directions. *Journal of Human Stress, 4*(1), 3–15.

RAJECKI, D. W. (1990). *Attitudes: Themes and advances* (2nd ed.). Sunderland, MA: Sinauer Associates.

RAMA, S., BALLENTINE, R., & AJAYA, S. (1976). *Yoga and psychotherapy: The evolution of consciousness.* Honesdale, PA: Himalayan International Institute.

RAMACHANDRAN, V. (1988). Perceiving shape from shading. *Scientific American, 259*(2), 76–83.

RANDI, J. (1982). *Flim-flam.* Buffalo, NY: Prometheus.

RAPOPORT, J. L. (1989). The biology of obsessions and compulsions. *Scientific American, 260*(3), 83–89.

RASKIN, M., BALI, L. R., & PEEKE, H. (1980). Muscle biofeedback and transcendental meditation: A controlled evaluation of efficacy in the treatment of chronic anxiety. *Archives of General Psychiatry, 37*(1), 93–97.

RATHUS, S. A. (1992). *Understanding child development* (2nd ed.). New York: Holt, Rinehart and Winston.

RATTNER, A. (1990). Social indicators and crime rate forecasting. *Social Indicators Research, 22*, 83–95.

RAZ, S., & RAZ, N. (1990). Structural brain abnormalities in the major psychoses: A quantitative review of the evidence from computerized imaging. *Psychological Bulletin, 208*, 93–108.

READ, J. D., & BRUCE, D. (1982). Longitudinal tracking of difficult memory retrievals. *Cognitive Psychology, 14*, 280–300.

REBOK, G. W. (1987). *Life-span cognitive development.* New York: Holt, Rinehart and Winston.

RECHTSCHAFFEN, A., GILLILAND, M. A., BERGMANN, B. M., & WINTER, J. B. (1983). Physiological correlates of prolonged sleep deprivation in rats. *Science, 221*, 182–184.

REED L., & LEIDERMAN, P. H. (1983). Is imprinting an appropriate model for human infant attachment? *International Journal of Behavioral Development, 6*, 51–69.

REGIER, D. A., NARROW, W. E., RAE, D. S., MANDERSCHEID, R. W., LOCKE, B. Z., & GOODWIN, F. K. (1993). The de facto US mental and addictive disorders service system. *Archives of General Psychiatry, 50*, 85–93.

REIFMAN, A. S., LARRICK, R. P., & FEIN, S. (1991). Temper and temperature on the diamond: The heat-aggression relationship in major league baseball. *Personality and Social Psychology Bulletin, 17*, 580–585.

REINISCH, J. M., & SANDERS, S. A. (1992). Effects of prenatal exposure to diethylstil-bestrol (DES) on hemispheric laterality and spatial ability in human males. *Hormones and Behavior, 26*(1), 62–75.

REINISCH, J. M., ZIEMBA, D. M., & SANDERS, S. A. (1991). Hormonal contributions to sexually dimorphic behavioral development in humans. Special issue: Neuroendocrine effects on brain development and cognition. *Psychoneuroendocrinology, 16*(1–3), 213–278.

REISENZEIN, R. (1983). The Schachter theory of emotion: Two decades later. *Psychological Bulletin, 94*, 239–264.

REISMAN, J. E. (1987). Touch, motion, and perception. In P. Salapatek & L. Cohen (Eds.), *Handbook of infant perception. Vol. 1:From sensation to perception.* New York: Academic Press.

REISS, T. L. (1986). *Journey into sexuality: An exploratory voyage.* Englewood Cliffs, NJ: Prentice Hall.

REMINGTON, D. W., FISHER, A. G., & PARENT, E. A. (1984). *How to lower your fat thermostat.* Provo, UT: Vitality House.

REST, J. R., TURIEL, E., & KOHLBERG, L. (1969). Relations between level of moral judgment and preference and comprehension of the moral judgments of others. *Journal of Personality, 37*, 225–252.

RESTON, J., JR. (1981). *Our father who art in hell.* New York: Times Books.

REUDER, M. E. (1984). Phrenology. In R. J. Corsini (Ed.), *Encyclopedia of psychology* (Vol. 3, pp. 39–40). New York: Wiley.

RHINE, J. B. (1972). Parapsychology and man. *Journal of Parapsychology, 36*(2), 101–121.

RHODES, A. J. (1961). *Virus infections and congenital*

malformations. Paper delivered at the First Conference on Congenital Malformations, Philadelphia.

RHODES, N., & WOOD, W. (1992). Self-esteem and intelligence affect influenceability: The mediating role of message reception. *Psychological Bulletin, 111,* 156–171.

RICCIUTI, H. N. (1993). Nutrition and mental development. *Current Directions in Psychological Science, 2,* 43–47.

RICE, M. E., QUINSEY, V. L., & HARRIS, G. T. (1991). Sexual recidivism among child molesters released from a maximum security psychiatric institution. *Journal of Consulting and Clinical Psychology, 59,* 381–386.

RICE, M. L. (1989). Children's language acquisition. *American Psychologist, 44,* 149–156.

RICHARDS, D. D., & GOLDFARB, J. (1986). The episodic memory model of conceptual development: An integrative viewpoint. *Cognitive Development, 1,* 183–219.

RICHARDS, L., ROLLERSON, B., & PHILLIPS, J. (1991). Perceptions of submissiveness: Implications for victimization. *The Journal of Psychology, 125,* 407–411.

RICHARDS, R., KINNEY, K. K., BENET, J., & MERZEL, A. P. C. (1988). Assessing everyday creativity: Characteristics of the lifetime creativity scales and validation with three large samples. *Journal of Personality and Social Psychology, 54,* 476–485.

RICHMOND-ABBOTT, M. (1983). *Masculine and feminine sex roles over the life cycle.* Reading, MA: Addison-Wesley.

RIESEN, A. H. (1950). Arrested vision. *Scientific American, 183,* 16–19.

RIGER, S. (1991). Gender dilemmas in sexual harrassment policies and procedures. *American Psychologist, 46,* 497–505.

RILEY, V. (1981). Psychoneuroendocrine influences on immunocompetence and neoplasia. *Science, 212,* 1100–1109.

RIMM, D. C., & MASTERS, J. C. (1979). *Behavior therapy: Techniques and empirical findings* (2nd ed.). New York: Academic Press.

ROBARCHEK, S. A., & DENTAN, R. (1987). Blood drunkenness and the bloodthirsty Semai: Unmasking another anthropological myth. *American Anthropologist, 89,* 356–363.

ROBBINS, L. N., HELZER, J. E., WEISSMAN, M. M., ORVASCHEL, H., GRUENBERG, E., BURKE, J. D., & REGIER, D. A. (1984). Lifetime prevalence of specific psychiatric disorders in three sites. *Archives of General Psychiatry, 41,* 949–958.

ROBBINS, M., & JENSON, G. (1978). Multiple orgasm in males. *Journal of Sex Research, 14,* 21–26.

ROBERTS, E. QUOTED BY P. JACOBS & S. LANDAU (1971). *To serve the devil* (Vol. 2, p. 71). New York: Vintage Books.

ROBICSEK, F. (1992, Sept./Oct.). Sacred smoke. *Utne Reader,* pp. 90–91.

ROBIN, E. (1986, December). Hysterectomies and blood transfusions. *Stanford Magazine,* pp. 20–21.

ROBINS, C. J. (1988). Attributions and depression: Why is the literature so inconsistent? *Journal of Personality and Social Psychology, 54,* 880–889.

ROBINS, L. N., & REGIER, D. A. (1991). *Psychiatric disorders in America: The epidemiological catchment area.* New York: The Free Press.

ROBINSON, L. A., BERMAN, J. S., & NEIMEYER, R. A. (1990). Psychotherapy for the treatment of depression: A comprehensive review of controlled outcome research. *Psychological Bulletin, 108,* 30–49.

RODGERS, J. (1984, October). Life on the cutting edge. *Psychology Today,* pp. 56–67.

RODGERS, J. E. (1992). *Psychosurgery: Damaging the brain to save the mind.* New York: HarperCollins.

RODGERS, R., & HUNTER, J. E. (1991). Impact of management by objectives on organizational productivity. *Journal of Applied Psychology, 76,* 322–336.

RODIN, J. (1981). Current status of the internal-external hypothesis for obesity: What went wrong? *American Psychologist, 36,* 361–372.

RODIN, J. (1984, December). A sense of control: *Psychology Today* conversation. *Psychology Today,* pp. 38–42.

RODIN, J. (1985). Insulin levels, hunger and food intake: An example of feedback loops in body weight regulation. *Health Psychology, 4,* 1–18.

RODIN J., & SALOVEY, P. (1989). Health psychology. In M. R. Rosenzweig & L. W. Porter (Eds.), *Annual review of psychology* (pp. 533–580). Palo Alto, CA: Annual Reviews Inc.

ROEDIGER, H. L. (1980). The effectiveness of four mnemonics in ordering recall. *Journal of Experimental Psychology: Human Learning and Memory, 6,* 558–567.

ROELEVALD, N., VINGERHOETS, E., ZIELHUIS, G., & GABREELS, F. (1992). Mental retardation associated with parental smoking and alcohol consumption before, during, and after pregnancy. *Preventive Medicine, 21,* 110–119.

ROFF, J. D., & KNIGHT, R. (1981). Family characteristics, childhood symptoms, and adult outcome in schizophrenia. *Journal of Abnormal Psychology, 90,* 510–520.

ROGERS, C. R. (1961). *On becoming a person.* Boston: Houghton Mifflin.

ROGERS, C. R. (1964). Toward a science of the person. In F. W. Wann (Ed.), *Behaviorism and phenomenology: Contrasting bases for modern psychology* (pp. 109–140). Chicago: Phoenix Books, University of Chicago Press.

ROGERS, C. R. (1980). *A way of being.* Boston: Houghton Mifflin.

ROHNER, R. (1986). *The warmth dimension.* Newbury Par, CA: Sage.

ROKEACH, M. P., SMITH P. W., & EVANS, R. E. (1960). Two kinds of prejudice or one? In M. Rokeach (Ed.), *The open and closed mind.* New York: Basic Books.

ROSCH, E. H. (1973). Natural categories. *Cognitive Psychology, 4,* 328–350.

ROSE, R. J., KOSKENVUO, M., KAPRIO, J., SARNA, S., & LANGINVAINIO, H. (1988). Shared genes, shared experiences, and similarity of personality: Data from 14,288 adult Finnish co-twins. *Journal of Personality and Social Psychology, 54,* 161–171.

ROSENBAUM, M. B., & LURIGIO, A. J. (1985, June). Crime stoppers: Paying the price. *Psychology Today,* pp. 56–61.

ROSENFELD, A., & STARK, E. (1987, May). The prime of our lives. *Psychology Today,* pp. 62–72.

ROSENFELD, D., FOLGER, R., & ADELMAN, H. F. (1980). When rewards reflect competence: A qualification of the overjustification effect. *Journal of Personality and Social Psychology, 39,* 368–376.

ROSENFELD, P., GLACALONE, R. A., & TEDESCHI, J. T. (1983). Cognitive dissonance vs. impression management. *Journal of Social Psychology, 120,* 203–211.

ROSENHAN, D. (1973). On being sane in insane places. *Science, 197,* 250–258.

ROSENTHAL, N. E., SACK, D. A., GILLIN, J. C., LEWRY, A. J., GOODWIN, F. K., DAVENPORT, Y., MUELLER, P. S., NEWSOME, D. A., & WEHR, T. A. (1984). Seasonal-affective disorder: A description of the syndrome and preliminary finding with light therapy. *Archives of General Psychiatry, 41,* 72–80.

ROSENTHAL, T. L., & STEFFEK, B. D. (1991). Modeling methods. In F. H. Kanfer & A. P. Goldstein (Eds.), *Helping people change.* Elmsford, NY: Pergamon.

ROSENZWEIG, M. R., BENNET, E. L., & DIAMOND, M. C. (1972). Brain changes in response to experience. *Scientific American, 226,* 22–29.

ROSEWICZ, B. (1983, January 31). Study finds grim link between liquor and crime: Figures far worse than officials expected. *Detroit Free Press,* pp. 1A, 4A.

ROSOW, I. (1963). Adjustment of the normal aged: Concept and measurement. In R. Williams, C. Tibbitts, & W. Donahue (Eds.), *Processing of aging* (Vol. 2). New York: Atherton.

ROSS, B. M., & MILLSOM, C. (1970). Repeated memory of oral prose in Gahana and New York. *International Journal of Psychology, 5,* 173–181.

ROSS, C. A., HEBER, S., NORTON, G. R., & ANDERSON, G. (1989). Differences between multiple personality disorder and other diagnostic groups on structured interview. *Journal of Nervous and Mental Disorders, 177,* 487–491.

ROSS, J., & LAWRENCE, K. A. (1968). Some observations on memory artifice. *Psychonomic Science, 13*(2), 107–108.

ROTH, T., & ZORICK, F. (1983). The use of hypnotics in specific disorders of initiating and maintaining sleep. In M. H. Chase & E. D. Weitzman (Eds.), *Sleep disorders: Basic and clinical research.* New York: Spectrum

ROTHBART, M. K. (1992). Temperament and the development of inhibited approach. *Child Development, 34,* 99–110.

ROTHENBERG, P. S. (1992). *Race, class, and gender in the United States: An integrated study.* New York: St. Martin's Press.

ROTTER, J. B. (1954). *Social learning and clinical psychology.* Englewood Cliffs, NJ: Prentice Hall.

ROTTER, J. B. (1990). Internal versus external control of reinforcement: A case history of a variable. *American Psychologist, 45,* 489–493.

RUBENSTEIN, C. (1983, July). The modern art of courtly love. *Psychology Today,* pp. 40–49.

RUBIN, J., PROVENZANO, F., & LURIA, Z. (1974). The eye of the beholder: Parents' views on sex of newborns. *American Journal of Orthopsychiatry, 44,* 512–519.

RUBIN, L. B. (1992). The empty nest. In J. M. Henslin (Ed.), *Marriage and family in a changing society* (4th ed., pp. 261–270). New York: Free Press.

RUBIN, Z. (1970). Measurement of romantic love. *Journal of Personality and Social Psychology, 16,* 265–273.

RUBLE, D. N., BALABAN, T., & COOPER, J. (1981). Gender constancy and the effect of sex-typed televised commercials. *Child Development, 52,* 667–673.

RUMBAUGH, D. M., ET AL. (1974). Lana (chimpanzee) learning language: A progress report. *Brain & Language, 1*(2), 205–212.

RUSHTON, J. P. (1989). Genetic similarity, human altruism, and group selection. *Behavioral and Brain Sciences, 12,* 503–559.

RUSHTON, J. P. (1991). Is altruism innate? *Psychological Inquiry, 2,* 141–143.

RUSSELL, D. (1984). The prevalence and seriousness of incestuous abuse: Stepfathers versus biological fathers. *Child Abuse and Neglect, 8,* 15–22.

RUSSELL, M. J. (1976). Human olfactory communication. *Nature, 260,* 520–522.

RUZOVSKY, F. A. (1984). *Consent to treatment: A practical guide.* Boston: Little, Brown.

SAAL, F. E., & KNIGHT, P. A. (1988). *Industrial/organizational psychology: Science and practice.* Belmont, CA: Wadsworth.

SABINI, J., & SILVER, M. (1993). Critical thinking and obedience to authority. In J. Chaffee (Ed.), *Critical *thinking (2nd ed.)* (pp. 367–376). Palo Alto, CA: Houghton Mifflin.

SACERDOTE, P. (1978). Teaching self-hypnosis to patients with chronic pain. *Journal of Human Stress, 4,* 18–21.

SACHS, J. S. (1967). Recognition memory for syntactic and semantic aspects of connected discourse. *Perception and Psychophysics, 2,* 437–442.

SACHS, L. B., FEUERSTEIN, M., & VITALE, J. H. (1977). Hypnotic self-regulation of chronic pain. *American Journal of Clinical Hypnosis, 20*(2), 106–113.

SACK, R. L., LEWY, A. J., WHITE, D. M., SINGER, C. M., FIREMAN, M. J., & VANDIVER, R. (1990). Morning vs. evening light treatment for winter depression. *Archives of General Psychiatry, 47,* 343–351.

SACKHEIM, H. A. (1988). Mechanisms of action of electroconvulsive therapy. In A. J. Frances & R. E. Hales (Eds.), *Review of psychiatry* (Vol. 7). Washington, DC: American Psychiatric Press.

SADKER, M., & SADKER, D. (1985, February). Sexism in the school room of the 80's. *Psychology Today,* pp. 54–57.

SAGI, A., & HOFFMAN, M. L. (1976). Empathetic distress in the newborn. *Developmental Psychology, 12,* 175–176.

SALHOLZ, E., WRIGHT, L., & CRANDALL, R. (1992, May 18). A new challenge for Ueberroth. *Newsweek,* p. 45.

SANDAY, P. (1981). The socio-cultural context of rape: A cross-cultural study. *Journal of Social Issues, 37,* 5–27.

SANDERS, M. S., & MCCORMICK, E. J. (1993). *Human factors in engineering and design* (7th ed.). New York: McGraw-Hill.

SANDERS, S. H. (1985). Chronic pain: Conceptualization and epidemiology. *Annals of Behavioral Medicine, 7*(3), 3–5.

SARAFINO, E. P. (1990). *Health Psychology: Biopsychosocial interactions.* New York: Wiley.

SARASON, I. G. (1982). Three lacunae of cognitive therapy. In M. R. Goldfried (Ed.), *Converging themes in psychotherapy* (pp. 353–364). New York: Springer-Verlag.

SARASON, I. G., & SARASON, B. R. (1993). *Abnormal psychology: The problem of maladaptive behavior* (7th ed.). Englewood Cliffs, NJ: Prentice Hall.

SARBIN, T. R. (1988). Self deception in the claims of hypnosis subjects. In J. Lockard & D. Paulhus (Eds.), *Self deception: An adaptive mechanism.* Englewood Cliffs, NJ: Prentice-Hall.

SARBIN, T. R. (1992). Accounting for "dissociative" actions without invoking mentalistic constructs. *Consciousness and Cognition, 1*(1), 54–58.

SATINOFF, E. (1974). Neural integration of thermoregulatory responses. In L. V. Di Cara (Ed.), *Limbic and autonomic nervous system research.* New York: Plenum.

SATINOFF, E., LIRAN, J., & CLAPMAN, R. (1982). Aberrations of circadian body temperature rhythms in rats with medial preoptic lesions. *American Journal of Physiology, 242,* R352–R357.

SATIR, V. (1976). *Conjoint family therapy.* Palo Alto, CA: Science and Behavior Books.

SAVAGE-RUMBAUGH, E. S. (1986). *Ape language: From conditioned response to symbol.* New York: Columbia University Press.

SAVAGE-RUMBAUGH, E. S. (1990). Language acquisition in a nonhuman species: Implications for the innateness debate. *Developmental Psychobiology, 23,* 599–620.

SAVAGE-RUMBAUGH, E. S., RUMBAUGH, D. M., & BOYSEN, S. (1980). Do apes use language? *American Scientist, 68*(1), 49–61.

SAVIN-WILLIAMS, R., & SMALL, S. (1986). The timing of puberty and its relationship to adolescent and par-

ent perceptions of family interactions. *Developmental Psychology, 22,* 322–347.

SAXE, G. B. (1991). *Culture and cognitive development: Studies in mathematical understanding.* Hillsdale, NJ: Erbaum.

SAYETTE, M. A., & MAYNE, T. J. (1990). Survey of current clinical and research trends in clinical psychology. *American Psychologist, 45,* 1263–1266.

SCHACHTER, S. (1959). *The psychology of affiliation.* Stanford, CA: Stanford University Press.

SCHACHTER, S. (1971). *Emotion, obesity, and crime.* New York: Academic Press.

SCHACHTER, S. (1978). Pharmacological and psychological determinants of smoking. *Annals of International Medicine, 88,* 104–114.

SCHACHTER, S., & GROSS, L. P. (1968). Manipulated time and eating behavior. *Journal of Personality and Social Psychology, 10,* 98–106.

SCHACHTER, S., & SINGER, J. E. (1962). Cognitive, social, and physiological determinants of emotional state. *Psychological Review, 69,* 379–399.

SCHAEFER, E. S. (1960, August). *Converging conceptual models for maternal behavior and for child behavior.* Paper presented at the Conference on Research on Parental Attitudes and Child Behavior, Washington University, St. Louis.

SCHAIE, K. W. (1984). Midlife influences upon intellectual functioning in old age. *International Journal of Behavioral Development, 7,* 463–478.

SCHAIE, K. W. (1988). Ageism in psychological research. *American Psychologist, 43,* 179–183.

SCHAIE, K. W., & GEIWITZ, J. (1982). *Adult development and aging.* Boston: Little, Brown.

SCHLEIFER, S., KELLER, S., MCKEGNEY, F., & STEIN, M. (1980). *Bereavement and lymphocyte function.* Paper presented at the annual meeting of the American Psychiatric Association, Montreal.

SCHLOSSBERG, N. K. (1987, May). Taking the mystery out of change. *Psychology Today,* pp. 74–75.

SCHMITT, E. (1990, February 9). Two in three military women report harassment. *New York Times,* pp. 14, 20.

SCHNEIDER, B. H., & BYRNE, B. M. (1987). Individualizing social skills training for behavior-disordered children. *Journal of Consulting and Clinical Psychology, 55,* 444–445.

SCHOEN, E. J. (1990). The status of circumcision of newborns. *New England Journal of Medicine, 322,* 1308–1312.

SCHOEN, E. J., ANDERSON, G., BOHON, C. ET AL. (1989). Report of the task force on circumcision. *Pediatrics, 84,* 388–391.

SCHOEN, E. J., & FISCHELL, A. (1991). Pain in neonatal circumcision. *Clinical Pediatrics, 30,* 429–432.

SCHOENLEIN, R. W., PETEANU, L. A., MATHIES, R. A., & SHANK, C. V. (1991). The first step in vision: Femtosecond isomerization of rhodopsin. *Science, 254,* 412–415.

SCHOFIELD, W. (1964). *Psychotherapy: The purchase of friendship.* Englewood Cliffs, NJ: Prentice Hall.

SCHORR, L. B., & SCHORR, D. (1990). *Within our reach: Breaking the cycle of disadvantage and despair.* New York: Doubleday.

SCHREIBER, F. R. (1973). *Sybil.* New York: Warner Books.

SCHULTZ, D. P. (1969). *A history of modern psychology.* New York: Academic Press.

SCHWARTZ, B. (1982). *Diets don't work.* Houston, TX: Breakthru Publishing.

SCHWARTZ, D. H., MCCLANE, S., HERNANDEZ, L., & HOEBEL, B. (1989). Feeding increases extracellular serotonin in the lateral hypothalamus of the rat as measured by microdialysis. *Brain Research, 479,* 349–354.

SCHWARTZ, S. H., & INBAR-SABAN, N. (1988). Value self-confrontation as a method to aid in weight loss. *Journal of Personality and Social Psychology, 54,* 396–404.

SCHWEBEL, A. I. (1982). Radio psychologists: A community psychology/psycho-educational mode. *Journal of Community Psychology, 10*(2), 180–184.

SCHWEIGER, U. (1991). Menstrual function and luteal-phase deficiency in relation to weight changes and dieting. *Clinical Obstetrics and Gynecology, 34,* 191–197.

SCOTT, K. G., & CARRAN, D. T. (1987). The epidemiology and prevention of mental retardation. *American Psychologist, 42,* 801–804.

SCOVILLE, W. B., & MILNER, B. (1957). Loss of recent memory after bilateral hippocampal lesions. *Journal of Neurology, Neurosurgery, and Psychiatry, 20,* 11–21.

SCRIBNER, S. (1977). Modes of thinking and ways of speaking: Culture and logic reconsidered. In P. N. Johnson-Laird & P. C. Wason (Eds.), *Thinking: Readings in cognitive science* (pp. 324–339). New York: Cambridge University Press.

SEAMON, G., & GAZZANIGA, M. S. (1973). Coding strategies and cerebral laterality effects. *Cognitive Psychology, 5,* 249–256.

SEECH, Z. (1987). *Logic in everyday life: Practical reasoning skills.* Belmont, CA: Wadsworth.

SEGAL, M. W. (1974). Alphabet and attraction: An unobtrusive measure of the effect of propinquity in a field setting. *Journal of Personality and Social Psychology, 30,* 654–657.

SEGALL, M. H., CAMPBELL, D. T., & HERSKOVITS, M. J. (1966). *The influence of culture on visual perception.* New York: Bobbs-Merrill.

SEGALL, M. H., DASEN, P. R., BERRY, J. W., & PORTINGA, Y. H. (1990). *Human behavior in global perspective: An introduction to cross-cultural psychology.* Elmsford, NY: Pergamon Press.

SEGHAL, S., EWING, C., WARING, P., FINDLAY, R., BEAN, X., & TAEUSCH, H. W. (1993). Morbidity of low-birthweight infants with intrauterine cocaine exposure. *Journal of the National Medical Association, 85,* 20–24.

SELIGMAN, M. E. P. (1991). *Learned optimism.* New York: Knopf.

SELKOE, D. J. (1991). Amyloid protein and Alzheimer's disease. *Scientific American, 265*(5), 68–78.

SELKOE, D. J. (1992). Aging brain, aging mind. *Scientific American, 267*(3), 134–143.

SELYE, H. (1956). *The stress of life.* New York: McGraw-Hill.

SELYE, H. (1974). *Stress without distress.* New York: Harper & Row.

SERPELL, R. (1976). *Culture's influence on behavior.* London: Methuen.

Sexual disorders—Part II. (1990). *Harvard Medical School Mental Health Letter, 6*(7), 1–4.

SHAKLEE, B. D. (1992). Identification of young gifted students. *Journal for the Education of the Gifted, 15*(2), 134–144.

SHANAB, M. E., & YAHYA, K. A. (1977). A behavioral study of obedience in children. *Journal of Personality and Social Psychology, 35*(7), 530–536.

SHAPIRO, J. P. (1979). "Fear of success" imagery as a reaction to sex-role inappropriate behavior. *Journal of Personality Assessment, 43,* 33–38.

SHATZ, C. J. (1992). The developing brain. *Scientific American, 267*(3), 60–67.

SHAVIT, H., & SHOUVAL, R. (1980). Self-esteem and cognitive consistency on self-other evaluations. *Journal of Experimental Social Psychology, 16,* 417–425.

SHAW, M. E. (1981). *Group dynamics: The psychology*

of small group behavior (3rd ed.). New York: McGraw-Hill.

SHEA, J. D. (1981). Changes in interpersonal distances and categories of play behavior in the early weeks of preschool. *Developmental Psychology, 17,* 417–425.

SHEEHY, G. (1976). *Passages: Predictable crises of adult life.* New York: Dutton.

SHELDON, W. H., & STEVENS, S. S. (1942). *Varieties of human temperament: A psychology of constitutional differences.* New York: Harper.

SHEPARD, R. N. (1967). Recognition memory for words, sentences and pictures. *Journal of Verbal Learning and Verbal Behavior, 6,* 156–163.

SHEPARD, R. N., & CHIPMAN, S. (1970). Second-order isomorphism of internal representation: Shapes of states. *Cognitive Psychology, 1,* 1–17.

SHEPARD, R. N., & METZLER, J. (1971). Mental rotation of three-dimensional objects. *Science, 171,* 701–703.

SHEPPARD, R. Z. (1988, April 18). A piece of the true couch. *Time,* pp. 85–86.

SHERIDAN, M. (1975). Talk time for hospitalized children. *Social Work, 20,* 40–44.

SHERIF, M. (1966). *In common predicament: Social psychology of intergroup conflict and cooperation.* Boston: Houghton Mifflin.

SHERIF, M., HARVEY, L. J., WHITE, B. J., HOOD, W. R., & SHERIF, C. W. (1988). *The Robber's Cave experiment: Intergroup conflict and cooperation.* Middletown, CT: Wesleyan University Press.

SHNEIDMAN, E. S. (1969). Fifty-eight years. In E. S. Shneidman (Ed.), *On the nature of suicide* (pp. 1–30). San Francisco: Jossey-Bass.

SHNEIDMAN, E. S. (1987, March). At the point of no return. *Psychology Today,* pp. 58–63.

SHODELL, M. (1984). The clouded mind. *Science, 84,* 68–72.

SHOFIELD, J. (1982). *Black and white in school.* New York: Praeger.

SHOTLAND, R. L., & STEBBINS, C. A. (1980). Bystander response to rape: Can a victim attract help? *Journal of Applied Social Psychology, 10,* 510–527.

SIEGEL, A., & BRUTUS, M. (1990). Neural substrates of aggression and range in the cat. *Progress in Psychobiology and Physiological Psychology, 14,* 135–143.

SIEGEL, D. J., & PIOTROWSKI, R. J. (1985). Reliability of K-ABC subtest composites. *Journal of Psychoeducational Assessment, 3*(1), 73–76.

SIEGEL, D. L. (1990). Women's reproductive changes: A marker not a turning point. *Generations, 14*(3), 31–32.

SIEGEL, R. K. (1989). *Life in pursuit of artificial paradise.* New York: Dutton.

SIEGELMAN, M. (1987). Empirical input. In L. Diamant (Ed.), *Male and female homosexuality: Psychological approaches* (pp. 37–48). Washington, DC: Hemisphere.

SIEGLER, R. S. (1983). Information processing approaches to development. In W. Kessen (Ed.), *Handbook of child psychology: Vol. 1. History, theory and methods.* New York: Wiley.

SIEGLER, R. S. (1991). *Children's thinking* (2nd ed.). Englewood Cliffs, NJ: Prentice Hall.

SILVA, A. J., PAYLOR, R., WEHNER, J. M., & TONEGWA, S. (1992). Impaired spatial learning in a-calcium-calmodulin kinase II mutant mice. *Science, 257,* 206–211.

SILVA, A. J., STEVENS, C. F., TONEGAWA, S., & WANG, Y. (1992). Deficient hippocampal long-term potentiation in a-calcium-calmodulin kinase II mutant mice. *Science, 257,* 201–206.

SILVERMAN, L. H. (1980). A comprehensive report of studies using the subliminal psychodynamic activation method. *Psychological Research Bulletin, Lund University, 20*(3).

SILVERMAN, L. H., & LACHMANN, F. M. (1985). The therapeutic properties of unconscious oneness fantasies: Evidence and treatment implications. *Contemporary Psychoanalysis, 21*(1), 91–115.

SIMKIN, J. S., & YONTEF, G. M. (1984). Gestalt therapy. In R. Corsini (Ed.), *Current psychotherapies* (3rd ed.). Itasca, IL: Peacock.

SIMMONS, D. D. (1987). Self-reports of eating behavior, goals, imagery, and health status: Principal components and sex differences. *Journal of Psychology, 121,* 57–60.

SIMON, C. W., & EMMONS, W. H. (1956). Responses to material presented during various stages of sleep. *Journal of Experimental Psychology, 51,* 89–97.

SIMON, R., & HUGHES, C. C. (Eds.). (1985). *The culture-bound syndromes.* Dordrecht: Reidel.

SIMPSON, J. A. (1990). Influence of attachment styles on romantic relationships. *Journal of Personality and Social Psychology, 59,* 971–980.

SINGER, B., & BENASSI, V. A. (1981). Occult beliefs. *American Scientist, 69*(1), 49–55.

SINGER, J. L., SINGER, D. G., & RAPACZYNSKI, W. S. (1984). Family patterns and television viewing as predictors of children's beliefs and aggression. *Journal of Communication, 34*(2), 73–89.

SINOWAY, C. G., RAUPP, C. D., & NEWMAN, J. (1985, August). *Binge eating and bulimia: Comparing incidence and characteristics across universities.* Poster presented at the meeting of the American Psychological Association, Los Angles.

SKEELS, H. M. (1966). Adult status of children with contrasting early life experiences: A follow-up study. *Monographs of the Society for Research in Child Development, 31* (Serial No. 105).

SKEELS, H. M., & DYE, H. B. (1939). A study of the effects of differential stimulation on mentally retarded children. *Proceedings of the American Association for Mental Deficiency, 44,* 114–136.

SKINNER, B. F. (1948). Superstition in the pigeon. *Journal of Experimental Psychology, 38,* 168–172.

SKINNER, B. F. (1971). *Beyond freedom and dignity.* New York: Bantam.

SKINNER, B. F. (1979). *The shaping of a behaviorist.* New York: Knopf.

SKINNER, B. F. (1981). Selection by consequences. *Science, 213,* 501–504.

SKINNER, B. F. (1985). *What is wrong with daily life in the Western World?* Paper presented at the annual convention of the American Psychological Association, Los Angles.

SKINNER, B. F. (1990). Can psychology be a science of mind? *American Psychologist, 45,* 1206–1210.

SMITH, A. (1982). *Powers of mind.* New York: Summit.

SMITH, D. (1982). Trends in counseling and psychotherapy. *American Psychologist, 37*(3), 802–809.

SMITH, D. E. P., OLSON, M., BARGER, F., & MCCONNELL, J. V. (1981). The effects of improved auditory feedback on the verbalizations of an autistic child. *Journal of Autism and Developmental Disorders, 11*(4), 449–454.

SMITH, E. M., NORTH, C. S., MCCOOL, R. E., & SHEA, J. M. (1990). Acute postdisaster psychiatric disorders: Identification of persons at risk. *American Journal of Psychiatry, 147,* 202–206.

SMITH, J. C., ELLENBERGER, H. H., BALLANYI, K., RICHTER, D. W., & FELDMAN, J. L. (1991). Pre-Botzinger complex: A brainstem region that may generate respiratory rhythm in mammals. *Science, 254,* 726–729.

SMITH, M. L., & GLASS, G. V. (1977). Meta-analysis of psychotherapy outcome studies. *American Psychologist, 32,* 752–760.

SMITH, S. M., & SHAFFER, D. R. (1991). Celebrity and cajolery: Rapid speech may promote or inhibit persuasion through its impact on message elaboration. *Personality and Social Psychology Bulletin, 17,* 663–669.

SNAREY, J. R. (1985). Cross-cultural universality of social-moral development: A critical review of Kohlbergian research. *Psychological Bulletin, 97,* 202–233.

SNAREY, J. R. (1987, June). A question of morality. *Psychology Today,* pp. 6–7.

SNAREY, J., & KELJO, K. (1991). In a gemeinschaft voice: The cross-cultural expansion of moral development theory. In W. M. Kurtines, & J. Gewirtz (Eds.), *Moral behavior and development* (Vol. 1). Hillsdale, NJ: Erlbaum.

SNYDER, C. R. (1988, August). *Reality negotiation: From excuses to hope.* Symposium conducted at the annual meeting of the American Psychological Association, Atlanta.

SNYDER, M., TANKE, E. D., & BERSCHEID, E. (1977). Social perception and interpersonal behavior: On the self-fulfilling nature of social stereotypes. *Journal of Personality and Social Psychology, 35,* 656–666.

SNYDER, S. H. (1980). Brain peptides as neurotransmitters. *Science, 209*(4460), 976–983.

SNYDER, S. H. (1984). Cholinergic mechanisms in affective disorders. *New England Journal of Medicine, 311*(4), 254–255.

SOKOLOV, E. N. (1977). Brain functions: Neuronal mechanisms of learning and memory. *Annual Review of Psychology, 20,* 85–112.

SOLOMON, G. F., AMKRAUT, A. A., & KASPER, P. (1974). Immunity, emotions, and stress: With special reference to the mechanisms of stress effects on the immune system. *Psychotherapy & Psychosomatics, 23,* 209–217.

SOLOMON, R. L. (1980). The opponent-process theory of acquired motivation: The costs of pleasure and the benefits of pain. *American Psychologist, 35,* 691–712.

SOLOMON, R. L. (1982). The opponent process in acquired motivation. In D. W. Pfaff (Ed.), *The physiological mechanisms of motivation.* New York: Springer-Verlag.

SOMMER, R. (1969). *Personal space.* Englewood Cliffs, NJ: Prentice Hall.

SOMMERS, D., & ECK, A. (1977). Occupational mobility in the American labor force. *Monthly Labor Review, 100*(1), 3–19.

SOUCHEK, A. W. (1986). A comparison of dynamic stereoscopic acuities in both the primary and secondary positions of gaze. In preparation.

SAPANOS, N. P., BURGESS, C. A., CROSS, P. A., & MACLEOD, G. (1992). Hypnosis, reporting bias, and suggested negative hallucinations. *Journal of Abnormal Psychology, 101,* 192–199.

SPANOS, N. P., & CHAVES, J. F. (1988). *Hypnosis: The cognitive-behavioral perspective.* New York: Prometheus.

SPANOS, N. P., WEEKES, J. R., & BERTRAND, L. D. (1985). Multiple personalities: A social psychological perspective. *Journal of Abnormal Psychology, 94,* 362–376.

SPEARMAN, C. (1972). *The abilities of man.* New York: Macmillan.

SPECTOR, J. P., & CAREY, M. P. (1990). Incidence and prevalence of the sexual dysfunctions: A critical review of the empirical literature. *Archives of Sexual Behavior, 19,* 389–408.

SPELKE, E. S. (1988). Where perceiving ends and thinking begins: The apprehension of objects in infance. In A. Yonas (Ed.), *Minnesota symposia on child psychology: Vol. 20. Perceptual development in infancy.* Hillsdale, NJ: Erlbaum.

SPENCE, J. T. (1984). Masculinity, femininity, and gender-related traits: A conceptual analysis and critique of current research. In B. A. Maker & W. B. Maker (Eds.), *Progress in experimental personality research: Normal personality processes* (Vol. 13). New York: Academic Press.

SPENCE, J. T. (1991). Do the BSRI and PAQ measure the same or different concepts? *Psychology of Women Quarterly, 15,* 141–165.

SPERLING, G. (1960). The information available in brief visual presentations. *Psychological Monographs, 74* (Whole No. 498).

SPERRY, R. W. (1968). Hemisphere deconnection and unity in conscious awareness. *American Psychologist, 23,* 723–733.

SPIEGEL, D. (1985, Winter). Trance, trauma, and testimony. *Stanford Magazine,* pp. 4–6.

SPIELMAN, A., & HERRERA, C. (1991). Sleep disorders. In S. A. Ellman & J. S. Antrobus (Eds.), *The mind in sleep: Psychology and psychophysiology* (2nd ed., pp. 25–80). New York: Wiley.

SPINETTA, J. J., ELLIOTT, E. S., HENNESSEY, J. S., KNAPP, V. S., SHEPOSH, J. P., SPARTA, S. N., & SPRIGLE, R. P. (1982). The pediatric psychologist's role in catastrophic illness: Research and clinical issues. In J. M. Tuma (Ed.), *Handbook for the practice of pediatric psychology* (pp. 165–277). New York: Wiley-Interscience.

SPITZ, R. A., & WOLF, K. M. (1946). The smiling response: A contribution to the ontogenesis of social relations. *Genetic Psychology Monographs, 34,* 57–123.

SPITZER, M. W., & SEMPLE, M. N. (1991). Intraural phase coding in auditory midbrain: Influence of dynamic stimulus features. *Science, 254,* 721–724.

SPITZER, R. L. (1988). On pseudo-science in science, logic in remission and psychiatric diagnoses. In J. Rubinstein & B. Slife (Eds.), *Taking sides: Clashing views on controversial psychological issues* (5th ed., pp. 235–248). Guilford, CT: Dushkin.

SPIVEY, C. B., & PRENTICE-DUNN, S. (1990). Assessing the directionality of deindividuated behavior: Effects of deindividuation, modeling, and private self-consciousness on aggressiveness and prosocial responses. *Basic and Applied Social Psychology, 11,* 387–403.

SPRECHER, S. (1986). The relation between inequity and emotions in close relationships. *Social Psychology Quarterly, 49,* 309–321.

SPRINGER, S. P., & DEUTSCH, G. (1981). *Left brain, right brain.* San Francisco: Freeman.

SQUIRE, L. R., & ZOLA-MORGAN, S. (1991). The medial temporal lobe memory system. *Science, 253,* 1380–1386.

STAATS, A. W., & STAATS, C. K. (1958). Attitudes established by classical conditioning. *Journal of Experimental Psychology, 57,* 37–40.

STABENAU, J. R., & POLLIN, W. (1969). The pathogenesis of schizophrenia: 11 contributions from the NIMH study of 16 pairs of monozygotic twins discordant for schizophrenia. In D. V. Sanker (Ed.), *Schizophrenia: Current concepts and research* (pp. 336–351). Hicksville, NY: PJD Publications.

STANDING, L. (1973). Learning 10,000 pictures. *Quarterly Journal of Experimental Psychology, 25,* 207–222.

STANDING, L., CONEZIO, J., & HABER, R. N. (1970). Perception and memory for pictures: Single-trial learning of 2500 visual stimuli. *Psychonomic Science, 19,* 73–74.

STANLEY, B. G., SCHWARTZ, D. H., HERNANDEQ, L., LEI-

BOWITZ, S. F., & HOEBEL, B. G. (1989). Patterns of extracellular 5-hydroxyindoleacetic acid (5-HIAA) in the paraventricular hypothalamus (PVN): Relation to circadian rhythm and deprivation-induced eating behavior. *Pharmacology, Biochemistry, and Behavior, 33,* 257–260.

STARK, E. (1984a, February). Hypnosis on trial. *Psychology Today,* pp. 34–36.

STARK, E. (1984b, October). To sleep, perchance to dream. *Psychology Today,* p. 16.

STARKER, S. (1982). *Fantastic thought: All about dreams: daydreams, and hypnosis.* Englewood Cliffs, NJ: Prentice Hall.

Statistical abstract of the United States. (1990). Worldwide homicide rates. *United States Census Bureau.* Washington, DC: U.S. Government Printing Office.

Statistical abstract of the United States. (1992). Mean income by gender and race. *United States Census Bureau.* Washington, DC: U.S. Government Printing Office.

STEHLING, M. K., TURNER, R., & MANSFIELD, P. (1991). Echo-planar imaging: Magnetic resonance imaging in a fraction of a second. *Science, 254,* 43–50.

STEIN, A. P. (1991). The Chlamydia epidemic: Teenagers at risk. *Medical Aspects of Human Sexuality, 25,* 26–33.

STEIN, M. (1983). *Psychosocial perspectives on aging and the immune response.* Paper presented at Academy of Behavioral Medicine Research, Reston, VA.

STEINHART, P. (1986, March). Personal boundaries. *Audubon,* pp. 8–11.

STENGEL, R. (1987, September 14). At issue: Freedom for the irrational. *Time,* p. 88.

STEPHAN, W., BERSCHEID, E., & WALSTER, E. (1971). Sexual arousal and heterosexual perception. *Journal of Personality and Social Psychology, 20*(1), 93–101.

STERN, M. (1980). *Sex in USSR.* New York: Times Books.

STERNBACH, R. A. (1974). *Pain patients: Traits and treatment.* New York: Academic Press.

STERNBACH, R. A. (1978). Treatment of the chronic pain patient. *Journal of Human Stress, 4*(3), 11–15.

STERNBERG, R. J. (1985). *Beyond IQ: A triarchic theory of human intelligence.* New York: Cambridge University Press.

STEVENS-SIMON, C., & WHITE, M. (1991). Adolescent pregnancy. *Pediatric Annals, 20,* 322–331.

STIFTER, C. A., & FOX, N. A. (1990). Infant reactivity: Physiological correlates of newborn and 5-month temperament. *Developmental Psychology, 26,* 582–588.

STILES, W. B., SHAPIRO, D. A., & ELLIOTT, R. (1986, February). "Are all psychotherapies equivalent?" *American Psychologist, 41*(2), 165–180.

STINE, G. J. (1993). *Acquired immune deficiency syndrome: Biological, medical, social, and legal issues.* Englewood Cliffs, NJ: Prentice Hall.

STINNETT, N. (1992). Strong families. In J. M. Henslin (Ed.), *Marriage and family in a changing society* (4h ed., pp. 496–507). New York: Free Press.

STODDARD, S. (1978). *The hospice movement: A better way of caring for the dying.* New York: Vintage Books.

STOLER, P. (1984, October 1). Ali fights a new round. *Time,* p. 60.

STOLLER, R. J. (1969). Parental influences in male transsexualism. In R. Green & J. Money (Eds.), *Transsexualism and sex reassignment.* Baltimore: The Johns Hopkins University Press.

STONE, J. (1988, August). Sex and the single gorilla. *Discover,* pp. 78–81.

STONE, J. L., & CHURCH, J. (1973). *Childhood and ado-*

lescence: A psychology of the growing person (3rd ed.). New York: Random House.

STONE, N., FROMME, M., & KAGEN, D. (1985). *Cocaine: Seduction and solution.* New York: Pinnacle.

STONER, J. A. (1961). *A comparison of individual and group decisions involving risk.* Unpublished master's thesis, School of Industrial Management, MIT, Cambridge, MA.

STRACK, F., MARTIN, L. L., & STEPPER, S. (1988). Inhibiting and facilitating conditions of the human smile: A nonobstrusive test of the facial feedback hypothesis. *Journal of Personality and Social Psychology, 54,* 768–777.

STRASBURGER, L. H. (1992). Should psychotherapist-patient sex be a crime? *The Harvard Mental Health Letter, 8*(9), 8.

STRASBURGER, L. H. (1993). Should psychotherapist-patient sex be a crime? *Harvard Mental Health Letter, 8*(9), 8.

STRATHMAN, A. J., PETTY, R. E., GLEICHER, F. H., & BOZZOLO, A. M. (1988, August). *Interpersonal judgments under scrutiny: The effects of self-monitoring.* Paper presented at the annual meeting of the American Psychological Association, Atlanta.

STRATTON, G. (1896). Some preliminary experiments on vision without inversion of the retinal image. *Psychological Review, 3,* 611–617.

STRAUS, M. A., GELLES, R. J., & STEINMETZ, S. K. (1980). *Behind closed doors: Violence in the American family.* Garden City, NY: Anchor Press.

STREISSGUTH, A. P., AASE, J. M., CLARREN, S. K., RANDELS, S. P., LADUE, R. A., & SMITH, D. F. (1991). Fetal alcoholism syndrome in adolescents and adults. *Journal of the American Medical Association, 265,* 1961–1967.

STREISSGUTH, A. P., MARTIN, D. C., BARR, H. M., SANDMAN, B. M., KIRCHNER, G. L., & DARBY, B. L. (1984). Intrauterine alcohol and nicotine exposure: Attention and reaction time in 4-year-old children. *Developmental Psychology, 20,* 533–542.

STRICKLAND, B. R. (1978). Internal–external expectancies and health-related behaviors. *Journal of Counsulting and Clinical Psychology, 46,* 1192–1211.

STRICKLAND, B. R. (1992). Women and depression. *Current Directions in Psychological Science, 1*(4), 132–135.

STRUCKMAN, T., & JOHNSON, C. (1988). Forced sex on dates: It happens to men too. *Journal of Sex Research, 24,* 234–240.

STROMEYER, C. F. (1970, November). Eidetikers. *Psychology Today,* pp. 77–80.

STROOP, J. R. (1935). Studies of interference in serial verbal reactions. *Journal of Experimental Psychology, 18,* 643–662.

SUEDFELD, P. (1975). The benefits of boredom: Sensory deprivation reconsidered. *American Scientist, 63*(1), 60–69.

SUEDFELD, P. (1982). Aloneness as a healing experience. In L. A. Peplau & D. Perlman (Eds.), *Loneliness: A sourcebook of current theory, research, and therapy.* New York: Wiley.

SUEDFELD, P., & BAKER-BROWN, G. (1986). Restricted environmental stimulation therapy and aversion conditioning in smoking cessation: Active and placebo effects. *Behavior Research and Therapy, 24,* 421–428.

SUEDFELD, P., & BEST, J. A. Satiation and sensory deprivation combined in smoking therapy: Some case studies and unexpected side-effects. *International Journal of the Addictions, 12,* 337–359.

SUEDFELD, P., RANK, D., & BORRIE, R. (1976). Frequency of exposure and evaluation of candidates and campaign speeches. *Journal of Applied Social Psychology, 5,* 118–126.

SUGARMAN, S. (1987). *Piaget's construction of the child's reality.* Cambridge, England? Cambridge University Press.

SUINN, R. M. (1987). Abnormal psychology: New challenges and basic foundations. In I. Cohen (Ed.), *G. Stanley Hall lecture series* (pp. 91–136). Washington, DC: American Psychological Association.

SUOMI, S., & HARLOW, H. (1972). Social rehabilitation of isolate-reared monkeys. *Developmental Psychology, 6*(3), 487–496.

SUOMI, S., & HARLOW, H. (1978). Early experience and social development in Rhesus monkeys. In M. Lamb (Ed.), *Social and personality development.* New York: Holt, Rinehard and Winston.

SUPER, C. M. (1981). Cross-cultural research on infancy. In H. C. Triandis & A. Heron (Eds.), *Handbook of cross-cultural psychology: Vol. 4. Developmental psychology.* Boston: Allyn & Bacon.

SUPER, C., & HARKNESS, S. (1986). The developmental niche: A conceptualization at the interface of society and the individual. *International Journal of Behavioral Development, 9*(4), 545–570.

SUZDAK, P. D., GLOWA, J. R., CRAWLEY, J. N., SCHWARTZ, R. D., SKOLNICK, P., & PAUL, S. M. (1986). A selective imidazobenzodiazepine antagonist of ethanol in the rat. *Science, 234,* 1243–1247.

SWAP, W. C. (1977). Interpersonal attraction and repeated exposure to rewarders and punishers. *Personality and Social Psychology Bulletin, 3,* 248–251.

SZAPOCNIK, J., & KURTINES, W. M. (1993). Family psychotherapy and cultural diversity: Opportunities for theory, research, and applications. *American Psychologist, 48*(4), 400–407.

SZASZ, T. S. (1960). The myth of mental illness. *American Psychologist, 15,* 113–118.

SZASZ, T. S. (1987). *Insanity: The idea and its consequences.* New York: Wiley.

TANABE, T., INO, M., & TAKAGI, S. F. (1975). Discrimination of odors in olfactory bulb, pyriform-amygdaloid areas, and orbitofrontal cortex of the monkey. *Journal of Neurophysiology, 38,* 1284–1296.

TANNER, J. M. (1982). *Growth at adolescence* (2nd ed.), Oxford, CT: Scientific Publications.

TART, C. T. (1975). *States of consciousness.* New York: Dutton.

TAUSIG, M. (1982). Measuring life events. *Journal of Health and Social Behavior, 23,* 52–64.

TAVRIS, C. (1989). *Anger: The misunderstood emotion* (2nd ed.). New York: Simon & Schuster.

TAVRIS, C. (1992). *The mismeasure of woman.* New York: Simon & Schuster.

TAVRIS, C, & OFIR, C. (1984). *The longest war: Sex differences in perspective.* San Diego: Harcourt Brace Jovanovich.

TAYLOR, D. T., BERRY, P. C., & BLOCK, C. H. (1958). Does group participation when brainstorming facilitate or inhibit creative thinking? *Administrator's Science Quarterly, 3,* 23–47.

TAYLOR, S. E., COLLINS, R., SKOKAN, L., & ASPINWALL, L. (1988, August). *Illusions, reality and adjustment in coping with victimizing events.* Paper presented at the annual meeting of the American Psychological Association, Atlanta.

TEDRICK, D. (1985, May 25). Bank of sperm from "intelligent" men produces first baby. *Hartford Courant,* p. C-16.

TEEVAN, R. C., & MCGHEE, P. E. (1972). Childhood development of fear of failure motivation. *Journal of Personality and Social Psychology, 21,* 345–348.

TEGHTSOONIAN, M., & BECKWITH, J. B. (1976). Children's size judgments when size and distance vary: Is there a developmental trend to overconstancy? *Journal of Experimental Child Psychology, 22*(2), 23–39.

TEICHER, M. H., GLOD, C., & COLE, J. O. (1990). Emergence of intense suicidal preoccupation during fluoxetine treatment. *American Journal of Psychiatry, 147,* 207–210.

TELLEGEN, A, LYKKEN, D. T., BOUCHARD, T. J., WILCOX, K. J., SEGAL, N. L., & RICH, S. (1988). Personality similarity in twins reared apart and together. *Journal of Personality and Social Psychology, 54,* 1031–1039.

TELLER, D. Y., PEEPLES, D. R., & SEKEL, M. (1978). Discrimination of chromatic from white light by two-month-old human infants. *Vision research, 18*(1), 41–48.

TENNOV, D. (1979). *Love and limerence.* New York: Stein & Day.

TERMAN, L. M. (1916). *The measurement of intelligence.* Boston: Houghton Mifflin.

TERMAN, L. M. (1954). Scientists and nonscientists in a group of 800 gifted men. *Psychological Monographs, 68*(7), 1–44.

TERMAN, M., & LINK, M. (1989, January/February). Fighting the winter blues with bright light. *Psychology Today,* pp. 18–21.

TERRANCE, H. S. (1979, November). How Nim Chimpsky changed my mind. *Psychology Today,* pp. 65–76.

TESCH, S. A., & GENNELO, K. (1985, August). *Age, intimacy, and affect in young men and women.* Paper presented at the annual meeting of the American Psychological Association, Los Angeles.

TESSER, A., & SHAFFER, D. R. (1990). Attitudes and attitude change. *Annual Review of Psychology, 41,* 479–523.

THASE, M. S., FRANK, E., & KUPFER, D. J. (1985). Biological processes in major depression. In E. E. Beckham & W. R. Leber (Eds.), *Handbook of depression: Treatment, assessment, and research* (pp. 816–913). Homewood, IL: Dorsey Press.

THATCHER, R. W., WALKER, R. A., & GUIDICE, S. (1987). Human cerebral hemispheres develop at different rates and ages. *Science, 236,* 110–113.

THIEMAN, T. J., & CLARY, E. G. (1988, August). *Teaching ethically informed decision-making by experiment.* Paper presented at the annual meeting of the American Psychological Association, Atlanta.

THIGPEN, C. H., & CLECKLEY, H. M. (1984). On the incidence of multiple personality disorder: A brief communication. *International Journal of Clinical and Experimental Hypnosis, 32,* 63–66.

THOMA, S. J. (1986). Estimating gender differences in the comprehension and preference of moral issues. *Developmental Review, 6,* 165–180.

THOMAS, A., & CHESS, S. (1977). *Temperament and development.* New York: Brunner/Mazel.

THOMAS, A., & CHESS, S. (1987). Roundtable: What is temperament: Four approaches. *Child Development, 58,* 505–529.

THOMAS, A., & CHESS, S. (1991). Temperament in adolescence and its functional significance. In R. M. Lerner, A. C. Petersen, & J. Brooks-Gunn (Eds.), *Encyclopedia of adolescence* (Vol. 2). New York: Garland.

THOMPSON, D. (1988, September 19). The environment: Cleaning up the mess. *Time,* pp. 22–24.

THOMPSON, J. K., JARVIE, G. J., LAHEY, B. B., & CURETON, K. J. (1982). Exercise and obesity: Etiology, physiology, and intervention. *Psychological Bulletin, 91,* 55–79.

THOMPSON, J. W., & BLAINE, J. D. (1987). Use of ECT in the U. S. in 1975 and 1980. *American Journal of Psychiatry, 144,* 557–562.

THOMPSON, L. A., DETTERMAN, D. K., & PLOMIN, R. (1991). Associations between cognitive abilities and scholastic achievement: Genetic overlap but environmental differences. *Psychological Science, 2,* 158–165.

THOMPSON, R. A. (1991). Construction and reconstruction of early attachments: Taking perspective on attachment theory and research. In D. P. Keating & H. G. Rosen (Eds.), *Constructivist perspectives on atypical development.* Hillsdale, NJ: Erlbaum.

THORNDIKE, E. L. (1898). Animal intelligence. *Psychological Review Monograph, 2*(8).

THORNDIKE, E. L. (1901). The mental life of the monkeys. *Psychological Review Monograph, 3*(15).

THORNDIKE, E. L. (1931). *Human learning.* New York: Century.

THURSTONE, L. L. (1938). *Primary mental abilities.* Chicago: University of Chicago Press.

TIFFANY, S. T., MARFIN, E. M., & BAKER, T. B. (1986). Treatments for cigarette smoking: An evaluation of the contributions of aversion and counseling procedures. *Behavior Research & Therapy, 24,* 437–452.

TOBIN, J., WU, D., & DAVIDSON, D. (1989). *Preschool in three cultures: Japan, China, and the United States.* New Haven: Yale University Press.

TOCH H. (1980). *Violent men.* Cambridge, MA: Schenkman.

TODD, T. C., & STANTON, M. D. (1983). Research on marital and family therapy: Answers, issues, and recommendations for the future. In B. B. Wolman & G. Stricker (Eds.), *Handbook of marital and family therapy* (pp. 91–115), New York: Plenum.

TOLMAN, E. C., & HONZIK, C. H. (1930). Introduction and removal of reward, and maze performance in rats. *University of California Publications in Psychology, 4,* 257–275.

TOMKINS, S. S. (1962). *Affect, imagery, consciousness, the positive effects* (Vol. 1). New York: Springer.

TOMKINS, S. S. (1980). Affect as amplification: Some modifications in theory. In R. Plutchik & H. Kellerman (Eds.), *Emotion: Theory, research and experience* (Vol.1). New York: Academic Press.

TOOBY, J., & COSMIDES, L. (1989). Evolutionary psychologists need to distinghish between the evolutionary process, ancestral selection pressures, and psychological mechanisms. *Behavioral and Brain Sciences, 12,* 724–725.

TORREY, E. F. (1986). Geographic variations in schizophrenia. In C. Shagass, R. C. Josiassen, W. H. Bridger, K. J. Weiss, D. Stoff, & G. M. Simpson (Eds.), *Biological psychiatry,* (pp. 1080–1082). New York: Elsevier.

TORREY, E. F. (1988). *Surviving schizophrenia: A family manual.* New York: Harper & Row.

TORREY, E. F. (1992a). Are we overestimating the genetic contribution to schizophrenia? *Schizophrenic Bulletin, 18*(2), 159–170.

TORREY, E. F. (1992b). *Freudian fraud: The malignant effect of Freud's theory on American thought and culture.* New York: HarperCollins.

TOUFEXIS, A. (1993, April 19). Seeking the roots of violence. *Time,* pp. 52–54.

TREHUB, S. E., SCHNIEDER, B. A., THORPE, L. A., & JUDGE, P. (1991). Observational measures of auditory sensitivity in early infancy. *Developmental Psychology, 27,* 40–49.

TRIANDIS, H. (1989). The self and social behavior in differing cultural contexts. *Psychological Review, 96,* 506–520.

TRIANDIS, H. C. (1990). Theoretical concepts that are applicable to the analysis of ethnocentrism. In R. W. Brislin (Ed.), *Applied cross-cultural psychology* (pp. 34–55). Newbury Park, CA: Sage.

TRICKETT, P. K., & PUTNAM, F. W. (1993). Impact of child sexual abuse on females: Toward a developmental psychobiological integration. *Psychological Science, 4*(2), 81–87.

TRIMBLE, J. E., BOLEK, C. S., & NIEMCRYK, S. J. (1993). Ethnic and multicultural drug abuse: Perspectives on current research. Binshamton, NY: Haworth Press.

TROLL, S. J., MILLER, J., & ATCHLEY, R. C. (1979). *Families in later life*. Belmont, CA: Wadsworth.

TRONICK, E. Z. (1989). Emotions and emotional communication in infants. *American Psychologist, 44*, 112–119.

TROTTER, R. J. (1987, January). The play's the thing. *Psychology Today*, pp. 27–34.

TULVING, E. (1972). Episodic and semantic memory. In E. Tulving & W. Donaldson (Eds.), *Organization of memory*. New York: Academic Press.

TULVING, E. (1985). How many memory systems are there? *American Psychologist, 40*(4), 385–398.

TULVING, E. (1986). What kind of hypothesis is the distinction between episodic and semantic memory? *Journal of Experimental Psychology: Learning, Memory, and Cognition, 12*, 307–311.

TULVING, E., & THOMSON, D. M. (1973). Encoding specificity and retrieval processes in episodic memory. *Psychological Review, 80*, 352–373.

TURK, D. C., MEICHENBAUM, D. H., & GENEST, M. (1983). *Pain and behavioral medicine: A cognitive-behavioral perspective*. New York: Guilford Press.

TURNBULL, C. M. (1961). Some observations regarding the experiences and behavior of the Bamputi pygmies. *American Journal of Psychology, 74*, 304–308.

TURNER, J. C. (1987). *Rediscovering the social group*. New York: Basil Blackwell.

TURNER, J. S., & RUBINSON, L. (1993). *Contemporary human sexuality*. Englewood Cliffs, NJ: Prentice Hall.

TURNER, R. H., & KILLIAN, L. (1987). *Collective behavior* (3rd ed.). Englewood Cliffs, NJ: Prentice Hall.

TURNER, R. J., & WAGONFIELD, M. O. (1967). Occupational mobility and schizophrenia. *American Sociological Review, 32*, 104–113.

TVERSKY, A., & KAHNEMAN, D. (1974). Judgment under uncertainty: Heuristics and biases. *Science, 185*, 1123–1131.

TVERSKY, A., & KAHNEMAN, D. (1981). The framing of decisions and the psychology of choice. *Science, 211*, 453–458.

ULRICH, R. E. (1991). Animal rights, animals wrongs and the question of balance. *Psychological Science, 2*, 197–201.

ULRICH, R. E., STACHNIK, T. J., & STAINTON, N. R. (1963). Student acceptance of generalized personality interpretations. *Psychological Reports, 13*, 831–834.

ULRICH, R. S., SIMONS, R. F., LOSITO, B. D., FIORITO, E. ET AL. (1991). Stress recovery during exposure to natural and urban environments. *Journal of Environmental Psychology, 11*, 201–230.

UNDERWOOD, S. L., & ALEXANDER, P. P. (1988, August). *Body image: Reformulation and assessment*. Paper presented at the annual meeting of the American Psychological Association, Atlanta.

UNGER, R., & CRAWFORD M. (1992). *Women and gender: A feminist psychology*. New York: McGraw-Hill.

United States Census Bureau. (1990). *Statistical abstract of the United States 1990*. Washington, DC: U.S. Government Printing Office.

United States Census Bureau. (1991, January 11). Reported in the *New York Times*, p. 1.

VALENSTEIN, E. S. (1973). *Brain control*. New York: Wiley.

VALENSTEIN, E. S. (1987). *Great and desperate cures: The rise and decline of psychosurgery and other radical treatments for mental illness*. New York: Basic Books.

VALLIANT, G. E., & VALLIANT, C. O. (1990). Natural history of male psychological health: XII. A 45-year study of predictors of successful aging at age 65. *American Journal of Psychiatry, 147*, 31–37.

VAN DYKE, C., & BYCK, R. (1982). Cocaine. *Scientific American, 10*, 128.

VAN WYK, P. (1984). Psychosocial development of heterosexual, bisexual, and homosexual behavior. *Archives of Sexual Behavior, 13*, 505–544.

VAN YPEREN, N. W., & BUUNK, B. P. (1990). A longitudinal study of equity and satisfaction in intimate relationships. *European Journal of Social Psychology, 20*, 287–309.

VANIJZENDOORN, M. H., & KROONENBERG, P. M. (1988). Cross-cultural patterns of attachment: a meta-analysis of the Strange Situation. *Child Develpment, 59*, 147–156.

VASTA, R., HAITH, M. M., & MILLER, S. A. (1992). *Child psychology: The modern science*. New York: Wiley.

VAUGHN, C., SNYDER, K., JONES, S., FREEMAN, W., & FALLOON. I. (1984). Family factors in schizophrenic relapse: A replication in California of British research in expressed emotion. *Archives of General Psychiatry, 41*, 1169–1177.

VENTURA, J., NUECHTERLEIN, K. H., LUKOFF, D., & HARDESTY, J. P. (1989). A prospective study of stressful life events and schizophrenic relapse. *Journal of Abnormal Psychology, 98*, 407–411.

VERNOY, M. W., & LURIA, S. M. (1977). Perception of, and adaptation to, a three-dimensional curvative distortion. *Perception and Psychophysics, 22*(3), 245–248.

VERPLANKEN, B. (1991). Persuasive communication of risk information: A test of cue versus message processing effects in a field experiment. *Personality and Social Psychology Bulletin, 17*, 188–193.

VERVALIN, C. H. (1978). Just what is creativity? In G. A. Davis & J. A. Scott (Eds.), *Training creative thinking*. Huntington, NY: Krieger.

VESSELS, J. (1985, January). Kodo's kitten. *National Geographic*, pp. 110–114.

VICTOR, M., & WOLFE, S. M. (1973). Causation and treatment of the alcohol withdrawal syndrome. In P. G. Bourne & R. Fox (Eds.), *Alcoholism: Progress in research and treatment* (pp. 137–169). New York: Academic Press.

VILBERG, T. R., & KEESEY, R. E. (1990). Ventromedial hypothalamic lesions abolish compensatory reduction in energy expenditure to weight loss. *American Journal of Physiology, 258*, 476–480.

VIRKKUNEN, M., NUUTILA, A., GOODWIN, F. K., & LINNOILA, M. (1987). Cerebrospinal fluid monoamine metabolite levels in male arsonists. *Archives of General Psychiatry, 44*, 241–247.

VITO, C. C., & FOX, T. O. (1981). Androgen and estrogen receptors in embryonic and neonatal rat brain. *Developmental Brain Research, 2*(1), 97–110.

VOELLER, B. (1991). AIDS and heterosexual anal intercourse. *Archives of Sexual Behavior, 20*, 233–269.

VOKEY, J. R., & READ, J. D. (1985). Subliminal messages: Between the devil and the media. *American Psychologist, 40*, 1231–1239.

VOLVAKA, J. (1990). Aggression, electroencephalography, and evoked potentials: A critical review. *Neuropsychiatry, Neuropsychology, and Behavioral Neurology, 3*, 249–259.

WABER, D. (1977). Sex differences in mental abilities, hemispheric lateralization and rate of physical growth at adolescence. *Developmental Psychology, 13*, 29–38.

WADSWORTH, B. (1981, September). Misinterpretations of Piaget's theory. *Educational Digest, 47*, 56–58.

WAGNER, D. A. (1982). Ontogeny in the study of culture and cognition. In D. A. Wagner & H. W. Stevenson (Eds.), *Cultural perspectives on child development* (pp. 105–123). San Francisco: Freeman.

WAID, W. M., & ORNE, M. T. (1982). The physiological detection of deception. *American Scientist, 70*, 402–409.

WALD, G. (1964). The receptors for human color vision. *Science, 145*, 1007–1017.

WALDROP, M. M. (1988). Toward a unified theory of cognition. *Science, 241*, 27–29.

WALFORD, R. L. (1983). *Maximum life span*. New York: Norton.

WALKER, L. J. (1984). Sex differences in the development of moral reasoning: A critical review. *Child Development, 55*, 677–691.

WALKER, L. J. (1991). Sex differences in moral development. In W. M. Kurtines & J. Gewirtz (Eds.), *Moral behavior and development* (Vol. 2). Hillsdale, NJ: Erlbaum.

WALLACE, B., & FISHER, L. E. (1983). *Consciousness and behavior*. Boston: Allyn & Bacon.

WALLACE, M. (1969, November 25). *New York Times*, p. 16.

WALLACE, R. K., DILLBECK, M., JACOBE, E., & HARRINGTON, B. (1982). The effects of transcendental meditation and TM-Sidhi program on the aging process. *International Journal of Neuroscience, 16*, 53–58.

WALLERSTEIN, J. S., & BLAKESLEE, S. (1989). *Second chances: Men, women, and children a decade after divorce*. New York: Ticknor & Fields.

WALLERSTEIN, J. S., & KELLY, J. B. (1980). *Surviving the breakup: How children and parents cope with divorce*. New York: Basic Books.

WALLERSTEIN, J. S., & KELLY, J. B. (1992). How children react to parental divorce. In J. M. Henslin (Ed.), *Marriage and family in a changing society* (4th ed., pp. 397–409). New York: Free Press.

WALLERSTEIN, J. S., CORBIN, S. B., & LEWIS, J. M. (1988). Children of divorce: A ten-year-study. In E. M. Hetherington & J. Arasteh (Eds.), *Impact of divorce, single-parenting, and step-parenting on children* (pp. 198–214). Hillsdale, NJ:

WALLSTON, K. A., MAIDES, S., & WALLSTON, B. S. (1976). Health-related information seeking as a function of health-related locus of control and health value. *Journal of Research in Personality, 10*, 215–222.

WALSH, M. R. (1987). *The psychology of women: Ongoing debates*. New Haven, CT: Yale University Press.

WALSTER, E., & WALSTER, G. W. (1978). *A new look at love*. Reading, MA: Addison-Wesley.

WARD, S., CHAPMAN, K., COHN, E., WHITE, S., & WILLIAMS, K. (1991). Acquaintance rape and the college social scene. *Family Relations, 40*, 65–71.

WARGA, C. (1987). Pain's gatekeeper. *Psychology Today*, pp. 50–56.

WARREN, R. M. (1970). Perceptual restoration of missing speech sounds. *Science, 167*, 392–393.

WATERMAN, A. S. (1982). Identify development from adolescence to adulthood: An extension of theory and a review of research. *Developmental Psychology, 18*, 341–358.

WATERMAN, C. K., & FOSS-GOODMAN, D. (1984). Child molesting: Variables relating to attribution of fault to victims, offenders, and nonparticipating parents. *Journal of Sex Research, 20*, 329–349.

WATSON, J. (1913). Psychology as the behaviorist views it. *Psychological Review, 20*, 158–177.

WATSON, J. B. (1930). *Behaviorism*. Chicago: Phoenix.

WATSON, J. B., & RAYNER, R. (1920). Conditioned emotional reactions. *Journal of Experimental Psychology, 3*, 1–14.

WAUGH, N. C., & NORMAN, D. A. (1965). Primary memory. *Psychological Review, 72*(2), 89–104.

WEBB, W. B. (1992). *Sleep the gentle tyrant* (2nd ed.). Bolton, MA: Anker.

WEBB, W. B. (1983). Theories in modern sleep research. In A. Mayes (Ed.), *Sleep mechanisms and functions*. Wokingham, England: Van Nostrand Reinhold.

WEBB, W. B. (1988). An objective behavioral model of sleep. *Sleep, 11*, 488–496.

WEBB, W., & CARTWRIGHT, R. D. (1978). Sleep and dreams. In M. Rosenzweig & L. Porter (Eds.), *Annual review of psychology* (Vol. 29, pp. 223–252). Palo Alto, CA: Annual Reviews Inc.

WEGMAN, W. E. (1986). Annual summary of vital statistics—1985. *Pediatrics, 78*, 983–984.

WEHR, T. A., JACOBSEN, F. M., SACK, D. A., ARENDT, J., TAMARKIN, L., & ROSENTHAL, N. E. (1986). Phototherapy of seasonal affective disorders. *Archives of General Psychiatry, 43*, 870–875.

WEHR, T. A., SACK, D. A., & ROSENTHAL, N. E. (1987). Seasonal affective disorder with summer depression and winter hypomania. *American Journal of Psychiatry, 144*, 1602–1603.

WEHREN, A., & DE LISI, R. (1983). The development of gender understanding: Judgments and explanations. *Child Development, 54*, 1568–1578.

WEIL, A. (1972). *The natural mind: A new way of looking at drugs and the higher consciousness*. Boston: Houghton Mifflin.

WEIL, A. (1980). *The marriage of the sun and moon: A quest for unity in consciousness*. Boston: Houghton Mifflin.

WEIL, A. (1985). *Health and healing: Understanding conventional and alternative medicine*. Boston: Houghton Mifflin.

WEIL, A., & ROSEN, W. (1983). *Chocolate to morphine: Understanding mind active drugs*. Boston: Houghton Mifflin.

WEIL, A., & ROSEN, W. (1993). *From chocolate to morphine: Everyday mind-altering drugs*. Boston: Houghton Mifflin.

WEINBERG, G. M. (1973). *Society and the healthy homosexual*. New York: Anchor.

WEINBERGER, D. R., WAGNER, R. J., & WYATT, R. L. (1983). Neuropathological studies of schizophrenia: A selective review. *Schizophrenia Bulletin, 9*, 198–212.

WEINER, B. (1972). *Theories of motivation*. Chicago: Rand-McNally.

WEINER, B. (1982). The emotional consequences of causal attributions. In M. S. Clark & S. T. Fiske (Eds.), *Affect and cognition*. Hillsdale, NJ: Erlbaum.

WEINER, B. (1985). An attributional theory of achievement, motivation, and emotion. *Psychological Review, 92*, 548–573.

WEINGARTEN, J. P., CHANG, P. K., & McDONALD, T. J. (1985). Comparison of the metabolic and behavioral disturbances following paraventricular and ventromedial hypothalamic lesions. *Brain Research Bulletin, 14*, 551–559.

WEINGARTNER, H., ADELFRIS, W., EICH, J. E., & MURPHY, D. L. (1976). Encoding specificity in alcohol state-dependent learning. *Journal of Experimental Psychology: Human Learning and Memory, 2*, 83–87.

WEINRAUB, M., CLEMENS, L. P., SOCKLOFF, A., ETHRIDGE, T., GRACELY, E., & MYERS, B. (1984). The development of sex role stereotypes in the third year: Relationship to gender labeling, gender identity, sex-typed toy preference and family characteristics. *Child Development, 55*, 1493–1503.

WEINSTEIN, L. N., SCHWARTZ, D. G., & ELLMAN, S. J. (1991). Sleep mentation as affected by REM deprivation: a new look. In S. A. Ellman & J. S. Antrobus (Eds.), *The mind in sleep: Psychology and psychophysiology* (2nd ed., pp. 377–395). New York: Wiley.

WEINSTEIN, L. N., SCHWARTZ, D. G., & ARKIN, A. M. (1991). Qualitative aspects of sleep mentation. In S. A. Ellman & J. S. Antrobus (Eds.), *The mind in sleep: Psychology and psychophysiology* (2nd ed., pp. 172–213). New York: Wiley.

WEIR, P. (1990). Hypnosis and the treatment of burned patients: A review of the literature. *Australian Journal of Clinical Hypnotherapy and Hypnosis, 11*, 11–15.

WEIS, C. R., ROUNDS, J. B., & ZARICHNY, K. T. (1985, August). *Longitudinal investigation of a cognitive-behavioral intervention for premenstrual distress*. Paper presented at the meeting of the American Psychological Association, Los Angeles.

WEISENBERG, M. (1980). The regulation of pain. *Annals of the New York Academy of Sciences, 340*, 102–114.

WEISS, R. F. (1990). Shadows of thoughts revealed. *Science News, 138*, 297.

WEISS, R. F., BOYER, J. L., LOMBARDO, J. P., & STITCH, M. H. (1973). Altruistis drive and altruistic reinforcement. *Journal of Personality and Social Psychology, 25*, 390–400.

WEISS, R. L. (1975). *Marital separation*. New York: Basic Books.

WEISS, R. L. (1990). *Going it alone: The family life and social situation of the single parent*. New York: Basic Books.

WEISSKOPF-JOELSON, E., & ELISEO, T. S. (1961). An experimental study of the effectiveness of brainstorming. *Journal of Applied Psychology, 45*, 45–49.

WEITZ, D. (1991, April/May). Chemical lobotomies. *Canadian Dimension*, pp. 12–19.

WEITZMAN, L. (1985). *The divorce revolution*. New York: Free Press.

WELLBORN, S. N. (1987, April 13). How genes shape personality. *U.S. News and World Report*, pp. 58–62.

WELLS, M. (1988, January). A schizophrenic's voices. *Psychology Today*, pp. 76–79.

WERNER, J. S., & WOOTEN, B. R. (1979). Human infant color vision and color perception. *Infant Behavior and Development, 2*(3), 241–273.

WHEELER, D. L. (1993, March 10). Psychologist deflates the modern craze of "baby bonding." *The Chronicle of Higher Education*, pp. A6, A13.

WHITE, G. L., & SHAPIRO, D. (1987). Don't I know you? Antecedents and social consequences of perceived familiarity. *Journal of Experimental Social Psychology, 23*, 75–92.

WHITE, S., & DEBLASSIE, R. (1992). Adolescent sexual behavior. *Adolescence, 27*, 183–191.

WHITFIELD, J. C., & EVANS, E. F. (1965). Responses of auditory and cortical neurons to stimuli of changing frequency. *Journal of Neurophysiology, 28*, 655–672.

WHITLEY, B. E. (1987). The effects of discredited eyewitness testimony: A meta-analysis. *Journal of Social Psychology, 127*, 209–214.

WHITTAKER, J. O., & MEADE, R. D. (1967). Social pressure in the modification and distortion of judgment: A cross-cultural study. *International Journal of Psychology, 2*, 109–113.

WHITTY, C. W. M., & ZANGWILL, O. L. (1977). Traumatic amnesia. In C. W. M. Whitty & O. L. Zangwill (Eds.), *Amnesia* (2nd ed.). London: Butterworths.

WHORF, B. (1956). *Language, thought, and reality*. Cambridge, MA: MIT Press.

WHYTE, M. K. (1992, March–April). Choosing mates—the American way. *Society*, pp. 71–77.

WICKER, A. W. (1969). Attitudes versus actions: The relationship of verbal and overt behavioral responses to attitude objects. *Journal of Social Issues, 25*, 41–78.

WIDER, D. A., & THOMPSON, J. E. (1988). Assimilation and contrast effects in the judgments of groups. *Journal of Personality and Social Psychology, 54*, 62–73.

WILDER, D. A. (1990). Some determinants of the persuasive power of in-groups and out-groups: Organization of information and attribution of independence. *Journal of Personality and Social Psychology, 59*, 1202–1213.

WILKES, J. (1986, January). A study in hypnosis: A conversation with Ernest R. Hilgard. *Psychology Today*, pp. 23–27.

WILLIAMS, D. E., & PAGE, M. M. (1989). A multi-dimensional measure of Maslow's hierarchy of needs. *Journal of Research in Personality, 23*, 192–213.

WILLIAMS, R. B. (1984). Type A behavior and coronary heart disease: Something old, something new. *Behavioral Medicine Update, 6*(3), 29–33.

WILSON, E. O. (1975). *Sociobiology: The new synthesis*. Cambridge, MA: Harvard University Press.

WILSON, E. O. (1978). *On human nature*. Cambridge, MA: Harvard University Press.

WILSON, G. T., O'LEARY, K. D., & NATHAN, P. (1992). *Abnormal psychology*. Englewood Cliffs, NJ: Prentice Hall.

WINETT, R. A. (1973). Parameters of deposit contracts in the modification of smoking. *Psychological Record, 23*, 49–60.

WINNUBST, J. A. M., BUUNK, B. P., & MARCELISSEN, F. H. G. (1988). Social support and stress: Perspectives and processes. In S. Fisher & J. Reason (Eds.), *Handbook of life stress, cognition and health*. New York: Wiley.

WISE, R. A. (1984). Neural mechanisms of the reinforcing action of cocaine. *National Institute on Drug Abuse: Research Monograph Series, 50*, 15–33.

WIXTED, J. T., & EBBESEN, E. B. (1991). On the form of forgetting. *Psychological Science, 2*, 409–415.

WOBER, M. (1971). Towards an understanding of the Kiganda concept of intelligence. In J. W. Berry & P. R. Dasen (Eds.), *Culture and cognition: Readings in cross cultureal psychology*. London: Methuen & Co., Ltd.

WOLF, N. (1991). The beauty myth: How images of beauty are used against women. New York: Wm. Morrow.

WOLFERS, O. (1992, March). Same abuse, different parent. *Social Work Today*, pp. 13–15.

WOLFF, P. (1969). The natural history of crying and vocalization in early infancy. In B. M. Foss (Ed.), *Determinants of infant behavior* (Vol. IV). London: Methuen.

WOLPE, J. (1976). Behavior therapy and its malcontent: II. Multimodal electricism, cognitive exclusivism, and "exposure" empiricism. *Journal of Behavior Therapy and Experimental Psychiatry, 7*, 109–116.

WOLPE, J. (1989). The derailment of behavior therapy: A tale of conceptual misdirection. *Journal of Behavior Therapy and Experimental Psychiatry, 20*, 3–15.

WOLPE, J. (1990). *The practice of behavior therapy* (4th ed.). Elmsford, NY: Pergamon.

WOOD, J. V., SALTZBERG, J. A., NEALE, J. M., STONE, A. A., & RACHMIEL, T. B. (1990). Self-focused attention, coping responses, and distressed mood in everyday life. *Journal of Personality and Social Psychology, 58*, 1027–1036.

WOOD, W. (1982). Retrieval of attitude-relevant information from memory: Effects on susceptibility to persuasion and on intrinsic motivation. *Journal of Personality and Social Psychology, 42*, 798–810.

WOOD, W., & EAGLY, A. H. (1981). Steps in the positive

analysis of causal attributions and message comprehension. *Journal of Personality and Social Psychology, 4,* 246–259.

WOOD, W., WONG, F. Y., & CHACHERE, J. G. (1991). Effects of media violence on viewers' aggression in unconstrained social interaction. *Psychological Bulletin, 109,* 371–383.

WOODEN, K. (1981). *The children of Jonestown.* New York: McGraw-Hill.

WORCHEL, S., COOPER, J., & GOETHALS, G. R. (1992). *Understanding social psychology* (5th ed.). Chicago: Dorsey.

World Health Organization. (1979). *Schizophrenia: An international follow-up study.* New York: Wiley.

World Health Organization. (1983). *Depressive disorders in different cultures: Report of the WHO collaborative study of standardized assessment of depressive disorders.* Geneva: Author.

World health statistics. (1992). Reported AIDS cases (WHO). *World health statistical annual.* Washington, DC: World Resources Institute.

WURTMAN, J. (1987). Eating sweets when depressed or tense. *Harvard Medical School Mental Health Letter, 3,* 8.

WURTMAN, R. J., & WURTMAN, J. J. (1989). Carbohydrates and depression. *Scientific American, 260*(1), 68–75.

WYER, R. W., & SRULL, T. K. (1980). Category accessibility and social perception: Some implications for the study of person memory and interpersonal judgments. *Journal of Personality and Social Psychology, 28,* 841–856.

WYNNE, E. A. (1988). The great tradition in education: Transmitting moral values. In J. Rubinstein & R. Slife (Eds.), *Taking sides: Clashing views on controversial psychological issues* (pp. 145–153). Guilford, CT: Dushkin.

YATES, A. (1990). Current perspectives on eating disorders: II. Treatment, outcome, and research directions. *Journal of the American Academy of Child and Adolescent Psychiatry, 29,* 1–9.

YOUNG, L. (1992). Sexual abuse and the problem of embodiment. *Child Abuse and Neglect, 16,* 89–100.

YOUNG, T. (1802). Color vision. *Philosophical Transactions of the Royal Society,* p. 12.

YUDOLFSKY, S., & SILVER, J. (1987). Treating perform-

ance anxiety. *Harvard Medical School Mental Health Letter, 4*(6), 8.

ZAIDEL, E. (1975). A technique for presenting lateralized visual input with prolonged exposure. *Vision Research, 15,* 283–289.

ZAJONC, R. B., SHAVER, P., TAVRIS, C., & VAN KREVELD, D. (1972). Exposure, satiation, and stimulus discriminability. *Journal of Personality and Social Psychology, 21,* 270–280.

ZANOT, E. J., PINCUS, J. D., & LAMP, E. J. (1983). Public perceptions of subliminal advertising. *Journal of Advertising, 12*(1), 39–45.

ZAVIACIC, M., ZAVIACICOVA, A., HOLOMAN, I., & MOLCAN, J. (1988). Female urethral expulsions evoked by local digital stimulation of the G-spot: Differences in the response patterns. *Journal of Sex Research, 24,* 311–318.

ZEIGARNIK, B. V. (1927). Untersuchungen zur Handlungsund Affektpsychologie, Herausgegeben von K. Lewin, 3. Das Behalten erledigter und unerledigter Handlungen. *Psychologische Forschung, 9,* 1–85.

ZELLNER, M. (1970). Self-esteem, reception, and influenceability. *Journal of Personality and Social Psychology, 15,* 87–93.

ZIGLER, E., & HODAPP, R. M. (1986). *Understanding mental retardation.* New York: Cambridge University Press.

ZILBERGELD, B. (1986). Psychabuse. *Science 86, 7*(5), 48–53.

ZILBERGELD, B., & EVANS, M. (1980). The inadequacy of Masters and Johnson. *Psychology Today, 14,* 29–43.

ZILLMAN, D., & WEAVER, J. B. (1989). Poronography and men's sexual callousness toward women. In D. Zillman & J. Bryant (Eds.), *Pornography: Research advances and policy considerations.* Hillsdale, NJ: Erlbaum.

ZIMBARDO, P. (1993). *Stanford prison experiment: A 20-year retrospective.* Invited presentation at the meeting of the Western Psychological Association, Phoenix, AZ.

ZIMBARDO, P. G. (1970). The human choice: Individuation, reason, and order versus deindividuation, impulse, and chaoe. In W. J. Arnold & D. Levine (Eds.), *Nebraska symposium on motivation.* Lincoln: University of Nebraska Press.

ZIMBARDO, P. G., & LEIPPE, M. R. (1991). *The psychology of attitude change and social influence.* New York: McGraw-Hill.

ZIMBARDO, P. G., EBBESON, E. B., & MASLACH, C. (1977). *Influencing attitudes and changing behavior.* Reading, MA: Addison-Wesley.

ZIMMERMAN, D. (1985, January 10). Talking gorilla mourns dead pet. *USA Today,* p. 10.

ZOLA-MORGAN, S., SQUIRE, L. R., & MISHKIN, M. (1982). The neuroanatomy of amnesia: Amygdala-hippocampus versus temporal stem. *Science, 218,* 1337–1339.

ZOLLINGER, T. W., PHILLIPS, R. L., & KUZMA, J. W. (1984). Breast cancer survival rates among Seventh-day Adventists and non-Seventh-day Adventists. *American Journal of Epidemiology, 119,* 503–509.

ZUBIN, J. (1986). Implications of the vulnerability model for DSM-IV with special reference to schizophrenia. In T. Millon & G. L. Klerman (Eds.), *Contemporary directions in psychopathology: Toward the DSM-IV.* New York: Guilford Press.

ZUCKERMAN, M. (1979). Sensation seeking: *Beyond the optimal level of arousal.* Hillsdale, NJ: Erlbaum.

ZUCKERMAN, M. (1990). The psychophysiology of sensation seeking. *Journal of Personality, 58,* 313–345.

ZUCKERMAN, M., EYSENCK, S., & EYSENCK, H. J. (1978). Sensation seeking in England and America: Cross-cultural, age, and sex comparison. *Journal of Consuling and Clinical Psychology, 46,* 139–149.

ZUCKERMAN, M., KUHLMAN, D. M., & CAMAC, C. (1988). What lies beyond E and N? Factor analyses of scales believed to measure basic dimensions of personality. *Journal of Personality and Social Psychology, 54,* 96–107.

ZUCKERMAN, M., MURTAUGH, T., & SIEGEL, V. (1974). Sensation seeking and cortical augmenting-reducing. *Psychophysiology, 11,* 533–542

ZUCKERMAN, M., & WHEELER, L. (1975). To dispel fantasies about the fantasy-based measure of fear of success. *Psychological Bulletin, 82,* 932–946.

ZUGER, B. (1989). Homosexuality in families of boys with early effeminate behavior: An epidemiological study. *Archives of Sexual Behavior, 18,* 155–165.

Photo Credits

Chapter 1 *Opener*: Dale O'Dell/The Stock Market. *Page 4*: From *Obedience to Authority* by Stanley Milgram, copyright © 1974 by Stanley Milgram, reprinted with permission of Harper & Row Publishers, Inc. *Page 8* (top): Ken Lax/Photo Researchers. *Page 8* (bottom): Jeff Greenberg/Photo Researchers. *Page 10*: Jeff Greenberg/Photo Researchers. *Page 13*: Bob Daemmrich/The Image Works, Inc. *Page 20*: Baron Hugo Van Lawick/National Geographic Society. *Page 23*: Dr. Monte Buchsbaum, Mount Sinai Medical Center. *Page 26*: Rafael Macia/Photo Researchers. *Page 27*: Courtesy Foundation for Biomedical Research.

Chapter 2 *Opener*: Custom Medical Stock Photo. *Page 42*: Richard Hutchings/Photo Researchers. *Page 43*: Frank Siteman/Stock, Boston. *Page 49*: John David Fleck/Gamma Liaison. *Page 50*: John Dominis/Life Magazine/Time, Inc. *Page 53*: Fred McConnaughey/Photo Researchers. *Page 55* (bottom): Courtesy Warren Anatomical Museum, Harvard Medical School. *Page 55* (top left): Bob Daemmrich/The Image Works. *Page 57* (top): Courtesy Drs. David Hubel and Torsten Wiesel. *Page 57*: The British Museum of Natural History. *Page 60*: Lawrence Migdale/Photo Researchers. *Figure 2.20*: Dr. Colin Chumbley/Science Photo Library/Photo Researchers. *Page 63*: Roy Morsch/The Stock Market. *Page 66* (top): Mulvehill/The Image Works. *Page 66* (bottom): Courtesy James Olds, California Institute of Technology. *Page 68* (top): Mehau Kulyk/ Science Photo Library/Photo Researchers. *Page 69* (top): Science Photo Library/Photo Researchers. *Page 69* (bottom): Michael W. Vannier, M. D., Mallinckrodt Institute of Radiology at Washington University. *Page 69* (top): Dan McCoy/Rainbow.

Chapter 3 *Opener*: COMSTOCK, Inc. *Page 74*: Rollie McKenna/Photo Researchers. *Page 77*: Blair Seitz/Photo Researchers. *Page 78*: George Goodwin/Monkmeyer Press Photo. *Figure 3.7*: Boehringer Ingelheim International GMBH/Lennart Nilsson. *Figure 3.8 a and b*: Gerry Ellis Nature Photography. *Page 85* (bottom): Bob Daemmrich/The Image Works. *Page 90*: Robert S. Preston, courtesy of Prof. J. E. Hawkins, Kresge Hearing Research Institute, University of Michigan Medical School. *Page 91*: George Azar/The Image Works. *Page 95*: Omikron/Photo Researchers. *Page 96* (left): Marcello Bertinetti/Photo Researchers. *Page 96* (right): Mark and Judy Vernoy. *Page 98*: Tony Freeman/PhotoEdit. *Page 101*: William Sallaz/Duomo. *Page 102*: Jeff Lowenthal/Woodfin Camp & Associates. *Page 105*: B. Nation/Sygma. *Page 106*: American Museum of Natural History. Photo no. 316359.

Chapter 4 *Opener*: Dag Sundberg/The Image Bank. *Page 110*: Michael Ventura/Bruce Coleman, Inc. *Page 112* (top): Copyright © 1955 M. C. Escher Foundation/Cordon Art Baarn-Holland. All rights reserved. *Page 112* (bottom): Jan Halaska/Photo Researchers. *Page 113*: Duomo. *Page 122*: Enrico Ferorelli. *Page 120*: Baron Wolman/Woodfin Camp & Associates. *Figure 4.8*: Mimi Forsyth/Monkmeyer Press Photo. *Page 126*: E. R. Degginger/Bruce Coleman, Inc. *Page 132*: Courtesy Alan Hein, Massachusetts Institute of Technology. *Page 133* (bottom right): Karl Gehring/Gamma Liaison. *Page 133* (top): Kaiser Porcelain, Ltd., London, England. *Page 133* (bottom left): Karl Gehring/Gamma Liaison. *Page 135* (top): Marc Romanelli/The Image Bank. *Page 135* (bottom): Eric. L. Wheater/The Image Bank.

Chapter 5 *Opener*: Bill Longcore/Photo Researchers. *Page 142*: Michael A. Donato/The Image Bank. *Page 146* (left): Bob Daemmrich/Stock, Boston. *Page 146* (center): David Wells/The Image Works. *Page 146* (right): Kevin Horan/Stock, Boston. *Page 146* (bottom): Courtesy of Lamont Lindstrom. *Figure 5.2*: Grant Le Duc/Monkmeyer Press Photo. *Page 153*: Edmund Apel/Photo Researchers. *Page 154*: Chagall, Marc. *I and the Vil-*

lage. 1911. Oil on canvas, 6' 3 5/8" x 59 5/8". The Museum of Modern Art, New York. Mrs. Simon Guggenheim Fund. *Page 158* (top): Bettmann Archive. *Page 158* (bottom and middle): Bella C. Landauer Collection/The New York Historical Society. *Page 162*: Mark Walker/The Picture Cube. *Page 164*: Robert Brenner/PhotoEdit. *Page 168*: Dr. Ronald K. Siegal. *Page 173*: Bob Daemmrich/Stock, Boston.

Chapter 6 *Opener*: Mug Shots/The Stock Market. *Page 180*: Ronald H. Cohn/The Gorilla Foundation. *Page 182*: Joan Baron/The Stock Market. *Page 186*: Alan Carey/The Image Works. *Page 187*: James Balog/Black Star. *Page 191*: Courtesy of The B. F. Skinner Foundation. *Page 193*: Sygma. *Page 194*: Owen Franken/Stock, Boston. *Page 196* (left): Dan McCoy/Rainbow. *Page 196* (right): Acey Harper/Picture Group. *Page 198*: Calvin and Hobbes, copyright © 1987 Watterson. Reprinted with permission of Universal Press Syndicate. All rights reserved. *Page 202*: Will & Deni McIntyre/Photo Researchers. *Page 204*: Reprinted with permission of the American Philosophical Society Library. *Page 206* (top): Courtesy Albert Bandura, Stanford University. *Page 206* (bottom): Erika Stone/Photo Researchers. *Page 208*: From the research of Patricia Greenfield and Carla Childs. Photo by Lauren Greenfield.

Chapter 7 *Opener*: Phil Prosen/The Image Bank. *Page 212* UPI/Bettman Newsphotos. *Page 214*: Bill Gallery/Stock, Boston. *Page 216*: Rick Maiman/Sygma. *Page 217*: Billy E. Barnes/Stock, Boston. *Page 221* (top left): COMSTOCK, Inc. *Page 221* (top right): Ulrike Welsch/Ulrike Welsch Photography. *Page 221* (bottom left): Chuck Fishman/Woodfin Camp & Associates. *Page 221* (bottom right): Nancy Bates/The Picture Cube. *Page 225* (left): Zapruder Film: copyright © 1967 LMH Co. c/o James Lorin Silverberg, Esq. Washington, D.C. (202) 332-7978. All rights reserved. *Page 225* (right): NASA. *Page 228*: M. & E. Bernheim/Woodfin Camp & Associates. *Page 231*: Hazel Hankin/Stock, Boston. *Page 237* (top): Dan McCoy/Black Star. *Page 237* (bottom): Ira Wyman/Sygma. *Page 237* (middle): Dan McCoy/Black Star.

Chapter 8 *Opener*: Terry Why/Index Stock. *Page 246*: Courtesy Jerry Ohlinger's. *Page 250*: Christina Thompson/Woodfin Camp & Associates. *Figure 8.1 and page 258*: Len Speier. *Page 263*: Mike Clemmer/Picture Group. *Page 265*: Ed Kashi/Gamma Liaison. *Page 267* (top right): Shelly Katz/Black Star. *Page 267* (top center): Georges Merillon/Gamma Liaison. *Page 267* (top left): Bernard Gottfryd/Woodfin Camp & Associates. *Page 267* (bottom left): William Sallaz/Duomo. *Page 267* (middle left): John Barrett/Globe Photos, Inc. *Page 267* (middle center): A. Tannenbaum/Sygma. *Page 267* (bottom right): David Gamble/Sygma. *Page 267* (middle right): Luc Novovitch/Gamma Liaison. *Page 270*: Jim Harrison/Stock, Boston. *Page 273*: The Psychological Corporation. *Page 275*: G. Goodwin/Monkmeyer Press Photo. *Page 276*: Steve Leonard/Black Star.

Chapter 9 *Opener*: Jon Feingersh/The Stock Market. *Page 286*: Jacques Chenet/Woodfin Camp & Associates. *Page 290*: Michael Salas/The Image Bank. *Figure 9.3*: David M. Phillips/Photo Researchers. *Figure 9.4b*: Lennart Nilsson from *A Child is Born*, Dell Publishing Co., Inc. *Figure 9.4c*: Petit Format, Nestle/Science Source/Photo Researchers. *Figure 9.4d*: Harriet Gans/The Image Works. *Figure 9.8*: Dr. James Hanson. *Page 301* (top): Elizabeth Crews/The Image Works. *Page 301* (center): David Schaefer/Monkmeyer Press Photo. *Figure 9.10*: Gary Hutchings. *Page 301* (bottom): Michael Heron/Woodfin Camp & Associates. *Figure 9.11*: David Linton from *Scientific American*. *Page 305*: Bob Daemmrich/The Image Works. *Figure 9.15a*: Michael Newman/PhotoEdit. *Figure 9.15b*: Dion Ogust/The Image Works. *Figure 9.15c*: Myrleen Ferguson/PhotoEdit. *Figure 9.15d*: Marc Romanelli/The Image Bank. *Page 313*: Jeffry Myers/Stock, Boston. *Page 317*: Larry Lawfer/The Picture Cube. *Page 318*: Spencer

Grant/Monkmeyer Press Photo. *Figure 9.18*: From A. N. Meltzoff and M.K. Moore, *Science*, 1977, 198, 75-78. Copyright © 1977 AAAS.

Chapter 10   *Opener*: R. Llewellyn/SUPERSTOCK. *Page 326*: Karen Huffman. *Page 329*: Diego Goldberg/Sygma. *Page 331*: Camilla Smith/ Rainbow. *Page 337* (bottom center): Karen Huffman. *Page 334*: Tom McCarthy/PhotoEdit. *Page 337* (top left): The Production Co./The Image Bank. *Page 337* (bottom right): Jocelyn Boutin/The Picture Cube. *Page 337* (top): Jeff Greenberg/Photo Researchers. *Page 342* and Figure 10.3: Nina Leen/Life Magazine, copyright ©Time, Inc. *Page 346* (left): J. Wishnetsky/COMSTOCK, Inc. *Page 346* (right): Camilla Smith/Rainbow. *Page 350*: Bob Daemmrich/The Image Works. *Page 351*: Bob Shaw/The Stock Market. *Page 353* (bottom): Dennis Brack/Black Star.

Chapter 11   *Opener*: Walter Bibikow/The Image Bank. *Page 358*: Barbara Campbell/Gamma Liaison. *Page 360* (top left): Rameshwar Das/Monkmeyer Press Photo. *Page 360* (top right): Bob Daemmrich/The Image Works. *Page 360* (bottom left): D. & I. MacDonald/The Picture Cube. *Page 360* (bottom right): Grant Le Duc/Monkmeyer Press Photo. *Page 360* (center): Janeart Ltd./The Image Bank. *Page 361* (top): Special Collections, Morris Library, Southern Illinois University. *Page 361* (bottom): Ira Wyman/Sygma. *Page 363*: M. Milner/Sygma. *Page 369*: Barbara Alper/ Stock, Boston. *Page 375* (left): Bill Gallery/Stock, Boston. *Page 375* (right): Bob Daemmrich/The Image Works. *Page 385*: Courtesy The AIDS Action Committee. *Page 391*: Markel/Gamma Liaison. *Page 393*: Les Stone/Sygma. *Page 395*: Andrew Kaiser/Sipa Press.

Chapter 12   *Opener*: John Kelly/The Image Bank. *Page 402*: Ronald H. Cohn/The Gorilla Foundation. *Figure 12.2b*: Courtesy of Professor Philip Teitelbaum, University of Pennsylvania. *Page 408*: Don Klumpp/The Image Bank. *Page 409*: Georges de Keerle/Gamma Liaison. *Figure 12.4*: Courtesy of Dean Robert M. Block, University of Wisconsin. *Figure 12.5*: Reprinted by permission of the publishers from Henry A. Murray, Thematic Aperception Test, Harvard University Press, Cambridge, MA, copyright © 1943 by the President and Fellows of Harvard College, 1971 by Henry A. Murray. *Page 414*: Owen Franken/Stock, Boston. *Page 416*: Tom Bledsoe/Photo Researchers. *Page 419*: Audrey Gottlieb/Monkmeyer Press Photo. *Page 420*: Jeffry Myers/The Stock Market. *Page 422*: Douglas Mason/Woodfin Camp & Associates. *Page 426*: Mike Abramson/Woodfin Camp & Associates. *Page 431*: Roger Dollarhide/Monkmeyer Press Photo. *Figure 12.17*: Courtesy of Dr. Paul Ekman, Human Interaction Lab.

Chapter 13   *Opener*: Mike Hewitt/Tony Stone World Wide. *Page 442*: Alvis Upitis/The Image Bank. *Page 446*: Lawrence Migdale/Photo Researchers. *Page 447*: Richard Hutchings/PhotoEdit. *Page 448* (top): Courtesy American Cancer Society. *Page 449*: Lester Sloan/Woodfin Camp & Associates. *Page 451*: Mark Reinstein/The Image Works. *Page 453* (top): Willie Hill/The Image Works. *Page 453* (bottom): Liane Enkelis/Stock, Boston. *Page 457*: A. Operti/Courtesy the American Museum of Natural History. *Page 459* (top): Jeffrey D. Smith/Woodfin Camp & Associates. *Page 459* (bottom): Boehringer Ingelheim International GmbH. *Page 460*: American Heart Association. *Page 463*: Alon Reininger/Woodfin Camp & Associates. *Page 465*: Sidney Harris. *Page 467*: Bob Daemmrich/ The Image Works. *Page 469* (top): Jean-Yves Russzniewski/Photo Researchers. *Page 469* (bottom): Margaret Durrance/Photo Researchers.

Chapter 14   *Opener*: Marc Romanelli/The Image Bank. *Page 474*: From *Bergasse 19*; the photographs of Edmund Engelman. *Page 477* (left to right): AP/Wide World Photos; Courtesy Mark Vernoy; Courtesy Judy Vernoy; T. S. LotterbeckGlobe Photos, Inc.; Courtesy Karen Huffman. *Page 480*: Lester Sloan/Woodfin Camp & Associates. *Page 484*: Margaret Miller/ Photo Researchers. *Figure 14.7*: The Brooklyn Museum. *Page 490*: Courtesy Karen Huffman. *Page 492*: Michael Rougier/Life Magazine, ©Time, Inc. *Page 498*: Bettmann Archive. *Figure 14.10*: Sepp Seitz/Woodfin Camp & Associates. *Figure 14.11*: Reprinted by permission of the publishers from Henry A Murray, Thematic Apperception Test, Harvard University Press, Cambridge, MA, copyright © 1943 by the President and Fellow of Harvard College, 1971 by Henry A . Murray.

Chapter 15   *Opener*: Louise Williams/Science Photo Library/Photo Researchers. *Page 510*: David Gifford/Science Photo Library/Photo Researchers. *Page 511*: Will McIntyre/Photo Researchers. *Page 515* (top): Photo by John Verrano. *Page 515* (bottom): Bettmann Archive. *Page 516*: Painting by Charles Muller/The Bettmann Archive. *Page 521*: Sidney Harris. *Page 523*: Art Wilkinson/Woodfin Camp & Associates. *Figure 15.3a and b*: Nancy C. Andreasen, M.D., Ph.D., The University of Iowa Hospitals and Clinics. *Page 525*: Dr. Monte Buchsbaum, Mount Sinai Medical Center. *Figure 15.3c*: Science Source/Photo Researchers. *Page 534*: Steve Weinrebe/Stock, Boston. *Page 539*: Courtesy Jerry Ohlinger's. *Page 541*: Bettmann Archive. *Page 543*: Mark M. Walker/The Picture Cube.

Chapter 16   *Opener*: Paul Micich/The Image Bank. *Page 550*: Photofest. *Figure 16.2a*: Courtesy Jerry Ohlinger's. *Figure 16.2b*: Museum of Modern Art Film Stills Archive. *Page 559*: Pool/Gamma Liaison. *Page 561*: PEANUTS reprinted by permission of UFS, Inc. *Page 563*: Biomedical Communications/Photo Researchers. *Page 566* (left): Jacques Chenet/Woodfin Camp & Associates. *Page 566* (right): Dr. R. Nesse copyright ©Andrew Sacks/Black Star. *Page 568*: Courtesy Jerry Ohlinger's. *Page 571*: J. Pickerell/The Image Works. *Page 572*: Bob Daemmrich/The Image Works. *Page 576*: Illustration by Theo Rudnak; courtesy Newsweek. *Page 577*: James Wilson/Woodfin Camp & Associates. *Page 579* (left): Paul Fusco/ Magnum Photos, Inc. *Page 579* (right): Audrey Gottlieb/Monkmeyer Press Photo. *Page 582*: J. L. Dugast/Sygma.

Chapter 17   *Opener*: Peter Till/The Image Bank. *Page 588*: Bettmann Archive. *Page 590*: William Vandivert. *Page 592*: David Pollack/The Stock Market. *Page 593*: Reprinted with special permission of King Features Syndicate. *Page 594*: Weinberg-Clark/The Image Bank. *Page 600 and 602*: Courtesy of Professor Phillip E. Zimbardo, Standford University. *Page 603*: Courtesy Jerry Ohlinger's. *Page 608*: Jean-Marc Loubat/Photo Researchers. *Page 612* (top left): Marc & Evelyne Bernheim/Woodfin Camp & Associates. *Page 612* (top right): Eric Robert/Sygma. *Page 612* (bottom): Bill Ellzey/COMSTOCK, Inc. *Page 617*: Nancy Sheehan/The Picture Cube. *Page 620* (top): Movie Stills Archive. *Page 620* (bottom): Phototheque. *Page 621*: Courtesy Karen Huffman.

Chapter 18   *Opener*: Guido Rossi/The Image Bank. *Page 626*: John T. Barr/Gamma Liaison. *Page 631*: Tomas Muscionico/Contact. *Page 632* (top): Bob Daemmrich/The Image Works. *Page 632* (bottom): Michael Newman/PhotoEdit. *Page 634* (left): Michael Kienitz/Picture Group. *Page 634* (right): Anna Flynn/Stock, Boston. *Page 636* (bottom): Courtesy Dr. Kathleen Navarre, Delta College. *Figure 18.6a*: AP/Wide World. *Figure 18.6b*: Bettmann Archive. *Figure 18.6c*: Woolaroc Museum, Bartlesville, Oklahoma. *Figure 18.6d*: Chris Morris/Black Star. *Page 643*: Spencer Grant/The Picture Cube. *Page 645*: Arthur Leipzig.

Appendix B   *Page A-12* (left): Department of Health and Human Services. *Page A-12* (right): Dan Bubnick/Woodfin Camp & Associates.

Timeline (in order of appearance)   *1879*: Bettmann Archive. *1882*: Archives of the History of American Psychology. *1890*: Bettmann Archive. *1891*: Wellesley College. *1892*: Archives of the History of American Psychology. *1898*: Teachers College. *1900*: Archiv/Photo Researchers. *1905*: Archives of the History of American Psychology. *1906*: Bettmann Archive. *1908*: Archives of the History of American Psychology. *1913*: Bettmann Archive. *1914*: Bettmann Archive. *1916*: Archives of the History of American Psychology. *1924*: Archives of the History of American Psychology. *1925*: Courtesy Swarthmore College Archives, Friends Historical Library, Swarthmore College. *1927*: Archives of the History of American Psychology. *1932*: Jean Piaget Society. *1938*: Photo by K. Bendo. *1945*: Bettmann Archive. *1946*: Courtesy Dr. Solomon Asch. *1950*: Photo by Jon Erikson. *1954*: Bettmann Archive. *1954*: Bettmann Archive. *1954*: Courtesy Kenneth Clark. *1957*: Karen Zebulon. *1958*: Bettmann Archive. *1961*: Courtesy John Berry. *1961*: Delacorte Press Photo by Antony di Gesu. *1963*: Courtesy Albert Bandura. *1963*: HGSE . *1965*: Archives of the History of American Psychology.

Text and Illustration Credits

Chapter 1 Table 1.2: Plous, S. "An attitude survey of animal rights activists" *American Psychological Society,* 1991. Copyright © 1991 American Psychological Society. Reprinted by permission of the American Psychological Society and S. Plous.

Chapter 2 Figure 2.21: Kimura, D. "Sex differences in the brain" *Scientific American,* 1992. From *Sex Differences in the Brain* by D. Kimura. Copyright © 1992 by Scientific American, Inc. All rights reserved.; Figure 2.22: Kimura, D. "Sex differences in the brain" *Scientific American,* 1992. From *Sex Differences in the Brain* by D. Kimura. Copyright © 1992 by Scientific American, Inc. All rights reserved.

Chapter 4 Figure 4.4: Luria, A. R. *Cognitive development: Its cultural and social foundations* Harvard University Press, 1976. Reprinted by permission of the publishers from *Cognitive Development: Its Cultural and Social Foundations* by A. R. Luria, Cambridge, Mass.: Harvard University Press. Copyright © 1976 by the President and Fellows of Harvard College.; Page 122: From *Drugs affecting the central nervous system,* A. Burger (Ed.), Marcel Dekker, Inc., New York 1968. Reprinted from *Drugs affecting the central nervous system,* pp. 184–185, by courtesy of Marcel Dekker, Inc.; Figure 4.11: Commanding Officer, *Naval Submarine Medical Research Laboratory* United States Navy, 1958. By permission of the Commanding Officer, Naval Submarine Medical Research Laboratory, Naval Submarine Base, New London, Groton, CT.

Chapter 5 "Try This Yourself," Page 149: Adapted from "Industrial Time Clocks—Often at Odds with Those Inside a Worker's Body," by Nancy J. Perry, of November 28, 1982. Copyright © 1982 by The New York Times Company. Reprinted by permission.; Figure 5.5: Adapted from Williams, R. L., Karacan, I., & Hursch, C. J. (1974). *Electroencephalography (EEG) of human sleep: Clinical applications.* New York: Wiley. Reprinted by permission of John Wiley & Sons, Inc.; Table 5.1: From *Can't get enough shut-eye? There's help,* K. Peterson. Copyright © 1984, *USA Today.* Reprinted with permission.; Figure 5.9: From *Divided Consciousness: Multiple Controls in Human Thought and Action,* E. R. Hilgard, Copyright © 1977 by John Wiley & Sons, Inc., New York. Reprinted by permission of John Wiley & Sons, Inc.; "Try This Yourself," Page 175: From "Systematic hypertension and the relaxation response," by H. Benson. *New England Journal of Medicine, 296,* (1977). Reprinted with permission of New England Journal of Medicine.

Chapter 6 Page 180: Patterson, F., and Linden, E. *The Education of Koko* Holt, Rinehart, & Winston, 1981. From The *Education of Koko* by F. Patterson, and E. Linden. Copyright © 1981 by Holt, Rinehart, & Winston. Reprinted by permission.; Figure 6.6: Kiewra, K. A., & DuBois, N. F. Using a *Spatial System* for *Teaching Operant Conditioning* / Lawrence Erlbaum Associates, Inc., 1992. Kiewra, K. A., & DuBois, N. F. (1992). "Using a spatial system of teaching operant conditioning," *Teaching of Psychology,* **19**(1), 43. Figure #1 on page 43. Copyright © 1992 by Lawrence Erlbaum Associates, Inc. Reprinted by permission.

Chapter 7 Figure 7.2: Postman, L., and Phillips, L. W. "Short-term temporal changes in free recall." *Experimental Psychology Society,* 1965. Reprinted by permission of the Experimental Psychology Society.; Figure 7.3: Collins, A. M., and Quillian, M. R. *"Retrieval Time From Semantic Memory,"* Academic Press, 1969. From A. M. Collins, & M. R. Quillian, "Retrieval time from semantic memory," *Journal of Verbal Learning and Verbal Behavior.* Copyright © 1969 by Academic Press. Reprinted by permission of Academic Press and the author.; Figure 7.4: Bahrick, H. P., Bahrick, P. O., & Wittlinger, R. P. "Those unforgettable High-School days" *Psychology Today,* 1971. Reprinted with permission from *Psychology Today Magazine.* Copyright © 1974.; Figure 7.6 a,b: Murdock, B. B., Jr. "The Serial effect of free recall" *American Psychological Association,* 1962. Murdock, B. B., Jr. (1962). The serial effect of free recall. *Journal of Experimental Psychology,* 64(5), 482–488, figure 1 page 483. Copyright © 1962 by the American Psychological Association. Reprinted/Adapted by permission of the author.; Figure 7.7: Peterson, L. R., and Peterson, M. J. "Short-term retention of individual verbal items," American Psychological Association, 1959. Peterson, L. R., & Peterson, M. J. (1959). Short-term retention of individual verbal items. *Journal of Experimental Psychology,* 8(3), 193–198. Copyright © 1959 by the American Psychological Association. Reprinted/Adapted by the permission of the author.

Chapter 8 Page 246: Clarke, A. C. *2001: A space odyssey* Arthur C. Clarke and Polaris Productions, 1968. From *2001: A Space Odyssey* by Arthur C. Clarke. Copyright © 1968 by Arthur C. Clarke and Polaris Productions. Reprinted by arrangement with New America Library, New York, NY.; "Try This Yourself," Page 250: Shepard, R. N., and Metzler, J. "Mental rotation of three-dimensional objects," *American Association for the Advancement of Science,* 1971. Copyright © 1971 by the AAAS.; "Try This Yourself, " Page 256: Luchins, A. S., and Luchins, E. H. "New experimental attempts at preventing mechanization in problem solving," *Journal of General Psychology,* 1950. *Journal of General Psychology,* 42, Page 280. Reprinted with permission of the Helen Dwight Reid Educational Foundation. Published by Heldref Publications, 4000 Albemarle St., N.W., Washington, D. C. 20015. Copyright © 1950.

Chapter 9 Figure 9.2: From Schaie, K. W., and Strothers, C. R. (1968). A cross-sequential study of age changes in cognitive behavior. *Psychological Bulletin, 70,* 671–680. Copyright © 1968 by the American Psychological Association. Reprinted/Adapted by permission of the author.; Figure 9.5: From *Child Development: A Topical Approach,* A. Clarke-Stewart, S. Friedman, and J. Koch. Copyright © 1985 by John Wiley & Sons, Inc., New York. Reprinted by permission of John Wiley & Sons, Inc.; Figure 9.13: From Tanner, J. M., Whitehouse, R. N., & Takaislu, M. (1966). Male/female growth spurt chart. *Archives of Diseases in Childhood, 41,* 454–471. Reprinted by permission.; Figure 9.14: Chart of elderly achievers (Figure 10.5) from *The Brain: A User's Manual* by The Diagram Group. Reprinted by permission of the Putnam Publishing Group from The Brain: A User's Manual by the Diagram Group. Copyright © 1982 by Diagram Visual Information Ltd.; Figure 9.17: Adapted from Table 8.6 p. 322 in *Child Development: A Topical Approach,* A. Clarke-Stewart, S. Friedman, & J. Koch. Copyright © 1985 by John Wiley & Sons, Inc., New York. Reprinted by permission of John Wiley & Sons, Inc.

Chapter 10 Table 10.1: Adapted table of Kohlberg chapter, Rest, J. (Ed.) (1969). *Handbook of Socialization Theory and Research,* D. A. Goslin (Ed.). Reprinted by permission of Houghton Mifflin Company.; Figure 10.1: From Colby, A., Kohlberg, L., Gibbs, J., & Leiberman, M. (1983).

Name Index

Subject Index